2000

OurSundayVisitor's

CATHOLIC ALMANAC

Matthew Bunson
General Editor

Our Sunday Visitor Publishing Division
Our Sunday Visitor, Inc.
Huntington, Indiana 46750

STAFF OF OUR SUNDAY VISITOR'S CATHOLIC ALMANAC

Robert Lockwood
Publisher

Greg Erlandson
Editor-in-Chief

Matthew E. Bunson
General Editor

Cathy Dee
Production Editor

Contributors to the 2000 Edition
Mrs. Helen Alvaré
Rev. Clyde Crews
Mrs. Barbara Fraze
Most Rev. Wilton Gregory
Brother Jeffrey Gros, F.S.C.
Rev. Alfred McBride, O.Praem.
Rev. Ronald Roberson, C.S.P.
Mr. William Ryan
Mr. Russell Shaw

Special Consultant
Rev. Felician Foy, O.F.M.

Assistant
Amy Thomas

Cover Designer
Rebecca Heaston

ACKNOWLEDGMENTS: Catholic News Service, for coverage of news and documentary texts; *The Documents of Vatican II*, ed. W. M. Abbott (Herder and Herder, America Press: New York 1966), for quotations of Council documents; *Annuario Pontificio* (1999); *Statistical Yearbook of the Church* (1999); *L'Osservatore Romano* (English editions); *The Official Catholic Directory* — excerpts of statistical data and other material, reprinted with permission of *The Official Catholic Directory*, © 1999 by Reed Reference Publishing, a division of Reed Publishing (U.S.A.), Inc. Trademark used under license from Reed Publishing (Nederland) B.V.; *The Papal Encyclicals*, 5 vols., ed. C. Carlen (Pierian Press, Ann Arbor, Mich.); Newsletter of the U.S. Bishops' Committee on the Liturgy; The United States Catholic Mission Assoc. (3029 Fourth St. N.E., Washington, D.C. 20017), for U.S. overseas mission compilations and statistics; *Catholic Press Directory* (1999); *Annuaire Directiore* 1998-1999, Canadian Conference of Catholic Bishops, for latest available Canadian Catholic statistics; Rev. Thomas J. Reese, S.J., for names of dioceses for which U.S. bishops were ordained; other sources as credited in particular entries. Special thanks are owed to His Excellency Most Reverend John P. Foley, President of the Pontifical Council for Social Communications; Most Reverend Wilton Gregory, Bishop of Belleville and Vice-President of the NCCB; Helen Alvaré of the Secretariat for Pro-Life Activities, NCCB/USCC; Suzanne Lea; and Lisa Grote and Henry O'Brien, of Our Sunday Visitor, for their invaluable assistance in the preparation of this work.

2000 Catholic Almanac

Editorial Note: This edition of the *Catholic Almanac* includes an extensive revision and updating of longstanding material and introduces sections with revised material in order to reflect current developments in the life of the Church. Comments and suggestions should be addressed to the editorial offices of the *Catholic Almanac*: 9165 W. Desert Inn Rd., N-202, Las Vegas, NV 89117. E-mail: almanac@osv.com.

TABLE OF CONTENTS

INDEX

THE GREAT JUBILEE OF THE YEAR 2000

PRAYER OF HIS HOLINESS POPE JOHN PAUL II FOR THE CELEBRATION OF THE GREAT JUBILEE OF THE YEAR 2000

1. Blessed are You, Father,
who, in Your infinite love,
gave us Your only-begotten Son.
By the power of the Holy Spirit He became incarnate
in this spotless womb of the Virgin Mary
and was born in Bethlehem
two thousand years ago.
He became our companion on life's path
and gave new meaning to our history,
the journey we make together
in toil and suffering, in faithfulness and love,
towards the new heaven and the new earth
where You, once death has been vanquished,
will be all in all.
Praise and glory to You, Most Holy Trinity,
You alone are God most high!
2. By Your Grace, O Father, may the Jubilee Year
be a time of deep conversion
and of joyful return to You.
May it be a time of reconciliation between people,
and of peace restored among nations,
a time when swords are beaten into ploughshares
and the clash of arms gives way to songs of peace.
Father, grant that we may live this Jubilee Year
docile to the voice of the Spirit,
faithful to the way of Christ,
diligent in listening to Your Word
and in approaching the wellsprings of grace.
Praise and glory to You, Most Holy Trinity,
You alone are God most high!
3. Father, by the power of the Spirit,
strengthen the Church's commitment
    to the new evangelization
and guide our steps along the pathways of the world,
to proclaim Christ by our lives,
and to direct our earthly pilgrimage
towards the City of heavenly light.
May Christ's followers show forth their love
for the poor and the oppressed;
may they be one with those in need
and abound in works of mercy;
may they be compassionate towards all,
that they themselves may obtain indulgence
    and forgiveness from You.
Praise and glory to You, Most Holy Trinity,
You alone are God most high!
4. Father, grant that Your Son's disciples,
purified in memory
and acknowledging their failings,
may be one, that the world may believe.
May dialogue between the followers
    of the great religions prosper,
and may all people discover
the joy of being Your children.
May the intercession of Mary,
Mother of Your faithful people,
in union with the prayers of the Apostles,
    the Christian martyrs,
and the righteous of all nations in every age,
make the Holy Year a time of renewed hope
    and of joy in the Spirit

for each of us and for the whole Church.
Praise and glory to You, Most Holy Trinity,
You alone are God most high!
5. To You, Almighty Father,
Creator of the universe and of mankind,

through Christ, the Living One,
Lord of time and history,
in the Spirit who makes all things holy,
be praise and honor and glory
now and forever. Amen!

THE SIGNIFICANCE OF THE JUBILEE HOLY YEAR
FOR THE CHURCH IN THE UNITED STATES

By Most Reverend Wilton D. Gregory, Bishop of Belleville, Vice-President of the NCCB

The Church's hopes for the year 2000 are expressed in Pope John Paul's apostolic letter *On the Coming of the Third Millennium* (*Tertio Millennio Adveniente* [TMA]) and in his bull promulgating the Jubilee Year *The Mystery of the Incarnation* (*Incarnationis Mysterium* [IM]). These two documents invite us to reflect on our history as a faith community and on our hopes for the future.

"Do as much as possible to ensure that the great challenge of the year 2000 is not overlooked, for this challenge certainly involves a special grace of the Lord for the Church and for the whole of humanity." (TMA, 55)

Pope John Paul II has extended an invitation to Catholics around the world to fix a particular Christian focus on the observances of the year 2000. This extraordinary time in our history, resulting from our use of the contemporary calendar, provides the Church with a special opportunity — a once in a lifetime moment. The passing of a 1,000-year mark is an extraordinary moment in time. Few people experience such an event over the length and breath of history. Historians tell us that only one generation in every 40 or 50 generations is privileged to cross the threshold into a new millennium. We, standing at this time in history, become part of this privileged generation. Pope John Paul II re-echoes this sentiment: "Humanity, upon reaching this goal (the 21st century), will leave behind not just a century, but a millennium" (TMA, 33). The wonder [of the Jubilee Year] "will be celebrated simultaneously in Rome and in all the particular Churches around the world...."(IM 2).

As Catholics, we have a story to tell the rest of the world. It holds the key to the deeply religious significance of the year 2000. We celebrate 2,000 years of Christ's presence in human history. We celebrate the 2,000 years of Christianity beginning "with the redemption accomplished by Christ in his death and resurrection" (IM, 6). It is an invitation to "lift (our) eyes of faith to embrace new horizons in proclaiming the Kingdom of God" (IM 2). The 2,000 years which have passed since the birth of Christ "represent an extraordinarily great Jubilee [an outward jubilation of joy], not only for Christians, but indirectly for the whole of humanity, given the prominent role played by Christianity during these two millennia" (TMA 15).

The message that the United States Catholic Bishops' subcommittee on the Third Millennium invites us all to grasp during this jubilee year is expressed in the theme "Open Wide the Doors to Christ — Evangelize, Reconcile, Celebrate." This image refers both to the ancient symbol or "significant sign" of the Church's observance of Holy Years — the special Holy Doors of the four basilicas in Rome (cf. IM 8), as well as the theological basis for this unique Holy Year:

conversion/atonement, pilgrimage and the Incarnate God: Jesus Christ.

As a Jubilee Holy Year, there is a natural development from passing through the threshold of the Holy Year Door — confessing that Jesus Christ is Lord, and crossing the threshold into a new millennium. It is through Christ, the doorway to the Father, that we enter into life with God. Faith in Jesus Christ becomes the means by which we pass into the third millennium of Christianity. "To focus upon the door is to recall the responsibility of every believer to cross its threshold" (IM 8). It is to strengthen faith in Christ in order to live the new life which has been given us, the freedom to choose and the courage to leave something behind — our old selves ... as we enter into the jubilee of the third Christian millennium. "The jubilee year, a great anniversary of Christianity, is a time to let faith be refreshed, 'let hope increase and let charity exert itself still more' " (IM 11) (*Parish Guide*, p. 1).

The year 2000 brings us an unprecedented chance to renew our efforts of evangelization in the world today and to embrace the spirit of reconciliation with God and each other. It is a time and a unique opportunity to deepen our spiritual life — to be the holy people God calls us to be. It "requires effort and commitment to live the beatitudes" (*Called and Gifted for the Third Millennium*, p. 3) and to undertake a spirit of conversion leading to healing and reconciliation. The Jubilee is a "summons to conversion of heart through a change in life" (IM 12).

Looking at the experience of life in our contemporary society, the Jubilee Holy Year suggests a framework with four characteristics for the new millennium. These four characteristics respond to present-day needs: the need to be rooted in life, the need for hope, the need for community, and the need to undertake responsible action. The Jubilee Year challenges us to place Jesus Christ at the center of our lives, to see that Jesus Christ is the only real foundation in which to root our lives. Placing Christ as the foundation of life calls us to conversion and gives us the ability to be hopeful people.

At the end of the 20th century, there is a strong desire among people to be connected. The Christian community, our parishes, and small church communities can be a response to this need. The celebration of the Great Jubilee is not a celebration of individuals, but of individuals within a faith community for "the Christian is not alone on the path of conversion" (IM 10). These communities are places where we must be challenged to make the Gospel come alive in society, especially to be challenged to live just and charitable lives. A sign of the "mercy of God which is especially necessary today is the sign of charity, which opens our eyes to the needs of those who are poor and excluded" (IM 12). The sins of injustice "offend the holiness and justice of God and scorn God's personal friendship" (IM 10) with us.

The biblical roots of jubilee speak in a most persuasive manner to the justice demands of the Great Jubilee. Luke 4: 18-19, echoing Isaiah 61:2, proclaims the commission of being a jubilee people: "The spirit of the Lord is upon me, because He has anointed me to bring glad tidings to the poor. He has sent me to proclaim liberty to captives and recovery of sight to the blind, to let the oppressed go free, and to proclaim a year acceptable to the Lord."

"Seven weeks of years shall you count — seven times seven years — so that the seven cycles amount to forty-nine years. Then, on the tenth day of the seventh month let the trumpet resound; on this, the Day of Atonement, the trumpet blast shall re-echo throughout your land. This fiftieth year you shall make sacred by proclaiming liberty in the land for all its inhabitants. It shall be a jubilee for you, when every one of you shall return to your own property, every one to your own family estate. In this fiftieth year, your year of jubilee, you shall not sow, nor shall you reap the aftergrowth or pick the grapes from the untrimmed vines. Since this is the jubilee, which shall be sacred for you, you may not eat of its produce, except as taken directly from the field" (Lev. 25: 8-12).

The Jubilee ought to be a time where the power and presence of the Holy Spirit will be felt more "deeply impelling Christians to preach the Gospel with new power, giving hope of liberation to the marginalized and the oppressed" (A. Dulles, "John Paul II and the Advent of the New Millennium," *America* 175:19, 11). It should be a time of freedom from bondage, and a time of restoration and of forgiveness of debts. A year of the Lord's favor.

PASTORAL RESPONSE

During the Great Jubilee of the Year 2000, which begins in Rome on Christmas Eve, 1999, and in the local churches on Christmas Day 1999, dioceses, parishes, families and individuals are invited to observe the year in a number of ways.

The Pledge for Justice and Charity in the New Millennium

As a way of inaugurating the Great Jubilee Year 2000 and signaling an attitude for justice and peace in the forthcoming new millennium, Catholics are invited to participate in the "Pledge for Justice and Charity" (see bottom of next page).

The National Day of Reconciliation and Pardon (Lent 2000)

The Church's tradition regarding the Holy Year as well as the season of Lent is to call us to repentance and conversion. Parishes and dioceses throughout the United States are invited to participate in a special day of reconciliation and healing on April 8, 2000, Saturday of the Fourth Week of Lent. On this day the bishops' subcommittee on the Third Millennium invites churches to hold special celebrations of the Sacrament of Reconciliation and to prepare for this day with a catechesis on the sacrament.

Participate in the Diocesan Eucharistic Congress/Eucharistic Day

Each diocese is invited to convene a diocesan Eucharistic Congress or celebrate a special Eucharistic Liturgy on the Feast of Corpus Christi (June 24-25, 2000) or on a more appropriate day. Pope John Paul II has called this Jubilee to be one especially focused on the Eucharist.

Convene a Parish Mission

Another suggestion for an activity that a parish may wish to undertake is to reinstate the tradition of the parish mission. Missions have been undertaken typically during Advent and Lent as opportunities for personal conversion and growth in faith.

Undertake a Personal Pilgrimage

One of the key elements of the Church's commemoration of Holy Years throughout history has been pilgrimage. In past these pilgrimages were primarily to Rome. Now the church urges each person to make a pilgrimage during the Jubilee Year. This pilgrimage may be to Rome or the Holy Land, to the diocesan cathedral or other designated churches or to a particular shrine. These pilgrimages can be undertaken alone, as a family, a youth group, or a parish community or diocesan church.

Join a Small Christian Community or Faith-sharing Group

Catholics are invited to join a small community or faith group for reflection and prayer during the Great Jubilee. Hopefully, a positive experience of this type of faith sharing will encourage participants to continue them into the new millennium.

Welcome — Outreach Sunday

The Jubilee Year should be marked by a great desire to proclaim the person of Jesus Christ and his message of salvation. This year provides us with a wonderful opportunity to initiate special occasions for evangelization and outreach to the unchurched or alienated. We encourage every parish to sponsor a "Welcome Sunday" during one of the Sundays in Advent in 2000 to welcome people to church for the new millennium. There can be a time for a special welcome to "come and see" the richness of faith in Jesus Christ. Mary is a wonderful model of "hospitality" as she welcomed God into her life and as she extended herself in visiting her cousin Elizabeth.

The Jubilee Days — Days of Celebration and Mission

In addition to these suggestions for marking the year 2000, the Vatican has designated a number of "Jubilee Days" throughout the year to commemorate and celebrate people's vocation and work in life. We propose that these days have two foci: first to honor and remember a particular group of people for what they have contributed to the life of the Church and the world and second as a day to reflect on the challenges people face in living the Gospel in the new millennium.

As these and other initiates are planned for Jubilee Year 2000, there are a number of pastoral principles to keep in mind. One of the most important includes creating time for personal reflection, meditation, and prayer. A second concern is that the Church's celebration of the year 2000 is about helping people deepen their spiritual life, rather than merely creating more programs. Third, the great Jubilee Year will provide an excellent moment for ecumenical collaboration and partnership. We hope that the themes of Jubilee be woven into present church life as we celebrate 2,000 years of Christ's presence in human history.

"For I know well the plans I have in mind for you, says the LORD, plans for your welfare, not for woe! Plans to give you a future full of hope." (Jer 29: 11)

THE GREAT JUBILEE OF THE YEAR 2000

By Russell Shaw

"Contemplating the mystery of the Incarnation of the Son of God, the Church prepares to cross the threshold of the third millennium.... The whole of human history in fact stands in reference to him: our own time and the future of the world are illumined by his presence."

Jesus Christ ... the Incarnation and the Redemption: this is the Person and these the mysteries at the heart of the Church's observance of the Great Jubilee of the Year 2000 and the start of the third millennium of the Christian era. The words above come from *Incarnationis Mysterium (The Mystery of the Incarnation)*, Pope John Paul II's "bull of indiction" formally proclaiming the Jubilee. Dated November 29, 1998, the document is addressed to "all the faithful journeying toward the third millennium."

Preparing the Church for the third millennium has been a priority for John Paul from the beginning of his pontificate. His first encyclical, *Redemptor Hominis*, dated March 4, 1979, opened with the ringing declaration, "The Redeemer of man, Jesus Christ, is the center of the universe and of history," and went on to point out that the world was rapidly approaching the year 2000, seen as a moment of profound symbolic importance for the Church and the human race.

John Paul has returned to this theme many times since. In 1994, in an apostolic letter called *Tertio Millennio Adveniente (On the Coming of the Third Millennium)*, he set out the rationale for the Church's observance in detail, together with the elements of a plan for both the preparatory period and the Great Jubilee itself. Since then the Church throughout the world has been involved in planning, with an elaborate program of religious events and spiritual exercises of all kinds now scheduled to take place during the year in Rome and many other places.

The most intensive preparations have taken place in the three years immediately preceding the Jubilee, with each dedicated in particular to reflection on one of the Persons of the Trinity—in 1997 Christ, the Second Person of the Trinity made man; in 1998 the Holy Spirit; and in 1999 God the Father. Also closely linked to the millennium preparations has been a series of regional assemblies of the world Synod of Bishops—for Africa in 1994, for America (North, Central, and South) in 1997, for Asia and for Oceania, both in 1998, and for Europe, scheduled in October, 1999. A general assembly of the Synod is planned for October 2000, in Rome.

Why is the Church, under the leadership of Pope John Paul, giving so much attention to the year 2000? He answered that question in *Incarnationis Mysterium*: "Jesus is the genuine newness which surpasses all human expectations and as such he remains for ever, from age to age. The Incarnation of the Son of God and the salvation which he has accomplished by his Death and Resurrection are therefore the true criterion for evaluating all that happens in time and every effort to make life more human."

Evangelization is central to the pope's thinking about the third millennium. He wants the Great Jubilee to give new impetus to Catholics' efforts to preach the Gospel to the world. In *Incarnationis Mysterium*, as elsewhere, he related this project to the Second Vatican Council (1962-65), which he said "shed new light upon the missionary task of the Church" and where "the Church became more deeply conscious both of the mystery which she herself is and of the apostolic mission entrusted to her by the Lord.

"The journey of believers towards the third millennium is in no way weighed down by the weariness which the burden of 2000 years of history could bring with it," he added. "Rather, Christians feel invigorated, in the knowledge that they bring to the world the true light, Christ the Lord. Proclaiming Jesus of Nazareth, true God and perfect Man, the Church opens to all people the prospect of being 'divinized' and thus of becoming more human. This is the one path which can lead the world to discover its lofty calling and to achieve it fully in the salvation wrought by God."

History of the Jubilee

The Great Jubilee of the Year 2000 will be unique in many ways, but it stands in continuity with an ancient tradition that goes back to Old Testament times.

The word "jubilee" comes from the Hebrew word *jobel*, for a ram's horn—the instrument used to announce and inaugurate the celebration. The word passed through the Greek *iobelaios* or *iobelos*, which became linked to the Latin *jubilo* ("to shout") and the forms *jubilatio* and *jubilaeum*.

In ancient Israel, jubilees — "sabbatical years" — were observed every seven years, with a jubilee of special solemnity every 50 years. For example, Leviticus 25:10 prescribes: "And you shall hallow the fiftieth year, and proclaim liberty throughout the land to all its inhabitants; it shall be a jubilee for you, when each of you shall return to his property and each of you shall return to his family." According to Jewish law, the elements of the jubilee included the reuniting of families, the return of ancestral land to its original owners, the freeing of Hebrew slaves, and the forgiveness of debts. "The prescriptions of the jubilee year largely remained ideals — more a hope than an actual fact," Pope John Paul remarked in *Tertio Millennio Adveniente*; but the ideals were taken seriously and can be seen has having a kind of prophetic character pointing to "the freedom which would be won by the coming Messiah."

Although the idea of marking every 50th year in a solemn manner was familiar to medieval writers before 1300, the first Jubilee of the Christian era of which there is a precise record was instituted by Pope

Boniface VIII in that year. In a bull issued February 22, the pope granted "great remissions and indulgences for sins" to penitent pilgrims who visited Rome, confessed their sins, and visited the basilicas of St. Peter and St. Paul daily for a specified time— 15 days in the case of visitors, 30 days in the case of residents of the city. It is estimated that an average of 200,000 pilgrims were in Rome during most of the year. Dante, said to have been one of them, included a description of the throngs going to and from St. Peter's across the Castel Sant'Angelo bridge in his *Divine Comedy*.

The Jubilee of 1300 was a great success, and subsequent popes continued the custom, with the interval between the observances eventually being set at — ordinarily — 25 years. But this pattern was not invariable. During the 19th century there was only one Jubilee, in 1825, with the observances that otherwise would have taken place in 1800, 1850 and 1875 omitted because of political conflicts and disruptions. Pope Leo XIII observed the Jubilee of the year 1900, although it was, as one historian remarks, "shorn of much of its splendor" by the pope's status as "prisoner of the Vatican" due to the seizure of the Papal States and most of Rome in 1870 by the Italian authorities.

As the Jubilee developed, the basilicas of St. John Lateran and St. Mary Major were added to the list of Roman pilgrimage sites along with St. Peter's and St. Paul's. The Jubilee indulgence (in Catholic doctrine, "indulgence" signifies the remission of temporal punishment due to sins that have been forgiven) granted to penitent pilgrims remained a central part of the observance.

The Program of the Jubilee Year

According to Pope John Paul in *Mysterium Incarnationis*, the Great Jubilee of the Year 2000 will have "two centers," Rome and the Holy Land — Rome because that is where "Providence chose to place the See of the Successor of Peter," the Holy Land because of its association with the Incarnation: "It was there that Jesus was born and died." The Great Jubilee also will be celebrated in dioceses around the world. The observance begins on Christmas Eve of 1999 and will close on the Feast of the Epiphany, January 6, 2001.

The official commencement of the Great Jubilee will be marked by the opening of the "Holy Door" in St. Peter's Basilica in Rome — a ceremony likely to be viewed by hundreds of millions of people via television. The door, one of the basilica's main entrances, is kept sealed between Holy Years. During the Christmas Eve liturgy, the Holy Father will approach it and tap it three times with a silver hammer while singing "Open unto me the gates of justice." At the third blow the door will open and the pope will enter the church. In similar ceremonies on Christmas Day, cardinals will open the Holy Doors of the other patriarchal basilicas, except for the Basilica of St. Paul Outside the Walls, where the Holy Door will be opened on January 18, 2000, during an ecumenical celebration marking the start of the annual Week of Prayer for Christian Unity. *Mysterium Incarnationis* recommends that diocesan bishops similarly preside over solemn liturgies in their cathedrals on Christmas Day to mark the inauguration of the Jubilee.

The ritual of opening the Holy Door is an ancient one, with the earliest known reference to it dating from around the year 1437. In connection with the Jubilee of 1450, a Florentine merchant, Giovanni Rucellai, described the unwalling of the Holy Door of the Lateran basilica. Of that basilica's five doors, he wrote, one "is always walled up except during the Jubilee Year, when it is broken down at Christmas when the Jubilee commences. The devotion which the populace has for the bricks and mortar of which it is composed is such that at the unwalling, the fragments are immediately carried off by the crowd, and the foreigners take them home as so many sacred relics…. Out of devotion every one who gains the indulgence passes through that door, which is walled up again as soon as the Jubilee is ended."

The symbolism of the Holy Door is said by some to be linked to the ancient custom of "sanctuary" — seeking refuge in a church — and by others to the expulsion of Adam and Eve from Paradise and the reconciliation of penitents. Pope John Paul emphasized its Christological significance: "It evokes the passage from sin to grace which every Christian is called to accomplish. Jesus said: 'I am the door' (Jn 10:7), in order to make it clear that no one can come to the Father except through him."

He added: "To focus upon the door is to recall the responsibility of every believer to cross its threshold. To pass through that door means to confess that Jesus Christ is Lord; it is to strengthen faith in him in order to live the new life which he has given us. It is a decision which presumes freedom to choose and also the courage to leave something behind, in the knowledge that what is gained is divine life (cf. Mt 13.44-46). It is in this spirit that the Pope will be the first to pass through the Holy Door…. Crossing its threshold, he will show to the Church and to the world the Holy Gospel, the wellspring of life and hope for the coming third millennium."

During the year that follows, events of all kinds will take place in Rome as part of the celebration of the Great Jubilee. The aim is to focus attention on the spiritual meaning of the observance and to encourage participation by many different groups. The highlights will include: a study conference on the implementation of Vatican Council II (Feb. 25-27); a public "request for pardon" during an Ash Wednesday penitential procession led by the pope (Mar. 8); an ecumenical service for the "new martyrs" of the 20th century (May 7); a day of prayer for interreligious collaboration (June 11); an international Eucharistic Congress (June 18-25); the 15th World Youth Day (Aug. 19-20); an international Marian-Mariological congress (September 15-24); a general assembly of the world Synod of Bishops (Oct.); a day of Jewish-Christian dialogue (Oct. 3); the third Worldwide Encounter of the Holy Father with Families (Oct. 14-15); a congress on missions (Oct. 20-22); and a world congress of the laity (Nov. 24-26). There will be events for many special groups, from the sick and the elderly to athletes, entertainers, and the police.

The Holy Land also will be the site of many pilgrimages and other events. In the bull of indiction, Pope John Paul expresses the hope that the Great Jubilee will "serve to advance mutual dialogue when all of us together — Jews, Christians and Moslems — will exchange the greeting of peace in Jerusalem." The Pope himself is expected to go to the Holy Land, perhaps in connection with the Feast of the Annunciation, Mar. 25, when the Basilica of the Annunciation in Nazareth will be the site of a special liturgical celebration linked via satellite with celebrations in the Basilica of St. Mary Major in Rome and other major Marian shrines around the world. The celebration will emphasize the dignity of women in light of Mary's mission as Mother of Christ.

The Pilgrimage and the Jubilee

As many as 30 million pilgrims are expected to visit Rome during the Jubilee Year. Like much else connected with the observance, pilgrimage is an ancient custom with deep spiritual meaning. Pope John Paul in *Incarnationis Mysterium* likened it to "the situation of many who readily describes his life as a journey."

"Pilgrimages have always been a significant part of the life of the faithful, assuming different cultural forms in different ages," he wrote. "A pilgrimage evokes the believer's personal journey in the footsteps of the Redeemer: it is an exercise of practical asceticism, of repentance for human weaknesses, of constant vigilance over one's own frailty, of interior preparation for a change of heart. Through vigils, fasting and prayer, the pilgrim passes along the path of Christian perfection, striving to attain, with the support of God's grace, 'the state of the perfect man, to the measure and full maturity of Christ' (Eph 4.13)."

The Jubilee Indulgence

Pope John Paul calls the indulgence one of the "constitutive elements" of the Jubilee, and links it to the sacrament of Penance and conversion. "From the first centuries ... the Church has always been profoundly convinced that pardon, freely granted by God, implies in consequence a real change of life, the gradual elimination of evil within, a renewal in our way of living," he said in *Incarnationis Mysterium*.

But even pardoned sin has "enduring consequences," he noted, and these underline the need for purification. "It is precisely in this context that the indulgence becomes important.... With the indulgence, the repentant sinner receives a remission of the temporal punishment due for the sins already forgiven as regards the fault," he said.

Published at the same time as the bull of indiction was a document of the Apostolic Penitentiary setting out conditions for gaining the Jubilee Indulgence. Clearly, the aim is to make the indulgence as widely available as possible. Not only is the plenary indulgence, in keeping with long tradition, available to pilgrims to Rome, but it also can be gained by persons who perform prescribed acts of a spiritual and charitable nature in their own communities. The indulgence also can be applied "in suffrage" to the souls of the deceased.

To gain the indulgence, it is necessary to make a sacramental confession "during a suitable period of time," although people are encouraged to receive the sacrament not just once but frequently. Having made a sacramental confession, penitents can receive or apply the plenary indulgence as often as once a day (but no more often). They must participate in the Eucharist on the same day the prescribed works are performed; prayer for the intentions of the pope also is required.

Confessors are authorized to commute from the prescribed works and the required conditions in the case of persons "legitimately impeded" from carrying them out — for example, cloistered religious, the ill and infirm who cannot leave their homes. Such persons are asked at least to unite themselves spiritually with those who perform the prescribed work in the usual manner and to offer their prayers and sufferings to God.

For others, the Jubilee indulgence can be gained on the following conditions.

In Rome, by making a pilgrimage to one of the patriarchal basilicas (St. Peter's, the Lateran, St. Mary Major, St. Paul's), and there participating in Mass or some other liturgical celebration, or visiting one of the basilicas, individually or with a group, and spending time in Eucharistic adoration and prayer, ending with the Our Father, recitation of a creed, and prayer to the Blessed Virgin. The indulgence also can be gained, under the same conditions, at the Basilica of the Holy Cross in Jerusalem, the Basilica of St. Lawrence in Campo Verano, the Shrine of Our Lady of Divine Love, and the Catacombs.

In the Holy Land, under the same conditions, by visiting the Basilica of the Holy Sepulchre in Jerusalem, the Basilica of the Nativity in Bethlehem, or the Basilica of the Annunciation in Nazareth.

In other ecclesiastical territories (dioceses, etc.), by making a pilgrimage to the local cathedral or some other church or place designated by the ordinary or visiting it alone or in a group, under the same conditions as those prescribed for those in Rome.

In any place, by visiting persons who are "in need or difficulty" (the sick, the imprisoned, the elderly living alone, the handicapped, etc.) "as if making a pilgrimage to Christ present in them," and fulfilling the usual spiritual and sacramental conditions and saying the usual prayers. The plenary indulgence can be gained each time — though no more often than once a day — such a visit is made. It also can be gained through "actions which express in a practical and generous way the penitential spirit" of the Jubilee (examples given are abstaining for at least one whole day from smoking or alcohol, or fasting or abstaining from meat according to the usual rules), and giving a proportionate sum of money to the poor, making a "significant contribution" to religious or social works (especially those benefiting abandoned children, young people in trouble, the needy elderly, or the poor and needy abroad), devoting free time to community service, or "other similar forms of personal sacrifice."

Debt Reduction

As forgiveness of debts was an element of the Jubilee observance in ancient Israel, so Pope John Paul often has urged that wealthy nations and international financial institutions forgive or significantly reduce the international debt of poor countries in connection with the Great Jubilee. He returned to this subject in *Incarnationis Mysterium*, observing that the debt of some countries is "so huge that repayment is practically impossible."

"It is clear ... that there can be no real progress without effective cooperation between the peoples of every language, race, nationality and religion," he wrote. "The abuses of power which result in some dominating others must stop: such abuses are sinful and unjust. Whoever is concerned to accumulate treasure only on earth (cf. Mt 6:19) 'is not rich in the sight of God' (Lk 12:21)."

Calling for "a new culture of international solidarity and cooperation" based on an economic model according to which all benefit, the pope said: "There should be no more postponement of the time when the poor Lazarus can sit beside the rich man to share the same banquet and be forced no more to feed on the scraps that fall from the table (cf. Lk. 16.19-31). Extreme poverty is a source of violence, bitterness and scandal; and to eradicate it is to do the work of justice and therefore the work of peace."

All Need to Repent

Pope John Paul repeatedly has emphasized that the Great Jubilee of the Year 2000 is a time of celebration — celebration of the Incarnation and of humankind's redemption by Jesus Christ. But he also has pointed out that, for followers of Christ, to celebrate redemption from sin involves repentance. *Incarnationis Mysterium* spoke of the need for a corporate "purification of memory ... an act of courage and humility in recognizing the wrongs done by those whose who have borne or bear the name of Christian."

The Church's holiness is a fact, John Paul said, manifest not only in the saints and blessed — although certainly in them — but also in the lives of countless unknown Christians which testify that "perfection is possible." In a special way he singled out the martyrs — including the new martyrs of the 20th century — for their testimony to faith.

"This century now drawing to a close has known very many martyrs, especially because of Nazism, Communism, and racial or tribal conflicts," he said. "People from every sector of society have suffered for their faith.... From the psychological point of view, martyrdom is the most eloquent proof of the truth of the faith, for faith can give a human face even to the most violent of deaths and show its beauty even in the midst of the most atrocious persecutions."

Along with the evidence of holiness, however, the pope also has made it a point to acknowledge histori-cal "counter-testimony"— the errors and faults of Christians past and present. "As the Successor of Peter," he said in the bull of indiction, "I ask that in this year of mercy the Church, strong in the holiness which she receives from her Lord, should kneel before God and implore forgiveness for the past and present sins of her sons and daughters."

Earlier, in *Tertio Millennio Adveniente*, he spelled out some of the varieties of wrongdoing he had in mind. These include offenses against Christian unity, "intolerance and even the use of violence in the service of truth," and the contributions made by contemporary Christians to such "evils of our day" as religious indifference, confusion about fundamental matters like respect for human life and the family, secularism and ethical relativism, weakened faith and a "crisis of obedience vis-à-vis the Church's Magisterium," acquiescence in human rights violations by totalitarian regimes, failure to know and practice the Church's social doctrine, and inadequate "reception" of Vatican Council II.

Even so, Pope John Paul's approach to the Great Jubilee of the Year 2000 is profoundly optimistic. He sees this as being, in God's providential plan, an immensely hopeful moment for the Church and the world — an opportunity for a deeper commitment to the realization of God's redemptive will accomplished in and through Jesus Christ. Always, in speaking of the Jubilee, he holds up the Blessed Virgin as model. In *Incarnationis Mysterium* he wrote: "Called to be the Mother of God, from the day of the virginal conception Mary lived the fullness of her motherhood, crowning it on Calvary at the foot of the Cross. There, by the wondrous gift of Christ, she also became the Mother of the Church, and showed to everyone the way that leads to the Son.... May she deign to intercede intensely for the Christian people, so that abundant grace and mercy may be theirs, as they rejoice at the 2,000 years since the birth of their Savior."

This Jubilee Pledge for Charity, Justice and Peace is being offered to individuals, families and parishes as a sign of commitment in preparation for the Millennium:

Jubilee Pledge for Charity, Justice and Peace
— A Catholic Commitment for the New Millennium

This pledge is being promoted by a variety of U.S. Catholic Conference offices and other organizations as a practical response to the Holy Father's designation of 1999 as "the year of charity."
The Jubilee of our Lord's birth calls us "to bring glad tidings to the poor, to proclaim liberty to captives, recovery of sight to the blind, and release to prisoners" (Lk. 4:18).
As disciples of Jesus in the new Millennium, I/we pledge to:
Pray regularly for greater justice and peace.
Learn more about Catholic social teaching and its call to protect human life, stand with the poor, and care for creation.
Reach across boundaries of religion, race, ethnicity, gender, and disabling conditions.
Live justly in family life, school, work, the marketplace, and the political arena.
Serve those who are poor and vulnerable, sharing more time and talent.
Give more generously to those in need at home and abroad.
Advocate public policies that protect human life, promote human dignity, preserve God's creation, and build peace.
Encourage others to work for greater charity, justice, and peace.

(Signature)_____

Love for others, and in the first place love for the poor, in whom the Church sees Christ himself, is made concrete in the promotion of justice.
Pope John Paul II, *Centesimus Annus*, 1991

Papal Anniversary — Archbishop Agostino Cacciavillan, papal nuncio to the U.S., celebrated the 20th anniversary of the Holy Father's pontificate at an Oct.18 Mass attended by a large congregation at the national Shrine of the Immaculate Conception in Washington. He called his pontificate "a great gift from the Holy Spirit."

Time for Trust — The time has come for Christians and Jews to "finally and definitively" put aside feelings of mistrust and resentment toward each other, said Cardinal Edward I. Cassidy, president of the Pontifical Council for Promoting Christian Unity, in a keynote address during the Fifth Biennial Conference on Christianity and the Holocaust. "Christians and Jews have at last a new opportunity of contributing together to the well-being of the societies of which we are both members and, indeed, to the world in which we live.... We are no longer simply called to reconciliation but to genuine partnership." The conference was held Oct. 18 and 19 in Plainsboro, N.J.

Veto, Again — Adamant in his pro-abortion stance, President Clinton vetoed again Oct. 15 a measure that would have outlawed partial birth abortions.

Killing Condemned — The murder Oct. 23 of New York Dr. Barnett Slepian, who performed abortions, was condemned as barbaric by Bishop Henry J. Mansell of Buffalo. He said in a statement that such an act "is totally contradictory to the values and ideals of people truly interested in life, and certainly to the pro-life movement."

Maryknoll at U.N. — The United Nations granted special consultative status to the Maryknoll Fathers and Brothers and the Maryknoll Sisters. The status gives Maryknoll special opportunities and responsibilities with the U.N., especially with the Economic and Social Council, its regional commissions and ad hoc committees. Father John McAuley said: "Maryknoll has the grass-roots experience to contribute to the ongoing initiatives of the U.N."

Honored — Honored during the month were:
• Cardinal Vinko Puljic of Sarajevo, with the 1998 Notre Dame Award for his ecumenical efforts to oppose ethnic and religious division in Bosnia-Herzegovina, Oct. 7;
• Medical Missionary of Mary Sister Bernadette Kenny, with the Lumen Christi Award of the Catholic Church Extension Society, for bringing "health care and hope" to some of the people of Appalachia for 18 years, Oct. 12;
• Maryknoll Father Roy Bourgeois, with the 1998 Adela Dwyer/ St. Thomas of Villanova Peace Award of Villanova University for eight years of effort to close the School of the Americas, Oct. 13;
• Cardinal Jean-Marie Lustiger and Rabbi Rene-Samuel Sirat, former chief rabbi of France, with the *Nostra Aetate* Award of the Center for Christian-Jewish Understanding at Sacred Heart University, Fairfield, Conn., for work in Christian-Jewish relations, Oct. 20;
• Former Senate Majority Leader George Mitchell, with the Robert F. Drinan, S.J., Public Service Award of Georgetown University's Law School, for involvement in negotiating the Good Friday peace accord in Northern Ireland, Oct. 23;
• Biblical scholar Father Raymond Brown, S.S., with the Washington Theological Union's Distinguished Service Award, posthumously, Oct. 29.

Promotion But Not Ordination of Women — In two separate documents released Oct. 13, committees of the national Conference of Catholic Bishops called for advancing the cause of women in the Church but explained why that does not include their ordination to the priesthood. "From Words to Deeds: Continuing Reflections on the Role of Women in the Church," was the work of the Committee on Women in Society and the Church. It deals with what has been done and remains to be done in three areas:
• appreciating and incorporating the gifts of women in the Church;
• appointing women to Church leadership positions;
• promoting collaboration between men and women in the Church.

The second document, from the Committee on Doctrine, is entitled "Ten Frequently Asked Questions about the Reservation of Priestly Ordination to Men." It says: "The Church has no authority to confer priestly ordination on women," and that this is a teaching "to be held definitively by all the faithful as belonging to the deposit of faith."

INTERNATIONAL

Catholic Truth Society — The British publisher of the famous *Penny Catechism* celebrated its 100th anniversary early in the month.

ETA Ceasefire — The bishops of the three Basque provinces and the neighboring region of Navarre expressed hope that a temporary ETA ceasefire might become permanent and lead to a peaceful political settlement with the Spanish government

Bethlehem University Anniversary — Alumni, faculty members and students participated in ceremonies Oct. 4 to 11 commemorating the 25th anniversary of the university. Founded by Pope Paul VI and under the administration of the De La Salle Brothers of the Christian Schools, the institution grew from a three-classroom, six-instructor staff and a student body of 100 to university status with six academic departments and a student body of 2,050.

Islamic Bill Opposed — The Pakistani bishops' national Commission on Justice and Peace denounced a bill that would Islamize the nation's constitution. In a statement issued Oct. 10, the commission said the proposed constitutional amendment was "bound to cause a concentration of power opposite to the principles of democratic governance." It would make the Koran, the Islamic holy book, and the *Sunna*, Islamic tradition, the supreme law of the land, and would increase the government's power to enforce harsh Islamic law.

Anti-Christian Violence in India — More than 4,000 persons took part in street demonstrations in New Delhi Oct. 3 to protest against anti-Christian attacks in the nation. More than 40 such attacks, including the rape of four nuns, took place in recent months. Archbishop Alan de Lastic of Delhi said Christians were "beginning to feel threatened for the first time since India's independence in 1947."

Nuncio Backs Activists — Catholic activists for land reform in Honduras had the support of the apostolic nuncio, Archbishop Luigi Conti. He said he "fully supported" several Jesuit priests and other church activists accused of stirring up indigenous communities. "They're being accused of international terrorism; but, if what they are doing in support of the indigenous people is terrorism, then I say it's welcome here," he told Catholic News Service in an interview Oct. 18. The accusations came after activists seized the famous Mayan ruins at Copan and began a hunger strike at two embassies in Tegucigalpa. "Some people say the Jesuits are behind the protests, but that's without foundation," said the nuncio; "it's completely false. And it's an insult to the indigenous, treating them as it they were children who have to be led around by the hand."

Chinese Government Not Sincere — Despite China's signing of an international human rights covenant and its serving as host to a meeting on human rights, Christians in mainland China doubted the government's sincerity about religious freedom. Vice Premier Oian Oichen hailed what he called the extensive rights and freedoms enjoyed in China at the opening Oct. 20 of the International Symposium on "World Human Rights Toward the 21st Century," attended by some 100 academics and government officials from 17 countries. The two-day symposium in Beijing was run by the quasi-official China Society for Human Rights Studies and the U.N. Association of China to mark the 50th anniversary of the Universal Declaration on Human Rights. On the day the meeting opened, however, an underground priest in eastern China said Beijing's signing of the International Covenant on Civil and Political Rights Oct. 5 was a perfunctory response to world pressure. But signing the covenant, he said, was "better than not signing it since, at least, the government might be more careful about violating what it had promised." So stated a report by UCA News, an Asian church agency based in Thailand. An underground Catholic in northern China who spoke to UCA News soon after Beijing signed the covenant was less hopeful, saying he felt pessimistic about the status of religious freedom in the country. "'Even if the officials do not crack down on us for religious reasons, they can do so with many other excuses" about our violations of the law, he said.

Status of Jerusalem — This was the subject of an address delivered by Archbishop Jean-Louis Tauran Oct. 25 at a meeting of representatives of bishops' conferences in Jerusalem. He said: "In at least three respects, Jerusalem differs from most other places: the city is holy to the adherents of three religions, it is the subject of conflicting claims by two peoples, and its population is heterogeneous to a considerable degree.... Looking to Jerusalem, the Holy See continues to ask that it be protected by a special internationally guaranteed statute ... In the Holy See's view:

• "The historical and material characteristics of the city, as well as its religious and cultural characteristics, must be preserved; and perhaps today it is necessary to speak of restoring and safeguarding those still existing.

• "There must be equality of rights and treatment for those belonging to the communities of the three religions found in the city, in the context of the freedom of spiritual, cultural, civic and economic activities.

• "The holy places situated in the city must be preserved, and the rights of freedom of religion and worship, and of access, for residents and pilgrims alike, whether from the Holy Land itself or from other parts of the world, must be safeguarded."

Vatican's U.N. Concerns — These were among the subjects of statements to U.N. agencies during the month:

• Sanctions: That "appropriate and effective structures be found within the United Nations to alleviate the adverse impact of sanctions on innocent and vulnerable citizens."

• Women: The Holy See remains concerned about the needs of women identified at the 1995 Beijing Conference on Women and intends to monitor closely preparations for the relevant review scheduled to take place in the year 2000.

• Nuclear Arms: "The modernization programs of those who already have nuclear weapons, combined with the acquiring of nuclear weapons by other states, and research now going on in still others, plunge the world into more danger than existed even during the Cold War."

• Child Soldiers: "Now is the moment to tell those who commit the abomination of sending children into combat that they commit a serious crime against the fundamental rights of the child, and that the international community cannot and will not tolerate such crimes."

Dialogue for Austria — About 300 persons — bishops, priests, religious, lay persons — from throughout the country took part in the Dialogue for Austria which ended toward the end of the month. Delegates supported a variety of proposals including: admitting married men to the Latin-rite priesthood, ordaining women to the diaconate, allowing lay persons a voice in the appointment of bishops, better communications between lay persons and priests and between bishops and Vatican agencies, and substantial changes in moral norms regarding marriage and other matters. Pope John Paul told Austrian bishops during their *ad limina* visit to the Vatican that such proposals "have been made in your country and have had a receptive audience beyond its borders.... One cannot help being saddened at the erroneous conceptions of faith and morality, as well as certain matters of church discipline."

Youth Meetings — Thousands of youths attended two international youth meetings during the month in Chile.

• More than 700 youth ministers from 22 countries took part Oct. 3 to 10 in the Second Latin American Youth Congress on the theme, "Young People with Christ Transforming Latin America with Justice and Hope." Congress proposals for youth ministry in Latin America called for more educational opportunities for young people; encouragement of youths to be more critical of their surroundings; adoption of a "preferential option for the poor and the youth"; promotion of family values; space for the spiritual side of youth ministry; greater participation of youths in political and social organizations; and strengthening the role of young persons within the Church.

• Two hundred thousand youths attended Oct. 11 the opening Mass of a five-day Continental Youth and Young Adult Gathering. Cardinal Angelo Sodano, Pope John Paul's representative to the gathering, called on the youths to give shape to their "thirst for truth, peace and freedom ... and enthusiasm for living, and for opening new horizons for the Church and for the Americas.... You must assume the challenge of living with Christ in your spirit."

NOVEMBER 1998

VATICAN

Hurricane Aid — Pope John Paul sent a message of condolence Nov. 3 to victims of Hurricane Mitch in Honduras, saying he wanted to give them "a message of encouragement, solidarity and closeness, beseeching the Lord to give them the strength and hope necessary to face this dramatic moment" of tragedy and need. The storm took a toll of perhaps 6,000 lives and millions of dollars in property damage. Similar messages along with emergency relief supplies were sent to the stricken Central American nation from many quarters.

Ambassador to U.S. Reassigned — Archbishop Agostino Cacciavillan, papal nuncio to the United States since June 13, 1990, was reassigned Nov. 5 to be president of the Administration of the Patrimony of the Holy See.

Attend to the Family — "Among the primary missions of the ecclesial community is attention to the family," the pope told visiting Bulgarian bishops Nov. 7. "Marriage is the institution at the base of society and the Church. It is important that younger generations discover day there is in constructing a durable relation with a person.... It is indispensable that the education of children be founded on the teaching of a hierarchy of truly authentic values and not be dictated by trends or by purely personal interest."

Two days later, at a meeting with Italian bishops, the pope underlined his support of the family and warned about attacks on the family "on the cultural, political, legislative and administrative levels." He said the weakness of government policy on the family in Italy left families "too often not economically or socially supported in an adequate manner."

Moratorium Proposals — In remarks made Nov. 6, the pope said: "I am pleased that the proposal for reducing the foreign debt of the poorest countries and for a moratorium on executions, at least for the Jubilee Year, is supported by people who hold high office and who can therefore help ensure that these proposals are welcomed."

Bioethic Concern — The discovery of a medical technique using primordial human cells to repair damaged organs and tissues drew a cautionary response from Bishop Elio Sgreccia, vice president of the Pontifical Academy for Life and an expert on bioethics. In an interview Nov. 10, he said the technique raises serious moral considerations about the protection of the rights of human embryos and fetuses, as well as morally objectionable in-vitro fertilization for creating human embryos.

Memorial Mass — Pope John Paul celebrated his annual memorial Mass Nov. 10 for the cardinals and bishops who died during the past year.

Pope Can't Dissolve Valid Marriage —A front-page article in the Nov. 11 edition of *L'Osservatore Romano* said the bond of the sacrament of matrimony is so strong and so holy that not even the pope can dissolve a valid and consummated marriage between baptized Catholics. Some theologians, motivated by a desire to ease suffering in irregular marital situations, have said that "new pastoral circumstances would legitimate the extension" of papal powers to include dissolving Catholic marriages. "The Church," however, "has reached the certainty and has repeatedly affirmed that its power has its impassable limit at a marriage concluded and consummated, which is, therefore, intrinsically and extrinsically indissoluble." The Church's position is "founded on Sacred Scripture and has been offered many times explicitly and formally by the magisterium. Therefore, ... it must be accepted and firmly held." Any extension of papal power would betray the Church's firm belief that Christian marriage is indissoluble by divine law. "The limit placed by divine design even on the power of the supreme pontiff is, in fact, an expression of the greatness of the mystery of matrimony."

Charity Extends Faith — Pope John Paul urged the Pontifical Council *"Cor Unum,"* the Vatican's coordinating agency for charitable activities, to emphasize that charity is an extension of faith and to "intensify our generosity toward those in need." Two days after the close of its Nov. 11 to 14 meeting, the council announced its agencies had raised $800,000 in 1998 for disaster relief in more than 30 countries in Africa, Asia and Latin America, as well as for flood victims in southern Italy. Another $450,000 was collected for projects for "human and Christian promotion" in about 20 counties.

Missionary Concern — The past and future of missionary activity by members of religious orders were among topics discussed during the plenary meeting of the Congregation for the Evangelization of Peoples Nov. 17 to 20. Archbishop Marcello Zago, secretary of the congregation, said religious orders founded for the purpose of missionary work were insisting that the main focus of their members' energies were on evangelizing non-Christians.

Australian Bishops and Vatican Officials — The bishops of Australia and the heads of major Vatican departments met in joint discussions Nov. 17 to 20 on a variety of subjects, including: social teaching and practice; internal church policies; abortion; the breakup of marriage; the roles and missions of bishops, priests and religious; liturgy and the sacraments, with special focus on the sacrament of penance; evangelization and the role of lay persons in the Church. Cardinal Edward B. Clancy of Sydney told *Catholic News Service* Nov. 21 the meeting emphasized "the necessity to preach the doctrine of the Church in all its authenticity and its purity, without any distortion by trends and preferences and expectations of our secular society."

Preparation for 2000 — The final year of preparation for Holy Year 2000 should be a time for a pilgrimage of charity, of sharing with the poor and of dialogue with all people, said Pope John Paul Nov. 29, the first Sunday of Advent and the beginning of the new church year.

General Audience Topics:

• Just as Jesus' body was glorified in the Resurrection, so too will our bodies be glorified when they are raised from the dead (Nov. 4).
• Signs of hope at the end of this century include advances in science, medicine and technology, as well as a sense of responsibility for the environment and concern for peace and justice (Nov. 18).

• Signs of hope found in the Church are connected with the outpouring of the Holy Spirit which the Church experienced at the Second Vatican Council (Nov. 25).

Jubilee 2000 Proclaimed

As he announced the beginning of the third year of preparation for Jubilee 2000, Pope John Paul presented Nov. 29 the Bull of Indiction formally proclaiming the event. In the bull, entitled *Incarnationis Mysterium* ("Mystery of the Incarnation"), the Holy Father said:

"I ... decree that the Great Jubilee of the Year 2000 will begin on Christmas Eve 1999 with the opening of the holy door of St. Peter's Basilica in the Vatican, a few hours before the inaugural celebration planned for Jerusalem and Bethlehem, and the opening of the holy door in each of the other Patriarchal Basilicas of Rome. At St. Paul's Basilica, the holy door will be opened on Tuesday, 18 January, when the Week of Prayer for Christian Unity begins, as a way of emphasizing the distinctive ecumenical character of this Jubilee.

"I also decree that in the particular churches the Jubilee will begin on the most holy day of the Nativity of the Lord Jesus, with a solemn Eucharistic Liturgy presided over by the diocesan bishop in the cathedral."

Accompanying the bull were a description and salient conditions of the Jubilee Indulgence, which is one of the distinctive signs of the celebration.

Special Synod of Bishops

A Special Synod for Oceania was held from November 12 to December 12, 1998, with the theme "Jesus Christ and the Peoples of Oceania: Walking His Way, Telling His Truth, Living His Life." (For details, see Special Report.)

NATIONAL

Aid for Mitch Victims — Catholic Relief Services and on-site diocesan agencies were among organizations seeking and providing emergency aid for victims of Hurricane Mitch which devastated El Salvador, Guatemala, Honduras and Nicaragua. Thousands of people and millions in damage were reported in perhaps the worst combination of winds and rain in Central American history.

Don't Blend In — Christians should not blend in with everything else," Bishop J. Terry Steib of Memphis told a gathering of black Catholics in Philadelphia Nov. 5. Rather, Christians should affect society "positively, just as seasoning brings out the best flavor in food." But, if seasoning has flavor, it has no value.... If Christians make no effort to have an effect on the world around them, they are of little value to God. If we are too much like the world, we are worthless."

Basilica and Shrine — St. Joseph's Church in Webster, Mass., the oldest Polish-American church in New England, entered the second month of its history as a minor basilica. The church was founded in no 1887.

The Shrine of the Little Flower in the Church of St. Thérèse in Royal Oak, Mich., was declared a national shrine by the bishops' Administrative Board.

Helping People — While announcing the "Helping People Help Themselves" theme of the 1998 Catholic Campaign for Human Development, Bishop Ricardo Ramirez of Las Cruces, N.M., reported that the 1997 campaign brought in a record $14 million. One-fourth of the collection remained in the dioceses of origin. The national share funded 300 projects in 46 states, the District of Columbia, Puerto Rico and the U.S. Virgin Islands.

In another development, the Catholic Church Extension Society reported it distributed an unprecedented $15 million to the poorest 75 U.S. dioceses in fiscal year 1997-98.

Catholic University President — Vincentian Father David O'Connell, 43, was inaugurated as the new president of The Catholic University of America Nov. 19. He said in an address during ceremonies that he would work to uphold and strengthen the university's Catholic identity as it looks toward the third millennium. "Our greatest strength is our Catholic identity, for it gives form and substance, shape and direction to all that we do as a university," he told an assembly of 2,500 people.

Death Video by Kevorkian — The national Catholic Association for Communicators sharply questioned the decision of CBS's "60 Minutes" to air videotape of Dr. Jack Kevorkian killing a terminally ill man by lethal injection. "What we had was a cold, calculated decision to broadcast a real murder on national television," said Unda-USA President Frank Morock. It was estimated that 22 million people viewed the show Nov. 22. Morock said: "Unda-USA questions three aspects of the broadcast segment: its conscious decision to air the actual murder; its pre-broadcast promotion and hype of the segment; and its decision not to turn the tape over to legal authorities prior to the broadcast if it believed the crime of murder was committed." CBS News "compromised its journalistic integrity by allowing itself to be used to further the philosophy of Mr. Kevorkian." ... The program could have raised the issue and had a thorough discussion on it, consistent with its own internal journalistic standards, without the need for showing the actual murder."

School of the Americas — More than 2,300 people took part Nov. 22 in a protest demonstration against continuing operation of the U.S. Army School of the Americas at Fort Benning, Ga. Some graduates of the school for the training of Latin American soldiers had been implicated in violations of human rights in their various countries.

Health Plan for Suicide — The director of the Oregon Catholic Conference charged Nov. 23 that state health officials exceeded their authority when they made doctor-assisted suicide a procedure covered by the state's health plan for the poor. Robert Castagna, director, asked health plan administrators to withhold funds for the procedure. "The Oregon Catholic Conference asserts that the commission's February 1998 decision to add physician-assisted suicide under the euphemism of 'physician aid in dying' to the prioritized list of health services of the Oregon Health Plan exceeded the statutory authority of the agency and is invalid," Castagna said through an aide. Despite his objections, the state Office of Medical Assistance Programs appeared ready to put the health plan decision into effect by allocating money for that purpose.

Funding for Social Change — Partners for the Common Good 2000 announced that its fund to promote economic justice and social change through member religious institutions had surpassed $8.5 million. Established in 1994 by the Christian Brothers Investment Service, Partners for the Common Good 2000 had attracted investments ranging from $25,000 to a half million dollars from 99 religious investors nationwide — 68 congregations of sisters, 19 congregations of brothers and priests, eight Catholic health care systems, three Protestant denominations and Christian Brothers Investment Service. "Thanks to the generous investments of the religious community, we have been able to support women micro-entrepreneurs, low-income housing, minority-owned businesses, low-income credit unions, and other projects that advance the common good," said Dominican Sister Carol Costen, head of the fund.

Groups for Spiritual Support — Homosexual persons need a support group that encourages them to live "chaste lives in a spiritual way," said the founder and director of the Courage ministry for homosexual men and women. Oblate Father John F. Harvey told attendants at a two-day meeting in New York: "You need more than a relationship with a confessor or therapist. You need a spiritual support group to learn how to be chaste in a spiritual way — what the Gospels describe as 'purity of one's heart.' "

School Voucher Program — The U.S. Supreme Court decided Nov. 9 not to review the constitutionality of a Milwaukee school voucher program.

In Philadelphia, Cardinal Anthony J. Bevilacqua expressed disappointment over the Pennsylvania Legislature's failure to act on proposed school-choice legislation. "I am distressed that our lawmakers have failed to provide children and their parents with the fundamental right to freely choose their education," he said.

Critical Votes — On two critical issues on state ballots, voters in Michigan turned down an assisted-suicide proposal, and in Alaska and Hawaii rejected a move to legalize same-sex marriages.

Partial-Birth Abortion Rulings — U.S. District Judge Donald Graham ruled Nov. 24 in Miami against the constitutionality of Florida's ban on partial-birth abortion. Judges in nine states had already ruled against such bans, and enforcement of bans had already been halted in nine other states.

Bishops' Meeting

About 250 bishops attended the annual meeting of the national Conference of Catholic Bishops and the U.S. Catholic Conference Nov. 16 to19 in Washington. They approved a variety of items, including the following: a document challenging Catholics to improve application of the Church's social teaching in public life; $400,000 for emergency aid to hurricane-stricken areas of Central America, the Dominican Republic and Haiti; a statement on moral principles involved in the crisis in Iraq; revised guidelines for diocesan vocations offices; a 12-point statement of principles relating to the treatment of persons with disabilities; five proposed canon-law decrees regarding clerical garb, priests' councils, registration of the baptism of an adopted child; engagements and preparations for marriage; a pastoral reflection of the obligations of lay persons in the world at the turn of the millennium; authorization for a 1999 budget of $46.8 million; two Spanish-language liturgical texts for funeral rites.

The bishops also approved a rule under which each province of bishops can decide to transfer observance of the solemnity of the Ascension from Thursday to the Seventh Sunday of Easter.

Among elections of conference officers were those of Bishops Joseph A. Fiorenza and Wilton D. Gregory to three-year terms as president and vice president, respectively.

INTERNATIONAL

Rosary Day — Thousands of Mexicans gathered to pray the Rosary for world peace in 8,000 sites across the country Oct. 31, according to a delayed report. Joining them in prayer were tens of thousands of other people throughout the world in celebration of the Day of the Rosary.

Book Could Mislead — A recently published book by a retired Australian bishop might mislead readers because of its ambiguity regarding certain church issues, said the Central Commission of the nation's bishops' conference. "From a strictly doctrinal point of view, it cannot be accused of explicitly deviating from any of the teachings of the Church…. It is, however, ambiguous on a number of (unstated) issues and runs the risk of misleading its readers. For this reason, it is not a book we can recommend." The book, entitled *The Love That Dares To Question: A Bishop Challenges His Church,"* was written by 71-year-old Bishop John Heaps.

Rwandan Tribunal — The Vatican called Nov. 3 for "more efficiency and more speed" in the work of the International Tribunal set up to try Rwandans responsible for the 1994 genocide in their country and surrounding areas. Archbishop Renato R. Martino told a plenary session of the U.N. General Assembly that the tribunal's role was "important and irreplaceable…. Any delay leading to a culture of impunity might seriously and adversely affect the healing process, and could become the source of further vengeance and violence," he said.

Muslim Dialogue — Muslim leaders throughout the world should follow the Vatican's lead and create a dialogue structure to conduct talks with Christians and Jews, said Abdelouhab Maalmi, Moroccan ambassador to the Holy See, Nov. 5. He said that coordinating Islamic positions for interfaith dialogue would help to ensure that no religion would become a "source of intolerance or a pretext for violence…. In our opinion, if dialogue is to be effective, we must look at how the Vatican has formulated a doctrine of dialogue and official structures charged with putting it into action….On the Muslim side, there should be a reference directory elaborated at the level of the Organization of Islamic Congress, and an agency of the same organization entrusted with following, proposing and coordinating the various dialogue initiatives between Islam and the other monotheistic religions." The ambassador also said: "The Muslim world … expects from the Holy See firm and clear positions against the systematic 'Judaization' of the Holy City, which is occurring to the detriment of the Christian and Muslim religions."

Support for Wye Memorandum — The Vatican nuncio to the United Nations, Archbishop Renato R. Martino, appealed to the international community to support implementation of the Wye agreement between Israelis and Palestinians despite acts of extremists. Archbishop Martino said the Wye Memorandum, named for the Wye Plantation in Maryland where the agreement was negotiated, gave hope of wiping out some of the injustices suffered by Palestinians through Israel's anti-terrorism measures.

Speaking a week after two Palestinians carried out a bombing that killed themselves and injured 24 others in Jerusalem, the nuncio acknowledged "the difficulties posed by extremists seeking to destroy the prospects for peace and stability." But he said retaliatory border closings damaged both the Palestinian economy and their freedom of worship, and served "only to exacerbate the tensions already present.... It is the sincere wish of the Holy See that the seeds of a solution will not be crushed by extremism or terrorism." He expressed hope that "security for the citizens of Israel" and respect for the rights of the Palestinians, including their "right to a homeland," would be achieved. He warned that "the security of the people of Israel would be guaranteed only when the rights of the Palestinians to freedom of worship and access to education, medical care and employment are assured."

Archbishop Martino made his comments Nov. 9 in a statement to the U.N. General Assembly committee reviewing operations of the U.N. Relief and Works Agency for Palestine Refugees in the Near East. He also said the Vatican, operating through the Pontifical Mission for Palestine and other agencies, had been working for nearly 50 years in the same area with the U.N. agency to assist needy Palestinians "on the basis of need, not creed."

Religious Freedom Threatened — Representatives of 54 governments called for steps to counter growing threats to religious freedom and cautioned against granting privileges to traditional religious communities at cost to new groups. Msgr. Werner Freistetter, a Vatican delegate to the Warsaw meeting, said states needed to "get accustomed" to a current increase in religious groups and ensure the "broadest possible religious freedom" without allowing its misuse. A report for the 54-nation Organization on Security and Cooperation in Europe said official investigations into minority faiths had been used to "incite discrimination." It also said registration laws were being used to restrict religious groups and even arrest their members. Offending states included Macedonia, post-communist Russia and Uzbekistan. National parliaments in France, Belgium and Germany had launched investigations into minority groups, making them targets of public backlash. The report was issued at the close of an Oct. 26-to-Nov. 6 meeting on humanitarian issues outlined in the 1975 Helsinki Final Act and later documents of the Organization on Security and Cooperation in Europe. Member states of the organization include the United States and Canada.

Mass and Aid for Mitch Victims — A public memorial Mass Nov. 16 at Ottawa's Notre Dame Cathedral for victims of Hurricane Mitch was attended by the ambassadors of five Central American nations. In a homily delivered during the Mass, Archbishop Marcel Gervais of Ottawa announced that an aid campaign launched by the Canadian Catholic Organization for Development and Peace had raised an aid fund of two million dollars.

Food for North Korea — Buddhist, Catholic and Protestant groups contributed more than half of all donations received from nongovernmental sources to aid famine-stricken North Koreans, reported Kim Seung-kuen, an official of the Korea national Red Cross. The report came from UCA News, a church news agency based in Thailand.

New Office — Human Life International extended its outreach to 89 countries Nov. 16 with the dedication of a new office at Piazzale Gregorio VII 22, Rome. "The Rome office will become an extension of our main office in Front Royal, Va., and it will become the location most enabling us to powerfully influence the Church throughout the world in the most direct and effective way possible," said Redemptorist Father Richard Welch, president of the organization.

Siberian Church Registration — Russia's Siberian Catholics cleared an important bureaucratic hurdle by obtaining registration as a religious organization with the federal government, reported Bishop Joseph Werth, apostolic administrator of Siberia. "It is a vital step for us," he said in a Nov. 24 interview from Novosibirsk, the capital of Siberia. Registration of the Siberian Apostolic Administration, which covers seven time zones, is required by a controversial law on religion enacted in 1998 over the objections of the Holy See and the United States. Every religious organization in Russia must register first on a national level and then parish by parish.

Basic Christian Communities — The bishops of Argentina established norms for basic Christian communities late in the month, reminding them that they must be united with the Church and "become the family of God, a community that lives faith, hope and charity in visible union with the bishops." They "must not be isolated organizations, but ones that are respectful of the pastoral guidelines designed by the local bishop and in coordination with him on behalf of the poor."

The diocese should do an inventory of all church buildings, sell some and invest the proceeds in human resources and social and spiritual programs.

Tragic Sudan

"This is probably the most tragic experience I have had in all of my visits to Africa.... It is tragic that people who are already impoverished are reduced to brutal conditions (and) ... are forced to live in this dehumanizing condition." So stated Bishop John H. Ricard about his visit Nov. 4 at a Catholic Relief Services supplementary feeding center in Mapourdit, Sudan. He witnessed the poverty, hunger to the point of famine, and civil-war devastation of people suffering the extremes of human endurance with no end in sight. One of the primary causes of the disastrous state of the nation, especially the southern part, was and continues to be the 40-year civil war between the Muslim-controlled government of the northern part of the country and the Christian-animist region of the south.

Two months before Bishop Ricard's visit, the Sudanese bishops' conference issued a statement in which they decried the "ethnic cleansing." They said: "We noted with the greatest concern the devastating consequences of the ongoing civil war on civilian population and property, as represented by the continuing loss of innocent lives and destruction of property." They expressed concern also about the war-connected violation of human rights, including "extrajudicial punishment, disappearances, slavery and slavery-related practices, tortures, and restrictions on freedom of worship and expression."

DECEMBER 1998

VATICAN

No Holocaust Secrets — Responding to renewed criticism of its archival secrecy, the Holy See said there was "nothing to add" to published documents on the Vatican and the Holocaust. "Exhaustive scrutiny of documents from the Vatican Archives allows the affirmation that there is nothing — I repeat: nothing — to add to that which is already published," spokesman Joaquin Navarro-Valls said in a Dec. 3 statement. "Whoever makes insinuations contrary to those that the Holy See has already reaffirmed many times must justify them with concrete proof," he wrote. "This, naturally, has never happened."

New Nuncio to U.S. — Pope John Paul II appointed Colombian Archbishop Gabriel Montalvo, president since 1993 of the Pontifical Ecclesiastical Academy, to succeed Archbishop Agostino Cacciavillan as the Holy See's nuncio to the United States. The appointment was announced Dec. 7.

Traditional Visit — On the feast of the Immaculate Conception, Dec. 8, the pope made a traditional visit to Rome's Piazza di Spagna to pray at the base of a monument erected there to commemorate the proclamation of the dogma by Pope Pius IX.

Embryo Cloning — Cloning human embryos to produce cells for the therapeutic treatment of other people boils down to "producing human beings for sacrifice.... The existence of the cloned embryo will be deliberately crushed, and that is simply monstrous," said Franciscan Father Gino Concetti, writing in the Dec. 11 edition of *L'Osservatore Romano.* He and Bishop Elio Sgreccia, vice president of the Pontifical Academy for Life, harshly criticized the recommendation of a British government advisory board to permit the cloning of embryos so their cells could be used to generate tissues and organs for use by other patients. "The therapeutic aim of the operation would succeed by sacrificing the embryo cloned in the laboratory," Father Concetti wrote. That the embryo is a human being is clear from the fact that, if it were implanted in a woman's womb, it could develop into an infant. He quoted another critic of the proposal who called the process "technological cannibalism."

Vatican-Croatian Agreement — Pope John Paul told a delegation of Croatian diplomats Dec. 15 that their government and the Holy See had reached an agreement a day earlier on the legal and economic status of the Church, and on the restitution of church property once held by communists. "With this agreement," said the pope, "there is an effort to address the injustices caused in the past by the confiscation of church goods, and to furnish the Catholic Church with the necessary means to develop its pastoral activity."

U.N. Year of Older Persons — The 1999 celebration of the Year of Older Persons should find Catholics making a new commitment not only to care for the elderly, but also to learn from them. So stated a document issued by the Pontifical Council for the Laity. "The elderly are bearers of religious and moral values which represent a rich spiritual patrimony for the life of Christian communities, families and the world." The council said the growing number of people over the age of 70 and the spread of a culture which seems to appreciate only productivity call for action by the Church. It noted that "a society which bases everything on efficiency and the glossy image of eternal youth excludes from its relational networks those who no longer have such prerequisites," but still have much to offer society.

In a related development, Archbishop Karl-Joseph Rauber, nuncio to Hungary, told participants in a U.N.-sponsored conference that the aging of the European population required a new commitment to solidarity and to strengthening traditional families. European countries will face a new "gerontological transition" after the year 2000 when so-called "baby boomers" will begin retirement. "According to forecasts," the archbishop said, "we will come to a point where only a third of the population will be working full-time and will be burdened with the social expenses for the two-thirds of the population who are not yet or who are no longer in the work force.... Solidarity of the family and of society are needed to face the problems of population aging." He called attention to the fact that governments and societies will not be able to meet the challenges of their aging without a huge contribution from families, society's traditional means of caring for the very young and the very old. The archbishop's talk was released by the Vatican Dec. 16.

Homosexual Marriage — Writing in the Dec. 16 edition of *L'Osservatore Romano,* Father Gino Concetti decried proposed legislation in The Netherlands that would allow homosexual marriage. "From a moral point of view," he said, "homosexual unions constitute a moral disorder," and to permit homosexual marriage "means not only to distort the public's vocabulary, but also and above all to upset the original statute of marriage and of the family, sanctified at the dawn of creation of man and woman by the Author himself." He noted: "In Europe, as in North America, the battle for the legalization of homosexual unions knows no truce.... Movements and elite groups exercise strong pressure on parliaments and governments to introduce a new model of the family, which coexists with the model of the family consecrated by millennia of history."

Solidarity Needed — A new international policy of solidarity and cooperation is needed to give people hope as they enter the third millennium, the pope said. "Tragic situations of injustice, extreme poverty and violations of human rights are still an open wound in the side of humanity," he said Dec. 17 in a brief address to four new ambassadors to the Holy See. It is imperative that humanity make a new commitment to solidarity "so that all peoples will know a new hope" and may live "in societies that are more just."

Iraq Bombing — After four days of intense bombing of Iraq by U.S. and British planes, Pope John Paul said Dec. 20 he was saddened and disappointed at the raids, saying the attacks represented a failure of international order. "The Christmas atmosphere intensifies the pain over what has happened in these last few days to the Iraqi population, whose drama should leave no one indifferent. Along with my deep sadness for the situation of these people, there is also bitterness in seeing how often are disappointed the hopes placed in the validity and strength of international law and in the international organizations called to guarantee its application." The pope also repeated an earlier statement: "War has never been and will never be an adequate means to a solution of the problems between nations!"

The attacks were also criticized by the head of Iraq's largest Catholic community. Chaldean-rite Patriarch Raphael I Bidawid said he was disappointed at the failure of diplomacy to avert more violence against his country: "We see this as a campaign of hatred. It is simply vengeance, nothing more than that."

Missionaries Killed — A Colombian priest and nun were murdered in a late December ambush in the mountains of Bolivia, raising to 39 the number of missionaries killed in 1998, reported Fides, the news agency of the Congregation for the Evangelization of Peoples. The casualties were Redemptorist Father Alvaro Lopez Sora and Teresita Missionary Sister Celina Posada.

Christmas Message

"May the joy of Christmas, which sings of the birth of the Savior, instill in all trust in the power of truth and of patient perseverance in doing good," was the Holy Father's Christmas message of hope. He prayed for:

• those working for peace in the Middle East;
• consensus concerning the need for urgent and adequate measures to halt the production and sale of arms;
• the defense of human life;
• the end to the death penalty;
• freedom of children and adolescents from all forms of exploitation;
• restraint of the bloodied hand of those responsible for genocide and crimes of war;
• attention to environmental issues;
• protection of creation and of human dignity.

The papal message to the City and the World (*Urbi et Orbi*) in 58 languages, was broadcast on 45 national television networks.

NATIONAL

School Vouchers — Vouchers and other options to expand parental choice in education, already available for preschoolers and college students, would not be "such a radical departure ... for elementary and secondary education," said former U.S. Secretary for Education William J. Bennett. "We already have vouchers" for preschool up to kindergarten and "grades 13 through 16 and beyond" through Pell grants and federal day-care funds. "So, interesting and somewhat puzzling, elementary and secondary education is the exception to the more general rule." Bennett, speaking Dec. 2 in Philadelphia, added: "School choice works. It decreases the gap between minorities and whites; it decreases the gap between rich and poor. School choice narrows the gap between kids who start with a lot and kids who start with little."

Kids at Risk — Sister Mary Rose McGeady, president of Covenant House, warned at the agency's annual candlelight vigil Dec. 3 in New York that "the crisis of children-at-risk and homeless youths keeps growing. There are so many kids teetering on the edge of survival." She asked: "Do you know, as we speak, over 300,000 kids are sleeping on the streets of America tonight?" According to its annual report, in

1997 Covenant House served 13,000 young people through its shelters and Rights of Passage programs, 14,500 through its Community Service Centers and 21,000 through outreach workers on the streets; its 800 phone number received 87,000 calls. Covenant House was operating shelters in New York and 10 other cities in the United States, and programs had been launched in Mexico, Guatemala, Honduras and Nicaragua.

Youth Ministry — About 1,300 youth ministers from throughout the U.S. attended the three-day national Conference on Catholic Youth Ministry early in the month in Cincinnati. Participants called attention to the thirst of young Catholics for "teaching that matters, service that matters (and) faith that matters."

Priest Suspended — A priest already removed as a parish administrator by Bishop Matthew H. Clark of Rochester for defying church teachings was suspended from the priesthood, as of Dec. 7. Accordingly, Father James Callan lost authorization to function as a priest, celebrate Mass or administer the sacraments. He was removed from Corpus Christi Parish in August for publicly defying church teaching on the liturgical role of women, ministry to gay Catholics, and intercommunion with non-Catholics. Since then, Father Callan repeatedly stated he would not back down on any stands he had taken.

Rebuilding Central America — Caritas, an international network of Catholic relief agencies, pledged $500,000 to help rebuild hurricane-shattered Central America. At a Dec.8 news conference in Miami, Caritas representatives emphasized the importance of continuing long-term assistance to Honduras, El Salvador, Nicaragua and Guatemala in a way that would rebuild infrastructures and improve the economic prospects "of the poorest of the poor."

Embryo Research — A Catholic official urged Congress to continue its ban on funding human embryo research, saying that "in trying to serve humanity we should not support actions that are fundamentally wrong.... Scientific progress must not come at the expense of human dignity," argued Richard Doerflinger, associate director for policy development for the bishops' Secretariat for Pro-Life Activities. He addressed the U.S. Senate's Appropriations Subcommittee on Labor, Health and Education, in the wake of November reports that two U.S. research teams had developed ways of collecting human embryonic stem cells, which are believed to be capable of developing into any of the various types of body cells.

Catholic Charities Tops — *Smart Money* magazine ranked Catholic Charities agencies Number One in the nation for their collection and allocation of 90.9 percent of their income on programs.

K. of C. Scholarships — For the 1998-99 academic year, the Supreme Council of the Knights of Columbus awarded $1.2 million in scholarships, and Knights at all levels awarded $8 million in scholarships, reported Supreme Knight Virgil C. Dechant Dec. 21.

Strictures Extended — Pope John Paul approved a 10-year extension in the U.S. of modifications in church law making it easier for bishops to impose penalties on clergy for sexual abuse of a minor. Penalties could include return of an ordained person to the lay state and loss of all clerical rights and privileges. The changes in law were originally approved Apr. 25, 1994.

Trappist Anniversary — Monks at the Abbey of Gethsemani, Ky., marked the 150th anniversary of their order's first monastery in the United States, founded in 1848 by 44 monks from the Abbey of Melleray in France. The U.S. monastery is a place of retreat for several thousand persons a year.

Anti-Gay Violence Protested — In a full-page ad in *The New York Times* Dec. 30, nearly 2,000 U.S. Catholics or Catholic organizations pledged themselves to work to end anti-gay violence. The signers, including nine bishops, urged all Catholics to "weed out violent perceptions and behaviors," and called on church leaders to "speak boldly when the rights of gay and lesbian people are destroyed and when they are maligned by politicians and other religious leaders." The pledge was sparked by the murder in October of 21-year-old Matthew Shepard near Laramie, Wyoming.

Refugee Decision — Bishop Nicholas A. DiMarzio, chairman of the bishops' Committee on Migration, praised the U.S. decision Dec. 30 to grant temporary protected status to some 150,000 Hondurans and Nicaraguans living in the United States illegally. He said it was unfortunate, however, that an estimated half-million Salvadorans and Guatemalans, whose countries were also severely damaged by Hurricane Mitch in October, were not given the same protection. Under temporary protected status, Hondurans and Nicaraguans who entered the U.S. illegally before Dec. 30 could register to live and work here for the next 18 months and send part of their earnings to relatives in their homelands.

Bombing Iraq — The head of the U.S. Archdiocese for Military Services said Dec. 30 that the bombing of Iraq "should cause serious moral concern for all Americans." In a statement sent to all Catholic chaplains, Archbishop Edwin F. O'Brien warned that military personnel "are not exempt from making conscientious decisions" if they are ordered to take an action they regard as a clear "violation of the moral law." He also said: "I join the bishops of our country as well as the concerned voices of the Holy See and other hierarchies in calling on our President and his advisers to initiate no further military action in the Middle East."

Top 1998 News Stories
Leading news stories of the year cited in the 37th annual survey of editors of Catholic News Service client newspapers were as follows:
1. Assisted suicide/euthanasia; Oregon law and Dr. Jack Kevorkian.
2. Clinton-Lewinski affair.
3. Hurricane destruction in Central America.
4. Pope John Paul's visit to Cuba.
5. Partial-birth abortion and related developments.
6. The Holy Father's 20th anniversary as pope.
7. Efforts for peace in Northern Ireland.
8. Preparations for the Millennium and Jubilee 2000.
9. and 10., tie: Doctrinal disputes; Murder of Guatemalan Bishop Juan Gerardi Conedra.
Pope John Paul II was chosen as the top news-maker.

INTERNATIONAL

Rights Still Violated — In a pastoral letter issued Dec. 1, bishops of the Philippines said seemingly endless violations of human rights in their country made commemoration of the 50th anniversary of the Universal Declaration of Human Rights "almost farcical." To prove their point, they cited "a long litany of injustice including: kidnappings, electoral fraud, corruption in government and the judicial system, curtailment of workers' rights to strike and to bargain collectively, abuses by government-sanctioned paramilitary groups and extrajudicial killings by government and rebel forces."

World Council of Churches Assembly — Four thousand delegates from its 332 member churches attended the 50th annual assembly of the World Council of Churches Dec. 3 to 14 at the University of Zimbabwe in Harare. The Vatican was represented by a 23-member delegation headed by Bishop Mario Joseph Conti of Aberdeen, Scotland, a member of the Pontifical Council for Promoting Christian Unity. He commented about a proposal made during the assembly for the setting-up of a forum that would "provide opportunities for worship, exploration of matters of common Christian concern, and development of enhanced mutual understanding" among WCC members and nonmembers, such as the Catholic Church. He said: "No one expects the Catholic Church to enter the council in its present structure," and the proposed forum aims "to see whether there is another way" the Church could play a more active role. He also said he found the work of the WCC, as reflected in the assembly, "very positive," especially in terms of its achievements in the social field.

RU-486 Opposed — Catholics should oppose plans by leading political parties to approve use of the abortion pill RU-486, "an instrument of death" that should not be allowed in German society. So stated Cardinal Joachim Meisner of Cologne in a Dusseldorf newspaper article Dec. 5. He said the pill is not a medicine, but rather the exact opposite, "a chemical instrument of death specially designed for unborn children."

Three-Way Talks Needed — Talks must begin among representatives of Jerusalem's three monotheistic religions, said Auxiliary Bishop Kamal Hanna Bathis at a Dec. 9 meeting. "We have to start such a dialogue without delay as an expression of our good will and to begin the education of our faithful toward openness and dialogue.... Religion, particularly monotheism, must never be the cause of divisions between persons.... Sincere dialogue between religions means an openness to believers of other religions, combined with full fidelity to one's own religious faith. This will never open the way for violence nor for fanaticism and religious extremism."

Declaration of Human Rights — "The universality of human rights has been recognized and reemphasized," Archbishop Renato R. Martino told Catholic News Service as celebrations Dec. 10 and 11 marked the 50th anniversary of the Universal Declaration of Human Rights. Speeches during the celebration also showed that the principles of the declaration stand in harmony with Catholic thought about the "inherent rights" that are not bestowed by others but are "imprinted in the human being at birth." The Holy See's nuncio to the United Nations also said that, while it was inspiring to hear every nation speaking for human rights, he was afraid there might be hypocrisy and only "lip service" in some cases, especially regarding religious rights.

Free Contraceptives for Teens — Cardinal Thomas Winning of Glasgow condemned a British company's plan to offer free contraceptives to teenagers in one of its stores. He told *The Catholic Times* newspaper in Manchester that the Boots plan was "absolutely disgraceful and totally unacceptable.... It erodes the principles of morality and undermines the role and authority of parents. The place has gone sex-mad. There is no doubt that this will start encouraging (teens) to start experimenting with sex."

Nobel Laureates — As they received the 1998 Nobel Peace Prize Dec. 10 in Oslo, two Northern Irelanders promised support for the Good Friday Agreement they helped forge with the aim of undoing 30 years of conflict in the British province. The prize winners were Catholic nationalist leader John Hume and Protestant union leader David Trimble. Hume said: "The Good Friday Agreement now opens a new future for all the people of Ireland, a future built on respect for diversity and for political difference."

Guadalupe Call for Renewal — During celebration of the feast of Our Lady of Guadalupe, Dec. 12, Archbishop Norberto Rivera Carrera of Mexico City said Christianity must re-awaken today as it did among the country's indigenous population 500 years ago, following Mary's appearance to Blessed Juan Diego. Mary came, he said, to bring peace, "which is not the absence of pain or suffering, but rather accepting each other as we are, with greatness and misery, having and lacking; this is to have love present."

Murder Investigation Stymied — Eight months after the murder of Auxiliary Bishop Juan Gerardi Conedra of Guatemala City, a growing sense of frustration surrounded the unresolved investigation. As of mid-December, the government's chief inspector resigned, judicial proceedings against the only remaining suspect were suspended, and rumors abounded of other untested leads. The involvement of government officials in the case was not free of suspicion.

Attack on Iraq Condemned — The Middle East Council of Churches condemned the U.S.-led military attack on Iraq, calling Operation Desert Fox "a clear example of an impatient and unclear policy.... The MECC condemns the use of military power when it is still possible for peaceful resolution of conflict," said the Rev. Riad Jarjour, general secretary, on Dec. 17. The council "has consistently and persistently called upon international leaders to resolve the eight-year conflict with Iraq ... through diplomacy, negotiations and talks." The statement also called for an end to Iraqi "obstinacy" in refusing U.N. inspectors access for site inspections.

Social Services in Cuba — Such services were reported to be increasing somewhat with expanded aid from U.S. Catholics. Church and Cuban officials attributed this largely to the influence of Pope John Paul's visit to the communist-ruled country the previous January. But the road to full respect for religious freedom was still a long one, they said in interviews with Catholic News Service. Officials said the Church still needed greater autonomy to run its humanitarian and social service programs, improved access to the mass media and stepped-up contacts of Cuban Catholics with Catholics in other parts of the world. "The pope came to confirm the path of social involvement that the Cuban church was taking," said Orlando Marquez Hidalgo, spokesman for the bishops' conference. Evidence of a sort of normalization in church-state relations was cited in "a more fluid dialogue and better personal relations"; also, in the government-granted permission for the public celebration of Mass on Christmas Day.

Israelis and Americans Criticized — In his annual Christmas message, Latin-rite Patriarch Michel Sabbah criticized Israelis and Americans for the current situation in the Middle East. He denounced the recent U.S.-British attack on Iraq, noting that the Iraqi people "remain hostage to political world conflicts.... We affirm that no reasons whatsoever can justify and tranquilize the conscience of those who impose death upon a whole people.... We hope that the grace of Christmas may enlighten their minds and hearts and help them find other ways to resolve the conflict without imposing death on the people." The patriarch expressed concern over mounting tensions between Christians and Muslims in Nazareth, blaming a "foreign hand" (unidentified) for fomenting the discord. He said the conflicts were neither "spontaneous nor natural."

German Catholic Statistics — Fewer German Catholics were leaving the Church, while more were being baptized or returning to parishes across the country, according to 1998 figures released by the bishops' conference. The number of people leaving the Church in 1997 decreased seven percent in comparison with 1996 statistics. "This marks an ongoing trend over a period of years," the conference reported. Compared with statistics from 1992, the number of Catholics leaving the Church decreased by 36 percent over a five-year period. During 1997, more than 15,000 adults and young people over the age of 14 either joined or returned to the Church. The number of baptisms rose by 4,000 over 1996 figures. Catholics accounted for 33.4 percent of the total population of 82 million people.

Chiapas Conflict Issues

As Mexicans recalled the beginning of an armed rebellion in the southern state of Chiapas five years earlier this New Year's Day, bishops of the diocese most affected by the conflict warned that failure to resolve it was costing more lives. Bishop Samuel Ruiz Garcia and Coadjutor Bishop Raul Vera Lopez of San Cristobal de las Casas said in a pastoral letter Dec. 24 that suspension of peace talks in 1996 and "frozen political postures have made the possibility of seeking a solution to the causes of the armed conflict more distant." The 1994 revolt by the Zapatista national Liberation Army put Mexico's reality on public display, the bishops said. While a truce between Zapatistas and the Mexican army had held with only sporadic violations since 1994, church and human rights groups accused the state and federal governments of supporting armed civilian groups in attacking Zapatista supporters. Among issues in the conflict were violations of human rights, poverty, land and political reform, and neglect of the needs of indigenous peoples. Two days before the bishops issued their letter, 5,000 people attended a Mass in Acteal to mark the first anniversary of the massacre of 45 unarmed indigenous peasants by members of an armed paramilitary group.

JANUARY 1999

VATICAN

World Day of Peace — Pope John Paul began the new year with an appeal for peace around the globe and a look back at the causes of war in this century. At Mass, he emphasized respect for human rights as an essential element of lasting peace, the theme of his World Day of Peace message. While expressing hope that the international community might overcome the "great and difficult" problems that give birth to conflict, the Pontiff said the 20th century was marked by moral failure on a continuing worldwide scale. "When we turn our gaze to the events of the century about to end, the two world wars pass before our eyes: the cemeteries, the graves of those who died, the destroyed families, the crying and desperation, the misery and suffering," he said. In reviewing events of the last 100 years, the pope said Christians should look at the world situation with hope and realism. Hope comes from the belief that the world has been liberated from sin by Christ crucified, while realism forces people to recognize that, "unfortunately, humanity gives in to the influence of evil…. However, aided by grace, humanity continually gets up again and, guided by the strength of redemption, proceeds toward good."

Bishops Ordained — The pope ordained nine bishops, including new heads of dioceses in Sudan and Vietnam, Jan. 6, the feast of the Epiphany. During the Mass of ordination, he said: "The Church continues through the centuries the mission of its Lord; its primary commitment is to help all men and women know the face of the Father by reflecting the light of Christ, the light of the peoples, the light of love, of truth and of peace."

Moral Renewal Responsibility — The Church in the United States must use its personnel and resources to aid the moral renewal of society, particularly in respect for the human person, said the pope Jan. 8 in an address at the North American College in Rome. He said the Church in the U.S. "enjoys unparalleled resources for proclaiming the Gospel and for bringing the rich inheritance of the Church's moral and social teaching to the great debates which are shaping your nation's future. The great challenge now facing America's Catholics in every sector of national life and culture is to bear a united and convincing public witness to those truths about the human person and human community which are revealed by God, accessible to reason and embodied in the founding documents of your Republic."

Christian-Muslim Relations — Christians and Muslims are called by their respective faiths to love one another, to care for the poor and to respect human dignity, said Cardinal Francis Arinze, president of the Pontifical Council for Interreligious Dialogue. In an annual message to Muslims marking the end of Ramadan, he said Jan. 8: "God's love for humanity is universal, going beyond political frontiers, beyond the differences of race, culture or religion, beyond political or ideological options, independent of any particular social situation…. We are, therefore, invited on the basis of our belief to love one another. True love is indeed at the heart of the believer's way of acting."

Infants Baptized — Pope John Paul baptized 19 babies in a two-hour liturgy Jan. 10. During the ceremony, he said: "I hope the baptism received today by these little ones can make them courageous witnesses to the Gospel throughout their lives. This will be possible, thanks to their own constant commitment. But you parents will also have to work at educating them. From you, may they learn early to love Christ, to pray to him without ceasing, and to imitate him and continually follow his call."

Violence in Africa — Amid reports of massacres, kidnappings and ethnic conflict, the pope called for an end to brutal violence in Africa. In his annual address to diplomats Jan. 11, he said "Africa remains a continent at risk. Of its 53 states, 17 are experiencing military conflicts, either internally or with other states." He pointed to civil war and the threat of widespread famine in Sudan, new tensions between Ethiopia and Eritrea, and fighting in Sierra Leone "where the people are still the victims of merciless struggles." The pope also called attention to renewed fighting in Angola and the struggles of Burundi and Rwanda to rebuild their countries and reconcile their peoples in the wake of ethnic war.

Another Dialogue — A Vatican commission and a group of Liberal and Reform rabbis from Great Britain reported agreement to begin preparations for the start of a theological dialogue. Dominican Father Remi Hoeckman, secretary of the commission, said: "What they want and what we want coincide: a religious dialogue, a theological dialogue looking at the challenges facing society from the basis of our religious faiths."

Christianity To Impact Europe's Future — Christianity, which has left its imprint on European culture, must be allowed to impact its future as well, the pope said in an address Jan. 14 at a symposium sponsored by the Pontifical Council for Culture. "In a world where difficulties are numerous, the message of Christ opens an infinite horizon and brings incomparable energies: light for intelligence, strength for will and love for hearts." He said that, even though all Europeans are not Christians, the peoples and cultures of the continent "have been deeply marked by the Gospels…. This constitutes our common roots where we can find the values capable of guiding our thoughts, our projects and our actions."

Vatican Secret Archives — The holdings of the Vatican Secret Archives should be preserved and studied, Pope John Paul said Jan. 15 during a meeting with personnel of the Vatican Secret Archives and the Vatican Library. The holdings contain "the memory of the Church and, therefore, the continuity of its apostolic service through the centuries with its lights and shadows;" and the triumphs and failures should be "known and made known, without fear and with sincere gratitude to the Lord, who does not cease to guide his Church."

Week of Prayer for Unity — Every Christian has an obligation to pray and work for Christian unity so that the faith truly will be a light to all peoples. So stated the Holy Father on the eve of the annual Week of Prayer for Christian Unity, Jan. 18 to 25. He said God's plan is for his Church to be a "sign and instrument of unity for all humankind.... Every baptized person is called to contribute" to the search for Christian unity "with unceasing prayer and fraternal charity."

Marriage Laws Promote Love — The Church's laws regarding marriage are pastoral means to protect individuals, promote true married love and safeguard God's design for matrimony, Pope John Paul said Jan. 21 in an address to personnel of the Roman Rota. "Conjugal love is not only or even especially a feeling; instead, it is essentially a commitment to another person, a commitment which is assumed with a precise act of the will." These laws are based on an authentic understanding of conjugal love "between two persons of equal dignity, but who are distinct and complementary in their sexuality." The pope said church action is needed to counteract "a widespread deterioration of the natural and religious meaning of marriage" as seen in the growing number of couples who live together without marriage and in "the insistent public opinion campaigns aimed at obtaining conjugal dignity for unions between persons of the same sex."

Exorcism Ritual — The Congregation for Divine Worship and the Sacraments published Jan. 26 a revised Rite of Exorcisms to take the place of the version dating from 1614. The new 84-page compendium of prayers, Scriptural readings and directives does not contain any substantial changes in the rite.

Papal Intercession — Following intercession by the pope, Missouri Gov. Mel Carnahan commuted the death sentence of murderer Darrell Mease to life imprisonment, Jan. 28.

Our Lady of Guadalupe — Before leading the recitation of the Angelus on Sunday, Jan. 31, the Holy Father spoke briefly to the many faithful gathered in St. Peter's Square about his recent visit to the United States. He also spoke to the young members of Rome's Catholic Action, who released a pair of doves as a sign of their hope for peace in the world. The Holy Father declared: "Let us entrust the destiny of the American peoples and their new evangelization to Our Lady of Guadalupe, patroness of Mexico and of the entire continent.... The two doves we will release in a few moments are meant as a wish for peace for Rome and the whole world, which we entrust to the Blessed Virgin's intercession.

General Audience Topics:
- God's revelation of himself as Father is connected with his interventions in history, culminating in the saving mission of his Son, Jesus Christ (Jan. 13).
- In the history of the Chosen People, God revealed that he was their Father in a special way by establishing a covenant with them (Jan. 20).

Visits to Mexico City, St. Louis
Pope John Paul, on the 85th foreign trip of his pontificate, visited Mexico Jan. 22 to 26 and spent 30 hours in St. Louis Jan 26 and 27.

The Pontiff's principal action in Mexico was the combined signing and proclamation of an apostolic exhortation entitled *Ecclesia in America,* based on and responsive to deliberations and recommendations of the 1997 Special Assembly for America of the Synod of Bishops. A new evangelization and focus on human dignity and rights are central themes of the document: "The new and unique situation in which

the world and the Church find themselves at the threshold of the third millennium, and the urgent needs which result, mean that the mission of evangelization today calls for a new program which can be defined overall as a new evangelization." The exhortation covers many issues of church life, such as spirituality and conversion; study of Scripture, popular piety and inculturation of the Gospel; the roles of bishops, priests, deacons, religious and lay persons; the need to foster vocations to the priesthood; youth ministry, ecumenism and renewal of parishes. The document applies social teaching of the Church to challenging social issues like corruption in public life, the drug trade, the environment, the arms race and globalization. The Holy Father was greeted enthusiastically by hundreds of thousands of people during his visit.

Outstanding events of the St. Louis visit were the rally of 20,000 youths in the Kiel Center and the Mass celebrated before 100,000 people in the Trans World Dome, during which the pope called on Catholics to embrace the upcoming millennium as a time for "far-reaching spiritual renewal" and a "springtime of faith."(See Special Reports.)

NATIONAL
Death Penalty Opposed — Cardinal Adam F. Maida of Detroit praised the citizens of Michigan Jan. 1 for defeating an assisted-suicide referendum in 1998 and warned against moves toward legalizing the death penalty in the state. "Michigan has a long and proud tradition of having rejected such a penalty from the earliest days of our history," he said. "What a tragedy it would be if we were to begin the third millennium of Christianity by reducing ourselves to an endorsement of capital punishment." The cardinal also spoke about abortion, racism, prejudice, assistance to poor families and "educational justice for parents." His address was delivered shortly before the inauguration of Gov. John Engler and other state officials.

Ten Million Helped — Local Catholic Charities agencies provided social and emergency services to more than 10.6 million people in 1997, according to an annual survey by Catholic Charities USA. Of the total, 3.8 million received social services such as counseling, respite care and refugee resettlement, while 6.8 million got emergency assistance of food, shelter and other crisis services. Poverty was a factor in both conditions; 66 percent of those receiving social services and 84 percent of those getting emergency services reported incomes below the poverty level.

Catholics in Congress — One hundred and fifty-three Catholics — 25 Senators, 128 Representatives — from 37 states and two territories were among members of the 106th Congress. Baptists and Methodists had the second and third largest representations, with 69 and 59 members, respectively.

Shea Medalist — John M. Howe, professor of history at Texas Tech University, Lubbock, was announced Jan. 9 the winner of the John Gilmary Shea Prize for his book *Church Reform and Social Change in Eleventh-Century Italy: Dominic of Sora and His Patrons.* The award is sponsored by the American Catholic Historical Association.

Respect in Dialogue — "Dialogue is only fruitful when there's great respect on all sides," said Cardinal

Francis E. George of Chicago during a symposium on "The Catholic Faith and the Secular Academy" at the University of Chicago Divinity School. He gave the keynote talk opening the symposium, which was co-sponsored by the national Catholic Common Ground Initiative and the Lumen Christi Institute of the University of Chicago. His address focused mainly on the role of the Catholic faith in the world and dialogue within the Church, a major concern of the Catholic Common Ground Initiative founded by his predecessor, the late Cardinal Joseph L. Bernardin. Cardinal George said the Initiative had been instrumental in highlighting the constructive aspects of disagreement.

Study of Communion Services — Prompted by the concerns of diocesan liturgy directors, the bishops' Committee on the Liturgy announced plans to study the growing practice of weekday parish Communion services in the absence of a priest. Father James P. Moroney, executive director of the Secretariat for the Liturgy, said that 1974 norms governing a weekday worship service with distribution of Communion outside Mass needed updating and expansion to reflect experience since that time.

Saints' Names Required — People in the Archdiocese of Santa Fe were being reminded of the importance of selecting a saint's name for themselves or their children when approaching the sacraments of baptism and confirmation. "There will be no 'Crystals' or 'Fifis' as names for baptism or confirmation," said Archbishop Michael J. Sheehan. "I have a special ruling to invoke our saints as heroes." In 1997, he mandated in the sacramental policies of the archdiocese that people must have a saint's name for baptism and confirmation.

New York Teacher Contract — A new contract negotiated for teachers in parish schools of the New York Archdiocese, subject to confirmation late in the month, would offer significant financial benefits for teachers and achieve policy goals sought by the archdiocese. Negotiators agreed on a three-year contract, retroactive to September, providing for raises of three percent for the current year, three percent for the next year and four percent for the third year. In addition, the archdiocese committed itself to bring salaries of elementary school teachers up to the level of those teaching in parish high schools over a 12-year period. The contract would cover about 3,000 teachers in 234 elementary schools and 14 parish-operated high schools. It would bring elementary teacher salaries up to a range of $25,851 to $37,710. High school salaries would be raised this year to a range of $27,906 to $38,971, and in the third year would be in the range of $29,893 to $41,745.

New Nuncio Arrives — Archbishop Gabriel Montalvo, 69, a veteran of more than 40 years in the diplomatic service of the Holy See, arrived in Washington Jan. 16 to take up his duties as Nuncio of the Holy See to the United States.

Franciscan Centers for Social Concerns — The Franciscans of Holy Name Province announced the establishment of two centers for social concerns at St. Bonaventure University and Siena College, to train students for advocacy and direct service to the poor. Both schools are in the state of New York.

Racism Rejected — The Catholic Church rejects racism "as foreign to the mind of Christ," said Archbishop Daniel E. Pilarczyk of Cincinnati in a reflection for Dr. Martin Luther King, Jr., Day. He wrote in the Jan. 15 edition of *The Catholic Telegraph*: "Our relationship with God the Father and our relationship with our human brothers and sisters are so linked together that Scripture says, 'The one who does not love does not know God' (1 Jn 4:8). The ground is, therefore, removed from every theory or practice which leads to a distinction between persons or peoples in the matter of human dignity or the rights that flow from it."

In another statement, Father Bryan Massingale said the profound "estrangement" between black and white cultures in the United States impedes the growth of the Church in the African-American community. "The greatest obstacle to evangelizing African-Americans is the radical cultural divide" between blacks and whites, he said Jan.21 during a national consultation sponsored by the National Black Catholic Congress in Baltimore. He cited two world views that threaten each other. One is the fact that African-Americans share "a common experience of being treated as less than fully human," and of "indignities traceable to the simple fact that they are black." White culture, on the other hand, views itself as "the norm by which all other frames of reference are measured" and "sees itself as dominant."

March for Life — Thousands of people across the country took part in pro-life demonstrations marking the 26th anniversary of the Roe v. Wade and Doe v. Bolton Supreme Court decisions which legalized abortion on demand. The principal demonstration was the March for Life in Washington Jan. 22.

INTERNATIONAL

Northern Ireland Impasse — The impasse over the decommissioning of weapons in Northern Ireland should not be an obstacle to implementing the 1998 Good Friday Agreement, said Archbishop Sean Brady of Armagh. "I would appeal to all sides not to allow the decommissioning issue to become an obstacle to the implementation of the agreement. The sooner the assembly and the executive (council) are up and running, the sooner trust will be given a chance to grow, he said Jan. 1. He added it was important "that there are many issues, apart from decommissioning, which will cause difficulties and which will not be satisfactorily dealt with unless some degree of mutual trust and confidence is established." Everyone agrees "that it is the decommissioning mind-set which is important. It is the outcome of the process which is really essential. It is the change of attitude of those who have been prepared to use arms to achieve political ends which is absolutely necessary."

Austrians Not Paying Church Tax — The number of persons discontinuing tax payments to the Catholic Church in Austria increased in 1998. At the same time, a survey indicated that only one in five Austrians said they felt linked to any church, compared to 50 percent before the outbreak of recent controversies in the Church. More than 33,400 Catholics discontinued "church tax" payment between January and November, 1998, a rise of 15 percent over the previous year, according to data presented at a bishops' conference Jan. 4 and 5 in Linz. It was not known how many Catholics discontinued payment because of economic difficulties or how many stopped the practice in protest against internal conflicts, said Margareta Matich, speaking for the Vienna Archdiocese. She noted that the numbers released in January indicated a "real increase" over 1997, when more than 29,000 Austrians discontinued payment.

Dominican Sisters in Vietnam — Despite 10 years of hardship and trial, Dominican Sisters were continuing a discreet and low-key ministry in the Lang Son Diocese of communist-controlled Vietnam, said a local leader of the religious order. The nun recently told UCA News, an Asian church news agency based in Thailand, that during the previous decade her congregation had sent groups of nuns back to the Lang Son Diocese which the order had left some 45 years earlier. Regarding their ministry, she said: "Since our sisters do not have the government's official permission to work publicly, they have to stay in peoples' homes, live among the ordinary people and not wear the habit." Most of the time, the sisters walk through the hills and valleys, bringing consecrated hosts to the faithful in remote sub-parishes, teaching catechism to children and caring for the sick and the poor. The ministry is only for those "sisters who can endure hardship and sacrifice. Otherwise, they cannot stay long in such a remote place with very little church support."

Underground Catholics Attacked in China — In mid-January, UCA News received reports of violence and harassment against Catholic peasants in the Baoding Diocese around Christmas time. Father Peter Hu Duo, just released from a re-education-through-labor camp, was arrested and seriously beaten by government personnel Dec. 20 in Xushui County. Also reported was an attack Dec. 24 by a masked mob on three Catholic leaders of Liangzhuang village in the same area; the men had to be hospitalized after being gagged, blindfolded and beaten with electric batons and other implements.

Role of Lay Movements — More than 300 representatives of 85 lay movements and several dioceses in France discussed ways in which they should operate in the Church in the 21st century. "We are living out a great ecclesial moment," said Bishop Jean-Paul Jaeger of Arras, president of the bishops' Commission for Lay Movements at a Jan. 16-to-17 conference in Paris. Bishop Claude Dagens of Angouleme, commenting on evangelization in the next century, warned against the danger of "privatizing faith." He also spoke of the challenges posed by young people with their "key questions of life, death and freedom," questions to which all lay movements should be able to respond. He suggested that the main contemporary task is "to transform humanity from within," to work for change by cooperating with and transforming the valid initiatives already in process in society. The Church, said the bishop, is among the organizations active for change and in need of constant evangelization.

"Funeral Stone of Debt" — The head of the Latin America Bishops' Council opened a conference on foreign debt with a call for world financial leaders to remove the "funeral stone" of indebtedness from poor countries. "The debt is not one more problem for us to face; it is the problem," said Bishop Oscar Andres Rodriguez of Tegucigalpa. "The foreign debt is like a funeral stone over Honduras. It doesn't let us resurrect to a better life. It is indispensable that the stone be removed.... We need to break this vicious cycle of unsustainable debt, whose shadow extends over us like a nightmare." The three-day conference, attended by more than 100 participants, was sponsored by the worldwide Jubilee 2000 Campaign.

Earthquake in Colombia — The president of the Colombian bishops' conference and Pope John Paul called for solidarity with victims of the Jan. 25 earthquake which devastated 20 towns and villages in five provinces and took a toll of an estimated 500 dead and nearly 2,000 injured.

Safe Return Urged for Refugees — Bishops of Croatia and Bosnia-Herzegovina issued a joint statement late in the month in which they said refugees from Bosnia should be allowed to return home in safety. "Due to political, economic and security reasons," however, "many Catholic faithful who have endured all the horrors of the war are now being forced to emigrate." It was estimated that two million people were forced from their homes by the fighting and ethnic cleansing campaigns that marked the war in Bosnia. A peace treaty signed in Dayton, Ohio, in November, 1995, led to a ceasefire but little or no relief for many displaced persons.

Violence in Africa — Catholics were the targets of violence during the month, reported MISNA, the Rome-based missionary news service.

• In Angola, a priest and two catechists were murdered the night of Jan. 4-5 in Catchiungo by an unidentified group of armed men.

• In the Democratic Republic of the Congo, government soldiers sacked several Catholic institutions in the nation's capital and attempted to break into the Vatican nunciature, Jan 12.

• In Sierra Leone, an archbishop and four Xaverian missionaries were kidnapped but managed to escape their captors Jan. 22.

Christians Unprotected in India — Major superiors of women religious in India criticized government failure to protect minority Christians from attacks by tribal militants and Hindu fundamentalists. A memorandum signed by 238 members of the Women's Section of the Conference of Religious of India described the attacks on Christians as "a systematically planned campaign" to create "a sense of fear and insecurity," reported UCA News, an Asian church news agency based in Thailand. The Jan. 20-24 national Assembly of Women Religious Superiors also expressed shock over the burning alive of an Australian Protestant missionary and his two sons in the state of Orissa Jan. 23.

Third Millennium Challenges

Poverty, secularism, the shortage of priests and the widening gap between rich and poor countries will be among major challenges to the Church in the third millennium, according to a draft document of the Latin American Bishops' Council (CELAM). In addition to analysis of global economic conditions, the document described various facets of the Church in Latin America. The Church, it said, "tends to lose credibility and membership when it presents itself as a hierarchical and authoritarian structure," but "conserves its respect when it becomes involved with the promotion and the defense of human rights, is committed to social justice and gives witness to what it believes." The document also described Catholics who do not identify with the hierarchy and church teaching as "Christians without a church."

of 110,795. U.S. diocesan newspaper circulation had the strongest increase, 193,712, to a total of 5,472,955. The circulation of U.S. national newspapers declined to 196,650, from 201,678. U.S. magazine circulation dropped by 1.2 percent, for a total of 13,801,728. (See separate article for additional statistics.)

Men's Rally — Catholic men attending a Mar. 20 rally in Cincinnati were urged to renew their commitments to family and Church. The event, organized by the Catholic Men's Fellowship of Greater Cincinnati, drew about 10,000 men from Ohio, Kentucky, Indiana, Illinois and West Virginia.

Another Minor Basilica — The church at Belmont Abbey, N.C., was officially proclaimed Mar. 22 the minor Basilica of Mary, Help of Christians.

Health-Care Protocol — Cardinal Anthony J,. Bevilacqua of Philadelphia released a protocol for evaluating collaborative relationships between Catholic and non-Catholic health-care facilities. The protocol, issued after extended consultation with local Catholic providers and sponsoring religious congregations, became diocesan law Mar. 25. Its three stated aims are:

• "to preserve the Catholic identity and ensure the continuation of the mission of health-care apostolates" in the Philadephia archdiocese;

• "to promote cooperation of all parties involved in the Catholic health-care apostolate" in the archdiocese;

• "to further the healing ministry that embodies the Gospel message of Jesus Christ as reflected in the values and teachings of the Catholic Church" and in the "Ethical and Religious Directives for Catholic Health-Care Services" of the U.S. bishops.

The protocol provided for the establishment of an Archdiocesan Catholic Health-Care Review Committee to review proposed agreements that would result in a major alliance or affiliation agreement, and to make appropriate recommendations to the archbishop.

Pilgrimage Guidelines — The U.S. bishops' Administrative Board approved a set of "guidelines intended as a practical tool to help those traveling to the Holy Land on pilgrimage to enrich their experience by gaining an appreciation for the living reality of the Christian — as well as Muslim and Jewish — communities there." The guidelines were issued Mar. 26 by the Committee on International Policy, headed by Archbishop Theodore E. McCarrick of Newark. The bishops said in a statement: "We want to encourage Catholics undertaking visits to the Holy Land to do so in the spirit of true pilgrims, to walk prayerfully and devoutly in the steps of our Lord and with openness to the movement of the spirit of Jesus in their lives."

NATO Bombing

In a statement issued shortly after NATO forces began bombing Yugoslavian targets Mar. 24, Bishop Joseph A. Fiorenza said the U.S. bishops regretted that the Kosovo situation had deteriorated to the point of prompting a NATO bombing campaign, and prayed that a political solution might be achieved "as soon as possible." The president of the bishops' conference said Yugoslavia's attacks against civilians were "morally unacceptable" and that the situation in Kosovo required a serious response by the international community. He also said the bombing campaign posed "difficult moral and policy questions on which persons of good will may disagree." But "it seems clear to us that the humanitarian objective — protecting civilian populations ... from further indiscriminate attacks — is a legitimate one.... What is less clear are the consequences of the use of force."

INTERNATIONAL

Women's Issues — Conflict over "reproductive health" that arose in connection with the 1995 World Conference on Women at Beijing was renewed at the Mar. 1-12 meeting of the U.N. Commission on the Status of Women. Many delegates continued to push for abortion and other "reproductive rights," while Vatican observers continued to insist on a different and broader approach to women's health. "It looks like the old issues are going to surface again," said Kathryn Hauwa Hoomkwap, a Nigerian who served on the Vatican Delegation to Beijing. She said in an interview with Catholic News Service that some commission members were trying to go even further than at Beijing in support of efforts for the acceptance of measures not adopted there.

Guatemalan Abuse Report — The bishops of Guatemala welcomed a truth commission's report that accused the government of waging genocide against its indigenous population during the country's 36-year-long civil war. The findings "lay before the eyes of Guatemala and the world the deep abyss of dehumanization and deterioration of moral values into which our country has fallen," said a statement circulated by the bishops' conference. The report showed that "the suffering of the victims, the disregard for human dignity, the loss of moral conscience on the part of the aggressors, urge us to find the necessary paths that lead to a respect for human rights, ... a culture of mutual respect ... and national reconciliation in Guatemala." The Commission for Historical Clarification blamed the armed forces for 93 percent of an estimated 200,000 killings.

Alcoholism in France — French bishops declared alcoholism an illness presenting a serious threat to health which can be cured only through individual and community effort. In a mid-month document, their conference reported that each year 40,000 persons die from alcohol-related illnesses, traffic accidents, suicides or incidents at work — making alcohol's death toll in France five times higher than that of illegal hard drugs such as heroin. The bishops said all members of society must consider their views and behavior in order "to avoid becoming accomplices" in problems created by overconsumption of alcohol, and pointed to the family for its "premier role in the prevention of risks regarding alcohol."

Violence of Indian Extremists — Church leaders in India said a recent surge in anti-Christian violence was an extremist response by better-off Indians to Christian efforts to empower the poorest people in the country. In early March interviews, Catholic and other Christian pastors expressed hope that dialogue and "good sense" would quell the attacks, in which 25 church workers were killed and many institutions damaged. Fifty attacks were reported in the first 10 weeks of 1999. Despite the violence, pastors said Christians would not turn their backs on the poor; neither would they give up their constitutional right to evangelize.

In a related development, Prime Minister Atal Behari Vajpayee yielded to objections of his cabinet and withdrew plans to proclaim the year 2000 the "Year of Christ."

Armed Forces Agreement Opposed — Columban Father Shay Cullen urged Filipino senators not to ratify the Visiting Forces Agreement with the United States, saying it was "against the common good, again the people and against our heritage." He did so Mar. 11 in testimony before a senate committee. He told the senators about the sexual exploitation he had witnessed around the former U.S. Subic Bay Naval Base in the northern Philippines, according to UCA News, an Asian church agency based in Thailand. He told the senators that, in the nearly 30 years he lived around the base, he saw almost irreversible damage to the social, cultural, economic and spiritual lives of the people, which he blamed on personnel of the base. "The very worst of these social evils was the sexual exploitation of impoverished women and children," he said.

Child-Soldiers Rescued — A church-run agency in Sierra Leone was reported working with UNICEF to help former child-soldiers. "The public is presently contacting us to trace lost children, and we have succeeded in reuniting 47 children with their families," said Father Theophilus Momoh, director of Children Associated with the War, an agency of the Archdiocese of Freetown and Bo. He said Nigerian-led West African Peacekeeping Forces had rescued the children from rebels and handed them over to UNICEF, which in turn arranged with local nongovernmental organizations, like Children Associated with the War, to take care of them. "From the end of January, we have accepted 97 children," Father Momoh said. "We are trying to make them feel at home, since they have been traumatized." He also said that nearly 2,200 children had been abducted by rebels.

Religious Discrimination in Europe — A number of East and West European countries were discriminating against religious minorities, according to a report from the Austrian-based International Helsinki Federation for Human Rights. Among findings were:
- violations of legal guarantees of religious freedom in Russia;
- harassment of new religious movements in Germany;
- structural support for the Orthodox Church in Romania but denial of recognition of other religious groups.

The federation's report on religious freedom in 18 countries was released several days before its Mar. 22 date of delivery to the Organization for Security and Cooperation in Europe.

La Civilta Cattolica Anniversary — The 150th anniversary of the Jesuit magazine, published "in harmony with the Holy See," was marked with celebrations that began Mar. 22.

Theologians Supported — Jesuit provincials of South Asia affirmed support for two theologians working to make God's word relevant in the Asian mode, and urged the Vatican not to view theologizing in the Asian context with mistrust. "We, like many of our fellow Jesuits, are pained by the atmosphere of suspicion, not to say mistrust, created by recent decisions of the Congregation for the Doctrine of the Faith" concerning writings of Fathers Anthony de Mello and Jacques Dupuis, said some 20 provincials in a statement. They viewed suspicion of their confreres as "a disservice to the whole Church." They also said that decisions made "unilaterally without a dialogue with the Asian churches" reflected a "lack of appreciation of differences and of proper procedures." In June, 1998, the congregation issued a notification that some writings by the late Father de Mello were "incompatible with the Catholic faith and can cause harm." In November, the congregation launched an initial inquiry regarding the book *Toward a Christian Theology of Religious Pluralism,* by Father Dupuis.

Day of the Unborn — A decree by President Carlos Saul Menem of Argentina, declaring Mar. 25 a national day of commemoration of the unborn child, was applauded by Archbishop Renato R. Martino, Vatican nuncio to the United Nations. He said he knew of no other country that had given this kind of recognition to the unborn. "This is very important because a head of state has had the courage to say this, going against the trend of political correctness."

RU-486 — Canada's Catholic Organization for Life and Family urged the federal government not to allow the abortion-inducing RU-486 pill into the country. In a Mar. 26 letter to Health Minister Allan Rock, Archbishop Adam Exner of Vancouver said: "This pill is not a therapeutic drug but one which destroys the unborn child and has serious health risks for women. While the Supreme Court of Canada struck down the abortion law in 1988 because of procedural flaws, it also clearly recognized that the state has an interest in the unborn child that relates to a pressing and substantial concern in a free and democratic society." The pill, first produced and marketed in France, has been approved legally in the United States, Great Britain, Sweden and China.

Marriage in Jeopardy

The survival of marriage and the family is under attack in contemporary society, said Cardinal George Basil Hume of Westminster in an address at the annual general meeting of LIFE, one of Britain's largest pro-life organizations. He said: "The idea of marriage as a permanent, life-long commitment is often regarded as unrealistic, and even undesirable because it limits future choices. And the notion of confining sexual relationships to marriage is seen by many as an unattainable fantasy. The link between life and love is broken.... We have elevated freedom of choice to the seeming exclusion of other values. In the endless obsession with sex in so much of the media today we see the peddling of unreal fantasies about what makes for human happiness....It is almost taken for granted that there need by no connection at all between the unitive and the procreative aspects of sexual intimacy." The ideals of the Church, in which marriage involves an exclusive commitment, are under siege in today's society. "What is needed is a change of mind and heart. We are engaged, like it or not, in a battle for the future survival of marriage and the family. It demands that we challenge some prevailing attitudes and assumptions."

APRIL 1999

VATICAN

Long Pontificate — On Apr. 3, after 20 years and five months, Pope John Paul's pontificate became the 10th longest in the history of the Church. (The exact length of St. Peter's's pontificate is not known.)

John Paul II's pontificate is now the longest of the 20th century, exceeding Pope Pius XII (1939-1958), Pope Pius XI (1922-39), and Pope Paul VI (1963-1978). Pope Leo XIII (1878-1903) began his reign in the 19th century and finished it in the 20th. The longest reigning pontiff was Pope Pius IX, from 1846 to 1878 (32 years).

Norms for Economic Justice — The Holy See's envoy to U.N. offices in Geneva said Apr. 8 that enforceable global norms are needed to guarantee economic justice. "The engagement in the fight against poverty and for development should respect ... the real dignity of man as a responsible being in a brotherly community," Bishop Giuseppe Bertello said at a special U.N. meeting on human rights. He noted that the world is better informed than ever about abuses of human rights, including the right to economic self-determination, but it appears to be no better prepared than before to address them. "In an ever-more interdependent world, the big challenges posed by the globalization of commerce, the system of monetary and financial exchange, the participation in new technologies require multilateral collaboration and, above all, demand a political will capable of exploring new strategies for putting to work projects which respond to the real needs of populations, and not only to the interests of a minority."

For Greater Respect — The Pontifical Biblical Commission's study of how the New Testament portrays the Jewish people and their sacred writings should reinforce the Church's teaching that a lack of respect for them is anti-Christian, said the commission's secretary. Scholars appointed by the pope met Apr. 12-16 to discuss a rough draft of a document entitled "The Jewish People and Their Scriptures in the Christian Bible." Jesuit Father Albert Vanhoye said the document was being developed in light of current church teaching about Judaism, which emphasizes "fraternal ties and the abolition of any feeling of contempt or hatred which might insert itself in the Christian conscience in an abnormal way, as has unfortunately happened. Now there is a very decisive effort on the part of the Church against any sentiment of disrespect or scorn."

Thanks — The pope thanked a group of U.S. benefactors for their continued generosity as they presented a list of more than $2 million worth of grants to church projects this year. "I deeply appreciate this commitment of solidarity with our brothers and sisters throughout the world," he told visiting members of the Philadelphia-based Papal Foundation Apr. 14. He added that people throughout the world "look in hope to the Church's witness to the Gospel and her efforts to promote justice, reconciliation and fraternal cooperation among members of the human family."

Diplomacy Nets a Bishop — In the wake of a diplomatic mission to Vietnam, the pope named a Vietnam bishop Apr. 15 with the government's assent.

Msgr. Celestine Migliore said the nomination was "a good sign because it indicates that other announcements of this sort are forthcoming, and it shows that the attitude of the government (toward the Church) is positive and constructive."

Prevention of Child Exploitation — Norms for preventing the involvement of children in prostitution, slavery and armed conflict must be adopted and enforced throughout the world. So stated Bishop Giuseppe Bertello, envoy of the Holy See to U.N. offices in Geneva, in remarks released Apr. 16 at the Vatican. He told a special U.N. session on human rights that accepting such guidelines would be "an ethical leap, reminding society that it must protect and sustain with all its means the still fragile personality of the child.....The abuse of children, sexually exploited for commercial purposes, is a grave crime and is regarded as such by public opinion because the most authentic part of a small being, his innocence, is thereby devastated.... Evil transforms beauty into horror and savage oppression."

Three Canonizations — During ceremonies in St. Peter's Square Apr. 18, the pope canonized two priests and a nun: Marcellin Champagnat, French founder of the Marist Brothers, who died in 1840; Giovanni Calabria, Italian founder of the male and female branches of the Poor Servants of Divine Providence, who died in 1954; Agostina Pietrantoni, an Italian Sister of Charity, who was murdered in 1894. Their canonizations raised to 283 the number of saints canonized by Pope John Paul.

Prayers for Columbine High School Victims — Pope John Paul offered his prayers and expressed his hope that the shootings by two teen-age gunmen in Columbine High School, Colorado, would convince Americans of the need to teach moral values to young people. The pope's shock and sadness over the shootings Apr. 20 that left at least 15 people dead and 20 critically injured was conveyed in a message to Archbishop Charles J. Chaput of Denver.

Youth Ministry — The pope told visiting Canadian bishops Apr. 22 about the need to pay close attention to the pastoral care of young people. "From infancy through adolescence," he said, "Christian communities and educators must take care to develop an organic catechesis, so that young people may come to know the broad outlines of the Christian mystery.... I invite the faithful to mobilize themselves without end to transmit the faith and Christian values to children." Noting that the bishops had reported difficulties in their dioceses with the pastoral care of adolescents, he encouraged adults engaged in ministry to them "not to despair if they do not immediately see the fruits of their action. May they never forget that they are the instruments through which the Holy Spirit acts mysteriously."

Esteem for Art and Artists — In an open letter meant "to help consolidate a more constructive partnership between art and the Church," Pope John Paul affirmed the Church's esteem for artists and the spiritual value of art. "Even beyond its typically religious expressions, true art has a close affinity with the world of faith — so that, even in situations where culture and the Church are far apart, art remains a kind of bridge to religious experience." The 39-page message, published Apr. 23, explored art's theological, historical and aesthetic significance, focusing particularly on sacred Christian art but also embracing other forms. All forms had the potential to make the spiritual more comprehensible, he said.

Ordinations — The Holy Father ordained 31 deacons to the priesthood for the Diocese of Rome Apr. 25, the World Day of Prayer for Vocations.

General Audience Topics:
• "The law God gives his people is ... the expression of that fatherly love which shows the right path for human conduct and the condition for inheriting the divine promises" (Apr. 7).
• The "Gospel message, confirmed by the witness of a sensible charity, is the most effective way for people to understand something of God's goodness and gradually to recognize his merciful face" (Apr. 14).
• Because God is the father of all peoples, human beings are brothers and sisters who must learn to respect each other and settle their differences through dialogue (Apr. 21).
• Hope that the Jewish-Christian dialogue "will help create a new civilization founded on the one, holy and merciful God, and fostering a humanity reconciled in love" (Apr. 28).

Easter Message
Pope John Paul's Easter message recalled the saving mystery of the death and resurrection of Christ and appealed for the relief of thousands of ethnic Albanians forced to leave Kosovo as refugees bereft of virtually everything except the will to survive. He said:

"From the risen Lord, I invoke the precious gift of peace, above all for the devastated land of Kosovo, where tears and blood continue to mingle in a tragic spectacle of hatred and violence. I think of those who have been killed, of those made homeless, of those who have been torn from their families, of those being forced to flee.... How can we be insensitive to the sorrowing flood of men and women from Kosovo?... I feel duty-bound to make a heartfelt appeal to the authorities of the Federal Republic of Yugoslavia to allow a humanitarian corridor to be opened in order for help to be brought to the mass of people gathered at the border of Kosovo."

The Holy Father also spoke about war, social tensions and obstacles to peace in countries of Asia, Africa and Latin America.

Celebration of the Easter Liturgy climaxed events of Holy Week which included the Thursday Masses of Chrism and the Last Supper, the Stations of the Cross and Solemn Liturgy of the Passion on Good Friday and the rites of the Easter Vigil.

NATIONAL
New Evangelization Effort — Following up on the success of an archdiocesan Reconciliation Weekend in March, Cardinal Anthony J. Bevilacqua of Philadelphia announced Apr. 1 a continuation of the concerted effort to draw Catholics back to the Church. "Our evangelization efforts over the past year have shown us that there is a great hunger for God in the archdiocese," he said. He noted that the Disciples in Mission program, developed by the Paulist national Catholic Evangelization Association, "will help us to feed that hunger." It was estimated that 100,000 persons received the sacrament of reconciliation during the weekend.

End the Death Penalty — In a statement entitled "Good Friday Appeal to End the Death Penalty," the Administrative Board of the U.S. Catholic Conference appealed to "all people of good will, and especially Catholics, to work to end capital punishment." At a San Antonio conference sponsored by Religious Organizing against the Death Penalty Project and the San Antonio Peace Center, it was reported that at least 23 innocent persons had mistakenly been executed in this century and at least 74 had been released from death row after their convictions were reversed.

NCEA Convention — More than 13,000 persons attended the 96th annual convention of the national Catholic Educational Association Apr. 6-9 in New Orleans. The association reported that Catholic school enrollment in the previous six years had grown by more than 81,000 to a total of 2,648,844 students. Another report, on Catholic high schools, dispelled some popular myths that they catered only to elite and rich Catholic students. The association's C. Albert Koob Merit Award was presented to Howard Jenkins, superintendent of schools in the Archdiocese of New Orleans for 26 years.

CRS Donations — Actor Paul Newman donated $250,000 to Catholic Relief Services to assist Kosovar refugees and others suffering from the current crisis in the Balkans. A similar donation was made later by Bob and Dolores Hope.

Black Catholic Worship — Community, culture, education and holiness of life are the four main factors which will help shape the African-American Catholic community as it enters the next century, according to Benedictine Father Cyprian Davis. He gave the keynote address Apr. 11 at the 11th Workshop on Pastoring in African-American Parishes sponsored by the national Black Catholic Congress. He also said that the "new Catholic immigrants" are no longer people from Ireland or southern Europe, as in the past, but are Africans and French- and Spanish-speaking blacks from the Caribbean and Latin America.

Kevorkian Murder Sentence — Pro-life advocates applauded the 10-25-year sentence given Jack Kevorkian for second degree murder in the death of Thomas Youk. "This sentence affirms that people with disabilities deserve the same quality of justice as those who are able-bodied," said an Apr. 13 statement by David O'Steen, executive director of the national Right to Life Committee. He added his hope that "this will serve as a deterrent against pushing people with disabilities farther down the slippery slope toward a 'duty to die.' " Judie Brown, president of the American Life League, said: "Thomas Youk's value and dignity as a fellow human being was denied by Kevorkian and others. Youk was deemed less than whole because of his condition. Thus, Kevorkian murdered Youk and, as a result, received just punishment." The death of Youk, who suffered from Lou Gehrig's disease, was videotaped and televised nationally in November, 1998, on the CBS program, "60 Minutes."

Seminarians — The Center for Applied Research in the Apostolate reported that there were 3,386 post-college seminarians and 1,556 college-level seminarians at the start of the 1998-99 academic year. The college figure was 40 seminarians higher than in the previous year; the post-college figure was 228 higher. The simultaneous increase in college and post-college figures was the first since 1983-84. CARA also reported a continuing rise in lay ministry formation, estimating that more than 30,000 people were enrolled in professional ministry formation programs across the country in 1998-99, three times as many as in 1985-86. The CARA report, entitled "Catholic Ministry Formation Enrollments: Statistical Overview for 1998-1999," was published in mid-April.

Alarm over Catholic-Jewish Relations — A "signal of alarm" sounded by Cardinal Edward I. Cassidy Mar. 23 at negative responses to Catholic efforts at dialogue prompted Rabbi A. James Rudin, interreligious affairs director of the American Jewish Committee, to call for consultation with his colleagues during the month.

Koinonia — Catholic and Lutheran representatives held extensive discussions about *koinonia*, or communion, as it relates to ordained ministry and church unity efforts, during an Apr. 15-18 dialogue session in Chicago. It was the second meeting in the current 10th round of talks between representatives of the Evangelical Lutheran Church in America and the national Conference of Catholic Bishops. Auxiliary Bishop Richard J. Sklba of Milwaukee, co-chair of the dialogue, said participants in the dialogue made "a very meticulous review of the concept and the pastoral and theological concerns of *koinonia* in each of our respective traditions, and particularly in the last few decades of documentation."

Anti-Singer Protest — More than 250 demonstrators, including the head of the national Catholic Office for Persons with Disabilities, lined the sidewalks in front of Princeton University Apr. 17 to protest the appointment of Peter Singer as the tenured chair at the university's Center for Human Values. Singer was known in the United States as a leader in the animal rights movement through his book, *Animal Liberation*. His views on human rights, however, were another matter, especially his justification of infanticide and euthanasia for the disabled. In his writings, he favored killing of severely disabled babies, as well as those with Down Syndrome who "would need more care and attention than a normal child."

Columbine Victims — Four of the 13 persons killed in the Apr. 20 shootings at Columbine High School, Littleton, Colo., were members of the local parish of St. Frances Cabrini. Prayers for them, their slain schoolmates and families were offered by people of the community and of the whole country during a sad period of mourning.

Advocacy Goes with Help — Jesuit Father Fred Kammer, president of Catholic Charities USA, told employees of Catholic Charities of the Milwaukee Archdiocese that advocacy on behalf of the poor is integral to helping them. "Without the doing of justice, Christ is unknown," he said in a talk at Alverno College. "We believe it's not enough to feed one hungry family after another. From the very beginning, advocacy was part of our mission.... We have to be people who put our lives on the line for the people we care for, we have to speak out for them."

Interfaith Healing Service — Cardinal John J. O'Connor of New York presided over an interfaith prayer service Apr. 20 in St. Patrick's Cathedral as a healing response to tensions ignited by the police killing of Amadou Diallo, a young Muslim immigrant from Guinea. The cardinal hoped the service, of prayer rather than protest, would begin "a new look at racial justice in our society." Participants in the service included Muslims, Jews, Protestants, Orthodox and Catholics, as well as civic and business people.

Debt Relief — "A Jubilee Call for Debt Forgiveness" was issued Apr. 23 by the Administrative Board of the U.S. Catholic Conference. The statement urged policy makers to take a new view of debt relief, with emphasis on its relationshiop to human development. "Debt cannot be mere numbers on a page or credit card bills.... It is about how children live and die half a world away. It is about poverty and people. It is about what kind of world we live in," the bishops said.

Desecration of the Eucharist

The rector of the Palm Beach diocesan cathedral re-blessed its altar and tabernacle Apr. 11, three days after thieves ripped the tabernacle from its moorings, left it smashed in a drainage ditch, and scattered consecrated hosts on the ground. Msgr. Thomas Klinzing said the sight of the hosts scattered about was almost more than he could bear. "I asked myself the question, 'Have we all lost the sense of the sacred? Is faith dead?' The desecration of the tabernacle and hosts into a drainage ditch is a blasphemy, and it tears at my heart."

INTERNATIONAL

Jesuits Refused Registration — Jesuit officials denounced the Russian government's rejection Apr. 1 of the order's application for registration as an independent legal body under the religion law of 1997. Ministry of Justice officials recommended registration as part of the local apostolic administration. The Jesuits contended that such registration would deprive the order of its independence.

Political Correctness in Germany — Cardinal Joseph Ratzinger, in an interview published Apr. 4 in the Berlin-based *Welt am Sonntag*, said Germany was undergoing a religious crisis and therefore was confronting issues such as abortion with "political correctness" rather than moral consideration. "This situation creates the possibility that God will be considered a distant hypothesis (in Germany), and that everything that concerns religion will be pushed into the realm of the subjective." He said agnosticism and atheism had more current influence than they had before the end of the Cold War.

Genocide Charge against Bishop — The arrest Apr. 4 of Rwandan Bishop Augustin Misago of Gikongoro on allegations of complicity in the 1994 genocide of Tutsis was part of a government attempt to discredit the Church, said a report by *Fides*, the news agency of the Congregation for the Evangelization of Peoples.

Admit Having Hurt Catholics — While Romania's Orthodox bishops did what they felt was necessary to keep their church going under communism, they should admit that their collaboration hurt people, especially the nation's Eastern-rite Catholics. Shortly before the beginning of Pope John Paul's visit to the country, Orthodox Metropolitan Nicolae Cornjeanu of Tumisiara detailed the extent of his own collaboration and apologized for not helping his persecuted Eastern-rite Catholic neighbors. In an interview circulating during the month, he said he was named a bishop in 1962 when the communists were in complete control of Romania. To accept leadership of a diocese meant going along with the government and with its efforts to control religious life. "I could have acted differently, but at that time I thought that for the good of the (Orthodox) Church I had to make compromises with the regime.... Now I must confess my sins with all sincerity. I did not fulfill my obligations as a bishop, because I did not protest against the regime."

Catholics Persecuted — Catholics loyal to the pope in southeastern China were suffering under suppression by the government, said Hong Kong Catholics with mainland connections. Earlier in the year, they said, the government leveled 13 churches built by underground Catholics in Fuzhou Diocese, in Fujian province.

Second Irish Seminary To Close — Father Liam Power, spokesman for the Diocese of Waterford and Lismore, announced that beginning in June St. John's College in Waterford would no longer accept candidates for the priesthood; it would become the second Irish seminary to announce closing in less than a year because of declining enrollment.

Poor Evangelization in Mexico — Mexican bishops criticized evangelization efforts as "insufficient" and called for a "society of solidarity" to defend human life and the rights of all. The Church had fallen into a "superficial evangelization," they said at the end of a plenary meeting. Church teachings remained prominent in popular traditions and opinion, but had yet to touch the lives of most Mexicans or to "transform unjust social structures." They sought to declare a "clear yes" to truth, life and participation while saying "no" to corruption, lies, apathy, easy money and consumerism. The bishops' statement noted: "A society of solidarity can be built only on the promotion and defense of rights, without forgetting that each right brings with it a corresponding obligation. We dream of a society in which no institution or agency makes attacks against life or against the right of all men and women to seek God according to the dictates of their own conscience."

Bewildering Decision of Planned Parenthood — A Catholic aid agency criticized a decision by Planned Parenthood to send thousands of condoms and contraceptives to refugees in Albania. A spokeswoman for CAFOD, the overseas aid and development agency of the Bishops' Conference of England and Wales, said she was astonished that the International Planned Parenthood Federation was sending $60,000 in "emergency supplies" to five camps in the region. "The idea that what these people need is contraception is bewildering," said Fiona Fox.

Doomsday Cults — Church and civic experts in South Korea warned of an increase in the number of doomsday cult followers who believe the world will end before the new millennium. The Church should intensify its teaching on the true meaning of salvation and redemption in order to prevent the spread of such cults, said Father John Kim Mong-eun, director of the Catholic Academy for Korean Culture. "The doomsday cults would no longer prevail if orthodox Christian churches performed their roles and duties," Father Kim told UCA News, an Asian church agency based in Thailand.

Solidarity Needed in Indonesia — Indonesian bishops called on Catholics nationwide to join with people of other religions to develop the kind of solidarity needed to cope with sectarian riots and other crises affecting the nation. "Together with the whole nation, we should be committed to restore all damage and wounds caused by egotism, narrow-minded group interests, manipulations, efforts to marginalize others and fierce revenge," they said in a pastoral letter. "Our togetherness with the whole nation is valuable and could become a greater force to combat immorality and to build up the future. We are citizens of this nation and have a duty to maintain its security."

Action against Anti-Christian Campaign — The bishops of India outlined an action plan to counteract a nationwide anti-Christian campaign, suggesting a strengthening of spirituality, promoting interreligious dialogue and solidarity, improving communications and increasing social involvement by Catholics. Atrocities against Christians and opposition to church preparations for Jubilee 2000 celebrations were dominant subjects of consideration at the Apr. 15-16 meeting of officials of the bishops' conference. They said the Church faced "a moment of trial and suffering" because of violence during the past year, and warned of fundamentalists' "long-term, determined plans" to attack the Church. They called attention to an increase in attacks on Christians since a pro-Hindu government came to power in March, 1998, and cited 116 anti-Christian attacks and five killings since January 1998. The bishops said that continued atrocities "should not in any way deter us from our mission to spread the Good News and to serve the poor." The bishops noted that atrocities had "brought blessings for us" in that they helped Christians to deepen their faith and engender "a readiness to suffer with Christian hope and greater unity." The violence also made the Church and Christian values "better known all over the country," they said. Meanwhile, Hindu fundamentalists were conducting a pamphlet campaign throughout the country depicting Christians as anti-nationals who should be ousted from the country.

Crisis in Australia — The bishops of Australia endorsed a statement signed by their representatives and Vatican officials that spoke of a "crisis of faith" in their country. Accordingly, they said it was time for Catholics to engage in "prayer, reflection, discernment, responsibility and action to which the pope calls us." At a meeting Apr. 5-15 in Sydney, they also released a pastoral letter accepting the pope's "personal directive that use of the Third Rite of Reconciliation, or general absolution, (a bone of contention) in Australia, be kept strictly within the conditions laid down by church law." The bishops said they wanted to address "conflicting reports ... that have caused confusion, hurt and ager for many" in Australia. At the Special Assembly of the Synod of Bishops for Oceania and a meeting with the Vatican, their representatives consistently and forcefully indicated the great strengths of the Australian church and the admirable dedication of the clergy, religious and lay people in so many fields." Meanwhile, friction continued to develop over widespread use of the Third Rite of Reconciliation and the circulation of negative allegations about church abuses.

JUNE 1999

VATICAN

Eucharistic Congress — The Vatican announced that the International Eucharistic Congress of Jubilee Year 2000 would be held June 18-25 with opening and closing ceremonies to be held at the Basilica of St. John Lateran. The announcement represented "a call to pastors and the faithful to give greater value to every Eucharistic celebration," said an article in *L'Osservatore Romano*.

Christian-Buddhist Opportunities — Buddhist and Christian beliefs do not mix, but Buddhism's increasing popularity in Europe offers opportunities to explore common values of the two faiths, according to a statement issued June 4 by the Pontifical Council for Interreligious Dialogue. "The presence of Buddhism in Europe can become an important occasion to review elements of the Christian tradition such as mystical experience, the dimension of silence, respect toward creation (and) the life of charity and compassion." The statement summarized conclusions reached during a four-day conference of Eastern European Buddhist and Catholic representatives, especially that "the face of Europe in the coming centuries certainly will be marked by the meeting between Christian tradition and the great religions and cultures of the Middle and Far East."

Catholic-Orthodox Meeting Postponed — In a letter published June 4, Pope John Paul expressed regret over a year-long postponement of a Catholic-Orthodox dialogue meeting, because of the inability of Orthodox delegates to attend due to the war in Yugoslavia. "The postponement of the plenary session ... has made it evident that historical events can place conditions even on theological dialogue," he wrote in the letter to Cardinal Edward I. Cassidy, president of the Pontifical Council for Promoting Christian Unity. He said the dialogue in the 1990s had set aside discussion of strictly theological issues in order to examine "difficult questions arising from historical events," including the formation of Eastern Catholic churches and their re-emergence in Eastern Europe after 50 years of suppression by communist governments. It was time, he said, to return to the dialogue commission's original set of theological topics aimed at the full unity of the churches "so that the witness of the followers of Christ in the contemporary world would shine more brightly."

AIDS Care — The growing gap between rich and poor in the world is glaringly evident in the care provided to people with AIDS, the president of the Vatican's health-care council told the World Health Organization. "The abyss which separates rich populations from the poor is particularly deep and dramatic in matters of health." Governments and health-care institutions must therefore commit themselves "to making medications and the most advanced treatment fully accessible to all those suffering from AIDS, not only the wealthiest or citizens of the most developed countries," said Archbishop Javier Lozano Barragan. "The precarious health situation of a large part of the world at the threshold of the third millennium is in marked contrast to the abundance of scientific and technical means" available, he noted. According to a statistical study commissioned by the Pontifical Council for the Pastoral Care of Health Workers, Catholic hospitals, clinics and hospices were responsible for nearly 25 percent of all medical care provided worldwide to persons with HIV-AIDS.

Cloister Rules — New rules for nuns living in cloistered convents were issued early in the month by the Congregation for Institutes of Consecrated Life and for Societies of Apostolic Life. The regulations cover the authority of superiors regarding those who may enter or leave the cloister, the use of television and other media, and additional matters. The rules are related to the "real separation from the world, silence and solitude" which "express and protect the integrity of the wholly contemplative life." The rules are the subject of an "Instruction on the Contemplative Life and on the Enclosure of Nuns."

Trip to Poland — Pope John Paul visited his native Poland June 5-17. (See Special Reports.)

Christianity Is the Religion of Love — So stated Pope John Paul marking the June 11 feast of the Sacred Heart of Jesus and the 100th anniversary of Pope Leo XIII's consecration of humankind to the Sacred Heart. He said the Sacred Heart is the symbol of God's love for all people and a reminder that followers of Christ must be people who love God and love others as he did. "The heart of the Savior calls us to return to the love of the Father, who is the source of every authentic love.... His heart particularly reveals the generosity of God toward sinners. God, reacting to sin, does not lessen his love but increases it in a movement of mercy which becomes the initiative of redemption."

Justification Statement — Cardinal Edward I. Cassidy, the Vatican's chief ecumenist, and the Rev. Dr. Ishmael Noko, general secretary of the Lutheran World Federation, announced June 11 that "The Joint Declaration on the Doctrine of Justification" would be signed formally Oct. 31, 1999, in Augsburg, Germany.

Women in Charitable Work — Women delegates to the general assembly of Caritas Internationalis asked Catholic Charities organizations to involve more women in decision-making and to focus more programs on improving the lot of women. In soup kitchens and refugee camps, orphanages and health clinics, women comprise the majority of Catholic Charities employees and volunteers. But, when it comes to the governing and coordinating structures of Catholic aid programs, women "are almost invisible at the national, regional and international levels," said a report to the June 14-19 assembly at the Vatican. "We do not see the advancement of women within Caritas as a seeking after power (nor) as a need to dominate or control," the report said. "It is the special quality of service and caring which women bring that we wish to advance."

Tourism Is More Than Dollars — Msgr. Piero Monni, Vatican observer at the World Tourism Organization's June 15-18 conference in Nice, said profit cannot be the only consideration in tourism. If competition and profit are the only concerns, companies and governments can lose sight of the needs of the people who are tourists and those who live in tourist places. He called for a code of conduct for tour agencies and their clients, closer monitoring of the impact of tourist facilities on the environment, and studies on the impact of tourism on local cultures before a big push is made to advertise an area as a holiday destination.

Common Celebration of Jubilee 2000 — "The Jubilee offers us [Catholics and Orthodox] an occasion to raise up to the Lord a common and universal hymn of praise," Pope John Paul said June 28 as he welcomed visiting representatives of Ecumenical Orthodox Patriarch Bartholomew of Constantinople. They were at the Vatican to participate in the celebration of the feast of Sts. Peter and Paul, patrons of the Roman Church.

Pilgrimage — "Concerning Pilgrimage to the Places Linked to the History of Salvation" is the title of a papal letter released June 30.

General Audience Topics:

• Reflections on his June 5-17 visit to Poland, June 23. (See separate article.)
• Meaning of the pallium, a vestment for metropolitan archbishops symbolic of their union with the Church of Rome (June 30).

Lay Movements Need Guidance
Bishops are responsible for the guidance and discernment of the potential of new movements of the laity to serve the good of people, parishes and the Church. This was the major point stressed during a June 16-19 meeting attended by 100 bishops and cardinals. Movements under consideration included Charismatic Renewal, Focolare, L'Arche, Communion and Liberation, and the Neocatechumenal Way. Cardinal Joseph Ratzinger, head of the Congregation for the Doctrine of the Faith, said: "Bishops have the task of discernment to help the movements find the right path to peaceful unity and to help pastors be open to letting themselves be surprised by these groups which arise from the Holy Spirit." Cardinal J. Francis Stafford, president of the Pontifical Council for the Laity, said "the experience of new and traditionally undefined charisms within the Church has been unsettling to some pastors and bishops. For others, it has been an enormous gift…. Some of the unease is legitimate…. There are growing pains within these new ecclesial expressions" which need correction. The bishop's task, said Cardinal Ratzinger, is to build the local church as a family where everyone works together instead of allowing it to become a "marketplace" where the faithful choose one community over another. "The challenge today is to ensure that the faithful do nor retreat into closed groups, but that they enlighten all and speak to everyone."

NATIONAL

No Assisted Suicide in California or Maryland — The California General Assembly ended its session June 4 without acting on legislation which would have allowed terminally ill Californians to seek assisted suicide. Eight days earlier, Maryland Governor Parris Glendening signed into law a bill making Maryland the 37th state to ban the practice. Oregon remained alone in permitting assisted suicide.

Kosovo Aid — The American Jewish Committee gave Catholic Relief Services $100,000 for aid in Kosovo, June 7. Cardinal Anthony J. Bevilacqua announced June 29 that the Archdiocese of Phila-

delphia had raised $700,000 for the same purpose.

No Rebaptism — The North American Orthodox-Catholic Theological Consultation issued a challenge to Orthodox churches to repudiate rebaptism of Catholics who become Orthodox. In an agreed statement released June 8, the group called for a formal withdrawal of the 1755 decree of the Patriarch of Constantinople on rebaptism. Later patriarchal decrees said rebaptism is not needed, but the 1755 decree was never rescinded. The statement said mutual recognition of baptism "is fully consistent with the perennial teaching of both churches," and that the theory and practice of rebaptism, though upheld only by a minority within the Orthodox churches, presents "a fundamental obstacle" to Christian unity.

Worry about Universities — Vatican officials are "worried about (U.S.) universities floating away" from their Catholic identity, as had already happened in Canada and Europe, said theologian Monika Hellwig early in the month after an April meeting with personnel of the Congregation for Catholic Education. Backgrounding her remarks were differences of views about norms for governing Catholic institutions of higher learning, and a trend toward their independence dating from 1967.

Refugees and Migrants — Of all the popes in history, John Paul has devoted the most time and attention to the issue of refugees and displaced migrants. So stated Father Richard Ryscavage, director of Jesuit Refugee Service, during the June 10-13 meeting of the Catholic Theological Society of America. Besides intensifying focus on refugees and migrants, he said, the pope has contributed two new insights which are not welcomed by the community of nations. "First, he believes it is becoming increasingly difficult to distinguish between refugees, internally displaced people and economic migrants." Secondly, "international law, treaties and international organizations need greater scrutiny and reform in order to protect people on the move."

Missionaries of Charity in Asbury Park — Four of Mother Teresa's Missionaries of Charity opened a residence in Asbury Park, N.J., to begin work among poor people in the community. Welcoming them June 6, the feast of Corpus Christi, Bishop John M. Smith of Trenton said: "I think the presence of the Missionaries of Charity will help many to see the presence of Jesus, if not in the Eucharist, then in the love and concern you show to the needy and the poor."

Healing Outreach — The Church must take the lead in healing racial and ethnic divisions by reaching out to persons scarred by insensitivity and benign neglect, said a panel of speakers during the annual meeting of the national Council for Catholic Evangelization June 16-19 in New Orleans. Panelists — Vietnamese and Native American priests, an African-American lay person and a Hispanic deacon — spoke from personal experiences of racism.

Youth Conference — More than 2,500 teen-agers from 24 states and Canada attended the "Goin' Home to My Father's House" conference June 18-20 on the campus of the Franciscan University of Steubenville, Ohio.

Synagogue Attacks Decried —Cardinal William H. Keeler, in the name of his fellow bishops June 22, expressed "solidarity with our Jewish brothers and sisters who have been the victims of senseless violence" in the form of arson attacks on three synagogues in Sacramento. He said the bishops condemned such terrorism and "the targeting of religious sites and the repositories of religious knowledge, culture and tradition." Bishop William K. Weigand of Sacramento said: "Acts like these make it painfully clear that one of the challenges (in the new millennium) will continue to be combating religious and racial prejudice and hatred."

Bishops' Meeting — The National Conference of Catholic Bishops held a closed-door, retreat-type of meeting June 18-22 in Tucson, with discussions focusing on the challenge of episcopal leadership in the new millennium.

Abuse of Human Rights — Abuse of human rights around the world grew worse over the last decade, according to Amnesty International's annual report. Ethnic cleansing in Yugoslavia, slavery in Sudan, torture and disappearances in Mexico, and executions in the United States were among violations of rights included in the report, released June 16 in Washington. William F. Schultz, executive director of Amnesty International USA, said at a press conference that, of 142 nations surveyed, the percentage of countries where torture and other abuses occurred increased from 55 percent to 66 percent between 1988 and 1998. The number of countries responsible for deaths from torture and for the "disappearances" of individuals also increased dramatically over the decade.

Mass Information for Travelers — The Catholic Communications Campaign announced June 21 it would help publicize a service already providing times-of-Mass information for travelers around the United States, by dialing 1-800-Mass-Times. With very little promotion, as many as 100,000 people had already used the service in the course of a year, according to its founder, Robert Hummel.

Health Care Won't Be Abandoned — Despite "concerted efforts to diminish, if not completely destroy, our Catholic health care systems, here and throughout the United States, we will not abandon health care.... We will not turn our backs on the needy.... We will not forget the poor." So stated Cardinal John J. O'Connor June 27 at a Mass for health-care personnel in New York's St. Patrick's Cathedral.

K. of C. Donations, Services — The Knights of Columbus fraternal service organization announced new records for charitable giving in 1998: nearly $111 million in donations and more than 55 million hours in volunteer services.

Women in Diocesan Positions — The bishops' Committee on Women in Society and in the Church released a report June 30 indicating that women held nearly 47 percent of diocesan administrative and professional positions in 1998.

Common Ground Initiative
In a speech written shortly before his death on June 17, British Cardinal George Basil Hume called on American Catholics to end divisions in their ranks and to focus attention on "Christ as the Way, the Truth and the Life." The speech was read by Archbishop Oscar H. Lipscomb, chairman of the Catholic Common Ground Initiative, June 25 before a packed audience at the Washington Theological Union. Cardinal Hume wrote, in part:

• "The mission of the Church is weakened, both locally and nationally, if it is a divided Church. I believe unity in the Church in the next millennium will be dependent on two essentials: the primacy of spirituality in the lives of individuals and society, and a rediscovery of the centrality of Christ as the Way, the Truth, and the Life."

• "The Catholic Common Ground Initiative is an attempt to look both at what unites us and what is needed for the Church of the future, the Church of the third millennium."

• "It is a search for the common ground where we all stand, not the different pieces of land from where we can proclaim differing opinions.... That common ground must be faithful to the Church's teaching. That is part of the foundation and bedrock on which we must stand together."

• "There are many outstanding issues in the Church today where dialogue is important," the cardinal also said, citing the role of women, the role of lay persons, liturgy, religious education and questions of faith, morals and church authority."

The Catholic Common Ground Initiative was launched by Cardinal Joseph L. Bernardin shortly before his death in 1996.

INTERNATIONAL

Sudan Worse than Kosovo — A Sudanese bishop was joined by three Congressmen in urging the U.S. government to increase efforts to bring about peace in Sudan and to end atrocities against civilians in the southern part of the country. "What is happening in Sudan ... makes Kosovo look like a Sunday-school picnic.... Everything that we've heard from the administration about why we're in Kosovo — the human rights violations, the terrible atrocities — everything is true in Sudan, only more so," said Rep. Thomas Tancredo, R-Colo., at a June 8 press conference in Washington. His remarks were echoed by visiting Bishop Macram Gassis of el Obeid, Sudan.

Don't Blame All Serbs — "The great tragedy of the war in Yugoslavia does not only consist in the great material misery, but also in the deep wound between peoples, which risks staying open for numerous future generations," said the secretaries-general of the European bishops' conferences. They called on "political and military authorities not to condemn the whole Serb people today by reason of the cruelty of their political leaders, but to include them in the aid effort." The statement came in the wake of a June 19-23 meeting in Dubrovnik, Croatia, of the Council of Catholic Episcopates of Europe.

Day of Prayer for Peace — The Syro-Malabar Church, based in southern India, observed a day of prayer for peace June 20 as India and Pakistan continued combat along their disputed border in Kashmir. Syro-Malabar Archbishop Varkey Vithayathil said the fighting, in addition to its death toll, wasted money needed by the region's desperately poor people.

No Clearance for Abortion — In a letter authorized by Pope John Paul, the bishops of Germany were told June 22 that a certificate issued to pregnant women counseled at church-run facilities should bear the message, "This certificate cannot be used to obtain legal abortions."

Stop Arms Sales — Congolese Cardinal Frederic Etsou-Nzabi-Bamungwabi told Catholic News Service June 24: "If the United States would not give arms to Uganda, Burundi and Rwanda, they would not have taken over parts of the Congo.... What is going on with the support of the United States and other countries is perpetuating the war in Congo."

Priesthood Celebration in the Holy Land — Seven hundred and fifty priests from around the world gathered in the Holy Land June 22-27 to celebrate their priesthood and prepare for the Church's celebration of Holy Year 2000. The international gathering was the fourth of its kind sponsored by the Congregation for the Clergy. Latin-rite Patriarch Michael Sabah of Jerusalem welcomed the priests, saying it was appropriate for them to renew their priestly lives in contact with the Holy Land. "Everywhere you go, continue to announce the Life and the Resurrection," he said. Cardinal Bernardin Gantin, dean of the College of Cardinals, noted the great importance of priests' service to the needs of the faithful. "Christ did not come to be served, but to serve," he said. "Men expect priests who really serve, who are coherent with their identity. The priest should be recognized as the other Christ."

The most dramatic event of the gathering was the celebration of Mass June 25 by 520 priests on six boats on the Sea of Galilee.

Medical Guidelines Opposed — Seven days after the British Medical Association proposed new guidelines June 23 that would give legal protection to doctors who starve and dehydrate their patients to death, Cardinal Thomas Winning of Glasgow spoke out against them in a statement issued through *The Catholic Herald* newspaper in London. Although the guidelines are not legally binding, he called them "sinister" and "worrying," saying: They "will cause very real anxiety among thousands of patients and their families. There can be no justification for starving and dehydrating people to death. That this should go on in national Health Service hospitals with the full approval of the British Medical Association is almost beyond belief. In essence, the guidelines give doctors the power of life or death over stroke victims, accident victims, the elderly and those with Alzheimer's disease."

First Church in Kazakhstan — The first Catholic church opened in Astana, a year after the city was inaugurated as the ex-Soviet Republic's capital. The Mass of dedication was celebrated by Cardinal Joachim Meisner of Cologne June 27. He said in a homily that the opening of the church would give the Christian cross a "permanent presence" in the capital.

G-7 Cologne Initiative — The Cologne Initiative issued by seven industrialized democracies to provide debt relief for the world's poorest countries was called significant but still "short of the amount needed," said Archbishop Theodore E. McCarrick, chairman of the U.S. bishops' Committee on International Policy. "It is an important step forward to securing access to education, health care, sanitation and other basic needs for millions of people suffering under the burden of debt." The agreement "will provide more debt relief to a wider range of countries than under existing programs," but it "still falls short of the amount needed to make a major difference for the 45 countries in greatest need." The Cologne Initiative was issued by the heads of government of Britain, France, Germany, Italy, Canada, the United States and Japan on the first day of a June 18-20 summit meeting of the Group of Seven, or G-7 (to become G-8 with the later addition of Russia).Under the plan, some 33 debtor nations meeting required conditions could reduce their external debt over the next few years by as much as $70 billion of the $127 billion they owe to industrialized nations and such financial institutions as the World Bank and the International Monetary Fund.

The U.S. bishops' conference along with similar conferences in other countries were supportive of moves toward debt reduction for poor nations for several reasons, among them the Jubilee Year 2000 effort for the forgiveness of crushing and unpayable debt.

The Church in Latin America
The Church in Latin America faces serious challenges in the form of economic injustice, political corruption, aggressive sects and its own failure to grow, according to the immediate past president of the Latin American Bishops' Council (CELAM). Archbishop Oscar Rodriguez Maradiaga of Tegucigalpa, Honduras, presented a grim picture of the state of the Church in Latin America in a June 25 talk to a conference at John Carroll University in Cleveland. He said some church communities "maintain a preconciliar model of church that is characterized, among other things, by clericalism and vertical structures, fundamentalist doctrine, a closed moral viewpoint and a centralized view of the parish." In some cases, "support for base Christian communities has been the fruit of a passing pastoral fancy, rather than deep conviction." In other areas, "the aggressive presence of sects and the new religious movements ... (has) led to the disintegration of the family and communities, and constitutes a serious danger to peoples' freedom and dignity." Liturgical celebrations, "in general, are not very creative, participatory or inculturated.... The religious expressions of simple people and native groups are still not valued and are often disdained." The archbishop cited the need for cooperation "in proclaiming the Good News through integral evangelization, to love and respect diverse cultures and make every effort to deeply inculturate the Gospel." He said family ministry "must be renovated and made more dynamic, in order to respond to the challenges of the day: strengthening the institution of the family, supporting couples who are having difficulties, welcoming and providing guidance for families in irregular situations, pastoral attention to the role of men as husbands and fathers, preparation of young people for marriage, fostering the spirituality of marriage." The Church's "greatest challenge ... is posed by the near absence of committed lay Christians in social and political life.... Those who take up this challenge have shown themselves to have a weak Christian identity, due to a lack of formation specifically oriented toward political and social commitment."

On the positive side, however, Archbishop Maradiaga said there is "a greater presence of lay people in the life of the Church, which is a sign that people are becoming more aware of the dignity, vocation and mission conferred on every person by baptism."

JULY 1999

VATICAN

Budget Surplus — The Vatican reported a 1998 budget surplus of $1.5 million, lower than in recent years due to a variety of circumstances.

Remarks to Religious — At a time when so many societies are suffering from division, violence, hatred and selfishness, communities of religious women must be models of love and caring, Pope John Paul II said July 5 in a message to representatives of the Adorers of the Blood of Christ. "In your daily relationships, let yourselves be guided by a gaze of supernatural tenderness toward each of your sisters and toward everyone you meet," he said.

The Church relies on Benedictine monasteries to provide "witnesses of a humble and tenacious fidelity to the word of God," the Holy Father said in a July 7 letter marking the 1,500th anniversary of the founding of the Subiaco monastery by St. Benedict. He said Benedictines should return to the initial experience of St. Benedict and his rule, and realize how much the world needs the straightforward witness of lives devoted to listening to God's word, prayer and building a community marked by brotherhood.

During a July 18 visit to a Carmelite monastery in the Alpine village of Quart, the pope said: "A monastery is an authentic center of spiritual energy which draws sustenance from the springs of contemplation."

Debt Impedes Development — "The weight of debt condemns the poorest countries to permanent underdevelopment," said Archbishop Giuseppe Bertello at a U.N. meeting on economics. In remarks released July 13, he said: "International public opinion in general, and the churches and numerous non-governmental organizations in particular, are more and more sensitive" to questions of debt "and demand for the third millennium that a solution be found for the most indebted countries." The community of nations "possesses the effective means to combat misery" and can make debt alleviation and equitable development its priorities if it wishes to do so. "In an ever-more interdependent world, a new culture of international solidarity is called for." Archbishop Bertello was the Holy See's observer to Geneva-based U.N. agencies.

European Synod — The Vatican released in midmonth a lengthy working paper for the Special Assembly of the Synod of Bishops for Europe, to be held in October. The paper noted topics of concern, including material progress and spiritual values, solidarity, religious freedom, threats to faith in the forms of relativism, indifferentism and agnosticism. "Jesus Christ alive in his Church," along with living faith, is a basic theme of the document, which seeks to proclaim that "the hope of Europe is in the Cross of Christ."

Mother Teresa's Cause — The process for the beatification of Mother Teresa of Calcutta got under way during the month with the setting up by Archbishop Henry Sebastian D'Sousa of special tribunals to gather information regarding her life, work and evidence of sanctity.

Heaven and Hell — Heaven "is not an abstraction nor a physical place amid the clouds, but a living and personal relationship with the Holy Trinity.... When this world has passed away, those who accepted God in their lives and were sincerely open to his love, at least at the moment of death, will enjoy that fullness of communion with God which is the goal of human existence."

So stated the pope at a general audience July 21. He added that it is possible to get a taste of heaven on earth. Through the sacraments, especially the Eucharist, and through acts of self-giving in charity one can experience some of the happiness and peace which will reach its culmination in final, complete communion with God in heaven.

Hell is real and eternal, and the end chosen by those who turn away from God, said an editorial in the July 17 edition of the Jesuit magazine, *La Civilta Cattolica*. Church teaching clarifies the nature of hell by maintaining that it "is not a 'place,' but a 'state,' a 'way of being' in which a person suffers the penalty of the (self-chosen) privation of God." This punishment is accompanied by "a 'penalty of the senses,' which is expressed with the image of 'fire,' but which has nothing to do with the fire which we have experienced." This punishment is eternal, "not because this is what God wants, but by the decision that man makes consciously in life and confirms at the point of death — for God or against God," forever.

Concerning the Elderly — Society should re-examine its views concerning the elderly and should adjust its relations with them accordingly, Pope John Paul said July 25. "In industrially and technologically developed societies, the condition of the elderly is ambivalent," he noted, explaining that elderly persons are becoming less integrated into family and social life. The situation highlights "the characteristic imbalance of a social model dominated by the economy and by profit, which tends to penalize 'nonproductive' groups, assigning value to people ... for their utility."

NATIONAL

Reconsecration after Murder — More than 1,000 parishioners crowded into St. Matthew Church in Forestville, Conn., July 1 to witness ceremonies for reconsecration of the church following the murder of Father Robert J. Lysz. Father Lysz was bludgeoned to death June 24.

His body, under a pile of vestments in a side aisle of the church, was discovered the next day by parishioners waiting for him to celebrate the 7:30 a.m. Mass. The reconsecration of the church was conducted by Auxiliary Bishop Peter A. Rosazza of Hartford. A man with no permanent address was arrested and charged with murder and third-degree burglary.

Stem-Cell Research — Catholics were among ethicists, scientists, politicians and religious leaders urging Congress to continue the existing ban on federally funded human embryo research; they said it violates existing law and is unethical and scientifically unnecessary. Dr. Edmund Pellegrino, professor of medicine and medical ethics at Georgetown University Medical Center, one of the signers of a July 1 statement, said he was not opposed to stem-cell research itself, but to the "deliberate production of living human embryos for the purpose of harvesting embryonic stem cells" which "effectively ends the life of a new human being at its most vulnerable stage of existence."

Executions Increasing — The number of executions in the United States continued to rise at a record pace as Catholics and others around the country raised their voices against the death penalty. Despite pleas from many bishops and lay persons, inmates in Missouri, Pennsylvania, Oklahoma, Alabama, Arizona and Florida were put to death in late June or early July, bringing to 58 the number of people executed in 1999 and to 558 the number killed since capital punishment was reinstated in 1976.

Ministry to Homosexuals — The Congregation for the Doctrine of the Faith barred Salvatorian Father Robert Nugent and School Sister of Notre Dame Jeannine Gramick "from any pastoral work involving homosexual persons." (See Special Report for details.)

Jubilee Justice — More than 3,000 persons took part in the National Catholic Gathering for Jubilee Justice July 15-18 in Los Angeles. "Open the Doors to Christ" was the theme of the gathering. Accordingly, Cardinal Roger M. Mahony said in a homily during the concluding Mass that Catholics are called to "build a culture of life and love to replace the violence, divisions and emptiness that diminishes so many lives.... We believe every person is precious, no matter how young or how old, how rich or how poor; regardless of race, gender, ethnicity or immigration status; whether they are in Kosovo, East Los Angeles, or even on death row...."

Prayer for Crash Victims — Catholics joined their countrymen of other faiths in prayer for the casualties of the July 16 plane crash which claimed the lives of John F. Kennedy, Jr., his wife Carolyn and sister-in-law Lauren Bessette.

Bishop Resigned — Bishop Patrick Ziemann of Santa Rosa resigned from his diocese because of a sexual affair with one of his diocesan priests.

Low Givers — Among Catholics, the higher the income, the lower the giving, percentage-wise. So reported Charles Zech, a professor of economics at Villanova University and author of *Why Catholics Don't Give ... And What Can Be Done About It.* He told Catholic News Service July 28 that, "among low-income people, Catholic giving is not much different from Protestant giving. But, as income increases, the gap between the two increases, so the biggest gap between Catholic giving and Protestant giving is at the highest income levels.... Overall, Catholics give half as much as Protestants. At the highest levels, it's probably about a third as much." Backgrounding Zech's comments was a national study of church giving conducted from 1992 to 1995.

INTERNATIONAL

Holy See Attacked — The role of the Holy See at the United Nations came under attack at the Cairo Plus Five conference which reviewed the implementation of the final document of the U.N. conference on population and development held in Cairo in 1994. At issue were conflicting positions regarding reproductive rights, contraception, abortion, methods of AIDS prevention, parental rights and responsibilities, and conscience rights of medical staff. Britain's Secretary of State for International Development, Clare Short, broadsided the Catholic Church, saying it was

on a "morally destructive" course, according to the July 10 edition of *The Tablet.* In New York, John Klink, one of the Holy See's negotiators, was confronted by opponents of its positions. The International Planned Parenthood Federation had already called for the Holy See's ouster from participation at U.N. conferences. Archbishop Renato Martino, head of the Holy See's delegation, said in an address July 2 that the Holy See would continue its involvement in the work of the United Nations to help in "finding answers, solving problems and sharing ideas" on population and development." *The Tablet* noted: "Sources in Rome are said to have interpreted Clare Short's remarks not as an attack on the Holy See's status in the United Nations, but as a criticism of the Vatican's position on contraception and abortion, and therefore an attack on the fundamental right to free speech."

Landless Suffer Violence — The Brazilian bishops' conference called for an end to violence in rural areas of the country in the wake of reports of brutal imprisonment and torture of landless peasants by representatives of the judicial system. Brazilian society cannot remain indifferent to the "ever-growing poverty and agony of its people," the bishops said in a statement issued early in the month.

Division Remains in Nicaragua — Twenty years after the Sandinista revolution, signs remained of the divide it caused in the Church. "The tensions remain; there is still a kind of cold war" between the hierarchy and some groups of Catholics, said Vida Luz Meneses, director of the ecumenical Valdivieso Study Center in Managua. But Bishop Juan Mata Guevara of Esteli said that, since the Sandinista Front lost power to a more conservative regime in 1990, the Church has been gradually reuniting.

Caribbean Youths Challenged — Bishop Robert Rivas of Kingstown, St. Vincent and the Grenadines told young people July 18 that they "must go and live the Good News and touch the lives" of their peers. Speaking at a youth assembly in Willemstad, Curacao, he said the Church "has taken a preferential option for young people," and that his dream was to see Catholic youths "give service as strong, vibrant, zealous missionaries ... to build the Church of the Caribbean" through work in justice and peace, evangelization, youth ministry, teaching and counseling.

Vision of Mexico — The bishops were reported to be working on a document that would outline their vision of the "Mexico we long for," with formal proposals for "achieving unity, cohesion and dialogue among Mexicans, so as to overcome the crises and defeat the economic and political threats of the next millennium."

Chinese Order Defied — Despite a government warning, 4,000 Catholics in eastern China bade farewell publicly to an underground priest who suffered from a tonic spasm for 13 years but kept celebrating Mass every day until he died. Father Matthias Chen Xizhi of Wenzhou Diocese died July 23 in a Catholic home in Wenzhou at the age of 85, reported UCA News, a church news agency based in Thailand. He continued his ministry until his death because people preferred his Masses over those celebrated by priests of the government-approved church, according to a local Catholic. Father Chen often insisted there was "nothing called retirement" unless it was retirement to "the bosom of God."

AUGUST 1999

VATICAN

Vacation Time — People should use summer vacations to enjoy moments of peace and closeness with their families and with God, Pope John Paul II said Aug. 1 at Castel Gandolfo. Vacations should be "a time of human recharging," an opportunity "to find yourself and others in a more balanced and serene way."

Tribute to Paul VI — The Holy Father paid tribute to Pope Paul VI on Aug. 6, the 21st anniversary of his death, calling him an "unforgettable predecessor in the See of Peter," whose "profound spiritual conviction guided his entire ecclesial mission."

Reorganization in Kazakhstan — The pope reorganized church jurisdictions in Kazakhstan by dividing the country into one diocese and three separate apostolic administrations.

Youth for the New Millennium — In a video message dated Aug. 7 during a European youth pilgrimage to Santiago de Compostela, the pope said: "The Church looks to you; it counts on you....Yours is the generation called to transmit the gift of faith in the new millennium."

NATIONAL

No Electronic Sacraments — The bishops' Secretariat for the Liturgy said in its (delayed) May-June newsletter that no sacrament can be received by electronic communication. Liturgical celebrations "depend on the physical presence of the gathered faithful" and "require the physical presence of the bishop, priest, deacon or other approved presiding minister.... Electronic communication via telephone, television, video conference or Internet is not sufficient for the celebration of the sacraments."

Black Catholics Are Unique — In the United States, "black Catholics are a unique group," with education and income levels well above the average for all African-Americans, said Father Clarence Williams, author of *Recovering from Everyday Racisms* and principal celebrant of a Mass at the African-American World Festival, held July 31-Aug. 1 in Milwaukee. He attributed this to "the Catholic advantage" of parochial schools.

Knights against Capital Punishment — Bishop Joseph A. Fiorenza, president of the National Conference of Catholic Bishops, urged the Knights of Columbus Aug. 3 to take up the cause to abolish the death penalty with the same enthusiasm they had been devoting to fighting abortion. He made the appeal during the Knights' international convention in Minneapolis.

U.S. Refugee Policy Wanting — Bishop Nicholas A. De Marzio, chairman of the bishops' Migration Committee, testified at a Senate hearing Aug. 4 that, despite a Clinton administration plan to increase to 90,000 the number of refugees allowed to enter the country next year, "U.S. leadership in the area of refugee protection is in decline." He recommended that the U.S. open its doors to a larger share of the world's refugees, that it begin resettling more of the thousands of refugee children and teen-agers without known relatives, that changes made to the asylum program in 1996 be re-evaluated, and that the State Department improve its system of processing the applications of asylum applicants. As recently as 1980, the U.S. admitted 207,000 refugees, Bishop Marzio said. For the past three years, the ceiling was 78,000.

Observance of the Ascension — Bishop Joseph A. Fiorenza, president of the National Conference of Catholic Bishops, issued a formal decree Aug. 6 authorizing "each ecclesiastical province to transfer the Solemnity of the Ascension (from Thursday to the following Sunday) ... by the affirmative vote of two-thirds of the bishops of the respective ecclesiastical province." In nearly a decade of debate on the issue, bishops from Eastern states consistently favored keeping Ascension as a holy day of obligation on Thursday, while those from Western states preferred moving it to Sunday.

Latino Radio Group — A group of Catholic communicators announced formation of the Latino Catholic Communications Consortium to produce and distribute radio programs to the U.S. Latino community. With funding support from a number of religious organizations and help from the U.S. Catholic Conference, the consortium planned to make available: programming from Radio Paz in Miami; more than 800 international programs produced by HTN Productions in San Antonio; segments from Latin America and the United States produced in collaboration with Maryknoll World Productions, New York; and catechetical programming produced by the Diocese of Orlando. Consortium plans were announced by Family Theater Productions in Hollywood.

Harvard Divinity School Head — Father J. Bryan Hehir was named the first Catholic head of the Harvard Divinity School Aug. 12. A Harvard graduate, he was a professor of religion and social studies since 1992. He was also a writer of scholarly articles and a consultant to the National Conference of Catholic Bishops and the U.S. Catholic Conference.

INTERNATIONAL

Assisi Churches Reopened — Almost two years after suffering earthquake damage and in time for traditional Franciscan celebrations Aug. 2, open again were the Basilica of St. Mary of the Angels and the Portiuncula Chapel, where St. Francis founded the Franciscan Order and St. Clare professed her vows.

False Abuse Claims — Egyptian Coptic Catholic Auxiliary Bishop Youhanna Golta said false reports of Christians being forced to convert to Islam were contributing to a worsening of the Muslim-Christian climate in Egypt. "Conversions to Islam are often presented as the results of Muslim pressure, but that is wrong," he said.

Famine and Persecution — More than 250,000 people in Sudan's Bahr el Ghazal region were facing the prospect of famine due to continuing drought, Bishop Cesare Mazzolari reported during the July 26-Aug. 8 meeting in Nairobi of the Association of Member Episcopal Conferences in Eastern Africa.

No Papal Visit to Hong Kong — Beijing's refusal to allow Pope John Paul to visit Hong Kong called the territory's special autonomy into question and raised fears of religious repression, said Hong Kong's leading English daily.

DEATHS

SEPTEMBER 1998 TO AUGUST 1999

Atkins, C. Clyde, 84, Mar. 15, 1999, Coral Gables, Fla.; federal judge; founding member of the Miami Catholic Lawyers Guild, board member of the Catholic Welfare Bureau; first Florida Catholic to become a federal judge, in 1966.

Ball, William Bentley, 82, Jan. 10, 1999, Sanibel Island, Fla.; Catholic attorney and champion of religious rights; argued cases in front of the Supreme Court 10 times, including cases involving state financial aid to Catholic schools, tax status of religious institutions, and the rights of Amish children involving education.

Barturen, José Manuel, 72, Nov. 25, 1998, New Rochelle; promoter of Opus Dei in the United States; student of Josémaria Escriva, founder of Opus Dei; established the first Opus Dei student residence in New York City.

Buckley, Cornelius M., 77, Nov. 20, 1998, Danvers, Mass.; news editor at *The Pilot,* Boston archdiocesan newspaper; served as editor for 30 years; publicist for the Society for the Propagation of the Faith.

Carasco Briseno, Bartolome, 80, Jan. 7, 1999, Oaxaca, Mexico; archbishop. of Oaxaca; ord. bp. of Huejutla, 1963-76; bp. of Tapachula, 1976; abp. of Oaxaca, 1976-93; revered as a defender of human rights and the poor.

Cargas, Harry James, 66, Aug. 18, 1998, St. Louis, Mo.; Catholic Holocaust scholar; professor of religion, language and literature at Webster University in St. Louis; author of 32 books; lecturer and writer on the Holocaust, including the book *Conversations with Elie Wiesel.*

Crucitti, Prof. Francesco, 67, Aug. 26, 1998, Rome, Italy; Italian physician, director of the Institute of Clinical Surgery, Catholic University of the Sacred Heart; papal surgeon; attended Pope John Paul II in 1981, following the assassination attempt on the pontiff, and operated on the Holy Father in 1992 and 1996.

Cullman, Oscar, 96, Jan. 16, 1999, Chamonix, France; Lutheran theologian, ecumenist, and biblical scholar; served as professor at the Universities of Basel and Paris; author of *Christ and Time* and *Peter, Disciple-Apostle-Martyr*; invited guest at Vatican Council II; close friend and advisor to Pope Paul VI; honored for his commitment to ecumenism by Pope John Paul II.

De Souza, Archbishop Isidore, 64, Mar. 13, 1999; archbishop of Cotonou, Benin and head of the bishop's conference of French-speaking West Africa; major figure in the transition of Benin to democracy, including leadership of the national Conference supervising democratic elections.

DiMaggio, Joe (Joseph Paul DiMaggio), 84, Mar. 8, 1999, Hollywood, Fla.; American baseball player, called "Joltin' Joe" and the "Yankee Clipper," who spent his entire career (1936–51) with the New York Yankees; set a major-league record in 1941 by hitting safely in 56 straight games; married briefly to Marilyn Monroe; inducted 1955 into the Baseball Hall of Fame; funeral in Sts. Peter and Paul Church, San Francisco; raised millions for the Joe DiMaggio Children's Hospital.

Donohue, Francis J., 74, Jan. 22, Miami, Fla.; press editor and former priest; editor of the Savannah edition of the Georgia Bulletin and the Southern Cross; later assisted the Miami archdiovese communications department.

Duhart, Bishop Clarence, 86, Sept. 21, 1998, Bangkok, Thailand; American founder of the Redemptorist Mission in Thailand; established first mission of the Redemptorists in Thailand in 1948, spending his remaining years in the missions; retired in 1975 in favor of a native local bishop.

Finn, Hugh, 44, Oct. 9, 1998, Manassas, Va.; Catholic layman removed from his feeding tube; former television news anchor rendered comatose by a car accident; his wife obtained a court order to remove him from the feeding tube with the support of Archbishop Thomas Kelly of Louisville.

Flannery, Fr. Edward, 86, Oct. 19, 1998, Washington, D.C.; leader in Catholic-Jewish relations; author of *The Anguish of the Jews: Twenty-Three Centuries of Anti-Semitism*; first secretary for Catholic-Jewish relations of the NCCB; honored by both Jewish and Catholic leaders, including Rabbi James Rudin, of the American Jewish Committee and Abraham Foxman of the Anti-Defamation League.

Frawley, Patrick J., K.M., 75, Nov. 3, 1998, Santa Monica, Calif.; Catholic businessman and publisher; chairman and CEO of Schick, from 1958-70; chairman of the Twin Circle Publishing Co.; promoted centers for treatment of alcohol, drug, and tobacco additction; member of the Knights of Malta.

Freking, Frederick W., 85, Nov. 28, 1998, La Crosse, Wis.; retired bishop. of La Crosse; ord. bp. of Salina, Nov. 30, 1957; app. bp. of La Crosse, Dec. 30, 1964, installed Feb. 24, 1965; resigned May 10, 1983.

Ghedighian, Patriarch Hemaiagh, 93, Nov. 28, 1998, Beirut, Lebanon; Armenian Catholic patriarch; served for decades as spiritual leader of Armenian Catholics, including during the civil wars of Lebanon; known for his spirituality and humility.

Grillmeier, Cardinal Alois, S.J., 88, Sept. 13, 1998, Munich, Germany; Jesuit cardinal and theologian; entered Society of Jesus, 1929; ord. priest June 24, 1937; taught fundamental and dogmatic theology and the history of theology at various ecclesiastical institutes; author of a number of books on dogmatic theology and the history of theology; member of the theological commission of the Second Vatican Council; cardinal Nov. 26, 1994; deacon, St. Nicholas in Prison.

Guitton, Jean, 97, Mar. 21, 1999, Paris, France; philosopher, scholar, and intellectual; observer at Vatican Council II, called by Pope John Paul II "one of the greatest thinkers of our century"; the first lay person invited to Vatican II, he delivered a memorable appeal for ecumenism; advised popes Pius XII, Paul VI, and John Paul II; author of over 30 scholarly works, including a biography of Paul VI.

Hume, Cardinal Basil — See Special Report in the Church Hierarchy section.

Kennedy, John F., Jr., 38, July 16, 1999; son of President John F. Kennedy and Jacqueline Kennedy Onassis; born 17 days after the election of his father in 1960; graduated Brown University; assistant district attorney for New York City, 1989-1994; founder of *George* magazine, 1995; married Carolyn Bessette, 1996; killed with his wife and her sister in a plane crash; buried at sea.

strengthen my brothers and sisters in the faith and to proclaim the Gospel to all people."

"Through the new evangelization the Church wishes to reveal her identity more clearly: to be closer to Christ and to his Word; to demonstrate that she is authentic and free from worldly influences; to be of greater service to the human person from a Gospel perspective; to be a leaven of the unity and not the division of humanity, which is opening to new, broader and still emerging horizons."

January 23

During morning Mass at the Basilica of Our Lady of Guadalupe, which concluded the Special Assembly for America of the Synod of Bishops.

"I have come here to place at the feet of the *mestiza* Virgin of Tepeyac ... the apostolic exhortation *Ecclesia in America,* which incorporates the contributions and pastoral suggestions of that Synod, entrusting to the Mother and Queen of this continent the future of its evangelization."

"The Church in America is the Church of Hope."

"If the Church in America has many reasons to rejoice, she also faces serious problems and important challenges."

The Gospel of Life: "The Church must proclaim the Gospel of life and speak out with prophetic voice against the culture of death. May the Continent of Hope also be the Continent of Life! This is our cry: Life with dignity for all! For all who have been conceived in their mother's womb, for street children, for indigenous peoples and Afro-Americans, for immigrants and refugees, for the young deprived of opportunity, for the old, for those who suffer any kind of poverty or marginalization."

"The time has come to banish ... from the continent every attack against life" — violence, terrorism, drug trafficking, torture. "There must be an end to the unnecessary recourse to the death penalty! No more exploitation of the weak, racial discrimination or ghettoes of poverty! Never again!"

Appeal to Mary: "O Lady and Mother of America! Strengthen the faith of our brothers and sisters so that in all areas of social, professional, cultural and political life they may act in accord with the truth and the new law which Jesus brought to humanity. Look with mercy on the distress of those suffering from hunger, loneliness, rejection or ignorance. Make us recognize them as your favorite children and give us the fervent charity to help them in their needs."

"Holy Virgin of Guadalupe, Queen of Peace! Save the nations and peoples of this continent. Teach everyone, political leaders and citizens, to live in true freedom and to act according to the requirements of justice and respect for human rights, so that peace may thus be established once and for all."

At an evening gathering of the Diplomatic Corps at the Presidential Residence.

"A social system must be promoted which allows all peoples to take an active part in furthering their integral progress; otherwise, many of these peoples could find themselves prevented from achieving it."

Primacy of the Human Person: "Contemporary progress, unparalleled in the past, must enable all human beings to see their dignity safeguarded and to be offered a deeper awareness of the greatness of their own destiny."

"The Church tirelessly proclaims that the human person must be the center of every civil and social order, of every system of technological and economic development.... This is the conviction that the Church would like to put on the table of the United Nations, or to express in the amicable dialogue she maintains with you, the members of the Diplomatic Corps, and with the authorities you represent in various parts of the world."

"This continent could be the 'Continent of Hope' if the human communities and their ruling classes which comprise it were to adopt a common ethical foundation. The Catholic Church and the other great religious confessions in America can contribute specific elements to this common ethic, elements which free consciences from being limited by ideas deriving from mere incidental consensus."

January 24

During morning Mass at the Hermanos Rodriguez Speedway.

May the light of Christ "illumine Mexican society, its families, schools and universities, its fields and its cities. May the values of the Gospel inspire its leaders to serve their fellow citizens with constant concern for those most in need."

The Light of Faith: "Faith in Christ is an integral part of the Mexican nation, indelibly inscribed in its history. Do not let this light of faith be extinguished! Mexico still needs it in order to build a more just and fraternal society with those who have nothing and hope for a better future."

"The world today sometimes forgets the transcendent values of the human person: his dignity and freedom, his inviolable right to life and the priceless gift of the family, in a social climate of solidarity. Human relations are not always based on the principles of charity and mutual aid. On the contrary, other criteria prevail, endangering the harmonious development and integral progress of individuals and peoples. For this reason Christians must be the 'soul' of this world. May they fill it with spirit, infuse life into it and cooperate in building a new society governed by love and truth."

"Bring Christ's word to those who still do not know it! Have the courage to bear witness to the Gospel in the streets and squares, in the valleys and mountains of this nation! Promote the new evangelization according to the Church's guidelines."

During an evening visit to the Adolfo Lopez Mateos Hospital, the pope visited a number of patients and delivered a written message.

"For Christians ... suffering is a mystery, often inscrutable to reason. It is part of the mystery of the human person, which is only explained in Jesus Christ, the one who reveals to man his own identity. Only through him will we find the meaning of all that is human."

Suffering with Jesus: "There is a close relationship between Jesus' Cross — a symbol of supreme suffering and the price of our true freedom — and our pains, sufferings, afflictions, hardships and anguish which can weigh on our souls or take root in our bodies. Suffering is transformed and elevated, when in those moments we become aware of God's closeness and solidarity. This is the certainty that gives inner peace and spiritual joy to the person who suffers generously and offers his pain 'as a living sacrifice, holy and acceptable to God' (Rom 12:1). The person who suffers in this way is not a burden to others, but by his own suffering contributes to the salvation of all."

January 25

During a multicultural extravaganza of all generations of the century at Aztec Stadium.

"You are called to become newly aware of having been entrusted with a rich human and religious tradition. It is your task to transmit this heritage of values to the new generations in order to nourish their vitality and hope, making them share in the Christian faith that shaped their past and must mark their future."

Building the New World: "The forthcoming new era must lead to a strengthening of America's faith in Jesus Christ. It is this faith, lived each day by many believers, which will motivate and inspire the necessary measures to overcome the deficiencies in the community's social progress, especially that of the rural and indigenous peoples; to overcome the corruption that affects so many institutions and citizens; to eliminate drug trafficking ...; to end the violence that sets brothers and social classes against one another, leading to bloodshed. Only faith in Christ can give rise to culture opposed to selfishness and death."

"America, Land of Christ and Mary! You have an important role in building the new world that the Second Vatican Council wanted to promote. You must be committed to making the truth prevail over the many forms of deceit, so that good may triumph over evil, justice over injustice, honesty over corruption. Accept without reservation the council's vision of the human being, created by God and redeemed by Jesus Christ. In this way, you will attain the full truth of moral values despite the illusion of temporary, precarious and subjective certitudes."

Challenge: "Every Christian is called to proclaim Christ, to witness to him and to make him present everywhere in the various cultures and ages of history."

"Anyone who follows the Gospel as a guide and norm of life cannot remain passive, but must share and spread Christ's light, even to the point of self-sacrifice."

"In the Lord's name," he challenged all his hearers but especially the young, "go with determination and evangelize your surroundings so that they may become more human, fraternal and united, more respectful of the nature entrusted to us. Share your faith and ideas of life with all the peoples of the continent, not by useless confrontation, but by the witness of your life. Show that Christ has the words of eternal life which can save people of yesterday, today and tomorrow. Reveal to your brothers and sisters the divine and human face of Jesus Christ, the Alpha and the Omega, the Beginning and the End, the First and the Last of all creation and all history, even of the history you are writing with your own lives."

January 26

At departures for St.Louis.

"At the end of my pastoral visit, I would like to reaffirm my full confidence in the future of this people, a future in which Mexico, ever more evangelized and Christian, can become a reference point in America and the world, a country where democracy — stronger and more deeply rooted, clearer and more effective each day, with the joyous and peaceful coexistence of her peoples — may always live under the tender gaze of her Queen and Mother, Our Lady of Guadalupe."

On arival at the St Louis Lambert International Airport, in response to a greeting by President Clinton.

A Culture of Life: America faces a conflict between "a culture that affirms, cherishes and celebrates the gift of life, and a culture that seeks to declare entire groups of human beings — the unborn, the terminally ill, the handicapped, and others considered 'unuseful' — to be outside the boundaries of legal protection. Because of the seriousness of the issues involved, and because of America's great impact on the world as a whole, the resolution of this new time of testing will have profound consequences for the century whose threshold we are about to cross. My fervent prayer is that, through the grace of God at work in the lives of Americans of every race, ethnic group, economic condition and creed, America will resist the culture of death and choose to stand steadfastly on the side of life. To choose life ... involves rejecting every form of violence: the violence of poverty and hunger which oppresses so many human beings; the violence of armed conflict which does not resolve but only increases divisions and tensions; the violence of particularly abhorrent weapons such as anti-personnel mines; the violence of drug trafficking; the violence of racism; and the violence of mindless damage to the natural environment."

At an afternoon encounter with young people at Kiel Center.

"Youth is a marvelous gift of God. It is a time of special energies, special opportunities and special responsibilities. Christ and the Church need your special talents. Use well the gifts the Lord has given you!"

The Time Is Now: "This is the time of your training, of your physical, intellectual, emotional and spiritual development. But this does not mean that you can put off until later your meeting with Christ and your sharing in the Church's mission. Even though you are young, the time for action is now! Jesus does not have contempt for your youth. He does not set you aside for a later time when you will be older and your training will be complete. Your training will never be finished. Christians are always in training. You are ready for what Christ wants of you now. He wants you ... to be the light of the world, as only young people can be light. It is time to let your light shine!"

"Wherever I go, I challenge young people — as a friend — to live in the light and truth of Jesus Christ."

"Through prayer you will learn to become the light of the world, because in prayer you become one with the source of our true light, Jesus himself."

Special Mission: "Each of you has a special mission in life and you are each called to be a disciple of Christ. Many of you will serve God in the vocation of Christian married life; some of you will serve him as dedicated single persons; some as priests and religious. But all of you must be the light of the world. To those of you who think that Christ may be inviting you to follow him in the priesthood or the consecrated life, I make this personal appeal ... to open your hearts generously to him. Do not delay your response. The

Lord will help you to follow your vocation courageously."

January 27

During morning Mass at the Trans World Dome.

"Today, American Catholics are seriously challenged to know and cherish [their] immense heritage of holiness and service. Out of that heritage, you must draw inspiration and strength for the new evangelization so urgently needed at the approach of the third Christian millennium."

The New Evangelization: "As the new evangelization unfolds, it must include a special emphasis on the family and the renewal of Christian marriage. In their primary mission of communicating love to each other, of being co-creators with God of human life and of transmitting the love of God to their children, parents must know that they are fully supported by the Church and by society. The new evangelization must bring a fuller appreciation of the family as the primary and most vital foundation of society, the first school of social virtue and solidarity.

"The new evangelization must also bring out the truth that 'the Gospel of God's love for man, the Gospel of the dignity of the person and the Gospel of life are a single and indivisible Gospel' (Encyclical Letter, *The Gospel of Life*). As believers, how can we fail to see that abortion, euthanasia and assisted suicide are a terrible rejection of God's gift of life and love? ... How can we fail to feel the duty to surround the sick and those in distress with the warmth of our affection and the support that will help them always to embrace life?

"The new evangelization calls for followers of Christ who are unconditionally pro-life, who will proclaim, celebrate and serve the Gospel of life in every situation. A sign of hope is the increasing recognition that the dignity of human life must never be taken away, even in the case of someone who has done great evil. Modern society has the means of protecting itself, without definitively denying criminals the chance to reform. I renew the appeal I made most recently at Christmas for a consensus to end the death penalty, which is both cruel and unnecessary."

"As the new millennium approaches, there remains another great challenge facing ... the whole country: to put an end to every form of racism, a plague which your bishops have called one of the most persistent and destructive evils of the nation."

Come Back to the Father: "In the name of Jesus, the Good Shepherd, I wish to make an appeal to Catholics throughout the United States and wherever my voice or words may reach — especially to those who for one reason or another are separated from the practice of their faith. On the eve of the Great Jubilee of the 2,000th anniversary of the Incarnation, Christ is seeking you out and inviting you back to the community of faith. Is this not the moment for you to experience the joy of returning to the Father's house? In some cases, there may still be obstacles to Eucharistic participation; in some cases there may be memories to be healed. In all cases there is the assurance of God's love and mercy."

At evening prayer in the Basilica of St. Louis before departure for Rome.

America's Responsibility: "At the end of this century — at once marked by unprecedented progress and by a tragic toll of human suffering — radical changes in world politics leave America with a heightened responsibility to be for the world an example of a genuinely free, democratic, just and humane society."

"America first proclaimed its independence on the basis of self-evident moral truths. America will remain a beacon of freedom for the world as long as it stands by those moral truths which are the very heart of its historical experience. And so, America: If you want peace, work for justice. If you want justice, defend life. If you want life, embrace the truth revealed by God."

POPE JOHN PAUL II IN ROMANIA

Pope John Paul, on the 86th pastoral pilgrimage of his pontificate, spent the weekend of May 7-9, 1999, in Romania.

His actions and addresses during the visit were related to a variety of subjects, principally: commitment to the Catholic-Romanian Orthodox quest for unity and communion; the shared experience of the churches under communist repression; mutual forgiveness and reconciliation for wrongs done; the development of a society free of the dominance of atheistic communism. Outstanding events were the papal address to the Romanian Orthodox Holy Synod; the attendance of the pope and Patriarch Teoctist at each other's liturgies and their exchange of the kiss of peace; and the favorable reaction by scores of thousands of Romanians to the papal visit.

Following are excerpts from several of the pope's addresses.

May 7

At welcoming ceremonies on arrival at Bucharest's Baneasa Airport.

"I trust that my visit will help heal the wounds inflicted on the relations between our churches in the last 50 years and will open a season of trusting mutual collaboration."

"I am among you as a pilgrim of faith and hope."

"My visit is meant to strengthen those ties between Romania and the Holy See which were so important for the history of Christianity in the region."

Shared Suffering: "Dear brothers and sisters of Romania! In this century now drawing to a close, your country has experienced the horrors of harsh totalitarian systems, sharing the sufferings that were the lot of many other European countries. The communist regime suppressed the Church of the Byzantine-Romanian rite united with Rome and persecuted bishops and priests, men and women religious and lay people, many of whom paid with blood for their fidelity to Christ. Some survived the tortures and are still with us."

"I would also like to give due recognition to the members of the Romanian Orthodox Church and of other churches and religious communities who suffered similar persecutions and grave restrictions. Death united our brothers and sisters in faith in the heroic witness of martyrdom; they have left us an unforgettable lesson of love for Christ and his Church."

In response to a greeting by Romanian Orthodox Patriarch Teoctist.

"I particularly hope that a growing understanding between all who are honored by the name Christian — Orthodox, Catholics of the various rites and Protestants of different denominations — may be a leaven of unity and harmony in your homeland and on the whole European continent."

At lunch with members of the Episcopal Conference.

"Be the image of Christ for your faithful. Be so especially as builders of communion.... The bishop is the guarantor of communion, and his fatherly role must help the community to grow as a family, by reflecting in some way the very fatherhood of God."

Communion: "Many are the forms and requirements of the communion that bishops are called to foster. The communion that joins them to other bishops and in particular to the Bishop of Rome, the Successor of Peter, is fundamental. This communion should be lived more concretely with the brother-bishops of their own country, so that it becomes a source of mutual enrichment. This is particularly true when, as is the case with Romania, the Church's tradition is expressed in different rites, each of which contributes its own history, culture and holiness."

"Communion must mark the relations of the faithful among themselves, with the priests and with the bishop. It must be promoted in every way" — affecting "men and women religious, the promotion of vocations to the priesthood and religious life, lay persons, and the 'fundamental challenge' of the new generation."

Restitution: Turning to the question of restitution of Catholic properties confiscated during the communist regime, the pope said: "While acknowledging that it would be difficult to return to the pre-existing situation, it is a duty in justice to return the schools and confiscated property, thereby enabling the Church to carry out her mission ... in the area of education. Without doubt, this would be a great benefit to society as a whole."

"The restitution of property is an issue that frequently surfaces, especially for the Catholic Church of the Byzantine-Romanian rite, which is still deprived of many worship sites she had at her disposal before her suppression.... I know that the hierarchs are not requesting the simultaneous restitution of all the property confiscated, but would like to have those which are most needed for liturgical functions. In this regard, I have followed with great interest the work of the Joint Commission of the Romanian Orthodox Church and the Greek Catholic Church on the above-mentioned questions."

"This [interreligious] dialogue is situated in the broader horizon of the ecumenical commitment to which the whole Church is called. We must do all that we can with an open heart and perseverance, in both theological and practical dialogue with the other churches and Christian communities, seeing as our goal the unity of all Christ's disciples."

"Along with intra-ecclesial and ecumenical concerns, the Catholic Church's efforts in Romania must respond to precise expectations in the social field" — regarding the family, respect for life, the needs of the poorest and most marginalized, and the reconstruction of society.

At the presidential palace after a private meeting with President Emil Constantinescu and family, to civil and political authorities, representatives of various religious communities and the diplomatic corps.

"I come to your land as a pilgrim of peace, brotherhood and understanding within nations, between peoples and the disciples of Christ.... I hope that the pastors and faithful will commit themselves in turn to concrete dialogue and mutual acceptance, which will show that fraternal charity in Christ is not an empty phrase but an essential element of the Church and of Christian life."

Society in Transition: "Romania is going through a period of transition which is crucial for its future, for its more active involvement in the construction of Europe and for its presence on the international scene. My thoughts turn to those who are undergoing trials, especially those who are seriously affected by the economic crisis and those in situations of poverty or illness, as well as the families who are finding it difficult to provide for their needs. I invite all Romanians to show their solidarity, thus offering concrete proof that living in the same region creates strong ties of brotherhood.... Each person is responsible for his brothers and sisters, and for the country's future."

"Forty years of atheistic communism have left after-effects and scars on your people's flesh and memory, and have created a climate of distrust. None of this can disappear without a real effort of conversion by citizens in their personal lives and in their relations with the national community as a whole."

"I encourage the people of Romania to work on building a society at the service of all, and to let Christ's message touch them, ... showing how Christian spiritual, moral and human values hold an important place in the life of a country."

May 8

At the Divine Liturgy in the Byzantine-Romanian rite at St. Joseph's Latin-rite Cathedral in Bucharest.

Forgiveness and Reconciliation: "For Christians, these are days of forgiveness and reconciliation. Without this witness, the world will not believe. How can we credibly speak of God who is love if there is no respite from conflict? Heal the wounds of the past with love. May your shared suffering not lead to separation but accomplish the miracle of reconciliation. Is not this the marvel that the world expects from believers? You too ... are called to make your valuable contribution to the ecumenical dialogue in truth and in charity, according to the directives of the Second Vatican Council and the Church's magisterium."

At the Romanian Orthodox Patriarchal Palace, to the bishops of the Romanian Orthodox Holy Synod.

Fraternal Dialogue: "It is my turn, as a pilgrim of love, to pay homage to this land steeped in the blood of ancient and recent martyrs.... I come to meet a people who welcomed the Gospel, assimilated it, defended it against repeated attacks and now considers it an integral part of their cultural heritage."

"I am pleased that, in practical terms, it has been possible to begin a fraternal dialogue here in Romania on the problems which still divide us. The Greek-Catholic Church of Romania suffered violent repression in recent decades, and her rights were scorned and violated. Her children suffered greatly, some even bearing the supreme witness of bloodshed. The end of persecution brought freedom, but the problem of ecclesial structures still awaits a definitive solution. May dialogue be the way to heal the wounds that are still open and to resolve the difficulties which still exist."

"The Orthodox Churches and the Catholic Church have come a long way on the road to reconciliation. I would like to offer God my deep and heartfelt gratitude for all that has been achieved; and I want to thank you, venerable Brothers in Christ, for the efforts you have made on this path."

For Restoration of Unity: "Your Beatitude, dear Brothers in the episcopate: Let us restore visible unity to the Church, or this world will be deprived of a witness that only the disciples of God's Son ... can offer it, so that it may be prompted to open itself to faith. And, what can encourage the people of today to believe in him, if we continue to tear the seamless garment of the Church, if we do not succeed in receiving the miracle of unity from God by working to remove the obstacles which prevent its full manifestation? Who will forgive us for this lack of witness? I have sought unity with all my strength, and I will continue to do all I can until the end to make it one of the priority concerns of the churches and of those who govern them in the apostolic ministry."

May 9

At the Divine Liturgy celebrated by Romanian Orthodox Patriarch Teoctist and the bishops of the Holy Synod.

Jubilee Challenges: "May a single hymn of praise to the name of the Lord rise from the Romanian Orthodox Church and the Romanian Catholic Church! May it form a symphony of voices to express the heartfelt brotherhood of mutual relations and to implore the full communion of all believers. The Romanian Orthodox Church and the Catholic Church, founded on the apostolic succession, have the same Word of the Lord preserved in Holy Scripture and the same sacraments. In particular, they have kept the same priesthood and celebrate the one sacrifice of Christ, through which he builds up and gives growth to his Church."

"The Great Jubilee of the Year 2000 urges Christians to look at the future with a better awareness of the challenges they will face in the new millennium. One that stands out is the search for unity among all believers in Christ. I hope that the third Christian millennium will find us, if not completely united, at least closer to full communion."

At Mass in Podul Izvor Park.

Do Not Be Afraid: "Dear Catholics of Romania: I know well how you suffered during the years of the harsh communist regime. I also know how courageously you have persevered in your fidelity to Christ and his Gospel. Now, as we stand on the threshold of the third millennium, be not afraid. Open the doors of our heart to Christ the Savior. He loves you and is close to you. He calls you to a renewed commitment to evangelization. Faith is a gift from God and a heritage of incomparable value to be preserved and spread. In defending and furthering common values, always be open to active cooperation with all the ethnic, social and religious groups that make up your country. May your every decision be motivated by hope and love."

At his departure for Rome May 9.

Millennial Hope: The Holy Father expressed "the hope that the new millennium opening before us will be a time of renewed communion between the Christian churches and the discovery of brotherhood among peoples. This is the dream I take with me as I leave this land so dear to me."

The pope also said: "You who have been freed from the nightmare of communist dictatorship, do not let yourselves be deceived by the false and dangerous dreams of consumerism. They also destroy the future. Jesus enables you to dream of a new Romania, a land where East and West can meet in brotherhood. This Romania is entrusted to your hands. Boldly build it together. The Lord is entrusting it to you. Entrust yourselves to him, knowing that 'unless the Lord builds the house, those who build it labor in vain.'"

PAPAL REFLECTIONS ON THE ROMANIAN VISIT

The pope reflected on his visit to Romania during his general audience of May 12, 1999. In part, he said as follows.

"My thoughts keep returning with deep emotion to the visit God enabled me to make to Romania a few days ago. This was an event of historic importance because it was my first visit to a country where the majority of the Christians are Orthodox. I thank God ... that this should take place shortly before the Year 2000, offering Catholics and our Orthodox brothers and sisters to take a particularly significant step together on the way toward full unity, in fidelity to the spirit of the Great Jubilee which is now at hand."

"With this journey I wanted to pay homage to the Romanian people and to their Christian roots which, according to tradition, date back to the preaching of the Gospel by the Apostle Andrew, brother of Simon Peter."

"This journey gave me an opportunity to experience what a blessing it is for Christians to breathe with the two 'lungs' of the Eastern and Western traditions. I realized this during the solemn and moving liturgical celebrations, for I had the joy of presiding at the Eucharist in the Greek-Catholic rite; I attended the Divine Liturgy for my Orthodox brethren, led by the Patriarch ... and was able to pray with them; and, lastly, I celebrated Mass in the Roman rite with the faithful of the Latin Church."

Meeting with Patriarch and Synod

"Particularly desired and important was the meeting with Patriarch Teoctist and the Holy Synod of the Romanian Orthodox Church. On Saturday afternoon (May 8), they welcomed me at the Patriarchate with great cordiality and I found in his Beatitude and in the other members of the Holy Synod fraternal understanding and a sincere desire for full communion according to the Lord's will. On this occasion I wanted to assure the Romanian Orthodox Church, involved in an important work of renewal, of the affection and collaboration of the Catholic Church. Fraternal love is the soul of dialogue and is the path for overcoming the remaining obstacles and difficulties in order to reach full Christian unity. God has already worked marvels on this journey of reconciliation. We must press ahead with confident enthusiasm, because Europe and the world have greater need than ever for the visible witness of the brotherhood of all who believe in Christ."

"Ecumenical commitment does not lessen but rather strengthens the task of Peter's successor as Pastor of the Catholic Church. I carried out my ministry especially by meeting the Romanian Episcopal Conference, composed of bishops of the Latin and Greek-Catholic rites.... I urged them to proclaim the Gospel without tiring, to be builders of communion, to provide for the formation of their priests and of the many who are called to the consecrated life, as well as the laity. I encouraged them to promote the pastoral care of young people and school children, and to make every effort to defend the family, to protect life and serve the poor."

"The Romanian nation arose with evangelization, and in the Gospel it will find the light and strength to fulfill its vocation as a crossroads of peace in the coming millennium."

FOR PEACE IN THE BALKANS: Joint Pope-Patriarch Declaration

Pope John Paul and Romanian Orthodox Patriarch Teoctist signed May 8, 1999, a joint declaration on the urgent need for peace in the Balkans. They said:

"Fathers and servants of our communities, united with all those whose mission is to proclaim to today's world the One who 'has called us to live in peace' (1 Cor 7:15), and especially united with the pastors or our Churches in the Balkans, we wish:

• "to express our human and spiritual solidarity with all those who, driven from their homes and land and separated from their loved ones, are undergoing the cruel reality of emigration, as well as with the victims of the deadly bombings and all people prevented from living in tranquillity and peace;

• "to appeal in God's name to all those who in one

way or another are responsible for the current tragedy, that they will have the courage to return to dialogue and find the right conditions for achieving a just and lasting peace that will permit the displaced persons to return to their homes; to end the sufferings of all who live in the Federal Republic of Yugoslavia — Serbs, Albanians and people of other nationalities; and to lay the foundations for a new social harmony among all peoples of the Federation;

• "to encourage the international community and its institutions to use all their legal resources to help the parties in conflict resolve their differences in accordance with the conventions in force, especially those regarding respect for the basic rights of the person and cooperation between sovereign states;

• "to support all humanitarian organizations, especially those of Christian inspiration, which are involved in relieving the suffering of the present time, while insisting that nothing be allowed to hinder their efforts to help all who are suffering great hardships, regardless of nationality, language or religion;

• "lastly, to appeal to Christians of all denominations to be concretely committed and united in a unanimous and ceaseless prayer for peace and understanding between peoples, entrusting these intentions to the Blessed Virgin so that she will intercede with her Son 'who is our peace' (Eph 2:14).

"In the name of God, Father of all mankind, we insistently ask the parties involved in the conflict to lay down their arms once and for all, and we vigorously urge them to make prophetic gestures so that a new art of living in the Balkans, marked by respect for all, by brotherhood and by social harmony, can grow in this beloved land. This will be a powerful sign in the world's eyes and will show that the territory of the Federal Republic of Yugoslavia, together with all of Europe, can become a place of peace, freedom and harmony for everyone who lives there."

POPE JOHN PAUL II IN POLAND

Pope John Paul made a 13-day pilgrimage to Poland June 5-17, 1999. It was the 87th foreign trip of his pontificate and the busiest of his visits to his homeland, with stops in 21 cities and towns, the celebration of solemn Masses, participation in Liturgies of the Word, the delivery of 40 or more addresses, meetings, and many public appearances. He was seen by perhaps five million people who attended public functions and by several times that many via television.

Following are: (1) the pontiff's own reflections on the visit, made during a general audience of June 23 and reported in the June 30, English-language edition of *L'Osservatore Romano;* (2) events and excerpts from selected addresses.

PAPAL REFLECTIONS

"Today I would like to reflect again on the pilgrimage to Poland which I had the joy of making from the 5th to the 17th of this month. My seventh and longest pastoral visit to my country took place 20 years after my first journey from 2 to 10 June, 1979. On the eve of the Great Jubilee of the Year 2000, I shared with the Church in Poland in the celebrations to mark the millennium of two events which are at the root of her history: the canonization of St. Adalbert and the es-

tablishment of the country's first metropolitan see, Gniezno, with its three suffragan dioceses of Kolobrzeg, Krakow and Wroclaw. I was also able to conclude the nation's Second Plenary Synod and to proclaim a new saint as well as numerous new blesseds, exemplary witnesses of God's love."

Theme: God's Love and Beatitudes

" 'God is love' was the theme of my apostolic journey, which became a great hymn of praise to the heavenly Father and to the wonderful works of his mercy. For this reason, I never stop thanking him, the Lord of the world and of history, who once again allowed me to cross the land of my ancestors as a pilgrim of faith and hope, and in particular as a pilgrim of his love."

"The overall theme of these days was the Gospel text of the Beatitudes, which shows us God's love in the unmistakable features of Christ's face. What a joy it was for me, in St. Adalbert's footsteps, to proclaim the eight Beatitudes, as I meditated on the history of my ancestors! My brief stops in Gdansk, Pelplin and Elblag in the Baltic region, where Adalbert was martyred, were dedicated to the memory of this great bishop and martyr. The legacy of Adalbert has always been guarded by the Polish people and has borne wonderful fruits of witness th roughout Poland's history."

Heroic Witnesses of Faith

"In this regard, I had the opportunity to visit cities which preserve an indelible memory of the destruction, mass executions and deportations of the Second World War. Only faith in God, who is love and mercy, made possible their material and moral resurgence. In Bydgoszcz, where Cardinal Wyszynski built the church dedicated to 'The Holy Polish Brethren Martyrs,' I celebrated Mass for the martyrs, commemorating the 'unknown soldiers' of God's cause and those who died in this century. In Turon I beatified Father Wincenty Frelichowski (1913-45), who was a peacemaker in his pastoral ministry and later in the concentration camp; until his death, he bore witness to God's love among the typhus victims of the Dachau concentration camp.

"In Warsaw I beatified 108 martyrs, including bishops, priests, religious and lay people, victims of the concentration camps during the Second World War. In the capital, I also beatified Edmund Bojanowski — an organizer of educational and charitable works and precursor of the [Second Vatican] Council's teaching on the lay apostolate — and Sister Regina Protmann, who combined the contemplative life with caring for the sick and teaching children and young girls. In Stary Sacz I canonized Sister Kinga, an outstanding 13th-century figure, a model of charity both as the wife of the Polish Prince Boleslaus and, after his death, as a Poor Clare nun.

"These heroic witnesses of faith show that the *traditio* of God's word, heard and put into practice, has been handed down from Adalbert to this day, and should be courageously incarnated in today's society as it prepares to cross the threshold of the third millennium."

Devotion to the Sacred Heart and Mary

"In Poland, faith was nourished and greatly supported by devotion to the Sacred Heart and to the Blessed Virgin Mary. Veneration of the divine Heart of Jesus had special prominence in this pilgrimage; in the background was the consecration of the human race to the Sacred Heart which my revered predecessor, Leo XIII, performed for the first time exactly 100 years ago. Humanity needs to enter the new millennium with trust in God's merciful love. However, this will only be possible if we turn to Christ the Savior, the inexhaustible source of life and holiness.

"And then, what can we say of my compatriots' filial affection for their Queen, Mary most holy? In Lichen I blessed the large new shrine dedicated to her; and in some cities, including my birthplace, I crowned revered images of the Blessed Virgin. In Sandomierz I celebrated the Eucharist in honor of the Immaculate Heart of the Blessed Virgin Mary.

"I would also like to recall my prayer meetings in Elk, Zamosc, Warsaw-Praga, Lowicz, Sosnowiec, Gliwice and in my native town of Wadowice, as well as my visit to the monastery in Wigry.

"Before my return, I knelt in front of the venerable icon of Our Lady of Czestochowa at Jasna Gora; it was a moment of deep spiritual feeling. I renewed the entrustment of my life and my Petrine ministry to her.... To her I consecrated the Church in Poland and throughout the world. To her I prayed for the precious gift of peace for all humanity and solidarity among peoples."

Twenty Years of Change

"During my journey, I had several occasions to thank God for the changes which have occurred in Poland over the last 20 years in the name of freedom and solidarity. I did this at Gdansk, the city which symbolizes the Solidarity Movement. I did it especially when I spoke to the Polish Parliament, where I recalled the peaceful struggles of the '80s and the revolution of '89. The moral principles of those struggles must continue to inspire political life, so that democracy will be based on strong ethical values: the family, human life, work, education, care of the weak. At the same time as elections were being held for the European Parliament, I prayed for the 'old' continent, that it might continue to be a beacon of civilization and authentic progress, rediscovering its spiritual roots and making the very most of the peoples' potential from the Urals to the Atlantic.

"In addition, at the two meetings with the academic world, in Turon and Warsaw, I was able to emphasize how relations between the Church and the world of science have improved, to the great advantage of both. Nor can I forget the prayer at Radzymin in memory of the war of 1920 and the 'Miracle of the Vistula' (when outnumbered Polish soldiers turned back an invasion by Russian forces).

"At other events, I raised my voice in defense of the weakest persons and groups. While the Church performs works of mercy, she encourages justice and solidarity after the example of saints like Queen Hedwig and Albert Chmielowski, models of sharing with the most needy. Progress cannot be made at the expense of the poor or of economically weaker groups, or at the expense of the natural environment."

Development and Evangelization

"There was also an opportunity to stress that the Church makes her contribution to the integral development of the nation, first of all, by the formation of consciences. The Church exists to evangelize, that is, to proclaim to all that 'God is love' and to enable every person to meet him. The Second Plenary Synod renewed this commitment according to the Second Vatican Council and in the light of the signs of the times, calling all believers to generous co-responsibility.

"Evangelization is not credible if as Christians we do not love one another according to the Lord's commandment. In Siedlce and Warsaw, in memory of the Blessed Martyrs of Podlasie, I prayed with the Greek-Catholic faithful that the divisions of the second millennium would be overcome. I also wanted to meet my brothers of other confessions, to strengthen the bonds of unity. At a shared ecumenical liturgy in Drohiczyn, this prayer involved the Orthodox, Lutheran and other non-Catholic ecclesial communities. The need for unity in the Church is felt by all; we must work for its full realization, ready to admit our faults and to forgive one another.

"In the morning of the last day of my pilgrimage, I was able to celebrate the Eucharist in Wawel Cathedral. Thus, as I left my beloved city of Krakow, I could thank God for the millennium of that archdiocese. "Dear Brothers and Sisters, let us praise the Lord together for these days of grace."

ITINERARY AND TALKS

June 5

At Rebiechowo Airport, Gdanz, during welcoming ceremonies with church and state dignitaries.

Freedom's Task and Challenge: "I am pleased that this pilgrimage to my homeland begins in Gdansk, a city which has a place forever in the history of Poland, of Europe, and perhaps even of the whole world. In fact, it was here that the voice of consciences was heard in a particular way, calling for respect for human dignity, especially of workers, a voice calling for freedom, justice and solidarity between people. This cry of consciences roused from slumber rang out with such force as to make room for the yearned-for freedom, a freedom which has become and continues to be for us a great task and a challenge for today and the future. It was precisely in Gdansk that a new Poland was born, which gives us so much and of which we are so proud. I notice with joy that our country has made great progress on the path of economic development. Thanks to the efforts of all its citizens, Poland can look to the future with hope. In the last few years, our country has earned particular recognition and the respect of other nations of the world. For all of this, blessed be God and Father of our Lord Jesus Christ! Pray unceasingly that Poland's material development will increase at an equal rate with its spiritual development."

During an afternoon Mass at Sopot Racetrack.

Heritage of St. Adalbert: "Today ... we are preparing together to enter the third millennium. We want to enter it with God, as a people which has placed its trust in love and has loved the truth. As a people that wishes to live in the spirit of truth."

"Much has changed and is still changing in Poland. The centuries pass, and Poland grows amid changing destinies, like a great, historic oak tree with healthy roots. Let us thank divine Providence for blessing this 1,000-year process of growth with the presence of St. Adalbert and with his martyr's death on the Baltic. This is a great heritage which we pass on toward the future. Through the work of St. Adalbert and all the patron saints of Poland gathered around the Mother of God, may the fruits of the Redemption endure and take deeper roots among generations to come. May the men and women of the third millennium take up the mission handed on 1,000 years ago by St. Adalbert and in turn pass it on to the coming generations."

June 6

During Mass at Pelplin.

Martyrs of Pelplin: "In this land, there is a long tradition of listening to the word of God and of witness given to the Word, who in Christ became Incarnate.... An eloquent and tragic symbol of this continuity was the so-called 'Autumn of Pelplin,' the 60th anniversary of which occurs this year. At that time, 24 courageous priests, teachers at the major seminary and members of the bishop's staff, bore witness to their faithful service of the Gospel by the sacrifice of suffering and death. In the time of the [World War II] Occupation, 303 pastors were taken from the land of Pelplin and, at the cost of their lives, heroically testified to the message of hope in the dramatic period of the war and the Occupation. If today we remember these martyred priests, it is because it was from their lips that our generation heard the word of God and, thanks to their witness, experienced its power."

During Sacred Heart devotions in Elblag.

"Let us make acts of reparation to the divine Heart for the sins committed by us and by our fellow men. Let us make reparation for rejecting God's goodness and love. Let us draw close each day to this fount from which flows springs of living water."

June 7

At the blessing of a new church at the shrine of Mary at Lichen.

"Mother of the divine Son, watch over us, watch over our unshakeable fidelity to God, to the Cross, to the Gospel and to the holy Church, as you have done since the first moments of our Christian history. Defend this nation which for a thousand years has walked the path of the Gospel. Grant that we live, grow and persevere in faith until the end."

During a Mass for Martyrs and the crowning of an image of Our Lady of Fair Love at Bydgoszcz, where 25 percent of the population was exterminated by the Nazis in the fist days of World Wear II.

A Great Martyrology: The first church built after World War II bears the name, "The Holy Polish Brethren Martyrs." It "commemorates all the nameless Poles who during the more than 1,000-year history of Polish Christianity gave their lives for the Gospel of Christ and for the homeland, beginning with St. Adalbert. Significant too is the fact that Father Jerzy Popieluszko (a social justice activist killed by government personnel) set out from this very church on his last journey."

"Our century has written a great martyrology. How many martyrs there were during the time of the Second World War and under communist totalitarianism!. They suffered and gave their lives in the death camps of Hitler or those of the Soviets. Now is the time to remember them all."

At a meeting in Torun with the rectors of academic institutions.

Challenge to Scientific Freedom: "Scholarship today ... faces great challenges. The unprecedented development of the sciences and technological progress are raising fundamental questions about the limits of experimentation, the meaning and direction of technological development, the limits of man's tampering with nature and the natural environment. This progress gives rise to both wonderment and fear. Man is becoming ever more fearful of the products of his own intelligence and freedom. He feels endangered. Hence, it is more important and timely than ever to recall the fundamental truth that the world is a gift of God the Creator, who is love, and that man as a creature is called to a prudent and responsible dominion over the world of nature, and not its heedless destruction.... Authentic freedom of scientific research cannot prescind from the criterion of truth and of goodness. Concern for the moral conscience and the sense of individual responsibility has today become a fundamental imperative for men and women of science. It is precisely here that both the future of contemporary science and, in some sense, the future of humanity are being d decided."

During Sacred Heart devotions and ceremonies for the beatification of Father Stefan Wincenty Frelichowski in Torun:

Martyr Priest: "We bow in faith before the great mystery of the love of the divine Heart, and we give it honor and glory. Hail, O Jesus; hail, O Heart divine of the Son of Man, which has so loved us men and women."

"Let us share the peace of God with others, as did the blessed priest and martyr Wincenty Frelichowski. Thus we will become a source of peace in the world, in society, in the environment in which we live and work. I make this appeal to everyone without exception" — to priests, parents, educators, young people, societies and nations."

[Father Frelichowski was born Jan. 22, 1913; was ordained to the priesthood Mar. 14, 1937; served as secretary to his bishop and in pastoral ministry before being arrested by Nazi personnel Sept. 11, 1939, and subsequently sent to the concentration camps of Stuthoff, Sachsenhausen and Dachau — where he ministered clandestinely to fellow prisoners; his final ministry was to typhus victims, from whom he contracted the disease and died Feb. 23, 1945, at the age of 32.]

June 8

At Mass in honor of St. Hedwig in Elk, attended by a large number of Lithuanians.

Human Person Comes First: "We must recall that the country's economic development must take into consideration the greatness, dignity and vocation of man, who was made in the image and likeness of God? (cf. Gn 1:26). Development and economic progress must never be at the expense of men and women, hindering the meeting of their fundamental needs. The human person must be the subject of development, that is, its most important point of reference. Development and economic progress cannot be pursued at whatever cost! That would not be worthy of man. The Church of today proclaims and seeks to exercise a preferential option for the poor. This is not just a passing feeling for immediate action, but a real and persevering will to work for the good of those who are in need and who often have no hope for a better future."

The Holy Father spent the night at Elk and June 9 at the former Camaldolese monastery in Wigry.

June 10

At a Mass honoring the already beatified (1996) 13 martyrs of Pratulin in the Diocese of Siedlce:

Faithful Servants: "Today we venerate the martyrs of Podlasie and we adore the Cross of Pratulin, the silent witness of their identity. They held this Cross in their hands and they bore it in the depth of their hearts as a sign of love of the Father and of the unity of the Church of Christ.

"It was here that the confessors of Christ belonging to the Greek-Catholic Church, Bl. Wincenty Lewoniuk and his 12 companions, were martyred" [shot to death by Russian soldiers].

"As faithful servants of the Lord, trusting in his grace, they bore witness to their membership of the Catholic Church in fidelity to their Eastern tradition. With a gesture so generous, the Martyrs of Pratulin defended not only the holy place of worship in front of which they were slaughtered but also the Church of Christ entrusted to the Apostle Peter, of which they felt themselves to be the living stones."

"More than ever now there is a need for genuine witness of faith made visible through the life of the lay disciples of Christ, men and women, young and old. There is a need for committed witness to fidelity to the Church and responsibility toward the Church."

At an ecumenical prayer service with representatives of the Orthodox, Lutheran and other ecclesial communities of Poland, in Drohiczyn:

Mutual Love: "The forging of unity is 'a duty of the Christian conscience enlightened by faith and guided by love,' since to believe in Christ means to desire unity; to desire unity means to desire the Church; to desire the Church means to desire the communion of grace which corresponds to the Father's plan from all eternity?" [Encyclical Letter *Ut Unum Sint*, "That All May Be One"].

"At the threshold of a new period of history, we must all examine our consciences regarding responsibility for the present divisions. We must admit the faults committed and pardon each other in turn. In fact, we have received the new commandment of mutual love, which has its source in the love of Christ."

"Love should lead us to reflect together on the past, so that we may move forward with perseverance and courage on the path toward unity."

"Love is the only power that opens hearts to the word of Jesus and to the grace of Redemption. It is the only power able to lead us to share as brothers all that we are and all that we have through Christ's will. It is a powerful stimulus to dialogue, in which we listen to each other and come to know each other."

"On the eve of the third millennium, we must move more quickly toward full and fraternal reconciliation, so that in the next millennium with joined hands we can witness to salvation before a world which eagerly awaits this sign of unity."

June 11

The pope, after a privately celebrated Mass and a courtesy visit to President Aleksander Kwasniewski, addressed the Polish Parliament, other members of the government and the diplomatic corps.

Build on Spiritual Values: "As we rejoice together at the positive changes taking place in Poland before our eyes, we cannot fail to recognize as well that in a free society there must also be values which guarantee the supreme good of man in his totality. Every economic change must help to build a world that is more human and more just. To Polish politicians and to all those involved in political life, I would express the hope that you not stint in your efforts to build a state which cares particularly for the family, for human life, for the education of the young, which respects the right to work, which considers the essential problems of the entire nation, and which is sensitive to the real needs of people, especially the poor and weak."

"The Church warns against a reduced vision of Europe which would see it solely in its economic and political aspects, as she does against a consumerist model of life. If we wish Europe's new unity to last, we must build on the basis of the spiritual values which were once its foundation, keeping in mind the wealth and diversity of the cultures and traditions of individual nations. This must be the great European Community of the Spirit. Here I renew my appeal to the Old Continent: 'Europe, open the doors to Christ!' "

"Poland is fully entitled to take part in the world's general process of development and progress, and especially in that of Europe. The integration of Poland with the European Union has been supported by the Holy See from the beginning. The Polish nation's historical experience and its spiritual and cultural wealth can contribute effectively to the common good of the entire human family, especially in consolidating peace and security in Europe."

At a prayer service honoring the Martyrs of Pratulin in the church of the Eastern-rite Basilian Order of St. Josaphat in Warsaw:

Guard Eastern Tradition: "Dear Brothers and Sisters! Zealously guard your [Eastern-rite] tradition as a unique spiritual patrimony. This is the strength of your lives and your work. Remember the great witness of fidelity to Christ, to the Church and to the Successor of St. Peter borne by your confreres. They preferred to lose their lives rather than be separated from the Apostolic See. Their sufferings and martyrdom are an inexhaustible source of grace for your Church now and for the future, You must preserve in your hearts this great patrimony of faith, prayer and witness, in order to hand it on to the coming generations."

Addressing members of the Polish Bishops' Conference, the pope said in part:

Beatitudes for Guidance: "The essence of the apostolate of all members of the Church is the spreading of the truth about God's love. Do all that you can to see that this truth is proclaimed, accepted and realized in the life of pastors and all believers."

"The Sermon on the Mount is the program for the whole Church. The community of the New Covenant is formed when it is based upon the law of love written in every human heart.... The Gospel Beatitudes are in a sense the concrete form of this law, and at the same time they ensure a true and lasting happiness which springs from purity and peace of heart, the fruits of reconciliation with God and men."

"The greatest pastoral duty of each of you is to care for the unerring transmission of the Deposit of Faith."

"On the threshold of the third millennium, the Church in Poland faces new historic changes. Poland enters the 21st century as a free and sovereign country. This freedom, if it is not to be abused, requires people aware not only of their rights but also of their duties; generous people motivated by love of the homeland and a spirit of service, who in a bond of fraternity want to build the common good and contribute to a properly ordered freedom in every aspect of personal, family and social life.... Freedom demands constant reference to the truth of the Gospel and to stable and well-established moral norms which enable people to distinguish between good and evil. This is especially important in our own day, when Poland is going through a time of reform."

In the afternoon, the pope visited and prayed at Warsaw's Holocaust Monument and the monument commemorating Poles deported to Siberia by tsarist and communist regimes. Then he spoke during concluding ceremonies of the Second Plenary Synod of Poland.

Synod Accomplishments: "The approved documents (of the Synod) express a common concern for the renewal of Christian life in the Polish Church in the spirit of the Second Vatican Council, and also point the way for future work."

"The formation of a new society based upon respect for human rights, truth and freedom, requires from all the daughters and sons of the Church an awareness that can be the starting point for wider responsibility in the Church. It is good that, in a situation such as this, the Plenary Synod recognized that its fundamental task was to work for the rebuilding and deepening of this awareness in the Church among both laity and clergy."

"Thanks to the work of the Synod, the Church is called to grow stronger as a community of believers, and this can be done chiefly through a well-informed sharing in the Church's life, in accordance with the charism proper to each person's state of life and with the principle of subsidiarity. The Synod, therefore, will accomplish its task in so far as it succeeds in reviving in the hearts of all — clergy and laity — the sense of responsibility for the Church and the desire to work together for the realization of the Church's saving mission."

June 12

At Mass in honor of the Immaculate Heart of Mary, in Sandomierz:

Destructive Culture of Death: " Purity of heart is first and foremost a gift of God."

"This message about purity of heart is very timely. The culture of death wants to destroy purity of heart. One of its strategies is deliberately to create doubt about the value of the human attitude which we call the virtue of chastity. This is something particularly dangerous when the attack is aimed at the sensitive consciences of children and young people. A culture which in this way impairs or even destroys a correct relationship between individuals, is a culture of death, for man cannot live without true love."

At a Liturgy of the Word in Zamosc:

Respect for Nature and Life: "Every action which ignores God's rights over his world, as well as the rights of man bestowed upon him by the Creator, is in conflict with the commandment of love.... We need to realize, therefore, that there can be a grave sin against the natural environment, one which weighs on our consciences and which calls for grave responsibility toward God the Creator."

"In speaking of responsibility before God, we know that it is not just a matter of what is nowadays called ecology. It is not enough to seek the cause of the world's destruction only in excessive industrialization, uncritical applications in industry and agriculture of scientific and technological advances, or in an unbridled pursuit of wealth without concern for the future effects of all these actions. Although it cannot be denied that these actions do cause great harm, it is easy to see that their source is deeper; it lies in man's very attitude. It appears that what is most dangerous for creation and for man is lack of respect for the laws of nature and the disappearance of a sense of the value of life."

June 13

At Mass and the beatification of 108 martyrs of World War II, Sister Regina Protmann, and Edmund Bojanowski, in Warsaw:

Beatifications: "Today we are celebrating the victory of those who in our century gave their lives for Christ, gave their temporal lives, in order to possess life forever in his glory."

"These blessed martyrs are today inscribed in the history of holiness of the people of God on pilgrimage for over 1,000 years in the land of Poland."

"If we rejoice today for the beatification of 108 martyrs ... we do so above all because they bear witness to the victory of Christ, the gift which restores hope."

"Though we see in history the painful signs of evil, we are certain that in the end evil will not prevail over the fate of man and the world. This certainty arises from faith in God's mercy."

[The 108 Polish Martyrs of World War II suffered death between 1938 and 1945 because of their practice of the faith: three bishops, 52 diocesan priests, 26 priests of religious orders, three students for the priesthood, seven religious brothers and eight sisters, and nine lay persons.

[Sister Regina Protmann (1552-1613), Polish founder of the contemplative-active Sisters of St. Catherine of Alexandria. In 1999, sisters of the institute were active in nine countries on three continents.

[Edmund Bojanowski (Nov. 14, 1814-Aug. 17, 1871), social service worker especially for abandoned children, founder of the Sisters Servants of Mary Immaculate. More than 3,300 Sisters Servants were working in Poland and abroad in 1999.]

During a Liturgy of the Word in Warsaw-Praga:

The Eucharist: "Before offering his life on the cross for the salvation of man, the Son of God offered it sacramentally. He gives his Body and Blood to the disciples so that, in consuming them, they may share in the fruits of his saving death.... Christ left the Apostles this sacramental sign of love. He said to them: 'Do this in memory of me' (cf. 1 Cor 11:24). The Apostles did this and, passing on the Gospel to their disciples, they passed on the Eucharist as well. From the Last Supper onwards, the Church has been built and formed through the Eucharist. The Church celebrates the Eucharist and the Eucharist forms the Church. This has always been the case wherever new generations of Christ's disciples gradually became the Church. This has always been the case on Polish soil too, and so it is today as we approach the threshold of the third millennium; to those who will come after us, we pass on the Gospel and the Eucharist."

"The celebration of the Eucharist is most important for the Church and for her individual members. It is 'the source and summit of the Christian life' " (*Lumen Gentium*, no. 11).

"The unity in love which springs from the Eucharist is not only an expression of human solidarity, but is a sharing in the very love of God. Upon this unity, the Church is built. It is this which determines the success of her saving mission."

June 14

At Mass in Lowicz:

Family and Education: "The family is called upon to educate its children. The first place where the educational process of a young person begins is the family home. All children have the natural, inalienable right to have their own family, parents, brothers and sisters, among whom they come to the realization that they are persons needing love and capable of loving others, their loved ones. May the Holy Family of Nazareth always be the example for you, the family in which Christ grew up with his mother Mary and putative father Joseph. Since parents give life to their own children, they have the right to be recognized as the first and principal educators. They also have the duty to create a family atmosphere filled with love and respect for God and neighbor, which favors the personal and social education of their children."

"In this responsible duty of education, the family must receive assistance. It needs help and expects it from the Church and from the State. It is not a matter of replacing the family in its duties, but of harmoniously uniting everyone in this great task."

"I therefore speak to ... all who are involved in catechesis: Open wide the doors of the Church so that everyone, and in particular the young, can draw abundantly upon and profit from her enormous spiritual wealth."

During a Liturgy of the Word in Sosnowiec:

Meaning of Work: "We cannot forget the divine perspective of sharing in the work of creation, which confers upon all human effort true meaning and dignity. Without this perspective, work can easily lose its subjective dimension. When this happens, the man who does the work is no longer important, and all that matters is the material worth of what is produced. Man is no longer regarded as a craftsman, as one who creates, but as an instrument of production."

"The structures of the State and the economy have an influence on attitudes toward work, but the dignity of work depends upon the human conscience. It is here that it is given its ultimate value. In the conscience, the voice of the Creator is heard incessantly, a voice pointing to what is the true good for man and the world entrusted to him. Those who have lost the right judgment of conscience can transform the blessing of work into a curse."

"Wisdom is needed to discover ever anew the supernatural dimension of work, given as a task to man by the Creator. A correctly formed conscience is needed to discern the absolute value of one's work."

"If man can discern in the work of his hands the sign of God's blessing, he will have no doubt that this same God exists — is near — and cares constantly for man's journey, especially when he crosses the great wilderness of daily problems and nagging worries."

June 15

Because of an attack of flu, the pope was unable to celebrate Mass and preach in Krakow. Cardinal Angelo Sodano, secretary of state, was the principal celebrant of the Mass. The Holy Father's address was read by Cardinal Franciszek Macharski, archbishop of Krakow.

The Church in Krakow: "The roots of the Church in Krakow are profoundly fixed in the apostolic tradition, in the prophetic mission and in the witness of martyrdom. Entire generations made this tradition, mission and martyrdom their own, and built their faith on them in the course of a millennium. Thanks to this point of reference, the Church in Krakow has always been in close union with the universal Church, and at the same time it developed its own historical character and wrote its own history as a unique and unrepeatable community of men and women sharing in the saving mission of Christ.

"By staying in the current of the universal Church and simultaneously preserving its own unique character, this community gave shape to the history and culture of the City of Krakow, of the region and, it is possible to say, of the whole of Poland."

June 16

Canonization: At a morning Mass in Stary Sqcz, the Holy Father canonized Bl. Kinga (Kunigunda) (1234-92), Hungarian princess known for her generosity to the poor, who founded a Poor Clare convent in the city and later became a member of the order. He challenged his brothers and sisters: "Do not be afraid to aspire to holiness. Do not be afraid to be saints. Make of this century now drawing to a close and of the new millennium an era of saintly men and women."

Nostalgia: In the evening, he spoke nostalgically during a Liturgy of the Word in Wadowice, the city of his birth where, he said, "Here everything began: my life, my studies, the theater, the priesthood."

June 17

Prayer at Jasna Gora: The Holy Father celebrated Mass privately in the St. Stanislaus Chapel of the Wawel Cathedral in Krakow, and then made a private pilgrimage to the Shrine of Our Lady of Jasna Gora in Czestochowa. At the shrine, he prayed: "I implore you, Mother of Jasna Gora, Queen of Poland, to embrace my entire country with your maternal heart. Increase its courage and spiritual strength so that it will be able to fulfill the great responsibility it faces. May the Polish nation cross the threshold of the third millennium with faith, hope and love, and adhere even more strongly to your Son, Jesus Christ, and to his Church, built on the foundation of the Apostles."

The Pope visited the burial site of his mother, father and brother in Rakowice Cemetery before departing for Rome late in the afternoon.

SPECIAL REPORTS

PAPAL ENCYCLICAL: *FIDES ET RATIO*

Dated Sept. 14, 1998, and publicly released on Oct. 15, Pope John Paul II's 13th encyclical, Fides et Ratio, *powerfully expresses his convictions about the importance of philosophical enquiry. The encyclical, addressed to the bishops of the world and setting out a broad panorama of the history of ideas, concerns the relationships between faith and reason, theology and philosophy. An unofficial summary follows.*

Introduction

1. The more human beings know reality and the world around them, the more they know themselves. In various cultures all over the world, people have sought answers to fundamental questions: Who am I? Where have I come from and where am I going? Why is there such a thing as evil? What comes after this life? 2. In the paschal mystery, the Church has received the gift of the ultimate truth about human life and the duty of serving humanity through the "*diakonia* of the truth," looking to the time when truth's fullness will appear in the final revelation of God.

3. Philosophy is concerned with life's meaning and is one of the noblest of human tasks. Every people has a native wisdom that tends to develop in philosophical ways. 4. It is "philosophical pride" to identify any one system as final and definitive; every system must recognize the primacy of enquiry. Beyond different schools, there is a core of insights and principles constituting a spiritual heritage of humanity and an implicit philosophy shared by all.

5. The Church views philosophy as an indispensable help for deeper understanding of faith and for communicating the gospel. Now, though, the search for ultimate truth often seems to be neglected. Modern philosophy and science have achieved much; but modern thought seems to have forgotten the quest for transcendent truth while concentrating on the limitations of the human capacity to know truth. Different forms of agnosticism and relativism are the re-

sult. There is a "lack of confidence in truth" which reduces everything to opinion and doubts philosophy's ability to give definitive answers.

6. We bishops have the duty of bearing witness to the truth. Here I shall concentrate upon the theme of truth and faith. Philosophy, which forms thought and culture, must recover its original vocation.

Chapter One: The Revelation of God's Wisdom

7. The Church bears a message that originates in God himself. Knowledge of God perfects our knowledge of life's meaning. 8. The First Vatican Council in the constitution *Dei Filius* replied to the rationalism of the time. 9. It taught that philosophical truth and revealed truth are neither the same nor mutually exclusive. 10. The Second Vatican Council in the dogmatic constitution on revelation *Dei Verbum* stressed the salvific character of God's revelation in history. 11. Revelation comes to fulfillment in the words and deeds of Jesus of Nazareth. 12. Here we have the ultimate truth about human life and the goal of history, without which our existence is an insoluble riddle. 13. Yet God's revelation remains irreducibly mysterious, and can be understood coherently only by faith. Freedom is not just part of the act of faith but is essential to it; but decisions against God are not genuine expressions of freedom.

14. The teaching of Vatican I and Vatican II confronts philosophy with a new consideration: While revelation cannot be ignored if the mystery of human life is to be understood, knowledge derived from revelation nevertheless refers back constantly to the mystery of God, which the human mind can only receive and embrace in faith; the truth contained in revelation challenges the human mind to constant effort. 15. Philosophy and theology, different as they are in methods and content, are alike in being concerned with the ultimate purpose of human existence.

Chapter II: *Credo Ut Intellegam*

16. Sacred Scripture, especially the Wisdom literature, makes clear the deep relationship between the knowledge of faith and the knowledge of reason. The world and history cannot be fully understood apart from faith in God who is at work in them. Reason and faith cannot be separated the human capacity to know oneself, the world, and God. 17. Hence there is no reason for competition between faith and reason; "each contains the other," while also having its own field of action.

18. In the Bible, the "fool" is someone who loses sight of these matters and strays from the truth about the origin and destiny of things. 19. The Book of Wisdom speaks of God as revealing himself in nature as its creator. 20. This makes clear the value of reason, whose achievements have their true meaning "only...within the larger horizon of faith."

21. The struggle to understand God's mysterious design is wearying, but believers can continue because confident that God has created them for this. 22. The first chapter of Romans, declaring that we can come to knowledge of God through creation, in effect "affirms the human capacity for metaphysical enquiry." Original sin has wounded reason so that the search for truth is difficult, but Christ's coming has "redeemed reason from its weakness."

23. The New Testament, especially the Pauline epistles, points to the opposition between worldly wisdom and God's wisdom revealed in Christ. The salvific message of the Cross reduces human logic to futility while giving the ultimate answer to questions about life's meaning. "The preaching of Christ crucified and risen is the reef upon which the link between faith and philosophy can break up, but it is also the reef beyond which the two can set forth upon the boundless ocean of truth."

Chapter III: *Intellego Ut Credam*

24. The human heart contains "a seed of desire and nostalgia for God." Human beings have sought God in different ways at different times, and especially philosophy has done so. 25. Neither in matters of theory nor in practical, ethical matters are people indifferent to whether what they know is true. It is essential to choose and pursue true values, for only thus do people fully realize themselves by being true to their nature.

26. Truth begins with a question: Does life have meaning? Where is it going? Suffering and death make it urgent to find the answer. 27. Neither philosophers nor ordinary people can avoid questions like this. Human beings seek a final explanation, a supreme value, which puts an end to all questioning. 28. Thus one might define a human being as "the one who seeks the truth." 29. It is unthinkable that a search so deeply rooted in human nature should be useless. Only the sense that the answer can be found leads people to take the first step — for instance, by undertaking scientific research. The same is true of the search for answers to ultimate questions.

30. There are different modes of truth — experimental truth proper to everyday life and to scientific research, philosophical truth attained by speculative intellect, and religious truth. 31. For any individual, truths he or she simply believes far outnumber truths he or she has personally verified. 32. In believing, one trusts oneself to knowledge others have acquired. So human perfection involves "a dynamic relationship of faithful self-giving with others." The martyrs, aware of finding the truth about life in their encounter with Christ, testify to this.

33. From what has been said it follows that people are on a journey of discovery, a search for truth, that cannot be halted. Christian faith offers them the possibility of reaching the goal, which faith recognizes as residing in Jesus Christ, the Truth. 34. The truth revealed in Christ is not opposed to philosophical truth. Rather, the two modes of knowledge lead to the fullness of truth. The unity of truth is a fundamental premise of reasoning; and what reason naturally seeks can be found only through Christ. 35. On the basis of these considerations we turn to the relationship between revealed truth and philosophy.

Chapter IV: The Relationship Between Faith and Reason

36. From the start, the Christian proclamation of the gospel engaged the philosophical currents of the time. St. Paul's encounter with the Epicurean and Stoic philosophers in Athens is an instance. One of classical philosophy's major concerns was to purify thinking about God of mythological elements, and on that basis the Fathers of the Church entered into fruitful dialogue with ancient philosophy. 37. Christianity was careful not to confuse philosophy with gnosticism and esoteric knowledge; and this caution, expressed by Paul in Colossians, also is relevant to the forms of esoteric superstition that are widespread today.

38. Still, the urgent task for the first Christians was proclamation of and personal encounter with the risen Christ leading to conversion and the request for baptism. At first therefore they saw no need at first to look into philosophy, though pioneers like St. Justin and Clement of Alexandria did have some interest in philosophical thought. 39. Origen responds to philosophical attacks on Christianity by beginning to construct an early form of Christian theology from Platonic elements. 40. St. Augustine is of particular importance in the work of christianizing Platonic and Neo-Platonic thought. He produced the first great synthesis of philosophy and theology. 41. In sum, the originality of the Fathers lay in welcoming reason while infusing it with riches from revelation.

42. The interaction of faith and philosophically trained reason is especially noteworthy in Scholastic theology. St. Anselm of Canterbury points out that the intellect seeks that which it loves, and the more it loves, the more it desires to know. 43. St. Thomas Aquinas occupies a special place, not only because of what he taught but because of his dialogue with the Arab and Jewish thought of his time. He recognized that nature, philosophy's proper concern, can help us understand divine revelation. For his grasp of the relationship between faith and reason the Church proposes him as a model of how to do theology. 44. Another of his great insights concerns the role of wisdom, as a gift of the Holy Spirit, alongside philosophical and theological wisdom. His realism recognizes the objectivity of truth and produces "not merely a philosophy of 'what seems to be' but a philosophy of 'what is.'"

45. With the rise of the first universities, theology

came more directly into contact with other forms of learning and scientific research. The exaggerated rationalism of some thinkers led to a philosophy cut off from faith. One consequence of this separation was growing distrust of reason itself.

46. Much of the history of modern philosophy is a movement away from Christian revelation, to the point of opposing it. This process reached a peak in the last century, when idealism sought to treat the contents of faith as "dialectical structures" comprehensible by reason while atheistic humanism regarded faith as contrary to reason. A positivist mentality took hold in science, so that some scientists seem now to aspire to "a quasi-divine power over nature and even over the human being." In our times, nihilism — "a philosophy of nothingness" — has arisen from the crisis of rationalism and holds a certain attraction for people. 47. The role of philosophy itself has changed in modern times. No longer thought of as universal wisdom and learning, it is simply one of many fields of human knowing, in some ways consigned to a marginal role. As I pointed out in my first encyclical (*Redemptor Hominis*), modes of thought have emerged which are directed to utilitarian ends and to power. 48. Faith and reason are impoverished without each other. Hence my strong and insistent appeal for a recovery of their profound unity, without compromising the autonomy of either.

Chapter V: The Magisterium's Interventions in Philosophical Matters

49. "The Church has no philosophy of her own nor does she canonize any one particular philosophy in preference to others." Nor is it the Magisterium's role to correct philosophical mistakes. But the Magisterium does have an obligation to respond when philosophical opinions threaten the right understanding of revelation. 50. In this discernment, bishops are to be witnesses to the truth, carrying on a ministry that philosophers should appreciate. 51. This work is not primarily negative. The Magisterium aims to "prompt, promote and encourage" philosophical enquiry.

52. The Magisterium often has addressed philosophical errors. Since the middle of the nineteenth century it has censured such errors as fideism and radical traditionalism on the one hand and rationalism and ontologism on the other. The positive elements of this debate were drawn together in the dogmatic constitution *Dei Filius* of Vatican Council I, still a reference point for correct Christian thinking about philosophical research. 53. But the Magisterium's pronouncements have especially addressed the need for philosophical knowledge in order to understand faith. Vatican I affirmed that faith and reason are both inseparable and distinct. 54. In the present century, the Magisterium often has revisited these themes — for example, in the pronouncements of Pope St. Pius X regarding the philosophical bases of Modernism, in the rejection of Marxist philosophy and atheistic communism, and in Pope Pius XII's warnings against evolutionism, existentialism, and historicism.

55. Today, problems of former times have returned in a new mode — no longer the views of particular individuals and groups, but convictions so widespread they constitute virtually "the common mind." This is true, for instance, of the deep-seated distrust of reason, which leads some to speak of the "end of metaphysics." In theology, too, there has been a resurgence of rationalism and of fideism, one sign of which is the tendency to treat Scripture as the sole criterion of truth. 56. In the face of this "widespread distrust of universal and absolute statements," I encourage philosophers, whether Christian or not, to trust in the power of reason and not set overly modest goals for their philosophizing.

57. Along with pointing out philosophical mistakes, the Magisterium stresses the basic principles of a renewal of philosophical enquiry. Pope Leo XIII took a step of historic importance with his encyclical *Aeterni Patris*, especially its insistence on the incomparable value of the philosophy of St. Thomas. 58. This stimulated many studies of Thomas and other Scholastic writers and a rediscovery of the riches of Medieval thought. Throughout the century, and notably at Vatican II, the Church was served by thinkers who were products of the revival of Thomistic philosophy. 59. But this resurgence was not limited to Thomism and Neo-Thomism. Other Catholic philosophers, adopting more recent currents of thought, have done important work on various questions.

60. Vatican II offers rich teaching concerning philosophy, especially *Gaudium et Spes's* treatment of biblical anthropology and its analysis of atheism. Its teaching about the human person — that Christ "fully reveals man to himself and brings to light his most high calling" — is a constant point of reference for my teaching. The Council also dealt with the philosophical education of candidates for the priesthood, and its recommendations have implications for Christian education as a whole.

61. In the years since Vatican II, however, many Catholic faculties showed a diminished interest in the study of Scholastic philosophy and philosophy generally. It is a matter of "surprise and displeasure" that not a few theologians share this lack of interest. Vatican II's invitation to theologians to use the human sciences was not an authorization to marginalize philosophy and replace it with something else in pastoral formation. 62. "The study of philosophy is fundamental and indispensable to the structure of theological studies and to the formation of candidates for the priesthood." 63. These considerations make clear my responsibility to state principles and criteria for a harmonious, creative relationship between theology and philosophy.

Chapter VI: The Interaction Between Philosophy and Theology

64. For some of its tasks, theology must refer to philosophy. 65. Philosophy makes its specific contribution to the *auditus fidei* (the "hearing" of faith) by studying the structure of human knowledge and communication, especially language. 66. With regard to the *intellectus fidei* (the "knowledge" of faith), without philosophy's contribution certain issues of both dogmatic and moral theology could not even be discussed. 67. Fundamental theology's concern is to expound the relationship between faith and philosophical thought. Although faith, a gift of God, is not based on reason, it cannot dispense with it. 68. Moral theology may have an even greater need of philosophy. It requires a sound philosophical vision of human nature and society as well as the general principles of ethical decision-making. 69. Theol-

ogy also should make use of other kinds of knowledge, including the sciences, but this should not mean rejecting philosophy.
70. Insofar as human cultures embody the values of older traditions, they point to God's manifestation in nature. 71. The cultural context permeates the living of Christian faith while at the same time faith shapes the culture. The gospel prompts cultures to open themselves to its truth and develop in new ways. 72. There are new tasks of inculturation today, as the gospel gradually comes into contact with cultures previously beyond Christian influence. This is especially so in the East, and particularly India, from whose rich spiritual heritage Christians should draw elements compatible with faith. But even as it engages these cultures, the Church cannot abandon her heritage of Greco-Latin thought. All this holds true also for the cultures of China, Japan, and other Asian countries as well as Africa.
73. The relationship between theology and philosophy is circular. Theology's source is God's revealed word, which it seeks to understand better. But since God's word is Truth, the human search for truth — philosophy — helps us understand revelation better. 74. The fruitfulness of this relationship is confirmed by great Christian theologians who also were distinguished philosophers.
75. Different stances toward faith are possible for philosophy. One of these is autonomy — complete independence of revelation. The demand for valid autonomy should be respected, but there also is a version of philosophical self-sufficiency that, refusing the truth offered by divine revelation, precludes access to deeper knowledge of truth. 76. Christian philosophy represents a second possible stance. The term should not be taken to mean that the Church has an "official philosophy." Rather, it indicates a way of philosophizing with two aspects: faith's purifying of reason and revelation's proposal of truths that reason might not otherwise have discovered — the idea of a free, personal God, the reality of sin, the person as a spiritual being, etc. 77. There is also the "stance" involved in theology's calling upon philosophy for help. If theologians refused that help, they would be at risk of doing philosophy themselves — badly — while if philosophers shunned theology they would have to master the contents of Christian faith on their own.
78. These reflections show why the Magisterium repeatedly has praised St. Thomas's thought and made him guide and model for theology. The aim is not to take a position on properly theological questions or "demand adherence to particular theses"; it is to show how he is "an authentic model for all who seek the truth."
79. Finally, I shall consider certain requirements which theology and, more fundamentally, the word of God today make of philosophy. Christian revelation is the point where philosophy and theology engage each other; theologians should be guided by "the authority of truth alone" for the sake of the encounter of faith and culture and understanding between believers and non-believers.

Chapter VII: Current Requirements and Tasks

80. It is basic to the "philosophy" of the Bible that the world and human life have meaning and look to-

ward fulfillment in Jesus Christ. The mystery of the Incarnation is the central point of reference for understanding human existence, the world, and God himself. 81. Today, however, there is a crisis of meaning. Living in a "maelstrom of data and facts," people wonder if it makes sense even to raise the question of meaning. Skepticism, indifference, and nihilism arise from this. Philosophy must recover its "sapiential dimension" as a search for ultimate meaning. This need is all the greater because of the immense of expansion of technology, which, unless ordered to something greater than a merely utilitarian end, threatens to destroy the human race.
82. Philosophy must affirm the human capacity to know the truth. Scripture takes it for granted that people can know truth, and theology needs the contribution of a philosophy which does not reject the idea of objective truth. 83. There also is need for a philosophy with a genuinely metaphysical dimension, capable of transcending empirical data so as to reach what is absolute, ultimate, and foundational. 84. Current developments in hermeneutics and the analysis of language make the importance of metaphysics still more evident. While such studies can be helpful for the understanding of faith, some scholars in these fields put forward views that obscure faith's contents.
85. Human beings can achieve unified, organic knowledge. But today the "segmentation of knowledge" keeps people from interior unity. In this situation, it is significant that some philosophers are promoting a recovery of the great tradition of philosophy. It is on the basis of this tradition that a new, constructive mode of thinking can develop. This is true also for theology.
86. There are a number of dangers in some currents of thought today. The first is eclecticism — the use of ideas from different philosophies, without concern for their internal coherence; an extreme form of this is the rhetorical misuse of philosophical terms by some theologians, a form of manipulation unhelpful to the search for truth. 87. Often lying hidden in eclecticism is historicism, whose fundamental claim is that a philosophy's truth depends on its relevance to a certain historical period: what was true in one period may not be true in another. Historicism in theology tends to appear mainly as "modernism," one form of which is the substitution of relevance for truth. 88. Scientism, another threat, denies the validity of any forms of knowledge except those of positive science: religious, theological, ethical, and aesthetic knowledge are "mere fantasy." One result is to make people think that whatever is technically possible is morally licit. 89. No less dangerous is pragmatism, which rules out theoretical considerations or judgments based on ethical principles. This gives rise to a view of democracy according to which the admissibility of a line of action is decided, not by unchanging values, but by majority vote.
90. These positions lead to a more general view that provides the framework for many philosophies: nihilism. It not only conflicts with revelation but denies the very identity of the human being, erasing the human likeness to God and leading people either to "a destructive will to power" or "a solitude without hope."
91. Some call this the age of postmodernity. According to some postmodern currents of thought, the

age of certainty is over and people must learn to live with a complete absence of meaning in which everything is provisional. The terrible experience of evil in our times helps account for this nihilism. Certainly it has destroyed rationalist optimism, which took for granted reason's triumphant progress in history. In fact, "now, at the end of this century, one of our greatest threats is the temptation to despair."

92. Theology faces a dual task today: to renew its methods in order to serve evangelization more effectively, while at the same time considering the ultimate truth entrusted to it by revelation. The latter task, theology's prime concern, also challenges philosophy. To believe that universally valid truth can be known does not lead to intolerance; rather, it is essential to dialogue.

93. Theology's chief purpose is to provide an understanding of revelation and the content of faith. Contemplation of the mystery of the Triune God is at its very heart. It begins with reflection upon the mystery of Incarnation and God's *kenosis* ("emptying").

There is a basic and urgent need for careful analysis of the relevant texts, and here certainly there are problems that cannot be solved without the help of philosophy. 94. One problem is the relationship between meaning and truth. To interpret the sources of revelation, the theologian must ask what truth a text intends to communicate within the limits of language. There is a pressing need in analyzing biblical texts, especially the gospels, to consider the relationship between fact and meaning from the philosophical point of view.

95. Again, there is the question of how to reconcile the absoluteness and universality of truth with the historically and culturally conditioned character of the formulas that express that truth. A hermeneutic open to metaphysics can show how to move from the circumstances in which texts developed to the truth they express.

96. Here one glimpses the solution to another problem: the permanent validity of the language of dogmatic definitions. This is a complex subject; but, across cultures, propositions expressing certain basic concepts do retain their truth. Philosophy can be very helpful to a better understanding of the relationship between conceptual language and truth. 97. Again, philosophy's contribution is needed by dogmatic theology. The temptation to understand truths of faith only in functional terms — for example, a Christology "from below" or an ecclesiology developed solely on the model of civil society — should be resisted. The *intellectus fidei* must turn to the philosophy of being as found in the Christian metaphysical tradition. 98. These considerations apply equally to moral theology. Faced with contemporary challenges in the social, economic, political, and scientific fields, people's ethical consciences are disoriented. In the encyclical *Veritatis Splendor* I stressed the fundamental place of truth in the moral field. Moral theology needs the support of a philosophical ethics, neither subjectivist nor utilitarian, which looks to the truth of the good.

99. Theological work in the Church is first of all at the service of the proclamation of the faith (*kerygma*) and catechesis. Catechesis has philosophical implications that require exploration in light of faith. The reciprocity between the theological disciplines and philosophy can be fruitful for the communication and understanding of faith.

Conclusion

100. The Church is convinced that faith and reason influence and support each other. 101. Today, theology and philosophy need to recover their relationship. 102. A philosophy that is true wisdom will help people see that their humanity is affirmed by opening themselves to Christ. 103. Philosophy also has an important contribution to make to the new evangelization through its shaping of culture. 104. Christian philosophers can develop the ground for mutual understanding and dialogue with non-believers.

105. I ask theologians to give particular attention to the philosophical implications of the word of God, and to enter into a critical dialogue with contemporary philosophy and the philosophical tradition. I encourage those responsible for priestly formation to attend to the philosophical preparation of those who will proclaim the gospel and, especially, those who will do theological research and teaching.

106. I appeal to philosophers and teachers of philosophy to be open to the urgent questions that arise from the word of God. Alert to the link between truth and goodness, they can formulate the genuine ethics that is now so badly needed. Expressing my admiration and encouragement to those engaged in scientific research, I urge them to situate the achievements of science and technology in a context of wisdom linked to philosophical and ethical values.

107. I ask everyone to reflect on the human search for truth and meaning. Some philosophical systems have led people to believe they are their own absolute masters. But a human being can only find fulfillment in entering the truth and knowing and loving God.

108. Finally, I turn to Mary, Seat of Wisdom. There is a deep harmony between her vocation and the vocation of philosophy. As she lost none of her humanity and freedom by assenting to Gabriel's word, so philosophical enquiry surrenders none of its autonomy but reaches its highest expression in heeding the summons of the gospel's truth. "May Mary, Seat of Wisdom, be a sure haven for all who devote their lives to the search for wisdom."

EXCERPTS FROM *FIDES ET RATIO*

Following are excerpts from the encyclical Fides et Ratio (Faith and Reason).

No. 1. [A] cursory glance at ancient history shows clearly how in different parts of the world, with their different cultures, there arise at the same time the fundamental questions which pervade human life: Who am I? Where have I come from and where am I going? Why is there evil? What is there after this life? These are the questions which we find in the sacred writings of Israel, as also in the Veda and the Avesta; we find them in the writings of Confucius and Lao-Tze, and in the preaching of Tirthankara and Buddha; they appear in the poetry of Homer and in the tragedies of Euripides and Sophocles, as they do in the philosophical writings of Plato and Aristotle. They are questions which have their common source in the quest for meaning which has always compelled the human heart.

No. 12. In the Incarnation of the Son of God we see forged the enduring and definitive synthesis which the human mind of itself could not even have imagined: the Eternal enters time, the Whole lies hidden in the part, God takes on a human face. The truth communicated in Christ's Revelation is therefore no longer confined to a particular place or culture, but is offered to every man and woman.... Seen in any other terms, the mystery of personal existence remains an insoluble riddle.

No. 26. [T]he first absolutely certain truth of our life, beyond the fact that we exist, is the inevitability of our death. Given this unsettling fact, the search for a full answer is inescapable. Each of us has both the desire and the duty to know the truth of our own destiny...No. 27. No one can avoid this questioning, neither the philosopher nor the ordinary person. The answer we give will determine whether or not we think it possible to attain universal and absolute truth.... No. 28. Life in fact can never be grounded upon doubt, uncertainty or deceit; such an existence would be threatened constantly by fear and anxiety. One may define the human being, therefore, as the one who seeks the truth.

No. 36. One of the major concerns of classical philosophy was to purify human notions of God of mythological elements.... It was on this basis that the Fathers of the Church entered into fruitful dialogue which ancient philosophy, which offered new ways of proclaiming and understanding the God of Jesus Christ.

No. 43. A quite special place in this long development belongs to Saint Thomas, not only because of what he taught but also because of the dialogue which he undertook with the Arab and Jewish thought of his time. In an age when Christian thinkers were rediscovering the treasures of ancient philosophy, and more particularly of Aristotle, Thomas had the great merit of giving pride of place to the harmony which exists between faith and reason.... More radically, Thomas recognized that nature, philosophy's proper concern, could contribute to the understanding of divine Revelation.... This is why the Church has been justified in consistently proposing Saint Thomas as a master of thought and a model of the right way to do theology.

No. 55. Surveying the situation today, we see that the problems of other times have returned, but in a new key. It is no longer a matter of questions of interest only to certain individuals and groups, but convictions so widespread that they have become to some extent the common mind. An example of this is the deep-seated distrust of reason which has surfaced in the most recent developments of philosophical research, to the point where there is talk at times of "the end of metaphysics".... In theology too the temptations of other times have reappeared. In some contemporary theologies, for instance, a certain rationalism is gaining ground.... There are also signs of a resurgence of fideism, which fails to recognize the importance of rational knowledge and philosophical discourse for the understanding of faith, indeed for the very possibility of belief in God.

No. 57. Pope Leo XIII with his Encyclical Letter *Aeterni Patris* took a step of historic importance for the life of the Church.... More than a century later, many of the insights of his Encyclical Letter have lost none of their interest from either a practical or pedagogical point of view — most particularly, his insistence upon the incomparable value of the philosophy of Saint Thomas.

No. 61. In the years after the Second Vatican Council, many Catholic faculties were in some ways impoverished by a diminished sense of the study not just of Scholastic philosophy but more generally of the study of philosophy itself. I cannot fail to note with surprise and displeasure that this lack of interest in the study of philosophy is shared by not a few theologians....

No. 62. I wish to repeat clearly that the study of philosophy is fundamental and indispensable to the structure of theological studies and to the formation of candidates for the priesthood.

No. 72. Today, as the Gospel gradually comes into contact with cultural worlds which once lay beyond Christian influence, there are new tasks of inculturation.... My thoughts turn immediately to the lands of the East, so rich in religious and philosophical traditions of great antiquity. Among these lands, India has a special place.... In this work of discernment, which finds its inspiration in the Council's Declaration *Nostra Aetate*, certain criteria will have to be kept in mind. The first of these is the universality of the human spirit, whose basic needs are the same in the most disparate cultures. The second, which derives from the first, is this: in engaging great cultures for the first time, the Church cannot abandon what she has gained from her inculturation in the world of Greco-Latin thought.... Thirdly, care will need to be taken lest, contrary to the very nature of the human spirit, the legitimate defense of the uniqueness and originality of Indian thought be confused with the idea that a particular cultural tradition should remain closed in its difference and affirm itself by opposing other traditions.

No. 105. In concluding this Encyclical Letter, my thoughts turn particularly to theologians.... I urge them to recover and express to the full the metaphysical dimension of truth in order to enter into a demanding critical dialogue with both contemporary philosophical thought and with the philosophical tradition....

No. 106. I appeal also to philosophers, and to all teachers of philosophy, asking them to have the courage to recover ... the range of authentic wisdom and truth — metaphysical truth included — which is proper to philosophical enquiry.... Finally, I cannot fail to address a word to scientists.... I would urge them to continue their efforts without ever abandoning the sapiential horizon within which scientific and technological achievements are wedded to the philosophical and ethical values which are the distinctive and indelible mark of the human person.

SYNOD FOR OCEANIA

by Russell Shaw

"Jesus Christ and the Peoples of Oceania: Walking His Way, Telling His Truth and Living His Life" was the theme of the Special Assembly of the Synod of Bishops for Oceania that was held November 22 to December 12 at the Vatican.

Taking part in the assembly were 154 persons, including 117 voting members. The participants included bishops of the region and heads of major Vatican offices, several invited bishops from outside the region, religious superiors, auditors, experts, and four representatives of other Christian churches.

The assembly for Oceania was one in a series of five regional assemblies of the Synod of Bishops convened by Pope John Paul II in preparation for the Jubilee Year 2000. Previous sessions for Africa, America, and Asia were held April 10 to May 8, 1994, November 16 to December 12, 1997, and April 19 to May 14, 1998, while an assembly for Europe is expected to take place late in 1999.

A General Assembly of the Synod on the theme "The Bishop: Evangelizer of Jesus Christ For the Hope of the World" is planned in Rome in October of the year 2000. Earlier general assemblies have considered the laity (1987), priests (1990), and persons in consecrated life (1994).

The common focus of the regional assemblies is the program of new evangelization that Pope John Paul has declared central to the efforts of the Church in the Third Millennium. Oceania covers one-third of the earth's surface, but there are only 29 million people in the region, and many of them live on small islands separated by vast distances. Of the 8 million Catholics, 5 million are in Australia.

The synod opening Mass November 22 in St. Peter's Basilica was marked by the use of numerous native elements in the liturgy including music and dance. In his homily Pope John Paul welcomed the representatives of "that far-flung portion of the Church, which extends over the immense spaces of Oceania" and encouraged them to consider how the Gospel can best be proclaimed amid "the diversity of cultures and human, social and religious traditions, and in the remarkable variety of their peoples."

At the start of the working sessions, Archbishop Barry James Hickey of Perth, Australia, relator or recording secretary for the assembly, presented a panorama treatingf the challenge of secularism and "post-Christian" modernity said now to face Christians in many parts of the region.

Confronted with this challenge, he said, two "almost incompatible" responses were possible for the Church: either to "make friends with modernity" by largely accepting its values or for the most part to reject the secular culture by reaffirming traditional Christian values and beliefs on such issues as contraception. He said the division existing within the Church between different groups of Catholics holding these opposed points of view "affects theology, liturgy, catechetics, seminary formation, religious life, lay leadership and, inevitably, vocations."

The discussion which followed was described by participants as pastorally oriented and good-natured, without the theological tensions that had marked some previous synod assemblies. The wide-ranging nature of the debate was indicated by the message which the participants issued at the conclusion of the assembly.

"During our sessions the words of the commission of Jesus to preach the Gospel to every creature recurred often and focused our attention on the role of the bishop as teacher of the faith. We know that we are not alone in this, and we recognize the key role of catechists, parish communities, Catholic schools, seminaries, universities, lay formation programs and the media," the message said.

"Time after time, matters of social justice were raised and intimately linked to the establishment of God's kingdom. Major concerns included the issues of refugees and migration, environment, unemployment, development funding, health care, sexual abuse and the economy. The sacredness of life, the dignity of the human person, both women and men, and the common good of all peoples were integral to all our considerations.

"Above all, the need for holiness in leaders and the faithful was stressed. If the Church is to be a teacher, she must first be a witness."

According to reports, one issue which came up many times during the discussion was the shortage of priests and what to do about it. In Oceania as a whole there are about 1,575 Catholics per priest, but in the Pacific region the figure climbs to about 2,500 per priest. The result, speakers said, was that some isolated, hard-to-reach communities of Catholics must go for months, even years, without the Eucharist. One solution for such places urged by some speakers was the ordination as priests of mature married men, the so-called *viri probati* who have been cited for years in discussions of this question as potential candidates.

But there was no clear consensus on the issue, and the closing message of the assembly skirted the question, as did the "propositions" or recommendations submitted to the pope as a basis for his post-synodal apostolic exhortation, expected in the year 2000. The message put it this way:

"The Eucharist must stand at the heart of our sacramental life and our faith. For this reason, concern was expressed about the non-availability of the Eucharist in some areas. Given the centrality of the Eucharist, the ordained priesthood grows in importance; and this consideration led to other questions touching on the issue of priestly celibacy, vocations, formation and ongoing support for priests."

Similarly, none of the propositions directly advocated the ordination of married men, even though one did ask for continued dialogue about the problem of communities cut off from the Eucharist and sacraments for long periods of time because of a shortage of priests. Another proposition warmly commended priestly celibacy.

Others among the 48 propositions turned over to the pope dealt with such matters as the role of women in the Church and the use of gender-inclusive language in liturgical translations, pastoral care of divorced and remarried Catholics and of priests who have quit the active ministry, the need for catechesis concerning the sacrament of Penance, sexual abuse by Church personnel, more collegiality in the appointment of bishops and the approval of liturgical texts, ecumenism, new lay movements, inculturation, the protection of human life, social doctrine and development, and discrimination against indigenous peoples.

Even so, there were some complaints that the assembly had not given enough attention to evangelization. The missionary news agency Fides in an editorial complimented the participants for having faced many serious regional issues, but it added:

"The person who should have been the protagonist of the synod — 'Jesus Christ: Walking His Way, Telling His Truth, Living His Life' — risked being submerged in a flood of concern over ecclesiastical structures.... An amazing amount of space was given to questions of balance and power (the relationships of priest-laity, men-women and pope-bishops) and to the internal elements of the Church (sacraments, liturgy and traditions), and very little space to the Church's mission to the people of Oceania."

Even on the question of women, Fides remarked, the assembly should have spent more time on ways of upholding women's dignity in the cultures of Oceania and less time on their functions in the Church. The editorial called the latter "an interesting problem, but a bit clerical and not very responsive to the urgent concerns of the world."

In his homily at the closing Mass, nevertheless, Pope John Paul took note of the assembly's broad agenda and praised its deliberations. He said:

"You have come from Australia, New Zealand, the Pacific islands, Papua New Guinea and Solomon Islands, bringing the spiritual wealth of your peoples as well as the problems they encounter.

"In fact, how can we not point out that even in your societies religion faces threats and attempts to isolate it? How can we not stress that at times some people would like to reduce it to an individual experience that can have no influence on social life?

"You have spoken about the consequences of colonization and immigration, the living conditions of ethnic minorities and the faith problems of young people. The challenges of modernity and secularization were also highlighted....

"You have dialogued with one another and have united around the basic theme: Jesus Christ is also the way to follow, the truth to proclaim and the life to live for the peoples of Oceania. The new evangelization follows this program throughout the world."

DOCTRINAL MEETING IN MENLO PARK

(From: Catholic News Service.) From Feb. 9-12, 1999, a meeting was held at the Vallombrosa Center in Menlo Park, Calif., that included representatives of the Congregation for the Doctrine of the Faith and the chairpeople and members of the doctrinal commissions and conference presidents or their representatives from the United States, Canada, Australia, New Zealand, Papua New Guinea and Solomon Islands, and the Pacific region.

Chief among the participants were Cardinal Joseph Ratzinger, Prefect of the Congregation for the Doctrine of the Faith; Cardinal Aloysius Ambrozic of Toronto; Archbishop Tarcisio Bertone, secretary of the same congregation; Archbishop William Levada of San Francisco; Archbishop Daniel Pilarczyk of Cincinnati; Archbishop Michel Marie Calvet of New Caledonia; Archbishop Eric D'Arcy of Australia; Archbishop Adrian Smith of New Zealand; and Fr. Gilles Langevin, S.J. and Fr. Augustine DiNoia, O.P. staff to the Canadian and U.S. Doctrinal Commissions respectively.

The conference was sponsored by the Congregation for the Doctrine of the Faith as an expression of episcopal collegiality and was the next in a series of meetings between Congregation officials and representatives of doctrinal commissions throughout the Church. Previous gatherings were held in Latin America (Bogota, 1984 and Guadalajara, 1996), Africa (Kinshasa, 1987), Europe (Vienna, 1989), and Asia (Hong Kong, 1993).

The primary focus of the meetings is to examine the way in which doctrinal unity expresses and fosters ecclesial communion in both the local church and the universal church and at the same time contributes to a vigorous witness to the faith in diverse cultures. At Vallambrosa, the participating bishops reported on the doctrinal situation in their particular regions as well as on the ways in which effective collaboration between doctrinal commissions and the Congregation for the Doctrine of the Faith might be enhanced.

Among the topics discussed were: the authority of the Church's magisterium; the importance of the profession of faith; the ecclesial role of the theologian; and dialogue between bishops and theologians. Other relevant topics included the implications of feminism for Catholic thought and the pastoral care of homosexual persons.

From the presentations of the various representatives concerning the doctrinal situation in their particular regions, several points of consensus were established:

Cultural pluralism is profoundly present, although taking different forms, throughout the areas represented;

More effective doctrinal formation is very important. A new evangelization is urgently required even within the Church;

Developments in medical technology pose many urgent and important questions for the Church in the area of bioethics. What is needed is a renewed and deepened understanding of Christian anthropology to provide the adequate foundation for the proclamation and comprehension of the Church's teaching in those areas;

The artificiality for the Christian of the separation between faith and morality was discussed by the participants. The division between doctrine and moral life is seen as a serious problem;

In the resolution of doctrinal and moral questions as well as in other areas, the importance of the role of Catholic theologians in the life of the Church and in effective collaboration with the hierarchy was noted;

The Catholic theologian, like all members of the Catholic faithful, receives revelation and grace through the mediation of the Church.

As a result of discussions, the conference issued a set of concrete proposals:

It is the bishops who have the primary as teachers of the Catholic faith;

In certain geographical areas the formation of joint doctrinal commissions serving two or more episcopal conferences should be seriously considered;

With regard to membership in doctrinal commissions, it should be noted that only bishops and those who are equivalent to bishops under canon law can be full members;

The doctrinal commissions should make use of the documents issued by the Holy See, especially those published by the Congregation for the Doctrine of the Faith;

In order to ensure the exchange of information regarding the life and teaching of the Church, it would important to evaluate and to enhance communications and coordination on all levels — whether between dioceses, within the structures of the episcopal conferences, among various conferences of bishops and with the Congregation for the Doctrine of the Faith;

Doctrinal commissions should send their publications to the Congregation for the Doctrine of the Faith on an annual basis and, depending on the nature of the documents, those of other commissions as well;

It is strongly recommended that every doctrinal commission send an annual report on the doctrinal situation of its region to the Congregation for the Doctrine of the Faith;

The doctrinal commission should prepare a special report for submission to the Congregation of the Doctrine of the Faith on the occasion of the *ad limina* visit of the members of the bishops' conference;

Collaboration between the Congregation for the Doctrine of the Faith and the doctrinal commissions becomes particularly relevant with respect to the examination of publications presenting doctrinal problems;

Doctrinal commissions should be available to assist local bishops in the work of evaluating books and other publications which have been submitted for the *imprimatur;*

The doctrinal commission can also be of assistance to local bishops when, as required by canon law, a theologian requests the *mandatum* from the competent ecclesiastical authority in order to teach theology in a Catholic college or university;

The doctrinal commission should be consulted by the other commissions of the conference of bishops in the process of drafting any documents for publication which have doctrinal aspect or implications.

Following the conference, Cardinal Ratzinger delivered a lecture on culture and truth in Pope John Paul II's encyclical *Fides et Ratio.*

LITTLETON TRAGEDY

On Apr. 20, 1999, two students at Columbine High School in Littleton, Colorado, Dylan Klebold and Eric Harris launched the bloodiest school massacre in American history, systematically shooting their fellow classmates and finally committing suicide at the climax of a siege of the school by police authorities.

The shootings left twelve students and one teacher dead and the school scarred with physical, emotional, and spiritual scars. The massacre sparked a national debate about the roots of school violence and the absence of religion in public schools as well as predictable calls for stricter gun control legislation. Archbishop Charles Chaput, O.F.M. Cap., of Denver, issued a statement about the tragedy, and messages were received from the Holy Father (see below) and from Cardinal Francis Stafford, Archbishop Emeritus of Denver and now President of the Pontifical Council of the Family. Following are Archbishop Chaput's statement at the April 22 prayer service at Civic Center Park and the message of condolence from the Holy Father:

Archbishop Chaput's statement:

The news of the terrible experience of yesterday was communicated to me when I was in Wichita, Kansas, for a Church gathering. The reality of what happened here didn't hit home until this morning when I visited a large number of students from Columbine High School and then had the privilege of spending some time with the families of two students who were killed.

They taught me something.

The students who gathered to encourage each other taught me again the importance of our sharing this experience together and encouraging one another. They spoke individually, one by one, and encouraged their fellow students to hope for the future.

When I met with the families of the students who had been killed, they taught me to trust, to trust God. Because in the midst of their great suffering, suffering that is beyond my imagination, they had a certain confidence that God would care for them and care for the children they had lost.

Violence is pervasive in our society — in our homes, in our schools, on our streets, in our cars as we drive home from work, in the media, in music, in video games. It's in some ways a very unconscious part of our lives, but a very real part of our lives.

The causes of this violence are hostility, hatred, racism, despair, indifference and a growing coarsening of our views of the value of human life.

We need to change.

We sometimes talk easily about our society needing to change. But societies change when our families are changed. And our families are changed when we as individuals have an experience of conversion to non-violence and to love within our own hearts.

It is not enough for us to speak about society, or our communities. We need to speak about ourselves.

I ask you to join me in praying today and throughout this week in a very special way for the families that have been affected by this violence in such a personal way. But I also ask you to pray that each of us, including myself, will experience a deep conversion in our hearts towards love and non-violence in all our relationships with others.

Pope John Paul II's Message of Condolence:

The following message was received by Archbishop Charles J. Chaput from the Holy See via Angelo Cardinal Sodano, Secretary of State:

Your Excellency,

I have been directed to send you the following message:

"His Holiness Pope John Paul II has been deeply shocked by news of the terrible tragedy which has caused many deaths and injuries at a school near Denver and he asks you to convey to the families and school community the assurance of his prayerful closeness at this very difficult time. He com-

mends the victims to Almighty God and invokes divine strength and comfort on the injured and on all affected by this awful event. He expresses the earnest hope that American society as a whole will react to this latest act of violence among the young by committing itself to promoting and transmitting the moral vision and the values which alone can ensure respect for the inviolable dignity of human life.

BAN ON TWO RELIGIOUS FROM MINISTRY TO HOMOSEXUALS

(Courtesy, Vatican Information Service)

On July 13, 1999 the Congregation for the Doctrine of the Faith made public a Notification regarding Sr. Jeannine Gramick S.S.N.D. and Fr. Robert Nugent S.D.S., founders of the "New Ways Ministry" organization in the archdiocese of Washington, U.S.A.

For more than 20 years the two religious have been involved in pastoral activities directed towards homosexual persons; they are also the authors of the books, Building Bridges: Gay and Lesbian Reality and the Catholic Church and Voices of Hope: A Collection of Positive Catholic Writings on Gay and Lesbian Issues. Owing to serious questions concerning their willingness to adhere to the teachings of the Church concerning homosexuality, an inquiry was launched in 1984. After fifteen years of investigation into their activities and writings, the Congregation for the Doctrine of the Faith issued its Notification. The document was signed by Cardinal Joseph Ratzinger and Archbishop Tarcisio Bertone S.D.B., emeritus of Vercelli, respectively prefect and secretary of the congregation, and was issued in English, Italian, Spanish, French, German and Portuguese.

Following are excerpts from the document:

"From the beginning, in presenting the Church's teaching on homosexuality, Father Nugent and Sister Gramick have continually called central elements of that teaching into question. For this reason, in 1984, James Cardinal Hickey, the Archbishop of Washington, following the failure of a number of attempts at clarification, informed them that they could no longer undertake their activities in that Archdiocese. At the same time, the Congregation for Institutes of Consecrated Life and for Societies of Apostolic Life ordered them to separate themselves totally and completely from 'New Ways Ministry.'

"Despite this action by the Holy See, Father Nugent and Sister Gramick continued their involvement in activities organized by 'New Ways Ministry,' though removing themselves from leadership positions. They also continued to maintain and promote ambiguous positions on homosexuality and explicitly criticized documents of the Church's Magisterium on this issue."

"In 1988, the Holy See established a Commission under the Presidency of Adam Cardinal Maida to study and evaluate their public statements and activities and to determine whether these were faithful to Catholic teaching on homosexuality.

"After the publication of Building Bridges, which summarized the activities and thinking (of the two religious), the investigation of the Commission focused primarily on this book.... The Commission found serious deficiencies in their writings and pas-

toral activities, which were incompatible with the fullness of Christian morality.

"In 1995, the Congregation for Institutes of Consecrated Life and for Societies of Apostolic Life transferred the entire case to the competence of the Congregation for the Doctrine of the Faith. At this point, with the hope that Father Nugent and Sister Gramick would be willing to express their assent to Catholic teaching on homosexuality and to correct the errors in their writings, the Congregation undertook another attempt at resolution by inviting them to respond unequivocally to certain questions regarding their position on the morality of homosexual acts and on the homosexual inclination.

"Their responses, dated February 22, 1996, were not sufficiently clear to dispel the serious ambiguities of their position. In these, Sister Gramick and Father Nugent demonstrated a clear conceptual understanding of the Church's teaching on homosexuality, but refrained from professing any adherence to that teaching. Furthermore, the publication, in 1995, of their book Voices of Hope: A Collection of Positive Catholic Writings on Gay and Lesbian Issues had made it clear that there was no change in their opposition to fundamental elements of the Church's teaching.

"The Congregation decided that the case should be resolved according to the procedure outlined in its 'Regulations for Doctrinal Examination' (chapter 4).

"Each was asked to respond to the contestatio personally and independently from the other, to allow them the greatest freedom in expressing their individual positions.

"In the Ordinary Sessions of May 6 and May 20, 1998, the Members of the Congregation carefully evaluated the responses.... (They) were unanimous in their decision that the responses of the two, while containing certain positive elements, were unacceptable. In each case, Father Nugent and Sister Gramick had sought to justify the publication of their books and neither had expressed personal adherence to the Church's teaching on homosexuality in sufficiently unequivocal terms. Thus, it was decided that they should be asked to formulate a public declaration.... In this declaration they were asked to express their interior assent to the teaching of the Catholic Church on homosexuality and to acknowledge that the two above-mentioned books contained errors.

"Sister Gramick, while expressing her love for the Church, simply refused to express any assent whatsoever to the teaching of the Church on homosexuality. Father Nugent was more responsive, but not unequivocal in his statement of interior assent to the teaching of the Church. It was decided by the Members of the Congregation, therefore, that Father Nugent should be given yet another opportunity to express unequivocal assent.... His response, dated January 25, 1999, showed that this attempt had not met with success. Father Nugent would not sign the declaration he had received and responded by formulating an alternative text which modified the Congregation's declaration on certain important points. In particular, he would not state that homosexual acts are intrinsically disordered and he added a section which

calls into question the definitive and unchangeable nature of Catholic doctrine in this area.

"The ambiguities and errors of the approach of Father Nugent and Sister Gramick have caused confusion among the Catholic people and have harmed the community of the Church. For these reasons, Sister Jeannine Gramick, S.S.N.D., and Father Robert Nugent, S.D.S., are permanently prohibited from any pastoral work involving homosexual persons and are ineligible, for an undetermined period, for any office in their respective religious institutes."

ANGLICAN-ROMAN CATHOLIC DIALOGUE: THE GIFT OF AUTHORITY

Courtesy, Br. Jeffrey Gros, FSC, Associate Director, Secretariat for Ecumenical and Interreligious Affairs
In May, 1999, the Anglican Roman Catholic International Commission II issued its report The Gift of Authority. *The report covered those areas of authority that were not treated in its two authority texts in the* Final Report *(1982). The following is a summary:*

The agreed statement, the fourth of the second phase of the Anglican-Roman Catholic International Commission (ARCIC II) and the fourth text on authority in this history of this ongoing international dialogue (the Venice Statement of 1976 and the Elucidation and Windsor Statement of 1981) has a retrospective introduction in three sections, after an introduction: authority in the Church, the exercise of authority in the Church, and agreement in the exercise of authority: steps toward visible unity. The framework is the "Yes" of God to us in Jesus Christ, and the "Amen" of the Church (2Cor. 1:18-20). The theological themes touched upon are local church, Tradition and apostolicity, Scripture, reception and re-reception of apostolic Tradition and catholicity. The exercise of authority covers mission and unity, synodality, perseverance in the truth through teaching and memory, primacy through collegiality and conciliarity, and freedom of conscience. It is the belief of the dialogue "that if this statement about the nature of authority in the manner of its exercise is accepted and acted upon, this issue will no longer be a cause for continued breach of communion between our two churches." (51)

Building upon previous ARCIC texts on authority, this agreed statement explicates further how the Church may teach *infallibly*. The dialogue approaches the topic of the teaching role of the Bishop of Rome by first addressing the themes of conciliarity, the *indefectibility* of the Church, the roles of laity and ordained ministry, synodality and past agreements on *episcopé*. It then states its agreement on papal *infallibility* without using the term itself: "Every solemn definition pronounced from the chair of Peter in the church of Peter and Paul may, however, express only the faith of

the Church... When the Faith is articulated in this way, the Bishop of Rome proclaims the faith of the local churches. It is thus *wholly reliable* teaching of the whole Church that is operative in the judgment of the universal primate.... The reception of the primacy of the Bishop of Rome entails the recognition of the specific ministry of the universal primate. We believe that this is a gift to be received by all of the churches." (47) The dialogue then states: "This form of authoritative teaching has no stronger guarantee from the Spirit than have the solemn definitions of ecumenical councils."

Questions are addressed to both communions, such as the following: For Anglicans "Is the Communion also open to the acceptance of instruments of oversight which would allow decisions to be reached that, in certain circumstances, would bind the whole Church?... Above all, how will Anglicans address the question of universal primacy as it is emerging from their life together and from ecumenical dialogue?" (56)

For Catholics: "Is there are at all levels effective participation of clergy as well as lay people in emerging synodal bodies? ... Has enough provision been made to ensure consultation between the Bishop of Rome and the local churches prior to making of important decisions affecting either a local church or the whole Church?"

The principal enunciated for the practical recommendation is that "there is no turning back in our journey toward full ecclesial communion. In light of our agreement the Commission believes our two communions should make more visible the *koinonia* we already have. Theological dialogue... is not itself sufficient... Anglicans and Roman Catholic bishops should find ways of cooperating and developing relationships of mutual accountability in their exercise of oversight... Meeting regularly together at regional and local levels and participation of bishops from one communion in the international meetings of bishops of the other... Wherever possible, bishops should take the opportunity of reaching an acting together in matters of faith and morals." (58-59)

CLARIFICATION ON THE DOCTRINE OF JUSTIFICATION

Courtesy, Vatican Information Service
The Pontifical Council for Promoting Christian Unity today issued on June 22, 1999 a communiqué stating that, "due to various erroneous interpreta-

tions by the communications media following the publication of a Joint Declaration of the Catholic Church and the Lutheran World Federation on the Doctrine of Justification together with an Official

Common Statement and an Annex it seemed appropriate to underline the correct meaning of the above-mentioned texts."

" 'The ecumenical dialogue carried out since Vatican Council II has led to a significant convergence regarding the doctrine of justification. This (convergence) allows an agreement on fundamental truths regarding the doctrine of justification to be formulated in this Joint Declaration.'

"Consequently 'the teaching of the Lutheran Churches, as presented in this Declaration, does not fall under the condemnations of the Council of Trent'. 'However, this does not remove anything from the seriousness of the doctrinal condemnations associated with the doctrine of justification. Some of these (condemnations) did not simply lack foundation. For us they still hold 'the significance of salutary warnings' to which we must pay heed, both in doctrine and in practice'."

" 'This Joint Declaration, just as the dialogues themselves, is based on the conviction that overcoming condemnations and controversial questions is not equivalent to taking separation and condemnations lightly, nor does it mean renouncing the past of each of our Churches. Nonetheless, it (the Declaration) is convinced that new methods of evaluation are emerging in the history of our Churches and developments are taking place which

not only permit but demand that the divisive questions and the condemnations be checked and examined from a new perspective.'

"'Together we confess that the sinner is justified through faith in the salvific action of God in Christ. This salvation is given to him by the Holy Spirit in baptism which is the foundation of his whole Christian life.' "

" 'Immediately when the Holy Spirit starts in us His work of regeneration and renewal, by means of the Word and the holy Sacraments, it is certain that we can and must collaborate by means of the power of the Holy Spirit.' "

" 'If, therefore, we say that we are without sin, we are not in the right.... In this way, Lutherans and Catholics can together comprehend the Christian as 'simul justus et peccator,' despite the different ways they have of approaching the question.'

"As regards the question of 'concupiscence,' understood by the Lutherans as the desire of the human being who seeks himself and which, consequently, they consider a sin; for Catholics this is an inclination that arises from sin and induces to sin but is not itself sin because 'sin is personal in nature and, as such, leads to a separation from God'.

"Consequently, there has been no denial of the past, but rather a common step forward in understanding the mystery of Christ's salvation."

LIFE ISSUES

THE PRO-LIFE MOVEMENT AT THE THRESHOLD OF THE THIRD MILLENNIUM

By Helen Alvaré, Director of Planning and Information, Secretariat for Pro-Life Activities, NCCB/USCC

Living the Gospel of Life: A Challenge to American Catholics

The following are excerpts from the Pro-Life statement by Catholic Bishops of the United States and approved by a vote of 217-30 during their November, 1998 meetings in Washington, D.C.

"... The nobility of the American experiment flows from its founding principles, not from its commercial power. In this century alone, hundreds of thousands of Americans have died defending those principles. Hundreds of thousands more have lived lives of service to those principles — both at home and on other continents — teaching, advising and providing humanitarian assistance to people in need. As Pope John Paul has observed, 'At the center of the moral vision of [the American] founding documents is the recognition of the rights of the human person ...' The greatness of the United States lies 'especially [in its] respect for the dignity and sanctity of human life in all conditions and at all stages of development'... This nobility of the American spirit endures today in those who struggle for social justice and equal opportunity for the disadvantaged. The United States has thrived because, at its best, it embodies a commitment to human freedom, human rights and human dignity.

"But success often bears the seeds of failure. U.S. economic and military power has sometimes led to

grave injustices abroad. At home, it has fueled self-absorption, indifference and consumerist excess. Overconfidence in our power, made even more pronounced by advances in science and technology, has created the illusion of a life without natural boundaries and actions without consequences. The standards of the marketplace, instead of being guided by sound morality, threaten to displace it. We are now witnessing the gradual restructuring of American culture according to ideals of utility, productivity and cost-effectiveness. It is a culture where moral questions are submerged by a river of goods and services and where the misuse of marketing and public relations subverts public life.

"The losers in this ethical sea change will be those who are elderly, poor, disabled and politically marginalized.... As we tinker with the beginning, the end and even the intimate cell structure of life, we tinker with our own identity as a free nation dedicated to the dignity of the human person ... Today, when the inviolable rights of the human person are proclaimed and the value of life publicly affirmed, the most basic human right, 'the right to life, is being denied or trampled upon, especially at the more significant moments of existence: the moment of birth and the moment of death' " (Pope John Paul II, The Gospel of Life [*Evangelium Vitae*], 18).

"The culture of death extends beyond our shores: famine and starvation, denial of health care and development around the world, the deadly violence of armed conflict and the scandalous arms trade that spawns such conflict. Our nation is witness to domestic violence, the spread of drugs, sexual activity which poses a threat to lives, and a reckless tampering with the world's ecological balance ... Yet abortion and euthanasia have become preeminent threats to human dignity because they directly attack life itself, the most fundamental human good and the condition for all others ...

"Every Catholic, without exception, should remember that he or she is called by our Lord to proclaim His message. Some proclaim it by word, some by action and all by example. But every believer shares responsibility for the Gospel. Every Catholic is a missionary of the Good News of human dignity redeemed through the cross ...

"Nations are not machines or equations. They are like ecosystems. A people's habits, beliefs, values and institutions intertwine like a root system. Poisoning one part will eventually poison it all. As a result, bad laws and bad court decisions produce degraded political thought and behavior, and vice versa. So it is with the legacy of Roe vs. Wade. Roe effectively legalized abortion throughout pregnancy for virtually any reason, or none at all. It is responsible for the grief of millions of women and men, and the killing of millions of unborn children in the past quarter century ... Taking a distorted "right to privacy" to new heights, and developing a new moral calculus to justify it, Roe has spread through the American political ecology with toxic results.

"Thanks ultimately to Roe, some today speculate publicly and sympathetically why a number of young American women kill their newborn babies or leave them to die. Even the word "infanticide" is being replaced by new and less emotionally charged words like "neonaticide" (killing a newborn on the day of his or her birth) and "filicide" (killing the baby at some later point). Revising the name given to the killing reduces its perceived gravity. This is the ecology of law, moral reasoning and language in action ...

"Opposition to abortion and euthanasia does not excuse indifference to those who suffer from poverty, violence and injustice. Any politics of human life must work to resist the violence of war and the scandal of capital punishment. Any politics of human dignity must seriously address issues of racism, poverty, hunger, employment, education, housing, and health care.

U.S. Abortion Practice

Since 1990 [federal government and private sources report that] the annual number of abortions performed in the United States has been declining. Numbers have fallen from 1.6 million in the late 1980's to approximately 1.3 million in 1997 (the most recent year measured).

This has corresponded with declines from 1995-99 in the percentages of U.S. voters who tell pollsters they are "pro-choice." As of 1999, approximately the same percentages self-identify as "pro-life" and "pro-choice"; young people and women have shifted their opinion toward pro-life disproportionately.

The number of facilities performing abortions is in decline. According to a 1998 study by the research affiliate of the nation's primary abortion provider, Planned Parenthood Federation of America between 1992 and 1996 there was a 14% decline. Since 1982, the total decline in the number of abortion providers is 33%.

KEY ABORTION DECISIONS BY THE SUPREME COURT

The key abortion-related decision was handed down by the Supreme Court in the case of Roe v. Wade and the companion case of Dole v. Bolton. The court ruled 7-to-2 Jan. 22, 1973:

(1) During the first three months of pregnancy, a woman's right to privacy is paramount; accordingly, she has an unrestricted right to abortion with the consent and cooperation of a physician.

(2) In the second trimester, the principle controlling legislation is the health or welfare of the mother.

(3) In the third trimester, the "state subsequent to viability," the controlling principles of legislation are the State's "interest in the potentiality of human life" and "the preservation of the life or health of the mother."

The decision legalized abortion nationwide; practically, on demand.

In the 22 years subsequent to the Roe v. Wade decision, an estimated 37 million legal abortions have been performed in the United States.

Webster v. Reproductive Health Services

The court upheld, July 3, 1989, 5-to-4, provisions of the Missouri law:

(l) forbidding public employees to perform or assist in abortions;

(2) barring the use of public facilities for abortion;

(3) requiring physicians to take steps to determine fetal viability when a woman 20 or more weeks pregnant seeks an abortion.

The court did not overturn Roe v. Wade because the case afforded no occasion to revisit the 1973 decision; neither did it rule on the preamble of the Missouri law, which states that human life begins at conception.

Rust v. Sullivan:

The U.S. Supreme Court ruled 5-to-4 May 23, 1991 that provisions of Title X (the National Family Planning Program) of the 1970 Public Health Service Act were in accord with the U.S. Constitution. Pertinent regulations forbade family planning clinics from counseling or advising abortion if they received federal funds disbursed under Title X.

The Court observed:

(1) Abortion cannot be equated with family planning. The family planning legislation of 1970 distinguished between abortion and family planning, and intended to restrict federal funding to planning human life, not destroying it.

(2) The admission of a legal right (in this case, abortion) does not necessarily imply a government duty to promote the right.

(3) The fact that abortion is a legal right does not mean the government and those who do not subscribe to this right have to pay for it.

The Court ruled that the government can establish rules for funding only family planning programs which do not "encourage, promote or advocate abortion."

Planned Parenthood v. Casey
On June 29, 1992, in a fragmented decision the Court upheld provisions as constitutional provisions of a 1989 Pennsylvania Abortion Control Law regulating the practice of abortion.

In five separate opinions, the court upheld these provisions:

Women seeking abortion must receive information about risks, fetal development and alternatives to abortion, and must wait at least 24 hours after receiving such information before having an abortion.

Medical offices must file detailed, confidential reports about each abortion performed.

Minors must get permission from one parent or a judge before having an abortion.

The Court struck down a requirement that married women notify their husbands before having an abortion.

The Court did not revisit or overturn the radical pro-abortion Roe v. Wade decision of 1973, not because Roe was rightly decided, but because women and couples, it claimed, had come to rely heavily on the availability of abortion.

Since Casey, the Supreme Court has not accepted for consideration any cases which touch upon the constitutionality of the abortion "right" itself.

FEDERAL LEGISLATION

Partial-Birth Abortion
Partial-birth abortion is a procedure in which a doctor partially delivers an intact, living infant in the breech position until all but the head is visible outside the mother's body, before he stabs the head, suctions the brain matter out of the cavity, and fully delivers the now-dead infant. There is a consensus in the mainstream medical community that such a procedure is never medically necessary. There are likely 5,000 to 10,000 performed annually in the United States.

Since 1995, Congress has attempted to ban this procedure. Twice the bill has passed both the House and Senate. But President Clinton has twice vetoed the bill, and the Senate has twice fallen three votes short of an override, so the procedure remains legal in most states. To date, over 20 states have passed bans on this procedure, but pro-abortion groups have succeeded in getting courts to enjoin the vast majority of such laws.

Child Custody Protection Act
A bill was introduced in 1998 to ban a non-parent from taking a minor across state lines for an abortion to evade her own state's parental involvement law. In 1998, the bill passed in the House, but the Senate voted to block floor action. The bill was re-introduced in both the House and Senate.

Mandatory Contraceptive Prescription Coverage
In 1998, Congress passed a one-year mandate requiring federal employee health benefit plans to cover contraceptive drug devices as part of any prescription drug coverage. Five specific "religious plans" were exempted as well as any other existing or future plan religiously opposed (as distinguished from those "morally" opposed only). An executive agency memorandum later defined "contraceptive" to include the "full range" of contraceptives approved for use by the FDA, including the "morning after" pill which acts primarily to destroy an already formed human embryo. Some members of the House and Senate are promising to attempt to pass a further law mandating *private* health insurance plans to provide the same coverage. Several states are considering similar legislation.

State Laws
In 1998 and 1999, an unusual number of stories appeared in the press nationally regarding botched, legal abortions. In response, more than 10 bills were introduced in state legislatures to upgrade safety regulations at abortion clinics. The majority of states regulate such clinics to a far lesser degree than other medical clinics.

UNITED NATIONS ABORTION POLICY

Cairo +5
Five years after a United Nations' summit in Cairo on Population and Development, representatives from many nations met at the Hague in Belgium to consider whether progress had been made on the "plan of action" adopted at Cairo. The conference, entitled "Cairo + 5," was largely dominated by the efforts of the United States and its allies to engraft certain "reproductive rights," including abortion, birth control, and sex education for minors as young as ten, into the Cairo document. Due to the efforts of delegations including the Holy See, such proposals were defeated.

The president vetoed a bill in 1998 which would have paid back dues owed by the U.S. to the U.N., because the bill contained a provision forbidding U.S. funding of organizations that perform elective abortions or that lobby foreign governments to change their abortion laws.

Emergency Contraception
Beginning in 1998, national abortion advocacy programs and "family planning" organizations began promoting strongly "emergency contraception," also called "morning after pills." These are drugs taken within 72 hours of intercourse with the primary and intended effect of preventing a human embryo from implanting and growing in the womb. Abortion advocates insist that "pregnancy" does not begin until an embryo is attached to the uterine wall, and publicly insist, therefore, that these drugs are contraceptive and not abortifacient.

RU-486
RU-486, the "abortion pill" invented in France, received preliminary FDA approval in 1996. Final approval, including review of marketing and labeling practices, is expected in 1999. RU-486 is used primarily in the first 7-9 weeks of pregnancy. Its U.S. patent is owned by the Population

Council, which has licensed the Danco Group to manufacture the drug. It is unclear what effect this will have upon abortion practice in the United Stets, since it involves a relatively onerous protocol and may or may not encourage more doctors to offer abortion services.

NEW REPRODUCTIVE TECHNOLOGIES

Embryo Experimentation

Since 1995, federal law has forbidden funding of harmful experiments upon human embryos. As of mid-1999, this ban is under renewed attack due to interest in the therapeutic potential of embryonic stem cells. Obtaining such cells requires destroying human embryos in the first weeks of development. Promising stem-cell research does *not* involve the destruction of human lives is simultaneously developing rapidly.

Cloning

In 1998, a Scottish doctor successfully cloned an adult lamb. Soon after, a U.S. doctor insisted that he intends to proceed to clone human beings. The Catholic Church condemns the cloning of humans (as distinguished from animals) as an offensive against human dignity, against the manner of procreation established by God, and against the dignity and love of husband and wife.

EUTHANASIA AND ASSISTED SUICIDE — KEY SUPREME COURT DECISIONS

Vacco v. Quill and Washington v. Glucksberg

On June 26, 1997, by a 9-0 vote, the U.S. Supreme Court upheld New York and Washington statutes that prohibited assisted suicide in all cases, including cases of terminal illness. The majority opinion rejected claims that a constitutional right to assisted suicide could be developed from Supreme Court precedents concerning abortion or the withdrawal of life-sustaining treatment.

Oregon

In 1997, Oregon voters decided to keep physician-assisted suicide legal in their state. In 1998, the state health plan agreed to subsidize lethal drugs used in committing suicide. Oregon is presently considering expanding its state law to allow physicians to kill directly those disabled patients who are physically unable to administer their own suicide drugs.

In 1998, the U.S. Attorney general announced that the federal Controlled Substance Act establishes no uniform national policy against the use of federally regulated drugs for assisted suicide. Such drugs may therefore be used to assist patients' suicides in any state which allows the practice under state law. In 1998, House and Senate committees passed legislation to reverse this ruling. New legislation has been introduced in 1999 which would affirm and support pain management as a legitimate purpose for use of federally controlled drugs, even when such use could unintentionally hasten death as a side effect. It would also provide that state laws prevent misuse of potentially dangerous drugs.

Dr. Kevorkian

In 1999, a Michigan jury convicted Dr. Jack Kevorkian of second degree murder and delivery of a controlled substance in the death of Thomas Youk. Mr. Youk's death was televised on the television program "60 Minutes" in November, 1998. Dr. Kevorkian was sentenced to between 10 and 25 years in prison.

Michigan Ballot Initiative

In November, 1998, Michigan voters rejected a ballot proposal to legalize assisted suicide by a resounding vote of 71 to 29%.

NATIONAL CONFERENCE OF CATHOLIC BISHOPS

MEETINGS OF U.S. BISHOPS 1998-1999

November 16-19, 1998

Presidential Address: Newly elected President of the NCCB/USCC, Bishop Joseph A. Fiorenza of Galveston-Houston, concluded the Bishops' Meeting with an inaugural address on Nov. 19. Bishop Fiorenza declared: "Bishop Pilla is a hard act to follow. I will try to the very best of my abilities to serve you, my brother bishops and this wonderful episcopal conference ... I have been a bishop for 19 years, and I know most of you rather well. I know and have experienced your passionate love for the Church, your dedication to the collegial mission of this conference and the enormous energy that you willingly expend in its service ... This moment in history finds us at the dawn of the final year of the second millennium. We have been preparing the Church for the Great Jubilee Year 2000 and the third millennium of Christian faith. The opportunities these events offer us to renew every diocese in the spirit of the Gospel are unlimited. If we take advantage of the graced moments they offer, we can realize the "new spring-time of Christianity that the Holy Father envisions ... The Church in the United States is strong, dynamic and wonderfully alive. Our parishes are vibrant and more people are more intimately involved in the mission of the Church than ever before."

Pro-Nuncio's Address: Archbishop Agostino Cacciavillan, Apostolic Pro-Nuncio to the United States, delivered his ninth and final address to the Fall meeting of the NCCB. Recalling with fondness his time in the United States, the archbishop declared: "It really was a privilege to serve here and to all I say goodbye with the assurance of unfailing fond memories"; he added that the recent actions of Pope John Paul II, in particular his canonization of Edith Stein and the issue of the encyclicals *Fides et Ratio* and the documents *Ad Tuendam Fidem* and *Dies Domini*, demonstrated that from the pope's "teachings, his person and life, two powerful appeals resonate: be courageous in truth and generous in love." Of St. Edith Stein, the archbishop noted that "Sister Teresa Benedicta ... says to us all: Don't accept anything as truth if it is without love. And don't accept anything as love if it is without truth. One without the other becomes a destructive lie." [Archbishop Cacciavillan was succeeded by Archbishop Gabriel Montalvo, who addressed the Spring meeting of the Bishops.]

Agenda

The bishops attending the meeting in Washington, D.C. acted on the following issues:

Pro-Life: Amended and then approved by a 217-30 vote the document *Living the Gospel of Life: A Challenge to American Catholics* (See Special Report below).

Budget: Authorized a budget of $46.8 million for 1999 and a diocesan assessment for 2000 of over $11 million.

Lay People: Approved a pastoral reflection on the obligations of Christian lay people in the world at the start of the millennium. (See Special Report below.)

Disabled Persons: Approved a 12-point statement of principles for how the Church should welcome and treat persons with disabilities. (See Special Report below.)

Ascension: Approved by a narrow margin a rule under which each province of bishops can decide to transfer the observance of Ascension from Thursday to the seventh Sunday of Easter.

Iraq: Agreed with Bishop Pilla's statement on the moral principles involved in the crisis in Iraq.

Canon Law: Approved five proposed decrees setting national norms in such areas of Canon Law as clerical garb, priests' councils, engagements, marriage preparation, and baptisms of adopted children.

NCCB/USCC: Voted on restructuring the NCCB/USCC for the coming millennium.

Hurricane Relief: Approved an emergency fund of $400,000 to hurricane relief in Central America, the Dominican Republic, and Haiti.

Vocations: Ratified revised guidelines for vocations directors, including the provision for full-time appointments.

Seminary Students: Began discussions on a set of nationwide standards for admitting seminary students who have left seminaries in the past.

University Norms: Began discussions on a new statement and U.S. norms for Catholic universities.

Funeral Rites: Approved two Spanish-language liturgical texts for funeral rites.

Pro-Nuncio: Bid farewell to the Pro-Nuncio, Archbishop Agostino Cacciavillan.

June 18-20, 1999

President's Address: Bishop Joseph Fiorenza delivered a homily on June 18 in which he declared: "During these few days together in the desert we are reflecting on 'The Challenge of Episcopal Leadership in the Third Millennium.' Apart from the challenges that we will face in the dioceses we serve in the third millennium, there will be challenges to us as an episcopal conference. The topics for each day of this special assembly will address both aspects of our episcopal service ... The millennium that we eagerly await will not be a utopia in which the darkness of sin and ignorance will be dispelled from the face of the earth. Rather, the millennium will be much like the dawn of every morning, which St. Gregory the Great said in a recent second reading holds the mixture of darkness and light ... Our ministry as bishops also will not be much different in 'Y2K,' although there will be new challenges because the people we serve will be greatly impacted by new and developing technologies which stun and dazzle the mind. However, human nature will not change ... Every member's participation and voice contributes to the building up of the Church in the United States. Our collective statements and pastoral programs are important to the universal Church... . At the dawn of the third millennium the Church in the United States is strong, dynamic and bursting with evangelical energy. By most measures, we are in much better shape than the Church in any other country."

Pro-Nuncio's Address: On June 21, Archbishop Gabriel Montalvo, Apostolic Pro-Nuncio to the United States, delivered an address to the bishops. Archbishop Montalvo states: "Speaking to this assembly from my heart and sharing with you on a rather personal level, I would also like to renew at this moment to the Holy Father my sense of profound gratitude for his having decided to entrust to me this task — which is one of great honor and responsibilities — of being his personal representative among you, dear bishops, and in your great country ... I think I can say to you, without presumption on my part, that I have the impression of finding myself in the midst of a Church full of vigor, rich in activity, ready to take initiative and looking for solutions to not a few problems which it must face ... It is no secret that on the level of faith and morals there cannot be divergences. One faith, one Lord! It is precisely for this reason that the Holy See is pleased to see the commitment and the will of the ecclesiastical hierarchy in this country to look for and to maintain the purity of doctrine ... America and the vigorous Catholic Church that lives and functions in it are continually a point of reference. What happens here has an influence and repercussion elsewhere. In this context, the words addressed by His Holiness to your president, Bishop Fiorenza, resound here with great force: 'America, be faithful to your vocation.' "

The bishops attending the meeting in Tucson took part in a retreat-style assembly reflecting on the theme "The Challenge of Episcopal Leadership in the Third Millennium."

(See also Special Supplement for the *Ad Limina Apostolorum* visits by the U.S. Bishops in 1998.)

108

DOCTRINE OF THE
CATHOLIC CHURCH

THE CATECHISM OF THE CATHOLIC CHURCH

By Russell Shaw

"The *Catechism of the Catholic Church* . . . is a statement of the Church's faith and of Catholic doctrine, attested to or illumined by Sacred Scripture, the Apostolic Tradition, and the Church's Magisterium. I declare it to be a sure norm for teaching the faith and thus a valid and legitimate instrument for ecclesial communion."

Thus Pope John Paul II in the Apostolic Constitution *Fidei Depositum* (The Deposit of Faith) formally presented the first official catechism or compendium of doctrine for the universal Church to have been published since the sixteenth century.

Fidei Depositum is dated October 11, 1992, the thirtieth anniversary of the opening of the Second Vatican Council (1962-65), and that date is significant. The predecessor of the *Catechism of the Catholic Church* is the *Roman Catechism* or *Catechism of the Council of Trent*, which was published by Pope St. Pius V in 1566 following the great reforming council held from 1545 to 1563. As the *Roman Catechism* sets forth the doctrine of the Church in light of the Council of Trent, so the *Catechism of the Catholic Church* sets forth the Church's teaching against the background of Vatican Council II.

History of the Catechism

In development since 1986, the definitive text of the *Catechism of the Catholic Church* was officially approved by Pope John Paul on June 25, 1992, with December 8 the date of formal promulgation.

Nine separate drafts of the *Catechism* were prepared. The document was written in French. In November, 1989, the commission of cardinals sent a draft text to all the bishops of the world asking for their comments and suggestions. Although this consultation produced a reaction generally favorable to the text, more than 24,000 individual amendments were submitted by the bishops, and these were reviewed by the commission, and helped to shape the further revision of the document.

The pope in *Fidei Depositum* described the Catechism as "a sure and authentic reference text" both for the teaching of Catholic doctrine and particularly for the preparation of local catechisms; he said the catechism was presented to "all the Church's Pastors and the Christian faithful" with these ends in view. Other purposes mentioned included helping Catholics to deepen their knowledge of the faith, supporting ecumenical efforts by "showing carefully the content and wondrous harmony of the catholic faith," and providing authoritative answers to anyone who wishes to know "what the Catholic Church believes."

Structure and Contents of the Catechism

The *Catechism* adopts the four-fold division of the *Roman Catechism*. The four parts or "pillars" deal with the Creed; the Sacred Liturgy, with special emphasis on the sacraments; the Christian way of life, analyzed according to the Ten Commandments; and Prayer, considered in the framework of the petitions of the Our Father.

Describing this organizational scheme, Pope John

Paul said: "The four parts are related one to another: the Christian mystery is the object of faith (first part); it is celebrated and communicated in liturgical actions (second part); it is present to enlighten and sustain the children of God in their actions (third part); it is the basis of our prayer, the privileged expression of which is the Our Father, and it represents the object of our supplication, our praise and our intercession (fourth part)."

The pope also stressed the Christocentric nature of Christian faith as it is presented in the *Catechism*. "In reading the *Catechism of the Catholic Church* we can perceive the wonderful unity of the mystery of God, his saving will, as well as the central place of Jesus Christ, the only-begotten Son of God, sent by the Father, made man in the womb of the Blessed Virgin Mary by the power of the Holy Spirit, to be our Savior. Having died and risen, Christ is always present in his Church, especially in the sacraments; he is the source of our faith, the model of Christian conduct, and the Teacher of our prayer."

The text of the *Catechism of the Catholic Church*, with extensive cross-references and sectional summaries, consists of 2,865 numbered paragraphs. Passages in large print set out its more substantive contents, while passages in small print provide background information and explanations; there are numerous cross-references in the margins directing readers to other passages that treat the same theme or related themes. Among the features of the catechism are the "In Brief" sections found throughout, which sum up the teaching of the preceding unit.

Outline of the Catechism

Prologue (1-25). The nature of catechesis is described, along with the aim of the present catechism and its intended readership, its structure, its use, and the desirability of adaptations for different cultures, age groups, etc.

Part One: The Profession of Faith (26-1065)

Section One discusses the nature of faith. "Faith is man's response to God, who reveals himself and gives himself to man, at the same time bringing man a superabundant light as he searches for the ultimate meaning of his life. Thus we shall consider first that search (Chapter One), then the divine Revelation by which God comes to meet man (Chapter Two), and finally the response of faith (Chapter Three)" (26). The topics discussed include knowledge of God; Divine Revelation and its transmission; Sacred Scripture; and faith as the human response to God. "We do not believe in formulas, but in those realities they express, which faith allows us to touch. . . . All the same, we do approach these realities with the help of formulations of the faith which permit us to express the faith and to hand it on, to celebrate it in community, to assimilate and live on it more and more" (170).

Section Two deals with the profession of Christian faith, with the treatment organized according to the articles of the Creed. The Creed used is the Apostles' Creed; its "great authority," says the *Catechism*, quoting St. Ambrose, arises from its being "the Creed of the Roman Church, the See of Peter, the first of the apostles" (194). Among the doctrines covered in the three chapters of this section are the Trinity, creation,

the angels, the creation of man, original sin, the Incarnation, the virgin birth, redemption, the Resurrection of Christ, the work of the Holy Spirit, the Church, the hierarchical constitution of the Church, the communion of saints, the Virgin Mary as Mother of Christ and Mother of the Church, the resurrection of the dead, judgment, heaven, and hell. "[T]he Creed's final 'Amen' repeats and confirms its first words: 'I believe.' To believe is to say 'Amen' to God's words, promises and commandments; to entrust oneself completely to him who is the 'Amen' of infinite love and perfect faithfulness. The Christian's everyday life will then be the 'Amen' to the 'I believe' of our baptismal profession of faith" (1064).

Part Two: The Celebration of the Christian Mystery (1066-1690)

Section One considers the sacramental economy. It explains that in this present "age of the Church," begun on Pentecost, "Christ now lives and acts in his Church, in a new way appropriate to this new age. He acts through the sacraments in what the common Tradition of the East and the West calls 'the sacramental economy'. . . the communication (or 'dispensation') of the fruits of Christ's Paschal Mystery in the celebration of the Church's 'sacramental' liturgy" (1076). Topics treated here are the Paschal Mystery and its sacramental celebration.

Section Two covers the seven sacraments of the Church. "Christ instituted the sacraments of the new law. . . . The seven sacraments touch all the stages and all the important moments of Christian life: they give birth and increase, healing and mission to the Christian's life of faith. There is thus a certain resemblance between the stages of natural life and the stages of the spiritual life" (1210). The presentation is organized in four chapters. These are: the sacraments of Christian initiation (Baptism, Confirmation, the Eucharist) in chapter one; the sacraments of healing (Penance and Reconciliation, the Anointing of the Sick) in chapter two; the "sacraments at the service of communion" (Holy Orders and Matrimony) in chapter three; and sacramentals and Christian funerals in chapter four.

Part Three: Life in Christ (1691-2557)

Section One is entitled "Man's Vocation: Life in the Spirit." Its three chapters discuss the dignity of the human person, the human community, and "God's Salvation: Law and Grace" (the moral law, grace and justification, the Church as teacher of moral truth). "Catechesis has to reveal in all clarity the joy and the demands of the way of Christ. . . . The first and last point of reference of this catechesis will always be Jesus Christ himself, who is 'they way, and the truth, and the life' " (1697-1698).

Section Two reflects on the contents of Christian moral life. The treatment is organized according to the Ten Commandments, with a chapter devoted to each commandment and its concrete applications. While the commandments admit of what is traditionally called light matter (venial sin), nevertheless, the text says: "Since they express man's fundamental duties towards God and towards his neighbor, the Ten Commandments reveal, in their primordial content, grave obligations. They are fundamentally immutable, and they oblige always and everywhere. No one can dispense from them. The Ten Commandments are engraved by God in the human heart" (2072).

Part Four: Christian Prayer (2558-2865)

Section One considers prayer in Christian life, underlining the relationship of this topic to the rest of the catechism: "The Church professes this mystery [of faith] in the Apostles' Creed (Part One) and celebrates it in the sacramental liturgy (Part Two), so that the life of the faithful may be conformed to Christ in the Holy Spirit to the glory of God the Father (Part Three). This mystery, then, requires that the faithful believe in it, that they celebrate it, and that they live from it in a vital and personal relationship with the living and true God. This relationship is prayer" (2558). The section then discusses the "revelation of prayer" in the Old Testament and now in the age of the Church, the tradition of prayer, and the life of prayer (kinds of prayer, problems and perseverance in prayer).

Section Two presents an extended reflection on the Our Father, considered as the model of prayer. Quoting Tertullian, the catechism says: "The Lord's Prayer 'is truly the summary of the whole Gospel.' 'Since the Lord . . . after handing over the practice of prayer, said elsewhere, 'Ask and you will receive,' and since everyone has petitions which are peculiar to his circumstances, the regular and appropriate prayer [the Lord's Prayer] is said first, as the foundation of further desires'" (2761).

Reception of the Catechism

Following the publication of the *Catechism of the Catholic Church*, Pope John Paul established an Interdicasterial Commission for the Catechism, under the chairmanship of Cardinal Ratzinger, responsible for overseeing translations of the volume and reviewing and approving suggested changes in the text. The commission approved the English translation of the catechism in February 1994, and it was published on June 22 of that year — in the United States, under the auspices of the National Conference of Catholic Bishops.

Pope John Paul presented the *editio typica* or normative Latin version of the catechism in a formal ceremony on September 8, 1997.

The following day, Cardinal Ratzinger presented the *editio typica* at a Vatican news conference. At the same time, he also introduced more than a hundred changes which had been approved for incorporation into the text. Most of the changes were of a minor, editorial nature. The most important was in paragraphs 2265-2267 of the catechism, where the treatment of capital punishment had been strengthened to reflect the discussion of the same topic in Pope John Paul's 1995 encyclical letter *Evangelium Vitae* (*The Gospel of Life*).

In the United States, the National Conference of Catholic Bishops in 1994 established an Ad Hoc Committee to Oversee the Use of the Catechism. It has an office and staff at NCCB headquarters in Washington, D.C. The committee reviews and approves materials that seek to make substantial direct use of the text of the *Catechism of the Catholic Church*, and also reviews catechetical series for their conformity with the catechism. In addition, the committee was mandated to conduct a feasibility study of a national catechism or catechetical series for the United States.

DOGMATIC CONSTITUTION ON THE CHURCH — *LUMEN GENTIUM*

Following are excerpts from the first two chapters of the "Dogmatic Constitution on the Church" (Lumen Gentium) promulgated by the Second Vatican Council. They describe the relation of the Catholic Church to the Kingdom of God, the nature and foundation of the Church, the People of God, the necessity of membership and participation in the Church for salvation. Additional subjects in the constitution are treated in other Almanac entries.

I. MYSTERY OF THE CHURCH

By her relationship with Christ, the Church is a kind of sacrament or sign of intimate union with God, and of the unity of all mankind (No. 1).

He (the eternal Father) planned to assemble in the holy Church all those who would believe in Christ. Already from the beginning of the world the foreshadowing of the Church took place. She was prepared for in a remarkable way throughout the history of the people of Israel and by means of the Old Covenant. Established in the present era of time, the Church was made manifest by the outpouring of the Spirit. At the end of time she will achieve her glorious fulfillment. Then all just men from the time of Adam, "from Abel, the just one, to the last of the elect," will be gathered together with the Father in the universal Church (No. 2).

When the work which the Father had given the Son to do on earth (cf. Jn. 17:4) was accomplished, the Holy Spirit was sent on the day of Pentecost in order that he might forever sanctify the Church, and thus all believers would have access to the Father through Christ in the one Spirit (cf. Eph. 2:18).

The Spirit dwells in the Church and in the hearts of the faithful as in a temple (cf. 1 Cor. 3:16; 6:19). . . . The Spirit guides the Church into the fullness of truth (cf. Jn. 16:13) and gives her a unity of fellowship and service. He furnishes and directs her with various gifts, both hierarchical and charismatic, and adorns her with the fruits of His grace (cf. Eph. 4:11-12; 1 Cor. 12:4; Gal. 5:22). By the power of the Gospel he makes the Church grow, perpetually renews her, and leads her to perfect union with her Spouse (No. 4).

Foundation of the Church

The mystery of the holy Church is manifest in her very foundation, for the Lord Jesus inaugurated her by preaching the Good News, that is, the coming of God's Kingdom, which, for centuries, had been promised in the Scriptures. . . . In Christ's word, in his works, and in his presence this Kingdom reveals itself to men.

The miracles of Jesus also confirm that the Kingdom has already arrived on earth.

Before all things, however, the Kingdom is clearly visible in the very Person of Christ, Son of God and Son of Man.

When Jesus rose up again after suffering death on

the cross for mankind, he manifested that he had been appointed Lord, Messiah, and Priest forever (cf. Acts 2:36; Heb. 5:6; 7:17-21), and he poured out on his disciples the Spirit promised by the Father (cf. Acts 2:33). The Church, consequently, equipped with the gifts of her Founder and faithfully guarding his precepts . receives the mission to proclaim and to establish among all peoples the Kingdom of Christ and of God. She becomes on earth the initial budding forth of that Kingdom. While she slowly grows, the Church strains toward the consummation of the Kingdom and, with all her strength, hopes and desires to be united in glory with her King (No. 5).

Figures of the Church

In the Old Testament the revelation of the Kingdom had often been conveyed by figures of speech. In the same way the inner nature of the Church was now to be made known to us through various images.

The Church is a sheepfold . . . a flock . . . a tract of land to be cultivated, the field of God . . . his choice vineyard . . . the true vine is Christ . . . the edifice of God . . . the house of God . . . the holy temple (whose members are) living stones . . . this holy city . . . a bride . . . our Mother . . . the spotless spouse of the spotless Lamb . . . an exile (No. 6).

In the human nature which he united to himself, the Son of God redeemed man and transformed him into a new creation (cf Gal. 6:15; 2 Cor. 5:17) by overcoming death through his own death and resurrection. By communicating his Spirit to his brothers, called together from all peoples, Christ made them mystically into his own body.

In that body, the life of Christ is poured into the believers, who, through the sacraments, are united in a hidden and real way to Christ who suffered and was glorified. Through baptism we are formed in the likeness of Christ.

Truly partaking of the body of the Lord in the breaking of the eucharistic bread, we are taken up into communion with him and with one another (No. 7).

One Body in Christ

As all the members of the human body, though they are many, form one body, so also are the faithful in Christ (cf. 1 Cor. 12:12). Also, in the building up of Christ's body there is a flourishing variety of members and functions. There is only one Spirit who . distributes his different gifts for the welfare of the Church (cf. 1 Cor. 12:1-11). Among these gifts stands out the grace given to the apostles. To their authority, the Spirit himself subjected even those who were endowed with charisms (cf. 1 Cor. 14). The head of this body is Christ (No. 7).

Mystical Body of Christ

Christ, the one Mediator, established and ceaselessly sustains here on earth his holy Church, the community of faith, hope, and charity, as a visible structure. Through her he communicates truth and grace to all. But the society furnished with hierarchical agencies and the Mystical Body of Christ are not to be considered as two realities, nor are the visible assembly and the spiritual community, nor the earthly Church and the Church enriched with heavenly things. Rather they form one interlocked reality which is comprised of a divine and a human element. For this reason . this

reality is compared to the mystery of the incarnate Word. Just as the assumed nature inseparably united to the divine Word serves him as a living instrument of salvation, so, in a similar way, does the communal structure of the Church serve Christ's Spirit, who vivifies it by way of building up the body (cf. Eph. 4:16).

This is the unique Church of Christ which in the Creed we avow as one, holy, catholic, and apostolic. After his Resurrection our Savior handed her over to Peter to be shepherded (Jn. 21:17), commissioning him and the other apostles to propagate and govern her (cf. Mt. 28:18, ff.). Her he erected for all ages as "the pillar and mainstay of the truth" (1 Tm. 3:15). This Church, constituted and organized in the world as a society, subsists in the Catholic Church, which is governed by the successor of Peter and by the bishops in union with that successor, although many elements of sanctification and of truth can be found outside of her visible structure. These elements, however, as gifts properly belonging to the Church of Christ, possess an inner dynamism toward Catholic unity.

The Church, embracing sinners in her bosom, is at the same time holy and always in need of being purified, and incessantly pursues the path of penance and renewal.

The Church, "like a pilgrim in a foreign land, presses forward, announcing the cross and death of the Lord until he comes" (cf. 1 Cor. 11:26) (No. 8).

II. THE PEOPLE OF GOD

At all times and among every people, God has given welcome to whosoever fears him and does what is right (cf. Acts 10:35). It has pleased God, however, to make men holy and save them not merely as individuals without any mutual bonds, but by making them into a single people, a people which acknowledges him in truth and serves him in holiness. He therefore chose the race of Israel as a people unto himself. With it he set up a covenant. Step by step he taught this people by manifesting in its history both himself and the decree of his will, and by making it holy unto himself. All these things, however, were done by way of preparation and as a figure of that new and perfect covenant which was to be ratified in Christ.

Christ instituted this New Covenant, that is to say, the New Testament, in his blood (cf. 1 Cor. 11:25), by calling together a people made up of Jew and Gentile, making them one, not according to the flesh but in the Spirit.

This was to be the new People of God . . . reborn . . . through the Word of the living God (cf. 1 Pt. 1:23). from water and the Holy Spirit (cf. Jn. 3:5-6) . . . "a chosen race, a royal priesthood, a holy nation, a purchased people. You who in times past were not a people, but are now the People of God" (1 Pt. 2:9-10).

That messianic people has for its head Christ. Its law is the new commandment to love as Christ loved us (cf. Jn. 13:34). Its goal is the Kingdom of God, which has been begun by God himself on earth, and which is to be further extended until it is brought to perfection by him at the end of time.

This messianic people, although it does not actually include all men, and may more than once look like a small flock, is nonetheless a lasting and sure seed of unity, hope, and salvation for the whole human race. Established by Christ as a fellowship of life, charity, and truth, it is also used by him as an instrument for the redemption of all, and is sent forth into the whole world as the light of the world and the salt of the earth (cf. Mt. 5:13-16).

Israel according to the flesh . . . was already called the Church of God (Neh. 13:1; cf. Nm. 20:4; Dt. 23:1, ff.). Likewise the new Israel . . . is also called the Church of Christ (cf. Mt. 16:18). For he has bought it for himself with his blood (cf. Acts 20:28), has filled it with his Spirit, and provided it with those means which befit it as a visible and social unity. God has gathered together as one all those who in faith look upon Jesus as the author of salvation and the source of unity and peace, and has established them as the Church, that for each and all she may be the visible sacrament of this saving unity (No. 9).

Priesthood

The baptized, by regeneration and the anointing of the Holy Spirit, are consecrated into a holy priesthood.

[All members of the Church participate in the priesthood of Christ, through the common priesthood of the faithful. See Priesthood of the Laity.]

Though they differ from one another in essence and not only in degree, the common priesthood of the faithful and the ministerial or hierarchical priesthood are nonetheless interrelated. Each of them in its own special way is a participation in the one priesthood of Christ (No. 10).

It is through the sacraments and the exercise of the virtues that the sacred nature and organic structure of the priestly community is brought into operation (No. 11). (See Role of the Sacraments.)

Prophetic Office

The holy People of God shares also in Christ's prophetic office. It spreads abroad a living witness to him, especially by means of a life of faith and charity and by offering to God a sacrifice of praise. . . . The body of the faithful as a whole, anointed as they are by the Holy One (cf. Jn. 2:20, 27), cannot err in matters of belief. Thanks to a supernatural sense of faith which characterizes the People as a whole, it manifests this unerring quality when, "from the bishops down to the last member of the laity," it shows universal agreement in matters of faith and morals.

God's People accepts not the word of men but the very Word of God (cf. 1 Thes. 2:13). It clings without fail to the faith once delivered to the saints (cf. Jude 3), penetrates it more deeply by accurate insights, and applies it more thoroughly to life. All this it does under the lead of a sacred teaching authority to which it loyally defers.

It is not only through the sacraments and Church ministries that the same Holy Spirit sanctifies and leads the People of God. . . . He distributes special graces among the faithful of every rank. By these gifts he makes them fit and ready to undertake the various tasks or offices advantageous for the renewal and upbuilding of the Church. These charismatic gifts . . . are to be received with thanksgiving and consolation, for they are exceedingly suitable and useful for the needs of the Church.

Judgment as to their genuineness and proper use belongs to those who preside over the Church, and to

whose special competence it belongs . . . to test all things and hold fast to that which is good (cf. 1 Thes. 5:12; 19-21) (No. 12).

All Are Called

All men are called to belong to the new People of God. Wherefore this People, while remaining one and unique, is to be spread throughout the whole world and must exist in all ages, so that the purpose of God's will may be fulfilled. In the beginning God made human nature one. After his children were scattered, he decreed that they should at length be united again (cf. Jn. 11:52). It was for this reason that God sent his Son. . . . that he might be Teacher, King, and Priest of all, the Head of the new and universal People of the sons of God. For this God finally sent his Son's Spirit as Lord and Lifegiver. He it is who, on behalf of the whole Church and each and every one of those who believe, is the principle of their coming together and remaining together in the teaching of the apostles and in fellowship, in the breaking of bread and in prayers (cf. Acts 2:42) (No. 13).

One People of God

It follows that among all the nations of earth there is but one People of God, which takes its citizens from every race, making them citizens of a Kingdom which is of a heavenly and not an earthly nature. For all the faithful scattered throughout the world are in communion with each other in the Holy Spirit. . . . the Church or People of God . foster(s) and take(s) to herself, insofar as they are good, the ability, resources and customs of each people. Taking them to herself, she purifies, strengthens, and ennobles them. . . . This characteristic of universality which adorns the People of God is a gift from the Lord himself. By reason of it, the Catholic Church strives energetically and constantly to bring all humanity with all its riches back to Christ its Head in the unity of his Spirit.

In virtue of this catholicity each individual part of the Church contributes through its special gifts to the good of the other parts and of the whole Church. Thus through the common sharing of gifts. The whole and each of the parts receive increase.

All men are called to be part of this catholic unity of the People of God. And there belong to it or are related to it in various ways, the Catholic faithful as well as all who believe in Christ, and indeed the whole of mankind. For all men are called to salvation by the grace of God (No. 13).

The Catholic Church

This sacred Synod turns its attention first to the Catholic faithful. Basing itself upon sacred Scripture and tradition, it teaches that the Church is necessary for salvation. For Christ, made present to us in his Body, which is the Church, is the one Mediator and the unique Way of salvation. In explicit terms he himself affirmed the necessity of faith and baptism (cf. Mk. 16:16; Jn. 3:5) and thereby affirmed also the necessity of the Church, for through baptism as through a door men enter the Church. Whosoever, therefore, knowing that the Catholic Church was made necessary by God through Jesus Christ, would refuse to enter her or to remain in her could not be saved.

They are fully incorporated into the society of the Church who, possessing the Spirit of Christ, accept her entire system and all the means of salvation given to her, and through union with her visible structure are joined to Christ, who rules her through the Supreme Pontiff and the bishops. This joining is effected by the bonds of professed faith, of the sacraments, of ecclesiastical government, and of communion. He is not saved, however, who, though he is part of the body of the Church, does not persevere in charity. He remains indeed in the bosom of the Church, but only in a "bodily" manner and not "in his heart."

Catechumens who, moved by the Holy Spirit, seek with explicit intention to be incorporated into the Church, are by that very intention joined to her. Mother Church already embraces them as her own (No. 14).

Other Christians, The Unbaptized

The Church recognizes that in many ways she is linked with those who, being baptized, are honored with the name of Christian, though they do not profess the faith in its entirety or do not preserve unity of communion with the successor of Peter.

We can say that in some real way they are joined with us in the Holy Spirit, for to them also he gives his gifts and graces, and is thereby operative among them with his sanctifying power (No. 15).

Finally, those who have not yet received the Gospel are related in various ways to the People of God. In the first place there is the people to whom the covenants and the promises were given and from whom Christ was born according to the flesh (cf. Rom. 9:4-5). On account of their fathers, this people remains most dear to God, for God does not repent of the gifts he makes nor of the calls he issues (cf. Rom. 11:28-29).

But the plan of salvation also includes those who acknowledge the Creator. In the first place among these are the Moslems. Nor is God himself far distant from those who in shadows and images seek the unknown God.

Those also can attain to everlasting salvation who through no fault of their own do not know the Gospel of Christ or his Church, yet sincerely seek God and, moved by grace, strive by their deeds to do his will as it is known to them through the dictates of conscience. Nor does divine Providence deny the help necessary for salvation to those who, without blame on their part, have not yet arrived at an explicit knowledge of God, but who strive to live a good life, thanks to his grace. Whatever goodness or truth is found among them is looked upon by the Church as a preparation for the Gospel. She regards such qualities as given by him who enlightens all men so that they may finally have life. (No. 16).

THE POPE, TEACHING AUTHORITY, COLLEGIALITY

The Roman Pontiff — the successor of St. Peter as the bishop of Rome and head of the Church on earth — has full and supreme authority over the universal Church in matters pertaining to faith and morals (teaching authority), discipline and government (jurisdictional authority).

The primacy of the pope is real and supreme power. It is not merely a prerogative of honor — that is, of his being regarded as the first among equals. Neither does primacy imply that the pope is just the presiding officer of the collective body of bishops. The pope is the head of the Church.

Catholic belief in the primacy of the pope was stated in detail in the dogmatic constitution on the Church, *Pastor Aeternus*, approved in 1870 by the fourth session of the First Vatican Council. Some elaboration of the doctrine was made in the Dogmatic Constitution on the Church which was approved and promulgated by the Second Vatican Council Nov. 21, 1964. The entire body of teaching on the subject is based on Scripture and tradition and the centuries-long experience of the Church.

Infallibility

The essential points of doctrine concerning infallibility in the Church and the infallibility of the pope were stated by the Second Vatican Council in the Dogmatic Constitution on the Church, as follows:

"This infallibility with which the divine Redeemer willed his Church to be endowed in defining a doctrine of faith and morals extends as far as extends the deposit of divine revelation, which must be religiously guarded and faithfully expounded. This is the infallibility which the Roman Pontiff, the head of the college of bishops, enjoys in virtue of his office, when, as the supreme shepherd and teacher of all the faithful who confirms his brethren in their faith (cf. Lk. 22:32), he proclaims by a definitive act some doctrine of faith or morals. Therefore his definitions, of themselves, and not from the consent of the Church, are justly styled irreformable, for they are pronounced with the assistance of the Holy Spirit, an assistance promised to him in blessed Peter. Therefore they need no approval of others, nor do they allow an appeal to any other judgment. For then the Roman Pontiff is not pronouncing judgment as a private person. Rather, as the supreme teacher of the universal Church, as one in whom the charism of the infallibility of the Church herself is individually present, he is expounding or defending a doctrine of Catholic faith.

"The infallibility promised to the Church resides also in the body of bishops when that body exercises supreme teaching authority with the successor of Peter. To the resultant definitions the assent of the Church can never be wanting, on account of the activity of that same Holy Spirit, whereby the whole flock of Christ is preserved and progresses in unity of faith.

"But when either the Roman Pontiff or the body of bishops together with him defines a judgment, they pronounce it in accord with revelation itself. All are obliged to maintain and be ruled by this revelation, which, as written or preserved by tradition, is transmitted in its entirety through the legitimate succession of bishops and especially through the care of the Roman Pontiff himself.

"Under the guiding light of the Spirit of truth, revelation is thus religiously preserved and faithfully expounded in the Church. The Roman Pontiff and the bishops, in view of their office and of the importance of the matter, strive painstakingly and by appropriate means to inquire properly into that revelation and to give apt expression to its contents. But they do not allow that there could be any new public revelation pertaining to the divine deposit of faith" (No. 25).

Authentic Teaching

The pope rarely speaks *ex cathedra* — that is, "from the chair" of St. Peter — for the purpose of making an infallible pronouncement. More often and in various ways he states authentic teaching in line with Scripture, tradition, the living experience of the Church, and the whole analogy of faith. Of such teaching, the Second Vatican Council said in its Dogmatic Constitution on the Church (No. 25):

"Religious submission of will and of mind must be shown in a special way to the authentic teaching authority of the Roman Pontiff, even when he is not speaking *ex cathedra*. That is, it must be shown in such a way that his supreme magisterium is acknowledged with reverence, the judgments made by him are sincerely adhered to, according to his manifest mind and will. His mind and will in the matter may be known chiefly either from the character of the documents, from his frequent repetition of the same doctrine, or from his manner of speaking."

With respect to bishops, the constitution states: "They are authentic teachers, that is, teachers endowed with the authority of Christ, who preach to the people committed to them the faith they must believe and put into practice. By the light of the Holy Spirit, they make that faith clear, bringing forth from the treasury of revelation new things and old (cf. Mt. 13:52), making faith bear fruit and vigilantly warding off any errors which threaten their flock (cf. 2 Tm. 4:1-4).

"Bishops, teaching in communion with the Roman Pontiff, are to be respected by all as witnesses to divine and Catholic truth. In matters of faith and morals, the bishops speak in the name of Christ and the faithful are to accept their teaching and adhere to it with a religious assent of soul."

Magisterium — Teaching Authority

Responsibility for teaching doctrine and judging orthodoxy belongs to the official teaching authority of the Church.

This authority is personalized in the pope, the successor of St. Peter as head of the Church, and in the bishops together and in union with the pope, as it was originally committed to Peter and to the whole college of apostles under his leadership. They are the official teachers of the Church.

Others have auxiliary relationships with the magisterium: theologians, in the study and clarification of doctrine; teachers — priests, religious, lay persons — who cooperate with the pope and bishops in spreading knowledge of religious truth; the faithful, who by their sense of faith and personal witness contribute to the development of doctrine and the establishment of its relevance to life in the Church and the world.

The magisterium, Pope Paul VI noted in an address at a general audience Jan. 11, 1967, "is a subordinate and faithful echo and secure interpreter of the divine word." It does not reveal new truths, "nor is it superior to sacred Scripture." Its competence extends to the limits of divine revelation manifested in Scripture and tradition and the living experience of the Church, with respect to matters of faith and morals and related subjects. Official teaching in these areas is infallible when it is formally defined, for belief and acceptance by all members of the Church, by the pope, acting in the capacity of supreme shepherd of the flock of Christ; also, when doctrine is proposed and taught with moral unanimity of bishops with the pope in a solemn collegial manner, as in an ecumenical council, and/or in the ordinary course of events. Even when not infallibly defined, official teaching in the areas of faith and morals is authoritative and requires religious assent.

The teachings of the magisterium have been documented in creeds, formulas of faith, decrees and enactments of ecumenical and particular councils, various kinds of doctrinal statements, encyclical letters and other teaching instruments. They have also been incorporated into the liturgy, with the result that the law of prayer is said to be a law of belief.

Collegiality

The bishops of the Church, in union with the pope, have supreme teaching and pastoral authority over the whole Church in addition to the authority of office they have for their own dioceses.

This collegial authority is exercised in a solemn manner in an ecumenical council and can be exercised in other ways as well, "provided that the head of the college calls them to collegiate action, or at least so approves or freely accepts the united action of the dispersed bishops that it is made a true collegiate act."

This doctrine is grounded on the fact that: "Just as, by the Lord's will, St. Peter and the other apostles constituted one apostolic college, so in a similar way the Roman Pontiff as the successor of Peter, and the bishops as the successors of the apostles are joined together."

Doctrine on collegiality was stated by the Second Vatican Council in the Dogmatic Constitution on the Church (Nos. 22 and 23).

(For coverage of the *Role of Mary in the Mystery of Christ and the Church,* Chapter VIII, *Lumen Gentium,* please see the section on the Blessed Virgin Mary.)

REVELATION

Following are excerpts from the "Dogmatic Constitution on Divine Revelation" (Dei Verbum) promulgated by the Second Vatican Council. They describe the nature and process of divine revelation, inspiration and interpretation of Scripture, the Old and New Testaments, and the role of Scripture in the life of the Church.

I. REVELATION ITSELF

God chose to reveal himself and to make known to us the hidden purpose of his will (cf. Eph. 1:9) by which through Christ, the Word made flesh, man has access to the Father in the Holy Spirit and comes to share in the divine nature (cf. Eph. 2:18; 2 Pt. 1:4). Through this revelation, therefore, the invisible God (cf. Col. 1:15; 1 Tm. 1:17). speaks to men as friends (cf. Ex. 33:11; Jn. 15:14-15) and lives among them (cf. Bar. 3:38) so that he may invite and take them into fellowship with himself. This plan of revelation is realized by deeds and words having an inner unity: the deeds wrought by God in the history of salvation manifest and confirm the teaching and realities signified by the words, while the words proclaim the deeds and clarify the mystery contained in them. By this revelation then, the deepest truth about God and the salvation of man is made clear to us in Christ, who is the Mediator and at the same time the fullness of all revelation (No. 2).

God from the start manifested himself to our first parents. Then after their fall his promise of redemption aroused in them the hope of being saved (cf. Gn. 3:15), and from that time on he ceaselessly kept the human race in his care, in order to give eternal life to those who perseveringly do good in search of salvation (cf. Rom. 2:6-7). He called Abraham in order to make of him a great nation (cf. Gn. 12:2). Through the patriarchs, and after them through Moses and the prophets, he taught this nation to acknowledge himself as the one living and true God and to wait for the Savior promised by him. In this manner he prepared the way for the Gospel down through the centuries (No. 3).

Revelation in Christ

Then, after speaking in many places and varied ways through the prophets, God "last of all in these days has spoken to us by his Son" (Heb. 1:1-2). Jesus perfected revelation by fulfilling it through his whole work of making himself present and manifesting himself: through his words and deeds, his signs and wonders, but especially through his death and glorious resurrection from the dead and final sending of the Spirit of truth. Moreover, he confirmed with divine testimony what revelation proclaimed: that God is with us to free us from the darkness of sin and death, and to raise us up to life eternal.

The Christian dispensation, therefore, as the new and definitive covenant, will never pass away, and we now await no further new public revelation before the glorious manifestation of our Lord Jesus Christ (cf. 1 Tm. 6:14; Ti. 2:13) (No. 4).

II. TRANSMISSION OF REVELATION

God has seen to it that what he had revealed for the salvation of all nations would abide perpetually in its full integrity and be handed on to all generations. Therefore Christ the Lord, in whom the full revelation of the supreme God is brought to completion (cf. 2 Cor. 1:20; 3:16; 4:6), commissioned the apostles to preach to all men that Gospel which is the source of all saving truth and moral teaching, and thus to impart to them divine gifts. This Gospel had been promised in former times through the prophets, and Christ himself fulfilled it and promulgated it with his own lips. This commission was faithfully fulfilled by the apostles who, by their oral preaching, by example, and by ordinances, handed on what they had received from Christ or what they had learned through the prompting of the Holy Spirit. The commission was fulfilled, too, by those apostles and apostolic men who under the inspiration of the same Holy Spirit committed the message of salvation to writing (No. 7).

Tradition

But in order to keep the Gospel forever whole and alive within the Church, the apostles left bishops as their successors, "handing over their own teaching role" to them. This sacred tradition, therefore, and sacred Scripture of both the Old and the New Testament are like a mirror in which the pilgrim Church on earth looks at God (No. 7).

The apostolic preaching, which is expressed in a special way in the inspired books, was to be preserved by a continuous succession of preachers until the end of time. Therefore the apostles, handing on what they themselves had received, warn the faithful to hold fast to the traditions which they have learned. Now what was handed on by the apostles includes everything which contributes to the holiness of life, and the increase in faith of the People of God; and so the Church, in her teaching, life, and worship, perpetuates and hands on to all generations all that she herself is, all that she believes (No. 8).

Development of Doctrine

This tradition which comes from the apostles develops in the Church with the help of the Holy Spirit. For there is a growth in the understanding of the realities and the words which have been handed down. This happens through the contemplation and study made by believers through the intimate understanding of spiritual things they experience, and through the preaching of those who have received through episcopal succession the sure gift of truth. For, as the centuries succeed one another, the Church constantly moves forward toward the fullness of divine truth until the words of God reach their complete fulfillment in her.

The words of the holy Fathers witness to the living presence of this tradition, whose wealth is poured into the practice and life of the believing and praying Church. Through the same tradition the Church's full canon of the sacred books is known, and the sacred writings themselves are more profoundly understood and unceasingly made active in her; . . . and the Holy Spirit, through whom the living voice of the Gospel resounds in the Church, and through her, in the world, leads unto all truth those who believe and makes the word of Christ dwell abundantly in them (cf. Col. 3:16) (No. 8).

Tradition and Scripture

Hence there exist a close connection and communication between sacred tradition and sacred Scripture. For both of them, flowing from the same divine wellspring, in a certain way merge into a unity and tend toward the same end. For sacred Scripture is the word of God inasmuch as it is consigned to writing under the inspiration of the divine Spirit. To the successors of the apostles, sacred tradition hands on in its full purity God's word, which was entrusted to the apostles by Christ the Lord and the Holy Spirit. Thus, led by the light of the Spirit of truth, these successors can in their preaching preserve this word of God faithfully, explain it, and make it more widely known. Consequently, it is not from sacred Scripture alone that the Church draws her certainty about every thing which has been revealed. Therefore both sacred tradition and sacred Scripture are to be accepted and venerated with the same sense of devotion and reverence (No. 9).

Sacred tradition and sacred Scripture form one sacred deposit of the word of God, which is committed to the Church (No. 10).

Teaching Authority of Church

The task of authentically interpreting the word of God, whether written or handed on, has been entrusted exclusively to the living teaching office of the Church, whose authority is exercised in the name of Jesus Christ. This teaching office is not above the word of God, but serves it, teaching only what has been handed on . . . it draws from this one deposit of faith everything which it presents for belief as divinely revealed.

It is clear, therefore, that sacred tradition, sacred Scripture, and the teaching authority of the Church . . . are so linked and joined together that one cannot stand without the others, and that all together and each in its own way under the action of the one Holy Spirit contribute effectively to the salvation of souls (No. 10).

III. INSPIRATION, INTERPRETATION

Those revealed realities contained and presented in sacred Scripture have been committed to writing under the inspiration of the Holy Spirit. Holy Mother Church, relying on the belief of the apostles, holds that the books of both the Old and New Testament in their entirety, with all their parts, are sacred and canonical because, having been written under the inspiration of the Holy Spirit (cf. Jn. 20:31; 2 Tm. 3:16; 2 Pt. 1:19-21; 3:15-16) they have God as their author and have been handed on as such to the Church herself. In composing the sacred books, God chose men and, while employed by him, they made use of their powers and abilities, so that, with him acting in them and through them, they, as true authors, consigned to writing everything and only those things which he wanted (No. 11).

Inerrancy

Therefore, since everything asserted by the inspired authors or sacred writers must be held to be asserted by the Holy Spirit, it follows that the books of Scripture must be acknowledged as teaching firmly, faithfully, and without error that truth which God wanted put into the sacred writings for the sake of our salvation. Therefore "all Scripture is inspired by God and useful for teaching, for reproving, for correcting, for instruction in justice; that the man of God may be perfect, equipped for every good work" (2 Tm. 3:16-17) (No. 11).

Literary Forms

However, since God speaks in sacred Scripture through men in human fashion, the interpreter of sacred Scripture, in order to see clearly what God wanted to communicate to us, should carefully investigate what meaning the sacred writers really intended, and what God wanted to manifest by means of their words.

The interpreter must investigate what meaning the sacred writer intended to express and actually expressed in particular circumstances as he used contemporary literary forms in accordance with the situation of his own time and culture. For the correct understanding of what the sacred author wanted to assert, due attention must be paid to the customary and characteristic styles of perceiving, speaking, and narrating which prevailed at the time of the sacred writer, and to the customs men normally followed at that period in their everyday dealings with one another (No. 12).

Analogy of Faith

No less serious attention must be given to the content and unity of the whole of Scripture, if the meaning of the sacred texts is to be correctly brought to light. The living tradition of the whole Church must be taken into account along with the harmony which exists between elements of the faith. All of what has been said about the way of interpreting Scripture is subject finally to the judgment of the Church, which carries out the divine commission and ministry of guarding and interpreting the word of God (No. 12).

IV. THE OLD TESTAMENT

In carefully planning and preparing the salvation of the whole human race, the God of supreme love, by a special dispensation, chose for himself a people to whom he might entrust his promises. First he entered into a covenant with Abraham (cf. Gn. 15:18) and, through Moses, with the people of Israel (cf. Ex. 24:8). To this people which he had acquired for himself, he so manifested himself through words and deeds as the one true and living God that Israel came to know by experience the ways of God with men. The plan of salvation, foretold by the sacred authors, recounted and explained by them, is found as the true word of God in the books of the Old Testament: these books, therefore, written under divine inspiration, remain permanently valuable (No. 14).

Principal Purpose

The principal purpose to which the plan of the Old Covenant was directed was to prepare for the coming both of Christ, the universal Redeemer, and of the messianic Kingdom. Now the books of the Old Testament, in accordance with the state of mankind before the time of salvation established by Christ, reveal to all men the knowledge of God and of man and the ways in which God deals with men. These books show us true divine pedagogy (No. 15).

The books of the Old Testament with all their parts, caught up into the proclamation of the Gospel, acquire and show forth their full meaning in the New Testament (cf. Mt. 5:17; Lk. 24:27; Rom. 16:25-26; 2 Cor. 3:14-16) and in turn shed light on it and explain it (No. 16).

V. THE NEW TESTAMENT

The word of God is set forth and shows its power in a most excellent way in the writings of the New Testament. For when the fullness of time arrived (cf. Gal. 4:4), the Word was made flesh and dwelt among us in the fullness of grace and truth (cf. Jn. 12:32). This mystery had not been manifested to other generations as it was now revealed to his holy apostles and prophets in the Holy Spirit (cf. Eph. 3:4-6), so that they might preach the Gospel, stir up faith in Jesus, Christ and Lord, and gather the Church together. To these realities, the writings of the New Testament stand as a perpetual and divine witness (No. 17).

The Gospels and Other Writings

The Gospels have a special preeminence for they

are the principal witness of the life and teaching of the incarnate Word, our Savior.

The Church has always and everywhere held and continues to hold that the four Gospels are of apostolic origin. For what the apostles preached afterwards they themselves and apostolic men, under the inspiration of the divine Spirit, handed on to us in writing: the foundation of faith, namely, the fourfold Gospel, according to Matthew, Mark, Luke, and John (No. 18).

The four Gospels . . . whose historical character the Church unhesitatingly asserts, faithfully hand on what Jesus Christ, while living among men, really did and taught for their eternal salvation until the day he was taken up into heaven (see Acts 1:1-2). Indeed, after the ascension of the Lord the apostles handed on to their hearers what he had said and done. The sacred authors wrote the four Gospels, selecting some things from the many which had been handed on by word of mouth or in writing, reducing some of them to a synthesis, explicating some things in view of the situation of their churches, and preserving the form of proclamation but always in such fashion that they told us the honest truth about Jesus. For their intention in writing was that we might know "the truth" concerning those matters about which we have been instructed (cf. Lk. 1:2-4) (No. 19).

Besides the four Gospels, the canon of the New Testament also contains the Epistles of St. Paul and other apostolic writings, composed under the inspiration of the Holy Spirit. In these writings those matters which concern Christ the Lord are confirmed, his true teaching is more and more fully stated, the saving power of the divine work of Christ is preached, the story is told of the beginnings of the Church and her marvelous growth, and her glorious fulfillment is foretold (No. 20).

VI. SCRIPTURE IN CHURCH LIFE

The Church has always venerated the divine Scriptures just as she venerates the body of the Lord. She has always regarded the Scriptures together with sacred tradition as the supreme rule of faith, and will ever do so. For, inspired by God and committed once and for all to writing, they impart the word of God himself without change, and make the voice of the Holy Spirit resound in the words of the prophets and apostles. Therefore, like the Christian religion itself, all the preaching of the Church must be nourished and ruled by sacred Scripture (No. 21).

Easy access to sacred Scripture should be provided for all the Christian faithful. That is why the Church from the very beginning accepted as her own that very ancient Greek translation of the Old Testament which is named after seventy men (the Septuagint); and she has always given a place of honor to other translations, Eastern and Latin, especially the one known as the Vulgate. But since the word of God should be available at all times, the Church with maternal concern sees to it that suitable and correct translations are made into different languages, especially from the original texts of the sacred books. And if, given the opportunity and the approval of Church authority, these translations are produced in cooperation with the separated brethren as well, all Christians will be able to use them (No. 22).

Biblical Studies, Theology

The constitution encouraged the development and progress of biblical studies "under the watchful care of the sacred teaching office of the Church."

It also noted: "Sacred theology rests on the written word of God, together with sacred tradition, as its primary and perpetual foundation," and that "the study of the sacred page is, as it were, the soul of sacred theology" (Nos. 23, 24).

(See separate article, Interpretation of the Bible.)

THE BIBLE

The Canon of the Bible is the Church's official list of sacred writings. These works, written by men under the inspiration of the Holy Spirit, contain divine revelation and, in conjunction with the tradition and teaching authority of the Church, constitute the rule of Catholic faith. The Canon was fixed and determined by the tradition and teaching authority of the Church.

The Catholic Canon

The Old Testament Canon of 46 books is as follows.

The Pentateuch, the first five books: Genesis (Gn.), Exodus (Ex.), Leviticus (Lv.), Numbers (Nm.), Deuteronomy (Dt.).

Historical Books: Joshua (Jos.), Judges (Jgs.), Ruth (Ru.) 1 and 2 Samuel (Sm.), 1 and 2 Kings (Kgs.), 1 and 2 Chronicles (Chr.), Ezra (Ezr.), Nehemiah (Neh.), Tobit (Tb.), Judith (Jdt.), Esther (Est.), 1 and 2 Maccabees (Mc.).

Wisdom Books: Job (Jb.), Psalms (Ps.), Proverbs (Prv.), Ecclesiastes (Eccl.), Song of Songs (Song), Wisdom (Wis.), Sirach (Sir.).

The Prophets: Isaiah (Is.), Jeremiah (Jer.), Lamentations (Lam.), Baruch (Bar.), Ezekiel (Ez.), Daniel (Dn.), Hosea (Hos.), Joel (Jl.), Amos (Am.), Obadiah (Ob.), Jonah (Jon.), Micah (Mi.), Nahum (Na.), Habakkuk (Hb.), Zephaniah (Zep.), Haggai (Hg.), Zechariah (Zec.) Malachi (Mal.).

The New Testament Canon of 27 books is as follows.

The Gospels: Matthew (Mt.), Mark (Mk.), Luke (Lk.), John (Jn.)

The Acts of the Apostles (Acts).

The Pauline Letters: Romans (Rom.), 1 and 2 Corinthians (Cor.), Galatians (Gal.), Ephesians (Eph.), Philippians (Phil.), Colossians (Col.), 1 and 2 Thessalonians (Thes.) 1 and 2 Timothy (Tm.), Titus (Ti.), Philemon (Phlm.), Hebrews (Heb.).

The Catholic Letters: James (Jas.), 1 and 2 Peter (Pt.), 1, 2, and 3 John (Jn.), Jude (Jude).

Revelation (Rv.).

Developments

The Canon of the Old Testament was firm by the fifth century despite some questioning by scholars. It was stated by a council held at Rome in 382, by African councils held in Hippo in 393 and in Carthage in 397 and 419, and by Innocent I in 405.

All of the New Testament books were generally known and most of them were acknowledged as inspired by the end of the second century. The Muratorian Fragment, dating from about 200, listed most of the books recognized as canonical in later decrees. Prior to the end of the fourth century, however, there was controversy over the inspired character of several works — the Letter to the Hebrews, James, Jude, 2 Peter, 2 and 3 John and Revelation. Controversy ended in the fourth century and these books, along with those about which there was no dispute, were enumerated in the canon stated by the councils of Hippo and Carthage and affirmed by Innocent I in 405.

The Canon of the Bible was solemnly defined by the Council of Trent in the dogmatic decree *De Canonicis Scripturis*, Apr. 8, 1546.

Hebrew and Other Canons

The Hebrew Canon of sacred writings was fixed by tradition and the consensus of rabbis, probably by about 100 A.D. by the Synod or Council of Jamnia and certainly by the end of the second or early in the third century. It consists of the following works in three categories.

The Law (Torah): the five books of Moses: Genesis, Exodus, Leviticus, Numbers, Deuteronomy.

The Prophets: former prophets — Joshua, Judges, 1 and 2 Samuel, 1 and 2 Kings; latter prophets — Isaiah, Jeremiah, Ezekiel, and 12 minor prophets (Hosea, Joel, Amos, Obadiah, Jonah, Micah, Nahum, Habakkuk, Zephaniah, Haggai, Zechariah, Malachi).

The Writings: 1 and 2 Chronicles, Ezra, Nehemiah, Job, Psalms, Proverbs, Ecclesiastes, Song of Songs, Ruth, Esther, Daniel.

This Canon, embodying the tradition and practice of the Palestine community, did not include a number of works contained in the Alexandrian version of sacred writings translated into Greek between 250 and 100 B.C. and in use by Greek-speaking Jews of the Dispersion (outside Palestine). The rejected works, called apocrypha and not regarded as sacred, are: Tobit, Judith, Wisdom, Sirach, Baruch, 1 and 2 Maccabees, the last six chapters of Esther and three passages of Daniel (3:24-90; 13; 14). These books have also been rejected from the Protestant Canon, although they are included in Bibles under the heading "Apocrypha."

The aforementioned books are held to be inspired and sacred by the Catholic Church. In Catholic usage, they are called deuterocanonical because they were under discussion for some time before questions about their canonicity were settled. Books regarded as canonical with little or no debate were called protocanonical. The status of both categories of books is the same in the Catholic Bible.

The Protestant Canon of the Old Testament is the same as the Hebrew.

The Old Testament Canon of some separated Eastern churches differs from the Catholic Canon.

Christians are in agreement on the Canon of the New Testament.

Languages

Hebrew, Aramaic and Greek were the original languages of the Bible. Most of the Old Testament books were written in Hebrew. Portions of Daniel, Ezra,

Jeremiah, Esther, and probably the books of Tobit and Judith were written in Aramaic. The Book of Wisdom, 2 Maccabees and all the books of the New Testament were written in Greek.

Manuscripts and Versions

The original writings of the inspired authors have been lost. The Bible has been transmitted through ancient copies called manuscripts and through translations or versions.

Authoritative Greek manuscripts include the Sinaitic and Vatican manuscripts of the fourth century and the Alexandrine of the fifth century A.D. The Septuagint and Vulgate translations are in a class by themselves.

The Septuagint version, a Greek translation of the Old Testament for Greek-speaking Jews, was begun about 250 and completed about 100 B.C. The work of several Jewish translators at Alexandria, it differed from the Hebrew Bible in the arrangement of books and included several, later called deuterocanonical, which were not acknowledged as sacred by the community in Palestine.

The Vulgate was a Latin version of the Old and New Testaments produced from the original languages by St. Jerome from about 383 to 404. It became the most widely used Latin text for centuries and was regarded as basic long before the Council of Trent designated it as authentic and suitable for use in public reading, controversy, preaching and teaching. Because of its authoritative character, it became the basis for many translations into other languages. A critical revision was completed by a pontifical commission in 1977.

Hebrew and Aramaic manuscripts of great antiquity and value have figured more significantly than before in recent scriptural work by Catholic scholars, especially since their use was strongly encouraged, if not mandated, in 1943 by Pius XII in the encyclical *Divino Afflante Spiritu*.

The English translation of the Bible in general use among Catholics until well into the 20th century was the Douay-Rheims, so called because of the places where it was prepared and published, the New Testament at Rheims in 1582 and the Old Testament at Douay in 1609. The translation was made from the Vulgate text. As revised and issued by Bishop Richard Challoner in 1749 and 1750, it became the standard Catholic English version for about 200 years.

A revision of the Challoner New Testament, made on the basis of the Vulgate text by scholars of the Catholic Biblical Association of America, was published in 1941 in the United States under the sponsorship of the Episcopal Committee of the Confraternity of Christian Doctrine.

New American Bible

A new translation of the entire Bible, the first ever made directly into English from the original languages under Catholic auspices, was projected in 1944 and completed in the fall of 1970 with publication of the *New American Bible*. The Episcopal Committee of the Confraternity of Christian Doctrine sponsored the NAB. The translators were members of the Catholic Biblical Association of America and scholars of other faiths. The typical edition was produced by St. Anthony Guild Press, Paterson, N.J.

The *Jerusalem Bible*, published by Doubleday &

Co., Inc., is an English translation of a French version based on the original languages.

Biblical translations approved for liturgical use by the National Conference of Catholic Bishops and the Holy See are the *New American Bible* (1970 edition), the *Revised Standard Version-Catholic Edition*, and the *Jerusalem Bible* (1966).

The Protestant counterpart of the *Douay-Rheims Bible* was the *King James Bible*, called the *Authorized Version* in England. Originally published in 1611 and in general use for more than three centuries, its several revisions include the *Revised Standard Version* and the *New Revised Standard Version*.

Biblical Federation

In November, 1966, Pope Paul VI commissioned the Secretariat for Promoting Christian Unity to start work for the widest possible distribution of the Bible and to coordinate endeavors toward the production of Catholic-Protestant Bibles in all languages.

The World Catholic Federation for the Biblical Apostolate, established in 1969, sponsors a program designed to create greater awareness among Catholics of the Bible and its use in everyday life.

The U. S. Center for the Catholic Biblical Apostolate is related to the Secretariat for Pastoral Research and Practices, National Conference of Catholic Bishops, 3211 Fourth St. N.E., Washington, DC 20017.

APOCRYPHA

In Catholic usage, Apocrypha are books which have some resemblance to the canonical books in subject matter and title but which have not been recognized as canonical by the Church. They are characterized by a false claim to divine authority; extravagant accounts of events and miracles alleged to be supplemental revelation; material favoring heresy (especially in "New Testament" apocrypha); minimal, if any, historical value. Among examples of this type of literature itemized by J. McKenzie, S.J., in *Dictio-*nary of the Bible* are: the Books of Adam and Eve, Martyrdom of Isaiah, Testament of the Patriarchs, Assumption of Moses, Sibylline Oracles; Gospel of James, Gospel of Thomas, Arabic Gospel of the Infancy, History of Joseph the Carpenter; Acts of John, Acts of Paul, Acts of Peter, Acts of Andrew, and numerous epistles.

Books of this type are called pseudepigrapha by Protestants.

In Protestant usage, some books of the Catholic Bible (deuterocanonical) are called apocrypha because their inspired character is rejected.

DEAD SEA SCROLLS

The Qumran Scrolls, popularly called the Dead Sea Scrolls, are a collection of manuscripts, all but one of them in Hebrew, found since 1947 in caves in the Desert of Juda west of the Dead Sea.

Among the findings were a complete text of Isaiah dating from the second century, B.C., more or less extensive fragments of other Old Testament texts (including the deuterocanonical Tobit), and a commentary on Habakkuk. Until the discovery of these materials, the oldest known Hebrew manuscripts were from the 10th century A.D.

Also found were messianic and apocalyptic texts, and other writings describing the beliefs and practices of the Essenes, a rigoristic Jewish sect.

The scrolls, dating from about the first century before and after Christ, are important sources of information about Hebrew literature, Jewish history during the period between the Old and New Testaments, and the history of Old Testament texts. They established the fact that the Hebrew text of the Old Testament was fixed before the beginning of the Christian era and have had definite effects in recent critical studies and translations of the Old Testament. Together with other scrolls found at Masada, they are still the subject of intensive study.

BOOKS OF THE BIBLE

OLD TESTAMENT BOOKS

Pentateuch

The Pentateuch is the collective title of the first five books of the Bible. Substantially, they identify the Israelites as Yahweh's Chosen People, cover their history from Egypt to the threshold of the Promised Land, contain the Mosaic Law and Covenant, and disclose the promise of salvation to come. Principal themes concern the divine promise of salvation, Yahweh's fidelity and the Covenant. Work on the composition of the Pentateuch was completed in the sixth century.

Genesis: The book of origins, according to its title in the Septuagint. In two parts, covers: religious prehistory, including accounts of the origin of the world and man, the original state of innocence and the fall, the promise of salvation, patriarchs before and after the Deluge, the Tower of Babel narrative, genealogies (first 11 chapters); the Covenant with Abraham and patriarchal history from Abraham to Joseph (balance of the 50 chapters). Significant are the themes of Yahweh's universal sovereignty and mercy.

Exodus: Named with the Greek word for departure, is a religious epic which describes the oppression of the 12 tribes in Egypt and their departure, liberation or passover therefrom under the leadership of Moses; Yahweh's establishment of the Covenant with them, making them his Chosen People, through the mediation of Moses at Mt. Sinai; instructions concerning the tabernacle, the sanctuary and Ark of the Covenant; the institution of the priesthood. The book is significant because of its theology of liberation and redemption. In Christian interpretation, the Exodus is a figure of baptism.

Leviticus: Mainly legislative in theme and purpose, contains laws regarding sacrifices, ceremonies of ordination and the priesthood of Aaron, legal purity, the holiness code, atonement, the redemption of offerings and other subjects. Summarily, Levitical laws provided directives for all aspects of religious observance and for the manner in which the Israelites were to conduct themselves with respect to Yahweh and each other. Leviticus was the liturgical handbook of the priesthood.

Numbers: Taking its name from censuses recounted

at the beginning and near the end, is a continuation of Exodus. It combines narrative of the Israelites' desert pilgrimage from Sinai to the border of Canaan with laws related to and expansive of those in Leviticus.

Deuteronomy: The concluding book of the Pentateuch, recapitulates, in the form of a testament of Moses, the Law and much of the desert history of the Israelites; enjoins fidelity to the Law as the key to good or bad fortune for the people; gives an account of the commissioning of Joshua as the successor of Moses. Notable themes concern the election of Israel by Yahweh, observance of the Law, prohibitions against the worship of foreign gods, worship of and confidence in Yahweh, the power of Yahweh in nature. The Deuteronomic Code or motif, embodying all of these elements, was the norm for interpreting Israelite history.

Joshua, Judges, Ruth

Joshua: Records the fulfillment of Yahweh's promise to the Israelites in their conquest, occupation and division of Canaan under the leadership of Joshua. It also contains an account of the return of Transjordanian Israelites and of a renewal of the Covenant. It was redacted in final form probably in the sixth century or later.

Judges: Records the actions of charismatic leaders, called judges, of the tribes of Israel between the death of Joshua and the time of Samuel, and a crisis of idolatry among the people. The basic themes are sin and punishment, repentance and deliverance; its purpose was in line with the Deuteronomic motif, that the fortunes of the Israelites were related to their observance or non-observance of the Law and the Covenant. It was redacted in final form probably in the sixth century.

Ruth: Named for the Gentile (Moabite) woman who, through marriage with Boaz, became an Israelite and an ancestress of David (her son, Obed, became his grandfather). Themes are filial piety, faith and trust in Yahweh, the universality of messianic salvation. Dates ranging from c. 950 to the seventh century have been assigned to the origin of the book, whose author is unknown.

Historical Books

These books, while they contain a great deal of factual material, are unique in their preoccupation with presenting and interpreting it, in the Deuteronomic manner, in primary relation to the Covenant on which the nation of Israel was founded and in accordance with which community and personal life were judged.

The books are: Samuel 1 and 2, from the end of Judges (c. 1020) to the end of David's reign (c. 961); Kings 1 and 2, from the last days of David to the start of the Babylonian Exile and the destruction of the Temple (587); Chronicles 1 and 2, from the reign of Saul (c. 1020-1000) to the return of the people from the Exile (538); Ezra and Nehemiah, covering the reorganization of the Jewish community after the Exile (458-397); Maccabees 1 and 2, recounting the struggle against attempted suppression of Judaism (168-142).

Three of the books listed below — Tobit, Judith and Esther — are categorized as religious novels.

Samuel 1 and 2: A single work in concept and contents, containing episodic history of the last two Judges, Eli and Samuel, the establishment and rule of the monarchy under Saul and David, and the political consequences of David's rule. The royal messianic dynasty of David was the subject of Nathan's oracle in 2 Sm. 7. The books were edited in final form probably late in the seventh century or during the Exile.

Kings 1 and 2: Cover the last days of David and the career of Solomon, including the building of the Temple and the history of the kingdom during his reign; stories of the prophets Elijah and Elisha; the history of the divided kingdom to the fall of Israel in the North (721) and the fall of Judah in the South (587), the destruction of Jerusalem and the Temple. They reflect the Deuteronomic motif in attributing the downfall of the people to corruption of belief and practice in public and private life. They were completed probably in the sixth century.

Chronicles 1 and 2: A collection of historical traditions interpreted in such a way as to present an ideal picture of one people governed by divine law and united in one Temple worship of the one true God. Contents include genealogical tables from Adam to David, the careers of David and Solomon, coverage of the kingdom of Judah to the Exile, and the decree of Cyrus permitting the return of the people and rebuilding of Jerusalem. Both are related to and were written about 400 by the same author, the Chronicler, who composed Ezra and Nehemiah.

Ezra and Nehemiah: A running account of the return of the people to their homeland after the Exile and of practical efforts, under the leadership of Ezra and Nehemiah, to restore and reorganize the religious and political community on the basis of Israelite traditions, divine worship and observance of the Law. Events of great significance were the building of the second Temple, the building of a wall around Jerusalem and the proclamation of the Law by Ezra. This restored community was the start of Judaism. Both are related to and were written about 400 by the same author, the Chronicler, who composed Chronicles 1 and 2.

Tobit: Written in the literary form of a novel and having greater resemblance to wisdom than to historical literature, narrates the personal history of Tobit, a devout and charitable Jew in exile, and persons connected with him, viz., his son Tobiah, his kinsman Raguel and Raguel's daughter Sarah. Its purpose was to teach people how to be good Jews. One of its principal themes is patience under trial, with trust in divine Providence which is symbolized by the presence and action of the angel Raphael. It was written about 200.

Judith: Recounts, in the literary form of a historical novel or romance, the preservation of the Israelites from conquest and ruin through the action of Judith. The essential themes are trust in God for deliverance from danger and emphasis on observance of the Law. It was written probably during the Maccabean period.

Esther: Relates, in the literary form of a historical novel or romance, the manner in which Jews in Persia were saved from annihilation through the central role played by Esther, the Jewish wife of Ahasuerus; a fact commemorated by the Jewish feast of Purim. Like Judith, it has trust in divine Providence as its theme and indicates that God's saving will is sometimes realized by persons acting in unlikely ways. It may have been written near the end of the fourth century.

Maccabees 1 and 2: While related to some extent because of common subject matter, are quite different from each other.

The first book recounts the background and events of the 40-year (175-135) struggle for religious and political freedom led by Judas Maccabaeus and his brothers against the Hellenist Seleucid kings and some Hellenophiles among the Jews. Victory was symbolized by the rededication of the Temple. Against the background of opposition between Jews and Gentiles, the author equated the survival of belief in the one true God with survival of the Jewish people, thus identifying religion with patriotism. It was written probably near the year 100.

The second book supplements the first to some extent, covering and giving a theological interpretation to events from 180 to 162. It explains the feast of the Dedication of the Temple, a key event in the survival of Judaism which is commemorated in the feast of Hanukkah; stresses the primacy of God's action in the struggle for survival; and indicates belief in an afterlife and the resurrection of the body. It was completed probably about 124.

Wisdom Books

With the exceptions of Psalms and the Song of Songs, the titles listed under this heading are called wisdom books because their purpose was to formulate the fruits of human experience in the context of meditation on sacred Scripture and to present them as an aid toward understanding the problems of life. Hebrew wisdom literature was distinctive from pagan literature of the same type, but it had limitations; these were overcome in the New Testament, which added the dimensions of the New Covenant to those of the Old. Solomon was regarded as the archetype of the wise man.

Job: A dramatic, didactic poem consisting mainly of several dialogues between Job and his friends concerning the mystery involved in the coexistence of the just God, evil and the suffering of the just. It describes an innocent man's experience of suffering and conveys the truth that faith in and submission to God rather than complete understanding, which is impossible, make the experience bearable; also, that the justice of God cannot be defended by affirming that it is realized in this world. Of unknown authorship, it was composed between the seventh and fifth centuries.

Psalms: A collection of 150 religious songs or lyrics reflecting Israelite belief and piety dating from the time of the monarchy to the post-Exilic period, a span of well over 500 years. The psalms, which are a compendium of Old Testament theology, were used in the temple liturgy and for other occasions. They were of several types suitable for the king, hymns, lamentations, expressions of confidence and thanksgiving, prophecy, historical meditation and reflection, and the statement of wisdom. About one-half of them are attributed to David; many were composed by unknown authors.

Proverbs: The oldest book of the wisdom type in the Bible, consisting of collections of sayings attributed to Solomon and other persons regarding a wide variety of subjects including wisdom and its nature, rules of conduct, duties with respect to one's neighbor, the conduct of daily affairs. It reveals many details of Hebrew life. Its nucleus dates from the period before the Exile. The extant form of the book dates probably from the end of the fifth century.

Ecclesiastes: A treatise about many subjects whose unifying theme is the vanity of strictly human efforts and accomplishments with respect to the achievement of lasting happiness; the only things which are not vain are fear of the Lord and observance of his commandments. The pessimistic tone of the book is due to the absence of a concept of afterlife. It was written by an unknown author probably in the third century.

Song of Songs: A collection of love lyrics reflecting various themes, including the love of God for Israel and the celebration of ideal love and fidelity between man and woman. It was written by an unknown author after the Exile.

Wisdom: Deals with many subjects including the reward of justice; praise of wisdom, a gift of Yahweh proceeding from belief in him and the practice of his Law; the part played by him in the history of his people, especially in their liberation from Egypt; the folly and shame of idolatry. Its contents are taken from the whole sacred literature of the Jews and represent a distillation of its wisdom based on the law, beliefs and traditions of Israel. The last of the Old Testament books, it was written in the early part of the first century before Christ by a member of the Jewish community at Alexandria.

Sirach: Resembling Proverbs, is a collection of sayings handed on by a grandfather to his grandson. It contains a variety of moral instruction and eulogies of patriarchs and other figures in Israelite history. Its moral maxims apply to individuals, the family and community, relations with God, friendship, education, wealth, the Law, divine worship. Its theme is that true wisdom consists in the Law. (It was formerly called Ecclesiasticus, the Church Book, because of its extensive use by the Church for moral instruction.) It was written in Hebrew between 200 and 175, during a period of strong hellenistic influence, and was translated into Greek after 132.

The Prophets

These books and the prophecies they contain "express judgments of the people's moral conduct, on the basis of the Mosaic alliance between God and Israel. They teach sublime truths and lofty morals. They contain exhortations, threats, announcements of punishment, promises of deliverance. In the affairs of men, their prime concern is the interests of God, especially in what pertains to the Chosen People through whom the Messiah is to come; hence their denunciations of idolatry and of that externalism in worship which exclude the interior spirit of religion. They are concerned also with the universal nature of the moral law, with personal responsibility, with the person and office of the Messiah, and with the conduct of foreign nations" (The Holy Bible, Prophetic Books, CCD Edition, 1961; Preface). There are four major (Isaiah, Jeremiah, Ezekiel, Daniel) and 12 minor prophets (distinguished by the length of books), Lamentations and Baruch. Earlier prophets, mentioned in historical books, include Samuel, Gad, Nathan, Elijah and Elisha.

Before the Exile, prophets were the intermediaries through whom God communicated revelation to the people. Afterwards, prophecy lapsed and the written word of the Law served this purpose.

Isaiah: Named for the greatest of the prophets whose career spanned the reigns of three Hebrew kings from 742 to the beginning of the seventh century, in a period of moral breakdown in Judah and threats of invasion by foreign enemies. It is an anthology of poems and oracles credited to him and a number of followers deeply influenced by him. Of special importance are the prophecies concerning Immanuel (6 to 12), including the prophecy of the virgin birth (7:14). Chapters 40 to 55, called Deutero-Isaiah, are attributed to an anonymous poet toward the end of the Exile; this portion contains the Songs of the Servant. The concluding part of the book (56-66) contains oracles by later disciples. One of many themes in Isaiah concerned the saving mission of the remnant of Israel in the divine plan of salvation.

Jeremiah: Combines history, biography and prophecy in a setting of crisis caused by internal and external factors, viz., idolatry and general infidelity to the Law among the Israelites and external threats from the Assyrians, Egyptians and Babylonians. Jeremiah prophesied the promise of a new covenant as well as the destruction of Jerusalem and the Temple. His career began in 626 and ended some years after the beginning of the Exile. The book, the longest in the Bible, was edited in final form after the Exile.

Lamentations: A collection of five laments or elegies over the fall of Jerusalem and the fate of the people in Exile, written by an unknown eyewitness. They convey the message that Yahweh struck the people because of their sins and reflect confidence in his love and power to restore his converted people.

Baruch: Against the background of the already-begun Exile, it consists of an introduction and several parts: an exile's prayer of confession and petition for forgiveness and the restoration of Israel; a poem praising wisdom and the Law of Moses; a lament in which Jerusalem, personified, bewails the fate of her people and consoles them with the hope of blessings to come; and a polemic against idolatry. Although ascribed to Baruch, Jeremiah's secretary, it was written by several authors, probably in the second century.

Ezekiel: Named for the priest-prophet who prophesied in Babylon from 593 to 571, during the first phase of the Exile. To prepare his fellow early exiles for the impending fall of Jerusalem, he reproached the Israelites for past sins and predicted woes to come upon them. After the destruction of the city, the burden of his message was hope and promise of restoration. Ezekiel had great influence on the religion of Israel after the Exile.

Daniel: The protagonist is a young Jew, taken early to Babylon where he lived until about 538, who figured in a series of edifying stories which originated in Israelite tradition. The stories, whose characters are not purely legendary but rest on historical tradition, recount the trials and triumphs of Daniel and his three companions, and other episodes including those concerning Susannah, Bel, and the Dragon. The book is more apocalyptic than prophetic: it envisions Israel in glory to come and conveys the message that men of faith can resist temptation and overcome adversity. It states the prophetic themes of right conduct, divine control of men and events, and the final triumph of the kingdom. It was written by an unknown author in the 160s to give moral support to Jews during the persecutions of the Maccabean period.

Hosea: Consists of a prophetic parallel between Hosea's marriage and Yahweh's relations with his people. As the prophet was married to a faithless wife whom he would not give up, Yahweh was bound in Covenant with an idolatrous and unjust Israel whom he would not desert but would chastise for purification. Hosea belonged to the Northern Kingdom of Israel and began his career about the middle of the eighth century. He inaugurated the tradition of describing Yahweh's relation to Israel in terms of marriage.

Joel: Is apocalyptic and eschatological regarding divine judgment, the Day of the Lord, which is symbolized by a ravaging invasion of locusts, the judgment of the nations in the Valley of Josaphat and the outpouring of the Spirit in the messianic era to come. Its message is that God will vindicate and save Israel, in view of the prayer and repentance of the people, and will punish their enemies. It was composed about 400.

Amos: Consists of an indictment against foreign enemies of Israel; a strong denunciation of the people of Israel, whose infidelity, idolatry and injustice made them subject to divine judgment and punishment; and a messianic oracle regarding Israel's restoration. Amos prophesied in the Northern Kingdom of Israel, at Bethel, in the first half of the eighth century; chronologically, he was the first of the canonical prophets.

Obadiah: A 21-verse prophecy, the shortest and one of the sternest in the Bible, against the Edomites, invaders of southern Judah and enemies of those returning from the Exile to their homeland. It was probably composed in the fifth century.

Jonah: A parable of divine mercy with the theme that Yahweh wills the salvation of all, not just a few, men who respond to his call. Its protagonist is a disobedient prophet; forced by circumstances beyond his control to preach penance among Gentiles, he is highly successful in his mission but baffled by the divine concern for those who do not belong to the Chosen People. It was written after the Exile, probably in the fifth century.

Micah: Attacks the injustice and corruption of priests, false prophets, officials and people; announces judgment and punishment to come; foretells the restoration of Israel; refers to the saving remnant of Israel. Micah was a contemporary of Isaiah.

Nahum: Concerns the destruction of Nineveh in 612 and the overthrow of the Assyrian Empire by the Babylonians.

Habakkuk: Dating from about 605-597, concerns sufferings to be inflicted by oppressors on the people of Judah because of their infidelity to the Lord. It also sounds a note of confidence in the Lord, the Savior, and declares that the just will not perish.

Zephaniah: Exercising his ministry in the second half of the seventh century, during a time of widespread idolatry, superstition and religious degradation, he prophesied impending judgment and punishment for Jerusalem and its people. He prophesied too that a holy remnant of the people (*anawim*, mentioned also by Amos) would be spared. Zephaniah was a forerunner of Jeremiah.

Haggai: One of the first prophets after the Exile, Haggai in 520 encouraged the returning exiles to re-establish their community and to complete the second Temple (dedicated in 515), for which he envisioned greater glory, in a messianic sense, than that enjoyed by the original Temple of Solomon.

Zechariah: A contemporary of Haggai, he prophesied in the same vein. A second part of the book, called Deutero-Zechariah and composed by one or more unknown authors, relates a vision of the coming of the Prince of Peace, the Messiah of the Poor.

Malachi: Written by an anonymous author, presents a picture of life in the post-Exilic community between 516 and the initiation of reforms by Ezra and Nehemiah about 432. Blame for the troubles of the community is placed mainly on priests for failure to carry out ritual worship and to instruct the people in the proper manner; other factors were religious indifference and the influence of doubters who were scandalized at the prosperity of the wicked. The vision of a universal sacrifice to be offered to Yahweh (1:11) is interpreted in Catholic theology as a prophecy of the sacrifice of the Mass. Malachi was the last of the minor prophets.

DATES OF THE OLD TESTAMENT

c. 1800 - c. 1600 B.C.: Period of the patriarchs (Abraham, Isaac, Jacob).

c. 1600: Israelites in Egypt.

c. 1250: Exodus of Israelites from Egypt.

c. 1210: Entrance of Israelites into Canaan.

c. 1210-c. 1020: Period of the Judges.

c. 1020-c. 1000: Reign of Saul, first king.

c. 1000-c. 961: Reign of David.

c. 961-922: Reign of Solomon. Temple built during his reign.

922: Division of the Kingdom into Israel (North) and Judah (South).

721: Conquest of Israel by Assyrians.

587-538: Conquest of Judah by Babylonians.

Babylonian Captivity and Exile. Destruction of Jerusalem and the Temple, 587. Captivity ended with the return of exiles, following the decree of Cyrus permitting the rebuilding of Jerusalem.

515: Dedication of the second Temple.

458-397: Restoration and reform of the Jewish religious and political community; building of the Jerusalem wall, 439. Leaders in the movement were Ezra and Nehemiah.

168-142: Period of the Maccabees; war against Syrians.

142: Independence granted to Jews by Demetrius II of Syria.

135-37: Period of the Hasmonean dynasty.

63: Beginning of Roman rule.

37-4: Period of Herod the Great.

NEW TESTAMENT BOOKS

Gospels

The term Gospel is derived from the Anglo-Saxon *god-spell* and the Greek *euangelion*, meaning good news, good tidings. In Christian use, it means the good news of salvation proclaimed by Christ and the Church, and handed on in written form in the Gospels of Matthew, Mark, Luke and John.

The initial proclamation of the coming of the king-dom of God was made by Jesus in and through his Person, teachings and actions, and especially through his Passion, death and resurrection. This proclamation became the center of Christian faith and the core of the oral Gospel tradition with which the Church spread the good news by apostolic preaching for some 30 years before it was committed to writing by the Evangelists.

Nature of the Gospels

The historical truth of the Gospels was the subject of an instruction issued by the Pontifical Commission for Biblical Studies Apr. 21, 1964.

The sacred writers selected from the material at their disposal (the oral Gospel tradition, some written collections of sayings and deeds of Jesus, eyewitness accounts) those things which were particularly suitable to the various conditions (liturgical, catechetical, missionary) of the faithful and the aims they had in mind, and they narrated these things in such a way as to correspond with those circumstances and their aims.

The life and teaching of Jesus were not simply reported in a biographical manner for the purpose of preserving their memory but were "preached" so as to offer the Church the basis of doctrine concerning faith and morals.

In their works, the Evangelists presented the true sayings of Jesus and the events of his life in the light of the better understanding they had following their enlightenment by the Holy Spirit. They did not transform Christ into a "mythical" Person, nor did they distort his teaching. Passion narratives are the core of all the Gospels, covering the suffering, death and resurrection of Jesus as central events in bringing about and establishing the New Covenant. Leading up to them are accounts of the mission of John the Baptizer and the ministry of Jesus, especially in Galilee and finally in Jerusalem before the Passion. The infancy of Jesus is covered by Luke and Matthew with narratives inspired in part by appropriate Old Testament citations.

Matthew, Mark and Luke, while different in various respects, have so many similarities that they are called Synoptic; their relationships are the subject of the Synoptic Problem.

Matthew: Written probably between 80 and 100 for Jewish Christians with clear reference to Jewish background and identification of Jesus as the divine Messiah, the fulfillment of the Old Testament. Distinctive are the use of Old Testament citations regarding the Person, activity and teaching of Jesus, and the presentation of doctrine in sermons and discourses.

Mark: Most likely the first of the Gospels, dating from about 70. Written for Gentile Christians, it is noted for the realism and wealth of concrete details with which it reveals Jesus as Son of God and Savior more by his actions and miracles than by his discourses. Theologically, it is less refined than the other Gospels.

Luke: Written about 75 for Gentile Christians. It is noted for the universality of its address, the insight it provides into the Christian way of life, the place it gives to women, the manner in which it emphasizes Jesus' friendship with sinners and compassion for the suffering.

John: Edited and arranged in final form probably

between 90 and 100, this is the most sublime and theological of the Gospels, and is different from the Synoptics in plan and treatment. Combining accounts of signs with longer discourses and reflections, it progressively reveals the Person and mission of Jesus — as Word, Way, Truth, Life, Light — in line with the purpose, "to help you believe that Jesus is the Messiah, the Son of God, so that through this faith you may have life in his name" (Jn. 20:31). There are questions about the authorship but no doubt about the Johannine authority and tradition behind the Gospel.

Acts of the Apostles

Written by Luke about 75 as a supplement to his Gospel. It describes the origin and spread of Christian communities through the action of the Holy Spirit from the resurrection of Christ to the time when Paul was placed in custody in Rome in the early 60s.

Letters (Epistles)

These letters, many of which antedated the Gospels, were written in response to existential needs of the early Christian communities for doctrinal and moral instruction, disciplinary action, practical advice, and exhortation to true Christian living.

Pauline Letters

These letters, which comprise approximately one-fourth of the New Testament, are primary and monumental sources of the development of Christian theology. Several of them may not have had Paul as their actual author, but evidence of the Pauline tradition behind them is strong. The letters to the Colossians, Philippians, Ephesians and Philemon have been called the "Captivity Letters" because of a tradition that they were written while Paul was under house arrest or another form of detention.

Romans: Written about 57 probably from Corinth on the central significance of Christ and faith in him for salvation, and the relationship of Christianity to Judaism; the condition of mankind without Christ; justification and the Christian life; duties of Christians.

Corinthians 1: Written near the beginning of 57 from Ephesus to counteract factionalism and disorders, it covers community dissension, moral irregularities, marriage and celibacy, conduct at religious gatherings, the Eucharist, spiritual gifts (charisms) and their function in the Church, charity, the resurrection of the body.

Corinthians 2: Written later in the same year as 1 Cor., concerning Paul's defense of his apostolic ministry, and an appeal for a collection to aid poor Christians in Jerusalem.

Galatians: Written probably between 54 and 55 to counteract Judaizing opinions and efforts to undermine his authority, it asserts the divine origin of Paul's authority and doctrine, states that justification is not through Mosaic Law but through faith in Christ, insists on the practice of evangelical virtues, especially charity.

Ephesians: Written probably between 61 and 63, mainly on the Church as the Mystical Body of Christ.

Philippians: Written between 56 and 57 or 61 and 63 to warn the Philippians against enemies of their faith, to urge them to be faithful to their vocation and unity of belief, and to thank them for their kindness to him while he was being held in detention.

Colossians: Written probably while he was under house arrest in Rome from 61 to 63, to counteract the influence of self-appointed teachers who were watering down doctrine concerning Christ. It includes two highly important Christological passages, a warning against false teachers, and an instruction on the ideal Christian life.

Thessalonians 1 and 2: Written within a short time of each other probably in 51 from Corinth, mainly on doctrine concerning the Parousia, the second coming of Christ.

Timothy 1 and 2, Titus: Written between 65 and 67, or perhaps in the 70s, giving pastoral counsels to Timothy and Titus, who were in charge of churches in Ephesus and Crete, respectively. 1 Tm. emphasizes pastoral responsibility for preserving unity of doctrine; 2 Tm. describes Paul's imprisonment in Rome.

Philemon: A private letter written between 61 and 63 to a wealthy Colossian concerning a slave, Onesimus, who had escaped from him; Paul appealed for kind treatment of the man.

Hebrews: Dating from sometime between 70 and 96, a complex theological treatise on Christology, the priesthood and sacrifice of Christ, the New Covenant, and the pattern for Christian living. Critical opinion is divided as to whether it was addressed to Judaeo or Gentile Christians.

Catholic Letters

These seven letters have been called "catholic" because it was thought for some time, not altogether correctly, that they were not addressed to particular communities.

James: Written sometime before 62 in the spirit of Hebrew wisdom literature and the moralism of Tobit. An exhortation to practical Christian living, it is also noteworthy for the doctrine it states on good works and its citation regarding anointing of the sick.

Peter 1 and 2: The first letter may have been written between 64 and 67 or between 90 and 95; the second may date from 100 to 125. Addressed to Christians in Asia Minor, both are exhortations to perseverance in the life of faith despite trials and difficulties arising from pagan influences, isolation from other Christians and false teaching.

John 1: Written sometime in the 90s and addressed to Asian churches, its message is that God is made known to us in the Son and that fellowship with the Father is attained by living in the light, justice and love of the Son.

John 2: Written sometime in the 90s and addressed to a church in Asia, it commends the people for standing firm in the faith and urges them to perseverance.

John 3: Written sometime in the 90s, it appears to represent an effort to settle a jurisdictional dispute in one of the churches.

Jude: Written probably about 80, it is a brief treatise against erroneous teachings and practices opposed to law, authority and true Christian freedom.

Revelation

Written in the 90s along the lines of Johannine thought, it is a symbolic and apocalyptic treatment of things to come and of the struggle between the Church and evil combined with warning but hope and assurance to the Church regarding the coming of the Lord in glory.

INTERPRETATION OF THE BIBLE

According to the Dogmatic Constitution on Divine Revelation (Dei Verbum) issued by the Second Vatican Council, "the interpreter of Sacred Scripture, in order to see clearly what God wanted to communicate to us, should carefully investigate what meaning the sacred writers really intended, and what God wanted to manifest by means of their words" (No. 12).

Hermeneutics, Exegesis

This careful investigation proceeds in accordance with the rules of hermeneutics, the normative science of biblical interpretation and explanation. Hermeneutics in practice is called exegesis.

The principles of hermeneutics are derived from various disciplines and many factors which have to be considered in explaining the Bible and its parts. These include: the original languages and languages of translation of the sacred texts, through philology and linguistics; the quality of texts, through textual criticism; literary forms and genres, through literary and form criticism; cultural, historical, geographical and other conditions which influenced the writers, through related studies; facts and truths of salvation history; the truths and analogy of faith.

Distinctive to biblical hermeneutics, which differs in important respects from literary interpretation in general, is the premise that the Bible, though written by human authors, is the work of divine inspiration in which God reveals his plan for the salvation of men through historical events and persons, and especially through the Person and mission of Christ.

Textual, Form Criticism

Textual criticism is the study of biblical texts, which have been transmitted in copies several times removed from the original manuscripts, for the purpose of establishing the real state of the original texts. This purpose is served by comparison of existing copies; by application to the texts of the disciplines of philology and linguistics; by examination of related works of antiquity; by study of biblical citations in works of the Fathers of the Church and other authors; and by other means of literary study.

Since about 1920, the sayings of Christ have been a particular object of New Testament study, the purpose being to analyze the forms of expression used by the Evangelists in order to ascertain the words actually spoken by him.

Literary Criticism

Literary criticism aims to determine the origin and kinds of literary composition, called forms or genres, employed by the inspired authors. Such determinations are necessary for decision regarding the nature and purpose and, consequently, the meaning of biblical passages. Underlying these studies is the principle that the manner of writing was conditioned by the intention of *the* authors, the meaning they wanted to convey, and the then-contemporary literary style, mode or medium best adapted to carry their message — e.g., true history, quasi-historical narrative, poems, prayers, hymns, psalms, aphorisms, allegories, discourses. Understanding these media is necessary for the valid interpretation of their message.

Literal Sense

The key to all valid interpretation is the literal sense of biblical passages. Regarding this matter and the relevance to it of the studies and procedures described above, Pius XII wrote the following in the encyclical *Divino Afflante Spiritu:*

"What the literal sense of a passage is, is not always as obvious in the speeches and writings of ancient authors of the East as it is in the works of our own time. For what they wished to express is not to be determined by the rules of grammar and philology alone nor solely by the context; the interpreter must, as it were, go back wholly in spirit to those remote centuries of the East and with the aid of history, archeology, ethnology, and other sciences accurately determine what modes of writing, so to speak, the authors of that ancient period would be likely to use and in fact did use. In explaining the Sacred Scripture and in demonstrating and proving its immunity from all error [the Catholic interpreter] should make a prudent use of this means, determine to what extent the manner of expression or literary mode adopted by the sacred writer may lead to a correct and genuine interpretation; and let him be convinced that this part of his office cannot be neglected without serious detriment to Catholic exegesis."

The literal sense of the Bible is the meaning in the mind of and intended by the inspired writer of a book or passage of the Bible. This is determined by the application to texts of the rules of hermeneutics. It is not to be confused with word-for-word literalism.

Typical Sense

The typical sense is the meaning which a passage has not only in itself but also in reference to something else of which it is a type or foreshadowing. A clear example is the account of the Exodus of the Israelites: in its literal sense, it narrates the liberation of the Israelites from death and oppression in Egypt; in its typical sense, it foreshadowed the liberation of men from sin through the redemptive death and resurrection of Christ. The typical sense of this and other passages emerged in the working out of God's plan of salvation history. It did not have to be in the mind of the author of the original passage.

Accommodated Senses

Accommodated, allegorical and consequent senses are figurative and adaptive meanings given to books and passages of the Bible for moral and other purposes. Such interpretations involve the danger of stretching the literal sense beyond proper proportions. Hermeneutical principles require that interpretations like these respect the integrity of the literal sense of the passages in question.

In the Catholic view, the final word on questions of biblical interpretation belongs to the teaching authority of the Church. In other views, generally derived from basic principles stated by Martin Luther, John Calvin and other reformers, the primacy belongs to individual judgment acting in response to the inner testimony of the Holy Spirit, the edifying nature of biblical subject matter, the sublimity and simplicity of the message of salvation, the intensity with which Christ is proclaimed.

Biblical Studies

The first center for biblical studies, in some strict sense of the term, was the School of Alexandria, founded in the latter half of the second century. It was noted for allegorical exegesis. Literal interpretation was a hallmark of the School of Antioch.

St. Jerome, who produced the Vulgate, and St. Augustine, author of numerous commentaries, were the most important figures in biblical studies during the patristic period. By the time of the latter's death, the Old and New Testament canons had been stabilized. For some centuries afterwards, there was little or no progress in scriptural studies, although commentaries were written, collections were made of scriptural excerpts from the writings of the Fathers of the Church, and the systematic reading of Scripture became established as a feature of monastic life.

Advances were made in the 12th and 13th centuries with the introduction of new principles and methods of scriptural analysis stemming from renewed interest in Hebraic studies and the application of dialectics.

By the time of the Reformation, the Bible had become the first book set in movable type, and more than 100 vernacular editions were in use throughout Europe.

The Council of Trent

In the wake of the Reformation, the Council of Trent formally defined the Canon of the Bible; it also reasserted the authoritative role of tradition and the teaching authority of the Church as well as Scripture with respect to the rule of faith. In the heated atmosphere of the 16th and 17th centuries, the Bible was turned into a polemical weapon; Protestants used it to defend their doctrines, and Catholics countered with citations in support of the dogmas of the Church. One result of this state of affairs was a lack of substantial progress in biblical studies during the period.

Rationalists from the 18th century on and later Modernists denied the reality of the supernatural and doctrine concerning inspiration of the Bible, which they generally regarded as a strictly human production expressive of the religious sense and experience of mankind. In their hands, the tools of positive critical research became weapons for biblical subversion.

The defensive Catholic reaction to their work had the temporary effect of alienating scholars of the Church from solid advances in archeology, philology, history, textual and literary criticism.

Catholic Developments

Major influences in bringing about a change in Catholic attitude toward use of these disciplines in biblical studies were two papal encyclicals and two institutes of special study, the *École Biblique*, founded in Jerusalem in 1890, and the Pontifical Biblical Institute established in Rome in 1909. The encyclical *Providentissimus Deus*, issued by Leo XIII in 1893, marked an important breakthrough; in addition to defending the concept of divine inspiration and the formal inspiration of the Scriptures, it encouraged the study of allied and ancillary sciences and techniques for a more fruitful understanding of the sacred writings. The encyclical *Divino Afflante Spiritu*, by Pope Pius XII 50 years later, gave encouragement for the use of various forms of criticism as tools of biblical research. A significant addition to documents on the subject is "The Interpretation of the Bible in the Church," published by the Pontifical Biblical Commission in November, 1993. It presents an overview of approaches to the Bible and probes the question: "Which hermeneutical theory best enables a proper grasp of the profound reality of which Scripture speaks and its meaningful expression for people today?"

The documents encouraged the work of scholars and stimulated wide communication of the fruits of their study.

Great changes in the climate and direction of biblical studies have occurred in recent years. One of them has been an increase in cooperative effort among Catholic, Protestant, Orthodox and Jewish scholars. Their common investigation of the Dead Sea Scrolls is well-known. Also productive has been the collaboration of Catholics and Protestants in turning out various editions of the Bible.

The development and results of biblical studies in this century have directly and significantly affected all phases of the contemporary renewal movement in the Church. Their influence on theology, liturgy, catechetics, and preaching indicate the importance of their function in the life of the Church.

APOSTLES AND EVANGELISTS

The Apostles were the men selected, trained and commissioned by Christ to preach the Gospel, to baptize, to establish, direct and care for his Church as servants of God and stewards of his mysteries. They were the first bishops of the Church.

St. Matthew's Gospel lists the Apostles in this order: Peter, Andrew, James the Greater, John, Philip, Bartholomew, Thomas, Matthew, James the Less, Jude, Simon and Judas Iscariot. Matthias was elected to fill the place of Judas. Paul became an Apostle by a special call from Christ. Barnabas was called an Apostle.

Two of the Evangelists, John and Matthew, were Apostles. The other two, Luke and Mark, were closely associated with the apostolic college.

Andrew: Born in Bethsaida, brother of Peter, disciple of John the Baptist, a fisherman, the first Apostle

called; according to legend, preached the Gospel in northern Greece, Epirus and Scythia, and was martyred at Patras about 70; in art, is represented with an x-shaped cross, called St. Andrew's Cross; is honored as the patron of Russia and Scotland; Nov. 30.

Barnabas: Originally called Joseph but named Barnabas by the Apostles, among whom he is ranked because of his collaboration with Paul; a Jew of the Diaspora, born in Cyprus; a cousin of Mark and member of the Christian community at Jerusalem, influenced the Apostles to accept Paul, with whom he became a pioneer missionary outside Palestine and Syria, to Antioch, Cyprus and southern Asia Minor; legend says he was martyred in Cyprus during the Neronian persecution; June 11.

Bartholomew (Nathaniel): A friend of Philip; according to various traditions, preached the Gospel in

Ethiopia, India, Persia and Armenia, where he was martyred by being flayed and beheaded; in art, is depicted holding a knife, an instrument of his death; Aug. 24 (Roman Rite), Aug. 25 (Byzantine Rite).

James the Greater: A Galilean, son of Zebedee, brother of John (with whom he was called a "Son of Thunder"), a fisherman; with Peter and John, witnessed the raising of Jairus's daughter to life, the transfiguration, the agony of Jesus in the Garden of Gethsemani; first of the Apostles to die, by the sword in 44 during the rule of Herod Agrippa; there is doubt about a journey legend says he made to Spain and also about the authenticity of relics said to be his at Santiago de Compostela; in art, is depicted carrying a pilgrim's bell; July 25 (Roman Rite), Apr. 30 (Byzantine Rite).

James the Less: Son of Alphaeus, called "Less" because he was younger in age or shorter in stature than James the Greater; one of the Catholic Epistles bears his name; was stoned to death in 62 or thrown from the top of the temple in Jerusalem and clubbed to death in 66; in art, is depicted with a club or heavy staff; May 3 (Roman Rite), Oct. 9 (Byzantine Rite).

John: A Galilean, son of Zebedee, brother of James the Greater (with whom he was called a "Son of Thunder"), a fisherman, probably a disciple of John the Baptist, one of the Evangelists, called the "Beloved Disciple"; with Peter and James the Greater, witnessed the raising of Jairus's daughter to life, the transfiguration, the agony of Jesus in the Garden of Gethsemane; Mary was commended to his special care by Christ; the fourth Gospel, three Catholic Epistles and Revelation bear his name; according to various accounts, lived at Ephesus in Asia Minor for some time and died a natural death about 100; in art, is represented by an eagle, symbolic of the sublimity of the contents of his Gospel; Dec. 27 (Roman Rite), May 8 (Byzantine Rite).

Jude Thaddeus: One of the Catholic Epistles, the shortest, bears his name; various traditions say he preached the Gospel in Mesopotamia, Persia and elsewhere, and was martyred; in art, is depicted with a halberd, the instrument of his death; Oct. 28 (Roman Rite), June 19 (Byzantine Rite).

Luke: A Greek convert to the Christian community, called "our most dear physician" by Paul, of whom he was a missionary companion; author of the third Gospel and Acts of the Apostles; the place — Achaia, Bithynia, Egypt — and circumstances of his death are not certain; in art, is depicted as a man, a writer, or an ox (because his Gospel starts at the scene of temple sacrifice); Oct. 18.

Mark: A cousin of Barnabas and member of the first Christian community at Jerusalem; a missionary companion of Paul and Barnabas, then of Peter; author of the Gospel which bears his name; according to legend, founded the Church at Alexandria, was bishop there and was martyred in the streets of the city; in art, is depicted with his Gospel and a winged lion, symbolic of the voice of John the Baptist crying in the wilderness, at the beginning of his Gospel; Apr. 25.

Matthew: A Galilean, called Levi by Luke and John and the son of Alphaeus by Mark, a tax collector, one of the Evangelists; according to various accounts, preached the Gospel in Judea, Ethiopia, Persia and Parthia, and was martyred; in art, is depicted with a spear, the instrument of his death, and as a winged man in his role as Evangelist; Sept. 21 (Roman Rite), Nov. 16 (Byzantine Rite).

Matthias: A disciple of Jesus whom the faithful 11 Apostles chose to replace Judas before the Resurrection; uncertain traditions report that he preached the Gospel in Palestine, Cappadocia or Ethiopia; in art, is represented with a cross and a halberd, the instruments of his death as a martyr; May 14 (Roman Rite), Aug. 9 (Byzantine Rite).

Paul: Born at Tarsus, of the tribe of Benjamin, a Roman citizen; participated in the persecution of Christians until the time of his miraculous conversion on the way to Damascus; called by Christ, who revealed himself to him in a special way; became the Apostle of the Gentiles, among whom he did most of his preaching in the course of three major missionary journeys through areas north of Palestine, Cyprus, Asia Minor and Greece; 14 epistles bear his name; two years of imprisonment at Rome, following initial arrest in Jerusalem and confinement at Caesarea, ended with martyrdom, by beheading, outside the walls of the city in 64 or 67 during the Neronian persecution; in art, is depicted in various ways with St. Peter, with a sword, in the scene of his conversion; June 29 (with St. Peter), Jan. 25 (Conversion).

Peter: Simon, son of Jonah, born in Bethsaida, brother of Andrew, a fisherman; called Cephas or Peter by Christ who made him the chief of the Apostles and head of the Church as his vicar; named first in the listings of Apostles in the Synoptic Gospels and the Acts of the Apostles; with James the Greater and John, witnessed the raising of Jairus's daughter to life, the transfiguration, the agony of Jesus in the Garden of Gethsemane; was the first to preach the Gospel in and around Jerusalem and was the leader of the first Christian community there; established a local church in Antioch; presided over the Council of Jerusalem in 51; wrote two Catholic Epistles to the Christians in Asia Minor; established his see in Rome where he spent his last years and was martyred by crucifixion in 64 or 65 during the Neronian persecution; in art, is depicted carrying two keys, symbolic of his primacy in the Church; June 29 (with St. Paul), Feb. 22 (Chair of Peter).

Philip: Born in Bethsaida; according to legend, preached the Gospel in Phrygia where he suffered martyrdom by crucifixion; May 3 (Roman Rite), Nov. 14 (Byzantine Rite).

Simon: Called the Cananean or the Zealot; according to legend, preached in various places in the Middle East and suffered martyrdom by being sawed in two; in art, is depicted with a saw, the instrument of his death, or a book, symbolic of his zeal for the Law; Oct. 28 (Roman Rite), May 10 (Byzantine Rite).

Thomas (Didymus): Notable for his initial incredulity regarding the Resurrection and his subsequent forthright confession of the divinity of Christ risen from the dead; according to legend, preached the Gospel in places from the Caspian Sea to the Persian Gulf and eventually reached India where he was martyred near Madras; Thomas Christians trace their origin to him; in art, is depicted kneeling before the risen Christ, or with a carpenter's rule and square; feast, July 3 (Roman Rite), Oct. 6 (Byzantine Rite).

Judas: The Gospels record only a few facts about

Judas, the Apostle who betrayed Christ. The only non-Galilean among the Apostles, he was from Carioth, a town in southern Judah. He was keeper of the purse in the apostolic band. He was called a petty thief by John. He voiced dismay at the waste of money, which he said might have been spent for the poor, in connection with the anointing incident at Bethany. He took the initiative in arranging the betrayal of Christ. Afterwards, he confessed that he had betrayed an innocent man and cast into the Temple the money he had re-

ceived for that action. Of his death, Matthew says that he hanged himself; the Acts of the Apostles states that he swelled up and burst open; both reports deal more with the meaning than the manner of his death — the misery of the death of a sinner.

The consensus of speculation over the reason why Judas acted as he did in betraying Christ focuses on disillusionment and unwillingness to accept the concept of a suffering Messiah and personal suffering of his own as an Apostle.

APOSTOLIC FATHERS, FATHERS, DOCTORS OF THE CHURCH

The writers listed below were outstanding and authoritative witnesses to authentic Christian belief and practice, and played significant roles in giving them expression.

Apostolic Fathers

The Apostolic Fathers were Christian writers of the first and second centuries whose writings echo genuine apostolic teaching. Chief in importance are: St. Clement (d.c. 97), bishop of Rome and third successor of St. Peter in the papacy; St. Ignatius (50-c. 107), bishop of Antioch and second successor of St. Peter in that see, reputed to be a disciple of St. John; St. Polycarp (69-155), bishop of Smyrna and a disciple of St. John. The authors of the Didache and the Epistle of Barnabas are also numbered among the Apostolic Fathers.

Other early ecclesiastical writers included: St. Justin, martyr (100-165), of Asia Minor and Rome, a layman and apologist; St. Irenaeus (130-202), bishop of Lyons, who opposed Gnosticism; and St. Cyprian (210-258), bishop of Carthage, who opposed Novatianism.

Fathers and Doctors

The Fathers of the Church were theologians and writers of the first eight centuries who were outstanding for sanctity and learning. They were such authoritative witnesses to the belief and teaching of the Church that their unanimous acceptance of doctrines as divinely revealed has been regarded as evidence that such doctrines were so received by the Church in line with apostolic tradition and Sacred Scripture. Their unanimous rejection of doctrines branded them as heretical. Their writings, however, were not necessarily free of error in all respects.

The greatest of these Fathers were: Sts. Ambrose, Augustine, Jerome and Gregory the Great in the West; Sts. John Chrysostom, Basil the Great, Gregory of Naziansus and Athanasius in the East.

The Doctors of the Church were ecclesiastical writers of eminent learning and sanctity who have been given this title because of the great advantage the Church has derived from their work. Their writings, however, were not necessarily free of error in all respects.

Albert the Great, St. (c. 1200-1280): Born in Swabia, Germany; Dominican; bishop of Regensburg (1260-1262); wrote extensively on logic, natural sciences, ethics, metaphysics, Scripture, systematic theology; contributed to development of Scholasticism; teacher of St. Thomas Aquinas; canonized and proclaimed doctor, 1931; named patron of natural scien-

tists, 1941; called *Doctor Universalis, Doctor Expertus*; Nov. 15.

Alphonsus Liguori, St. (1696-1787): Born near Naples, Italy; bishop of Saint Agatha of the Goths (1762-1775); founder of the Redemptorists; in addition to his principal work, *Theologiae Moralis*, wrote on prayer, the spiritual life and doctrinal subjects in response to controversy; canonized, 1839; proclaimed doctor, 1871; named patron of confessors and moralists, 1950; Aug. 1.

Ambrose, St. (c. 340-397): Born in Trier, Germany; bishop of Milan (374-397); one of the strongest opponents of Arianism in the West; his homilies and other writings — on faith, the Holy Spirit, the Incarnation, the sacraments and other subjects — were pastoral and practical; influenced the development of a liturgy at Milan which was named for him; Father and Doctor of the Church; Dec. 7.

Anselm, St. (1033-1109): Born in Aosta, Piedmont, Italy; Benedictine; archbishop of Canterbury (1093-1109); in addition to his principal work, *Cur Deus Homo*, on the atonement and reconciliation of man with God through Christ, wrote about the existence and attributes of God and defended the *Filioque* explanation of the procession of the Holy Spirit from the Father and the Son; proclaimed doctor, 1720; called Father of Scholasticism; Apr. 21.

Anthony of Padua, St. (1195-1231): Born in Lisbon, Portugal; first theologian of the Franciscan Order; preacher; canonized, 1232; proclaimed doctor, 1946; called Evangelical Doctor; June 13.

Athanasius, St. (c. 297-373): Born in Alexandria, Egypt; bishop of Alexandria (328-373); participant in the Council of Nicaea I while still a deacon; dominant opponent of Arians whose errors regarding Christ he refuted in *Apology Against the Arians*, Discourses against the Arians and other works; Father and Doctor of the Church; called Father of Orthodoxy; May 2.

Augustine, St. (354-430): Born in Tagaste, North Africa; bishop of Hippo (395-430) after conversion from Manichaeism; works include the autobiographical and mystical *Confessions, City of God,* treatises on the Trinity, grace, passages of the Bible and doctrines called into question and denied by Manichaeans, Pelagians and Donatists; had strong and lasting influence on Christian theology and philosophy; Father and Doctor of the Church; called Doctor of Grace; Aug. 28.

Basil the Great, St. (c. 329-379): Born in Caesarea, Cappadocia, Asia Minor; bishop of Caesarea (370-379); wrote three books; *Contra Eunomium,* in refutation of Arian errors; a treatise on the Holy Spirit;

many homilies; and several rules for monastic life, on which he had lasting influence; Father and Doctor of the Church; called Father of Monasticism in the East; Jan. 2.

Bede the Venerable, St. (c. 673-735): Born in Northumberland, England; Benedictine; in addition to his principal work, *Ecclesiastical History* of the English Nation (covering the period 597-731), wrote scriptural commentaries; regarded as probably the most learned man in Western Europe of his time; called Father of English History; May 25.

Bernard of Clairvaux, St. (c. 1090-1153): Born near Dijon, France; abbot; monastic reformer, called the second founder of the Cistercian Order; mystical theologian with great influence on devotional life; opponent of the rationalism brought forward by Abélard and others; canonized, 1174; proclaimed doctor, 1830; called Mellifluous Doctor because of his eloquence; Aug. 20.

Bonaventure, St. (c. 1217-1274): Born near Viterbo, Italy; Franciscan; bishop of Albano (1273-1274); cardinal; wrote *Itinerarium Mentis in Deum, De Reductione Artium ad Theologiam, Breviloquium,* scriptural commentaries, additional mystical works affecting devotional life and a life of St. Francis of Assisi; canonized, 1482; proclaimed doctor, 1588; called Seraphic Doctor; July 15.

Catherine of Siena, St. (c. 1347-1380): Born in Siena, Italy; member of the Third Order of St. Dominic; mystic; authored a long series of letters, mainly concerning spiritual instruction and encouragement, to associates, and *Dialogue,* a spiritual testament in four treatises; was active in support of a crusade against the Turks and efforts to end war between papal forces and the Florentine allies; had great influence in inducing Gregory XI to return himself and the Curia to Rome in 1377, to end the Avignon period of the papacy; canonized, 1461; proclaimed the second woman doctor, Oct. 4, 1970; Apr. 29.

Cyril of Alexandria, St. (c. 376-444): Born in Egypt; bishop of Alexandria (412-444); wrote treatises on the Trinity, the Incarnation and other subjects, mostly in refutation of Nestorian errors; made key contributions to the development of Christology; presided at the Council of Ephesus, 431; proclaimed doctor, 1882; June 27.

Cyril of Jerusalem, St. (c. 315-386): Bishop of Jerusalem from 350; vigorous opponent of Arianism; principal work, Catecheses, a pre-baptismal explanation of the creed of Jerusalem; proclaimed doctor, 1882; Mar. 18.

Ephraem, St. (c. 306-373): Born in Nisibis, Mesopotamia; counteracted the spread of Gnostic and Arian errors with poems and hymns of his own composition; wrote also on the Eucharist and Mary; proclaimed doctor, 1920; called Deacon of Edessa and Harp of the Holy Spirit; June 9.

Francis de Sales, St. (1567-1622): Born in Savoy; bishop of Geneva (1602-1622); spiritual writer with strong influence on devotional life through treatises such as *Introduction to a Devout Life,* and *The Love of God;* canonized, 1665; proclaimed doctor, 1877; patron of Catholic writers and the Catholic press; Jan. 24.

Gregory Nazianzen, St. (c. 330-c. 390): Born in Arianzus, Cappadocia, Asia Minor; bishop of Constantinople (381-390); vigorous opponent of Arianism; in addition to five theological discourses on the Nicene Creed and the Trinity for which he is best known, wrote letters and poetry; Father and Doctor of the Church; called the Christian Demosthenes because of his eloquence and, in the Eastern Church, the Theologian; Jan. 2.

Gregory I, the Great, St. (c. 540-604): Born in Rome; pope (590-604): wrote many scriptural commentaries, a compendium of theology in the *Book of Morals* based on Job, Dialogues concerning the lives of saints, the immortality of the soul, death, purgatory, heaven and hell, and 14 books of letters; enforced papal supremacy and established the position of the pope vis-á-vis the emperor; worked for clerical and monastic reform and the observance of clerical celibacy; Father and Doctor of the Church; Sept. 3.

Hilary of Poitiers, St. (c. 315-368): Born in Poitiers, France; bishop of Poitiers (c. 353-368); wrote *De Synodis,* with the Arian controversy in mind, and *De Trinitate,* the first lengthy study of the doctrine in Latin; introduced Eastern theology to the West; contributed to the development of hymnology; proclaimed doctor, 1851; called the Athanasius of the West because of his vigorous defense of the divinity of Christ against Arians; Jan. 13.

Isidore of Seville, St. (c. 560-636): Born in Cartagena, Spain; bishop of Seville (c. 600-636); in addition to his principal work, *Etymologiae,* an encyclopedia of the knowledge of his day, wrote on theological and historical subjects; regarded as the most learned man of his time; proclaimed doctor, 1722; Apr. 4.

Jerome, St. (c. 343-420): Born in Stridon, Dalmatia; translated the Old Testament from Hebrew into Latin and revised the existing Latin translation of the New Testament to produce the Vulgate version of the Bible; wrote scriptural commentaries and treatises on matters of controversy; regarded as Father and Doctor of the Church from the eighth century; called Father of Biblical Science; Sept. 30.

John Chrysostom, St. (c. 347-407): Born in Antioch, Asia Minor; archbishop of Constantinople (398-407); wrote homilies, scriptural commentaries and letters of wide influence in addition to a classical treatise on the priesthood; proclaimed doctor by the Council of Chalcedon, 451; called the greatest of the Greek Fathers; named patron of preachers, 1909; called Golden-Mouthed because of his eloquence; Sept. 13.

John Damascene, St. (c. 675-c. 749): Born in Damascus, Syria; monk; wrote Fountain of Wisdom, a three-part work including a history of heresies and an exposition of the Christian faith, three discourses against the Iconoclasts, homilies on Mary, biblical commentaries and treatises on moral subjects; proclaimed doctor, 1890; called Golden Speaker because of his eloquence; Dec. 4.

John of the Cross, St. (1542-1591): Born in Old Castile, Spain; Carmelite; founder of Discalced Carmelites; one of the greatest mystical theologians, wrote *The Ascent of Mt. Carmel; The Dark Night of the Soul, The Spiritual Canticle, The Living Flame of Love;* canonized, 1726; proclaimed doctor, 1926; called Doctor of Mystical Theology; Dec. 14.

Lawrence of Brindisi, St. (1559-1619): Born in Brindisi, Italy; Franciscan (Capuchin); vigorous preacher of strong influence in the post-Reformation period; 15 tomes of collected works include scriptural commentaries, sermons, homilies and doctrinal writings; canonized, 1881; proclaimed doctor, 1959; July 21.

Leo I, the Great, St. (c. 400-461): Born in Tuscany, Italy; pope (440-461); wrote the *Tome* of Leo, to explain doctrine concerning the two natures and one Person of Christ, against the background of the Nestorian and Monophysite heresies; other works included sermons, letters and writings against the errors of Manichaeism and Pelagianism; was instrumental in dissuading Attila from sacking Rome in 452; proclaimed doctor, 1574; Nov. 10.

Peter Canisius, St. (1521-1597): Born in Nijmegen, Holland; Jesuit; wrote popular expositions of the Catholic faith in several catechisms which were widely circulated in 20 editions in his lifetime alone; was one of the moving figures in the Counter-Reformation period, especially in southern and western Germany; canonized and proclaimed doctor, 1925; Dec. 21.

Peter Chrysologus, St. (c. 400-450): Born in Imola, Italy; served as archbishop of Ravenna (c. 433-450); his sermons and writings, many of which were designed to counteract Monophysitism, were pastoral and practical; proclaimed doctor, 1729; July 30.

Peter Damian, St. (1007-1072): Born in Ravenna, Italy; Benedictine; cardinal; his writings and sermons, many of which concerned ecclesiastical and clerical reform, were pastoral and practical; proclaimed doctor, 1828; Feb. 21.

Robert Bellarmine, St. (1542-1621): Born in Tuscany, Italy; Jesuit; archbishop of Capua (1602-1605); wrote *Controversies*, a three-volume exposition of doctrine under attack during and after the Reformation, two catechisms and the spiritual work, *The Art of Dying Well*; was an authority on ecclesiology and Church-state relations; canonized, 1930; proclaimed doctor, 1931; Sept. 17.

Teresa of Jesus (Ávila), St. (1515-1582): Born in Ávila, Spain; entered the Carmelite Order, 1535; in the early 1560s, initiated a primitive Carmelite reform which greatly influenced men and women religious, especially in Spain; wrote extensively on spiritual and mystical subjects; principal works included her *Autobiography, Way of Perfection, The Interior Castle, Meditations on the Canticle, The Foundations, Visitation of the Discalced Nuns*; canonized, 1622; proclaimed first woman doctor, Sept. 27, 1970; Oct. 15.

Thérèse of Lisieux, St. (1873-1897): Born in Alençon, Normandy, France; entered the Carmelites at Lisieux in 1888, lived for only nine more years, dying on September 30, 1897 from tuberculosis. Trusting completely in God, a path she described as the "little way," she lived a seemingly ordinary life of a nun, but her spiritual advancement was such that her superiors instructed her to write an autobiography in 1895 (*The Story of a Soul*). One of the most popular and respected saints throughout the 20th century, she was canonized on May 17, 1925. Pope John Paul II declared her the third woman doctor on Oct. 20, 1997 in the letter *Divini amoris scientia*; Oct. 1.

Thomas Aquinas, St. (1225-1274): Born near Naples, Italy; Dominican; teacher and writer on virtually the whole range of philosophy and theology; principal works were *Summa contra Gentiles*, a manual and systematic defense of Christian doctrine, and *Summa Theologiae*, a new (at that time) exposition of theology on philosophical principles; canonized, 1323; proclaimed doctor, 1567; called *Doctor Communis, Doctor Angelicus*, the Great Synthesizer because of the way in which he related faith and reason, theology and philosophy (especially that of Aristotle), and systematized the presentation of Christian doctrine; named patron of Catholic schools and education, 1880; Jan. 28.

CREEDS

Creeds are formal and official statements of Christian doctrine. As summaries of the principal truths of faith, they are standards of orthodoxy and are useful for instructional purposes, for actual profession of the faith and for expression of the faith in the liturgy.

The classical creeds are the Apostles' Creed and the Creed of Nicaea-Constantinople. Two others are the Athanasian Creed and the Creed of Pius IV.

Apostles' Creed

Text: *I believe in God, the Father almighty, Creator of heaven and earth.*

And in Jesus Christ, his only Son, our Lord; who was conceived by the Holy Spirit, born of the Virgin Mary, suffered under Pontius Pilate, was crucified, died, and was buried. He descended into hell; the third day he arose again from the dead; he ascended into heaven, sits at the right hand of God, the Father almighty; from thence he shall come to judge the living and the dead.

I believe in the Holy Spirit, the holy Catholic Church, the communion of saints, the forgiveness of sins, the resurrection of the body, and life everlasting. Amen.

Background: The Apostles' Creed reflects the teaching of the Apostles but is not of apostolic origin. It probably originated in the second century as a rudimentary formula of faith professed by catechumens before the reception of baptism. Baptismal creeds in fourth-century use at Rome and elsewhere in the West closely resembled the present text, which was quoted in a handbook of Christian doctrine written between 710 and 724. This text was in wide use throughout the West by the ninth century. The Apostles' Creed is common to all Christian confessional churches in the West, but is not used in Eastern Churches.

Nicene Creed

The following translation of the Latin text of the creed was prepared by the International Committee on English in the Liturgy.

Text: *We believe in one God, the Father, the Almighty, maker of heaven and earth, of all that is seen and unseen.*

We believe in one Lord, Jesus Christ, the only Son of God, eternally begotten of the Father, God from God, Light from Light, true God from true God, begotten, not made, one in Being with the Father.

Through him all things were made. For us men and for our salvation he came down from heaven: by the power of the Holy Spirit he was born of the Virgin Mary, and became man. For our sake he was crucified under Pontius Pilate; he suffered, died, and was buried. On the third day he rose again in fulfillment of the Scriptures; he ascended into heaven and is seated at the right hand of the Father. He will come again in glory to judge the living and the dead, and his kingdom will have no end.

We believe in the Holy Spirit, the Lord, the giver of life, who proceeds from the Father and the Son. With the Father and the Son he is worshipped and glorified. He has spoken through the prophets.

We believe in one holy catholic and apostolic Church. We acknowledge one baptism for the forgiveness of sins. We look for the resurrection of the dead, and the life of the world to come. Amen.

Background: The Nicene Creed (Creed of Nicaea-Constantinople) consists of elements of doctrine contained in an early baptismal creed of Jerusalem and enactments of the Council of Nicaea (325) and the Council of Constantinople (381).

Its strong trinitarian content reflects the doctrinal errors, especially of Arianism, it served to counteract. Theologically, it is much more sophisticated than the Apostles' Creed.

Since late in the fifth century, the Nicene Creed has been the only creed in liturgical use in the Eastern Churches. The Western Church adopted it for liturgical use by the end of the eighth century.

The Athanasian Creed

The Athanasian Creed, which has a unique structure, is a two-part summary of doctrine concerning the Trinity and the Incarnation-Redemption bracketed at the beginning and end with the statement that belief in the cited truths is necessary for salvation; it also contains a number of anathemas or condemnatory clauses regarding doctrinal errors. Although attributed to St. Athanasius, it was probably written after his death, between 381 and 428, and may have been authored by St. Ambrose. It is not accepted in the East; in the West, it formerly had place in the Roman-Rite Liturgy of the Hours and in the liturgy for the Solemnity of the Holy Trinity.

Creed of Pius IV

The Creed of Pius IV, also called the Profession of Faith of the Council of Trent, was promulgated in the bull *Injunctum Nobis*, Nov. 13, 1564. It is a summary of doctrine defined by the council concerning: Scripture and tradition, original sin and justification, the Mass and sacraments, veneration of the saints, indulgences, the primacy of the See of Rome. It was slightly modified in 1887 to include doctrinal formulations of the First Vatican Council.

CHRISTIAN MORALITY

By Fr. Alfred McBride, O.Praem.

"Incorporated into Christ by Baptism, Christians are 'dead to sin and alive in Christ Jesus . . . ' " (Rom 6:11).

CHRISTIAN MORALITY IS LIFE IN CHRIST

The third part of the *Catechism* focuses on Christian morality. After the creed as faith professed, and sacraments as faith celebrated, the *Catechism* turns our attention to the faith lived. It deals with this issue in two major sections. The first section establishes the context for Christian morality. The second section analyzes the ten commandments. This approach preserves the *Catechism's* resolute insistence on the primacy of God's initiative through Revelation, salvation, and grace followed by our human response in faith, celebration, and Christian witness. Hence morality does not begin with the rules but with the call to life in Christ and the Holy Spirit. Covenant love comes first, then the response of Christian affection in the life of the commandments. This saves us both from legalism and from piety without practical witness.

The following excerpt from the *Catechism of the Catholic Church* sets the vision for the Christian moral life:

LIFE IN CHRIST

1691 "Christian, recognize your dignity and, now that you share in God's own nature, do not return to your former base condition by sinning. Remember who is your head and of whose body you are a member. Never forget that you have been rescued from the power of darkness and brought into the light of the Kingdom of God."[1]

1692 The Symbol of the faith confesses the greatness of God's gifts to man in his work of creation, and even more in redemption and sanctification. What faith confesses, the sacraments communicate: by the sacraments of rebirth, Christians have become "children of God,"[2] "partakers of the divine nature."[3] Coming to see in the faith their new dignity, Christians are called to lead henceforth a life "worthy of the gospel of Christ."[4] They are made capable of doing so by the grace of Christ and the gifts of his Spirit, which they receive through the sacraments and through prayer.

1693 Christ Jesus always did what was pleasing to the Father,[5] and always lived in perfect communion with him. Likewise Christ's disciples are invited to live in the sight of the Father "who sees in secret,"[6] in order to become "perfect as your heavenly Father is perfect."[7]

1694 Incorporated into Christ by Baptism, Christians are "dead to sin and alive to God in Christ Jesus" and so participate in the life of the Risen Lord.[8] Following Christ and united with him,[9] Christians can strive to be "imitators of God as beloved children, and walk in love"[10] by conforming their thoughts, words and actions to the "mind . . . which is yours in Christ Jesus,"[11] and by following his example.[12]

1695 "Justified in the name of the Lord Jesus Christ and in the Spirit of our God,"[13] "sanctified . . . [and] called to be saints,"[14] Christians have become the temple of the Holy Spirit.[15] This "Spirit of the Son" teaches them to pray to the Father[16] and, having become their life, prompts them to act so as to bear "the fruit of the Spirit"[17] by charity in action. Healing the wounds of sin, the Holy Spirit renews us interiorly through a spiritual transformation.[18] He enlightens and strengthens us to live as "children of light" through "all that is good and right and true."[19]

1696 The way of Christ "leads to life"; a contrary way "leads to destruction."[20] The Gospel parable of the two ways remains ever present in the catechesis of the Church; it shows the importance of moral decisions for our salvation: "There are two ways, the one of life, the other of death; but between the two, there is a great difference."[21]

1697 Catechesis has to reveal in all clarity the joy and the demands of the way of Christ.[22] Catechesis for the "newness of life"[23] in him should be:

a catechesis of the Holy Spirit, the interior Master of life according to Christ, a gentle guest and friend who inspires, guides, corrects, and strengthens this life;

a catechesis of grace, for it is by grace that we are saved and again it is by grace that our works can bear fruit for eternal life;

a catechesis of the beatitudes, for the way of Christ is summed up in the beatitudes, the only path that leads to the eternal beatitude for which the human heart longs;

a catechesis of sin and forgiveness, for unless man acknowledges that he is a sinner he cannot know the truth about himself, which is a condition for acting justly; and without the offer of forgiveness he would not be able to bear this truth;

a catechesis of the human virtues which causes one to grasp the beauty and attraction of right dispositions towards goodness;

a catechesis of the Christian virtues of faith, hope, and charity, generously inspired by the example of the saints; -a catechesis of the twofold commandment of charity set forth in the Decalogue;

an ecclesial catechesis, for it is through the manifold exchanges of "spiritual goods" in the "communion of saints" that Christian life can grow, develop, and be communicated.

1698 The first and last point of reference of this catechesis will always be Jesus Christ himself, who is "the way, and the truth, and the life."[24] It is by looking to him in faith that Christ's faithful can hope that he himself fulfills his promises in them, and that, by loving him with the same love with which he has loved them, they may perform works in keeping with their dignity: "I ask you to consider that our Lord Jesus Christ is your true head, and that you are one of his members. He belongs to you as the head belongs to its members; all that is his is yours: his spirit, his heart, his body and soul, and all his faculties. You must make use of all these as of your own, to serve, praise, love, and glorify God. You belong to him, as members belong to their head. And so he longs for you to use all that is in you, as if it were his own, for the service and glory of the Father."[25] "For to me, to live is Christ."[26]

FOOTNOTES

1. *St. Leo the Great, Sermo 22 in nat. Dom. 3: PL 54, 192C.* 2. *Jn 1:12; 1 Jn 3:1.* 3. *2 Pet 1:4.* 4. *Phil 1:27.* 5. *Cf. Jn 8:29.* 6. *Mt 6:6.* 7. *Mt 5:48.* 8, *Rom 6:11 and cf. 6:5; cf. Col 2:12.* 9. *Cf. Jn 15:5.* 10. *Eph 5:1-2.* 11. *Phil 2:5.* 12. *Cf. Jn 13:12-16.* 13. *1 Cor 6:11.* 14. *1 Cor 1:2.* 15. *Cf. 1 Cor 6:19.* 16. *Cf. Gal 4:6.* 17. *Gal 5:22, 25.* 18. *Cf. Eph 4:23.* 19. *Eph 5:8, 9.* 20. *Mt 7:13; cf. Deut 30: 15-20.* 21. *Didache 1, 1: SCh 248, 140.* 22 .*Cf. John Paul II, CT 29.* 23. *Rom 6:4.* 24. *Jn 14:6.* 25. *St. John Eudes, Tract. de admirabili corde Jesu, 1, 5.* 26. *Phil 1:21.*

THE TEN COMMANDMENTS

Any discussions of the commandments should begin with the scene at Sinai where God gave them to us. Read Exodus 19:3-6; 20:1-17. The first event is a covenant experience. God tells Moses how much he has loved the Israelites, is delivering them from slavery by "raising them up on eagles' wings," and is bringing them to freedom. God then offers them a binding covenant of love. He will be their only God and they will be his chosen people. It's like a marriage experience, an exchange of vows between God and Israel.

The next section shows God telling them how to live out the love they have pledged. He gives them the Ten Commandments as the means to live the covenant, to express the love they have promised. The *Catechism* points out that the Ten Commandments are privileged expressions of the natural law, made known to us by reason as well as Divine Revelation. We are obliged in obedience to observe these laws of love, both in serious and light matters. Love is in the details as well as the large matters. We must remember that what God has commanded, he makes possible by his grace.

Jesus set the tone for understanding the importance of the commandments. When a rich young man came to him and asked him what he should do to enter eternal life, Jesus replied, "if you wish to enter into life, keep the commandments" (Mt 19:17). In another case, someone asked him which were the greatest commandments, Jesus replied, "you shall love the Lord, your God, with all your heart, with all your soul, and with all your mind. This is the greatest and first commandment. The second is like it: You shall love your neighbor as yourself" (Mt 22:37-39). The first three commandments deal with Christ's call to God with all our being. The last seven commandments show us how to love our neighbors as we love ourselves.

The following excerpt from the *Catechism of the Catholic Church* shows how Jesus taught the importance of the Ten Commandments:

"Teacher, what must I do . . .?"

2052 "Teacher, what good deed must I do, to have eternal life?" To the young man who asked this question, Jesus answers first by invoking the necessity to recognize God as the "One there is who is good," as the supreme Good and the source of all good. Then Jesus tells him: "If you would enter life, keep the commandments." And he cites for his questioner the precepts that concern love of neighbor: "You shall not kill, You shall not commit adultery, You shall not steal, You shall not bear false witness, Honor your father and mother." Finally Jesus sums up these commandments positively: "You shall love your neighbor as yourself."[1]

2053 To this first reply Jesus adds a second: "If you would be perfect, go, sell what you possess and give to the poor, and you will have treasure in heaven; and come, follow me."[2] This reply does not do away with the first: following Jesus Christ involves keeping the

Commandments. The Law has not been abolished,[3] but rather man is invited to rediscover it in the person of his Master who is its perfect fulfillment. In the three synoptic Gospels, Jesus' call to the rich young man to follow him, in the obedience of a disciple and in the observance of the Commandments, is joined to the call to poverty and chastity.[4] The evangelical counsels are inseparable from the Commandments.

2054 Jesus acknowledged the Ten Commandments, but he also showed the power of the Spirit at work in their letter. He preached a "righteousness [which] exceeds that of the scribes and Pharisees"[5] as well as that of the Gentiles.[6] He unfolded all the demands of the Commandments. "You have heard that it was said to the men of old, 'You shall not kill.' . . . But I say to you that every one who is angry with his brother shall be liable to judgment."[7]

2055 When someone asks him, "Which commandment in the Law is the greatest?"[8] Jesus replies: "You shall love the Lord your God with all your heart, and with all your soul, and with all your mind. This is the greatest and first commandment. And a second is like it: You shall love your neighbor as yourself. On these two commandments hang all the Law and the prophets."[9] The Decalogue must be interpreted in light of this twofold yet single commandment of love, he fullness of the Law: "The commandments: 'You shall not commit adultery, You shall not kill, You shall not steal, You shall not covet,' and any other commandment, are summed up in this sentence: You shall love your neighbor as yourself.' Love does no wrong to a neighbor; therefore love is the fulfilling of the law."[10]

FOOTNOTES

1. *Mt 19:16-19.* 2. *Mt 19:21.* 3. *Cf. Mt 5:17.* 4. *Cf. Mt 19:6-12, 21, 23-29.* 5. *Mt 5:20.* 6.*Cf. Mt 5:46-47.* 7. *Mt 5:21-22.* 8. *Mt 22:36.* 9. *Mt 22:37-40; cf. Deut 6:5; Lev 19:18.* 10. *Rom 13:9-10.*

In the traditional Catholic enumeration and according to Dt. 5:6-21, the Commandments are:

1. "I, the Lord, am your God You shall not have other gods besides me. You shall not carve idols."
2. "You shall not take the name of the Lord, your God, in vain."
3. "Take care to keep holy the Sabbath day."
4. "Honor your father and your mother."
5. "You shall not kill."
6. "You shall not commit adultery."
7. "You shall not steal."
8. "You shall not bear dishonest witness against your neighbor."
9. "You shall not covet your neighbor's wife."
10. "You shall not desire your neighbor's house or field, nor his male or female slave, nor his ox or ass,

nor anything that belongs to him" (summarily, his goods).

Another version of the Commandments, substantially the same, is given in Ex. 20:1-17.

The traditional enumeration of the Commandments in Protestant usage differs from the above. Thus: two commandments are made of the first, as above; the third and fourth are equivalent to the second and third, as above, and so on; and the 10th includes the ninth and 10th, as above.

Love of God and Neighbor

The first three of the commandments deal directly with man's relations with God, viz.: acknowledgment of one true God and the rejection of false gods and idols; honor due to God and his name; observance of the Sabbath as the Lord's day.

The rest cover interpersonal relationships, viz.: obedience due to parents and, logically, to other persons in authority, and the obligations of parents to children and of persons in authority to those under their care; respect for life and physical integrity; fidelity in marriage, and chastity; justice and rights; truth; internal respect for faithfulness in marriage, chastity, and the goods of others.

Perfection in Christian Life

The moral obligations of the Ten Commandments are complemented by others flowing from the twofold law of love, the whole substance and pattern of Christ's teaching, and everything implied in full and active membership and participation in the community of salvation formed by Christ in his Church. Some of these matters are covered in other sections of the *Almanac* under appropriate headings.

Precepts of the Church

The purpose of the precepts of the Church, according to the *Catechism of the Catholic Church*, is "to guarantee to the faithful the indispensable minimum in the spirit of prayer and moral effort, in the growth and love of God and neighbor" (No. 2041).

1. Attendance at Mass on Sundays and holy days of obligation. (Observance of Sundays and holy days of obligation involves refraining from work that hinders the worship due to God.)
2. Confession of sins at least once a year. (Not required by the precept in the absence of serious sin.)
3. Reception of the Eucharist at least during the Easter season (in the U.S., from the first Sunday of Lent to Trinity Sunday).
4. Keep holy the holy days of obligation.
5. Observance of specified days of fasting and abstinence.

There is also an obligation to provide for the material needs of the Church.

CATHOLIC MORAL TEACHINGS OF POPE JOHN PAUL II

On Aug. 6, 1993, Pope John Paul II published his tenth encyclical, Veritatis Splendor (The Splendor of the Truth) *regarding the fundamental truths of the Church's moral teachings. On Mar. 25, 1995, he published his eleventh encyclical,* Evangelium Vitae (The Gospel of Life), *concerning the value and inviolability of human life. The following material is adapted*

from The Encyclicals of John Paul II, *with the kind permission of Rev. J. Michael Miller, C.S.B.*

Veritatis Splendor (The Splendor of the Truth)

On Aug. 6, 1993, John Paul II signed his tenth encyclical, *Veritatis Splendor,* regarding certain fundamental truths of the Church's moral teaching.[1] Undoubtedly it is the pope's most complex and most discussed document. Since its publication, the encyclical has generated a great deal of comment in the media and among theologians. This is not surprising, since *Veritatis Splendor* is the first-ever papal document on the theological and philosophical foundations of Catholic moral teaching. In this encyclical the pope affirms that divine revelation contains "a specific and determined moral content, universally valid and permanent" (§37.1), which the Magisterium has the competence to interpret and teach.

Six years later, in the apostolic letter *Spiritus Domini* (1987), John Paul had publicly announced his intention to publish a document which would treat "more fully and more deeply the issues regarding the very foundations of moral theology" (§5.1). For several reasons the encyclical's preparation took longer than was first anticipated. First, the pope widely consulted bishops and theologians throughout the world, and various drafts were drawn up. Second, he thought that it was fitting for the encyclical "to be preceded by the *Catechism of the Catholic Church*, which contains a complete and systematic exposition of Christian moral teaching" (§5.3). The *Catechism*, published in 1992, gives a full presentation of the Church's moral doctrine, including that on particular questions, and expounds it in a positive way. *Veritatis Splendor*, on the other hand, limits itself to dealing with the fundamental principles underlying all moral teaching.

But why does John Paul think that an encyclical on moral issues will serve the Church and the world on the threshold of the third millennium? According to him, reflection on the ethical implications of Christian faith, lived from the beginning as the "way" (Acts 22:4), belongs to the full proclamation of the Gospel. Moreover, he is convinced that society is in the throes of a *"crisis of truth"* (§32.2). This crisis has the "most serious implications for the moral life of the faithful and for communion in the Church, as well as for a just and fraternal social life" (§5.2).

The dechristianization of many cultures involves not only a loss of faith but also *"a decline or obscuring of the moral sense"* (§106.2). This new moral situation brings with it "the *confusion between good and evil*, which makes it impossible to build up and to preserve the moral order" (§93.1). The ethical bewilderment of some Catholics has led to "the spread of numerous doubts and objections of a human and psychological, social and cultural, religious and even properly theological nature, with regard to the Church's moral teachings" (§4.2). In an increasingly secular world, believers are "making judgments and decisions [that] often appear extraneous or even contrary to those of the Gospel" (§88.2). Moreover, dissent from Catholic moral teaching often entails "an overall and systematic calling into question of traditional moral doctrine" (§4.2). Thus, as a service to the ethical and spiritual welfare of individuals and cultures, John Paul addresses the basic moral principles handed down by the Christian Tradition.

In order to meet his goal, the pope responds in a constructive way to the contemporary moral crisis by proclaiming "the splendor of the truth." When he announced the forthcoming publication of *Veritatis Splendor*, he described the encyclical's purpose: "It reaffirms the dignity of the human person, created in

God's image, and proposes anew the genuine concept of human freedom, showing its essential and constitutive relationship with the truth in accordance with Christ's words: 'The truth will make you free!' (Jn 8:32)."[2] On another occasion, John Paul said that he intended the encyclical to be "a proclamation of truth and a hymn to freedom: values felt strongly by contemporary man and deeply respected by the Church."[3] His primary aim, then, is not to censure specific dissident moral opinions but to proclaim that Christ is "the true and final answer to the problem of morality" (§85).

John Paul sets several specific objectives for the encyclical. First, he wishes *"to reflect on the whole of the Church's moral teaching"*, with the precise goal of recalling certain fundamental truths of Catholic doctrine which, in the present circumstances, risk being distorted or denied" (§4.2, cf. §30.1). Second, he aims to show the faithful "the inviting splendor of that truth which is Jesus Christ himself" (§83.2). Christ alone is the answer to humanity's questions, "the only response fully capable of satisfying the desire of the human heart" (§7.1). Third, if the present crisis is to be successfully resolved, the Magisterium must authoritatively discern *"interpretations of Christian morality which are not consistent with 'sound teaching'* (2 Tim 4:3)" (§29.4, cf. §27.4). This pastoral discernment of the pope and bishops is necessary as a way of assuring *"the right of the faithful* to receive Catholic doctrine in its purity and integrity" (§113.2).

The pope addresses *Veritatis Splendor* specifically to his brother bishops. He intends them to be the first, but not exclusive, recipients of the encyclical. John Paul reminds them of their responsibility to safeguard and find "ever new ways of speaking with love and mercy" about *"the path of the moral life"* (§3.1,2).

John Paul II's training in ethics and moral theology is clearly evident in *Veritatis Splendor*. The encyclical's exposition is sometimes highly technical, especially in its analyses and responses to opinions contrary to Church teaching. While some commentators have voiced disagreement about the accuracy of the pope's descriptions of the ethical positions with which he disagrees, they respect his desire to be fair-minded. As we shall see, whenever John Paul deals with an opinion he disagrees with, he first takes great pains to point out what is positive in the view. Only after doing this does he then examine its weaknesses. When unmasking theological and philosophical ideas incompatible with revealed truth, he scrupulously avoids imposing "any particular theological system, still less a philosophical one" (§29.4).

Throughout the encyclical the pope repeatedly draws inspiration from the Bible. Chapter one, structured around the encounter of Jesus with the rich young man (Mt 19:16-21), establishes a biblical foundation for fundamental moral principles. In this chapter the pope wishes to apply the theological method proposed by the Second Vatican Council: "Sacred Scripture remains the living and fruitful source of the Church's moral doctrine" (§28.2, cf. §5.3). Chapter two, on the other hand, uses Scripture chiefly to corroborate positions advanced on the basis of the natural moral law. The beginning of chapter three returns to a more biblical approach; it discusses discipleship in terms of the Paschal Mystery and of martyrdom as the supreme expression of following Christ.

More so than in his other encyclicals, in *Veritatis Splendor* John Paul relies considerably on the teaching of Saint Thomas Aquinas, referring to him directly at least 20 times, and on the teaching of Saint Augustine, citing him 16 times. The pope also mines extensively the documents of Vatican II, especially *Gaudium et Spes,* which he cites more than 25 times. Except for one reference to Saint Alphonsus Liguori and a single direct citation of John Henry Newman, the pope mentions no moral philosopher or theologian after the Middle Ages.

FOOTNOTES

1. *Acta Apostolicae Sedis,* 85 (1993), 1133-1228.
2. Angelus, October 3, 1993, *L'Osservatore Romano,* 40 (1993), 1. 3. Angelus, October 17, 1993, *L'Osservatore Romano,* 42 (1993), 1.

Evangelium Vitae (The Gospel of Life)

"The *Gospel of life* is at the heart of Jesus' message" (§1.1). With these words Pope John Paul II begins his eleventh encyclical, *Evangelium Vitae,* published on March 25, 1995.[1] He aptly chose the feast of the Annunciation, which celebrates Mary's welcoming of the Son of God who took flesh in her womb, to issue a document dedicated to the value and inviolability of human life. By taking up the cause of the "great multitude of weak and defenseless human beings" (§5.4), especially unborn children and those at the end of life, the pope continues the defense of human dignity dealt with in his three social encyclicals. *Evangelium Vitae* is an anguished and vigorous response to *"scientifically and systematically programmed threats"* against life (§17.2), assaults which have repercussions on Church teaching, touching upon "the core of her faith in the redemptive Incarnation of the Son of God" (§3.1).

For John Paul, the cause of life is the cause of the Gospel entrusted to the Church, which is duty-bound to raise her voice in the defense of life. His encyclical is a "pressing appeal addressed to each and every person, in the name of God: *respect, protect, love and serve life, every human life!"* (§5.5).

Preparations for the encyclical began in April 1991, when the pope called a special meeting in Rome of the College of Cardinals to discuss current threats to human life. After their deliberations, the cardinals asked him "to reaffirm with the authority of the Successor of Peter the value of human life and its inviolability" (§5.1). As a first response to their request, the pope wrote a personal letter to every bishop, seeking contributions to the planned document. They replied with valuable suggestions, and he incorporated many of their proposals into the encyclical. *Evangelium Vitae,* then, is the fruit of genuine epis-copal collegiality. By taking an active part in its preparation, the bishops "bore witness to their unanimous desire to share in the doctrinal and pastoral mission of the Church with regard to the *Gospel of life"* (§5.2).

Unlike *Veritatis Splendor,* which was directed primarily to bishops, John Paul intends *Evangelium Vitae* to be read also by the lay faithful, indeed by all people of good will. Concern for the sacredness of human life is not just a matter for Catholics. "The value at stake," writes the pope, "is one which every human being can grasp by the light of reason" (§101.2). The essential truths of the Gospel of life "are written in the heart of every man and woman," echoing in every human conscience "from the time of creation itself" (§29.3). He insists that anyone who is sincerely open to truth and goodness can discover "the sacred value of human life from its very beginning until its end, and can affirm the right of every human being to have this primary good respected to the highest degree" (§2.2).

The encyclical's style is typically Wojtylan. It intersperses rigorous analysis with prayers and exhortations. As can be seen from the more than three hundred biblical quotations and references, Scripture accompanies the pope's presentation from start to finish, giving *Evangelium Vitae* an inspirational tone and familiar style. He also relies heavily on the Church Fathers. The eighteen patristic quotations that appear in the encyclical reinforce the truths that God is the origin of life, that human beings share in divine life, and that Jesus gave his life so that others might live. As is customary, John Paul frequently cites the documents of the Second Vatican Council – here, more than twenty-five times. He also makes use of the *Catechism of the Catholic Church,* citing it on ten occasions.

Of particular significance in *Evangelium Vitae* are the pope's three authoritative doctrinal pronouncements: on the direct and voluntary killing of innocent human life (cf. §57.4), on abortion (cf. §62.3), and on euthanasia (cf. §65.3). In each of these formal statements John Paul recalls, through his ordinary magisterium, that a specific proposition is taught infallibly by the ordinary and universal Magisterium of the College of Bishops in communion with the Successor of Peter. He does not, therefore, call upon the charism which belongs to the Petrine ministry to teach infallibly, as this was defined at the First Vatican Council (1870). Rather, the pope "confirms" or "declares" (as in the case of abortion) a doctrine already taught by the bishops as belonging to the Catholic faith. Thus, there is nothing "new" in the Pope's affirmations, but merely the reiteration of teaching about which a consensus exists in the Episcopal College.

FOOTNOTES

1. *Acta Apostolicae Sedis,* 87 (1995), 401-522.

CATHOLIC SOCIAL DOCTRINE

Nature of the Doctrine

Writing in *Christianity and Social Progress,* Pope John XXIII made the following statement about the nature and scope of the Church's social doctrine as stated in the encyclicals in particular and related writings in general:

"What the Catholic Church teaches and declares regarding the social life and relationships of men is beyond question for all time valid.

"The cardinal point of this teaching is that individual men are necessarily the foundation, cause, and end of all social institutions insofar as they are social by nature, and raised to an order of existence that transcends and subdues nature.

"Beginning with this very basic principle whereby the dignity of the human person is affirmed and defended, Holy Church — especially during the last century and with the assistance of learned priests and laymen, specialists in the field — has arrived at clear social teachings whereby the mutual relationships of men are ordered. Taking general norms into account, these principles are in accord with the nature of things and the changed conditions of man's social life, or with the special genius of our day. Moreover, these norms can be approved by all."

Background

While social concerns have always been a part of the Church's teachings, Catholic social doctrine has been the subject of much consideration since the end of the last century and has been formulated in a progressive manner in a number of authoritative documents starting with the encyclical *Rerum Novarum* ("On Capital and Labor") issued by Leo XIII in 1891. Owing to its significance, the encyclical was called by Pope John XXIII the magna carta of Catholic social doctrine.

Other outstanding examples are the encyclicals: *Quadragesimo Anno* ("On Reconstruction of the Social Order") by Pius XI in 1931; *Mater et Magistra* ("Christianity and Social Progress") and *Pacem in Terris* ("Peace on Earth"), by John XXIII in 1961 and 1963, respectively; *Populorum Progressio* ("Development of Peoples"), by Paul VI in 1967; *Laborem Exercens* ("On Human Work"), *Sollicitudo Rei Socialis* ("On Social Concerns") and *Centesimus Annus* ("The 100th Year") by John Paul II in 1981, 1987 and 1991, respectively. Among many other accomplishments of ideological importance in the social field, Pius XII made a distinctive contribution with his formulation of a plan for world peace and order in Christmas messages from 1939 to 1941, and in other documents.

Of particular significance to the contemporary application of social doctrine are the document *Gaudium et Spes* (Pastoral Constitution on the Church in the Modern World) issued by the Second Vatican Council and Pope John Paul II's encyclical letters, *Laborem Exercens* ("On Human Work"), *Sollicitudo Rei Socialis* ("On Social Concerns"), and *Centesimus Annus* ("The 100th Year").

These documents represent the most serious attempts in modern times to systematize the social implications of divine revelation as well as the socially relevant writings of the Fathers and Doctors of the Church. Their contents are theological penetrations into social life, with particular reference to human rights, the needs of the poor and those in underdeveloped countries, and humane conditions of life, freedom, justice and peace. In some respects, they read like juridical documents; essentially, however, they are Gospel-oriented and pastoral in intention.

Gaudium et Spes

Gaudium et Spes (Pastoral Constitution on the Church in the Modern World) was the last document issued by Vatican Council II (Dec. 7, 1965). The document has as its purpose to search out the signs of God's presence and meaning in and through the events of this time in human history. Accordingly, it deals with the situation of men in present circumstances of pro-

found change, challenge and crisis on all levels of life. It is evenly divided into two main parts: the Church's teaching on humanity in the modern era and urgent problems of the times.

Part One

The first part begins: "The joys and the hopes, the griefs and the anxieties of this age" (No. 1) — a clear indication that the Council Fathers were aware both of the positive nature of the modern world and its many dangers and travails. Further, the council places great emphasis throughout on the human existence, a stress that was quite innovative in its presentation: "According to the almost unanimous opinion of believers and unbelievers alike, all things on earth should be related to man as their center and crown" (No. 12). Having developed an analysis of humanity, the document then offered a thorough summary of traditional Church teaching on human life, complete with discussion of sin, the union of body and soul, and the moral conscience.

There is, as well, a genuinely realistic appraisal of contemporary society, noting the pervasiveness of atheism, adding that its spread can be attributed in part to the fault and carelessness of those within the Church whose actions and failures "must be said to conceal rather than reveal the authentic face of God and religion" (No. 19). Toward the fuller understanding of the place of the Church in the modern world, *Gaudium et Spes* emphasizes the harmony that should exist between the Catholic faith and scientific progress because "earthly matters and the concerns of faith derive from the same God" (No. 36). This does not mean, however, that there ought to be no qualifying elements or restraints to science; the Council Fathers add to this positive statement the provision that such research, "within every branch of learning," must be "carried out in a genuinely scientific manner and in accord with moral norms" (No. 36). Finally, the first part makes an ecumenical gesture, noting that the Church "holds in high esteem the things which other Christian Churches or ecclesial communities have done. . . ." (No. 40).

Part Two

Part Two offers the practical application of the Church's teaching and message enunciated in Part One. Most pressing is the council's concern for the family, and its treatment of family life and marriage is the most detailed and extensive in the history of the councils of the Church. This leads to study of the deeply troubling presence of contraception. The council reiterates Church instruction in an affirmation of opposition to contraception that would receive even fuller expression in three years in the encyclical *Humanae Vitae*. In the matter of abortion, the document states clearly: ". . . from the moment of its conception life must be guarded with the greatest care, while abortion and infanticide are unspeakable crimes" (No. 51). In its study of culture, in which the council reminds all humanity that culture and civilization are creations of man, it points out his responsibility over it and his duty to seek that which is above, which entails an "obligation to work with all men in constructing a more human world" (No. 57). Here we have a powerful preface or introduction to the next concerns voiced in *Gaudium et Spes*: the questions of economic life, political systems, and war. In building upon earlier social encyclicals, *Gaudium et Spes* discusses economics as vital to human progress and social development, striking the important balance (developed so masterfully in the later writings of Pope John Paul II) between the rights of an individual to possess goods and the obligation to aid the poor (Nos. 63-72). While declaring the autonomous and independent nature of the Church and politics, the Council Fathers do

acknowledge: "There are, indeed, close links between earthly affairs and those aspects of man's condition which transcend this world. The Church herself employs the things of time to the degree that her own proper mission demands" (No. 76). The document goes on to state that "the arms race is an utterly treacherous trap for humanity" (No. 81) and "It is our clear duty, then, to strain every muscle as we work for the time when all war can be completely outlawed by international consent" (No. 82).

SOCIAL DOCTRINE UNDER POPE JOHN PAUL II

Background

Throughout his pontificate, Pope John Paul II has traveled the globe speaking out on all matters of the Church's social teachings and has written a number of important encyclicals that are reflective not only of the Church's traditions of social doctrine but that seek to utilize the teachings of the faith to offer specific points of reflection and solutions to the many pressing problems of the late 20th century. Rooted in Christian anthropology and Tradition, Scripture, and Magisterium, John Paul's writings have encompassed economic ethics, the rights and dignity of the worker, the primacy of the human person, the place of the family in society and the Church, and the integrative teachings of the Church in the areas of moral and pastoral theology. The three main expressions of his social teachings have been the encyclicals: *Laborem Exercens* (1981); *Sollicitudo Rei Socialis* (1987); and *Centesimus Annus* (1991).

SOCIAL ENCYCLICALS OF POPE JOHN PAUL II

(The following material is adapted from The Encyclicals of John Paul II, *with the kind permission of the Rev. J. Michael Miller, C.S.B.)*

Laborem Exercens

Fascinated as he is by commemorative events, Pope John Paul II marked the ninetieth anniversary of Leo XIII's *Rerum Novarum* (1891) by publishing his first social encyclical, *Laborem Exercens*, on Sept. 14, 1981.[1] Before him, Pius XI in *Quadragesimo Anno* (1931), John XXIII in *Mater et Magistra* (1961), and Paul VI in *Octogesima Adveniens* (1971) had observed the anniversary of Leo's ground-breaking encyclical with documents of their own.

Laborem Exercens is a very personal document. The encyclical has solid roots in the pope's own experience as a worker. It reflects his familiarity with various worlds of work: in mines and factories, in artistic and literary production, in scholarship and pastoral ministry. More particularly, *Laborem Exercens* has its origins in the long debate carried on by the Archbishop of Kracow with Marxist intellectuals. The topics chosen, which include the struggle between capital and labor, ownership of the means of production, and solidarity, as well as the terminology of the encyclical, bear ample witness to this background of controversy. Here, however, he is less concerned with economic systems than with the human person as a "worker." Furthermore, John Paul intended his letter to encourage the Solidarity union movement, which

in the early 1980s was the primary motor for effecting social and political change in a Poland under a totalitarian regime.

The style of encyclical is distinctively Wojtylan. It reveals the pope's preference for combining a phenomenological description of experience with philosophical-theological meditation. While he cites the Second Vatican Council's *Gaudium et Spes*, John Paul never directly quotes from any previous social encyclical, not even from *Rerum Novarum*. The encyclical's footnotes are almost entirely biblical, indicating that its primary inspiration is Sacred Scripture. As in his two previous encyclicals, *Redemptor Hominis* (1979) and *Dives in Misericordia* (1980), the pope relies heavily upon the plastic and descriptive language of the Bible, especially from the opening chapters of Genesis, to develop his theme. The encyclical unfolds the meaning of the human vocation to work in light of the biblical text on "subduing the earth" (cf. Gen 1:28). This call to exercise dominion is to be carried out by those created "in the image of God" (Gen 1:27) through their work, which the pope qualifies as *"one of the characteristics that distinguish* man from the rest of creatures" (preface).

Unlike earlier social encyclicals which dealt with a wide range of different questions, *Laborem Exercens* is sharply focused. John Paul chooses a very specific theme — the dignity and role of human work — and explores its many ramifications: "Through work man must earn his daily bread and contribute to the continual advance of science and technology and, above all, to elevating unceasingly the cultural and moral level of the society within which he lives in community with those who belong to the same family" (preface). At the present moment, he believes, the world is faced with important choices. It is "on the eve of new developments in technological, economic, and political conditions which, according to many experts, will influence the world of work and production no less than the industrial revolution of the last century" (§1.3).

A crisis in the meaning of human work is a crucial factor contributing to society's current plight. "Work, as human issue, is at the very center of the 'social question' " (§2.1). Moreover, the pope adds, "human work is *a key*, probably *the essential key*, to the whole social question" (§3.2). It is a problem with ramifications which extend beyond the so-called "working class"; the dimensions of the crisis are universal. Therefore he does not confine his encyclical to a reflection on the work only of industrial or agricultural workers. Instead, he extends it to encompass the work done by every sector of society: management, white-collar workers, scientists, intellectuals, artists, women in the home. "Each and every individual, to the proper extent and in an incalculable number of ways, takes part in the giant process whereby man 'subdues the earth' through his work" (§4.4). To use a favorite expression of the pope's, the world's "workbench" includes all those who labor for their daily bread — all men and women.

As in his two previous encyclicals, John Paul takes up the "way" of the human person, this time with regard to his fundamental activity of work. *Laborem Exercens* is yet another chapter in the pope's book on Christian anthropology. Moreover, since work is a great gift and good for humanity, his tone throughout the encyclical is constructive and exhortatory.

Footnote
1. *Acta Apostolicae Sedis,* 73 (1981), 577-647.

Sollicitudo Rei Socialis
Although signed on Dec. 30, 1987, Pope John Paul II's encyclical "on social concern" was not officially published until Feb. 19, 1988.[1] Like *Laborem Exercens* (1981), this second social encyclical commemorates a previous papal document. *Sollicitudo Rei Socialis* marks the twentieth anniversary of Paul VI's *Populorum Progressio* (1967). But more than merely recalling the relevance and doctrine of Pope Paul's encyclical, it highlights new themes and responds to the problems of development in the Third World which had emerged in the intervening twenty years.

John Paul writes as a teacher, explaining why the proclamation of the Church's social doctrine belongs to her evangelizing mission. He also writes as an informed witness to the increasing injustice and poverty in the world. Lastly, he writes as a defender of human dignity and inalienable rights, and of every person's transcendent vocation to communion with the Triune God.

In some ways *Sollicitudo Rei Socialis* echoes *Laborem Exercens* (1981). John Paul's use of Sacred Scripture, for example, is similar in that he frequently quotes from the opening chapters of Genesis. The differences between the two social encyclicals, however, are noteworthy. Whereas in *Laborem Exercens* (1981) the pope never directly cites *Rerum Novarum* (1891), the encyclical of Leo XIII which it commemorates, throughout *Sollicitudo Rei Socialis* John Paul quotes or refers to *Populorum Progressio* more than forty times. It is his constant point of reference. Second, to support his presentation, the pope marshals statements taken from earlier writings and discourses of his own pontificate, as well as the social teaching of the Second Vatican Council expressed in *Gaudium et Spes.* Third, more than in any other encyclical, John Paul makes use of documents published by the Roman Curia. Especially notable are his six references to the *Instruction on Christian Freedom and Liberation* (1986) issued by the Congregation for the Doctrine of the Faith. He also cites two publications of the Pontifical Commission "Iustitia et Pax": *At the Service of the Human Community: An Ethical Approach to the International Debt Question* (1986) and *The Church and the Housing Problem* (1987).

While *Sollicitudo Rei Socialis* perceptively analyzes the economic, political, social, and cultural dimensions of world development, its perspective is primarily ethical and theological. John Paul rereads *Populorum Progressio* through a moral-spiritual lens. His main concern is to form the consciences of individual men and women, to help them in their task of promoting authentic development "in the light of faith and of the Church's Tradition" (§41.7).

Footnote
1. *Acta Apostolicae Sedis,* 80 (1988), 513-586.

Centesimus Annus
Pope John Paul II issued his ninth encyclical, *Centesimus Annus,* on May 1, 1991.[1] Not surprisingly, the pope chose to mark the centenary of Leo XIII's *Rerum Novarum* (1891) with a document of his own. In the four years since the signing of *Sollicitudo Rei Socialis* (1987) the Berlin Wall had collapsed, and in the light of this event John Paul offers his "rereading" of *Rerum Novarum.* His purpose is twofold. He wishes to recall Leo's contribution to the development of the Church's social teaching and to honor the popes who drew upon the encyclical's "vital energies" in their social teaching.

Centesimus Annus has some interesting peculiarities. First, among all John Paul's encyclicals, it relies the least on citing Sacred Scripture. Its few biblical references are primarily exhortatory or illustrative. For his sources the pope depends mostly on *Rerum Novarum* and on the social encyclicals of his predecessors, as well as on earlier documents and discourses of his own Magisterium. Second, much of the encyclical's content is conditioned by current geopolitical affairs. Indeed, the encyclical reads as if the pope had *Rerum Novarum* in one hand and a diary of the 1989 events sweeping eastern Europe in the other.

Despite the opinions of some commentators, John Paul's primary interest is not to pass judgment on either failed socialism or contemporary capitalism. Above all, in keeping with his desire to articulate a Christian anthropology, he recalls the need for Catholic social doctrine to have a *"correct view of the human person* and of his unique value" (§11.3). Without such a view, he believes, it is impossible to solve today's social, economic, and political problems. The Church's distinctive contribution to meeting these challenges is her vision of the transcendent dignity of the human person created in God's image and redeemed by Christ's blood.

The pope's rereading of Leo XIII encompasses three time frames: "looking back" at *Rerum Novarum* itself, "looking around" at the contemporary situation, and "looking to the future" (§3.1). In looking back, John Paul confirms the enduring principles of Leo's encyclical, principles that belong to the Church's doctrinal inheritance. His "pastoral solicitude" also impels the pope to analyze recent political events from the perspective of the Gospel "in order to discern the new requirements of evangelization" (§3.5).

Even more clearly than in his two previous social encyclicals, *Laborem Exercens* (1981) and *Sollicitudo Rei Socialis* (1987), John Paul clearly distinguishes the authentic doctrine contained in the Church's social teaching from the analysis of contingent historical events. This analysis, he states, "is not meant to pass definitive judgments, since this does not fall *per se* within the Magisterium's specific domain" (§3.5). Whatever comes within the doctrinal sphere, however, "pertains to the Church's evangelizing mission and is an essential part of the Christian message" (§5.5).

Footnote

1. *Acta Apostolicae Sedis,* 83 (1991), 793-867.

SOCIO-ECONOMIC STATEMENTS BY U.S. BISHOPS

Over a period of nearly 80 years, the bishops of the United States have issued a great number of socio-economic statements reflecting papal documents in a U.S. context.

One such statement, entitled "Economic Justice for All: Social Teaching and the U.S. Economy" was issued in November, 1986. It's contents are related in various ways with the subsequently issued encyclical letter, *Centesimus Annus.* Principles drawn from the bishops' document are given in the following excerpt entitled "A Catholic Framework for Economic Life." Another significant statement, entitled "The Harvest of Justice Is Sown in Peace" (1993) follows.

A Catholic Framework for Economic Life

As followers of Jesus Christ and participants in a powerful economy, Catholics in the United States, are called to work for greater economic justice in the face of persistent poverty, growing income gaps and increasing discussion of economic issues in the United States and around the world. We urge Catholics to use the following ethical framework for economic life as principles for reflection, criteria for judgment and directions for action. These principles are drawn directly from Catholic teaching on economic life.

1. The economy exists for the person, not the person for the economy.
2. All economic life should be shaped by moral principles. Economic choices and institutions must be judged by how they protect or undermine the life and dignity of the human person, support the family and serve the common good.
3. A fundamental moral measure of an economy is how the poor and vulnerable are faring.
4. All people have a right to life and to secure the basic necessities of life (e.g., food, clothing, shelter, education, health care, safe environment, economic security).
5. All people have the right to economic initiative, to productive work, to just wages and benefits, to decent working conditions as well as to organize and join unions or other associations.
6. All people, to the extent they are able, have a corresponding duty to work, a responsibility to provide for the needs of their families and an obligation to contribute to the broader society.
7. In economic life, free markets have both clear advantages and limits; government has essential responsibilities and limitations; voluntary groups have irreplaceable roles, but cannot substitute for the proper working of the market and the just policies of the state.
8. Society has a moral obligation, including governmental action where necessary, to assure opportunity, meet basic human needs and pursue justice in economic life.
9. Workers, owners, managers, stockholders and consumers are moral agents in economic life. By our choices, initiative, creativity and investment, we enhance or diminish economic opportunity, community life and social justice.

10. The global economy has moral dimensions and human consequences. Decisions on investment, trade, aid and development should protect human life and promote human rights, especially for those most in need wherever they might live on this globe.

The Harvest of Justice Is Sown in Peace

The National Conference of Catholic Bishops, at a meeting Nov. 17, 1993, issued a statement entitled "The Harvest of Justice Is Sown in Peace," marking the 10th anniversary of their earlier pastoral letter, "The Challenge of Peace: God's Promise and Our Response."

The Challenge of Peace

"The challenge of peace today is different, but no less urgent" than in 1983, and the threat of global nuclear war "may seem more remote than at any time in the nuclear age." Questions of peace and war, however, cannot be addressed "without acknowledging that the nuclear question remains of vital political and moral significance."

The statement outlines an agenda for action to guide future advocacy efforts of the bishops' national conference. It also urges that the cause of peace be reflected constantly in liturgical prayers of petition, preaching and Catholic education at all levels.

Confronting the temptation to isolationism in U.S. foreign policy is among "the major challenges peacemakers face in this new era."

Factors in a vision for peace include a commitment to the universal common good and recognition of the imperative of human solidarity.

Nonviolent revolutions in some countries "challenge us to find ways to take into full account the power of organized, active nonviolence."

With respect to just war criteria, the statement says that "important work needs to be done in refining, clarifying and applying the just war tradition to the choices facing our decision-makers in this still violent and dangerous world."

Subjects of concern include humanitarian intervention, deterrence, conscientious objection and the development of peoples.

Presumption against Force

"Our conference's approach, as outlined in 'The Challenge of Peace,' can be summarized in this way:

"1) In situations of conflict our constant commitment ought to be, as far as possible, to strive for justice through nonviolent means.

"2) But when sustained attempts at nonviolent action fail to protect the innocent against fundamental injustice, then legitimate political authorities are permitted as a last resort to employ limited force to rescue the innocent and establish justice."

Lethal Force

"Whether lethal force may be used is governed by the following criteria:

"Just cause: Force may be used only to correct a grave, public evil, i.e., aggression or massive violation of the basic rights of whole populations.

"Comparative justice: While there may be rights and wrongs on all sides of a conflict, to override the presumption against the use of force, the injustice suffered by one party must significantly outweigh that suffered by the other.

"Legitimate authority: Only duly constituted public authorities may use deadly force or wage war.

"Right intention: Force may be used only in a truly just cause and solely for that purpose.

"Probability of Success: Arms may not be used in a futile cause or in a case where disproportionate measures are required to achieve success.

"Proportionality: The overall destruction expected from the use of force must be outweighed by the good to be achieved.

"Last Resort: Force may be used only after all peaceful alternatives have been seriously tried and exhausted.

"These criteria [of just war], taken as a whole, must be satisfied in order to override the strong presumption against the use of force."

Just War

"The just-war tradition seeks also to curb the violence of war through restraint on armed combat between the contending parties by imposing the following moral standards for the conduct of armed conflict:

"Noncombatant Immunity: Civilians may not be the object of direct attack, and military personnel must take due care to avoid and minimize indirect harm to civilians.

"Proportionality: In the conduct of hostilities, efforts must be made to attain military objectives with no more force than is militarily necessary and to avoid disproportionate collateral damage to civilian life and property.

"Right Intention: Even in the midst of conflict, the aim of political and military leaders must be peace with justice so that acts of vengeance and indiscriminate violence, whether by individuals, military units or governments, are forbidden."

Structures for Justice and Peace

Quoting an address given by Pope John Paul in August, 1993, in Denver, the statement said:

" 'The international community ought to establish more effective structures for maintaining and promoting justice and peace. This implies that a concept of strategic interest should evolve which is based on the full development of peoples — out of poverty and toward a more dignified existence, out of injustice and exploitation toward fuller respect for the human person and the defense of universal rights.'

"As we consider a new vision of the international community, five areas deserve special attention: (1) strengthening global institutions; (2) securing human rights; (3) promoting human development; (4) restraining nationalism and eliminating religious violence; and (5) building cooperative security."

Humanitarian Intervention

"Pope John Paul, citing the 'conscience of humanity and international humanitarian law,' has been outspoken in urging that 'humanitarian intervention be obligatory where the survival of populations and entire ethnic groups is seriously compromised. This is a duty for nations and the international community.' He elaborated on this right and duty of humanitarian intervention in his 1993 annual address to the diplomatic corps (accredited to the Holy See):

" 'Once the possibilities afforded by diplomatic negotiations and the procedures provided for by international agreements and organizations have been put into effect, and that [sic], nevertheless, populations are succumbing to the attacks of an unjust aggressor, states no longer have a 'right to indifference.' It seems clear that their duty is to disarm this aggressor if all other means have proved ineffective. The principles of the sovereignty of states and of noninterference in their internal affairs — which retain all their value — cannot constitute a screen behind which torture and murder may be carried out.' "

(For the annual NCCB Labor Day Statement, please see p. 447.)

THE BLESSED VIRGIN MARY

ROLE OF MARY IN THE MYSTERY OF CHRIST AND THE CHURCH

The following excerpts are from Chapter VIII of the Second Vatican Council's Constitution on the Church, Lumen Gentium.

Preface

Wishing in his supreme goodness and wisdom to effect the redemption of the world, "when the fullness of time came, God sent his Son, born of a woman, that we might receive the adoption of sons" (Gal. 4:4-5). "He for us men, and for our salvation, came down from heaven, and was incarnate by the Holy Spirit from the Virgin Mary." This divine mystery of salvation is revealed to us and continued in the Church, which the Lord established as his own body. In this Church, adhering to Christ the head and having communion with all his saints, the faithful must also venerate the memory "above all of the glorious and perpetual Virgin Mary. Mother of our God and Lord Jesus Christ." (52)

At the message of the angel, the Virgin Mary received the Word of God in her heart and in her body, and gave Life to the world. Hence, she is acknowledged and honored as being truly the Mother of God and Mother of the Redeemer. Redeemed in an especially sublime manner by reason of the merits of her Son, and united to him by a close and indissoluble tie, she is endowed with the supreme office and dignity of being the Mother of the Son of God. As a result, she is also the favorite daughter of the Father and the temple of the Holy Spirit. Because of this gift of sublime grace, she far surpasses all other creatures, both in heaven and on earth.

At the same time, however, because she belongs to the offspring of Adam, she is one with all human beings in their need for salvation. Indeed, she is "clearly the Mother of the members of Christ since she cooperated out of love so that there might be born in the Church the faithful, who are members of Christ their head. Therefore, she is also hailed as a pre-eminent and altogether singular member of the Church, and as the Church's model and excellent exemplar in faith and charity. Taught by the Holy Spirit, the Catholic Church honors her with filial affection and piety as a most beloved Mother. (53)

This sacred synod intends to describe with diligence the role of the Blessed Virgin in the mystery of the Incarnate Word and the Mystical Body. It also wishes to describe the duties of redeemed mankind toward the Mother of God, who is the Mother of Christ and Mother of men, particularly of the faithful.

The synod does not, however, have it in mind to give a complete doctrine on Mary, nor does it wish to decide those questions which have not yet been fully illuminated by the work of theologians. (54)

II. The Role of the Blessed Virgin in the Economy of Salvation

The Father of mercies willed that the consent of the predestined Mother should precede the Incarnation so that, just as a woman contributed to death, so also a woman should contribute to life. This contrast was verified in outstanding fashion by the Mother of Jesus. She gave to the world that very Life which renews all things, and she was enriched by God with gifts befitting such a role.

It is no wonder, then, that the usage prevailed among the holy Fathers whereby they called the Mother of God entirely holy and free from all stain of sin, fashioned by the Holy Spirit into a kind of new substance and new creature. Adorned from the first instant of her conception with the splendors of an entirely unique holiness, the Virgin of Nazareth is, on God's command, greeted by an angel messenger as "full of grace" (cf. Lk. 1:28). To the heavenly messenger she replies: "Behold the handmaid of the Lord; be it done to me according to thy word" (Lk. 1:38).

By thus consenting to the divine utterance, Mary, a daughter of Adam, became the Mother of Jesus. Embracing God's saving will with a full heart and impeded by no sin, she devoted herself totally as a handmaid of the Lord to the person and work of her Son. In subordination to him and along with him, by the grace of almighty God she served the mystery of redemption.

Rightly, therefore, the holy Fathers see her as used by God not merely in a passive way but as cooperating in the work of human salvation through free faith and obedience. (56)

This union of the Mother with the Son in the work of salvation was manifested from the time of Christ's virginal conception up to his death. It is shown first of all when Mary, arising in haste to go to visit Elizabeth, was greeted by her as blessed because of her belief in the promise of salvation, while the precursor leaped for joy in the womb of his mother (cf. Lk. 1:41-45). This association was shown also at the birth of our Lord, who did not diminish his Mother's virginal integrity but sanctified it, when the Mother of God joyfully showed her first-born Son to the shepherds and the Magi.

When she presented him to the Lord in the Temple, making the offering of the poor, she heard Simeon foretelling at the same time that her Son would be a sign of contradiction and that a sword would pierce the Mother's soul, that out of many hearts thoughts might be revealed (cf. Lk. 2:34-35). When the Child Jesus was lost and they had sought him sorrowing, his parents found him in the temple, taken up with things which were his Father's business. They did not understand the reply of the Son. But his Mother, to be sure, kept all these things to be pondered over in her heart (cf. Lk. 2:41-51). (57)

In the public life of Jesus, Mary made significant appearances. This was so even at the very beginning, when she was moved with pity at the marriage feast of Cana, and her intercession brought about the beginning of the miracles by Jesus the Messiah (Cf. Jn. 2:1-11). In the course of her Son's preaching, she received his praise when, in extolling a kingdom beyond the calculations and bonds of flesh and blood, he declared blessed (cf. Mk. 3:35 par.; Lk. 11:27-28) those who heard and kept the word of the Lord as she was faithfully doing (cf. Lk. 2:19, 51).

Thus, the Blessed Virgin advanced in her pilgrimage of faith and loyally persevered in her union with her Son unto the cross. There she stood, in keeping with the divine plan (cf. Jn. 19:25), suffering grievously with her only-begotten Son. There she united herself with a maternal heart to his sacrifice, and lovingly consented to the immolation of this Victim whom she herself had brought forth. Finally, the same Christ Jesus dying on the cross gave her as a mother to his disciple. This he did when he said: "Woman, behold your son" (Jn. 19:26-27). (58)

But since it pleased God not to manifest solemnly the mystery of the salvation of the human race until he poured forth the Spirit promised by Christ, we see the apostles before the day of Pentecost "continuing with one mind in prayer with the women and Mary, the Mother of Jesus, and with his brethren" (Acts 1:14). We see Mary prayerfully imploring the gift of the Spirit, who had already overshadowed her in the Annunciation.

Finally, preserved free from all guilt of original sin, the Immaculate Virgin was taken up body and soul into heavenly glory upon the completion of her earthly sojourn. She was exalted by the Lord as Queen of all, in order that she might be the more thoroughly conformed to her Son, the Lord of lords (cf. Rev. 19:16) and the conqueror of sin and death. (59)

III. The Blessed Virgin and the Church

We have but one Mediator, as we know from the words of the Apostle: "For there is one God, and one Mediator between God and men, himself man, Christ Jesus, who gave himself as a ransom for all" (1 Tim. 2:5-6). The maternal duty of Mary toward men in no way obscures or diminishes this unique mediation of Christ, but rather shows its power. For all the saving influences of the Blessed Virgin on men originate, not from some inner necessity, but from the divine pleasure. They flow forth from the superabundance of the merits of Christ, rest on his mediation, depend entirely on it, and draw all their power from it. In no way do they impede the immediate union of the faithful with Christ. Rather, they foster this union. (60)

In an utterly singular way, she (Mary) cooperated by her obedience, faith, hope and burning charity in the Savior's work of restoring supernatural life to souls. For this reason she is a mother to us in the order of grace. (61)

This maternity of Mary in the order of grace began with the consent which she gave in faith at the Annunciation and which she sustained without wavering beneath the cross. This maternity will last without interruption until the eternal fulfillment of all the elect. For, taken up to heaven, she did not lay aside this saving role, but by her manifold acts of intercession continues to win for us gifts of eternal salvation.

By her maternal charity, Mary cares for the brethren of her Son who still journey on earth surrounded by dangers and difficulties until they are led to their happy fatherland. Therefore, the Blessed Virgin is invoked by the Church under the titles of Advocate, Auxiliatrix, Adjutrix and Mediatrix. These, however, are to be so understood that they neither take away nor add anything to the dignity and efficacy of Christ the one Mediator.

For no creature could ever be classed with the Incarnate Word and Redeemer. But, just as the priesthood of Christ is shared in various ways both by sacred ministers and by the faithful; and as the one goodness of God is in reality communicated diversely to his creatures: so also the unique mediation of the Redeemer does not exclude but rather gives rise among creatures to a manifold cooperation which is but a sharing in this unique source.

The Church does not hesitate to profess this subordinate role of Mary. She experiences it continuously and commends it to the hearts of the faithful so that, encouraged by this maternal help, they may more closely adhere to the Mediator and Redeemer. (62)

Through the gift and role of divine maternity, Mary is united with her Son, the Redeemer, and with his singular graces and offices. By these, the Blessed Virgin is also intimately united with the Church. As St. Ambrose taught, the Mother of God is a model of the Church in the matter of faith, hope and charity, and perfect union with Christ. For in the mystery of the Church, herself rightly called Mother and Virgin, the Blessed Virgin stands out in eminent and singular fashion as exemplar of both virginity and motherhood. (63)

In the most holy Virgin, the Church has already reached that perfection whereby she exists without spot or wrinkle (cf. Eph. 5:27). Yet, the followers of Christ still strive to increase in holiness by conquering sin. And so they raise their eyes to Mary who shines forth to the whole community of the elect as a model of the virtues. Devotedly meditating on her and contemplating her in the light of the Word made man, the Church with reverence enters more intimately into the supreme mystery of the Incarnation and becomes ever increasingly like her Spouse. (64)

The Church in her apostolic work looks to her who brought forth Christ, conceived by the Holy Spirit and born of the Virgin, so that through the Church Christ may be born and grow in the hearts of the faithful also. The Virgin Mary in her own life lived as an example of that maternal love by which all should be fittingly animated who cooperate in the apostolic mission of the Church on behalf of the rebirth of men. (65)

IV. Devotion to the Blessed Virgin in the Church

Mary was involved in the mystery of Christ. As the most holy Mother of God she was, after her Son, exalted by divine grace above all angels and men. Hence, the Church appropriately honors her with special reverence. Indeed, from most ancient times the Blessed Virgin has been venerated under the title of "God-bearer." In all perils and needs, the faithful; have fled prayerfully to her protection. Especially after the Council of Ephesus the cult of the people of God toward Mary wonderfully increased in veneration and love, in invocation and imitation, according to her own prophetic words: "All generations shall call me blessed; because he who is mighty has done great things for me" (Lk. 1:48).

As it has always existed in the Church, this cult (of Mary) is altogether special, Still, it differs essentially from the cult of adoration which is offered to the Incarnate Word, as well as to the Father and the Holy Spirit. Yet, devotion to Mary is most favorable to this supreme cult. The Church has endorsed many forms of piety toward the Mother of God, provided that they were within the limits of sound and orthodox doctrine. These forms have varied according to the circumstances of time and place, and have reflected the diversity of native characteristics and temperament among the faithful. While honoring Christ's Mother, these devotions cause her Son to be rightly known, loved and glorified, and all his commands observed. Through him all things have their beginning (cf. Col. 1: 15-16) and in him "it has pleased (the eternal Father) that . all his fullness should dwell" (Col. 1:19). (66)

This most holy synod deliberately teaches this Catholic doctrine. At the same time, it admonishes all the sons of the Church that the cult, especially the liturgical cult, of the Blessed Virgin, be generously fostered. It charges that practices and exercises of

devotion toward her be treasured as recommended by the teaching authority of the Church in the course of centuries.

This synod earnestly exhorts theologians and preachers of the divine word that, in treating of the unique dignity of the Mother of God, they carefully and equally avoid the falsity of exaggeration on the one hand and the excess of narrow-mindedness on the other.

Let the faithful remember, moreover, that true devotion consists neither in fruitless and passing emotion, nor in a certain vain credulity. Rather, it proceeds from the true faith, by which we are led to know the excellence of the Mother of God, and are moved to a filial love toward our Mother and to the imitation of her virtues. (67)

REDEMPTORIS MATER

Redemptoris Mater (*Mother of the Redeemer*), Pope John Paul II's sixth encyclical letter, is a "reflection on the role of Mary in the mystery of Christ and on her active and exemplary presence in the life of the Church." The letter was published Mar. 25, 1987.

Central to consideration of Mary is the fact that she is the Mother of God (*Theotokos*), since by the power of the Holy Spirit she conceived in her virginal womb and brought into the world Jesus Christ, the Son of God, who is of one being with the Father and the Holy Spirit.

Mary was preserved from original sin in view of her calling to be the Mother of Jesus. She was gifted in grace beyond measure. She fulfilled her role in a unique pilgrimage of faith. She is the Mother of the Church and the spiritual mother of all people.

The following excerpts are from the English text provided by the Vatican and circulated by the CNS Documentary Service, *Origins*, Apr. 9, 1987 (Vol. 16, No. 43). Subheads have been added. Quotations are from pertinent documents of the Second Vatican Council.

Mary's Presence in the Church

Mary, through the same faith which made her blessed, especially from the moment of the Annunciation, is present in the Church's mission, present in the Church's work of introducing into the world the kingdom of her Son.

This presence of Mary finds as many different expressions in our day just as it did throughout the Church's history. It also has a wide field of action: through the faith and piety of individual believers; through the traditions of Christian families or "domestic churches," of parish and missionary communities, religious institutes and dioceses; through the radiance and attraction of the great shrines where not only individuals or local groups, but sometimes whole nations and societies, even whole continents, seek to meet the Mother of the Lord, the one who is blessed because she believed, is the first among believers, and therefore became the Mother of Emmanuel.

This is the message of the land of Palestine, the spiritual homeland of all Christians, because it was the homeland of the Savior of the world and of his Mother.

This is the message of the many churches in Rome and throughout the world which have been raised up

in the course of the centuries by the faith of Christians. This is the message of centers like Guadalupe, Lourdes, Fátima and others situated in the various countries. Among them, how could I fail to mention the one in my own native land, Jasna Gora? One could perhaps speak of a specific "geography" of faith and Marian devotion which includes all of these special places of pilgrimage where the people of God seek to meet the Mother of God in order to find, within the radius of the maternal presence of her "who believed," a strengthening of their own faith.

Mary and Ecumenism

"In all of Christ's disciples the Spirit arouses the desire to be peacefully united, in the manner determined by Christ, as one flock under one shepherd." The journey of the Church, especially in our own time, is marked by the sign of ecumenism: Christians are seeking ways to restore that unity which Christ implored from the Father for his disciples on the day before his passion.

Christians must deepen in themselves and each of their communities that "obedience of faith" of which Mary is the first and brightest example.

Christians know that their unity will be truly rediscovered only if it is based on the unity of their faith. They must resolve considerable discrepancies of doctrine concerning the mystery and ministry of the Church, and sometimes also concerning the role of Mary in the work of salvation.

Mary, who is still the model of this pilgrimage, is to lead them to the unity which is willed by their one Lord, and which is so much desired by those who are attentively listening to what "the Spirit is saying to the churches" today.

A Hopeful Sign

Meanwhile, it is a hopeful sign that these churches and ecclesial communities are finding agreement with the Catholic Church on fundamental points of Christian belief, including matters relating to the Virgin Mary. For they recognize her as the Mother of the Lord and hold that this forms part of our faith in Christ, true God and true man. They look to her who at the foot of the cross accepted as her son the Beloved Disciple (John), the one who in his turn accepted her as his Mother.

On the other hand, I wish to emphasize how profoundly the Catholic Church, the Orthodox Church and the ancient churches of the East feel united by love and praise of the *Theotokos*. Not only "basic dogmas of the Christian faith concerning the Trinity and God's Word made flesh of the Virgin Mary were defined in ecumenical councils held in the East," but also in their liturgical worship "the Eastern Christians pay high tribute, in very beautiful hymns, to Mary ever-Virgin. God's most holy Mother."

The churches which profess the doctrine of Ephesus proclaim the Virgin as "true Mother of God" since "our Lord Jesus Christ, born of the Father before time began according to his divinity, in the last days he himself, for our sake and for our salvation, was begotten of Mary the Virgin Mother of God according to his humanity." The Greek Fathers and the Byzantine tradition, contemplating the Virgin in the light of the Word made flesh, have sought to penetrate the depth of that bond which unites Mary, as the Mother of God, to Christ and the Church. The Virgin is a permanent presence in the whole reality of the salvific mystery.

Marian Mediation

The Church knows and teaches with St. Paul that there is only one mediator: "For there is one God, and there is one mediator between God and men, the man Christ Jesus, who gave himself as a ransom for all" (1 Tm. 2:5-6). "The maternal role of Mary toward people in no way obscures or diminishes the unique mediation of Christ, but rather shows its power." It is mediation in Christ.

The Church knows and teaches that "all the saving influences of the Blessed Virgin on mankind originate . from the divine pleasure. They flow forth from the superabundance of the merits of Christ, rest on his mediation, depend entirely on it and draw all their power from it. In no way do they impede the immediate union of the faithful with Christ. Rather, they foster this union." This saving influence is sustained by the Holy Spirit, who, just as he overshadowed the Virgin Mary when he began in her the divine motherhood, in a similar way constantly sustains her solicitude for the brothers and sisters of her Son.

Mediation and Motherhood

In effect, Mary's mediation is intimately linked with her motherhood. It possesses a specifically maternal character, which distinguishes it from the mediation of the other creatures who in various and always subordinate ways share in the one mediation of Christ, although her own mediation is also a shared mediation. In fact, while it is true that "no creature could ever be classed with the Incarnate Word and Redeemer," at the same time "the unique mediation of the Redeemer does not exclude but rather gives rise among creatures a manifold cooperation which is but a sharing in this unique source." Thus "the one good-

ness of God is in reality communicated diversely to his creatures."

Subordinate Mediation

The teaching of Vatican II presents the truth of Mary's mediation as "a sharing in the one unique source that is the mediation of Christ himself." Thus we read: "The Church does not hesitate to profess this subordinate role of Mary. She experiences it continuously and commends it to the hearts of the faithful so that, encouraged by this maternal help, they may more closely adhere to the Mediator and Redeemer."

This role is at the same time special and extraordinary. It flows from her divine motherhood and can be understood and lived in faith only on the basis of the full truth of this motherhood. Since by virtue of divine election Mary is the earthly Mother of the Father's consubstantial Son and his "generous companion" in the work of redemption, "she is a Mother to us in the order of grace." This role constitutes a real dimension of her presence in the saving mystery of Christ and the Church.

Mary is honored in the Church "with special reverence. Indeed, from most ancient times the Blessed Virgin Mary has been venerated under the title of 'God-bearer.' In all perils and needs, the faithful have fled prayerfully to her protection." This cult is altogether special; it bears in itself and expresses the profound link which exists between the Mother of Christ and the Church. As Virgin and Mother, Mary remains for the Church a "permanent model." It can therefore be said that, especially under this aspect, namely, as a model or rather as a "figure," Mary, present in the mystery of Christ, remains constantly present also in the mystery of the Church. For the Church too is "called mother and virgin," and these names have a profound biblical and theological justification.

Mary and Women

This Marian dimension of Christian life takes on special importance in relation to women and their status. In fact, femininity has a unique relationship with the Mother of the Redeemer, a subject which can be studied in greater depth elsewhere. . . . The figure of Mary of Nazareth sheds light on womanhood as such by the very fact that God, in the sublime event of the incarnation of his Son, entrusted himself to the ministry, the free and active ministry, of a woman.

. . . Women, by looking to Mary, find in her the secret of living their femininity with dignity and of achieving their own true advancement. In the light of Mary, the Church sees in the face of women the reflection of a beauty which mirrors the loftiest sentiments of which the human heart is capable: the self-offering totality of love; the strength that is capable of bearing the greatest sorrows; limitless fidelity and tireless devotion to work; the ability to combine penetrating intuition with words of support and encouragement.

APPARITIONS OF THE BLESSED VIRGIN MARY

Seven of the best known apparitions are described. **Banneux**, near Liège, Belgium: Mary appeared eight times between Jan. 15 and Mar. 2, 1933, to an 11-year-old peasant girl, Mariette Beco, in a garden

behind the family cottage in Banneux. She called herself the Virgin of the Poor, the Sick, and the Indifferent. A small chapel was blessed Aug. 15, 1933.

Approval of devotion to Our Lady of Banneux was given in 1949 by Bishop Louis J. Kerkhofs of Liège, and a statue of that title was solemnly crowned in 1956.

Beauraing, Belgium: Mary appeared 33 times between Nov. 29, 1932, and Jan. 3, 1933, to five children in the garden of a convent school in Beauraing. A chapel was erected on the spot. Reserved approval of devotion to Our Lady of Beauraing was given Feb. 2, 1943, and final approbation July 2, 1949, by Bishop Charue of Namur (d. 1977).

Fátima, Portugal: Mary appeared six times between May 13 and Oct. 13, 1917, to three children (Lucia dos Santos, 10, who is now a Carmelite nun; Francisco Marto, 9, who died in 1919; and his sister Jacinta, 7, who died in 1920) in a field called Cova da Iria near Fátima. She recommended frequent recitation of the Rosary; urged works of mortification for the conversion of sinners; called for devotion to herself under the title of her Immaculate Heart; asked that the people of Russia be consecrated to her under this title, and that the faithful make a Communion of reparation on the first Saturday of each month.

The apparitions were declared worthy of belief in October, 1930, and devotion to Our Lady of Fátima was authorized under the title of Our Lady of the Rosary. In October, 1942, Pius XII consecrated the world to Mary under the title of her Immaculate Heart. Ten years later, in the first apostolic letter addressed directly to the peoples of Russia, he consecrated them in a special manner to Mary.

Guadalupe, Mexico: Mary appeared four times in 1531 to an Indian, Juan Diego (declared Blessed in 1990), on Tepeyac hill outside of Mexico City, and instructed him to tell Bishop Zumarraga of her wish that a church be built there. The bishop complied with the request about two years later, after being convinced of the genuineness of the apparition by the evidence of a miraculously painted life-size figure of the Virgin on the mantle of the Indian. The mantle bearing the picture has been preserved and is enshrined in the Basilica of Our Lady of Guadalupe. The shrine church, originally dedicated in 1709 and subsequently enlarged, has the title of basilica.

Benedict XIV, in a 1754 decree, authorized a Mass and Office under the title of Our Lady of Guadalupe for celebration on Dec. 12, and named Mary the patroness of New Spain. Our Lady of Guadalupe was designated patroness of Latin America by St. Pius X in 1910 and of the Americas by Pius XII in 1945.

La Salette, France: Mary appeared as a sorrowing and weeping figure Sept. 19, 1846, to two peasant children, Melanie Matthieu, 15, and Maximin Giraud, 11, at La Salette. The message she confided to them, regarding the necessity of penance, was communicated to Pius IX in 1851 and has since been known as the "secret" of La Salette. Bishop de Bruillard of Grenoble declared in 1851 that the apparition was credible, and devotion to Mary under the title of Our Lady of La Salette was authorized. A Mass and Office with this title were authorized in 1942. The shrine church was given the title of minor basilica in 1879.

Lourdes, France: Mary, identifying herself as the Immaculate Conception, appeared 18 times between Feb. 11 and July 16, 1858, to 14-year-old Bernadette Soubirous (canonized in 1933) at the grotto of Massabielle near Lourdes. Her message concerned the necessity of prayer and penance for the conversion of peoples. Mary's request that a chapel be built at the grotto and spring was fulfilled in 1862. Devotion under the title of Our Lady of Lourdes was authorized, and a Feb. 11 feast commemorating the apparitions was instituted by Leo XIII. St. Pius X extended this feast throughout the Church in 1907. The Church of Notre Dame was made a basilica in 1870, and the Church of the Rosary was built later. The underground Church of St. Pius X, with a capacity of 20,000 persons, was consecrated Mar. 25, 1958. Plans were announced in 1994 for renovation and reconstruction of the Lourdes sanctuary.

Our Lady of the Miraculous Medal, France: Mary appeared three times in 1830 to Catherine Labouré (canonized in 1947) in the chapel of the motherhouse of the Daughters of Charity of St. Vincent de Paul, Rue de Bac, Paris. She commissioned Catherine to have made the medal of the Immaculate Conception, now known as the Miraculous Medal, and to spread devotion to her under this title. In 1832, the medal was struck.

EVENTS AT MEDJUGORJE

The alleged apparitions of the Blessed Virgin Mary to six young people of Medjugorje, Bosnia-Herzogovina, have been the source of interest and controversy since they were first reported in June 1981, initially in the neighboring hillside field, subsequently in the village church of St. James and even in places far removed from Medjugorje.

Reports say the alleged visionaries have seen, heard, and even touched Mary during visions, and that they have variously received several or all of 10 secret messages related to coming world events and urging a quest for peace through penance and personal conversion. An investigative commission appointed by former local Bishop Pavao Zanic of Mostar-Duvno reported in March, 1984, that the authenticity of the apparitions had not been verified. He called the apparitions a case of "collective hallucination" exploited by local Franciscan priests at odds with him over control of a parish.

Former Archbishop Frane Franic of Split-Makarska, on the other hand, said in December, 1985: "Speaking as a believer and not as a bishop, my personal conviction is that the events at Medjugorje are of supernatural inspiration." He based his conviction on the observations of spiritual benefits related to the reported events, such as the spiritual development of the six young people, the increases in Mass attendance and sacramental practice at the scene of the apparitions, and the incidence of reconciliation among people.

On Jan. 29, 1987, the bishops of Yugoslavia (by a vote of 19 to 1) declared: "On the basis of research conducted so far, one cannot affirm that supernatural apparitions are involved" at Medjugorje. Currently, the events at Medjugorje are under on-going investigation by the Holy See to determine their authenticity. Nevertheless, the site of Medjugorje remains a popular destination for Catholic pilgrims from Europe and the United States.

A

Abbacy Nullius: A non-diocesan territory whose people are under the pastoral care of an abbot acting in general in the manner of a bishop.

Abbess: The female superior of a monastic community of nuns; e.g., Benedictines, Poor Clares, some others. Elected by members of the community, an abbess has general authority over her community but no sacramental jurisdiction.

Abbey: See Monastery.

Abbot: The male superior of a monastic community of men religious; e.g., Benedictines, Cistercians, some others. Elected by members of the community, an abbot has ordinary jurisdiction and general authority over his community. Eastern Rite equivalents of an abbot are a hegumen and an archimandrite. A regular abbot is the head of an abbey or monastery. An abbot general or archabbot is the head of a congregation consisting of several monasteries. An abbot primate is the head of the modern Benedictine Confederation.

Abiogenesis: The term used to describe the spontaneous generation of living matter from non-living matter.

Ablution: A term derived from Latin, meaning washing or cleansing, and referring to the cleansing of the hands of a priest celebrating Mass, after the offering of gifts; and to the cleansing of the chalice with water and wine after Communion.

Abnegation: The spiritual practice of self-denial (or mortification), in order to atone for past sins or in order to join oneself to the passion of Christ. Moritifcation can be undertaken through fasting, abstinence, or refraining from legitimate pleasure.

Abortion: Abortion is not only "the ejection of an immature fetus" from the womb, but is "also the killing of the same fetus in whatever way at whatever time from the moment of conception it may be procured." (This clarification of Canon 1398, reported in the Dec. 5, 1988, edition of *L'Osservatore Romano*, was issued by the Pontifical Council for the Interpretation of Legislative Texts — in view of scientific developments regarding ways and means of procuring abortion.) Accidental expulsion, as in cases of miscarriage, is without moral fault. Direct abortion, in which a fetus is intentionally removed from the womb, constitutes a direct attack on an innocent human being, a violation of the Fifth Commandment. A person who procures a completed abortion is automatically excommunicated (Canon 1398 of the *Code of Canon Law*); also excommunicated are all persons involved in a deliberate and successful effort to bring about an abortion. Direct abortion is not justifiable for any reason, e.g.: therapeutic, for the physical and/or psychological welfare of the mother; preventive, to avoid the birth of a defective or unwanted child; social, in the interests of family and/or community. Indirect abortion, which occurs when a fetus is expelled during medical or other treatment of the mother for a reason other than procuring expulsion, is permissible under the principle of double effect for a proportionately serious reason; e.g., when a medical or surgical procedure is necessary to save the life of the mother.

Abrogation: The Abolition or elimination of a law by some official action. In Canon Law, abrogation occurs through a direct decree of the Holy See or by the enactment of a later or subsequent law contrary to the former law.

Absolute: (1) A term in philosophy, first introduced at the end of the 18th century and used by Scholasticism, that signifies the "perfect being" (i.e., God), who relies upon no one for existence. Modern philosophical thought has added two new concepts: a) the Absolute is the sum of all being; b) the Absolute has no relationship with any other things; the Absolute is thus unknowable. These concepts are agnostic and contrary to Catholicism, which holds that God is the cause of all being (and hence not the sum) and is knowable by his creatures, at least in part. (2) Certain truths, revealed by God, which are unchanging.

Absolution, Sacramental: The act by which bishops and priests, acting as agents of Christ and ministers of the Church, grant forgiveness of sins in the sacrament of penance. The essential formula of absolution is: "I absolve you from your sins; in the name of the Father, and of the Son, and of the Holy Spirit. Amen." The power to absolve is given with ordination to the priesthood and episcopate. Priests exercise this power in virtue of authorization (faculties) granted by a bishop, a religious superior or canon law. Authorization can be limited or restricted regarding certain sins and penalties or censures. In cases of necessity, and also in cases of the absence of their own confessors, Eastern and Latin Rite Catholics may ask for and receive sacramental absolution from an Eastern or Latin Rite priest; so may Polish National Catholics, according to a Vatican decision issued in May, 1993. Any priest can absolve a person in danger of death; in the absence of a priest with the usual faculties, this includes a laicized priest or a priest under censure. (See additional entry under Sacraments.)

Abstinence: 1. The deliberate deprivation by a person of meat or of foods prepared with meat on those days prescribed by the Church as penitential (Ash Wednesday, Good Friday, and all Fridays of the year which are not solemnities — in the United States, not all Fridays of the year but only the Fridays of Lent). Those fourteen years of age and above are bound by the discipline. (2) Sexual Abstinence is the willing refrain from sexual intercourse; total abstinence is observed in obedience to the Sixth Commandment by single persons and couples whose marriages are not recognized by the Church as valid; periodic abstinence or periodic continence is observed by a married couple for regulating conception by natural means or for ascetical motives.

Adoration: The highest act and purpose of religious worship, which is directed in love and reverence to God alone in acknowledgment of his infinite perfection and goodness, and of his total dominion over creatures. Adoration, which is also called latria, consists of internal and external elements, private and social prayer, liturgical acts and ceremonies, and especially sacrifice.

Adultery: Marital infidelity. Sexual intercourse between a married person and another to whom one is not married, a violation of the obligations of the marital covenant, chastity and justice; any sin of impurity (thought, desire, word, action) involving a married person who is not one's husband or wife has the nature of adultery.

Advent Wreath: A wreath of laurel, spruce, or similar foliage with four candles which are lighted successively in the weeks of Advent to symbolize the approaching celebration of the birth of Christ, the Light of the World, at Christmas. The wreath originated among German Protestants.

Agape: A Greek word, meaning love, love feast, designating the meal of fellowship eaten at some gatherings of early Christians. Although held in some places in connection with the Mass, the agape was not part of the Mass, nor was it of universal institution and observance. It was infrequently observed by the fifth century and disappeared altogether between the sixth and eighth centuries.

Age of Reason: (1) The time of life when one begins to distinguish between right and wrong, to understand an obligation and take on moral responsibility; seven years of age is the presumption in church law. (2) Historically, the 18th century period of Enlightenment in England and France, the age of the Encyclopedists and Deists. According to a basic thesis of the Enlightenment, human experience and reason are the only sources of certain knowledge of truth; consequently, faith and revelation are discounted as valid sources of knowledge, and the reality of supernatural truth is called into doubt and/or denied.

Aggiornamento: An Italian word having the general meaning of bringing up to date, renewal, revitalization, descriptive of the processes of spiritual renewal and institutional reform and change in the Church; fostered by the Second Vatican Council.

Agnosticism: A theory which holds that a person cannot have certain knowledge of immaterial reality, especially the existence of God and things pertaining to him. Immanuel Kant, one of the philosophical fathers of agnosticism, stood for the position that God, as well as the human soul, is unknowable on speculative grounds; nevertheless, he found practical imperatives for acknowledging God's existence, a view shared by many agnostics. The First Vatican Council declared that the existence of God and some of his attributes can be known with certainty by human reason, even without divine revelation. The word agnosticism was first used, in the sense given here, by T. H. Huxley in 1869.

Agnus Dei: A Latin phrase, meaning Lamb of God. (1) A title given to Christ, the Lamb (victim) of the Sacrifice of the New Law (on Calvary and in Mass). (2) A prayer said at Mass before the reception of Holy Communion. (3) A sacramental. It is a round paschal-candle fragment blessed by the pope. On one side it bears the impression of a lamb, symbolic of Christ. On the reverse side, there may be any one of a number of impressions; e.g., the figure of a saint, the name and coat of arms of the reigning pope. The _agnus dei_ may have originated at Rome in the fifth century. The first definite mention of it dates from about 820.

Akathist Hymn: The most profound and famous expression of Marian devotion in churches of the Byzantine Rite. It consists of 24 sections, 12 of which relate to the Gospel of the Infancy and 12 to the mysteries of the Incarnation and the virginal motherhood of Mary. In liturgical usage, it is sung in part in Byzantine churches on the first four Saturdays of Lent and in toto on the fifth Saturday; it is also recited in private devotion. It is of unknown origin prior to 626, when its popularity increased as a hymn of thanksgiving after the successful defense and liberation of Constantinople, which had been under siege by Persians and Avars. Akathist means "without sitting," indicating that the hymn is recited or sung while standing. Pope John Paul, in a decree dated May 25, 1991, granted a plenary indulgence to the faithful of any rite who recite the hymn in a church or oratory, as a family, in a religious community or in a pious association — in conjunction with the usual conditions of freedom from attachment to sin, reception of the sacraments of penance and the Eucharist, and prayers for the intention of the pope (e.g., an Our Father, the Apostles' Creed and an aspiration). A partial indulgence can be gained for recitation of the hymn in other circumstances.

Alleluia: An exclamation of joy derived from Hebrew, "All hail to him who is, praise God," with various use in the liturgy and other expressions of worship.

Allocution: A formal type of papal address, as distinguished from an ordinary sermon or statement of views.

Alms: An act, gift or service of compassion, motivated by love of God and neighbor, for the help of persons in need; an obligation of charity, which is measurable by the ability of one person to give assistance and by the degree of another's need. Almsgiving, along with prayer and fasting, is regarded as a work of penance as well as an exercise of charity. (See Mercy, Works of.)

Alpha and Omega: The first and last letters of the Greek alphabet, used to symbolize the eternity of God (Rv. 1:8) and the divinity and eternity of Christ, the beginning and end of all things (Rv. 21:6; 22:13). Use of the letters as a monogram of Christ originated in the fourth century or earlier.

Amen: A Hebrew word meaning truly, it is true. In the Gospels, Christ used the word to add a note of authority to his statements. In other New Testament writings, as in Hebrew usage, it was the concluding word to doxologies. As the concluding word of prayers, it expresses assent to and acceptance of God's will.

Anamnesis: A prayer recalling the saving mysteries of the death and resurrection of Jesus, following the consecration at Mass in the Latin Rite.

Anaphora: A Greek term for the Canon or Eucharistic Prayer of the Mass.

Anathema: A Greek word with the root meaning of cursed or separated and the adapted meaning of excommunication, used in church documents, especially the canons of ecumenical councils, for the condemnation of heretical doctrines and of practices opposed to proper discipline.

Anchorite: A kind of hermit living in complete isolation and devoting himself exclusively to exercises of religion and severe penance according to a rule and way of life of his own devising. In early Christian times, anchorites were the forerunners of the monastic life. The closest contemporary approach to the life of an anchorite is that of Carthusian and Camaldolese hermits.

Angels: Purely spiritual beings with intelligence and free will whose name indicates their mission as servants and messengers of God. They were created before the creation of the visible universe. Good angels enjoy the perfect good of the beatific vision. They

can intercede for persons. The doctrine of guardian angels, although not explicitly defined as a matter of faith, is rooted in long-standing tradition. No authoritative declaration has ever been issued regarding choirs or various categories of angels: seraphim, cherubim, thrones, dominations, principalities, powers, virtues, archangels and angels. Archangels commemorated in the liturgy are: Michael, leader of the angelic host and protector of the synagogue; Raphael, guide of Tobiah and healer of his father; Gabriel, angel of the Incarnation. Fallen angels, the chief of whom is called the Devil or Satan, rejected the love of God and were therefore banished from heaven to hell. They can tempt persons to commit sin.

Angelus: A devotion which commemorates the Incarnation of Christ. It consists of three versicles, three Hail Marys and a special prayer, and recalls the announcement to Mary by the Archangel Gabriel that she was chosen to be the Mother of Christ, her acceptance of the divine will, and the Incarnation (Lk. 1:26-38). The Angelus is recited in the morning, at noon and in the evening. The practice of reciting the Hail Mary in honor of the Incarnation was introduced by the Franciscans in 1263. The *Regina Caeli*, commemorating the joy of Mary at Christ's Resurrection, replaces the Angelus during the Easter season.

Anger (Wrath): Passionate displeasure arising from some kind of offense suffered at the hands of another person, frustration or other cause, combined with a tendency to strike back at the cause of the displeasure; a violation of the Fifth Commandment and one of the capital sins if the displeasure is out of proportion to the cause and/or if the retaliation is unjust.

Anglican Orders: Holy orders conferred according to the rite of the Anglican Church, which Leo XIII declared null and void in the bull *Apostolicae Curae*, Sept. 13, 1896. The orders were declared null because they were conferred according to a rite that was substantially defective in form and intent, and because of a break in apostolic succession that occurred when Matthew Parker became head of the Anglican hierarchy in 1559. In making his declaration, Pope Leo cited earlier arguments against validity made by Julius III in 1553 and 1554 and by Paul IV in 1555. He also noted related directives requiring absolute ordination, according to the Catholic ritual, of convert ministers who had been ordained according to the Anglican Ordinal.

Anglican Use Parishes: In line with Vatican-approved developments since 1980, several Anglican use parishes have been established in the United States with the right to continue using some elements of Anglican usage in their liturgical celebrations. A Vatican document dated Mar. 31, 1981, said: "In June, 1980, the Holy See, through the Congregation for the Doctrine of the Faith, agreed to the request presented by the bishops of the United States of America in behalf of some clergy and laity formerly or actually belonging to the Episcopal (Anglican) Church for full communion with the Catholic Church. The Holy See's response to the initiative of these Episcopalians includes the possibility of a 'pastoral provision' which will provide, for those who desire it, a common identity reflecting certain elements of their own heritage."

Animals: Creatures of God, they are entrusted to human stewardship for appropriate care, use for human needs, as pets, for reasonable experimentation for the good of people. They should not be subject to cruel treatment.

Annulment: A decree issued by an appropriate Church authority or tribunal that a sacrament or ecclesiastical act is invalid and therefore lacking in all legal or canonical consequences.

Antichrist: The "deceitful one," the "antichrist" (2 Jn. 7), adversary of Christ and the kingdom of God, especially in the end time before the second coming of Christ. The term is also used in reference to anti-Christian persons and forces in the world.

Antiphon: (1) A short verse or text, generally from Scripture, recited in the Liturgy of the Hours before and after psalms and canticles. (2) Any verse sung or recited by one part of a choir or congregation in response to the other part, as in antiphonal or alternate chanting.

Anti-Semitism: A prejudice against Jews, and often accompanied by persecution. The prejudice has existed historically from the time of the ancient Persian Empire and survives even to the present day. It has been condemned consistently by the Church as being in opposition to scriptural principles and Christian charity.

Apologetics: The science and art of developing and presenting the case for the reasonableness of the Christian faith, by a wide variety of means including facts of experience, history, science, philosophy. The constant objective of apologetics, as well as of the total process of pre-evangelization, is preparation for response to God in faith; its ways and means, however, are subject to change in accordance with the various needs of people and different sets of circumstances.

Apostasy: (1) The total and obstinate repudiation of the Christian faith. An apostate automatically incurs a penalty of excommunication. (2) Apostasy from orders is the unlawful withdrawal from or rejection of the obligations of the clerical state by a man who has received major orders. An apostate from orders is subject to a canonical penalty. (3) Apostasy from the religious life occurs when a Religious with perpetual vows unlawfully leaves the community with the intention of not returning, or actually remains outside the community without permission. An apostate from religious life is subject to a canonical penalty.

Apostolate: The ministry or work of an apostle. In Catholic usage, the word is an umbrella-like term covering all kinds and areas of work and endeavor for the service of God and the Church and the good of people. Thus, the apostolate of bishops is to carry on the mission of the Apostles as pastors of the People of God: of priests, to preach the word of God and to carry out the sacramental and pastoral ministry for which they are ordained; of religious, to follow and do the work of Christ in conformity with the evangelical counsels and their rule of life; of lay persons, as individuals and/or in groups, to give witness to Christ and build up the kingdom of God through practice of their faith, professional competence and the performance of good works in the concrete circumstances of daily life. Apostolic works are not limited to those done within the Church or by specifically Catholic groups, although some apostolates are officially assigned to certain persons or groups and are

under the direction of church authorities. Apostolate derives from the commitment and obligation of baptism, confirmation, holy orders, matrimony, the duties of one's state in life, etc.

Apostolic Succession: Bishops of the Church, who form a collective body or college, are successors to the Apostles by ordination and divine right; as such they carry on the mission entrusted by Christ to the Apostles as guardians and teachers of the deposit of faith, principal pastors and spiritual authorities of the faithful. The doctrine of apostolic succession is based on New Testament evidence and the constant teaching of the Church, reflected as early as the end of the first century in a letter of Pope St. Clement to the Corinthians. A significant facet of the doctrine is the role of the pope as the successor of St. Peter, the vicar of Christ and head of the college of bishops. The doctrine of apostolic succession means more than continuity of apostolic faith and doctrine; its basic requisite is ordination by the laying on of hands in apostolic succession.

Archives: Documentary records, and the place where they are kept, of the spiritual and temporal government and affairs of the Church, a diocese, church agencies like the departments of the Roman Curia, bodies like religious institutes, and individual parishes. The collection, cataloguing, preserving, and use of these records are governed by norms stated in canon law and particular regulations. The strictest secrecy is always in effect for confidential records concerning matters of conscience, and documents of this kind are destroyed as soon as circumstances permit.

Ark of the Covenant: The sacred chest of the Israelites in which were placed and carried the tablets of stone inscribed with the Ten Commandments, the basic moral precepts of the Old Covenant (Ex. 25: 10-22; 37:1-9). The Ark was also a symbol of God's presence. The Ark was probably destroyed with the Temple in 586 B.C.

Asceticism: The practice of self-discipline. In the spiritual life, asceticism — by personal prayer, meditation, self-denial, works of mortification, and outgoing interpersonal works — is motivated by love of God and contributes to growth in holiness.

Ashes: Religious significance has been associated with their use as symbolic of penance since Old Testament times. Thus, ashes of palm blessed on the previous Sunday of the Passion are placed on the foreheads of the faithful on Ash Wednesday to remind them to do works of penance, especially during the season of Lent, and that they are dust and unto dust will return. Ashes are a sacramental.

Aspergillum: A vessel or device used for sprinkling holy water. The ordinary type is a metallic rod with a bulbous tip which absorbs the water and discharges it at the motion of the user's hand.

Aspersory: A portable metallic vessel, similar to a pail, for carrying holy water.

Aspiration (Ejaculation): Short exclamatory prayer; e.g., My Jesus, mercy.

Atheism: Denial of the existence of God, finding expression in a system of thought (speculative atheism) or a manner of acting (practical atheism) as though there were no God. The Second Vatican Council, in its Pastoral Constitution on the Church in the Modern World (*Gaudium et Spes*, Nos. 19 to 21), noted that a profession of atheism may represent an explicit denial of God, the rejection of a wrong notion of God, an affirmation of man rather than of God, an extreme protest against evil. It said that such a profession might result from acceptance of such propositions as: there is no absolute truth; man can assert nothing, absolutely nothing, about God; everything can be explained by scientific reasoning alone; the whole question of God is devoid of meaning.

Atonement: The redemptive activity of Christ, who reconciled man with God through his Incarnation and entire life, and especially by his suffering and Resurrection. The word also applies to prayer and good works by which persons join themselves with and take part in Christ's work of reconciliation and reparation for sin.

Attributes of God: Perfections of God. God possesses — and is — all the perfections of being, without limitation. Because he is infinite, all of these perfections are one, perfectly united in him. Because of the limited power of human intelligence, divine perfections — such as omnipotence, truth, love, etc. — are viewed separately, as distinct characteristics, even though they are not actually distinct in God.

Authority, Ecclesiastical: The authority exercised by the Church, and particularly by the pope and the bishops; it is delegated by Jesus Christ to St. Peter. This authority extends to all those matters entrusted to the Apostles by Christ, including teaching of the Faith, the liturgy and sacraments, moral guidance, and the administration of discipline.

Avarice (Covetousness): A disorderly and unreasonable attachment to and desire for material things; called a capital sin because it involves preoccupation with material things to the neglect of spiritual goods and obligations of justice and charity.

Ave Maria: See **Hail Mary.**

B

Baldacchino: A canopy over an altar.

Baptism: See Sacraments.

Beatification: A preliminary step toward canonization of a saint. It begins with an investigation of the candidate's life, writings and heroic practice of virtue, and, except in the case of martyrs, the certification of one miracle worked by God through his or her intercession. If the findings of the investigation so indicate, the pope decrees that the Servant of God may be called Blessed and may be honored locally or in a limited way in the liturgy. Additional procedures lead to canonization. (See separate entry).

Beatific Vision: The intuitive, immediate and direct vision and experience of God enjoyed in the light of glory by all the blessed in heaven. The vision is a supernatural mystery.

Beatitude: A literary form of the Old and New Testaments in which blessings are promised to persons for various reasons. Beatitudes are mentioned 26 times in the Psalms, and in other books of the Old Testament. The best known Beatitudes — identifying blessedness with participation in the kingdom of God and his righteousness, and descriptive of the qualities of Christian perfection — are those recounted in Mt. 5:3-12 and Lk. 6:20-23. The Beatitudes are of central importance in the teaching of Jesus.

Benedictus: The canticle or hymn of Zechariah at the circumcision of St. John the Baptist (Lk. 1:68-79). It is an expression of praise and thanks to God for sending John as a precursor of the Messiah. The Benedictus is recited in the Liturgy of the Hours as part of the Morning Prayer.

Biglietto: A papal document of notification of appointment to the cardinalate.

Biretta: A stiff, square hat with three ridges on top worn by clerics in church and on other occasions.

Blasphemy: Any internal or external expression of hatred, reproach, insult, defiance or contempt with respect to God and the use of his name, principally, and to the Church, saints and sacred things, secondarily; a serious sin, directly opposed to the second commandment. Blasphemy against the Spirit is the deliberate refusal to accept divine mercy, rejection of forgiveness of sins and of the promise of salvation. The sin that is unforgivable because a person refuses to seek or accept forgiveness.

Blessing: Invocation of God's favor, by official ministers of the Church or by private individuals. Blessings are recounted in the Old and New Testaments, and are common in the Christian tradition. Many types of blessings are listed in the Book of Blessings of the Roman Ritual. Private blessings, as well as those of an official kind, are efficacious. Blessings are imparted with the Sign of the Cross and appropriate prayer.

Bride of Christ: A metaphorical title that denotes the intimate union that Christ enjoys with his Church; the title is mentioned specifically in the NT (2 Cor. 11:2).

Brief, Apostolic: A papal letter, less formal than a bull, signed for the pope by a secretary and impressed with the seal of the Fisherman's Ring. Simple apostolic letters of this kind are issued for beatifications and with respect to other matters.

Bull, Apostolic: Apostolic letter, a solemn form of papal document, beginning with the name and title of the pope (e.g., John Paul II, Servant of the Servants of God), dealing with an important subject, sealed with a *bulla* or red-ink imprint of the device on the *bulla.* Bulls are issued to confer the titles of bishops and cardinals, to promulgate canonizations, to proclaim Holy Years and for other purposes. A collection of bulls is called a *bullarium.*

Burial, Ecclesiastical: Interment with ecclesiastical rites, a right of the Christian faithful. The Church recommends burial of the bodies of the dead, but cremation is permissible if it does not involve reasons against church teaching. Ecclesiastical burial is in order for catechumens; for unbaptized children whose parents intended to have them baptized before death; and even, in the absence of their own ministers, for baptized non-Catholics unless it would be considered against their will.

Burse, Financial: A special fund maintained by a diocese, religious institute, or private foundation usually endowed by a private benefactor; it often has the purpose of making possible the education of candidates for the priesthood.

C

Calumny (Slander): Harming the name and good reputation of a person by lies; a violation of obligations of justice and truth. Restitution is due for calumny.

Calvary: A knoll about 15 feet high just outside the western wall of Jerusalem where Christ was crucified, so called from the Latin calvaria (skull) which described its shape.

Canon: A Greek word meaning rule, norm, standard, measure. (1) The word designates the Canon of Sacred Scripture, which is the list of books recognized by the Church as inspired by the Holy Spirit. (2) The term also designates the canons (Eucharistic Prayers, anaphoras) of the Mass, the core of the eucharistic liturgy. (3) Certain dignitaries of the Church have the title of Canon, and some religious are known as Canons. (See Bible.)

Canonization: An infallible declaration by the pope that a person, who died as a martyr and/or practiced Christian virtue to a heroic degree, is now in heaven and is worthy of honor and imitation by all the faithful. Such a declaration is preceded by the process of beatification and another detailed investigation concerning the person's reputation for holiness, writings, and (except in the case of martyrs) a miracle ascribed to his or her intercession after death. The pope can dispense from some of the formalities ordinarily required in canonization procedures (equivalent canonization), as Pope John XXIII did in the canonization of St. Gregory Barbarigo on May 26, 1960. A saint is worthy of honor in liturgical worship throughout the universal Church. From its earliest years the Church has venerated saints. Public official honor always required the approval of the bishop of the place. Martyrs were the first to be honored. St. Martin of Tours, who died in 397, was an early non-martyr venerated as a saint. The earliest canonization by a pope with positive documentation was that of St. Ulrich (Uldaric) of Augsburg by John XV in 993. Alexander III reserved the process of canonization to the Holy See in 1171. In 1588 Sixtus V established the Sacred Congregation of Rites for the principal purpose of handling causes for beatification and canonization: this function is now the work of the Congregation for the Causes of Saints. The official listing of saints and blessed is contained in the Roman Martyrology (being revised and updated) and related decrees issued after its last publication. Butler's unofficial *Lives of the Saints* (1956) contains 2,565 entries. The Church regards all persons in heaven as saints, not just those who have been officially canonized. (See Beatification, Saints, Canonizations by Leo XIII and His Successors.)

Canon Law: The Code of Canon Law (*Corpus Iuris Canonici*) enacted and promulgated by ecclesiastical authority for the orderly and pastoral administration and government of the Church. A revised Code for the Latin Rite, effective Nov. 27, 1983, consists of 1,752 canons in seven books under the titles of general norms, the people of God, the teaching mission of the Church, the sanctifying mission of the Church, temporal goods of the Church, penal law and procedural law. The antecedent of this Code was promulgated in 1917 and became effective in 1918; it consisted of 2,414 canons in five books covering general rules, ecclesiastical persons, sacred things, trials, crimes and punishments. There is a separate Code of the Canons of Eastern Churches, in effect since Oct. 1, 1991.

Canticle: A scriptural chant or prayer differing from the psalms. Three of the canticles prescribed for use in the Liturgy of the Hours are: the *Magnificat*, the Canticle of Mary (Lk. 1:46-55); the *Benedictus*, the Canticle of Zechariah (Lk. 1:68-79); and the *Nunc Dimittis*, the Canticle of Simeon (Lk. 2:29-32).

Capital Punishment: Punishment for crime by means of the death penalty. The political community, which has authority to provide for the common good, has the right to defend itself and its members against unjust aggression and may in extreme cases punish with the death penalty persons found guilty before the law of serious crimes against individuals and a just social order. Such punishment is essentially vindictive. Its value as a crime deterrent is a matter of perennial debate. The prudential judgment as to whether or not there should be capital punishment belongs to the civic community. The U.S. Supreme Court, in a series of decisions dating from June 29, 1972, ruled against the constitutionality of statutes on capital punishment except in specific cases and with appropriate consideration, with respect to sentence, of mitigating circumstances of the crime. Pope John Paul II, in his encyclical letter *Evangelium Vitae* ("The Gospel of Life"), wrote: "There is a growing tendency, both in the Church and in civil society, to demand that it (capital punishment) be applied in a very limited way or even that it be abolished completely." Quoting the *Catechism of the Catholic Church*, the pope wrote: " 'If bloodless means are sufficient to defend human lives against an aggressor and to protect public order and the safety of persons, public authority must limit itself to such means, because they better correspond to the concrete conditions of the common good and are more in conformity to the dignity of the human person.' "

Capital Sins: Sins which give rise to other sins: pride, avarice, lust, wrath (anger), gluttony, envy, sloth.

Cardinal Virtues: The four principal moral virtues are prudence, justice, temperance and fortitude.

Casuistry: In moral theology, the application of moral principles to specific cases. Casuistry can be of assistance because it takes the abstract and makes it practical in a particular situation. It has definite limitations and does not replace the conscience in the decision-making process; additionally, it must be aligned with the cardinal virtue of prudence.

Catacombs: Underground Christian cemeteries in various cities of the Roman Empire and Italy, especially in the vicinity of Rome; the burial sites of many martyrs and other Christians.

Catechesis: The whole complex of church efforts to make disciples of Christ, involving doctrinal instruction and spiritual formation through practice of the faith.

Catechism: A systematic presentation of the fundamentals of Catholic doctrine regarding faith and morals. Sources are Sacred Scripture, tradition, the magisterium (teaching authority of the Church), the writings of Fathers and Doctors of the Church, liturgy. The new *Catechism of the Catholic Church*, published Oct. 11, 1992, consists of four principal sections: the profession of faith, (the Creed), the sacraments of faith, the life of faith (the Commandments) and the prayer of the believer (the Lord's Prayer). The 16th century Council of Trent mandated publication of the *Roman Catechism*. Catechisms such as these two are useful sources for other catechisms serving particular needs of the faithful and persons seeking admission to the Catholic Church.

Catechumen: A person preparing in a program (catechumenate) of instruction and spiritual formation for baptism and reception into the Church. The Church has a special relationship with catechumens. It invites them to lead the life of the Gospel, introduces them to the celebration of the sacred rites, and grants them various prerogatives that are proper to the faithful (one of which is the right to ecclesiastical burial). (See Rite of Christian Initiation of Adults, under Baptism.)

Cathedra: A Greek word for chair, designating the chair or seat of a bishop in the principal church of his diocese, which is therefore called a cathedral.

Cathedraticum: The tax paid to a bishop by all churches and benefices subject to him for the support of episcopal administration and for works of charity.

Catholic: A Greek word, meaning universal, first used in the title Catholic Church in a letter written by St. Ignatius of Antioch about 107 to the Christians of Smyrna.

Celebret: A Latin word, meaning "Let him celebrate," the name of a letter of recommendation issued by a bishop or other superior stating that a priest is in good standing and therefore eligible to celebrate Mass or perform other priestly functions.

Celibacy: The unmarried state of life, required in the Roman Church of candidates for holy orders and of men already ordained to holy orders, for the practice of perfect chastity and total dedication to the service of people in the ministry of the Church. Celibacy is enjoined as a condition for ordination by church discipline and law, not by dogmatic necessity. In the Roman Church, a consensus in favor of celibacy developed in the early centuries while the clergy included both celibates and men who had been married once. The first local legislation on the subject was enacted by a local council held in Elvira, Spain, about 306; it forbade bishops, priests, deacons and other ministers to have wives. Similar enactments were passed by other local councils from that time on, and by the 12th century particular laws regarded marriage by clerics in major orders to be not only unlawful but also null and void. The latter view was translated by the Second Lateran Council in 1139 into what seems to be the first written universal law making holy orders an invalidating impediment to marriage. In 1563 the Council of Trent ruled definitely on the matter and established the discipline in force in the Roman Church. Some exceptions to this discipline have been made in recent years. A number of married Protestant and Episcopalian (Anglican) clergymen who became converts and were subsequently ordained to the priesthood have been permitted to continue in marriage. Married men over the age of 35 can be ordained to the permanent diaconate. Eastern Church discipline on celibacy differs from that of the Roman Church. In line with legislation enacted by the Synod of Trullo in 692 and still in force, candidates for holy orders may marry before becoming deacons and may continue in marriage thereafter, but marriage after ordination is forbidden. Bishops of Eastern Catholic Churches in the U.S., however, do not ordain married candidates for the priesthood. Bishops of Eastern Catholic Churches are unmarried.

Cenacle: The upper room in Jerusalem where Christ ate the Las Supper with his Apostles.

Censer: A metal vessel with a perforated cover and suspended by chains, in which incense is burned. It is used at some Masses, Benediction of the Blessed Sacrament and other liturgical functions.

Censorship of Books: An exercise of vigilance by the Church for safeguarding authentic religious teaching. Pertinent legislation in a decree issued by the Congregation for the Doctrine of the Faith Apr. 9, 1975, is embodied in the Code of Canon Law (Book III, Title IV). The legislation deals with requirements for pre-publication review and clearance of various types of writings on religious subjects. Permission to publish works of a religious character, together with the apparatus of reviewing them beforehand, falls under the authority of the bishop of the place where the writer lives or where the works are published. Clearance for publication is usually indicated by the terms *Nihil obstat* ("Nothing stands in the way") issued by the censor and *Imprimatur* ("Let it be printed") authorized by the bishop. The clearing of works for publication does not necessarily imply approval of an author's viewpoint or his manner of handling a subject.

Censures: Sanctions imposed by the Church on baptized Roman Catholics 18 years of age or older for committing certain serious offenses and for being or remaining obstinate therein: (1) excommunication (exclusion from the community of the faithful, barring a person from sacramental and other participation in the goods and offices of the community of the Church), (2) suspension (prohibition of a cleric to exercise orders) and (3) interdict (deprivation of the sacraments and liturgical activities). The intended purposes of censures are to correct and punish offenders; to deter persons from committing sins which, more seriously and openly than others, threaten the common good of the Church and its members; and to provide for the making of reparation for harm done to the community of the Church. Censures may be incurred automatically (*ipso facto*) on the commission of certain offenses for which fixed penalties have been laid down in church law (*latae sententiae*); or they may be inflicted by sentence of a judge (*ferendae sententiae*). Automatic excommunication is incurred for the offenses of abortion, apostasy, heresy and schism. Obstinacy in crime — also called contumacy, disregard of a penalty, defiance of church authority — is presumed by law in the commission of offenses for which automatic censures are decreed. The presence and degree of contumacy in other cases, for which judicial sentence is required, is subject to determination by a judge. Absolution can be obtained from any censure, provided the person repents and desists from obstinacy. Absolution may be reserved to the pope, the bishop of a place, or the major superior of an exempt clerical religious institute. In danger of death, any priest can absolve from all censures; in other cases, faculties to absolve from reserved censures can be exercised by competent authorities or given to other priests. The penal law of the Church is contained in Book VI of the Code of Canon Law.

Ceremonies, Master of: One who directs the proceedings of a rite or ceremony during the function.

Chamberlain (*Camerlengo*): (1) the Chamberlain of the Holy Roman Church is a cardinal with special responsibilities, especially during the time between the death of one pope and the election of his successor; among other things, he safeguards and administers the goods and revenues of the Holy See and heads particular congregations of cardinals for special purposes. (See also Papal Election.) (2) the Chamberlain of the College of Cardinals has charge of the property and revenues of the College and keeps the record of business transacted in consistories. (3) the Chamberlain of the Roman Clergy is the president of the secular clergy of Rome.

Chancellor: Notary of a diocese, who draws up written documents in the government of the diocese; takes care of, arranges and indexes diocesan archives, records of dispensations and ecclesiastical trials.

Chancery: (1) A branch of church administration that handles written documents used in the government of a diocese. (2) The administrative office of a diocese, a bishop's office.

Chant: A type of sacred singing. It is either recitative in nature with a short two-to-six tones for an accentus, or melodic in one of three styles (syllabic, neumatic, or melismatic).

Chapel: A building or part of another building used for divine worship; a portion of a church set aside for the celebration of Mass or for some special devotion.

Chaplain: A priest — or, in some instances, a properly qualified religious or lay person — serving the pastoral needs of particular groups of people and institutions, such as hospitals, schools, correctional facilities, religious communities, the armed forces, etc.

Chaplet: A term, meaning little crown, applied to a rosary or, more commonly, to a small string of beads used for devotional purposes; e.g., the Infant of Prague chaplet.

Chapter: A general meeting of delegates of religious orders for elections and the handling of other important affairs of their communities.

Charismatic Renewal: A movement which originated with a handful of Duquesne University students and faculty members in the 1966-67 academic year and spread from there to Notre Dame, Michigan State University, the University of Michigan, other campuses and cities throughout the U.S., and to well over 100 other countries. Scriptural keys to the renewal are: Christ's promise to send the Holy Spirit upon the Apostles; the description, in the Acts of the Apostles, of the effects of the coming of the Holy Spirit upon the Apostles on Pentecost; St. Paul's explanation, in the Letter to the Romans and 1 Corinthians, of the charismatic gifts (for the good of the Church and persons) the Holy Spirit would bestow on Christians; New Testament evidence concerning the effects of charismatic gifts in and through the early Church. The personal key to the renewal is baptism in the Holy Spirit. This is not a new sacrament but the personally experienced actualization of grace already sacramentally received, principally in baptism and confirmation. The experience of baptism in the Holy Spirit is often accompanied by the reception of one or more charismatic gifts. A characteristic form of the renewal is the weekly prayer meeting, a gathering which includes periods of spontaneous prayer, singing, sharing of experience and testimony, fellowship and teaching. (See also Index.)

Charisms: Gifts or graces given by God to persons for the good of others and the Church. Examples are special gifts for apostolic work, prophecy, healing, discernment of spirits, the life of evangelical poverty, here-and-now witness to faith in various circumstances of life. The Second Vatican Council made the following statement about charisms in the Dogmatic Constitution on the Church (No. 12): "It is not only through the sacraments and Church ministries that the same Holy Spirit sanctifies and leads the People of God and enriches it with virtues. Allotting his gifts 'to everyone according as he will' (1 Cor. 12:11), he distributes special graces among the faithful of every rank. By these gifts he makes them fit and ready to undertake the various tasks or offices advantageous for the renewal and upbuilding of the Church, according to the words of the Apostle: 'The manifestation of the Spirit is given to everyone for profit' (1 Cor. 12:7). These charismatic gifts, whether they be the most outstanding or the more simple and widely diffused, are to be received with thanksgiving and consolation, for they are exceedingly suitable and useful for the needs of the Church. Still, extraordinary gifts are not to be rashly sought after, nor are the fruits of apostolic labor to be presumptuously expected from them. In any case, judgment as to their genuineness and proper use belongs to those who preside over the Church, and to whose special competence it belongs, not indeed to extinguish the Spirit, but to test all things and hold fast to that which is good" (cf. 1 Thes. 5:12; 19-21).

Charity: Love of God above all things for his own sake, and love of one's neighbor as oneself because and as an expression of one's love for God; the greatest of the three theological virtues. The term is sometimes also used to designate sanctifying grace.

Chastity: Properly ordered behavior with respect to sex. In marriage, the exercise of the procreative power is integrated with the norms and purposes of marriage. Outside of marriage, the rule is self-denial of the voluntary exercise and enjoyment of the procreative faculty in thought, word or action. The vow of chastity, which reinforces the virtue of chastity with the virtue of religion, is one of the three vows professed publicly by members of institutes of consecrated life.

Chirograph or Autograph Letter: A letter written by a pope himself, in his own handwriting.

Chrism: A mixture of olive or other vegetable oil and balsam (or balm), that is consecrated by a bishop for use in liturgical anointings: Baptism, Confirmation, Holy Orders, the blessing of an altar.

Christ: The title of Jesus, derived from the Greek translation *Christos* of the Hebrew term Messiah, meaning the Anointed of God, the Savior and Deliverer of his people. Christian use of the title is a confession of belief that Jesus is the Savior.

Christianity: The sum total of things related to belief in Christ — the Christian religion, Christian churches, Christians themselves, society based on and expressive of Christian beliefs, culture reflecting Christian values.

Christians: The name first applied about the year 43 to followers of Christ at Antioch, the capital of Syria. It was used by the pagans as a contemptuous term. The word applies to persons who profess belief in the divinity and teachings of Christ and who give witness to him in life.

Circumcision: A ceremonial practice symbolic of initiation and participation in the covenant between God and Abraham.

Circumincession: The indwelling of each divine Person of the Holy Trinity in the others.

Clergy: Men ordained to holy orders and commissioned for sacred ministries and assigned to pastoral and other duties for the service of the people and the Church. (1) Diocesan or secular clergy are committed to pastoral ministry in parishes and in other capacities in a particular church (diocese) under the direction of their bishop, to whom they are bound by a promise of obedience. (2) Regular clergy belong to religious institutes (orders, congregations, societies — institutes of consecrated life) and are so called because they observe the rule (*regula*, in Latin) of their respective institutes. They are committed to the ways of life and apostolates of their institutes. In ordinary pastoral ministry, they are under the direction of local bishops as well as their own superiors.

Clericalism: A term generally used in a derogatory sense to mean action, influence and interference by the Church and the clergy in matters with which they allegedly should not be concerned. Anticlericalism is a reaction of antipathy, hostility, distrust and opposition to the Church and clergy arising from real and/or alleged faults of the clergy, overextension of the role of the laity, or for other reasons.

Cloister: Part of a monastery, convent or other house of religious reserved for use by members of the institute. Houses of contemplative Religious have a strict enclosure.

Code: A digest of rules or regulations, such as the Code of Canon Law.

Code of Canon Law: See Canon Law.

Collegiality: A term in use especially since the Second Vatican Council to describe the authority exercised by the College of Bishops. The bishops of the Church, in union with and subordinate to the pope — who has full, supreme and universal power over the Church which he can always exercise independently — have supreme teaching and pastoral authority over the whole Church. In addition to their proper authority of office for the good of the faithful in their respective dioceses or other jurisdictions, the bishops have authority to act for the good of the universal Church. This collegial authority is exercised in a solemn manner in an ecumenical council and can also be exercised in other ways sanctioned by the pope. Doctrine on collegiality was set forth by the Second Vatican Council in *Lumen Gentium* (the Dogmatic Constitution on the Church). (See separate entry.) By extension, the concept of collegiality is applied to other forms of participation and co-responsibility by members of a community.

Communicatio in Sacris: The reception of the Church's sacraments by non-members or the reception by Catholics of sacraments in non-Catholic Churches.

Communion of Saints: "The communion of all the faithful of Christ, those who are pilgrims on earth, the dead who are being purified, and the blessed in heaven, all together forming one Church; in this communion, the merciful love of God and his saints is always (attentive) to our prayers" (Paul VI, *Creed of the People of God*).

Communism: The substantive principles of modern communism, a theory and system of economics and social organization, were stated about the middle of the 19th century by Karl Marx, author of *The Communist Manifesto* and, with Friedrich Engels, *Das Kapital*. The elements of communist theory include: radical materialism; dialectical determinism; the inevitability of class struggle and conflict, which is to be furthered for the ultimate establishment of a worldwide, classless society; common ownership of productive and other goods; the subordination of all persons and institutions to the dictatorship of the collectivity; denial of the rights, dignity and liberty of persons; militant atheism and hostility to religion, utilitarian morality. Communism in theory and practice has been the subject of many papal documents and statements. Pius IX condemned it in 1846. Leo XIII dealt with it at length in the encyclical letter *Quod Apostolici Muneris* in 1878 and *Rerum Novarum* in 1891. Pius XI wrote on the same subject in the encyclicals *Quadragesimo Anno* in 1931 and *Divini Redemptoris* in 1937. These writings have been updated and developed in new directions by Pius XII, John XXIII, Paul VI and John Paul II.

Compline: The night prayer of the Church that completes the daily cursus (course) of the Liturgy of the Hours (Divine Office).

Concelebration: The liturgical act in which several priests, led by one member of the group, offer Mass together, all consecrating the bread and wine. Concelebration has always been common in churches of Eastern Rite. In the Roman Rite, it was long restricted, taking place only at the ordination of bishops and the ordination of priests. The Constitution on the Sacred Liturgy issued by the Second Vatican Council set new norms for concelebration, which is now relatively common in the Roman Rite.

Concordance, Biblical: An alphabetical verbal index enabling a user knowing one or more words of a scriptural passage to locate the entire text.

Concordat: A church-state treaty with the force of law concerning matters of mutual concern — e.g., rights of the Church, arrangement of ecclesiastical jurisdictions, marriage laws, education. Approximately 150 agreements of this kind have been negotiated since the Concordat of Worms in 1122.

Concupiscence: Any tendency of the sensitive appetite. The term is most frequently used in reference to desires and tendencies for sinful sense pleasure.

Confession: Sacramental confession is the act by which a person tells or confesses his sins to a priest who is authorized to give absolution in the sacrament of penance.

Confessor: A priest who administers the sacrament of penance. The title of confessor, formerly given to a category of male saints, was suppressed with publication of the calendar reform of 1969.

Confraternity: An association whose members practice a particular form of religious devotion and/or are engaged in some kind of apostolic work.

Congregation: (1) The collective name for the people who form a parish. (2) One of the chief administrative departments of the Roman Curia. (3) An unofficial term for a group of men and women who belong to a religious community or institute of consecrated life.

Conscience: Practical judgment concerning the moral goodness or sinfulness of an action (thought, word, desire). In the Catholic view, this judgment is made by reference of the action, its attendant circumstances and the intentions of the person to the requirements of moral law as expressed in the Ten Commandments, the summary law of love for God and neighbor, the life and teaching of Christ, and the authoritative teaching and practice of the Church with respect to the total demands of divine Revelation. A person is obliged: (1) to obey a certain and correct conscience; (2) to obey a certain conscience even if it is inculpably erroneous; (3) not to obey, but to correct, a conscience known to be erroneous or lax; (4) to rectify a scrupulous conscience by following the advice of a confessor and by other measures; (5) to resolve doubts of conscience before acting. It is legitimate to act for solid and probable reasons when a question of moral responsibility admits of argument (see Probabiliorism and Probabilism).

Conscience, Examination of: Self-examination to determine one's spiritual state before God, regarding one's sins and faults. It is recommended as a regular practice and is practically necessary in preparing for the sacrament of penance. The particular examen is a regular examination to assist in overcoming specific faults and imperfections.

Consequentialism: A moral theory, closely associated with proportionalism and utilitarianism, that holds that the preferable action is one that brings about the best consequences. Preferred results, rather than the objective truth and intentionality, are the object of actions based on consequentialism. While traditional moral theology acknowledges that consequences are important in determining the rightness of an act, importance is also placed on the intrinsic morality of the act and the agent's intention.

Consistory: An assembly of cardinals presided over by the pope.

Constitution: (1) An apostolic or papal constitution is a document in which a pope enacts and promulgates law. (2) A formal and solemn document issued by an ecumenical council on a doctrinal or pastoral subject, with binding force in the whole Church; e.g., the four constitutions issued by the Second Vatican Council on the Church, liturgy, Revelation, and the Church in the modern world. (3) The constitutions of institutes of consecrated life and societies of apostolic life spell out details of and norms drawn from the various rules for the guidance and direction of the life and work of their members.

Consubstantiation: A theory which holds that the Body and Blood of Christ coexist with the substance of bread and wine in the Holy Eucharist. This theory, also called impanation, is incompatible with the doctrine of transubstantiation.

Contraception: Anything done by positive interference to prevent sexual intercourse from resulting in conception. Direct contraception is against the order of nature. Indirect contraception — as a secondary effect of medical treatment or other action having a necessary, good, non-contraceptive purpose — is permissible under the principle of the double effect. The practice of periodic continence is not contraception because it does not involve positive inter-

ference with the order of nature. (See *Humanae Vitae*, other entries.)

Contrition: Sorrow for sin coupled with a purpose of amendment. Contrition arising from a supernatural motive is necessary for the forgiveness of sin. (1) Perfect contrition is total sorrow for and renunciation of attachment to sin, arising from the motive of pure love of God. Perfect contrition, which implies the intention of doing all God wants done for the forgiveness of sin (including confession in a reasonable period of time), is sufficient for the forgiveness of serious sin and the remission of all temporal punishment due for sin. (The intention to receive the sacrament of penance is implicit — even if unrealized, as in the case of some persons — in perfect contrition.) (2) Imperfect contrition or attrition is sorrow arising from a quasi-selfish supernatural motive; e.g., the fear of losing heaven, suffering the pains of hell, etc. Imperfect contrition is sufficient for the forgiveness of serious sin when joined with absolution in confession, and sufficient for the forgiveness of venial sin even outside of confession.

Contumely: Personal insult, reviling a person in his presence by accusation of moral faults, by refusal of recognition or due respect; a violation of obligations of justice and charity.

Conversion: In a general sense, the turning away from someone or something and the moving toward another person or thing. In Christian belief, conversion is the embrace of Jesus Christ and a rejection of all that keeps one from God.

***Corpus Iuris Canonici*:** See Canon Law.

Council: A formal meeting of Church leaders, summoned by a bishop or appropriate Church leader, with the general purpose of assisting the life of the Church through deliberations, decrees, and promulgations. Different councils include: **diocesan** councils (synod), a gathering of the officials of an individual diocese; **provincial** councils, the meeting of the bishops of a province; **plenary** councils, the assembly of the bishops of a country; and **ecumenical** councils, a gathering of all the bishops in the world under the authority of the Bishop of Rome.

Counsels, Evangelical: Gospel counsels of perfection, especially voluntary poverty, perfect chastity and obedience, which were recommended by Christ to those who would devote themselves exclusively and completely to the immediate service of God. Religious (members of institutes of consecrated life) bind themselves by public vows to observe these counsels in a life of total consecration to God and service to people through various kinds of apostolic works.

Counter-Reformation: The period of approximately 100 years following the Council of Trent (1545-63), which witnessed a reform within the Church to stimulate genuine Catholic life and to counteract effects of the Reformation.

Covenant: A bond of relationship between parties pledged to each other. God-initiated covenants in the Old Testament included those with Noah, Abraham, Moses, Levi, David. The Mosaic (Sinai) covenant made Israel God's Chosen People on terms of fidelity to true faith, true worship, and righteous conduct according to the Decalogue. The New Testament covenant, prefigured in the Old Testament, is the bond people have with God through Christ. All people are called to be parties to this perfect and everlasting covenant, which was mediated and ratified by Christ. The marriage covenant seals the closest possible relationship between a man and a woman.

Creation: The production by God of something out of nothing. The biblical account of creation is contained in the first two chapters of Genesis.

Creator: God, the supreme, self-existing Being, the absolute and infinite First Cause of all things.

Creature: Everything in the realm of being is a creature, except God.

Cremation: The reduction of a human corpse to ashes by means of fire. Cremation is not in line with Catholic tradition and practice, even though it is not opposed to any article of faith. The Congregation for the Doctrine of the Faith, under date of May 8, 1963, circulated among bishops an instruction which upheld the traditional practices of Christian burial but modified anti-cremation legislation. Cremation may be permitted for serious reasons, of a private as well as public nature, provided it does not involve any contempt of the Church or of religion, or any attempt to deny, question, or belittle the doctrine of the resurrection of the body. In a letter dated Mar. 21, 1997, and addressed to Bishop Anthony M. Pilla, president of the National Conference of Catholic Bishops, the Congregation for Divine Worship and the Discipline of the Sacraments granted "a particular permission to the diocesan bishops of the United States of America. By this, local Ordinaries (heads of dioceses) are authorized . . . to permit that the funeral liturgy, including where appropriate the celebration of the Eucharist, be celebrated in the presence of the cremated remains instead of the natural body." Bishop Pilla asked bishops not to use this indult until appropriate texts and ritual directives are approved by the Vatican. (See Burial, Ecclesiastical).

Crib: Also Crèche, a devotional representation of the birth of Jesus. The custom of erecting cribs is generally attributed to St. Francis of Assisi, who in 1223 obtained from Pope Honorius III permission to use a crib and figures of the Christ Child, Mary, St. Joseph, and others, to represent the mystery of the Nativity.

Crosier: The bishop's staff, symbolic of his pastoral office, responsibility and authority; used at liturgical functions.

Crypt: An underground or partly underground chamber; e.g., the lower part of a church used for worship and/or burial.

Cura Animarum: A Latin phrase, meaning care of souls, designating the pastoral ministry and responsibility of bishops and priests.

Curia: The personnel and offices through which (1) the pope administers the affairs of the universal Church, the Roman Curia (see p. 268), or (2) a bishop the affairs of a diocese, diocesan curia. The principal officials of a diocesan curia are the vicar general of the diocese, the chancellor, officials of the diocesan tribunal or court, examiners, consultors, auditors, notaries.

Custos: A religious superior who presides over a number of convents collectively called a custody. In some institutes of consecrated life a custos may be the deputy of a higher superior.

D

Dean: (1) A priest with supervisory responsibility over a section of a diocese known as a deanery. The post-Vatican II counterpart of a dean is an episcopal vicar. (2) The senior or ranking member of a group.

Decision: A judgment or pronouncement on a cause or suit, given by a church tribunal or official with judicial authority. A decision has the force of law for concerned parties.

Declaration: (1) An ecclesiastical document which presents an interpretation of an existing law. (2) A position paper on a specific subject; e.g., the three declarations issued by the Second Vatican Council on religious freedom, non-Christian religions, and Christian education.

Decree: An edict or ordinance issued by a pope and/or by an ecumenical council, with binding force in the whole Church; by a department of the Roman Curia, with binding force for concerned parties; by a territorial body of bishops, with binding force for persons in the area; by individual bishops, with binding force for concerned parties until revocation or the death of the bishop. The nine decrees issued by the Second Vatican Council were combinations of doctrinal and pastoral statements with executive orders for action and movement toward renewal and reform in the Church.

Dedication of a Church: The ceremony whereby a church is solemnly set apart for the worship of God. The custom of dedicating churches had an antecedent in Old Testament ceremonies for the dedication of the Temple, as in the times of Solomon and the Maccabees. The earliest extant record of the dedication of a Christian church dates from early in the fourth century, when it was done simply by the celebration of Mass. Other ceremonies developed later. A church can be dedicated by a simple blessing or a solemn consecration. The rite of consecration is generally performed by a bishop.

Deposit of the Faith: The body of saving truth, entrusted by Christ to the Apostles and handed on by them to the Church to be preserved and proclaimed. As embodied in Revelation and Tradition the term is very nearly coextensive with objective revelation, in that it embraces the whole of Christ's teaching. But the term of deposit highlights particular features of the apostolic teaching implying that this teaching is an inexhaustible store that rewards and promotes reflection and study so that new insights and deeper penetration might be made into the mystery of the divine economy of salvation. Although our understanding of this teaching can develop, it can never be augmented in its substance; the teaching is a divine trust, that cannot be altered, modified, or debased. The term *depositum fidei* first entered official Catholic teaching with the Council of Trent, but its substance is well-attested in the Scriptures and the Fathers.

Despair: Abandonment of hope for salvation arising from the conviction that God will not provide the necessary means for attaining it, that following God's way of life for salvation is impossible, or that one's sins are unforgivable; a serious sin against the Holy Spirit and the theological virtues of hope and faith, involving distrust in the mercy and goodness of God and a denial of the truths that God wills the salvation of all persons and provides sufficient grace for it. Real despair is distinguished from unreasonable fear with respect to the difficulties of attaining salvation, from morbid anxiety over the demands of divine justice, and from feelings of despair.

Detraction: Revelation of true but hidden faults of a person without sufficient and justifying reason; a violation of requirements of justice and charity, involving the obligation to make restitution when this is possible without doing more harm to the good name of the offended party. In some cases, e.g., to prevent evil, secret faults may and should be disclosed.

Devil: (1) Lucifer, Satan, chief of the fallen angels who sinned and were banished from heaven. Still possessing angelic powers, he can cause such diabolical phenomena as possession and obsession, and can tempt men to sin. (2) Any fallen angel.

Devotion: (1) Religious fervor, piety; dedication. (2) The consolation experienced at times during prayer; a reverent manner of praying.

Devotions: Pious practices of members of the Church include not only participation in various acts of the liturgy but also in other acts of worship generally called popular or private devotions. Concerning these, the Second Vatican Council said in the Constitution on the Sacred Liturgy (*Sacrosanctum Concilium*, No. 13): "Popular devotions of the Christian people are warmly commended, provided they accord with the laws and norms of the Church. Such is especially the case with devotions called for by the Apostolic See. Devotions proper to the individual churches also have a special dignity. These devotions should be so drawn up that they harmonize with the liturgical seasons, accord with the sacred liturgy, are in some fashion derived from it, and lead the people to it, since the liturgy by its very nature far surpasses any of them." Devotions of a liturgical type are Exposition of the Blessed Sacrament, recitation of Evening Prayer and Night Prayer of the Liturgy of the Hours. Examples of paraliturgical devotion are a Bible Service or Vigil, and the Angelus, Rosary and Stations of the Cross, which have a strong scriptural basis.

Diocese: A particular church, a fully organized ecclesiastical jurisdiction under the pastoral direction of a bishop as local Ordinary.

Discalced: Of Latin derivation and meaning without shoes, the word is applied to religious orders or congregations whose members go barefoot or wear sandals.

Disciple: A term used sometimes in reference to the Apostles but more often to a larger number of followers (70 or 72) of Christ mentioned in Lk. 10:1.

Disciplina Arcani: A Latin phrase, meaning discipline of the secret and referring to a practice of the early Church, especially during the Roman persecutions, to: (1) conceal Christian truths from those who, it was feared, would misinterpret, ridicule and profane the teachings, and persecute Christians for believing them; (2) instruct catechumens in a gradual manner, withholding the teaching of certain doctrines until the catechumens proved themselves of good faith and sufficient understanding.

Dispensation: The relaxation of a law in a particular case. Laws made for the common good sometimes work undue hardship in particular cases. In such cases, where sufficient reasons are present, dispensations may be granted by proper authorities. Bishops, religious superiors and others may dispense from certain laws; the pope can dispense from all ecclesiastical laws. No one has authority to dispense from obligations of the divine law.

Divination: Attempting to foretell future or hidden things by means of things like dreams, necromancy, spiritism, examination of entrails, astrology, augury, omens, palmistry, drawing straws, dice, cards, etc. Practices like these attribute to created things a power which belongs to God alone and are violations of the First Commandment.

Divine Praises: Fourteen praises recited or sung at Benediction of the Blessed Sacrament in reparation for sins of sacrilege, blasphemy and profanity. Some of these praises date from the end of the 18th century: *Blessed be God. / Blessed be his holy Name. / Blessed be Jesus Christ, true God and true Man. / Blessed be the Name of Jesus. / Blessed be his most Sacred Heart. / Blessed be his most Precious Blood. / Blessed be Jesus in the most holy Sacrament of the Altar. / Blessed be the Holy Spirit, the Paraclete. / Blessed be the great Mother of God, Mary most holy. / Blessed be her holy and Immaculate Conception. / Blessed be her glorious Assumption. / Blessed be the name of Mary, Virgin and Mother. / Blessed be St. Joseph, her most chaste Spouse. / Blessed be God in his Angels and in his Saints.*

Double Effect Principle: Actions sometimes have two effects closely related to each other, one good and the other bad, and a difficult moral question can arise: Is it permissible to place an action from which two such results follow? It is permissible to place the action, if: the action is good in itself and is directly productive of the good effect; the circumstances are good; the intention of the person is good; the reason for placing the action is proportionately serious to the seriousness of the indirect bad effect.

Doxology: (1) The lesser doxology, or ascription of glory to the Trinity, is the Glory be to the Father. The first part dates back to the third or fourth century, and came from the form of baptism. The concluding words, As it was in the beginning, etc., are of later origin. (2) The greater doxology, Glory to God in the highest, begins with the words of angelic praise at the birth of Christ recounted in the Infancy Narrative (Lk. 2:14). It is often recited at Mass. Of early Eastern origin, it is found in the Apostolic Constitutions in a form much like the present. (3) The formula of praise at the end of the Eucharistic Prayer at Mass, sung or said by the celebrant while he holds aloft the paten containing the consecrated host in one hand and the chalice containing the consecrated wine in the other.

Dulia: A Greek term meaning the veneration or homage, different in nature and degree from that given to God, paid to the saints. It includes honoring the saints and seeking their intercession with God.

Duty: A moral obligation deriving from the binding force of law, the exigencies of one's state in life, and other sources.

E

Easter Controversy: A three-phase controversy over the time for the celebration of Easter. Some early Christians in the Near East, called Quartodecimans, favored the observance of Easter on the 14th day of

Nisan, the spring month of the Hebrew calendar, whenever it occurred. Against this practice, Pope St. Victor I, about 190, ordered a Sunday observance of the feast. The Council of Nicaea, in line with usages of the Church at Rome and Alexandria, decreed in 325 that Easter should be observed on the Sunday following the first full moon of spring. Uniformity of practice in the West was not achieved until several centuries later, when the British Isles, in delayed compliance with measures enacted by the Synod of Whitby in 664, accepted the Roman date of observance. Unrelated to the controversy is the fact that some Eastern Christians, in accordance with traditional calendar practices, celebrate Easter at a different time than the Roman and Eastern Churches.

Easter Duty: The serious obligation binding Catholics of Roman Rite, to receive the Eucharist during the Easter season (in the U.S.), from the first Sunday of Lent to and including Trinity Sunday).

Easter Water: Holy water blessed with special ceremonies and distributed on the Easter Vigil; used during Easter Week for blessing the faithful and homes.

Ecclesiology: Study of the nature, constitution, members, mission, functions, etc., of the Church.

Ecology: The natural environment of the total range of creation — mineral, vegetable, animal, human — entrusted to people for respect, care and appropriate use as well as conservation and development for the good of present and future generations.

Ecstasy: An extraordinary state of mystical experience in which a person is so absorbed in God that the activity of the exterior senses is suspended.

Economy, Divine: The fulfillment of God's plan of salvation. It was fully developed in his divine mind from eternity, and fully revealed in Jesus Christ. Before the Incarnation it was known only obscurely, but after the ascension of Christ and the coming of the Holy Spirit at Pentecost, it became the substance of apostolic preaching and is preserved in its integrity for each new generation.

Ecumenism: The movement of Christians and their churches toward the unity willed by Christ. The Second Vatican Council called the movement "those activities and enterprises which, according to various needs of the Church and opportune occasions, are started and organized for the fostering of unity among Christians" (Decree on Ecumenism, No. 4). Spiritual ecumenism, i.e., mutual prayer for unity, is the heart of the movement. The movement also involves scholarly and pew-level efforts for the development of mutual understanding and better interfaith relations in general, and collaboration by the churches and their members in the social area. (See Index for other entries.)

Elevation: The raising of the host after consecration at Mass for adoration by the faithful. The custom was introduced in the Diocese of Paris about the close of the 12th century to offset an erroneous teaching of the time which held that transubstantiation of the bread did not take place until after the consecration of the wine in the chalice. The elevation of the chalice following the consecration of the wine was introduced in the 15th century.

Encyclical: The highest form of papal teaching document. It is normally addressed to all the bishops and/or to all the faithful.

Envy: Sadness over another's good fortune because it is considered a loss to oneself or a detraction from one's own excellence; one of the seven capital sins, a violation of the obligations of charity.

Epiclesis: An invocation of the Holy Spirit, to bless the offerings consecrated at Mass; before the consecration in the Latin Rite, after the consecration in Eastern usage.

Epikeia: A Greek word meaning reasonableness and designating a moral theory and practice, a mild interpretation of the mind of a legislator who is prudently considered not to wish positive law to bind in certain circumstances.

Episcopate: (1) The office, dignity and sacramental powers bestowed upon a bishop at his ordination. (2) The body of bishops collectively.

Equivocation: (1) The use of words, phrases, or gestures having more than one meaning in order to conceal information which a questioner has no strict right to know. It is permissible to equivocate (have a broad mental reservation) in some circumstances. (2) A lie, i.e., a statement of untruth. Lying is intrinsically wrong. A lie told in joking, evident as such, is not wrong.

Eschatology: Doctrine concerning the last things: death, judgment, heaven and hell, and the final state of perfection of the people and kingdom of God at the end of time.

Eternity: The interminable, perfect possession of life in its totality without beginning or end; an attribute of God, who has no past or future but always is. Man's existence has a beginning but no end and is, accordingly, called immortal.

Ethics: Moral philosophy, the science of the morality of human acts deriving from natural law, the natural end of man, and the powers of human reason. It includes all the spheres of human activity — personal, social, economic, political, etc. Ethics is distinct from but can be related to moral theology, whose primary principles are drawn from divine revelation.

Euthanasia: Mercy killing, the direct causing of death for the purpose of ending human suffering. Euthanasia is murder and is totally illicit, for the natural law forbids the direct taking of one's own life or that of an innocent person. The use of drugs to relieve suffering in serious cases, even when this results in a shortening of life as an indirect and secondary effect, is permissible under conditions of the double-effect principle. It is also permissible for a seriously ill person to refuse to follow — or for other responsible persons to refuse to permit — extraordinary medical procedures even though the refusal might entail shortening of life.

Evangelization: Proclamation of the Gospel, the Good News of salvation in and through Christ, among those who have not yet known or received it; and efforts for the progressive development of the life of faith among those who have already received the Gospel and all that it entails. Evangelization is the primary mission of the Church, in which all members of the Church are called to participate.

Evolution: Scientific theory concerning the development of the physical universe from unorganized matter (inorganic evolution) and, especially, the development of existing forms of vegetable, animal and human life from earlier and more primitive organisms (organic evolution). Various ideas about evolution were advanced for some centuries before scientific evidence in support of the main-line theory of organic evolution, which has several formulations, was discovered and verified in the second half of the 19th century and afterwards. This evidence — from the findings of comparative anatomy and other sciences — confirmed evolution of species and cleared the way to further investigation of questions regarding the processes of its accomplishment. While a number of such questions remain open with respect to human evolution, a point of doctrine not open to question is the immediate creation of the human soul by God. For some time, theologians regarded the theory with hostility, considering it to be in opposition to the account of creation in the early chapters of Genesis and subversive of belief in such doctrines as creation, the early state of man in grace, and the fall of man from grace. This state of affairs and the tension it generated led to considerable controversy regarding an alleged conflict between religion and science. Gradually, however, the tension was diminished with the development of biblical studies from the latter part of the 19th century onwards, with clarification of the distinctive features of religious truth and scientific truth, and with the refinement of evolutionary concepts. So far as the Genesis account of creation is concerned, the Catholic view is that the writer(s) did not write as a scientist but as the communicator of religious truth in a manner adapted to the understanding of the people of his time. He used anthropomorphic language, the figure of days and other literary devices to state the salvation truths of creation, the fall of man from grace, and the promise of redemption. It was beyond the competency and purpose of the writer(s) to describe creation and related events in a scientific manner.

Excommunication: A penalty or censure by which a baptized Roman Catholic is excluded from the communion of the faithful, for committing and remaining obstinate in certain serious offenses specified in canon law; e.g. heresy, schism, apostasy, abortion. As by baptism a person is made a member of the Church in which there is a communication of spiritual goods, so by excommunication he is deprived of the same spiritual goods until he repents and receives absolution. Even though excommunicated, a person is still responsible for fulfillment of the normal obligations of a Catholic. (See Censures).

Ex Opere Operantis: A term in sacramental theology meaning that the effectiveness of sacraments depends on the moral rectitude of the minister or participant. This term was applied to rites of the O.T. in contrast with those of the N.T. when it was first advanced in the thirteenth century.

Ex Opere Operato: A term in sacramental theology meaning that sacraments are effective by means of the sacramental rite itself and not because of the worthiness of the minister or participant.

Exorcism: (1) Driving out evil spirits; a rite in which evil spirits are charged and commanded on the authority of God and with the prayer of the Church to depart from a person or to cease causing harm to a person suffering from diabolical possession or obsession. The sacramental is officially administered by a priest delegated for the purpose by the bishop of the place. Elements of the rite include the Litany of Saints; recitation of the Our Father, one or more

creeds, and other prayers; specific prayers of exorcism; the reading of Gospel passages and use of the Sign of the Cross. On Jan. 26, 1999, the Congregation for Divine Worship and the Discipline of the Sacraments published a new rite of exorcism in the Roman Ritual. [See Special Report for additional details.] (2) Exorcisms which do not imply the conditions of either diabolical possession or obsession form part of the ceremony of baptism and are also included in formulas for various blessings; e.g., of water.

Exposition of the Blessed Sacrament: "In churches where the Eucharist is regularly reserved, it is recommended that solemn exposition of the Blessed Sacrament for an extended period of time should take place once a year, even though the period is not strictly continuous. Shorter expositions of the Eucharist (Benediction) are to be arranged in such a way that the blessing with the Eucharist is preceded by a reasonable time for readings of the word of God, songs, prayers and a period for silent prayer." So stated Vatican directives issued in 1973.

F

Faculties: Grants of jurisdiction or authority by the law of the Church or superiors (pope, bishop, religious superior) for exercise of the powers of holy orders; e.g., priests are given faculties to hear confessions, officiate at weddings; bishops are given faculties to grant dispensations, etc.

Faith: In religion, faith has several aspects. Catholic doctrine calls faith the assent of the mind to truths revealed by God, the assent being made with the help of grace and by command of the will on account of the authority and trustworthiness of God revealing. The term faith also refers to the truths that are believed (content of faith) and to the way in which a person, in response to Christ, gives witness to and expresses belief in daily life (living faith). All of these elements, and more, are included in the following statement: " 'The obedience of faith' (Rom. 16:26; 1:5; 2 Cor. 10:5-6) must be given to God who reveals, an obedience by which man entrusts his whole self freely to God, offering 'the full submission of intellect and will to God who reveals' (First Vatican Council, Dogmatic Constitution on the Catholic Faith, Chap. 3), and freely assenting to the truth revealed by him. If this faith is to be shown, the grace of God and the interior help of the Holy Spirit must precede and assist, moving the heart and turning it to God, opening the eyes of the mind, and giving 'joy and ease to everyone in assenting to the truth and believing it' " (Second Council of Orange, Canon 7) (Second Vatican Council, Constitution on Revelation, *Dei Verbum*, No. 5). Faith is necessary for salvation.

Faith, Rule of: The norm or standard of religious belief. The Catholic doctrine is that belief must be professed in the divinely revealed truths in the Bible and tradition as interpreted and proposed by the infallible teaching authority of the Church.

Fast, Eucharistic: Abstinence from food and drink, except water and medicine, is required for one hour before the reception of the Eucharist. Persons who are advanced in age or suffer from infirmity or illness, together with those who care for them, can receive Holy Communion even if they have not abstained from food and drink for an hour. A priest celebrating two or three Masses on the same day can eat and drink something before the second or third Mass without regard for the hour limit.

Father: A title of priests, who are regarded as spiritual fathers because they are the ordinary ministers of baptism, by which persons are born to supernatural life, and because of their pastoral service to people.

Fear: A mental state caused by the apprehension of present or future danger. Grave fear does not necessarily remove moral responsibility for an act, but may lessen it.

First Friday: A devotion consisting of the reception of Holy Communion on the first Friday of nine consecutive months in honor of the Sacred Heart of Jesus and in reparation for sin. (See Sacred Heart, Promises.)

First Saturday: A devotion tracing its origin to the apparitions of the Blessed Virgin Mary at Fátima in 1917. Those practicing the devotion go to confession and, on the first Saturday of five consecutive months, receive Holy Communion, recite five decades of the Rosary, and meditate on the mysteries for 15 minutes.

Fisherman's Ring: A signet ring (termed in Italian the *pescatorio*) engraved with the image of St. Peter fishing from a boat, and encircled with the name of the reigning pope. It is not worn by the pope. It is used to seal briefs, and is destroyed after each pope's death.

Forgiveness of Sin: Catholics believe that sins are forgiven by God through the mediation of Christ in view of the repentance of the sinner and by means of the sacrament of penance. (See Penance, Contrition).

Fortitude: Courage to face dangers or hardships for the sake of what is good; one of the four cardinal virtues and one of the seven gifts of the Holy Spirit.

Forty Hours Devotion: A Eucharistic observance consisting of solemn exposition of the Blessed Sacrament coupled with special Masses and forms of prayer, for the purposes of making reparation for sin and praying for God's blessings of grace and peace. The devotion was instituted in 1534 in Milan. St. John Neumann of Philadelphia was the first bishop in the U.S. to prescribe its observance in his diocese. For many years in this country, the observance was held annually on a rotating basis in all parishes of a diocese. Simplified and abbreviated Eucharistic observances have taken the place of the devotion in some places.

Forum: The sphere in which ecclesiastical authority or jurisdiction is exercised. (1) External: Authority is exercised in the external forum to deal with matters affecting the public welfare of the Church and its members. Those who have such authority because of their office (e.g., diocesan bishops) are called ordinaries. (2) Internal: Authority is exercised in the internal forum to deal with matters affecting the private spiritual good of individuals. The sacramental forum is the sphere in which the sacrament of penance is administered; other exercises of jurisdiction in the internal forum take place in the non-sacramental forum.

Freedom, Religious: The Second Vatican Council declared that the right to religious freedom in civil society "means that all men are to be immune from coercion on the part of individuals or of social groups and of any human power, in such wise that in matters religious no one is to be forced to act in a manner contrary to his own beliefs. Nor is anyone to be restrained from acting in accordance with his own beliefs, whether privately or publicly, whether alone or in association with others, within due limits" of requirements for the common good. The foundation of this right in civil society is the "very dignity of the human person" (Declaration on Religious Freedom, *Dignitatis Humanae*, No. 2). The conciliar statement did not deal with the subject of freedom within the Church. It noted the responsibility of the faithful "carefully to attend to the sacred and certain doctrine of the Church" (No. 14).

Free Will: The faculty or capability of making a reasonable choice among several alternatives. Freedom of will underlies the possibility and fact of moral responsibility.

Friar: Term applied to members of mendicant orders to distinguish them from members of monastic orders. (See Mendicants.)

Fruits of the Holy Spirit: Charity, joy, peace, patience, kindness, goodness, generosity, gentleness, faithfulness, modesty, self-control, chastity.

Fruits of the Mass: The spiritual and temporal blessings that result from the celebration of the Holy Sacrifice of the Mass. The general fruits are shared by all the faithful, living and departed, while the special fruits are applied to the priest who celebrates it, to those for whose intention it is offered, and to all those who participate in its celebration.

Fundamental Option: The orientation of one's life either to God by obedience or against Him through disobedience. Catholic Tradition acknowledges that one free and deliberate act with knowledge renders one at odds with God. A prevalent and vague moral theory today asserts that one act cannot change one's option to God — no matter how grave — unless the action comes from the person's "center." Pope John Paul II cautioned against this ambiguous position in the encyclical *Veritatis Splendor* (1993).

G

Gehenna: Greek form of a Jewish name, Gehinnom, for a valley near Jerusalem, the site of Moloch worship; used as a synonym for hell.

Genuflection: Bending of the knee, a natural sign of adoration or reverence, as when persons genuflect with the right knee in passing before the tabernacle to acknowledge the Eucharistic presence of Christ.

Gethsemani: A Hebrew word meaning oil press, designating the place on the Mount of Olives where Christ prayed and suffered in agony the night before he died.

Gifts of the Holy Spirit: Supernatural habits disposing a person to respond promptly to the inspiration of grace; promised by Christ and communicated through the Holy Spirit, especially in the sacrament of confirmation. They are: wisdom, understanding, counsel, knowledge, fortitude, piety, and fear of the Lord.

Glorified Body: The definitive state of humanity in eternity. The risen Christ calls humanity to the glory of his resurrection; this is a theological premise that presupposes that, like Christ, all of his brothers and sisters will be transformed physically.

Gluttony: An unreasonable appetite for food and drink; one of the seven capital sins.

God: The infinitely perfect Supreme Being, uncaused and absolutely self-sufficient, eternal, the Creator and final end of all things. The one God subsists in three equal Persons, the Father and the Son and the Holy Spirit. God, although transcendent and distinct from the universe, is present and active in the world in realization of his plan for the salvation of human beings, principally through Revelation, the operations of the Holy Spirit, the life and ministry of Christ, and the continuation of Christ's ministry in the Church. The existence of God is an article of faith, clearly communicated in divine Revelation. Even without this Revelation, however, the Church teaches, in a declaration by the First Vatican Council, that human beings can acquire certain knowledge of the existence of God and some of his attributes. This can be done on the bases of principles of reason and reflection on human experience. Non-revealed arguments or demonstrations for the existence of God have been developed from the principle of causality; the contingency of human beings and the universe; the existence of design, change and movement in the universe; human awareness of moral responsibility; widespread human testimony to the existence of God.

Goods of Marriage: Three blessings — children, faithful companionship, and permanence — that were first enumerated by St. Augustine in a work on marriage.

Grace: A free gift of God to persons (and angels), grace is a created sharing or participation in the life of God. It is given to persons through the merits of Christ and is communicated by the Holy Spirit. It is necessary for salvation. The principal means of grace are the sacraments (especially the Eucharist), prayer and good works. (1) **Sanctifying or habitual grace** makes persons holy and pleasing to God, adopted children of God, members of Christ, temples of the Holy Spirit, heirs of heaven capable of supernaturally meritorious acts. With grace, God gives persons the supernatural virtues and gifts of the Holy Spirit. The sacraments of baptism and penance were instituted to give grace to those who do not have it; the other sacraments, to increase it in those already in the state of grace. The means for growth in holiness, or the increase of grace, are prayer, the sacraments, and good works. Sanctifying grace is lost by the commission of serious sin. Each sacrament confers sanctifying grace for the special purpose of the sacrament; in this context, grace is called sacramental grace. (2) **Actual grace** is a supernatural help of God which enlightens and strengthens a person to do good and to avoid evil. It is not a permanent quality, like sanctifying grace. It is necessary for the performance of supernatural acts. It can be resisted and refused. Persons in the state of serious sin are given actual grace to lead them to repentance.

Grace at Meals: Prayers said before meals, asking a blessing of God, and after meals, giving thanks to God. In addition to traditional prayers for these purposes, many variations suitable for different occasions are possible, at personal option.

Guilt: The condition of an individual who has committed some moral wrong and is liable to receive punishment.

H

Habit: (1) A disposition to do things easily, given with grace (and therefore supernatural) and/or acquired by repetition of similar acts. (2) The garb worn by Religious.

Hagiography: Writings or documents about saints and other holy persons.

Hail Mary: A prayer addressed to the Blessed Virgin Mary; also called the *Ave Maria* (Latin equivalent of Hail Mary) and the Angelic Salutation. In three parts, it consists of the words addressed to Mary by the Archangel Gabriel on the occasion of the Annunciation, in the Infancy Narrative (*Hail Mary, full of grace, the Lord is with you, blessed are you among women.*); the words addressed to Mary by her cousin Elizabeth on the occasion of the Visitation (*Blessed is the fruit of your womb.*); a concluding petition (*Holy Mary, Mother of God, pray for us sinners now and at the hour of our death. Amen.*). The first two salutations were joined in Eastern rite formulas by the sixth century, and were similarly used at Rome in the seventh century. Insertion of the name of Jesus at the conclusion of the salutations was probably made by Urban IV about 1262. The present form of the petition was incorporated into the breviary in 1514.

Heaven: The state of those who, having achieved salvation, are in glory with God and enjoy the beatific vision. The phrase, kingdom of heaven, refers to the order or kingdom of God, grace, salvation.

Hell: The state of persons who die in mortal sin, in a condition of self-alienation from God which will last forever.

Heresy: The obstinate post-baptismal denial or doubt by a Catholic of any truth which must be believed as a matter of divine and Catholic faith (Canon 751, of the Code of Canon Law). Formal heresy involves deliberate resistance to the authority of God who communicates revelation through Scripture and tradition and the teaching authority of the Church. Heretics automatically incur the penalty of excommunication (Canon 1364 of the Code of Canon Law). Heresies have been significant not only as disruptions of unity of faith but also as occasions for the clarification and development of doctrine. Heresies from the beginning of the Church to the 13th century are described in Dates and Events in Church History.

Hermit: See **Anchorite**.

Heroic Act of Charity: The completely unselfish offering to God of one's good works and merits for the benefit of the souls in purgatory rather than for oneself. Thus a person may offer to God for the souls in purgatory all the good works he performs during life, all the indulgences he gains, and all the prayers and indulgences that will be offered for him after his death. The act is revocable at will, and is not a vow. Its actual ratification depends on the will of God.

Heroic Virtue: The exemplary practice of the four cardinal virtues and three theological virtues; such virtue is sought in persons considered for sainthood.

Heterodoxy: False doctrine teaching or belief; a departure from truth.

Hierarchy: The hierarchy of order who carry out the sacramental, teaching, and pastoral ministry of the Church; the hierarchy consists of the pope, bishops, priests, and deacons; the pope and the bishops give pastoral governance to the faithful.

Holy Father: A title used for the pope; it is a shortened translation of the Latin title *Beatissimus Pater*, "Most Blessed Father" and refers to his position as the spiritual father of all the Christian faithful.

Holy See: (1) The diocese of the pope, Rome. (2) The pope himself and/or the various officials and bodies of the Church's central administration at Vatican City — the Roman Curia — which act in the name and by authority of the pope.

Holy Spirit: God the Holy Spirit, third Person of the Holy Trinity, who proceeds from the Father and the Son and with whom he is equal in every respect; inspirer of the prophets and writers of sacred Scripture; promised by Christ to the Apostles as their advocate and strengthener; appeared in the form of a dove at the baptism of Christ and as tongues of fire at his descent upon the Apostles; soul of the Church and guarantor, by his abiding presence and action, of truth in doctrine; communicator of grace to human beings, for which reason he is called the sanctifier.

Holy Water: Water blessed by the Church and used as a sacramental, a practice which originated in apostolic times.

Holy Year: A year during which the pope grants the plenary Jubilee Indulgence to the faithful who fulfill certain conditions. For those who make a pilgrimage to Rome during the year, the conditions are reception of the sacraments of penance and the Eucharist, visits and prayer for the intention of the pope in the basilicas of St. Peter, St. John Lateran, St. Paul and St. Mary Major. For those who do not make a pilgrimage to Rome, the conditions are reception of the sacraments and prayer for the pope during a visit or community celebration in a church designated by the bishop of the locality. Pope Boniface VIII formally proclaimed the first Holy Year on Feb. 22, 1300, and the first three Holy Years were observed in 1300, 1350 and 1390. Subsequent ones were celebrated at 25-year intervals except in 1800 and 1850 when, respectively, the French invasion of Italy and political turmoil made observance impossible. Pope Paul II (1464-1471) set the 25-year timetable. In 1500, Pope Alexander VI prescribed the start and finish ceremonies — the opening and closing of the Holy Doors in the major basilicas on successive Christmas Eves. All but a few of the earlier Holy Years were classified as ordinary. Several — like those of 1933 and 1983-84 to commemorate the 1900th and 1950th anniversaries of the death and resurrection of Christ — were in the extraordinary category. Pope John Paul has designated Jubilee Year 2000 to be a Holy Year ending the second and beginning the third millennium of Christianity.

Homosexuality: The condition of a person whose sexual orientation is toward persons of the same rather than the opposite sex. The condition is not sinful in itself. Homosexual acts are seriously sinful in themselves; subjective responsibility for such acts, however, may be conditioned and diminished by compulsion and related factors.

Hope: The theological virtue by which a person firmly trusts in God for the means and attainment salvation.

Hosanna: A Hebrew word, meaning *O Lord, save, we pray.*

Host, The Sacred: The bread under whose appearances Christ is and remains present in a unique manner after the consecration which takes place during Mass. (See Transubstantiation.)

Human Dignity: The inherent worth of all human persons as they are made in God's image and likeness and they alone — of all God's creatures on earth — have an immortal soul.

Humanism: A world view centered on man. Types of humanism which exclude the supernatural are related to secularism.

Humility: A virtue which induces a person to evaluate himself or herself at his or her true worth, to recognize his or her dependence on God, and to give glory to God for the good he or she has and can do.

Hyperdulia: The special veneration accorded the Blessed Virgin Mary because of her unique role in the mystery of Redemption, her exceptional gifts of grace from God, and her pre-eminence among the saints. Hyperdulia is not adoration; only God is adored.

Hypostatic Union: The union of the human and divine natures in the one divine Person of Christ.

I

Icons: Byzantine-style paintings or representations of Christ, the Blessed Virgin and other saints, venerated in the Eastern Churches where they take the place of statues.

Idolatry: Worship of any but the true God; a violation of the First Commandment.

IHS: In Greek, the first three letters of the name of Jesus — Iota, Eta, Sigma.

Immaculate Conception: The doctrine that affirms that "the Blessed Virgin Mary was preserved, in the first instant of her conception, by a singular grace and privilege of God omnipotent and because of the merits of Jesus Christ the Savior of the human race, free from all stain of Original Sin," as stated by Pope Pius IX in his declaration of the dogma, Dec. 8, 1854. Thus, Mary was conceived in the state of perfect justice, free from Original Sin and its consequences, in virtue of the redemption achieved by Christ on the cross.

Immortality: The survival and continuing existence of the human soul after death.

Imprimatur: See Censorship of Books.

Impurity: Unlawful indulgence in sexual pleasure. (See Chastity.)

Imputability: A canonical term for the moral responsibility of a person for an act that he or she has performed.

Incardination: The affiliation of a priest to his diocese. Every secular priest must belong to a certain diocese. Similarly, every priest of a religious community must belong to some jurisdiction of his community; this affiliation, however, is not called incardination.

Incarnation: (1) The coming-into-flesh or taking of human nature by the Second Person of the Trinity. He became human as the Son of Mary, being miraculously conceived by the power of the Holy Spirit, without ceasing to be divine. His divine Person hypostatically unites his divine and human natures. (2) The supernatural mystery coextensive with Christ from the moment of his human conception and continuing through his life on earth; his sufferings and death; his resurrection from the dead and ascension to glory with the Father; his sending, with the Father, of the Holy Spirit upon the Apostles and the Church; and his unending mediation with the Father for the salvation of human beings.

Incense: A granulated substance which, when burnt, emits an aromatic smoke. It symbolizes the zeal with which the faithful should be consumed, the good odor of Christian virtue, the ascent of prayer to God. An incense boat is a small vessel used to hold incense which is to be placed in the censer.

Incest: Sexual intercourse with relatives by blood or marriage; a sin of impurity and also a grave violation of the natural reverence due to relatives. Other sins of impurity desire, etc.) concerning relatives have the nature of incest.

Inculturation: The correct and entirely appropriate adaptation of the Catholic liturgy and institutions to the culture, language, and customs of an indigenous or local people among whom the Gospel is first proclaimed. Pope John Paul II Feb. 15, 1982, at a meeting in Lagos with the bishops of Nigeria proclaimed: "An important aspect of your own evangelizing role is the whole dimension of the inculturation of the Gospel into the lives of your people. The Church truly respects the culture of each people. In offering the Gospel message, the Church does not intend to destroy or to abolish what is good and beautiful. In fact, she recognizes many cultural values and, through the power of the Gospel, purifies and takes into Christian worship certain elements of a people's customs."

Index of Prohibited Books: A list of books which Catholics were formerly forbidden to read, possess or sell, under penalty of excommunication. The books were banned by the Holy See after publication because their treatment of matters of faith and morals and related subjects were judged to be erroneous or serious occasions of doctrinal error. Some books were listed in the Index by name; others were covered under general norms. The Congregation for the Doctrine of the Faith declared June 14, 1966, that the Index and its related penalties of excommunication no longer had the force of law in the Church. Persons are still obliged, however, to take normal precautions against occasions of doctrinal error.

Indifferentism: A theory that any one religion is as true and good — or false — as any other religion, and that it makes no difference, objectively, what religion one professes, if any. The theory is completely subjective, finding its justification entirely in personal choice without reference to or respect for objective validity. It is also self-contradictory, since it regards as equally acceptable — or unacceptable — the beliefs of all religions, which in fact are not only not all the same but are in some cases opposed to each other.

Indulgence: According to The Doctrine and Practice of Indulgences, an apostolic constitution issued by Paul VI Jan. 1, 1967, an indulgence is the remission before God of the temporal punishment due for sins already forgiven as far as their guilt is concerned, which a follower of Christ — with the proper dispositions and under certain determined conditions — acquires through the intervention of the Church. An indulgence is partial or plenary, depending on whether it does away with either part or all of the temporal punishment due for sin. Both types of indulgences can always be applied to the dead by way of suffrage; the actual disposition of indulgences applied to the dead rests with God. Only one plenary indulgence can be gained in a single day. The Apostolic Penitentiary issued a decree Dec. 14, 1985, granting diocesan bishops the right to impart — three times a year on solemn feasts of their choice — the papal blessing with a plenary indulgence to those who cannot be physically present but who follow the sacred rites at which the blessing is imparted by radio or television transmission. In July, 1986, publication was announced of a new and simplified *Enchiridion Indulgentiarum*, in accord with provisions of the revised Code of Canon Law.

Indult: A favor or privilege granted by competent ecclesiastical authority, giving permission to do something not allowed by the common law of the Church.

Infallibility: 1) The inability of the Church to err in its teaching, in that she preserves and teaches the deposit of truth as revealed by Christ; 2) The inability of the Roman Pontiff to err when he teaches *ex cathedra* in matters of faith or morals, and indicates that the doctrine is to be believed by all the faithful; and 3) the inability of the college of bishops to err when speaking in union with the pope in matters of faith and morals, agreeing that a doctrine must be held by the universal Church, and the doctrine is promulgated by the Pontiff.

Infused Virtues: The theological virtues of faith, hope, and charity; principles or capabilities of supernatural action, they are given with sanctifying grace by God rather than acquired by repeated acts of a person. They can be increased by practice; they are lost by contrary acts. Natural-acquired moral virtues, like the cardinal virtues of prudence, justice, temperance, and fortitude, can be considered infused in a person whose state of grace gives them supernatural orientation.

Inquisition: A tribunal for dealing with heretics, authorized by Gregory IX in 1231 to search them out, hear and judge them, sentence them to various forms of punishment, and in some cases to hand them over to civil authorities for punishment. The Inquisition was a creature of its time when crimes against faith, which threatened the good of the Christian community, were regarded also as crimes against the state, and when heretical doctrines of such extremists as the Cathari and Albigensians threatened the very fabric of society. The institution, which was responsible for many excesses, was most active in the second half of the 13th century.

Inquisition, Spanish: An institution peculiar to Spain and the colonies in Spanish America. In 1478, at the urging of King Ferdinand, Pope Sixtus IV approved the establishment of the Inquisition for trying charges of heresy brought against Jewish (*Marranos*) and Moorish (*Moriscos*) converts. It acquired jurisdiction over other cases as well, however, and fell into disrepute because of irregularities in its functions, cruelty in its sentences, and the manner in which it served the interests of the Spanish crown more than the accused persons and the good of the Church. Protests by the Holy See failed to curb excesses of the Inquisition, which lingered in Spanish history until early in the 19th century.

I N R I: The first letters of words in the Latin inscription atop the cross on which Christ was crucified: *(I)esus (N)azaraenus, (R)ex (I)udaeorum* — Jesus of Nazareth, King of the Jews.

Insemination, Artificial: The implanting of human semen by some means other than consummation of natural marital intercourse. In view of the principle that procreation should result only from marital intercourse, donor insemination is not permissible.

In Sin: The condition of a person called spiritually dead because he or she does not possess sanctifying grace, the principle of supernatural life, action and merit. Such grace can be regained through repentance.

Instruction: A document containing doctrinal explanations, directive norms, rules, recommendations, admonitions, issued by the pope, a department of the Roman Curia or other competent authority in the Church. To the extent that they so prescribe, instructions have the force of law.

Intercommunion, Eucharistic Sharing: The common celebration and reception of the Eucharist by members of different Christian churches; a pivotal issue in ecumenical theory and practice. Catholic participation and intercommunion in the Eucharistic liturgy of another church without a valid priesthood and with a variant Eucharistic belief is out of order. Under certain conditions, other Christians may receive the Eucharist in the Catholic Church. (See additional Intercommunion entry). Intercommunion is acceptable to some Protestant churches and unacceptable to others.

Interdict: A censure imposed on persons for certain violations of church law. Interdicted persons may not take part in certain liturgical services, administer or receive certain sacraments.

Intinction: A method of administering Holy Communion under the dual appearances of bread and wine, in which the consecrated host is dipped in the consecrated wine before being given to the communicant. The administering of Holy Communion in this manner, which has been traditional in Eastern-Rite liturgies, was authorized in the Roman Rite for various occasions by the Constitution on the Sacred Liturgy promulgated by the Second Vatican Council.

Irenicism: Peace-seeking, conciliation, as opposed to polemics; an important element in ecumenism, provided it furthers pursuit of the Christian unity willed by Christ without degenerating into a peace-at-any-price disregard for religious truth.

Irregularity: A permanent impediment to the lawful reception or exercise of holy orders. The Church instituted irregularities — which include apostasy, heresy, homicide, attempted suicide — out of reverence for the dignity of the sacraments.

J

Jehovah: The English equivalent of the Hebrew *Adonai* ("my Lord") used out of fear and reverence for the Holy Name of Yahweh. *Jehovah* uses the consonants YHWH and the vowels of *Adonai* (a, o, a). Scholars today maintain that *Jehovah* is a false derivation.

Jesus: The name of Jesus, meaning "God saves," expressing the identity and mission of the second Person of the Trinity become man; derived from the Aramaic and Hebrew Yeshua and Joshua, meaning Yahweh is salvation.

Jesus Prayer: A prayer of Eastern origin, dating back to the fifth century: *"Lord Jesus Christ, Son of God, have mercy on me (a sinner)."*

Judgment: (1) **Last or final judgment**: Final judgment by Christ, at the end of the world and the general resurrection. (2) **Particular judgment**: The judgment that takes place immediately after a person's death, followed by entrance into heaven, hell or purgatory.

Jurisdiction: Right, power, authority to rule. Jurisdiction in the Church is of divine institution; has pastoral service for its purpose; includes legislative, judicial and executive authority; can be exercised only by persons with the power of orders. (1) Ordinary jurisdiction is attached to ecclesiastical offices by law; the officeholders, called Ordinaries, have authority over those who are subject to them. (2) Delegated jurisdiction is that which is granted to persons rather than attached to offices. Its extent depends on the terms of the delegation.

Justice: One of the four cardinal virtues by which a person gives to others what is due to them as a matter of right. (See Cardinal Virtues.)

Justification: The act by which God makes a person just, and the consequent change in the spiritual status of a person, from sin to grace; the remission of sin and the infusion of sanctifying grace through the merits of Christ and the action of the Holy Spirit.

K

Kenosis: A term from the Greek for "emptying" that denotes Christ's emptying of Himself in his free renunciation of his right to divine status, by reason of the Incarnation, particularly as celebrated in the kenotic hymn (Phil 2:6-11), where it is said that Christ "emptied himself," taking the form of a slave, born in the likeness of man totally integrated with his divinity.

Kerygma: Proclaiming the word of God, in the manner of the Apostles, as here and now effective for salvation. This method of preaching or instruction, centered on Christ and geared to the facts and themes of salvation history, is designed to dispose people to faith in Christ and/or to intensify the experience and practice of that faith in those who have it.

Keys, Power of the: Spiritual authority and jurisdiction in the Church, symbolized by the keys of the kingdom of heaven. Christ promised the keys to St. Peter, as head-to-be of the Church (Mt. 16:19), and commissioned him with full pastoral responsibility to feed his lambs and sheep (Jn. 21:15-17), The pope, as the successor of St. Peter, has this power in a primary and supreme manner. The bishops of the Church also have the power, in union with and subordinate to the pope. Priests share in it through holy orders and the delegation of authority. Examples of the application of the Power of the Keys are the exercise of teaching and pastoral authority by the pope and bishops, the absolving of sins in the sacrament of penance, the granting of indulgences, the imposing of spiritual penalties on persons who commit certain serious sins.

Kingdom of God: God's sovereign lordship or rule

over salvation history, leading to the eschatological goal of eternal life with God.

Koinonia: A term from the Greek word for "community, fellowship, or association" that was used by St. Luke for the fellowship of believers who worshipped together and held all their possessions in common (Acts 2:42-47); it is also used of fellowship with God (1 Jn. 1:3, 6), with the Son (1 Cor. 1:9), and with the Holy Spirit (2 Cor. 13:13; Phil. 2:1). St. Paul used *koinonia* to denote the intimate union of the believer with Christ and the community that exists among all the faithful themselves (Rom. 15:26; 2 Cor. 6:14).

L

Laicization: The process by which a man ordained to holy orders is relieved of the obligations of orders and the ministry and is returned to the status of a lay person.

Languages of the Church: The languages in which the Church's liturgy is celebrated. These include Ge'ez, Syriac, Greek, Arabic, and Old Slavonic in the Eastern Churches. In the West, there is, of course, Latin and the various vernaculars. The Eastern Rites have always had the vernacular. The first language in church use, for divine worship and the conduct of ecclesiastical affairs, was Aramaic, the language of the first Christians in and around Jerusalem. As the Church spread westward, Greek was adopted and prevailed until the third century when it was supplanted by Latin for official use in the West. In the Western Church, Latin prevailed as the general official language until the promulgation on Dec. 4, 1963, of the Constitution on the Sacred Liturgy (*Sacrosanctum Concilium*) by the second session of the Second Vatican Council. Since that time, vernacular languages have come into use in the Mass, administration of the sacraments, and the Liturgy of the Hours. Latin, however, remains the official language for documents of the Holy See, administrative and procedural matters.

Latria: Greek-rooted Latin term that refers to that form of praise due to God alone.

Law: An ordinance or rule governing the activity of things. (1) **Natural law**: Moral norms corresponding to man's nature by which he orders his conduct toward God, neighbor, society and himself. This law, which is rooted in human nature, is of divine origin, can be known by the use of reason, and binds all persons having the use of reason. The Ten Commandments are declarations and amplifications of natural law. The primary precepts of natural law, to do good and to avoid evil, are universally recognized, despite differences with respect to understanding and application resulting from different philosophies of good and evil. (2) **Divine positive law**: That which has been revealed by God. Among its essentials are the twin precepts of love of God and love of neighbor, and the Ten Commandments. (3) **Ecclesiastical law**: That which is established by the Church for the spiritual welfare of the faithful and the orderly conduct of ecclesiastical affairs. (See Canon Law.) (4) **Civil law**: That which is established by a socio-political community for the common good.

Liberalism: A multiphased trend of thought and movement favoring liberty, independence and progress in moral, intellectual, religious, social, eco-nomic and political life. Traceable to the Renaissance, it developed through the Enlightenment, the rationalism of the 19th century, and modernist- and existentialist-related theories of the 20th century. Evaluations of various kinds of liberalism depend on the validity of their underlying principles. Extremist positions — regarding subjectivism, libertinarianism, naturalist denials of the supernatural, and the alienation of individuals and society from God and the Church — were condemned by Gregory XVI in the 1830s, Pius IX in 1864, Leo XIII in 1899, and St. Pius X in 1907. There is, however, nothing objectionable about forms of liberalism patterned according to sound principles of Christian doctrine.

Liberation Theology: Deals with the relevance of Christian faith and salvation — and, therefore, of the mission of the Church — to efforts for the promotion of human rights, social justice and human development. It originated in the religious, social, political and economic environment of Latin America, with its contemporary need for a theory and corresponding action by the Church, in the pattern of its overall mission, for human rights and integral personal and social development. Some versions of liberation theology are at variance with the body of church teaching because of their ideological concept of Christ as liberator, and also because they play down the primary spiritual nature and mission of the Church. Instructions from the Congregation for the Doctrine of the Faith — "On Certain Aspects of the Theology of Liberation" (Sept. 3, 1984) and "On Christian Freedom and Liberation" (Apr. 5, 1986) — contain warnings against translating sociology into theology and advocating violence in social activism.

Life in Outer Space: Whether rational life exists on other bodies in the universe besides earth, is a question for scientific investigation to settle. The possibility can be granted, without prejudice to the body of revealed truth.

Limbo: The limbo of the fathers was the state of rest and natural happiness after death enjoyed by the just of pre-Christian times until they were admitted to heaven following the Ascension of Christ.

Litany: A prayer in the form of responsive petition; e.g., St. Joseph, pray for us, etc. Examples are the litanies of Loreto (Litany of the Blessed Mother), the Holy Name, All Saints, the Sacred Heart, the Precious Blood, St. Joseph, Litany for the Dying.

Logos: A Greek term for "word, speech, or reason." It is most commonly identified with the title given to Jesus in John's Gospel, though not exclusive to that Gospel; In the N.T., however, the term reflects more the influence of Hellenistic philosophy: St. Paul uses logos as interchangeable with *sophia*, wisdom (1 Cor. 1:24). The *Logos* is the Wisdom of God made manifest in the Son. As a name for the Second Person of the Trinity, the Incarnate Word, the term receives new meaning in the light of the life, death, and resurrection of Jesus Christ.

Loreto, House of: A Marian shrine in Loreto, Italy, consisting of the home of the Holy Family which, according to an old tradition, was transported in a miraculous manner from Nazareth to Dalmatia and finally to Loreto between 1291 and 1294. Investigations conducted shortly after the appearance of the structure in Loreto revealed that its dimensions matched those of the house of the Holy Family missing from its place of enshrinement in a basilica at Nazareth. Among the many popes who regarded it with high honor was John XXIII, who went there on pilgrimage Oct. 4, 1962. The house of the Holy Family is enshrined in the Basilica of Our Lady.

Love: A devotion to a person or object that has been categorized by Greek philosophy into four types: *storge* (one loves persons and things close to him); *philia* (the love of friends); *eros* (sexual love and that of a spiritual nature); *agape* (a self-giving to one in need). Christian charity is love, but not all love is true charity.

Lust: A disorderly desire for sexual pleasure; one of the seven capital sins.

M

Magi: In the Infancy Narrative of St. Matthew's Gospel (2:1-12), three wise men from the East whose visit and homage to the Child Jesus at Bethlehem indicated Christ's manifestation of himself to non-Jewish people. The narrative teaches the universality of salvation. The traditional names of the Magi are Caspar, Melchior and Balthasar.

Magisterium: The Church's teaching authority, instituted by Christ and guided by the Holy Spirit, which seeks to safeguard and explain the truths of the faith. The Magisterium is exercised in two ways. The extraordinary Magisterium is exercised when the pope and ecumenical councils infallibly define a truth of faith or morals that is necessary for one's salvation and that has been constantly taught and held by the Church. Ordinary Magisterium is exercised when the Church infallibly defines truths of the Faith as taught universally and without dissent; which must be taught or the Magisterium would be failing in its duty; is connected with a grave matter of faith or morals; and which is taught authoritatively. Not everything taught by the Magisterium is done so infallibly; however, the exercise of the Magisterium is faithful to Christ and what He taught.

Magnificat: The canticle or hymn of the Virgin Mary on the occasion of her visitation to her cousin Elizabeth (Lk. 1:46-55). It is an expression of praise, thanksgiving and acknowledgment of the great blessings given by God to Mary, the Mother of the Second Person of the Blessed Trinity made Man. The *Magnificat* is recited in the Liturgy of the Hours as part of the Evening Prayer.

Martyr: A Greek word, meaning witness, denoting one who voluntarily suffered death for the faith or some Christian virtue.

Martyrology: A catalogue of martyrs and other saints, arranged according to the calendar. The Roman Martyrology contains the official list of saints venerated by the Church. Additions to the list are made in beatification and canonization decrees of the Congregation for the Causes of Saints.

Mass for the People: On Sundays and certain feasts throughout the year pastors are required to offer Mass for the faithful entrusted to their care. If they cannot offer the Mass on these days, they must do so at a later date or provide that another priest offer the Mass.

Materialism: Theory which holds that matter is the only reality, and everything in existence is merely a manifestation of matter; there is no such thing as spirit, and the supernatural does not ex-

ist. Materialism is incompatible with Christian doctrine.

Meditation: Mental, as distinguished from vocal, prayer, in which thought, affections, and resolutions of the will predominate. There is a meditative element to all forms of prayer, which always involves the raising of the heart and mind to God.

Mendicants: A term derived from Latin and meaning beggars, applied to members of religious orders without property rights; the members, accordingly, worked or begged for their support. The original mendicants were Franciscans and Dominicans in the early 13th century; later, the Carmelites, Augustinians, Servites and others were given the mendicant title and privileges, with respect to exemption from episcopal jurisdiction and wide faculties for preaching and administering the sacrament of penance. The practice of begging is limited at the present time, although it is still allowed with the permission of competent superiors and bishops. Mendicants are supported by free will offerings and income received for spiritual services and other work.

Mercy, Divine: The love and goodness of God, manifested particularly in a time of need.

Mercy, Works of: Works of corporal or spiritual assistance, motivated by love of God and neighbor, to persons in need. (1) **Corporal works:** feeding the hungry, giving drink to the thirsty, clothing the naked, visiting the imprisoned, sheltering the homeless, visiting the sick, burying the dead. (2) **Spiritual works:** counseling the doubtful, instructing the ignorant, admonishing sinners, comforting the afflicted, forgiving offenses, bearing wrongs patiently, praying for the living and the dead.

Merit: In religion, the right to a supernatural reward for good works freely done for a supernatural motive by a person in the state of and with the assistance of grace. The right to such reward is from God, who binds himself to give it. Accordingly, good works, as described above, are meritorious for salvation.

Metanoia: A term from the Greek *metanoein* ("to change one's mind, repent, be converted") that is used in the N.T. for conversion. It entails the repentance of sin and the subsequent turning toward the Lord. *Metanoia* is fundamental to the Christian life and is necessary for spiritual growth.

Metaphysics: The branch of philosophy (from the Greek *meta* — after + *physika* — physics) dealing with first things, including the nature of being (ontology), the origin and structure of the world (cosmology), and the study of the reality and attributes of God (natural theology). Metaphysics has long been examined by Catholic philosophers, most especially in the writings of St. Augustine and St. Thomas Aquinas.

Millennium: A thousand-year reign of Christ and the just upon earth before the end of the world. This belief of the Millenarians, Chiliasts, and some sects of modern times is based on an erroneous interpretation of Rv. 20.

Miracles: Observable events or effects in the physical or moral order of things, with reference to salvation, which cannot be explained by the ordinary operation of laws of nature and which, therefore, are attributed to the direct action of God. They make known, in an unusual way, the concern and intervention of God in human affairs for the salvation of men.

Mission: (1) Strictly, it means being sent to perform a certain work, such as the mission of Christ to redeem mankind, the mission of the Apostles and the Church and its members to perpetuate the prophetic, priestly and royal mission of Christ. (2) A place where: the Gospel has not been proclaimed; the Church has not been firmly established; the Church, although established, is weak. (3) An ecclesiastical territory with the simplest kind of canonical organization, under the jurisdiction of the Congregation for the Evangelization of Peoples. (4) A church or chapel without a resident priest. (5) A special course of sermons and spiritual exercises conducted in parishes for the purpose of renewing and deepening the spiritual life of the faithful and for the conversion of lapsed Catholics.

Modernism: The "synthesis of all heresies," which appeared near the beginning of the 20th century. It undermines the objective validity of religious beliefs and practices which, it contends, are products of the subconscious developed by mankind under the stimulus of a religious sense. It holds that the existence of a personal God cannot be demonstrated, the Bible is not inspired, Christ is not divine, nor did he establish the Church or institute the sacraments. A special danger lies in modernism, which is still influential, because it uses Catholic terms with perverted meanings. St. Pius X condemned 65 propositions of modernism in 1907 in the decree *Lamentabili* and issued the encyclical *Pascendi* to explain and analyze its errors.

Monastery: The dwelling place, as well as the community thereof, of monks belonging to the Benedictine and Benedictine-related orders like the Cistercians and Carthusians; also, the Augustinians and Canons Regular. Distinctive of monasteries are: their separation from the world; the enclosure or cloister; the permanence or stability of attachment characteristic of their members; autonomous government in accordance with a monastic rule, like that of St. Benedict in the West or of St. Basil in the East; the special dedication of its members to the community celebration of the liturgy as well as to work that is suitable to the surrounding area and the needs of its people. Monastic superiors of men have such titles as abbot and prior; of women, abbess and prioress. In most essentials, an abbey is the same as a monastery.

Monk: A member of a monastic order — e.g., the Benedictines, the Benedictine-related Cistercians and Carthusians, and the Basilians, who bind themselves by religious profession to stable attachment to a monastery, the contemplative life and the work of their community. In popular use, the title is wrongly applied to many men religious who really are not monks.

Monotheism: Belief in and worship of one God.

Morality: Conformity or difformity of behavior to standards of right conduct. (See Moral Obligations, Commandments of God, Precepts of the Church, Conscience, Law.)

Mortification: Acts of self-discipline, including prayer, hardship, austerities and penances undertaken for the sake of progress in virtue.

Motu Proprio: A Latin phrase designating a document issued by a pope on his own initiative. Documents of this kind often concern administrative matters.

Mystagogy: Experience of the mystery of Christ, especially through participation in the liturgy and the sacraments.

Mysteries of Faith: Supernatural truths whose existence cannot be known without revelation by God and whose intrinsic truth, while not contrary to reason, can never be wholly understood even after revelation. These mysteries are above reason, not against reason. Among them are the divine mysteries of the Trinity, Incarnation and Eucharist. Some mysteries — e.g., concerning God's attributes — can be known by reason without revelation, although they cannot be fully understood.

N

Natural Law: See Law.

Natural Theology: The field of knowledge that relies upon human reason and the observation of nature, instead of revelation, to determine the existence and attributes of God.

Necromancy: Supposed communication with the dead; a form of divination.

Neo-Scholasticism: A movement begun in the late 19th century that had as its aim the restoration of Scholasticism for use in contemporary philosophy and theology. Great emphasis was placed upon the writings of such Scholastic masters as Peter Lombard, St. Albert the Great, St. Anselm, St. Bonaventure, Bl. John Duns Scotus, and especially St. Thomas Aquinas. The movement began at the Catholic University of Louvain, in Belgium, and then found its way into theological centers in Italy, France, and Germany. Particular attention was given to the philosophical and theological works of St. Thomas Aquinas, from which arose a particular school of neo-Thomism; the movement was strongly reinforced by Pope Leo XIII who issued the encyclical *Aeterni Patris* (1879) mandating that Scholasticism, in particular Thomism, be the foundation for all Catholic philosophy and theology taught in Catholic seminaries, universities, and colleges. Neo-Scholasticism was responsible for a true intellectual renaissance in 20th-century Catholic philosophy and theology. Among its foremost modern leaders were Jacques Maritain, Étienne Gilson, M. D. Chenu, Henri de Lubac, and Paul Claudel.

Nihil Obstat: See Censhorship of Books.

Non-Expedit: A Latin expression. It is not expedient (fitting, proper), used to state a prohibition or refusal of permission.

Novena: A term designating public or private devotional practices over a period of nine consecutive days; or, by extension, over a period of nine weeks, in which one day a week is set aside for the devotions.

Novice: A man or woman preparing, in a formal period of trial and formation called a novitiate, for membership in an institute of consecrated life. The novitiate lasts a minimum of 12 and a maximum of 24 months; at its conclusion, the novice professes temporary promises or vows of poverty, chastity and obedience. Norms require that certain periods of time be spent in the house of novitiate; periods of apostolic work are also required, to acquaint the novice with the apostolate(s) of the institute. A novice is not bound by the obligations of the professed members of the institute, is free to leave at any time, and may be discharged at the discretion of competent superiors. The superior of a novice is a master of novices or director of formation.

Nun: (1) Strictly, a member of a religious order of women with solemn vows (*moniales*). (2) In general, all women religious, even those in simple vows who are more properly called sisters.

Nunc Dimittis: The canticle or hymn of Simeon at the sight of Jesus at the Temple on the occasion of his presentation (Lk. 2:29-32). It is an expression of joy and thanksgiving for the blessing of having lived to see the Messiah. It is prescribed for use in the Night Prayer of the Liturgy of the Hours.

O

Oath: Calling upon God to witness the truth of a statement. Violating an oath, e.g., by perjury in court, or taking an oath without sufficient reason, is a violation of the honor due to God.

Obedience: Submission to one in authority. General obligations of obedience fall under the Fourth Commandment. The vow of obedience professed by religious is one of the evangelical counsels.

Obsession, Diabolical: The extraordinary state of one who is seriously molested by evil spirits in an external manner. Obsession is more than just temptation.

Occasion of Sin: A person, place, or thing that is a temptation to sin. An occasion may be either a situation that always leads to sin or one that usually leads to sin.

Octave: A period of eight days given over to the celebration of a major feast such as Easter.

Oils, Holy: The oils blessed by a bishop at the Chrism Mass on Holy Thursday or another suitable day, or by a priest under certain conditions. (1) The oil of catechumens (olive or vegetable oil), used at baptism; also, poured with chrism into the baptismal water blessed in Easter Vigil ceremonies. (2) Oil of the sick (olive or vegetable oil) used in anointing the sick. (3) Chrism (olive or vegetable oil mixed with balm), which is ordinarily consecrated by a bishop, for use at baptism, in confirmation, at the ordination of a priest and bishop, in the dedication of churches and altars.

Ontologism: A philosophical theory (the name is taken from the Greek for being and study) that posits that knowledge of God is immediate and intuitive; it stipulates further that all other human knowledge is dependent upon this. It was condemned in 1861 by Pope Pius IX. (See also Ontology.)

Ontology: A branch of metaphysics that studies the nature and relations of existence.

Oratory: A chapel.

Ordinariate: An ecclesiastical jurisdiction for special purposes and people. Examples are military ordinariates for armed services personnel (in accord with provisions of the apostolic constitution *Spirituali militum curae*, Apr. 21, 1986) and Eastern-Rite ordinariates in places where Eastern-Rite dioceses do not exist.

Ordination: The consecration of sacred ministers for divine worship and the service of people in things pertaining to God. The power of ordination comes from Christ and the Church, and must be conferred by a minister capable of communicating it.

Organ Transplants: The transplanting of organs from one person to another is permissible provided it is done with the consent of the concerned parties and does not result in the death or essential mutilation of the donor. Advances in methods and technology have increased the range of transplant possibilities in recent years.

Original Sin: The sin of Adam (Gn. 2:8-3:24), personal to him and passed on to all persons as a state of privation of grace. Despite this privation and the related wounding of human nature and weakening of natural powers, original sin leaves unchanged all that man himself is by nature. The scriptural basis of the doctrine was stated especially by St. Paul in 1 Cor. 15:21ff., and Rom. 5:12-21. Original sin is remitted by baptism and incorporation in Christ, through whom grace is given to persons. Pope John Paul, while describing original sin during a general audience Oct. 1, 1986, called it "the absence of sanctifying grace in nature which has been diverted from its supernatural end."

O Salutaris Hostia: The first three Latin words, *O Saving Victim*, of a Benediction hymn.

Ostpolitik: Policy adopted by Pope Paul VI in an attempt to improve the situation of Eastern European Catholics through diplomatic negotiations with their governments.

Oxford Movement: A movement in the Church of England from 1833 to about 1845 which had for its objective a threefold defense of the Church as a divine institution, the apostolic succession of its bishops, and the *Book of Common Prayer* as the rule of faith. The movement took its name from Oxford University and involved a number of intellectuals who authored a series of influential Tracts for Our Times. Some of its leading figures — e.g., F. W. Faber, John Henry Newman and Henry Edward Manning — became converts to the Catholic Church. In the Church of England, the movement affected the liturgy, historical and theological scholarship, the status of the ministry, and other areas of ecclesiastical life.

P

Paganism: A term referring to non-revealed religions, i.e., religions other than Christianity, Judaism, and Islam.

Palms: Blessed palms are a sacramental. They are blessed and distributed on the Sunday of the Passion in commemoration of the triumphant entrance of Christ into Jerusalem. Ashes of the burnt palms are used on Ash Wednesday.

Pange Lingua: First Latin words, *Sing, my tongue*, of a hymn in honor of the Holy Eucharist, used particularly on Holy Thursday and in Eucharistic processions.

Pantheism: Theory that all things are part of God, divine, in the sense that God realizes himself as the ultimate reality of matter or spirit through being and/ or becoming all things that have been, are, and will be. The theory leads to hopeless confusion of the Creator and the created realm of being, identifies evil with good, and involves many inherent contradictions.

Papal Election: The pope is elected by the College of Cardinals during a secret conclave which begins no sooner than 15 days and no later than 20 days after the death of his predecessor. Cardinals under the age of 80, totaling no more than 120, are eligible to take part in the election by secret ballot. Election is by a two-thirds vote of participating cardinals. New legislation regarding papal elections and church government during a vacancy of the Holy See was promulgated by Pope John Paul Feb. 23, 1996, in the apostolic constitution *Universi Dominici Gregis* ("Shepherd of the Lord's Whole Flock").

Paraclete: A title of the Holy Spirit meaning, in Greek, Advocate, Consoler.

Parental Duties: All duties related to the obligation of parents to provide for the welfare of their children. These obligations fall under the Fourth Commandment.

Parish: A community of the faithful served by a pastor charged with responsibility for providing them with full pastoral service. Most parishes are territorial, embracing all of the faithful in a certain area of a diocese: some are personal or national, for certain classes of people, without strict regard for their places of residence.

Parousia: The coming, or saving presence, of Christ which will mark the completion of salvation history and the coming to perfection of God's kingdom at the end of the world.

Particular Church: A term used since Vatican II that denotes certain divisions of the Universal Church. Examples include dioceses, vicariates, and prelatures.

Paschal Candle: A large candle, symbolic of the risen Christ, blessed and lighted on the Easter Vigil and placed at the altar until Pentecost. It is ornamented with five large grains of incense, representing the wounds of Christ, inserted in the form of a cross; the Greek letters Alpha and Omega, symbolizing Christ the beginning and end of all things, at the top and bottom of the shaft of the cross; and the figures of the current year of salvation in the quadrants formed by the cross.

Paschal Precept: Church law requiring reception of the Eucharist in the Easter season (see separate entry) unless, for a just cause, once-a-year reception takes place at another time.

Passion of Christ: Sufferings of Christ, recorded in the four Gospels.

Pastor: An ordained minister charged with responsibility for the doctrinal, sacramental and related service of people committed to his care; e.g., a bishop for the people in his diocese, a priest for the people of his parish.

Pater Noster: The initial Latin words, *Our Father*, of the Lord's Prayer.

Peace, Sign of: A gesture of greeting — e.g., a handshake — exchanged by the ministers and participants at Mass.

Pectoral Cross: A cross worn on a chain about the neck and over the breast by bishops and abbots as a mark of their office.

Penance or Penitence: (1) The spiritual change or conversion of mind and heart by which a person turns away from sin, and all that it implies, toward God, through a personal renewal under the influence of the Holy Spirit. Penance involves sorrow and contrition for sin, together with other internal and external acts of atonement. It serves the purposes of reestablishing in one's life the order of God's love and commandments, and of making satisfaction to God for sin. (2) Penance is a virtue disposing a person to turn to God in sorrow for sin and to carry out works of amendment and atonement. (3) The sacrament of penance and sacramental penance.

People of God: A name for the Church in the sense that it is comprised by a people with Christ as its head, the Holy Spirit as the condition of its unity, the law of love as its rule, and the kingdom of God as its destiny. Although it is a scriptural term, it was given new emphasis by the Second Vatican Council's Dogmatic Constitution on the Church (*Lumen Gentium*).

Perjury: Taking a false oath, lying under oath, a violation of the honor due to God.

Persecution, Religious: A campaign waged against a church or other religious body by persons and governments intent on its destruction. The best known campaigns of this type against the Christian Church were the Roman persecutions which occurred intermittently from about 54 to the promulgation of the Edict of Milan in 313. More Catholics have been persecuted in the 20th century than in any other period in history.

Personal Prelature: A special-purpose jurisdiction — for particular pastoral and missionary work, etc. — consisting of secular priests and deacons and open to lay persons willing to dedicate themselves to its apostolic works. The prelate in charge is an Ordinary, with the authority of office; he can establish a national or international seminary, incardinate its students and promote them to holy orders under the title of service to the prelature. The prelature is constituted and governed according to statutes laid down by the Holy See. Statutes define its relationship and mode of operation with the bishops of territories in which members live and work. Opus Dei is a personal prelature.

Peter's Pence: A collection made each year among Catholics for the maintenance of the pope and his works of charity. It was originally a tax of a penny on each house, and was collected on St. Peter's day, whence the name. It originated in England in the 8th century.

Petition: One of the four purposes of prayer. In prayers of petition, persons ask of God the blessings they and others need.

Pharisees: Influential class among the Jews, referred to in the Gospels, noted for their self-righteousness, legalism, strict interpretation of the Law, acceptance of the traditions of the elders as well as the Law of Moses, and beliefs regarding angels and spirits, the resurrection of the dead and judgment. Most of them were laymen, and they were closely allied with the Scribes; their opposite numbers were the Sadducees. The Pharisaic and rabbinical traditions had a lasting influence on Judaism following the destruction of Jerusalem in 70 A.D.

Pious Fund: Property and money originally accumulated by the Jesuits to finance their missionary work in Lower California. When the Jesuits were expelled from the territory in 1767, the fund was appropriated by the Spanish Crown and used to support Dominican and Franciscan missionary work in Upper and Lower California. In 1842 the Mexican government took over administration of the fund, incorporated most of the revenue into the national treasury, and agreed to pay the Church interest of six per cent a year on the capital so incorporated. From 1848 to 1967 the fund was the subject of lengthy negotiations between the U.S. and

Mexican governments because of the latter's failure to make payments as agreed. A lump-sum settlement was made in 1967 with payment by Mexico to the U.S. government of more than $700,000, to be turned over to the Archdiocese of San Francisco.

Polytheism: Belief in and worship of many gods or divinities, especially prevalent in pre-Christian religions.

Poor Box: Alms-box; found in churches from the earliest days of Christianity.

Pope: A title from the Italian word *papa* (from Greek *pappas*, father) used for the Bishop of Rome, the Vicar of Christ and successor of St. Peter, who exercises universal governance over the Church.

Portiuncula: (1) Meaning little portion (of land), the Portiuncula was the chapel of Our Lady of the Angels near Assisi, Italy, which the Benedictines gave to St. Francis early in the 13th century. He repaired the chapel and made it the first church of the Franciscan Order. It is now enshrined in the Basilica of St. Mary of the Angels in Assisi. (2) The plenary Portiuncula Indulgence, or Pardon of Assisi, was authorized by Honorius III. Originally, it could be gained for the souls in purgatory only in the chapel of Our Lady of the Angels; by later concessions, it could be gained also in other Franciscan and parish churches. The indulgence (applicable to the souls in purgatory) can be gained from noon of Aug. 1 to midnight of Aug. 2, once each day. The conditions are, in addition to freedom from attachment to sin: reception of the sacraments of penance and the Eucharist on or near the day and a half; a visit to a parish church within the day and a half, during which the Our Father, Creed and another prayer are offered for the intentions of the pope.

Positivism: The philosophy that teaches that the only reality is that which is perceived by the senses; the only truth is that which is empirically verified. It asserts that ideas about God, morality, or anything else that cannot be scientifically tested are to be rejected as unknowable.

Possession, Diabolical: The extraordinary state of a person who is tormented from within by evil spirits who exercise strong influence over his powers of mind and body. (See also Exorcism.)

Postulant: One of several names used to designate a candidate for membership in a religious institute during the period before novitiate.

Poverty: (1) The quality or state of being poor, in actual destitution and need, or being poor in spirit. In the latter sense, poverty means the state of mind and disposition of persons who regard material things in proper perspective as gifts of God for the support of life and its reasonable enrichment, and for the service of others in need. It means freedom from unreasonable attachment to material things as ends in themselves, even though they may be possessed in small or large measure. (2) One of the evangelical counsels professed as a public vow by members of an institute of consecrated life. It involves the voluntary renunciation of rights of ownership and of independent use and disposal of material goods; or, the right of independent use and disposal, but not of the radical right of ownership. Religious institutes provide their members with necessary and useful goods and services from common resources. The manner in which goods are received and/or handled by religious is determined

by poverty of spirit and the rule and constitutions of their institute.

Pragmatism: Theory that the truth of ideas, concepts and values depends on their utility or capacity to serve a useful purpose rather than on their conformity with objective standards; also called utilitarianism.

Prayer: The raising of the mind and heart to God in adoration, thanksgiving, reparation and petition. Prayer, which is always mental because it involves thought and love of God, may be vocal, meditative, private and personal, social, and official. The official prayer of the Church as a worshiping community is called the liturgy.

Precepts: Commands or orders given to individuals or communities in particular cases; they establish law for concerned parties. Preceptive documents are issued by the pope, departments of the Roman Curia and other competent authority in the Church.

Presence of God: A devotional practice of increasing one's awareness of the presence and action of God in daily life.

Presumption: A sin against hope, by which a person striving for salvation (1) either relies too much on his own capabilities or (2) expects God to do things which he cannot do, in keeping with his divine attributes, or does not will to do, according to his divine plan. Presumption is the opposite of despair.

Preternatural Gifts: Exceptional gifts, beyond the exigencies and powers of human nature, enjoyed by Adam in the state of original justice: immunity from suffering and death, superior knowledge, integrity or perfect control of the passions. These gifts were lost as the result of original sin; their loss, however, implied no impairment of the integrity of human nature.

Pride: Unreasonable self-esteem; one of the seven capital sins.

Prie-Dieu: A French phrase, meaning pray God, designating a kneeler or bench suitable for kneeling while at prayer.

Priesthood: (1) The common priesthood of the non-ordained faithful. In virtue of baptism and confirmation, the faithful are a priestly people who participate in the priesthood of Christ through acts of worship, witness to the faith in daily life, and efforts to foster the growth of God's kingdom. (2) The ordained priesthood, in virtue of the sacrament of orders, of bishops, priests and deacons, for service to the common priesthood.

Primary Option: The life-choice of a person for or against God which shapes the basic orientation of moral conduct. A primary option for God does not preclude the possibility of serious sin.

Prior: A superior or an assistant to an abbot in a monastery.

Privilege: A favor, an exemption from the obligation of a law. Privileges of various kinds, with respect to ecclesiastical laws, are granted by the pope, departments of the Roman Curia and other competent authority in the Church.

Probabiliorism: The moral system asserting that the more probable opinion of a varied set of acceptable positions regarding the binding character of a law should be accepted. If the reasons for being free from a law are more probably true, one is freed from the law's obligations. Probabiliorism, however, maintained that if it was probable that the law did not bind, one still had to follow it unless it was more probable that the law did not bind.

Probabilism: A moral system for use in cases of conscience which involve the obligation of doubtful laws. There is a general principle that a doubtful law does not bind. Probabilism, therefore, teaches that it is permissible to follow an opinion favoring liberty, provided the opinion is certainly and solidly probable. Probabilism may not be invoked when there is question of: a certain law or the certain obligation of a law; the certain right of another party; the validity of an action; something which is necessary for salvation.

Pro-Cathedral: A church used as a cathedral.

Promoter of the Faith (*Promotor fidei*): An official of the Congregation for the Causes of Saints, whose role in beatification and canonization procedures is to establish beyond reasonable doubt the validity of evidence regarding the holiness of prospective saints and miracles attributed to their intercession.

Prophecy: (1) The communication of divine revelation by inspired intermediaries, called prophets, between God and his people. Old Testament prophecy was unique in its origin and because of its ethical and religious content, which included disclosure of the saving will of Yahweh for the people, moral censures and warnings of divine punishment because of sin and violations of the Law and Covenant, in the form of promises, admonitions, reproaches and threats. Although Moses and other earlier figures are called prophets, the period of prophecy is generally dated from the early years of the monarchy to about 100 years after the Babylonian Exile. From that time on, the written Law and its interpreters supplanted the prophets as guides of the people. Old Testament prophets are cited in the New Testament, with awareness that God spoke through them and that some of their oracles were fulfilled in Christ. John the Baptist is the outstanding prophetic figure in the New Testament. Christ never claimed the title of prophet for himself, although some people thought he was one. There were prophets in the early Church, and St. Paul mentioned the charism of prophecy in 1 Cor. 14:1-5. Prophecy disappeared after New Testament times. Revelation is classified as the prophetic book of the New Testament. (2) In contemporary non-scriptural usage, the term is applied to the witness given by persons to the relevance of their beliefs in everyday life and action.

Proportionalism: The moral theory that asserts that an action is judged on whether the evils resulting are proportionate to the goods that result. If the evils outweigh the goods, the act is objectionable; if the opposite is true, the act is permissible. Proportionalism differs from consequentialism in that the former admits that the inherent morality of the act and the agent's intention must also be considered. Proportionalism is rejected by critics as it does not offer an objective criterion for determining when evils are proportionate or disproportionate. It also fails to consider the intrinsic nature of human acts and does nothing to assist Christians to grow in virtue.

Province: (1) A territory comprising one archdiocese called the metropolitan see and one or more dioceses called suffragan sees. The head of the archdio-

cese, an archbishop, has metropolitan rights and responsibilities over the province. (2) A division of a religious order under the jurisdiction of a provincial superior.

Prudence: Practical wisdom and judgment regarding the choice and use of the best ways and means of doing good; one of the four cardinal virtues.

Punishment Due for Sin: The punishment which is a consequence of sin. It is of two kinds: (1) Eternal punishment is the punishment of hell, to which one becomes subject by the commission of mortal sin. Such punishment is remitted when mortal sin is forgiven. (2) Temporal punishment is a consequence of venial sin and/or forgiven mortal sin; it is not everlasting and may be remitted in this life by means of penance. Temporal punishment unremitted during this life is remitted by suffering in purgatory.

Purgatory: The state or condition of those who have died in the state of grace but with some attachment to sin, and are purified for a time before they are admitted to the glory and happiness of heaven. In this state and period of passive suffering, they are purified of unrepented venial sins, satisfy the demands of divine justice for temporal punishment due for sins, and are thus converted to a state of worthiness of the beatific vision.

Q

Quadragesima: From the Latin for fortieth, the name given to the forty penitential days of Lent.

Quinquennial Report: A report on the current state of a diocese that must be compiled and submitted by a bishop to the Holy See every five years in anticipation of the *ad liminal* visit.

Quinque Viae: From the Latin for the "five ways," the five proofs for the existence of God that were proposed by St. Thomas Aquinas in his *Summa Theologiae* (Part I, question 2, article 3). The five ways are: 1) all the motion in the world points to an unmoved Prime Mover; 2) the subordinate agents in the world imply the First Agent; 3) there must be a Cause Who is not perishable and Whose existence is underived; 4) the limited goodness in the world must be a reflection of Unlimited Goodness; 5) all things tend to become something, and that inclination must have proceeded from some Rational Planner.

R

Racism: A theory which holds that any one or several of the different races of the human family are inherently superior or inferior to any one or several of the others. The teaching denies the essential unity of the human race, the equality and dignity of all persons because of their common possession of the same human nature, and the participation of all in the divine plan of redemption. It is radically opposed to the virtue of justice and the precept of love of neighbor. Differences of superiority and inferiority which do exist are the result of accidental factors operating in a wide variety of circumstances, and are in no way due to essential defects in any one or several of the branches of the one human race. The theory of racism, together with practices related to it, is incompatible with Christian doctrine.

Rash Judgment: Attributing faults to another without sufficient reason; a violation of the obligations of justice and charity.

Rationalism: A theory which makes the mind the measure and arbiter of all things, including religious truth. A product of the Enlightenment, it rejects the supernatural, divine revelation, and authoritative teaching by any church.

Recollection: Meditation, attitude of concentration or awareness of spiritual matters and things pertaining to salvation and the accomplishment of God's will.

Relativism: Theory which holds that all truth, including religious truth, is relative, i.e., not absolute, certain or unchanging; a product of agnosticism, indifferentism, and an unwarranted extension of the notion of truth in positive science. Relativism is based on the tenet that certain knowledge of any and all truth is impossible. Therefore, no religion, philosophy or science can be said to possess the real truth; consequently, all religions, philosophies and sciences may be considered to have as much or as little of truth as any of the others.

Relics: The physical remains and effects of saints, which are considered worthy of veneration inasmuch as they are representative of persons in glory with God. Catholic doctrine proscribes the view that relics are not worthy of veneration. In line with norms laid down by the Council of Trent and subsequent enactments, discipline concerning relics is subject to control by the Congregations for the Causes of Saints and for Divine Worship and the Discipline of the Sacraments.

Religion: The adoration and service of God as expressed in divine worship and in daily life. Religion is concerned with all of the relations existing between God and human beings, and between humans themselves because of the central significance of God. Objectively considered, religion consists of a body of truth which is believed, a code of morality for the guidance of conduct, and a form of divine worship. Subjectively, it is a person's total response, theoretically and practically, to the demands of faith; it is living faith, personal engagement, self-commitment to God. Thus, by creed, code and cult, a person orders and directs his or her life in reference to God and, through what the love and service of God implies, to all people and all things.

Reliquary: A vessel for the preservation and exposition of a relic; sometimes made like a small monstrance.

Reparation: The making of amends to God for sin committed; one of the four ends of prayer and the purpose of penance.

Requiem: A Mass offered for the repose of the soul of one who has died in Christ. Its name is derived from the first word of the Gregorian (Latin) entrance chant (or Introit) at Masses for the dead: *Requiem aeternam dona eis, Domine* ("Eternal rest grant unto them, O Lord"). The revised Rite for Funerals refers to the requiem as the Mass of Christian Burial; however, it would not be uncommon to hear people employ the former usage.

Rescript: A written reply by an ecclesiastical superior regarding a question or request; its provisions bind concerned parties only. Papal dispensations are issued in the form of rescripts.

Reserved Censure: A sin or censure, absolution from which is reserved to religious superiors, bishops, the pope, or confessors having special faculties. Reservations are made because of the serious nature and social effects of certain sins and censures.

Restitution: An act of reparation for an injury done to another. The injury may be caused by taking and/or retaining what belongs to another or by damaging either the property or reputation of another. The intention of making restitution, usually in kind, is required as a condition for the forgiveness of sins of injustice, even though actual restitution is not possible.

Ring: In the Church a ring is worn as part of the insignia of bishops, abbots, et al.; by sisters to denote their consecration to God and the Church. The wedding ring symbolizes the love and union of husband and wife.

Ritual: A book of prayers and ceremonies used in the administration of the sacraments and other ceremonial functions. In the Roman Rite, the standard book of this kind is the Roman Ritual.

Rogito: The official notarial act or document testifying to the burial of a pope.

Rosary: A form of mental and vocal prayer centered on mysteries or events in the lives of Jesus and Mary. Its essential elements are meditation on the mysteries and the recitation of a number of decades of Hail Marys, each beginning with the Lord's Prayer. Introductory prayers may include the Apostles' Creed, an initial Our Father, three Hail Marys and a Glory be to the Father; each decade is customarily concluded with a Glory be to the Father; at the end, it is customary to say the Hail, Holy Queen and a prayer from the liturgy for the feast of the Blessed Virgin Mary of the Rosary. The Mysteries of the Rosary, which are the subject of meditation, are: (1) *Joyful* — the Annunciation to Mary that she was to be the Mother of Christ, her visit to Elizabeth, the birth of Jesus, the presentation of Jesus in the Temple, the finding of Jesus in the Temple. (2) *Sorrowful* —Christ's agony in the Garden of Gethsemani, scourging at the pillar, crowning with thorns, carrying of the cross to Calvary, and crucifixion. (3) *Glorious* — the Resurrection and Ascension of Christ, the descent of the Holy Spirit upon the Apostles, Mary's Assumption into heaven and her crowning as Queen of angels and men. The complete Rosary, called the Dominican Rosary, consists of 15 decades. In customary practice, only five decades are usually said at one time. Rosary beads are used to aid in counting the prayers without distraction. The Rosary originated through the coalescence of popular devotions to Jesus and Mary from the 12th century onward. Its present form dates from about the 15th century. Carthusians contributed greatly toward its development; Dominicans have been its greatest promoters.

S

Sabbath: The seventh day of the week, observed by Jews and Sabbatarians as the day for rest and religious observance.

Sacrarium: A basin with a drain leading directly into the ground; standard equipment of a sacristy.

Sacred Heart, Enthronement of the: An acknowledgment of the sovereignty of Jesus Christ over the Christian family, expressed by the installation of an image or picture of the Sacred Heart in a place of honor in the home, accompanied by an act of consecration.

Sacred Heart, Promises: Twelve promises to persons having devotion to the Sacred Heart of Jesus, which were communicated by Christ to St. Margaret Mary Alacoque in a private revelation in 1675: (1) *I will give them all the graces necessary in their state in life.* (2) *I will establish peace in their homes.* (3) *I will comfort them in all their afflictions.* (4) *I will be their secure refuge during life and, above all, in death.* (5) *I will bestow abundant blessing upon all their undertakings.* (6) *Sinners shall find in my Heart the source and the infinite ocean of mercy.* (7) *By devotion to my Heart tepid souls shall grow fervent.* (8) *Fervent souls shall quickly mount to high perfection.* (9) *I will bless every place where a picture of my Heart shall be set up and honored.* (10) *I will give to priests the gift of touching the most hardened hearts.* (11) *Those who promote this devotion shall have their names written in my Heart, never to be blotted out.* (12) *I will grant the grace of final penitence to those who communicate (receive Holy Communion) on the first Friday of nine consecutive months.*

Sacrilege: Violation of and irreverence toward a person, place or thing that is sacred because of public dedication to God; a sin against the virtue of religion. Personal sacrilege is violence of some kind against a cleric or religious, or a violation of chastity with a cleric or religious. Local sacrilege is the desecration of sacred places. Real sacrilege is irreverence with respect to sacred things, such as the sacraments and sacred vessels.

Sacristy: A utility room where vestments, church furnishings and sacred vessels are kept and where the clergy vest for sacred functions.

Sadducees: The predominantly priestly party among the Jews in the time of Christ, noted for extreme conservatism, acceptance only of the Law of Moses, and rejection of the traditions of the elders. Their opposite numbers were the Pharisees.

Saints, Cult of: The veneration, called *dulia*, of holy persons who have died and are in glory with God in heaven; it includes honoring them and petitioning them for their intercession with God. Liturgical veneration is given only to saints officially recognized by the Church; private veneration may be given to anyone thought to be in heaven. The veneration of saints is essentially different from the adoration given to God alone; by its very nature, however, it terminates in the worship of God. (See also Dulia and Latria.)

Salvation: The liberation of persons from sin and its effects, reconciliation with God in and through Christ, the attainment of union with God forever in the glory of heaven as the supreme purpose of life and as the God-given reward for fulfillment of his will on earth. Salvation-in-process begins and continues in this life through union with Christ in faith professed and in action; its final term is union with God and the whole community of the saved in the ultimate perfection of God's kingdom. The Church teaches that: God wills the salvation of all men; men are saved in and through Christ; membership in the Church established by Christ, known and understood as the community of salvation, is necessary for salvation; men with this knowledge and understanding

who deliberately reject this Church, cannot be saved. The Catholic Church is the Church founded by Christ. (See below, Salvation outside the Church.)

Salvation History: The facts and the record of God's relations with human beings, in the past, present and future, for the purpose of leading them to live in accordance with his will for the eventual attainment after death of salvation, or everlasting happiness with him in heaven. The essentials of salvation history are: God's love for all human beings and will for their salvation; his intervention and action in the world to express this love and bring about their salvation; the revelation he made of himself and the covenant he established with the Israelites in the Old Testament; the perfecting of this revelation and the new covenant of grace through Christ in the New Testament; the continuing action-for-salvation carried on in and through the Church; the communication of saving grace to people through the merits of Christ and the operations of the Holy Spirit in the here-and-now circumstances of daily life and with the cooperation of people themselves.

Salvation outside the Church: The Second Vatican Council covered this subject summarily in the following manner: "Those also can attain to everlasting salvation who through no fault of their own do not know the Gospel of Christ or his Church, yet sincerely seek God and, moved by grace, strive by their deeds to do his will as it is known to them through the dictates of conscience. Nor does divine Providence deny the help necessary for salvation to those who, without blame on their part, have not yet arrived at an explicit knowledge of God, but who strive to live a good life, thanks to his grace. Whatever good or truth is found among them is looked upon by the Church as a preparation for the Gospel. She regards such qualities as given by him who enlightens all men so that they may finally have life" (Dogmatic Constitution on the Church, *Lumen Gentium*, No. 16).

Sanctifying Grace: See Grace.

Satanism: Worship of the devil, a blasphemous inversion of the order of worship which is due to God alone.

Scandal: Conduct which is the occasion of sin to another person.

Scapular: (1) A part of the habit of some religious orders like the Benedictines and Dominicans; a nearly shoulder-wide strip of cloth worn over the tunic and reaching almost to the feet in front and behind. Originally a kind of apron, it came to symbolize the cross and yoke of Christ. (2) Scapulars worn by lay persons as a sign of association with religious orders and for devotional purposes are an adaptation of monastic scapulars. Approved by the Church as sacramentals, they consist of two small squares of woolen cloth joined by strings and are worn about the neck. They are given for wearing in a ceremony of investiture or enrollment. There are nearly 20 scapulars for devotional use: the five principal ones are generally understood to include those of Our Lady of Mt. Carmel (the brown Carmelite Scapular), the Holy Trinity, Our Lady of the Seven Dolors, the Passion, the Immaculate Conception.

Scapular Medal: A medallion with a representation of the Sacred Heart on one side and of the Blessed Virgin Mary on the other. Authorized by St. Pius X in 1910, it may be worn or carried in place of a scapular by persons already invested with a scapular.

Scapular Promise: According to a legend of the Carmelite Order, the Blessed Virgin Mary appeared to St. Simon Stock in 1251 at Cambridge, England, and declared that wearers of the brown Carmelite Scapular would be the beneficiaries of her special intercession. The scapular tradition has never been the subject of official decision by the Church. Essentially, it expresses belief in the intercession of Mary and the efficacy of sacramentals in the context of truly Christian life.

Schism: Derived from a Greek word meaning separation, the term designates formal and obstinate refusal by a baptized Catholic, called a schismatic, to be in communion with the pope and the Church. The canonical penalty is excommunication. One of the most disastrous schisms in history resulted in the definitive separation of the Church in the East from union with Rome about 1054.

Scholasticism: The term usually applied to the Catholic theology and philosophy which developed in the Middle Ages. (See also Neo-Scholasticism.)

Scribes: Hebrew intellectuals noted for their knowledge of the Law of Moses, influential from the time of the Exile to about 70 A.D. Many of them were Pharisees. They were the antecedents of rabbis and their traditions, as well as those o the Pharisees, had a lasting influence on Judaism following the destruction of Jerusalem in 70 A.D.

Scruple: A morbid, unreasonable fear and anxiety that one's actions are sinful when they are not, or more seriously sinful than they actually are. Compulsive scrupulosity is quite different from the transient scrupulosity of persons of tender or highly sensitive conscience, or of persons with faulty moral judgment.

Seal of Confession: The obligation of secrecy which must be observed regarding knowledge of things learned in connection with the confession of sin in the sacrament of penance. The seal covers matters whose revelation would make the sacrament burdensome. Confessors are prohibited, under penalty of excommunication, from making any direct revelation of confessional matter; this prohibition holds, outside of confession, even with respect to the person who made the confession unless the person releases the priest from the obligation. Persons other than confessors are obliged to maintain secrecy, but not under penalty of excommunication. General, non-specific discussion of confessional matter does not violate the seal.

Secularism: A school of thought, a spirit and manner of action which ignores and/or repudiates the validity or influence of supernatural religion with respect to individual and social life.

See: Another name for diocese or archdiocese.

Seminary: A house of study and formation for men, called seminarians, preparing for the priesthood. Traditional seminaries date from the Council of Trent in the middle of the 16th century; before that time, candidates for the priesthood were variously trained in monastic schools, universities under church auspices, and in less formal ways.

Sermon on the Mount: A compilation of sayings of Our Lord in the form of an extended discourse in Matthew's Gospel (5:1 to 7:27) and, in a shorter discourse, in Luke (6:17-49). The passage in Matthew, called the "Constitution of the New Law," summa-

rizes the living spirit of believers in Christ and members of the kingdom of God. Beginning with the Beatitudes and including the Lord's Prayer, it covers the perfect justice of the New Law, the fulfillment of the Old Law in the New Law of Christ, and the integrity of internal attitude and external conduct with respect to love of God and neighbor, justice, chastity, truth, trust and confidence in God.

Seven Last Words of Christ: Words of Christ on the cross. (1) *"Father, forgive them; for they do not know what they are doing."* (2) To the penitent thief: *"I assure you: today you will be with me in Paradise."* (3) To Mary and his Apostle John: *"Woman, there is your son There is your mother."* (4) *"My God, my God, why have you forsaken me?"* (5) *"I am thirsty."* (6) *"Now it is finished."* (7) *"Father, into your hands I commend my spirit."*

Shrine, Crowned: A shrine approved by the Holy See as a place of pilgrimage. The approval permits public devotion at the shrine and implies that at least one miracle has resulted from devotion at the shrine. Among the best known crowned shrines are those of the Virgin Mary at Lourdes and Fátima. Shrines with statues crowned by Pope John Paul in 1985 in South America were those of Our Lady of Coromoto, patroness of Venezuela, in Caracas, and Our Lady of Carmen of Paucartambo in Cuzco, Peru.

Shroud of Turin: A strip of brownish linen cloth, 14 feet, three inches in length and three feet, seven inches in width, bearing the front and back imprint of a human body. A tradition dating from the 7th century, which has not been verified beyond doubt, claims that the shroud is the fine linen in which the body of Christ was wrapped for burial. The early history of the shroud is obscure. It was enshrined at Lirey, France, in 1354 and was transferred in 1578 to Turin, Italy, where it has been kept in the cathedral down to the present time. Scientific investigation, which began in 1898, seems to indicate that the markings on the shroud are those of a human body. The shroud, for the first time since 1933, was placed on public view from Aug. 27 to Oct. 8, 1978, and was seen by an estimated 3.3 million people. Scientists conducted intensive studies of it thereafter, finally determining that the material of the shroud dated from between 1260 and 1390. The shroud, which had been the possession of the House of Savoy, was willed to Pope John Paul II in 1983.

Sick Calls: When a person is confined at home by illness or other cause and is unable to go to church for reception of the sacraments, a parish priest should be informed and arrangements made for him to visit the person at home. Such visitations are common in pastoral practice, both for special needs and for providing persons with regular opportunities for receiving the sacraments. If a priest cannot make the visitation, arrangements can be made for a deacon or Eucharistic minister to bring Holy Communion to the homebound or bedridden person.

Sign of the Cross: A sign, ceremonial gesture or movement in the form of a cross by which a person confesses faith in the Holy Trinity and Christ, and intercedes for the blessing of himself or herself, other persons and things. In Roman-Rite practice, a person making the sign touches the fingers of the right hand to forehead, below the breast, left shoulder and right shoulder while saying: *"In the name of the Father,* *and of the Son, and of the Holy Spirit."* The sign is also made with the thumb on the forehead, the lips, and the breast. For the blessing of persons and objects, a large sign of the cross is made by movement of the right hand. In Eastern-Rite practice, the sign is made with the thumb and first two fingers of the right hand joined together and touching the forehead, below the breast, the right shoulder and the left shoulder; the formula generally used is the doxology, *"O Holy God, O Holy Strong One, O Immortal One."* The Eastern manner of making the sign was general until the first half of the 13th century; by the 17th century, Western practice involved the whole right hand and the reversal of direction from shoulder to shoulder.

Signs of the Times: Contemporary events, trends and features in culture and society, the needs and aspirations of people, all the factors that form the context in and through which the Church has to carry on its saving mission. The Second Vatican Council spoke on numerous occasions about these signs and the relationship between them and a kind of manifestation of God's will, positive or negative, and about subjecting them to judgment and action corresponding to the demands of divine revelation through Scripture, Christ, and the experience, tradition and teaching authority of the Church.

Simony: The deliberate intention and act of selling and/or buying spiritual goods or material things so connected with the spiritual that they cannot be separated therefrom; a violation of the virtue of religion, and a sacrilege, because it wrongfully puts a material price on spiritual things, which cannot be either sold or bought. In church law, actual sale or purchase is subject to censure in some cases. The term is derived from the name of Simon Magus, who attempted to buy from Sts. Peter and John the power to confirm people in the Holy Spirit (Acts 8:4-24).

Sin: (1) Actual sin is the free and deliberate violation of God's law by thought, word or action. (a) Mortal sin — involving serious matter, sufficient reflection and full consent — results in the loss of sanctifying grace and alienation from God, and renders a person incapable of performing meritorious supernatural acts and subject to everlasting punishment. (b) Venial sin — involving less serious matter, reflection and consent — does not have such serious consequences. (2) Original sin is the sin of Adam, with consequences for all human beings. (See separate entry.)

Sins against the Holy Spirit: Despair of salvation, presumption of God's mercy, impugning the known truths of faith, envy at another's spiritual good, obstinacy in sin, final impenitence. Those guilty of such sins stubbornly resist the influence of grace and, as long as they do so, cannot be forgiven.

Sins, Occasions of: Circumstances (persons, places, things, etc.) which easily lead to sin. There is an obligation to avoid voluntary proximate occasions of sin, and to take precautions against the dangers of unavoidable occasions.

Sins That Cry to Heaven for Vengeance: Willful murder, sins against nature, oppression of the poor, widows and orphans, defrauding laborers of their wages.

Sister: Any woman religious, in popular speech; strictly, the title applies only to women religious belonging to institutes whose members never professed solemn vows. Most of the institutes whose members are properly called Sisters were established during and since the 19th century. Women religious with solemn vows, or belonging to institutes whose members formerly professed solemn vows, are properly called nuns.

Sisterhood: A generic term referring to the whole institution of the life of women religious in the Church, or to a particular institute of women religious.

Situation Ethics: A subjective, individualistic ethical theory which denies the binding force of ethical principles as universal laws and preceptive norms of moral conduct, and proposes that morality is determined only by situational conditions and considerations and the intention of the person. It has been criticized for ignoring the principles of objective ethics. (See also Consequentialism and Proportionalism.)

Slander: Attributing to a person faults which he or she does not have; a violation of the obligations of justice and charity, for which restitution is due.

Sloth (Acedia): One of the seven capital sins; spiritual laziness, involving distaste and disgust for spiritual things; spiritual boredom, which saps the vigor of spiritual life. Physical laziness is a counterpart of spiritual sloth.

Sorcery: A kind of black magic in which evil is invoked by means of diabolical intervention; a violation of the virtue of religion.

Soteriology: The division of theology which treats of the mission and work of Christ as Redeemer.

Species, Sacred: The appearances of bread and wine (color, taste, smell, etc.) which remain after the substance has been changed at the Consecration of the Mass into the Body and Blood of Christ. (See Transubstantiation.)

Spiritism: Attempts to communicate with spirits and departed souls by means of seances, table tapping, ouija boards, and other methods; a violation of the virtue of religion. Spiritualistic practices are noted for fakery.

Stational Churches, Days: Churches, especially in Rome, where the clergy and lay people were accustomed to gather with their bishop on certain days for the celebration of the liturgy. The 25 early titular or parish churches of Rome, plus other churches, each had their turn as the site of divine worship in practices which may have started in the third century. The observances were rather well developed toward the latter part of the 4th century, and by the fifth they included a Mass concelebrated by the pope and attendant priests. On some occasions, the stational liturgy was preceded by a procession from another church called a *collecta*. There were 42 Roman stational churches in the 8th century, and 89 stational services were scheduled annually in connection with the liturgical seasons. Stational observances fell into disuse toward the end of the Middle Ages. Some revival was begun by John XXIII in 1959 and continued by Paul VI and John Paul II.

Stations (Way) of the Cross: A form of devotion commemorating the Passion and death of Christ, consisting of a series of meditations (stations): (1) his condemnation to death, (2) taking up of the cross, (3) the first fall on the way to Calvary, (4) meeting his Mother, (5) being assisted by Simon of Cyrene and (6) by the woman Veronica who wiped his face, (7) the second fall, (8) meeting the women of Jerusalem,

(9) the third fall, (10) being stripped and (11) nailed to the cross, (12) his death, (13) the removal of his body from the cross and (14) his burial. Depictions of these scenes are mounted in most churches, chapels and in some other places, beneath small crosses. A person making the Way of the Cross passes before these stations, or stopping points, pausing at each for meditation. If the stations are made by a group of people, only the leader has to pass from station to station. A plenary indulgence is granted to the faithful who make the stations, under the usual conditions: freedom from all attachment to sin, reception of the sacraments of penance and the Eucharist, and prayers for the intentions of the pope. Those who are impeded from making the stations in the usual manner can gain the same indulgence if, along with the aforementioned conditions, they spend at least a half hour in spiritual reading and meditation on the passion and death of Christ. The stations originated remotely from the practice of Holy Land pilgrims who visited the actual scenes of incidents in the Passion of Christ. Representations elsewhere of at least some of these scenes were known as early as the 5th century. Later, the stations evolved in connection with and as a consequence of strong devotion to the Passion in the 12th and 13th centuries. Franciscans, who were given custody of the Holy Places in 1342, promoted the devotion widely; one of them, St. Leonard of Port Maurice, became known as the greatest preacher of the Way of the Cross in the 18th century. The general features of the devotion were fixed by Clement XII in 1731.

Statutes: Virtually the same as decrees (see separate entry), they almost always designate laws of a particular council or synod rather than pontifical laws.

Stigmata: Marks of the wounds suffered by Christ in his crucifixion, in hands and feet by nails, and side by the piercing of a lance. Some persons, called stigmatists, have been reported as recipients or sufferers of marks like these. The Church, however, has never issued any infallible declaration about their possession by anyone, even in the case of St. Francis of Assisi whose stigmata seem to be the best substantiated and may be commemorated in the Roman-Rite liturgy. Ninety percent of some 300 reputed stigmatists have been women. Judgment regarding the presence, significance, and manner of causation of stigmata should depend, among other things, on irrefutable experimental evidence.

Stipend, Mass: An offering given to a priest for applying the fruits of the Mass according to the intention of the donor. The offering is a contribution to the support of the priest. The disposition of the fruits of the sacrifice, in line with doctrine concerning the Mass in particular and prayer in general, is subject to the will of God. Mass offerings and intentions were the subjects of a decree approved by John Paul II and made public Mar. 22, 1991: (1) Normally, no more than one offering should be accepted for a Mass; the Mass should be offered in accord with the donor's intention; the priest who accepts the offering should celebrate the Mass himself or have another priest do so. (2) Several Mass intentions, for which offerings have been made, can be combined for a "collective" application of a single Mass only if the previous and explicit consent of the donors is obtained. Such Masses are an exception to the general rule.

Stole Fee: An offering given on certain occasions;

e.g., at a baptism, wedding, funeral, for the support of the clergy who administer the sacraments and perform other sacred rites.

Stoup: A vessel used to contain holy water.

Suffragan See: Any diocese, except the archdiocese, within a province.

Suicide: The taking of one's own life; a violation of God's dominion over human life. Ecclesiastical burial is denied to persons while in full possession of their faculties; it is permitted in cases of doubt.

Supererogation: Actions which go beyond the obligations of duty and the requirements enjoined by God's law as necessary for salvation. Examples of these works are the profession and observance of the evangelical counsels of poverty, chastity, and obedience, and efforts to practice charity to the highest degree.

Supernatural: Above the natural; that which exceeds and is not due or owed to the essence, exigencies, requirements, powers and merits of created nature. While human beings have no claim on supernatural things and do not need them in order to exist and act on a natural level, they do need them in order to exist and act in the higher order or economy of grace established by God for their salvation. God has freely given them certain things which are beyond the powers and rights of their human nature. Examples of the supernatural are: grace, a kind of participation by human beings in the divine life, by which they become capable of performing acts meritorious for salvation; divine revelation by which God manifests himself to them and makes known truth that is inaccessible to human reason alone; faith, by which they believe divine truth because of the authority of God who reveals it through Sacred Scripture and tradition and the teaching of his Church.

Suspension: A censure by which a cleric is forbidden to exercise some or all of his powers of orders and jurisdiction, or to accept the financial support of his benefices.

Syllabus, The: (1) When not qualified, the term refers to the list of 80 errors accompanying Pope Pius IX's encyclical *Quanta Cura*, issued in 1864. (2) The Syllabus of St. Pius X in the decree *Lamentabili*, issued by the Holy Office July 4, 1907, condemning 65 heretical propositions of modernism. This schedule of errors was followed shortly by that pope's encyclical *Pascendi*, the principal ecclesiastical document against modernism, issued Sept. 8, 1907.

Synod, Diocesan: Meeting of representative persons of a diocese — priests, religious, lay persons — with the bishop, called by him for the purpose of considering and taking action on matters affecting the life and mission of the Church in the diocese. Persons taking part in a synod have consultative status; the bishop alone is the legislator, with power to authorize synodal decrees. According to canon law, every diocese should have a synod every 10 years.

T

Tabernacle: The receptacle in which the Blessed Sacrament is reserved in churches, chapels, and oratories. It is to be immovable, solid, locked, and located in a prominent place.

Te Deum: The opening Latin words, *Thee, God*, of a hymn of praise and thanksgiving prescribed for use in the Office of Readings of the Liturgy of the Hours on many Sundays, solemnities and feasts.

Temperance: Moderation, one of the four cardinal virtues.

Temptation: Any enticement to sin, from any source: the strivings of one's own faculties, the action of the devil, other persons, circumstances of life, etc. Temptation itself is not sin. Temptation can be avoided and overcome with the use of prudence and the help of grace.

Thanksgiving: An expression of gratitude to God for his goodness and the blessings he grants; one of the four ends of prayer.

Theism: A philosophy which admits the existence of God and the possibility of divine revelation; it is generally monotheistic and acknowledges God as transcendent and also active in the world. Because it is a philosophy rather than a system of theology derived from revelation, it does not include specifically Christian doctrines, like those concerning the Trinity, the Incarnation and Redemption.

Theodicy: From the Greek for God (*theos*) and judgment (*dike*), the study of God as he can be known by natural reason, rather than from supernatural revelation. First used by Gottfried Leibnitz (1646-1716), its primary objective is to make God's omnipotence compatible with the existence of evil.

Theological Virtues: The virtues which have God for their direct object: faith, or belief in God's infallible teaching; hope, or confidence in divine assistance; charity, or love of God. They are given to a person with grace in the first instance, through baptism and incorporation in Christ.

Theology: Knowledge of God and religion, deriving from and based on the data of divine Revelation, organized and systematized according to some kind of scientific method. It involves systematic study and presentation of the truths of divine Revelation in Sacred Scripture, tradition, and the teaching of the Church. Theology has been divided under various subject headings. Some of the major fields have been: dogmatic (systematic theology), moral, pastoral, historical, ascetical (the practice of virtue and means of attaining holiness and perfection), sacramental, and mystical (higher states of religious experience). Other subject headings include ecumenism (Christian unity, interfaith relations), ecclesiology (the nature and constitution of the Church), and Mariology (doctrine concerning the Blessed Virgin Mary), etc.

Theotokos: From the Greek for God-bearer, the preeminent title given to the Blessed Mother in the Oriental Church. This title has very ancient roots, stretching as far back as the third century but it did not became official in the Church until the Council of Ephesus in 431.

Thomism: The philosophy based on St. Thomas Aquinas (1224/5-1274), which is mandated to be the dominant philosophy used in Catholic educational institutions. (See also Neo-Scholasticism and Scholasticism.)

Tithing: Contribution of a portion of one's income, originally one-tenth, for purposes of religion and charity. The practice is mentioned 46 times in the Bible. In early Christian times, tithing was adopted in continuance of Old Testament practices of the Jewish people, and the earliest positive church legislation on the subject was enacted in 567. Catholics are bound in conscience to contribute to the support of their church, but the manner in which they do so is not fixed by law. Tithing, which amounts to a pledged contribution of a portion of one's income, has aroused new attention in recent years in the United States.

Titular Sees: Dioceses where the Church once flourished but which now exist only in name or title. Bishops without a territorial or residential diocese of their own; e.g., auxiliary bishops, are given titular sees. There are more than 2,000 titular sees; 16 of them are in the United States.

Transfinalization, Transignification: Terms coined to express the sign value of consecrated bread and wine with respect to the presence and action of Christ in the Eucharistic sacrifice and the spiritually vivifying purpose of the Eucharistic banquet in Holy Communion. The theory behind the terms has strong undertones of existential and "sign" philosophy, and has been criticized for its openness to interpretation at variance with the doctrine of transubstantiation and the abiding presence of Christ under the appearances of bread and wine after the sacrifice of the Mass and Communion have been completed. The terms, if used as substitutes for transubstantiation, are unacceptable; if they presuppose transubstantiation, they are acceptable as clarifications of its meaning.

Transubstantiation: "The way Christ is made present in this sacrament (Holy Eucharist) is none other than by the change of the whole substance of the bread into his Body, and of the whole substance of the wine into his Blood (in the Consecration at Mass), this unique and wonderful change the Catholic Church rightly calls transubstantiation" (encyclical *Mysterium Fidei* of Paul VI, Sept. 3, 1965). The first official use of the term was made by the Fourth Council of the Lateran in 1215. Authoritative teaching on the subject was issued by the Council of Trent.

Treasury of the Church: The superabundant merits of Christ and the saints from which the Church draws to confer spiritual benefits, such as indulgences.

Triduum: A three-day series of public or private devotions.

U-Z

Ultramontanism: The movement found primarily in France during the 19th century that advocated a strong sense of devotion and service to the Holy See. Generally considered a reaction to the anti-papal tendencies of Gallicanism, its name was derived from the Latin for "over the mountains," a reference to the Alps, beyond which rested Rome and the Holy See.

Unction: From the Latin, *ungere*, meaning to anoint or smear, a term used to denote the Sacrament of the Sick (or the Anointing of the Sick); it was more commonly termed Extreme Unction and was given as an anointing to a person just before death.

Universal Law: See Law.

Urbi et Orbi: A Latin phrase meaning "To the City and to the World" that is a blessing given by the Holy Father. Normally, the first *Urbi et Orbi* delivered by a pontiff is immediately after his election by the College of Cardinals. This is a blessing accompanied by a short address to the crowds in St. Peter's Square and to the world; frequently, as with Pope John Paul II in 1978, it is delivered in as many languages as possible. The pope also delivers an *Urbi et Orbi* each year at Christmas and at Easter.

Usury: Excessive interest charged for the loan and use of money; a violation of justice.

Vagi: A Latin word meaning wanderers that is used to describe any homeless person with no fixed residence.

Veni Creator Spiritus: A Latin phrase, meaning "Come, Creator Spirit" that is part of a hymn sung to the Holy Spirit. The hymn invokes the presence of the Holy Spirit and was perhaps first composed by Rabanus Maurus (776-856). The hymn is commonly sung as part of the Divine Office, papal elections, episcopal consecrations, ordinations, councils, synods, canonical elections, and confirmations.

Venial Sin: See under Sin.

Veronica: A word resulting from the combination of a Latin word for true, *vera*, and a Greek word for image, *eikon*, designating a likeness of the face of Christ or the name of a woman said to have given him a cloth on which he caused an imprint of his face to appear. The veneration at Rome of a likeness depicted on cloth dates from about the end of the 10th century; it figured in a popular devotion during the Middle Ages, and in the Holy Face devotion practiced since the 19th century. A faint, indiscernible likeness said to be of this kind is preserved in St. Peter's Basilica. The origin of the likeness is uncertain, and the identity of the woman is unknown. Before the 14th century, there were no known artistic representations of an incident concerning a woman who wiped the face of Christ with a piece of cloth while he was carrying the cross to Calvary.

Vespers: From the Latin for evening, the evening service of the Divine Office, also known as Evening Prayer, or among Anglicans as Evensong.

Viaticum: Holy Communion given to those in danger of death. The word, derived from Latin, means provision for a journey through death to life hereafter.

Vicar Forane: A Latin term meaning "deputy outside" that is applied to the priest given authority by the local bishop over a certain area or region of the diocese.

Vicar General: A priest or bishop appointed by the bishop of a diocese to serve as his deputy, with ordinary executive power, in the administration of the diocese.

Vicar, Judicial: The title given to the chief judge and head of the tribunal of a diocese.

Virginity: Observance of perpetual sexual abstinence. The state of virginity, which is embraced for the love of God by religious with a public vow or by others with a private vow, was singled out for high praise by Christ (Mt. 19:10-12) and has always been so regarded by the Church. In the encyclical *Sacra Virginitas*, Pius XII stated: "Holy virginity and that perfect chastity which is consecrated to the service of God is without doubt among the most perfect treasures which the founder of the Church has left in heritage to the society which he established." Paul VI approved in 1970 a rite in which women can consecrate their virginity "to Christ and their brethren" without becoming members of a religious institute. The *Ordo Consecrationis Virginum*, a revision of a rite promulgated by Clement VII in 1596, is traceable to the Roman liturgy of about 50

Virtue: A habit or established capability for performing good actions. Virtues are natural (acquired and increased by repeating good acts) and/or supernatural (given with grace by God).

Visions: A charism by which a specially chosen individual is able to behold a person or something that is naturally invisible. A vision should not be confused with an illusion or hallucination. Like other charisms, a vision is granted for the good of people; it should be noted, however, that they are not essential for holiness or salvation. Many saints throughout history have beheld visions, among them St. Thomas Aquinas, St. Teresa of Ávila, St. John of the Cross, and St. Francis of Assisi.

Vocation: A call to a way of life. Generally, the term applies to the common call of all persons, from God, to holiness and salvation. Specifically, it refers to particular states of life, each called a vocation, in which response is made to this universal call; viz., marriage, the religious life and/or priesthood, the single state freely chosen or accepted for the accomplishment of God's will. The term also applies to the various occupations in which persons make a living. The Church supports the freedom of each individual in choosing a particular vocation, and reserves the right to pass on the acceptability of candidates for the priesthood and religious life. Signs or indicators of particular vocations are many, including a person's talents and interests, circumstances and obligations, invitations of grace and willingness to respond thereto.

Vow: A promise made to God with sufficient knowledge and freedom, which has as its object a moral good that is possible and better than its voluntary omission. A person who professes a vow binds himself or herself by the virtue of religion to fulfill the promise. The best known examples of vows are those of poverty, chastity and obedience professed by religious (see Evangelical Counsels, individual entries). Public vows are made before a competent person, acting as an agent of the Church, who accepts the profession in the name of the Church, thereby giving public recognition to the person's dedication and consecration to God and divine worship. Vows of this kind are either solemn, rendering all contrary acts invalid as well as unlawful; or simple, rendering contrary acts unlawful. Solemn vows are for life; simple vows are for a definite period of time or for life. Vows professed without public recognition by the Church are called private vows. The Church, which has authority to accept and give public recognition to vows, also has authority to dispense persons from their obligations for serious reasons.

Witness, Christian: Practical testimony or evidence given by Christians of their faith in all circumstances of life — by prayer and general conduct, through good example and good works, etc.; being and acting in accordance with Christian belief; actual practice of the Christian faith.

Zeal: The expression of charity that permits one to serve God and others fully with the objective of furthering the Mystical Body of Christ.

Zucchetto: A small skullcap worn by ecclesiastics, most notably prelates and derived from the popular Italian vernacular term *zucca*, meaning a pumpkin, and used as slang for head. The Holy Father wears a white zucchetto made of watered silk; cardinals use scarlet, and bishops use purple. Priests of the monsignorial rank may wear black with purple piping. All others may wear simple black.

The calendar of the Roman Church consists of an arrangement throughout the year of a series of liturgical seasons, commemorations of divine mysteries and commemorations of saints for purposes of worship.

The key to the calendar is the central celebration of the Easter Triduum, commemorating the supreme saving act of Jesus in his death and resurrection to which all other observances and acts of worship are related.

The purposes of this calendar were outlined in the Constitution on the Sacred Liturgy (*Sacrosanctum Concilium*, Nos. 102-105) promulgated by the Second Vatican Council.

"Within the cycle of a year . . . (the Church) unfolds the whole mystery of Christ, not only from his incarnation and birth until his ascension, but also as reflected in the day of Pentecost, and the expectation of a blessed, hoped-for return of the Lord.

Recalling thus the mysteries of redemption, the Church opens to the faithful the riches of her Lord's powers and merits, so that these are in some way made present at all times, and the faithful are enabled to lay hold of them and become filled with saving grace (No. 102).

In celebrating this annual cycle of Christ's mysteries, holy Church honors with special love the Blessed Mary, Mother of God" (No. 103).

The Church has also included in the annual cycle days devoted to the memory of the martyrs and the other saints (who) sing God's perfect praise in heaven and offer prayers for us. By celebrating the passage of these saints from earth to heaven the Church proclaims the paschal mystery as achieved in the saints who have suffered and been glorified with Christ; she proposes them to the faithful as examples who draw all to the Father through Christ, and through their merits she pleads for God's favors (No. 104).

In the various seasons of the year and according to her traditional discipline, the Church completes the formation of the faithful by means of pious practices for soul and body, by instruction, prayer, and works of penance and mercy (No. 105).

THE ROMAN CALENDAR

Norms for a revised calendar for the Western Church as decreed by the Second Vatican Council were approved by Paul VI in the *motu proprio Mysterii Paschalis* dated Feb. 14, 1969. The revised calendar was promulgated a month later by a decree of the Congregation for Divine Worship and went into effect Jan. 1, 1970, with provisional modifications. Full implementation of all its parts was delayed in 1970 and 1971, pending the completion of work on related liturgical texts. The U.S. bishops ordered the calendar into effect for 1972.

The Seasons

Advent: The liturgical year begins with the first Sunday of Advent, which introduces a season of four weeks or slightly less duration with the theme of expectation of the coming of Christ. During the first two weeks, the final coming of Christ as Lord and Judge at the end of the world is the focus of attention. From Dec. 17 to 24, the emphasis shifts to anticipa-

THE CHURCH CALENDAR

tion of the celebration of his Nativity on the solemnity of Christmas.

Advent has four Sundays. Since the 10th century, the first Sunday has marked the beginning of the liturgical year in the Western Church. In the Middle Ages, a kind of pre-Christmas fast was in vogue during the season.

Christmas Season: The Christmas season begins with the vigil of Christmas and lasts until the Sunday after Jan. 6, inclusive.

The period between the end of the Christmas season and the beginning of Lent belongs to the Ordinary Time of the year. Of variable length, the pre-Lenten phase of this season includes what were formerly called the Sundays after Epiphany and the suppressed Sundays of Septuagesima, Sexagesima and Quinquagesima.

Lent: The penitential season of Lent begins on Ash Wednesday, which occurs between Feb. 4 and Mar. 11, depending on the date of Easter, and lasts until the Mass of the Lord's Supper (Holy Thursday). It has six Sundays. The sixth Sunday marks the beginning of Holy Week and is known as Passion (formerly called Palm) Sunday.

The origin of Lenten observances dates back to the fourth century or earlier.

Easter Triduum: The Easter Triduum begins with evening Mass of the Lord's Supper and ends with Evening Prayer on Easter Sunday.

Easter Season: The Easter season whose theme is resurrection from sin to the life of grace, lasts for 50 days, from Easter to Pentecost. Easter, the first Sunday after the first full moon following the vernal equinox, occurs between Mar. 22 and Apr. 25. The terminal phase of the Easter season, between the solemnities of the Ascension of the Lord and Pentecost, stresses anticipation of the coming and action of the Holy Spirit.

Ordinary Time: The season of Ordinary Time begins on Monday (or Tuesday if the feast of the Baptism of the Lord is celebrated on that Monday) after the Sunday following Jan. 6 and continues until the day before Ash Wednesday, inclusive. It begins again on the Monday after Pentecost and ends on the Saturday before the first Sunday of Advent. It consists of 33 or 34 weeks. The last Sunday is celebrated as the Solemnity of Christ the King. The overall purpose of the season is to elaborate the themes of salvation history.

The various liturgical seasons are characterized in part by the scriptural readings and Mass prayers assigned to each of them. During Advent, for example, the readings are messianic; during the Easter season, from the Acts of the Apostles, chronicling the Resurrection and the original proclamation of Christ by the Apostles, and from the Gospel of John; during Lent, baptismal and penitential passages. Mass prayers reflect the meaning and purpose of the various seasons.

Commemorations of Saints

The commemorations of saints are celebrated concurrently with the liturgical seasons and feasts of our Lord. Their purpose is to illustrate the paschal mysteries as reflected in the lives of saints, to honor them as heroes of holiness, and to appeal for their intercession.

In line with revised regulations, some former feasts

were either abolished or relegated to observance in particular places by local option for one of two reasons: (1) lack of sufficient historical evidence for observance of the feasts; (2) lack of universal significance.

The commemoration of a saint, as a general rule, is observed on the day of death (*dies natalis*, day of birth to glory with God in heaven). Exceptions to this rule include the feasts of St. John the Baptist, who is honored on the day of his birth; Sts. Basil the Great and Gregory Nazianzen, and the brother Saints, Cyril and Methodius, who are commemorated in joint feasts. Application of this general rule in the revised calendar resulted in date changes of some observances.

Sundays and Other Holy Days

Sunday is the original Christian feast day and holy day of obligation because of the unusually significant events of salvation history which took place and are commemorated on the first day of the week viz., the Resurrection of Christ, the key event of his life and the fundamental fact of Christianity; and the descent of the Holy Spirit upon the Apostles on Pentecost, the birthday of the Church. The transfer of observance of the Lord's Day from the Sabbath to Sunday was made in apostolic times. The Mass and Liturgy of the Hours (Divine Office) of each Sunday reflect the themes and set the tones of the various liturgical seasons.

Holy days of obligation are special occasions on which Catholics who have reached the age of reason are seriously obliged, as on Sundays, to assist at Mass: they are also to refrain from work and involvement with business which impede participation in divine worship and the enjoyment of appropriate rest and relaxation.

The holy days of obligation observed in the United States are: Christmas, the Nativity of Jesus, Dec. 25; Solemnity of Mary the Mother of God, Jan. 1; Ascension of the Lord; Assumption of Blessed Mary the Virgin, Aug. 15; All Saints' Day, Nov. 1; Immaculate Conception of Blessed Mary the Virgin, Dec. 8.

The precept to attend Mass is abrogated in the U.S. whenever the Solemnity of Mary, the Assumption, or All Saints falls on a Saturday or Monday (1991 decree of U.S. bishops; approved by Holy See July 4, 1992, and effective Jan. 1, 1993).

In addition to these, there are four other holy days of obligation prescribed in the general law of the Church which are not so observed in the U.S.: Epiphany, Jan. 6; St. Joseph, Mar. 19; Corpus Christi; Sts. Peter and Paul, June 29. The solemnities of Epiphany and Corpus Christi are transferred to a Sunday in countries where they are not observed as holy days of obligation.

Solemnities, Feasts, Memorials

Categories of observances according to dignity and manner of observance are: solemnities, principal days in the calendar (observance begins with Evening Prayer I of the preceding day; some have their own vigil Mass); feasts (celebrated within the limits of the natural day); obligatory memorials (celebrated throughout the Church); optional memorials (observable by choice).

Fixed observances are those which are regularly celebrated on the same calendar day each year.

TABLE OF MOVABLE FEASTS

Year	Ash Wed.	Easter	Ascension	Pentecost	Weeks of Ordinary Time				First Sunday of Advent
					Before Lent		After Pent.		
					Week	Ends	Week	Ends	
2000	Mar. 8	Apr. 23	June 1	June 11	9	Mar. 7	10	June 12	Dec. 3
2001	Feb. 28	Apr. 15	May 24	June 3	8	Feb. 27	9	June 4	Dec. 2
2002	Feb. 13	Mar. 31	May 9	May 19	5	Feb. 12	7	May 20	Dec. 1
2003	Mar. 5	Apr. 20	May 29	June 8	8	Mar. 4	10	June 9	Nov. 30
2004	Feb. 25	Apr. 11	May 20	May 30	7	Feb. 24	9	May 31	Nov. 28
2005	Feb. 9	Mar. 27	May 5	May 15	5	Feb. 8	7	May 16	Nov. 27
2006	Mar. 1	Apr. 16	May 25	June 4	8	Feb. 28	9	June 5	Dec. 3
2007	Feb. 21	Apr. 8	May 17	May 27	7	Feb. 20	8	May 28	Dec. 2
2008	Feb. 6	Mar. 23	May 1	May 11	4	Feb. 5	6	May 12	Nov. 30
2009	Feb. 25	Apr. 12	May 21	May 31	7	Feb. 24	9	June 1	Nov. 29
2010	Feb. 17	Apr. 4	May 13	May 23	6	Feb. 16	8	May 24	Nov. 28
2011	Mar. 9	Apr. 24	June 2	June 12	9	Mar. 8	11	June 13	Nov. 27
2012	Feb. 22	Apr. 8	May 17	May 27	7	Feb. 21	8	May 28	Dec. 2
2013	Feb. 13	Mar. 31	May 9	May 19	5	Feb. 12	7	May 20	Dec. 1
2014	Mar. 5	Apr. 20	May 29	June 8	8	Mar. 4	10	June 9	Nov. 30
2015	Feb. 18	Apr. 5	May 14	May 24	6	Feb. 17	8	May 25	Nov. 29
2016	Feb. 10	Mar. 27	May 5	May 15	5	Feb. 9	7	May 16	Nov. 27
2017	Mar. 1	Apr. 16	May 25	June 4	8	Feb. 28	9	June 5	Dec. 3
2018	Feb. 14	Apr. 1	May 10	May 20	6	Feb. 13	7	May 21	Dec. 2
2019	Mar. 6	Apr. 21	May 30	June 9	8	Mar. 5	10	June 1	Dec. 1
2020	Feb. 26	Apr. 12	May 21	May 31	7	Feb. 25	9	June 1	Nov. 29
2021	Feb. 17	Apr. 4	May 13	May 23	6	Feb. 16	8	May 24	Nov. 28

Movable observances are those which are not observed on the same calendar day each year. Examples of these are Easter (the first Sunday after the first full moon following the vernal equinox), Ascension (40 days after Easter), Pentecost (50 days after Easter), Trinity Sunday (first after Pentecost), Christ the King (last Sunday of the liturgical year).

Weekdays, Days of Prayer

Weekdays are those on which no proper feast or vigil is celebrated in the Mass or Liturgy of the Hours (Divine Office). On such days, the Mass may be that of the preceding Sunday, which expresses the liturgical spirit of the season, an optional memorial, a votive Mass, or a Mass for the dead. Weekdays of Advent and Lent are in a special category of their own.

Days of Prayer: Dioceses, at times to be designated by local bishops, should observe "days or periods of prayer for the fruits of the earth, prayer for human rights and equality, prayer for world justice and peace, and penitential observance outside of Lent." So stated the Instruction on Particular Calendars (No. 331) issued by the Congregation for the Sacraments and Divine Worship June 24, 1970.

These days are contemporary equivalents of what were formerly called ember and rogation days.

Ember days originated at Rome about the fifth century, probably as Christian replacements for seasonal festivals of agrarian cults. They were observances of penance, thanksgiving, and petition for divine blessing on the various seasons; they also were occasions of special prayer for clergy to be ordained. These days were observed four times a year.

Rogation days originated in France about the fifth century. They were penitential in character and also occasions of prayer for a bountiful harvest and protection against evil.

Days and Times of Penance

Fridays throughout the year and the season of Lent are penitential times.

• **Abstinence**: Catholics in the United States, from the age of 14 throughout life, are obliged to abstain from meat on Ash Wednesday, the Fridays of Lent and Good Friday. The law forbids the use of meat, but not of eggs, the products of milk or condiments made of animal fat. Permissible are soup flavored with meat, meat gravy and sauces. The obligation to abstain from meat is not in force on days celebrated as solemnities (e.g., Christmas, Sacred Heart).

• **Fasting**: Catholics in the United States, from the day after their 18th birthday to the day after their 59th birthday, are also obliged to fast on Ash Wednesday and Good Friday. The law allows only one full meal a day, but does not prohibit the taking of some food in the morning and evening, observing as far as quantity and quality are concerned approved local custom. The order of meals is optional; i.e., the full meal may be taken in the evening instead of at midday. Also: (1) The combined quantity of food taken at the two lighter meals should not exceed the quantity taken at the full meal. (2) The drinking of ordinary liquids does not break the fast.

• **Obligation**: There is a general obligation to do penance for sins committed and for the remission of punishment due because of sin. Substantial observance of fasting and abstinence, prescribed for the community of the Church, is a matter of serious obligation; it allows, however, for alternate ways of doing penance (e.g., works of charity, prayer and prayer-related practices, almsgiving).

Readings at Mass

Scriptural readings for Mass on Sundays and holy days are indicated under the appropriate dates in the calendar pages for the year 2000. The B cycle is prescribed for Sunday Masses in liturgical year 2000, beginning Dec. 3, 1999. The C cycle is prescribed for liturgical year 2001, beginning Dec. 2, 2000. Weekday cycles of readings are the second and first, respectively, for liturgical years 2000 and 2001.

Monthly Prayer Intentions

Intentions chosen and recommended by Pope John Paul II to the prayers of the faithful and circulated by the Apostleship of Prayer are given for each month of the calendar. He has expressed his desire that all Catholics make these intentions their own "in the certainty of being united with the Holy Father and praying according to his intentions and desires."

Celebrations in U.S. Particular Calendar

The General Norms for the Liturgical Year and the Calendar, issued in 1969 and published along with the General Roman Calendar for the Universal Church, noted that the calendar consists of the General Roman Calendar used by the entire Church and of particular calendars used in particular churches (nations or dioceses) or in families of religious.

The particular calendar for the U.S. contains the following celebrations. **January**: 4, Elizabeth Ann Seton; 5, John Neumann; 6, Bl. André Bessette. **March**: 3, Bl. Katharine Drexel. **May**: 15, Isidore the Farmer. **July**: 1, Bl. Junípero Serra; 4, Independence Day; 14, Bl. Kateri Tekakwitha. **August**: 18, Jane Frances de Chantal. **September**: 9, Peter Claver. **October**: 6, Bl. Marie-Rose Durocher; 19, Isaac Jogues and John de Brébeuf and Companions; 20, Paul of the Cross. **November**: 13, Frances Xavier Cabrini; 18, Rose Philippine Duchesne; 23, Bl. Miguel Agustín Pro; Fourth Thursday, Thanksgiving Day. **December**: 9, Bl. Juan Diego; 12, Our Lady of Guadalupe.

THE PILGRIMAGE IN THE GREAT JUBILEE

This is the title of a document issued Apr. 28, 1998, by the Pontifical Council for Migrants and Travelers. It said in part as follows:

"The fundamental goal of the present historical pilgrimage of the Church is the Jubilee of the Year 2000.... This itinerary should not be spatial but rather interior and vital, in the reconquest of the great values of the biblical Jubilee Year. With the sounding of the horn marking this date in Israel, slaves became free again, debts were condoned such that everyone would find again personal dignity and social solidarity, the earth spontaneously offered its gifts to everyone, reminding us that at its origin is the Creator.

"A 'pilgrimage of brotherhood' is the meaning of the jubilee of mercy that appears at the horizon of the third millennium, point of arrival for the creation of a human society that is more just, in which the public debts of developing nations will be condoned and a more equitable distribution of land will be accomplished in the spirit of the biblical prescription.

"Lived as a celebration of one's own faith, for the Christian a pilgrimage is a manifestation of worship to be accomplished faithfully according to tradition....

"Pilgrimages lead to the tent of meeting with the word of God, ... to the tent of meeting with the Church, ... to the tent of meeting with humankind, ... to moments of living together with people of different ages and formation, ... to the tent of personal meeting with God and with oneself, ... to the tent of meeting with Mary, Mother of the Lord."

2000 CALENDAR

JANUARY

Prayer Intentions: That believers in Christ may increasingly live in communion and reciprocal respect for one another (General). That the International Year for the Culture of Peace may be a source of authentic peace for all men and women (Mission).

1 Sat. Solemnity of Mary, Mother of God. Not observed this year in the U.S. as a holy day of obligation. (Nm 6: 22-27; Gal 4:4-7; Lk 2:16-21)

2 Sun. Epiphany of the Lord (U.S.); solemnity. (Is 60:1-6; Eph 3:2-3a, 5-6; Mt 2:1-12.).

3 Mon. Weekday.

4 Tues. St. Elizabeth Ann Seton, religious; memorial (in U.S.).

5 Wed. St. John Neumann, bishop; memorial (in U.S.).

6 Thurs. Weekday. Bl. André Bessette, religious; optional memorial.

7 Fri. Weekday. St. Raymond of Peñafort, priest; option memorial.

8 Sat. Weekday.

9 Sun. Baptism of the Lord, feast. (Is 42:1-4, 6-7 or Is 55: 1-11; Acts 10:34-38 or 1 Jn 5:19; Mk 1:7-11.).

10 Mon. Weekday. (First Week in Ordinary Time.).

11 Tues. Weekday.

12 Wed. Weekday

13 Thurs. Weekday. St. Hilary, bishop-doctor; optional memorial.

14 Fri. Weekday.

15 Sat. Weekday.

16 Second Sunday in Ordinary Time. (1 Sm 3:3b-10, 19; 1 Cor 6:13c-15a, 17-20; Jn 1:35-42.).

17 Mon. St. Anthony, abbot; memorial.

18 Tues. Weekday.

19 Wed. Weekday.

20 Thurs. Weekday. St. Fabian, pope-martyr, or St. Sebastian, martyr; optional memorials

21 Fri. St. Agnes, virgin-martyr; memorial.

22 Sat. Weekday. St. Vincent, deacon-martyr; optional memorial.

23 Third Sunday in Ordinary Time. (Jn 3:1-5, 10; 1 Cor 7:29-31; Mk 1: 14-20).

24 Mon. St. Francis de Sales, bishop-doctor; memorial.

25 Tues. Conversion of St. Paul, apostle; feast.

26 Wed. Sts. Timothy and Titus, bishops; memorial.

27 Thurs. Weekday. St. Angela Merici, virgin; optional memorial.

28 Fri. St. Thomas Aquinas, priest-doctor; memorial.

29 Sat. Weekday.

30 Fourth Sunday in Ordinary Time. (Dt 18:15-20; 1 Cor 7:32-35; Mk 1:21-28).

31 Mon. St. John Bosco, priest; memorial).

Holy Year Events in Rome: World Day of Peace, Jan. 1; Children's Day, Jan. 2; Ordinations of Bishops, Jan. 6; Celebration of the Sacrament of Baptism for Children, Jan. 9; Week of Prayer for Christian Unity beginning Jan. 18 with Opening of the Holy Door at the Basilica of St. Paul Outside-the-Walls and an Ecumenical Celebration; Divine Liturgy in the East Syrian rite (Chaldean and Malabarese), Jan. 28.

Other Events: National Prayer Vigil for Life, Jan. 21-22; March for Life in Washington, D.C., Jan. 22, Anniversary of Roe v. Wade, the pro-abortion decision of the U.S. Supreme Court; Catholic Schools Week, beginning Jan. 31.

FEBRUARY

Prayer Intentions: That Christian communities may welcome all consecrated vocations, however diverse they may be (General). That pilgrims visiting Rome, Jerusalem and other Christian sanctuaries may become messengers of the "Good News" of hope (Mission).

1 Tues. Weekday.

2 Wed. Presentation of the Lord; feast.

3 Thurs. Weekday. St. Blase, bishop-martyr or St. Ansgar, bishop; optional memorials.

4 Fri. Weekday.

5 Sat. St. Agatha, virgin-martyr; memorial.

6 Fifth Sunday in Ordinary Time. (Jb 7:1-4, 6-7; 1 Cor 9:16-19, 22-23; Mk 1:29-39.)

7 Mon. Weekday.

8 Tues. Weekday. St. Jerome Emiliani, priest; optional memorial.

9 Wed. Weekday.

10 Thurs. St. Scholastica, virgin; memorial.

11 Fri. Weekday. Our Lady of Lourdes; optional memorial.

12 Sat. Weekday.

13 Sixth Sunday in Ordinary Time. (Lv 13: 1-2, 44-46; 1 Cor 10:31 11:1; Mk 1:40-45.)

14 Mon. Sts. Cyril, monk, and Methodius, bishop; memorial.

15 Tues. Weekday.

16 Wed. Weekday.

17 Thurs. Seven Founders of the Order of Servites, religious; optional memorial.

18 Fri. Weekday.

19 Sat. Weekday.

20 Seventh Sunday in Ordinary Time. (Is 43:18-19, 21-22, 24b-25; 2 Cor 1:18-22; Mk 2:1-12.)

21 Mon. Weekday. St. Peter Damian, bishop-doctor; optional memorial.

22 Tues. Chair of Peter, apostle; feast.

23 Wed. St. Polycarp, bishop-martyr; memorial.

24 Thurs. Weekday.

25 Fri. Weekday.

26. Sat. Weekday.

27 Eighth Sunday in Ordinary Time. (Hos 2:16b, 17b, 21-22; 2 Cor 3:1b-6; Mk 2:18-22.)

28 Mon. Weekday.

29 Tues. Weekday.

Holy Year Events in Rome: Jubilee Celebrations of: Consecrated Life, Feb. 2; the Sick and Health Care Workers, with Celebration of the Sacrament of Anointing of the Sick, Feb. 11; Artists, Feb. 18; Permanent Deacons, Feb. 20; the Roman Curia, Feb. 22. Also, Celebration of the Divine Liturgy in the Syro-Antiochene rite (Maronite), Feb. 9, and a Study Convention on the Implementation of the Second Vatican Ecumenical Council, Feb. 25-27.

The blessing of candles for use during the year takes place on the feast of the Presentation. The blessing of throats takes place on the optional memorial of St. Blase.

Saints commemorated during the month include St. Scholastica, sister of St. Benedict and an important figure in contemplative life for women; Feb. 10; Cyril and Methodius, apostles to the Slavs, Feb. 14; and Polycarp, a disciple of the apostles, Feb. 23.

MARCH

Prayer Intentions: That the Holy Year, a favorable time for repentance and mercy, may foster in us deep and lasting conversion (General). That the Virgin Mary may protect and sustain missionaries in their apostolic work (Mission).

1 Wed. Weekday.
2 Thurs. Weekday.
3 Fri. Bl. Katharine Drexel, virgin; optional memorial.
4 Sat. Weekday.
5 **Ninth Sunday in Ordinary Time.** (Dt 5:12-15; 2 Cor 4:6-11; Mk 2: 23-3:6 or 2:23-28.)
6 Mon. Weekday.
7 Tues. Sts. Perpetua and Felicity, martyrs; memorial.
8 Ash Wednesday. Beginning of Lent. Fast and abstinence.(Jl 2:12-18; 2 Cor 5:20-6:2; Mt 6:1-6, 16-18.)
9 Thurs. Lenten Weekday. St. Frances of Rome, religious; optional memorial.
10 Fri. Lenten Weekday. Abstinence.
11 Sat. Lenten Weekday.
12 **First Sunday of Lent.** (Gn 9:8-15; 1Pt 3:18-22; Mk 1:12-15.)
13 Mon. Lenten Weekday.
14 Tues. Lenten Weekday.
15 Wed. Lenten Weekday.
16 Thurs. Lenten Weekday.
17 Fri. Lenten Weekday. St. Patrick, bishop; optional memorial. Abstinence.
18 Sat. Lenten Weekday. St. Cyril of Jerusalem, bishop-doctor; optional memorial.
19 **Second Sunday of Lent.** (Gn 22:1-2, 9a, 10-13, 15-18; Rom 8:31b 34; Mk 9:2-10.)
20 Mon. St. Joseph, husband of the Blessed Virgin Mary; solemnity.
21 Tues. Lenten Weekday.
22 Wed. Lenten Weekday.
23 Thurs. Lenten Weekday. St. Turibius de Mogrovejo, bishop; optional memorial.
24 Fri. Lenten Weekday. Abstinence.
25 Sat. Annunciation of the Lord; solemnity.
26 **Third Sunday of Lent.** (Ex 20:1-17 or 20:1-3, 7-8, 12-17; 1 Cor 1:22-25; Jn 2:13-25 or Ex 17:3-7; Rom 5:1-2, 5-8; Jn 4:5-42 or 4:5-15, 19b-26, 39a; 40-42.).
27 Mon. Lenten Weekday.
28 Tues. Lenten Weekday.
29 Wed. Lenten Weekday.
30 Thurs. Lenten Weekday.
31 Fri. Lenten Weekday. Abstinence.

Holy Year Events in Rome: In various churches, penitential and other celebrations (of the Eucharist, the Rosary, Way of the Cross), and the Rite of Election and Enrollment of Catechumens' Names, Mar. 12; the Jubilee of Craftsmen on the Solemnity of St. Joseph, Mar. 20; on the Solemnity of the Annunciation of the Lord, Mar. 25, a liturgical celebration of the link between the Basilica of St. Mary Major and other major Marian shrines of the world.

On Ash Wednesday, Mar. 8, ashes are blessed and imposed on the forehead of the faithful to remind them of their obligation to do penance for sin and to seek spiritual renewal by means of prayer, fasting, good works, and by bearing with patience and for God's purposes the trials and difficulties of everyday life.

APRIL

Prayer Intentions: That, through Christians' generous welcome, refugees and immigrants may experience the goodness of God the Father (General). That the peoples of Africa, torn by discord and wars, may find in the Gospel the strength to repress any urge to revenge and violence, and to open their hearts to mercy and reconciliation (Mission).

1 Sat. Lenten Weekday.
2 Fourth Sunday of Lent. (2 Chr 36:14-16, 19-23; Eph 2:4-10; Jn 3:14-21 or 1 Sm 16:1b, 6-7, 10-13a; Eph 5:8-14; Jn 9:1-41 or 9:1, 6-9, 13-17, 34-38.).
3 Mon. Lenten Weekday.
4 Tues. Lenten Weekday. St. Isidore of Seville, bishop-doctor; optional memorial.
5 Wed. Lenten Weekday. St. Vincent Ferrer, priest; optional memorial.
6 Thurs. Lenten Weekday.
7 Fri. Lenten Weekday. St. John Baptist de la Salle, priest; optional memorial. Abstinence.
8 Sat. Lenten Weekday.
9 Fifth Sunday of Lent. (Jer 31:31-34; Heb 5:7-9; Jn 12:20-33 or Ez 37:12-14; Rom 8:8-11; Jn 11:1-45 or 11:3-7, 17, 20-27, 33b-45.)
10 Mon. Lenten Weekday.
11 Tues. Lenten Weekday. St. Stanislaus, bishop-martyr; optional memorial.
12 Wed. Lenten Weekday.
13 Thurs. Lenten Weekday. St. Martin I, pope-martyr; optional memorial.
14 Fri. Lenten Weekday. Abstinence.
15 Sat. Lenten Weekday.
16 **Palm Sunday of the Lord's Passion.** (Mk 11:1-10 or Jn 12:12-16; Is 50:4-7; Phil 2:6-11; Mk 14:1 15:47 or 15:1-39.)
17 Monday of Holy Week.
18 Tuesday of Holy Week.
19 Wednesday of Holy Week.
20 Holy Thursday. Chrism Mass. The Easter Triduum begins with the evening Mass of the Lord's Supper.
21 Good Friday. Fast and abstinence.
22 Holy Saturday. Easter Vigil.
23 **Easter Sunday; solemnity.** (Acts 10:34a, 37-43; Col 3:1-4 or Cor 5:6b-8; Jn 20:1-9 or Mk 16:1-7 or (at an afternoon Mass) Lk 24:13-35.)
24 Easter Monday; solemnity.
25 Easter Tuesday; solemnity.
26 Easter Wednesday; solemnity.
27 Easter Thursday; solemnity.
28 Easter Friday; solemnity.
29 Easter Saturday; solemnity.
30 **Second Sunday of Easter.** (Acts 4:32-35; 1 Jn 5:1-6; Jn 20:19-31.)

Holy Year Events in Rome: Rite of Giving the Creed and the Lord's Prayer to Catechumens, Apr. 9; Celebration of the Sacrament of Penance with individual confession, Apr. 18; Holy Thursday Masses of Chrism and the Lord's Supper, Apr. 20; Good Friday Celebration of the Passion and Way of the Cross, Apr. 21; celebration of the Resurrection, Apr. 22-23 — Easter Vigil of the Holy Night: Service of Light; Liturgy of the Word; Baptismal Liturgy (with Rite of Christian Initiation of Adults); Eucharistic Liturgy, and Mass during the day with the Pope's Message to the City of Rome and the World; Mass for newly baptized adults, Apr. 30.

MAY

Prayer Intentions. That Mary, Mother of the Lord, may be the model of faithfulness and generosity in following Christ (General). That the Jubilee remembrance of the new martyrs may bring about a renewed missionary spring (Mission).

1 Mon. Easter Weekday. St. Joseph the Worker; optional memorial.
2 Tues. St. Athanasius, bishop-doctor; memorial.
3 Wed. Sts. Philip and James, apostles; feast.
4 Thurs. Easter Weekday.
5 Fri. Easter Weekday.
6 Sat. Easter Weekday.
7 **Third Sunday of Easter.** (Acts 3:13-15, 17-19; 1 Jn 2:1-5a. Lk 24:35-48.)
8 Mon. Easter Weekday.
9 Tues. Easter Weekday.
10 Wed. Easter Weekday.
11 Thurs. Easter Weekday.
12 Fri. Easter Weekday. Sts. Nereus and Achilleus or St. Pancras, martyrs; optional memorials.
13 Sat. Easter Weekday.
14 **Fourth Sunday of Easter.** (Acts 4:8-12; 1 Jn 3:1-2; Jn 10:11-18.)
15 Mon. Easter Weekday. St. Isidore the Farmer; optional memorial.
16 Tues. Easter Weekday.
17 Wed. Easter Weekday.
18 Thurs. Easter Weekday. St. John I, pope-martyr; optional memorial.
19 Fri. Easter Weekday.
20 Sat. Easter Weekday. St. Bernardine of Siena, priest; optional memorial.
21 **Fifth Sunday of Easter.** (Acts 9:26-31; 1 Jn 3:18-24; Jn 15:1-8.).
22 Mon. Easter Weekday.
23 Tues. Easter Weekday.
24 Wed. Easter Weekday.
25 Thurs. Easter Weekday. St. Bede the Venerable, priest-doctor; St. Gregory VII, pope; St. Mary Magdalene de Pazzi, virgin; optional memorials.
26 Fri. St. Philip Neri, priest; memorial.
27 Sat. Easter Weekday. St. Augustine of Canterbury; optional memorial.
28 **Sixth Sunday or Easter.** (Acts 10:25-26, 34-35, 44-48; 1 Jn 4:7-10; Jn 15:9-17.)
29 Mon. Easter Weekday.
30 Tues. Easter Weekday.
31 Wed. Visitation of the Blessed Virgin Mary; feast.

Holy Year Events in Rome: Jubilee Celebrations of: Workers, on the Memorial of St. Joseph, the Worker, May 1; Clergy, on the Pope's 80th Birthday, May 18; Scientists, May 25; the Diocese of Rome, May 28. Also: an Ecumenical Service for the "New Martyrs," May 7; Priestly Ordinations on the World Day of Prayer for Vocations, May 14; the Divine Liturgy in the Alexandrian-Ethiopian Rite, May 26.

Traditionally, the month of May has been observed as a time of special devotion to the Blessed Mother, with daily praying of the Rosary, which links the mysteries of her life with those of Christ her Son. One of her feasts, observed May 31, commemorates the visitation to Elizabeth. The scriptural background of the mysteries of the Rosary are a rich source of meditation and inspiration.

JUNE

Prayer Intentions: That Christ, adored and celebrated in the Eucharist, may increasingly be welcomed and shared as Bread of Life for the good of the world (General). That in China priests, men and women religious, and lay persons may be animated by an apostolic and Catholic spirit (Mission).

1 **Thurs. Ascension of the Lord; solemnity. Holy day of obligation.** (Acts 1:1-11; Eph 1:17-23 or Eph 4:1-13 or 4:1-7, 11-13; Mk 16:15-20.) In eight Western states and Hawaii, celebration of the solemnity is transferred to June 4.
2 Fri. Easter Weekday. Sts. Marcellinus and Peter, martyrs; optional memorial.
3 Sat. Sts. Charles Lwanga and Companions, martyrs; memorial.
4 **Seventh Sunday of Easter.** (Acts 1:15-17, 20a, 20c-26; 1 Jn 4:11-16; Jn 17:1b-19.)
5 Mon. St. Boniface, bishop-martyr; memorial.
6 Tues. Easter Weekday. St. Norbert, bishop; optional memorial.
7 Wed. Easter Weekday.
8 Thurs. Easter Weekday.
9 Fri. Easter Weekday. St. Ephraem, deacon-doctor; optional memorial.
10 Sat. Easter Weekday.
11 **Pentecost Sunday; solemnity.**(Acts 2:1-11; 1 Cor 12:3b-7, 12-13 or Gal 5:16-15; Jn 20:19-23 or Jn 15:26-27; 16:12-15.)
12 Mon. Weekday. (Tenth Week in Ordinary Time.)
13 Tues. St. Anthony of Padua, priest-doctor; memorial.
14 Wed. Weekday.
15 Thurs. Weekday.
16 Fri. Weekday
17 Sat. Weekday.
18 **Sunday. The Holy Trinity; solemnity.** (Dt 4:32-34, 39-40; Rom 8:14-17; Mt 28:16-20.)
19 Mon. Weekday. St. Romuald, abbot; optional memorial.
20 Tues. Weekday.
21 Wed. St. Aloysius Gonzaga, religious; memorial.
22 Thurs. Weekday. St. Paulinus of Nola, bishop, or St. John Fisher, bishop-martyr, and St. Thomas More, martyr; optional memorials.
23 Fri. Weekday.
24 Sat. Birth of John the Baptist; solemnity.
25 **Sun. Most Holy Body and Blood of Christ; solemnity.** (Ex 24:32-34, 39-40; Rom 8:14-17; Mt. 28:16-20.).
26 Mon. Weekday. (Twelfth Sunday in Ordinary Time.)
27 Tues. Weekday. St. Cyril of Alexandria, bishop-doctor; optional memorial.
28 Wed. St. Irenaeus, bishop-martyr; memorial.
29 Thurs. Sts. Peter and Paul, apostles; solemnity.
30 Fri. Most Sacred Heart of Jesus; solemnity.

Holy Year Events in Rome: World Day of Social Communications, with the Jubilee of Journalists, June 4; Day of Prayer for Collaboration among the Different Religions, on the Solemnity of Pentecost, June 11; Celebration of the International Eucharistic Congress, June 18-25.

Significant Feasts: Ascension of the Lord, Pentecost Sunday, the Holy Trinity, the Most Holy Body and Blood of Christ, and the most Sacred Heart of Jesus. The Solemnity of Sts. Peter and Paul is a major feast of the Church of Rome.

JULY

Prayer Intentions: That followers of the various religions may grow in respecting one another and collaborating to consolidate justice and peace in the world (General). That all those tried by sickness and loneliness may offer their suffering with Christ for the conversion of the world (Mission).

1 Sat. Immaculate Heart of Mary; memorial. [Bl.Junípero Serra; optional memorial in U.S.]
2 **Thirteenth Sunday in Ordinary Time.** (Wis. 1:1-15, 2:23-24; 2 Cor 8:7, 9, 13-15; Mk 5:21-43 or 5:21-24.)
3 Mon. St. Thomas, apostle; feast.
4 Tues. Weekday. Independence Day; proper Mass in U.S. St. Elizabeth of Portugal, religious; optional memorial.
5 .Wed. Weekday. St. Anthony Mary Zaccaria, priest; optional memorial.
6 Thurs. Weekday. St. Maria Goretti, virgin-martyr; optional, memorial.
7 Fri. Weekday.
8 Sat. Weekday.
9 **Fourteenth Sunday in Ordinary Time.** (Ez 2:2-5; 2 Cor 12:7-10; Mk 9:18-26.)
10 Mon. Weekday.
11 Tues. St. Benedict, abbot; memorial.
12 Wed. Weekday.
13 Thurs. Weekday. St. Henry; optional memorial.
14 Fri. Bl. Kateri Tekakwitha, virgin; memorial.
15 Sat. St. Bonaventure, bishop-doctor; memorial.
16 **Fifteenth Sunday in Ordinary Time.** (Am 7:5-12; Eph. 1:3-14; Mk 6:7-13.)
17 Mon. Weekday.
18 Tues. Weekday.
19 Wed. Weekday.
20 Thurs. Weekday.
21 Fri. Weekday. St. Lawrence of Brindisi, priest-doctor; optional memorial.
22 Sat. Mary Magdalene; memorial.
23 **Sixteenth Sunday in Ordinary Time.** (Jer 23:1-6; Eph 2:13-18; Mk 6:30-34.)
24 Mon. Weekday.
25 Tues. St. James, apostle; feast.
26 Wed. Sts. Joachim and Anne, parents of the Blessed Virgin Mary; memorial.
27 Thurs. Weekday.
28 Fri. Weekday.
29 Sat. St. Martha; memorial.
30 **Seventeenth Sunday in Ordinary Time.** (2 Kgs 4:42-44; Eph 4:1-6; Jn 6:1-15.)
31 Mon. St. Ignatius of Loyola, priest; memorial.

Holy Year Events in Rome: Station Masses of the Jubilee on all Sundays of the month; Jubilee Celebration in Prisons, July 9.

Significant Feasts: Blessed Junípero Serra, whose optional memorial may be observed July 1, founder of California missions; St. Thomas, apostle, pioneer evangelist of India, July 3; St. Benedict, founder of monasticism in Western Europe, patron saint of Europe, July 11; St. Bonaventure, called the second founder of the Franciscan Order, July 15; St. Ignatius of Loyola, founder of the Society of Jesus (Jesuits), July 31.

Holy Year pilgrims are expected to strain tourist facilities in and around Rome. Hopefully advance planning will be adequate for what might possibly be the greatest influx of visitors to the Eternal City in history.

AUGUST

Prayer Intentions: That all young Christians may unite in testifying that Jesus Christ is the eternal Son of God come to dwell among us (General). That the Churches of Oceania may work with true missionary spirit for the propagation of the kingdom of God (Mission).

1 Tues. St. Alphonsus Liguori, bishop-doctor; memorial.
2 Wed. Weekday. St. Eusebius of Vercelli, bishop, and St. Peter Julian Eymard, priest; optional memorials.
3 Thurs. Weekday.
4 Fri. St. John Maria Vianney, priest; memorial.
5 Sat. Weekday. Dedication of the Basilica of St. Mary in Rome; optional memorial.
6 **Sun. Transfiguration of the Lord; feast.** (Dn 7:9-10, 13-14; 2 Pt 1:16-19; Mk 9:2-10.)
7 Mon. Weekday. Sts. Sixtus II, pope-martyr, and Companions, martyrs; optional memorial. (Eighteenth Week in Ordinary Time.)
8 Tues. St. Dominic, priest; memorial.
9 Wed. Weekday.
10 Thurs. St. Lawrence, deacon-martyr; memorial.
11 Fri. St. Clare, virgin; memorial..
12 Sat. Weekday,
13 **Nineteenth Sunday in Ordinary Time.** (1Kgs 19:4-8; Eph 4:30   5:2; Jn 6:41-51.)
14 Mon. St. Maximilian Kolbe, priest-martyr; memorial.
15 Tues. Assumption of the Blessed Virgin Mary; solemnity. Holy day of obligation. (Rv 11:19a; 12:1-6a, 10ab; 1 Cor 15:20-27; Lk 1:39-56.)
16 Wed. Weekday. St. Stephen of Hungary; optional memorial.
17 Thurs. Weekday.
18 Fri. Weekday. St. Jane Frances de Chantal, religious; optional memorial.
19 Sat. Weekday. St.John Eudes, priest; optional memorial.
20 **Twentieth Sunday in Ordinary Time.** (Prv 9:1-6; Eph 5:15-20; Jn 6:51-58.)
21 Mon. St. Pius X, pope; memorial.
22 Tues. Queenship of the Blessed Virgin Mary; memorial.
23 Wed. Weekday. St. Rose of Lima, virgin; optional memorial.
24 Thurs. St. Bartholomew, apostle; feast.
25 Fri. Weekday. St. Louis or St. Joseph Calasanz, priest; optional memorials.
26 Sat. Weekday.
27 **Twenty-First Sunday in Ordinary Time.** (Jos 24:1-2a, 15-17, 18b; Eph 5:21-32 or 5:2a, 25-32; Jn 6:60-69.)
28 Mon. St. Augustine, bishop-doctor; memorial.
29 Tues. Beheading of John the Baptist, martyr; memorial.
30 Wed. Weekday.
31 Thurs. Weekday.

Holy Year Events in Rome: Prayer Vigil of the Feast of the Transfiguration, Aug. 5; Incense Rite of the Coptic Liturgy, Aug. 14; Fifteenth World Youth Day, Aug. 15-20.

Significant Feasts: Solemnity of the Assumption of the Blessed Virgin Mary, Aug. 15; St. Bernard of Clairvaux, Aug. 20; Queenship of Mary, Aug. 22; St. Monica, mother of St. Augustine, Aug. 27; St. Augustine, Father and Doctor of the Church, Aug.28.

SEPTEMBER

Prayer Intentions: That scientists and academics may find in the search for truth the way to God, the heavenly Father (General). That Muslim-Christian relationships may be marked by mutual understanding and respect (Mission).

1 Fri. Weekday.
2 Sat. Weekday.
3 **Twenty-Second Sunday in Ordinary Time.** (Dt 4:1-2, 6-8; Jas. 1:17-18, 21b-22, 27; Mk 7:1-8, 14-15, 21-23.
4 Mon. Weekday. In U.S., Labor Day proper Mass, For the Blessing of Human Labor.
5 Tues. Weekday.
6 Wed. Weekday.
7 Thurs. Weekday.
8 Fri. Birth of the Blessed Virgin Mary; feast.
9 Sat. St. Peter Claver, priest; memorial.
10 **Twenty-Third Sunday in Ordinary Time.** (Is 35: 4-7a; Jas 2:1-5; Mk 7:31-37.)
11 Mon. Weekday.
12 Tues. Weekday.
13 Wed. St. John Chrysostom, bishop-doctor; memorial.
14 Thurs. Exaltation of the Holy Cross. Feast.
15 Fri. Our Lady of Sorrows; memorial.
16 Sat. Sts. Cornelius, pope-martyr, and St. Cyprian, bishop-martyr; memorial.
17 **Twenty-Fourth Sunday in Ordinary Time.** (Is 50:5-9a; Jas 2:14-18; Mk 8:27-35.)
18 Mon. Weekday.
19 Tues. Weekday. St. Januarius, bishop-martyr; optional memorial.
20 Wed. St. Andrew Kim, priest-martyr, and Sts. Paul Chong Hasang and their Companions, martyrs; memorial.
21 Thurs. St. Matthew, apostle; feast.
22 Fri. Weekday.
23 Sat. Weekday.
24 **Twenty-Fifth Sunday in Ordinary Time.** (Wis 2:12, 17-20; Jas 3:16-4:3; Mk 9:30-37.)
25 Mon. Weekday.
26 Tues. Sts. Cosmas and Damian, martyrs; optional memorial.
27 Wed. St.Vincent de Paul, priest; memorial.
28 Thurs. Weekday. St. Wenceslaus, martyr, or St. Lawrence Ruiz and Companions, martyrs; optional memorials.
29 Fri. Michael, Gabriel and Raphael, archangels; feast.
30 Sat. St. Jerome, priest-doctor; memorial.

Holy Year Events in Rome: Prayer Vigil of the Feast of the Transfiguration, Aug. 5; Incense Rite of the Coptic Liturgy, Aug. 14; Fifteenth World Youth Day, Aug. 15-20.

Significant Feasts: Solemnity of the Assumption of the Blessed Virgin Mary, Aug. 15; St. Bernard of Clairvaux, leader of monasticism, Aug. 20; Queenship of Mary, Aug. 22; St. Monica, mother of St. Augustine, Aug. 27; St. Augustine, profoundly influential Father and Doctor of the Church, Aug.28.

OCTOBER

Prayer Intentions: That young married couples may be sustained by the example of their parents and other families (General). That cooperation among local churches may multiply missionary initiatives (Mission).

1 **Twenty-Sixth Sunday in Ordinary Time.** (Nm 11:25-29; Jas 5:1-6; Mk 9:38-43, 45, 47-48.)
2 Mon. Guardian Angels; memorial.
3 Tues. Weekday.
4 Wed. St. Francis of Assisi, religious; memorial.
5 Thurs. Weekday.
6 Fri. Weekday. St. Bruno, priest, or Bl. Marie-Rose Durocher, virgin; optional memorials.
7 Sat. Our Lady of the Rosary; feast.
8 **Twenty-Seventh Sunday in Ordinary Time.** (Gn 2:18-24; Heb 2:9-11; Mk 10:2-16 or 10:2-12.)
9 Mon. Weekday. St, Denis, bishop-martyr, and his Companions, martyrs, or St. John Leonard, priest; optional memorials.
10 Tues. Weekday.
11 Wed. Weekday.
12 Thurs. Weekday.
13 Fri. Weekday.
14 Sat. Weekday. St. Callistus I, pope-martyr; optional memorial.
15 **Twenty-Eighth Sunday in Ordinary Time.** (Wis 7:7-11; Heb 4:12-13; Mk 10:17-30 or 10:17-27.)
16 Mon. Weekday, St. Hedwig, religious, or St. Margaret Mary Alacoque, virgin; optional memorials.
17 Tues. St. Ignatius of Antioch, bishop-martyr; memorial.
18 Wed. St. Luke, evangelist; feast.
19 Thurs. Sts. Isaac Jogues and John de Brebeuf, priests-martyrs, and Companions, martyrs; memorial.
20 Fri. Weekday. St. Paul of the Cross, priest; optional memorial.
21 Sat. Weekday.
22 **Twenty Ninth Sunday in Ordinary Time.** (Is 53:10-11; Heb. 4:14-16; Mk 10:35-45 or 10:42-45.)
23 Mon. Weekday. St. John of Capistrano, priest; optional memorial.
24 Tues. Weekday. St. Anthony Mary Claret, bishop; optional memorial.
25 Wed. Weekday.
26 Thurs. Weekday.
27 Fri. Weekday.
28 Sat. Sts. Simon and Jude, apostles; feast.
29 **Thirtieth Sunday in Ordinary Time.** (Jer 31:7-9; Heb 5:1-6; Mk 10:46-52.)
30 Mon. Weekday.
31 Tues. Weekday.

Holy Year Events in Rome: Celebration of the Birth of Mary, Sept. 8; Jubilees of University Teachers (Sept. 10) and Senior Citizens (Sept. 17); Feast of the Exaltation of the Holy Cross, with Celebrations in the Basilica of the Holy Cross in Jerusalem and the Basilica of St. John Lateran in Rome, Sept. 14; Vespers in the Armenian Rite and the Rite of Antasdan, Sept. 14; International Marian-Mariological Congress, Sept. 15-24.

Significant Feasts: The archangels, Michael, Gabriel and Rafael, Sept. 29; and St. Jerome, Sept. 30.

NOVEMBER

Prayer Intentions: That politicians and economists may attend to the welfare of all people, especially the most poverty-stricken (General). That reflection on the missionary role of religious institutes may foster vocations to the consecrated life (Mission).

1 **Wed. All Saints; solemnity. Holy day of obligation.**
2 Thurs. Commemoration of All the Faithful Departed (All Souls Day).
3 Fri. Weekday. St. Martin de Porres, religious; optional memorial.
4 Sat. St. Charles Borromeo, bishop; memorial.
5 **Thirty-First Sunday in Ordinary Time.** (Dt 6:2-6; Heb 7:23-28; Mk 12:28b-34.)
6 Mon. Weekday.
7 Tues. Weekday.
8 Wed. Weekday.
9 Thurs. Dedication of the Lateran Basilica in Rome; feast.
10 Fri. St. Leo the Great, pope; memorial.
11 Sat. St. Martin of Tours, bishop; memorial.
12 **Thirty-Second Sunday in Ordinary Time.** (1 Kgs 17:10-16; Heb 9:24-28; Mk 12:38-44 or 12:41-44.)
13 Mon. St. Frances Xavier Cabrini, virgin; memorial.
14 Tues. Weekday.
15 Wed. Weekday. St. Albert the Great, bishop-doctor; optional memorial.
16 Thurs. Weekday. St. Margaret of Scotland or St. Gertrude the Great, virgin; optional memorials.
17 Fri. St. Elizabeth of Hungary, religious; memorial.
18 Sat. Weekday. Dedication of the Basilicas of the Apostles Peter and Paul in Rome, or St. Rose Philippine Duchesne, religious; optional memorials.
19 **Thirty-Third Sunday in Ordinary Time.** (Dan 12:1-3;Heb 10:11-14, 18; Mk 13:24-32.)
20 Mon. Weekday.
21 Tues. Presentation of the Blessed Virgin Mary; memorial.
22 Wed. St. Cecilia, virgin-martyr; memorial.
23 Thurs. Thanksgiving Day in U.S.; proper Mass. [Bl. Miguel Agustin Pro, priest-martyr, optional memorial in U.S.; St. Clement I, pope-martyr, or St. Columban, abbot; optional memorials.]
24 Fri. St. Andrew Dung-Lac, priest-martyr, and Companions, martyrs; memorial.
25 Sat. Weekday.
26 **Sun. Christ the King; solemnity.** (Dan 7:13-14; Rv 1:5-8; Jn 18:33b-37.)
27 Mon. Weekday. (Thirty-Fourth Week in Ordinary Time.)
28 Tues. Weekday.
29 Wed. Weekday.
30 Thurs. St. Andrew, apostle; feast.

Holy Year Events in Rome: Celebration in the Ambrosian Rite, Nov. 4; Jubilee of Persons in Public Life, Nov. 5; Day of Thanksgiving for the Gifts of Creation, Nov. 12; Jubilees of the Agricultural World (Nov. 12) and of the Military and Police (Nov. 19); Divine Liturgy in the Syro-Antiochene Rite (Syrian and Malankarese), Nov. 21; World Congress for the Apostolate of the Laity, Nov. 24-26.

Significant Feasts: All Saints and All Souls, Nov. 1 and 2, respectively.

DECEMBER

Prayer Intentions: That celebration of the Jubilee may lead men and women of good will to protect and promote human life (General). That children may be respected in their dignity, and that all child abuse may stop (Mission).

1 Fri. Weekday.
2 Sat. Weekday.
3 **First Sunday of Advent.** (Jer 33:14-16. 1Thes 3:12   42; Lk 21:25-28,34-36.).
4 Mon. Advent Weekday. St. John of Damascus, priest-doctor; optional memorial.
5 Tues. Advent Weekday.
6 Wed. Advent Weekday. St. Nicholas, bishop; optional memorial.
7 Thurs. St. Ambrose, bishop-doctor; memorial.
8 **Fri. Immaculate Conception of the Blessed Virgin Mary; solemnity. Holy day of obligation.** (Gn 3:9-15, 20; Eph 1:3-6, 11-12; Lk 1:26-38.).
9 Sat Advent Weekday. Bl.. Juan Diego; optional memorial.
10 **Second Sunday of Advent.** (Bar 5:1-9; Phil 1:4-6, 8-11; Lk 3:1-6.)
11 Mon. Advent Weekday. St. Damasus I, pope; optional memorial.
12 Tues. Our Lady of Guadalupe; feast.
13 Wed. St. Lucy, virgin-martyr; memorial.
14 Thurs. St. John of the Cross, priest-doctor; memorial.
15 Fri. Advent Weekday.
16 Sat. Advent Weekday.
17 **Third Sunday of Advent.** (Zep 3:14-18a; Phil 4:4-7; Lk 3:10-18.)
18 Mon. Advent Weekday.
19 Tues. Advent Weekday.
20 Wed. Advent Weekday.
21 Thurs. Advent Weekday. St. Peter Canisius, priest-doctor; optional memorial.
22 Fri. Advent Weekday.
23 Sat. Advent Weekday. St. John of Kanty, priest; optional memorial.
24 **Fourth Sunday of Advent.** (Mi 5:1a; Heb 10:5-10; Lk 1:39-45.)
25 **Mon. Christmas. Birth of the Lord; solemnity. Holy day of obligation.** (Vigil Is 62:1-5; Acts 13:16-17, 22-25; Mt 1:1-25 or 1:18-25. Midnight Is 9:1-6; Ti 2:11-14; Lk 2:1-14. At Dawn Is 62:11-12; Ti 3:4-7; Lk 2:15-20. During the Day Is 52:7-10; Heb 1:1-6; Jn 1:1-18 or 1:1-5, 9-14.)
26 Tues. St. Stephen, first martyr; memorial.
27 Wed. St. John, apostle-evangelist; memorial.
28 Thurs. Holy Innocents; feast.
29 Fri. Fifth Day in the Octave of Christmas. St. Thomas Becket, bishop-martyr; optional memorial.
30 Sat. Sixth Day in the Octave of Christmas.
31 **Sun. The Holy Family; feast.** (Sir 3:2-6, 12-14 or 1 Sam 1:20-22, 24-28; Col 3:12-21 or Col 3:12-17 or 1 Jn 3:1-2, 21-24; Lk 2:41-52.)

Holy Year Events in Rome: Celebration in the Mozarabic Rite, Dec. 16; Jubilee of Entertainment World, Dec. 17; Christmas Masses and Papal Message, Dec. 24-25; Prayer Vigil for Passage to the New Millennium, Dec. 31.

January 2001: Closing of the Holy Doors in the Holy Land, local Roman Churches, St. Peter's Basilica and Closing of the Jubilee, Jan. 5-6.

HOLY DAYS AND OTHER OBSERVANCES

The following list includes the six holy days of obligation observed in the United States and additional observances of devotional and historical significance. The dignity or rank of observances is indicated by the terms: **solemnity** (highest in rank); **feast; memorial** (for universal observance); **optional memorial** (for celebration by choice).

All Saints, Nov. 1, holy day of obligation, solemnity. Commemorates all the blessed in heaven, and is intended particularly to honor the blessed who have no special feasts. The background of the feast dates to the fourth century when groups of martyrs, and later other saints, were honored on a common day in various places. In 609 or 610, the Pantheon, a pagan temple at Rome, was consecrated as a Christian church for the honor of Our Lady and the martyrs (later all saints). In 835, Gregory IV fixed Nov. 1 as the date of observance.

All Souls, Commemoration of the Faithful Departed, Nov. 2. The dead were prayed for from the earliest days of Christianity. By the sixth century it was customary in Benedictine monasteries to hold a commemoration of deceased members of the order at Pentecost. A common commemoration of all the faithful departed on the day after All Saints was instituted in 998 by St. Odilo, of the Abbey of Cluny, and an observance of this kind was accepted in Rome in the 14th century.

Annunciation of the Lord (formerly, Annunciation of the Blessed Virgin Mary), Mar. 25, solemnity. A feast of the Incarnation which commemorates the announcement by the Archangel Gabriel to the Virgin Mary that she was to become the Mother of Christ (Lk. 1:26-38), and the miraculous conception of Christ by her. The feast was instituted about 430 in the East. The Roman observance dates from the seventh century, when celebration was said to be universal.

Ascension of the Lord, movable observance held 40 days after Easter, holy day of obligation, solemnity. Commemorates the Ascension of Christ into heaven 40 days after his Resurrection from the dead (Mk. 16:19; Lk. 24:51; Acts 1:2). The feast recalls the completion of Christ's mission on earth for the salvation of all people and his entry into heaven with glorified human nature. The Ascension is a pledge of the final glorification of all who achieve salvation. Documentary evidence of the feast dates from early in the fifth century, but it was observed long before that time in connection with Pentecost and Easter.

Ash Wednesday, movable observance, six and one-half weeks before Easter. It was set as the first day of Lent by Pope St. Gregory the Great (590-604) with the extension of an earlier and shorter penitential season to a total period including 40 weekdays of fasting before Easter. It is a day of fast and abstinence. Ashes, symbolic of penance, are blessed and distributed among the faithful during the day. They are used to mark the forehead with the Sign of the Cross, with the reminder: "Remember you are dust, and to dust you will return," or: "Turn away from sin and be faithful to the Gospel."

Assumption, Aug. 15, holy day of obligation, solemnity. Commemorates the taking into heaven of Mary, soul and body, at the end of her life on earth, a truth of faith that was proclaimed a dogma by Pius XII on Nov. 1, 1950. One of the oldest and most solemn feasts of Mary, it has a history dating back to at least the seventh century when its celebration was already established at Jerusalem and Rome.

Baptism of the Lord, movable, usually celebrated on the Sunday after January 6, feast. Recalls the baptism of Christ by John the Baptist (Mk. 1:9-11), an event associated with the liturgy of the Epiphany. This baptism was the occasion for Christ's manifestation of himself at the beginning of his public life.

Birth of Mary, Sept. 8, feast. This is a very old feast which originated in the East and found place in the Roman liturgy in the seventh century.

Candlemas Day, Feb. 2. See Presentation of the Lord.

Chair of Peter, Feb. 22, feast. The feast, which has been in the Roman calendar since 336, is a liturgical expression of belief in the episcopacy and hierarchy of the Church.

Christmas, Birth of Our Lord Jesus Christ, Dec. 25, holy day of obligation, solemnity. Commemorates the birth of Christ (Lk. 2:1-20). This event was originally commemorated in the East on the feast of Epiphany or Theophany. The Christmas feast itself originated in the West; by 354 it was certainly kept on Dec. 25. This date may have been set for the observance to offset pagan ceremonies held at about the same time to commemorate the birth of the sun at the winter solstice. There are texts for three Christmas Masses at midnight, dawn, and during the day.

Christ the King, movable, celebrated on the last Sunday of the liturgical year, solemnity. Commemorates the royal prerogatives of Christ and is equivalent to a declaration of his rights to the homage, service and fidelity of all people in all phases of individual and social life. Pius XI instituted the feast Dec. 11, 1925.

Conversion of St. Paul, Jan. 25, feast. An observance mentioned in some calendars from the 8th and 9th centuries. Pope Innocent III (1198-1216) ordered its observance with great solemnity.

Corpus Christi (The Body and Blood of Christ), movable, celebrated on the Thursday (or Sunday, as in the U.S.) following Trinity Sunday, solemnity. Commemorates the institution of the Holy Eucharist (Mt. 26:26-28). The feast originated at Liège in 1246 and was extended throughout the Church in the West by Urban IV in 1264. St. Thomas Aquinas composed the Liturgy of the Hours for the feast.

Cross, The Holy, Sept. 14, feast. Commemorates the finding of the Cross on which Christ was crucified, in 326 through the efforts of St. Helena, mother of Constantine; the consecration of the Basilica of the Holy Sepulchre nearly 10 years later: and the recovery in 628 or 629 by Emperor Heraclius of a major portion of the cross which had been removed by the Persians from its place of veneration at Jerusalem. The feast originated in Jerusalem and spread through the East before being adopted in the West. General adoption followed the building at Rome of the Basilica of the Holy Cross "in Jerusalem," so called because it was the place of enshrinement of a major portion of the cross of crucifixion.

Dedication of St. John Lateran, Nov. 9, feast. Commemorates the first public consecration of a church, that of the Basilica of the Most Holy Savior by Pope St. Sylvester about 324. The church, as well as the Lateran Palace, was the gift of Emperor Constantine. Since the 12th century it has been known as St. John Lateran, in honor of John the Baptist after whom the adjoining baptistery was named. It was rebuilt by Innocent X (1644-55), reconsecrated by Benedict XIII in 1726, and enlarged by Leo XIII (1878-1903). This basilica is regarded as the church of highest dignity in Rome and throughout the Roman rite.

Dedication of St. Mary Major, Aug. 5, optional memorial. Commemorates the rebuilding and dedication by Pope Sixtus III (432-40) of a church in honor of Blessed Mary the Virgin. This is the Basilica of St. Mary Major on the Esquiline Hill in Rome. An earlier building was erected during the pontificate of Liberius (352-66); according to legend, it was located on a site covered by a miraculous fall of snow seen by a nobleman favored with a vision of Mary.

Easter, movable celebration held on the first Sunday after the full moon following the vernal equinox (between Mar. 22 and Apr. 25), solemnity with an octave. Commemorates the Resurrection of Christ from the dead (Mk. 16:1-7). The observance of this mystery, kept since the first days of the Church, extends throughout the Easter season which lasts until the feast of Pentecost, a period of 50 days. Every Sunday in the year is regarded as a "little" Easter. The date of Easter determines the dates of movable feasts, such as Ascension and Pentecost, and the number of weeks before Lent and after Pentecost.

Easter Vigil, called by St. Augustine the "Mother of All Vigils," the night before Easter. Ceremonies are all related to the Resurrection and renewal-in-grace theme of Easter: blessing of the new fire, procession with the Easter Candle, singing of the Easter Proclamation (*Exsultet*), Liturgy of the Word with at least three Old Testament readings, the Litany of Saints, blessing of water, baptism of converts and infants, renewal of baptismal promises, Liturgy of the Eucharist. The vigil ceremonies are held after nightfall on Saturday.

Epiphany of the Lord, Jan. 6 or (in the U.S.) a Sunday between Jan. 2 and 8, solemnity. Commemorates the manifestations of the divinity of Christ. It is one of the oldest Christian feasts, with an Eastern origin traceable to the beginning of the third century and antedating the Western feast of Christmas. Originally, it commemorated the manifestations of Christ's divinity — or Theophany — in his birth, the homage of the Magi, and baptism by John the Baptist. Later, the first two of these commemorations were transferred to Christmas when the Eastern Church adopted that feast between 380 and 430. The central feature of the Eastern observance now is the manifestation or declaration of Christ's divinity in his baptism and at the beginning of his public life. The Epiphany was adopted by the Western Church during the same period in which the Eastern Church accepted Christmas. In the Roman rite, commemoration is made in the Mass of the homage of the wise men from the East (Mt. 2:1-12).

Good Friday, the Friday before Easter, the second day of the Easter Triduum. Liturgical elements of the observance are commemoration of the Passion and Death of Christ in the reading of the Passion (accord-

ing to John), special prayers for the Church and people of all ranks, the veneration of the Cross, and a Communion service. The celebration takes place in the afternoon, preferably at 3:00 p.m.

Guardian Angels, Oct. 2, memorial. Commemorates the angels who protect people from spiritual and physical dangers and assist them in doing good. A feast in their honor celebrated in Spain in the 16th century was placed in the Roman calendar in 1615 and Oct. 2 was set as the date of observance. Earlier, guardian angels were honored liturgically in conjunction with the feast of St. Michael.

Holy Family, movable observance on the Sunday after Christmas, feast. Commemorates the Holy Family of Jesus, Mary and Joseph as the model of domestic society, holiness and virtue. The devotional background of the feast was very strong in the 17th century. In the 18th century, in prayers composed for a special Mass, a Canadian bishop likened the Christian family to the Holy Family. Leo XIII consecrated families to the Holy Family. In 1921, Benedict XV extended the Divine Office and Mass of the feast to the whole Church.

Holy Innocents, Dec. 28, feast. Commemorates the infants who suffered death at the hands of Herod's soldiers seeking to kill the child Jesus (Mt. 2:13-18). A feast in their honor has been observed since the fifth century.

Holy Saturday, the day before Easter. The Sacrifice of the Mass is not celebrated, and Holy Communion may be given only as Viaticum. If possible the Easter fast should be observed until the Easter Vigil.

Holy Thursday, the Thursday before Easter. Commemorates the institution of the sacraments of the Eucharist and holy orders, and the washing of the feet of the Apostles by Jesus at the Last Supper. The Mass of the Lord's Supper in the evening marks the beginning of the Easter Triduum. Following the Mass, there is a procession of the Blessed Sacrament to a place of reposition for adoration by the faithful. Usually at an earlier Mass of Chrism, bishops bless oils (of catechumens, chrism, the sick) for use during the year. (For pastoral reasons, diocesan bishops may permit additional Masses, but these should not overshadow the principal Mass of the Lord's Supper.)

Immaculate Conception, Dec. 8, holy day of obligation, solemnity. Commemorates the fact that Mary, in view of her calling to be the Mother of Christ and in virtue of his merits, was preserved from the first moment of her conception from original sin and was filled with grace from the very beginning of her life. She was the only person so preserved from original sin. The present form of the feast dates from Dec. 8, 1854, when Pius IX defined the dogma of the Immaculate Conception An earlier feast of the Conception, which testified to long-existing belief in this truth, was observed in the East by the eighth century, in Ireland in the ninth, and subsequently in European countries. In 1846, Mary was proclaimed patroness of the U.S. under this title.

Immaculate Heart of Mary, Saturday following the second Sunday after Pentecost, memorial. On May 4, 1944, Pius XII ordered this feast observed throughout the Church in order to obtain Mary's intercession for "peace among nations, freedom for the Church, the conversion of sinners, the love of purity and the practice of virtue." Two years earlier, he consecrated the entire human race to Mary under this title. Devotion to Mary under the title of her Most Pure Heart originated during the Middle Ages. It was given great impetus in the 17th century by the preaching of St. John Eudes, who was the first to celebrate a Mass and Divine Office of Mary under this title. A feast, celebrated in various places and on different dates, was authorized in 1799.

Joachim and Ann, July 26, memorial. Commemorates the parents of Mary. A joint feast, celebrated Sept. 9, originated in the East near the end of the sixth century. Devotion to Ann, introduced in the eighth century at Rome, became widespread in Europe in the 14th century; her feast was extended throughout the Latin Church in 1584. A feast of Joachim was introduced in the West in the 15th century.

John the Baptist, Birth, June 24, solemnity. The precursor of Christ, whose cousin he was, was commemorated universally in the liturgy by the fourth century. He is the only saint, except the Blessed Virgin Mary, whose birthday is observed as a feast. Another feast, on Aug. 29, commemorates his passion and death at the order of Herod (Mk. 6:14-29).

Joseph, Mar. 19, solemnity. Joseph is honored as the husband of the Blessed Virgin Mary, the patron and protector of the universal Church and workman. Devotion to him already existed in the eighth century in the East, and in the 11th in the West. Various feasts were celebrated before the 15th century when Mar. 19 was fixed for his commemoration; this feast was extended to the whole Church in 1621 by Gregory XV. In 1955, Pius XII instituted the feast of St. Joseph the Workman for observance May 1; this feast, which may be celebrated by local option, supplanted the Solemnity or Patronage of St. Joseph formerly observed on the third Wednesday after Easter. St. Joseph was proclaimed protector and patron of the universal Church in 1870 by Pius IX.

Michael, Gabriel and Raphael, Archangels, Sept. 29, feast. A feast bearing the title of Dedication of St. Michael the Archangel formerly commemorated on this date the consecration in 530 of a church near Rome in honor of Michael, the first angel given a liturgical feast. For a while, this feast was combined with a commemoration of the Guardian Angels. The separate feasts of Gabriel (Mar. 24) and Raphael (Oct. 24) were suppressed by the calendar in effect since 1970 and this joint feast of the three archangels was instituted.

Octave of Christmas, Jan. 1. See Solemnity of Mary, Mother of God.

Our Lady of Guadalupe, Dec. 12, feast (in the U.S.). Commemorates under this title the appearances of the Blessed Virgin Mary in 1531 to an Indian, Juan Diego, on Tepeyac hill outside Mexico City (see Apparitions of the Blessed Virgin Mary). The celebration, observed as a memorial in the U.S., was raised to the rank of feast at the request of the National Conference of Catholic Bishops. Approval was granted in a decree dated Jan. 8, 1988.

Our Lady of Sorrows, Sept. 15, memorial. Recalls the sorrows experienced by Mary in her association with Christ: the prophecy of Simeon (Lk. 2:34-35), the flight into Egypt (Mt. 2:13-21), the three-day separation from Jesus (Lk. 2:41-50), and four incidents connected with the Passion: her meeting with Christ

on the way to Calvary, the crucifixion, the removal of Christ's body from the cross, and his burial (Mt. 27:31-61; Mk. 15:20-47; Lk. 23:26-56; Jn. 19:17-42). A Mass and Divine Office of the feast were celebrated by the Servites, especially, in the 17th century, and in 1814 Pius VII extended the observance to the whole Church.

Our Lady of the Rosary, Oct. 7, memorial. Commemorates the Virgin Mary through recall of the mysteries of the Rosary which recapitulate events in her life and the life of Christ. The feast was instituted in 1573 to commemorate a Christian victory over invading the forces of the Ottoman Empire at Lepanto in 1571, and was extended throughout the Church by Clement XI in 1716.

Passion Sunday (formerly called Palm Sunday), the Sunday before Easter. Marks the start of Holy Week by recalling the triumphal entry of Christ into Jerusalem at the beginning of the last week of his life (Mt. 21:1-9). A procession and other ceremonies commemorating this event were held in Jerusalem from very early Christian times and were adopted in Rome by the ninth century, when the blessing of palm for the occasion was introduced. Full liturgical observance includes the blessing of palm and a procession before the principal Mass of the day. The Passion, by Matthew, Mark or Luke, is read during the Mass.

Pentecost, also called **Whitsunday**, movable celebration held 50 days after Easter, solemnity. Commemorates the descent of the Holy Spirit upon the Apostles, the preaching of Peter and the other Apostles to Jews in Jerusalem, the baptism and aggregation of some 3,000 persons to the Christian community (Acts 2:1-41). It is regarded as the birthday of the Catholic Church. The original observance of the feast antedated the earliest extant documentary evidence from the third century.

Peter and Paul, June 29, solemnity. Commemorates the martyrdoms of Peter by crucifixion and Paul by beheading during the Neronian persecution. This joint commemoration of the chief Apostles dates at least from 258 at Rome.

Presentation of the Lord (formerly called Purification of the Blessed Virgin Mary, also Candlemas), Feb. 2, feast. Commemorates the presentation of Jesus in the Temple — according to prescriptions of Mosaic law (Lv. 12:2-8; Ex. 13:2; Lk. 2:22-32) — and the purification of Mary 40 days after his birth. In the East, where the feast antedated fourth century testimony regarding its existence, it was observed primarily as a feast of Our Lord; in the West, where it was adopted later, it was regarded more as a feast of Mary until the calendar in effect since 1970. Its date was set for Feb. 2 after the celebration of Christmas was fixed for Dec. 25, late in the fourth century. The blessing of candles, probably in commemoration of Christ who was the Light to enlighten the Gentiles, became common about the 11th century and gave the feast the secondary name of Candlemas.

Queenship of Mary, Aug. 22, memorial. Commemorates the high dignity of Mary as Queen of heaven, angels and men. Universal observance of the memorial was ordered by Pius XII in the encyclical *Ad Caeli Reginam*, Oct. 11, 1954, near the close of a Marian Year observed in connection with the centenary of the proclamation of the dogma of the Immacu-

late Conception and four years after the proclamation of the dogma of the Assumption. The original
date of the memorial was May 31.

Resurrection. See **Easter.**

Sacred Heart of Jesus, movable observance held
on the Friday after the second Sunday after Pentecost
(Corpus Christi, in the U.S.), solemnity. The object
of the devotion is the divine Person of Christ, whose
heart is the symbol of his love for all people — for
whom he accomplished the work of Redemption. The
Mass and Office now used on the feast were prescribed by Pius XI in 1929. Devotion to the Sacred
Heart was introduced into the liturgy in the 17th century through the efforts of St. John Eudes who composed an Office and Mass for the feast. It was furthered as the result of the revelations of St. Margaret
Mary Alacoque after 1675 and by the work of St.
Claude de la Colombière, S.J. In 1765, Clement XIII
approved a Mass and Office for the feast, and in 1856
Pius IX extended the observance throughout the Roman rite.

Solemnity of Mary, Mother of God, Jan. 1, holy
day of obligation, solemnity. The calendar in effect
since 1970, in accord with Eastern tradition, reinstated
the Marian character of this commemoration on the
octave day of Christmas. The former feast of the Circumcision, dating at least from the first half of the
sixth century, marked the initiation of Jesus (Lk. 2:21)
in Judaism and by analogy focused attention on the
initiation of persons in the Christian religion and their

incorporation in Christ through baptism. The feast of
the Solemnity supplants the former feast of the Maternity of Mary observed on Oct. 11.

Transfiguration of the Lord, Aug. 6, feast. Commemorates the revelation of his divinity by Christ to
Peter, James and John on Mt. Tabor (Mt. 17:1-9). The
feast, which is very old, was extended throughout the
universal Church in 1457 by Callistus III.

Trinity, The Holy, movable observance held on the
Sunday after Pentecost, solemnity. Commemorates
the most sublime mystery of the Christian faith, i.e.,
that there are Three Divine Persons — Father, Son
and Holy Spirit — in one God (Mt. 28:18-20). A votive Mass of the Most Holy Trinity dates from the
seventh century; an Office was composed in the 10th
century; in 1334, John XXII extended the feast to the
universal Church.

Visitation, May 31, feast. Commemorates Mary's
visit to her cousin Elizabeth after the Annunciation and before the birth of John the Baptist, the
precursor of Christ (Lk. 1:39-47). The feast had a
medieval origin and was observed in the Franciscan
Order before being extended throughout the
Church by Urban VI in 1389. It is one of the feasts
of the Incarnation and is notable for its recall of
the *Magnificat*, one of the few New Testament canticles, which acknowledges the unique gifts of God
to Mary because of her role in the redemptive work
of Christ. The canticle is recited at Evening Prayer
in the Liturgy of the Hours.

ASPECTS OF THE HOLY YEAR CALENDAR

*The following are excerpts from the document on
the Holy Year Calendar for 2000, issued on May 2,
1998, Solemnity of the Ascension of the Lord, by Cardinal Roger Etchegaray, President of the Central
Committee and the Presidential Council for the Jubilee, and Crescenzio Sepe, General Secretary of the
Central Committee and the Presidential Council.*

Foreword

1. The Holy Year of 2000, when the Church will
celebrate the second millennium of the birth of Jesus,
her Lord and Saviour, is a "year of jubilee" and also a
"liturgical year." These two aspects cannot be separated, but must vivify that unique period of time in
which the chronological date, inherent in the number
2000, and the mystical date, that of the sacramental
celebration of the mystery of Christ, are harmoniously
welded together.

Characteristics of the 2000 Calendar

The "Calendar of the Holy Year 2000" is an instrument which, following the rhythm of the liturgical
year, indicates the principal celebrations which will
occur in the "jubilee year": from Midnight Mass on
the Birth of the Lord (Dec. 24, 1999), when the Holy
Year will be inaugurated, until Jan. 6, 2001, the Solemnity of the Epiphany, when the Great Jubilee will
be closed in Rome.

Catechetical, missionary and social aspects are underlined in the Calendar. In the midst of these, provision is made for particularly intense celebrations in
order to sensitize Christians and public opinion to
these important themes of ecclesiastical Magisterium.

A **"Sacramental" Calendar** — The liturgical year
is the celebration, during the solar year, of the entire
mystery of Christ.

A **Roman Calendar** — The "Calendar of the Holy
Year of 2000" is eminently Roman. From the time
when access by the faithful to Jerusalem and the holy
places was difficult, Rome became the principal place
of pilgrimage.

A **Universal Calendar** — The singular position of
the City of Rome, episcopal seat of the Roman Pontiff, and the fact that, for the first time ever, the Jubilee will be celebrated simultaneously in Rome, the
Holy Land and in the local Churches, indicates that
the Calendar is addressed not only to the Roman
Church, but to the Church as a whole.

An **Ecumenical Calendar** — "From an *ecumenical point of view*, this will certainly be a very important year for Christians to look together to Christ the
one Lord, deepening our commitment to become one
in him, in accordance with his prayer to the Father."
(n. 41).

A **Calendar Attentive to Popular Piety** — A liturgical calendar, because of its nature, does not contain references to pious exercises. But the "Calendar
of the Holy Year of 2000" does, because many of the
exercises of the "Jubilee Year" processions, penitential celebrations, Eucharistic adoration, the Way of
the Cross, all have a popular basis.

A **Calendar Attentive to the Figure and Mission
of the Mother of Jesus** — Mary of Nazareth has
played an essential role in the event commemorated
in the Grand Jubilee of the Year 2000 the Incarnation
of the Word and the birth of Christ.

The nature and purpose of the liturgy, along with norms for its revision, were the subject matter of *Sacrosanctum Concilium* (the Constitution on the Sacred Liturgy) promulgated by the Second Vatican Council. The principles and guidelines stated in this document, the first issued by the Council, are summarized here and/or are incorporated in other Almanac entries on liturgical subjects.

Nature and Purpose of Liturgy

The paragraphs under this and the following subhead are quoted directly from *Sacrosanctum Concilium* (Constitution on the Sacred Liturgy).

"It is through the liturgy, especially the divine Eucharistic Sacrifice, that 'the work of our redemption is exercised.' The liturgy is thus the outstanding means by which the faithful can express in their lives, and manifest to others, the mystery of Christ and the real nature of the true Church " (No. 2).

"The liturgy is considered as an exercise of the priestly office of Jesus Christ. In the liturgy the sanctification of man is manifested by signs perceptible to the senses, and is effected in a way which is proper to each of these signs; in the liturgy full public worship is performed by the Mystical Body of Jesus Christ, that is, by the Head and his members.

"From this it follows that every liturgical celebration, because it is an action of Christ the priest and of his Body the Church, is a sacred action surpassing all others. No other action of the Church can match its claim to efficacy, nor equal the degree of it" (No. 7).

"The liturgy is the summit toward which the activity of the Church is directed; at the same time it is the fountain from which all her power flows. For the goal of apostolic works is that all who are made sons of God by faith and baptism should come together to praise God in the midst of his Church, to take part in her sacrifice, and to eat the Lord's Supper.

"From the liturgy, therefore, and especially from the Eucharist, as from a fountain, grace is channeled into us; and the sanctification of men in Christ and the glorification of God, to which all other activities of the Church are directed as toward their goal, are most powerfully achieved" (No. 10).

Full Participation

"Mother Church earnestly desires that all the faithful be led to that full, conscious, and active participation in liturgical celebrations which is demanded by the very nature of the liturgy. Such participation by the Christian people as 'a chosen race, a royal priesthood, a holy nation, a purchased people' (1 Pt. 2:9; cf. 2:4-5), is their right and duty by reason of their baptism.

"In the restoration and promotion of the sacred liturgy, this full and active participation by all the people is the aim to be considered before all else; for it is the primary and indispensable source from which the faithful are to derive the true Christian spirit" (No. 14).

"In order that the Christian people may more securely derive an abundance of graces from the sacred liturgy, holy Mother Church desires to undertake with great care a general restoration of the liturgy itself. For the liturgy is made up of unchangeable elements divinely instituted, and elements sub-

LITURGICAL LIFE OF THE CHURCH

ject to change. The latter not only may but ought to be changed with the passing of time if features have by chance crept in which are less harmonious with the intimate nature of the liturgy, or if existing elements have grown less functional.

"In this restoration, both texts and rites should be drawn up so that they express more clearly the holy things which they signify. Christian people, as far as possible, should be able to understand them with ease and to take part in them fully, actively, and as befits a community " (No. 21).

Norms

Norms regarding the reforms concern the greater use of Scripture; emphasis on the importance of the sermon or homily on biblical and liturgical subjects; use of vernacular languages for prayers of the Mass and for administration of the sacraments; provision for adaptation of rites to cultural patterns.

Approval for reforms of various kinds — in liturgical texts, rites, etc. — depends on the Holy See, regional conferences of bishops and individual bishops, according to provisions of law. No priest has authority to initiate reforms on his own. Reforms may not be introduced just for the sake of innovation, and any that are introduced in the light of present-day circumstances should embody sound tradition.

To assure the desired effect of liturgical reforms, training and instruction are necessary for the clergy, religious and the laity. The functions of diocesan and regional commissions for liturgy, music and art are to set standards and provide leadership for instruction and practical programs in their respective fields.

Most of the constitution's provisions regarding liturgical reforms have to do with the Roman rite. The document clearly respects the equal dignity of all rites, leaving to the Eastern Churches control over their ancient liturgies.

(For coverage of the Mystery of the Eucharist, see The Mass; Other Sacraments, see also separate entries.)

Sacramentals

Sacramentals, instituted by the Church, "are sacred signs which bear a resemblance to the sacraments: they signify effects, particularly of a spiritual kind, which are obtained through the Church's intercession. By them men are disposed to receive the chief effect of the sacraments, and various occasions in life are rendered holy" (No. 60).

"Thus, for well-disposed members of the faithful, the liturgy of the sacraments and sacramentals sanctifies almost every event in their lives; they are given access to the stream of divine grace which flows from the paschal mystery of the passion, death, and resurrection of Christ, the fountain from which all sacraments and sacramentals draw their power. There is hardly any proper use of material things which cannot thus be directed toward the sanctification of men and the praise of God" (No. 61).

Some common sacramentals are priestly blessings, blessed palm, candles, holy water, medals, scapulars, prayers and ceremonies of the Roman Ritual.

Liturgy of the Hours

The Liturgy of the Hours (Divine Office) is the public prayer of the Church for praising God and sanctify-

ing the day. Its daily celebration is required as a sacred obligation by men in holy orders and by men and women religious who have professed solemn vows. Its celebration by others is highly commended and is to be encouraged in the community of the faithful.

"By tradition going back to early Christian times, the Divine Office is arranged so that the whole course of the day and night is made holy by the praises of God. Therefore, when this wonderful song of praise is worthily rendered by priests and others who are deputed for this purpose by Church ordinance, or by the faithful praying together with the priest in an approved form, then it is truly the voice of the bride addressing her bridegroom; it is the very prayer which Christ himself, together with his Body, addresses to the Father" (No. 84).

"Hence all who perform this service are not only fulfilling a duty of the Church, but also are sharing in the greatest honor accorded to Christ's spouse, for by offering these praises to God they are standing before God's throne in the name of the Church their Mother" (No. 85).

Revised Hours

The Liturgy of the Hours, revised since 1965, was the subject of Pope Paul VI's apostolic constitution *Laudis Canticum*, dated Nov. 1, 1970. The master Latin text was published in 1971; its four volumes have been published in authorized English translation since May 1975.

One-volume, partial editions of the Liturgy of the Hours containing Morning and Evening Prayer and other elements, have been published in approved English translation.

The revised Liturgy of the Hours consists of:

• Office of Readings, for reflection on the word of God. The principal parts are three psalms, biblical and non-biblical readings.

• Morning and Evening Prayer, called the "hinges" of the Liturgy of the Hours. The principal parts are a hymn, two psalms, an Old or New Testament canticle, a brief biblical reading, Zechariah's canticle (the *Benedictus*, morning) or Mary's canticle (the *Magnificat*, evening), responsories, intercessions and a concluding prayer.

• Daytime Prayer. The principal parts are a hymn, three psalms, a biblical reading and one of three concluding prayers corresponding to the time of day.

• Night Prayer: The principal parts are one or two psalms, a brief biblical reading, Simeon's canticle (*Nunc Dimittis*), a concluding prayer and an antiphon in honor of Mary.

In the revised Liturgy of the Hours, the hours are shorter than they had been, with greater textual variety, meditation aids, and provision for intervals of silence and meditation. The psalms are distributed over a four-week period instead of a week; some psalms, entirely or in part, are not included. Additional canticles from the Old and New Testaments are assigned for Morning and Evening Prayer. Additional scriptural texts have been added and variously arranged for greater internal unity, correspondence to readings at Mass, and relevance to events and themes of salvation history. Readings include some of the best material from the Fathers of the Church and other authors, and improved selections on the lives of the saints.

The book used for recitation of the Office is the Breviary.

For coverage of the Liturgical Year, see Church Calendar.

Sacred Music

"The musical tradition of the universal Church is a treasure of immeasurable value, greater even than that of any other art. The main reason for this pre-eminence is that, as sacred melody united to words, it forms a necessary or integral part of the solemn liturgy.

"Sacred music increases in holiness to the degree that it is intimately linked with liturgical action, winningly expresses prayerfulness, promotes solidarity, and enriches sacred rites with heightened solemnity. The Church indeed approves of all forms of true art, and admits them into divine worship when they show appropriate qualities" (No. 112).

The constitution decreed:

• Vernacular languages for the people's parts of the liturgy, as well as Latin, may be used.

• Participation in sacred song by the whole body of the faithful, and not just by choirs, is to be encouraged and brought about.

• Provisions should be made for proper musical training for clergy, religious and lay persons.

• While Gregorian Chant has a unique dignity and relationship to the Latin liturgy, other kinds of music are acceptable.

• Native musical traditions should be used, especially in mission areas.

• Various instruments compatible with the dignity of worship may be used.

Gregorian Chant: A form and style of chant called Gregorian was the basis and most highly regarded standard of liturgical music for centuries. It originated probably during the formative period of the Roman liturgy and developed in conjunction with Gallican and other forms of chant. Gregory the Great's connection with it is not clear, although it is known that he had great concern for and interest in church music. The earliest extant written versions of Gregorian Chant date from the ninth century. A thousand years later, the Benedictines of Solesmes, France, initiated a revival of chant which gave impetus to the modern liturgical movement.

Sacred Art and Furnishings

"Very rightly the fine arts are considered to rank among the noblest expressions of human genius. This judgment applies especially to religious art and to its highest achievement, which is sacred art. By their very nature both of the latter are related to God's boundless beauty, for this is the reality which these human efforts are trying to express in some way. To the extent that these works aim exclusively at turning men's thoughts to God persuasively and devoutly, they are dedicated to God and to the cause of his greater honor and glory" (No. 122).

The objective of sacred art is "that all things set apart for use in divine worship should be truly worthy, becoming, and beautiful, signs and symbols of heavenly realities. The Church has always reserved to herself the right to pass judgment upon the arts, deciding which of the works of artists are in accordance with faith, piety, and cherished traditional laws, and thereby suited to sacred purposes.

"Sacred furnishings should worthily and beautifully serve the dignity of worship" (No. 122).

According to the constitution:

• Contemporary art, as well as that of the past, shall "be given free scope in the Church, provided that it adorns the sacred buildings and holy rites with due honor and reverence" (No. 123).

• Noble beauty, not sumptuous display, should be sought in art, sacred vestments and ornaments.

• "Let bishops carefully exclude from the house of God and from other sacred places those works of artists which are repugnant to faith, morals, and Christian piety, and which offend true religious sense either by their distortion of forms or by lack of artistic worth, by mediocrity or by pretense.

• "When churches are to be built, let great care be taken that they be suitable for the celebration of liturgical services and for the active participation of the faithful" (No. 124).

• "The practice of placing sacred images in churches so that they may be venerated by the faithful is to be firmly maintained. Nevertheless, their number should be moderate and their relative location should reflect right order. Otherwise they may create confusion among the Christian people and promote a faulty sense of devotion" (No. 125).

• Artists should be trained and inspired in the spirit and for the purposes of the liturgy.

• The norms of sacred art are to be revised. "These laws refer especially to the worthy and well-planned construction of sacred buildings, the shape and construction of altars, the nobility, location, and security of the Eucharistic tabernacle, the suitability and dignity of the baptistery, the proper use of sacred images, embellishments, and vestments" (No. 128).

RITES

Rites are the forms and ceremonial observances of liturgical worship coupled with the total expression of the theological, spiritual and disciplinary heritages of particular churches of the East and the West.

Different rites have evolved in the course of church history, giving to liturgical worship and church life in general forms and usages peculiar and proper to the nature of worship and the culture of the faithful in various circumstances of time and place. Thus, there has been development since apostolic times in the prayers and ceremonies of the Mass, in the celebration of the sacraments, sacramentals and the Liturgy of the Hours, and in observances of the liturgical calendar. The principal sources of rites in present use were practices within the patriarchates of Rome (for the West) and Antioch, Alexandria and Constantinople (for the East). Rites are identified as Eastern or Western on the basis of their geographical area of origin in the Roman Empire.

Eastern and Roman Rites

Eastern rites are proper to Eastern Catholic Churches (see separate entry). The principal rites are Byzantine, Alexandrian, Antiochene, Armenian and Chaldean.

The Latin or Roman rite prevails in the Western Church. It was derived from Roman practices and the use of Latin from the third century onward, and has been the rite in general use in the West since the eighth century. Other rites in limited use in the Western Church have been the Ambrosian (in the Archdiocese of Milan), the Mozarabic (in the Archdiocese of Toledo), the Lyonnais, the Braga, and rites peculiar to some religious orders like the Dominicans, Carmelites and Carthusians.

The purpose of the revision of rites in progress since the Second Vatican Council is to renew them, not to eliminate the rites of particular churches or to reduce all rites to uniformity. The Council reaffirmed the equal dignity and preservation of rites as follows.

"It is the mind of the Catholic Church that each individual church or rite retain its traditions whole and entire, while adjusting its way of life to various needs of time and place. Such individual churches, whether of the East or the West, although they differ somewhat among themselves in what are called rites (that is, in liturgy, ecclesiastical discipline and spiritual heritage), are, nevertheless, equally entrusted to the pastoral guidance of the Roman Pontiff, the divinely appointed successor of St. Peter in supreme government over the universal Church. They are, consequently, of equal dignity, so that none of them is superior to the others by reason of rite."

Determination of Rite

Determination of a person's rite is regulated by church law. Through baptism, a child becomes a member of the rite of his or her parents. If the parents are of different rites, the child's rite is decided by mutual consent of the parents; if there is lack of mutual consent, the child is baptized in the rite of the father. A candidate for baptism over the age of 14 can choose to be baptized in any approved rite. Catholics baptized in one rite may receive the sacraments in any of the approved ritual churches; they may transfer to another rite only with the permission of the Holy See and in accordance with other provisions of the Code of Canon Law.

MASS, EUCHARISTIC SACRIFICE AND BANQUET

Declarations of Vatican II

The Second Vatican Council made the following declarations among others with respect to the Mass:

"At the Last Supper, on the night when he was betrayed, our Savior instituted the Eucharistic Sacrifice of his Body and Blood. He did this in order to perpetuate the Sacrifice of the Cross throughout the centuries until he should come again, and so to entrust to his beloved spouse, the Church, a memorial of his death and resurrection: a sacrament of love, a sign of unity, a bond of charity, a paschal banquet in which Christ is consumed, the mind is filled with grace, and a pledge of future glory is given to us" (*Sacrosanctum Concilium*, Constitution on the Sacred Liturgy, No. 47).

". . . As often as the Sacrifice of the Cross in which 'Christ, our Passover, has been sacrificed' (1 Cor. 5:7) is celebrated on an altar, the work of our redemption is carried on. At the same time, in the sacrament of the Eucharistic bread the unity of all believers who form one body in Christ (cf. 1 Cor. 10:17) is both expressed and brought about. All men are called to this union with Christ." (*Lumen Gentium*, Dogmatic Constitution on the Church, No. 3).

". . . The ministerial priest, by the sacred power he enjoys, molds and rules the priestly people. Acting in the person of Christ, he brings about the Eucharistic Sacrifice, and offers it to God in the name of all the people. For their part, the faithful join in the offering of the Eucharist by virtue of their royal priesthood ." (Ibid., No. 10).

Declarations of Trent

Among its decrees on the Holy Eucharist, the Council of Trent stated the following points of doctrine on the Mass.

1. There is in the Catholic Church a true sacrifice, the Mass instituted by Jesus Christ. It is the sacrifice of his Body and Blood, Soul and Divinity, himself, under the appearances of bread and wine.

2. This Sacrifice is identical with the Sacrifice of the Cross, inasmuch as Christ is the Priest and Victim in both. A difference lies in the manner of offering, which was bloody upon the Cross and is bloodless on the altar.

3. The Mass is a propitiatory Sacrifice, atoning for the sins of the living and dead for whom it is offered.

4. The efficacy of the Mass is derived from the Sacrifice of the Cross, whose superabundant merits it applies to men.

5. Although the Mass is offered to God alone, it may be celebrated in honor and memory of the saints.

6. Christ instituted the Mass at the Last Supper.

7. Christ ordained the Apostles priests, giving them power and the command to consecrate his Body and Blood to perpetuate and renew the Sacrifice.

ORDER OF THE MASS

The Mass consists of two principal divisions called the **Liturgy of the Word**, which features the proclamation of the Word of God, and the **Eucharistic Liturgy**, which focuses on the central act of sacrifice in the Consecration and on the Eucharistic Banquet in Holy Communion. (Formerly, these divisions were called, respectively, the **Mass of the Catechumens** and the **Mass of the Faithful**.) In addition to these principal divisions, there are ancillary introductory and concluding rites.

The following description covers the Mass as celebrated with participation by the people. This Order of the Mass was approved by Pope Paul VI in the apostolic constitution *Missale Romanum* dated Apr. 3, 1969, and promulgated in a decree issued Apr. 6, 1969, by the Congregation for Divine Worship. The assigned effective date was Nov. 30, 1969.

Introductory Rites

Entrance: The introductory rites begin with the singing or recitation of an entrance song consisting of one or more scriptural verses stating the theme of the mystery, season or feast commemorated in the Mass.

Greeting: The priest and people make the Sign of the Cross together. The priest then greets them in one of several alternative ways and they reply in a corresponding manner.

Introductory Remarks: At this point, the priest or another of the ministers may introduce the theme of the Mass.

Penitential Rite: The priest and people together acknowledge their sins as a preliminary step toward worthy celebration of the sacred mysteries.

This rite includes a brief examination of conscience, a general confession of sin and plea for divine mercy in one of several ways, and a prayer for forgiveness by the priest.

Glory to God: A doxology, a hymn of praise to God, sung or said on festive occasions.

Opening Prayer: A prayer of petition offered by the priest on behalf of the worshiping community.

I. Liturgy of the Word

Readings: The featured elements of this liturgy are readings of passages from the Bible. If three readings are in order, the first is usually from the Old Testament, the second from the New Testament (Letters, Acts, Revelation), and the third from one of the Gospels; the final reading is always a selection from a Gospel. The first reading(s) is (are) concluded with the formula, "The Word of the Lord" (effective Feb. 28, 1993; optional before that date), to which the people respond, "Thanks be to God." The Gospel reading is concluded with the formula, "The Gospel of the Lord," (effective as above), to which the people respond, "Praise to you, Lord Jesus Christ." Between the readings, psalm verses are sung or recited. A Gospel acclamation is either sung or omitted.

Homily: An explanation, pertinent to the mystery being celebrated and the special needs of the listeners, of some point in either the readings from sacred Scripture or in another text from the Ordinary or Proper parts of the Mass; it is a proclamation of the Good News for a response of faith.

Creed: The Nicene profession of faith, by priest and people, on certain occasions.

Prayer of the Faithful: Litany-type prayers of petition, with participation by the people. Called general intercessions, they concern needs of the Church, the salvation of the world, public authorities, persons in need, the local community.

II. Eucharistic Liturgy

Presentation and Preparation of Gifts: Presentation to the priest of the gifts of bread and wine, principally, by participating members of the congregation. Preparation of the gifts consists of the prayers and ceremonies with which the priest offers bread and wine as the elements of the sacrifice to take place during the Eucharistic Prayer and of the Lord's Supper to be shared in Holy Communion.

Washing of Hands: After offering the bread and wine, the priest cleanses his fingers with water in a brief ceremony of purification.

Pray, Brothers and Sisters: Prayer that the sacrifice to take place will be acceptable to God. The first part of the prayer is said by the priest; the second, by the people.

Prayer over the Gifts: A prayer of petition offered by the priest on behalf of the worshiping community.

Eucharistic Prayer

Preface: A hymn of praise, introducing the Eucharistic Prayer or Canon, sung or said by the priest following responses by the people. The Order of the Mass contains a variety of prefaces, for use on different occasions.

Holy, Holy, Holy; Blessed is He: Divine praises sung or said by the priest and people.

Eucharistic Prayer (Canon): Its central portion is the Consecration, when the essential act of sacrificial offering takes place with the changing of bread and wine into the Body and Blood of Christ. The various parts of the prayer, which are said by the celebrant only, commemorate principal mysteries of salvation history and include petitions for the Church, the living and dead, and remembrances of saints.

Doxology: A formula of divine praise sung or said by the priest while he holds aloft the chalice containing the consecrated wine in one hand and the paten containing the consecrated host in the other.

Communion Rite

Lord's Prayer: Sung or said by the priest and people.

Prayer for Deliverance from evil: Called an embolism because it is a development of the final petition of the Lord's Prayer; said by the priest. It concludes with a memorial of the return of the Lord to which the people respond, "For the kingdom, the power, and the glory are yours, now and forever."

Prayer for Peace: Said by the priest, with corresponding responses by the people. The priest can, in accord with local custom, bid the people to exchange a greeting of peace with each other.

Lamb of God (*Agnus Dei*): A prayer for divine mercy sung or said while the priest breaks the consecrated host and places a piece of it into the consecrated wine in the chalice.

Communion: The priest, after saying a preparatory prayer, administers Holy Communion to himself and then to the people, thus completing the sacrifice-banquet of the Mass. (This completion is realized even if the celebrant alone receives the Eucharist.) On giving the Eucharist to each person under both species separately, the priest or eucharistic minister says, "The Body of Christ," "The Blood of Christ." The customary response is "Amen." If the Eucharist is given by intinction (in which the host is dipped into the consecrated wine), the priest says, "The Body and Blood of Christ."

Communion Song: Scriptural verses or a suitable hymn sung or said during the distribution of Holy Communion. After Holy Communion is received, some moments may be spent in silent meditation or in the chanting of a psalm or hymn of praise.

Prayer after Communion: A prayer of petition offered by the priest on behalf of the worshiping community.

Concluding Rite

Announcements: Brief announcements to the people are in order at this time.

Dismissal: Consists of a final greeting by the priest, a blessing, and a formula of dismissal. This rite is omitted if another liturgical action immediately follows the Mass; e.g., a procession, the blessing of the body during a funeral rite.

Some parts of the Mass are changeable with the liturgical season or feast, and are called the proper of the Mass. Other parts are said to be common because they always remain the same.

Additional Mass Notes

Catholics are seriously obliged to attend Mass in a worthy manner on Sundays and holy days of obligation. Failure to do so without a proportionately serious reason is gravely wrong.

It is the custom for priests to celebrate Mass daily whenever possible. To satisfy the needs of the faithful on Sundays and holy days of obligation, they are authorized to say Mass twice (**bination**) or even three times (**trination**). Bination is also permissible on weekdays to satisfy the needs of the faithful. On Christmas every priest may say three Masses.

The **fruits of the Mass**, which in itself is of infinite value, are: **general**, for all the faithful; **special (ministerial)**, for the intentions or persons specifically intended by the celebrant; **most special (personal)**, for the celebrant himself. On Sundays and certain other days pastors are obliged to offer Mass for their parishioners, or to have another priest do so. If a priest accepts a stipend or offering for a Mass, he is obliged in justice to apply the Mass for the intention of the donor. Mass may be applied for the living and the dead, or for any good intention.

Mass can be celebrated in several ways: e.g., with people present, without their presence (privately), with two or more priests as co-celebrants (con-celebration), with greater or less solemnity.

Some of the various types of Masses are: **for the dead** (Funeral Mass or Mass of Christian Burial, Mass for the Dead — formerly called Requiem Mass); **ritual**, in connection with celebration of the sacraments, religious profession, etc.; **nuptial**, for married couples, with or after the wedding ceremony; votive, to honor a Person of the Trinity, a saint, or for some special intention.

Places, Altars for Mass

The ordinary place for celebrating the Eucharist is a church or other sacred place, at a fixed or movable altar.

The altar is a table at which the Eucharistic Sacrifice is celebrated.

A fixed altar is attached to the floor of the church. It should be of stone, preferably, and should be consecrated. The Code of Canon Law orders observance of the custom of placing under a fixed altar relics of martyrs or other saints.

A movable altar can be made of any solid and suitable material, and should be blessed or consecrated.

Outside of a sacred place, Mass may be celebrated in an appropriate place at a suitable table covered with a linen cloth and corporal. An altar stone containing the relics of saints, which was formerly prescribed, is not required by regulations in effect since the promulgation Apr. 6, 1969, of *Institutio Generalis Missalis Romani*.

LITURGICAL VESTMENTS

In the early years of the Church, vestments worn by the ministers at liturgical functions were the same as the garments in ordinary popular use. They became distinctive when their form was not altered to correspond with later variations in popular style. Liturgical vestments are symbolic

of the sacred ministry and add appropriate decorum to divine worship.

Mass Vestments

Alb: A body-length tunic of white fabric; a vestment common to all ministers of divine worship.

Amice: A rectangular piece of white cloth worn about the neck, tucked into the collar and falling over the shoulders; prescribed for use when the alb does not completely cover the ordinary clothing at the neck.

Chasuble: Originally, a large mantle or cloak covering the body, it is the outer vestment of a priest celebrating Mass or carrying out other sacred actions connected with the Mass.

Chasuble-Alb: A vestment combining the features of the chasuble and alb; for use with a stole by concelebrants and, by way of exception, by celebrants in certain circumstances.

Cincture: A cord which serves the purpose of a belt, holding the alb close to the body.

Dalmatic: The outer vestment worn by a deacon in place of a chasuble.

Stole: A long, band-like vestment worn by a priest about the neck and falling to about the knees. A deacon wears a stole over the left shoulder, crossed and fastened at his right side.

The material, form and ornamentation of the aforementioned and other vestments are subject to variation and adaptation, according to norms and decisions of the Holy See and concerned conferences of bishops. The overriding norm is that they should be appropriate for use in divine worship. The customary ornamented vestments are the chasuble, dalmatic and stole.

The minimal vestments required for a priest celebrating Mass are the alb, stole, and chasuble.

Liturgical Colors

The colors of outer vestments vary with liturgical seasons, feasts and other circumstances. The colors and their use are:

Green: For the season of Ordinary Time; symbolic of hope and the vitality of the life of faith.

Violet (Purple): For Advent and Lent; may also be used in Masses for the dead; symbolic of penance. (See below, Violet for Advent.)

Red: For the Sunday of the Passion, Good Friday, Pentecost; feasts of the Passion of Our Lord, the Apostles and Evangelists, martyrs; symbolic of the supreme sacrifice of life for the love of God.

Rose: May be used in place of purple on the Third Sunday of Advent (formerly called Gaudete Sunday) and the Fourth Sunday of Lent (formerly called Laetare Sunday); symbolic of anticipatory joy during a time of penance.

White: For the seasons of Christmas and Easter; feasts and commemorations of Our Lord, except those of the Passion; feasts and commemorations of the Blessed Virgin Mary, angels, saints who are not martyrs, All Saints (Nov. 1), St. John the Baptist (June 24), St. John the Evangelist (Dec. 27), the Chair of St. Peter (Feb. 22), the Conversion of St. Paul (Jan. 25). White, symbolic of purity and integrity of the life of faith, may generally be substituted for other colors, and can be used for funeral and other Masses for the dead.

Options are provided regarding the color of vestments used in offices and Masses for the dead. The newsletter of the U.S. Bishops' Committee on the Liturgy, in line with No. 308 of the General Instruction of the Roman Missal, announced in July 1970: "In the dioceses of the United States, white vestments may be used, in addition to violet (purple) and black, in offices and Masses for the dead."

On more solemn occasions, better than ordinary vestments may be used, even though their color (e.g., gold) does not match the requirements of the day.

Violet for Advent: Violet is the official liturgical color for the season of Advent, according to the September 1988, edition of the newsletter of the U.S. Bishops' Committee on the Liturgy. Blue was being proposed in order to distinguish between the Advent season and the specifically penitential season of Lent. The newsletter said, however, that "the same effect can be achieved by following the official color sequence of the Church, which requires the use of violet for Advent and Lent, while taking advantage of the varying shades which exist for violet. Light blue vestments are not authorized for use in the United States."

Considerable freedom is permitted in the choice of colors of vestments worn for votive Masses.

Other Vestments

Cappa Magna: Flowing vestment with a train, worn by bishops and cardinals.

Cassock: A non-liturgical, full-length, close-fitting robe for use by priests and other clerics under liturgical vestments and in ordinary use; usually black for priests, purple for bishops and other prelates, red for cardinals, white for the pope. In place of a cassock, priests belonging to religious institutes wear the habit proper to their institute.

Cope: A mantle-like vestment open in front and fastened across the chest; worn by sacred ministers in processions and other ceremonies, as prescribed by appropriate directives.

Habit: The ordinary (non-liturgical) garb of members of religious institutes, analogous to the cassock of diocesan priests; the form of habits varies from institute to institute.

Humeral Veil: A rectangular vestment worn about the shoulders by a deacon or priest in Eucharistic processions and for other prescribed liturgical ceremonies.

Mitre: A headdress worn at some liturgical functions by bishops, abbots and, in certain cases, other ecclesiastics.

Pallium: A circular band of white wool about two inches wide, with front and back pendants, marked with six crosses, worn about the neck. It is a symbol of the fullness of the episcopal office. Pope Paul VI, in a document issued July 20, 1978, on his own initiative and entitled *Inter Eximia Episcopalis*, restricted its use to the pope and archbishops of metropolitan sees. In 1984, Pope John Paul II decreed that the pallium would ordinarily be conferred by the pope on the solemnity of Sts. Peter and Paul, June 29. The pallium is made from the wool of lambs blessed by the pope on the feast of St. Agnes (Jan. 21).

Rochet: A knee-length, white linen-lace garment of prelates worn under outer vestments.

Surplice: a loose, flowing vestment of white fabric with wide sleeves. For some functions, it is interchangeable with an alb.

Zucchetto: A skullcap worn by bishops and other prelates.

SACRED VESSELS, LINENS
Vessels

Paten and Chalice: The principal sacred vessels required for the celebration of Mass are the paten (plate) and chalice (cup) in which bread and wine, respectively, are offered, consecrated and consumed. Both should be made of solid and noble material which is not easily breakable or corruptible. Gold coating is required of the interior parts of sacred vessels subject to rust. The cup of a chalice should be made of non-absorbent material.

Vessels for containing consecrated hosts (see below) can be made of material other than solid and noble metal — e.g., ivory, more durable woods — provided the substitute material is locally regarded as noble or rather precious and is suitable for sacred use.

Sacred vessels should be blessed, according to prescribed requirements.

Vessels, in addition to the paten, for containing consecrated hosts are:

Ciborium: Used to hold hosts for distribution to the faithful and for reservation in the tabernacle.

Luna, Lunula, Lunette: A small receptacle which holds the sacred host in an upright position in the monstrance.

Monstrance, Ostensorium: A portable receptacle so made that the sacred host, when enclosed therein, may be clearly seen, as at Benediction or during extended exposition of the Blessed Sacrament.

Pyx: A watch-shaped vessel used in carrying the Eucharist to the sick.

Linens

Altar Cloth: A white cloth, usually of linen, covering the table of an altar. One cloth is sufficient. Three were used according to former requirements.

Burse: A square, stiff flat case, open at one end, in which the folded corporal can be placed; the outside is covered with material of the same kind and color as the outer vestments of the celebrant.

Corporal: A square piece of white linen spread on the altar cloth, on which rest the vessels holding the Sacred Species — the consecrated host(s) and wine — during the Eucharistic Liturgy. The corporal is used whenever the Blessed Sacrament is removed from the tabernacle; e.g., during Benediction the vessel containing the Blessed Sacrament rests on a corporal.

Finger Towel: A white rectangular napkin used by the priest to dry his fingers after cleansing them following the offering of gifts at Mass.

Pall: A square piece of stiff material, usually covered with linen, which can be used to cover the chalice at Mass.

Purificator: A white rectangular napkin used for cleansing sacred vessels after the reception of Communion at Mass.

Veil: The chalice intended for use at Mass can be covered with a veil made of the same material as the outer vestments of the celebrant.

THE CHURCH BUILDING

A church is a building set aside and dedicated for purposes of divine worship, the place of assembly for a worshiping community.

A Catholic church is the ordinary place in which the faithful assemble for participation in the Eucharistic Liturgy and other forms of divine worship.

In the early years of Christianity, the first places of assembly for the Eucharistic Liturgy were private homes (Acts 2:46; Rom. 16:5; 1 Cor. 16:5; Col. 4:15) and, sometimes, catacombs. Church building began in the latter half of the second century during lulls in persecution and became widespread after enactment of the Edict of Milan in 313, when it finally became possible for the Church to emerge completely from the underground. The oldest and basic norms regarding church buildings date from about that time.

The essential principle underlying all norms for church building was reformulated by the Second Vatican Council, as follows: "When churches are to be built, let great care be taken that they be suitable for the celebration of liturgical services and for the active participation of the faithful" (*Sacrosanctum Concilium*, Constitution on the Sacred Liturgy, No. 124).

This principle was subsequently elaborated in detail by the Congregation for Divine Worship in a document entitled *Institutio Generalis Missalis Romani*, which was approved by Paul VI Apr. 3 and promulgated by a decree of the congregation dated Apr. 6, 1969. Coverage of the following items reflects the norms stated in Chapter V of this document.

Main Features

Sanctuary: The part of the church where the altar of sacrifice is located, the place where the ministers of the liturgy lead the people in prayer, proclaim the word of God and celebrate the Eucharist. It is set off from the body of the church by a distinctive structural feature — e.g., elevation above the main floor — or by ornamentation. (The traditional communion rail, removed in recent years in many churches, served this purpose of demarcation.) The customary location of the sanctuary is at the front of the church; it may, however, be centrally located.

Altar: The main altar of sacrifice and table of the Lord is the focal feature of the sanctuary and entire church. It stands by itself, so that the ministers can move about it freely, and is so situated that they face the people during the liturgical action. In addition to this main altar, there may also be others; in new churches, these are ideally situated in side chapels or alcoves removed to some degree from the body of the church.

Adornment of the Altar: The altar table is covered with a suitable linen cloth. Required candelabra and a cross are placed upon or near the altar in plain sight of the people and are so arranged that they do not obscure their view of the liturgical action.

Seats of the Ministers: The seats of the ministers should be so arranged that they are part of the seating arrangement of the worshiping congregation and suitably placed for the performance of ministerial functions. The seat of the celebrant or chief concelebrant should be in a presiding position.

Ambo, Pulpit, Lectern: The stand at which scriptural lessons and psalm responses are read, the word of God preached, and the prayer of the faithful offered. It is so placed that the ministers can be easily seen and heard by the people.

Places for the People: Seats and kneeling benches (pews) and other accommodations for the people are so arranged that they can participate in the most appropriate way in the liturgical action and have freedom of movement for the reception of Holy Communion. Reserved seats are out of order.

Place for the Choir: Where it is located depends on the most suitable arrangement for maintaining the unity of the choir with the congregation and for providing its members maximum opportunity for carrying out their proper function and participating fully in the Mass.

Tabernacle: The best place for reserving the Blessed Sacrament is in a chapel suitable for the private devotion of the people. If this is not possible, reservation should be at a side altar or other appropriately adorned place. In either case, the Blessed Sacrament should be kept in a tabernacle, i.e., a safe-like, secure receptacle.

Statues: Images of the Lord, the Blessed Virgin Mary and the saints are legitimately proposed for the veneration of the faithful in churches. Their number and arrangement, however, should be ordered in such a way that they do not distract the people from the central celebration of the Eucharistic Liturgy. There should be only one statue of one and the same saint in a church.

General Adornment and Arrangement of Churches: Churches should be so adorned and fitted out that they serve the direct requirements of divine worship and the needs and reasonable convenience of the people.

Other Items

Ambry: A box containing the holy oils, attached to the wall of the sanctuary in some churches.

Baptistry: The place for administering baptism. Some churches have baptisteries adjoining or near the entrance, a position symbolizing the fact that persons are initiated in the Church and incorporated in Christ through this sacrament. Contemporary liturgical practice favors placement of the baptistery near the sanctuary and altar, or the use of a portable font in the same position, to emphasize the relationship of baptism to the Eucharist, the celebration in sacrifice and banquet of the death and resurrection of Christ.

Candles: Used more for symbolical than illuminative purposes, they represent Christ, the light and life of grace, at liturgical functions. They are made of beeswax. (See Index: Paschal Candle.)

Confessional, Reconciliation Room: A booth-like structure for the hearing of confessions, with separate compartments for the priest and penitents and a grating or screen between them. The use of confessionals became general in the Roman rite after the Council of Trent. Since the Second Vatican Council, there has been a trend in the U.S. to replace or supplement confessionals with small reconciliation rooms so arranged that priest and penitent can converse face-to-face.

Crucifix: A cross bearing the figure of the body of Christ, representative of the Sacrifice of the Cross.

Cruets: Vessels containing the wine and water used at Mass. They are placed on a credence table in the sanctuary.

Holy Water Fonts: Receptacles containing holy water, usually at church entrances, for the use of the faithful.

Sanctuary Lamp: A lamp which is kept burning continuously before a tabernacle in which the Blessed Sacrament is reserved, as a sign of the Real Presence of Christ.

LITURGICAL DEVELOPMENTS

The principal developments covered in this article are enactments of the Holy See and actions related to their implementation in the United States.

Modern Movement

Origins of the modern movement for renewal in the liturgy date back to the 19th century. The key contributing factor was a revival of liturgical and scriptural studies. Of special significance was the work of the Benedictine monks of Solesmes, France, who aroused great interest in the liturgy through the restoration of Gregorian Chant. St. Pius X approved their work in a *motu proprio* of 1903 and gave additional encouragement to liturgical study and development.

St. Pius X did more than any other single pope to promote early first Communion and the practice of frequent Communion, started the research behind a revised breviary, and appointed a group to investigate possible revisions in the Mass.

The movement attracted some attention in the 1920s and 30s but made little progress.

Significant pioneering developments in the U.S. during the 20s, however, were the establishment of the Liturgical Press, the beginning of publication of *Orate Fratres* (now Worship), and the inauguration of the League of the Divine Office by the Benedictines at St. John's Abbey, Collegeville, Minn. Later events of influence were the establishment of the Pius X School of Liturgical Music at Manhattanville College of the Sacred Heart and the organization of a summer school of liturgical music at Mary Manse College by the Gregorian Institute of America. The turning point toward real renewal was reached during and after World War II.

Pius XII gave it impetus and direction, principally through the background teaching in his encyclicals on the Mystical Body (*Mystici Corporis Christi*, 1943), Sacred Liturgy (*Mediator Dei*, 1947), and On Sacred Music (*Musicae sacrae*, 1955), and by means of specific measures affecting the liturgy itself. His work was continued during the pontificates of his successors. The Second Vatican Council, in virtue of *Sacrosanctum Concilium*, the Constitution on the Sacred Liturgy, inaugurated changes of the greatest significance.

Before and After Vatican II

The most significant liturgical changes made in the years immediately preceding the Second Vatican Council were the following:

(1) Revision of the rites of Holy Week, for universal observance from 1956.

(2) Modification of the Eucharistic fast and permission for afternoon and evening Mass, in effect from 1953 and extended in 1957.

(3) The Dialogue Mass, introduced in 1958.

(4) Use of popular languages in administration of the sacraments.

(5) Calendar-missal-breviary reform, in effect from Jan. 1, 1961.

(6) Seven-step administration of baptism for adults, approved in 1962.

The Constitution on the Sacred Liturgy, *Sacrosanctum Concilium*, approved (2,174 to 4) and promulgated by the Second Vatican Council Dec. 4, 1963, marked the beginning of a profound renewal in the Church's corporate worship. Implementation of some of its measures was ordered by Paul VI Jan. 25, 1964, in the *motu proprio Sacram Liturgiam*. On Feb. 29, a special commission, the Consilium for Implementing the Constitution on the Sacred Liturgy, was formed to supervise the execution of the entire program of liturgical reform. Implementation of the program on local and regional levels was left to bishops acting through their own liturgical commissions and in concert with their fellow bishops in national conferences.

Liturgical reform in the United States has been carried out under the direction of the Liturgy Committee, National Conference of Catholic Bishops. Its secretariat, established early in 1965, is located at 3211 Fourth St. N.E., Washington, D.C. 20017.

Stages of Development

Liturgical development after the Second Vatican Council proceeded in several stages. It started with the formulation of guidelines and directives, and with the translation into vernacular languages of virtually unchanged Latin ritual texts. Then came structural changes in the Mass, the sacraments, the calendar, the Divine Office and other phases of the liturgy. These revisions were just about completed with the publication of a new order for the sacrament of penance in February 1974. A continuing phase of development, in progress from the beginning, involves efforts to deepen the liturgical sense of the faithful, to increase their participation in worship and to relate it to full Christian life.

Texts and Translations

The master texts of all documents on liturgical reform are in Latin. Effective dates of their implementation have depended on the completion and approval of appropriate translations into vernacular languages. English translations were made by the International Committee for English in the Liturgy.

The principal features of liturgical changes and the effective dates of their introduction in the United States are covered below under topical headings. (For expanded coverage of various items, especially the sacraments, see additional entries.)

The Mass

A new Order of the Mass, supplanting the one authorized by the Council of Trent in the 16th century, was introduced in the U.S. Mar. 22, 1970. It had been approved by Paul VI in the apostolic constitution *Missale Romanum*, dated Apr. 3, 1969.

Preliminary and related to it were the following developments.

Mass in English: Introduced Nov. 29, 1964. In the same year, Psalm 42 was eliminated from the prayers at the foot of the altar.

Incidental Changes: The last Gospel (prologue of John) and vernacular prayers following Mass were eliminated Mar. 7, 1965. At the same time, provision was made for the celebrant to say aloud some prayers formerly said silently.

Rubrics: An instruction entitled *Tres Abhinc Annos*, dated May 4 and effective June 29, 1967, simplified directives for the celebration of Mass, approved the practice of saying the canon aloud, altered the Communion and dismissal rites, permitted purple instead of black vestments in Masses for the dead, discontinued wearing of the maniple, and approved in principle the use of vernacular languages for the canon, ordination rites, and lessons of the Divine Office when read in choir.

Eucharistic Prayers (Canons): The traditional Roman Canon in English was introduced Oct. 22, 1967. Three additional Eucharistic prayers, authorized May 23, 1968, were approved for use in English the following Aug. 15.

The customary Roman Canon, which dates at least from the beginning of the fifth century and has remained substantially unchanged since the seventh century, is the first in the order of listing of the Eucharistic prayers. It can be used at any time, but is the one of choice for most Sundays, some special feasts like Easter and Pentecost, and for feasts of the Apostles and other saints who are commemorated in the canon. Any preface can be used with it.

The second Eucharistic prayer, the shortest and simplest of all, is best suited for use on weekdays and various special circumstances. It has a preface of its own, but others may be used with it. This canon bears a close resemblance to the one framed by St. Hippolytus about 215.

The third Eucharistic prayer is suitable for use on Sundays and feasts as an alternative to the Roman Canon. It can be used with any preface and has a special formula for remembrance of the dead.

The fourth Eucharistic prayer, the most sophisticated of them all, presents a broad synthesis of salvation history. Based on the Eastern tradition of Antioch, it is best suited for use at Masses attended by persons versed in Sacred Scripture. It has an unchangeable preface.

Five additional Eucharistic prayers — three for Masses with children and two for Masses of reconciliation — were approved in 1974 and 1975, respectively, by the Congregation for the Sacraments and Divine Worship.

Use of the Eucharistic Prayers for Various Needs and Occasions, was approved by the U.S. bishops in 1994, confirmed by the appropriate Vatican congregations May 9, 1995, and ratified for use beginning Oct. 1, 1995.

Lectionary: A new compilation of scriptural readings and psalm responsories for Mass was published in 1969. The Lectionary contains a three-year cycle of readings for Sundays and solemn feasts, a two-year weekday cycle, and a one-year cycle for the feasts of saints, in addition to readings for a variety of votive Masses, ritual Masses and Masses for various needs. There are also responsorial psalms to follow the first readings and gospel or alleluia versicles.

A second edition of the Lectionary, substantially the same as the first, was published in 1981. New features included an expanded introduction, extensive scriptural references and additional readings for a number of solemnities and feasts.

Volume One of a new Lectionary for the Mass was decreed by Bishop Anthony Pilla of Cleveland, president of the NCCB, as permissible for use as of the first Sunday of Advent, Nov. 29, 1998. The first new Lectionary since 1973, Volume One contains the readings for Sundays, solemnities and feasts of the Lord. Volume Two, containing the readings for weekdays, feasts of saints, and various other occasions, was given final approval on June 19, 1998, by the NCCB but still required confirmation by the Holy See.

Sacramentary (Missal): The Vatican Polyglot Press began distribution in June 1970, of the Latin text of a new Roman Missal, the first revision published in 400 years. The English translation was authorized for optional use beginning July 1, 1974; the mandatory date for use was Dec. 1, 1974.

The Sacramentary is the celebrant's Mass book of entrance songs, prayers, prefaces and Eucharistic prayers, including special common sets of texts for various commemorations and intentions — dedication of churches, Mary, the apostles, martyrs, doctors of the Church, virgins, holy men and women, the dead, other categories of holy persons, administration of certain sacraments, special intentions.

Study of the Mass: The Bishops' Committee on the Liturgy, following approval by the National Conference of Catholic Bishops in May 1979, began a study of the function and position of elements of the Mass, including the Gloria, the sign of peace, the penitential rite and the readings. Major phases of the study have been completed, and work is still under way toward completion of the project.

Mass for Special Groups: Reasons and norms for the celebration of Mass at special gatherings of the faithful were the subject of an instruction issued May 15, 1969. Two years earlier, the U.S. Bishops' Liturgy Committee went on record in support of the celebration of Mass in private homes under appropriate conditions.

Sunday Mass on Saturday: The Congregation for the Clergy, under date of Jan. 10, 1970, granted the request that the faithful, where bishops consider it pastorally necessary or useful, may satisfy the precept of participating in Mass in the late afternoon or evening hours of Saturdays and the days before holy days of obligation. This provision is stated in Canon 1248 of the Code of Canon Law.

Bination and Trination: Canon 905 of the Code of Canon Law provides that local ordinaries may permit priests to celebrate Mass twice a day (bination), for a just cause; in cases of pastoral need, they may permit priests to celebrate Mass three times a day (trination) on Sundays and holy days of obligation.

Mass in Latin: According to notices issued by the Congregation for Divine Worship June 1, 1971, and Oct. 28, 1974: (1) Bishops may permit the celebration of Mass in Latin for mixed-language groups. (2) Bishops may permit the celebration of one or two Masses in Latin on weekdays or Sundays in any church, irrespective of mixed-language groups involved (1971). (3) Priests may celebrate Mass in Latin when people are not present. (4) The approved revised Order of the Mass is to be used in Latin as well as vernacular languages. (5) By way of exception, bishops may permit older and handicapped priests to use the Council of Trent's Order of the Mass in private celebration of the holy Sacrifice. (See Permission for Tridentine Mass.)

Mass Obligation Waived: The Congregation for Bishops approved July 4, 1992, a resolution of the U.S. bishops to waive the Mass attendance obligation for the holy days of Mary, the Mother of God

(Jan. 1), the Assumption of Mary (Aug. 15) and All Saints (Nov. 1) when these solemnities fall on Saturday or Monday.

Inter-Ritual Concelebration: The Apostolic Delegation (now Nunciature) in Washington, D.C., announced in June 1971, that it had received authorization to permit priests of Roman and Eastern rites to celebrate Mass together in the rite of the host church. It was understood that the inter-ritual concelebrations would always be "a manifestation of the unity of the Church and of communion among particular churches."

Ordo of the Sung Mass: In a decree dated June 24 and made public Aug. 24, 1972, the Congregation for Divine Worship issued a new *Ordo of the Sung Mass* — containing Gregorian chants in Latin — to replace the *Graduale Romanum*.

Mass for Children: Late in 1973, the Congregation for Divine Worship issued special guidelines for children's Masses, providing accommodations to the mentality and spiritual growth of pre-adolescents while retaining the principal parts and structures of the Mass. The Directory for Masses with Children was approved by Paul VI Oct. 22 and was dated Nov. 1, 1973. Three Eucharistic prayers for Masses with children were approved by the congregation in 1974; English versions were approved June 5, 1975. Their use, authorized originally for a limited period of experimentation, was extended indefinitely Dec. 15, 1980.

Lectionary for Children: A lectionary for Masses with children, with an announced publication date of September 1993, was authorized for use by choice beginning Nov. 28, 1993.

Sacraments

The general use of English in administration of the sacraments was approved for the U.S. Sept. 14, 1964. Structural changes of the rites were subsequently made and introduced in the U.S. as follows.

Pastoral Care of the Sick: Revised rites, covering also administration of the Eucharist to sick persons, were approved Nov. 30, 1972, and published Jan. 18, 1973. The effective date for use of the provisional English prayer formula was Dec. 1, 1974. The mandatory effective date for use of the ritual, Pastoral Care of the Sick in English, was Nov. 27, 1983.

Baptism: New rites for the baptism of infants, approved Mar. 19, 1969, were introduced June 1, 1970.

Rite of Christian Initiation of Adults: Revised rites were issued Jan. 6, 1972, for the Christian initiation of adults — affecting preparation for and reception of baptism, the Eucharist and confirmation; also, for the reception of already baptized adults into full communion with the Church. These rites, which were introduced in the U.S. on the completion of English translation, nullified a seven-step baptismal process approved in 1962. On Mar. 8, 1988, the National Conference of Catholic Bishops was notified that the Congregation for Divine Worship had approved the final English translation of the Rite of Christian Initiation of Adults. The mandatory date for putting the rite into effect was Sept. 1, 1988.

Confirmation: Revised rites, issued Aug. 15, 1971, became mandatory in the U.S. Jan. 1, 1973. The use of a stole by persons being confirmed should be avoided, according to an item in the December 1984,

edition of the Newsletter of the Bishops' Committee on the Liturgy. The item said: "The distinction between the universal priesthood of all the baptized and the ministerial priesthood of the ordained is blurred when the distinctive garb (the stole) of ordained ministers is used in this manner."

A decree regarding the proper age for confirmation, approved by the U.S. bishops in June 1993, was ratified by the Congregation for Bishops Feb. 8, 1994. The decree reads: "In accord with prescriptions of canon 891, the National Conference of Catholic Bishops hereby decrees that the sacrament of confirmation in the Latin rite shall be conferred between the age of discretion, which is about the age of seven, and 18 years of age, within the limits determined by the diocesan bishop and with regard for the legitimate exceptions given in canon 891, namely, when there is danger of death or where, in the judgment of the minister, grave cause urges otherwise." The decree became effective July 1, 1994, and continued in effect until July 1, 1999.

Special Ministers of the Eucharist: The designation of lay men and women to serve as special ministers of the Eucharist was authorized by Paul VI in an "Instruction on Facilitating Communion in Particular Circumstances" (*Immensae Caritatis*), dated Jan. 29 and published by the Congregation for Divine Worship Mar. 29, 1973. Provisions concerning them are contained in Canons 230 and 910 of the Code of Canon Law.

Qualified lay persons may serve as special ministers for specific occasions or for extended periods in the absence of a sufficient number of priests and deacons to provide reasonable and appropriate service in the distribution of Holy Communion, during Mass and outside of Mass (to the sick and shut-ins). Appointments of ministers are made by priests with the approval of the appropriate bishop.

The Newsletter of the U.S. Bishops' Committee on the Liturgy stated in its February 1988, edition: "When ordinary ministers (bishops, priests, deacons) are present during a Eucharistic celebration, whether they are participating in it or not, and are not prevented from doing so, they are to assist in the distribution of Communion. Accordingly, if the ordinary ministers are in sufficient number, special ministers of the Eucharist are not allowed to distribute Communion at that Eucharistic celebration." Pope John Paul approved this decision and ordered it published June 15, 1987.

Holy Orders: Revised ordination rites for deacons, priests and bishops, validated by prior experimental use, were approved in 1970. The sacrament of holy orders underwent further revision in 1972 with the elimination of the Church-instituted orders of porter, reader, exorcist, acolyte and subdeacon, and of the tonsure ceremony symbolic of entrance into the clerical state. The former minor orders of reader and acolyte were changed from orders to ministries.

Matrimony: A revised rite for the celebration of marriage was promulgated by the Congregation for Divine Worship and the Discipline of the Sacraments Mar. 19, 1969, and went into effect June 1, 1970. A second typical edition of the order of celebration, with revisions in accord with provisions of the Code of Canon Law promulgated in 1983, was approved and published in 1990 (*Notitiae*, Vol. 26, No.6). The date for implementation was reported to be dependent on the completion of required translations and appropriate formalities.

Penance: Ritual revision of the sacraments was completed with the approval by Paul VI Dec. 2, 1973, of new directives for the sacrament of penance or reconciliation. The U.S. Bishops' Committee on the Liturgy set Feb. 27, 1977, as the mandatory date for use of the new rite. The committee also declared that it could be used from Mar. 7, 1976, after adequate preparation of priests and people. Earlier, authorization was given by the Holy See in 1968 for the omission of any reference to excommunication or other censures in the formula of absolution unless there was some indication that a censure had actually been incurred by a penitent.

Additional Developments

Music: An instruction on Music in the Liturgy, dated Mar. 5 and effective May 14, 1967, encouraged congregational singing during liturgical celebrations and attempted to clarify the role of choirs and trained singers. More significantly, the instruction indicated that a major development under way in the liturgy was a gradual erasure of the distinctive lines traditionally drawn between the sung liturgy and the spoken liturgy, between what had been called the high Mass and the low Mass.

In the same year, the U.S. Bishops' Liturgy Committee approved the use of contemporary music, as well as guitars and other suitable instruments, in the liturgy. The Holy See authorized in 1968 the use of musical instruments other than the organ in liturgical services, "provided they are played in a manner suitable to worship."

Calendar: A revised liturgical calendar approved by Paul VI Feb. 14 and made public May 9, 1969, went into effect in the U.S. in 1972. Since that time, memorials and feasts of beatified persons and saints have been added.

Communion in Hand: Since 1969, the Holy See has approved the practice of in-hand reception of the Eucharist in regions and countries where it had the approval of the appropriate episcopal conferences. The first grant of approval was to Belgium, in May 1969. Approval was granted the United States in June 1977.

Liturgy of the Hours: The background, contents, scope and purposes of the revised Divine Office, called the Liturgy of the Hours, were described by Paul VI in the apostolic constitution *Laudis Canticum*, dated Nov. 1, 1970. A provisional English version, incorporating basic features of the master Latin text, was published in 1971. The four complete volumes of the Hours in English have been published since May 1975. One-volume, partial editions have also been published in approved form. Nov. 27, 1977, was set by the Congregation for Divine Worship and the National Conference of Catholic Bishops as the effective date for exclusive use in liturgical worship of the translation of the Latin text of the Liturgy of the Hours approved by the International Committee on English in the Liturgy.

Holy Week: The English version of revised Holy Week rites went into effect in 1971. They introduced concelebration of Mass, placed new emphasis on commemorating the institution of the priesthood on Holy Thursday and modified Good Friday prayers for other Christians, Jews and other non-Christians.

In another action, the Congregation for Divine Worship released Feb. 20, 1988, a "Circular Letter concerning the Preparation and Celebration of the Easter Feasts." It called the feasts the "summit of the whole liturgical year," and criticized practices which dilute or change appropriate norms for their celebration. Singled out for blame for the abuse or ignorance of norms was the "inadequate formation given to the clergy and the faithful regarding the paschal mystery as the center of the liturgical year and of Christian life." The document set out the appropriate norms for the Lenten season, Holy Week, the Easter Triduum, Easter and the weeks following. It was particularly insistent on the proper celebration of the Easter Vigil, to take place after nightfall on Saturday and before dawn on Sunday.

Oils: The Congregation for Divine Worship issued a directive in 1971 permitting the use of other oils — from plants, seeds or coconuts — instead of the traditional olive oil in administering some of the sacraments. The directive also provided that oils could be blessed at other times than at the usual Mass of Chrism on Holy Thursday, and authorized bishops' conferences to permit priests to bless oils in cases of necessity.

Dancing and Worship: Dancing and worship was the subject of an essay which appeared in a 1975 edition of *Notitiae* (11, pp. 202-205), the official journal of the Congregation for the Sacraments and Divine Worship. The article was called a "qualified and authoritative sketch," and should be considered "an authoritative point of reference for every discussion of the matter."

The principal points of the essay were:

• "The dance has never been made an integral part of the official worship of the Latin Church."

• "If the proposal of the religious dance in the West is really to be made welcome, care will have to be taken that in its regard a place be found outside of the liturgy, in assembly areas which are not strictly liturgical. Moreover, the priests must always be excluded from the dance."

Mass for Deceased Non-Catholic Christians: The Congregation for the Doctrine of the Faith released a decree June 11, 1976, authorizing the celebration of public Mass for deceased non-Catholic Christians under certain conditions: "(1) The public celebration of the Masses must be explicitly requested by the relatives, friends, or subjects of the deceased person for a genuine religious motive. (2) In the Ordinary's judgment, there must be no scandal for the faithful."

Environment and Art in Catholic Worship: A booklet with this title was issued by the U.S. Bishops' Committee on the Liturgy in March 1978. Work is under way on a new edition.

Doxology: The bishops' committee called attention in August 1978, to the directive that the Doxology concluding the Eucharistic Prayer is said or sung by the celebrant (concelebrants) alone, to which the people respond, "Amen."

Churches, Altars, Chalices: The Newsletter of the U.S. Bishops' Committee on the Liturgy reported in November 1978, that the Congregation for Divine Worship had given provisional approval of a new English translation for the rite of dedicating churches and altars, and of a new form for the blessing of chalices.

Eucharistic Worship: This was the subject of two documents issued in 1980. *Dominicae Coenae* was a letter addressed by Pope John Paul to bishops throughout the world in connection with the celebration of Holy Thursday; it was dated Feb. 24 and released Mar.18. It was more doctrinal in content than the "Instruction on Certain Norms concerning Worship of the Eucharistic Mystery" (*Inaestimabile Donum*, "The Priceless Gift"), which was approved by the Pope Apr. 17 and published by the Congregation for the Sacraments and Divine Worship May 23. Its stated purpose was to reaffirm and clarify teaching on liturgical renewal contained in enactments of the Second Vatican Council and in several related implementing documents.

Tridentine Mass: The celebration of Mass according to the 1962 typical (master) edition of the Roman Missal — the so-called Tridentine Mass — was authorized by Pope John Paul under certain conditions. So stated a letter from the Congregation for Divine Worship, dated Oct. 3, 1984. The letter said the Pope wished to be responsive to priests and faithful who remained attached to the so-called Tridentine rite. The principal condition for the celebration was: "There must be unequivocal, even public, evidence that the priest and people petitioning have no ties with those who impugn the lawfulness and doctrinal soundness of the Roman Missal promulgated in 1970 by Pope Paul VI." (This, in particular, with reference to the followers of dissident Archbishop Marcel Lefebvre.)

Six guidelines for celebration of the Tridentine Mass were contained in the letter regarding its "wide and generous" use, for two purposes: to win back Lefebvre followers and to clear up misunderstandings about liberal permission for use of the Tridentine rite. The letter, from the Pontifical Commission *Ecclesia Dei*, said in part:

• The Tridentine Mass can be celebrated in a parish church, so long as it provides a pastoral service and is harmoniously integrated into the parish liturgical schedule.

• When requested, the Mass should be offered on a regular Sunday and holyday basis, "at a central location, at a convenient time" for a trial period of several months, with "adjustment" later if needed.

• Celebrants of the Mass should make it clear that they acknowledge the validity of the postconciliar liturgy.

• Although the commission has the authority to grant use of the Tridentine rite to all groups that request it, the commission "would much prefer that such faculties be granted by the Ordinary himself so that ecclesial communion can be strengthened."

• While the new Lectionary in the vernacular can be used in the Tridentine Mass, as suggested by the Second Vatican Council, it should not be "imposed on congregations that decidedly wish to maintain the former liturgical tradition in its integrity."

• Older and retired priests who have asked permission to celebrate Mass according to the Tridentine rite should be given the chance to do so for groups that request it.

Spanish: In accord with decrees of the Congregation for Divine Worship, Spanish was approved as a liturgical language in the U.S. (Jan. 19, 1985). The *texto unico* of the Ordinary of the Mass became mandatory in the U.S. Dec. 3, 1989. Spanish translations of Proper-of-the-Mass texts proper to U.S. dioceses were approved Mar. 12, 1990. An approved Spanish version of the Rite for the Christian Initiation of Adults was published in 1991. The Institute of Hispanic Liturgy opened its national office June 1, 1995, on the campus of the Catholic University of America in Washington.

Funeral Rites: A revised Order of Christian Funerals became mandatory in the U.S. Nov. 2, 1989.

Permission for the presence of cremated human remains in the funeral liturgy, including the Eucharist, was granted in 1997 to local bishops in the U.S. by the Congregation for Divine Worship and the Discipline of the Sacraments. Adaptations to existing rites are under study.

Popular Piety and Liturgy: The relation of popular piety to the liturgy was the subject of remarks by Pope John Paul II at a meeting with a group of Italian bishops Apr. 24, 1986. He said, in part:

"An authentic liturgical ministry will never be able to neglect the riches of popular piety, the values proper to the culture of a people, so that such riches might be illuminated, purified and introduced into the liturgy as an offering of the people."

Extended Eucharistic Exposition: In response to queries, the Secretariat of the U.S. Bishops' Committee on the Liturgy issued an advisory stating that liturgical law permits and encourages in parish churches:

• a. exposition of the Blessed Sacrament for an extended period of time once a year, with consent of the local Ordinary and only if suitable numbers of the faithful are expected to be present;

• b. exposition ordered by the local Ordinary, for a grave and general necessity, for a more extended period of supplication when the faithful assemble in large numbers.

With regard to perpetual exposition, this form is generally permitted only in the case of those religious communities of men or women who have the general practice of perpetual Eucharistic adoration or adoration over extended periods of time.

The Secretariat's advisory appeared in the June-July 1986, edition of the Newsletter of the Bishops' Committee on the Liturgy.

Native American Languages: The Newsletter of the U.S. Bishops' Committee on the Liturgy reported in December 1986, and May 1987, respectively, that the Congregation for Divine Worship had authorized Mass translations in Navajo and Choctaw. Lakota was approved as a liturgical language in 1989.

Communion Guidelines: In 1986 and again in 1996, the U.S. bishops' approved the insertion of advisories in missalettes and similar publications, stating that: (1) The Eucharist is to be received by Catholics only, except in certain specific cases. (2) To receive Communion worthily, a person must be in the state of grace (i.e., free of serious sin) and observe the eucharistic fast (See separate entry).

Unauthorized Eucharistic Prayers: The May 1987, Newsletter of the U.S. Bishops' Committee on the Liturgy restated the standing prohibition against the use of any Eucharistic Prayers other than those contained in the Sacramentary. Specifically, the article referred to the 25 unauthorized prayers in a volume entitled Spoken Visions.

Homilist: According to the Pontifical Commission for the Authentic Interpretation of Canon Law, the diocesan bishop cannot dispense from the requirement of Canon 767, par. 1, that the homily in the liturgy be reserved to a priest or deacon. Pope John Paul approved this decision June 20, 1987.

Concerts in Churches: In a letter released Dec. 5, 1987, the Congregation for Divine Worship declared that churches might be used on a limited basis for concerts of sacred or religious music, but not for concerts featuring secular music.

Blessings: A revised Book of Blessings was ordered into use beginning Dec. 3, 1989.

Litany of the Blessed Virgin Mary: "Queen of Families," a new invocation was reported by the U.S. bishops in 1996, for insertion between "Queen of the Rosary" and "Queen of Peace."

Inclusive Language: "Criteria for the Evaluation of Inclusive Language Translations of Scriptural Texts Proposed for Liturgical Use" was issued by the U.S. bishops in November 1990. The criteria distinguish between non-use of vertical inclusiveness in references to God and use of horizontal, gender-inclusive terms (he/she, man/woman and the like) where appropriate in references to persons.

POPE JOHN PAUL II ON LITURGICAL RENEWAL

(Courtesy, L'Osservatore Romano.) On Sept. 10, 1998, Pope John Paul received the bishops of the Northwestern United States during their ad limina visit to Rome. He used the occasion to address the bishops about the current state of liturgical renewal in the Church. Following are the opening remarks from his address:

The 2000th anniversary of the Birth of the Savior is a call to all Christ's followers to seek a genuine conversion to God and a great advance in holiness. Since the liturgy is such a central part of the Christian life, I wish today to consider some aspects of the liturgical renewal so vigorously promoted by the Second Vatican Council as the prime agent of the wider renewal of Catholic life.

To look back over what has been done in the field of liturgical renewal in the years since the Council is, first, to see many reasons for giving heartfelt thanks and praise to the Most Holy Trinity for the marvelous awareness which has developed among the faithful of their role and responsibility in this priestly work of Christ and his Church. It is also to realize that not all changes have always and everywhere been accompanied by the necessary explanation and catechesis; as a result, in some cases there has been a misunderstanding of the very nature of the liturgy, leading to abuses, polarization, and sometimes even grave scandal. After the experience of more than thirty years of liturgical renewal, we are well placed to assess both the strengths and weaknesses of what has been done, in order more confidently to plot our course into the future which God has in mind for his cherished People.

The challenge now is to move beyond whatever misunderstandings there have been and to reach the proper point of balance, especially by entering more deeply into the contemplative dimension of worship, which includes the sense of awe, reverence and adoration which are fundamental attitudes in our relationship with God. This will happen only if we recognize that the liturgy has dimensions *both* local *and* universal, time-bound *and* eternal, horizontal *and* vertical, subjective *and* objective. It is precisely these tensions which give to Catholic worship its distinctive character. The universal Church is united in the one great act of praise; but it is always the worship of a particular community in a particular culture. It is the eternal worship of Heaven, but it is also steeped in time. It gathers and builds a human community,

but it is also "the worship of the divine majesty" (*Sacrosanctum Concilium,* 33). It is subjective in that it depends radically upon what the worshippers bring to it; but it is objective in that it transcends them as the priestly act of Christ himself, to which he associates us but which ultimately does not depend upon us (*ibid.,* 7). This is why it is so important that liturgical law be respected. The priest, who is the servant of the liturgy, not its inventor or producer, has a particular responsibility in this regard, lest he empty liturgy of its true meaning or obscure its sacred character. The core of the mystery of Christian worship is the sacrifice of Christ offered to the Father and the work of the Risen Christ who sanctifies his People through the liturgical signs. It is therefore essential that in seeking to enter more deeply into the contemplative depths of worship the inexhaustible mystery of the priesthood of Jesus Christ be fully acknowledged and respected. While all the baptized share in that one priesthood of Christ, not all share in it in the same manner. The ministerial priesthood, rooted in Apostolic Succession, confers on the ordained priest faculties and responsibilities which are different from those of the laity but which are at the service of the common priesthood and are directed at the unfolding of the baptismal grace of all Christians (cf. *Catechism of the Catholic Church,* No. 1547). The priest therefore is not just one who presides, but one who acts in the person of Christ.

Only by being radically faithful to this doctrinal foundation can we avoid one-dimensional and unilateral interpretations of the Council's teaching. The sharing of all the baptized in the one priesthood of Jesus Christ is the key to understanding the Council's call for "full, conscious and active participation" in the liturgy (*Sacrosanctum Concilium,* 14). Full participation certainly means that every member of the community has a part to play in the liturgy; and in this respect a great deal has been achieved in parishes and communities across your land. But full participation does not mean that everyone does everything, since this would lead to a *clericalizing* of the laity and a *laicizing* of the priesthood; and this was not what the Council had in mind. The liturgy, like the Church, is intended to be hierarchical and polyphonic, respecting the different roles assigned by Christ and allowing all the different voices to blend in one great hymn of praise.

The sacraments are actions of Christ and his Church (itself a kind of sacrament) which signify grace, cause it in the act of signifying it, and confer it upon persons properly disposed to receive it. They perpetuate the redemptive activity of Christ, making it present and effective. They infallibly communicate the fruit of that activity — namely grace — to responsive persons with faith. Sacramental actions consist of the union of sensible signs (matter of the sacraments) with the words of the minister (form of the sacraments).

Christ himself instituted the seven sacraments of the New Law by determining their essence and the efficacy of their signs to produce the grace they signify.

Christ is the principal priest or minister of every sacrament; human agents — an ordained priest, baptized persons contracting marriage with each other, any person conferring emergency baptism in a proper manner — are secondary ministers. Sacraments have efficacy from Christ, not from the personal dispositions of their human ministers.

Each sacrament confers sanctifying grace for the special purpose of the sacrament; this is, accordingly, called sacramental grace. It involves a right to actual graces corresponding to the purposes of the respective sacraments.

Baptism, confirmation and the Eucharist are sacraments of initiation; penance (reconciliation) and anointing of the sick, sacraments of healing; order and matrimony, sacraments for service.

While sacraments infallibly produce the grace they signify, recipients benefit from them in proportion to their personal dispositions. One of these is the intention to receive sacraments as sacred signs of God's saving and grace-giving action. The state of grace is also necessary for fruitful reception of the Holy Eucharist, confirmation, matrimony, holy orders and anointing of the sick. Baptism is the sacrament in which grace is given in the first instance and original sin is remitted. Penance is the secondary sacrament of reconciliation, in which persons guilty of serious sin after baptism are reconciled with God and the Church, and in which persons already in the state of grace are strengthened in that state.

Role of Sacraments

The Second Vatican Council prefaced a description of the role of the sacraments with the following statement concerning participation by all the faithful in the priesthood of Christ and the exercise of that priesthood by receiving the sacraments (Dogmatic Constitution on the Church, *Lumen Gentium*, Nos. 10 and 11).

"The baptized by regeneration and the anointing of the Holy Spirit are consecrated into a spiritual house and a holy priesthood. Thus through all those works befitting Christian men they can offer spiritual sacrifice and proclaim the power of him who has called them out of darkness into his marvelous light (cf. 1 Pt. 2:4-10)."

"Though they differ from one another in essence and not only in degree, the common priesthood of the faithful and the ministerial or hierarchical priesthood (of those ordained to holy orders) are nonetheless interrelated. Each of them in its own special way is a participation in the one priesthood of Christ. The ministerial priest, by the sacred power he enjoys, molds and rules the priestly people. Acting in the

THE SACRAMENTS OF THE CHURCH

Person of Christ, he brings about the Eucharistic Sacrifice, and offers it to God in the name of all the people. For their part, the faithful join in the offering of the Eucharist by virtue of their royal priesthood. They likewise exercise that priesthood by receiving the sacraments, by prayer and thanksgiving, by the witness of a holy life, and by self-denial and active charity."

"It is through the sacraments and the exercise of the virtues that the sacred nature and organic structure of the priestly community is brought into operation."

Baptism: "Incorporated into the Church through baptism, the faithful are consecrated by the baptismal character to the exercise of the cult of the Christian religion. Reborn as sons of God, they must confess before men the faith which they have received from God through the Church."

Confirmation: "Bound more intimately to the Church by the sacrament of confirmation, they are endowed by the Holy Spirit with special strength. Hence they are more strictly obliged to spread and defend the faith both by word and by deed as true witnesses of Christ.

Eucharist: "Taking part in the Eucharistic Sacrifice, which is the fount and apex of the whole Christian life, they offer the divine Victim to God, and offer themselves along with It. Thus, both by the act of oblation and through holy Communion, all perform their proper part in this liturgical service, not, indeed, all in the same way but each in that way which is appropriate to himself. Strengthened anew at the holy table by the Body of Christ, they manifest in a practical way that unity of God's People which is suitably signified and wondrously brought about by this most awesome sacrament."

Penance: "Those who approach the sacrament of penance obtain pardon from the mercy of God for offenses committed against him. They are at the same time reconciled with the Church, which they have wounded by their sins, and which by charity, example, and prayer seeks their conversion."

Anointing of the Sick: "By the sacred anointing of the sick and the prayer of her priests, the whole Church commends those who are ill to the suffering and glorified Lord, asking that he may lighten their suffering and save them (cf. Jas. 5:14-16). She exhorts them, moreover, to contribute to the welfare of the whole People of God by associating themselves freely with the passion and death of Christ (cf. Rom. 8:17; Col. 1:24; 2 Tm. 2:11-12; 1 Pt. 4:13)."

Holy Orders: "Those of the faithful who are consecrated by holy orders are appointed to feed the Church in Christ's name with the Word and the grace of God."

Matrimony: "Christian spouses, in virtue of the sacrament of matrimony, signify and partake of the mystery of that unity and fruitful love which exists between Christ and his Church (cf. Eph. 5:32). The spouses thereby help each other to attain to holiness in their married life and by the rearing and education of their children. And so, in their state and way of life, they have their own special gift among the People of God (cf. 1 Cor. 7:7).

"For from the wedlock of Christians there comes the family, in which new citizens of human society are born. By the grace of the Holy Spirit received in baptism these are made children of God, thus perpetuating the People of God through the centuries. The family is, so to speak, the domestic Church. In it parents should, by their word and example, be the first preachers of the faith to their children. They should encourage them in the vocation which is proper to each of them, fostering with special care any religious vocation."

"Fortified by so many and such powerful means of salvation, all the faithful, whatever their condition or state, are called by the Lord, each in his own way, to that perfect holiness whereby the Father himself is perfect."

Baptism

Baptism is the sacrament of spiritual regeneration by which a person is incorporated in Christ and made a member of his Mystical Body, given grace, and cleansed of original sin. Actual sins and the punishment due for them are remitted also if the person baptized was guilty of such sins (e.g., in the case of a person baptized after reaching the age of reason). The theological virtues of faith, hope and charity are given with grace. The sacrament confers a character on the soul and can be received only once.

The matter is the pouring of water. The form is: "I baptize you in the name of the Father and of the Son and of the Holy Spirit."

The minister of solemn baptism is a bishop, priest or deacon, but in case of emergency anyone, including a non-Catholic, can validly baptize. The minister pours water on the forehead of the person being baptized and says the words of the form while the water is flowing. The water used in solemn baptism is blessed during the rite.

Baptism is conferred in the Roman rite by immersion or infusion (pouring of water), depending on the directive of the appropriate conference of bishops, according to the Code of Canon Law. The Church recognizes as valid baptisms properly performed by non-Catholic ministers. The baptism of infants has always been considered valid and the general practice of infant baptism was well established by the fifth century. Baptism is conferred conditionally when there is doubt about the validity of a previous baptism.

Baptism is necessary for salvation. If a person cannot receive the baptism of water described above, this can be supplied by baptism of blood (martyrdom suffered for the Catholic faith or some Christian virtue) or by baptism of desire (perfect contrition joined with at least the implicit intention of doing whatever God wills that people should do for salvation).

A sponsor is required for the person being baptized. (See Godparents, below).

A person must be validly baptized before he or she can receive any of the other sacraments.

Christian Initiation of Infants: Infants should be solemnly baptized as soon after birth as conveniently possible. In danger of death, anyone may baptize an infant. If the child survives, the ceremonies of solemn baptism should be supplied.

The sacrament is ordinarily conferred by a priest or deacon of the parents' parish.

Catholics 16 years of age and over who have received the sacraments of confirmation and the Eucharist and are practicing their faith are eligible to be sponsors or godparents. Only one is required. Two, one of each sex, are permitted. A non-Catholic Christian cannot be a godparent for a Catholic child, but may serve as a witness to the baptism. A Catholic may not be a godparent for a child baptized in a non-Catholic religion, but may be a witness.

"Because of the close communion between the Catholic Church and the Eastern Orthodox churches," states the 1993 Directory on Ecumenism, "it is permissible for a just cause for an Eastern faithful to act as godparent together with a Catholic godparent at the baptism of a Catholic infant or adult, so long as there is provision for the Catholic education of the person being baptized and it is clear that the godparent is a suitable one.

"A Catholic is not forbidden to stand as godparent in an Eastern Orthodox Church if he/she is so invited. In this case, the duty of providing for the Christian education binds in the first place the godparent who belongs to the church in which the child is baptized."

The role of godparents in baptismal ceremonies is secondary to the role of the parents. They serve as representatives of the community of faith and with the parents request baptism for the child and perform other ritual functions. Their function after baptism is to serve as proxies for the parents if the parents should be unable or fail to provide for the religious training of the child.

At baptism every child should be given a name with Christian significance, usually the name of a saint, to symbolize newness of life in Christ.

Christian Initiation of Adults: According to the *Ordo Initiationis Christianae Adultorum* ("Rite of the Christian Initiation of Adults") issued by the Congregation for Divine Worship under date of Jan. 6, 1972, and put into effect in revised form Sept. 1, 1988, adults are prepared for baptism and reception into the Church in several stages:

• An initial period of inquiry, instruction and evangelization.

• The catechumenate, a period of at least a year of formal instruction and progressive formation in and familiarity with Christian life. It starts with a statement of purpose and includes a rite of election.

• Immediate preparation, called a period of purification and enlightenment, from the beginning of Lent to reception of the sacraments of initiation — baptism, confirmation, Holy Eucharist — during ceremonies of the Easter Vigil. The period is marked by scrutinies, formal giving of the creed and the Lord's Prayer, the choice of a Christian name, and a final statement of intention.

• A mystagogic phase whose objective is greater familiarity with Christian life in the Church through observances of the Easter season and association with the community of the faithful, and through extended formation for about a year.

National Statutes for the Catechumenate were approved by the National Conference of Catholic Bishops Nov. 11, 1986, and were subsequently ratified by the Vatican.

The priest who baptizes a catechumen can also administer the sacrament of confirmation.

A sponsor is required for the person being baptized.

The *Ordo* also provides a simple rite of initiation for adults in danger of death and for cases in which all stages of the initiation process are not necessary, and guidelines for: (1) the preparation of adults for

the sacraments of confirmation and Holy Eucharist in cases where they have been baptized but have not received further formation in the Christian life; (2) for the formation and initiation of children of catechetical age.

The Church recognizes the right of anyone over the age of seven to request baptism and to receive the sacrament after completing a course of instruction and giving evidence of good will. Practically, in the case of minors in a non-Catholic family or environment, the Church accepts them when other circumstances favor their ability to practice the faith — e.g., well-disposed family situation, the presence of another or several Catholics in the family. Those who are not in such favorable circumstances are prudently advised to defer reception of the sacrament until they attain the maturity necessary for independent practice of the faith.

Reception of Baptized Christians: Procedure for the reception of already baptized Christians into full communion with the Catholic Church is distinguished from the catechumenate, since they have received some Christian formation. Instruction and formation are provided as necessary, however; and conditional baptism is administered if there is reasonable doubt about the validity of the person's previous baptism.

In the rite of reception, the person is invited to join the community of the Church in professing the Nicene Creed and is asked to state: "I believe and profess all that the holy Catholic Church believes, teaches, and proclaims as revealed by God." The priest places his hand on the head of the person, states the formula of admission to full communion, confirms (in the absence of a bishop), gives a sign of peace, and administers Holy Communion during a Eucharistic Liturgy.

Confirmation

Confirmation is the sacrament by which a baptized person, through anointing with chrism and the imposition of hands, is endowed with the fullness of baptismal grace; is united more intimately to the Church; is enriched with the special power of the Holy Spirit; is committed to be an authentic witness to Christ in word and action. The sacrament confers a character on the soul and can be received only once.

According to the apostolic constitution *Divinae Consortium Naturae* dated Aug. 15, 1971, in conjunction with the *Ordo Confirmationis* ("Rite of Confirmation"): "The sacrament of confirmation is conferred through the anointing with chrism on the forehead, which is done by the imposition of the hand (matter of the sacrament), and through the words: '*N, receive the seal of the Holy Spirit, the Gift of the Father*'" (form of the sacrament). On May 5, 1975, bishops' conferences in English-speaking countries were informed by the Congregation for Divine Worship that Pope Paul had approved this English version of the form of the sacrament: "*Be sealed with the gift of the Holy Spirit.*"

The ordinary minister of confirmation in the Roman rite is a bishop. Priests may be delegated for the purpose. A pastor can confirm a parishioner in danger of death, and a priest can confirm in ceremonies of Christian initiation and at the reception of a baptized Christian into union with the Church.

Ideally, the sacrament is conferred during the Eucharistic Liturgy. Elements of the rite include renewal of the promises of baptism, which confirmation ratifies and completes, and the laying on of hands by the confirming bishop and priests participating in the ceremony.

"The entire rite," according to the *Ordo*; "has a twofold meaning. The laying of hands upon the candidates, done by the bishop and the concelebrating priests, expresses the biblical gesture by which the gift of the Holy Spirit is invoked. The anointing with chrism and the accompanying words clearly signify the effect of the Holy Spirit. Signed with the perfumed oil by the bishop's hand, the baptized person receives the indelible character, the seal of the Lord, together with the Spirit who is given and who conforms the person more perfectly to Christ and gives him the grace of spreading the Lord's presence among men."

A sponsor is required for the person being confirmed. Eligible is any Catholic 16 years of age or older who has received the sacraments of confirmation and the Eucharist and is practicing the faith. The baptismal sponsor, preferably, can also be the sponsor for confirmation. Parents may present their children for confirmation but cannot be sponsors.

In the Roman rite, it has been customary for children to receive confirmation within a reasonable time after first Communion and confession. There is a trend, however, to defer confirmation until later when its significance for mature Christian living becomes more evident. In the Eastern rites, confirmation is administered at the same time as baptism.

Eucharist

The Holy Eucharist is a sacrifice (see The Mass) and the sacrament in which Christ is present and is received under the appearances of bread and wine.

The matter is bread of wheat, unleavened in the Roman rite and leavened in the Eastern rites, and wine of grape. The form consists of the words of consecration said by the priest at Mass: "This is my body. This is the cup of my blood" (according to the traditional usage of the Roman rite).

Only a priest can consecrate bread and wine so they become the body and blood of Christ. After consecration, however, the Eucharist can be administered by deacons and, for various reasons, by religious and lay persons.

Priests celebrating Mass receive the Eucharist under the species of bread and wine. In the Roman rite, others receive under the species of bread only, i.e., the consecrated host, or in some circumstances they may receive under the species of both bread and wine. In Eastern-rite practice, the faithful generally receive a piece of consecrated leavened bread which has been dipped into consecrated wine (i.e., by intinction).

Conditions for receiving the Eucharist, commonly called Holy Communion, are the state of grace, the right intention and observance of the Eucharistic fast.

The faithful of Roman rite are required by a precept of the Church to receive the Eucharist at least once a year, ordinarily during the Easter time.

(See Eucharistic Fast, Mass, Transubstantiation, Viaticum.)

First Communion and Confession: Children are to be prepared for and given opportunity for receiving both sacraments (Eucharist and reconciliation, or penance) on reaching the age of discretion, at which time they become subject to general norms concerning confession and Communion. This, together with a stated preference for first confession before first Communion, was the central theme of a document entitled *Sanctus Pontifex* and published May 24, 1973, by the Congregation for the Discipline of the Sacraments and the Congregation for the Clergy, with the approval of Pope Paul VI.

What the document prescribed was the observance of practices ordered by St. Pius X in the decree *Quam Singulari* of Aug. 8, 1910. Its purpose was to counteract pastoral and catechetical experiments virtually denying children the opportunity of receiving both sacraments at the same time. Termination of such experiments was ordered by the end of the 1972-73 school year.

At the time the document was issued, two- or three-year experiments of this kind — routinely deferring reception of the sacrament of penance until after the first reception of Holy Communion — were in effect in more than half of the dioceses of the U.S. They have remained in effect in many places, despite the advisory from the Vatican.

One reason stated in support of such experiments is the view that children are not capable of serious sin at the age of seven or eight, when Communion is generally received for the first time, and therefore prior reception of the sacrament of penance is not necessary. Another reason is the purpose of making the distinctive nature of the two sacraments clearer to children.

The Vatican view reflected convictions that the principle and practice of devotional reception of penance are as valid for children as they are for adults, and that sound catechetical programs can avoid misconceptions about the two sacraments.

A second letter on the same subject and in the same vein was released May 19, 1977, by the aforementioned congregations. It was issued in response to the question:

" 'Whether it is allowed after the declaration of May 24, 1973, to continue to have, as a general rule, the reception of first Communion precede the reception of the sacrament of penance in those parishes in which this practice developed in the past few years.'

"The Sacred Congregations for the Sacraments and Divine Worship and for the Clergy, with the approval of the Supreme Pontiff, reply: Negative, and according to the mind of the declaration.

"The mind of the declaration is that one year after the promulgation of the same declaration, all experiments of receiving first Communion without the sacrament of penance should cease so that the discipline of the Church might be restored, in the spirit of the decree, *Quam Singulari*."

The two letters from the Vatican congregations have not produced uniformity of practice in this country. Simultaneous preparation for both sacraments is provided in some dioceses where a child has the option of receiving either sacrament first, with the counsel of parents, priests and teachers. Programs in other dioceses are geared first to reception of Communion and later to reception of the sacrament of reconciliation.

Commentators on the letters note that: they are disciplinary rather than doctrinal in content; they are subject to pastoral interpretation by bishops; they cannot be interpreted to mean that a person who is not guilty of serious sin must be required to receive the sacrament of penance before (even first) Communion.

Canon 914 of the Code of Canon Law states that sacramental confession should precede first Communion.

Holy Communion under the Forms of Bread and Wine (by separate taking of the consecrated bread and wine or by intinction, the reception of the host dipped in the wine): Such reception is permitted under conditions stated in instructions issued by the Congregation for Divine Worship (May 25, 1967; June 29, 1970), the General Instruction on the Roman Missal (No. 242), and directives of bishops' conferences and individual bishops.

Accordingly, Communion can be administered in this way to: persons being baptized, received into communion with the Church, confirmed, receiving anointing of the sick; couples at their wedding or jubilee; religious at profession or renewal of profession; lay persons receiving an ecclesiastical assignment (e.g., lay missionaries); participants at concelebrated Masses, retreats, pastoral commission meetings, daily Masses and, in the U.S., Masses on Sundays and holy days of obligation.

A communicant has the option of receiving the Eucharist under the form of bread alone or under the forms of bread and wine.

Holy Communion More Than Once a Day: A person who has already received the Eucharist may receive it (only) once again on the same day only during a Eucharistic celebration in which the person participates. A person in danger of death who has already received the Eucharist once or twice is urged to receive Communion again as Viaticum. Pope John Paul approved this decision, in accord with Canon 917, and ordered it published July 11, 1984.

Holy Communion and Eucharistic Devotion outside of Mass: These were the subjects of an instruction (*De Sacra Communione et de Cultu Mysterii Eucharistici extra Missam*) dated June 21 and made public Oct. 18, 1973, by the Congregation for Divine Worship.

Holy Communion can be given outside of Mass to persons unable for a reasonable cause to receive it during Mass on a given day. The ceremonial rite is modeled on the structure of the Mass, consisting of a penitential act, a scriptural reading, the Lord's Prayer, a sign or gesture of peace, giving of the Eucharist, prayer and final blessing. Viaticum and Communion to the sick can be given by extraordinary ministers (authorized lay persons) with appropriate rites.

Forms of devotion outside of Mass are exposition of the Blessed Sacrament (by men or women religious, especially, or lay persons in the absence of a priest; but only a priest can give the blessing), processions and congresses with appropriate rites.

Intercommunion: Church policy on intercommunion was stated in an "Instruction on the Admission of Other Christians to the Eucharist," dated June 1 and made public July 8, 1972, against the background of the Decree on Ecumenism approved by the Second Vatican Council, and the Directory on Ecumenism issued by the Secretariat for Promoting Christian Unity in 1967, 1970 and 1993.

Basic principles related to intercommunion are:
• "There is an indissoluble link between the mystery of the Church and the mystery of the Eucharist, or between ecclesial and Eucharistic communion; the celebration of the Eucharist of itself signifies the fullness of profession of faith and ecclesial communion" (1972 Instruction).

• "Eucharistic communion practiced by those who are not in full ecclesial communion with each other cannot be the expression of that full unity which the Eucharist of its nature signifies and which in this case does not exist; for this reason such communion cannot be regarded as a means to be used to lead to full ecclesial communion" (1972 Instruction).

• The question of reciprocity "arises only with those churches which have preserved the substance of the Eucharist, the sacrament of orders and apostolic succession" (1967 Directory).

• "A Catholic cannot ask for the Eucharist except from a minister who has been validly ordained" (1967 Directory).

The policy distinguishes between separated Eastern Christians and other Christians.

With Separated Eastern Christians (e.g., Orthodox): These may be given the Eucharist (as well as penance and anointing of the sick) at their request. Catholics may receive these same sacraments from priests of separated Eastern churches if they experience genuine spiritual necessity, seek spiritual benefit, and access to a Catholic priest is morally or physically impossible. This policy (of reciprocity) derives from the facts that the separated Eastern churches have apostolic succession through their bishops, valid priests, and sacramental beliefs and practices in accord with those of the Catholic Church.

With Other Christians (e.g., members of Reformation-related churches, others): Admission to the Eucharist in the Catholic Church, according to the Directory on Ecumenism, "is confined to particular cases of those Christians who have a faith in the sacrament in conformity with that of the Church, who experience a serious spiritual need for the Eucharistic sustenance, who for a prolonged period are unable to have recourse to a minister of their own community and who ask for the sacrament of their own accord; all this provided that they have proper dispositions and lead lives worthy of a Christian." The spiritual need is defined as "a need for an increase in spiritual life and a need for a deeper involvement in the mystery of the Church and its unity."

Circumstances under which Communion may be given to other properly disposed Christians are danger of death, imprisonment, persecution, grave spiritual necessity coupled with no chance of recourse to a minister of their own community.

Catholics cannot ask for the Eucharist from ministers of other Christian churches who have not been validly ordained to the priesthood.

Penance

Penance is the sacrament by which sins committed after baptism are forgiven and a person is reconciled with God and the Church.

Individual and integral confession and absolution are the only ordinary means for the forgiveness of serious sin and for reconciliation with God and the Church.

(Other than ordinary means are perfect contrition and general absolution without prior confession, both of which require the intention of subsequent confession and absolution.)

A revised ritual for the sacrament — *Ordo Paenitentiae*, published by the Congregation of Divine Worship Feb. 7, 1974, and made mandatory in the U.S. from the first Sunday of Lent, 1977 — reiterates standard doctrine concerning the sacrament; emphasizes the social (communal and ecclesial) aspects of sin and conversion, with due regard for personal aspects and individual reception of the sacrament; prescribes three forms for celebration of the sacrament; and presents models for community penitential services.

The basic elements of the sacrament are sorrow for sin because of a supernatural motive, confession (of previously unconfessed mortal or grave sins, required; of venial sins also, but not of necessity), and reparation (by means of prayer or other act enjoined by the confessor), all of which comprise the matter of the sacrament; and absolution, which is the form of the sacrament.

The traditional words of absolution — *"I absolve you from your sins in the name of the Father, and of the Son, and of the Holy Spirit"* — remain unchanged at the conclusion of a petition in the new rite that God may grant pardon and peace through the ministry of the Church.

The minister of the sacrament is an authorized priest — i.e., one who, besides having the power of orders to forgive sins, also has faculties of jurisdiction granted by an ecclesiastical superior and/or by canon law.

The sacrament can be celebrated in three ways.

• For individuals, the traditional manner remains acceptable but is enriched with additional elements including: reception of the penitent and making of the Sign of the Cross; an exhortation by the confessor to trust in God; a reading from Scripture; confession of sins; manifestation of repentance; petition for God's forgiveness through the ministry of the Church and the absolution of the priest; praise of God's mercy, and dismissal in peace. Some of these elements are optional.

• For several penitents, in the course of a community celebration including a Liturgy of the Word of God and prayers, individual confession and absolution, and an act of thanksgiving.

• For several penitents, in the course of a community celebration, with general confession and general absolution. In extraordinary cases, reconciliation may be attained by general absolution without prior individual confession as, for example, under these circumstances: (1) danger of death, when there is neither time nor priests available for hearing confessions; (2) grave necessity of a number of penitents who, because of a shortage of confessors, would be deprived of sacramental grace or Communion for a lengthy period of time through no fault of their own. Persons receiving general absolution are obliged to be properly disposed and resolved to make an individual confession of the grave sins from which they have been absolved; this confession should be made as soon as the opportunity to confess presents itself and before any second reception of general absolution.

Norms regarding general absolution, issued by the Congregation for the Doctrine of the Faith in 1972, are not intended to provide a basis for convoking large gatherings of the faithful for the purpose of imparting general absolution, in the absence of extraordinary circumstances. Judgment about circumstances that warrant general absolution belongs principally to the bishop of the place, with due regard for related decisions of appropriate episcopal conferences.

Communal celebrations of the sacrament are not held in connection with Mass.

The place of individual confession, as determined by episcopal conferences in accordance with given norms, can be the traditional confessional or another appropriate setting.

A precept of the Church obliges the faithful guilty of grave sin to confess at least once a year.

The Church favors more frequent reception of the sacrament not only for the reconciliation of persons guilty of serious sins but also for reasons of devotion. Devotional confession — in which venial sins or previously forgiven sins are confessed — serves the purpose of confirming persons in penance and conversion.

Penitential Celebrations: Communal penitential celebrations are designed to emphasize the social dimensions of Christian life — the community aspects and significance of penance and reconciliation.

Elements of such celebrations are community prayer, hymns and songs, scriptural and other readings, examination of conscience, general confession and expression of sorrow for sin, acts of penance and reconciliation, and a form of non-sacramental absolution resembling the one in the penitential rite of the Mass.

If the sacrament is celebrated during the service, there must be individual confession and absolution of sin.

(See Absolution, Confession, Confessional, Confessor, Contrition, Faculties, Forgiveness of Sin, Power of the Keys, Seal of Confession, Sin.)

Anointing of the Sick

This sacrament, promulgated by St. James the Apostle (Jas. 5:13-15), can be administered to the faithful after reaching the age of reason who begin to be in danger because of illness or old age. By the anointing with blessed oil and the prayer of a priest, the sacrament confers on the person comforting grace; the remission of venial sins and inculpably unconfessed mortal sins, together with at least some of the temporal punishment due for sins; and, sometimes, results in an improved state of health.

The matter of this sacrament is the anointing with blessed oil (of the sick — olive oil, or vegetable oil if necessary) of the forehead and hands; in cases of necessity, a single anointing of another portion of the body suffices. The form is: "Through this holy anointing and his most loving mercy, may the Lord assist you by the grace of the Holy Spirit so that, when you have been freed from your sins, he may save you and in his goodness raise you up."

Anointing of the sick, formerly called extreme unction, may be received more than once, e.g., in new or continuing stages of serious illness. Ideally, the sacrament should be administered while the recipient is conscious and in conjunction with the sacraments of penance and the Eucharist. It should be administered in cases of doubt as to whether the person has reached the age of reason, is dangerously ill or dead.

The sacrament can be administered during a communal celebration in some circumstances, as in a home for the aged.

Holy Orders

Order is the sacrament by which the mission given by Christ to the Apostles continues to be exercised in the Church until the end of time; it is the sacrament of apostolic mission. It has three grades: episcopacy, priesthood and diaconate. The sacrament confers a character on the soul and can be received only once. The minister of the sacrament is a bishop.

Order, like matrimony but in a different way, is a social sacrament. As the Second Vatican Council declared in *Lumen Gentium*, the Dogmatic Constitution on the Church:

"For the nurturing and constant growth of the People of God, Christ the Lord instituted in his Church a variety of ministries, which work for the good of the whole body. For those ministers who are endowed with sacred power are servants of their brethren, so that all who are of the People of God, and therefore enjoy a true Christian dignity, can work toward a common goal freely and in an orderly way, and arrive at salvation" (No. 18).

Bishop: The fullness of the priesthood belongs to those who have received the order of bishop. Bishops, in hierarchical union with the pope and their fellow bishops, are the successors of the Apostles as pastors of the Church: they have individual responsibility for the care of the local churches they serve and collegial responsibility for the care of the universal Church (see Collegiality). In the ordination or consecration of bishops, the essential form is the imposition of hands by the consecrator(s) and the assigned prayer in the preface of the rite of ordination.

"With their helpers, the priests and deacons, bishops have taken up the service of the community presiding in place of God over the flock whose shepherds they are, as teachers of doctrine, priests of sacred worship, and officers of good order" (No. 20).

Priests: A priest is an ordained minister with the power to celebrate Mass, administer the sacraments, preach and teach the word of God, impart blessings, and perform additional pastoral functions, according to the mandate of his ecclesiastical superior.

Concerning priests, the Second Vatican Council stated in *Lumen Gentium* (No. 28):

"The divinely established ecclesiastical ministry is exercised on different levels by those who from antiquity have been called bishops, priests, and deacons. Although priests do not possess the highest degree of the priesthood, and although they are dependent on the bishops in the exercise of their power, they are nevertheless united with the bishops in sacerdotal dignity. By the power of the sacrament of orders, and in the image of Christ the eternal High Priest (Hb. 5:1-10; 7:24; 9:11-28), they are consecrated to preach the Gospel, shepherd the faithful, and celebrate divine worship as true priests of the New Testament.

"Priests, prudent cooperators with the episcopal order as well as its aides and instruments, are called to serve the People of God. They constitute one priesthood with their bishop, although that priesthood is comprised of different functions."

In the ordination of a priest of Roman rite, the essential matter is the imposition of hands on the heads of those being ordained by the ordaining bishop. The essential form is the accompanying prayer in the preface of the ordination ceremony. Other elements in the rite are the presentation of the implements of sacrifice — the chalice containing the wine and the paten containing a host — with accompanying prayers.

Deacon: There are two kinds of deacons: those who receive the order and remain in it permanently, and those who receive the order while advancing to priesthood. The following quotation — from Vatican II's Dogmatic Constitution on the Church (*Lumen Gentium*, No. 29) — describes the nature and role of the diaconate, with emphasis on the permanent diaconate.

"At a lower level of the hierarchy are deacons, upon whom hands are imposed 'not unto the priesthood, but unto a ministry of service.' For strengthened by sacramental grace, in communion with the bishop and his group of priests, they serve the People of God in the ministry of the liturgy, of the word, and of charity. It is the duty of the deacon, to the extent that he has been authorized by competent authority, to administer baptism solemnly, to be custodian and dispenser of the Eucharist, to assist at and bless marriages in the name of the Church, to bring Viaticum to the dying, to read the sacred Scripture to the faithful, to instruct and exhort the people, to preside at the worship and prayer of the faithful, to administer sacramentals, and to officiate at funeral and burial services. (Deacons are) dedicated to duties of charity and administration."

"The diaconate can in the future be restored as a proper and permanent rank of the hierarchy. It pertains to the competent territorial bodies of bishops, of one kind or another, to decide, with the approval of the Supreme Pontiff, whether and where it is opportune for such deacons to be appointed for the care of souls. With the consent of the Roman Pontiff, this diaconate will be able to be conferred upon men of more mature age, even upon those living in the married state. It may also be conferred upon suitable young men. For them, however, the law of celibacy must remain intact" (No. 29).

The Apostles ordained the first seven deacons (Acts 6:1-6): Stephen, Philip, Prochorus, Nicanor, Timon, Parmenas, Nicholas.

Former Orders, Ministries: With the revision of the sacrament of order which began in 1971, the orders of subdeacon, acolyte, exorcist, lector and porter were abolished because they and their respective functions had fallen into disuse or did not require ordination. The Holy See started revision of the sacrament of order in 1971. In virtue of an indult of Oct. 5 of that year, the bishops of the United States were permitted to discontinue ordaining porters and exorcists. Another indult, dated three days later, permitted the use of revised rites for ordaining acolytes and lectors.

To complete the revision, Pope Paul VI abolished Sept. 14, 1972, the orders of porter, exorcist and subdeacon; decreed that laymen, as well as candidates for the diaconate and priesthood, can be installed (rather than ordained) in the ministries (rather than orders) of acolyte and lector; reconfirmed the suppression of tonsure and its replacement with a service of dedication to God and the Church; and stated that a man enters the clerical state on ordination to the diaconate.

The abolished orders were:

• Subdeacon, with specific duties in liturgical worship, especially at Mass. The order, whose first extant mention dates from about the middle of the third century, was regarded as minor until the 13th century; afterwards, it was called a major order in the West but not in the East.

• Acolyte, to serve in minor capacities in liturgical worship; a function now performed by Mass servers.

• Exorcist, to perform services of exorcism for expelling evil spirits; a function which came to be reserved to specially delegated priests.

• Lector, to read scriptural and other passages during liturgical worship; a function now generally performed by lay persons.

• Porter, to guard the entrance to an assembly of Christians and to ward off undesirables who tried to gain admittance; an order of early origin and utility but of present insignificance.

Permanent Diaconate

Restoration of the permanent diaconate in the Roman rite — making it possible for men to become deacons permanently, without going on to the priesthood — was promulgated by Pope Paul VI June 18, 1967, in a document entitled *Sacrum Diaconatus Ordinem* ("Sacred Order of the Diaconate").

The Pope's action implemented the desire expressed by the Second Vatican Council for reestablishment of the diaconate as an independent order in its own right not only to supply ministers for carrying on the work of the Church but also to complete the hierarchical structure of the Church of Roman rite.

Permanent deacons have been traditional in the Eastern Church. The Western Church, however, since the fourth or fifth century, generally followed the practice of conferring the diaconate only as a sacred order preliminary to the priesthood, and of restricting the ministry of deacons to liturgical functions.

The Pope's document, issued on his own initiative, provided:

• Qualified unmarried men 25 years of age or older may be ordained deacons. They cannot marry after ordination.

• Qualified married men 35 years of age or older may be ordained deacons. The consent of the wife of a prospective deacon is required. A married deacon cannot remarry after the death of his wife.

• Preparation for the diaconate includes a course of study and formation over a period of at least three years.

• Candidates who are not members of religious institutes must be affiliated with a diocese. Reestablishment of the diaconate among religious is reserved to the Holy See.

• Deacons will practice their ministry under the direction of a bishop and with the priests with whom they will be associated. (For functions, see also the description of deacon, under Holy Orders.)

Restoration of the permanent diaconate in the United States was approved by the Holy See in October 1968. Shortly afterwards the U.S. bishops established a committee for the permanent diaconate, which was chaired by Bishop Edward U. Kmiec of Nashville in 1997. The committee operates through a secretariat, with offices at 3211 Fourth St. N. E., Washington, D.C. 20017. Deacon John Pistone is executive director.

Status and Functions

The 1999 *Official Catholic Directory* reports that in the United States there were a total of 12,675 permanent deacons (the highest total for any single country), an increase of 428 from the previous year and an increase of 3,610 from 1989. According to a study conducted by CARA (Center for Applied Research in the Apostolate) based at Georgetown University and released under the title "Catholic Ministry Formation Enrollments, 1997-1998," enrollment in permanent diaconate programs was about 2,620 in 136 diocesan programs in the United States. Three-fourths were between the ages of 40 and 59; 17% were age 60 or over; and 10% were 39 and under. Five out of six were Caucasian; 13% were Hispanic; 2% were African-American; Native-Americans and Asian-Americans were each 1%. Ninety-seven percent of all candidates were married.

Training programs of spiritual, theological and pastoral formation are based on guidelines emanating from the National Conference of Catholic Bishops.

Deacons have various functions, depending on the nature of their assignments. Liturgically, they can officiate at baptisms, weddings, wake services and funerals, can preach and distribute Holy Communion. Some are engaged in religious education work. All are intended to carry out works of charity and pastoral service of one kind or another.

The majority of deacons, the majority of whom are married, continue in their secular work. Their ministry of service is developing in three dimensions: of liturgy, of the word, and of charity. Depending on the individual deacon's abilities and preference, he is assigned by his bishop to either a parochial ministry or to another field of service. Deacons are active in a variety of ministries including those to prison inmates and their families, the sick in hospitals, nursing homes and homes for the aged, alienated youth, the elderly and the poor, and in various areas of legal service to the indigent, of education and campus ministry.

National Association of Diaconate Directors: Membership organization of directors, vicars and other staff personnel of diaconate programs. Established in 1977 to promote effective communication and facilitate the exchange of information and resources of members; to develop professional expertise and promote research, training and self evaluation; to foster accountability and seek ways to promote means of implementing solutions to problems. The association is governed by an executive board of elected officers. Officers include Deacons: Maurice Reed of Green Bay, pres., 1997-98; Peter D'Heilly of St.Paul-Minneapolis, president-elect; Thomas Welch, exec. dir. Office: 1337 W. Ohio St., Chicago, Il 60622.

(See also Special Report for coverage of the recent decree from the Congregation for the Doctrine of the Faith on the shared ministry.)

MATRIMONY

Coverage of the sacrament of matrimony is given in the following articles: Marriage Doctrine, Humanae Vitae, Marriage Laws, Mixed Marriages, and Pastoral Ministry for Divorced and Remarried.

Marriage Doctrine

The following excerpts, stating key points of doctrine on marriage, are from *Gaudium et Spes*, (Nos. 48 to 51) promulgated by the Second Vatican Council.

Conjugal Covenant

The intimate partnership of married life and love has been established by the Creator and qualified by his laws. It is rooted in the conjugal covenant of irrevocable personal consent.

God himself is the author of matrimony, endowed as it is with various benefits and purposes. All of these have a very decisive bearing on the continuation of the human race, on the personal development and eternal destiny of the individual members of a family, and on the dignity, stability, peace, and prosperity of the family itself and of human society as a whole. By their very nature, the institution of matrimony itself and conjugal love are ordained for the procreation and education of children, and find in them their ultimate crown.

Thus a man and a woman render mutual help and service to each other through an intimate union of their persons and of their actions. Through this union they experience the meaning of their oneness and attain to it with growing perfection day by day. As a mutual gift of two persons, this intimate union, as well as the good of the children, imposes total fidelity on the spouses and argues for an unbreakable oneness between them (No. 48).

Sacrament of Matrimony

Christ the Lord abundantly blessed this many-faceted love. The Savior of men and the Spouse of the Church comes into the lives of married Christians through the sacrament of matrimony. He abides with them thereafter so that, just as he loved the Church and handed himself over on her behalf, the spouses may love each other with perpetual fidelity through mutual self-bestowal.

Graced with the dignity and office of fatherhood and motherhood, parents will energetically acquit themselves of a duty which devolves primarily on them; namely, education, and especially religious education.

The Christian family, which springs from marriage as a reflection of the loving covenant uniting Christ with the Church, and as a participation in that covenant, will manifest to all men the Savior's living presence in the world, and the genuine nature of the Church (No. 48).

Conjugal Love

The biblical Word of God several times urges the betrothed and the married to nourish and develop their wedlock by pure conjugal love and undivided affection.

This love is an eminently human one since it is directed from one person to another through an affec-

tion of the will. It involves the good of the whole person. Therefore it can enrich the expressions of body and mind with a unique dignity, ennobling these expressions as special ingredients and signs of the friendship distinctive of marriage. This love the Lord has judged worthy of special gifts, healing, perfecting, and exalting gifts of grace and of charity.

Such love, merging the human with the divine, leads the spouses to a free and mutual gift of themselves, a gift proving itself by gentle affection and by deed. Such love pervades the whole of their lives. Indeed, by its generous activity it grows better and grows greater. Therefore it far excels mere erotic inclination, which, selfishly pursued, soon enough fades wretchedly away.

This love is uniquely expressed and perfected through the marital act. The actions within marriage by which the couple are united intimately and chastely are noble and worthy ones. Expressed in a manner which is truly human, these actions signify and promote that mutual self-giving by which spouses enrich each other with a joyful and a thankful will.

Sealed by mutual faithfulness and hallowed above all by Christ's sacrament, this love remains steadfastly true in body and in mind, in bright days or dark. It will never be profaned by adultery or divorce. Firmly established by the Lord, the unity of marriage will radiate from the equal personal dignity of wife and husband, a dignity acknowledged by mutual and total love.

The steady fulfillment of the duties of this Christian vocation demands notable virtue. For this reason, strengthened by grace for holiness of life, the couple will painstakingly cultivate and pray for constancy of love, largeheartedness, and the spirit of sacrifice (No. 49).

Fruitfulness of Marriage

Marriage and conjugal love are by their nature ordained toward the begetting and educating of children. Children are really the supreme gift of marriage and contribute very substantially to the welfare of their parents. God himself wished to share with man a certain special participation in his own creative work. Thus he blessed male and female, saying: "Increase and multiply" (Gn. 1:28).

Hence, while not making the other purposes of matrimony of less account, the true practice of conjugal love, and the whole meaning of the family life which results from it, have this aim: that the couple be ready with stout hearts to cooperate with the love of the Creator and the Savior, who through them will enlarge and enrich his own family day by day.

Parents should regard as their proper mission the task of transmitting human life and educating those to whom it has been transmitted. They should realize that they are thereby cooperators with the love of God the Creator, and are, so to speak, the interpreters of that love. Thus they will fulfill their task with human and Christian responsibility (No. 50).

Norms of Judgment

They will thoughtfully take into account both their own welfare and that of their children, those already born and those who may be foreseen. For this accounting they will reckon with both the material and the spiritual conditions of the times as well as of their state in life. Finally, they will consult the interests of the family group, of temporal society, and of the Church herself.

The parents themselves should ultimately make this judgment in the sight of God. But in their manner of acting, spouses should be aware that they cannot proceed arbitrarily. They must always be governed according to a conscience dutifully conformed to the divine law itself, and should be submissive toward the Church's teaching office, which authentically interprets that law in the light of the Gospel. That divine law reveals and protects the integral meaning of conjugal love, and impels it toward a truly human fulfillment.

Marriage, to be sure, is not instituted solely for procreation. Rather, its very nature as an unbreakable compact between persons, and the welfare of the children, both demand that the mutual love of the spouses, too, be embodied in a rightly ordered manner, that it grow and ripen. Therefore, marriage persists as a whole manner and communion of life, and maintains its value and indissolubility, even when offspring are lacking — despite, rather often, the very intense desire of the couple (No. 50).

Love and Life

This Council realizes that certain modern conditions often keep couples from arranging their married lives harmoniously, and that they find themselves in circumstances where at least temporarily the size of their families should not be increased. As a result, the faithful exercise of love and the full intimacy of their lives are hard to maintain. But where the intimacy of married life is broken off, it is not rare for its faithfulness to be imperiled and its quality of fruitfulness ruined. For then the upbringing of the children and the courage to accept new ones are both endangered.

To these problems there are those who presume to offer dishonorable solutions. Indeed, they do not recoil from the taking of life. But the Church issues the reminder that a true contradiction cannot exist between the divine laws pertaining to the transmission of life and those pertaining to the fostering of authentic conjugal love.

Church Teaching

For God, the Lord of Life, has conferred on men the surpassing ministry of safeguarding life — a ministry which must be fulfilled in a manner which is worthy of men. Therefore from the moment of its conception life must be guarded with the greatest care, while abortion and infanticide are unspeakable crimes. The sexual characteristics of man and the human faculty of reproduction wonderfully exceed the dispositions of lower forms of life. Hence the acts themselves which are proper to conjugal love and which are exercised in accord with genuine human dignity must be honored with great reverence (No. 51).

Therefore when there is question of harmonizing conjugal love with the responsible transmission of life, the moral aspect of any procedure does not depend solely on the sincere intentions or on an evaluation of motives. It must be determined by objective standards. These, based on the nature of the human person and his acts, preserve the full sense of mutual self-giving and human procreation in the context of true love. Such a goal cannot be achieved unless the virtue of conjugal chastity is sincerely practiced. Relying on these principles, sons of the Church may not undertake methods of regulating procreation which are found blameworthy by the teaching authority of the Church in its unfolding of the divine law.

Everyone should be persuaded that human life and the task of transmitting it are not realities bound up with this world alone. Hence they cannot be measured or perceived only in terms of it, but always have a bearing on the eternal destiny of men (No. 51).

Humanae Vitae

Marriage doctrine and morality were the subjects of the encyclical letter Humanae Vitae ("Of Human Life"), issued by Pope Paul VI, July 29, 1968. Humanae Vitae was given reaffirmation and its teaching restated and defended by Pope John Paul II in his encyclical Evangelium Vitae (The Gospel of Life, 1995). Following are a number of key excerpts from Humanae Vitae, which was framed in the pattern of traditional teaching and statements by the Second Vatican Council.

Each and every marriage act ("quilibet matrimonii usus") must remain open to the transmission of life (No. 11).

Indeed, by its intimate structure, the conjugal act, while most closely uniting husband and wife, capacitates them for the generation of new lives according to laws inscribed in the very being of man and of woman. By safeguarding both these essential aspects, the unitive and the procreative, the conjugal act preserves in its fullness the sense of true mutual love and its ordination toward man's most high calling to parenthood (No. 12).

It is, in fact, justly observed that a conjugal act imposed upon one's partner without regard for his or her condition and lawful desires is not a true act of love, and therefore denies an exigency of right moral order in the relationships between husband and wife. Hence, one who reflects well must also recognize that a reciprocal act of love which jeopardizes the responsibility to transmit life — which God the Creator, according to particular laws, inserted therein — is in contradiction with the design constitutive of marriage and with the will of the Author of life. To use this divine gift, destroying, even if only partially, its meaning and its purpose, is to contradict the nature both of man and of woman and of their most intimate relationship, and therefore it is to contradict also the plan of God and his will (No. 13).

Forbidden Actions

The direct interruption of the generative process already begun, and, above all, directly willed and procured abortion, even if for therapeutic reasons, are to be absolutely excluded as licit means of regulating birth.

Equally to be excluded is direct sterilization, whether perpetual or temporary, whether of the man or of the woman. Similarly excluded is every action which, either in anticipation of the conjugal act, or in its accomplishment, or in the development of its natural consequences, proposes, whether as an end or as a means, to render procreation impossible.

To justify conjugal acts made intentionally infecund, one cannot invoke as valid reasons the lesser evil, or the fact that such acts would constitute a whole together with the fecund acts already performed or to follow later and hence would share in one and the same moral goodness. In truth, if it is sometimes licit to tolerate a lesser evil in order to avoid a greater evil or to promote a greater good, it is not licit, even for the gravest reasons, to do evil so that good may follow therefrom; that is, to make into the object of a positive act of the will something which is intrinsically disorder, and hence unworthy of the human person, even when the intention is to safeguard or promote individual, family or social well-being.

Consequently, it is an error to think that a conjugal act which is deliberately made infecund, and so is intrinsically dishonest, could be made honest and right by the ensemble of a fecund conjugal life (No. 14).

If, then, there are serious motives to space out births, which derive from the physical or psychological conditions of husband and wife, or from external conditions, the Church teaches that it is then licit to take into account the natural rhythms immanent in the generative functions, for the use of marriage in the infecund periods only, and in this way to regulate birth without offending earlier stated principles (No. 16).

Pastoral Concerns

We do not at all intend to hide the sometimes serious difficulties inherent in the life of Christian married persons; for them, as for everyone else, "the gate is narrow and the way is hard that leads to life." But the hope of that life must illuminate their way, as with courage they strive to live with wisdom, justice and piety in this present time, knowing that the figure of this world passes away.

Let married couples then, face up to the efforts needed, supported by the faith and hope which "do not disappoint because God's love has been poured into our hearts through the Holy Spirit, who has been given to us." Let them implore divine assistance by persevering prayer; above all, let them draw from the source of grace and charity in the Eucharist. And, if sin should still keep its hold over them, let them not be discouraged but rather have recourse with humble perseverance to the mercy of God, which is poured forth in the sacrament of penance (No. 25).

Marriage Laws

The Catholic Church claims jurisdiction over its members in matters pertaining to marriage. which is a sacrament. Church legislation on the subject is stated principally in 111 canons of the Code of Canon Law.

Marriage laws of the Church provide juridical norms in support of the marriage covenant. In 10 chapters, the revised Code covers: pastoral directives for preparing men and women for marriage; impediments in general and in particular; matrimonial consent; form for the celebration of marriage; mixed marriages; secret celebration of marriage; effects of marriage; separation of spouses, and convalidation of marriage.

Catholics are bound by all marriage laws of the Church. Non-Catholics, whether baptized or not, are not considered bound by these ecclesiastical laws except in cases of marriage with a Catholic. Certain natural laws, in the Catholic view, bind all men and women, irrespective of their religious beliefs; accordingly, marriage is prohibited before the time of puberty, without knowledge and free mutual consent, in the case of an already existing valid marriage bond, in the case of antecedent and perpetual impotence.

Formalities

These include, in addition to arrangements for the time and place of the marriage ceremony, doctrinal and moral instruction concerning marriage and the recording of data which verifies in documentary form the eligibility and freedom of the persons to marry. Records of this kind, which are confidential, are preserved in the archives of the church where the marriage takes place.

Premarital instructions are the subject matter of Pre-Cana Conferences.

Marital Consent

Matrimonial consent can be invalidated by an essential defect, substantial error, the strong influence of force and fear, the presence of a condition or intention against the nature of marriage.

Form of Marriage

A Catholic is required, for validity and lawfulness, to contract marriage — with another Catholic or with a non-Catholic — in the presence of a competent priest or deacon and two witnesses.

There are two exceptions to this law. A Roman-rite Catholic (since Mar. 25, 1967) or an Eastern-rite Catholic (since Nov. 21, 1964) can contract marriage validly in the presence of a priest of a separated Eastern-rite Church, provided other requirements of law are complied with. With permission of the competent Roman-rite or Eastern-rite bishop, this form of marriage is lawful, as well as valid. (See Eastern-rite Laws, below.)

With these two exceptions, and aside from cases covered by special permission, the Church does not regard as valid any marriages involving Catholics which take place before non-Catholic ministers of religion or civil officials.

(An excommunication formerly in force against Catholics who celebrated marriage before a non-Catholic minister was abrogated in a decree issued by the Sacred Congregation for the Doctrine of the Faith on Mar. 18, 1966.)

The ordinary place of marriage is the parish of either Catholic party or of the Catholic party in case of a mixed marriage.

Church law regarding the form of marriage does not affect non-Catholics in marriages among themselves. The Church recognizes as valid the marriages of non-Catholics before ministers of religion and civil officials, unless they are rendered null and void on other grounds.

The canonical form is not to be observed in the case of a marriage between a non-Catholic and a baptized Catholic who has left the Church by a formal act.

Impediments

Diriment Impediments to marriage are factors which render a marriage invalid.

• age, which obtains before completion of the 14th year for a woman and the 16th year for a man;

• impotency, if it is antecedent to the marriage and permanent (this differs from sterility, which is not an impediment);
• the bond of an existing valid marriage;
• disparity of worship, which obtains when one party is a Catholic and the other party is unbaptized;
• sacred orders;
• religious profession of the perpetual vow of chastity;
• abduction, which impedes the freedom of the person abducted;
• crime, variously involving elements of adultery, promise or attempt to marry, conspiracy to murder a husband or wife;
• blood relationship in the direct line (father-daughter, mother-son, etc.) and to the fourth degree inclusive of the collateral line (brother-sister, first cousins);
• affinity, or relationship resulting from a valid marriage, in any degree of the direct line;
• public honesty, arising from an invalid marriage or from public or notorious concubinage; it renders either party incapable of marrying blood relatives of the other in the first degree of the direct line.
• legal relationship arising from adoption; it renders either party incapable of marrying relatives of the other in the direct line or in the second degree of the collateral line.

Dispensations from Impediments: Persons hindered by impediments cannot marry unless they are dispensed therefrom in view of reasons recognized in canon law. Local bishops can dispense from the impediments most often encountered (e.g., disparity of worship) as well as others.

Decision regarding some dispensations is reserved to the Holy See.

Separation

A valid and consummated marriage of baptized persons cannot be dissolved by any human authority or any cause other than the death of one of the persons.

In other circumstances:

• 1. A valid but unconsummated marriage of baptized persons, or of a baptized and an unbaptized person, can be dissolved:

a. by the solemn religious profession of one of the persons, made with permission of the pope. In such a case, the bond is dissolved at the time of profession, and the other person is free to marry again.

b. by dispensation from the pope, requested for a grave reason by one or both of the persons. If the dispensation is granted, both persons are free to marry again.

Dispensations in these cases are granted for reasons connected with the spiritual welfare of the concerned persons.

• 2. A legitimate marriage, even consummated, of unbaptized persons can be dissolved in favor of one of them who subsequently receives the sacrament of baptism. This is the Pauline Privilege, so called because it was promulgated by St. Paul (1 Cor. 7:12-15) as a means of protecting the faith of converts. Requisites for granting the privilege are:

a. marriage prior to the baptism of either person;
b. reception of baptism by one person;
c. refusal of the unbaptized person to live in peace

with the baptized person and without interfering with his or her freedom to practice the Christian faith. The privilege does not apply if the unbaptized person agrees to these conditions.

• 3. A legitimate and consummated marriage of a baptized and an unbaptized person can be dissolved by the pope in virtue of the Privilege of Faith, also called the Petrine Privilege.

Civil Divorce

Because of the unity and the indissolubility of marriage, the Church denies that civil divorce can break the bond of a valid marriage, whether the marriage involves two Catholics, a Catholic and a non-Catholic, or non-Catholics with each other.

In view of serious circumstances of marital distress, the Church permits an innocent and aggrieved party, whether wife or husband, to seek and obtain a civil divorce for the purpose of acquiring title and right to the civil effects of divorce, such as separate habitation and maintenance, and the custody of children. Permission for this kind of action should be obtained from proper church authority. The divorce, if obtained, does not break the bond of a valid marriage.

Under other circumstances — as would obtain if a marriage was invalid (see Annulment, below) — civil divorce is permitted for civil effects and as a civil ratification of the fact that the marriage bond really does not exist.

Annulment

This is a decision by a competent church authority — e.g., a bishop, a diocesan marriage tribunal, the Roman Rota — that an apparently valid marriage was actually invalid from the beginning because of the unknown or concealed existence, from the beginning, of a diriment impediment, an essential defect in consent, radical incapability for marriage, or a condition placed by one or both of the parties against the very nature of marriage.

Eastern-rite Laws

Marriage laws of the Eastern Church differ in several respects from the legislation of the Roman rite. The regulations in effect since May 2, 1949, were contained in the *motu proprio Crebre Allatae* issued by Pius XII the previous February.

According to both the Roman Code of Canon Law and the Oriental Code, marriages between Roman-rite Catholics and Eastern-rite Catholics ordinarily take place in the rite of the groom and have canonical effects in that rite.

Regarding the form for the celebration of marriages between Eastern Catholics and baptized Eastern non-Catholics, the Second Vatican Council declared: "By way of preventing invalid marriages between Eastern Catholics and baptized Eastern non-Catholics, and in the interests of the permanence and sanctity of marriage and of domestic harmony, this sacred Synod decrees that the canonical 'form' for the celebration of such marriages obliges only for lawfulness. For their validity, the presence of a sacred minister suffices, as long as the other requirements of law are honored" (Decree on Eastern Catholic Churches, No. 18).

Marriages taking place in this manner are lawful,

as well as valid, with permission of a competent Eastern-rite bishop.

The Rota

The Roman Rota is the ordinary court of appeal for marriage, and some other cases, which are appealed to the Holy See from lower church courts. Appeals are made to the Rota if decisions by diocesan and archdiocesan courts fail to settle the matter in dispute. Pope John Paul II, at annual meetings with Rota personnel, speaks about the importance of the court's actions in providing norms of practice for other tribunals.

Mixed Marriages

"Mixed Marriages" (*Matrimonia Mixta*) was the subject of: (1) a letter issued under this title by Pope Paul VI Mar. 31, 1970, and (2) a statement, Implementation of the Apostolic Letter on Mixed Marriages, approved by the National Conference of Catholic Bishops Nov. 16, 1970.

One of the key points in the bishops' statement referred to the need for mutual pastoral care by ministers of different faiths for the sacredness of marriage and for appropriate preparation and continuing support of parties to a mixed marriage.

Pastoral experience, which the Catholic Church shares with other religious bodies, confirms the fact that marriages of persons of different beliefs involve special problems related to the continuing religious practice of the concerned persons and to the religious education and formation of their children.

Pastoral measures to minimize these problems include instruction of a non-Catholic party in essentials of the Catholic faith for purposes of understanding. Desirably, some instruction should also be given the Catholic party regarding his or her partner's beliefs.

Requirements

The Catholic party to a mixed marriage is required to declare his (her) intention of continuing practice of the Catholic faith and to promise to do all in his (her) power to share his (her) faith with children born of the marriage by having them baptized and raised as Catholics. No declarations or promises are required of the non-Catholic party, but he (she) must be informed of the declaration and promise made by the Catholic.

Notice of the Catholic's declaration and promise is an essential part of the application made to a bishop for (1) permission to marry a baptized non-Catholic, or (2) a dispensation to marry an unbaptized non-Catholic.

A mixed marriage can take place with a Nuptial Mass. (The bishops' statement added this caution: "To the extent that Eucharistic sharing is not permitted by the general discipline of the Church, this is to be considered when plans are being made to have the mixed marriage at Mass or not.")

The ordinary minister at a mixed marriage is an authorized priest or deacon, and the ordinary place is the parish church of the Catholic party. A non-Catholic minister may not only attend the marriage ceremony but may also address, pray with and bless the couple.

For appropriate pastoral reasons, a bishop can grant a dispensation from the Catholic form of marriage and can permit the marriage to take place in a non-Catholic church with a non-Catholic minister as the officiating minister. A priest may not only attend such a ceremony but may also address, pray with and bless the couple.

"It is not permitted," however, the bishops' statement declared, "to have two religious services or to have a single service in which both the Catholic marriage ritual and a non-Catholic marriage ritual are celebrated jointly or successively."

Pastoral Ministry for Divorced and Remarried

Ministry to divorced and remarried Catholics is a difficult field of pastoral endeavor, situated as it is in circumstances tantamount to the horns of a dilemma.

At Issue

On the one side is firm church teaching on the permanence of marriage and norms against reception of the Eucharist and full participation in the life of the Church by Catholics in irregular unions.

On the other side are men and women with broken unions followed by second and perhaps happier attempts at marriage which the Church does not recognize as valid and which may not be capable of being validated because of the existence of an earlier marriage bond.

Factors involved in these circumstances are those of the Church, upholding its doctrine and practice regarding the permanence of marriage, and those of many men and women in irregular second marriages who desire full participation in the life of the Church.

Sacramental participation is not possible for those whose first marriage was valid, although there is no bar to their attendance at Mass, to sharing in other activities of the Church, or to their efforts to have children baptized and raised in the Catholic faith.

An exception to this rule is the condition of a divorced and remarried couple living in a brother-sister relationship.

There is no ban against sacramental participation by separated or divorced persons who have not attempted a second marriage, provided the usual conditions for reception of the sacraments are in order.

Unverified estimates of the number of U.S. Catholics who are divorced and remarried vary between six and eight million.

Tribunal Action

What can the Church do for them and with them in pastoral ministry, is an old question charged with new urgency because of the rising number of divorced and remarried Catholics.

One way to help is through the agency of marriage tribunals charged with responsibility for investigating and settling questions concerning the validity or invalidity of a prior marriage. There are reasons in canon law justifying the Church in declaring a particular marriage null and void from the beginning, despite the short- or long-term existence of an apparently valid union.

Decrees of nullity (annulments) are not new in the history of the Church. If such a decree is issued, a man or woman is free to validate a second marriage and live in complete union with the Church.

The 1998 *Statistical Yearbook* of the Church, reported that in 1998 U.S. tribunals issued 54,013 annulments (in ordinary and documentary processes). The canonical reasons were: invalid consent (39,276), impotence (3), other impediments (2,731), defect of form (12,003). Worldwide, 73,108 decrees or declarations of nullity were issued in 1997. The 1996 *Statistical Yearbook of the Church*, reported that in 1996 U.S. tribunals issued 55,700 annulments (in ordinary and documentary processes). The canonical reasons were: invalid consent (41,680), impotence (5), other impediments (3.039), defect of form (10,986). Worldwide, 75,019 decrees or declarations of nullity were issued in 1996.

Reasons behind Decrees

Pastoral experience reveals that some married persons, a short or long time after contracting an apparently valid marriage, exhibit signs that point back to the existence, at the time of marriage, of latent and serious personal deficiencies which made them incapable of valid consent and sacramental commitment.

. Such deficiencies might include gross immaturity and those affecting in a serious way the capacity to love, to have a true interpersonal and conjugal relationship, to fulfill marital obligations, to accept the faith aspect of marriage.

Psychological and behavioral factors like these have been given greater attention by tribunals in recent years and have provided grounds for numerous decrees of nullity.

Decisions of this type do not indicate any softening of the Church's attitude regarding the permanence of marriage. They affirm, rather, that some persons who have married were really not capable of doing so.

Serious deficiencies in the capacity for real interpersonal relationship in marriage were the reasons behind a landmark decree of nullity issued in 1973 by the Roman Rota, the Vatican high court of appeals in marriage cases. Pope John Paul referred to such deficiencies — the "grave lack of discretionary judgment," incapability of assuming "essential matrimonial rights and obligations," for example — in an address Jan. 26, 1984, to personnel of the Rota.

The tribunal way to a decree of nullity regarding a previous marriage, however, is not open to many persons in second marriages — because grounds are either lacking or, if present, cannot be verified in tribunal process.

Unacceptable Solutions

One unacceptable solution of the problem, called "good conscience procedure," involves administration of the sacraments of penance and the Eucharist to divorced and remarried Catholics unable to obtain a decree of nullity for a first marriage who are living in a subsequent marriage "in good faith."

This procedure, despite the fact that it has no standing or recognition in church law, is being advocated and practiced by some priests and remarried Catholics.

This issue was addressed by the Congregation for the Doctrine of the Faith in a letter to bishops dated Oct. 14, 1994, and published with the approval of Pope John Paul II. The letter said in part:

"Pastoral solutions in this area have been suggested according to which divorced-and-remarried members of the faithful could approach holy Communion in specific cases when they considered themselves authorized according to a judgment of conscience to do so. This would be the case, for example, when they had been abandoned completely unjustly although they sincerely tried to save the previous marriage; or when they are convinced of the nullity of their previous marriage although (they are) unable to demonstrate it in the external forum; or when they have gone through a long period of reflection and penance; or also when for morally valid reasons they cannot satisfy the obligation to separate.

"In some places it has also been proposed that, in order objectively to examine their actual situation, the divorced-and-remarried would have to consult a prudent and experienced priest. This priest, however, would have to respect their eventual decision in conscience to approach holy Communion, without this implying an official authorization.

"In these and similar cases, it would be a matter of a tolerant and benevolent pastoral solution in order to do justice to the different situations of the divorced-and-remarried.

"Even if analogous solutions have been proposed by a few fathers of the Church and in some measure were practiced, nevertheless these never attained the consensus of the fathers and in no way came to constitute the common doctrine of the Church nor to determine her discipline. It falls to the universal magisterium, in fidelity to sacred Scripture and tradition, to teach and to interpret authentically the deposit of faith."

Conditions for Receiving Communion

Practically speaking, "when for serious reasons — for example, for the children's upbringing — a man and a woman cannot satisfy the obligation to separate," they may be admitted to Communion if "they take on themselves the duty to live in complete continence, that is, by abstinence from the acts proper to married couples. In such a case they may receive holy Communion as long as they respect the obligation to avoid giving scandal."

The teaching of the Church on this subject "does not mean that the Church does not take to heart the situation of those faithful who, moreover, are not excluded from ecclesial communion. She is concerned to accompany them pastorally and invite them to share in the life of the Church in the measure that is compatible with the dispositions of divine law, from which the Church has no power to dispense. On the other hand, it is necessary to instruct these faithful so that they do not think their participation in the life of the Church is reduced exclusively to the question of the reception of the Eucharist. The faithful are to be helped to deepen their understanding of the value of sharing in the sacrifice of Christ in the Mass, or spiritual communion, of prayer, of meditation on the word of God, and of works of charity and justice."

SAINTS OF THE CHURCH

Biographical sketches of additional saints and blessed are under other Almanac entries. See Index, under the name of each saint for the Apostles, Evangelists, Doctors of the Church, and Fathers of the Church. For Beatification and Canonization procedures, see those entries in the Glossary.

An asterisk with a feast date indicates that the saint is listed in the General Roman Calendar or the proper calendar for U.S. dioceses. For rank of observances, see listing in calendar for current year on preceding pages.

Adalbert (956-997): Born in Bohemia; bishop of Prague; Benedictine; missionary in Poland, Prussia and Hungary; martyred by Prussians near Danzig; Apr. 23.*

Adjutor (d. 1131): Norman knight; fought in First Crusade; monk-recluse after his return; Apr. 30.

Agatha (d. c. 250): Sicilian virgin-martyr; her intercession credited in Sicily with stilling eruptions of Mt. Etna; patron of nurses; Feb. 5.*

Agnes (d. c. 304): Roman virgin-martyr; martyred at age of 10 or 12; patron of young girls; Jan. 21.*

Aloysius Gonzaga (1568-1591): Italian Jesuit; died while nursing plague-stricken; canonized 1726; patron of youth; June 21.*

Amand (d. c. 676): Apostle of Belgium; b. France; established monasteries throughout Belgium; Feb. 6.

Andre Bessette, Bl. (Bro. Andre) (1845-1937): Canadian Holy Cross Brother; prime mover in building of St. Joseph's Oratory, Montreal; beatified May 23, 1982; Jan. 6* (U.S.).

Andre Grasset de Saint Sauveur, Bl. (1758-1792): Canadian priest; martyred in France, Sept. 2, 1792, during the Revolution; one of a group called the Martyrs of Paris who were beatified in 1926; Sept. 2.

Andrew Bobola (1592-1657): Polish Jesuit; joined Jesuits at Vilna; worked for return of Orthodox to union with Rome; martyred; canonized 1938; May 16.

Andrew Corsini (1302-1373): Italian Carmelite; bishop of Fiesoli; mediator between quarrelsome Italian states; canonized 1629; Feb. 4.

Andrew Dung-Lac and Companions (d. 18th-19th c.): Martyrs of Vietnam. Total of 117 included 96 Vietnamese, 11 Spanish and 10 French missionaries (8 bishops; 50 priests, including Andrew Dung-Lac; 1 seminarian, 58 lay persons). Canonized June 19, 1988; inscribed in General Roman Calendar, 1989, as a memorial. Nov. 24.*

Andrew Fournet (1752-1834): French priest; co-founder with St. Jeanne Elizabeth Bichier des Anges of the Daughters of the Holy Cross of St. Andrew; canonized 1933; May 13.

Andrew Kim, Paul Chong and Companions (d. between 1839-1867): Korean martyrs (103) killed in persecutions of 1839, 1846, 1866, and 1867; among them were Andrew Kim, the first Korean priest, and Paul Chong, lay apostle; canonized May 6, 1984, during Pope John Paul II's visit to Korea; entered into General Roman Calendar, 1985, as a memorial. Sept. 20.*

Angela Merici (1474-1540): Italian secular Franciscan; foundress of Company of St. Ursula, 1535, the first teaching order of women Religious in the Church; canonized 1807; Jan. 27.*

Angelico, Bl. (Fra Angelico; John of Faesulis)

(1387-1455): Dominican; Florentine painter of early Renaissance; proclaimed blessed by John Paul II, Feb. 3, 1982; patron of artists; Feb. 18.

Anne Marie Javouhey, Bl. (1779-1851): French virgin; foundress of Institute of St. Joseph of Cluny, 1812; beatified 1950; July 15.

Ansgar (801-865): Benedictine monk; b. near Amiens; archbishop of Hamburg; missionary in Denmark, Sweden, Norway and northern Germany; apostle of Scandinavia; Feb. 3.*

Anthony (c. 251-c. 354): Abbot; Egyptian hermit; patriarch of all monks; established communities for hermits which became models for monastic life, especially in the East; friend and supporter of St. Athanasius in the latter's struggle with the Arias; Jan. 17.*

Anthony Claret (1807-1870): Spanish bishop; founder of Missionary Sons of the Immaculate Heart of Mary (Claretians), 1849; archbishop of Santiago, Cuba, 1851-57; canonized 1950; Oct. 24.*

Anthony Gianelli (1789-1846): Italian bishop; founded the Daughters of Our Lady of the Garden, 1829; bishop of Bobbio, 1838; canonized 1951; June 7.

Anthony Zaccaria (1502-1539): Italian priest; founder of Barnabites (Clerks Regular of St. Paul), 1530; canonized 1897; July 5.*

Apollonia (d. 249): Deaconess of Alexandria; martyred during persecution of Decius; her patronage of dentists and those suffering from toothaches probably rests on tradition that her teeth were broken by her persecutors; Feb. 9.

Augustine of Canterbury (d. 604 or 605): Italian missionary; apostle of the English; sent by Pope Gregory I with 40 monks to evangelize England; arrived there 597; first archbishop of Canterbury; May 27.*

Bartolomea Capitania (1807-1833): Italian foundress with Vincenza Gerosa of the Sisters of Charity of Lovere; canonized 1950; July 26.

Beatrice da Silva Meneses (1424-1490): Foundress, b. Portugal; founded Congregation of the Immaculate Conception, 1484, in Spain; canonized 1976; Sept. 1.

Benedict Joseph Labré (1748-1783): French layman; pilgrim-beggar; noted for his piety and love of prayer before the Blessed Sacrament; canonized 1883; Apr. 16.

Benedict of Nursia (c. 480-547): Abbot; founder of monasticism in Western Europe; established monastery at Monte Cassino; proclaimed patron of Europe by Paul VI in 1964; July 11.*

Benedict the Black *(il Moro)* (1526-1589): Sicilian Franciscan; born a slave; joined Franciscans as lay brother; appointed guardian and novice master; canonized 1807; Apr. 3.

Bernadette Soubirous (1844-1879): French peasant girl favored with series of visions of Blessed Virgin Mary at Lourdes (see Lourdes Apparitions); joined Institute of Sisters of Notre Dame at Nevers, 1866; canonized 1933; Apr. 16.

Bernard of Montjoux (or Menthon) (d. 1081): Augustinian canon; probably born in Italy; founded Alpine hospices near the two passes named for him; patron of mountaineers; May 28.

Bernardine of Feltre, Bl. (1439-1494): Italian Franciscan preacher; a founder of montes pietatis; Sept. 28.

Bernardine of Siena (1380-1444): Italian Fran-

ciscan; noted preacher and missioner; spread of devotion to Holy Name is attributed to him; represented in art holding to his breast the monogram IHS; canonized 1450; May 20.*

Blase (d. c. 316): Armenian bishop; martyr; the blessing of throats on his feast day derives from tradition that he miraculously saved the life of a boy who had half-swallowed a fish bone; Feb. 3.*

Boniface (Winfrid) (d. 754): English Benedictine; bishop; martyr; apostle of Germany; established monastery at Fulda which became center of missionary work in Germany; archbishop of Mainz; martyred near Dukkum in Holland; June 5.*

Brendan (c. 489-583): Irish abbot; founded monasteries; his patronage of sailors probably rests on a legend that he made a seven-year voyage in search of a fabled paradise; called Brendan the Navigator; May 16.

Bridget (Brigid) (c. 450-525): Irish nun; founded religious community at Kildare, the first in Ireland; patron, with Sts. Patrick and Columba, of Ireland; Feb. 1.

Bridget (Birgitta) (c. 1303-1373): Swedish mystic; widow; foundress of Order of Our Savior (Brigittines); canonized 1391; patroness of Sweden; July 23.*

Bruno (1030-1101): German monk; founded Carthusians, 1084, in France; Oct. 6.*

Cabrini, Mother: See **Frances Xavier Cabrini.**

Cajetan (Gaetano) **of Thiene** (1480-1547): Italian lawyer; religious reformer; a founder of Oratory of Divine Love, forerunner of the Theatines; canonized 1671; Aug. 7.*

Callistus I (d. 222): Pope, 217-222; martyr; condemned Sabellianism and other heresies; advocated a policy of mercy toward repentant sinners; Oct. 14.*

Camillus de Lellis (1550-1614): Italian priest; founder of Camillians (Ministers of the Sick); canonized 1746; patron of the sick and of nurses; July 14.*

Casimir (1458-1484): Polish prince; grand duke of Lithuania; noted for his piety; buried at cathedral in Vilna, Lithuania; canonized 1521; patron of Poland and Lithuania; Mar. 4.*

Cassian of Tangier (d. 298): Roman martyr; an official court stenographer who declared himself a Christian; patron of stenographers; Dec. 3.

Catherine Labouré (1806-1876): French Religious; favored with series of visions soon after she joined Sisters of Charity of St. Vincent de Paul in Paris in 1830; first Miraculous Medal (see Index) struck in 1832 in accord with one of the visions; canonized 1947; Nov. 28.

Catherine of Bologna (1413-1463): Italian Poor Clare; mystic, writer, artist canonized 1712; patron of artists; May 9.

Cecilia (2nd-3rd century): Roman virgin-martyr; traditional patroness of musicians; Nov. 22.*

Charles Borromeo (1538-1584): Italian cardinal; nephew of Pope Pius IV; cardinal bishop of Milan; influential figure in Church reform in Italy; promoted education of clergy; canonized 1610; Nov. 4.*

Charles Lwanga and Companions (d. between 1885 and 1887): Twenty-two Martyrs of Uganda, many of them pages of King Mwanga of Uganda, who were put to death because they denounced his corrupt lifestyle; canonized 1964; first martyrs of black Africa; June 3.*

Charles of Sezze (1616-1670): Italian Franciscan lay brother who served in humble capacities; canonized 1959; Jan. 6.

Christopher (3rd cent.): Early Christian martyr inscribed in Roman calendar about 1550; feast relegated to particular calendars because of legendary nature of accounts of his life; traditional patron of travelers; July 25.

Clare (1194-1253): Foundress of Poor Clares; b. at Assisi; was joined in religious life by her sisters, Agnes and Beatrice, and eventually her widowed mother Ortolana; canonized 1255; patroness of television; Aug. 11.*

Claude de la Colombiere (1641-1682): French Jesuit; spiritual director of St. Margaret Mary Alacoque; instrumental in spreading devotion to the Sacred Heart; beatified, 1929; canonized May 31, 1992; Feb. 15.

Clement Hofbauer (1751-1820): Redemptorist priest, missionary; born in Moravia; helped spread Redemptorists north of the Alps; canonized 1909; Mar. 15.

Clement I (d. c. 100): Pope, 88-97; third successor of St. Peter; wrote important letter to Church in Corinth settling disputes there; venerated as a martyr; Nov. 23.*

Columba (521-597): Irish monk; founded monasteries in Ireland; missionary in Scotland; established monastery at Iona which became the center for conversion of Picts, Scots, and Northern English; Scotland's most famous saint; patron saint of Ireland (with Sts. Patrick and Brigid); June 9.

Columban (545-615): Irish monk; scholar; founded monasteries in England and Brittany (famous abbey of Luxeuil), forced into exile because of his criticism of Frankish court; spent last years in northern Italy where he founded abbey at Bobbio; Nov. 23.*

Conrad of Parzham (1818-1894): Bavarian Capuchin lay brother; served as porter at the Marian shrine of Altotting in Upper Bavaria for 40 years; canonized 1934; Apr. 21.

Contardo Ferrini, Bl. (1859-1902): Italian secular Franciscan; model of the Catholic professor; beatified 1947; patron of universities; Oct. 20.

Cornelius (d. 253): Pope, 251-253; promoted a policy of mercy with respect to readmission of repentant Christians who had fallen away during the persecution of Decius (lapsi); banished from Rome during persecution of Gallus; regarded as a martyr; Sept. 16 (with Cyprian).*

Cosmas and Damian (d. c. 303): Arabian twin brothers, physicians; martyred during Diocletian persecution; patrons of physicians; Sept. 26.*

Crispin and Crispinian (3rd cent.): Early Christian martyrs; said to have met their deaths in Gaul; patrons of shoemakers, a trade they pursued; Oct. 25.

Crispin of Viterbo (1668-1750): Capuchin brother; canonized June 20, 1982; May 21.

Cyprian (d. 258): Early ecclesiastical writer; b. Africa; bishop of Carthage, 249-258; supported Pope St. Cornelius concerning the readmission of Christians who had apostatized in time of persecution; erred in his teaching that baptism administered by heretics and schismatics was invalid; wrote De Unitate; Sept. 16 (with St. Cornelius).*

Cyril and Methodius (9th century): Greek missionaries, bothers; venerated as apostles of the Slavs; Cyril (d. 869) and Methodius (d. 885) began their missionary work in Moravia in 863; developed a Slavonic alphabet; used the vernacular in the liturgy, a practice that was eventually approved; declared patrons of Europe with St. Benedict, Dec. 31, 1980; Feb. 14.*

Damasus I (d. 384): Pope, 366-384; opposed Arians and Apollinarians; commissioned St. Jerome to work on Bible translation; developed Roman liturgy; Dec. 11.*

Damian: See **Cosmas and Damian.**

Damien of Molokai (d. 1889): The so-called leper priest of Molokai; originally from Belgium, Damien devoted over twenty years to the care of the lepers in Hawaii, ultimately dying from the same disease. He was beatified by Pope John Paul II in 1996.

David (5th or 6th cent.): Nothing for certain known of his life; said to have founded monastery at Menevia; patron saint of Wales; Mar. 1.

Denis and Companions (d. 3rd cent.): Denis, bishop of Paris, and two companions identified by early writers as Rusticus, a priest, and Eleutherius, a deacon; martyred near Paris; Denis is popularly regarded as the apostle and a patron saint of France; Oct. 9.*

Dismas (1st cent.): Name given to repentant thief (Good Thief) to whom Jesus promised salvation (Lk. 23:40-43); regarded as patron of prisoners; Mar. 25 (observed on second Sunday of October in U.S. prison chapels).

Dominic (Dominic de Guzman) (1170-1221): Spanish priest; founded the Order of Preachers (Dominicans), 1215, in France; preached against the Albigensian heresy; a contemporary of St. Francis of Assisi; canonized 1234; Aug. 8.*

Dominic Savio (1842-1857): Italian youth; pupil of St. John Bosco; died before his 15th birthday; canonized 1954; patron of choir boys; May 6.

Duns Scotus, John (d. 1308): Scottish Franciscan; theologian; advanced theological arguments for doctrine of the Immaculate Conception; proclaimed blessed; cult solemnly confirmed by John Paul II, Mar. 20, 1993; Nov. 8.

Dunstan (c. 910-988): English monk; archbishop of Canterbury; initiated reforms in religious life; counselor to several kings; considered one of greatest Anglo-Saxon saints; patron of goldsmiths, locksmiths, jewelers (trades in which he is said to have excelled); May 19.

Dymphna (dates unknown): Nothing certain known of her life; according to legend, she was an Irish maiden murdered by her heathen father at Gheel near Antwerp, Belgium, where she had fled to escape his advances; her relics were discovered there in the 13th century; since that time cures of mental illness and epilepsy have been attributed to her intercession; patron of those suffering from mental illness; May 15.

Edith Stein, St. (1891-1942): German Carmelite (Teresa Benedicta of the Cross); born of Jewish parents; author and lecturer; baptized in Catholic Church, 1922; arrested with her sister Rosa in 1942 and put to death at Auschwitz; beatified 1987, by Pope John Paul II during his visit to West Germany. Aug. 10. She was canonized by Pope John Paul II on Oct. 11, 1998.

Edmund Campion (1540-1581): English Jesuit; convert 1573; martyred at Tyburn; canonized 1970, one of the Forty English and Welsh Martyrs; Dec. 1.

Edward the Confessor (d. 1066): King of England, 1042-66; canonized 1161; Oct. 13.

Eligius (c. 590-660): Bishop; born in Gaul; founded monasteries and convents; bishop of Noyon and Tournai; famous worker in gold and silver; Dec. 1.

Elizabeth Ann Seton (1774-1821): American foundress; convert, 1805; founded Sisters of Charity in the U.S.; beatified 1963; canonized Sept. 14, 1975; the first American-born saint; Jan. 4 (U.S.).*

Elizabeth of Hungary (1207-1231): Became secular Franciscan after death of her husband in 1227; devoted life to poor and destitute; a patron of the Secular Franciscan Order; canonized 1235; Nov. 17.*

Elizabeth of Portugal (1271-1336): Queen of Portugal; b. Spain; retired to Poor Clare convent as a secular Franciscan after the death of her husband; canonized 1626; July 4.*

Emily de Rodat (1787-1852): French foundress of the Congregation of the Holy Family of Villefranche; canonized 1950; Sept. 19.

Emily de Vialar (1797-1856): French foundress of the Sisters of St. Joseph of the Apparition; canonized 1951; June 17.

Erasmus (Elmo) (d. 303): Life surrounded by legend; martyred during Diocletian persecution; patron of sailors; June 2.

Ethelbert (552-616): King of Kent, England; baptized by St. Augustine of Canterbury, 597; issued legal code; furthered spread of Christianity; Feb. 26.

Euphrasia Pelletier (1796-1868): French Religious; founded Sisters of the Good Shepherd at Angers, 1829; canonized 1940; Apr. 24.

Eusebius of Vercelli (283-370): Italian bishop; exiled from his see (Vercelli) for a time because of his opposition to Arianism; considered a martyr because of sufferings he endured; Aug. 2.*

Fabian (d. 250): Pope, 236-250; martyred under Decius; Jan. 20.*

Felicity: See **Perpetua and Felicity**.

Ferdinand III (1198-1252): King of Castile and Leon; waged successful crusade against Muhammadans in Spain; founded university at Salamanca; canonized 1671; May 30.

Fiacre (Fiachra) (d. c. 670): Irish hermit; patron of gardeners; Aug. 30.

Fidelis of Sigmaringen (Mark Rey) (1577-1622): German Capuchin; lawyer before he joined the Capuchins; missionary to Swiss Protestants; stabbed to death by peasants who were told he was agent of Austrian emperor; Apr. 24.*

Frances of Rome (1384-1440): Italian model for housewives and widows; happily married for 40 years; after death of her husband in 1436 joined community of Benedictine Oblates she had founded; canonized 1608; patron of motorists; Mar. 9.*

Frances Xavier Cabrini (Mother Cabrini) (1850-1917): American foundress; b. Italy; founded the Missionary Sisters of the Sacred Heart, 1877; settled in the U.S. 1889; became an American citizen at Seattle 1909; worked among Italian immigrants; canonized 1946, the first American citizen so honored; Nov. 13 (U.S.).*

Francis Borgia (1510-1572): Spanish Jesuit; joined Jesuits after death of his wife in 1546; became general of the Order, 1565; Oct. 10.

Francis Caracciolo (1563-1608): Italian priest; founder with Father Augustine Adorno of the Clerics Regular Minor (Adorno Fathers); canonized 1807; declared patron of Italian chefs, 1996; June 4.

Francis Fasani (1681-1742): Italian Conventual Franciscan; model of priestly ministry, especially in service to poor and imprisoned; canonized 1986; Nov. 27.

Francis of Assisi (Giovanni di Bernardone) (1181/82-1226): Founder of the Franciscans, 1209; received stigmata 1224; canonized 1228; one of best known and best loved saints; patron of Italy, Catholic Action and ecologists; Oct. 4.*

Francis of Paola (1416-1507): Italian hermit: founder of Minim Friars; Apr. 2.*

Francis Xavier (1506-1552): Spanish Jesuit; missionary to Far East; canonized 1602; patron of foreign missions; considered one of greatest Christian missionaries; Dec. 3.*

Francis Xavier Bianchi (1743-1815): Italian Barnabite; acclaimed apostle of Naples because of his work there among the poor and abandoned; canonized 1951; Jan. 31.

Gabriel of the Sorrowful Mother (Francis Possenti) (1838-1862): Italian Passionist; died while a scholastic; canonized 1920; Feb. 27.

Gaspar (Caspar) **del Bufalo** (1786-1836): Italian priest; founded Missionaries of the Precious Blood, 1815; canonized 1954; Jan. 2.

Gemma Galgani (1878-1903): Italian laywoman; visionary; subject of extraordinary religious experiences; canonized 1940; Apr. 11.

Genesius (d. c. 300): Roman actor; according to legend, was converted while performing a burlesque of Christian baptism and was subsequently martyred; patron of actors; Aug. 25.

Geneviève (422-500): French nun; a patroness and protectress of Paris; events of her life not authenticated; Jan. 3.

George (d. c. 300): Martyr, probably during Diocletian persecution in Palestine; all other incidents of his life, including story of the dragon, are legendary; patron of England; Apr. 23.*

Gerard Majella (1725-1755): Italian Redemptorist lay brother; noted for supernatural occurrences in his life including bilocation and reading of consciences; canonized 1904; patron of mothers; Oct. 16.

Gertrude (1256-1302): German mystic; writer; helped spread devotion to the Sacred Heart; Nov. 16.*

Gregory VII (Hildebrand) (1020?-1085): Pope, 1075-1085; Benedictine monk; adviser to several popes; as pope, strengthened interior life of Church and fought against lay investiture; driven from Rome by Henry IV; died in exile; canonized 1584; May 25.*

Gregory Barbarigo (1626-1697): Italian cardinal; noted for his efforts to bring about reunion of separated Christians; canonized 1960; June 18.

Gregory of Nyssa (c. 335-395): Bishop; theologian; younger brother of St. Basil the Great; Mar. 9.

Gregory Thaumaturgus (c. 213-268): Bishop of Neocaesarea; missionary, famed as wonder worker; Nov. 17.

Gregory the Illuminator (257-332): Martyr; bishop; apostle and patron saint of Armenia; helped free Armenia from the Persians; Sept. 30.

Hedwig (1174-1243): Moravian noblewoman; married duke of Silesia, head of Polish royal family; fostered religious life in country; canonized 1266; Oct. 16.*

Helena (250-330): Empress; mother of Constantine the Great; associated with discovery of the True Cross; Aug. 18.

Henry (972-1024): Bavarian emperor; cooperated with Benedictine abbeys in restoration of ecclesiastical and social discipline; canonized 1146; July 13.*

Herman Joseph (1150-1241): German Premonstratensian; his visions were the subjects of artists; writer; cult approved, 1958; Apr. 7.

Hippolytus (d. c. 236): Roman priest; opposed Pope St. Callistus I in his teaching about the readmission to the Church of repentant Christians who had apostatized during time of persecution; elected antipope; exiled to Sardinia; reconciled before his martyrdom; important ecclesiastical writer; Aug. 13* (with Pontian).

Hubert (d. 727): Bishop; his patronage of hunters is based on legend that he was converted while hunting; Nov. 3.

Hugh of Cluny (the Great) (1024-1109): Abbot of Benedictine foundation at Cluny; supported popes in efforts to reform ecclesiastical abuses; canonized 1120; Apr. 29.

Ignatius of Antioch (d. c. 107): Early ecclesiastical writer; martyr; bishop of Antioch in Syria for 40 years; Oct. 17.*

Ignatius of Laconi (1701-1781): Italian Capuchin lay brother whose 60 years of religious life were spent in Franciscan simplicity; canonized 1951; May 11.

Ignatius of Loyola (1491-1556): Spanish soldier; renounced military career after recovering from wounds received at siege of Pampeluna (Pamplona) in 1521; founded Society of Jesus (Jesuits), 1534, at Paris; wrote The Book of Spiritual Exercises; canonized 1622; July 31.*

Irenaeus of Lyons (130-202): Early ecclesiastical writer; opposed Gnosticism; bishop of Lyons; traditionally regarded as a martyr; June 28.*

Isidore the Farmer (d. 1170): Spanish layman; farmer; canonized 1622; patron of farmers; May 15 (U.S.).*

Jane Frances de Chantal (1572-1641): French widow; foundress, under guidance of St. Francis de Sales, of Order of the Visitation; canonized 1767; Dec. 12* (General Roman Calendar); Aug. 18* (U.S.).

Januarius (Gennaro) (d. 304): Bishop of Benevento; martyred during Diocletian persecution; fame rests on liquefaction of some of his blood preserved in a phial at Naples, an unexplained phenomenon which has occurred regularly several times each year for over 400 years; Sept. 19.*

Jeanne Delanoue (1666-1736): French foundress of Sisters of St. Anne of Providence, 1704; canonized 1982; Aug. 16.

Jeanne (Joan) **de Lestonnac** (1556-1640): French foundress; widowed in 1597; founded the Religious of Notre Dame 1607; canonized 1947; Feb. 2.

Jeanne de Valois (Jeanne of France) (1464-1505): French foundress; deformed daughter of King Louis XI; was married in 1476 to Duke Louis of Orleans who had the marriage annulled when he ascended the throne as Louis XII; Jeanne retired to life of prayer; founded contemplative Annonciades of Bourges, 1504; canonized 1950; Feb. 5.

Jeanne-Elizabeth Bichier des Ages (1773-1838): French Religious; co-founder with St. Andrew

Fournet of Daughters of the Cross of St. Andrew, 1807; canonized 1947; Aug. 26.

Jeanne Jugan, Bl. (1792-1879): French Religious; foundress of Little Sisters of the Poor; beatified Oct. 3, 1982; Aug. 30.

Jerome Emiliani (1481-1537): Venetian priest; founded Somascan Fathers, 1532, for care of orphans; canonized 1767; patron of orphans and abandoned children; Feb. 8.*

Joan Antida Thouret (1765-1826): French Religious; founded, 1799, congregation now known as Sisters of Charity of St. Joan Antida; canonized 1934; Aug. 24.

Joan of Arc (1412-1431): French heroine, called The Maid of Orleans, La Pucelle; led French army in 1429 against English invaders besieging Orleans; captured by Burgundians the following year; turned over to ecclesiastical court on charge of heresy, found guilty and burned at the stake; her innocence was declared in 1456; canonized 1920; patroness of France; May 30.

Joaquina de Vedruna de Mas (1783-1854): Spanish foundress; widowed in 1816; after providing for her children, founded the Carmelite Sisters of Charity; canonized 1959; Aug. 28.

John I (d. 526): Pope, 523-526; martyr; May 18.*

John Baptist de la Salle (1651-1719): French priest; founder of Brothers of the Christian Schools, 1680; canonized 1900; patron of teachers; Apr. 7.*

John Berchmans (1599-1621): Belgian Jesuit scholastic; patron of Mass servers; canonized 1888; Aug. 13.

John (Don) Bosco (1815-1888): Italian priest; founded Salesians, 1859, for education of boys; co-founder of Daughters of Mary Help of Christians for education of girls; canonized 1934; Jan. 31.*

John Capistran (1386-1456): Italian Franciscan; preacher; papal diplomat; canonized 1690; declared patron of military chaplains, Feb. 10, 1984. Oct. 23.*

John de Ribera (1532-1611): Spanish bishop and statesman; archbishop of Valencia, 1568-1611, and viceroy of that province; canonized 1960; Jan. 6.

John Eudes (1601-1680): French priest; founder of Sisters of Our Lady of Charity of Refuge, 1642, and Congregation of Jesus-Mary (Eudists), 1643; canonized 1925; Aug. 19.*

John Fisher (1469-1535): English prelate; theologian; martyr; bishop of Rochester, cardinal; refused to recognize validity of Henry VIII's marriage to Anne Boleyn; upheld supremacy of the pope; beheaded for refusing to acknowledge Henry as head of the Church; canonized 1935; June 22 (with St. Thomas More).*

John Francis Regis (1597-1640): French Jesuit priest; preached missions among poor and unlettered; canonized 1737; patron of social workers, particularly medical social workers, because of his concern for poor and needy and sick in hospitals; July 2.

John Gualbert (d. 1073): Italian priest; founder of Benedictine congregation of Vallombrosians, 1039; canonized 1193; July 12.

John Kanty (Cantius) (1395-1473): Polish theologian; canonized 1767; Dec. 23.*

John Leonardi (1550-1609): Italian priest; worked among prisoners and the sick; founded Clerics Regular of the Mother of God; canonized 1938; Oct. 9.*

John Nepomucene (1345-1393): Bohemian priest;

regarded as a martyr; canonized 1729; patron of Czechoslovakia; May 16.

John Nepomucene Neumann (1811-1860): American prelate; b. Bohemia; ordained in New York 1836; missionary among Germans near Niagara Falls before joining Redemptorists, 1840; bishop of Philadelphia, 1852; first bishop in U.S. to prescribe Forty Hours devotion in his diocese; beatified 1963; canonized June 19, 1977; Jan. 5 (U.S.).*

John of Ávila (1499-1569): Spanish priest; preacher; ascetical writer; spiritual adviser of St. Teresa of Jesus (Ávila); canonized 1970; May 10.

John of Britto (1647-1693): Portuguese Jesuit; missionary in India where he was martyred; canonized 1947; Feb. 4.

John of God (1495-1550): Portuguese founder; his work among the sick poor led to foundation of Brothers Hospitallers of St. John of God, 1540, in Spain; canonized 1690; patron of sick, nurses, hospitals; Mar. 8.*

John of Matha (1160-1213): French priest; founder of the Order of Most Holy Trinity, whose original purpose was the ransom of prisoners from the Muslems; Feb. 8.

John Ogilvie (1579-1615): Scottish Jesuit; martyr; canonized 1976, the first canonized Scottish saint since 1250 (Margaret of Scotland); Mar. 10.

John Vianney (Curé of Ars) (1786-1859): French parish priest; noted confessor, spent 16 to 18 hours a day in confessional; canonized 1925; patron of parish priests; Aug. 4.*

Josaphat Kuncevyc (1584-1623): Basilian monk; b. Poland; archbishop of Polotsk, Lithuania; worked for reunion of separated Eastern Christians with Rome; martyred by mob of schismatics; canonized 1867; Nov. 12.*

Joseph Benedict Cottolengo (1786-1842): Italian priest; established Little Houses of Divine Providence (Piccolo Casa) for care of orphans and the sick; canonized 1934; Apr. 30.

Joseph Cafasso (1811-1860): Italian priest; renowned confessor; promoted devotion to Blessed Sacrament; canonized 1947; June 23.

Joseph Calasanz (1556-1648): Spanish priest; founder of Piarists (Order of Pious Schools); canonized 1767; Aug. 25.*

Joseph of Cupertino (1603-1663): Italian Franciscan; noted for remarkable incidents of levitation; canonized 1767; Sept. 18.

Joseph Pignatelli (1737-1811): Spanish Jesuit; left Spain when Jesuits were banished in 1767; worked for revival of the Order; named first superior when Jesuits were reestablished in Kingdom of Naples, 1804; canonized 1954; Nov. 28.

Juan Diego, Bl. (16th cent.): Mexican Indian, convert; indigenous name according to tradition Cuauhtlatohuac ("The eagle who speaks"); favored with apparitions of Our Lady (see Index: Our Lady of Guadalupe) on Tepeyac hill; beatified, 1990; Dec. 9* (U.S.).

Julia Billiart (1751-1816): French foundress; founded Sisters of Notre Dame de Namur, 1804; canonized 1969; Apr. 8.

Justin de Jacobis (1800-1860): Italian Vincentian; bishop; missionary in Ethiopia; canonized 1975; July 31.

Justin Martyr (100-165): Early ecclesiastical writer; Apologies for the Christian Religion, Dialog with the Jew Tryphon; martyred at Rome; June 1.*

Kateri Tekakwitha, Bl. (1656-1680): "Lily of the Mohawks." Indian maiden born at Ossernenon (Auriesville), N.Y.; baptized Christian, Easter, 1676, by Jesuit missionary Father Jacques de Lambertville; lived life devoted to prayer, penitential practices and care of sick and aged in Christian village of Caughnawaga near Montreal where her relics are now enshrined; beatified June 22, 1980; July 14* (in U.S.).

Katharine Drexel, Bl. (1858-1955): Philadelphia-born heiress; devoted wealth to founding schools and missions for Indians and Blacks; foundress of Sisters of Blessed Sacrament for Indians and Colored People, 1891; beatified 1988; Mar. 3* (U.S.).

Ladislaus (1040-1095): King of Hungary; supported Pope Gregory VII against Henry IV; canonized 1192; June 27.

Lawrence (d. 258): Widely venerated martyr who suffered death, according to a long-standing but unverifiable legend, by fire on a gridiron; Aug. 10.*

Lawrence (Lorenzo) **Ruiz and Companions** (d. 1630s): Martyred in or near the city of Nagasaki, Japan; Lawrence Ruiz, first Filipino saint, and 15 companions (nine Japanese, four Spaniards, one Italian and one Frenchman); canonized 1987; Sept. 28.*

Leonard Murialdo (1828-1900): Italian priest; educator; founder of Pious Society of St. Joseph of Turin, 1873; canonized 1970; Mar. 30.

Leonard of Port Maurice (1676-1751): Italian Franciscan; ascetical writer; preached missions throughout Italy; canonized 1867; patron of parish missions; Nov. 26.

Leopold Mandic (1866-1942): Croatian-born Franciscan priest; noted confessor; spent most of his priestly life in Padua, Italy; canonized 1983; July 30.

Louis IX (1215-1270): King of France, 1226-1270; participated in Sixth Crusade; patron of Secular Franciscan Order; canonized 1297; Aug. 25.*

Louis de Montfort (1673-1716): French priest; founder of Sisters of Divine Wisdom, 1703, and Missionaries of Company of Mary, 1715; wrote True Devotion to the Blessed Virgin; canonized 1947; Apr. 28.*

Louis Zepherin Moreau, Bl. (d. 1901): Canadian bishop; headed St. Hyacinthe, Que., diocese, 1876-1901; beatified 1987; May 24.

Louise de Marillac (1591-1660): French foundress, with St. Vincent de Paul, of the Sisters of Charity; canonized 1934; Mar. 15.

Lucy (d. 304): Sicilian maiden; martyred during Diocletian persecution; one of most widely venerated early virgin-martyrs; patron of Syracuse, Sicily; invoked by those suffering from eye diseases; Dec. 13.*

Lucy Filippini (1672-1732): Italian educator; helped improve status of women through education; considered a founder of the Religious Teachers Filippini, 1692; canonized 1930; Mar. 25.

Madeleine Sophie Barat (1779-1865): French foundress of the Society of the Sacred Heart of Jesus; canonized 1925; May 25.

Malachy (1095-1148): Irish bishop; instrumental in establishing first Cistercian house in Ireland, 1142; canonized 1190; Nov. 3 (See Index: Prophecies of St. Malachy).

Marcellinus and Peter (d.c. 304): Early Roman martyrs; June 2.*

Margaret Clitherow (1556-1586): English martyr; convert shortly after her marriage; one of Forty Martyrs of England and Wales; canonized 1970; Mar. 25.

Margaret Mary Alacoque (1647-1690): French Religious; spread devotion to Sacred Heart in accordance with revelations made to her in 1675 (see Sacred Heart); canonized 1920; Oct. 16.*

Margaret of Cortona (1247-1297): Secular Franciscan; reformed her life in 1273 following the violent death of her lover; canonized 1728; May 16.

Margaret of Hungary (1242-1270): Contemplative; daughter of King Bela IV of Hungary; lived a life of self-imposed penances; canonized 1943; Jan. 18.

Margaret of Scotland (1050-1093): Queen of Scotland; noted for solicitude for the poor and promotion of justice; canonized 1250; Nov. 16.*

Maria Goretti (1890-1902): Italian virgin-martyr; a model of purity; canonized 1950; July 6.*

Mariana Paredes of Jesus (1618-1645): South American recluse; Lily of Quito; canonized, 1950; May 28.

Marie-Leonie Paradis, Bl. (1840-1912): Canadian Religious; founded Little Sisters of the Holy Family, 1880; beatified 1984; May 4.

Marie-Rose Durocher, Bl. (1811-1849): Canadian Religious; foundress of Sisters of Holy Names of Jesus and Mary; beatified 1982; Oct. 6* (in U.S.).

Martha (1st cent.): Sister of Lazarus and Mary of Bethany; Gospel accounts record her concern for homely details; patron of cooks; July 29.*

Martin I (d. 655): Pope, 649-55; banished from Rome by emperor in 653 because of his condemnation of Monothelites; considered a martyr; Apr. 13.*

Martin of Tours (316-397): Bishop of Tours; opposed Arianism and Priscillianism; pioneer of Western monasticism, before St. Benedict; Nov. 11.*

Mary Domenica Mazzarello (1837-1881): Italian foundress, with St. John Bosco, of the Daughters of Mary Help of Christians, 1872; canonized 1951; May 14.

Mary Josepha Rossello (1811-1881): Italian-born foundress of the Daughters of Our Lady of Mercy; canonized 1949; Dec. 7.

Mary Magdalen Postel (1756-1846): French foundress of the Sisters of Christian Schools of Mercy, 1807; canonized 1925; July 16.

Mary Magdalene (1st cent.): Gospels record her as devoted follower of Christ to whom he appeared after the Resurrection; her identification with Mary of Bethany (sister of Martha and Lazarus) and the woman sinner (Lk 7:36-50) has been questioned; July 22.*

Mary Magdalene dei Pazzi (1566-1607): Italian Carmelite nun; recipient of mystical experiences; canonized 1669; May 25.*

Mary Michaela Desmaisières (1809-1865): Spanish-born foundress of the Institute of the Handmaids of the Blessed Sacrament, 1848; canonized 1847; Aug. 24.

Maximilian Kolbe (1894-1941): Polish Conventual Franciscan; prisoner at Auschwitz who heroically offered his life in place of a fellow prisoner; beatified 1971, canonized 1982; Aug. 14.*

Methodius: See Index.

Miguel Febres Cordero (1854-1910): Ecuadorean Christian Brother; educator; canonized 1984; Feb. 9.

Miguel Pro, Bl. (1891-1927): Mexican Jesuit; joined Jesuits, 1911; forced to flee because of religious persecution; ordained in Belgium, 1925; returned to Mexico, 1926, to minister to people despite government prohibition; unjustly accused of assassination plot against president; arrested and executed; beatified 1988. Nov. 23* (U.S.).

Monica (332-387): Mother of St. Augustine; model of a patient mother; her feast is observed in the Roman calendar the day before her son's; Aug. 27.*

Nereus and Achilleus (d. c. 100): Early Christian martyrs; soldiers who, according to legend, were baptized by St. Peter; May 12.*

Nicholas of Flüe (1417-1487): Swiss layman; at the age of 50, with the consent of his wife and 10 children, he retreated from the world to live as a hermit; called Brother Claus by the Swiss; canonized 1947; Mar. 21.

Nicholas of Myra (4th cent.): Bishop of Myra in Asia Minor; one of most popular saints in both East and West; most of the incidents of his life are based on legend; patron of Russia; Dec. 6.*

Nicholas of Tolentino (1245-1305): Italian hermit; famed preacher; canonized 1446; Sept. 10.

Nicholas Tavelic and Companions (Deodatus of Aquitaine, Peter of Narbonne, Stephen of Cuneo) (d. 1391): Franciscan missionaries; martyred by Muslims in the Holy Land; canonized 1970; Nov. 14.

Norbert (1080-1134): German bishop; founded Canons Regular of Premontre (Premonstratensians, Norbertines), 1120; promoted reform of the clergy; devotion to Blessed Sacrament; canonized 1582; June 6.*

Odilia (d. c. 720): Benedictine abbess; according to legend she was born blind, abandoned by her family and adopted by a convent of nuns where her sight was miraculously restored; patroness of blind; Dec. 13.

Oliver Plunket (1629-1681): Irish martyr; theologian; archbishop of Armagh and primate of Ireland; beatified 1920; canonized, 1975; July 1.

Pancras (d. c. 304): Roman martyr; May 12.*

Paola Frassinetti (1809-1882): Italian Religious; foundress, 1834, of Sisters of St. Dorothy; canonized 1984; June 11.

Paschal Baylon (1540-1592): Spanish Franciscan lay brother; spent life as door-keeper in various Franciscan friaries; defended doctrine of Real Presence in Blessed Sacrament; canonized 1690; patron of all Eucharistic confraternities and congresses, 1897; May 17.

Patrick (389-461): Famous missionary of Ireland; began missionary work in Ireland about 432; organized the Church there and established it on a lasting foundation; patron of Ireland, with Sts. Bridget and Columba; Mar. 17.*

Paul Miki and Companions (d. 1597): Martyrs of Japan; Paul Miki, Jesuit, and twenty-five other priests and laymen were martyred at Nagasaki; canonized 1862, the first canonized martyrs of the Far East; Feb. 6.*

Paul of the Cross (1694-1775): Italian Religious; founder of the Passionists; canonized 1867; Oct 19* (Oct. 20, U.S.*).

Paulinus of Nola (d. 451): Bishop of Nola (Spain); writer; June 22.*

Peregrine (1260-1347): Italian Servite; invoked

against cancer (he was miraculously cured of cancer of the foot after a vision); canonized 1726; May 1.

Perpetua and Felicity (d. 203): Martyrs; Perpetua was a young married woman; Felicity was a slave girl; Mar. 7.*

Peter Chanel (1803-1841): French Marist; missionary to Oceania, where he was martyred; canonized 1954; Apr. 28.*

Peter Fourier (1565-1640): French priest; co-founder with Alice LeClercq (Mother Teresa of Jesus) of the Augustinian Canonesses of Our Lady, 1598; canonized 1897; Dec. 9.

Peter Gonzalez (1190-1246): Spanish Dominican; worked among sailors; court chaplain and confessor of King St. Ferdinand of Castile; patron of sailors; Apr. 14.

Peter Julian Eymard (1811-1868): French priest; founder of the Congregation of the Blessed Sacrament (men), 1856, and Servants of the Blessed Sacrament (women), 1864; dedicated to Eucharistic apostolate; canonized 1962; Aug. 2.*

Peter Nolasco (c. 1189-1258): Born in Langueduc area of present-day France; founded the Mercedarians (Order of Our Lady of Mercy), 1218, in Spain; canonized 1628; Jan. 31.

Peter of Alcantara (1499-1562): Spanish Franciscan; mystic; initiated Franciscan reform; confessor of St. Teresa of Jesus (Ávila); canonized 1669; Oct. 22 (in U.S.).

Philip Benizi (1233-1285): Italian Servite; noted preacher, peacemaker; canonized 1671; Aug. 23.

Philip Neri (1515-1595): Italian Religious; founded Congregation of the Oratory; considered a second apostle of Rome because of his mission activity there; canonized 1622; May 26.*

Philip of Jesus (1517-157): Mexican Franciscan; martyred at Nagasaki, Japan; canonized 1862; patron of Mexico City; Feb. 6.*

Pio, Padre, Bl.

Pius V (1504-1572): Pope, 1566-1572; enforced decrees of Council of Trent; organized expedition against Turks resulting in victory at Lepanto; canonized 1712; Apr. 30.*

Polycarp (2nd cent.): Bishop of Smyrna; ecclesiastical writer; martyr; Feb. 23.*

Pontian (d. c. 235): Pope, 230-235; exiled to Sardinia by the emperor; regarded as a martyr; Aug. 13 (with Hippolytus).*

Rafaela Maria Porras y Ayllon (1850-1925): Spanish Religious; founded the Handmaids of the Sacred Heart, 1877; canonized 1977; Jan. 6.

Raymond Nonnatus (d. 1240): Spanish Mercedarian; cardinal; devoted his life to ransoming captives from the Moors; Aug. 31.

Raymond of Peñafort (1175-1275): Spanish Dominican; confessor of Gregory IX; systematized and codified canon law, in effect until 1917; master general of Dominicans, 1238; canonized 1601; Jan. 7.*

Rita of Cascia (1381-1457): Widow; cloistered Augustinian Religious of Umbria; invoked in impossible and desperate cases; May 22.

Robert Southwell (1561-1595): English Jesuit; poet; martyred at Tyburn; canonized 1970, one of the Forty English and Welsh Martyrs; Feb. 21.

Roch (1350-1379): French layman; pilgrim; devoted life to care of plague-stricken; widely venerated; invoked against pestilence; Aug. 17.

Romuald (951-1027): Italian monk; founded Camaldolese Benedictines; June 19.*

Rose of Lima (1586-1617): Peruvian Dominican tertiary; first native-born saint of the New World; canonized 1671; Aug. 23.*

Scholastica (d. c. 559): Sister of St. Benedict; regarded as first nun of the Benedictine Order; Feb. 10.*

Sebastian (3rd cent.): Roman martyr; traditionally pictured as a handsome youth with arrows; martyred; patron of athletes, archers; Jan. 20.*

Seven Holy Founders of the Servants of Mary (Buonfiglio Monaldo, Alexis Falconieri, Benedict dell'Antello, Bartholomew Amidei, Ricovero Uguccione, Gerardino Sostegni, John Buonagiunta Monetti): Florentine youths who founded Servites, 1233, in obedience to a vision; canonized 1888; Feb. 17.*

Sharbel Makhlouf (1828-1898): Lebanese Maronite monk-hermit; canonized 1977; Dec. 24.

Sixtus II and Companions (d. 258): Sixtus, pope 257-258, and four deacons, martyrs; Aug. 7.*

Stanislaus (1030-1079): Polish bishop; martyr; canonized 1253; Apr. 11.*

Stephen (d. c. 33): First Christian martyr; chosen by the Apostles as the first of the seven deacons; stoned to death; Dec. 26.*

Stephen (975-1038): King; apostle of Hungary; welded Magyars into national unity; canonized 1083; Aug. 16.*

Sylvester I (d. 335): Pope 314-335; first ecumenical council held at Nicaea during his pontificate; Dec. 31.*

Tarcisius (d. 3rd cent.): Early martyr; according to tradition, was martyred while carrying the Blessed Sacrament to some Christians in prison; patron of first communicants; Aug. 15.

Teresa Margaret Redi (1747-1770): Italian Carmelite; lived life of prayer and austere penance; canonized 1934; Mar. 11.

Teresa of Jesus Jornet Ibars (1843-1897): Spanish Religious; founded the Little Sisters of the Abandoned Aged, 1873; canonized 1974; Aug. 26.

Thérèse Couderc (1805-1885): French Religious; foundress of the Religious of Our Lady of the Retreat in the Cenacle, 1827; canonized 1970; Sept. 26.

Thomas Becket (1118-1170): English martyr; archbishop of Canterbury; chancellor under Henry II; murdered for upholding rights of the Church; canonized 1173; Dec. 29.*

Thomas More (1478-1535): English martyr; statesman, chancellor under Henry VIII; author of Utopia; opposed Henry's divorce, refused to renounce authority of the papacy; beheaded; canonized 1935; June 22 (with St. John Fisher).*

Thorlac (1133-1193): Icelandic bishop; instituted reforms; although his cult was never officially approved, he was declared patron of Iceland, Jan. 14, 1984; Dec. 23.

Timothy (d. c. 97): Bishop of Ephesus; disciple and companion of St. Paul; martyr; Jan. 26.*

Titus (d. c. 96): Bishop; companion of St. Paul; recipient of one of Paul's epistles; Jan. 26.*

Titus Brandsma, Bl. (1881-1942): Dutch Carmelite priest; professor, scholar, journalist; denounced Nazi persecution of Jews; arrested by Nazis, Jan. 19, 1942; executed by lethal injection at Dachau, July 26, 1942; beatified 1985; July 26.

Valentine (d. 269): Priest, physician; martyred at Rome; legendary patron of lovers; Feb. 14.

Vicenta Maria Lopez y Vicuna (1847-1896): Spanish foundress of the Daughters of Mary Immaculate for domestic service; canonized 1975; Dec. 26.

Vincent (d. 304): Spanish deacon; martyr; Jan. 22.*

Vincent de Paul (1581?-1660): French priest; founder of Congregation of the Mission (Vincentians, Lazarists) and co-founder of Sisters of Charity; declared patron of all charitable organizations and works by Leo XIII; canonized 1737; Sept. 27.*

Vincent Ferrer (1350-1418): Spanish Dominican; famed preacher; Apr. 5.*

Vincent Pallotti (1795-1850): Italian priest; founded Society of the Catholic Apostolate (Pallottines), 1835; Jan. 22.

Vincent Strambi (1745-1824): Italian Passionist; bishop; reformer; canonized 1950; Sept. 25.

Vincenza Gerosa (1784-1847): Italian co-foundress of the Sisters of Charity of Lovere; canonized 1950; June 28.

Vitus (d.c. 300): Martyr; died in Lucania, southern Italy; regarded as protector of epileptics and those suffering from St. Vitus Dance (chorea); June 15.

Walburga (d. 779): English-born Benedictine Religious; belonged to group of nuns who established convents in Germany at the invitation of St. Boniface; abbess of Heidenheim; Feb. 25.

Wenceslaus (d. 935): Duke of Bohemia; martyr; patron of Bohemia; Sept. 28.*

Zita (1218-1278): Italian maid; noted for charity to poor; patron of domestics; Apr. 27.

SAINTS — PATRONS AND INTERCESSORS

A patron is a saint who is venerated as a special intercessor before God. Most patrons have been so designated as the result of popular devotion and long-standing custom. In many cases, the fact of existing patronal devotion is clear despite historical obscurity regarding its origin. The Church has made official designation of relatively few patrons; in such cases, the dates of designation are given in parentheses in the list below. The theological background of the patronage of saints includes the dogmas of the Mystical Body of Christ and the Communion of Saints. Listed are patron saints of occupations and professions, and saints whose intercession is sought for special needs.

Academics: Thomas Aquinss.

Accomodations: Gertrude of Nivelles.

Accountants: Matthew.

Actors: Genesius.

Adopted children: Clotilde; Thomas More.

Advertisers: Bernardine of Siena (May 20, 1960).

Alcoholics: John of God; Monica

Alpinists: Bernard of Montjoux (or Menthon) (Aug. 20, 1923).

Altar servers: John Berchmans.

Anesthetists: René Goupil.

Animals: Francis of Assisi.

Archaeologists: Damasus.

Archers: Sebastian.

Architects: Thomas, Apostle.

Art: Catherine of Bologna.

Artists: Luke, Catherine of Bologna, Bl. Angelico (Feb. 21, 1984).

Astronauts: Joseph Cupertino.

Astronomers: Dominic.

Athletes: Sebastian.

Authors: Francis de Sales.

Aviators: Our Lady of Loreto (1920), Thérèse of Lisieux, Joseph of Cupertino.

Bakers: Elizabeth of Hungary, Nicholas.

Bankers: Matthew.

Barbers: Cosmas and Damian, Louis.

Barren women: Anthony of Padua, Felicity.

Basket-makers: Anthony, Abbot.

Bees: Ambrose.

Birth: Margaret.

Beggars: Martin of Tours.

Blacksmiths: Dunstan.

Blind: Odilia, Raphael.

Blood banks: Januarius.

Bodily ills: Our Lady of Lourdes.

Bookbinders: Peter Celestine.

Bookkeepers: Matthew.

Booksellers: John of God.

Boy Scouts: George.

Brewers: Augustine of Hippo, Luke, Nicholas of Myra.

Bricklayers: Stephen.

Brides: Nicholas of Myra.

Bridges: John of Nepomucene.

Broadcasters: Gabriel.

Brushmakers: Anthony, Abbot.

Builders: Vincent Ferrer.

Bus drivers: Christopher.

Butchers: Anthony (Abbot), Luke.

Butlers: Adelelm.

Cabdrivers: Fiacre.

Cabinetmakers: Anne.

Cancer patients: Peregrine.

Canonists: Raymond of Peñafort.

Carpenters: Joseph.

Catechists: Viator, Charles Borromeo, Robert Bellarmine.

Catholic Action: Francis of Assisi (1916).

Catholic Press: Francis de Sales.

Chandlers: Ambrose, Bernard of Clairvaux.

Chaplains: John of Capistrano.

Charitable societies: Vincent de Paul (May 12, 1885).

Chastity: Thomas Aquinas.

Childbirth: Raymond Nonnatus; Gerard Majella.

Children: Nicholas of Myra.

Children of Mary: Agnes, Maria Goretti.

Choirboys: Dominic Savio (June 8, 1956), Holy Innocents.

Church: Joseph (Dec. 8, 1870).

Circus people: Julian the Hospitaller.

Clerics: Gabriel of the Sorrowful Mother.

Colleges: Thomas Aquinas.

Comedians: Vitus.

Communications personnel: Bernardine.

Confessors: Alphonsus Liguori (Apr. 26, 1950), John Nepomucene.

Converts: Helena; Vladimir.

Convulsive children: Scholastica.

Cooks: Lawrence, Martha.

Coopers: Nicholas of Myra.
Coppersmiths: Maurus.
Dairy workers: Brigid.
Dancers: Vitus.
Deaf: Francis de Sales.
Dentists: Apollonia.
Desperate situations: Gregory of Neocaesarea, Jude Thaddeus, Rita of Cascia.
Dietitians (in hospitals): Martha.
Diplomats: Gabriel.
Divorce: Helena.
Drug addiction: Maximilian Kolbe.
Dyers: Maurice, Lydia.
Dying: Joseph.
Ecologists: Francis of Assisi (Nov. 29, 1979).
Ecumenists: Cyril and Methodius.
Editors: John Bosco.
Emigrants: Frances Xavier Cabrini (Sept. 8, 1950).
Endurance: Pantaleon.
Engineers: Ferdinand III.
Epilepsy, Motor Diseases: Vitus, Willibrord.
Eucharistic congresses and societies: Paschal Baylon (Nov. 28, 1897).
Expectant mothers: Raymond Nonnatus, Gerard Majella.
Eye diseases: Lucy.
Falsely accused: Raymond Nonnatus.
Farmers: George, Isidore.
Farriers: John the Baptist.
Firemen: Florian.
Fire prevention: Catherine of Siena.
First communicants: Tarcisius.
Fishermen: Andrew.
Florists: Thérèse of Lisieux.
Forest workers: John Gualbert.
Foundlings: Holy Innocents.
Friendship: John the Divine.
Fullers: Anastasius the Fuller, James the Less.
Funeral directors: Joseph of Arimathea, Dismas.
Gardeners: Adelard, Tryphon, Fiacre, Phocas.
Glassworkers: Luke.
Goldsmiths: Dunstan, Anastasius.
Gravediggers: Anthony, Abbot.
Greetings: Valentine.
Grocers: Michael.
Grooms: King Louis IX of France.
Hairdressers: Martin de Porres.
Happy meetings: Raphael.
Hatters: Severus of Ravenna, James the Less.
Headache sufferers: Teresa of Jesus (Ávila).
Heart patients: John of God.
Homeless: Margaret of Cortona; Benedict Joseph Labré.
Horses: Giles; Hippolytus.
Housekeepers: Zita.
Hospital administrators: Basil the Great, Frances X. Cabrini.
Hospitals: Camillus de Lellis and John of God (June 22, 1886), Jude Thaddeus.
Housewives: Anne.
Hunters: Hubert, Eustachius.
Infantrymen: Maurice.
Innkeepers: Amand, Martha, Julian the Hospitaller.
Innocence: Hallvard.
Invalids: Roch.
Janitors: Theobald.
Jewelers: Eligius, Dunstan.

Journalists: Francis de Sales (Apr. 26, 1923).
Jurists: John Capistran.
Laborers: Isidore, James, John Bosco.
Lawyers: Ivo (Yves Helory), Genesius, Thomas More.
Learning: Ambrose.
Librarians: Jerome.
Lighthouse keepers: Venerius (Mar. 10, 1961).
Linguists: Gottschalk.
Locksmiths: Dunstan.
Lost souls: Nicholas of Tolentino.
Lovers: Raphael; Valentine.
Lunatics: Christina.
Maids: Zita.
Marble workers: Clement I.
Mariners: Michael, Nicholas of Tolentino.
Medical record librarians: Raymond of Peñafort.
Medical social workers: John Regis.
Medical technicians: Albert the Great.
Mentally ill: Dymphna.
Merchants: Francis of Assisi, Nicholas of Myra.
Messengers: Gabriel.
Metal workers: Eligius.
Military chaplains: John Capistran (Feb. 10, 1984).
Millers: Arnulph, Victor.
Missions, foreign: Francis Xavier (Mar. 25, 1904), Thérèse of Lisieux (Dec. 14, 1927).
Missions, black: Peter Claver (1896, Leo XIII), Benedict the Black.
Missions, parish: Leonard of Port Maurice (Mar. 17, 1923).
Monks: Benedict of Nursia.
Mothers: Monica.
Motorcyclists: Our Lady of Grace.
Motorists: Christopher, Frances of Rome.
Mountaineers: Bernard of Montjoux (or Menthon).
Musicians: Gregory the Great, Cecilia, Dunstan.
Mystics: John of the Cross.
Notaries: Luke, Mark.
Nuns: Bridget.
Nurses: Camillus de Lellis and John of God (1930, Pius XI), Agatha, Raphael.
Nursing and nursing service: Elizabeth of Hungary, Catherine of Siena.
Orators: John Chrysostom (July 8, 1908).
Organ builders: Cecilia.
Orphans: Jerome Emiliani.
Painters: Luke.
Paratroopers: Michael.
Pawnbrokers: Nicholas.
Plumbers: Vincent Ferrer.
Pharmacists: Cosmas and Damian, James the Greater.
Pharmacists (in hospitals): Gemma Galgani.
Philosophers: Justin.
Physicians: Pantaleon, Cosmas and Damian, Luke, Raphael.
Pilgrims: James the Greater.
Plasterers: Bartholomew.
Poets: David, Cecilia.
Poison sufferers: Benedict.
Policemen: Michael.
Poor: Lawrence, Anthony of Padua.
Poor souls: Nicholas of Tolentino.
Popes: Gregory I the Great.
Porters: Christopher.
Possessed: Bruno, Denis.
Postal employees: Gabriel.
Priests: Jean-Baptiste Vianney (Apr. 23, 1929).
Printers: John of God, Augustine of Hippo, Genesius.

Prisoners: Dismas, Joseph Cafasso.
Protector of crops: Ansovinus.
Public relations: Bernardine of Siena (May 20, 1960).
Public relations (of hospitals): Paul, Apostle.
Publishers: John the Divine.
Race relations: Martin de Porres.
Radiologists: Michael (Jan. 15, 1941).
Radio workers: Gabriel.
Refugees: Alban.
Retreats: Ignatius Loyola (July 25, 1922).
Rheumatism: James the Greater.
Saddlers: Crispin and Crispinian.
Sailors: Cuthbert, Brendan, Eulalia, Christopher, Peter Gonzalez, Erasmus, Nicholas.
Scholars: Bede the Venerable; Brigid.
Schools, Catholic: Thomas Aquinas (Aug. 4, 1880), Joseph Calasanz (Aug. 13, 1948).
Scientists: Albert (Aug. 13, 1948).
Sculptors: Four Crowned Martyrs.
Seamen: Francis of Paola.
Searchers of lost articles: Anthony of Padua.
Secretaries: Genesius.
Secular Franciscans: Louis of France, Elizabeth of Hungary.
Seminarians: Charles Borromeo.
Servants: Martha, Zita.
Shepherds: Drogo.
Shoemakers: Crispin and Crispinian.
Sick: Michael, John of God and Camillus de Lellis (June 22, 1886).
Silversmiths: Andronicus.
Singers: Gregory, Cecilia.
Single mothers: Margaret of Cortona.
Single women: Catherine of Alexandria.
Skaters: Lidwina.
Skiers: Bernard of Montjoux (or Menthon).
Social workers: Louise de Marillac (Feb. 12, 1960).
Soldiers: Hadrian, George, Ignatius, Sebastian, Martin of Tours, Joan of Arc.
Speleologists: Benedict.
Stamp collectors: Gabriel.
Stenographers: Genesius, Cassian.
Stonecutters: Clement.
Stonemasons: Stephen.
Stress: Walter of Portnoise.
Students: Thomas Aquinas.
Surgeons: Cosmas and Damian, Luke.
Swimmers: Adjutor.
Swordsmiths: Maurice.
Tailors: Homobonus.
Tanners: Crispin and Crispinian, Simon.
Tax collectors: Matthew.
Teachers: Gregory the Great, John Baptist de la Salle (May 15, 1950).
Telecommunications workers: Gabriel (Jan. 12, 1951).
Television: Clare of Assisi (Feb. 14, 1958).
Television workers: Gabriel.
Thieves: Dismas.
Theologians: Augustine, Alphonsus Liguori.
Throat ailments: Blase.
Torture victims: Alban; Eustachius; Regina; Vincent; Victor of Marseilles.
Toymakers: Claude.
Travelers: Anthony of Padua, Nicholas of Myra, Christopher, Raphael.
Travel hostesses: Bona (Mar. 2, 1962).
Truck drivers: Christopher.

Universities: Blessed Contardo Ferrini.
Veterinarians: Blaise.
Vocations: Alphonsus.
Whales: Brendan the Voyager.
Watchmen: Peter of Alcantara.
Weavers: Paul the Hermit, Anastasius the Fuller, Anastasia.
Wine merchants: Amand.
Wineries: Morand; Vincent.
Women in labor: Anne.
Workingmen: Joseph.
Writers: Francis de Sales (Apr. 26, 1923), Lucy.
Yachtsmen: Adjutor.
Young girls: Agnes.
Youth: Aloysius Gonzaga (1729, Benedict XIII; 1926, Pius XI), John Berchmans, Gabriel of the Sorrowful Mother.

Patron Saints of Places

Albania: Our Lady of Good Counsel.
Alsace: Odilia.
Americas: Our Lady of Guadalupe, Rose of Lima.
Angola: Immaculate Heart of Mary (Nov. 21, 1984).
Argentina: Our Lady of Lujan.
Armenia: Gregory Illuminator.
Asia Minor: John, Evangelist.
Australia: Our Lady Help of Christians.
Belgium: Joseph.
Bohemia: Wenceslaus, Ludmilla.
Bolivia: Our Lady of Copacabana *"Virgen de la Candelaria."*
Borneo: Francis Xavier.
Brazil: Nossa Senhora de Aparecida, Immaculate Conception, Peter of Alcantara.
Canada: Joseph, Anne.
Chile: James the Greater, Our Lady of Mt. Carmel.
China: Joseph.
Colombia: Peter Claver, Louis Bertran.
Corsica: Immaculate Conception.
Cuba: Our Lady of Charity.
Czechoslovakia: Wenceslaus, John Nepomucene, Procopius.
Denmark: Ansgar, Canute.
Dominican Republic: Our Lady of High Grace, Dominic.
East Indies: Thomas, Apostle.
Ecuador: Sacred Heart.
El Salvador: Our Lady of Peace (Oct. 10, 1966).
England: George.
Equatorial Guinea: Immaculate Conception (May 25, 1986).
Europe: Benedict (1964), Cyril and Methodius, co-patrons (Dec. 31, 1980).
Finland: Henry.
France: Our Lady of the Assumption, Joan of Arc, Thérèse (May 3, 1944).
Germany: Boniface, Michael.
Gibraltar: Blessed Virgin Mary under title, "Our Lady of Europe" (May 31, 1979).
Greece: Nicholas, Andrew.
Holland: Willibrord.
Hungary: Blessed Virgin, "Great Lady of Hungary," Stephen, King.
Iceland: Thorlac (Jan. 14, 1984).
India: Our Lady of Assumption.
Ireland: Patrick, Brigid and Columba.
Italy: Francis of Assisi, Catherine of Siena.
Japan: Peter Baptist.
Korea: Joseph and Mary, Mother of the Church.

Lesotho: Immaculate Heart of Mary.
Lithuania: Casimir, Bl. Cunegunda.
Luxembourg: Willibrord.
Malta: Paul, Our Lady of the Assumption.
Mexico: Our Lady of Guadalupe.
Monaco: Devota.
Moravia: Cyril and Methodius.
New Zealand: Our Lady Help of Christians.
Norway: Olaf.
Papua New Guinea (including northern Solomon Islands): Michael the Archangel (May 31, 1979).
Paraguay: Our Lady of Assumption (July 13, 1951).
Peru: Joseph (Mar. 19, 1957).
Philippines: Sacred Heart of Mary.
Poland: Casimir, Bl. Cunegunda, Stanislaus of Cracow, Our Lady of Czestochowa.
Portugal: Immaculate Conception, Francis Borgia, Anthony of Padua, Vincent of Saragossa, George.
Russia: Andrew, Nicholas of Myra, Thérèse of Lisieux.
Scandinavia: Ansgar.
Scotland: Andrew, Columba.
Silesia: Hedwig.
Slovakia: Our Lady of Sorrows.
South Africa: Our Lady of Assumption (Mar. 15, 1952).
South America: Rose of Lima.
Solomon Islands: BVM, under title Most Holy Name of Mary (Sept. 4, 1991).
Spain: James the Greater, Teresa.
Sri Lanka (Ceylon): Lawrence.
Sweden: Bridget, Eric.
Tanzania: Immaculate Conception (Dec. 8, 1964).
United States: Immaculate Conception (1846).
Uruguay: Blessed Virgin Mary under title *"La Virgen de los Treinte y Tres"* (Nov. 21, 1963).
Venezuela: Our Lady of Coromoto.
Wales: David.
West Indies: Gertrude.

Emblems, Portrayals of Saints

Agatha: Tongs, veil.
Agnes: Lamb.
Ambrose: Bees, dove, ox, pen.
Andrew: Transverse cross.
Anne, Mother of the Blessed Virgin: Door.
Anthony of Padua: Infant Jesus, bread, book, lily.
Augustine of Hippo: Dove, child, shell, pen.
Bartholomew: Knife, flayed and holding his skin.
Benedict: Broken cup, raven, bell, crosier, bush.
Bernard of Clairvaux: Pen, bees, instruments of the Passion.
Bernardine of Siena: Tablet or sun inscribed with IHS.
Blase: Wax, taper, iron comb.
Bonaventure: Communion, ciborium, cardinal's hat.
Boniface: Oak, ax, book, fox, scourge, fountain, raven, sword.
Bridget of Sweden: Book, pilgrim's staff.
Bridget of Kildare: Cross, flame over her head, candle.
Catherine of Ricci: Ring, crown, crucifix.
Catherine of Siena: Stigmata, cross, ring, lily.
Cecilia: Organ.
Charles Borromeo: Communion, coat of arms with word "Humilitas."
Christopher: Giant, torrent, tree, Child Jesus on his shoulders.
Clare of Assisi: Monstrance.
Cosmas and Damian: A phial, box of ointment.
Cyril of Alexandria: Blessed Virgin holding the Child Jesus, pen.

Cyril of Jerusalem: Purse, book.
Dominic: Rosary, star.
Edmund the Martyr: Arrow, sword.
Elizabeth of Hungary: Alms, flowers, bread, the poor, a pitcher.
Francis of Assisi: Wolf, birds, fish, skull, the Stigmata.
Francis Xavier: Crucifix, bell, vessel.
Genevieve: Bread, keys, herd, candle.
George: Dragon.
Gertrude: Crown, taper, lily.
Gervase and Protase: Scourge, club, sword.
Gregory I (the Great): Tiara, crosier, dove.
Helena: Cross.
Ignatius of Loyola: Communion, chasuble, book, apparition of Our Lord.
Isidore: Bees, pen.
James the Greater: Pilgrim's staff, shell, key, sword.
James the Less: Square rule, halberd, club.
Jerome: Lion.
John Berchmans: Rule of St. Ignatius, cross, rosary.
John Chrysostom: Bees, dove, pen.
John of God: Alms, a heart, crown of thorns.
John the Baptist: Lamb, head on platter, skin of an animal.
John the Evangelist: Eagle, chalice, kettle, armor.
Josaphat Kuncevyc: Chalice, crown, winged deacon.
Joseph, Spouse of the Blessed Virgin: Infant Jesus, lily, rod, plane, carpenter's square.
Jude: Sword, square rule, club.
Justin Martyr: Ax, sword.
Lawrence: Cross, book of the Gospels, gridiron.
Leander of Seville: A pen.
Liberius: Pebbles, peacock.
Longinus: In arms at foot of the cross.
Louis IX of France: Crown of thorns, nails.
Lucy: Cord, eyes on a dish.
Luke: Ox, book, brush, palette.
Mark: Lion, book.
Martha: Holy water sprinkler, dragon.
Mary Magdalene: Alabaster box of ointment.
Matilda: Purse, alms.
Matthew: Winged man, purse, lance.
Matthias: Lance.
Maurus: Scales, spade, crutch.
Meinrad: Two ravens.
Michael: Scales, banner, sword, dragon.
Monica: Girdle, tears.
Nicholas: Three purses or balls, anchor or boat, child.
Patrick: Cross, harp, serpent, baptismal font, demons, shamrock.
Paul: Sword, book or scroll.
Peter: Keys, boat, cock.
Philip, Apostle: Column.
Philip Neri: Altar, chasuble, vial.
Rita of Cascia: Rose, crucifix, thorn.
Roch: Angel, dog, bread.
Rose of Lima: Crown of thorns, anchor, city.
Sebastian: Arrows, crown.
Simon Stock: Scapular.
Teresa of Jesus (Ávila): Heart, arrow, book.
Thérèse of Lisieux: Roses entwining a crucifix.
Thomas, Apostle: Lance, ax.
Thomas Aquinas: Chalice, monstrance, dove, ox, person trampled under foot.
Vincent de Paul: Children.
Vincent Ferrer: Pulpit, cardinal's hat, trumpet, captives.

FIRST CENTURY

c. 33: First Christian Pentecost; descent of the Holy Spirit upon the disciples; preaching of St. Peter in Jerusalem; conversion, baptism and aggregation of some 3,000 persons to the first Christian community.

St. Stephen, deacon, was stoned to death at Jerusalem; he is venerated as the first Christian martyr.

c. 34: St. Paul, formerly Saul the persecutor of Christians, was converted and baptized. After three years of solitude in the desert, he joined the college of the apostles; he made three major missionary journeys and became known as the Apostle to the Gentiles; he was imprisoned twice in Rome and was beheaded there between 64 and 67.

39: Cornelius (the Gentile) and his family were baptized by St. Peter; a significant event signalling the mission of the Church to all peoples.

42: Persecution of Christians in Palestine broke out during the rule of Herod Agrippa; St. James the Greater, the first apostle to die, was beheaded in 44; St. Peter was imprisoned for a short time; many Christians fled to Antioch, marking the beginning of the dispersion of Christians beyond the confines of Palestine. At Antioch, the followers of Christ were called Christians for the first time.

49: Christians at Rome, considered members of a Jewish sect, were adversely affected by a decree of Claudius which forbade Jewish worship there.

51: The Council of Jerusalem, in which all the apostles participated under the presidency of St. Peter, decreed that circumcision, dietary regulations, and various other prescriptions of Mosaic Law were not obligatory for Gentile converts to the Christian community. The crucial decree was issued in opposition to Judaizers who contended that observance of the Mosaic Law in its entirety was necessary for salvation.

64: Persecution broke out at Rome under Nero, the emperor said to have accused Christians of starting the fire which destroyed half of Rome.

64 or 67: Martyrdom of St. Peter at Rome during the Neronian persecution. He established his see and spent his last years there after preaching in and around Jerusalem, establishing a see at Antioch, and presiding at the Council of Jerusalem.

70: Destruction of Jerusalem by Titus.

88-97: Pontificate of St. Clement I, third successor of St. Peter as bishop of Rome, one of the Apostolic Fathers. The First Epistle of Clement to the Corinthians, with which he has been identified, was addressed by the Church of Rome to the Church at Corinth, the scene of irregularities and divisions in the Christian community.

95: Domitian persecuted Christians, principally at Rome.

c. 100: Death of St. John, apostle and evangelist, marking the end of the Age of the Apostles and the first generation of the Church.

By the end of the century, Antioch, Alexandria and Ephesus in the East and Rome in the West

DATES AND EVENTS
IN CATHOLIC HISTORY

were established centers of Christian population and influence.

SECOND CENTURY

c. 107: St. Ignatius of Antioch was martyred at Rome. He was the first writer to use the expression, "the Catholic Church."

112: Emperor Trajan, in a rescript to Pliny the Younger, governor of Bithynia, instructed him not to search out Christians but to punish them if they were publicly denounced and refused to do homage to the Roman gods. This rescript set a pattern for Roman magistrates in dealing with Christians.

117-38: Persecution under Hadrian. Many Acts of Martyrs date from this period.

c. 125: Spread of Gnosticism, a combination of elements of Platonic philosophy and Eastern mystery religions. Its adherents claimed that its secret-knowledge principle provided a deeper insight into Christian doctrine than divine revelation and faith. One gnostic thesis denied the divinity of Christ; others denied the reality of his humanity, calling it mere appearance (Docetism, Phantasiasm).

c. 144: Excommunication of Marcion, bishop and heretic, who claimed that there was total opposition and no connection at all between the Old Testament and the New Testament, between the God of the Jews and the God of the Christians; and that the Canon (list of inspired writings) of the Bible consisted only of parts of St. Luke's Gospel and 10 letters of St. Paul. Marcionism was checked at Rome by 200 and was condemned by a council held there about 260, but the heresy persisted for several centuries in the East and had some adherents as late as the Middle Ages.

c. 155: St. Polycarp, bishop of Smyrna and disciple of St. John the Evangelist, was martyred.

c. 156: Beginning of Montanism, a form of religious extremism. Its principal tenets were the imminent second coming of Christ, denial of the divine nature of the Church and its power to forgive sin, and excessively rigorous morality. The heresy, preached by Montanus of Phrygia and others, was condemned by Pope St. Zephyrinus (199-217).

161-80: Reign of Marcus Aurelius. His persecution, launched in the wake of natural disasters, was more violent than those of his predecessors.

165: St. Justin, an important early Christian writer, was martyred at Rome.

c. 180: St. Irenaeus, bishop of Lyons and one of the great early theologians, wrote *Adversus Haereses*. He stated that the teaching and tradition of the Roman See was the standard for belief.

196: Easter Controversy, concerning the day of celebration — a Sunday, according to practice in the West, or the 14th of the month of Nisan (in the Hebrew calendar), no matter what day of the week, according to practice in the East. The controversy was not resolved at this time. The *Didache*, whose extant form dates from the second century, is an important record of Christian belief, practice and governance in the first century.

Latin was introduced as a liturgical language in the West. Other liturgical languages were Aramaic and Greek.

The Catechetical School of Alexandria, founded about the middle of the century, gained increasing influence on doctrinal study and instruction, and interpretation of the Bible.

THIRD CENTURY

202: Persecution under Septimius Severus, who wanted to establish a simple common religion in the Empire.

206: Tertullian, a convert since 197 and the first great ecclesiastical writer in Latin, joined the heretical Montanists; he died in 230.

215: Death of Clement of Alexandria, teacher of Origen and a founding father of the School of Alexandria.

217-35: St. Hippolytus, the first antipope; he was reconciled to the Church while in prison during persecution in 235.

232-54: Origen established the School of Caesarea after being deposed in 231 as head of the School of Alexandria; he died in 254. A scholar and voluminous writer, he was one of the founders of systematic theology and exerted wide influence for many years.

c. 242: Manichaeism originated in Persia: a combination of errors based on the assumption that two supreme principles (good and evil) are operative in creation and life, and that the supreme objective of human endeavor is liberation from evil (matter). The heresy denied the humanity of Christ, the sacramental system, the authority of the Church (and state), and endorsed a moral code which threatened the fabric of society. In the 12th and 13th centuries, it took on the features of Albigensianism and Catharism.

249-51: Persecution under Decius. Many of those who denied the faith (*lapsi*) sought readmission to the Church at the end of the persecution in 251. Pope St. Cornelius agreed with St. Cyprian that lapsi were to be readmitted to the Church after satisfying the requirements of appropriate penance. Antipope Novatian, on the other hand, contended that persons who fell away from the Church under persecution and/or those guilty of serious sin after baptism could not be absolved and readmitted to communion with the Church. The heresy was condemned by a Roman synod in 251.

250-300: Neo-Platonism of Plotinus and Porphyry gained followers.

251: Novatian, an antipope, was condemned at Rome.

256: Pope St. Stephen I upheld the validity of baptism properly administered by heretics, in the Rebaptism Controversy.

257: Persecution under Valerian, who attempted to destroy the Church as a social structure.

258: St. Cyprian, bishop of Carthage, was martyred.

c. 260: St. Lucian founded the School of Antioch, a center of influence on biblical studies.

Pope St. Dionysius condemned Sabellianism, a form of modalism (like Monarchianism and

Patripassianism). The heresy contended that the Father, Son and Holy Spirit are not distinct divine persons but are only three different modes of being and self-manifestations of the one God. St. Paul of Thebes became a hermit.

261: Gallienus issued an edict of toleration which ended general persecution for nearly 40 years.

c. 292: Diocletian divided the Roman Empire into East and West. The division emphasized political, cultural and other differences between the two parts of the Empire and influenced different developments in the Church in the East and West. The prestige of Rome began to decline.

FOURTH CENTURY

303: Persecution broke out under Diocletian; it was particularly violent in 304.

305: St. Anthony of Heracles established a foundation for hermits near the Red Sea in Egypt.

c. 306: The first local legislation on clerical celibacy was enacted by a council held at Elvira, Spain; bishops, priests, deacons and other ministers were forbidden to have wives.

311: An edict of toleration issued by Galerius at the urging of Constantine the Great and Licinius officially ended persecution in the West; some persecution continued in the East.

313: The Edict of Milan issued by Constantine and Licinius recognized Christianity as a lawful religion in the Roman Empire.

314: A council of Arles condemned Donatism, declaring that baptism properly administered by heretics is valid, in view of the principle that sacraments have their efficacy from Christ, not from the spiritual condition of their human ministers. The heresy was condemned again by a council of Carthage in 411.

318: St. Pachomius established the first foundation of the cenobitic (common) life, as compared with the solitary life of hermits in Upper Egypt.

325: Ecumenical Council of Nicaea (I). Its principal action was the condemnation of Arianism, the most devastating of the early heresies, which denied the divinity of Christ. The heresy was authored by Arius of Alexandria, a priest. Arians and several kinds of Semi-Arians propagandized their tenets widely, established their own hierarchies and churches, and raised havoc in the Church for several centuries. The council contributed to formulation of the Nicene Creed (Creed of Nicaea-Constantinople); fixed the date for the observance of Easter; passed regulations concerning clerical discipline; adopted the civil divisions of the Empire as the model for the jurisdictional organization of the Church.

326: With the support of St. Helena, the True Cross on which Christ was crucified was doscovered.

337: Baptism and death of Constantine.

c. 342: Beginning of a 40-year persecution in Persia.

343-44: A council of Sardica reaffirmed doctrine formulated by Nicaea I and declared also that bishops had the right of appeal to the pope as the highest authority in the Church.

361-63: Emperor Julian the Apostate waged an unsuccessful campaign against the Church in an attempt to restore paganism as the religion of the Empire.

c. 365: Persecution of orthodox Christians under Emperor Valens in the East.

c. 376: Beginning of the barbarian invasion in the West.

379: Death of St. Basil, the Father of Monasticism in the East. His writings contributed greatly to the development of rules for the life of Religious.

381: Ecumenical Council of Constantinople (I). It condemned various brands of Arianism as well as Macedonianism, which denied the divinity of the Holy Spirit; contributed to formulation of the Nicene Creed; approved a canon acknowledging Constantinople as the second see after Rome in honor and dignity.

382: The Canon of Sacred Scripture, the official list of the inspired books of the Bible, was contained in the Decree of Pope St. Damasus and published by a regional council of Carthage in 397; the Canon was formally defined by the Council of Trent in the 16th century.

382-c. 406: St. Jerome translated the Old and New Testaments into Latin; his work is called the Vulgate version of the Bible.

396: St. Augustine became bishop of Hippo in North Africa.

FIFTH CENTURY

410: Visigoths under Alaric sacked Rome and the last Roman legions departed Britain. The decline of imperial Rome dates approximately from this time.

430: St. Augustine, bishop of Hippo for 35 years, died. He was a strong defender of orthodox doctrine against Manichaeism, Donatism and Pelagianism. The depth and range of his writings made him a dominant influence in Christian thought for centuries.

431: Ecumenical Council of Ephesus. It condemned Nestorianism, which denied the unity of the divine and human natures in the Person of Christ; defined Theotokos (Bearer of God) as the title of Mary, Mother of the Son of God made Man; condemned Pelagianism. The heresy of Pelagianism, proceeding from the assumption that Adam had a natural right to supernatural life, held that man could attain salvation through the efforts of his natural powers and free will; it involved errors concerning the nature of original sin, the meaning of grace and other matters. Related Semi-Pelagianism was condemned by a council of Orange in 529.

432: St. Patrick arrived in Ireland. By the time of his death in 461 most of the country had been converted, monasteries founded and the hierarchy established.

438: The Theodosian Code, a compilation of decrees for the Empire, was issued by Theodosius II; it had great influence on subsequent civil and ecclesiastical law.

451: Ecumenical Council of Chalcedon. Its principal action was the condemnation of Monophysitism (also called Eutychianism), which denied the humanity of Christ by holding that he had only one, the divine, nature.

452: Pope St. Leo the Great persuaded Attila the Hun to spare Rome.

455: Vandals under Geiseric sacked Rome.

484: Patriarch Acacius of Constantinople was excommunicated for signing the *Henoticon*, a document which capitulated to the Monophysite heresy. The excommunication triggered the Acacian Schism which lasted for 35 years.

494: Pope St. Gelasius I declared in a letter to Emperor Anastasius that the pope had power and authority over the emperor in spiritual matters.

496: Clovis, King of the Franks, was converted and became the defender of Christianity in the West. The Franks became a Catholic people.

SIXTH CENTURY

520: Irish monasteries flourished as centers for spiritual life, missionary training, and scholarly activity.

529: The Second Council of Orange condemned Semi-Pelagianism.

c. 529: St. Benedict founded the Monte Cassino Abbey. Some years before his death in 543 he wrote a monastic rule which exercised tremendous influence on the form and style of religious life. He is called the Father of Monasticism in the West.

533: John II became the first pope to change his name. The practice did not become general until the time of Sergius IV (1009).

533-34: Emperor Justinian promulgated the *Corpus Iuris Civilis* for the Roman world; like the Theodosian Code, it influenced subsequent civil and ecclesiastical law.

c. 545: Death of Dionysius Exiguus who was the first to date history from the birth of Christ, a practice which resulted in use of the B.C. and A.D. abbreviations. His calculations were at least four years late.

553: Ecumenical Council of Constantinople (II). It condemned the Three Chapters, Nestorian-tainted writings of Theodore of Mopsuestia, Theodoret of Cyrus and Ibas of Edessa.

585: St. Columban founded an influential monastic school at Luxeuil.

589: The most important of several councils of Toledo was held. The Visigoths renounced Arianism, and St. Leander began the organization of the Church in Spain.

590-604: Pontificate of Pope St. Gregory I the Great. He set the form and style of the papacy which prevailed throughout the Middle Ages; exerted great influence on doctrine and liturgy; was strong in support of monastic discipline and clerical celibacy; authored writings on many subjects. Gregorian Chant is named in his honor.

596: Pope St. Gregory I sent St. Augustine of Canterbury and 40 monks to do missionary work in England.

597: St. Columba died. He founded an important monastery at Iona, established schools and did notable missionary work in Scotland. By the end of the century, monasteries of nuns were common; Western monasticism was flourishing; monasticism in the East, under the influence of Monophysitism and other factors, was losing its vigor.

SEVENTH CENTURY

613: St. Columban established the influential monastery of Bobbio in northern Italy; he died there in 615.

622: The *Hegira* (flight) of Mohammed from Mecca to Medina signalled the beginning of Islam which, by the end of the century, claimed almost all of the southern Mediterranean area.

628: Heraclius, Eastern Emperor, recovered the True Cross from the Persians.

649: A Lateran council condemned two erroneous formulas (Ecthesis and Type) issued by emperors Heraclius and Constans II as means of reconciling Monophysites with the Church.

664: Actions of the Synod of Whitby advanced the adoption of Roman usages in England, especially regarding the date for the observance of Easter. (See Easter Controversy.)

680-81: Ecumenical Council of Constantinople (III). It condemned Monothelitism, which held that Christ had only one will, the divine; censured Pope Honorius I for a letter to Sergius, bishop of Constantinople, in which he made an ambiguous but not infallible statement about the unity of will and/or operation in Christ.

692: Trullan Synod. Eastern-Church discipline on clerical celibacy was settled, permitting marriage before ordination to the diaconate and continuation in marriage afterwards, but prohibiting marriage following the death of the wife thereafter. Anti-Roman canons contributed to East-West alienation.

During the century, the monastic influence of Ireland and England increased in Western Europe; schools and learning declined; regulations regarding clerical celibacy became more strict in the East.

EIGHTH CENTURY

711: Muslims began the conquest of Spain.

726: Emperor Leo III, the Isaurian, launched a campaign against the veneration of sacred images and relics; called Iconoclasm (image-breaking), it caused turmoil in the East until about 843.

731: Pope Gregory III and a synod at Rome condemned Iconoclasm, with a declaration that the veneration of sacred images was in accord with Catholic tradition. Venerable Bede issued his *Ecclesiastical History of the English People.*

732: Charles Martel defeated the Muslims at Poitiers, halting their advance in the West.

744: The Monastery of Fulda was established by St. Sturmi, a disciple of St. Boniface; it was influential in the evangelization of Germany.

754: A council of more than 300 Byzantine bishops endorsed Iconoclast errors. This council and its actions were condemned by the Lateran synod of 769.

Stephen II (III) crowned Pepin ruler of the Franks. Pepin twice invaded Italy, in 754 and 756, to defend the pope against the Lombards. His land grants to the papacy, called the Donation of Pepin, were later extended by Charlemagne (773) and formed part of the States of the Church.

c. 755: St. Boniface (Winfrid) was martyred. He was

called the Apostle of Germany for his missionary work and organization of the hierarchy there.

781: Alcuin was chosen by Charlemagne to organize a palace school, which became a center of intellectual leadership.

787: Ecumenical Council of Nicaea (II). It condemned Iconoclasm, which held that the use of images was idolatry, and Adoptionism, which claimed that Christ was not the Son of God by nature but only by adoption. This was the last council regarded as ecumenical by Orthodox Churches.

792: A council at Ratisbon condemned Adoptionism. The famous *Book of Kells* ("The Great Gospel of Columcille") dates from the early eighth or late seventh century.

NINTH CENTURY

800: Charlemagne was crowned Emperor by Pope Leo III on Christmas Day.
Egbert became king of West Saxons; he unified England and strengthened the See of Canterbury.

813: Emperor Leo V, the Armenian, revived Iconoclasm, which persisted until about 843.

814: Charlemagne died.

843: The Treaty of Verdun split the Frankish kingdom among Charlemagne's three grandsons.

844: A Eucharistic controversy involving the writings of St. Paschasius Radbertus, Ratramnus and Rabanus Maurus occasioned the development of terminology regarding the doctrine of the Real Presence.

846: Muslims invaded Italy and attacked Rome.

847-52: Period of composition of the False Decretals, a collection of forged documents attributed to popes from St. Clement (88-97) to Gregory II (714-731). The Decretals, which strongly supported the autonomy and rights of bishops, were suspect for a long time before being repudiated entirely about 1628.

848: The Council of Mainz condemned Gottschalk for heretical teaching regarding predestination. He was also condemned by the Council of Quierzy in 853.

857: Photius displaced Ignatius as patriarch of Constantinople. This marked the beginning of the Photian Schism, a confused state of East-West relations which has not yet been cleared up by historical research. Photius, a man of exceptional ability, died in 891.

865: St. Ansgar, apostle of Scandinavia, died.

869: St. Cyril died and his brother, St. Methodius (d. 885), was ordained a bishop. The Apostles of the Slavs devised an alphabet and translated the Gospels and liturgy into the Slavonic language.

869-70: Ecumenical Council of Constantinople (IV). It issued a second condemnation of Iconoclasm, condemned and deposed Photius as patriarch of Constantinople and restored Ignatius to the patriarchate. This was the last ecumenical council held in the East. It was first called ecumenical by canonists toward the end of the 11th century.

871-c. 900: Reign of Alfred the Great, the only English king ever anointed by a pope at Rome.

TENTH CENTURY

910: William, duke of Aquitaine, founded the Benedictine Abbey of Cluny, which became a center of monastic and ecclesiastical reform, especially in France.

915: Pope John X played a leading role in the expulsion of Saracens from central and southern Italy.

955: St. Olga, of the Russian royal family, was baptized.

962: Otto I, the Great, crowned by Pope John XII, revived Charlemagne's kingdom, which became the Holy Roman Empire.

966: Mieszko, first of a royal line in Poland, was baptized; he brought Latin Christianity to Poland.

988: Conversion and baptism of St. Vladimir and the people of Kiev which subsequently became part of Russia.

993: John XV was the first pope to decree the official canonization of a saint — Bishop Ulrich (Uldaric) of Augsburg — for the universal Church.

997: St. Stephen became ruler of Hungary. He assisted in organizing the hierarchy and establishing Latin Christianity in that country.

999-1003: Pontificate of Sylvester II (Gerbert of Aquitaine), a Benedictine monk and the first French pope.

ELEVENTH CENTURY

1009: Beginning of lasting East-West Schism in the Church, marked by dropping of the name of Pope Sergius IV from the Byzantine diptychs (the listing of persons prayed for during the liturgy). The deletion was made by Patriarch Sergius II of Constantinople.

1012: St. Romuald founded the Camaldolese Hermits.

1025: The Council of Arras, and other councils later, condemned the Cathari (Neo-Manichaeans, Albigenses).

1027: The Council of Elne proclaimed the Truce of God as a means of stemming violence; it involved armistice periods of varying length, which were later extended.

1038: St. John Gualbert founded the Vallombrosians.

1043-59: Constantinople patriarchate of Michael Cerularius, the key figure in a controversy concerning the primacy of the papacy. His and the Byzantine synod's refusal to acknowledge this primacy in 1054 widened and hardened the East-West Schism in the Church.

1047: Pope Clement II died; he was the only pope ever buried in Germany.

1049-54: Pontificate of St. Leo IX, who inaugurated a movement of papal, diocesan, monastic and clerical reform.

1054: Start of the Great Schism between the Eastern and Western Churches; it marked the separation of Orthodox Churches from unity with the pope.

1055: Condemnation of the Eucharistic doctrine of Berengarius.

1059: A Lateran council issued new legislation regarding papal elections; voting power was entrusted to the Roman cardinals.

1066: Death of St. Edward the Confessor, king of England from 1042 and restorer of Westminster Abbey.

Defeat, at Hastings, of Harold by William, Duke of Normandy (later William I), who subsequently exerted strong influence on the lifestyle of the Church in England.

1073-85: Pontificate of St. Gregory VII (Hildebrand). A strong pope, he carried forward programs of clerical and general ecclesiastical reform and struggled against German King Henry IV and other rulers to end the evils of lay investiture. He introduced the Latin liturgy in Spain and set definite dates for the observance of ember days.

1077: Henry IV, excommunicated and suspended from the exercise of imperial powers by Gregory VII, sought absolution from the pope at Canossa. Henry later repudiated this action and in 1084 forced Gregory to leave Rome.

1079: The Council of Rome condemned Eucharistic errors (denial of the Real Presence of Christ under the appearances of bread and wine) of Berengarius, who retracted.

1084: St. Bruno founded the Carthusians.

1097-99: The first of several Crusades undertaken between this time and 1265. Recovery of the Holy Places and gaining free access to them for Christians were the original purposes, but these were diverted to less worthy objectives in various ways. Results included: a Latin Kingdom of Jerusalem, 1099-1187; a military and political misadventure in the form of a Latin Empire of Constantinople, 1204-1261; acquisition, by treaties, of visiting rights for Christians in the Holy Land. East-West economic and cultural relationships increased during the period. In the religious sphere, actions of the Crusaders had the effect of increasing the alienation of the East from the West.

1098: St. Robert founded the Cistercians.

TWELFTH CENTURY

1108: Beginnings of the influential Abbey and School of St. Victor in France.

1115: St. Bernard established the Abbey of Clairvaux and inaugurated the Cistercian Reform.

1118: Christian forces captured Saragossa, Spain; the beginning of the Muslim decline in that country.

1121: St. Norbert established the original monastery of the Praemonstratensians near Laon, France.

1122: The Concordat of Worms (*Pactum Callixtinum*) was formulated and approved by Pope Callistus II and Emperor Henry V to settle controversy concerning the investiture of prelates. The concordat provided that the emperor could invest prelates with symbols of temporal authority but had no right to invest them with spiritual authority, which came from the Church alone, and that the emperor was not to interfere in papal elections. This was the first concordat in history.

1123: Ecumenical Council of the Lateran (I), the first of its kind in the West. It endorsed provisions of the Concordat of Worms concerning the investiture of prelates and approved reform measures in 25 canons.

1139: Ecumenical Council of the Lateran (II). It adopted measures against a schism organized by antipope Anacletus and approved 30 canons related to discipline and other matters; one of the canons stated that holy orders is an invalidating impediment to marriage.

1140: St. Bernard met Abelard in debate at the Council of Sens. Abelard, whose rationalism in theology was condemned for the first time in 1121, died in 1142 at Cluny.

1148: The Synod of Rheims enacted strict disciplinary decrees for communities of women Religious.

1152: The Synod of Kells reorganized the Church in Ireland.

1160: Gratian, whose *Decretum* became a basic text of canon law, died.

Peter Lombard, compiler of the Four Books of Sentences, a standard theology text for nearly 200 years, died.

1170: St. Thomas Becket, archbishop of Canterbury, who clashed with Henry II over church-state relations, was murdered in his cathedral.

1171: Pope Alexander III reserved the process of canonization of saints to the Holy See.

1179: Ecumenical Council of the Lateran (III). It enacted measures against Waldensianism and Albigensianism (see year 242 regarding Manichaeism), approved reform decrees in 27 canons, provided that popes be elected by a two-thirds vote of the cardinals.

1184: Waldenses and other heretics were excommunicated by Pope Lucius III.

THIRTEENTH CENTURY

1198-1216: Pontificate of Innocent III, during which the papacy reached its medieval peak of authority, influence and prestige in the Church and in relations with civil rulers.

1208: Innocent III called for a crusade, the first in Christendom itself, against the Albigensians; their beliefs and practices threatened the fabric of society in southern France and northern Italy.

1209: Verbal approval was given by Innocent III to a rule of life for the Order of Friars Minor, started by St. Francis of Assisi.

1212: The Second Order of Franciscans, the Poor Clares, was founded.

1215: Ecumenical Council of the Lateran (IV). It ordered annual reception of the sacraments of penance and the Eucharist; defined and made the first official use of the term transubstantiation to explain the change of bread and wine into the body and blood of Christ; adopted additional measures to counteract teachings and practices of the Albigensians and Cathari; approved 70 canons.

1216: Formal papal approval was given to a rule of life for the Order of Preachers, started by St. Dominic.

The Portiuncula Indulgence was granted by the Holy See at the request of St. Francis of Assisi.

1221: Rule of the Third Order Secular of St. Francis

(Secular Franciscan Order) approved verbally by Honorius III.

1226: Death of St. Francis of Assisi.

1231: Pope Gregory IX authorized establishment of the Papal Inquisition for dealing with heretics. It was a creature of its time, when crimes against faith and heretical doctrines of extremists like the Cathari and Albigenses threatened the good of the Christian community, the welfare of the state and the very fabric of society. The institution, which was responsible for excesses in punishment, was most active in the second half of the century in southern France, Italy and Germany.

1245: Ecumenical Council of Lyons (I). It confirmed the deposition of Emperor Frederick II and approved 22 canons.

1247: Preliminary approval was given by the Holy See to a Carmelite rule of life.

1270: St. Louis IX, king of France, died. Beginning of papal decline.

1274: Ecumenical Council of Lyons (II). It accomplished a temporary reunion of separated Eastern Churches with the Roman Church; issued regulations concerning conclaves for papal elections; approved 31 canons. Death of St. Thomas Aquinas, Doctor of the Church, of lasting influence.

1280: Pope Nicholas III, who made the Breviary the official prayer book for clergy of the Roman Church, died.

1281: The excommunication of Michael Palaeologus by Pope Martin IV ruptured the union effected with the Eastern Church in 1274.

FOURTEENTH CENTURY

1302: Pope Boniface VIII issued the bull *Unam Sanctam*, concerning the unity of the Church and the temporal power of princes, against the background of a struggle with Philip IV of France; it was the most famous medieval document on the subject.

1309-77: For a period of approximately 70 years, seven popes resided at Avignon because of unsettled conditions in Rome and other reasons; see separate entry.

1311-12: Ecumenical Council of Vienne. It suppressed the Knights Templar and enacted a number of reform decrees.

1321: Dante Alighieri died a year after completing the *Divine Comedy*.

1324: Marsilius of Padua completed *Defensor Pacis*, a work condemned by Pope John XXII as heretical because of its denial of papal primacy and the hierarchical structure of the Church, and for other reasons. It was a charter for conciliarism (an ecumenical council is superior to the pope in authority).

1337-1453: Period of the Hundred Years' War, a dynastic struggle between France and England.

1338: Four years after the death of Pope John XXII, who had opposed Louis IV of Bavaria in a years-long controversy, electoral princes declared at the Diet of Rhense that the emperor did not need papal confirmation of his title and right to rule. Charles IV later (1356) said the same thing in a *Golden Bull*, eliminating papal rights in the election of emperors.

1347-50: The Black Death swept across Europe, killing perhaps one-fourth to one-third of the total population; an estimated 40 per cent of the clergy succumbed.

1374: Petrarch, poet and humanist, died.

1377: Return of the papacy from Avignon to Rome. Beginning of the Western Schism; see separate entry.

FIFTEENTH CENTURY

1409: The Council of Pisa, without canonical authority, tried to end the Western Schism but succeeded only in complicating it by electing a third claimant to the papacy; see Western Schism.

1414-18: Ecumenical Council of Constance. It took successful action to end the Western Schism involving rival claimants to the papacy; rejected the teachings of Wycliff; condemned Hus as a heretic. One decree — passed in the earlier stages of the council but later rejected — asserted the superiority of an ecumenical council over the pope (conciliarism).

1431: St. Joan of Arc was burned at the stake.

1431-45: Ecumenical Council of Florence (also called Basle-Ferrara-Florence). It affirmed the primacy of the pope against the claims of conciliarists that an ecumenical council is superior to the pope. It also formulated and approved decrees of union with several separated Eastern Churches — Greek, Armenian, Jacobite — which failed to gain general or lasting acceptance.

1438: The Pragmatic Sanction of Bourges was enacted by Charles VII and the French Parliament to curtail papal authority over the Church in France, in the spirit of conciliarism. It found expression in Gallicanism and had effects lasting at least until the French Revolution.

1453: The fall of Constantinople to the Turks.

c. 1456: Gutenberg issued the first edition of the Bible printed from movable type, at Mainz, Germany.

1476: Pope Sixtus IV approved observance of the feast of the Immaculate Conception on Dec. 8 throughout the Church.

1478: Pope Sixtus IV, at the urging of King Ferdinand of Spain, approved establishment of the Spanish Inquisition for dealing with Jewish and Moorish converts accused of heresy. The institution, which was peculiar to Spain and its colonies in America, acquired jurisdiction over other cases as well and fell into disrepute because of its procedures, cruelty and the manner in which it served the Spanish crown, rather than the accused and the good of the Church. Protests by the Holy See failed to curb excesses of the Inquisition, which lingered in Spanish history until early in the 19th century.

1492: Columbus discovered the Americas.

1493: Pope Alexander VI issued a Bull of Demarcation which determined spheres of influence for the Spanish and Portuguese in the Americas. The Renaissance, a humanistic movement which originated in Italy in the 14th century, spread to France, Germany, the Low Countries and England. A transitional period between the medieval world and the modern secular world, it introduced profound changes which affected literature and the other arts, general culture, politics and religion.

SIXTEENTH CENTURY

1512-17: Ecumenical Council of the Lateran (V). It stated the relation and position of the pope with respect to an ecumenical council; acted to counteract the Pragmatic Sanction of Bourges and exaggerated claims of liberty by the Church in France; condemned erroneous teachings concerning the nature of the human soul; stated doctrine concerning indulgences. The council reflected concern for abuses in the Church and the need for reforms but failed to take decisive action in the years immediately preceding the Reformation.

1517: Martin Luther signalled the beginning of the Reformation by posting 95 theses at Wittenberg. Subsequently, he broke completely from doctrinal orthodoxy in discourses and three published works (1519 and 1520); was excommunicated on more than 40 charges of heresy (1521); remained the dominant figure in the Reformation in Germany until his death in 1546.

1519: Zwingli triggered the Reformation in Zurich and became its leading proponent there until his death in combat in 1531.

1524: Luther's encouragement of German princes in putting down the two-year Peasants' Revolt gained political support for his cause.

1528: The Order of Friars Minor Capuchin was approved as an autonomous division of the Franciscan Order; like the Jesuits, the Capuchins became leaders in the Counter-Reformation.

1530: The Augsburg Confession of Lutheran faith was issued; it was later supplemented by the Smalkaldic Articles, approved in 1537.

1533: Henry VIII divorced Catherine of Aragon, married Anne Boleyn, was excommunicated. In 1534 he decreed the Act of Supremacy, making the sovereign the head of the Church in England, under which Sts. John Fisher and Thomas More were executed in 1535. Despite his rejection of papal primacy and actions against monastic life in England, he generally maintained doctrinal orthodoxy until his death in 1547.

1536: John Calvin, leader of the Reformation in Switzerland until his death in 1564, issued the first edition of Institutes of the Christian Religion, which became the classical text of Reformed (non-Lutheran) theology.

1540: The constitutions of the Society of Jesus (Jesuits), founded by St. Ignatius of Loyola, were approved.

1541: Start of the 11-year career of St. Francis Xavier as a missionary to the East Indies and Japan.

1545-63: Ecumenical Council of Trent. It issued a great number of decrees concerning doctrinal matters opposed by the Reformers, and mobilized the Counter-Reformation. Definitions covered the Canon of the Bible, the rule of faith, the nature of justification, grace, faith, origi-

nal sin and its effects, the seven sacraments, the sacrificial nature of the Mass, the veneration of saints, use of sacred images, belief in purgatory, the doctrine of indulgences, the jurisdiction of the pope over the whole Church. It initiated many reforms for renewal in the liturgy and general discipline in the Church, the promotion of religious instruction, the education of the clergy through the foundation of seminaries, etc. Trent ranks with Vatican II as the greatest ecumenical council held in the West.

1549: The first Anglican Book of Common Prayer was issued by Edward VI. Revised editions were published in 1552, 1559 and 1662 and later.

1553: Start of the five-year reign of Mary Tudor who tried to counteract actions of Henry VIII against the Roman Church.

1555: Enactment of the Peace of Augsburg, an arrangement of religious territorialism rather than toleration, which recognized the existence of Catholicism and Lutheranism in the German Empire and provided that citizens should adopt the religion of their respective rulers.

1558: Beginning of the reign (to 1603) of Queen Elizabeth I of England and Ireland, during which the Church of England took on its definitive form.

1559: Establishment of the hierarchy of the Church of England, with the consecration of Matthew Parker as archbishop of Canterbury.

1563: The first text of the 39 Articles of the Church of England was issued. Also enacted were a new Act of Supremacy and Oath of Succession to the English throne.

1570: Elizabeth I was excommunicated. Penal measures against Catholics subsequently became more severe.

1571: Defeat of the Turkish armada at Lepanto staved off the invasion of Eastern Europe.

1577: The Formula of Concord, the classical statement of Lutheran faith, was issued; it was, generally, a Lutheran counterpart of the canons of the Council of Trent. In 1580, along with other formulas of doctrine, it was included in the Book of Concord.

1582: The Gregorian Calendar, named for Pope Gregory XIII, was put into effect and was eventually adopted in most countries: England delayed adoption until 1752.

SEVENTEENTH CENTURY

1605: The Gunpowder Plot, an attempt by Catholic fanatics to blow up James I of England and the houses of Parliament, resulted in an anti-Catholic Oath of Allegiance.

1610: Death of Matteo Ricci, outstanding Jesuit missionary to China, pioneer in cultural relations between China and Europe.

Founding of the first community of Visitation Nuns by Sts. Francis de Sales and Jane de Chantal.

1611: Founding of the Oratorians.

1613: Catholics were banned from Scandinavia.

1625: Founding of the Congregation of the Mission (Vincentians) by St. Vincent de Paul. He founded the Sisters of Charity in 1633.

1642: Death of Galileo, scientist, who was censured

by the Congregation of the Holy Office for supporting the Copernican theory of the sun-centered planetary system. The case against him was closed in his favor in 1992.

Founding of the Sulpicians by Jacques Olier.

1643: Start of publication of the Bollandist Acta Sanctorum, a critical work on lives of the saints.

1648: Provisions in the Peace of Westphalia, ending the Thirty Years' War, extended terms of the Peace of Augsburg (1555) to Calvinists and gave equality to Catholics and Protestants in the 300 states of the Holy Roman Empire.

1649: Oliver Cromwell invaded Ireland and began a severe persecution of the Church there.

1653: Pope Innocent X condemned five propositions of Jansenism, a complex theory which distorted doctrine concerning the relations between divine grace and human freedom. Jansenism was also a rigoristic movement which seriously disturbed the Church in France, the Low Countries and Italy in this and the 18th century.

1673: The Test Act in England barred from public office Catholics who would not deny the doctrine of transubstantiation and receive Communion in the Church of England.

1678: Many English Catholics suffered death as a consequence of the Popish Plot, a false allegation by Titus Oates that Catholics planned to assassinate Charles II, land a French army in the country, burn London, and turn over the government to the Jesuits.

1682: The four Gallican articles, drawn up by Bossuet, asserted political and ecclesiastical immunities of France from papal control. The articles, which rejected the primacy of the pope, were declared null and void by Pope Alexander VIII in 1690.

1689: The Toleration Act granted a measure of freedom of worship to other English dissenters but not to Catholics.

EIGHTEENTH CENTURY

1704: Chinese Rites — involving the Christian adaptation of elements of Confucianism, veneration of ancestors and Chinese terminology in religion — were condemned by Clement XI.

1720: The Passionists were founded by St. Paul of the Cross.

1724: Persecution in China.

1732: The Redemptorists were founded by St. Alphonsus Liguori.

1738: Freemasonry was condemned by Clement XII and Catholics were forbidden to join, under penalty of excommunication; the prohibition was repeated by Benedict XIV in 1751 and by later popes.

1760s: Josephinism, a theory and system of state control of the Church, was initiated in Austria; it remained in force until about 1850.

1764: Febronianism, an unorthodox theory and practice regarding the constitution of the Church and relations between Church and state, was condemned for the first of several times. Proposed by an auxiliary bishop of Trier using the pseudonym Justinus Febronius, it had the effects of minimizing the office of the pope and supporting national churches under state control.

1773: Clement XIV issued a brief of suppression against the Jesuits, following their expulsion from Portugal in 1759, from France in 1764 and from Spain in 1767. Political intrigue and unsubstantiated accusations were principal factors in these developments. The ban, which crippled the society, contained no condemnation of the Jesuit constitutions, particular Jesuits or Jesuit teaching. The society was restored in 1814.

1778: Catholics in England were relieved of some civil disabilities dating back to the time of Henry VIII, by an act which permitted them to acquire, own and inherit property. Additional liberties were restored by the Roman Catholic Relief Act of 1791 and subsequent enactments of Parliament.

1789: Religious freedom in the United States was guaranteed under the First Amendment to the Constitution.

Beginning of the French Revolution which resulted in: the secularization of church property and the Civil Constitution of the Clergy in 1790; the persecution of priests, religious and lay persons loyal to papal authority; invasion of the Papal States by Napoleon in 1796; renewal of persecution from 1797-1799; attempts to dechristianize France and establish a new religion; the occupation of Rome by French troops and the forced removal of Pius VI to France in 1798.

This century is called the age of Enlightenment or Reason because of the predominating rational and scientific approach of its leading philosophers, scientists and writers with respect to religion, ethics and natural law. This approach downgraded the fact and significance of revealed religion. Also characteristic of the Enlightenment were subjectivism, secularism and optimism regarding human perfectibility.

NINETEENTH CENTURY

1801: Concordat between Napoleon and Pope Pius VII is signed. It is soon violated by the Organic Articles issued by Napoleon in 1802.

1804: Napoleon crowns himself Emperor of the French with Pope Pius in attendance.

1809: Pope Pius VII was made a captive by Napoleon and deported to France where he remained in exile until 1814. During this time he refused to cooperate with Napoleon who sought to bring the Church in France under his own control, and other leading cardinals were imprisoned. The turbulence in church-state relations in France at the beginning of the century recurred in connection with the Bourbon Restoration, the July Revolution, the second and third Republics, the Second Empire and the Dreyfus case.

1814: The Society of Jesus, suppressed since 1773, was restored.

1817: Reestablishment of the Congregation for the Propagation of the Faith (Propaganda) by Pius VII was an important factor in increasing missionary activity during the century.

1820: Year's-long persecution, during which thousands died for the faith, ended in China. Thereafter, communication with the West remained cut off until about 1834. Vigorous missionary work got under way in 1842.

1822: The Pontifical Society for the Propagation of the Faith, inaugurated in France by Pauline Jaricot for the support of missionary activity, was established.

1829: The Catholic Emancipation Act relieved Catholics in England and Ireland of most of the civil disabilities to which they had been subject from the time of Henry VIII.

1832: Gregory XVI, in the encyclical *Mirari vos*, condemned indifferentism, one of the many ideologies at odds with Christian doctrine which were proposed during the century.

1833: Start of the Oxford Movement which affected the Church of England and resulted in some notable conversions, including that of John Henry Newman in 1845, to the Catholic Church.

Bl. Frederic Ozanam founded the Society of St. Vincent de Paul in France. The society's objectives are works of charity.

1848: *The Communist Manifesto*, a revolutionary document symptomatic of socio-economic crisis, was issued.

1850: The hierarchy was reestablished in England and Nicholas Wiseman made the first archbishop of Westminster. He was succeeded in 1865 by Henry Manning, an Oxford convert and proponent of the rights of labor.

1853: The Catholic hierarchy was reestablished in Holland.

1854: Pius IX proclaimed the dogma of the Immaculate Conception in the bull Ineffabilis Deus.

1858: The Blessed Virgin Mary appeared to St. Bernadette at Lourdes, France.

1864: Pius IX issued the encyclical *Quanta cura* and the *Syllabus of Errors* in condemnation of some 80 propositions derived from the scientific mentality and rationalism of the century. The subjects in question had deep ramifications in many areas of thought and human endeavor; in religion, they explicitly and/or implicitly rejected divine revelation and the supernatural order.

1867: The first volume of *Das Kapital* was published. Together with the Communist First International, formed in the same year, it had great influence on the subsequent development of communism and socialism.

1869: The Anglican Church was disestablished in Ireland.

1869-70: Ecumenical Council of the Vatican (I). It defined papal primacy and infallibility in a dogmatic constitution on the Church; covered natural religion, revelation, faith, and the relations between faith and reason in a dogmatic constitution on the Cathoic faith.

1870-71: Victor Emmanuel II of Sardinia, crowned king of Italy after defeating Austrian and papal forces, marched into Rome in 1870 and expropriated the Papal States after a plebiscite in which Catholics, at the order of Pius IX, did not vote. In 1871, Pius IX refused to accept a Law of Guarantees. Confiscation of church property and hindrance of ecclesiastical administration by the regime followed.

1871: The German Empire, a confederation of 26 states, was formed. Government policy launched a *Kulturkampf* whose May Laws of 1873 were designed to annul papal jurisdiction in Prussia and other states and to place the Church under imperial control. Resistance to the enactments and the persecution they legalized forced the government to modify its anti-Church policy by 1887.

1878: Beginning of the pontificate of Leo XIII, who was pope until his death in 1903. Leo is best known for the encyclical *Rerum novarum*, which greatly influenced the course of Christian social thought and the labor movement. His other accomplishments included promotion of Scholastic philosophy and the impetus he gave to scriptural studies.

1881: The first International Eucharistic Congress was held in Lille, France.

Alexander II of Russia was assassinated. His policies of Russification — as well as those of his two predecessors and a successor during the century — caused great suffering to Catholics, Jews and Protestants in Poland, Lithuania, the Ukraine and Bessarabia.

1882: Charles Darwin died. His theory of evolution by natural selection, one of several scientific highlights of the century, had extensive repercussions in the faith-and-science controversy.

1887: The Catholic University of America was founded in Washington, D.C.

1893: The U.S. apostolic delegation was set up in Washington, D.C.

TWENTIETH CENTURY

1901: Restrictive measures in France forced the Jesuits, Benedictines, Carmelites and other religious orders to leave the country. Subsequently, 14,000 schools were suppressed; religious orders and congregations were expelled; the concordat was renounced in 1905; church property was confiscated in 1906. For some years the Holy See, refusing to comply with government demands for the control of bishops' appointments, left some ecclesiastical offices vacant.

1903-14: Pontificate of St. Pius X. He initiated the codification of canon law, 1904; removed the ban against participation by Catholics in Italian national elections, 1905; issued decrees calling upon the faithful to receive Holy Communion frequently and daily, and stating that children should begin receiving the Eucharist at the age of seven, 1905 and 1910, respectively; ordered the establishment of the Confraternity of Christian Doctrine in all parishes throughout the world, 1905; condemned Modernism in the decree *Lamentabili* and the encyclical *Pascendi*, 1907.

1908: The United States and England, long under the jurisdiction of the Congregation for the Propagation of the Faith as mission territories, were removed from its control and placed under the common law of the Church.

1910: Laws of separation were enacted in Portugal, marking a point of departure in church-state relations.

1911: The Catholic Foreign Mission Society of America — Maryknoll, the first U.S.-founded society of its type — was established.

1914: Start of World War I, which lasted until 1918.

1914-22: Pontificate of Benedict XV. Much of his pontificate was devoted to seeking ways and means of minimizing the material and spiritual havoc of World War I. In 1917 he offered his services as a mediator to the belligerent nations, but his pleas for settlement of the conflict went unheeded.

1917: The Blessed Virgin Mary appeared to three children at Fatima, Portugal.

A new constitution, embodying repressive laws against the Church, was enacted in Mexico. Its implementation resulted in persecution in the 1920s and 1930s.

Bolsheviks seized power in Russia and set up a communist dictatorship. The event marked the rise of communism in Russian and world affairs. One of its immediate, and lasting, results was persecution of the Church, Jews and other segments of the population.

1918: The Code of Canon Law, in preparation for more than 10 years, went into effect in the Western Church.

1919: Benedict XV stimulated missionary work through the decree *Maximum Illud*, in which he urged the recruiting and training of native clergy in places where the Church was not firmly established.

1920-22: Ireland was partitioned by two enactments of the British government which (1) made the six counties of Northern Ireland part of the United Kingdom in 1920 and (2) gave dominion status to the Irish Free State in 1922. The Irish Free State became an independent republic in 1949.

1922-39: Pontificate of Pius XI. He subscribed to the Lateran Treaty, 1929, which settled the Roman Question created by the confiscation of the Papal States in 1871; issued the encyclical *Casti connubii*, 1930, an authoritative statement on Christian marriage; resisted the efforts of Benito Mussolini to control Catholic Action and the Church, in the encyclical *Non abbiamo bisogno*, 1931; opposed various fascist policies; issued the encyclicals *Quadragesimo anno*, 1931, developing the social doctrine of Leo XIII's *Rerum novarum*, and *Divini Redemptoris*, 1937, calling for social justice and condemning atheistic communism; condemned anti-Semitism, 1937.

1926: The Catholic Relief Act repealed virtually all legal disabilities of Catholics in England.

1931: Leftists proclaimed Spain a republic and proceeded to disestablish the Church, confiscate church property, deny salaries to the clergy, expel the Jesuits and ban teaching of the Catholic faith. These actions were preludes to the civil war of 1936-1939.

1933: Emergence of Adolf Hitler to power in Germany. By 1935 two of his aims were clear, the elimination of the Jews and control of a single national church. Six million Jews were killed in the Holocaust. The Church was subject to repressive measures, which Pius XI protested futilely in the encyclical *Mit brennender sorge* in 1937.

1936-39: Civil war in Spain between the leftist Loyalist and rightist Franco forces. The Loyalists were defeated and one-man, one-party rule was established. Priests, Religious and lay persons fell victims to Loyalist persecution.

1939-45: World War II.

1939-58: Pontificate of Pius XII. He condemned communism, proclaimed the dogma of the Assumption of Mary in 1950, in various documents and other enactments provided ideological background for many of the accomplishments of the Second Vatican Council. (See Twentieth Century Popes.)

1940: Start of a decade of communist conquest in more than 13 countries, resulting in conditions of persecution for a minimum of 60 million Catholics as well as members of other faiths. Persecution diminished in Mexico because of non-enforcement of anti-religious laws still on record.

1950: Pius XII proclaimed the dogma of the Assumption of the Blessed Virgin Mary.

1957: The communist regime of China established the Patriotic Association of Chinese Catholics in opposition to the Church in union with the pope.

1958-63: Pontificate of John XXIII. His principal accomplishment was the convocation of the Second Vatican Council, the twenty-first ecumenical council in the history of the Church. (See Twentieth Century Popes.)

1962-65: Ecumenical Council of the Vatican (II). It formulated and promulgated 16 documents — two dogmatic and two pastoral constitutions, nine decrees and three declarations — reflecting pastoral orientation toward renewal and reform in the Church, and making explicit dimensions of doctrine and Christian life requiring emphasis for the full development of the Church and the better accomplishment of its mission in the contemporary world.

1963-78: Pontificate of Paul VI. His main purpose and effort was to give direction and provide guidance for the authentic trends of church renewal set in motion by the Second Vatican Council. (See Twentieth Century Popes.)

1978: The thirty-four-day pontificate of John Paul I. Start of the pontificate of John Paul II; see Index.

1983: The revised Code of Canon Law, embodying reforms enacted by the Second Vatican Council, went into effect in the Church of Roman Rite.

1985: Formal ratification of a Vatican-Italy concordat replacing the Lateran Treaty of 1929.

1989-91: Decline and fall of communist influence and control in Middle and Eastern Europe and the Soviet Union.

1991: The Code of Canon Law for Eastern Churches went into effect.

The Gulf War was waged to eject Saddam Hussein from Kuwait.

1992: Approval of the new *Catechism of the Catholic Church*.

The Vatican closed officially the case against Galileo Galilei.

1994: Initiation of celebration preparations of the start of the third Christian millennium in the year 2000.

1997: Pope John Paul II issued an apology for any anti-Semitism by Catholics; a conference on anti-Semitism was also held in Rome and a number of Catholic leaders in Europe issued apologies for historical anti-Semitism.

1998: Pope John Paul II visited Cuba and secured the release of over 300 political prisoners.
The Vatican issued a white paper on Anti-Semitism, titled: *We Remember: A Reflection on the Shoah.*

2000: The Catholic Church celebrates the Holy Year 2000 and the Jubilee; commencement of the third Christian millennium.

ECUMENICAL COUNCILS

An ecumenical council is an assembly of the college of bishops, with and under the presidency of the pope, which has supreme authority over the Church in matters pertaining to faith, morals, worship and discipline.

The Second Vatican Council stated: "The supreme authority with which this college (of bishops) is empowered over the whole Church is exercised in a solemn way through an ecumenical council. A council is never ecumenical unless it is confirmed or at least accepted as such by the successor of Peter. It is the prerogative of the Roman Pontiff to convoke these councils, to preside over them, and to confirm them" (Dogmatic Constitution on the Church, *Lumen Gentium*, No. 22).

Pope Presides

The pope is the head of an ecumenical council; he presides over it either personally or through legates. Conciliar decrees and other actions have binding force only when confirmed and promulgated by him. If a pope dies during a council, it is suspended until reconvened by another pope. An ecumenical council is not superior to a pope; hence, there is no appeal from a pope to a council.

Collectively, the bishops with the pope represent the whole Church. They do this not as democratic representatives of the faithful in a kind of church parliament, but as the successors of the Apostles with divinely given authority, care and responsibility over the whole Church.

All and only bishops are council participants with deliberative vote. The supreme authority of the Church can invite others and determine the manner of their participation.

Basic legislation concerning ecumenical councils is contained in Canons 337-41 of the Code of Canon Law. Basic doctrinal considerations were stated by the Second Vatican Council in the Dogmatic Constitution on the Church.

Background

Ecumenical councils had their prototype in the Council of Jerusalem in 51, at which the Apostles under the leadership of St. Peter decided that converts to the Christian faith were not obliged to observe all the prescriptions of Old Testament law (Acts 15). As early as the second century, bishops got together in regional meetings, synods or councils to take common action for the doctrinal and pastoral good of their communities of faithful. The expansion of such limited assemblies to ecumenical councils was a logical and historical evolution, given the nature and needs of the Church.

Emperors Involved

Emperors were active in summoning or convoking the first eight councils, especially the first five and the eighth. Among reasons for intervention of this kind were the facts that the emperors regarded themselves as guardians of the faith; that the settlement of religious controversies, which had repercussions in political and social turmoil, served the cause of peace in the state; and that the emperors had at their disposal ways and means of facilitating gatherings of bishops. Imperial actions, however, did not account for the formally ecumenical nature of the councils.

Some councils were attended by relatively few bishops, and the ecumenical character of several was open to question for a time. However, confirmation and de facto recognition of their actions by popes and subsequent councils established them as ecumenical.

Role in History

The councils have played a highly significant role in the history of the Church by witnessing to and defining truths of revelation, by shaping forms of worship and discipline, and by promoting measures for the ever-necessary reform and renewal of Catholic life. In general, they have represented attempts of the Church to mobilize itself in times of crisis for self-preservation, self-purification and growth.

The first eight ecumenical councils were held in the East; the other 13, in the West. The majority of separated Eastern Churches — e.g., the Orthodox — recognize the ecumenical character of the first seven councils, which formulated a great deal of basic doctrine. Other separated Eastern Churches acknowledge only the first two or first three ecumenical councils.

The 21 Councils

The 21 ecumenical councils in the history of the Church are listed below, with indication of their names or titles (taken from the names of the places where they were held); the dates; the reigning and/or approving popes; the emperors who were instrumental in convoking the eight councils in the East; the number of bishops who attended, when available; the number of sessions. Significant actions of the first 20 councils are indicated under appropriate dates in Dates and Events in Church History.

1. **Nicaea I,** 325: St. Sylvester I (Emperor Constantine I); attended by approximately 300 bishops; sessions held between May 20 or June 19 to near the end of August.

2. **Constantinople I,** 381: St. Damasus I (Emperor Theodosius I); attended by approximately 150 bishops; sessions held from May to July.

3. **Ephesus,** 431: St. Celestine I (Emperor

Theodosius II); attended by 150 to 200 bishops; five sessions held between June 22 and July 17.

4. Chalcedon, 451: St. Leo I (Emperor Marcian); attended by approximately 600 bishops; 17 sessions held between Oct. 8 and Nov. 1.

5. Constantinople II, 553: Vigilius (Emperor Justinian I); attended by 165 bishops; eight sessions held between May 5 and June 2.

6. Constantinople III, 680-681: St. Agatho, St. Leo II (Emperor Constantine IV); attended by approximately 170 bishops; 16 sessions held between Nov. 7, 680, and Sept. 6, 681.

7. Nicaea II, 787: Adrian I (Empress Irene); attended by approximately 300 bishops: eight sessions held between Sept. 24 and Oct. 23.

8. Constantinople IV, 869-870: Adrian II (Emperor Basil I); attended by 102 bishops; six sessions held between Oct. 5, 869, and Feb. 28, 870.

9. Lateran I, 1123: Callistus II; attended by approximately 300 bishops; sessions held between Mar. 8 and Apr. 6.

10. Lateran II, 1139: Innocent II; attended by 900 to 1,000 bishops and abbots; three sessions held in April.

11. Lateran III, 1179: Alexander III; attended by at least 300 bishops; three sessions held between Mar. 5 and 19.

12. Lateran IV, 1215: Innocent III; sessions held between Nov. 11 and 30.

13. Lyons I, 1245: Innocent IV; attended by approximately 150 bishops; three sessions held between June 28 and July 17.

14. Lyons II, 1274: Gregory X; attended by approximately 500 bishops; six sessions held between May 7 and July 17.

15. Vienne, 1311-1312: Clement V; attended by 132 bishops; three sessions held between Oct. 16, 1311, and May 6, 1312.

16. Constance, 1414-1418: Gregory XII, Martin V; attended by nearly 200 bishops, plus other prelates and many experts; 45 sessions held between Nov. 5, 1414, and Apr. 22, 1418.

17. Florence (also called Basel-Ferrara-Florence), 1431-c. 1445: Eugene IV; attended by many Latin-Rite and Eastern-Rite bishops; preliminary sessions were held at Basel and Ferrara before definitive work was accomplished at Florence.

18. Lateran V, 1512-1517: Julius II, Leo X; 12 sessions held between May 3, 1512, and Mar. 6, 1517.

19. Trent, 1545-1563: Paul III, Julius III, Pius IV; 25 sessions held between Dec. 13, 1545, and Dec. 4, 1563.

20. Vatican I, 1869-1870: Pius IX; attended by approximately 800 bishops and other prelates; four public sessions and 89 general meetings held between Dec. 8, 1869, and Sept. 1, 1870.

VATICAN II

The Second Vatican Council, which was forecast by Pope John XXIII Jan. 25, 1959, was held in four sessions in St. Peter's Basilica.

Pope John convoked it and opened the first session, which ran from Oct. 11 to Dec. 8, 1962. Following John's death June 3, 1963, Pope Paul VI reconvened the council for the other three sessions which ran from Sept. 29 to Dec. 4, 1963; Sept. 14 to Nov. 21, 1964; Sept. 14 to Dec. 8, 1965.

A total of 2,860 Fathers participated in council proceedings, and attendance at meetings varied between 2,000 and 2,500. For various reasons, including the denial of exit from Communist-dominated countries, 274 Fathers could not attend.

The council formulated and promulgated 16 documents — two dogmatic and two pastoral constitutions, nine decrees and three declarations — all of which reflect its basic pastoral orientation toward renewal and reform in the Church. Given below are the Latin and English titles of the documents and their dates of promulgation.

Lumen Gentium (Dogmatic Constitution on the Church), Nov. 21, 1964.

Dei Verbum (Dogmatic Constitution on Divine Revelation), Nov. 18, 1965.

Sacrosanctum Concilium (Constitution on the Sacred Liturgy), Dec. 4, 1963.

Gaudium et Spes (Pastoral Constitution on the Church in the Modern World), Dec. 7, 1965.

Christus Dominus (Decree on the Bishops' Pastoral Office in the Church), Oct. 28, 1965.

Ad Gentes (Decree on the Church's Missionary Activity), Dec. 7, 1965.

Unitatis Redintegratio (Decree on Ecumenism), Nov. 21, 1964.

Orientalium Ecclesiarum (Decree on Eastern Catholic Churches), Nov. 21, 1964.

Presbyterorum Ordinis (Decree on the Ministry and Life of Priests), Dec. 7, 1965.

Optatam Totius (Decree on Priestly Formation), Oct. 28, 1965.

Perfectae Caritatis (Decree on the Appropriate Renewal of the Religious Life), Oct. 28, 1965.

Apostolicam Actuositatem (Decree on the Apostolate of the Laity), Nov. 18, 1965.

Inter Mirifica (Decree on the Instruments of Social Communication), Dec. 4, 1963.

Dignitatis Humanae (Declaration on Religious Freedom), Dec. 7, 1965.

Nostra Aetate (Declaration on the Relationship of the Church to Non-Christian Religions), Oct. 28, 1965.

Gravissimum Educationis (Declaration on Christian Education), Oct. 28, 1965.

The key documents were the four constitutions, which set the ideological basis for all the others. To date, the documents with the most visible effects are those on the liturgy, the Church, the Church in the world, ecumenism, the renewal of religious life, the life and ministry of priests, the lay apostolate.

The main business of the council was to explore and make explicit dimensions of doctrine and Christian life requiring emphasis for the full development of the Church and the better accomplishment of its mission in the contemporary world.

Enactments of the Second Vatican Council have been points of departure for a wide variety of developments in the internal life of the Church and its mission in the world at large. Much effort has been made in the pontificate of Pope John Paul II to provide the interpretation and implementation of the conciliar documents with a more uniform and universal structure.

THE PAPACY AND THE HOLY SEE

POPE JOHN PAUL II

(Update courtesy of Russell Shaw; see many related entries under John Paul II in the Index.)

Cardinal Karol Wojtyla of Cracow was elected Bishop of Rome and 263rd successor of St. Peter as Supreme Pastor of the Universal Church on Oct. 16, 1978. He chose the name John Paul II in honor of his predecessor, Pope John Paul I, as well as Popes John XXIII and Paul VI. He was invested with the pallium, symbol of his office, on Oct. 22 in ceremonies attended by more than 250,000 people in St. Peter's Square.

From the start, Pope John Paul II has labored to keep the Church faithful to its tradition and to the teaching and spirit of Vatican Council II, while positioning it to meet the challenges of the Third Millennium. He is a staunch defender of the sanctity of human life — "from conception to natural death," he often says — and of marriage and the family. Opposition to totalitarianism and support for human rights make this activist, long-reigning pope a major figure on the world political scene.

He is the first non-Italian pope since Adrian VI (1522-23) and the first Polish pope ever. At his election, he was the youngest pope since Pius IX (1846-78). On May 24, 1998, he became the longest-reigning pope elected in the 20th century, surpassing the 19 years, seven months and seven days of Pius XII (1939-58). (Leo XIII, who died in 1903, was pope for 25 years.)

He is the most-traveled pope in history. Through June, 1998, he had covered almost 690,000 miles during 83 pastoral visits outside Italy and 132 within Italy. And almost certainly he is the pope most prolific in literary output, having issued (through mid-1998) 12 encyclicals, 10 apostolic exhortations, nine apostolic constitutions, and 34 apostolic letters.

By his 78th birthday John Paul had canonized 278 saints and declared over 800 persons blessed. He had held seven consistories in which he created 157 cardinals, not including two *in pectore* announced along with 20 others on Jan. 18 of this year. He also had convened five plenary meetings of the College of Cardinals and presided at 12 assemblies of the Synod of Bishops—five ordinary, one extraordinary, and six special.

Early Life

Karol Josef Wojtyla was born May 18, 1920, in Wadowice, an industrial town near Cracow. His parents were Karol Wojtyla, who had been an adminstrative officer in the Austrian army and was a lieutenant in the Polish army until his retirement in 1927, and Emilia Kaczorowska Wojtyla. His mother died in 1929 giving birth to a stillborn child. His older brother Edmund, a physician, died in 1932, and his father in 1941.

He attended schools in Wadowice and in 1938 enrolled in the faculty of philosophy of the Jagiellonian University in Cracow, moving there with his father that summer. At the university he also was active in the Studio 38 experimental theater group.

For young Wojtyla, as for countless others, life changed forever on Sept. 1, 1939, when World War II began. Nazi occupation forces closed the Jagiellonian University and the young man had to work in a quarry as a stone cutter and later in a chemical plant to avoid deportation to Germany. In February, 1940, he met Jan Tryanowski, a tailor who became his spiritual mentor and introduced him to the writings of St. John of the Cross and St. Teresa of Ávila. He also participated in underground theater groups, including the Rhapsodic Theater of Mieczyslaw Kotlarczyk.

In October, 1942, he began studies for the priesthood in the underground seminary maintained by Cardinal Adam Sapieha of Cracow. He was struck by an automobile Feb. 29, 1944, and hospitalized until Mar. 12. In Aug. of that year Cardinal Sapieha transferred him and the other seminarians to the Archbishop's Residence, where they lived and studied until war's end. Ordained a priest by the Cardinal on Nov. 1, 1946, he left Poland Nov. 15 to begin advanced studies in Rome at the Angelicum University (the Pontifical University of St. Thomas Aquinas).

He subsequently earned doctorates in theology and philosophy and was a respected moral theologian and ethicist.

Bishop and Cardinal

On July 4, 1958, Pope Pius XII named him Auxiliary Bishop to Archbishop Eugeniusz Baziak, Apostolic Administrator of Cracow. His book *Love and Responsibility* was published in 1960. (Earlier, he published poetry and several plays.) Following Archbishop Baziak's death in 1962, he became Vicar Capitular and then on Jan. 13, 1964, Archbishop of Cracow—the first residential head of the See permitted by the communist authorities since Cardinal Sapieha's death in 1951.

Archbishop Wojtyla attended all four sessions of the Second Vatican Council, from 1962 to 1965, and helped draft Schema XIII, which became *Gaudium et Spes*, the Pastoral Constitution on the Church in the Modern World. He also contributed to *Dignitatis Humanae* (the Declaration on Religious Freedom) and *Inter Mirifica* (the Decree on the Instruments of Social Communication).

Pope Paul VI created him a cardinal in the consistory of June 28, 1967, with the titular Roman church of S. Cesario in Palatio. Although scheduled to attend the first general assembly of the Synod of Bishops in Sept. in Oct. of that year, Cardinal Wojtyla did not go, as a sign of solidarity with Cardinal Stefan Wyszynski of Warsaw, Poland's primate, whom the communist government refused a passport. In October, 1969, however, he participated in the first extraordinary assembly of the synod. Earlier that year, with approval of the statutes of the Polish bishops' conference, he became its vice president.

In 1971 he took part in the second general assembly of the synod and was elected to the council of the secretary general of the synod. He continued to participate in synod assemblies and to serve on the synod

council up to his election as pope. May 8, 1972, saw the opening of the archdiocesan of synod of Cracow, which he had convened and would see conclude during his visit to Poland as Pope in 1979. Also in 1972 he published *Foundations of Renewal: A Study on the Implementation of the Second Vatican Council.*

Pope Paul died Aug. 6, 1978. Cardinal Wojtyla participated in the conclave that chose Cardinal Albino Luciani of Venice his successor on Aug. 26. When the new Pope, who had taken the name John Paul I, died unexpectedly on Sept. 28, Cardinal Wojtyla joined 110 other cardinals in that year's second conclave. He emerged on the second day of voting, Oct. 16, as Pope John Paul II.

Pontificate

Pope John Paul set out the major themes and program of his pontificate in his first encyclical, *Redemptor Hominis (The Redeemer of Man)*, dated Mar. 4, 1979, and published Mar. 15. "The Redeemer of Man, Jesus Christ, is the center of the universe and of history," he wrote. Throughout his pontificate he has emphasized preparation for the year 2000—which he proclaimed a Jubilee Year—and for the Third Millennium of the Christian era, with the aim of fostering a renewed commitment to evangelization among Catholics. He also has produced a significant body of magisterial teaching in such areas as Christian anthropology, sexual morality, and social justice, while working for peace and human rights throughout the world.

His pontificate has been uncommonly active and filled with dramatic events. Among the most dramatic are those associated with the fall of communism in Eastern Europe. Many students of that complex event credit John Paul with a central role. His visits to his Polish homeland in 1979 (June 2-10) and 1983 (June 16-23) bolstered Polish Catholicism and kindled Polish resistance to communism, while his determined support for the Solidarity labor movement gave his countrymen a vehicle for their resistance. The result was a growing nonviolent liberation movement leading to the dramatic developments of 1989—the collapse of communist regimes and the emergence of democracy in Poland and other countries, the fall of the Berlin Wall—and in time to the breakup of the Soviet Union and the end of the Cold War.

Dramatic in a much different way was the 1981 attempt on the Pope's life. At 5:19 p.m. on May 13, as he greeted crowds in St. Peter's Square before his Wednesday general audience, a Turkish terrorist named Mehmet Ali Agca shot John Paul at close range. Whether the assassin acted alone or at the behest of others—and which others—remain unanswered questions. Following a six-hour operation,

John Paul was hospitalized for 77 days at Gemelli Hospital. He visited Ali Agca in the Rebibbia prison on Dec. 27, 1983.

Although he resumed his activities vigorously after his recuperation, the Pope's health and strength have declined over the years. In July, 1992, he had colon surgery for the removal of a non-cancerous tumor; in November, 1993, his shoulder was dislocated in a fall; he suffered a broken femur in another fall in April, 1994; and in October, 1996, he had an appendectomy. For several years, too, the effects have been apparent of what the Vatican acknowledges to be a neurological condition (many observers take the ailment to be Parkinson's disease). John Paul nevertheless maintains what is by any standards a highly demanding schedule. Clearly, he wishes to lead the Church into the new millennium.

Foreign Pastoral Visits

As noted, his pastoral visits have been a striking feature of his pontificate. Many have been to nations in the Third World. His 88 trips outside Italy (through September, 1999) are as follows.

1979 Dominican Republic and Mexico, Jan. 5-Feb. 1; Poland, June 2-10; Ireland and the United States, Sept. 29-Oct. 7; Turkey, Nov. 28-30.

1980 Africa (Zaire, Congo Republic, Kenya, Ghana, Upper Volta, Ivory Coast), May 2-12; France, May 30-June 2; Brazil (13 cities), June 30-July 12; West Germany, Nov. 15-19.

1981 Philippines, Guam, and Japan, with stopovers in Pakistan and Alaska, Feb. 16-27.

1982 Africa (Nigeria, Benin, Gabon, Equatorial Guinea), Feb. 12-19; Portugal, May 12-15; Great Britain, May 28-June 2; Argentina, June 11-12; Switzerland, June 15; San Marino, Aug. 29; Spain, Oct. 31-Nov. 9.

198 Central America (Costa Rica, Nicaragua, Panama, El Salvador, Guatemala, Belize, Honduras) and Haiti, Mar. 2-10; Poland, June 16-23; Lourdes, France, Aug. 14-15; Austria, Sept. 10-13.

1984 South Korea, Papua New Guinea, Solomon Islands, Thailand, May 12; Switzerland, June 12-17; Canada, Sept. 9-20; Spain, Dominican Republic, and Puerto Rico, Oct. 10-12.

1985 Venezuela, Ecuador, Peru, Trinidad and Tobago, Jan. 26-Feb. 6; Belgium, The Netherlands, and Luxembourg, May 11-21; Africa (Togo, Ivory Coast, Cameroon, Central African Republic, Zaire, Kenya, and Morocco), Aug. 8-19; Liechtenstein, Sept. 8.

1986 India, Feb. 1-10; Colombia and Saint Lucia, July 1-7; France, Oct. 4-7; Oceania (Australia, New Zealand, Bangladesh, Fiji, Singapore, and Seychelles), Nov. 18-Dec. 1.

1987 Uruguay, Chile, and Argentina, Mar. 31-Apr. 12; West Germany, Apr. 30-May 4; Poland, June 8-14; the United States and Canada, Sept. 10-19.

1988 Uruguay, Bolivia, Peru, and Paraguay, May 7-18; Austria, June 23-27; Africa (Zimbabwe, Botswana, Lesotho, Swaziland, and Mozambique), Sept. 10-19; France, Oct. 8-11.

1989 Madagascar, Reunion, Zambia, and Malawi, Apr. 28-May 6; Norway, Iceland, Finland, Denmark, and Sweden, June 1-10; Spain, Aug. 19-

21; South Korea, Indonesia, East Timor, and Mauritius, Oct. 6-16.

1990 Africa (Cape Verde, Guinea Bissau, Mali, and Burkna Faso), Jan. 25-Feb. 1; Czechoslovakia, Apr. 21-22; Mexico and Curaçao, May 6-13; Malta, May 25-27; Africa (Tanzania, Burundi, Rwanda, and Ivory Coast), Sept. 1-10.

1991 Portugal, May 10-13; Poland, June 1-9; Poland and Hungary, Aug. 13-20; Brazil, Oct. 12-21.

1992 Africa (Senegal, The Gambia, Guinea), Feb. 10-26; Africa (Angola, São Tome, and Principe), June 4-10; Dominican Republic, Oct. 10-14.

1993 Africa (Benin, Uganda, Sudan), Feb. 2-10; Albania, Apr. 25; Spain, June 12-17; Jamaica, Mexico, Denver (U.S.A.), Aug. 9-15; Lithuania, Latvia, Estonia, Sept. 4-10.

1994 Zagreb, Croatia, Sept. 10.

1995 Philippines, Papua New Guinea, Australia, Sri Lanka, Jan. 12-21; Czech Republic and Poland, May 20-22; Belgium, June 3-4; Slovakia, June 30-July 3; Africa (Cameroon, South Africa, Kenya), Sept. 14-20; United Nations and United States, Oct. 4-8.

1996 Central America (Guatemala, Nicaragua, El Salvador), Feb. 5-11; Tunisia, Apr. 17; Slovenia, May 17-19; Germany, June 21-23; Hungary, Sept. 6-7; France, Sept. 19-22.

1997 Sarajevo, Apr. 12-13; Czech Republic, Apr. 25-27; Lebanon, May 10-11; Poland, May 31-June 10; France, Aug. 21-24; Brazil, Oct. 2-5.

1998 Cuba, Jan. 21-25; Nigeria, Mar. 21-23; Austria, June 19-21; Croatia, Oct. 3-4.

1999 Mexico, Jan. 22-25; St. Louis, United States, Jan. 26-27; Romania, May 2-5; Poland June, 5-17. (For details on the Holy Father's recent trips, please see the Papal Trips section under Special Reports.)

Notable among the Pope's pastoral visits have been journeys to celebrate World Youth Day with young people.

Encyclicals and Other Writings

As noted above, Pope John Paul's first encyclical, *Redemptor Hominis* (1979), set the tone for and in general terms indicated the subject matter of many of the documents to follow. These are infused with the Pope's distinctive personalism, which emphasizes the dignity and rights of the human person, most truly understood in the light of Christ, as the norm and goal of human endeavor.

His other encyclical letters to date are: *Dives in Misericordia* (*On the Mercy of God*), 1980; *Laborem Exercens* (*On Human Work*), 1981; *Slavorum Apostoli* (*The Apostles of the Slavs*, honoring Sts. Cyril and Methodius), 1985; *Dominum et Vivificantem* (*Lord and Giver of Life*, on the Holy Spirit), 1986; *Redemptoris Mater* (*Mother of the Redeemer*), 1987; *Sollicitudo Rei Socialis* (*On Social Concerns*), 1988; *Redemptoris Missio* (*Mission of the Redeemer*) and *Centesimus Annus* (*The Hundredth Year*, on the anniversary of Leo XIII's *Rerum Novarum*), both 1991; *Veritatis Splendor* (*The Splendor of Truth*), 1993; *Evangelium Vitae* (*The Gospel of Life*) and *Ut Unum Sint* (*That All May Be One*), 1995; *Fides et Ratio* (*Faith and Reason*), 1998.

Among his other publications are: *Catechesi Tradendae*, a post-synodal apostolic exhortation on catechesis, 1979; apostolic letter proclaiming Sts. Cyril and Methodius, together with St. Benedict, patrons of Europe, 1980; post-synodal apostolic exhortation *Familiaris Consortio*, on the family, 1981; apostolic letter *Caritatis Christi*, for the Church in China, 1982; letter for the 500th anniversary of the birth of Martin Luther, 1983; apostolic letter *Salvifici Doloris* ("On the Christian Meaning of Suffering"), apostolic exhortation *Redemptionis Donum*, to men and women religious, apostolic letters *Redemptionis Anno*, on Jerusalem, and *Les Grands Mysteres*, on Lebanon, and post-synodal apostolic exhortation *Reconciliatio et Poenitentia* ("Reconciliation and Penance"), all 1984.

Also: apostolic letter *Dilecti Amici*, on the occasion of the United Nations' International Year of Youth, 1985; apostolic letter *Euntes in Mundum*, for the millennium of Christianity in Kievan Rus', and apostolic letter *Mulieris Dignitatem* ("On the Dignity and Vocation of Women"), all 1988; post-synodal apostolic exhortation *Christifideles Laici* ("The Lay Members of Christ's Faithful People") and apostolic exhortation *Redemptoris Custos* ("On St. Joseph"), 1989; post-synodal apostolic exhortation *Pastores Dabo Vobis* ("I Give You Shepherds"), 1992; *Letter to Families*, for the International Year of the Family, Letter on the International Conference on Population and Development in Cairo, apostolic letter *Ordinatio Sacerdotalis* ("On Reserving Priestly Ordination to Men Alone"), and apostolic letter *Tertio Millennio Adveniente*, on preparation for the Jubilee Year 2000, and *Letter to Children in the Year of the Family*, all 1994.

Also: apostolic letter *Orientale Lumen* ("The Light of the East"), on Catholic-Orthodox relations, *Letter to Women*, post-synodal apostolic exhortation *Ecclesia in Africa*, and apostolic letter for the fourth centenary of the Union of Brest, all 1995; apostolic constitution *Universi Dominici Gregis* ("On the Vacancy of the Apostolic See and the Election of the Roman Pontiff"), post-synodal apostolic exhortation *Vita Consecrata* ("On the Consecrated Life and Its Mission in the Church and in the World"), and apostolic letter on the 350th anniversary of the Union of Uzhorod, all 1996; post-synodal apostolic exhortation, *A New Hope for Lebanon*, 1997; *Incarnationis Mysterium*, Bull of Indiction of the Great Jubilee of the Year 2000, 1998.

In his years as Pope he also has published two books: *Crossing the Threshold of Hope* (1994) and *Gift and Mystery: On the Fiftieth Anniversary of My Priestly Ordination* (1996).

Issues and Activities

Doctrinal Concerns: The integrity of Catholic doctrine has been a major concern of Pope John Paul. On Nov. 25, 1981, he appointed Archbishop— later, Cardinal—Joseph Ratzinger of Munich-Freising, a prominent theologian, Prefect of the Congregation for the Doctrine of the Faith. The congregation under Cardinal Ratzinger has published important documents on bioethics, on liberation theology (1984 and 1986), and on the Church's inability to ordain women as priests, the latter affirming that the teaching on this matter has been "set forth infallibly" (1995).

Catechism: One of Pope John Paul's most impor-

tant initiatives is the *Catechism of the Catholic Church*. The idea for this up-to-date compendium was broached at the extraordinary assembly of the Synod of Bishops held in 1985 to evaluate the implementation of Vatican Council II. The Pope approved, and the project went forward under a commission of cardinals headed by Cardinal Ratzinger. Published in 1992 by authorization of John Paul II (the original was in French, with the English translation appearing in 1994 and the authoritative Latin *editio typica* in 1997), this first catechism for the universal Church in four centuries is crucial to the hoped-for renewal of catechesis.

Canon Law: John Paul oversaw the completion of the revision of the Code of Canon Law begun in 1959 at the direction of Pope John XXIII. He promulgated the new code on Jan. 25, 1983; it went into effect on Nov. 27 of that year. In *Sacrae Disciplinae Leges*, the apostolic constitution accompanying the revised code, the Pope says it has "one and the same intention" as Vatican Council II — whose convening John XXIII announced at the same time — namely, "the renewal of Christian living."

On Apr. 18, 1990, John Paul promulgated the Code of Canons for the Eastern Churches. Although particular sections of the Eastern code appeared at various times dating back to 1949, this was the first time an integrated code of law for the Eastern Churches had been issued in its entirety.

Ecumenical and Interreligious Relations: Ecumenical and interreligious relations have received much attention from Pope John Paul II. Two of his major documents, the encyclical *Ut Unum Sint* and the apostolic letter *Orientale Lumen*, both published in 1995, deal with these matters. He has met frequently with representatives of other religious bodies, has spoken frequently about the quest for unity, and has called for Catholics and others to pray and work to this end.

Among the important actions in this area have been the signings of common declarations with the Ecumenical Patriarch of Constantinople His Holiness Dimitrios (Dec. 7, 1987) and his successor Bartholomew I (June 29, 1995), with the Archbishop of Canterbury and Primate of the Anglican Communion Dr. Robert Runcie (May 29, 1982, in Canterbury Cathedral and again Oct. 2, 1989 in Rome) and his successor Dr. George Leonard Carey (Dec. 6, 1996), with the Supreme Patriarch and Catholicos of All Armenians, His Holiness Karekin I (Dec. 14, 1996), and with His Holiness Aram I Keshishian, Catholicos of Cilicia of the Armenians (Jan. 26, 1997). On Oct. 5, 1991, for the first time since the Reformation, two Lutheran bishops joined the Pope and the Catholic bishops of Stockholm and Helsinki in an ecumenical prayer service in St. Peter's Basilica marking the sixth centenary of the canonization of St. Bridget of Sweden.

Pope John Paul has had Jewish friends since boyhood, and he has worked hard to strengthen Catholic-Jewish ties. The Holy See formally initiated diplomatic relations with the State of Israel at the level of apostolic nunciature and embassy on June 15, 1994. In Mar., 1998, the Commission for Religious Relations with the Jews published an important document on the roots of the World War II Jewish Holocaust entitled *We Remember: A Reflection on the 'Shoah.'*

In a letter dated Mar. 12 to the commission chairman, Cardinal Edward Idris Cassidy, the Pope expressed "fervent hope" that it would "help to heal the wounds of past misunderstandings and injustices."

Women's Concerns: Pope John Paul's insistence that, in fidelity to the will of Christ, the Church is unable to ordain women as priests has put him at odds with some feminists, as has his opposition to abortion and contraception. But it is clear from his writings that he is unusually sensitive to women's issues, and he is a strong defender of women's dignity and rights, about which he often has spoken. In 1995 he appointed a woman, Professor Mary Ann Glendon of the Harvard University law school, head of the Holy See's delegation to the fourth United Nations conference on women, held in Beijing Sept. 4-15, the first time a woman had been named to such a post.

World Affairs: At least since January of 1979, when he accepted a request for mediation in a border conflict between Argentina and Chile, John Paul II has worked for peace in many parts of the world. He has supported efforts to achieve reconciliation between conflicting parties in troubled areas like Lebanon, the Balkans, and the Persian Gulf, where he sought to avert the Gulf War of 1991. He has advocated religious liberty and human rights during pastoral visits to many countries, including Cuba and Nigeria in 1998. Among the notable ecumenical and interreligious events of the pontificate was the World Day of Prayer for Peace on Oct. 27, 1986, which he convoked in Assisi and attended along with representatives of numerous other churches and religious groups.

In 1984 the Holy See and the United States established diplomatic relations. (The Pope has met with Presidents Jimmy Carter, Ronald Reagan, George Bush, and Bill Clinton.) Relations with Poland were re-established in 1989. Diplomatic relations were established with the Soviet Union in 1990 and with the Russian Federation in 1992. Relations also have been established with other Eastern European countries and countries that were part of the former Soviet Union, with Mexico, and with other nations including Jordan, South Africa, and Libya. Working contacts of a "permanent and official character" were begun with the Palestine Liberation Organization in 1994.

Administration: Under Pope John Paul II the long-term financial problems of the Holy See have been addressed and brought under control. Finances were on the agenda at the first plenary assembly of the College of Cardinals, Nov. 5-9, 1979, and subsequent meetings of that body. A council of cardinals for the study of organizational and economic problems of the Holy See was established in 1981. In 1988, the Holy See's financial report (for 1986) was published for the first time, along with the 1988 budget. In April, 1991, a meeting of the presidents of episcopal conferences was held to discuss ways of increasing the Peter's Pence Collection taken in support of the Pope.

A reorganization of responsibilities of Vatican offices was carried out in 1984, and in 1988 an apostolic constitution, *Pastor Bonus*, on reform of the Roman Curia was issued. A Vatican labor office was instituted in 1989. Pope John Paul established a new Pontifical Academy of Social Sciences in 1994 and Pontifical Academy for Life in 1995. On Apr. 8, 1994, he celebrated Mass in the Sistine Chapel for the unveiling of the Michelangelo frescoes, which had been painstakingly cleaned and restored. The opening presentation of the Holy See's Internet site took place Mar. 24, 1997.

As Bishop of Rome, John Paul presided over a diocesan synod which concluded May 29, 1993. He also has visited numerous Roman parishes — 270 out of 328 by the time of his 78th birthday.

POPES OF THE ROMAN CATHOLIC CHURCH

Information includes the name of the pope, in many cases his name before becoming pope, his birthplace or country of origin, the date of accession to the papacy, and the date of the end of reign which, in all but a few cases, was the date of death. Double dates indicate date of election and date of solemn beginning of ministry as Pastor of the universal Church.

Source: Annuario Pontificio.

St. Peter (Simon Bar-Jona): Bethsaida in Galilee; d. c. 64 or 67.
St. Linus: Tuscany; 67-76.
St. Anacletus (Cletus): Rome; 76-88.
St. Clement: Rome; 88-97.
St. Evaristus: Greece; 97-105.
St. Alexander I: Rome; 105-115.
St. Sixtus I: Rome; 115-125.
St. Telesphorus: Greece; 125-136.
St. Hyginus: Greece; 136-140.
St. Pius I: Aquileia; 140-155.
St. Anicetus: Syria; 155-166.

St. Soter: Campania; 166-175.
St. Eleutherius: Nicopolis in Epirus; 175-189.
Up to the time of St. Eleutherius, the years indicated for the beginning and end of pontificates are not absolutely certain. Also, up to the middle of the 11th century, there are some doubts about the exact days and months given in chronological tables.
St. Victor I: Africa; 189-199.
St. Zephyrinus: Rome; 199-217.
St. Callistus I: Rome; 217-222.
St. Urban I: Rome; 222-230.
St. Pontian: Rome; July 21, 230, to Sept. 28, 235.
St. Anterus: Greece; Nov. 21, 235, to Jan. 3, 236.
St. Fabian: Rome; Jan. 10, 236, to Jan. 20, 250.
St. Cornelius: Rome; Mar., 251, to June, 253.
St. Lucius I: Rome; June 25, 253, to Mar. 5, 254.
St. Stephen I: Rome; May 12, 254, to Aug. 2, 257.
St. Sixtus II: Greece; Aug. 30, 257, to Aug. 6, 258.
St. Dionysius: birthplace unknown; July 22, 259, to Dec. 26, 268.

St. Felix I: Rome; Jan. 5, 269, to Dec. 30, 274.

St. Eutychian: Luni; Jan. 4, 275, to Dec. 7, 283.

St. Caius: Dalmatia; Dec. 17, 283, to Apr. 22, 296.

St. Marcellinus: Rome; June 30, 296, to Oct. 25, 304.

St. Marcellus I: Rome; May 27, 308, or June 26, 308, to Jan. 16, 309.

St. Eusebius: Greece; Apr. 18, 309, to Aug. 17, 309 or 310.

St. Melchiades (Miltiades): Africa; July 2, 311, to Jan. 11, 314.

St. Sylvester I: Rome; Jan. 31, 314, to Dec. 31, 335. (Most of the popes before St. Sylvester I were martyrs.)

St. Marcus: Rome; Jan. 18, 336, to Oct. 7, 336.

St. Julius I: Rome; Feb. 6, 337, to Apr. 12, 352.

Liberius: Rome; May 17, 352, to Sept. 24, 366.

St. Damasus I: Spain; Oct. 1, 366, to Dec. 11, 384.

St. Siricius: Rome; Dec. 15, or 22 or 29, 384, to Nov. 26, 399.

St. Anastasius I: Rome; Nov. 27, 399, to Dec. 19, 401.

St. Innocent I: Albano; Dec. 22, 401, to Mar. 12, 417.

St. Zozimus: Greece; Mar. 18, 417, to Dec. 26, 418.

St. Boniface I: Rome; Dec. 28 or 29, 418, to Sept. 4, 422.

St. Celestine I: Campania; Sept. 10, 422, to July 27, 432.

St. Sixtus III: Rome; July 31, 432, to Aug. 19, 440.

St. Leo I (the Great): Tuscany; Sept. 29, 440, to Nov. 10, 461.

St. Hilary: Sardinia; Nov. 19, 461, to Feb. 29, 468.

St. Simplicius: Tivoli; Mar. 3, 468, to Mar. 10, 483.

St. Felix III (II): Rome; Mar. 13, 483, to Mar. 1, 492. He should be called Felix II, and his successors of the same name should be numbered accordingly. The discrepancy in the numerical designation of popes named Felix was caused by the erroneous insertion in some lists of the name of St. Felix of Rome, a martyr.

St. Gelasius I: Africa; Mar. 1, 492, to Nov. 21, 496.

Anastasius II: Rome; Nov. 24, 496, to Nov. 19, 498.

St. Symmachus: Sardinia; Nov. 22, 498, to July 19, 514.

St. Hormisdas: Frosinone; July 20, 514, to Aug. 6, 523.

St. John I, Martyr: Tuscany; Aug. 13, 523, to May 18, 526.

St. Felix IV (III): Samnium; July 12, 526, to Sept. 22, 530.

Boniface II: Rome; Sept. 22, 530, to Oct. 17, 532.

John II: Rome; Jan. 2, 533, to May 8, 535. John II was the first pope to change his name. His given name was Mercury.

St. Agapitus I: Rome; May 13, 535, to Apr. 22, 536.

St. Silverius, Martyr: Campania; June 1 or 8, 536, to Nov. 11, 537 (d. Dec. 2, 537). St. Silverius was violently deposed in Mar., 537, and abdicated Nov. 11, 537. His successor, Vigilius, was not recognized as pope by all the Roman clergy until his abdication.

Vigilius: Rome; Mar. 29, 537, to June 7, 555.

Pelagius I: Rome; Apr. 16, 556, to Mar. 4, 561.

John III: Rome; July 17, 561, to July 13, 574.

Benedict I: Rome; June 2,.575, to July 30, 579.

Pelagius II: Rome; Nov. 26, 579, to Feb. 7, 590.

St. Gregory I (the Great): Rome; Sept. 3, 590, to Mar. 12, 604.

Sabinian: Blera in Tuscany; Sept. 13, 604, to Feb. 22, 606.

Boniface III: Rome; Feb. 19, 607, to Nov. 12, 607.

St. Boniface IV: Abruzzi; Aug. 25, 608, to May 8, 615.

St. Deusdedit (Adeodatus I): Rome; Oct. 19, 615, to Nov. 8, 618.

Boniface V: Naples; Dec. 23, 619, to Oct. 25, 625.

Honorius I: Campania; Oct. 27, 625, to Oct. 12, 638.

Severinus: Rome; May 28, 640, to Aug. 2, 640.

John IV: Dalmatia; Dec. 24, 640, to Oct. 12, 642.

Theodore I: Greece; Nov. 24, 642, to May 14, 649.

St. Martin I, Martyr: Todi; July, 649, to Sept. 16, 655 (in exile from June 17, 653).

St. Eugene I: Rome; Aug. 10, 654, to June 2, 657. St. Eugene I was elected during the exile of St. Martin I, who is believed to have endorsed him as pope.

St. Vitalian: Segni; July 30, 657, to Jan. 27, 672.

Adeodatus II: Rome; Apr. 11, 672, to June 17, 676.

Donus: Rome; Nov. 2, 676, to Apr. 11, 678.

St. Agatho: Sicily; June 27, 678, to Jan. 10, 681.

St. Leo II: Sicily; Aug. 17, 682, to July 3, 683.

St. Benedict II: Rome; June 26, 684, to May 8, 685.

John V: Syria; July 23, 685, to Aug. 2, 686.

Conon: birthplace unknown; Oct. 21, 686, to Sept. 21, 687.

St. Sergius I: Syria; Dec. 15, 687, to Sept. 8, 701.

John VI: Greece; Oct. 30, 701, to Jan. 11, 705.

John VII: Greece; Mar. 1, 705, to Oct. 18, 707.

Sisinnius: Syria; Jan. 15, 708, to Feb. 4, 708.

Constantine: Syria; Mar. 25, 708, to Apr. 9, 715.

St. Gregory II: Rome; May 19, 715, to Feb. 11, 731.

St. Gregory III: Syria; Mar. 18, 731, to Nov., 741.

St. Zachary: Greece; Dec. 10, 741, to Mar. 22, 752.

Stephen II (III): Rome; Mar. 26, 752, to Apr. 26, 757. After the death of St. Zachary, a Roman priest named Stephen was elected but died (four days later) before his consecration as bishop of Rome, which would have marked the beginning of his pontificate. Another Stephen was elected to succeed Zachary as Stephen II. (The first pope with this name was St. Stephen I, 254-57.) The ordinal III appears in parentheses after the name of Stephen II because the name of the earlier elected but deceased priest was included in some lists. Other Stephens have double numbers.

St. Paul I: Rome; Apr. (May 29), 757, to June 28, 767.

Stephen III (IV): Sicily; Aug. 1 (7), 768, to Jan. 24, 772.

Adrian I: Rome; Feb. 1 (9), 772, to Dec. 25, 795.

St. Leo III: Rome; Dec. 26 (27), 795, to June 12, 816.

Stephen IV (V): Rome; June 22, 816, to Jan. 24, 817.

St. Paschal I: Rome; Jan. 25, 817, to Feb. 11, 824.

Eugene II: Rome; Feb. (May), 824, to Aug., 827.

Valentine: Rome; Aug. 827, to Sept., 827.

Gregory IV: Rome; 827, to Jan., 844.

Sergius II: Rome; Jan., 844 to Jan. 27, 847.

St. Leo IV: Rome; Jan. (Apr. 10), 847, to July 17, 855.

Benedict III: Rome; July (Sept. 29), 855, to Apr. 17, 858.

St. Nicholas I (the Great): Rome; Apr. 24, 858, to Nov. 13, 867.

Adrian II: Rome; Dec. 14, 867, to Dec. 14, 872.

John VIII: Rome; Dec. 14, 872, to Dec. 16, 882.

Marinus I: Gallese; Dec. 16, 882, to May 15, 884.

St. Adrian III: Rome; May 17, 884, to Sept., 885. Cult confirmed June 2, 1891.

Stephen V (VI): Rome; Sept., 885, to Sept. 14, 891.

Formosus: Bishop of Porto; Oct. 6, 891, to Apr. 4, 896.

Boniface VI: Rome; Apr., 896, to Apr., 896.

Stephen VI (VII): Rome; May, 896, to Aug., 897.

Romanus: Gallese; Aug., 897, to Nov., 897.

Theodore II: Rome; Dec., 897, to Dec., 897.

John IX: Tivoli; Jan., 898, to Jan., 900.

Benedict IV: Rome; Jan. (Feb.), 900, to July, 903.

Leo V: Ardea; July, 903, to Sept., 903.

Sergius III: Rome; Jan. 29, 904, to Apr. 14, 911.

Anastasius III: Rome; Apr., 911, to June, 913.

Landus: Sabina; July, 913, to Feb., 914.

John X: Tossignano (Imola); Mar., 914, to May, 928.

Leo VI: Rome; May, 928, to Dec., 928.

Stephen VII (VIII): Rome; Dec., 928, to Feb., 931.

John XI: Rome; Feb. (Mar.), 931, to Dec., 935.

Leo VII: Rome; Jan. 3, 936, to July 13, 939.

Stephen VIII (IX): Rome; July 14, 939, to Oct., 942.

Marinus II: Rome; Oct. 30, 942, to May, 946.

Agapitus II: Rome; May 10, 946, to Dec., 955.

John XII (Octavius): Tusculum; Dec. 16, 955, to May 14, 964 (date of his death).

Leo VIII: Rome; Dec. 4 (6), 963, to Mar. 1, 965.

Benedict V: Rome; May 22, 964, to July 4, 966.

Confusion exists concerning the legitimacy of claims to the pontificate by Leo VIII and Benedict V. John XII was deposed Dec. 4, 963, by a Roman council. If this deposition was invalid, Leo was an antipope. If the deposition of John was valid, Leo was the legitimate pope and Benedict was an antipope.

John XIII: Rome; Oct. 1, 965, to Sept. 6, 972.

Benedict VI: Rome; Jan. 19, 973, to June, 974.

Benedict VII: Rome; Oct. 974, to July 10, 983.

John XIV (Peter Campenora): Pavia; Dec., 983, to Aug. 20, 984.

John XV: Rome; Aug., 985, to Mar. 996.

Gregory V (Bruno of Carinthia): Saxony; May 3, 996, to Feb. 18, 999.

Sylvester II (Gerbert): Auvergne; Apr. 2, 999, to May 12, 1003.

John XVII (Siccone): Rome; June 1003, to Dec., 1003.

John XVIII (Phasianus): Rome; Jan., 1004, to July, 1009.

Sergius IV (Peter): Rome; July 31, 1009, to May 12, 1012.

The custom of changing one's name on election to the papacy is generally considered to date from the time of Sergius IV. Before his time, several popes had changed their names. After his time, this became a regular practice, with few exceptions; e.g., Adrian VI and Marcellus II.

Benedict VIII (Theophylactus): Tusculum; May 18, 1012, to Apr. 9, 1024.

John XIX (Romanus): Tusculum; Apr. (May), 1024, to 1032.

Benedict IX (Theophylactus): Tusculum; 1032, to 1044.

Sylvester III (John): Rome; Jan. 20, 1045, to Feb. 10, 1045.

Sylvester III was an antipope if the forcible removal of Benedict IX in 1044 was not legitimate.

Benedict IX (second time): Apr. 10, 1045, to May 1, 1045.

Gregory VI (John Gratian): Rome; May 5, 1045, to Dec. 20, 1046.

Clement II (Suitger, Lord of Morsleben and Hornburg): Saxony; Dec. 24 (25), 1046, to Oct. 9, 1047.

If the resignation of Benedict IX in 1045 and his removal at the December, 1046, synod were not legitimate, Gregory VI and Clement II were antipopes.

Benedict IX (third time): Nov. 8, 1047, to July 17, 1048 (d. c. 1055).

Damasus II (Poppo): Bavaria; July 17, 1048, to Aug. 9, 1048.

St. Leo IX (Bruno): Alsace; Feb. 12, 1049, to Apr. 19, 1054.

Victor II (Gebhard): Swabia; Apr. 16, 1055, to July 28, 1057.

Stephen IX (X) (Frederick): Lorraine; Aug. 3, 1057, to Mar. 29, 1058.

Nicholas II (Gerard): Burgundy; Jan. 24, 1059, to July 27, 1061.

Alexander II (Anselmo da Baggio): Milan; Oct. 1, 1061, to Apr. 21, 1073.

St. Gregory VII (Hildebrand): Tuscany; Apr. 22 (June 30), 1073, to May 25, 1085.

Bl. Victor III (Dauferius; Desiderius): Benevento; May 24, 1086, to Sept. 16, 1087. Cult confirmed July 23, 1887.

Bl. Urban II (Otto di Lagery): France; Mar. 12, 1088, to July 29, 1099. Cult confirmed July 14, 1881.

Paschal II (Raniero): Ravenna; Aug. 13 (14), 1099, to Jan. 21, 1118.

Gelasius II (Giovanni Caetani): Gaeta; Jan. 24 (Mar. 10), 1118, to Jan. 28, 1119.

Callistus II (Guido of Burgundy): Burgundy; Feb. 2 (9), 1119, to Dec. 13, 1124.

Honorius II (Lamberto): Fiagnano (Imola); Dec. 15 (21), 1124, to Feb. 13, 1130.

Innocent II (Gregorio Papareschi): Rome; Feb. 14 (23), 1130, to Sept. 24, 1143.

Celestine II (Guido): Citta di Castello; Sept. 26 (Oct. 3), 1143, to Mar. 8, 1144.

Lucius II (Gerardo Caccianemici): Bologna: Mar. 12, 1144, to Feb. 15, 1145.

Bl. Eugene III (Bernardo Paganelli di Montemagno): Pisa; Feb. 15 (18), 1145, to July 8, 1153. Cult confirmed Oct. 3, 1872.

Anastasius IV (Corrado): Rome; July 12, 1153, to Dec, 3, 1154.

Adrian IV (Nicholas Breakspear): England; Dec. 4 (5), 1154, to Sept. 1, 1159.

Alexander III (Rolando Bandinelli): Siena; Sept. 7 (20), 1159, to Aug. 30, 1181.

Lucius III (Ubaldo Allucingoli): Lucca; Sept. 1 (6), 1181, to Sept. 25, 1185.

Urban III (Uberto Crivelli): Milan; Nov. 25 (Dec. 1), 1185, to Oct. 20, 1187.

Gregory VIII (Alberto de Morra): Benevento; Oct. 21 (25), 1187, to Dec. 17, 1187.

Clement III (Paolo Scolari): Rome; Dec. 19 (20), 1187, to Mar., 1191.

Celestine III (Giacinto Bobone): Rome; Mar. 30 (Apr. 14), 1191, to Jan. 8, 1198.

Innocent III (Lotario dei Conti di Segni); Anagni; Jan. 8 (Feb. 22), 1198, to July 16, 1216.

Honorius III (Cencio Savelli): Rome; July 18 (24), 1216, to Mar. 18, 1227.

Gregory IX (Ugolino, Count of Segni): Anagni; Mar. 19 (21), 1227, to Aug. 22, 1241.

Celestine IV (Goffredo Castiglioni): Milan; Oct. 25 (28), 1241, to Nov. 10, 1241.

Innocent IV (Sinibaldo Fieschi): Genoa; June 25 (28), 1243, to Dec. 7, 1254.

Alexander IV (Rinaldo, House of Ienne): Ienne (Rome); Dec. 12 (20), 1254, to May 25, 1261.

Urban IV (Jacques Pantal,on): Troyes; Aug. 29 (Sept. 4), 1261, to Oct. 2, 1264.

Clement IV (Guy Foulques or Guido le Gros): France; Feb. 5 (15), 1265, to Nov. 29, 1268.

Bl. Gregory X (Teobaldo Visconti): Piacenza; Sept. 1, 1271 (Mar. 27, 1272), to Jan. 10, 1276. Cult confirmed Sept. 12, 1713.

Bl. Innocent V (Peter of Tarentaise): Savoy; Jan. 21 (Feb. 22), 1276, to June 22, 1276. Cult confirmed Mar. 13, 1898.

Adrian V (Ottobono Fieschi): Genoa: July 11, 1276, to Aug. 18, 1276.

John XXI (Petrus Juliani or Petrus Hispanus): Portugal; Sept. 8 (20), 1276, to May 20, 1277. There is confusion in the numerical designation of popes named John. The error dates back to the time of John XV.

Nicholas III (Giovanni Gaetano Orsini): Rome; Nov. 25 (Dec. 26), 1277, to Aug. 22, 1280.

Martin IV (Simon de Brie): France; Feb. 22 (Mar. 23), 1281, to Mar. 28, 1285. The names of Marinus 1 (882-84) and Marinus II (942-46) were construed as Martin. In view of these two pontificates and the earlier reign of St. Martin I (649-55), this pope was called Martin IV.

Honorius IV (Giacomo Savelli): Rome; Apr. 2 (May 20), 1285, to Apr. 3, 1287.

Nicholas IV (Girolamo Masci): Ascoli; Feb. 22, 1288, to Apr. 4, 1292.

St. Celestine V (Pietro del Murrone): Isernia; July 5 (Aug. 29), 1294, to Dec. 13, 1294; d. May 19, 1296. Canonized May 5, 1313.

Boniface VIII (Benedetto Caetani): Anagni; Dec. 24, 1294 (Jan. 23, 1295), to Oct. 11, 1303.

Bl. Benedict XI (Niccolo Boccasini): Treviso; Oct. 22 (27), 1303, to July 7, 1304. Cult confirmed Apr. 24, 1736.

Clement V (Bertrand de Got): France; June 5 (Nov. 14), 1305, to Apr. 20, 1314. (First of Avignon popes.)

John XXII (Jacques d'Euse): Cahors; Aug. 7 (Sept. 5), 1316, to Dec. 4, 1334.

Benedict XII (Jacques Fournier): France; Dec. 20, 1334 (Jan. 8, 1335), to Apr. 25, 1342.

Clement VI (Pierre Roger): France; May 7 (19), 1342, to Dec. 6, 1352.

Innocent VI (Etienne Aubert): France; Dec. 18 (30), 1352, to Sept. 12, 1362.

Bl. Urban V (Guillaume de Grimoard): France; Sept. 28 (Nov. 6), 1362, to Dec. 19, 1370. Cult confirmed Mar. 10, 1870.

Gregory XI (Pierre Roger de Beaufort): France; Dec. 30, 1370 (Jan. 5, 1371), to Mar. 26, 1378. (Last of Avignon popes.)

Urban VI (Bartolomeo Prignano): Naples; Apr. 8 (18), 1378, to Oct. 15, 1389.

Boniface IX (Pietro Tomacelli): Naples; Nov. 2 (9), 1389, to Oct. 1, 1404.

Innocent VII (Cosma Migliorati): Sulmona; Oct. 17 (Nov. 11), 1404, to Nov. 6, 1406.

Gregory XII (Angelo Correr): Venice; Nov. 30 (Dec. 19), 1406, to July 4, 1415, when he voluntarily resigned from the papacy to permit the election of his successor. He died Oct. 18, 1417. (See the Western Schism.)

Martin V (Oddone Colonna): Rome; Nov. 11 (21), 1417, to Feb. 20, 1431.

Eugene IV (Gabriele Condulmer): Venice; Mar. 3 (11), 1431, to Feb. 23, 1447.

Nicholas V (Tommaso Parentucelli): Sarzana; Mar. 6 (19), 1447, to Mar. 24, 1455.

Callistus III (Alfonso Borgia): Jativa (Valencia); Apr. 8 (20), 1455, to Aug. 6, 1458.

Pius II (Enea Silvio Piccolomini): Siena; Aug. 19 (Sept. 3), 1458, to Aug. 14, 1464.

Paul II (Pietro Barbo): Venice; Aug. 30 (Sept. 16), 1464, to July 26, 1471.

Sixtus IV (Francesco della Rovere): Savona; Aug. 9 (25), 1471, to Aug. 12, 1484.

Innocent VIII (Giovanni Battista Cibo): Genoa; Aug. 29 (Sept. 12), 1484, to July 25, 1492.

Alexander VI (Rodrigo Borgia): Jativa (Valencia); Aug. 11 (26), 1492, to Aug. 18, 1503.

Pius III (Francesco Todeschini-Piccolomini): Siena; Sept. 22 (Oct. 1, 8), 1503, to Oct. 18, 1503.

Julius II (Giuliano della Rovere): Savona; Oct. 31 (Nov. 26), 1503, to Feb. 21, 1513.

Leo X (Giovanni de' Medici): Florence; Mar. 9 (19), 1513, to Dec. 1, 1521.

Adrian VI (Adrian Florensz): Utrecht; Jan. 9 (Aug. 31), 1522, to Sept. 14, 1523.

Clement VII (Giulio de' Medici): Florence; Nov. 19 (26), 1523, to Sept. 25, 1534.

Paul III (Alessandro Farnese): Rome; Oct. 13 (Nov. 3), 1534, to Nov. 10, 1549.

Julius III (Giovanni Maria Ciocchi del Monte): Rome; Feb. 7 (22), 1550, to Mar. 23, 1555.

Marcellus II (Marcello Cervini): Montepulciano; Apr. 9 (10), 1555, to May 1, 1555.

Paul IV (Gian Pietro Carafa): Naples; May 23 (26), 1555, to Aug. 18, 1559.

Pius IV (Giovan Angelo de' Medici): Milan; Dec. 25, 1559 (Jan. 6, 1560), to Dec. 9, 1565.

St. Pius V (Antonio-Michele Ghislieri): Bosco (Alexandria); Jan. 7 (17), 1566, to May 1, 1572. Canonized May 22, 1712.

Gregory XIII (Ugo Buoncompagni): Bologna; May 13 (25), 1572, to Apr. 10, 1585.

Sixtus V (Felice Peretti): Grottammare (Ripatransone); Apr. 24 (May 1), 1585, to Aug. 27, 1590.

Urban VII (Giambattista Castagna): Rome; Sept. 15, 1590, to Sept. 27, 1590.

Gregory XIV (Niccolo Sfondrati): Cremona; Dec. 5 (8), 1590, to Oct. 16, 1591.

Innocent IX (Giovanni Antonio Facchinetti): Bologna; Oct. 29 (Nov. 3), 1591, to Dec. 30, 1591.

Clement VIII (Ippolito Aldobrandini): Florence; Jan. 30 (Feb. 9), 1592, to Mar. 3, 1605.

Leo XI (Alessandro de' Medici): Florence; Apr. 1 (10), 1605, to Apr. 27, 1605.

Paul V (Camillo Borghese): Rome; May 16 (29), 1605, to Jan. 28, 1621.

Gregory XV (Alessandro Ludovisi): Bologna; Feb. 9 (14), 1621, to July 8, 1623.

Urban VIII (Maffeo Barberini): Florence; Aug. 6 (Sept. 29), 1623, to July 29, 1644.

Innocent X (Giovanni Battista Pamfili): Rome; Sept. 15 (Oct. 4), 1644, to Jan. 7, 1655.

Alexander VII (Fabio Chigi): Siena; Apr. 7 (18), 1655, to May 22, 1667.

Clement IX (Giulio Rospigliosi): Pistoia; June 20 (26), 1667, to Dec. 9, 1669.

Clement X (Emilio Altieri): Rome; Apr. 29 (May 11), 1670, to July 22, 1676.

Bl. Innocent XI (Benedetto Odescalchi): Como; Sept. 21 (Oct. 4), 1676, to Aug. 12, 1689. Beatified Oct. 7, 1956.

Alexander VIII (Pietro Ottoboni): Venice; Oct. 6 (16), 1689, to Feb. 1, 1691.

Innocent XII (Antonio Pignatelli): Spinazzola (Venosa); July 12 (15), 1691, to Sept. 27, 1700.

Clement XI (Giovanni Francesco Albani): Urbino; Nov. 23, 30 (Dec. 8), 1700, to Mar. 19, 1721.

Innocent XIII (Michelangelo dei Conti): Rome; May 8 (18), 1721, to Mar. 7, 1724.

Benedict XIII (Pietro Francesco - Vincenzo Maria - Orsini): Gravina (Bari); May 29 (June 4), 1724, to Feb. 21, 1730.

Clement XII (Lorenzo Corsini): Florence; July 12 (16), 1730, to Feb. 6, 1740.

Benedict XIV (Prospero Lambertini): Bologna; Aug. 17 (22), 1740, to May 3, 1758.

Clement XIII (Carlo Rezzonico): Venice; July 6 (16), 1758, to Feb. 2, 1769.

Clement XIV (Giovanni Vincenzo Antonio- Lorenzo - Ganganelli): Rimini; May 19, 28 (June 4), 1769, to Sept. 22, 1774.

Pius VI (Giovanni Angelo Braschi): Cesena; Feb. 15 (22), 1775, to Aug. 29, 1799.

Pius VII (Barnaba - Gregorio - Chiaramonti): Cesena; Mar. 14 (21), 1800, to Aug. 20, 1823.

Leo XII (Annibale della Genga): Genga (Fabriano); Sept. 28 (Oct. 5), 1823, to Feb. 10, 1829.

Pius VIII (Francesco Saverio Castiglioni): Cingoli; Mar. 31 (Apr. 5), 1829, to Nov. 30, 1830.

Gregory XVI (Bartolomeo Alberto - Mauro - Cappellari): Belluno; Feb. 2 (6), 1831, to June 1, 1846.

Pius IX (Giovanni M. Mastai-Ferretti): Senigallia; June 16 (21), 1846, to Feb. 7, 1878.

Leo XIII (Gioacchino Pecci): Carpineto (Anagni); Feb. 20 (Mar. 3), 1878, to July 20, 1903.

St. Pius X (Giuseppe Sarto): Riese (Treviso); Aug. 4 (9), 1903, to Aug. 20, 1914. Canonized May 29, 1954.

Benedit XV (Giacomo della Chiesa): Genoa; Sept. 3 (6), 1914, to Jan. 22, 1922.

Pius XI (Achille Ratti): Desio (Milan); Feb. 6 (12), 1922, to Feb. 10, 1939.

Pius XII (Eugenio Pacelli): Rome; Mar. 2 (12), 1939, to Oct. 9, 1958.

John XXIII (Angelo Giuseppe Roncalli): Sotto il Monte (Bergamo); Oct. 28 (Nov. 4), 1958, to June 3, 1963.

Paul VI (Giovanni Battista Montini): Concessio (Brescia); June 21 (30), 1963, to Aug. 6, 1978.

John Paul I (Albino Luciani): Forno di Canale (Belluno); Aug. 26 (Sept. 3), 1978, to Sept. 28, 1978.

John Paul II (Karol Wojtyla): Wadowice, Poland; Oct. 16 (22), 1978.

ANTIPOPES

This list of men who claimed or exercised the papal office in an uncanonical manner includes names, birthplaces and dates of alleged reigns.

Source: Annuario Pontificio

St. Hippolytus: Rome; 217-235; was reconciled before his death.

Novatian: Rome; 251.

Felix II: Rome; 355 to Nov. 22, 365.

Ursinus: 366-367.

Eulalius: Dec. 27 or 29, 418, to 419.

Lawrence: 498; 501-505.

Dioscorus: Alexandria; Sept. 22, 530, to Oct. 14, 530.

Theodore: ended alleged reign, 687.

Paschal: ended alleged reign, 687.

Constantine: Nepi; June 28 (July 5), 767, to 769.

Philip: July 31, 768; retired to his monastery on the same day.

John: ended alleged reign, Jan., 844.

Anastasius: Aug., 855, to Sept., 855; d. 880.

Christopher: Rome; July or Sept., 903, to Jan., 904.

Boniface VII: Rome; June, 974, to July, 974; Aug., 984, to July, 985.

John XVI: Rossano; Apr., 997, to Feb., 998.

Gregory: ended alleged reign, 1012.

Benedict X: Rome; Apr. 5, 1058, to Jan. 24, 1059.

Honorius II: Verona; Oct. 28, 1061, to 1072.

Clement III: Parma; June 25, 1080 (Mar. 24, 1084), to Sept. 8, 1100.

Theodoric: ended alleged reign, 1100; d. 1102.

Albert: ended alleged reign, 1102.

Sylvester IV: Rome; Nov. 18, 1105, to 1111.

Gregory VIII: France; Mar. 8, 1118, to 1121.

Celestine II: Rome; ended alleged reign, Dec., 1124.

Anacletus II: Rome; Feb. 14 (23), 1130, to Jan. 25, 1138.

Victor IV: Mar., 1138, to May 29, 1138; submitted to Pope Innocent II.

Victor IV: Montecelio; Sept. 7 (Oct. 4), 1159, to Apr. 20, 1164; he did not recognize his predecessor (Victor IV, above).

Paschal III: Apr. 22 (26), 1164, to Sept. 20, 1168.

Callistus III: Arezzo; Sept., 1168, to Aug. 29, 1178; submitted to Pope Alexander III.

Innocent III: Sezze; Sept. 29, 1179, to 1180.

Nicholas V: Corvaro (Rieti); May 12 (22), 1328, to Aug. 25, 1330; d. Oct. 16, 1333.

Four antipopes of the Western Schism:

Clement VII: Sept. 20 (Oct. 31), 1378, to Sept. 16, 1394.

Benedict XIII: Aragon; Sept. 28 (Oct. 11), 1394, to May 23, 1423.

Alexander V: Crete; June 26 (July 7), 1409, to May 3, 1410.

John XXIII: Naples; May 17 (25), 1410, to May 29, 1415. (Date of deposition by Council of Constance which ended the Western Schism; d. Nov. 22, 1419.)

Felix V: Savoy; Nov. 5, 1439 (July 24, 1440), to Apr. 7, 1449; d. 1451.

AVIGNON PAPACY

Avignon was the residence (1309-77) of a series of French popes (Clement V, John XXII, Benedict XII, Clement VI, Innocent VI, Urban V and Gregory XI). Prominent in the period were power struggles over the mixed interests of Church and state with the rulers of France (Philip IV, John II), Bavaria (Lewis IV),

England (Edward III); factionalism of French and Italian churchmen; political as well as ecclesiastical turmoil in Italy, a factor of significance in prolonging the stay of popes in Avignon. Despite some positive achievements, the Avignon papacy was a prologue to the Western Schism which began in 1378.

GREAT WESTERN SCHISM

The Great Western Schism was a confused state of affairs which divided Christendom into two and then three papal obediences from 1378 to 1417.

It occurred some 50 years after Marsilius theorized that a general (not ecumenical) council of bishops and other persons was superior to a pope and nearly 30 years before the Council of Florence stated definitively that no kind of council had such authority. It was a period of disaster preceding the even more disastrous period of the Reformation.

Urban VI, following the return of the papal residence to Rome after approximately 70 years at Avignon, was elected pope Apr. 8, 1378, and reigned until his death in 1389. He was succeeded by Boniface IX (1389-1404), Innocent VII (1404-1406) and Gregory XII (1406-1415). These four are considered the legitimate popes of the period.

Some of the cardinals who chose Urban pope, dissatisfied with his conduct of the office, declared that his election was invalid. They proceeded to elect Clement VII, who claimed the papacy from 1378 to 1394. He was succeeded by Benedict XIII.

Prelates seeking to end the state of divided papal loyalties convoked the Council of Pisa (1409) which, without authority, found Gregory XII and Benedict XIII, in absentia, guilty on 30-odd charges of schism and heresy, deposed them, and elected a third claimant to the papacy, Alexander V (1409-1410). He was succeeded by John XXIII (1410-1415).

The schism was ended by the Council of Constance (1414-1418). Although originally called into session in an irregular manner, the council, acquired authority after being convoked by Gregory XII in 1415. In its early irregular phase, it deposed John XXIII whose election to the papacy was uncanonical anyway. After being formally convoked, it accepted the abdication of Gregory in 1415 and dismissed the claims of Benedict XIII two years later, thus clearing the way for the election of Martin V on Nov. 11, 1417. The Council of Constance also rejected the theories of John Wycliff and condemned John Hus as a heretic.

POPES OF THE TWENTIETH CENTURY

LEO XIII

Leo XIII (Gioacchino Vincenzo Pecci) was born May 2, 1810, in Carpineto, Italy. Although all but three years of his life and pontificate were of the 19th century, his influence extended well into the 20th century.

He was educated at the Jesuit college in Viterbo, the Roman College, the Academy of Noble Ecclesiastics, and the University of the Sapienza. He was ordained to the priesthood in 1837.

He served as an apostolic delegate to two States of the Church, Benevento from 1838 to 1841 and Perugia in 1841 and 1842. Ordained titular archbishop of Damietta, he was papal nuncio to Belgium from Jan., 1843, until May, 1846; in the post, he had controversial relations with the government over education issues and acquired his first significant experience of industrialized society.

He was archbishop of Perugia from 1846 to 1878. He became a cardinal in 1853 and chamberlain of the Roman Curia in 1877. He was elected to the papacy Feb. 20, 1878. He died July 20, 1903.

Canonizations: He canonized 18 saints and beatified a group of English martyrs.

Church Administration: He established 300 new dioceses and vicariates; restored the hierarchy in Scotland, set up an English, as contrasted with the Portuguese, hierarchy in India; approved the action of the Congregation for the Propagation of the Faith in reorganizing missions in China.

Encyclicals: He issued 86 encyclicals, on subjects ranging from devotional to social. In the former category were Annum Sacrum, on the Sacred Heart, in 1899, and 11 letters on Mary and the Rosary.

Social Questions: Much of Leo's influence stemmed from social doctrine stated in numerous encyclicals, concerning liberalism, liberty, the divine origin of authority; socialism, in *Quod Apostolici Muneris*, 1878; the Christian concept of the family, in *Arcanum*, 1880; socialism and economic liberalism, relations between capital and labor, in *Rerum Novarum*, 1891. Two of his social encyclicals were against the African slave trade.

Interfaith Relations: He was unsuccessful in unity overtures made to Orthodox and Slavic Churches. He declared Anglican orders invalid in the apostolic bull Apostolicae Curae Sept. 13, 1896.

International Relations: Leo was frustrated in seeking solutions to the Roman Question arising from the seizure of church lands by the Kingdom of Italy in 1870. He also faced anticlerical situations in Belgium and France and in the Kulturkampf policies of Bismarck in Germany.

Studies: In the encyclical *Aeterni Patris* of Aug. 4, 1879, he ordered a renewal of philosophical and theological studies in seminaries along scholastic, and especially Thomistic, lines, to counteract influential trends of liberalism and Modernism. He issued guidelines for biblical exegesis in Providentissimus Deus Nov. 18, 1893, and established the Pontifical Biblical Commission in 1902.

In other actions affecting scholarship and study, he opened the Vatican Archives to scholars in 1883 and established the Vatican Observatory.

United States: He authorized establishment of the apostolic delegation in Washington, D.C., Jan. 24, 1893. He refused to issue a condemnation of the Knights of Labor. With a document entitled Testem Benevolentiae, he eased resolution of questions concerning what was called an American heresy in 1899.

ST. PIUS X

St. Pius X (Giuseppe Melchiorre Sarto) was born in 1835 in Riese, Italy. Educated at the college of Castelfranco and the seminary at Padua, he was ordained to the priesthood Sept. 18, 1858. He served as a curate in Trombolo for nine years before beginning an eight-year pastorate at Salzano. He was chancellor of the Treviso diocese from November, 1875, and bishop of Mantua from 1884 until 1893. He was cardinal-patriarch of Venice from that year until his election to the papacy by the conclave held from July 31 to Aug. 4, 1903.

Aims: Pius' principal objectives as pope were "to restore all things in Christ, in order that Christ may be all in all," and "to teach (and defend) Christian truth and law."

Canonizations, Encyclicals: He canonized four saints and issued 16 encyclicals. One of the encyclicals was issued in commemoration of the 50th anniversary of the proclamation of the dogma of the Immaculate Conception of Mary.

Catechetics: He introduced a whole new era of religious instruction and formation with the encyclical *Acerbo Nimis* of Apr. 15, 1905, in which he called for vigor in establishing and conducting parochial programs of the Confraternity of Christian Doctrine.

Catholic Action: He outlined the role of official Catholic Action in two encyclicals in 1905 and 1906. Favoring organized action by Catholics themselves, he had serious reservations about interconfessional collaboration.

He stoutly maintained claims to papal rights in the anticlerical climate of Italy. He authorized bishops to relax prohibitions against participation by Catholics in some Italian elections.

Church Administration: With the motu proprio *Arduum Sane* of Mar. 19, 1904, he inaugurated the work which resulted in the Code of Canon Law; the code was completed in 1917 and went into effect in the following year. He reorganized and strengthened the Roman Curia with the apostolic constitution *Sapienti Consilio* of June 29, 1908.

While promoting the expansion of missionary work, he removed from the jurisdiction of the Congregation for the Propagation of the Faith the Church in the United States, Canada, Newfoundland, England, Ireland, Holland and Luxembourg.

International Relations: He ended traditional prerogatives of Catholic governments with respect to papal elections, in 1904. He opposed anti-Church and anticlerical actions in several countries: Bolivia in 1905, because of anti-religious legislation; France in 1906, for its 1901 action in annulling its concordat with the Holy See, and for the 1905 Law of Separation by which it decreed separation of Church and state, ordered the confiscation of church property, and blocked religious education and the activities of religious orders; Portugal in 1911, for the separation of Church and state and repressive measures which resulted in persecution later.

In 1912 he called on the bishops of Brazil to work for the improvement of conditions among Indians.

Liturgy: "The Pope of the Eucharist," he strongly recommended the frequent reception of Holy Communion in a decree dated Dec. 20, 1905; in another decree, *Quam Singulari*, of Aug. 8, 1910, he called for the early reception of the sacrament by children.

He initiated measures for liturgical reform with new norms for sacred music and the start of work on revision of the Breviary for recitation of the Divine Office.

Modernism: Pius was a vigorous opponent of "the synthesis of all heresies," which threatened the integrity of doctrine through its influence in philosophy, theology and biblical exegesis. In opposition, he condemned 65 of its propositions as erroneous in the decree *Lamentabili* July 3, 1907; issued the encyclical Pascendi in the same vein Sept. 8, 1907; backed both of these with censures; and published the Oath against Modernism in September, 1910, to be taken by all the clergy. Ecclesiastical studies suffered to some extent from these actions, necessary as they were at the time.

Pius followed the lead of Leo XIII in promoting the study of scholastic philosophy. He established the Pontifical Biblical Institute May 7, 1909.

His death, Aug. 20, 1914, was hastened by the outbreak of World War I. He was beatified in 1951 and canonized May 29, 1954. His feast is observed Aug. 21.

BENEDICT XV

Benedict XV (Giacomo della Chiesa) was born Nov. 21, 1854, in Pegli, Italy.

He was educated at the Royal University of Genoa and Gregorian University in Rome. He was ordained to the priesthood Dec. 21, 1878.

He served in the papal diplomatic corps from 1882 to 1907; as secretary to the nuncio to Spain from 1882 to 1887, as secretary to the papal secretary of state from 1887, and as undersecretary from 1901.

He was ordained archbishop of Bologna Dec. 22, 1907, and spent four years completing a pastoral visitation there. He was made a cardinal just three months before being elected to the papacy Sept. 3, 1914. He died Jan. 22, 1922. Two key efforts of his pontificate were for peace and the relief of human suffering caused by World War I.

Canonizations: Benedict canonized three saints; one of them was Joan of Arc.

Canon Law: He published the Code of Canon Law, developed by the commission set up by St. Pius X, May 27, 1917; it went into effect the following year.

Curia: He made great changes in the personnel of the Curia. He established the Congregation for the Oriental Churches May 1, 1917, and founded the Pontifical Oriental Institute in Rome later in the year.

Encyclicals: He issued 12 encyclicals. Peace was the theme of three of them. In another, published two years after the cessation of hostilities, he wrote about child victims of the war. He followed the lead of Leo XIII in *Spiritus Paraclitus*, Sept. 15, 1920, on biblical studies.

International Relations: He was largely frustrated on the international level because of the events and attitudes of the war period, but the number of diplomats accredited to the Vatican nearly doubled, from 14 to 26, between the time of his accession to the papacy and his death.

Peace Efforts: Benedict's stance in the war was one of absolute impartiality but not of uninterested neutrality. Because he would not take sides, he was suspected by both sides and the seven-point peace plan he offered to all belligerents Aug. 1, 1917, was turned down. The points of the plan were: recognition of the moral force of right; disarmament; acceptance of arbitration in cases of dispute; guarantee of freedom of the seas; renunciation of war indemnities; evacuation and restoration of occupied territories; examination of territorial claims in dispute.

Relief Efforts: Benedict assumed personal charge of Vatican relief efforts during the war. He set up an international missing persons bureau for contacts between prisoners and their families, but was forced to close it because of the suspicion of warring nations that it was a front for espionage operations. He persuaded the Swiss government to admit into the country military victims of tuberculosis.

Roman Question: Benedict prepared the way for the meetings and negotiations which led to settlement of the question in 1929.

PIUS XI

Pius XI (Ambrogio Damiano Achille Ratti) was born May 31, 1857, in Desio, Italy.

Educated at seminaries in Seviso and Milan, and at the Lombard College, Gregorian University and Academy of St. Thomas in Rome, he was ordained to the priesthood in 1879.

He taught at the major seminary of Milan from 1882 to 1888. Appointed to the staff of the Ambrosian Library in 1888, he remained there until 1911, acquiring a reputation for publishing works on paleography and serving as director from 1907 to 1911. He then moved to the Vatican Library, of which he was prefect from 1914 to 1918. In 1919, he was named apostolic visitor to Poland in April, nuncio in June, and was made titular archbishop of Lepanto Oct. 28. He was made archbishop of Milan and cardinal June 13, 1921, before being elected to the papacy Feb. 6, 1922. He died Feb. 10, 1939.

Aim: The objective of his pontificate, as stated in the encyclical *Ubi Arcano*, Dec. 23, 1922, was to establish the reign and peace of Christ in society.

Canonizations: He canonized 34 saints, including the Jesuit Martyrs of North America, and conferred the title of Doctor of the Church on Sts. Peter Canisius, John of the Cross, Robert Bellarmine and Albertus Magnus.

Eastern Churches: He called for better understanding of the Eastern Churches in the encyclical *Rerum Orientalium* of Sept. 8, 1928, and developed facilities for the training of Eastern-Rite priests. He inaugurated steps for the codification of Eastern-Church law in 1929. In 1935 he made Syrian Patriarch Tappouni a cardinal.

Encyclicals: His first encyclical, *Ubi Arcano*, in addition to stating the aims of his pontificate, blueprinted Catholic Action and called for its development throughout the Church. In *Quas Primas*, Dec. 11, 1925, he established the feast of Christ the King for universal observance. Subjects of some of his other encyclicals were: Christian education, in *Rappresentanti in Terra*, Dec. 31, 1929; Christian marriage, in *Casti Connubii*, Dec. 31, 1930; social conditions and pressure for social change in line with the teaching in *Rerum Novarum*, in *Quadragesimo Anno*, May 15, 1931; atheistic Communism, in *Divini Redemptoris*, Mar. 19, 1937; the priesthood, in *Ad Catholici Sacerdotii*, Dec. 20, 1935.

Missions: Following the lead of Benedict XV, Pius called for the training of native clergy in the pattern of their own respective cultures, and promoted missionary developments in various ways. He ordained six native bishops for China in 1926, one for Japan in 1927, and others for regions of Asia, China and India in 1933. He placed the first 40 mission dioceses under native bishops, saw the number of native priests increase from about 2,600 to more than 7,000 and the number of Catholics in missionary areas more than double from nine million.

In the apostolic constitution *Deus Scientiarum Dominus* of May 24, 1931, he ordered the introduction of missiology into theology courses.

Interfaith Relations: Pius was negative to the ecumenical movement among Protestants but approved the Malines Conversations, 1921 to 1926, between Anglicans and Catholics.

International Relations: Relations with the Mussolini government deteriorated from 1931 on, as indicated in the encyclical *Non Abbiamo Bisogno*, when the regime took steps to curb liberties and activities of the Church; they turned critical in 1938 with the emergence of racist policies. Relations deteriorated also in Germany from 1933 on, resulting finally in condemnation of the Nazis in the encyclical *Mit Brennender Sorge*, March, 1937. Pius sparked a revival of the Church in France by encouraging Catholics to work within the democratic framework of the Republic rather than foment trouble over restoration of a monarchy. Pius was powerless to influence developments related to the civil war which erupted in Spain in July, 1936, sporadic persecution and repression by the Calles regime in Mexico, and systematic persecution of the Church in the Soviet Union. Many of the 10 concordats and two agreements reached with European countries after World War I became casualties of World War II.

Roman Question: Pius negotiated for two and one-half years with the Italian government to settle the Roman Question by means of the Lateran Agreement of 1929. The agreement provided independent status for the State of Vatican City; made Catholicism the official religion of Italy, with pastoral and educational freedom and state recognition of Catholic marriages, religious orders and societies; and provided a financial payment to the Vatican for expropriation of the former States of the Church.

PIUS XII

Pius XII (Eugenio Maria Giovanni Pacelli) was born Mar. 2, 1876, in Rome.

Educated at the Gregorian University and the Lateran University, in Rome, he was ordained to the priesthood Apr. 2, 1899.

He entered the Vatican diplomatic service in 1901, worked on the codification of canon law, and was appointed secretary of the Congregation for Ecclesiastical Affairs in 1914. Three years later he was ordained titular archbishop of Sardis and made apostolic nuncio to Bavaria. He was nuncio to Germany from 1920 to 1929, when he was made a cardinal, and took office as papal secretary of state in the following year. His diplomatic negotiations resulted in concordats between the Vatican and Bavaria (1924), Prussia (1929), Baden (1932), Austria and the German Republic (1933). He took part in negotiations which led to settlement of the Roman Question in 1929.

He was elected to the papacy Mar. 2, 1939. He died Oct. 9, 1958, at Castel Gandolfo after the 12th longest pontificate in history.

Canonizations: He canonized 34 saints, including Mother Frances X. Cabrini, the first U.S. citizen-Saint.

Cardinals: He raised 56 prelates to the rank of cardinal in two consistories held in 1946 and 1953. There were 57 cardinals at the time of his death.

Church Organization and Missions: He increased the number of dioceses from 1,696 to 2,048. He established native hierarchies in China (1946), Burma (1955) and parts of Africa, and extended the native structure of the Church in India. He ordained the first black bishop for Africa.

Communism: In addition to opposing and condemning Communism on numerous occasions, he decreed in 1949 the penalty of excommunication for all Catholics holding formal and willing allegiance to the Communist Party and its policies. During his reign the Church was persecuted in some 15 countries which fell under communist domination.

Doctrine and Liturgy: He proclaimed the dogma of the Assumption of the Blessed Virgin Mary Nov. 1, 1950 (apostolic constitution, *Munificentissimus Deus*).

In various encyclicals and other enactments, he provided background for the *aggiornamento* introduced by his successor, John XXIII: by his formulations of doctrine and practice regarding the Mystical Body of Christ, the liturgy, sacred music and biblical studies; by the revision of the Rites of Holy Week; by initiation of the work which led to the calendar-missal-breviary reform ordered into effect Jan. 1, 1961; by the first of several modifications of the Eucharistic fast; by extending the time of Mass to the evening. He instituted the feasts of Mary, Queen, and of St. Joseph the Worker, and clarified teaching concerning devotion to the Sacred Heart.

His 41 encyclicals and nearly 1,000 public addresses made Pius one of the greatest teaching popes. His concern in all his communications was to deal with specific points at issue and/or to bring Christian principles to bear on contemporary world problems.

Peace Efforts: Before the start of World War II, he tried unsuccessfully to get the contending nations — Germany and Poland, France and Italy — to settle their differences peaceably. During the war, he offered his services to mediate the widened conflict, spoke out against the horrors of war and the suffering it caused, mobilized relief work for its victims, proposed a five-point program for peace in Christmas messages from 1939 to 1942, and secured a generally open status for the city of Rome. He has been criticized in some quarters for not doing enough to oppose the Holocaust. This is a matter of historical debate, but it is a fact that through his direct intercession many thousands of Jews in Rome and Italy were saved from certain death, and he resisted wherever possible the threat of Nazism to human rights. Such were his contributions to assisting Jews that the rabbi of Rome, Dr. Abraham Zolli was converted to Catholicism, and upon his death, Pius was praised by Golda Meir for his efforts. After the war, he endorsed the principles and intent of the United Nations and continued efforts for peace.

United States: Pius appointed more than 200 of the 265 American bishops resident in the U.S. and abroad in 1958, erected 27 dioceses in this country, and raised seven dioceses to archiepiscopal rank.

JOHN XXIII

John XXIII (Angelo Roncalli) was born Nov. 25, 1881, at Sotte il Monte, Italy.

He was educated at the seminary of the Bergamo diocese and the Pontifical Seminary in Rome, where he was ordained to the priesthood Aug. 10, 1904.

He spent the first nine or 10 years of his priesthood as secretary to the bishop of Bergamo and as an instructor in the seminary there. He served as a medic and chaplain in the Italian army during World War I. Afterwards, he resumed duties in his own diocese until he was called to Rome in 1921 for work with the Society for the Propagation of the Faith.

He began diplomatic service in 1925 as titular archbishop of Areopolis and apostolic visitor to Bulgaria. A succession of offices followed: apostolic delegate to Bulgaria (1931-1935); titular archbishop of Mesembria, apostolic delegate to Turkey and Greece, administrator of the Latin vicariate apostolic of Istanbul (1935-1944); apostolic nuncio to France (1944-1953). On these missions, he was engaged in delicate negotiations involving Roman, Eastern-Rite and Orthodox relations; the needs of people suffering from the consequences of World War II; and unsettling suspicions arising from wartime conditions.

He was made a cardinal Jan. 12, 1953, and three days later was appointed patriarch of Venice, the position he held until his election to the papacy Oct. 28, 1958. He died of stomach cancer June 3, 1963.

John was a strong and vigorous pope whose influence far out-measured both his age and the shortness of his time in the papacy.

Second Vatican Council: John announced Jan. 25, 1959, his intention of convoking the 21st ecumenical council in history to renew life in the Church, to reform its structures and institutions, and to explore ways and means of promoting unity among Christians. Through the council, which completed its work two and one-half years after his death, he ushered in a new era in the history of the Church.

Canon Law: He established a commission Mar. 28, 1963, for revision of the Code of Canon Law. The revised Code was promulgated in 1983.

Canonizations: He canonized 10 saints and beatified Mother Elizabeth Ann Seton, the first native of the U.S. ever so honored. He named St. Lawrence of Brindisi a Doctor of the Church.

Cardinals: He created 52 cardinals in five consistories, raising membership of the College of Cardinals above the traditional number of 70; at one time in 1962, the membership was 87. He made the college more international in representation than it had ever been, appointing the first cardinals from the Philippines, Japan and Africa. He ordered episcopal ordination for all cardinals. He relieved the suburban bishops of Rome of ordinary jurisdiction over their dioceses so they might devote all their time to business of the Roman Curia.

Eastern Rites: He made all Eastern-Rite patriarchs members of the Congregation for the Oriental Churches.

Ecumenism: He assigned to the Second Vatican Council the task of finding ways and means of promoting unity among Christians. He established the

Vatican Secretariat for Promoting Christian Unity June 5, 1960. He showed his desire for more cordial relations with the Orthodox by sending personal representatives to visit Patriarch Athenagoras I June 27, 1961; approved a mission of five delegates to the General Assembly of the World Council of Churches which met in New Delhi, India, in November, 1961; removed a number of pejorative references to Jews in the Roman-Rite liturgy for Good Friday.

Encyclicals: Of the eight encyclicals he issued, the two outstanding ones were *Mater et Magistra* ("Christianity and Social Progress"), in which he recapitulated, updated and extended the social doctrine stated earlier by Leo XIII and Pius XI; and *Pacem in Terris* ("Peace on Earth"), the first encyclical ever addressed to all men of good will as well as to Catholics, on the natural-law principles of peace.

Liturgy: In forwarding liturgical reforms already begun by Pius XII, he ordered a calendar-missal-breviary reform into effect Jan. 1, 1961. He authorized the use of vernacular languages in the administration of the sacraments and approved giving Holy Communion to the sick in afternoon hours. He selected the liturgy as the first topic of major discussion by the Second Vatican Council.

Missions: He issued an encyclical on the missionary activity of the Church; established native hierarchies in Indonesia, Vietnam and Korea; and called on North American superiors of religious institutes to have one-tenth of their members assigned to work in Latin America by 1971.

Peace: John spoke and used his moral influence for peace in 1961 when tension developed over Berlin, in 1962 during the Algerian revolt from France, and later the same year in the Cuban missile crisis. His efforts were singled out for honor by the Balzan Peace Foundation. In 1963, he was posthumously awarded the U.S. Presidential Medal of Freedom.

PAUL VI

Paul VI (Giovanni Battista Montini) was born Sept. 26, 1897, at Concesio in northern Italy. Educated at Brescia, he was ordained to the priesthood May 29, 1920. He pursued additional studies at the Pontifical Academy for Noble Ecclesiastics and the Pontifical Gregorian University. In 1924 he began 30 years of service in the Secretariat of State; as undersecretary from 1937 until 1954, he was closely associated with Pius XII and was heavily engaged in organizing informational and relief services during and after World War II. He declined the offer of the cardinalate by Pope Pius XII.

Ordained archbishop of Milan Dec. 12, 1954, he was inducted into the College of Cardinals Dec. 15, 1958 by Pope John XXIII. Trusted by John, he was a key figure in organizing the first session of Vatican Council II and was elected to the papacy June 21, 1963, two days after the conclave began. He died of a heart attack Aug. 6, 1978.

Second Vatican Council: He reconvened the Second Vatican Council after the death of John XXIII, presided over its second, third and fourth sessions, formally promulgated the 16 documents it produced, and devoted the whole of his pontificate to the task of putting them into effect throughout the Church. The main thrust of his pontificate — in a milieu of cultural and other changes in the Church and the world — was to-

ward institutionalization and control of the authentic trends articulated and set in motion by the council.

Canonizations: He canonized 84 saints. They included groups of 22 Ugandan martyrs and 40 martyrs of England and Wales, as well as two Americans — Elizabeth Ann Bayley Seton and John Nepomucene Neumann.

Cardinals: He created 144 cardinals, and gave the Sacred College a more international complexion than it ever had before. He limited participation in papal elections to 120 cardinals under the age of 80.

Collegiality: He established the Synod of Bishops in 1965 and called it into session five times. He stimulated the formation and operation of regional conferences of bishops, and of consultative bodies on other levels.

Creed and Holy Year: On June 30, 1968, he issued a Creed of the People of God in conjunction with the celebration of a Year of Faith. He proclaimed and led the observance of a Holy Year from Christmas Eve of 1974 to Christmas Eve of 1975.

Diplomacy: He met with many world leaders, including Soviet President Nikolai Podgorny in 1967, Marshal Tito of Yugoslavia in 1971 and President Nicolas Ceausescu of Romania in 1973. He worked constantly to reduce tension between the Church and the intransigent regimes of Eastern European countries by means of a detente type of policy called *Ostpolitik.* He agreed to significant revisions of the Vatican's concordat with Spain and initiated efforts to revise the concordat with Italy. More than 40 countries established diplomatic relations with the Vatican during his pontificate.

Encyclicals: He issued seven encyclicals, three of which are the best known. In *Populorum Progressio* ("Development of Peoples") he appealed to wealthy countries to take "concrete action" to promote human development and to remedy imbalances between richer and poorer nations; this encyclical, coupled with other documents and related actions, launched the Church into a new depth of involvement as a public advocate for human rights and for humanizing social, political and economic policies. In *Sacerdotalis Caelibatus* ("Priestly Celibacy") he reaffirmed the strict observance of priestly celibacy throughout the Western Church. In *Humanae Vitae* ("Of Human Life") he condemned abortion, sterilization and artificial birth control, in line with traditional teaching and in "defense of life, the gift of God, the glory of the family, the strength of the people."

Interfaith Relations: He initiated formal consultation and informal dialogue on international and national levels between Catholics and non-Catholics — Orthodox, Anglicans, Protestants, Jews, Muslims, Buddhists, Hindus, and unbelievers. He and Greek Orthodox Patriarch Athenagoras I of Constantinople nullified in 1965 the mutual excommunications imposed by their respective churches in 1054.

Liturgy: He carried out the most extensive liturgical reform in history, involving a new Order of the Mass effective in 1969, a revised church calendar in 1970, revisions and translations into vernacular languages of all sacramental rites and other liturgical texts.

Ministries: He authorized the restoration of the permanent diaconate in the Roman Rite and the establishment of new ministries of lay persons.

Peace: In 1968, he instituted the annual observance of a World Day of Peace on New Year's Day as a means of addressing a message of peace to all the world's political leaders and the peoples of all nations. The most dramatic of his many appeals for peace and efforts to ease international tensions was his plea for "No more war!" before the United Nations Oct. 4, 1965.

Pilgrimages: A "Pilgrim Pope," he made pastoral visits to the Holy Land and India in 1964, the United Nations and New York City in 1965, Portugal and Turkey in 1967, Colombia in 1968, Switzerland and Uganda in 1969, and Asia, Pacific islands and Australia in 1970. While in Manila in 1970, he was stabbed by a Bolivian artist who made an attempt on his life.

Roman Curia: He reorganized the central administrative organs of the Church in line with provisions of the apostolic constitution, Regimini Ecclesiae Universae, streamlining procedures for more effective service and giving the agencies a more international perspective by drawing officials and consultors from all over the world. He also instituted a number of new commissions and other bodies. Coupled with curial reorganization was a simplification of papal ceremonies.

JOHN PAUL I

John Paul I (Albino Luciani) was born Oct. 17, 1912, in Forno di Canale (now Canale d'Agordo) in northern Italy. Educated at the minor seminary in Feltre and the major seminary of the Diocese of Belluno, he was ordained to the priesthood July 7, 1935. He pursued further studies at the Pontifical Gregorian University in Rome and was awarded a doctorate in theology. From 1937 to 1947 he was vice rector of the Belluno seminary, where he taught dogmatic and moral theology, canon law and sacred art. He was appointed vicar general of his diocese in 1947 and served as director of catechetics.

Ordained bishop of Vittorio Veneto Dec. 27, 1958, he attended all sessions of the Second Vatican Council, participated in three assemblies of the Synod of Bishops (1971, 1974 and 1977), and was vice president of the Italian Bishops' Conference from 1972 to 1975.

He was appointed archbishop and patriarch of Venice Dec. 15, 1969, and was inducted into the College of Cardinals Mar. 5, 1973.

He was elected to the papacy Aug. 26, 1978, on the fourth ballot cast by the 111 cardinals participating in the largest and one of the shortest conclaves in history. The quickness of his election was matched by the brevity of his pontificate of 33 days, during which he delivered 19 addresses. He died of a heart attack Sept. 28, 1978.

JOHN PAUL II

See separate entry.

PAPAL ENCYCLICALS — BENEDICT XIV (1740) TO JOHN PAUL II

(Source: *The Papal Encyclicals* [5 vols.], Claudia Carlen, I.H.M.; Pieran Press, Ann Arbor, Mich. Used with permission.)

An encyclical letter is a pastoral letter addressed by a pope to the whole Church. In general, it concerns matters of doctrine, morals or discipline, or significant commemorations. Its formal title consists of the first few words of the official text. Some encyclicals, notably *Pacem in terris* by John XXIII, *Ecclesiam Suam* by Paul VI and several by John Paul II, have been addressed to people of good will in general as well as to bishops and the faithful in communion with the Church.

An encyclical epistle resembles an encyclical letter but is addressed only to part of the Church.

The authority of encyclicals was stated by Pius XII in the encyclical *Humani generis* Aug. 12, 1950: "Nor must it be thought that what is contained in encyclical letters does not of itself demand assent, on the pretext that the popes do not exercise in them the supreme power of their teaching authority. Rather, such teachings belong to the ordinary magisterium, of which it is true to say: 'He who teaches you, hears me' (Lk. 10:16); for the most part, too, what is expounded and inculcated in encyclical letters already appertains to Catholic doctrine for other reasons."

The Second Vatican Council declared: "Religious submission of will and of mind must be shown in a special way to the authentic teaching authority of the Roman Pontiff, even when he is not speaking ex cathedra. That is, it must be shown in such a way that his supreme magisterium is acknowledged with reverence, the judgments made by him are sincerely adhered to, according to his manifest mind and will. His mind and will in the matter may be known chiefly either from the character of the documents (one of which could be an encyclical), from his frequent repetition of the same doctrine, or from his manner of speaking" (Dogmatic Constitution on the Church, *Lumen Gentium*, No. 25).

The following list contains the titles and indicates the subject matter of encyclical letters and epistles. The latter are generally distinguishable by the limited scope of their titles or contents.

Benedict XIV

(1740-1758)

1740: *Ubi primum* (On the duties of bishops), Dec. 3.

1741: *Quanta cura* (Forbidding traffic in alms), June 30.

1743: *Nimiam licentiam* (To the bishops of Poland: on validity of marriages), May 18.

1745: *Vix pervenit* (To the bishops of Italy: on usury and other dishonest profit), Nov. 1.

1748: *Magnae Nobis* (To the bishops of Poland: on marriage impediments and dispensations), June 29.

1749: *Peregrinantes* (To all the faithful: proclaiming a Holy Year for 1750), May 5.

Apostolica Constitutio (On preparation for the Holy Year), June 26.

1751: *A quo primum* (To the bishops of Poland: on Jews and Christians living in the same place), June 14.

1754: *Cum Religiosi* (To the bishops of the States of the Church: on catechesis), June 26.

Quod Provinciale (To the bishops of Albania: on Christians using Mohammedan names), Aug. 1.

1755: *Allatae sunt* (To missionaries of the Orient: on the observance of Oriental rites), July 26.

1756: *Ex quo primum* (To bishops of the Greek rite: on the Euchologion), Mar. 1.

Ex omnibus (To the bishops of France: on the apostolic constitution, *Unigenitus*), Oct. 16.

Clement XIII
(1758-1769)

1758: *A quo die* (Unity among Christians), Sept. 13.

1759: *Cum primum* (On observing canonical sanctions), Sept. 17.

Appetente Sacro (On the spiritual advantages of fasting), Dec. 20.

1761: *In Dominico agro* (On instruction in the faith), June 14.

1766: *Christianae republicae* (On the dangers of anti-Christian writings), Nov. 25.

1768: *Summa quae* (To the bishops of Poland: on the Church in Poland), Jan. 6.

Clement XIV
(1769-1774)

1769: *Decet quam maxime* (To the bishops of Sardinia: on abuses in taxes and benefices), Sept. 21.

Inscrutabili divinae sapientiae (To all Christians: proclaiming a universal jubilee), Dec.12.

Cum summi (Proclaiming a universal jubilee), Dec. 12.

1774: *Salutis nostra* (To all Christians: proclaiming a universal jubilee), Apr. 30.

Pius VI
(1775-1799)

1775: *Inscrutabile* (On the problems of the pontificate), Dec. 25.

1791: *Charitas* (To the bishops of France: on the civil oath in France), Apr. 13.

Pius VII
(1800-1823)

1800: *Diu satis* (To the bishops of France: on a return to Gospel principles), May 15.

Leo XII
(1823-1829)

1824: *Ubi primum* (To all bishops: on Leo XII's assuming the pontificate), May 5.

Quod hoc ineunte (Proclaiming a universal jubilee), May 24.

1825: *Charitate Christi* (Extending jubilee to the entire Church), Dec. 25.

Pius VIII
(1829-1830)

1829: *Traditi humilitati* (On Pius VIII's program for the pontificate), May 24.

Gregory XVI
(1831-1846)

1832: *Summo iugiter studio* (To the bishops of Bavaria: on mixed marriages), May 27.

Cum primum (To the bishops of Poland: on civil obedience), June 9.

Mirari vos (On liberalism and religious indifferentism), Aug. 15.

1833: *Quo graviora* (To the bishops of the Rhineland: on the "pragmatic Constitution"), Oct. 4.

1834: *Singulari Nos* (On the errors of Lammenais), June 25.

1835: *Commissum divinitus* (To clergy of Switzerland: on Church and State), May 17.

1840: *Probe nostis* (On the Propagation of the Faith), Sept. 18.

1841: *Quas vestro* (To the bishops of Hungary: on mixed marriages), Apr. 30.

1844: *Inter praecipuas* (On biblical societies), May 8.

Pius IX
(1846-1878)

1846: *Qui pluribus* (On faith and religion), Nov. 9.

1847: *Praedecessores Nostros* (On aid for Ireland), Mar. 25.

Ubi primum (To religious superiors: on discipline for religious), June 17.

1849: *Ubi primum* (On the Immaculate Conception), Feb. 2.

Nostis et Nobiscum (To the bishops of Italy: on the Church in the Pontifical States), Dec. 8.

1851: *Exultavit cor Nostrum* (On the effects of jubilee), Nov. 21.

1852: *Nemo certe ignorat* (To the bishops of Ireland: on the discipline for clergy), Mar. 25.

Probe noscitis Venerabiles (To the bishops of Spain: on the discipline for clergy), May 17.

1853: *Inter multiplices* (To the bishops of France: pleading for unity of spirit), Mar. 21.

1854: *Neminem vestrum* (To clergy and faithful of Constantinople: on the persecution of Armenians), Feb. 2.

Optime noscitis (To the bishops of Ireland: on the proposed Catholic university for Ireland), Mar. 20.

Apostolicae Nostrae caritatis (Urging prayers for peace), Aug. 1.

1855: *Optime noscitis* (To the bishops of Austria: on episcopal meetings), Nov. 5.

1856: *Singulari quidem* (To the bishops of Austria: on the Church in Austria), Mar. 17.

1858: *Cum nuper* (To the bishops of the Kingdom of the Two Sicilies: on care for clerics), Jan. 20.

Amantissimi Redemptoris (On priests and the care of souls), May 3.

1859: *Cum sancta mater Ecclesia* (Pleading for public prayer), Apr. 27.

Qui nuper (On Pontifical States), June 18.

1860: *Nullis certe verbis* (On the need for civil sovereignty), Jan. 19.

1862: *Amantissimus* (To bishops of the Oriental rite: on the care of the churches), Apr. 8.

1863: *Quanto conficiamur moerore* (To the bishops of Italy: on promotion of false doctrines), Aug. 10.

Incredibili (To the bishops of Bogota: on persecution in New Granada), Sept. 17.

1864: *Maximae quidem* (To the bishops of Bavaria: on the Church in Bavaria), Aug. 18.

Quanta cura (Condemning current errors), Dec. 8.

1865: *Meridionali Americae* (To the bishops of South America: on the seminary for native clergy), Sept. 30.

1867: *Levate* (On the afflictions of the Church), Oct. 27.

1870: *Respicientes* (Protesting the taking of the Pontifical States), Nov. 1.

1871: *Ubi Nos* (To all bishops: on Pontifical States), May 15.

Beneficia Dei (On the twenty-fifth anniversary of his pontificate), June 4.

Saepe Venerabiles Fratres (On thanksgiving for twenty-five years of pontificate), Aug. 5.

1872: *Quae in Patriarchatu* (To bishops and people of Chaldea: on the Church in Chaldea), Nov. 16.

1873: *Quartus supra* (To bishops and people of the Armenian rite: on the Church in Armenia), Jan. 6.

Etsi multa (On the Church in Italy, Germany and Switzerland), Nov. 21.

1874: *Vix dum a Nobis* (To the bishops of Austria: on the Church in Austria), Mar. 7.

Gravibus Ecclesiae (To all bishops and faithful: proclaiming a jubilee for 1875), Dec. 24.

1875: *Quod nunquam* (To the bishops of Prussia: on the Church in Prussia), Feb. 5.

Graves ac diuturnae (To the bishops of Switzerland: on the Church in Switzerland), Mar. 23.

Leo XIII
(1878-1903)

1878: *Inscrutabili Dei consilio* (On the evils of society), Apr. 21.

Quod Apostolici muneris (On socialism), Dec. 28.

1879: *Aeterni Patris* (On the restoration of Christian philosophy), Aug. 4.

1880: *Arcanum* (On Christian marriage), Feb. 10.

Grande munus (On Sts. Cyril and Methodius), Sept. 30.

Sancta Dei civitas (On mission societies), Dec. 3.

1881: *Diuturnum* (On the origin of civil power), June 29.

Licet multa (To the bishops of Belgium: on Catholics in Belgium), Aug. 3.

1882: *Etsi Nos* (To the bishops of Italy: on conditions in Italy), Feb. 15.

Auspicato concessum (On St. Francis of Assisi), Sept. 17.

Cum multa (To the bishops of Spain: on conditions in Spain), Dec. 8.

1883: *Supremi Apostolatus officio* (On devotion to the Rosary), Sept. 1.

1884: *Nobilissima Gallorum gens* (To the bishops of France: on the religious question), Feb. 8.

Humanum genus (On Freemasonry), Apr. 20.

Superiore anno (On the recitation of the Rosary), Aug. 30.

1885: *Immortale Dei* (On the Christian constitution of states), Nov. 1.

Spectata fides (To the bishops of England: on Christian education), Nov. 27.

Quod auctoritate (Proclamation of extraordinary Jubilee), Dec. 22.

1886: *Iampridem* (To the bishops of Prussia: on Catholicism in Germany), Jan. 6.

Quod multum (To the bishops of Hungary: on the liberty of the Church), Aug. 22.

Pergrata (To the bishops of Portugal: on the Church in Portugal), Sept. 14.

1887: *Vieben noto* (To the bishops of Italy: on the Rosary and public life), Sept. 20.

Officio sanctissimo (To the bishops of Bavaria: on the Church in Bavaria), Dec. 22.

1888: *Quod anniversarius* (On his sacerdotal jubilee), Apr. 1.

In plurimis (To the bishops of Brazil: on the abolition of slavery), May 5.

Libertas (On the nature of human liberty), June 20.

Saepe Nos (To the bishops of Ireland: on boycotting in Ireland), June 24.

Paterna caritas (To the Patriarch of Cilicia and the archbishops and bishops of the Armenian people: on reunion with Rome), July 25.

Quam aerumnosa (To the bishops of America: on Italian immigrants), Dec. 10.

Etsi cunctas (To the bishops of Ireland: on the Church in Ireland), Dec. 21.

Exeunte iam anno (On the right ordering of Christian life), Dec. 25.

1889: *Magni Nobis* (To the bishops of the United States: on the Catholic University of America), Mar. 7.

Quamquam pluries (On devotion to St. Joseph),Aug. 15.

1890: *Sapientiae Christianae* (On Christians as citizens), Jan. 10.

Dall'alto Dell'Apostolico seggio (To the bishops and people of Italy: on Freemasonry in Italy), Oct. 15.

Catholicae Ecclesiae (On slavery in the missions), Nov. 20.

1891: *In ipso* (To the bishops of Austria: on episcopal reunions in Austria), Mar. 3.

Rerum novarum (On capital and labor), May 15.

Pastoralis (To the bishops of Portugal: on religious union), June 25.

Pastoralis officii (To the bishops of Germany and Austria: on the morality of dueling), Sept. 12.

Octobri mense (On the Rosary), Sept. 22.

1892: *Au milieu des sollicitudes* (To the bishops, clergy and faithful of France: on the Church and State in France), Feb. 16.

Quarto abeunte saeculo (To the bishops of Spain, Italy, and the two Americas: on the Columbus quadricentennial), July 16.

Magnae Dei Matris (On the Rosary), Sept. 8.

Inimica vis (To the bishops of Italy: on Freemasonry), Dec. 8.

Custodi di quella fede (To the Italian people: on Freemasonry), Dec. 8.

1893: *Ad extremas* (On seminaries for native clergy), June 24.

Constanti Hungarorum (To the bishops of Hungary: on the Church in Hungary), Sept. 2.

Laetitiae sanctae (Commending devotion to the Rosary), Sept. 8.

Non mediocri (To the bishops of Spain: on the Spanish College in Rome), Oct. 25.

Providentissimus Deus (On the study of Holy Scripture), Nov. 18.

1894: *Caritatis* (To the bishops of Poland: on the Church in Poland), Mar. 19.

Inter graves (To the bishops of Peru: on the Church in Peru), May 1.

Litteras a vobis (To the bishops of Brazil: on the clergy in Brazil), July 2.

Iucunda semper expectatione (On the Rosary), Sept. 8.

Christi nomen (On the propagation of the Faith and Eastern churches), Dec. 24.

1895: *Longinqua* (To the bishops of the United States: on Catholicism in the United States), Jan. 6.

Permoti Nos (To the bishops of Belgium: on social conditions in Belgium), July 10.

Adiutricem (On the Rosary), Sept. 5.

1896: *Insignes* (To the bishops of Hungary: on the Hungarian millennium), May 1.

Satis cognitum (On the unity of the Church), June 29.

Fidentem piumque animum (On the Rosary), Sept. 20.

1897: *Divinum illud munus* (On the Holy Spirit), May 9.

Militantis Ecclesiae (To the bishops of Austria, Germany, and Switzerland: on St. Peter Canisius), Aug. 1.

Augustissimae Virginis Mariae (On the Confraternity of the Holy Rosary), Sept. 12.

Affari vos (To the bishops of Canada: on the Manitoba school question), Dec. 8.

1898: *Caritatis studium* (To the bishops of Scotland: on the Church in Scotland), July 25.

Spesse volte (To the bishops, priests, and people of Italy: on the suppression of Catholic institutions), Aug. 5.

Quam religiosa (To the bishops of Peru: on civil marriage law), Aug. 16.

Diuturni temporis (On the Rosary), Sept. 5.

Quum diuturnum (To the bishops of Latin America: on Latin American bishops' plenary council), Dec. 25.

1899: *Annum Sacrum* (On consecration to the Sacred Heart), May 25.

Depuis le jour (To the archbishops, bishops, and clergy of France: on the education of the clergy), Sept. 8.

Paternae (To the bishops of Brazil: on the education of the clergy), Sept. 18.

1900: *Omnibus compertum* (To the Patriarch and bishops of the Greek-Melkite rite: on unity among the Greek Melkites), July 21.

Tametsi futura prospicientibus (On Jesus Christ the Redeemer), Nov. 1.

1901: *Graves de communi re* (On Christian democracy), Jan. 18.

Gravissimas (To the bishops of Portugal: on religious orders in Portugal), May 16.

Reputantibus (To the bishops of Bohemia and Moravia: on the language question in Bohemia), Aug. 20.

Urbanitatis Veteris (To the bishops of the Latin church in Greece: on the foundation of a seminary in Athens), Nov. 20.

1902: *In amplissimo* (To the bishops of the United States: on the Church in the United States), Apr. 15.

Quod votis (To the bishops of Austria: on the proposed Catholic University), Apr. 30.

Mirae caritatis (On the Holy Eucharist), May 28.

Quae ad Nos (To the bishops of Bohemia and Moravia: on the Church in Bohemia and Moravia), Nov. 22.

Fin dal principio (To the bishops of Italy: on the education of the clergy), Dec. 8.

Dum multa (To the bishops of Ecuador: on marriage legislation), Dec. 24.

St. Pius X
(1903-1914)

1903: *E supremi* (On the restoration of all things in Christ), Oct. 4.

1904: *Ad diem illum laetissimum* (On the Immaculate Conception), Feb. 2.

Iucunda sane (On Pope Gregory the Great), Mar. 12.

1905: *Acerbo nimis* (On teaching Christian doctrine), Apr. 15.

Il fermo proposito (To the bishops of Italy: on Catholic Action in Italy), June 11.

1906: *Vehementer Nos* (To the bishops, clergy, and people of France: on the French Law of Separation), Feb. 11.

Tribus circiter (On the Mariavites or Mystic Priests of Poland), Apr. 5.

Pieni l'animo (To the bishops of Italy: on the clergy in Italy), July 28.

Gravissimo officio munere (To the bishops of France: on French associations of worship), Aug. 10.

1907: *Une fois encore* (To the bishops, clergy, and people of France: on the separation of Church and State), Jan. 6.

Pascendi dominici gregis (On the doctrines of the Modernists), Sept. 8.

1909: *Communium rerum* (On St. Anselm of Aosta), Apr. 21.

1910: *Editae saepe* (On St. Charles Borromeo), May 26.

1911: *Iamdudum* (On the Law of Separation in Portugal), May 24.

1912: *Lacrimabili statu* (To the bishops of Latin America: on the Indians of South America), June 7.

Singulari quadam (To the bishops of Germany: on labor organizations), Sept. 24.

Benedict XV
(1914-1922)

1914: *Ad beatissimi Apostolorum* (Appeal for peace), Nov. 1.

1917: *Humani generis Redemptionem* (On preaching the Word of God), June 15.

1918: *Quod iam diu* (On the future peace conference), Dec. 1.

1919: *In hac tanta* (To the bishops of Germany: on St. Boniface), May 14.

Paterno iam diu (On children of central Europe), Nov. 24.

1920: *Pacem, Dei munus pulcherrimum* (On peace and Christian reconciliation), May 23.

Spiritus Paraclitus (On St. Jerome), Sept. 15.

Principi Apostolorum Petro (On St. Ephrem the Syrian), Oct. 5.

Annus iam plenus (On children of central Europe), Dec. 1.

1921: *Sacra propediem* (On the Third Order of St. Francis), Jan. 6.

In praeclara summorum (To professors and students of fine arts in Catholic institutions of learning: on Dante), Apr. 30.

Fausto appetente die (On St. Dominic), June 29.

Pius XI
(1922-1939)

1922: *Ubi arcano Dei consilio* (On the peace of Christ in the Kingdom of Christ), Dec. 23.

1923: *Rerum omnium perturbationem* (On St. Francis de Sales), Jan. 26.

Studiorum Ducem (On St. Thomas Aquinas), June 29.

Ecclesiam Dei (On St. Josaphat), Nov. 12.

1924: *Maximam gravissimamque* (To the bishops, clergy, and people of France: on French diocesan associations), Jan. 18.

1925: *Quas primas* (On the feast of Christ the King), Dec. 11.

1926: *Rerum Ecclesiae* (On Catholic missions), Feb. 28.

Rite expiatis (On St. Francis of Assisi), Apr. 30.

Iniquis afflictisque (On the persecution of the Church in Mexico), Nov. 18.

1928: *Mortalium animos* (On religious unity), Jan. 6.

Miserentissimus Redemptor (On reparation to the Sacred Heart), May 8.

Rerum Orientalium (On the promotion of Oriental Studies), Sept. 8.

1929: *Mens Nostra* (On the promotion of Spiritual Exercises), Dec. 20.

Quinquagesimo ante (On his sacerdotal jubilee), Dec. 23.

Rappresentanti in terra (On Christian education), Dec. 31. [Latin text, *Divini illius magistri*, published several months later with minor changes.]

1930: *Ad salutem* (On St. Augustine), Apr. 20.

Casti connubii (On Christian Marriage), Dec. 31.

1931: *Quadragesimo anno* (Commemorating the fortieth anniversary of Leo XIII's *Rerum novarum*: on reconstruction of the soical order), May 15.

Non abbiamo bisogno (On Catholic Action in Italy), June 29.

Nova impendet (On the economic crisis), Oct. 2.

Lux veritatis (On the Council of Ephesus), Dec. 25.

1932: *Caritate Christi compulsi* (On the Sacred Heart), May 3.

Acerba animi (To the bishops of Mexico: on persecution of the Church in Mexico), Sept. 29.

1933: *Dilectissima Nobis* (To the bishops, clergy, and people of Spain: on oppression of the Church in Spain), June 3.

1935: *Ad Catholici sacerdotii* (On the Catholic priesthood), Dec. 20.

1936: *Vigilanti cura* (To the bishops of the United States: on motion pictures), June 29.

1937: *Mit brennender Sorge* (To the bishops of Germany: on the Church and the German Reich), Mar. 14.

Divini Redemptoris (On atheistic communism), Mar. 19.

Nos es muy conocida (To the bishops of Mexico: on the religious situation in Mexico), Mar. 28

Ingravescentibus malis (On the Rosary) Sept. 29.

Pius XII
(1939-1958)

1939: *Summi Pontificatus* (On the unity of human society), Oct. 20.

Sertum laetitiae (To the bishops of the United States: on the 150th anniversary of the establishment of the hierarchy in the United States), Nov. 1.

1940: *Saeculo exeunte octavo* (To the bishops of Portugal and its colonies: on the eighth centenary of the independence of Portugal), June 13.

1943: *Mystici Corporis Christi* (On the Mystical Body of Christ), June 29.

Divino afflante Spiritu (On promoting biblical studies, commemorating the fiftieth anniversary of *Providentissimus Deus*), Sept. 30.

1944: *Orientalis Ecclesiae* (On St. Cyril, Patriarch of Alexandria), Apr. 9.

1945: *Communium interpretes dolorum* (To the bishops of the world: appealing for prayers for peace during May), Apr. 15.

Orientales omnes Ecclesias (On the 350th anniversary of the reunion of the Ruthenian Church with the Apostolic See), Dec. 23.

1946: *Quemadmodum* (Pleading for the care of the world's destitute children), Jan. 6.

Deiparae Virginis Mariae (To all bishops: on the possibility of defining the Assumption of the Blessed Virgin Mary as a dogma of faith), May 1.

1947: *Fulgens radiatur* (On St. Benedict), Mar. 21.

Mediator Dei (On the sacred liturgy), Nov. 20.

Optatissima pax (Prescribing public prayers for social and world peace), Dec. 18.

1948: *Auspicia quaedam* (On public prayers for world peace and solution of the problem of Palestine), May 1.

In multiplicibus curis (On prayers for peace in Palestine), Oct. 24.

1949: *Redemptoris nostri cruciatus* (On the holy places in Palestine), Apr. 15.

1950: *Anni Sacri* (On the program for combatting atheistic propaganda throughout the world), Mar. 12.

Summi maeroris (On public prayers for peace), July 19.

Humani generis (Concerning some false opinions threatening to undermine the foundations of Catholic doctrine), Aug. 12.

Mirabile illud (On the crusade of prayers for peace), Dec. 6.

1951: *Evangelii praecones* (On the promotion of Catholic missions), June 2.

Sempiternus Rex Christus (On the Council of Chalcedon), Sept. 8.

Ingruentium malorum (On reciting the Rosary), Sept. 15.

1952: *Orientales Ecclesias* (On the persecuted Eastern Church), Dec. 15.

1953: *Doctor Mellifluus* (On St. Bernard of Clairvaux, the last of the fathers), May 24.

Fulgens corona (Proclaiming a Marian Year to commemorate the centenary of the definition of the dogma of the Immaculate Conception), Sept. 8.

1954: *Sacra virginitas* (On consecrated virginity), Mar. 25.

Ecclesiae fastos (To the bishops of Great Britain, Germany, Austria, France, Belgium, and Holland: on St. Boniface), June 5.

Ad Sinarum gentem (To the bishops, clergy, and people of China: on the supranationality of the Church), Oct. 7.

Ad Caeli Reginam (Proclaiming the Queenship of Mary), Oct. 11.

1955: *Musicae sacrae* (On sacred music), Dec. 25.

1956: *Haurietis aquas* (On devotion to the Sacred Heart), May 15.

Luctuosissimi eventus (Urging public prayers for peace and freedom for the people of Hungary), Oct. 28.

Laetamur admodum (Renewing exhortation for prayers for peace for Poland, Hungary, and especially for the Middle East), Nov. 1.

Datis nuperrime (Lamenting the sorrowful events in Hungary and condemning the ruthless use of force), Nov. 5.

1957: *Fidei donum* (On the present condition of the Catholic missions, especially in Africa), Apr. 21.

Invicti athletae (On St. Andrew Bobola), May 16.

Le pelerinage de Lourdes (Warning against materialism on the centenary of the apparitions at Lourdes), July 2.

Miranda prorsus (On the communications field: motion picture, radio, television), Sept. 8.

1958: *Ad Apostolorum Principis* (To the bishops of China; on Communism and the Church in China), June 29.

Meminisse iuvat (On prayers for persecuted Church), July 14.

John XXIII
(1958-1963)

1959: *Ad Petri Cathedram* (On truth, unity, and peace, in a spirit of charity), June 29.

Sacerdotii Nostri primordia (On St. John Vianney), Aug. 1.

Grata recordatio (On the Rosary: prayer for the Church, missions, international and social problems), Sept. 26.

Princeps Pastorum (On the missions, native clergy, lay participation), Nov. 28.

1961: *Mater et Magistra* (On Christianity and social progress), May 15.

Aeterna Dei sapientia (On fifteenth centenary of the death of Pope St. Leo I: the see of Peter as the center of Christian unity), Nov. 11.

1962: *Paenitentiam agere* (On the need for the practice of interior and exterior penance), July 1.

1963: *Pacem in terris* (On establishing universal peace in truth, justice, charity, and liberty), Apr. 11.

Paul VI
(1963-1978)

1964: *Ecclesiam Suam* (On the Church), Aug. 6.

1965: *Mense maio* (On prayers during May for the preservation of peace), Apr. 29.

Mysterium Fidei (On the Holy Eucharist), Sept. 3.

1966: *Christi Matri* (On prayers for peace during October), Sept. 15.

1967: *Populorum progressio* (On the development of peoples), Mar. 26.

Sacerdotalis caelibatus (On the celibacy of the priest), June 24.

1968: *Humanae vitae* (On the regulation of birth), July 25.

John Paul II
(1978-)

1979: *Redemptor hominis* (On redemption and dignity of the human race), Mar. 4

1980: *Dives in misericordia* (On the mercy of God), Nov. 30.

1981: *Laborem exercens* (On human work), Sept. 14.

1985: *Slavorum Apostoli* (Commemorating Sts. Cyril and Methodius, on the eleventh centenary of the death of St. Methodius), June 2.

1986: *Dominum et Vivificantem* (On the Holy Spirit in the life of the Church and the world), May 18.

1987: *Redemptoris Mater* (On the role of Mary in the mystery of Christ and her active and exemplary presence in the life of the Church), Mar. 25.

Sollicitudo Rei Socialis (On social concerns, on the twentieth anniversary of Populorum progressio), Dec. 30.

1991: *Redemptoris missio* (On the permanent validity of the Church's missionary mandate), Jan. 22.

Centesimus annus (Commemorating the centenary of *Rerum novarum* and addressing the social question in a contemporary perspective), May 1.

1993: *Veritatis Splendor* (Regarding fundamental questions on the Church's moral teaching), Aug. 6.

1995: *Evangelium Vitae* (On the value and inviolability of human life), Mar. 25.

Ut Unum Sint (On commitment to ecumenism), May 25.

1998: *Fides et Ratio* (On Faith and Reason), Oct. 1, 1998.

CANONIZATIONS BY LEO XIII AND HIS SUCCESSORS

Canonization (see entry in Glossary) is an infallible declaration by the pope that a person who suffered martyrdom and/or practiced Christian virtue to a heroic degree is in glory with God in heaven and is worthy of public honor by the universal Church and of imitation by the faithful.

Biographies of some of the saints listed below are given elsewhere in the Almanac. See Index.

Leo XIII
(1878-1903)

1881: Clare of Montefalco (d. 1308); John Baptist de Rossi (1698-1764); Lawrence of Brindisi (d. 1619).

1883: Benedict J. Labre (1748-1783).

1888: Seven Holy Founders of the Servite Order; Peter Claver (1581-1654); John Berchmans (1599-1621); Alphonsus Rodriguez (1531-1617).

1897: Anthony M. Zaccaria (1502-1539); Peter Fourier of Our Lady (1565-1640).

1900: John Baptist de La Salle (1651-1719); Rita of Cascia (1381-1457).

St. Pius X
(1903-1914)

1904: Alexander Sauli (1534-1593); Gerard Majella (1725-1755).

1909: Joseph Oriol (1650-1702); Clement M. Hofbauer (1751-1820).

Benedict XV
(1914-1922)

1920: Gabriel of the Sorrowful Mother (1838-1862); Margaret Mary Alacoque (1647-1690); Joan of Arc (1412-1431).

Pius XI
(1922-1939)

1925: Thérèse of Lisieux (1873-1897); Peter Canisius (1521-1597); Mary Magdalen Postel (1756-1846); Mary Magdalen Sophie Barat (1779-1865); John Eudes (1601-1680); John Baptist Vianney (Curé of Ars) (1786-1859).

1930: Lucy Filippini (1672-1732); Catherine Tomas

(1533-1574); Jesuit North American Martyrs; Robert Bellarmine (1542-1621); Theophilus of Corte (1676-1740).

1931: Albert the Great (1206-1280) (equivalent canonization).

1933: Andrew Fournet (1752-1834); Bernadette Soubirous (1844-1879).

1934: Joan Antida Thouret (1765-1826); Mary Michaeli (1809-1865); Louise de Marillac (1591-1660); Joseph Benedict Cottolengo (1786-1842); Pompilius M. Pirotti, priest (1710-1756); Teresa Margaret Redi (1747-1770); John Bosco (1815-1888); Conrad of Parzham (1818-1894).

1935: John Fisher (1469-1535); Thomas More (1478-1535).

1938: Andrew Bobola (1592-1657); John Leonardi (c. 1550-1609); Salvatore of Horta (1520-1567).

Pius XII
(1939-1958)

1940: Gemma Galgani (1878-1903); Mary Euphrasia Pelletier (1796-1868).

1943: Margaret of Hungary (d. 1270) (equvalent canonization).

1946: Frances Xavier Cabrini (1850-1917).

1947: Nicholas of Flüe (1417-1487); John of Britto (1647-1693); Bernard Realini (1530-1616); Joseph Cafasso (1811-1860); Michael Garicoits (1797-1863); Jeanne Elizabeth des Ages (1773-1838); Louis Marie Grignon de Montfort (1673-1716); Catherine Labouré (1806-1876).

1949: Jeanne de Lestonnac (1556-1640); Maria Josepha Rossello (1811-1880).

1950: Emily de Rodat (1787-1852); Anthony Mary Claret (1807-1870); Bartolomea Capitanio (1807-1833); Vincenza Gerosa (1784-1847) Jeanne de Valois (1461-1504); Vincenzo M. Strambi (1745-1824); Maria Goretti (1890-1902); Mariana Paredes of Jesus (1618-1645).

1951: Maria Domenica Mazzarello (1837-1881); Emilie de Vialar (1797-1856); Anthony M. Gianelli (1789-1846); Ignatius of Laconi (1701-1781); Francis Xavier Bianchi (1743-1815).

1954: Pope Pius X (1835-1914); Dominic Savio (1842-1857); Maria Crocifissa di Rosa (1813-1855); Peter Chanel (1803-1841); Gaspar del Bufalo (1786-1837); Joseph M. Pignatelli (1737-1811).

1958: Herman Joseph, O. Praem. (1150-1241) (equivalent canonization).

John XXIII
(1958-1963)

1959: Joaquina de Vedruna de Mas (1783-1854); Charles of Sezze (1613-1670).

1960: Gregory Barbarigo (1625-1697) (equivalent canonization); John de Ribera (1532-1611).

1961: Bertilla Boscardin (1888-1922).

1962: Martin de Porres (1579-1639); Peter Julian Eymard (1811-1868); Anthony Pucci, priest (1819-1892); Francis Mary of Camporosso (1804-1866).

1963: Vincent Pallotti (1795-1850).

Paul VI
(1963-1978)

1964: Charles Lwanga and Twenty-One Companions, Martyrs of Uganda (d. between 1885-1887).

1967: Benilde Romacon (1805-1862).

1969: Julia Billiart (1751-1816).

1970: Maria Della Dolorato Torres Acosta (1826-1887); Leonard Murialdo (1828-1900); Therese Couderc (1805-1885); John of Ávila (1499-1569); Nicholas Tavelic, Deodatus of Aquitaine, Peter of Narbonne and Stephen of Cuneo, martyrs (d. 1391); Forty English and Welsh Martyrs (d. 16th cent.).

1974: Teresa of Jesus Jornet Ibars (1843-1897).

1975: Vicenta Maria Lopez y Vicuna (1847-1890); Elizabeth Bayley Seton (1774-1821); John Masias (1585-1645); Oliver Plunket (1629-1681); Justin de Jacobis (1800-1860); John Baptist of the Conception (1561-1613).

1976: Beatrice da Silva (1424 or 1426-1490); John Ogilvie (1579-1615).

1977: Rafaela Maria Porras y Ayllon (1850-1925); John Nepomucene Neumann (1811-1860); Sharbel Makhlouf (1828-1898).

John Paul II
(1978-)

1982: Crispin of Viterbo (1668-1750); Maximilian Kolbe (1894-1941); Marguerite Bourgeoys (1620-1700); Jeanne Delanoue (1666-1736).

1983: Leopold Mandic (1866-1942).

1984: Paola Frassinetti (1809-1892); 103 Korean Martyrs (d. between 1839-1867); Miguel Febres Cordero (1854-1910).

1986: Francis Anthony Fasani (1681-1742); Giuseppe Maria Tomasi (1649-1713).

1987: Giuseppe Moscati (d. 1927); Lawrence (Lorenzo) Ruiz and Fifteen Companions, Martyrs of Japan (d. 1630s).

1988: Eustochia Calafato (1434-1485); 117 Martyrs of Vietnam (96 Vietnamese, 11 Spanish, 10 French; included 8 bishops, 50 priests, 1 seminarian, 58 lay persons); Roque Gonzalez (1576-1628), Alfonso Rodriguez (1598-1628) and Juan de Castillo (1596-1628), Jesuit martyrs of Paraguay; Rose Philippine Duchesne (1796-1852); Simon de Rojas (1552-1624); Magdalen of Canossa (1774-1835); Maria Rosa Molas y Vollve (d. 1876).

1989: Clelia Barbieri (1847-1870); Gaspar Bertoni (1777-1853); Richard Pampuri, religious (1897-1930); Agnes of Bohemia (1211-1282); Albert Chmielowski (1845-1916); Mutien-Marie Wiaux (1841-1917).

1990: Marguerite D'Youville (1701-1777).

1991: Raphael (Jozef) Kalinowski (1835-1907).

1992: Claude La Colombiere (1641-1682); Ezequiel Moreno y Diaz (1848-1905).

1993: Marie of St. Ignatius (Claudine Thevenet) (1774-1837); Teresa "de los Andes" (Juana Fernandez Solar) (1900-20); Enrique de Ossó y Cervelló (1840-96).

1995: Jan Sarkander (1576-1620), Zdislava of Lemberk (d. 1252); Marek Krizin (1588-1619), Stefan Pongracz (1582-1619), Melichar Grodziecky (1584-1619), martyrs of Kosice; Eugene de Mazenod (1782-1861).

1996: Jean-Gabriel Perboyre (1802-40), Juan Grande Roman (1546-1600) and Bro. Egidio Maria of St. Joseph (1729-1812).

1997: Hedwig (1371-1399), John Dukla, O.F.M. (d. 1484).

1998: Edith Stein (d. 1942).

1999: Marcellin Joseph Benoit Champagnat (1789-1840), Giovanni Calabria (1873-1954), Agostina

Livia Pietrantonio (1864-1894), Sr. Kunegunda Kinga.

BEATIFICATIONS BY POPE JOHN PAUL II, 1979-1998

1979: Margarret Ebner (Feb. 24); Francis Coll, O.P., Jacques Laval, S.S.Sp. (Apr. 29); Enrique de Ossó y Cervelló (Oct. 14; canonized June 16, 1993).
1980: José de Anchieta, Peter of St. Joseph Betancur, Francois de Montmorency Laval, Kateri Tekakwitha, Marie Guyart of the Incarnation (June 22); Don Luigi Orione, Bartolomea Longo, Maria Anna Sala (Oct. 26).
1981: Sixteen Martyrs of Japan (Lorenzo Ruiz and Companions) (Feb 18; canonized Oct. 18, 1987); Maria Repetto, Alan de Solminihac, Richard Pampuri(canonized, 1989), Claudine Thevenet (canonized 1993), Aloysius (Luigi) Scrosoppi (Oct. 4).
1982: Peter Donders, C.SS.R., Marie Rose Durocher, Andre Bessette, C.S.C., Maria Angela Astorch, Marie Rivier (May 23); Fra Angelico (equivalent beatification) (July); Jeanne Jugan, Salvatore Lilli and 7 Armenian Companions (Oct. 3); Sr. Angela of the Cross (Nov. 5).
1983: Maria Gabriella Sagheddu (Jan. 25); Luigi Versiglia, Callisto Caravario (May 15); Ursula Ledochowska (June 20); Raphael (Jozef) Kalinowski (canonized 1991), Bro. Albert (Adam Chmielowski), T.O.R. (June 22); Giacomo Cusmano, Jeremiah of Valachia, Domingo Iturrate Zubero (Oct. 30); Marie of Jesus Crucified (Marie Bouardy) (Nov. 13).
1984: Fr. William Repin and 98 Companions (Martyrs of Angers during French Revolution), Giovanni Mazzucconi (Feb. 19); Marie Leonie Paradis (Sept. 11); Federico Albert, Clemente Marchisio, Isidore of St. Joseph (Isidore de Loor), Rafaela Ybarra de Villalongo (Sept. 30); José Manyanet y Vives, Daniel Brottier, C.S.Sp., Sr. Elizabeth of the Trinity (Elizabeth Catez) (Nov. 25).
1985: Mercedes of Jesus (Feb. 1); Ana de los Angeles Monteagudo (Feb. 2); Pauline von Mallinckrodt, Catherine Troiani (Apr. 14); Benedict Menni, Peter Friedhofen (June 23); Anwarite Nangapeta (Aug. 15); Virginae Centurione Bracelli (Sept. 22); Diego Luis de San Vitores, S.J., Jose M. Rubio y Peralta, S.J., Francisco Garate, S.J. (Oct. 6); Titus Brandsma, O.Carm. (Nov. 3); Pio Campidelli, C.P., Marie Teresa of Jesus Gerhardinger, Rafqa Ar-Rayes (Nov. 17).
1986: Alphonsa Mattathupandatu of the Immaculate Conception, Kuriakose Elias Chavara (Feb. 8); Antoine Chevrier (Oct. 4); Teresa Maria of the Cross Manetti (Oct. 19).
1987: Maria Pilar of St. Francis Borgia, Teresa of the Infant Jesus, Maria Angeles of St. Joseph, Cardinal Marcellis Spinola y Maestre, Emmanuel Domingo y Sol (Mar. 29); Teresa of Jesus "de los Andes" (Apr. 3; canonized Mar. 21, 1993); Edith Stein (Teresa Benedicta of the Cross) (May 1; canonized, Oct. 1998); Rupert Meyer, S.J. (May 3); Pierre-Francois Jamet, Cardinal Andrea Carlo Ferrari, Benedicta Cambiagio Frassinello, Louis Moreau (May 10); Carolina Kozka, Michal Kozal (June 10); George Matulaitis (Matulewicz) (June

28); Marcel Callo, Pierino Morosini, Antonia Mesina (Oct. 4); Blandina Marten, Ulricke Nische, Jules Reche (Bro. Arnold) (Nov. 1); 85 Martyrs (d. between 1584-1689) of England, Scotland and Wales (Nov. 22).
1988: John Calabria (canonized, Apr. 18, 1999), Joseph Nascimbeni (Apr. 17); Pietro Bonilli, Kaspar Stangassinger, Francisco Palau y Quer, Savina Petrilli (Apr. 24), Laura Vicuna (Sept. 3); Joseph Gerard (Sept. 11); Miguel Pro, Giuseppe Benedetto Dusmet, Francisco Faa di Bruno, Junipero Serra, Frederick Jansoone, Josefa Naval Girbes (Sept. 25); Bernardo Maria Silvestrelli, Charles Houben, Honoratus Kozminski (Oct. 16); Niels Stensen (Nicolaus Steno) (Oct. 23); Katharine Drexel, 3 Missionary Martyrs of Ethiopia (Liberato Weiss, Samuel Marzorati, Michele Pio Fasoli) (Nov. 20).
1989: Martin of Saint Nicholas, Melchior of St. Augustine, Mary of Jesus of the Good Shepherd, Maria Margaret Caiani, Maria of Jesus Siedliska, Maria Catherine of St. Augustine (Apr. 23); Victoria Rasoamanarivo (Apr. 30); Bro. Scubilionis (John Bernard Rousseau) (May 2); Elizabeth Renzi, Antonio Lucci (June 17); Niceforo de Jesus y Maria (Vicente Diez Tejerina and 25 Companions (martyred in Spain), Lorenzo Salvi, Gertrude Caterina Comensoli, Francisca Ana Cirer Carbonell (Oct. 1); 7 Martyrs from Thailand (Philip Sipong, Sr. Agnes Phila, Sr. Lucia Khambang, Agatha Phutta, Cecilia Butsi, Bibiana Khampai, Maria Phon), Timothy Giaccardo, Mother Maria of Jesus Deluil-Martiny (Oct. 22); Giuseppe Baldo (Oct. 31).
1990: 9 Martyrs of Astoria during Spanish Civil War (De la Salle Brothers Cyrill Bertran, Marciano Jose, Julian Alfredo, Victoriano Pio, Benjamin Julian, Augusto Andres, Benito de Jesus, Aniceto Adolfo; and Passionist priest Innocencio Inmaculada), Mercedes Prat, Manuel Barbal Cosan (Brother Jaime), Philip Rinaldi (Apr. 29); Juan Diego (confirmation of Apr. 9 decree), 3 Child Martyrs (Cristobal, Antonio and Juan), Fr. Jose Maria de Yermo y Parres (May 6); Pierre Giorgio Frassati (May 20); Hanibal Maria Di Francia, Joseph Allamano (Oct. 7); Marthe Aimee LeBouteiller, Louise Therese de Montaignac de Chauvance, Maria Schinina, Elisabeth Vendramini (Nov. 4).
1991: Annunciata Cocchetti, Marie Therese Haze, Clara Bosatta (Apr. 21); Jozef Sebastian Pelczar (June 2); Boleslava Lament (June 5); Rafael Chylinski (June 9); Angela Salawa (Aug. 13); Edoardo Giuseppe Rosaz (July 14, Susa, Italy); Pauline of the Heart of Jesus in Agony Visentainer (Oct. 18, Brazil); Adolph Kolping (Oct. 27).
1992: Josephine Bakhita, Josemaria Escriva de Balaguer (May 17); Francesco Spinelli (June 21, Caravaggio, Italy); 17 Irish Martyrs, Rafael Arnáiz Barón, Nazaria Ignacia March Mesa, Léonie Françoise de Sales Aviat, and Maria Josefa Sancho de Guerra (Sept. 27); 122 Martyrs of Spanish Civil War, Narcisa Martillo Morán (Oct. 25); Cristóbal

Magellanes and 24 companions, Mexican martyrs, and Maria de Jesús Sacramentado Venegas (Nov. 22).

1993: Dina Belanger (Mar. 20); John Duns Scotus (Mar. 20, cult solemnly recognized); Mary Angela Truszkowska, Ludovico of Casoria, Faustina Kowalska, Paula Montal Fornés (Apr. 18); Stanislaus Kazimierczyk (Apr. 18, cult solemnly recognized); Maurice Tornay, Marie-Louise Trichet, Columba Gabriel and Florida Cevoli (May 16); Giuseppe Marello (Sept. 26); Eleven martyrs of Almeria, Spain, during Spanish Civil War (2 bishops, 7 brothers, 1 priest, 1 lay person); Victoria Diez y Bustos de Molina, Maria Francesca (Anna Maria) Rubatto; Pedro Castroverde, Maria Crucified (Elisabetta Maria) Satellico (Oct. 10).

1994: Isidore Bakanja, Elizabeth Canori Mora; Dr. Gianna Beretta Molla (Apr. 24); Nicolas Roland, Alberto Hurtado Cruchaga, Maria Rafols, Petra of St. Joseph Perez Florida, Josephine Vannini (Oct. 16); Magdalena Caterina Morano (Nov. 5); Hyacinthe Marie Cormier, Marie Poussepin, Agnes de Jesus Galand, Eugenia Joubert, Claudio Granzotto (Nov. 20).

1995: Peter ToRot (Jan. 17); Mother Mary of the Cross MacKillop (Jan. 19); Joseph Vaz (Jan. 21); Rafael Guizar Valencia, Modestino of Jesus and Mary, Genoveva Torres Morales, Grimoaldo of the Purification (Jan. 29); Johann Nepomuk von Tschiderer (Apr. 30); Maria Helena Stollenwerk, Maria Alvarado Cordozo, Giuseppina Bonino, Maria Domenica Brun Barbantini, Agostino Roscelli (May 7); Damien de Veuster (June 4); 109 Martyrs (64 from French Revolution – Martyrs of La Rochelle – and 45 from Spanish Civil War), Anselm Polanco Fontecha, Felipe Ripoll Morata, and Pietro Casini (Oct. 1); Mary Theresa Scherer, Maria Bernarda Butler and Marguerite Bays (Oct. 29).

1996: Daniel Comboni and Guido Maria Conforti (Mar. 17); Cardinal Alfredo Ildefonso Schuster, O.S.B., Filippo Smaldone and Gennaro Sarnelli (priests) and Candida Maria de Jesus Cipitria y Barriola, Maria Raffaella Cimatti, Maria Antonia Bandres (religious) (May 12), Bernhard Lichtenberg and Karl Leisner (June 23), Wincenty Lewoniuk and 12 companions, Edmund Rice, Maria Ana Mogas Fontcuberta and Marcelina Darowska (Oct 6); Otto Neururer, Jakob Gapp and Catherine Jarrige (Nov. 24).

1997: Bishop Florentino Asensio Barroso, Sr. Maria Encarnacion Rosal of the Sacred Heart, Fr. Gaetano Catanoso, Fr. Enrico Rebuschini and Ceferino Gimenez Malla, first gypsy beatified (May 4); Bernardina Maria Jablonska, Maria Karlowska (June 6); Frédéric Ozanam (Aug. 22); Bartholomew Mary Dal Monte (Sep. 27); Elías del Socorro Nieves, Domenico Lentini, Giovanni Piamarta, Emilie d'Hooghvorst, Maria Teresa Fasce (Oct. 12); John Baptist Scalabrini, Vilmos Apor, María Vicenta of St. Dorothy Chávez Orozco (Nov. 9).

1998: Bishop Vincent Bossilkov, María Sallés, Brigida of Jesus (Mar. 15); Fr. Cyprian Tansi (Mar. 22); Nimatullah al-Hardini, 11 Spanish nuns (May 10); Secondo Polla (May 23); Giovanni Maria Boccardo, Teresa Grillo Chavez, Teresa Bracco (May 24); Jakob Kern, Maria Restituta Kafka, and Anton Schwartz (June 21); Giuseppe Tovini (Sept. 20); Cardinal Alojzije Stepinac (Oct. 3); Antônio de Sant'Anna Galvão, Faustino Miguez, Zeferino Agostini, Mother Theodore Guérin (Oct. 25).

1999: Vicente Soler, and six Augustinian Recollect Companions, Manuel Martin Sierra, Nicolas Barre, Anna Schaeffer (Mar. 7); Padre Pio (May 2); Fr. Stefan Wincenty Frelichowski (June 7); 108 Polish Martyrs, Regina Protmann, Edmund Bojanowski (June 13).

ROMAN CURIA

The Roman Curia is the Church's network of central administrative agencies (called dicasteries) serving the Vatican and the local churches, with authority granted by the Pope.

The Curia evolved gradually from advisory assemblies or synods of the Roman clergy with whose assistance the popes directed church affairs during the first 11 centuries. Its original office was the Apostolic Chancery, established in the fourth century to transmit documents. The antecedents of its permanently functioning agencies and offices were special commissions of cardinals and prelates. Its establishment in a form resembling what it is now dates from the second half of the 16th century.

Pope Paul VI initiated a four-year reorganization study in 1963 which resulted in the constitution *Regimini Ecclesiae Universae*. The document was published Aug. 18, 1967, and went into full effect in March, 1968. Pope John Paul II, in the apostolic constitution *Pastor Bonus*, published June 28, 1988, and effective Mar. 1, 1989, ordered modifications of the Curia based on the broad outline of Paul VI's reorganization.

In accordance with Pope John Paul II's reform effective Mar. 1, 1989, and later revisions, the Curia consists of the Secretariat of State, nine congregations (governing agencies), three tribunals (judicial agencies), 11 councils (promotional agencies) and three offices (specialized service agencies). All have equal juridical status with authority granted by the Pope.

SECRETARIAT OF STATE

The Secretariat of State, *Palazzo Apostolico Vaticano*, Vatican City. Cardinal Angelo Sodano, Secretary of State; Most Rev. Giovanni Battista Re, Deputy for General Affairs; Most Rev. Jean Louis Tauran, Secretary for Relations with States.

The Secretariat of State provides the pope with the closest possible assistance in the care of the universal Church. It consists of two sections:

· The Section for General Affairs assists the Pope in expediting daily business of the Holy See. It coordinates curial operations; prepares drafts of documents entrusted to it by the pope; has supervisory duties over the *Acta Apostolicae Sedis, Annuario Pontificio,* the Vatican Press Office and the Central Statistics Office.

· The Section for Relations with States (formerly the Council for Public Affairs of the Church, a separate body) handles diplomatic and other relations with civil governments. Attached to it is a Council of Cardinals and Bishops.

Background: Evolved gradually from secretarial offices (dating back to the 15th century) and the Congregation for Extraordinary Ecclesiastical Affairs (dating back to 1793; restructured as the Council for the Public Affairs of the Church by Paul VI in 1967). John Paul II gave it its present form in his June 28, 1988, reform of the Curia.

CONGREGATIONS

Congregation for the Doctrine of the Faith: Piazza del S. Uffizio 11, 00193 Rome, Italy. Cardinal Joseph Ratzinger, prefect; Most Rev. Tarcisio Bertone, S.D.B., secretary.

Has responsibility to safeguard the doctrine of faith and morals. Accordingly, it examines doctrinal questions; promotes studies thereon; evaluates theological opinions and, when necessary and after prior consultation with concerned bishops, reproves those regarded as opposed to principles of the faith; examines books on doctrinal matters and can reprove such works, if the contents so warrant, after giving authors the opportunity to defend themselves. It examines matters pertaining to the Privilege of Faith (Petrine Privilege) in marriage cases, and safeguards the dignity of the sacrament of penance. Attached to the congregation are the Pontifical Biblical Commission and the Theological Commission.

Background: At the beginning of the 13th century, legates of Innocent III were commissioned as the Holy Office of the Inquisition to combat heresy; the same task was entrusted to the Dominican Order by Gregory IX in 1231 and to the Friars Minor by Innocent IV from 1243 to 1254. On July 21, 1542 (apostolic constitution *Licet*), Paul III instituted a permanent congregation of cardinals with supreme and universal competence over matters concerning heretics and those suspected of heresy. Pius IV, St. Pius V and Sixtus V further defined the work of the congregation. St. Pius X changed its name to the Congregation of the Holy Office. Paul VI (*motu proprio Integrae Servandae*, Dec. 7, 1965), began reorganization of the Curia with this body, to which he gave the new title, Congregation for the Doctrine of the Faith. Its orientation is not merely negative, in the condemnation of error, but positive, in the promotion of orthodox doctrine.

Congregation for the Oriental Churches: Palazzo del Bramante, Via della Conciliazione 34, 00193 Rome, Italy. Cardinal Achille Silvestrini, prefect; Most Rev. Miroslav Stefan Marusyn, secretary. Members include all patriarchs of the Eastern Catholic Churches and major archbishops.

Has competence in matters concerning the persons and discipline of Eastern Catholic Churches. It has jurisdiction over territories in which the majority of Christians belong to Eastern Churches (i.e., Egypt, the Sinai Peninsula, Eritrea, Northern Ethiopia, Southern Albania, Bulgaria, Cyprus, Greece, Iran, Iraq, Lebanon, Palestine, Syria, Jordan, Turkey, Afghanistan); also, over minority communities of Eastern

Church members no matter where they live.

Background: Established by Pius IX Jan. 6, 1862 (apostolic constitution *Romani Pontifices*), and united with the Congregation for the Propagation of the Faith. The congregation was made autonomous by Benedict XV May 1, 1917 (*motu proprio Dei Providentis*), and given wider authority by Pius XI Mar. 25, 1938 (motu proprio *Sancta Dei Ecclesia*).

Congregation for Divine Worship and the Discipline of the Sacraments: Piazza Pio XII 10, 00193 Rome, Italy. Cardinal Jorge Arturo Medina Estévez, prefect; Most Rev. Francesco Pio Tamburrino, O.S.B., secretary.

Supervises everything pertaining to the promotion and regulation of the liturgy, primarily the sacraments, without prejudice to the competencies of the Congregation for the Doctrine of the Faith. Attached to the congregation are special commissions treating causes of nullity of sacred ordinations and dispensations from obligations of sacred ordination of deacons and priests.

Background: Originally two separate congregations: the Congregation for Divine Worship (instituted by Paul VI, May 8, 1969) and the Congregation for the Discipline of the Sacraments (established by St. Pius X, June 29, 1908, to replace the Congregation of Rites instituted by Pope Sixtus V in 1588). They were united by Paul VI, July 11, 1975, as the Congregation for the Sacraments and Divine Worship; reestablished as separate congregations by John Paul II in an autograph letter of Apr. 5, 1984, and reunited anew by the same Pope, June 28, 1988 (apostolic constitution *Pastor Bonus*) as the Congregation for Divine Worship and the Discipline of the Sacraments.

Congregation for the Causes of Saints: Piazza Pio XII 10, 00193 Rome, Italy. Prefect, Most Rev. José Saraiva Martins, C.F.M.; Most Rev. Edward Nowak, secretary.

Handles matters connected with beatification and canonization causes (in accordance with revised procedures decreed in 1983), and the preservation of relics.

Background: Established by Sixtus V in 1588 as the Congregation of Rites; affected by legislation of Pius XI in 1930; title changed and functions defined by Paul VI, 1969 (apostolic constitution *Sacra Rituum Congregatio*). It was restructured and canonization procedures were revised by John Paul II in 1983 (apostolic constitution *Divinus Perfectionis Magister*).

Congregation for Bishops: Piazza Pio XII 10, 00193 Rome, Italy. Cardinal Lucas Moreira Neves, O.P., prefect; Most Rev. Francesco Monterisi, secretary.

Has functions related in one way or another to bishops and the jurisdictions in which they serve. It supervises the Pontifical Commission for Latin America. Attached to the congregation are a central coordinating office for Military Vicars (established Feb. 2, 1985) and an office for coordinating *ad limina* visits (established June 29, 1988).

Background: Established by Sixtus V Jan. 22, 1588 (apostolic constitution *Immensa*); given an extension of powers by St. Pius X June 20, 1908, and Pius XII Aug. 1, 1952 (apostolic constitution *Exsul Familia*); given present title (was known as Consistorial Congregation) by Paul VI (Aug. 1, 1967); competencies redefined by John Paul II, June 28, 1988.

Congregation for the Evangelization of Peoples: Piazza di Spagna 48, 00187 Rome, Italy. Cardinal Jozef Tomko, prefect; Most Rev. Marcello Zago, O.M.I., secretary; Most Rev. Charles A. Schleck, C.S.C., adjunct secretary.

Directs and coordinates missionary work throughout the world. Accordingly, it has competence over those matters which concern all the missions established for the spread of Christ's kingdom without prejudice to the competence of other congregations. These include: fostering missionary vocations; assigning missionaries to fields of work; establishing ecclesiastical jurisdictions and proposing candidates to serve them as bishops and in other capacities; encouraging the recruitment and development of indigenous clergy; mobilizing spiritual and financial support for missionary activity.

To promote missionary cooperation, the congregation has a Supreme Council for the Direction of Pontifical Missionary Works composed of the Missionary Union of the Clergy and Religious, the Society for the Propagation of the Faith, the Society of St. Peter the Apostle for Native Clergy, the Society of the Holy Childhood, and the International Center of Missionary Animation.

Background: Originated as a commission of cardinals by St. Pius V and Gregory XII for missions in East and West Indies, Italo-Greeks and for ecclesiastical affairs in Protestant territories of Europe; Clement VIII instituted a Congregation of the Propagation of the Faith in 1599 which ceased to exist after several years. Erected as a stable congregation by Gregory XV June 22, 1622 (apostolic constitution *Inscrutabili Divinae*); its functions were redefined by John Paul II, June 28, 1988.

Congregation for the Clergy: Piazza Pio XII 3, 00193 Rome, Italy. Cardinal Darío Castrillón Hoyos, prefect; Most Rev. Csaba Ternyák, secretary.

Has three offices with competencies concerning the life, discipline, rights and duties of the clergy; the preaching of the Word, catechetics, norms for religious education of children and adults; preservation and administration of the temporal goods of the Church. Attached to it are the International Council for Catechetics (established in 1973 by Paul VI) and the Institute *Sacrum Ministerium* for the permanent formation of the clergy (established in line with John Paul II's 1992 apostolic exhortation *Pastores Dabo Vobis*).

Background: Established by Pius IV Aug. 2, 1564 (apostolic constitution *Alias Nos*), under the title, Congregation of the Cardinals Interpreters of the Council of Trent; affected by legislation of Gregory XIII and Sixtus V; known as Congregation of the Council until Aug. 15, 1967, when Paul VI renamed it the Congregation for the Clergy and redefined its competency; John Paul II gave it added responsibilities June 28, 1988.

Congregation for Institutes of Consecrated Life and Societies of Apostolic Life: Piazza Pio XII 3, 00193 Rome, Italy. Cardinal Eduardo Martinez Somalo, prefect; Most. Rev. Piergiorgio Silvano Nesti, C.P., secretary.

Has competence over institutes of Religious, secular institutes, societies of the apostolic life and third (secular) orders. With two sections, the congregation has authority in matters related to the establishment,

general direction and suppression of the various institutes; general discipline in line with their rules and constitutions; the movement toward renewal and adaptation of institutes in contemporary circumstances; the setting up and encouragement of councils and conferences of major religious superiors for intercommunication and other purposes.

Background: Founded by Sixtus V May 27, 1586, with the title, Congregation for Consultations of Regulars; confirmed by the apostolic constitution *Immensa* Jan. 22, 1588; made part of the Congregation for Consultations of Bishops and other Prelates in 1601; made autonomous by St. Pius X in 1908 as Congregation of Religious; title changed to Congregation for Religious and Secular Institutes by Paul VI in 1967; given present title by John Paul II, June 28, 1988.

Congregation for Catholic Education (for Seminaries and Institutes of Study): Piazza Pio XII 3, 00193 Rome, Italy. Cardinal Pio Laghi, prefect; Most Rev. Giuseppe Pittau, S.J., secretary.

Has supervisory competence over institutions and works of Catholic education. It carries on its work through three offices. One office handles matters connected with the direction, discipline and temporal administration of seminaries, and with the education of diocesan clergy, religious and members of secular institutes. A second office oversees Catholic universities, faculties of study and other institutions of higher learning inasmuch as they depend on the authority of the Church; encourages cooperation and mutual assistance among Catholic institutions, and the establishment of Catholic hospices and centers on campuses of non-Catholic institutions. A third office is concerned in various ways with all Catholic schools below the college-university level, with general questions concerning education and studies, and with the cooperation of conferences of bishops and civil authorities in educational matters. The congregation supervises Pontifical Works for Priestly Vocations.

Background: The title (Congregation of Seminaries and Universities) and functions of the congregation were defined by Benedict XV Nov. 4, 1915; Pius XI, in 1931 and 1932, and Pius XII, in 1941 and 1949, extended its functions; Paul VI changed its title to Congregation for Catholic Education in 1967; given its present title by Pope John Paul II, June 28, 1988. Its work had previously been carried on by two other congregations erected by Sixtus V in 1588 and Leo XII in 1824.

Inter-Agency Curia Commissions

In accordance with provisions of the apostolic constitution *Pastor Bonus,* John Paul II established the following interdepartmental permanent commissions to handle matters when more than one agency of the Curia is involved in activities:

• For matters concerning appointments to local Churches and the setting up and alteration of them and their constitution (Mar. 22, 1989). Members include officials of the Secretariat of State and Congregation for Bishops. President, Cardinal Angelo Sodano, Secretary of State.

• For matters concerning members, individually or as a community, of Institutes of Consecrated Life founded or working in mission territories (Mar. 22,

1989). Members include officials of the Congregations for the Evangelization of Peoples and for Institutes of Consecrated Life and Societies of Apostolic Life. President: Cardinal Jozef Tomko, prefect of the Congregation for the Evangelization of Peoples.

• For the formation of candidates for Sacred Orders (Mar. 22, 1989). Members include officials of the Congregations for Catholic Education, for Institutes of Consecrated Life and Societies of Apostolic Life, for Evangelization of Peoples, for Oriental Churches. President: Cardinal Pio Laghi, prefect of the Congregation for Catholic Education.

• For promoting a more equitable distribution of priests throughout the world (July 20, 1991). Members include secretaries of congregations for Evangelization of Peoples, for the Clergy, Catholic Education, for the Institutes of Consecrated Life and Societies of Apostolic Life; and vice-president of Commission for Latin America. President: Cardinal Pio Laghi, prefect of the Congregation for Catholic Education.

• For the Church in Eastern Europe (Jan. 15, 1993), replacing the Pontifical Commission for Russia which was terminated. The commission is concerned with both Latin and Eastern-rite churches in territories of the former Soviet Union and other nations affected by the historical circumstances resulting from atheistic communism. It is responsible for promoting the apostolic mission of the Church and fostering ecumenical dialogue with the Orthodox and other Churches of the Eastern tradition. Members, under presidency of Cardinal Secretary of State, include the secretary and undersecretary of the Section for Relations with States and secretaries of Congregations for the Oriental Churches, for the Clergy, for Institutes of Consecrated Life and Societies of Apostolic Life, secretary of the Pontifical Council for Promoting Christian Unity. President, Cardinal Angelo Sodano.

TRIBUNALS

Apostolic Penitentiary: Piazza della Cancelleria 1, 00186 Rome, Italy. Cardinal William Wakefield Baum, major penitentiary; Msgr. Luigi de Magistris, regent.

Has jurisdiction for the internal forum only (sacramental and non-sacramental). It issues decisions on questions of conscience; grants absolutions, dispensations, commutations, sanations and condonations; has charge of non-doctrinal matters pertaining to indulgences.

Background: Origin dates back to the 12th century; affected by the legislation of many popes; radically reorganized by St. Pius V in 1569; jurisdiction limited to the internal forum by St. Pius X; Benedict XV annexed the Office of Indulgences to it Mar. 25, 1917.

Apostolic Signatura: Piazza della Cancelleria 1, 00186 Rome, Italy. Most Rev. Zenon Grocholewski, prefect; Most Rev. Francesco Saverio Salerno, secretary.

The principal concerns of this supreme court of the Church are to resolve questions concerning juridical procedure and to supervise the observance of laws and rights at the highest level. It decides the jurisdictional competence of lower courts and has jurisdiction in cases involving personnel and decisions of the Rota. It is the supreme court of the State of Vatican City.

Background: A permanent office of the Signatura has existed since the time of Eugene IV in the 15th century; affected by the legislation of many popes; reorganized by St. Pius X in 1908 and made the supreme tribunal of the Church.

Roman Rota: Piazza della Cancelleria 1, 00186 Rome, Italy. Most Rev. Mario Francesco Pompedda, dean.

The ordinary court of appeal for cases appealed to the Holy See. It is best known for its competence and decisions in cases involving the validity of marriage.

Background: Originated in the Apostolic Chancery; affected by the legislation of many popes; reorganized by St. Pius X in 1908; further revised by Pius XI in 1934; new norms approved and promulgated by John Paul II in 1982 and 1987.

PONTIFICAL COUNCILS

Pontifical Council for the Laity: Piazza S. Calisto 16, 00153 Rome, Italy. Cardinal James Francis Stafford, president; Most Rev. Stanislaw Rylko, secretary; Prof. Guzman Carriquiry, undersecretary.

Its competence covers the apostolate of the laity and their participation in the life and mission of the Church. Members are mostly lay people from different parts of the world and involved in different apostolates.

Background: Established on an experimental basis by Paul VI Jan. 6, 1967; given permanent status Dec. 10, 1976 (*motu proprio Apostolatus Peragendi*).

Pontifical Council for Promoting Christian Unity: Via dell' Erba 1, 00193 Rome, Italy. Cardinal Edward I. Cassidy, president; Cardinal Johannes Willebrands, president emeritus; Most Rev. Walter Kasper, secretary.

Handles relations with members of other Christian ecclesial communities; deals with the correct interpretation and execution of the principles of ecumenism; initiates or promotes Catholic ecumenical groups and coordinates on national and international levels the efforts of those promoting Christian unity; undertakes dialogue regarding ecumenical questions and activities with churches and ecclesial communities separated from the Apostolic See; sends Catholic observer-representatives to Christian gatherings, and invites to Catholic gatherings observers of other churches; orders into execution conciliar decrees dealing with ecumenical affairs. The **Commission for Religious Relations with the Jews** is attached to the secretariat.

Background: Established by John XXIII June 5, 1960, as a preparatory secretariat of the Second Vatican Council; raised to commission status during the first session of the council in the fall of 1962; status as a secretariat confirmed and functions defined by Paul VI in 1966 and 1967; made a pontifical council by John Paul II, June 28, 1988.

Pontifical Council for the Family: Piazza S. Calisto 16, 00153 Rome, Italy. Cardinal Alfonso López Trujillo, president; Most Rev. Francisco Gil Hellín, secretary.

Is concerned with promoting the pastoral care of families so they may carry out their educative, evangelizing and apostolic mission and make their influence felt in areas such as defense of human life and responsible procreation according to the teachings of the Church. Members, chosen by the Pope, are married couples and men and women from all parts of the world and representing different cultures. They meet in general assembly at least once a year.

Background: Instituted by John Paul II May 9, 1981, replacing the Committee for the Family established by Paul VI Jan. 11, 1973.

Pontifical Council for Justice and Peace: Piazza S. Calisto 16, 00153 Rome, Italy. Most Rev. François Xavier Nguyên Van Thuân, president; Most Rev. Diarmuid Martin, secretary.

Its primary competence is to promote justice and peace in the world according to the Gospels and social teaching of the Church.

Background: Instituted by Paul VI Jan. 6, 1967, on an experimental basis; reconstituted and made a permanent commission Dec. 10, 1976; its competence was redefined and it was made a pontifical council June 28, 1988, by John Paul II.

Pontifical Council "Cor Unum": Piazza S. Calisto 16, 00153 Rome, Italy. Most Rev. Paul Josef Cordes, president; secretary, Msgr. Karel Kasteel.

Its principal aims are to provide informational and coordinating services for Catholic aid and human development organizations and projects on a worldwide scale. Attached to the council are the John Paul II Foundation for the Sahel and *"Populorum Progressio."*

Background: Instituted by Paul VI July 15, 1971.

Pontifical Council for Pastoral Care of Migrants and Itinerant Peoples: Piazza S. Calisto 16, 00153 Rome, Italy. Most Rev. Stephen Fumio Hamao president; Most Rev. Emmanuel Milingo, special delegate; Most Rev. Francesco Gioia, O.F.M. Cap., secretary.

Is concerned with pastoral assistance to migrants, nomads, tourists, sea and air travelers.

Background: Instituted by Paul VI and placed under general supervision of Congregation for Bishops, Mar. 19, 1970; made autonomous as a pontifical council and renamed by John Paul II, June 28, 1988.

Pontifical Council for Pastoral Assistance to Health Care Workers: Via della Conciliazione 3, 00193 Rome, Italy. Most Rev. Javier Lozano Barragán, president; Most Rev. José Luis Redrado Marchite, O.H., secretary.

Its functions are to stimulate and foster the work of formation, study and action carried out by various international Catholic organizations in the health care field.

Background: Established in 1985 as a commission by John Paul II; made a council June 28, 1988.

Pontifical Council for the Interpretation of Legislative Texts: Piazza Pio XII 10, 00193 Rome, Italy. Most Rev. Julián Herranz, president; Most Rev. Bruno Bertagna, secretary.

Primary function is the authentic interpretation of the universal laws of the Church.

Background: Established by John Paul II, Jan. 2, 1984, as the Pontifical Commission for the Authentic Interpretation of the Code of Canon Law; name changed and given additional functions June 28, 1988. Its competency was extended in 1991 to include interpretation of Code of Canon Law of Oriental Church which was promulgated in 1990.

Pontifical Council for Interreligious Dialogue: Via dell' Erba 1, 00193 Rome, Italy. Cardinal Francis Arinze, president; Most Rev. Michael Louis Fitzgerald, M. Afr., secretary.

Its function is to promote studies and dialogue for the purpose of increasing mutual understanding and respect between Christians and non-Christians. The Commission for Religious Relations with Muslims is attached to the council.

Background: Established by Paul VI May 19, 1964, as the Secretariat for Non-Christians; given present title and functions by John Paul II, June 28, 1988.

Pontifical Council for Culture: Piazza S. Calisto 16, 00153 Rome, Italy. Cardinal Paul Poupard, president; Very Rev. Bernard Ardura, O. Praem., secretary.

Its functions are to foster the Church's and the Holy See's relations with the world of culture and to establish dialogue with those who do not believe in God or who profess no religion provided these are open to sincere cooperation. It consists of two sections: (1) faith and culture; (2) dialogue with cultures. Attached to it is the Coordinating Council for Pontifical Academies.

Background: Present council with expanded functions was instituted by John Paul II (motu proprio of Mar. 25, 1993) through the merger of the Pontifical Council for Culture (established May 20, 1982, by John Paul II) and the Pontifical Council for Dialogue with Non-Believers (established by Paul VI Apr. 9, 1965, as the secretariat for Non-Believers).

Pontifical Council for Social Communications: Palazzo S. Carlo, 00120 Vatican City. Most Rev. John P. Foley, president; Most Rev. Pierfranco Pastore, secretary; Mr. Hans-Peter Röthlin, undersecretary; Cardinal Andrzej M. Deskur, president emeritus.

Engaged in matters pertaining to instruments of social communication so that through them the message of salvation and human progress is fostered and carried forward in civil culture and mores.

Background: Instituted on an experimental basis by Pius XII in 1948; reorganized three times in the 1950s; made permanent commission by John XXIII Feb. 22, 1959; established as council and functions restated by John Paul II June 28, l988.

OFFICES

Apostolic Camera: Palazzo Apostolico, 00120 Vatican City. Cardinal Eduardo Martinez Somalo, chamberlain of the Holy Roman Church; Most Rev. Ettore Cunial, vice-chamberlain.

Administers the temporal goods and rights of the Holy See between the death of one pope and the election of another, in accordance with special laws.

Background: Originated in the 11th century; reorganized by Pius XI in 1934; functions redefined (especially of camerlengo) by subsequent legislation in 1945, 1962 and 1975.

Administration of the Patrimony of the Apostolic See: Palazzo Apostolico, 00120 Vatican City. Most Rev. Agostino Cacciavillan, president; Most Rev. Claudio Maria Celli, secretary.

Handles the estate of the Apostolic See under the direction of papal delegates acting ith ordinary or extraordinary authorization.

Background: Some of its functions date back to 1878; established by Paul VI Aug. 15, 1967.

Prefecture for the Economic Affairs of the Holy See: Largo del Colonnato 3, 00193 Rome, Italy. Most Rev.Sergio Sebastiani, pro-president; Msgr. Franco Croci, secretary.

A financial office which coordinates and supervises administration of the temporalities of the Holy See. Background: Established by Paul VI Aug. 15, 1967; functions redefined by John Paul II, June 28, 1988.

Other Curia Agencies

Prefecture of the Papal Household: Most Rev. James M. Harvey, prefect; Most Rev. Stanislaw Dziwisz, adjunct-prefect.

Oversees the papal chapel — which is at the service of the pope in his capacity as spiritual head of the Church — and the pontifical family — which is at the service of the pope as a sovereign. It arranges papal audiences, has charge of preparing non-liturgical elements of papal ceremonies, makes all necessary arrangements for papal visits and trips outside the Vatican, and settles questions of protocol connected with papal audiences and other formalities.

Background: Established by Paul VI Aug. 15, 1967, under the title, Prefecture of the Apostolic Palace; it supplanted the Sacred Congregation for Ceremonies founded by Sixtus V Jan. 22, 1588. The office was updated and reorganized under the present title by Paul VI, Mar. 28, 1968.

Office for Liturgical Celebrations of the Supreme Pontiff: Palazzo Apostolico Vaticano, 00120 Vatican City. Most Rev. Piero Marini, Master of Ceremonies.

Prepares everything necessary for liturgical and other sacred celebrations by the Pope or in his name; directs everything in accordance with prescriptions of liturgical law.

Background: Evolved gradually from the early office of Apostolic Master of Ceremonies; affected by legislation of Pope Paul IV in 1563 and Benedict XV in 1917; restructured by Paul VI in 1967; given its present title (formerly known as Prefecture of Pontifical Ceremonies) and constituted as an autonomous agency of the Roman Curia by John Paul II, June 28, 1988.

Vatican Press Office: Via della Conciliazione 54, 00120 Vatican City. Joaquin Navarro-Valls, director. Established Feb. 29, 1968, to replace service agencies formerly operated by *L'Osservatore Romano* and an office created for press coverage of the Second Vatican Council. New directives were issued in 1986.

Vatican Information Service (VIS): Via della Conciliazione 54, 00120 Vatican City. Established Mar. 28, 1990, within the framework but distinct from the Vatican Press Office. Furnishes information, in English, French and Spanish, on pastoral and magisterial activity of the Pope through use of electronic mail and fax.

Central Statistics Office: Palazzo Apostolico, 00120 Vatican City. Established by Paul VI Aug. 15, 1967; attached to the Secretariat of State. Compiles, systematizes and analyzes information on the status and condition of the Church.

COMMISSIONS AND COMMITTEES

Listed below are non-curial institutes which assist in the work of the Holy See. Some are attached to curial agencies, as indicated. Other institutes are listed elsewhere in the Almanac; see Index.

Pontifical Commission for the Cultural Heritage of the Church: Established by John Paul II, June 28, 1988, as Pontifical Commission for Preserving the Church's Patrimony of Art and History and attached to the Congregation for the Clergy; made autonomous and given present title Mar. 25, 1993. Most Rev. Francesco Marchisano, president.

Pontifical Commission for Sacred Archeology: Instituted by Pius IX Jan, 6, 1852. Most Rev. Francesco Marchisano, president.

Pontifical Biblical Commission: Instituted by Leo XIII Oct. 30, 1902; completely restructured by Paul VI June 27, 1971; attached to the Congregation for the Doctrine of the Faith. Cardinal Joseph Ratzinger, president.

Pontifical Commission for Latin America: Instituted by Pius XII Apr. 19, 1958; attached to the Congregation for Bishops July, 1969; restructured by John Paul II in 1988. Cardinal Lucas Moreira Neves, O.P., president.

Pontifical Commission for the Revision and Emendation of the Vulgate: Established in 1984 by John Paul II to replace the Abbey of St. Jerome instituted by Pius XI in 1933. Rev. Jean Mallet, O.S.B., director.

Pontifical Commission "Ecclesia Dei": Established by John Paul II, July 2, 1988, to facilitate the return to full ecclesial communion of priests, seminarians and religious who belonged to the fraternity founded by Marcel Lefebvre. Cardinal Angelo Felici, president.

International Theological Commission: Instituted by Paul VI Apr. 11, 1969, as an advisory adjunct of no more than 30 theologians to the Congregation for the Doctrine of the Faith; definitive statutes promulgated by John Paul II, Aug. 6, 1982. Cardinal Joseph Ratzinger, president; Rev. Georges Cottier, O.P., general secretary.

Commission for Religious Relations with the Jews: Instituted by Paul VI, Oct. 22, 1974, to promote and foster relations of a religious nature between Jews and Christians; attached to the Council for Promoting Christian Unity. Cardinal Edward I. Cassidy, president.

Commission for Religious Relations with Muslims: Instituted by Paul VI, Oct. 22, 1974, to promote, regulate and interpret relations between Catholics and Muslims; attached to the Council for Interreligious Dialogue. Cardinal Francis Arinze, president.

Pontifical Committee for International Eucharistic Congresses: Instituted, 1879, by Pope Leo XIII; established as a pontifical committee with new statutes by John Paul II, Feb. 11, 1986. Cardinal Edouard Gagnon, president.

Pontifical Committee for Historical Sciences: Instituted by Pius XII Apr. 7, 1954, as a continuation of a commission dating from 1883. Msgr. Walter Brandmüller, president.

Committee for the Grand Jubilee of the Holy Year 2000: Instituted by John Paul II Nov. 15, 1994. Cardinal Roger Etchegaray, president; Crescenzio Sepe, secretary.

Vatican II Archives: Preserves the documents of the Second Vatican Council. Msgr. Vincenzo Carbone, director.

Disciplinary Commission of the Roman Curia: Most Rev. Mario Francesco Pompedda, president.

Council of Cardinals for Study of Organizational

and Economic Problems of the Holy See: Council established in 1981 by Pope John Paul II; composed of approximately 15 cardinals from countries throughout the world (present membership includes U.S. Cardinal O'Connor).

Commission for the Protection of the Historical and Artistic Monuments of the Holy See: Instituted by Pius XI in 1923, reorganized by Paul VI in 1963. Cardinal Virgilio Noè, president.

Institute for Works of Religion: Instituted by Pius XII June 27, 1942, to bank and administer funds for works of religion; replaced an earlier administration established by Leo XIII in 1887; reorganized by John Paul II (chirograph of Mar. 1, 1990). Headed by a commission of Cardinals, including Cardinals Sodano and O'Connor.

Fabric of St. Peter: Administration, care and preservation of Vatican Basilica. Cardinal Virgilio Noè, Archpriest of the Patriarchal Vatican Basilica, president.

Office of Papal Charities (Apostolic Almoner): Distributes alms and aid to those in need in the name of the Pope. Most Rev. Oscar Rizzato, almoner.

Labor Office of the Apostolic See (ULSA - *Ufficio del Lavoro della Sede Apostolica*): Has competence in regard to those who work for the Apostolic See; charged with settling labor issues. Instituted by John

Paul II (motu proprio of Jan. 1, 1989); functions reaffirmed and definitive text of statutes approved by John Paul II (*motu proprio* of Sept. 30, 1994). Cardinal Jan Schotte, C.I.C.M., president.

Internationalization

As of May 15, 1999, principal officials of the Roman Curia were from the following countries: Italy (Cards. Antonetti, Cheli, Fagiolo, Felici, Laghi, Monduzzi, Noè, Silvestrini, Sodano; Abps. Bertone, Celli, Cunial, Lajolo, Marchiano, Ré, Sepe, Zago; Bps. Bertagna, Marini, Pastore, Sposito); France (Cards. Etchegaray, Poupard, Abp. Tauran); United States (Cards. Baum, Stafford, Szoka, Abps. Foley, Schleck, Bp. Harvey); Spain (Card. Martinez Somalo; Abp. Herranz); Argentina (Abp. Mejía); Germany (Card. Ratzinger, Bps. Cordes, Kasper); Poland (Abps. Grocholewski, Nowak, Bp. Dziwisz); Australia (Card. Cassidy); Belgium (Card. Schotte); Benin (Card. Gantin); Brazil (Cardinal Moreira Neves, Abp. Agnelo); Canada (Card. Gagnon); Chile (Card. Medina Estévez); Colombia (Cards. Castrillón Hoyos, Lopez Trujillo); England (Bp. Fitzgerald); Mexico (Abp. Lozano Barrágan); Nigeria (Card. Arinze); Portugal (Abp. Saraiva Martins); Slovakia (Card. Tomko); Switzerland (Card. Agustoni); Ukraine (Abp. Marusyn); Vietnam (Nguyên Van Thuân); Japan (Hamao).

VATICAN CITY STATE

The State of Vatican City (*Stato della Città del Vaticano*) is the territorial seat of the papacy. The smallest sovereign state in the world, it is situated within the city of Rome, embraces an area of 108.7 acres, and includes within its limits the Vatican Palace, museums, art galleries, gardens, libraries, radio station, post office, bank, astronomical observatory, offices, apartments, service facilities, St. Peter's Basilica, and neighboring buildings between the Basilica and Viale Vaticano. The extraterritorial rights of Vatican City extend to more than 10 buildings in Rome, including the major basilicas and office buildings of various congregations of the Roman Curia, and to the papal villas at **Castel Gandolfo** 15 miles southeast of the City of Rome. Castel Gandolfo is the summer residence of the Holy Father.

The government of Vatican City is in the hands of the reigning pope, who has full executive, legislative and judicial power. The administration of affairs, however, is handled by the **Pontifical Commission for the State of Vatican City** under Cardinal Edmund Casimir Szoka. The legal system is based on Canon Law; in cases where this code does not obtain, the laws of the City of Rome apply. The City is an absolutely neutral state and enjoys all the rights and privileges of a sovereign power. The citizens of Vatican City, and they alone, owe allegiance to the pope as a temporal head of state.

Cardinals of the Roman Curia residing outside Vatican City enjoy the privileges of extraterritoriality. The Secretary General for the Governorate of the Vatican City State is Most. Rev. Gianni Danzi.

The normal population is approximately 1,000. While the greater percentage is made up of priests

and religious, there are several hundred lay persons living in Vatican City. They are housed in their own apartments in the City and are engaged in secretarial, domestic, trade and service occupations. About 3,400 lay persons are employed by the Vatican.

Services of honor and order are performed by the Swiss Guards, who have been charged with responsibility for the personal safety of popes since 1506. Additional police and ceremonial functions are under the supervision of a special office. These functions were formerly handled by the Papal Gendarmes, the Palatine Guard of Honor, and the Guard of Honor of the Pope (Pontifical Noble Guard) which Pope Paul VI disbanded Sept. 14, 1970.

The **Basilica of St. Peter**, built between 1506 and 1626, is the largest church in Christendom (with the exception of the Basilica of Our Lady Queen of Peace in Ivory Coast) and the site of most papal ceremonies. The pope's own patriarchal basilica, however, is **St. John Lateran**, whose origins date back to 324.

St. Ann's, staffed by Augustinian Fathers, is the parish church of Vatican City. Its pastor is appointed by the pope following the recommendation of the prior general of the Augustinians and the archpriest of the Vatican Basilica.

The Church of **Santa Susanna** was designated as the national church for Americans in Rome by Pope Benedict XV Jan. 10, 1922, and entrusted to the Paulist Fathers, who have served there continuously since then except for several years during World War II.

Pastoral care in Vatican City State, which is separate from the diocese of Rome, is entrusted to the archpriest of St. Peter's Basilica, who is also vicar general for Vatican City and the papal villas at Castel Gandolfo (chirograph of Pope John Paul II, Jan. 14, 1991). Cardinal Virgilio Noè was appointed to the posts, July 1, 1991.

The Vatican Library (00120 Vatican City; Rev. Raffaele Farina, S.D.B., prefect; Rev. Ambrogio Piazzoni, vice-prefect) has among its holdings 150,000 manuscripts, about 1,000,000 printed books, and 7,500 incunabula. The **Vatican Secret Archives** (00120 Vatican City; Rev. Sergio Pagano, prefect), opened to scholars by Leo XIII in 1881, contain central church documents dating back to the time of Innocent III (1198-1216). Most Rev. Jorge María Mejía is librarian and archivist of the Holy Roman Church.

The independent temporal power of the pope, which is limited to the confines of Vatican City and small areas outside, was for many centuries more extensive than it is now. As late as the nineteenth century, the pope ruled 16,000 square miles of Papal States across the middle of Italy, with a population of over 3,000,000. In 1870 forces of the Kingdom of Italy occupied these lands which, with the exception of the small areas surrounding the Vatican and Lateran in Rome and the Villas of Castel Gandolfo, became part of the Kingdom by the Italian law of May 13, 1871.

The **Roman Question**, occasioned by this seizure and the voluntary confinement of the pope to the Vatican, was settled with ratification of the Lateran Agreement June 7, 1929, by the Italian government and Vatican City. The agreement recognized Catholicism as the religion of Italy and provided, among oter things, a financial indemnity to the Vatican in return for the former Papal States; it became Article 7 of the Italian Constitution Mar. 26, 1947.

The Lateran Agreement was superseded by a new concordat given final approval by the Italian Chamber of Deputies Mar. 20 and formally ratified June 3, 1985.

Papal Flag

The papal flag consists of two equal vertical stripes of yellow and white, charged with the insignia of the papacy on the white stripe — triple crown or tiara over two crossed keys, one of gold and one of silver, tied with a red cord and two tassels. The divisions of the crown represent the teaching, sanctifying and ruling offices of the pope. The keys symbolize his jurisdictional authority.

The papal flag is a national flag inasmuch as it is the standard of the Supreme Pontiff as the sovereign of the state of Vatican City. It is also universally accepted by the faithful as a symbol of the supreme spiritual authority of the Holy Father.

Vatican Radio

The declared purpose of Vatican Radio Station HVJ is "that the voice of the Supreme Pastor may be heard throughout the world by means of the ether waves, for the glory of Christ and the salvation of souls." Designed by Guglielmo Marconi, the inventor of radio, and supervised by him until his death, the station was inaugurated by Pope Pius XI in 1931. The original purpose has been extended to a wide variety of programming.

Vatican Radio operates on international wave lengths, transmits programs in 37 languages, and serves as a channel of communication between the Vatican, church officials and listeners in general in many parts of the world. The station broadcasts about 400 hours a week throughout the world.

The daily English-language program for North America is broadcast on 6095, 7305, 9600 kilohertz as well as via satellite INTELSAT 325,5° East (Atlantic) — 4097.75 Mhz — LHCP polarization.

Frequencies, background information and audio files can be obtained via the World Wide Web homepages www.wrn.org/vatican-radio and www.vatican.va.

The staff of 415 broadcasters and technicians includes 30 Jesuits. Studios and offices are at Palazzo Pio, Piazza Pia, 3, 00193 Rome. The transmitters are situated at Santa Maria di Galeria, a short distance north of Rome. Pres., Rev. Roberto Tucci, S.J.

1999 Vatican Stamps and Coins

The Vatican Philatelic and Numismatic Office (00120 Vatican City) scheduled the following issues of stamps and coins for 1999. Issue dates are given where available.

Stamps: The Popes and the Holy Years: 1300-2000 (second issue).
- Europe 1999 — Subject: Reservations and/or National Parks
- Holy Sites in Plestine.
- Towards the Holy Year 2000.
- Journeys of His Holiness John Paul II in the world (1998)
- Christian Solemnity of Christmas
- Opening of the Holy Door

Postal Stationery: Aerogramme — Subject: VIII Centenary of the Founding of the Holy Trinity Order
Postcards: The "Via Francigena," jubilee itinerary
Publications: Vaticano 1999
Coins: Series for XX year (1998) of the Pontificate of John Paul II; in eight values (L. 10, 20, 50, 100, 200, 500, 1,000 two metal, 1,000 — silver). Subject: From the justice of each comes peace for all.
- Gold Coins — Year XX (1998); issued in two coin values (L. 50,000 and L. 100,000) Subject: Towards the Holy Year 2000 (Basilica of St. Mary Major).
- Celebrative L. 500 Silver Coin. Subject: 70th Annversary of the Founding of the State of vatican City: 1929-1999.
- Diptych of L. 10,000 Silver Coins. Subject: Towards the Holy Year 2000 (Resurrection and Pentecost).
- Gold Coins — Year XXI (1999); issued in two coin values (L. 50,000 and L. 100,000) Subject: Towards the Holy Year 2000 (Basilica of St.Peter's Basilica in the Vatican).

Papal Audiences

General audiences are scheduled weekly, on Wednesday.

In Vatican City, they are held in the Audience Hall on the south side of St. Peter's Basilica or, weather permitting, in St. Peter's Square. The hall, which was opened in 1971, has a seating capacity of 6,800 and a total capacity of 12,000. Adiences have been held during the summer at Castel Gandolfo when the pope is there on a working vacation.

General audiences last from about 60 to 90 minutes, during which the pope gives a talk and his blessing. A résumé of the talk, which is usually in Italian, is given in several languages. rrangements for papal audiences are handled by an office of the Prefecture of the Apostolic Household.

American visitors can obtain passes for general audiences by applying to the Bishops' Office for United States Visitors to the Vatican, Casa Santa Maria, Via dell'Umilita, 30, 00187 Rome. Private and group audiences are reserved for dignitaries of various categories and for special occasions.

Publications

Acta Apostolicae Sedis, 00120 Vatican City: The only "official commentary" of the Holy See, was established in 1908 for the publication of activities of the Holy See, laws, decrees and acts of congregations and tribunals of the Roman Curia. The first edition was published in January, 1909. St. Pius X made AAS an official organ in 1908. Laws promulgated for the Church ordinarily take effect three months after the date of their publication in this commentary. The publication, mostly in Latin, is printed by the Vatican Press. The immediate predecessor of this organ was *Acta Sanctae Sedis*, founded in 1865 and given official status by the Congregation for the Propagation of the Faith in 1904.

Annuario Pontificio, 00120 Vatican City: The year-book of the Holy See. It is edited by the Central Statistics Office of the Church and is printed in Italian, with some portions in other languages, by the Vatican Press. It covers the worldwide organization of the Church, lists members of the hierarchy, and includes a wide range of statistical information. The publication of a statistical yearbook of the Holy See dates back to 1716, when a volume called *Notizie* appeared. Publication under the present title began in 1860, was suspended in 1870, and resumed again in 1872 under the title *Catholic Hierarchy*. This volume was printed privately at first, but has been issued by the Vatican Press since 1885. The title *Annuario Pontificio* was restored in 1912, and the yearbook was called an "official publication" until 1924.

L'Osservatore Romano, Via del Pellegrino, 00120 Vatican City: The daily newspaper of the Holy See. It began publication July 1, 1861, as an independent enterprise under the ownership and direction of four Catholic laymen headed by Marcantonio Pacelli, vice minister of the interior under Pope Pius IX and a grandfather of the late Pius XII. Leo XIII bought the publication in 1890, making it the "pope's" own newspaper.

The only official material in *L'Osservatore Romano* is that which appears under the heading, "*Nostre Informazioni*." This includes notices of appointments by the Holy See, the texts of papal encyclicals and addresses by the Holy Father and others, various types of documents, accounts of decisions and rulings of administrative bodies, and similar items. Additional material includes news and comment on develop-

ments in the Church and the world. Italian is the language most used. The editorial board is directed by Prof. Mario Agnes. A staff of about 15 reporters covers Rome news sources. A corps of correspondents provides foreign coverage.

A weekly roundup edition in English was inaugurated in 1968 (Msgr. Robert J. Dempsey, on leave from Chicago archdiocese, is editor). Other weekly editions are printed in French (1949), Italian (1950), Spanish (1969), Portuguese (1970) and German (1971). The Polish edition (1980) is published monthly. *L'Osservatore della Domenica* is published weekly as a supplement to the Sunday issue of the daily edition.

Vatican Television Center (*Centro Televisivo Vaticano*, CTV), Palazzo Belvedere, 00120 Vatican City: Instituted by John Paul II Oct. 23, 1983, with the rescript, *Ex Audentia*. Dr. Emilio Rossi is president of the administrative council.

Vatican Press, 00120 Vatican City: The official printing plant of the Vatican. The Vatican press was conceived by Marcellus II and Pius IV but was actually founded by Sixtus V on Apr. 27, 1587, to print the Vulgate and the writings of the Fathers of the Church and other authors. A Polyglot Press was established in 1626 by the Congregation for the Propagation of the Faith to serve the needs of the Oriental Church. St. Pius X merged both presses under the title Vatican Polyglot Press. It was renamed Vatican Press July 1, 1991, by John Paul II following restructuring. The plant has facilities for the printing of a wide variety of material in about 30 languages. Dir., Rev. Elio Torrigiani, S.D.B.

Vatican Publishing House (*Libreria Editrice Vaticana*), Piazza S. Pietro, 00120 Vatican City: Formerly an office of the Vatican Press to assist in the circulation of the liturgical and juridical publications of the Apostolic See, the congregations and later the *Acta Apostolicae Sedis*. In 1926, with the expansion of publishing activities and following the promulgation of the 1917 Code, the office was made an independent entity. An administrative council and editorial commission were instituted in 1983; in 1988 *Pastor Bonus* listed it among institutes joined to the Holy See; new statutes were approved by the Secretariat of State July 1, 1991. Chairman, Most Rev. Giovanni De Andrea.

Activities of the Holy See: An annual documentary volume covering the activities of the pope and of the congregations, commissions, tribunals and offices of the Roman Curia.

Statistical Yearbook of the Church: Issued by the Central Statistics Office of the Church, it contains principal data concerning the presence and work of the Church in the world. The first issue was published in 1972 under the title Collection of Statistical Tables, 1969. It is printed in corresponding columns of Italian and Latin. Some of the introductory material is printed in other languages.

DIPLOMATIC ACTIVITIES OF THE HOLY SEE

REPRESENTATIVES OF THE HOLY SEE

Representatives of the Holy See and their functions were the subject of a document entitled *Sollicitudo Omnium Ecclesiarum* which Pope Paul VI issued on his own initiative under the date of June 24, 1969.

Delegates and Nuncios

Papal representatives "receive from the Roman Pontiff the charge of representing him in a fixed way in the various nations or regions of the world.

"When their legation is only to local churches, they are known as apostolic delegates. When to this legation, of a religious and ecclesial nature, there is added diplomatic legation to states and governments, they receive the title of nuncio, pro-nuncio, and internuncio." An apostolic nuncio has the diplomatic rank of ambassador extraordinary and plenipotentiary. Traditionally, because the diplomatic service of the Holy See has the longest uninterrupted history in the world, a nuncio has precedence among diplomats in the country to which he is accredited and serves as dean of the diplomatic corps on state occasions. Since 1965 pro-nuncios, also of ambassadorial rank, have been assigned to countries in which this prerogative is not recognized. In recent years, the Vatican started to phase out the title of pro-nuncio. The title of nuncio (with an asterisk denoting he is not dean of the diplomatic corps) has been given to the majority of appointments of ambassadorial rank. See also: Other Representatives.

Service and Liaison

Representatives, while carrying out their general and special duties, are bound to respect the autonomy of local churches and bishops. Their service and liaison responsibilities include the following:

- Nomination of Bishops: To play a key role in compiling, with the advice of ecclesiastics and lay persons, and submitting lists of names of likely candidates to the Holy See with their own recommendations.
- Bishops: To aid and counsel local bishops without interfering in the affairs of their jurisdictions.
- Episcopal Conferences: To maintain close relations with them and to assist them in every possible way. (Papal representatives do not belong to these conferences.)
- Religious Communities of Pontifical Rank: To advise and assist major superiors for the purpose of promoting and consolidating conferences of men and women religious and to coordinate their apostolic activities.
- Church-State Relations: The thrust in this area is toward the development of sound relations with civil governments and collaboration in work for peace and the total good of the whole human family.mission of a papal representative begins with appointment and assignment by the pope and continues until termination of his mandate. He acts "under the guidance and according to the instructions of the cardinal secretary of state to whom he is di-

rectly responsible for the execution of the mandate entrusted to him by the Supreme Pontiff." Normally representatives are required to retire at age 75.

NUNCIOS AND DELEGATES

(Sources: *Annuario Pontificio, L'Osservatore Romano, Acta Apostolicae Sedis*, Catholic News Service.), as of July 30, 1999: country, rank of legation (corresponding to rank of legate unless otherwise noted), name of legate (archbishop unless otherwise noted) as available. An asterisk indicates a nuncio who is not presently dean of the diplomatic corps.

Delegate for Papal Legations: Archbishop Carlo M. Viganò, titular Archbishop of Ulpiana. The post was established in 1973 to coordinate papal diplomatic efforts throughout the world. The office entails responsibility for "following more closely through timely visits the activities of papal representatives . . . and encouraging their rapport with the central offices" of the Secretariat of State.

Albania: Tirana, Nunciature; Giovanni Bulaitis.*

Algeria: Algiers, Nunciature; Augustine Kasujja* (also Nuncio* to Tunisia).

Andorra: Nunciature; Lajos Kada (Also nuncio to Spain).

Angola: Luanda, Nunciature; Aldo Cavalli* (also Nuncio* to São Tome and Principe). Diplomatic relations established July, 1997.

Antigua and Barbuda: Nunciature; Eugenio Sbarbaro, Pro-Nuncio (resides in Port of Spain, Trinidad).

Antilles: Apostolic Delegation; Eugenio Sbarbaro (resides in Port of Spain, Trinidad).

Arabian Peninsula: Apostolic Delegation; Antonio Mario Veglio (also nuncio in Kuwait and Lebanon; resides in Lebanon).

Argentina: Buenos Aires, Nunciature; Ubaldo Calabresi.

Armenia: Nunciature; Peter Stephan Zurbriggen* (resides in Tbilisi, Georgia; also nuncio* to Georgia and Azerbaijan). (Diplomatic relations established May 23, 1992.)

Australia: Canberra, Nunciature; Francesco Canalini, Nuncio.

Austria: Vienna, Nunciature; Donato Squicciarini.

Azerbaijan: Nunciature; Peter Stephan Zurbriggen* (resides in Tbilisi, Georgia; also nuncio* to Georgia and Armenia). (Diplomatic relations established May 23, 1992.)

Bahamas: Nunciature; Eugenio Sbarbaro, Pro-Nuncio (resides in Port of Spain, Trinidad).

Bangladesh: Dhaka, Nunciature; Edward Joseph Adams.*

Barbados: Nunciature; Eugenio Sbarbaro, Pro-Nuncio (resides in Port of Spain, Trinidad).

Belarus: Nunciature; Dominik Hrusovský.*

Belgium: Brussels, Nunciature; Pier Luigi Celata (also Nuncio to Luxembourg).

Belize: Nunciature; Giacinto Berloco, Pro-Nuncio (resides in Port of Spain, Trinidad).

Benin (formerly Dahomey): Nunciature; André Dupuy* (resides in Accra, Ghana).

Bolivia: La Paz, Nunciature; vacant.

Bosnia and Herzegovina: Sarajevo; Nunciature; Giuseppe Leanza *

Botswana: See South Africa.

Brazil: Brasilia, Nunciature; Alfio Rapisarda.

Brunei: See Malaysia and Brunei.

Bulgaria: Sofia, Nunciature (reestablished, 1990); Blasco Francisco Collaço.*

Burkina Faso: Ouagadougou, Nunciature; Mario Zenari*(resides in Abidjan, Côte d'Ivoire).

Burma: See Myanmar.

Burundi: Bujumbura, Nunciature; Emil Paul Tscherrig.*

Cambodia: Nunciature; Adriano Bernardini* (resides in Bangkok, Thailand). Diplomatic relations established March, 1994.

Cameroon: Yaounde, Nunciature; Félix del Blanco Prieto* (also Nuncio to Equatorial Guinea).

Canada: Ottawa, Nunciature; Paolo Romeo.*

Cape Verde, Republic of: Nunciature; Jean-Paul Gobel * (resides in Dakar, Senegal).

Central African Republic: Bangui, Nunciature; vacant * (also Nuncio* to Chad).

Chad: Nunciature; vacant* (resides in Bangui, Central African Republic).

Chile: Santiago, Nunciature; Luigi Ventura.

China, Republic of: Taipei (Taiwan), Nunciature; vacant.

Colombia: Bogota, Nunciature; Beniamino Stella.

Comoros: See Madagascar.(formerly Zaire)

Congo (formerly Zaire): Kinshasa-Gombe, Nunciature; Francisco-Javier Lozano Sebastian.*

Congo: Brazzaville, Nunciature; Luigi Pezzuto* (also pro-nuncio to Gabon).

Costa Rica: San Jose, Nunciature; Antonio Sozzo.

Côte d'Ivoire (Ivory Coast): Abidjan, Nunciature; vacant (also nuncio* to Niger and Burkina Faso).

Croatia: Zagreb, Nunciature; Giulio Einaudi.

Cuba: Havana, Nunciature; Luiz Robles Díaz.*

Cyprus: Nicosia, Nunciature; Pietro Sambi (also Nuncio to Israel), Pro-Nuncio.

Czech Republic: Prague, Nunciature; Giovanni Coppa.

Denmark: Copenhagen, Nunciature; Piero Biggio * (also Nuncio* to Finland, Iceland, Norway and Sweden).

Djibouti: Apostolic Delegation; Silvano Tomasi, C.S. (resides in Addis Ababa, Ethiopia).

Dominica: Nunciature; Eugenio Sbarbaro, Pro-Nuncio (resides in Port-of-Spain, Trinidad).

Dominican Republic: Santo Domingo, Nunciature; Francois Bacque (also serves as Apostolic Delegate to Puerto Rico).

Ecuador: Quito, Nunciature; Alain Lebeaupin.

Egypt: Cairo, Nunciature; Paolo Giglio.*

El Salvador: San Salvador, Nunciature; Giacinto Berloco.

Equatorial Guinea: Santa Isabel, Nunciature; Felix del Blanco Prieto* (resides in Yaounde, Cameroon).

Eritrea: Nunciature: Silvano Tomasi, C.S.* (resides in Ethiopia). Diplomatic relations established July 15, 1995.

Estonia: Nunciature; Erwin Josef Ender* (resides in Vilna, Lithuania).

Ethiopia: Addis Ababa, Nunciature; Silvano Tomasi,

C.S.* (also nuncio* to Eritrea and apostolic delegate to Djibouti).

European Community: Brussels, Belgium, Nunciature; vacant.

Fiji: Nunciature; Patrick Coveney* (resides in Wellington, New Zealand).

Finland: Helsinki, Nunciature; Piero Biggio * (resides in Denmark).

France: Paris, Nunciature; Fortunato Baldelli.

Gabon: Libreville, Nunciature; Luigi Pezzuto* (resides in Congo).

Gambia: Nunciature; vacant* (resides in Freetown, Sierra Leone).

Georgia: Tbilisi, Nunciature; Peter Stephan Zurbriggen* (also nuncio* to Armenia and Azerbaijan). (Diplomatic relations established May 23, 1992.)

Germany: Bonn, Nunciature; Giovanni Lajolo.

Ghana: Accra, Nunciature; André Dupuy* (also Nuncio to Benin and Togo).

Great Britain: London, Nunciature; Pablo Puente* (also papal representative to Gibraltar).

Greece: Athens, Nunciature; Paul Fouad Tabet.*

Grenada: Nunciature; Eugenio Sbarbaro, Pro-Nuncio (resides in Port of Spain, Trinidad).

Guatemala: Guatemala City, Nunciature; Ramiro Moliner Inglés.

Guinea: Conakry, Nunciature; vacant*(resides in Freetown, Sierra Leone).

Guinea Bissau: Nunciature; Jean-Paul Gobel* (resides at Dakar, Senegal).

Guyana: Nunciature; Eugenio Sbarbaro (resides in Port of Spain, Trinidad).

Haiti: Port-au-Prince, Nunciature; Luigi Bonazzi.

Honduras: Tegucigalpa, Nunciature; vacant.

Hungary: Budapest, Nunciature; Karl-Josef Rauber (also nuncio* to Moldova).

Iceland: Nunciature; Piero Biggio * (resides in Denmark).

India: New Delhi, Nunciature; Lorenzo Baldisseri, Pro-Nuncio (also Pro-Nuncio to Nepal).

Indonesia: Jakarta, Nunciature; Renzo Fratini, Pro-Nuncio.

Iran: Teheran, Nunciature; Romeo Panciroli M.C.C.I.*

Iraq: Baghdad, Nunciature; Giuseppe Lazzarotto* (also nuncio to Jordan).

Ireland: Dublin, Nunciature; Luciano Storero.

Israel: Nunciature; Pietro Sambi (also Nuncio to Cyprus). Diplomatic relations established June 15, 1994.

Italy: Rome, Nunciature; Andrea Cordero Lanza di Montezemolo (also nuncio to San Marino).

Ivory Coast: See Côte d'Ivoire.

Jamaica: Nunciature; Eugenio Sbarbaro, Pro-Nuncio (resides in Port of Spain, Trinidad).

Japan: Tokyo, Nunciature; Ambrose de Paoli, Pro-Nuncio.

Jerusalem and Palestine: Apostolic Delegation (also Nuncio to Israel): Pietro Sambi.

Jordan: Nunciature; Giuseppe Lazzarotto* (also nuncio to Iraq).

Kazakhstan: Almaty, Nunciature; Marian Oleú* (also nuncio* to Kyrgyzstan, Tajikistan and Uzbekistan).

Kenya: Nairobi, Nunciature; Giovanni Tonucci.*

Kiribati: Nunciature; Patrick Coveney* (resides in Wellington, New Zealand).

Korea: Seoul, Nunciature; Giovanni Battista Morandini* (also nuncio* to Mongolia).

Kuwait: Al Kuwait, Nunciature; Antonio Maria Vegliò* (resides in Lebanon).

Kyrgyzstan: Nunciature; Marian Oles* (resides in Kazakhstan).

Laos: Apostolic Delegation; Luigi Bressan, (resides in Bangkok, Thailand).

Latvia: Nunciature; Erwin Josef Ender* (resides in Vilna, Lithuania).

Lebanon: Beirut, Nunciature; Antonio Maria Vegliò (also nuncio* to Kuwait and apostolic delegate to Arabian Peninsula).

Lesotho: Maseru, Nunciature; Manuel Monteiro de Castro (also nuncio to South Africa, Namibia, and Swaziland; resides in Pretoria, South Africa).

Liberia: Monrovia, Nunciature; vacant* (resides in Freetown, Sierra Leone).

Libya: Nunciature; Luigi Gatti* (resides in Malta). Diplomatic relations established in 1997.

Liechtenstein: Nunciature; Pier Giacomo De Nicolò (resides in Bern, Switzerland).

Lithuania: Vilnius, Nunciature; Erwin Josef Ender (also nuncio* to Estonia and Latvia.).

Luxembourg: Nunciature; Pier Luigi Celata (resides in Brussels, Belgium).

Macedonia: Nunciature; Edmond Farhat* (also nuncio to Slovenia; resides in Slovenia).

Madagascar: Antananarivo, Nunciature; vacant* (also Nuncio* to Seychelles, and Mauritius and Apostolic Delegate to Comoros and Reunion).

Malawi: Lilongwe, Nunciature; Orlando Antonini, Pro-Nuncio (resides in Lusaka, Zambia).

Malaysia and Brunei: Apostolic Delegation; vacant (resides in Bangkok, Thailand).

Mali: Nunciature; Jean-Paul Gobel* (resides in Dakar, Senegal).

Malta: La Valletta, Nunciature; Luigi Gatti (also nuncio* to Libya).

Marshall Islands: Nunciature; Patrick Coveney* (resides in Wellington, New Zealand).

Mauritania: Nouakchott, Apostolic Delegation; Jean-Paul Gobel (resides in Dakar, Senegal).

Mauritius: Port Louis, Nunciature; vacant* (resides in Antananarivo, Madagascar).

Mexico: Mexico City, Nunciature; Justo Mullor García* (diplomatic relations established 1992).

Micronesia, Federated States of: Nunciature; Patrick Coveney* (resides in Wellington, New Zealand).

Moldova: Nunciature; Karl-Josef Rauber* (resides in Budapest, Hungary). (Diplomatic relations established May 23, 1992.)

Mongolia: Nunciature; Giovanni Battista Morandini* (resides in Seoul, South Korea).

Morocco: Rabat, Nunciature; Domenico De Luca.*

Mozambique: Maputo, nunciature; Juliusz Janusz.* Diplomatic relations established 1995.

Myanmar (formerly Burma): Apostolic Delegation; vacant (resides in Bangkok, Thailand).

Namibia: Nunciature; Manuel Monteiro de Castro * (resides in Pretoria, South Africa).

Nauru: Nunciature; Patrick Coveney*(resides in Wellington, New Zealand).

Nepal: Nunciature; vacant, Pro-Nuncio (resides in New Delhi, India).

Netherlands: The Hague, Nunciature; Angelo Acerbi.*

New Zealand: Wellington, Nunciature; Patrick Coveney.* (He is also Nuncio* to Fiji, Kiribati, Marshall Islands, Federated States of Micronesia, Tonga, Vanuatu and Western Samoa; Apostolic Delegate to Pacific Islands).

Nicaragua: Managua, Nunciature; Luigi Travaglino.

Niger: Niamey, Nunciature; vacant* (resides in Abidjan, Côte d'Ivoire.)

Nigeria: Lagos, Nunciature; Osvaldo Padilla, Pro-Nuncio.

Norway: Nunciature; Piero Biggio * (resides in Denmark).

Pacific Islands: Apostolic Delegation; Patrick Coveney (resides in Wellington, New Zealand).

Pakistan: Islamabad, Nunciature; Alessandro D'Errico.

Palau, Republic of: Palau, Nunciature; vacant*.

Panama: Panama City, Nunciature; Bruno Musarò.

Papua New Guinea: Port Moresby; Nunciature; Hans Schwemmer (also Nuncio* to Solomon Islands).

Paraguay: Asuncion, Nunciature; Antonio Lucibello.

Peru: Lima, Nunciature; Rino Passigato.

Philippines: Manila, Nunciature; Antonio Franco.

Poland: Warsaw; Nunciature; Józef Kowalczyk.

Portugal: Lisbon, Nunciature; Edoardo Rovida.

Puerto Rico: See **Dominican Republic.**

Reunion: See **Madagascar.**

Romania: Bucharest, Nunciature. Jean-Claude Périsset*

Russia (Federation of): Moscow; John Bukovsky, S.V.D., Apostolic Nuncio; appointed Representative of the Holy See to Russian Federation, Dec, 20, 1994.

Rwanda: Kigali, Nunciature. Salvatore Pennacchio.

Santa Lucia: Nunciature; Eugenio Sbarbaro, Pro-Nuncio (resides in Port of Spain, Trinidad).

Saint Vincent and the Grenadines: Nunciature; Eugenio Sbarbaro, Pro-Nuncio (resides in Port of Spain, Trinidad).

San Marino: Nunciature; Andrea Cordero Lanza di Montezemolo.

São Tome and Principe: Nunciature; Aldo Cavalli* (also nuncio* to Angola, where he resides).

Senegal: Dakar, Nunciature; Jean-Paul Gobel* (also Pro-Nuncio to Cape Verde, Guinea-Bissau and Mali; Apostolic Delegate to Mauritania.)

Seychelles Islands: Nunciature; vacant* (resides in Antananarivo, Madagascar).

Sierra Leone: Freetown, Nunciature (1996); vacant* (also Nuncio* to Gambia, Guinea and Liberia).

Singapore: Nunciature; Adriano Bernardini* (He is also nuncio* to Cambodia and Thailand and apostolic delegate to Laos, Malaysia and Brunei, and Myanmar.)

Slovakia: Nunciature; Luigi Dossena.

Slovenia: Ljubljana, Nunciature; Edmond Farhat (also nuncio to Macedonia).

Solomon Islands: Nunciature; Hans Schwemmer (resides in Port Moresby, Papua New Guinea).

Somalia: Apostolic Delegation (est. 1992); Marco Dino Brogi, O.F.M. (resides in Sudan).

South Africa: Pretoria, Nunciature; Manuel Monteiro de Castro.* (He is also nuncio* to Namibia and Swaziland and apostolic delegate to Botswana.)

Spain: Madrid, Nunciature; Lajos Kada.

Sri Lanka: Colombo, Nunciature; Thomas Yeh Sheng-nan*

Sudan: Khartoum, Nunciature; Mario Dino Brogi, O.F.M., Pro-Nuncio (also Apostolic Delegate to Somalia).

Suriname: Nunciature; Eugenio Sbarbaro * (resides in Port of Spain, Trinidad).

Swaziland: Nunciature; Manuel Monteiro de Castro* (resides in Pretoria, South Africa).

Sweden: Nunciature; Piero Biggio* (resides in Denmark).

Switzerland: Bern, Nunciature; Pier Giacomo De Nicolò (also nuncio to Liechtenstein).

Syria: (Syrian Arab Republic): Damascus, Nunciature, Diego Causero.*

Tajikistan: Nunciature; Marian Oles* (resides in Kazakhstan). Diplomatic relations established June 15, 1996.

Tanzania: Dar-es-Salaam, Nunciature; vacant.*

Thailand: Bangkok, Nunciature; Adriano Bernardini* (also Nuncio* to Cambodia and Singapore and Apostolic Delegate to Laos, Malaysia, Brunei, Myanmar).

Togo: Lome, Nunciature; André Dupuy* (resides in Accra, Ghana).

Tonga: Nunciature; Patrick Coveney* (resides in Wellington, New Zealand).

Trinidad and Tobago: Port of Spain, Trinidad, Nunciature; Eugenio Sbarbaro, Pro-Nuncio (also Pro-Nuncio to Antigua and Barbuda, Bahamas, Barbados, Belize, Dominica, Grenada, Jamaica, Saint Lucia, Saint Vincent and the Grenadines, Suriname and Apostolic Delegate to Antilles).

Tunisia: Tunis, Nunciature; Augustine Kasujja* (resides in Algiers, Algeria).

Turkey: Ankara, Nunciature; Luigi Conti.*

Turkmenistan: Nunciature; Luigi Conti.* Diplomatic relations established July 10, 1996 (resides in Ankara, Turkey).

Ukraine: Kiev, Nunciature; vacant.*

Uganda: Kampala, Nunciature; Pro-Nuncio, Christophe Pierre.

United States of America: Washington, D.C., Nunciature; Gabriel Montalvo, Pro-Nuncio.

Uruguay: Montevideo, Nunciature; Francesco De Nittis.

Uzbekistan: Nunciature. Marian Oles* (resides in Kazakhstan).

Vanuatu: Nunciature; Patrick Coveney* (resides in Wellington, New Zealand).

Venezuela: Caracas, Nunciature; Leonardo Sandri.

Vietnam: Apostolic Delegation; Vacant.

Western Samoa: Nunciature; Patrick Coveney* (resides in Wellington, New Zealand).

Yemen: San'a, Nunciature; vacant* (relations established in 1998).

Yugoslavia: Belgrade, Nunciature; Santos Abril y Castello.

Zaire: See Congo: Lusaka, Nunciature; Giuseppe Leanza, Pro-Nuncio (also Pro-Nuncio to Malawi).

Zambia: Lusaka, Nunciature; vacant, Orlando Antonini, Pro-Nuncio (also Pro-Nuncio to Malawi).

Zimbabwe: Harare, Nunciature; Peter Paul Prabhu.*

Current Pro-Nuncio to the U.S.

The representative of the Pope to the Church in the United States is Archbishop Gabriel Montalvo. Archbishop Montalvo was born Jan. 27, 1930, in Bogota, Colombia. Ordained to the priesthood Jan. 18, 1953,

he earned a doctorate in canon law and entered the Vatican diplomatic service in 1957, serving in nunciatures in Bolivia, Argentina, and El Salvador. From 1964 to 1974, Archbishop Montalvo served in the Secretariat of State, Vatican City, where he dealt with matters affecting the Churches in eastern Europe. In 1974, he was named Apostolic Nuncio in Honduras and Nicaragua. He was named Titular Archbishop of Celene on June 30, 1974. In 1980, Archbishop Montalvo was named Pro-Nuncio in Algeria and Tunisia and Apostolic Delegate in Libya. In 1986, Archbishop Montalvo was named Apostolic Pro-Nuncio in Yugoslavia and subsequently Apostolic Nuncio in Belarus. In 1993 he was appointed President of the Pontifical Ecclesiastical Academy where diplomats in service to the Holy See are trained. On Dec. 7, 1998, Archbishop Montalvo was appointed pronuncio to the United States and permanent observer to the Organization of American States, succeeding Archbishop Agostino Cacciavillan.

The U.S. Apostolic Nunciature is located at 3339 Massachusetts Ave., N.W., Washington, D.C. 20008.

A Nuncio represents the Holy Father to both the hierarchy and Church of a particular nation and to that nation's civil government.

From 1893 to 1984, papal representatives to the Church in the U.S. were apostolic delegates (all archbishops): Francesco Satolli (1893-96), Sebastiano Martinelli, O.S.A., (1896-1902), Diomede Falconio, O.F.M. (1902-1911), Giovanni Bonzano (1911-22), Pietro Fumasoni-Biondi (1922-33), Amleto Cicognani (1933-58), Egidio Vagnozzi (1958-67), Luigi Raimondi (1967-73), Jean Jadot (1973-80), and Pio Laghi (1980-90) who was the first to hold the title Pro-Nuncio, beginning in 1984 (See Index, U.S.-Vatican Relations). Archbishop Agostino Cacciavillan was Pro-Nuncio and permanent observer to the Organization of American States from 1990 to 1998.

Other Representatives

(Sources: *Annuario Pontificio*; Catholic News Service.)

The Holy See has representatives to or is a regular member of a number of quasi-governmental and international organizations. Most Rev. Ernesto Gallina was appointed delegate to International Governmental Organizations Jan. 12, 1991.

Governmental Organizations: United Nations (Abp. Renato Raffaele Martino, permanent observer); UN Office in Geneva and Specialized Institutions (Abp. Giuseppe Bertello, permanent observer); International Atomic Energy Agency (Msgr. Dominique Rezeau, permanent representative); UN Office at Vienna and UN Organization for Industrial Development (Msgr. Dominique Rezeau, permanent observer); UN Food and Agriculture Organization (Abp. Agostino Marchetto, permanent observer); UN Educational, Scientific and Cultural Organization (Msgr. Lorenzo Frana, permanent observer); World Organization of Commerce (Abp. Giuseppe Bertolli); Council of Europe (Msgr. Michael Courtney, special representative with function of permanent observer); Council for Cultural Cooperation of the Council of Europe (Msgr. Michael Courtney, delegate); Organization of American States (Abp. Gabriel Montalvo, permanent observer, with personal title of Apostolic Nuncio); Organization for Security and Cooperation in Europe (Mario Zenari, permanent representative); International Institute for the Unification of Private Law (Prof. Tommaso Mauro, delegate); International Committee of Military Medicine (Rev. Luc Demaere, delegate), World Organization of Tourism (Msgr. Piero Monni, permanent observer); **Non-Governmental Organizations:** International Committee of Historical Sciences (Msgr. Victor Saxer); International Committee of the History of Art (Dr. Francesco Buranelli); International Committee of Anthropological and Ethnological Sciences; Committee for the Neutrality of Medicine; International Center of Study for the Preservation and Restoration of Cultural Goods (Dr. Francesco Buranelli); International Council of Monuments and Sites (Msgr. Lorenzo Frana, delegate); International Alliance on Tourism; World Association of Jurists; International Commission of the Civil State (Msgr. Michael Courtney); International Astronomical Union; International Institute of Administrative Sciences; International Technical Committee for Prevention and Extinction of Fires; World Medical Association; International Archives Council; World Trade Organization (Abp. Giuseppe Bertello).

DIPLOMATS TO THE HOLY SEE

(Sources: *Annuario Pontificio, L'Osservatore Romano*).

Listed below are countries maintaining diplomatic relations with the Holy See, dates of establishment (in some cases) and names of Ambassadors (as of Aug. 30, 1999). Leaders (. . . . .) indicate the post was vacant.

The senior member of the diplomatic corps at the Vatican is Jean Wagner of Luxembourg who was appointed in Nov. 7, 1981, and presented his credentials Jan. 18, 1982.

Albania (1991): Jul Loro Bushati.
Algeria (1972): Mohamed-Salah Dembri..
Andorra (1995): Manuel Mas Ribó.
Angola (1997): José Bernardo Domingos Quiosa.
Antigua and Barbuda (1986): . . . . .
Argentina: Esteban Juan Caselli.
Armenia (1992): Armen Sarkissian.
Australia (1973): Robert George Halverson.
Austria: Gustav Ortner.
Azerbaijan (1992): . . . . .
Bahamas (1979): . . . . .
Bangladesh (1972): Iftekhar Ahmed Chowdhury.
Barbados (1979): Peter Patrick Kenneth Simmons.
Belarus (1992): . . . . .
Belgium (1835): Thierry Muûls.
Belize (1983): . . . . .
Benin (formerly Dahomey) (1971): Corneille Mehissou.
Bolivia: Jorge Siles Salinas.
Bosnia and Herzegovina (1992): Dr. Vlatko Kraljevic.
Brazil: Dr. Marco Cesar Meira Naslausky.
Bulgaria (1990): Dr. Svetlozar Dimitrov Raev.
Burkina Faso (1973): Felipe Savadogo.
Burundi (1963): . . . . .
Cambodia (1994): . . . . .
Cameroon (1966): Jean Melaga.
Canada (1969): J. Fernand Tanguay.
Cape Verde (1976): Teófilo de Figueiredo Almeida.
Central African Republic (1975): . . . . .

Chad (1988): Abdallah Nassour Mahamat Ali.
Chile: Javier Luis Egaña Baraona.
China, Republic of (Taiwan) (1966): Raymond R.M. Tai.
Colombia: Dr. Guillermo León Escobar-Herrán.
Congo (formerly Zaire) (1963): . . . . .
Congo (1977): Pierre-Michel Nguimbi.
Costa Rica: Javier Guerra Laspiur.
Côte d'Ivoire (Ivory Coast) (1971): Simeon Aké
Croatia (1992): Dr. Marijan Sunjic.
Cuba: Hermes Herrera Hernández.
Cyprus (1973): Theophilos V. Theophilou.
Czech Republic (1929-50, reestablished, 1990, with Czech and Slovak Federative Republic; reaffirmed, 1993): Martin Stropnicky.
Denmark (1982): Jan Marcussen.
Dominica (1981): . . . . .
Dominican Republic: César Iván Feris Iglesias.
Ecuador: Alfredo Luna Tobar
Egypt (1966): Mohamed Hussein Said El-Sadre.
El Salvador: Roberto José Simán Jacir.
Equatorial Guinea (1981): . . . . .
Eritrea (1995): Abraha Woldemichael.
Estonia (1991): Margus Laidre.
Ethiopia (1969): Mulugeta Eteffa.
Fiji (1978): Filimone Jitoko.
Finland (1966): Olli Mennander.
France: Jean Guéguinou.
Gabon (1967): Eugène Milingout Mangaka.
Gambia, The (1978): John P. Boyang.
Georgia (1992): . . . . .
Germany: Jürgen Oesterhelt.
Ghana (1976): Agnes Yahan Aggrey-Orleans.
Great Britain (1982): Mark Pellew.
Greece (1980): Nikolaos Kalantzianos.
Grenada (1979): . . . . .
Guatemala: Sergio Iván Búcaro Hurtarte.
Guinea (1986): . . . . .
Guinea-Bissau (1986): . . . . .
Guyana (Cooperative Republic of): Laleshwar Kumar Narayan Singh.
Haiti: Marc A. Trouillot.
Honduras: Alejandro Emilio Valladares Lanza.
Hungary (1990): Pál Tar.
Iceland (1976): Hjalmar W.Hannesson.
India: Kizhakke Pisharath Balakrishnan.
Indonesia (1965): Irawan Abidin.
Iran (1966): Mohammad Hedi Abd Khoda'i.
Iraq (1966): Wissam Chawkat Al-Zahawi.
Ireland: Éamon Ó Tuathail.
Israel (1994): Aharon Lopez.
Italy: Alberto Bartoli.
Ivory Coast: See **Côte d'Ivoire.**
Jamaica (1979): Peter Carlisle Black.
Japan (1966): Hisakazu Tanaka.
Jordan (1994): Adnan Bahjat al Talhouni.
Kazakhstan (1992): . . . . .
Kenya (1965): Steven Loyatum.
Kiribati: Diplomatic relations established April, 1995.
Korea (1966): Bae Yang-il.
Kuwait (1969): Tarek Razzouqi.
Kyrgyzstan (1992): Apas Dschumagulov
Latvia (1991): Atis Sjanits.
Lebanon (1966): Youssef Arsanios.
Lesotho (1967): Miss Lebohang Nts'Inyi.
Liberia (1966): . . . . .

Libya: (1997): Husein-Fuad Mustafa Kabazi.
Liechtenstein (1985): Nikolaus de Liechtenstein.
Lithuania: Kazys Lozoraitis.
Luxembourg (1955): Jean Wagner.
Macedonia (1994): Dimitar Mircev.
Madagascar (1967): Malala-Zo Raolison Randrianjoa Ramahatafandry.
Malawi (1966): Geoffrey Gachuku Chipungu.
Mali (1979): N'Tji Laïco Traore.
Malta (1965): James Farrugia.
Marshall Islands (1993): . . . . .
Mauritius: Satcam Boolell.
Mexico (personal representative, 1990; diplomatic relations, 1992): Horacio Sánchez Unzueta.
Micronesia, Federated States (1994): . . . . .
Moldova (1992): . . . . .
Monaco: Jean- Claude Michel.
Mongolia (1992): Sukh-Ochir Bold.
Morocco: Abdelouhab Maalmi.
Mozambique: Diplomatic relations established December, 1995. . . .
Namibia: Diplomatic relations established September, 1995.
Nauru (1992): . . . . .
Nepal (1983): Novel Kishore Rai.
Netherlands (1967): Gijsbert Nicolaus Westerouen.
New Zealand (1973): Wilbur Dovey.
Nicaragua: Luvy Salerni Navas.
Niger (1971): . . . . .
Nigeria (1976): Isaac Agboola Aluko-Olokun.
Norway (1982): Bengt O. Johansen.
Order of Malta (see Index): Stefan Falez.
Pakistan (1965): S. M. Inamullah.
Palau, Republic of (1998): . . . . .
Panama: Mario Antonio Velásquez Fernández.
Papua New Guinea (1977): . . . . .
Paraguay: Luis Maria Ramirez Boettner.
Peru: Luis Solari Tudela.
Philippines (1951): Mrs. Henrietta Tambunting de Villa.
Poland (1989): Stefan Frankiewicz.
Portugal: António d'Oliveira Pinto da França.
Romania (1920; broken off, 1948; reestablished, 1990): Teodor Baconsky.
Rwanda (1964): Manzi Bakuramutsa.
Saint Lucia (1984): Desmond Arthur McNamara.
Saint Vincent and the Grenadines (1990): . . . . .
San Marino (1986): Giovanni Galassi.
São Tome and Principe (1984): . . . . .
Senegal (1966): Henri Antoine Turpin.
Seychelles (1984): . . . . .

Sierra Leone: Diplomatic relations established July 1996.
Singapore (1981): Eng Fong Pang.
Slovak Republic (1993; when it became independent republic): Dr. Marián Servátka.
Slovenia (1992): Karl Bonutti.
Solomon Islands (1984): . . . . .
South Africa (1994): Ruth Segomotsi Mompati.
Spain: Carlos Abella y Ramallo.
Sri Lanka (1975): H.M.G.S. Palihakkara.
Sudan (1972): Eltigani Salih Fidail.
Suriname (1994): Evert G. Azimullah.
Swaziland (1992): H.R.H. Prince David M. Dlamini.
Sweden (1982): Anders Thunborg.
Switzerland (1992): Claudio Caratsch, Ambassador with special mission to Holy See.
Syria (Arab Republic) (1966): Elias Najmeh.
Tajikistan: Diplomatic relations established June 15, 1996.
Tanzania (1968): Andrew Mhando Daraja.
Thailand (1969): Ronarong Nopakun.
Togo (1981): Elliot Latévi-Atcho Lawson.
Tonga (1994): . . . . .
Trinidad and Tobago (1978): . . . . .
Tunisia (1972): . . . . .
Turkey (1966): Altan Güven.
Turkmenistan: Diplomatic relations established July 10, 1996.
Uganda (1966): Tibamanya Mwene Mushanga.
Ukraine (1992): Nina Kovalska.
United States (1984): Corinne "Lindy" Boggs.
Uruguay: Felipe H. Paolillo.
Uzbekistan (1992): . . . . .
Vanuatu (1994): . . . . .
Venezuela: Alberto J. Vollmer Herrera.
Western Samoa (1994): . . . . .
Yemen: (1998): Mohy Al-Dhabbi.
Yugoslavia: Dojcilo Maslovaric.
Zaire: See Congo.
Zambia (1965): Dr. Moses Musonda.
Zimbabwe (1980): Joey Mazorodze Bimba.
Special Representatives
Russia (Federation of) (1989): Guennadi Uranov, Ambassador Extraordinary and Plenipotentiary.
United Nations (Center of Information of UN at the Holy See): Staffan de Mistura, director.
United Nations High Commission for Refugees: Ana Liria-Franch, delegate.
Organization for the Liberation of Palestine: Afif E. Safieh, director.

U.S. - HOLY SEE RELATIONS

The United States and the Holy See announced Jan. 10, 1984, the establishment of full diplomatic relations, thus ending a period of 117 years in which there was no formal diplomatic relationship. The announcement followed action by the Congress in November, 1983, to end a prohibition on diplomatic relations enacted in 1867.

William A. Wilson, President Reagan's personal representative to the Holy See from 1981, was confirmed as the U.S. ambassador by the Senate, on Mar. 7, 1984. He presented his credentials to Pope John Paul II on Apr. 9, 1984, and served until May 1986,

when he resigned. He was succeeded by Frank Shakespeare, 1986-89, and Thomas P. Melady, 1989-93. Raymond L. Flynn, Mayor of Boston, was appointed by President Bill Clinton and confirmed by the Senate in July, 1993. He served until 1997 when he was succeeded by Corinne Claiborne "Lindy" Boggs. She presented her credentials to Pope John Paul II on Dec. 16, 1997.

Archbishop (now Cardinal) Pio Laghi, apostolic delegate to the U.S. since 1980, was named first pronuncio by the Pope on Mar. 26, 1984. He served until 1990, when he was named prefect of the Congregation for Catholic Education; Archbishop Agostino Cacciavillan was appointed pro-nuncio on June 13, 1990. He served until he was named president of the Administration of the Patrimony of the Apostolic See (APSA) and was succeeded on Dec. 7, 1998 by Archbishop Gabriel Montalvo, the present pro-nuncio.

Nature of Relations

The nature of relations was described in nearly identical statements by John Hughes, a State Department spokesman, and the Holy See. Hughes said: "The United States of America and the Holy See, in the desire to further promote the existing mutual friendly relations, have decided by common agreement to establish diplomatic relations between them at the level of embassy on the part of the United States of America, and nunciature on the part of the Holy See, as of today, Jan. 10, 1984."

The Holy See statement said: "The Holy See and the United States of America, desiring to develop the mutual friendly relations already existing, have decided by common accord to establish diplomatic relations at the level of apostolic nunciature on the side of the Holy See and of embassy on the side of the United States beginning today, Jan. 10, 1984."

The establishment of relations was criticized as a violation of the separation-of-church-and-state principle by spokesmen for the National Council of Churches, the National Association of Evangelicals, the Baptist Joint Committee on Public Affairs, Seventh Day Adventists, Americans United for Separation of Church and State, and the American Jewish Congress.

Legal Challenge Dismissed

U.S. District Judge John P. Fullam, ruling May 7, 1985, in Philadelphia, dismissed a legal challenge to U.S.-Holy See relations brought by Americans United for Separation of Church and State. He stated that Americans United and its allies in the challenge lacked legal standing to sue, and that the courts did not have jurisdiction to intervene in foreign policy decisions of the executive branch of the U.S. government. Parties to the suit brought by Americans United were the National Association of Laity, the National Coalition of American Nuns and several Protestant church organizations. Bishop James W. Malone, president of the U.S. Catholic Conference, said in a statement: "This matter has been discussed at length for many years. It is not a religious issue but a public policy question which, happily, has now been settled in this context."

Russell Shaw, a conference spokesman, said the decision to send an ambassador to the Holy See was not a church-state issue and "confers no special privilege or status on the Church."

Earlier Relations

Official relations for trade and diplomatic purposes were maintained by the United States and the Papal States while the latter had the character of and acted like other sovereign powers in the international community.

Consular relations developed in the wake of an announcement, made by the papal nuncio in Paris to the American mission there Dec. 15, 1784, that the Papal States had agreed to open several Mediterranean ports to U.S. shipping.

U.S. consular representation in the Papal States began with the appointment of John B. Sartori, a native of Rome, in June, 1797. Sartori's successors as consuls were: Felix Cicognani, also a Roman, and Americans George W. Greene, Nicholas Browne, William C. Sanders, Daniel LeRoy, Horatio V. Glentworth, W.J. Stillman, Edwin C. Cushman, David M. Armstrong.

Consular officials of the Papal States who served in the U.S. were: Count Ferdinand Lucchesi, 1826 to 1829, who resided in Washington; John B. Sartori, 1829 to 1841, who resided in Trenton, N.J.; Daniel J. Desmond, 1841 to 1850, who resided in Philadelphia; Louis B. Binsse, 1850 to 1895, who resided in New York.

U.S. recognition of the consul of the Papal States did not cease when the states were absorbed into the Kingdom of Italy in 1871, despite pressure from Baron Blanc, the Italian minister. Binsse held the title until his death Mar. 28, 1895. No one was appointed to succeed him.

Diplomatic Relations

The U.S. Senate approved a recommendation, made by President James K. Polk in December, 1847, for the establishment of a diplomatic post in the Papal States. Jacob L. Martin, the first charge d'affaires, arrived in Rome Aug. 2, 1848, and presented his credentials to Pius IX Aug. 19. Martin, who died within a month, was succeeded by Lewis Cass, Jr. Cass became minister resident in 1854 and served in that capacity until his retirement in 1858.

John P. Stockton, who later became a U.S. Senator from New Jersey, was minister resident from 1858 to 1861. Rufus King was named to succeed him but, instead, accepted a commission as a brigadier general in the Army. Alexander W. Randall of Wisconsin took the appointment. He was succeeded in August, 1862, by Richard M. Blatchford who served until the following year. King was again nominated minister resident and served in that capacity until 1867 when the ministry was ended because of objections from some quarters in the U.S. and failure to appropriate funds for its continuation. J. C. Hooker, a secretary, remained in the Papal States until the end of March, 1868, closing the ministry and performing functions of courtesy.

Personal Envoys

Myron C. Taylor was appointed by President Franklin D. Roosevelt in 1939 to serve as his personal representative to Pope Pius XII and continued serving in that capacity during the presidency of Harry S. Truman until 1951. Henry Cabot Lodge was named to the post by President Richard M. Nixon in 1970, served also during the presidency of Gerald Ford, and represented President Carter at the canonization of St. John Neumann in 1977. Miami attorney David Walters served as the personal envoy of President Jimmy Carter to the Pope from July, 1977, until his resignation Aug. 16, 1978. He was succeeded by Robert F. Wagner who served from October, 1978, to the end of the Carter presidency in January, 1981. William A. Wilson, appointed by President Ronald Reagan in February, 1981, served as his personal envoy until 1984 when he was named ambassador to the Holy See.

None of the personal envoys had diplomatic status. President Harry S. Truman nominated Gen. Mark Clark to be ambassador to the Holy See in 1951, but withdrew the nomination at Clark's request because of controversy over the appointment. None of Truman's three immediate successors — Dwight D. Eisenhower, John F. Kennedy and Lyndon B. Johnson — had a personal representative to the Pope.

PONTIFICAL ACADEMIES

PONTIFICAL ACADEMY OF SCIENCES
(Sources: *Annuario Pontificio*, Catholic News Service.)

The Pontifical Academy of Sciences was constituted in its present form by Pius XI Oct. 28, 1936, in virtue of *In Multis Solaciis*, a document issued on his own initiative.

The academy is the only supranational body of its kind in the world with a pope-selected, life-long membership of outstanding mathematicians and experimental scientists regardless of creed from many countries. The normal complement of 70 members was increased to 80 in 1985-86 by John Paul II. There are additional honorary and supernumerary members.

The academy traces its origin to the *Linceorum Academia* (Academy of the Lynxes — its symbol) founded in Rome Aug. 17, 1603. Pius IX reorganized this body and gave it a new name — *Pontificia Accademia dei Nuovi Lincei* — in 1847. It was taken over by the Italian state in 1870 and called the *Accademia Nazionale dei Lincei*. Leo XIII reconstituted it with a new charter in 1887. Pius XI designated the Casina of Pope Pius IV in the Vatican Gardens as the site of academy headquarters in 1922 and gave it its present title and status in 1936. In 1940, Pius XII gave the title of Excellency to its members; John XXIII extended the privilege to honorary members in 1961.

Members in U.S.
Scientists in the U.S. who presently hold membership in the Academy are listed below according to year of appointment. Nobel prizewinners are indicated by an asterisk.

Franco Rasetti, professor emeritus of physics at Johns Hopkins University, Baltimore, Md. (Oct 28, 1936); Christian de Duve,* professor of biochemistry at the International Institute of Cellular and Molecular Pathology at Brussels, Belgium, and Rockefeller University, New York (Apr. 10, 1970); Marshall Warren Nirenberg,* director of Laboratory on genetics and biochemistry at the National Institutes of Health, Bethesda, Md. (June 24, 1974).

George Palade,* professor of cellular biology at University of California, San Diego and Victor Weisskopf, professor of physics at the Massachusetts Institute of Technology, Cambridge, Mass. (Dec. 2, 1975); David Baltimore,* professor of biology at the Massachusetts Institute of Technology, Cambridge, Mass.; Har Gobind Khorana,* professor of biochemistry, and Alexander Rich, professor of biophysics — both at the Massachusetts Institute of Technology, Cambridge, Mass. (Apr. 17, 1978).

Charles Townes,* professor emeritus of physics at the University of California at Berkeley (Jan. 26, 1983). Beatrice Mintz, senior member of the Cancer Research Institute of Philadelphia and Maxine Singer, biochemist, president of Carnegie Institution, Washington, D.C. (June 9, 1986).

Roald Z. Sagdeev, professor of physics at University of Maryland, College Park and Peter Hamilton Raven, professor of biology at the Missouri Botanical Garden of St. Louis, Mo. (Oct 4, 1990); Luis Angel Caffarelli, professor of mathematics at New York University and Luigi Luca Cavalli-Sforza, professor of genetics at Stanford University (Aug. 2, 1994).

Joshua Lederberg, professor of genetics at Rockefeller Univ., New York (Mar. 4, 1996), Joseph Edward Murray, professor of plastic surgery at Harvard Medical School, Cambridge, Mass., Paul Berg, professor of biochemistry at Stanford Univ. and Vera C. Rubin, professor of astronomy at Carnegie Institution of Washington (June 25, 1996); Gary S. Becker,* professor of economics at the University of Chicago (Mar. 3, 1997); and Chen-ning Yang,* professor of physics and director of the Institute of Theoretical Physics at the State University of New York at Stoney Brook (Apr. 18,1997),

There are also two honorary members from the U.S.: Stanley L, Jaki, O.S.B., professor of physics, history and philosophy at Seton Hall University, South Orange (Sept. 5, 1990) and Robert J. White, professor of neurosurgery at Case Western Reserve University, Cleveland (Mar. 29, 1994).

Members in Other Countries
Listing includes place and date of selection. Nobel prizewinners are indicated by an asterisk.

Armenia: Rudolf M. Muradian (Oct. 16, 1994).

Austria: Hans Tuppy (Apr. 10, 1970); Walter Thirring (June 9, 1986).

Belgium: Paul Adriaan Jan Janssen (June 25, 1990).

Brazil: Carlos Chagas, former president of the academy (Aug. 18, 1961); Johanna Döbereiner (Apr. 17, 1978); Crodowaldo Pavan (Apr. 17, 1978); Rudolf Muradian (Oct. 16, 1994).

Canada: Gerhard Herzberg* (Sept. 24, 1964); John Charles Polanyi* (June 9, 1986).

Chile: Héctor Rezzio Croxatto (Dec. 2, 1975).

Congo (formerly Zaire): Felix wa Kalengo Malu (Sept. 26, 1983).

Denmark: Aage Bohr* (Apr. 17, 1978).

France: Louis Leprince-Ringuet (Aug. 18, 1961); André Blanc-LaPierre (Apr. 17, 1978); Paul Germain (June 9, 1986); Jacques-Louis Lions (Oct. 4, 1990), Jean-Marie Lehn (May 30, 1996).

Germany: Rudolf L. Mössbauer* (Apr. 10, 1970); Manfred Eigen* (May 12, 1981); Wolf Joachim Singer (Sept. 18, 1992), Paul Joseph Crutzen (June 25, 1996), Yuri Ivanovich Manin (June 26, 1996).

Ghana: Daniel Adzei Bekoe (Sept. 26, 1983).

Great Britain: Hermann Alexander Brück (Apr. 5, 1955); George Porter* (June 24, 1974); Max Ferdinand Perutz* (May 12, 1981); Stephen Will-

iam Hawking (Jan. 9, 1986); Martin John Rees (June 25, 1990); Sir Richard Southwood (Sept. 18, 1992); Raymond Hide (June 25, 1996).
India: Mambillikalathil Govind Kumar Menon (May 12, 1981); Chintamani N.R. Rao (June 25, 1990).
Ireland: James Robert McConnell (June 25, 1990).
Israel: Michael Sela (Dec. 2, 1975).
Italy: Rita Levi-Montalcino* (June 24, 1974); Giampietro Puppi (Apr. 17, 1978); Nicola Cabibbo (June 9, 1986), President; Nicola Dallaporta (Oct. 5, 1989; honorary member); Bernardo Maria Colombo (Sept. 18, 1992).
Japan: Minoru Oda (Sept. 18, 1992).
Kenya: Thomas R. Odhiambo (May 12, 1981).
Mexico: Marcos Moshinsky (June 9, 1986).
Nigeria: Thomas Adeoye Lambo (June 24, 1974).
Poland: Stanislaw Lojasiewicz (Jan. 28, 1983); Czeslaw Olech (June 9, 1986); Michal Heller (Oct. 4, 1990); Andrzej Szezeklik (Oct. 16, 1994).
Russia: Vladimir Isaakovich Keilis-Borok (Oct. 16, 1994); Sergei Petrovich Novikov (June 25, 1996; also teaches at University of Maryland, U.S.A.).

Spain: Manuel Lora-Tamayo (Sept. 24, 1964).
Sweden: Sune Bergström* (Dec. 14, 1985); Kai Siegbahn* (Dec. 14, 1985).
Switzerland: Werner Arber* (May 12, 1981); Carlo Rubbia* (Dec. 14, 1985); Albert Eschenmoser (June 9, 1986).
Taiwan: Te-tzu Chang (Apr. 18, 1997).
Vatican City State: Cottier, Rev. George, O.P. (Oct. 28, 1992; honorary member); Msgr. Renato Dardozzi (July 1, 1997; honorary member); Rev. Enrico do Rovasenda, O.P. (Nov. 13, 1968; honorary member).
Venezuela: Marcel Roche (Apr. 10, 1970).
Ex officio members: Rev. George V. Coyne, S.J., director of Vatican Observatory (Sept. 2, 1978); Very Rev. Raffaele Farina, S.D.B., prefect of the Vatican Library (May 24, 1997); Very Rev. Sergio B. Pagano, prefect of the Secret Vatican Archives (Jan. 7, 1997). President: Nicola Cabibbo, professor of theoretical physics at Univ. of Rome (app. Apr. 6, 1993). Chancellor: Msgr. Marcelo Sánchez Sorondo.

PONTIFICAL ACADEMY OF SOCIAL SCIENCES

Founded by John Paul II, Jan. 1, 1994 (*motu proprio Socialium scientiarum investigationes*) to promote the study and the progress of social sciences, to advise the Vatican on social concerns and to foster research aimed at improving society. The number of members is not less than 20 nor more than 40. Two of the thirty members of the Academy (as of Jan. 1, 1996) were from the United States: Kenneth J. Arrow of Stanford University and Mary Ann Glendon of Harvard University. President, Prof. Edmond Malinvaud of France; Chancellor, Mons. Marcelo Sánchez Sorondo Address: Casino Pio IV, Vatican Gardens.

PONTIFICAL ACADEMY FOR LIFE

Established by John Paul II, Feb. 11, 1994 (*motu proprio Vitae Mysterium*) "to fulfill the specific task of study, information and formation on the principal problems of biomedicine and law relative to the promotion and defense of life, especially in the direct relationship they have with Christian morality and the directives of the Church's magisterium."
Members, appointed by the Pope without regard to religion or nationality, represent the various branches of "the biomedical sciences and those that are most closely related to problems concerning the promotion and protection of life." Membership, as of Jan. 1, 1999, included six from the United States: Prof. Carl Anderson, Vice-President of the Pontifical John Paul II Institute for Studies of Marriage and the Family. Mrs. Mercedes Arzu-Wilson, founder and president of the Foundations Family of the Americas and founder and director of the Commission at the World Organization for the Family; Dr. Thomas Hilgers, founder and director of the Institute "Paul VI," Omaha, Nebr.; Prof. Edmund Pellegrino, director of the Center for Advanced Studies in Ethics at Georgetown University, Washington; Mrs. Cristina de Vollmer, president of the World Organization for the Family; Dr. Denis Cavanaugh, professor of obstetrics and gynecology at the University of South Florida College of Medicine. President: Prof. Juan de Dios Vial Correa, physician and biologist. Address: Via della Conciliazione, 3, 00193 Rome, Italy.

HIERARCHY OF THE CATHOLIC CHURCH

ORGANIZATION AND GOVERNMENT

As a structured society, the Catholic Church is organized and governed along lines corresponding mainly to the jurisdictions of the pope and Bishops. The pope is the supreme head of the Church. He has primacy of jurisdiction as well as honor over the entire Church. Bishops, in union with and in subordination to the pope, are the successors of the Apostles for care of the Church and for the continuation of Christ's mission in the world. They serve the people of their own dioceses, or particular churches, with ordinary authority and jurisdiction. They also share, with the pope and each other, in common concern and effort for the general welfare of the whole Church.

Bishops of exceptional status are patriarchs of Eastern Catholic Churches who, subject only to the pope, are heads of the faithful belonging to their rites throughout the world.

Subject to the Holy Father and directly responsible to him for the exercise of their ministry of service to people in various jurisdictions or divisions of the Church throughout the world are: resident archbishops and metropolitans (heads of archdioceses), diocesan bishops, vicars and prefects apostolic (heads of vicariates apostolic and prefectures apostolic), certain abbots and prelates, apostolic administrators. Each of these, within his respective territory and according to the provisions of canon law, has ordinary jurisdiction over pastors (who are responsible for the administration of parishes), priests, religious and lay persons.

Also subject to the Holy Father are titular archbishops and bishops, religious orders and congregations of pontifical right, pontifical institutes and faculties, papal nuncios and apostolic delegates.

Assisting the pope and acting in his name in the central government and administration of the Church are cardinals and other officials of the Roman Curia.

THE HIERARCHY

The ministerial hierarchy is the orderly arrangement of the ranks and orders of the clergy to provide for the spiritual care of the faithful, the government of the Church, and the accomplishment of the Church's total mission in the world.

Persons belong to this hierarchy by virtue of ordination and canonical mission.

The term hierarchy is also used to designate an entire body or group of bishops; for example, the hierarchy of the Church, the hierarchy of the United States.

Hierarchy of Order: Consists of the pope, bishops, priests and deacons. Their purpose, for which they are ordained to holy orders, is to carry out the sacramental and pastoral ministry of the Church.

Hierarchy of Jurisdiction: Consists of the pope and bishops by divine institution, and other church officials by ecclesiastical institution and mandate, who have authority to govern and direct the faithful for spiritual ends.

The Pope

His Holiness the Pope is the Bishop of Rome, Vicar of Jesus Christ, successor of St. Peter, Prince of the

Apostles, Supreme Pontiff of the Universal Church, Patriarch of the West, Primate of Italy, Archbishop and Metropolitan of the Roman Province, Sovereign of the State of Vatican City, Servant of the Servants of God.

Cardinals

(See Index)

Patriarchs

Patriarch, a term which had its origin in the Eastern Church, is the title of a bishop who, second only to the pope, has the highest rank in the hierarchy of jurisdiction. He is the incumbent of one of the sees listed below. Subject only to the pope, a patriarch of the Eastern Church is the head of the faithful belonging to his rite throughout the world. The patriarchal sees are so called because of their special status and dignity in the history of the Church.

The Council of Nicaea (325) recognized three patriarchs — the Bishops of Alexandria and Antioch in the East, and of Rome in the West. The First Council of Constantinople (381) added the bishop of Constantinople to the list of patriarchs and gave him rank second only to that of the pope, the bishop of Rome and patriarch of the West; this action was seconded by the Council of Chalcedon (451) and was given full recognition by the Fourth Lateran Council (1215). The Council of Chalcedon also acknowledged patriarchal rights of the bishop of Jerusalem.

Eastern patriarchs are as follows: one of Alexandria, for the Copts; three of Antioch, one each for the Syrians, Maronites and Greek Melkites (the latter also has the personal title of Greek Melkite patriarch of Alexandria and of Jerusalem). The patriarch of Babylonia, for the Chaldeans, and the patriarch of Sis, or Cilicia, for the Armenians, should be called, more properly, *Katholikos* — that is, a prelate delegated for a universality of causes. These patriarchs are elected by bishops of their churches: they receive approval and the pallium, symbolic of their office, from the pope.

Latin Rite patriarchates were established for Antioch, Jerusalem, Alexandria and Constantinople during the Crusades; afterwards, they became patriarchates in name only. Jerusalem, however, was reconstituted as a patriarchate by Pius IX, in virtue of the bull *Nulla Celebrior* of July 23, 1847. In 1964, the Latin titular patriarchates of Constantinople, Alexandria and Antioch, long a bone of contention in relations with Eastern Churches, were abolished.

As of Aug. 15, 1998, the patriarchs in the Church were:

The Pope, Bishop of Rome, Patriarch of the West; Stephanos II Ghattas, C.M., of Alexandria, for the Copts; Ignace Antoine II Hayek, of Antioch, for the Syrians; Maximos V Hakim, of Antioch, for the Greek Melkites (he also has personal titles of Alexandria and Jerusalem for the Greek Melkites); Cardinal Nasrallah Pierre Sfeir, of Antioch, for the Maronites; Michael Sabbah, of Jerusalem, for the Latin Rite; Raphael I Bidawid, of Babylon, for the Chaldeans; Jean Pierre XVIII Kasparian, of Cilicia, for the Armenians.

The titular patriarchs (in name only) of the Latin Rite were: the patriarch of Lisbon (currently vacant); Cardinal Marco Cé, of Venice and Archbishop Raul Nicolau Gonsalves of the East Indies (archbishop of Goa and Damao, India). The patriarchate of the West Indies has been vacant since 1963.

Major Archbishops

An archbp. with the prerogatives but not the title of a patriarch. As of May 15, 1998, there was one major archbishop: Cardinal Myroslav Ivan Lubachivsky of the major archbp.ric of Lviv of the Ukrainian Catholic Church (Ukraine). The major archbishopric of Ernakulam-Angomaly of the Syro-Malabar Church (India) was vacant with the resignation Nov. 11, 1996, of Cardinal Anthony Padiyara.

Archbishops, Metropolitans

Archbishop: A bishop with the title of an archdiocese.

Coadj. Archbishop: An assistant archbishop with right of succession.

Metropolitan: Archbishop of the principal see, an archdiocese, in an ecclesiastical province consisting of several dioceses. He has the full powers of bishop in his own archdiocese and limited supervisory jurisdiction and influence over the other (suffragan) dioceses in the province. The pallium, conferred by the pope, is the symbol of his status as a metropolitan.

Titular Archbishop: Has the title of an archdiocese which formerly existed in fact but now exists in title only. He does not have ordinary jurisdiction over an archdiocese. Examples are archbishops in the Roman Curia, papal nuncios, apostolic delegates.

Archbishop *ad personam*: A title of personal honor and distinction granted to some bishops. They do not have ordinary jurisdiction over an archdiocese.

Primate: A title of honor given to the ranking prelate of some countries or regions.

Bishops

Diocesan Bishop: A bishop in charge of a diocese.

Coadj. Bishop: An assistant (auxiliary) bishop to a diocesan bishop, with right of succession to the see.

Titular Bishops: A bishop with the title of a diocese which formerly existed in fact but now exists in title only; an assistant (auxiliary) bishop to a diocesan bishop.

Episcopal Vicar: An assistant, who may or may not be a bishop, appointed by a residential bishop as his deputy for a certain part of a diocese, a determined type of apostolic work, or the faithful of a certain rite.

Eparch, Exarch: Titles of bishops of Eastern churches.

Nomination of Bishops: Nominees for episcopal ordination are selected in several ways. Final appointment and/or approval in all cases is subject to decision by the pope.

In the U.S., bishops periodically submit the names of candidates to the archbishop of their province. The names are then considered at a meeting of the Bishops of the province, and those receiving a favorable vote are forwarded to the pro-nuncio for transmission to the Holy See. Bishops are free to seek the counsel of priests, religious and lay persons with respect to nominees.

Eastern Catholic churches have their own procedures and synodal regulations for nominating and making final selection of candidates for episcopal ordination. Such selection is subject to approval by the pope. The Code of Canon Law concedes no rights or privileges to civil authorities with respect to the election, nomination, presentation or designation of candidates for the episcopate.

Ad Limina Visit: Diocesan bishops and apostolic vicars are obliged to make an ad limina visit ("to the threshold" of the Apostles) every five years to the tombs of Sts. Peter and Paul, have audience with the Holy Father and consult with appropriate Vatican officials. They are required to send a report on conditions in their jurisdiction to the Congregation for bishops approximately six — and not less than three — months in advance of the scheduled visit.

Others with Ordinary Jurisdiction

Ordinary: One who has the jurisdiction of an office: the pope, diocesan bishops, vicars general, prelates of missionary territories, vicars apostolic prefects apostolic, vicars capitular during the vacancy of a see, superiors general, abbots primate and other major superiors of men religious.

Some prelates and abbots, with jurisdiction like that of diocesan bishops, are pastors of the people of God in territories (prelatures and abbacies) not under the jurisdiction of diocesan bishops.

Vicar Apostolic: Usually a titular bishop who has ordinary jurisdiction over a mission territory.

Prefect Apostolic: Has ordinary jurisdiction over a mission territory.

Apostolic Administrator: Usually a bishop appointed to administer an ecclesiastical jurisdiction temporarily. Administrators of lesser rank are also appointed for special and more restricted supervisory duties.

Vicar General: A bishop's deputy for the administration of a diocese. Such a vicar does not have to be a bishop.

Prelates Without Jurisdiction

The title of protonotary apostolic was originally given by the fourth century or earlier to clergy who collected accounts of martyrdom and other church documents, or who served the Church with distinction in other ways. Other titles — e.g., domestic prelate, papal chamberlain, prelate of honor — are titles of clergy in service to the pope and the papal household, or of clergy honored for particular reasons. All prelates without jurisdiction are appointed by the pope, have designated ceremonial privileges and the title of Rev. Monsignor.

SYNOD OF BISHOPS

The Synod of Bishops was chartered by Pope Paul VI Sept. 15, 1965, in a document he issued on his own initiative under the title, *Apostolica Sollicitudo*. Provisions of this motu proprio are contained in Canons 342 to 348 of the Code of Canon Law. According to major provisions of the Synod charter:

• The purposes of the Synod are: "to encourage close union and valued assistance between the Sovereign Pontiff and the Bishops of the entire world; to insure that direct and real information is provided on questions and situations touching upon the internal action of the Church and its necessary activity in the world of today; to facilitate agreement on essential points of doctrine and on methods of procedure in the life of the Church."

• The Synod is a central ecclesiastical institution, permanent by nature.

• The Synod is directly and immediately subject to the Pope, who has authority to assign its agenda, to call it into session, and to give its members deliberative as well as advisory authority.

• In addition to a limited number of ex officio members and a few heads of male religious institutes, the majority of the members are elected by and representative of national or regional episcopal conferences. The Pope reserved the right to appoint the general secretary, special secretaries and no more than 15 per cent of the total membership.

The Pope is president of the Synod. The secretary general is Cardinal Jan Schotte, C.I.C.M., of Belgium. Address: Palazzo del Bramante, Via della Conciliazione 34, 00193 Rome, Italy.

An advisory council of 15 members (12 elected, three appointed by the pope) provides the secretariat with adequate staff for carrying on liaison with episcopal conferences and for preparing the agenda of synodal assemblies. Cardinal William H, Keeler, archbishop of Baltimore, is a member of the secretariat.

Assemblies

1. First Assembly: The first assembly was held from Sept. 29 to Oct. 29, 1967. Its objectives, as stated by Pope Paul VI, were "the preservation and strengthening of the Catholic faith, its integrity, its force, its development, its doctrinal and historical coherence." One result was a recommendation for the establishment of an international commission of theologians to assist the Congregation for the Doctrine of the Faith and to broaden approaches to theological research. Pope Paul set up the commission in 1969.

2. Pope-Bishop Relations: The second assembly held Oct. 11 to 28, 1969, was extraordinary in character. It opened the way toward greater participation by bishops with the pope and each other in the governance of the Church. Proceedings were oriented to three main points: (1) the nature and implications of collegiality; (2) the relationship of bishops and their conferences to the pope; (3) the relationships of bishops and their conferences to each other.

3. Priesthood and Justice: The ministerial priesthood and justice in the world were the principal topics under discussion at the second ordinary assembly, Sept. 30 to Nov. 6, 1971. In one report, the Synod emphasized the primary and permanent dedication of priests in the Church to the ministry of word, sacrament and pastoral service as a full-time vocation. In another report, the assembly stated: "Action on behalf of justice and participation in the transformation of the world fully appear to us as a constitutive dimension of the preaching of the Gospel; or, in other words, of the Church's mission for the redemption of the human race and its liberation from every oppressive situation."

4. Evangelization: The assembly of Sept. 27 to Oct. 26, 1974, produced a general statement on evangelization of the modern world, covering the need for it and its relationship to efforts for total human liberation from personal and social evil. The assembly observed: "The Church does not remain within merely political, social and economic limits (elements which she must certainly take into account) but leads towards freedom under all its forms — liberation from sin, from individual or collective selfishness — and to full communion with God and with men who are like brothers. In this way the Church, in her evangelical way, promotes the true and complete liberation of all men, groups and peoples."

5. Catechetics: The fourth ordinary assembly, Sept. 30 to Oct. 29, 1977, focused attention on catechetics, with special reference to children and young people. The participants issued a "Message to the People of God," the first synodal statement issued since inception of the body, and also presented to Pope Paul VI a set of 34 related propositions and a number of suggestions.

6. Family: "A Message to Christian Families in the Modern World" and a proposal for a "Charter of Family Rights" were produced by the assembly held Sept. 26 to Oct. 25, 1980. The assembly reaffirmed the indissolubility of marriage and the contents of the encyclical letter *Humanae Vitae* (see separate entry), and urged married couples who find it hard to live up to "the difficult but loving demands" of Christ not to be discouraged but to avail themselves of the aid of divine grace. In response to synodal recommendation, Pope John Paul issued a charter of family rights late in 1983.

7. Reconciliation: Penance and reconciliation in the mission of the Church was the theme of the assembly held Sept. 29 to Oct. 29, 1983. Sixty-three propositions related to this theme were formulated on a wide variety of subjects, including: personal sin and so-called systemic or institutional sin; the nature of serious sin; the diminished sense of sin and of the ned of redemption, related to decline in the administration and reception of the sacrament of penance; general absolution; individual and social reconciliation; violence and violations of human rights; reconciliation as the basis of peace and justice in society. In a statement issued Oct. 27, the Synod stressed the need of the world to become, increasingly, "a reconciled community of peoples," and said that "the Church, as sacrament of reconciliation to the world, has to be an effective sign of God's mercy."

8. Vatican II Review: The second extraordinary assembly was convened Nov. 24 to Dec. 8, 1985, for the purposes of: (1) recalling the Second Vatican Council; (2) evaluating the implementation of its enactments during the 20 years since its conclusion; (3) seeking ways and means of promoting renewal in the Church in accordance with the spirit and letter of the council. At the conclusion of the assembly the bishops issued two documents. (1) In A Message to the People of God, they noted the need for greater appreciation of the enactments of Vatican II and for greater efforts to put them into effect, so that all members of the Church might discharge their responsibility of proclaiming the good news of salvation. (2) In a Final Report, the first of its kind published by a synodal assembly, the bishops reflected on lights and shadows since Vatican II, stating that negative developments had come from partial and superficial interpretations of conciliar enactments and from incomplete or ineffective implementation thereof. The report also covered a considerable number of subjects discussed during the assembly, including the mystery of the Church, inculturation, the preferential (but not exclusive) option for the poor, and a suggestion for the development of a new universal catechism of the Catholic faith.

9. Vocation and Mission of the Laity in the Church and in the World 20 years after the Second Vatican Council: The seventh ordinary assembly, Oct. 1 to 30, 1987, said in a Message to the People of God: "The majority of the Christian laity live out their vocation as followers and disciples of Christ in all spheres of life which we call 'the world': the family, the field of work, the local community and the like. To permeate this day-to-day living with the spirit of Christ has always been the task of the lay faithful; and it should be with still greater force their challenge today. It is in this way that they sanctify the world and collaborate in the realization of the kingdom of God." The assembly produced a set of 54 propositions which were presented to the Pope for consideration in the preparation of a document of his own on the theme of the assembly. He responded with the apostolic exhortation, *Christifideles Laici,* "The Christian Faithful Laity," released by the Vatican Jan. 30, 1989.

10. Formation of Priests in Circumstances of the Present Day: The eighth general assembly, Sept. 30 to Oct. 28, 1990, dealt principally with the nature and mission of the priesthood; the identity, multi-faceted formation and spirituality of priests; and, in a Message to the People of God, the need on all levels of the Church for the promotion of vocations to the priesthood. Forty-one proposals were presented to the Pope for his consideration in preparing a document of his own on the theme of the assembly. Pope John Paul issued an apostolic exhortation entitled *Pastores Dabo Vobis* ("I Will Give You Shepherds") Apr. 7, 1992, in response to the Synods' recommendations.

11. The Consecrated Life and Its Role in the Church and in the World: The ninth general assembly was held Oct. 2 to 29, 1994. Pope John Paul's reflections on the proceedings of the assembly and the recommendations of the Bishops were the subjects of his apostolic exhortation entitled *Vita Consecrata* ("Consecrated Life"), issued Mar. 25, 1996. The document dealt with various forms of consecrated life: contemplative institutes, apostolic religious life, secular institutes, societies of apostolic life, mixed institutes and new forms of evangelical life.

12. The Tenth Ordinary General Assembly: The synod will assemble during the Great Jubilee in theYear 2000 on the topic "The Bishop: Servant of the Gospel of Jesus Christ for the Hope of the World."

Recent special assemblies of the Synod of Bishops: Special Synods have been held for Europe (Nov. 28 to Dec. 14, 1991; on the theme "So that we might be witnesses of Christ who has set us free"), for Africa (Apr. 10 to May 8, 1994; on the theme "The Church in Africa and Her Evangelizing Mission Towards the Year 2000: 'You Shall Be My Witnesses' (Acts 1:8)") and for Lebanon (Nov. 27 to Dec. 14, 1995; on the theme "Christ is Our

Hope: Renewed by His Spirit, in Solidarity We Bear Witness to His Love"), the Americas (Nov. 16 to Dec. 12, 1997; on the theme, "Encounter with the Living Jesus Christ: Way to Conversion, Community and Solidarity"), Asia (April 19 to May 14, 1998 on the theme "Jesus Christ the Savior and His Mission of Love and Service in Asia: '...That They May Have Life, and Have it Abundantly'"

(Jn 10:10), and Oceania (Nov. 12 to Dec. 12, 1998), with the theme "Jesus Christ and the Peoples of Oceania: Walking His Way, Telling His Truth, Living His Life" [See Special Report]. At the time of writing, preparations were under way for a special assembly for Europe (to be held from Oct. 1-23, 1999), on the theme "Jesus Christ, Alive in His Church, Source of Hope for Europe."

COLLEGE OF CARDINALS

Cardinals are chosen by the pope to serve as his principal assistants and advisers in the central administration of church affairs. Collectively, they form the College of Cardinals. Provisions regarding their selection, rank, roles and prerogatives are detailed in Canons 349 to 359 of the Code of Canon Law.

History of the College

The College of Cardinals was constituted in its present form and categories of membership in the 12th century. Before that time the pope had a body of advisers selected from among the bishops of dioceses neighboring Rome, priests and deacons of Rome. The college was given definite form in 1150, and in 1179 the selection of cardinals was reserved exclusively to the pope. Sixtus V fixed the number at 70, in 1586. John XXIII set aside this rule when he increased membership at the 1959 and subsequent consistories. The number was subsequently raised by Paul VI and by John Paul II. The number of cardinals entitle to participate in papal elections was limited to 120 by Paul VI in 1973. As of Aug. 30, 1999, 105 of the 154 cardinals were eligible to vote.

In 1567 the title of cardinal was reserved to members of the college; previously it had been used by priests attached to parish churches of Rome and by the leading clergy of other notable churches. The Code of Canon Law promulgated in 1918 decreed that all cardinals must be priests. Previously there had been cardinals who were not priests (e.g., Cardinal Giacomo Antonelli, d. 1876, Secretary of State to Pius IX, was a deacon). John XXIII provided in the motu proprio *Cum Gravissima* Apr. 15, 1962, that cardinals would henceforth be Bishops; this provision is included in the revised Code of Canon Law.

Age Limits

Pope Paul VI placed age limits on the functions of cardinals in the apostolic letter *Ingravescentem Aetatem,* dated Nov. 21, 1970, and effective as of Jan. 1, 1971. At 80, they cease to be members of curial departments and offices, and become ineligible to take part in papal elections. They retain membership in the College of Cardinals, however, with relevant rights and privileges.

Three Categories

All cardinals except Eastern patriarchs are aggregated to the clergy of Rome. This aggregation is signified by the assignment to each cardinal, except the patriarchs, of a titular church in Rome. The three categories of members of the college are cardinal Bishops, cardinal priests and cardinal deacons.

Cardinal Bishops include the six titular Bishops of the suburbicarian sees and Eastern patriarchs. First in rank are the titular Bishops of the suburbicarian sees, neighboring Rome: Ostia, Palestrina, Porto-Santa Rufina, Albano, Velletri-Segni, Frascati, Sabina-Poggio Mirteto. The dean of the college holds the title of the See of Ostia as well as his other suburbicarian see. These cardinal Bishops are engaged in full-time service in the central administration of church affairs in departments of the Roman Curia.

Full recognition is given in the revised Code of Canon Law to the position of Eastern patriarchs as the heads of sees of apostolic origin with ancient liturgies. They are assigned rank among the cardinals in order of seniority, following the suburbicarian titleholders.

Cardinal priests, who were formerly in charge of leading churches in Rome, are Bishops whose dioceses are outside Rome.

Cardinal deacons, who were formerly chosen according to regional divisions of Rome, are titular bishops assigned to full-time service in the Roman Curia.

The dean and sub-dean of the college are elected by the cardinal Bishops — subject to approval by the pope — from among their number. The dean, or the sub-dean in his absence, presides over the college as the first among equals. Cardinals Bernardin Gantin June 4, 1993 (papal approval June 5, 1993) and Joseph Ratzinger, Nov. 6, 1998 (papal approval Nov. 9, 1998) were elected dean and vice-dean, respectively,.

Selection and Duties

Cardinals are selected by the pope and are inducted into the college in appropriate ceremonies. Cardinals under the age of 80: elect the pope when the Holy See becomes vacant (see Index: Papal Election); and are major administrators of church affairs, serving in one or more departments of the Roman Curia. Cardinals in charge of agencies of the Roman Curia and Vatican City are asked to submit their resignation from office to the pope on reaching the age of 75. All cardinals enjoy a number of special rights and privileges. Their title, while symbolic of high honor, does not signify any extension of the powers of holy orders. They are called princes of the Church.

A cardinal *in pectore (petto)* is one whose selection has been made by the pope but whose name has not been disclosed; he has no title, rights or duties until such disclosure is made, at which time he takes precedence from the time of the secret selection.

BIOGRAPHIES OF CARDINALS

Biographies of the cardinals, as of Aug. 30, 1999, are given below in alphabetical order. For historical notes, order of seniority and geographical distribution of cardinals, see separate entries. An asterisk indicates cardinals ineligible to take part in papal elections.

Agustoni, Gilberto: b. July 26, 1922, Schaffhausen, Switzerland; ord. priest Apr. 20, 1946; called to Rome in 1950 to work under Cardinal Ottaviani in the Congregation for the Holy Office; a Prelate Auditor of the Roman Rota, 1970-86; ord. titular abp. of Caorle, Jan. 6, 1987; sec. of the Congregation for the Clergy, 1986-92; pro-prefect of the Apostolic Signatura, 1992-94; cardinal Nov. 26, 1994; deacon Sts. Urban and Laurence at Prima Porta. Prefect of Supreme Tribunal of Apostolic Signatura, 1994-98. Pefect emeritus of Supreme Tribunal of Apostolic Signatura. *Curial membership*: Bishops (congregations); Supreme Tribunal of the Apostolic Signatura Interpretation of Legislative (tribunal); Texts (council); APSA (office).

Ambrozic, Aloysius M.: b. Jan. 27, 1930, Gabrje, Slovenia (emigrated to Austria, 1945, and Canada, 1948); ord. priest June 4, 1955; taught Scripture, St. Augustine's Seminary, 1960-67; taught NT exegesis, Toronto School of Theology, 1970-76; aux. bp. of Toronto, March 26, 1976; co-adjutor of Toronto, May 22, 1986; abp. of Toronto, March 17, 1990; cardinal Feb. 21, 1998; titular church, Sts. Marcellinus and Peter. *Curial membership*: Clergy (congregation), Pastoral Care of Migrants and Itinerant People, Culture (councils).

Angelini,* Fiorenzo: b. Aug. 1, 1916, Rome, Italy; ord. priest Feb. 3, 1940; master of pontifical ceremonies, 1947-54; ord. bp. (titular see of Messene) July 29, 1956, and head of Rome Vicariate's section for apostolate to health care workers; abp, 1985; pres. of newly established Curia agency for health care workers; cardinal June 28, 1991, deacon, Holy Spirit (in Sassio). President of Pontifical Council for Pastoral Assistance to Health Care Workers, 1989-96.

Antonetti, Lorenzo: b. July 31, 1922, Romagnano Sesia, Italy; ord. priest, May 26, 1945; entered diplomatic service and served in Lebanon, Venezuela, first section for Extraordinary Affairs of the Secretariat of State, U.S., and France; ord. titular abp. of Roselle, May 12, 1968; apostolic nuncio to Nicaragua and Honduras, 1968-1973, and Zaire, 1973-77; secretary of the Administration of the Patrimony of the Apostolic See (APSA), 1977-88; apostolic nuncio to France, 1988-95; pro-president Admin. of the Patrimony of the Apostolic See, 1995-1998; pres. Administration of the Patrimony of the Apostolic See (APSA)., Feb. 23, 1998; cardinal, Feb. 21, 1998; deaconry, St. Agnes in Agone. President emeritus Administration of the Patrimony of the Apostolic See. *Curial membership*: Evangelization of Peoples (congregations), Economic Affairs of the Holy See, APSA (prefectures), Vatican City (commission).

Aponte Martínez, Luis: b. Aug. 4, 1922, Lajas, Puerto Rico; ord. priest Apr. 10, 1950; parish priest at Ponce; ord. titular bp. of Lares and aux. of Ponce, Oct. 12, 1960; bp. of Ponce, 1963-64; abp. of San Juan, Nov. 4, 1964; cardinal Mar. 5, 1973; titular church, St. Mary Mother of Providence (in Monte Verde). Abp. of San Juan.

Aramburu,* Juan Carlos: b. Feb. 11, 1912, Reduccion, Argentina; ord. priest in Rome, Oct. 28, 194; ord. titular bp. of Plataea and aux. of Tucuman, Argentina, Dec. 15, 1946; bp., 1953, and first abp., 1957, of Tucuman; titular abp. of Torri di Bizacena and coadj. abp. of Buenos Aires, June 14, 1967; abp. of Buenos Aires, Apr. 22, 1975 (resigned July 10, 1990); cardinal May 24, 1976; titular church, St. John Baptist of the Florentines. Abp. emeritus of Buenos Aires.

Araújo, Serafim Fernandes de: b. Aug. 13, 1924 Minas Novas, Brazil; ord. priest March 12, 1949; taught canon law at provincial seminary of Diamantina; titular bp. of Verinopolis and aux. bp. of Belo Horizonte, Jan. 19, 1959; co-adjutor abp. of Belo Horizonte, 1982; abp. Belo Horizonte Feb. 5, 1986; co-president of the Fourth General Conference of the Latin American Episcopate, 1992; cardinal, Feb. 21, 1998; titular church, St. Louis Marie Grignion de Montfort. Abp. of Belo Horizonte. *Curial membership*: Bishops (congregation); Latin America (commission), Justice and Peace (council).

Arinze, Francis: b. Nov. 1, 1932, Eziowelle, Nigeria; ord. priest Nov. 23, 1958; ord. titular bp. of Fissiana and aux. bp. of Onitsha, Aug. 29, 1965; abp. of Onitsha, 1967-84; pro-president of Secretariat for Non-Christians (now the Council for Interreligious Dialogue), 1984; cardinal May 25, 1985; deacon, St. John (della Pigna); transferred to the order of cardinal priests Jan. 29, 1996. President of Council for Interreligious Dialogue, 1985. *Curial membership*: Doctrine of the Faith, Oriental Churches, Evangelization of Peoples, Causes of Saints (congregations); Laity, Christian Unity, Culture (councils); International Eucharistic Congresses, Holy Year 2000 (committees).

Arns, Paulo Evaristo, O.F.M.: b. Sept. 14, 1921, Forquilhinha, Brazil; ord. priest Nov. 30, 1945; held various teaching posts; director of *Sponsa Christi*, monthly review for religious, and of the Franciscan publication center in Brazil; ord. titular bp. of Respetta and aux. bp. of São Paulo, July 3, 1966; abp. of São Paulo, Oct. 22, 1970; cardinal Mar. 5, 1973 (resigned April, 1998); titular church, St. Anthony of Padua (in Via Tuscolana). Abp. emeritus of São Paulo.

Bafile,* Corrado: b. July 4, 1903, L'Aquila, Italy; practiced law in Rome for six years before beginning studies for priesthood; ord. priest Apr. 11, 1936; served in Vatican secretariat of state, 1939-59; ord. titular abp. of Antiochia in Pisidia, Mar. 19, 1960; apostolic nuncio to Germany, 1960-75; pro-prefect of Congregation for Causes of Saints, July 18, 1975; cardinal May 24, 1976; deacon, S. Maria (in Portico); transferred to order of cardinal priests, June 22, 1987; prefect of Congregation for Causes of Saints, 1976-80.

Baum, William Wakefield: b. Nov. 21, 1926, Dallas, Tex.; moved to Kansas City, Mo., at an early age; ord. priest (Kansas City-St. Joseph diocese) May 12, 1951; executive director of U.S. Bishops commission for ecumenical and interreligious affairs, 1964-69; attended Second Vatican Council as *peritus* (expert adviser); ord. bp. of Springfield-Cape Girardeau, Mo., Apr. 6, 1970; abp. of Washington, D.C., 1973-80; cardinal May 24, 1976; titular church, Holy Cross (on the Via Flaminia); prefect of Congregation for Catholic Education (Seminaries and Institutes of Study), 1980-90. Major Penitentiary, 1990. *Curial membership*: Secretariat of State (second section); Doctrine of the Faith, Bishops, Oriental Churches, Causes of Saints, Institutes of Consecrated Life and Societies of Apostolic Life, Evangelization of Peoples (congregations); Texts (council); APSA (office).

Bertoli,* Paolo: b. Feb.1, 1908, Poggio Garfagnana, Italy; ord. priest Aug. 15, 1930; entered diplomatic service of the Holy See, serving in nunciatures in Yugoslavia, France, Haiti and Switzerland; ord. titular abp. of Nicomedia, May 11, 1952; apostolic delegate to Turkey (1952-53), nuncio to Colombia (1953-59), Lebanon (1959-60), France (1960-69); cardinal Apr. 28, 1969; prefect of Congregation for Causes of Saints, 1969-73; entered order of cardinal Bishops as titular bp. of Frascati, June 30, 1979; Chamberlain (Camerlengo) of Holy Roman Church, 1979-85.

Bevilacqua, Anthony Joseph: b. June 17, 1923, Brooklyn N.Y.; ord. priest (Brooklyn diocese) June 11, 1949; ord. titular bp. of Aquae Albae in Byzacena and aux. bp. of Brooklyn, Nov. 24, 1980; bp. of Pittsburgh Oct. 7, 1983, installed Dec. 12, 1983; abp. of Philadelphia, Feb. 11, 1988; cardinal June 28, 1991; titular church, Most Holy Redeemer and St. Alphonsus (on Via Merulana). Abp. of Philadelphia. *Curial membership*: Clergy, Causes of Saints (congregations); "Cor Unum," Migrants and Itinerant People (councils).

Biffi, Giacomo: b. June 13, 1928, Milan, Italy; ord. priest Dec. 23, 1950; ord. titular bp. of Fidene and aux. of Milan, Jan. 11, 1976; abp. of Bologna, Apr. 19, 1984; cardinal May 25, 1985; titular church, Sts. John the Evangelist and Petronius. Archbp. of Bologna. *Curial membership*: Divine Worship and Sacraments, Clergy, Catholic Education (congregations).

Canestri,* Giovanni: b. Sept. 30, 1918, Castelspina, Italy; ord. priest Apr. 12, 1941; spiritual director of Rome's seminary, 1959; ord. titular bp. of Tenedo and aux. to the cardinal vicar of Rome, July 30, 1961; bp. of Tortona, 1971-75; titular bp. of Monterano (personal title of archbp.) and vice regent of Rome, 1975-84; abp. of Cagliari, 1984-87; abp. of Genoa, July 6, 1987 (resigned Apr. 20, 1995); cardinal June 28, 1988; titular church, St. Andrew of the Valley. Abp. emeritus of Genoa.

Caprio,* Giuseppe: b. Nov. 15, 1914, Lapio, Italy; ord. priest Dec. 17, 1938; served in diplomatic missions in China (1947-51, when Vatican diplomats were expelled by communists), Belgium (1951-54), and South Vietnam (1954-56); internuncio in China with residence at Taiwan, 1959-67; ord. titular abp. of Apollonia, Dec. 17, 1961; pro-nuncio in India, 1967-69; secretary, 1969-77, and president, 1979-81, of Administration of Patrimony of Holy See; substitute secretary of state, 1977-79; cardinal deacon June 30, 1979; transferred to order of cardinal priests, November, 1990; titular church, St. Mary of Victory; president of Prefecture of Economic Affairs of the Holy See, 1981-90. Grand Master of Equestrian Order of the Holy Sepulchre, 1988-95.

Carles Gordó, Ricardo Maria: b. Sept. 24, 1926, Valencia, Spain; ord. priest June 29, 1951; ord. bp. of Tortosa, Aug. 3, 1969; abp. of Barcelona, Mar. 23, 1990; cardinal Nov. 26, 1994; titular church, St. Mary of Consolation in Tiburtino. Abp. of Barcelona. *Curial membership*: Catholic Education (congregation); Justice and Peace (council).

Carter,* Gerald Emmett: b. Mar. 1, 1912, Montreal, Canada; ord. priest May 22, 1937; founder and president of St. Joseph Teachers' College and co-founder and director of Thomas More Institute for adult education; ord. titular bp. of Altiburo and aux. bp. of London, Ont., Feb. 2, 1962; bp. of London, Ont., 1964-78; vice president, 1971-73, and president, 1975-77, of Canadian Conference of Catholic Bishops; abp. of Toronto, 1978-90; cardinal June 30, 1979; titular church, St. Mary (in Traspontina). Archbp. emeritus of Toronto.

Casoria,* Giuseppe: b. Oct. 1, 1908, Acerra, Italy; ord. priest Dec. 21, 1930; jurist; Roman Curia official from 1937; under-secretary, 1959-69, and secretary, 1969-73, of Congregation for Divine Worship and Sacraments; secretary of Congregation for Causes of Saints, 1973-81; ord. titular bp. of Vescovia with personal title of abp., Feb. 13, 1972; pro-prefect of Congregation for Divine Worship and Sacraments, 1981-83; cardinal deacon Feb. 2, 1983; transferred to order of cardinal priests Apr. 5, 1993; titular church, St. Joseph on Via Trionfale. Prefect of Congregation for Divine Worship and Sacraments, 1983-84.

Cassidy, Edward Idris: b. July 5, 1924, Sydney, Australia; ord. priest July 23, 1949; entered Vatican diplomatic service in 1955; served in nunciatures in India, Ireland, El Salvador and Argentina; ord. titular bp. of Amantia with personal title of abp., Nov. 15, 1970; pro-nuncio to Republic of China (Taiwan), 1970-79 and pro-nuncio to Bangladesh and apostolic delegate in Burma, 1973-79; pro-nuncio to Lesotho and apostolic delegate to southern Africa, 1979-84; pro-nuncio to the Netherlands, 1984-88; substitute of the Secretary of State for General Affairs, 1988-89; pres. of Pontifical Council for Promoting Christian Unity, 1989; cardinal June 28, 1991; deacon, St. Mary (in via Lata). President of Pontifical Council for Promoting Christian Unity. *Curial membership*: Secretariat of State (second section); Doctrine of the Faith, Divine Worship and Sacraments, Bishops, Oriental Churches, Evangelization of Peoples (congregations); Interreligious Dialogue, "Cor Unum" (councils); APSA (office); Latin America, Holy Year 2000 (committees).

Castillo Lara, Rosalio José, S.D.B.: b. Sept. 4, 1922, San Casimiro, Venezuela; ord. priest Sept. 4, 1949; ord. titular bp. of Precausa, May 24, 1973; coadj. bp. of Trujillo, 1973-76; abp. May 26, 1982; pro-pres. of Pontifical Commission for Revision of Code of Canon Law, 1982-84; pro-pres. of Commission for Authentic Interpretation of Code of Canon Law, 1984-85; cardinal May 25, 1985; deacon, Our Lady of Coromoto (in St. John of God); transferred to order of cardinal priests Jan. 29, 1996; pres. of Administration of Patrimony of the Holy See, 1989-95. President of the Pontifical Commission for the State of Vatican City State, 1990-97. *Curial membership*: Secretariat of State (second section); Institutes of Consecrated Life and Societies of Apostolic Life (congregations); Institute for Works of Religion (commission).

Castrillón Hoyos, Darío: b. July 4, 1929, Medellín, Colombia; ord. priest Oct. 26, 1952; served as curate in two parishes; dir. local Cursillo Movement; delegate for Catholic Action; taught canon law at the Free Civil University; gen. sec. of the Colombian Bishops' Conference; coadj. bp. of Pereira, June 2, 1971; bp. of Pereira, 1976-1992; gen. sec. of Latin American Episcopal Council (CELAM) 1983-87; pres. CELAM, 1987-91; abp. of Bucaramanga, 1992-96; pro-prefect Cong. for the Clergy, 1996-98; Pref. Cong. for the Clergy, 1998; cardinal, Feb. 21, 1998; deaconry, Holy Name of Mary on the Forum Traiani. Prefect of the Congregation for the Clergy. *Curial membership*: Evangelization of Peoples, Education (congregations); Social Communications, Texts (councils); APSA (office).

Cé, Marco: b. July 8, 1925, Izano, Italy; ord. priest Mar. 27, 1948; taught sacred scripture and dogmatic theology at seminary in his home diocese of Crema; rector of seminary, 1957; presided over diocesan liturgical commission, preached youth retreats; ord. titular bp. of Vulturia, May 17, 1970; aux. bp. of Bologna, 1970-76; gen. ecclesiastical assistant of Italian Catholic Action, 1976-78; patriarch of Venice, Dec. 7, 1978; cardinal June 30, 1979; titular church, St. Mark. Patriarch of Venice. *Curial membership*: Divine Worship and Sacraments, Oriental Churches (congregations).

Cheli,* Giovanni: b. October 4, 1918, Turin, Italy; ord. priest, June 21, 1942; entered Secretariat of State and diplomatic service; second secretary, apostolic nunciature in Guatemala, 1952-55; first secretary, apostolic nunciature in Madrid, Spain, 1955-62; counselor, nunciature in Rome, 1962-67; Council for Public Affairs of the Church, Vatican City, 1967-73; Permanent Observer of the Holy See to the United Nations, 1973-86; ord. titular abp. of Santa Giusta, Sept. 16, 1978; pres. Pontifical Council for the Pastoral Care of Migrants and Itinerant People, 1986-98; cardinal, Feb. 21, 1998; deaconry, Sts. Cosmas and Damian. President Emeritus Pontifical Council for the Pastoral Care of Migrants and Itinerant People.

Clancy, Edward Bede: b. Dec. 13, 1923, Lithgow, New South Wales, Australia; ord. priest July 23, 1949; ord. titular bp. of Ard Carna and aux. of Sydney, Jan. 19, 1974; abp. of Canberra, 1978-83; abp. of Sydney, Feb. 12, 1983; cardinal June 28, 1988; titular church, Holy Mary of Vallicella. Abp. of Sydney. *Curial membership*: Secretariat of State (second section); APSA (office).

Colasuonno, Francesco: b. Jan. 2, 1925, Grumo Appulia, Italy; ord. priest Sep. 28, 1947; taught in seminary of archdiocese of Bari; entered diplomatic service in 1958; served in section for Extraordinary Ecclesiastical Affairs of the Secretariat of State and in nunciatures in U.S., India, and Taiwan; ord. titular abp. of Truentum, Dec. 6, 1974; first apostolic delegate to Mozambique, 1974-81; apostolic delegate to Zimbabwe, 1981-85; apostolic pro-nuncio to Yugoslavia, 1985-86; headed Holy See delegation for permanent working contacts with Poland, 1986-90; representative to the USSR, 1990-94; nuncio to Italy, 1994-98, and San Marino, 1995-98; cardinal, Feb. 21, 1998. *Curial membership*: Oriental Churches (congregation); Promoting Christian Unity, Justice and Peace (councils).

Corripio Ahumada,* Ernesto: b. June 29, 1919, Tampico, Mexico; ord. priest Oct. 25, 1942, in Rome, where he remained until almost the end of World War II; taught and held various positions in local semi-

nary of Tampico, 1945-50; ord. titular bp. of Zapara and aux. bp. of Tampico, Mar. 19, 1953; bp. of Tampico, 1956-67; abp. of Antequera, 1967-76; abp. of Puebla de los Angeles, 1976-77; abp. of Mexico City and primate of Mexico, July 19, 1977 (resigned Sept. 29, 1994); cardinal June 30, 1979; titular church, Mary Immaculate al Tiburtino. Abp. emeritus of Mexico City. *Curial membership*: Clergy (congregation).

Daly,* Cahal Brendan: b. Oct. 1, 1917, Loughguile, Northern Ireland; ord. priest June 22, 1941; earned advanced degrees in philosophy and theology; 30 years of priestly life dedicated to teaching; attended Second Vatican Council as a theological adviser to members of Irish hierarchy; outspoken critic of violence in Northern Ireland; ord. bp. of Ardagh, July 16, 1967; bp. of Down and Connor, 1982-90; abp. of Armagh and primate of All Ireland, Nov. 6, 1990; cardinal June 28, 1991; titular church, St. Patrick. Abp. emeritus of Armagh (resigned Oct. 1, 1996).

Danneels, Godfried: b. June 4, 1933, Kanegem, Belgium; ord. priest Aug. 17, 1957; professor of liturgy and sacramental theology at Catholic University of Louvain, 1969-77; ord. bp. of Antwerp Dec. 18, 1977; app. abp. of Mechelen-Brussel, Dec. 19, 1979; installed Jan. 4, 1980; cardinal Feb. 2, 1983; titular church, St. Anastasia. Abp. of Mechelen-Brussel, military ordinary of Belgium. *Curial membership*: Secretariat of State (second section); Oriental Churches, Divine Worship and Sacraments, Evangelization of Peoples, Catholic Education (congregations).

Darmaatmadja, Julius Riyadi, S.J.: b. Dec. 20, 1934, Muntilan, Mageland, Central Java, Indonesia; entered Society of Jesus in 1957; ord. priest Dec. 18, 1969; ord. abp. of Semarang, June 29, 1983 (transferred to Jakarta Jan. 11, 1996); cardinal Nov. 26, 1994; titular church, Sacred Heart of Mary. Abp. of Jakarta, military ordinary of Indonesia (1984). *Curial membership*: Evangelization of Peoples (congregation); Interreligious Dialogue (council).

de Giorgi, Salvatore: b. Sep. 6, 1930 Vernole, Italy; ord. priest June 28, 1953; diocesan chaplain to the Teachers' Movement of Catholic Action; dir. Diocesan Pastoral Office; app. titular bp. of Tulana and aux. bp. of Oria, Nov. 21, 1973; bp. of Oria, March 17, 1978; abp. of Foggia, Apr. 4, 1981; abp. of Taranto, Oct. 10, 1987 (resigned, 1990); general president of Catholic Action, 1990-96; abp. of Palermo, Apr. 4, 1996; president of the Sicilian Episcopal Conference; cardinal Feb. 21, 1998; titular church, St. Mary in Ara Caeli. Abp. of Palermo. *Curial membership*: Laity, Family (councils).

Deskur, Andrzej Maria: b. Feb. 29, 1924, Sancygniow, Poland; ord. priest Aug. 20, 1950, in France; assigned to Vatican secretariat of state, 1952; undersecretary and later secretary of Pontifical Commission for Film, Radio and TV (Social Communications), 1954-73; ord. titular bp. of Tene, June 30, 1974; abp., 1980; president of Pontifical Commission for Social Communications, 1974-84; cardinal May 25, 1985; deacon, St. Cesario (in Palatio); transferred to order of cardinal priests Jan. 29, 1996. President emeritus of Council for Social Communications. *Curial membership*: Divine Worship and Sacraments, Causes of Saints (congregations); Health Care Workers (council); State of Vatican City (commission).

Dezza,* Paolo, S.J.: b. Dec. 13, 1901, Parma, Italy; entered Society of Jesus in 1918; ord. priest, Mar. 25, 1928; made solemn profession as Jesuit, 1935; served as rector of Pontifical Gregorian University; delegated as head of Society of Jesus by John Paul II Ocober, 1981, until the election of the new superior general; cardinal June 28, 1991, with permission to decline episcopal ordination; deacon, St. Ignatius of Loyola (a Campo Marzio).

do Nascimento, Alexandre: b. Mar. 1, 1925, Malanje, Angola; ord. priest Dec. 20, 1952, in Rome; professor of dogmatic theology in major seminary of Luanda, Angola; editor of *O Apostolada*, Catholic newspaper; forced into exile in Lisbon, Portugal, 1961-71; returned to Angola, 1971; professor at Pius XII Institute of Social Sciences; ord. bp. of Malanje, Aug. 31, 1975; abp. of Lubango and apostolic administrator of Onjiva, 1977-86; held hostage by Angolan guerrillas, Oct. 15 to Nov. 16, 1982; cardinal Feb. 2, 1983; titular church, St. Mark in Agro Laurentino. Abp. of Luanda, 1986. *Curial membership*: Evangelization of Peoples, Catholic Education (congregations).

Echeverría Ruiz,* Bernardino, O.F.M.: b. Nov. 12, 1912, Cotacachi, Ecuador; entered Franciscans 1928; ord. priest July 4, 1937; ord. bp. of Ambato Dec. 4, 1949; abp. of Guayaquil, 1969-89; apostolic administrator of Ibarra, 1989-95; cardinal Nov. 26, 1994; titular church, Sts. Nereus and Achilleus. Abp. emeritus of Guayaquil.

Etchegaray, Roger: b. Sept. 25, 1922, Espelette, France; ord. priest July 13, 1947; deputy director, 1961-66, and secretary general, 1966-70, of French Episcopal Conference; ord. titular bp. of Gemelle di Numidia and aux. of Paris, May 27, 1969; abp. of Marseilles, 1970-84; prelate of Mission de France, 1975-82; president of French Episcopal Conference, 1979-81; cardinal June 30, 1979; titular church, St. Leo I; president of Council *Cor Unum*, 1984-95. President of Council for Justice and Peace (1984-98) and President of Central Committee for the Jubilee of the Holy Year 2000 (1994-98); transferred to order of cardinal bishops, June 24, 1998 (suburbicarian see of Porto-Santa Rufina). President of the Central Committee for the Jubilee of the Holy Year 2000. *Curial membership*: Oriental Churches, Evangelization of Peoples, Catholic Education (congregations); Laity, Christian Unity, Social Communications, Interreligious Dialogue (councils).

Etsou-Nzabi-Bamungwabi, Frédéric, C.I.C.M.: b. Dec. 3, 1930, Mazalonga, Zaire; ord. priest July 13, 1958; educ. Catholic Institute of Paris (degree in sociology) and "Lumen Vitae" in Belgium (degree in pastoral theology); ord. titular bp. of Menefessi and coadj. abp. of Mbandaka-Bikora, Nov. 7, 1976; abp. of Mbandaka-Bikora, 1977-1990; abp. of Kinshasa, July 7, 1990; cardinal June 28, 1991; titular church, St. Lucy (a Piazza d'Armi). Abp. of Kinshasa. *Curial membership*: Evangelization of Peoples (congregation); Family (council).

Eyt, Pierre: b. June 4, 1934, Laruns, France; ord. priest June 29, 1961; chaplain of St. Louis of the French in Rome, 1963; taught theology at Catholic Institute in Toulouse, 1967-72; ord. coadj. abp. of Bordeaux, Sept. 28, 1986; abp. of Bordeaux, May 31, 1989; cardinal Nov. 26, 1994; titular church, Most Holy Trinity on Monte Pincio. Abp. of Bordeaux.

Curial membership: Doctrine of the Faith, Catholic Education (congregations).

Fagiolo,* Vincenzo: b. Feb. 5, 1918, Segni, Italy; ord. priest Mar. 6, 1943; prelate auditor of Roman Rota, 1967-71; ord. abp. of Chieti-Vasto, Dec. 19, 1971; resigned see July 15, 1984; secretary of Congregation for Institutes of Consecrated Life and Societies of Apostolic Life, 1984-90; president of the Pontifical Council for the Interpretation of Legislative Texts, 1991-94; cardinal Nov. 26, 1994; deacon, St. Theodore. President of Diciplinary Commission of the Roman Curia, Dec. 29, 1990.

Falcão, José Freire: b. Oct. 23, 1925, Erere, Brazil; ord. priest June 19, 1949; ord. titular bp. of Vardimissa and coadj. of Limoeiro do Norte, June 17, 1967; bp. of Limoeiro do Norte, Aug. 19, 1967; abp. of Teresina, Nov. 25, 1971; abp. of Brasilia, Feb. 15, 1984; cardinal June 28, 1988; titlar church, St. Luke (Via Prenestina). Abp. of Brasilia. *Curial membership*: Health Care Workers (council); Latin America (commission).

Felici,* Angelo: b. July 26, 1919, Segni, Italy; ord. priest Apr. 4, 1942; in Vatican diplomatic service from 1945; ord. titular bp. of Cesariana, with personal title of abp., Sept. 24, 1967; nuncio to Netherlands, 1967-76, Portugal, 1976-79, France, 1979-88; cardinal June 28, 1988; deacon, Sts. Blaise and Charles in Catinari, promoted to cardinal priest, Jan. 9, 1999. Prefect of Congregation for Causes of Saints, 1988-95. President of Pontifical Commission "Ecclesia Dei," 1995. *Curial membership*: Secretariat of State (second section); Oriental Churches, Bishops, Evangelization of Peoples, Clergy (congregations); Christian Unity (council).

Fresno Larraín,* Juan Francisco: b. July 26, 1914, Santiago, Chile; ord. priest Dec. 18, 1937; ord. bp. of Copiapo, Aug. 15, 1958; abp. of La Serena, 1967-83; abp. of Santiago, May 3, 1983 (resigned Mar. 30, 1990); cardinal May 25, 1985; titular church, St. Mary Immaculate of Lourdes (a Boccea). Abp. emeritus of Santiago.

Furno, Carlo: b. Dec. 2, 1921, Bairo Canavese, Italy; ord. priest June 25, 1944; entered diplomatic service of the Holy See in the 1950s; served in Colombia, Ecuador and Jerusalem; worked in Secretariat of State for 11 years and taught at Pontifical Ecclesiastical Academy, 1966-73; ord. titular bp. of Abari with personal title of abp., Sept. 16, 1973; nuncio in Peru, 1973-78, Lebanon, 1978-82, Brazil, 1982-92, Italy, 1992-94; cardinal Nov. 26, 1994; deacon, Sacred Heart of Christ the King. Grand Master of the Equestrian Order of the Holy Sepulchre, 1995; pontifical delegate for Patriarchal Basilica of St. Francis in Assisi, 1996; archpriest of the patriarchal basilica of Santa Maria Maggiore, Rome, 1998. *Curial membership*: Secretariat of State (second section); Oriental Churches, Bishops, Evangelization of Peoples (congregations); State of Vatican City, Institute for Works of Religion (commissions).

Gagnon,* Edouard, P.S.S.: b. Jan. 15, 1918, Port Daniel, Que., Canada; ord. priest Aug. 15, 1940; ord. bp. of St. Paul in Alberta Mar. 25, 1969 (resigned May 3, 1972); rector of Canadian College in Rome, 1972-77; vice president-secretary of Vatican Committee for the Family, 1973-80; titular abp. of Giustiniana Prima, July 7, 1983; pro-president of Pontifical Council for the Family, 1983; cardinal May

25, 1985; deacon, St. Elena (fuori Porta Prenestina); transferred to order of cardinal priests Jan. 29, 1996; titular church St. Marcellus; president of Pontifical Council for the Family, 1985-90. President of Pontifical Committee for International Eucharistic Congresses, 1991.

Gantin, Bernardin: b. May 8, 1922, Toffo, Dahomey (now Benin); ord. priest Jan. 14, 1951; ord. titular bp. of Tipasa di Mauritania and aux. bp. of Cotonou, Feb. 3, 1957; abp. of Cotonou, 1960-71; associate secretary (1971-73) and secretary (1973-75) of Congregation for Evangelization of Peoples; vice-president (1975) and president (1976-84) of Pontifical Commission for Justice and Peace; cardinal deacon June 27, 1977; transferred to order of priests June 25, 1984; titular church, Sacred Heart of Christ the King; titular bp. of suburbicarian see of Palestrina Sept 29, 1986, when he entered the order of cardinal bishops, and of Ostia June 5, 1993, when he became dean of the college of cardinals. Prefect of Congregation for Bishops, 1984-98; president of commission for Latin America, 1984-98; dean of college of cardinals, 1993. *Curial membership*: Secretariat of State (second section); Divine Worship and Sacraments, Causes of Saints, Evangelization of Peoples, Oriental Churches, Institutes of Consecrated Life and Societies of Apostolic Life, Catholic Education (congregations); Apostolic Signatura (tribunal).

George, Francis E., O.M.I.: b. Jan. 16, 1937, Chicago, Ill.; ord. priest Dec. 21, 1963; provincial of central region of Oblates of Mary Immaculate, 1973-74; vicar general, 1974-86; ord. bp. of Yakima, Sept. 21, 1990; abp. of Portland, Ore., Apr. 30, 1996, installed May 27, 1996; abp. of Chicago, Apr. 8, 1997, installed May 7, 1997; cardinal Feb. 21, 1998; titular church, St. Bartholomew on Tiber Island. Abp. of Chicago. *Curial membership*: Divine Worship and the Discipline of the Sacraments, Institutes of Consecrated Life and Societies of Apostolic Life (congregations); "Cor Unum" (council).

Giordano, Michele: b. Sept. 26, 1930, S. Arcangelo, Italy; ord. priest July 5, 1953; ord. titular bp. of LariCastello and aux. of Matera, Feb. 5, 1972; abp. of Matera and Irsina, 1974-87; abp. of Naples, May 9, 1987; cardinal June 28, 1988; titular church, St. Joachim. Abp. of Naples. *Curial membership*: Secretariat of State (second section); Divine Worship and Sacraments, Clergy (congregations); Health Care Workers (council).

Glemp, Józef: b. Dec. 18, 1929, Inowroclaw, Poland; assigned to forced labor on German farm in Rycerzow during Nazi occupation; ord. priest May 25, 1956; studied in Rome, 1958-64; received degree in Roman and canon law from Pontifical Lateran University; secretary of primatial major seminary at Gniezno on his return to Poland, 1964; spokesman for secretariat of primate of Poland and chaplain of primate for archdiocese of Gniezno, 1967; ord. bp. of Warmia, Apr. 21, 1979; abp. of Gniezno, 1981-92, with title of abp. of Warsaw and primate of Poland; cardinal Feb. 2, 1983; titular church, St. Mary in Trastevere. Abp. of Warsaw (Mar. 25, 1992), primate of Poland, ordinary for Eastern-rite faithful in Poland who do not have ordinaries of their own rites. *Curial membership*: Oriental Churches (congregation); Culture (council).

Gong Pin-mei,* Ignatius: b. Aug. 2, 1901,

P'ou-tong, China; ord. priest May 28, 1930; worked in schools and as a missionary; ord. bp. of Soochow Oct. 7, 1949; bp. of Shanghai July 15, 1950; imprisoned by Chinese communists in 1955 and sentenced to life imprisonment in 1960; paroled in 1985 after 30 years; pardoned and political rights restored Jan. 5, 1988, but was not permitted to function as a bp.; came to the United States in 1988; cardinal June 30, 1979 *in pectore*; name revealed and formally invested at June 28, 1991, public consistory; titular church, St. Sixtus. Bp. of Shanghai and apostolic administrator of Soochow. (Resides in U.S.)

González Martin,* Marcelo: b. Jan. 16, 1918, Villanubla, Spain; ord. priest June 29, 1941; taught theology and sociology at Valladolid diocesan seminary; founded organization for construction of houses for poor; ord. bp. of Astorga, Mar. 5, 1961; titular abp. of Case Mediane and coadj. of Barcelona, Feb. 21, 1966; abp. of Barcelona, 1967-71; abp. of Toledo, 1971-95; cardinal Mar. 5, 1973; titular church, St. Augustine. Abp. emeritus of Toledo.

Gouyon,* Paul: b. Oct. 24, 1910, Bordeaux, France; ord. priest Mar. 13, 1937; ord. bp. of Bayonne, Oct. 7, 1957; titular abp. of Pessinonte and coadj. abp. of Rennes, Sept. 6, 1963; abp. of Rennes, Sept. 4, 1964 (resigned Oct. 15, 1985); cardinal Apr. 28, 1969; titular church, Nativity of Our Lord Jesus Christ (Via Gallia). Abp. emeritus of Rennes.

Gröer,* Hans Hermann, O.S.B.: b. Oct. 13, 1919, Vienna, Austria; ord. priest Apr. 12, 1942; ord. abp. of Vienna, Sept. 14, 1986; cardinal June 28, 1988; titular church, Sts. Joachim and Anne al Tuscolano. Abp. emeritus of Vienna (resigned Sept. 14, 1995). *Curial membership*: Oriental Churches, Divine Worship and Sacraments, Institutes of Consecrated Life and Societies of Apostolic Life, Catholic Education (congregations).

Gulbinowicz, Henryk Roman: b. Oct. 17, 1928, Szukiszki, Poland; ord. priest June 18, 1950; ord. titular bp. of Acci and apostolic administrator of Polish territory in Lithuanian archdiocese of Vilnius (Vilna), Feb. 8, 1970; abp. of Wroclaw, Poland, Jan. 3, 1976; cardinal May 25, 1985; titular church, Immaculate Conception of Mary (a Grottarosa). Abp. of Wroclaw. *Curial membership*: Oriental Churches, Evangelization of Peoples, Clergy (congregations).

Hickey, James A.: b. Oct. 11, 1920, Midland, Mich.; ord. priest (Saginaw diocese) June 15, 1946; ord. titular bp. of Taraqua and aux. of Saginaw, Apr. 14, 1967; rector of North American College, Rome, 1969-74; bp. of Cleveland, 1974-80; app. of Washington, D.C., June 17, 1980, installed Aug. 5, 1980; cardinal June 28, 1988; titular church, St. Mary Mother of the Redeemer. Abp. of Washington, D.C. *Curial membership*: Causes of Saints, Institutes of Consecrated Life and Societies of Apostolic Life, Catholic Education, Clergy (congregations); Family (council).

Innocenti,* Antonio: b. Aug. 23, 1915, Poppi, Italy; ord. priest July 17, 1938; held curial and diplomatic positions; ord. titular bp. of Eclano with personal title of abp., Feb. 18, 1968; nuncio to Paraguay, 1967-73; secretary of Congregation for Causes of Saints, 1973-75; secretary of Congregation for Sacraments and Divine Worship, 1975-80; nuncio to Spain, 1980-85; cardinal deacon May 25, 1985; transferred to order of cardinal priests Jan. 29, 1996; titular church, St. Marie (in Aquiro); prefect of Congregation for the Clergy, 1986-91; president of Pontifical Commission for Preservation of Artistic Patrimony of the Church, 1988-91; president of Pontifical Commission "Ecclesia Dei," 1991-95.

Javierre Ortas, Antonio María, S.D.B.: b. Feb. 21, 1921, Sietamo, Spain; ord. priest Apr. 24, 1949; leading European writer on ecumenism; ord. titular bp. of Meta with personal title of abp., June 29, 1976; Secretary of Congregation for Catholic Education, 1976-88; cardinal June 28, 1988; deacon (Santa Maria Liberatrice a Monte Testaccio), promoted to cardinal priest, Jan. 9, 1999 (Santa Maria Liberatrice a Monte Testaccio; raised to presbyteral title). Librarian and Archivist of the Holy Roman Church, 1988-92. Prefect of Congregation for Divine Worship and the Sacraments, 1992-96. *Curial membership*: Doctrine of the Faith, Bishops, Catholic Education, Clergy (congregations); Apostolic Signatura (tribunal); Laity, Christian Unity, Interpretation of Legislative Texts (councils).

Keeler, William Henry: b. Mar. 4, 1931, San Antonio, Tex.; ord. priest (Harrisburg diocese) July 17, 1955; secretary to Bp. Leech at Vatican II, named *peritus* by Pope John XXIII; ord. titular bp. of Ulcinium and aux. bp. of Harrisburg, Sept. 21, 1979; bp. of Harrisburg, Nov. 10, 1983, installed Jan. 4, 1984; abp. of Baltimore, Apr. 6, 1989; cardinal Nov. 26, 1994; titular church, St. Mary of the Angels. Abp. of Baltimore. *Curial membership*: Oriental Churches (congregation); Christian Unity (council).

Kim Sou-hwan, Stephen: b. May 8, 1922, Tae Gu, Korea; ord. priest Sept. 15, 1951; ord. bp. of Masan, May 31, 1966; abp. of Seoul, Apr. 9, 1968(resigned May 29, 1998); cardinal Apr. 28, 1969; titular church, St. Felix of Cantalice (Centocelle). Abp. emeritus of Seoul, apostolic administrator emeritus of Pyeong Yang. *Curial membership*: Evangelization of Peoples (congregation).

Kitbunchu, Michael Michai: b. Jan. 25, 1929, Samphran, Thailand; ord. priest Dec. 20, 1959, in Rome; rector of metropolitan seminary in Bangkok, 1965-72; ord. abp. of Bangkok, June 3, 1973; cardinal Feb. 2, 1983, the first from Thailand; titular church, St. Laurence in Panisperna. Abp. of Bangkok. *Curial membership*: Evangelization of Peoples (congregation); Economic Affairs of the Holy See (office).

König,* Franz: b. Aug. 3, 1905, Rabenstein, Lower Austria; ord. priest Oct. 29, 1933; ord. titular bp. of Livias and coadj. bp. of Sankt Poelten, Aug. 31, 1952; abp. of Vienna, May 10, 1956 (resigned Sept. 16, 1985); cardinal Dec. 15, 1958; titular church, St. Eusebius; president of Secretariat (now Council) for Dialogue with Non-Believers, 1965-80. Abp. emeritus of Vienna.

Korec, Ján Chryzostom, S.J.: b. Jan. 22, 1924, Bosany, Slovakia; entered Society of Jesus in 1939; ord. priest Oct. 1, 1950; ord. bp. secretly Aug. 24, 1951; sentenced to 12 years in prison in 1960 for helping seminarians with their study and ordaining priests; paroled in 1968; appointed bp. of Nitra Feb. 6, 1990; cardinal June 28, 1991; titular church, Sts. Fabian and Venantius (a Villa Forelli). Bp. of Nitra. *Curial membership*: Institutes of Consecrated Life and Societies of Apostolic Life (Congregation); Culture (council).

Kozlowiecki,* Adam, S.J.: b. Apr. 1, 1911, Huta Komorowska, Poland; ord. priest June 24, 1937; ar-

rested by Nazi Gestapo with 24 fellow priests in Cracow in 1939 and sent to Auschwitz concentration camp; moved to Dachau six months later where he suffered throughout the war; sent to Rhodesia after the war and taught until 1950; appointed apostolic administrator of prefecture of Lusaka, 1950; appointed bp. and vicar apostolic, Sept. 11, 1955; appointed abp. of Lusaka, 1959; resigned, 1969, to allow a native African to receive the post; member Congregation for the Evangelization of People, 1970-91; cardinal, Feb. 21, 1998; titular church, St. Andrew on the Quirinal.

Kuharic,* Franjo: b. Apr. 15, 1919, Pribic, Croatia; ord. priest July 15, 1945; ord. titular bp. of Meta and aux. bp. of Zagreb, May 3, 1964; apostolic administrator of archdiocese of Zagreb, 1968-70; abp. of Zagreb, June 16, 1970; cardinal Feb. 2, 1983; titular church, St. Jerome of the Croats. Abp. emeritus of Zagreb (resigned July 5, 1997). *Curial membership*: Divine Worship and Sacraments, Clergy (congregations).

Laghi, Pio: b. May 21, 1922, Castiglione, Italy; ord. priest Apr. 20, 1946; entered diplomatic service of the Holy See in 1952; served in Nicaragua, the U.S. (as secretary of the apostolic delegation, 1954-61) and India; recalled to Rome and served on Council for Public Affairs of the Church; ord. titular abp. of Mauriana June 22, 1969; apostolic delegate to Jerusalem and Palestine, 1969-74; nuncio to Argentina, 1974-80; apostolic delegate, 1980-84, and first pro-nuncio, 1984-90 to the U.S.; pro-prefect of Congregation for Catholic Education, 1990-91; cardinal June 28, 1991; deacon, St. Mary Auxiliatrix (in Via Tuscolana). Prefect of Congregation for Catholic Education, 1991. Grand chancellor of Pontifical Gregorian University. Patron of Sovereign Military Order of Malta, 1993; protodeacon, Jan., 1999. *Curial membership*: Secretariat of State (second section); Bishops, Oriental Churches, Evangelization of Peoples, Causes of Saints, Institutes of Consecrated Life and Societies of Apostolic Life, Clergy (congregations);Texts (council).

Law, Bernard F.: b. Nov. 4, 1931, Torreon, Mexico, the son of U.S. Air Force colonel; ord. priest (Jackson diocese) May 21, 1961; editor of Natchez-Jackson, Miss., diocesan paper, 1963-68; director of NCCB Committee on Ecumenical and Interreligious Affairs, 1968-71; ord. bp. of Springfield-Cape Girardeau, Mo., Dec. 5, 1973; abp. of Boston, Jan. 11, 1984; cardinal May 25, 1985; titular church, St. Susanna. Abp. of Boston. *Curial membership*: Oriental Churches; Divine Worship and Sacraments, Institutes of Consecrated Life and Societies of Apostolic Life, Evangelization of Peoples, Catholic Education (congregations); Culture (council).

Lebrún Moratinos,* José Ali: b. Mar. 19, 1919, Puerto Cabello, Venezuela; ord. priest Dec. 19, 1943; ord. titular bp. of Arado and aux. bp. of Maracaibo, Sept. 2, 1956; first bp. of Maracay, 1958-62; bp. of Valencia, 1962-72; titular bp. of Voncario (personal title of abp.) and coadj. abp. of Caracas, Sept. 16, 1972; abp. of Caracas, 1980-95; cardinal Feb. 2, 1983; titular church, St. Pancratius. Abp. emeritus of Caracas. *Curial membership*: Secretariat of State (second section).

López Rodríguez, Nicolás de Jesús: b. Oct. 31, 1936, Barranca, Dominican Republic; ord. priest Mar.

18, 1961; sent to Rome for advanced studies at the Angelicum and Gregorian Univ.; served in various diocesan offices after returning to his home diocese of La Vega; ord. first bp. of San Francisco de Macoris Feb. 25, 1978; abp. of Santo Domingo, Nov. 15, 1981; cardinal June 28, 1991; titular church, St. ius X (alla Balduina). Abp. of Santo Domingo and Military Ordinary for Dominican Republic. *Curial membership*: Divine Worship and Sacraments, Clergy, Institutes of Consecrated Life and Societies of Apostolic Life (congregations); Social Communications (council); Latin America (commission) .

López Trujillo, Alfonso: b. Nov. 8, 1935, Villahermosa, Colombia; ord. priest Nov. 13, 1960, in Rome; returned to Colombia, 1963; taught at major seminary; was pastoral coordinator for 1968 International Eucharistic Congress in Bogota; vicar general of Bogota, 1970-72; ord. titular bp. of Boseta, Mar. 25, 1971; aux. bp. of Bogota, 1971-72; secretary-general of CELAM, 1972-78; helped organize 1979 Puebla Conference in which Pope John Paul II participated; app. coadj. abp. of Medellin, May 22, 1978; abp. of Medellin, June 2, 1979 (resigned Jan 9, 1991); president of CELAM, 1979-83; cardinal Feb. 2, 1983; titular church, St. Prisca. Abp. emeritus of Medellin. President of the Pontifical Council for the Family, 1990. *Curial membership*: Doctrine of the Faith, Causes of Saints, Bishops, Evangelization of Peoples (congregations); Latin America (commission).

Lorscheider, Aloisio, O.F.M.: b. Oct. 8, 1924, Estrela, Brazil; received in Franciscan Order, Feb. 1, 1942; ord. priest Aug. 22, 1948; professor of theology at the Antonianum, Rome, and director of Franciscan international house of studies; ord. bp. of Santo Angelo, Brazil, May 20, 1962; abp. of Fortaleza, 1973-95; president of CELAM, 1975-79; cardinal May 24, 1976; titular church, S. Pietro (in Montorio). Abp. of Aparecida, July 12, 1995. *Curial membership*: Institutes of Consecrated Life and Societies of Apostolic Life (congregation).

Lourdusamy, D. Simon: b. Feb. 5, 1924, Kalleri, India; ord. priest Dec. 21, 1951; ord. titular bp. of Sozusa and aux. of Bangalore, Aug. 22, 1962; titular abp. of Filippi and coadj. abp. of Bangalore, Nov. 9, 1964; abp. of Bangalore, 1968-71; associate secretary, 1971-73, and secretary, 1973-85, of Congregation for Evangelization of Peoples; cardinal May 25, 1985; deacon, St. Mary of Grace; transferred to the order of cardinal priests Jan. 29, 1996; prefect of Congregation for Oriental Churches, 1985-91. *Curial membership*: Evangelization of Peoples, Causes of Saints, (congregations); Apostolic Signatura (tribunal); Interreligious Dialogue, Family, Texts (councils); International Eucharistic Congresses (commission).

Lubachivsky,* Myroslav Ivan: b. June 24, 1914, Dolyna, Ukraine; ord. priest Sept. 21, 1938; began pastoral work in U.S., 1947; became U.S. citizen, 1952; ord. abp. of Ukrainian-rite archeparchy of Philadelphia, Nov. 12, 1979; coadj. abp. of Lviv of the Ukrainians, Mar. 27, 1980; abp. of Lviv and major abp. of Ukrainians, Sept. 7, 1984; cardinal May 25, 1985; titular church, St. Sofia (a Via Boccea). Major Abp. of Lviv of the Ukrainians.

Lustiger, Jean-Marie: b. Sept. 17, 1926, Paris, France, of Polish-Jewish parents who emigrated to France after World War I; taken in by Catholic family in Orleans when his parents were deported during Nazi occupation (his mother died in 1943 at Auschwitz); convert to Catholicism, baptized Aug. 25, 1940; active in Young Christian Students during university days; ord. priest Apr. 17, 1954; ord. bp. of Orleans, Dec. 8, 1979; abp. of Paris, Jan. 31, 1981; cardinal Feb. 2, 1983; titular church, St. Louis of France. Abp. of Paris, ordinary for Eastern-Rite faithful in France without ordinaries of their own. *Curial membership*: Secretariat of State (second section); Divine Worship and Sacraments, Bishops, Oriental Churches, Clergy, Institutes of Consecrated Life and Societies of Apostolic Life (congregations); Culture (council).

Macharski, Franciszek: b. May 20, 1927, Cracow, Poland; ord. priest Apr. 2, 1950; engaged in pastoral work, 1950-56; continued theological studies in Fribourg, Switzerland, 1956-60; taught pastoral theology at the Faculty of Theology in Kracow; app. rector of archdiocesan seminary at Kracow, 1970; ord. abp. of Kracow, Jan. 6, 1979, by Pope John Paul II; cardinal June 30, 1979; titular church, St. John at the Latin Gate. Abp. of Cracow. *Curial membership*: Secretariat of State (second section); Bishops, Clergy, Institutes of Consecrated Life and Societies of Apostolic Life, Catholic Education (congregations).

Mahony, Roger M.: b. Feb. 27, 1936, Hollywood, Calif.; ord. priest (Fresno diocese) May 1, 1962; ord. titular bp. of Tamascani and aux. bp. of Fresno, Mar. 19,1975; bp. of Stockton, Feb. 15, 1980, installed Apr. 25, 1980; abp. of Los Angeles, July 16, 1985, installed Sept. 5, 1985; cardinal June 28, 1991; titular church, Four Crowned Saints. Abp. of Los Angeles. *Curial membership*: Social Communications (council).

Maida, Adam Joseph: b. Mar. 18, 1930, East Vandergrift, Pa.; ord. priest (Pittsburgh diocese) May 26, 1956; ord. bp. of Green Bay, Jan. 25, 1984; app. abp. of Detroit, Apr. 28, 1990, installed June 12, 1990; cardinal Nov. 26, 1994; titular church, Sts. Vitalis, Valeria, Gervase and Protase. Abp. of Detroit. *Curial membership*: Clergy, Catholic Education (congregations); Migrants and Itinerant Peoples (council).

Margéot,* Jean: b. Feb. 3, 1916, Quatre-Bornes, Mauritius; ord. priest Dec. 17, 1938; ord. bp. of Port Louis, May 4, 1969; cardinal June 28, 1988; titular church, St. Gabriel the Archangel all'Acqua Traversa. Bp. emeritus of Port Louis (resigned Feb. 15, 1993).

Martinez Somalo, Eduardo: b. Mar. 31, 1927, Baños de Rio Tobia, Spain; ord. priest Mar. 19, 1950; ord. titular bp. of Tagora with personal title of abp., Dec. 13, 1975; in secretariat of state from 1956; substitute (assistant) secretary of state, 1979-88; cardinal June 28, 1988; deacon, Most Holy Name of Jesus, promoted to cardinal priest, Jan. 9, 1999; prefect of Congregation for Divine Worship and Sacraments, 1988-92. Prefect of Congregation for Institutes of Consecrated Life and Societies of Apostolic Life, Jan. 21, 1992; Chamberlain (Camerlengo) of the Holy Roman Church, Apr. 5, 1993; Protodeacon 1996-99. *Curial membership*: Secretariat of State (second section); Divine Worship and Sacraments, Bishops, Causes of Saints, Evangelization of Peoples, Clergy, Catholic Education (congregations); Texts (council); Latin America, Institute for Works of Religion (commissions).

Martini, Carlo Maria, S.J.: b. Feb. 15, 1927, Turin,

Italy; entered Jesuits Sept. 25, 1944; ord. priest July 13, 1952; biblical scholar; seminary professor, Chieri, Italy, 1958-61; professor and later rector, 1969-78, of Pontifical Biblical Institute; rector of Pontifical Gregorian University, 1978-79; author of theological, biblical and spiritual works; ord. abp. of Milan, Jan. 6, 1980, by Pope John Paul II; cardinal Feb. 2, 1983; titular church, St. Cecilia. Abp. of Milan. *Curial membership*: Secretariat of State (second section); Oriental Churches, Divine Worship and Sacraments, Institutes of Consecrated Life and Societies of Apostolic Life, Catholic Education (congregations); Culture (council); Cultural Heritage of the Church (commission).

Mayer,* Paul Augustin, O.S.B.: b. May 23, 1911, Altötting, Germany; ord. priest Aug. 25, 1935; rector of St. Anselm's Univ., Rome, 1949-66; secretary of Congregation for Religious and Secular Institutes, 1972-84; ord. titular bp. of Satriano with personal title of abp., Feb. 13, 1972; pro-prefect of Congregations for Sacraments and Divine Worship, 1984; cardinal May 25, 1985; deacon, St. Anselm; transferred to order of cardinal priests Jan. 29, 1996. Prefect of Congregation for Divine Worship and Sacraments, 1985-88; president of Pontifical Commission "Ecclesia Dei," 1988-91.

Medina Estévez, Jorge Arturo: b. December 23, 1926, Santiago, Chile; ord. priest June 12, 1954; ord. abp. Jan. 6, 1985, Santiago, Chile; appointed pro-Prefect, Congregation for Divine Worship and the Discipline of the Sacraments 1996-98; prefect of the Congregation for Divine Worship and the Discipline of the Sacraments, 1998; cardinal, Feb. 21, 1998; deaconry, St. Sabas. Prefect of the Congregation for Divine Worship and the Discipline of the Sacraments. *Curial membership*: Doctrine of the Faith, Bishops (congregations); Family, Texts (councils).

Meisner, Joachim: b. Dec. 25, 1933, Breslau, Silesia, Germany (present-day Wroclaw, Poland); ord. priest ec. 22, 1962; regional director of Caritas; ord. titular bp. of Vina and aux. of apostolic administration of Erfurt-Meiningen, E. Germany, May 17, 1975; bp. of Berlin, 1980-88; cardinal Feb. 2, 1983; titular church, St. Prudenziana. Abp. of Cologne, Dec. 20, 1988. *Curial membership*: Divine Worship and Sacraments, Bishops, Clergy (congregations); Interreligious Dialogue, Culture (councils); Economic Affairs of Holy See (office).

Monduzzi, Dino: b. Apr. 2, 1922, Brisighella, Italy; ord. priest July 22, 1945; director of Catholic Action in Calabria and Sardinia; served in Agrarian Reform Agency in Fucino; sec. in the Office of the Maestro di Camera 1959-67; sec. and regent of the Apostolic Palace 1967-86; ord. titular bp. of Capri Jan. 6, 1987; prefect of the Papal Household 1986-1998; cardinal, Feb. 21, 1998; deaconry, St. Sebastian on the Palatine. *Curial membership*: Divine Worship and the Discipline of the Sacraments, Causes of Saints (congregations).

Neves, Lucas Moreira, O.P.: b. Sept. 16, 1925, São Joao del Rei, Brazil; ord. priest July 9, 1950; ord. titular bp. of Feradi maggiore and aux. of São Paulo, Aug. 26, 1967; assigned to Vatican, 1974; vice president of Pontifical Commission for Laity, 1974-79; abp. Oct. 15, 1979; secretary of Congregation for Bishops, 1979-87; assigned titular see of Vescovia, Jan. 3, 1987; abp. of São Salvador da Bahia, 1987-

98; cardinal June 28, 1988; titular church, Sts. Boniface and Alexius; Prefect of Congregation of Bishops, 1998; transferred to order of cardinal bishops, June 25, 1998 (suburbicarian see of Sabina-Poggio Mireto); Prefect of Congregation of Bishops. *Curial membership*: Secretariat of State (second section); Institutes of Consecrated Life and Societies of Apostolic Life, Catholic Education (congregations); Family, Culture, Texts (councils).

Noè, Virgilio: b. Mar. 30, 1922, Zelata di Bereguardo, Italy; ord. priest Oct. 1, 1944; master of pontifical ceremonies and undersecretary of Congregation for Sacraments and Divine Worship, 1970-82; ord. titular bp. of Voncario with personal title of abp., Mar. 6, 1982; coadj. Archpriest of St. Peter's Basilica, 1989; vicar general of Vatican City State, Jan. 14, 1991; cardinal June 28, 1991; deacon, St. John Bosco (in Via Tuscolana). Archpriest of St. Peter's Basilica, Vicar General of Vatican City State and President of the Fabric of St. Peter, 1991. *Curial membership*: Divine Worship and Sacraments, Causes of Saints (congregations); Holy Year 2000 (committee).

Obando Bravo, Miguel, S.D.B.: b. Feb. 2, 1926, La Libertad, Nicaragua; ord. priest Aug. 10, 1958; ord. titular bp. of Puzia di Bizacena and aux. of Matagalpa, Mar. 31, 1968; abp. of Managua, Feb. 16, 1970; cardinal May 25, 1985; titular church, St. John the Evangelist (a Spinaceta). Abp. of Managua. *Curial membership*: Clergy, Institutes of Consecrated Life and Societies of Apostolic Life (congregations); Latin America (commission).

O'Connor, John J.: b. Jan. 15, 1920, Philadelphia, Pa.; ord. priest (Philadelphia archdiocese) Dec. 15, 1945; joined U.S. Navy and Marine Corps as a chaplain, 1952; overseas posts included service in South Korea and Vietnam; U.S. Navy chief of chaplains, 1975; retired from Navy June 1, 1979, with rank of rear admiral; ord. titular bp. of Curzola and aux. of military vicariate, May 27, 1979; bp. of Scranton, May 6, 1983; abp. of New York, Jan. 26, 1984; cardinal May 25, 1985; titular church, Sts. John and Paul. Abp. of New York. *Curial membership*: Secretariat of State (second section); Bishops, Oriental Churches, Evangelization of Peoples (congregations); Family, Health Care Workers, Migrants and Itinerant People (councils); Institute for Works of Religion (commission).

Oddi,* Silvio: b. Nov. 14, 1910, Morfasso, Italy; ord. priest May 21, 1933; ord. titular abp. of Mesembria, Sept. 27, 1953; served in Vatican diplomatic corps, 1953-69; apostolic delegate to Jerusalem, Palestine, Jordan and Cyprus, internuncio to the United Arab Republic, and nuncio to Belgium and Luxembourg; cardinal Apr. 28, 1969; titular church, St. Agatha of the Goths. Pontifical legate for Patriarchal Basilica of St. Francis in Assisi; prefect of Sacred Congregation for the Clergy, 1979-86.

Ortega y Alamino, Jaime Lucas: b. Oct. 18, 1936, Jagüey Grande, Cuba; ord. priest Aug. 2, 1964 detained in work camps (UMAP) 1966-67; parish priest; ord. bp. of Pinar del Rio, Jan. 14, 1979; app. abp. of Havana, Nov. 20, 1981; cardinal Nov. 26, 1994; titular church, Sts. Aquila and Priscilla. Abp. of Havana. *Curial membership*: Clergy (congregation); Health Care Workers (council); Latin America (commission).

Otunga, Maurice Michael: b. January, 1923, Chebukwa, Kenya; son of pagan tribal chief; baptized 1935, at age of 12; ord. priest Oct. 3, 1950, at Rome;

taught at Kisumu major seminary for three years; attaché in apostolic delegation at Mombasa, 1953-56; ord. titular bp. of Tacape and aux. of Kisumu, Feb. 25, 1957; bp. of Kisii, 1960-69; titular abp. of Bomarzo and coadj. of Nairobi, Nov. 15, 1969; abp. of Nairobi, Oct. 24, 1971 (resigned May 14, 1997); cardinal Mar. 5, 1973; titular church, St. Gregory Barbarigo. Abp. emeritus of Nairobi, military ordinary of Kenya, 1981. *Curial membership*: Institutes of Consecrated Life and Societies of Apostolic Life, Evangelization of Peoples (congregations).

Padiyara, Antony: b. Feb. 11, 1921, Manimala, India; raised in Syro-Malabar rite family; ord. priest for Latin rite diocese of Coimbatore, Dec. 19, 1945; first bp. of Ootacamund (Latin rite), Oct. 16, 1955; app. abp. of Changanacherry (Syro-Malabar rite), June 14, 1970, at which time he returned to the Syro-Malabar rite; abp. of Ernakulam, Apr. 23, 1985; cardinal June 28, 1988; titular church, St. Mary Queen of Peace (Monte Verde). First Major Abp. of Major Abp.ric of Ernakulam-Angamaly of Syro-Malabar Church (established Dec. 16, 1992); enthroned May 20, 1993; resigned Nov. 11,1996. Major abp. emeritus of Ernakulam-Angomaly of Syro Malabars. *Curial membership*: Oriental Churches (congregation).

Palazzini,* Pietro: b. May 19, 1912, Piobbico, Pesaro, Italy; ord. priest Dec. 6, 1934; assistant vice-rector of Pontifical Major Roman Seminary and vice-rector and bursar of Pontifical Roman Seminary for Juridical Studies; professor of moral theology at Lateran University; held various offices in Roman Curia; secretary of Congregation of Council (now Clergy), 1958-73; ord. titular abp. of Caesarea in Cappadocia, Sept. 21, 1962; author of numerous works on moral theology and law; cardinal Mar. 5, 1973; titular church, St. Jerome. Prefect of Congregation for Causes of Saints, 1980-88.

Pappalardo,* Salvatore: b. Sept. 23, 1918, Villafranca Sicula, Sicily; ord. priest Apr. 12, 1941; entered diplomatic service of secretariat of state, 1947; ord. titular abp. of Miletus, Jan. 16, 1966; pro-nuncio in Indonesia, 1966-69; president of Pontifical Ecclesiastical Academy, 1969-70; abp. of Palermo, Oct. 17, 1970; cardinal Mar. 5, 1973; titular church, St. Mary Odigitria of the Sicilians. Abp. emeritus of Palermo (resigned Apr. 4, 1996).

Paskai, László, O.F.M.: b. May 8, 1927, Szeged, Hungary; ord. priest Mar. 3, 1951; ord. titular bp. of Bavagaliana and apostolic administrator of Veszprem, Apr. 5, 1978; bp. of Veszprem Mar. 31, 1979; coadj. abp. of Kalocsa, Apr. 5, 1982; abp. of Esztergom (renamed Esztergom-Budapest, 1993), Mar. 3, 1987; cardinal June 28, 1988; titular church, St. Theresa (al Corso d'Italia). Abp. of Esztergom-Budapest. *Curial membership*: Oriental Churches, Institutes of Consecrated Life and Societies of Apostolic Life (congregations); Texts (council).

Pengo, Polycarp: b. August 5, 1944, Mwayze, Tanzania; ord. priest Aug. 5, 1971; taught moral theology at the major seminary in Kipalapala, Tanzania, 1977; rector of the major seminary in Segerea, 1978-83; ord. bp. of Nachingwea, Jan. 6, 1984; bp. of Tunduru-Masasi 1986-90; co-adjutor abp. of Dar-es-Salaam, Jan. 22, 1990; abp. of Dar-es-Salaam, July 22,1992, in succession to Laurean Cardinal Rugambwa; cardinal Feb. 21, 1998; titular church, Our Lady of La Salette. Abp. of Dar-es-Salaam. *Cu-*

rial membership: Evangelization of Peoples (congregation); Interreligious Dialogue (council).

Pham Dinh Tung,* Paul Joseph: b. June 15, 1919, Binh-Hoa, Vietnam; ord. priest June 6, 1949; ord. bp. of Bac Ninh, Aug. 15, 1963; apostolic administrator of Hanoi, June 18, 1990; abp. of Hanoi, Mar. 23, 1994; cardinal Nov. 26, 1994; titular church, St. Mary Queen of Peace in Ostia mare. Abp. of Hanoi. *Curial membership*: Evangelization of Peoples (congregation); "Cor Unum" (council).

Pimenta, Simon Ignatius: b. Mar. 1, 1920, Marol, India; ord. priest Dec. 21, 1949; ord. titular bp. of Bocconia and aux. of Bombay, June 29, 1971; coadj. abp. of Bombay, Feb. 26, 1977; abp. of Bombay, Sept. 11, 1978; cardinal June 28, 1988; titular church, Mary, Queen of the World (a Torre Spaccata). Abp. emeritus of Bombay (resigned Nov. 8, 1996). *Curial membership*: Evangelization of Peoples, Catholic Education (congregations); Economic Affairs of the Holy See (office).

Piovanelli, Silvano: b. Feb. 21, 1924, Ronta di Mugello, Italy; ord. priest July 13, 1947; ord. titular bp. of Tubune di Mauretania and aux. of Florence, June 24, 1982; abp. of Florence, Mar. 18, 1983; cardinal May 25, 1985; titular church, St. Mary of Graces (Via Trionfale). Abp. of Florence.

Poggi,* Luigi: b. Nov. 25, 1917, Piacenza, Italy; ord. priest July 28, 1940; studied diplomacy at the Pontifical Ecclesiastical Academy, 1944-46; started to work at Secretariat of State; ord. titular bp. of Forontoniana with personal title of abp., May 9, 1965; apostolic delegate for Central Africa, 1965; nuncio in Peru; recalled to Rome, 1973; negotiated with various Eastern bloc governments to improve situation of the Church; named head of Holy See's delegation for permanent contact with government of Poland, 1974; nuncio in Italy, 1986-92; pro-librarian and pro-archivist of the Holy Roman Church, 1992-94; cardinal Nov. 26, 1994; deacon, St. Mary in Domnica. Archivist and librarian of the Holy Roman Church (Nov. 26, 1994).

Poupard, Paul: b. Aug. 30, 1930, Bouzille, France; ord. priest Dec. 18, 1954; scholar; author of a number of works; ord. titular bp. of Usula and aux. of Paris, Apr. 6, 1979; title of abp. and pro-president of the Secretariat for Non-Believers, 1980; cardinal deacon May 25, 1985; transferred to order of cardinal priests Jan. 29, 1996; titular church, St. Praxedes; president of Pontifical Council for Dialogue with Non-Believers, 1985-93. President of Pontifical Council for Culture, 1988. *Curial membership*: Divine Worship and Sacraments, Evangelization of Peoples, Catholic Education (congregations); Interreligious Dialogue (council).

Primatesta,* Raúl Francisco: b. Apr. 14, 1919, Capilla del Senor, Argentina; ord. priest Oct. 25, 1942, at Rome; taught at minor and major seminaries of La Plata; contributed to several theology reviews; ord. titular bp. of Tanais and aux. of La Plata, Aug. 15, 1957; bp. of San Rafael, 1961-65; abp. of Cordoba, 1965-98; cardinal Mar. 5, 1973; titular church, Blessed Mary Sorrowful Virgin. Abp. emeritus of Cordoba, Argentina. *Curial membership*: Clergy (congregation).

Puljic, Vinko: b. Sept. 8, 1945, Prijecani, Bosnia-Herzegovina; ord. priest June 29, 1970; spiritual director of minor seminary of Zadar, 1978-87;

parish priest; app. vice-rector of Sarajevo major seminary, 1990; ord. abp. of Vrhbosna (Sarajevo), Jan. 6, 1991, in Rome; cardinal Nov. 26, 1994; titular church, St. Clare in Vigna Clara. Abp. of Sarajevo. *Curial membership*: Evangelization of Peoples (congregation); Interreligious Dialogue (council).

Ratzinger, Joseph: b. Apr. 16, 1927, Marktl am Inn, Germany; ord. priest June 29, 1951; professor of dogmatic theology at University of Regensburg, 1969-77; member of International Theological Commission, 1969-80; ord. abp. of Munich-Freising, May 28, 1977 (resigned Feb. 15, 1982); cardinal June 27, 1977; titular church, St. Mary of Consolation (in Tiburtina); transferred to order of cardinal bishops as titular bp. of suburbicarian see of Velletri-Segni, Apr. 5, 1993. Prefect of Congregation for Doctrine of the Faith, 1981; president of Biblical and Theological Commissions. Vice-dean of the Sacred College of Cardinals (Nov. 6, 1998, appr. Nov. 9, 1998). *Curial membership*: Secretariat of State (second section); Bishops, Divine Worship and Sacraments, Oriental Churches, Evangelization of Peoples, Catholic Education (congregations); Christian Unity, Culture (councils); Latin America (commission).

Razafindratandra, Armand Gaétan: b. Aug. 7, 1925, Ambohimalaza, Madagascar; ord. priest July 27, 1954; ord. bp. of Mahajanga, July 2, 1978; app. abp. of Antananarivo, Feb. 3, 1994, installed May 15, 1994; cardinal Nov. 26, 1994; titular church, Sts. Sylvester and Martin ai Monti. Abp. of Antananarivo and apostolic administrator of Miarinarivo. *Curial membership*: Evangelization of Peoples (congregation); Laity (council).

Righi-Lambertini,* Egano: b. Feb. 22, 1906, Casalecchio di Reno, Italy; ord. priest May 25, 1929; entered service of secretariat of state, 1939; served in diplomatic missions in France (1949-54), Costa Rica (1955), England (1955-57); first apostolic delegate to Korea, 1957-60; ord. titular abp. of Doclea, Oct. 28, 1960; apostolic nuncio in Lebanon, 1960-63, Chile, 1963-67, Italy, 1967-69; France, 1969-79; while nuncio in France he also served as special envoy at the Council of Europe, 1974-79; cardinal deacon June 30, 1979; transferred to order of cardinal priests, Nov. 26, 1990; titular church, Saint Mary (in Via).

Rivera Carrera, Norberto: b. June 6, 1942, La Purísima, Mexico; ord. priest July 3, 1966; taught dogmatic theology at the major seminary of Mexico City; professor of ecclesiology at Pontifical University of Mexico; bp. of Tehuacán, Nov. 5, 1985; abp. of Mexico City, June 13,1995; cardinal Feb. 21, 1998; titular church, St. Francis of Assisi at *Ripa Grande*. Abp. of Mexico City. *Curial membership*: Divine Worship and the Discipline of Sacraments (congregation), Family (council), Latin America (committee).

Rossi,* Opilio: b. May 14, 1910, New York, N.Y.; holds Italian citizenship; ord. priest for diocese of Piacenza (now Piacenza-Bobbio), Italy, Mar. 11, 1933; served in nunciatures in Belgium, The Netherlands, and Germany, 1938-53; ord. titular archbp. of Ancyra, Dec. 27, 1953; nuncio in Ecuador, 1953-59, Chile, 1959-61, Austria 1961-76; cardinal deacon May 24, 1976; transferred to order of cardinal priests, June 22, 1987; titular church, St. Lawrence (in Lucina); president of Pontifical Committee for International Eucharistic Congresses, 1983-90; president

of Commission for the Sanctuaries of Pompeii, Loreto and Bari, 1984-93.

Rouco Varela, Antonio María: b. Aug. 24, 1936, Villalba, Spain; ord. priest March 28, 1959; taught fundamental theology and canon law at the Mondoñedo seminary; adjunct professor at the University of Munich; taught ecclesiastical law at Pontifical University of Salamanca; vice-rector of Pontifical University of Salamanca; titular bp. of Gergis and aux. bp. of Santiago de Compostela, Sep. 17, 1976; abp. of Santiago de Compostela, My 9,1984; abp. of Madrid June 29, 1994; cardinal, Feb. 21, 1998, titular church, St. Laurence *in Damaso*. Abp. of Madrid. *Curial membership*: Clergy, Education (congregations); Texts, Culture (councils).

Ruini, Camillo: b. Feb. 19, 1931, Sassuolo, Italy; ord. priest Dec. 8, 1954; taught at seminaries in central Italy; ord. titular bp. of Nepte and aux. bp. of Reggio Emilia and Guastella, June 29, 1983; secretary general of Italian Bishops' Conference, 1986-91; abp. Jan. 17, 1991 and pro-vicar general of the Pope for the Rome diocese; pro-Archpriest of Patriarchal Lateran Archbasilica; cardinal June 28, 1991; titular church, St. Agnes outside the Wall. Vicar General of the Pope for the Diocese of Rome and Archpriest of Patriarchal Lateran Basilica, July 1, 1991; Grand Chancellor of Pontifical Lateran University; President of the Peregrinatio ad Petri Sedem, 1992-96. *Curial membership*: Bishops (congregation); Holy Year 2000 (committee).

Sabbattani,* Aurelio: b. Oct. 18, 1912, Casal Fiumanese, Italy; ord. priest July 26, 1935; jurist; served in various assignments in his native diocese of Imola and as judge and later an official of the regional ecclesiastical tribunal of Bologna; called to Rome in 1955 as prelate auditor of the Roman Rota; ord. titular abp. of Justinian Prima, July 25, 1965; prelate of Loreto, 1965-71; secretary of Supreme Tribunal of Apostolic Signatura and consultor of Secretariat of State, 1971; pro-prefect of Apostolic Signatura, 1982-83; cardinal deacon Feb. 2, 1983; transferred to order of cardinal priests Apr. 5, 1993; titular church, St. Apollinaris; prefect of Apostolic Signatura, 1983-88; archpriest of Patriarchal Vatican Basilica and president of the Fabric of St. Peter, 1983-91; former vicar general of the Pope for Vatican City.

Saldarini, Giovanni: b. Dec. 11, 1924, Cantu, Italy; ord. priest May 31, 1947; respected scripture scholar; taught scripture at Milan archdiocesan seminary, 1952-67; ord. titular bp. of Guadiaba and aux. bp. of Milan, Dec. 7, 1984; abp. of Turin Jan. 31, 1989; cardinal June 28, 1991 (resigned, June 19, 1999); titular church, Sacred Heart of Jesus (a Castro Pretorio). Abp. of Turin. *Curial membership*: Divine Worship and Sacraments, Evangelization of Peoples, Clergy (congregations).

Sales, Eugênio de Araújo: b. Nov. 8, 1920, Acari, Brazil; ord. priest Nov. 21, 1943; ord. titular bp. of Tibica and aux. bp. of Natal, Aug. 15, 1954; abp. of São Salvador, 1968-71; cardinal Apr. 28, 1969; titular church, St. Gregory VII. Abp. of Rio de Janeiro (1971), ordinary for Eastern Rite Catholics in Brazil without ordinaries of their own rites. *Curial membership*: Secretariat of State (second section); Oriental Churches, Divine Worship and Sacraments, Clergy, Evangelization of Peoples (congregations); Social Communications (council).

Sánchez, José T.: b. Mar. 17, 1920, Pandan, Philippines; ord. priest May 12, 1946; ord. titular bp. of Lesvi and coadj. bp. of Lucena, May 12, 1968; bp. of Lucena, 1976-82; abp. of Nueva Segovia Jan. 12, 1982 (resigned Mar. 22, 1986); secretary of Congregation for Evangelization of Peoples, 1985-91; cardinal June 28, 1991; deacon, St. Pius V (a Villa Carpegna); president of Commission for Preservation of Artistic and Historic Patrimony of the Holy See, 1991-93. Prefect of Congregation for the Clergy, 1991-96. *Curial membership*: Secretariat of State (second section); Bishops, Evangelization of Peoples (congregations); Texts (council); International Eucharistic Congresses, Latin America, Commission for the Sanctuaries of Pompeii, Loreto and Bari (commission).

Sandoval Íñiguez, Juan: b. Mar. 28, 1933, Yahualica, Mexico; ord. priest Oct. 27, 1957; ord. coadj. bp. of Ciudad Juárez, Apr. 30, 1988; bp. of Ciudad Juarez, July 11, 1992; app. abp. of Guadalajara, Apr. 21, 1994; cardinal Nov. 26, 1994; titular church, Our Lady of Guadalupe and St. Philip the Martyr on Via Aurelia. Abp. of Guadalajara. *Curial membership*: Institutes of Consecrated Life and Societies of Apostolic Life, Catholic Education (congregations); Latin America (commission).

Santos, Alexandre José Maria dos, O.F.M.: b. Mar. 18, 1924, Zavala, Mozambique; ord. priest July 25, 1953; first Mozambican black priest; ord. abp. of Maputo, Mar. 9, 1975; cardinal June 28, 1988; titular church, St. Frumentius (ai Prati Fiscali). Abp. of Maputo. *Curial membership*: Evangelization of Peoples (congregation).

Schönborn, Christoph, O.P.: b. January 22, 1945, Skalsko, Bohemia (fled to Austria in Sept. 1945); entered Dominican Order in 1963; ord. priest, 1970; student pastor in Graz University, 1973-75; associate professor of dogma in the Univeristy of Fribourg, 1976; professor for theology, 1978; professor for dogmatic theology, 1981-91; member of the Orthodox-Roman Catholic Dialogue Commission of Switzerland, 1980-87; member International Theological Commission, 1980-; member of the foundation, "Pro Oriente" since 1984; Secretary for the Draft-Commission of the *Catechism of the Catholic Church*, 1987-1992; ord. aux. bp. (Sutri) of Vienna, Sept. 29, 1991; Co-adjutor of Vienna, April 13, 1995; abp. of Vienna, Sept. 14, 1995; cardinal, Feb. 21, 1998; titular church, Jesus the Divine Worker. Abp. of Vienna. *Curial membership*: Doctrine of the Faith, Oriental Churches (congregations); Culture (council).

Schotte, Jan Pieter, C.I.C.M.: b. Apr. 29, 1928, Beveren-Leie, Belgium; entered Congregation of the Immaculate Heart of Mary (Scheut Missionaries) in 1946; ord. priest Aug. 3, 1952; taught canon law at Louvain and was rector of community's seminary in Washington, D.C.; general secretary of Congregation of the Immaculate Heart of Mary in Rome, 1967-72; secretary (1980) and vice-president (1983) of the Pontifical Commission of Justice and Peace; ord. titular bp. of Silli, Jan. 6, 1984; promoted to titular abp., Apr. 24, 1985; cardinal Nov. 26, 1994; deacon St. Julian of the Flemings. Secretary general of the Synod of Bishops since 1985; president of the Labor Office of the Holy See, 1989. *Curial membership*: Bishops, Evangelization of Peoples (congregations); Apostolic Signatura (tribunal); Latin America (commission).

Schwery, Henri: b. June 14, 1932, Saint-Leonard,

Switzerland; ord. priest July 7, 1957; director of minor seminary and later rector of the College in Sion; ord. bp. of Sion, Sept. 17, 1977; cardinal June 28, 1991; titular church, Protomartyrs (a via Aurelia Antica). Bp. emeritus of Sion (retired Apr. 1, 1995). *Curial membership*: Divine Worship and Sacraments, Causes of Saints, Clergy (congregations); Social Communications (council).

Sensi,* Giuseppe Maria: b. May 27, 1907, Cosenza, Italy; ord. priest Dec. 21, 1929; entered Vatican diplomatic service; served in nunciatures in Hungary, Switzerland, Belgium and Czechoslovakia, 1934-49; ord. titular abp. of Sardes, July 24, 1955; apostolic nuncio to Costa Rica, 1955; apostolic delegate to Jerusalem, 1956-62; nuncio to Ireland, 1962-67, and Portugal, 1967-76; cardinal deacon May 24, 1976; transferred to order of cardinal priests, June 22, 1987; titular church, Queen of Apostles.

Sfeir, Nasrallah Pierre: b. May 15, 1920, Reyfoun, in Maronite diocese of Sarba, Lebanon; ord. priest May 7, 1950; secretary of Maronite patriarchate, 1956-61; taught Arabic literature and philosphy at Marist Fathers College, Jounieh, 1951-61; ord. titular bp. of Tarsus for the Maronites, July 16, 1961; elected Patriarch of Antioch for Maronites, Apr. 19, 1986, granted ecclesial communion by John Paul II May 7, 1986; cardinal Nov. 26, 1994. Patriarch of Antioch for Maronites. *Curial membership*: Oriental Churches (congregation); Health Care Workers, Texts (councils).

Shan Kuo-hsi, Paul, S.J.: b. Dec. 2, 1923, Puyang, China; ord. priest March 18, 1955; director of the Chinese section of the Sacred Heart School in Cebu; socius of the novice master in Thu-duc, Vietnam; novice master and rector of manresa House, Chanhua, Taiwan; rector of St. Ignatius High School, Taipei, Taiwan; bp. of Hualien, November 15, 1979; bp. of Kaohsiung, Taiwan, 1991; cardinal, Feb. 21, 1998; titular church, St. Chrysogonus. Bp. of Kaohsiung. *Curial membership*: Evangelization of Peoples (congregation); Interreligious Dialogue, Social Communications (councils).

Shirayanagi, Peter Seiichi: b. June 17, 1928, Hachioji City, Japan; ord. priest Dec. 21, 1954; ord. titular bp. of Atenia and aux. bp. of Tokyo, May 8, 1966; titular abp. of Castro and coadj. abp. of Tokyo, Nov. 15, 1969; succeeded to see, Feb. 21, 1970; cardinal Nov. 26, 1994; titular church, St. Emerentiana in Tor Fiorenza. Abp. of Tokyo. *Curial membership*: Family, Interreligious Dialogue (councils).

Silvestrini, Achille: b. Oct. 25, 1923, Brisighella, Italy; ord. priest July 13, 1946; official in Secretariat of State from 1953; ord. titular bp. of Novaliciana with personal title of abp., May 27, 1979; undersecretary, 1973-79, and secretary, 1979-88, of the Council for Public Affairs of the Church (now the second section of the Secretariat of State); cardinal June 28, 1988; deacon, St. Benedict Outside St. Paul's Gate, promoted to cardinal priest, Jan. 9, 1999; prefect of Apostolic Signatura, 1988-91. Prefect of Congregation for Oriental Churches, 1991; Grand Chancellor of Pontifical Oriental Institute. *Curial membership*: Secretariat of State (second section); Doctrine of the Faith, Bishops, Causes of Saints, Evangelization of Peoples, Catholic Education (congregations); Christian Unity, Texts, Interreligious Dialogue (councils).

Simonis, Adrianus J.: b. Nov. 26, 1931, Lisse, Netherlands; ord. priest June 15, 1957; ord. bp. of Rotterdam, Mar. 20, 1971; coadj. abp. of Utrecht, June 27, 1983; abp. of Utrecht, Dec. 3, 1983; cardinal May 25, 1985; titular church, St. Clement. Abp. of Utrecht. *Curial membership:* Institutes of Consecrated Life and Societies of Apostolic Life, Catholic Education (congregations); Christian Unity (council).

Sin, Jaime L.: b. Aug. 31, 1928, New Washington, Philippines; ord. priest Apr. 3, 1954; diocesan missionary in Capiz, 1954-57; app. first rector of the St. Pius X Seminary, Roxas City, 1957; ord. titular bp. of Obba and aux. bp. of Jaro, Mar. 18, 1967; apostolic administrator of archdiocese of Jaro, June 20, 1970; titular abp. of Massa Lubrense and coadj. abp. of Jaro, Jan. 15, 1972; abp. of Jaro, 1972-74; abp. of Manila, Jan. 21, 1974; cardinal May 24, 1976; titular church, S. Maria (ai Monti). Abp. of Manila. *Curial membership:* Divine Worship and Sacraments, Clergy, Institutes of Consecrated Life and Societies of Apostolic Life (congregations); Social Communications (council).

Sladkevicius, Vincentas, M.I.C.: b. Aug. 20, 1920, Zasliai, Lithuania; ord. priest Mar. 25, 1944; ord. titular bp. of Abora and aux. of Kaisiadorys, Dec. 25, 1957, but was not permitted to exercise his office; under house arrest 1959-82; apostolic administrator of Kaisiadorys, 1982-89; cardinal June 28, 1988; titular church, Holy Spirit (alla Ferratella). Abp. of Kaunas (Mar. 10, 1989; resigned May 4, 1996). *Curial membership:* Catholic Education (congregation).

Sodano, Angelo: b. Nov. 23, 1927, Isola d'Asti, Italy; ord. priest Sept. 23, 1950; entered diplomatic service of the Holy See in 1959; served in Ecuador and Uruguay; ord. titular abp. of Nova di Cesare, Jan. 15, 1978; nuncio to Chile, 1978-88; secretary of the Council for Relations with States, 1988-90; pro-Secretary of State, 1990 (Dec. 1)-1991; cardinal June 28, 1991; titular church, S. Maria Nuova; transferred to order of cardinal Bishops, Jan 10, 1994, as titular bp. of suburbicarian see of Albano (while retaining title to S. Maria Nuova). Secretary of State, June 29, 1991. *Curial membership:* Doctrine of the Faith, Bishops, Oriental Churches (congregations); Institute for Works of Religion (commission).

Stafford, James Francis: b. July 26, 1932, Baltimore, Md.; ord. priest (Baltimore*) Dec. 15, 1957; ord. titular bp. of Respetta and aux. bp. of Baltimore, Feb. 29, 1976; app. bp. of Memphis, Nov. 17, 1982; app. abp. of Denver, June 3, 1986, installed July 30, 1986; app. President of Pontifical Council for the Laity, Aug. 20, 1996; cardinal Feb. 21, 1998; titular church, the church of Jesus, the Good Shepherd at Montagnola. President of Pontifical Council for the Laity. *Curial membership:* Doctrine of the Faith, Bishops (congregations); Texts (council).

Sterzinsky, Georg Maximilian: b. Feb. 9, 1936, Warlack, Germany; ord. priest June 29, 1960; vicar general to the apostolic administrator of Erfurt-Meiningen, 1981-89; ord. bp. of Berlin, Sept. 9, 1989; cardinal June 28, 1991; titular church, St. Joseph (all'Aurelio). Abp. of Berlin (June 27, 1994). *Curial membership:* Catholic Education (congregation); Migrants and Itinerant People (council).

Stickler,* Alfons, S.D.B.: b. Aug. 23, 1910, Neunkirchen, Austria; ord. priest Mar. 27, 1937; director of the Vatican Library, 1971; ord. titular bp. of Bolsena, Nov. 1, 1983, with personal title of abp.;

Pro-Librarian and Pro-Archivist, 1984; cardinal May 25, 1985; deacon, St. George (in Velabo); transferred to order of cardinal priests Jan. 29, 1996. Librarian and Archivist of the Holy Roman Church, 1985-88.

Suárez Rivera, Adolfo Antonio: b. Jan. 9, 1927, San Cristobal, Mexico; ord. priest Mar. 8, 1952; ord. bp. of Tepic, Aug. 15, 1971; bp. of Tlalnepantla, May 8, 1980; app. abp. of Monterrey, Nov. 8, 1983; cardinal Nov. 26, 1994; titular church, Our Lady of Guadalupe on Monte Mario. Abp. of Monterrey. *Curial membership:* Clergy (congregation); Latin America (commission).

Suquía Goicoechea,* Angel: b. Oct. 2, 1916, Zaldivia, Spain; ord. priest July 7, 1940; ord. bp. of Almeria, July 16, 1966; bp. of Malaga, 1969-73; abp. of Santiago de Compostela, 1973-83; abp. of Madrid, Apr. 12, 1983; cardinal May 25, 1985; titular church, Great Mother of God. Abp. emeritus of Madrid (retired July 28, 1994).

Swiàtek,* Kazimierz: b. Oct. 21, 1914, Walga, in apostolic administration of Estonia; ord. priest (of Pinsk, Belarus, clergy) Apr. 8, 1939; arrested by KGB Apr. 21, 1941, and imprisoned on death row until June 22, when he escaped during confusion of German invasion and returned to his parish; arrested again by KGB and imprisoned in Minsk until 1945; sentenced to 10 years of hard labor in concentration camps; released June 16, 1954; resumed pastoral work in cathedral parish in Pinsk; ord. abp. of Minsk-Mohilev, Belarus, May 21, 1991, and also appointed apostolic administrator of Pinsk; cardinal Nov. 26, 1994; titular church, St. Gerard Majella. Abp. of Minsk-Mohilev; apostolic administrator of Pinsk.

Szoka, Edmund C.: b. Sept. 14, 1927, Grand Rapids, Mich.; ord. priest (Marquette diocese), June 5, 1954; ord. first bp. of Gaylord, Mich., July 20, 1971; abp. of Detroit, 1981-90; cardinal June 28, 1988; titular church, Sts. Andrew and Gregory (al Monte Celio). President of Prefecture for Economic Affairs of the Holy See, 1990-97. Pres. Pont. Comm. for Vatican City State, 1997. *Curial membership:* Secretariat of State (second section); Causes of Saints, Bishops, Evangelization of Peoples, Clergy, Institutes of Consecrated Life and Societies of Apostolic Life (congregations).

Taofinu'u, Pio, S.M.: b. Dec. 9, 1923, Falealupo, W. Samoa; ord. priest Dec. 8, 1954; joined Society of Mary, 1955; ord. bp. of Apia (Samoa and Tokelau), May 29, 1968, the first Polynesian bp.; cardinal Mar. 5, 1973; titular church, St. Humphrey. Abp. of Samoa-Apia and Tokelau, Sept. 10, 1982 (title of see changed to Samoa-Apia, June 26, 1992).

Tettamanzi, Dionigi: b. March 14, 1934, Renate, Italy; ord. priest June 28, 1957; taught fundamental theology at the major seminary of Lower Venegono, pastoral theology at the Priestly Institute of Mary Immaculate and the Lombard Regional Institute of Pastoral Ministry, Milan; rector of the Pontifical Lombard Seminary, Rome; abp. of Ancona-Osimo July 1,1989 (resigned 1991); general secretary of the Italian Episcopal Conference 1991-95; Vice-President of the Italian Episcopal Conference May 25, 1995; abp. of Genoa Apr. 20, 1995; cardinal Feb. 21, 1998; titular church, Sts. Ambrose and Charles. Abp. of Genoa. *Curial membership:* Doctrine of the Faith, Catholic Education (congregations); Social Communications (council).

Thiandoum, Hyacinthe: b. Feb. 2, 1921, Poponguine, Senegal; ord. priest Apr. 18, 1949; studied at Gregorian University, Rome, 1951-53; returned to Senegal, 1953; ord. abp. of Dakar, May 20, 1962; cardinal May 24, 1976; titular church, S. Maria (del Popolo). Abp. of Dakar. *Curial membership*: Clergy, Institutes of Consecrated Life and Societies of Apostolic Life, Evangelization of Peoples (congregations); Social Communications (council).

Todea,* Alexandru: b. June 5, 1912, Teleac, Romania; ord. priest in the Byzantine Romanian rite Mar. 25, 1939; ord. bp. secretly (titular see of Cesaropoli), Nov. 19, 1950, by Abp. Gerald P. O'Hara, Vatican representative to Romania; arrested, 1951, and sentenced to life imprisonment; granted amnesty in 1964; abp. of Fagaras and Alba Julia, 1990-94; cardinal June 28, 1991; titular church, St. Athanasius. Abp. emeritus of Fagaras and Alba Julia of the Romanians.

Tomko, Jozef: b. Mar. 11, 1924, Udavske, Slovakia; ord. priest Mar. 12, 1949; ord. titular abp. of Doclea, Sept. 15, 1979; secretary-general of the Synod of Bishops, 1979-85; cardinal deacon May 25, 1985; transferred to order of cardinal priests Jan. 29, 1996; titular church, St. Sabina. Prefect of the Congregation for the Evangelization of Peoples, 1985; Grand Chancellor of Pontifical Urban University. *Curial membership*: Secretariat of State (second section); Docrine of the Faith, Divine Worship and Sacraments, Bishops, Clergy, Institutes of Consecrated Life and Societies of Apostolic Life, Catholic Education (congregations); Christian Unity, Interreligious Dialogue, Culture, Texts (councils); Latin America, State of Vatican City (commissions).

Tonino,* Ersilio: b. July 20, 1914, Centovera di San Giorgio Piacentino, Italy; ord. priest Apr. 18, 1937; vice-rector and later rector of the Piacenza seminary; taught Italian, Latin and Greek; editor of diocesan weekly; ord. bp. of Macerata-Tolentino, June 2, 1969; abp. of Ravenna-Cervia, Nov. 22, 1975 (retired Oct. 27, 1990); cardinal Nov. 26, 1994; titular church, Most Holy Redeemer in Val Melaina. Abp. emeritus of Ravenna-Cervia.

Tumi, Christian Wiyghan: b. Oct. 15, 1930, Kikaikelaki, Cameroon; ord. priest Apr. 17, 1966; ord. bp. of Yagoua, Jan. 6, 1980; coadj. abp. of Garoua, Nov. 19, 1982; abp. of Garoua, 1984-91; cardinal June 28, 1988; titular church, Martyrs of Uganda (a Poggio Ameno). Abp. of Douala, Aug. 31, 1991. *Curial membership*: Evangelization of Peoples, Catholic Education (congregations); Interreligious Dialogue, Culture (councils).

Turcotte, Jean-Claude: b. June 26, 1936, Montreal, Canada; ord. priest May 24, 1959; ord. titular bp. of Suas and aux. of Montreal, June 29, 1982; abp. of Montreal, Mar. 17, 1990; cardinal Nov. 26, 1994; titular church, Our Lady of the Blessed Sacrament and the Holy Canadian Martyrs. Abp. of Montreal. *Curial membership*: Causes of Saints (congregation); Social Communications (council).

Tzadua, Paulos: b. Aug. 25, 1921, Addifini, Ethiopia; ord. priest Mar. 12, 1944; ord. titular bp. of Abila di Palestina and aux. of Addis Ababa, May 20, 1973; abp. of Addis Ababa, Feb. 24, 1977; cardinal May 25, 1985; titular church, Most Holy Name of Mary (a Via Latina). Abp. of Addis Ababa. *Curial membership*: Oriental Churches (congregation).

Ursi,* Corrado: b. July 26, 1908, Andria, Italy; ord.

priest July 25, 1931; vice-rector and later rector of the Pontifical Regional Seminary of Molfetta, 1931-51; ord. bp. of Nardo, Sept. 30, 1951; abp. of Acerenza, Nov. 30, 1961; abp. of Naples, May 23, 1966 (resigned May 9, 1987); cardinal June 26, 1967; titular church, St. Callistus. Abp. emeritus of Naples.

Vachon,* Louis-Albert: b. Feb. 4, 1912, Saint-Frederic-de-Beauce, Que., Canada; ord. priest June 11, 1938; ord. titular bp. of Mesarfelta and aux. of Quebec, May 14, 1977; abp. of Quebec, Mar. 20, 1981 (resigned Mar. 17, 1990); cardinal May 25, 1985; titular church, St. Paul of the Cross (a Corviale). Abp. emeritus of Quebec.

Vargas Alzamora, Augusto, S.J.: b. Nov. 9, 1922, Lima, Peru; entered Society of Jesus Mar. 9, 1940; ord. priest July 15, 1955; ord. titular bp. of Cissi, Aug. 15, 1978; vicar apostolic of Jaen in Peru (or San Francisco Javier), 1978-85; abp. of Lima, De. 30, 1989; made passionate appeals against violence of the Sendero Luminoso; cardinal Nov. 26, 1994; titular see, St. Robert Bellarmine. Abp. of Lima. *Curial membership*: Institutes of Consecrated Life and Societies of Apostolic Life (congregation); Latin America (commission).

Vidal, Ricardo J.: b. Feb. 6, 1931, Mogpoc, Philippines; ord. priest Mar. 17, 1956; ord. titular bp. of Claterna and coadj. of Melalos, Nov. 30, 1971; abp. of Lipa, 1973-81; coadj. abp. of Cebu, Apr. 13, 1981; abp. of Cebu, Aug. 24, 1982; cardinal May 25, 1985; titular church, Sts. Peter and Paul (in Via Ostiensi). Abp. of Cebu. *Curial membership*: Evangelizaton of Peoples, Catholic Education (congregations); Health Care Workers (counci).

Vlk, Miloslav: b. May 17, 1932, Lisnice, Czech Republic; during communist persecution when theological studies were impossible he studied archival science at Charles University and worked in various archives in Bohemia; ord. priest June 23, 1968, during "Prague Spring"; sent to isolated parishes in Bohemian Forest by State authorities in 1971; state authorization to exercise his priestly ministry was cancelled in 1978; from then until 1986 he worked as a window-washer in Prague, carrying out his priestly ministry secretly among small groups. In 1989, he was permitted to exercise his priestly ministry for a "trial" year; the situation changed with the "velvet revolution"; ord. bp. of Ceske Budejovice, Mar. 31, 1990; abp. of Prague, Mar. 27, 1991; cardinal Nov. 26, 1994; titular church, Holy Cross in Jerusalem. Abp. of Prague, President of the Council of European Episcopal Conferences, 1993-. *Curial membership*: Oriental Churches (congregation); Social Communications (council).

Wamala, Emmanuel: b. Dec. 15, 1926, Kamaggwa, Uganda; ord. priest Dec. 21, 1957; ord. bp. of Kiyinda-Mityana, Nov. 22, 1981; coadj. abp. of Kampala, June 21, 1988; abp. of Kampala, Feb. 8, 1990; cardinal Nov. 26, 1994; titular church, St. Hugh. Abp. of Kampala. *Curial membership*: Evangelization of Peoples (congregation); "Cor Unum" (council).

Wetter, Friedrich: b. Feb. 20, 1928, Landau, Germany; ord. priest Oct. 10, 1953; ord. bp. of Speyer, June 29, 1968; abp. of Munich and Freising, Oct. 28, 1982; cardinal May 25, 1985; titular church, St. Stephen (al Monte Celio). Abp. of Munich and Freising. *Curial membership*: Evangelization of Peoples, Catholic Education (congregations).

Willebrands,* Johannes: b. Sept. 4, 1909, Bovenkarspel, The Netherlands; ord. priest May 26, 1934; ord. titular bp. of Mauriana, June 28, 1964; secretary of Secretariat for Christian Unity, 1960-69; cardinal Apr. 28, 1969; titular church, St. Sebastian (alle Catacombe); abp. of Utrecht, 1975-83; president of Council for Christian Unity, 1969-89. President emeritus of the Council for Promoting Christian Unity; Camerlengo of the College of Cardinals, 1988.

Williams, Thomas Stafford: b. Mar. 20, 1930, Wellington, New Zealand; ord. priest Dec. 20, 1959, in Rome; studied in Ireland after ordination, receiving degree in social sciences; served in various pastoral assignments on his return to New Zealand; missionary in Western Samoa to 1976; ord. abp. of Wellington, New Zealand, Dec. 20, 1979; cardinal Feb. 2, 1983; titular church, Jesus the Divine Teacher (at Pineda Sacchetti). Abp. of Wellington; Military Ordinary for New Zealand (1995). *Curial membership*: Evangelization of Peoples (congregation).

Winning, Thomas Joseph: b. June 3, 1925, Wishaw, Scotland; ord. priest Dec. 18, 1948; spiritual director of the Pontifical Scots College in Rome, 1961-66; returned to Scotland, 1966; served as parish priest,

episcopal vicar for marriage in Motherwell diocese and first president and officialis (1970-72) of the newly established Scottish National Tribunal, Glasgow; ord. titular bp. of Lugmad and aux. of Glasgow Nov. 30, 1971; abp. of Glasgow, Apr. 23, 1974; cardinal Nov. 26, 1994; titular church, St. Andrew delle Fratte. Abp. of Glasgow. *Curial membership*: Christian Unity, Family (councils).

Wu Cheng-chung, John Baptist: b. Mar. 26, 1925, Shui-Tsai, mainland China; ord. priest (for Hsinchu, Taiwan, diocese) July 6, 1952; ord. bp. of Hong Kong, July 25, 1975; cardinal June 28, 1988; titular church, Blessed Virgin Mary of Mount Carmel (a Mostacciano). Bp. of Hong Kong. *Curial membership*: Evangelization of Peoples (congregation); Interreligious Dialogue, Social Communications (councils).

Zoungrana,* Paul, M. Afr.: b. Sept 3, 1917, Ouagadougou, Upper Volta (now Burkina Faso); ord. priest May 2, 1942; ord. abp. of Ouagadougou at St. Peter's Basilica by John XXIII, May 8, 1960; cardinal Feb. 22, 1965; titular church, St. Camillus de Lellis. Abp. emeritus of Ouagadougou (resigned June 10, 1995).

CATEGORIES OF CARDINALS

As of Aug. 15, 1999
Information below includes categories of cardinals and dates of consistories at which they were created. Seniority or precedence usually depends on order of elevation.

One of these 154 cardinals one was named by John XXIII (consistory of Dec. 15, 1958); 23 by Paul VI (consistories of Feb. 22, 1965, June 26, 1967, Apr. 28, 1969, Mar. 5, 1973, May 24, 1976, and June 27, 1977); 131 by John Paul II (consistories of June 30, 1979, Feb. 2, 1983, May 25, 1985, June 28, 1988, June 28, 1991, Nov. 26, 1994, and Feb. 21, 1998).

Order of Bishops
Titular Bishops of Suburbicarian Sees: Bernardin Gantin, dean (June 27, 1977, Ostia and Palestrina); Joseph Ratzinger sub-dean (June 27, 1977, Velletri-Segni); Paolo Bertoli (Apr. 28, 1969, Frascati); Angelo Sodano (June 28, 1991, Albano); Roger Etchegaray (June 24, 1998, Porto-Santa Rufina); Lucas Moreira Neves, O.P. (June 25, 1998, Sabina-PoggioMireto).
Eastern Rite Patriarch: Nasrallah Pierre Sfeir (Nov. 26, 1994).

Order of Priests
1958 (Dec. 15): Franz König.
1965 (Feb. 22): Paul Zoungrana, M. Afr.
1967 (June 26): Corrado Ursi.
1969 (Apr. 28): Silvio Oddi, Paul Gouyon, Stephen Sou-hwan Kim, Eugênio de Araújo Sales, Johannes Willebrands.
1973 (Mar. 5): Pietro Palazzini, Luis Aponte Martinez, Raúl Francisco Primatesta, Salvatore Pappalardo, Marcelo González Martin, Maurice Otunga, Paulo Evaristo Arns, O.F.M., Pio Taofinu'u.
1976 (May 24): Opilio Rossi, Giuseppe Maria Sensi, Juan Carlos Aramburu, Corrado Bafile, Hyacinthe

Thiandoum, Jaime L. Sin, William W. Baum, Aloisio Lorscheider.
1979 (June 30): Giuseppe Caprio, Marco Cé, Egano Righi-Lambertini, Ernesto Corripio Ahumada, Gerald Emmett Carter, Franciszek Macharski, Ignatius Gong Pin-mei.
1983 (Feb. 2): Aurelio Sabattani, Franjo Kuharic, Giuseppe Casoria, José Ali Lebrún Moratinos, Michael Michai Kitbunchu, Alexandre do Nascimento, Alfonso López Trujillo, Godfried Danneels, Thomas Stafford Williams, Carlo Maria Martini, Jean-Marie Lustiger, Józef Glemp, Joachim Meisner.
1985 (May 25): Juan Francisco Fresno Larraín, Miguel Obando Bravo, S.D.B., Angel Suquía Goicoechea, Ricardo Vidal, Henryk Roman Gulbinowicz, Paulus Tzadua, Myroslav Ivan Lubachivsky, Louis-Albert Vachon, Friedrich Wetter, Silvano Piovanelli, Adrianus J. Simonis, Bernard F. Law, John J. O'Connor, Giacomo Biffi, Simon D. Lourdusamy, Francis A. Arinze, Antonio Innocenti, Paul Augustin Mayer, Jozef Tomko, Andrzej Maria Deskur, Paul Poupard, Rosalio José Castillo Lara, S.D.B., Edouard Gagnon, P.S.S., Alfons Stickler, S.D.B.
1988 (June 28): Antony Padiyara, José Freire Falcão, Michele Giordano, Alexandre José Maria dos Santos, O.F.M., Giovanni Canestri, Simon Ignatius Pimenta, Edward Bede Clancy, James Aloysius Hickey, Edmund C. Szoka, László Paskai, O.F.M., Christian Wiyghan Tumi, Hans Hermann Gröer, O.S.B., Vincentas Sladkevicius, M.I.C., Jean Margéot, John Baptist Wu Cheng-chung.
1991 (June 28): Alexandru Todea, Frédéric Etsou-Nzabi-Bamungwabi, C.I.C.M., Nicolás de Jesús López Rodríguez, Roger Mahony, Anthony J. Bevilacqua, Giovanni Saldarini, Cahal Brendan Daly, Camillo Ruini, Ján Chryzostom Korec, S.J., Henri Schwery, Georg Sterzinsky.

1994 (Nov. 26): Miroslav Vlk, Peter Seiichi Shirayanagi, Thomas Joseph Winning, Adolfo Antonio Suárez Rivera, Jaime Lucas Ortega y Alamino, Julius Riyadi Darmaatmadja, S.J., Pierre Eyt, Emmanuel Wamala, William Henry Keeler, Augusto Vargas Alzamora, S.J., Jean-Claude Turcotte, Ricardo Maria Carles Gordó, Adam Joseph Maida, Vinko Puljic, Armand Gaétan Razafindratandra, Paul Joseph Pham Dính Tung, Juan Sandoval Íñiguez, Bernardino Echeverría Ruiz, C.I.C.M., Kazimierz Swiàtek, Ersilio Tonino.
1998 (Feb. 21) Aloysius Ambrozic, Salvatore de Giorgi, Serafim Fernandes de Araújo, Francis George, O.M.I., Adam Kozlowiecki, S.J., Paul Shan Kuo-hsi, S.J., Polycarp Pengo, Norberto Rivera Carrera, Antonio Maria Rouco Varela, Christoph Schönborn, O.P., Dionigi Tettamanzi.

Order of Deacons

1988 (June 28): Eduardo Martinez Somalo, Achille Silvestrini, Angelo Felici, Antonio Maria Javierre Ortas, S.D.B.
1991 (June 28): Pio Laghi, Edward I. Cassidy, José T. Sánchez, Virgilio Noè, Fiorenzo Angelini, Paolo Dezza, S.J.
1994 (Nov. 26):Vincenzo Fagiolo, Carlo Furno, Jan Pieter Schotte, C.I.C.M., Gilberto Agustoni.
1998 (Feb. 21) Lorenzo Antonetti, Darío Castrillón Hoyos, Giovanni Cheli, Francesco Colasuonno, Jorge Medina Estévez, Dino Monduzzi, James Francis Stafford.

DISTRIBUTION OF CARDINALS

As of Aug.15, 1999, there were 154 cardinals from more than 60 countries or areas. Listed below are areas, countries, number and last names.

Europe — 81

Italy (38): Angelini, Antonetti, Bafile, Bertoli, Biffi, Canestri, Caprio, Casoria, Cé, Cheli, Colasuonno, de Giorgi, Dezza, Fagiolo, Felici, Furno, Giordano, Innocenti, Laghi, Martini, Monduzzi, Noè, Oddi, Palazzini, Pappalardo, Piovanelli, Poggi, Righi-Lambertini, Rossi, Ruini, Sabattani, Saldarini, Silvestrini, Sensi, Sodano,Tettamanzi,Tonino, Ursi.
Germany (5): Mayer, Meisner, Ratzinger, Sterzinsky, Wetter.
Spain (6): Carles Gordó, Gonzalez Martin, Javierre Ortas, Martinez Somalo, RoucoVarela, Suquia Goicoechea,
France (5): Etchegaray, Eyt, Gouyon, Lustiger, Poupard.
Poland (5): Deskur, Glemp, Gulbinowicz, Kozlowiecki, Macharski.
Austria (4): Gröer, König, Schönborn, Stickler.
Belgium (2): Danneels, Schotte.
Netherlands (2): Simonis, Willebrands.
Slovakia (2): Korec, Tomko.
Switzerland (2): Agustoni, Schwery.
One from each of the following countries: Belarus, Swiatek; Bosnia-Herzegovina, Puljic; Croatia, Kuharic; Czech Republic, Vlk; Hungary, Paskai; Ireland, Daly; Lithuania, Sladkevicius; Romania, Todea; Scotland, Winning; Ukraine, Lubachivsky.

Asia — 15

India (3): Lourdusamy, Padiyara, Pimenta.
Philippines (3): Sánchez, Sin, Vidal.

One from each of the following countries: China, Gong Pin-mei (exiled); Hong Kong, Wu Cheng-chung; Indonesia, Darmaatmadja; Japan, Shirayangi; Korea, Kim; Lebanon, Sfeir; Taiwan, Shan Kuo-hsi; Thailand, Kitbunchu; Vietnam, Pham Dinh Tung.

Oceania — 4

Australia (2): Cassidy, Clancy. One each from: New Zealand, Williams; Pacific Islands (Samoa), Taofinu'u.

Africa — 14

One from each of the following countries: Angola, do Nascimento; Benin, Gantin; Burkina Faso, Zoungrana; Cameroon, Tumi; Congo (formerly Zaire), Etsou-Nzabi-Bamungwabi; Ethiopia, Tzadua; Kenya, Otunga; Madagascar, Razafindratandra; Mauritius, Margeot; Mozambique, Santos; Nigeria, Arinze; Senegal, Thiandoum; Tanzania, Pengo; Uganda, Wamala.

North America – 21

United States (11): Baum, Bevilacqua; George, Hickey, Keeler, Law, Mahony, Maida, O'Connor, Stafford, Szoka.
Canada (5): Ambrozic, Carter, Gagnon, Turcotte, Vachon.
Mexico (4): Corripio Ahumada, Rivera Carrera, Sandoval Iñiguez, Suárez Rivera.
Puerto Rico (1): Aponte Martinez.

Central and South America – 19

Argentina (2): Aramburu, Primatesta.
Brazil (6): Arns, Falcão, Fernandes de Araújo, Lorscheider, Neves, Sales.
Chile (2): Fresno Larraín, Medina Estévez.
Colombia (2): Castrillón Hoyos, Lopez Trujillo.
Venezuela (2): Castillo Lara, Lebrún Moratinos.
One each fron the following countries: Cuba, Ortega y Alamino; Dominican Republic, Lopez Rodriguez; Ecuador, Echevarría Ruiz; Nicaragua, Obando Bravo; Peru, Vargas Alzamora.

Ineligible to Vote

As of August 30, 1999, 49 of the 154 cardinals were ineligible to take part in a papal election in line with the apostolic letter *Ingravescentem Aetetem* effective January 1, 1971, which limited the functions of cardinals after completion of their 80th year.
Cardinals affected are: Angelini, Aramburu, Bafile, Bertoli, Canestri, Caprio, Carter, Casoria, Daly, Dezza, Echevarría Ruiz, Fagiolo, Fresno Larrain, Gagnon, Gong Pin-mei, González Martin, Gouton, Innocenti, König, Kozlowiecki, Lubachivsky, Margeot, Mayer, Oddi, Palazzini, Poggi, Pappalardo, Righi-Lambertini, Rossi, Sabattini, Sensi, Stickler, Suguía Goicoechea, Swiatek, Todea, Tonino, Ursi, Vachon, Willebrands.
Cardinals who completed their 80th year in 1999 and who became ineligible to vote: Cheli, Corripio Ahumada, Felici, Gröer, Kuharic, Lebrún Moratinos, Pham Dinh Tung, Primatesta, Zoungrana.

Cardinals of the United States

As of August 30, 1999, the following cardinals were in service, according to their years of elevation (for biographies, see Index under individual names): 1976: **William W. Baum** (major penitentiary); 1985: **Bernard F. Law** (abp. of Boston), **John J. O'Connor** (abp. of New York); 1988: **James A. Hickey** (abp. of Washington), **Edmund C. Szoka** (governor of the Vatican City State); 1991: **Roger M. Mahony** (abp. of Los Angeles), **Anthony M. Bevilacqua** (abp. of Philadelphia); 1994: **William H. Keeler** (abp. of Baltimore), **Adam J. Maida** (abp. of Detroit); 1998: **Francis E. George, O.M.I.** (abp. of Chicago), **James F. Stafford** (president of the Pontifical Council for the Laity) [Myroslav Lubachivsky, major abp. of Lviv of the Ukrainians (Ukraine), was made a cardinal in 1985. He is a citizen of the United States and was metropolitan of the Philadelphia Ukrainian Rite Archeparchy, from 1979-81.]

U.S. Cardinals of the Past (according to year of elevation; for biographical data, see Index: Bishops, U.S., of the Past):

1875: John McCloskey; 1886: James Gibbons; 1911: John Farley, William O'Connell; 1921: Dennis Dougherty; 1924: Patrick Hayes, George Mundelein; 1946: John Glennon, Edward Mooney, Francis Spellman, Samuel Stritch; 1953: James F. McIntyre; 1958: John O'Hara, C.S.C., Richard Cushing; 1959: Albert Meyer, Aloysius Muench; 1961: Joseph Ritter; 1965: Lawrence J. Shehan; 1967: Francis Brennan, John P. Cody, Patrick A. O'Boyle, John J. Krol; 1969: John J. Wright, Terence J. Cooke, John F. Dearden, John J. Carberry; 1973: Humberto S. Medeiros, Timothy Manning; 1983: Joseph L. Bernardin.

Prelates who became cardinals after returning to their native countries: John Lefebvre de Chevrus, first bp. of Boston (1808-23) and apostolic administrator of New York (1810-15), elevated to the cardinalate, 1836, in France. Ignatius Persico, O.F.M. Cap., bp. of Savannah (1870-72), elevated to the cardinalate, 1893, in Italy; Diomede Falconio, O.F.M. ord. A priest Buffalo, N.Y.; missionary in U.S.; apostolic delegate to the U.S. (1902-11), elevated to cardinalate, 1911, in Italy.

CARDINAL BASIL HUME, O.S.B. (1923-1999)

Cardinal George Basil Hume, O.S.B., archbishop of Westminster and the most influential Catholic leader in Great Britain died on the evening June 17, 1999 from inoperable stomach cancer after an illness of several months. Respected and even revered as an eloquent spokesperson for conciliation, ecumenical dialogue, and compassion, Cardinal Hume served as archbishop of Westminster from 1976 until his death.

Early Career

Born on Mar. 2, 1923, at Newcastle-upon-Tyne, England, he was the son of William Errington Hume, a professor of medicine and a heart specialist, and Lady Marie Elizabeth Tisseyre, daughter of a distinguished military family of France; his father was an Anglican and his mother a Catholic. At the age of 13 he went to Ampleforth College, North Yorkshire, a private Catholic school, and then began monastic studies at Benedictine Abbey of St. Laurence at Ampleforth, 1941. He made his solemn perpetual vows as a Benedictine in 1945, and his subsequent studies for the priesthood brought him to Oxfords University and the University of Fribourg in Switzerland. He was ordained on July 23, 1950.

After teaching history and modern languages in the prestigious college of Ampleforth, Hume was elected abbot of Ampleforth in 1963, an office he held until 1976 when Pope Paul VI made the surprise announcement that he was to be the next Archbishop of Westminster. Consecrated on Mar. 25, 1976, he was elevated to the cardinalate on May 24, 1976 (with the titular church of St. Silvestro in Capite).

Archbishop OF Westminster

Known to many in London and across England simply as "Father Basil," the cardinal's time as archbishop is ranked as one of the most successful in the history of the Church in post-Reformation England. In 1982, he welcomed Pope John Paul II to Westminster Cathedral, the first pope ever to step foot on English soil. The papal visit helped advance the cause of ecumenical dialogue and was seen as an endorsement of

Hume's quiet, diplomatic style. In the 1970s and 1980s, Hume played a pivotal role in the effort to free the so-called "Guildford Four" and the "Maguire Seven" who had been accused wrongfully of terrorist crimes.

Prophetically, Hume spoke out in the early 1990s about what he saw as the mounting question of the burden of debt on the countries of the third world. In 1996, he hosted a seminar at Westminster that brought together Church leaders from the developing world with representatives from the World Bank and the International Monetary Fund.

One of the highlights of his tenure was the delicacy and sensitivity he displayed in his relations with the Anglican Church. After the decision of the Church of England to ordain women priests in 1992, Hume won approval from the Vatican to permit the ordination of married converted clergy. Nevertheless, Hume supported Catholic membership in the British Council of Churches and was an active, even leading participant in the Council for Christian Unity in Rome and the Anglican-Roman Catholic International Commission. He also was a devoted adherent of Interreligious Dialogue.

Death

In April, 1999, Cardinal Hume announced that he had been diagnosed with incurable stomach cancer. In a manner reminiscent of Cardinal Joseph Bernardin, Archbishop of Chicago, Hume spent his last days demonstrating serenity in the face of his illness and the true meaning of death in Christ. Shortly before his death, he was granted the Order of Merit by Queen Elizabeth II. The queen was represented at his funeral Mass in Westminster Cathedral on June 25 by the Duchess of Kent.

The Tablet, in its obituary on June 26, observed that: "It was among his greatest achievements that in an increasingly secular age and in a predominantly Anglican culture, he cut through the veils of cultural and religious prejudice to show the reality of the Roman Catholic faith.... He was always listened to, rarely wrong."

THE CHURCH IN COUNTRIES THROUGHOUT THE WORLD

(Principal sources for statistics: Statistical Yearbook of the Church, *1997 — the most recent edition;* Annuario Pontificio, *1999; and* Agenzia Internazionale FIDES. *Figures are as of Dec. 31, 1996, except for cardinals (as of Aug. 30, 1999) and others which are indicated. For 1997 developments, see Index entries for individual countries.) Readers are encouraged to consult as well the Special Reports for coverage of the various special synods held in Rome throughout 1998-99 on the concerns of the Church in different parts of the globe.*

An asterisk indicates that the country has full diplomatic relations with the Holy See (see Index: Diplomats to the Holy See).

Abbreviations (in order in which they appear): archd. — archdiocese; dioc. — diocese; ap. ex. — apostolic exarchate; prel. — prelature; abb. — abbacy; v.a. — apostolic vicariate; p.a. — apostolic prefecture; a.a. — apostolic administration; mil. ord. — military ordinariate; card. — cardinal; abp. — archbishops; bp. — bishops (diocesan and titular); priests (dioc. — diocesan or secular priests; rel. — those belonging to religious orders); p.d. — permanent deacons; sem. — major seminarians, diocesan and religious; bros. — brothers; srs. — sisters; bap. — baptisms; Caths. — Catholic population; tot. pop. — total population; (AD), apostolic delegate (see Index: Papal Representatives).

Afghanistan
Republic in south-central Asia; capital, Kabul. Christianity antedated Muslim conquest in the seventh century but was overcome by it. All inhabitants are subject to the law of Islam. Christian missionaries are prohibited.

Albania*
Archd., 2; dioc., 4; a.a. 1; abp., 2; bp., 4; parishes, 132; priests, 97 (29 dioc., 68 rel.); p.d.,1; sem., 49; bros., 13; srs., 277; bap., 7,523; Caths., 634,000 (16.5%); tot. pop., 3,420,000.

Republic in the Balkans, bordering the Adriatic Sea; capital, Tirana. Christianity was introduced in apostolic times. The northern part of the country remained faithful to Rome while the South broke from unity following the schism of 1054. A large percentage of the population was to become Muslim following the invasion (15th century) and long centuries of occupation by the Ottoman Turks. Many Catholics fled to southern Italy, Sicily and Greece. In 1945, at the time of the communist takeover, an estimated 68 percent of the population was Muslim; 19 percent was Orthodox and 13 percent, Roman Catholic. The Catholic Church prevailed in the North. During 45 years of communist dictatorship, the Church fell victim, as did all religions, to systematic persecution: non-Albanian missionaries were expelled; death, prison sentences and other repressive measures were enacted against Church personnel and laity; Catholic schools and churches were closed and used for other purposes, and lines of communication with the Holy See were cut off.

In 1967, the government, declaring it had eliminated all religion in the country, proclaimed itself the first atheist state in the world. The right to practice religion was restored in late 1990. In March 1991, a delegation from the Vatican was allowed to go to Albania; later in the year diplomatic relations were established with the Holy See at the request of the Albanian prime minister. Pope John Paul II made a one-day visit to the country Apr. 25, 1993, during which he ordained four bishops appointed by him in December 1992 to fill long-vacant sees. Restoration of the Church is a slow and difficult process. The first Albanian cardinal was named in November 1994.

In early 1997, rioting occurred after thousands of Albanians lost their investments in collapsed pyramid schemes, and in southern Albania, churches and mosques were looted an vandalized. Although Catholics are a minority, they are well respected, including for their work in the education and health fields. Albanians welcomed hundreds of thousands of ethnic Albanians from Kosovo during Yugoslav persecution in 1999.

Algeria*

Archd., 1; dioc., 3; abp., 2; bp., 2; parishes, 37; priests, 104 (43 dioc., 61 rel.); p.d., 1; sem., 1; bros., 13; srs., 177; bap., 9; Caths., 3,000 (.01%); tot. pop., 29,050,000.

Republic in northwest Africa: capital, Algiers. Christianity, introduced at an early date, succumbed to Vandal devastation in the fifth century and Muslim conquest in 709, but survived for centuries in small communities into the 12th century. Missionary work was unsuccessful except in service to traders, military personnel and captives along the coast. Church organization was established after the French gained control of the territory in the 1830s. A large number of Catholics were among the estimated million Europeans who left the country after it secured independence from France July 5, 1962. Islam is the state religion.

Armed Islamic militants and guerrillas have caused terror and unrest in Algeria since 1992. Among the more than 80,000 people killed were seven Trappist monks and the Catholic bishop of Oran, all in 1996.

Andorra*

Parishes, 7; priests, 19 (13 dioc., 6 rel.); p.d., 1; srs., 13; bap., 425; Caths., 59,000 (84.2%); tot. pop., 63,000.

Parliamentary state (1993) in the Pyrenees; capital, Andorra la Vella. From 1278-1993, it was a co-principality under the rule of the French head of state and the bishop of Urgel, Spain, who retain their titles. Christianity was introduced at an early date. Catholicism is the state religion. Ecclesiastical jurisdiction is under the Spanish Diocese of Urgel. The constitution calls for freedom of religion, but also guarantees "the Roman Catholic Church free and public exercise of its activities and the preservation of the relations of special cooperation with the state."

Angola*

Archd., 3; dioc., 12; card., 1; abp., 5; bp., 16; parishes, 246; priests, 472 (190 dioc., 282 rel.); p.d., 1; sem., 1,033; bros., 68; srs., 1,538; catechists, 24,423; bap., 169,124; Caths., 6,818,000 (58.9%); tot. pop., 11,570,000.

Republic in southwest Africa; capital, Luanda. Evan-

gelization by Catholic missionaries from Portugal, dating from 1491, reached high points in the 17th and 18th centuries. Independence from Portugal in 1975 and the long civil war that followed (peace accord signed in 1991) left the Church with a heavy loss of personnel through the departure of about half of the foreign missionaries and the persecution and martyrdom experienced by the Church during the war. Renewed fighting following elections in late 1992 brought repeated appeals for peace from the nation's bishops and religious in 1993 and 1994.

Despite another peace accord signed by the rebels and the government in late 1994, conditions have remained unsettled. One effect of the fighting was to cut off Church leaders from large groups of the faithful. In an attempt to encourage peace efforts, the Vatican established diplomatic relations with Angola in 1997. Attacks on Church workers, however, continued in 1998 and 1999.

Antigua and Barbuda*

Dioc., 1; bp., 1; parishes, 2; priests, 5 (3 dioc., 2 rel.); p.d., 4; sem., 2; bros., 5; srs., 9; catechists, 48; bap., 97; Caths., 8,000 (12.5%); tot. pop., 64,000.

Independent (1981) Caribbean island nation; capital, St. John's, Antigua. The Diocese of St. John's-Basseterre includes Antigua and Barbuda, St. Kitts and Nevis, Anguilla, the British Virgin Islands and Montserrat.

Argentina*

Archd., 14; dioc. (1997), 50; prel., 3; ap. ex., 2 (for Armenians of Latin America); mil. ord., 1; card., 2; abp., 21; bp., 84; parishes, 2,596; priests, 5,877 (3,532 dioc., 2,345 rel.); p.d., 421; sem., 2,043; bros., 848; srs., 10,773; bap., 569,455; catechists, 89,688; Caths., 32,088,000 (90%); tot. pop., 35,670,000

Republic in southeast South America, bordering on the Atlantic; capital, Buenos Aires. Priests were with the Magellan exploration party and the first Mass in the country was celebrated Apr. 1, 1519. Missionary work began in the 1530s, diocesan organization in the late 1540s, and effective evangelization about 1570. Independence from Spain was proclaimed in 1816. Since its establishment in the country, the Church has been influenced by Spanish cultural and institutional forces, antagonistic liberalism, government interference and opposition; the latter reached a climax during the last five years of the first presidency of Juan Peron (1946-55).

Widespread human rights violations, including the disappearance of thousands of people, marked the "Dirty War," the period of military rule from 1976 to December 1983, when an elected civilian government took over. In 1996 the Argentine bishops said they did not do enough to stop human rights violations during the "Dirty War." In the late 1990s, the bishops spoke out against government corruption and a severe government economic program.

Armenia*

Ord., 1 (for Catholic Armenians of Eastern Europe, with seat in Armenia); a.a., 1 (for Latin-rite Catholics, with seat in Georgia); parishes, 29; abp., 1; priests, 17 (1 dioc., 16 rel.); sem., 9; srs., 18; bap., 343; Caths., 147,000 (3.7%); tot. pop., 3,640,000.

Republic in Asia Minor; capital Yerevan. Part of the

USSR from 1920 until it declared its sovereignty in September 1991. Ancient Armenia, which also included territory annexed by Turkey in 1920, was Christianized in the fourth century. Diplomatic relations were established with the Holy See May 23, 1992.

Australia*

Archd., 7; dioc., 24; mil. ord., 1; card., 2; abp., 11; bp., 52; parishes, 1,408; priests, 3,429 (2,074 dioc., 1,355 rel.); p.d., 46; sem., 248; bros., 1,277; srs., 8,783; catechists, 22,226; bap., 70,495; Caths., 5,323,000 (28.7%); tot. pop. 18,530,000.

Commonwealth; island continent southeast of Asia; capital, Canberra. The first Catholics in the country were Irish under penal sentence, 1795-1804; the first public Mass was celebrated May 15, 1803. Official organization of the Church dates from 1820. The country was officially removed from mission status in March 1976.

As the 20th century neared its end, the Church in Australia was rocked by allegations of sexual abuse from previous decades. In 1996 the Australian bishops published a plan for dealing with such cases. In 1998 the bishops also apologized to former aboriginal children, saying their support of government policy in the 1970s might have contributed to separation of the children from their families.

In an unusual move, in mid-November 1998, just before the Synod of Bishops for Oceania at the Vatican and after the Australian bishops' "ad limina" visits, Vatican officials met with Church leaders from Australia to discuss doctrinal and pastoral issues. In December, the Vatican and representatives of Australian Church leaders signed a document, later endorsed by the Australian bishops' conference, that spoke of a "crisis of faith" in the Catholic Church on the continent.

Austria*

Archd., 2; dioc., 7; abb., 1; ord., 1; mil. ord.; card., 4; abp., 3; bp., 17; parishes, 3,055; priests, 4,793 (2,819 dioc., 1,974 rel.); p.d., 371; sem., 387; bros., 545; srs., 6,701; catechists, 3,980; bap., 67,110; Caths., 6,212,000 (76.9%); tot. pop., 8,070,000.

Republic in central Europe; capital, Vienna. Christianity was introduced by the end of the third century, strengthened considerably by conversion of the Bavarians from about 600, and firmly established in the second half of the eighth century. Catholicism survived and grew stronger as the principal religion in the country in the post-Reformation period, but suffered from Josephinism in the 18th century. Although liberated from much government harassment in the aftermath of the Revolution of 1848, the Church came under pressure again some 20 years later in the *Kulturkampf.* During this time the Church became involved with a developing social movement. The Church faced strong opposition from Socialists after World War I and suffered persecution from 1938 to 1945 during the Nazi regime. Some Church-state matters are regulated by a concordat originally concluded in 1934.

In recent years, the Church in Austria has been beset by internal difficulties, including the launch of a global movement seeking more lay participation in Church decision-making and changes in Church policy on ordination of women and priestly celibacy. In 1995, Cardinal Hans Hermann Gröer resigned as archbishop of Vienna amid charges of sexual misconduct. His successor, Cardinal Christoph Schönborn, has worked to restore a sense of unity to the Church.

Azerbaijan*

Independent republic (1991) on the Caspian Sea; formerly part of the USSR; capital, Baku. Islam is the prevailing religion. Soviet rulers destroyed Baku's one Catholic church in the late 1930s. A small Catholic community of Polish and Armenian origin near the capital is ministered to by missionaries. Latin-rite Catholics are under the apostolic administration of Caucasus (seat in Georgia) established in December 1993.

Bahamas*

Dioc., 1; bp., 1; parishes, 27; priests, 29 (13 dioc., 16 rel.); p.d., 9; sem., 7; bros., 1; srs., 27; catechists, 137; bap., 2,101; Caths., 31,000 (10.7%); tot. pop., 288,000.

Independent (July 10, 1973) island group consisting of some 700 (30 inhabited) small islands southeast of Florida and north of Cuba; capital, Nassau. On Oct. 12, 1492, Columbus landed on one of these islands, where the first Mass was celebrated in the New World. Organization of the Catholic Church in the Bahamas dates from about the middle of the 19th century.

Bahrain

Parish, 1; priests, 5 (2 dioc., 3 rel.); br., 1; srs., 73; bap., 188; Caths., 30,000 (20.6%); tot. pop., 620,000. (AD)

Island state in Persian Gulf; capital, Manama. Population is Muslim; Catholics are foreign workers. Under ecclesiastical jurisdiction of Arabia apostolic vicariate.

Bangladesh*

Archd., 1; dioc., 5; abp., 2; bp., 6; parishes, 76; priests, 268 (138 dioc., 130 rel.); sem., 108; bros., 60; srs., 976; catechists, 1,308; bap., 7,145; Caths., 248,000 (.20%); tot. pop. 122,010,000.

Formerly the eastern portion of Pakistan. Officially constituted as a separate nation Dec. 16, 1971; capital, Dhaka. Islam, the principal religion, was declared the state religion in 1988; freedom of religion is granted. Jesuit, Dominican and Augustinian missionaries were in the area in the 16th century. An apostolic vicariate (of Bengali) was established in 1834; the hierarchy was erected in 1950. Church-run humanitarian and development agencies have been instrumental in responding to natural disasters, such as flooding. The bishops have emphasized inculturation and Church social doctrine.

Barbados*

Dioc., 1; bp., 2; parishes, 6; priests, 12 (3 dioc., 9 rel.); p.d., 1; srs., 11; bap., 206; Caths., 10,000 (3.8%); tot. pop., 260,000.

Parliamentary democracy (independent since 1966), easternmost of the Caribbean islands; capital, Bridgetown. About 70 percent of the people are Anglicans.

Belarus*

Archd., 1; dioc., 2; card., 1; abp., 1; bp., 1; parishes, 357; priests, 254 (122 dioc., 132 rel.); sem., 193; bros., 11; srs., 283; bap., 7,338; Caths., 1,090,000 (12%); tot. pop., 10,220,000.

Independent republic (1991) in eastern Europe; former Soviet republic (Byelorussia); capital, Minsk. Slow recovery of the Church was reported after years of repression in the Soviet Union, although in the mid-1990s under the authoritarian rule of President Alexander Lukashenka, the Church encountered tensions, especially in refusal of permits for foreign religious workers.

Belgium*

Archd., 1; dioc., 7; mil. ord., 1; card., 2; abp., 4; bp., 21; parishes, 3,919; priests, 8,808 (5,442 dioc., 3,366 rel.); p.d., 516; sem., 320; bros., 1,497; srs., 17,734; catechists, 10,210; bap., 82,567; Caths., 8,274,000 (83.7%); tot. pop., 10,190,000.

Constitutional monarchy in northwestern Europe; capital, Brussels. Christianity was introduced about the first quarter of the fourth century and major evangelization was completed about 730. During the rest of the medieval period the Church had firm diocesan and parochial organization, generally vigorous monastic life and influential monastic and cathedral schools. Lutherans and Calvinists made some gains during the Reformation period but there was a strong Catholic restoration in the first half of the 17th century, when the country was under Spanish rule. Jansenism disturbed the Church from about 1640 into the 18th century. Josephinism, imposed by an Austrian regime, hampered the Church late in the same century. Repressive and persecutory measures were enforced during the Napoleonic conquest. Freedom came with separation of Church and state in the wake of the Revolution of 1830, which ended the reign of William I. Thereafter, the Church encountered serious problems with philosophical liberalism and political socialism. Except for one five-year period (1880-84), Belgium has had diplomatic relations with the Holy See since 1835.

Catholics have long been engaged in strong educational, social and political movements. In 1990, in an unprecedented political maneuver, King Baudouin temporarily gave up his throne, saying his Catholic conscience would not allow him to sign a law legalizing abortion. In the mid- and late-1990s, Church leaders expressed concern that the Church was characterized by indifference toward the papacy and dissent from Church teachings. Therapeutic in vitro fertilization for stable married couples continued at a leading Belgian Catholic hospital despite Vatican objections. A prominent pedophilia conviction of a priest added to many Belgian Catholics' lack of confidence in the Church.

Belize*

Dioc., 1; bp., 1; parishes, 13; priests, 38 (15 dioc., 23 rel.); p.d., 1; sem., 4; bros., 8; srs., 71; bap., 3,126; Caths., 133,000 (60%); tot. pop., 230,000.

Formerly British Honduras. Independent (Sept. 21, 1981) republic on eastern coast of Central America; capital, Belmopan. Its history has points in common with Guatemala, where evangelization began in the 16th century. The Church in Belize worked with refu-gees during the decades of Central American civil wars.

Benin*

Archd., 2; dioc., 7; card., 1; abp., 3; bp., 8; parishes, 172; priests, 361(254 dioc., 107 rel.); sem., 315; bros., 53; srs., 689; catechists, 7,740; bap., 52,395; Caths., 1,255,000 (21.5%); tot. pop., 5,830,000.

Formerly Dahomey. Democratic republic in west Africa, bordering on the Atlantic; capital, Porto Novo. Missionary work was very limited from the 16th to the 18th centuries. Effective evangelization dates from 1861. The hierarchy was established in 1955. In the 1970s, Benin's Marxist-Leninist government nationalized Catholic schools, expelled foreign missionaries and jailed some priests. After the government dropped the one-party system in 1989, Archbishop Isidore de Souza of Cotonou presided over the 1990 national conference that dew up a new constitution and prepared the way for elections. One challenge facing the Church as it entered the 21st century was maintaining peace with people of other faiths.

Bermuda

Dioc., 1; bp., 2; parishes, 6; priests, 8 (1 dioc., 7 rel.); srs., 4; bap., 109; Caths., 9,000 (16%); tot. pop., 58,000. (AD)

British dependency, consisting of 360 islands (20 of them inhabited), nearly 600 miles east of Cape Hatteras; capital, Hamilton. Catholics were not permitted until about 1800. Occasional pastoral care was provided the few Catholics there by visiting priests during the 19th century. Early in the 1900s priests from Nova Scotia began serving the area. An apostolic prefecture was set up in 1953. The first bishop assumed jurisdiction in 1956, when it was made an apostolic vicariate; diocese established, 1967.

Bhutan

Parishes, none; srs., 10; catechist, 2; bap., 3; Caths., 500 (approx.); tot. pop., 1,860,000.

Kingdom in the Himalayas, northeast of India; capital, Thimphu. Buddhism is the state religion; citizens of other faiths have freedom of worship but may not proselytize. Jesuits (1963) and Salesians (1965) were invited to country to direct schools. Salesians were expelled in February 1982, on disputed charges of proselytism. The only Catholic missionary allowed to stay in the country was Canadian Jesuit Father William Mackey, who served Catholics there from 1963 until his death in 1995. Ecclesiastical jurisdiction is under the Darjeeling (India) Diocese, which ordained the first native Bhutanese priest in 1995.

Bolivia*

Archd., 4; dioc., 6; prel., 2; v.a., 5; mil. ord. 1; v.a., 5; abp., 7; bp., 29; parishes, 542; priests, 1,058 (394 dioc., 664 rel.); p.d., 52; sem., 834; bros., 198; srs., 2,108; catechists, 7,129; bap., 176,897; Caths., 6,887,000 (88.6%); tot. pop., 7,770,000.

Republic in central South America; capital, Sucre; seat of government, La Paz. Catholicism, the official religion, was introduced in the 1530s, and the first diocese was established in 1552. Effective evangelization among the Indians, slow to start, reached high points in the middle of the 18th century and the beginning of the 19th centuries and was resumed about 1840. Independence from Spain was proclaimed in 1825, at the end of a campaign that started in 1809. Church-state relations are regulated by a 1951 concordat with the Holy See. In recent years, Catholics have worked against social poverty and corruption. In 1996, Pope John Paul II urged Bolivia to put its drug-trafficking "merchants of death" out of business.

Bosnia and Herzegovina*

Archd., 1; dioc., 2; card., 1; bp., 3; parishes, 281; priests, 559 (216 dioc., 343 rel.); sem., 168; bros., 14; srs., 542; bap., 7,207; Caths., 454,000 (17%); tot. pop., 3,780,000.

Independent republic (1992) in southeastern Europe; formerly part of Yugoslavia; capital Sarajevo. During the three years of fighting that erupted after Bosnia-Herzegovina declared its independence, some 450,000 Catholics were driven from their homes; many fled to Croatia or southern Bosnia. Sarajevo Cardinal Vinko Puljic, named a cardinal in 1994, has led the bishops in calls for the safe return of all refugees from the war and acknowledged that in some areas Croatian Catholics were responsible for atrocities. In 1999 the Vatican and Franciscan officials formally agreed to the hand over of seven parishes in the Diocese of Mostar, but the agreement was greeted in some areas with violence, and Church officials said many local people did not immediately accept the situation. The parish in Medjugorje, site of alleged Marian apparitions in 1981, remained the responsibility of the Franciscans.

Botswana

Dioc., 1; v.a.; bp., 1; parishes, 42; priests, 49 (7 dioc., 42 rel.); p.d., 1; sem., 15; bros., 5; srs., 42; catechists, 259; bap., 822; Caths., 53,000 (3.5%); tot. pop., 1,530,000. (AD)

Republic (independent since 1966) in southern Africa; capital, Gaborone. The first Catholic mission was opened in 1928 near Gaborone; earlier attempts at evangelization dating from 1879 were unsuccessful. The Church in Botswana gave strong support to tens of thousands of South African refugees from apartheid. As Botswana's diamond industry transformed it from a poor to wealthy country, Church leaders worked to minimize the effects of social changes such as pockets of unemployment and competition for jobs.

Brazil*

Archd., 38; dioc., 206; prel., 14; abb., 2; exarch.; mil. ord.; card., 6; abp., 51; bp., 311; parishes, 8,253; priests, 15,577 (8,204 dioc., 7,373 rel.); p.d., 818; sem., 7,298; bros., 2,268; srs., 35,852; bap., 2,173,036; catechists, 271,257; Caths., 137,570,000 (86%); tot. pop., 159,880,000.

Federal republic in northeastern South America; capital, Brasilia. One of several priests with the discovery party celebrated the first Mass in the country Apr. 26, 1500. Evangelization began some years later, and the first diocese was erected in 1551. During the colonial period, which lasted until 1822, evangelization made some notable progress — especially in the Amazon region between 1680 and 1750 — but was seriously hindered by government policy and the attitude of colonists regarding Amazon Indians the missionaries tried to protect from exploitation and sla-

very. The Jesuits were suppressed in 1782 and other missionaries expelled as well. Liberal anti-Church influence grew in strength. The government exercised maximum control over the Church. After the proclamation of independence from Portugal in 1822 and throughout the regency, government control was tightened and the Church suffered greatly from dissident actions of ecclesiastical brotherhoods, Masonic anticlericalism and general decline in religious life. Church and state were separated by the constitution of 1891, proclaimed two years after the end of the empire.

The Church carried into the 20th century problems associated with increasingly difficult political, economic and social conditions affecting the majority of the population. Many Afro-Brazilians indiscriminately mixed African-based rites such as candomble with Catholic rituals. In the second half of the 20th century, the bishops became know for their liberal stances on social and some theological issues. In the 1980s, Vatican officials had a series of meetings with Brazilian bishop to discuss liberation theology and other issues. The Brazilian bishops' conference took the lead in advocating for land reform in the country. Members of the Church's Pastoral Land Commission often faced threats, harassment and murder. The Church-founded Indigenous Missionary Council worked for the rights of the country's Indians. Each year, the bishops' Lenten campaign targeted a social issue, such as women's rights or economic reform.

Brunei

P.a.; parishes, 3; priests, 2 (1 dioc., 1 rel); srs., 1; sem., 2; Caths., 4,000 (1.2%); tot. pop., 310,000.

Independent state (1984) on the northern coast of Borneo; formal name, Brunei Darussalam; capital, Bandar Seri Begawan. Islam is the official religion; other religions are allowed with some restrictions. Most of the Catholics are technicians and skilled workers from other countries who are not permanent residents; under ecclesiastical jurisdiction of Miri Diocese, Malaysia.

Bulgaria*

Dioc., 2; ap. ex.; abp., 2; bp., 4; parishes, 53; priests, 44 (14 dioc., 30 rel.); sem., 9; p.d. 1; bros., 2; srs., 78; bap., 427; Caths., 85,000 (1%), tot. pop., 8,310,000.

Republic in southeastern Europe on the eastern part of the Balkan peninsula; capital, Sofia. Most of the population is Orthodox. Christianity was introduced before 343 but disappeared with the migration of Slavs into the territory. The baptism of Boris I about 865 ushered in a new period of Christianity, which soon became involved in switches of loyalty between Constantinople and Rome. Through it all the Byzantine, and later Orthodox, element remained stronger and survived under the rule of Ottoman Turks into the 19th century. The Byzantines are products of a reunion movement of the 19th century.

In 1947 the constitution of the new republic decreed the separation of Church and state. Catholic schools and institutions were abolished and foreign religious banished in 1948. A year later the apostolic delegate was expelled. Ivan Romanoff, vicar general of Plovdiv, died in prison in 1952. Bishop Eugene Bossilkoff, imprisoned in 1948, was sentenced to death in 1952;

his fate remained unknown until 1975, when the Bulgarian government informed the Vatican that he had died in prison shortly after being sentenced. He was beatified in 1998. Latin- and Eastern-rite apostolic vicars were permitted to attend the Second Vatican Council. All Church activity was under surveillance and/or control by the government, which professed to be atheistic. Pastoral and related activities were strictly limited. There was some improvement in Bulgarian-Vatican relations in 1975. In 1979, the Sofia-Plovdiv apostolic vicariate was raised to a diocese, and a bishop was appointed for the vacant see of Nicopoli. Diplomatic relations with the Holy See were established in 1990. In the late 1990s, the government instituted religion classes in state schools, but Church leaders complained they had no input into the curriculum and that teachers were predominantly Orthodox.

Burkina Faso*

Archd., 1; dioc., 10; card., 1; bp., 12; parishes, 115; priests, 518 (374 dioc., 144 rel.); sem., 425; bros., 144; srs., 992; catechists, 8,562; bap., 54,789; Caths., 1,145,000 (10.3%); tot. pop., 11,090,000.

Republic inland in West Africa; capital, Ouagadougou; formerly, Upper Volta. White Fathers (now known as Missionaries of Africa) started the first missions in 1900 and 1901. White Sisters began work in 1911. A minor and a major seminary were established in 1926 and 1942, respectively. The first native bishop in modern times from West Africa was ordained in 1956 and the first cardinal created in 1965. The hierarchy was established in 1955. In 1980 and 1990, Pope John Paul II's visits to the country were used to launch appeals for an end to desertification of sub-Saharan Africa and an end to poverty in the region. In later years, the pope encouraged increased evangelization and interreligious harmony.

Burma (See Myanmar)

Burundi*

Archd., 1; dioc., 6; abp., 3; bp., 8; parishes, 130; priests, 322 (245 dioc., 77 rel.); sem., 284; bros., 142; srs., 925; catechists, 4,231; bap., 115,309; Caths., 3,830,000 (62%); tot. pop., 6,190,000.

Republic since 1966, near the equator in east-central Africa; capital, Bujumbura. The first permanent Catholic mission station was established late in the 19th century. Large numbers were received into the Church following the ordination of the first Burundi priests in 1925. The first native bishop was appointed in 1959.

In 1972-73, the country was torn by tribal warfare between the Tutsis, the ruling minority, and the Hutus. In 1979, the government began expelling foreign missionaries, and in 1986, seminaries were nationalized. A gradual resumption of Church activity since 1987 has been hampered by continuing ethnic violence, which began in 1993 and left more than 150,000 Burundians dead. The bishops repeatedly have called for peace and for an end to sanctions imposed by the Organization of African Unity in 1996.

Cambodia*

V.a.; p.a., 2; bp., 2; parishes, none (there were 35 mission stations without resident priests) ; priests,

29 (3 dioc., 26 rel.); sem., 15; bros., 5; srs., 45; catechists, 11; baptisms, 50; Caths., 26,000 (.2%); tot. pop., 10,520,000.

Republic in Southeast Asia; capital Phnom Penh. Evangelization dating from the second half of the 16th century had limited results, more among Vietnamese than Khmers. Thousands of Catholics of Vietnamese origin were forced to flee in 1970 because of Khmer hostility. The status of the Church remained uncertain following the Khmer Rouge takeover in April 1975, the Vietnamese invasion in 1979 and the long civil war that followed. Foreign missionaries were expelled, local clergy and religious were sent to work the land and a general persecution followed. Religious freedom was re-established in 1990. Diplomatic relations with the Holy See were established in March 1994.

Cameroon*

Archd., 5; dioc., 17; card., 1; abp., 5; bp., 21; parishes, 671; priests, 1,110 (638 dioc., 472 rel.); p.d., 17; sem., 895; bros., 200; srs., 1,643; catechists, 14,848; bap., 83,712; Caths., 3,751,000 (26.9%); tot. pop., 13,940,000.

Republic in West Africa; capital, Yaounde. Effective evangelization began in 1890, although Catholics had been in the country long before that time. In the 40-year period from 1920 to 1960, the number of Catholics increased from 60,000 to 700,000. The first native priests were ordained in 1935. Twenty years later the first native bishops were ordained and the hierarchy established. The first Cameroonian cardinal (Christian Wiyghan Tumi) was named in 1988. Around that same time, unknown people began persecuting Church personnel. Among those murdered was Archbishop Yves Plumy of Garoua in 1991. Some felt the government did not do enough to investigate.

Canada* (See Catholic Church in Canada; see also Statistics of the Church in Canada.)

Cape Verde*

Dioc., 1; parishes, 31; priests, 47 (15 dioc., 32 rel.); sem., 16; bros., 6; srs., 104; catechists, 3,190; bap. , 9,278; Caths., 420,000 (96%); tot. pop., 438,000.

Independent (July 5, 1975) island group in the Atlantic 300 miles west of Senegal; formerly a Portuguese overseas province; capital, Praia, São Tiago Island. Evangelization began some years before the establishment of a diocese in 1532. The Church languished from the 17th to the 19th centuries, and for two long periods there was no resident bishop. Portugal's anti-clerical government closed the only minor seminary in 1910. Missionaries returned in the 1940s. They have faced massive emigration of youth because of perennial drought and a weak economy.

Central African Republic*

Archd., 1; dioc., 7; abp., 2; bp., 10; parishes, 115; priests, 283 (138 dioc., 145 rel.); sem., 114; bros., 59; srs., 370; catechists, 3,788; bap., 17,317; Caths., 688,000 (20.2%); tot. pop., 3,250,000.

Former French colony (independent since 1960) in central Africa; capital, Bangui. Effective evangelization dates from 1894. The region was organized as a mission territory in 1909. The first native priest was ordained in 1938. The hierarchy was organized in 1955. Pope John Paul II has urged the country's bishops to give hope to a people ruled by corrupt dictatorships and the military. The Church in the country also has expressed concern about the growing number of sects.

Chad*

Archd., 1; dioc., 6; abp., 1; bp., 6; parishes, 99; priests, 240 (109 dioc., 131 rel.); sem., 88; bros., 38; srs., 286; catechists, 7,195; bap., 14,614; Caths., 512,000 (7.6%); tot. pop., 6,700,000.

Republic (independent since 1960) in north-central Africa; former French possession; capital, N'Djamena. Evangelization began in 1929, leading to firm organization in 1947 and establishment of the hierarchy in 1955. Many catechists, who often were local community leaders, were killed during Chad's 1982-87 civil war. The Vatican established diplomatic relations with Chad in 1988. After the government established more freedoms in the early 1990s, the Church worked to teach people, including Catholics, that solidarity must extend across religious, ethnic and regional boundaries.

Chile*

Archd., 5; dioc., 17; prel., 2; v.a., 2; mil. ord.; card., 2; abp., 11; bp., 38; parishes, 926; priests, 2,266 (1,062 dioc., 1,204 rel.); p.d., 477; sem., 833; bros., 497; srs., 5,665; catechists, 40,069; bap., 175,932; Caths., 11,443,000 (78.2%); tot. pop., 14,620,000.

Republic on the southwest coast of South America; capital, Santiago. Priests were with the Spanish on their entrance into the territory early in the 16th century. The first parish was established in 1547 and the first diocese in 1561. Overall organization of the Church took place later in the century. By 1650, most of the peaceful Indians in the central and northern areas were evangelized. Missionary work was more difficult in the southern region. Church activity was hampered during the campaign for independence, 1810-18, and through the first years of the new government, to 1830. Later gains were made, into this century, but hindering factors were shortages of native clergy and religious and attempts by the government to control Church administration through the patronage system in force while the country was under Spanish control. Separation of Church and state was decreed in the constitution of 1925.

Church-state relations were strained during the regime of Marxist President Salvador Allende (1970-73). In the mid-1970s, the Archdiocese of Santiago established the Vicariate of Solidarity to counter human-rights abuses under the rule of Gen. Augusto Pinochet. The Chilean bishops issued numerous statements strongly critical of human rights abuses by the military dictator, who remained in power until 1990, when an elected president took office. The Church was praised for its role in educating and registering voters in the 1988 plebiscite that rejected another term for Pinochet. In 1999, when a British court ruled that Pinochet could be extradited from Britain to Spain to face trial for torture and murder, some Chilean bishops said the ruling damaged the Chilean democracy they had fought so hard to get.

China, People's Republic of

Archd., 20; dioc., 92; p.a., 29. No Roman Catholic statistics are available. In 1949 there were between 3,500,000-4,000,000 Catholics, about .7 per cent of the total population; current total is unknown. Tot. pop. 1,209,460,000. **Hong Kong:** *Dioc., 1; card., 1; bp., 2; parishes, 59; priests, 337 (71 dioc., 266 rel.); p.d., 3; sem., 19; bros., 73; srs., 559; catechists, 809; bap., 4,323; Caths., 240,000 (3.7%); tot. pop., 6,500,000.*

People's republic in eastern part of Asia; capital, Beijing. Christianity was introduced by Nestorians who had some influence on part of the area from 635 to 845 and again from the 11th century until 1368. John of Monte Corvino started a Franciscan mission in 1294; he was ordained an archbishop about 1307. Missionary activity involving more priests increased for a while thereafter, but the Franciscan mission ended in 1368. Jesuit Matteo Ricci initiated a remarkable period of activity in the 1580s. The Chinese-rites controversy, concerning the adaptation of rituals and other matters to Chinese traditions and practices, ran throughout the 17th century, ending in a negative decision by mission authorities in Rome. Francis de Capillas, the Dominican protomartyr of China, was killed in 1648. Persecution occurred several times in the 18th century and resulted in the departure of most missionaries from the country.

The Chinese door swung open again in the 1840s, and progress in evangelization increased with an extension of legal and social tolerance. At the turn of the 20th century, however, Christian missionary activity helped provoke the Boxer Rebellion.

Missionary work in the 1900s reached a new high. The hierarchy was instituted by Pope Pius XII, Apr. 11, 1946 (Apostolic Constitution *Quotidie Nos*). Then followed persecution initiated by communists, before and especially after they established the republic in 1949. The government began a savage persecution as soon as it came into power. Among its results were outlawed missionary work and pastoral activity; the expulsion of more than 5,000 foreign missionaries, 510 of whom were American; the arrest, imprisonment and harassment of Chinese Church officials; the forced closing of more than 4,000 schools, institutions and homes; denial of the free exercise of religion; the detention of hundreds of priests, religious and lay people in jail and their employment in slave labor; the proscription of Catholic movements for "counterrevolutionary activities" and "crimes against the new China."

The government formally established the Chinese Catholic Patriotic Association, independent of the Holy See, in July 1957. Relatively few priests and lay people joined the organization, which was condemned by Pius XII in 1958. The government formed the nucleus of what it hoped might become the hierarchy of a schismatic Chinese Church in 1958 by "electing" 26 bishops and having them consecrated validly but illicitly between Apr. 13, 1958, and Nov. 15, 1959, without the permission or approval of the Holy See. Additional bishops were subsequently ordained. Officially, members of the Patriotic Association spurn ties with the Vatican.

Growth of the underground Church has been reported for several years despite sometimes intense government persecution. Pope John Paul II's appointment of Hong Kong Archbishop John Baptist Wu Cheng-chung as a cardinal in 1988 was seen as significant, especially in light of the Hong Kong handover from British rule to China July 1, 1997. Some bishops who belong to the Patriotic Association are said to have secretly reconciled with the Vatican. Two Chinese bishops, recognized by the Patriotic Association but described as loyal to the pope, were denied visas to attend the 1998 Synod of Bishops for Asia. Chinese officials said visas were not granted because the Vatican and China do not have diplomatic relations; the Vatican's diplomatic relations with Taiwan remain the biggest stumbling block to Sino-Vatican ties.

Colombia*

Archd., 12; dioc., 43; prel., 2; v.a., 8; p.a., 5; mil. ord.; card., 2; abp., 16; bp., 73; parishes, 3,296; priests, 7,316 (5,053 dioc., 2,263 rel.); p.d., 119; sem., 4,165; bros., 786; srs., 17,983; catechists, 28,134; bap., 780,547; Caths., 32,503,000 (89.8%); tot. pop., 36,160,000.

Republic in northwest South America; capital, Bogotá. Evangelization began in 1508. The first two dioceses were established in 1534. Vigorous development of the Church was reported by the middle of the 17th century despite obstacles posed by the multiplicity of Indian languages, government interference through patronage rights, rivalry among religious orders and the small number of native priests among the predominantly Spanish clergy. Some persecution, including the confiscation of property, followed in the wake of the proclamation of independence from Spain in 1819. Guerrilla warfare aimed at Marxist-oriented radical social reform and redistribution of land, along with violence related to drug traffic, has plagued the country since the 1960s, posing problems for the Church, which backed reforms but rejected actions of radical groups. In the late 20th century, Church leaders often worked as mediators between the government and guerrillas, but Church leaders still suffered threats and attacks, including from paramilitaries.

Comoros

A.a.; parishes, 2; priests, 2 (rel.); bro., 1; srs., 8; catechists, 16; bap., 16; Caths., 3,000 (4.6%); tot. pop., 650,000. (AD)

Consists of main islands of Grande Comore, Anjouan and Moheli in Indian Ocean off southeast coast of Africa; capital, Moroni, Grande Comore Island. Former French territory; independent (July 6, 1975). The majority of the population is Muslim. An apostolic administration was established in 1975.

Congo, Democratic Republic of *

Archd., 6; dioc., 41; card., 1; abp., 9; bp., 50; parishes, 1,259; priests, 3,712 (2,347 dioc., 1,365 rel.); p.d., 1; sem., 2,952; bros., 1,469; srs., 6,425; catechists, 63,839; bap., 475,912; Caths., 24,391,000 (50.7%); tot. pop., 48,040,000.

Republic in south central Africa (formerly Zaire 1971-97); capital, Kinshasa. Christianity was introduced in 1484 and evangelization began about 1490. The first native bishop in black Africa was ordained in 1518. Subsequent missionary work was hindered by factors including 18th- and 19th-century

anticlericalism. Modern evangelization started in the second half of the 19th century. The hierarchy was established in 1959. In the civil disorders that followed independence in 1960, some missions and other Church installations were abandoned, thousands of people reverted to tribal religions and many priests and religious were killed.

Church-state tensions developed in the late 1980s and 1990s because of the Church's criticism of President Mobutu Sese Seko, who called a 1990 bishops' pastoral letter seditious. In 1992, after troops fired on thousands of protesters and killed 13, the government blamed priests who organized the march. In 1992, Archbishop Laurent Monswengo Pasinya was named president of a council charged with drafting a new constitution and overseeing a transition to democracy, but Mobutu supporters blocked effective change, and the archbishop resigned in 1994. As government and rebel forces battled in the Bukavu region of the country in 1996, Archbishop Christophe Munzihirwa Mwene Ngabo was killed in unclear circumstances. In 1997 the rebel forces of Laurent Kabila gained power, but renewed fighting by rebels opposing his government resulted in the deaths of thousands, including hundreds of church workers.

Congo, Republic of *

Archd., 1; dioc., 5; abp., 2; bp., 5; parishes, 126; priests, 274 (185 dioc., 89 rel.); sem., 246; bros., 54; srs., 267; catechists, 10,612; bap., 22,044; Caths., 1,564,000 (57%); tot. pop., 2,750,000.

Republic (independent since 1960) in west central Africa; former French possession; capital, Brazzaville. Small-scale missionary work with little effect preceded modern evangelization dating from the 1880s. The work of the Church has been affected by political instability, communist influence, tribalism and hostility to foreigners. The hierarchy was established in 1955. In 1992 Bishop Ernest Kombo of Owando was appointed chief organizer of the country's parliamentary elections. In 1994, the Church canceled independence day celebrations after more than 142 Catholics, mostly children, were crushed or suffocated in a rain-induced stampede at a Catholic church in Brazzaville. During renewed violence in the late 1990s, the bishops appealed for peace and stability.

Cook Islands

Dioc., 1; bp., 1; parishes, 15; priests, 8 (4 dioc., 4 rel.); bros., 5; srs., 10; bap., 74; Caths., 3,000 (15.7%); tot. pop., 18,000.

Self-governing territory of New Zealand, an archipelago of small islands in Oceania. Evangelization by Protestant missionaries started in 1821, resulting in a predominantly Protestant population. The first Catholic missionary work began in 1894. The hierarchy was established in 1966.

Costa Rica*

Archd., 1; dioc., 6; abp., 2; bp., 7; parishes, 241; priests, 746 (510 dioc., 236 rel.); sem., 233; bros., 46; srs., 923; catechists, 22,260; bap., 89,173; Caths., 2,891,000 (88%); tot. pop., 3,270,000.

Republic in Central America; capital, San José. Evangelization began about 1520 and proceeded by degrees to real development and organization of the

Church in the 17th and 18th centuries. The republic became independent in 1838. Twelve years later Church jurisdiction also became independent with the establishment of a diocese in the present capital.

Côte d'Ivoire (Ivory Coast)*

Archd., 4; dioc., 10; abp., 5; bp., 11; parishes, 243; priests, 685 (418 dioc., 267 rel.); p.d., 4; sem., 514; bros., 248; srs., 901; catechists, 12,665; bap., 52,977; Caths., 1,913,000 (13.3%); tot. pop., 14,300,000.

Republic in western Africa; capital, Abidjan. The Holy Ghost Fathers began systematic evangelization in 1895. The first native priests from the area were ordained in 1934. The hierarchy was set up in 1955; the first native cardinal (Bernard Yago) was named in 1983. In 1990 Pope John Paul II consecrated the continent's biggest, most costly and most controversial cathedral in Yamoussoukro. The pope only agreed to accept the cathedral after convincing the country's president to build an adjacent hospital and youth center.

Croatia*

Archd., 4; dioc., 9; mil. ord.; card., 1; abp., 8; bp., 15; parishes, 1,521; priests, 2,239 (1,436 dioc., 803 rel.); sem., 462; bros., 92; srs., 3,622; catechists, 1,190; bap., 52,205; Caths., 3,758,000 (83%); tot. pop., 4,500,000.

Independent (1991) republic in southeastern Europe; capital Zagreb; formerly a constituent republic of Yugoslavia. Christianity was introduced in the seventh century. On-again, off-again fighting from 1991 to 1995 pitted mostly Catholic Croats against mostly Orthodox Serbs. In 1995, Croatian bishops issued guidelines for rebuilding the nation that included suppressing feelings of vengeance toward Serbs. However, in 1996 the head of Croatia's Helsinki human rights committee criticized the bishops for taking a weak stance on Croat abuses after the 1995 Croatian recapture of the Serb-occupied Krajina region. Pope John Paul II's 1998 beatification of Croatian Cardinal Alojzije Stepinac generated controversy among some Serb and Jewish leaders, who considered the cardinal a Nazi sympathizer.

Cuba*

Archd., 3; dioc., 8; card., 1; abp., 2; bp., 11; parishes, 263; priests, 306 (164 dioc., 142 rel.); p.d., 36; sem., 77; bros., 32; srs., 501; catechists, 2,422; bap., 89,403; Caths. 4,825,000 (43.6%); tot. pop., 11,060,000.

Republic under Communist dictatorship, south of Florida; capital, Havana. Effective evangelization began about 1514, leading eventually to the predominance of Catholicism on the island. Native vocations to the priesthood and religious life were unusually numerous in the 18th century but declined in the 19th. The island became independent of Spain in 1902 following the Spanish-American War.

Fidel Castro took control of the government Jan. 1, 1959. In 1961, after Cuba was officially declared a socialist state, the University of Villanueva was closed, 350 Catholic schools were nationalized and 136 priests expelled. A greater number of foreign priests and religious had already left the country. Freedom of worship and religious instruction were limited to Church premises and no social action was permitted

by the Church, which survived under surveillance. A new constitution approved in 1976 guaranteed freedom of conscience but restricted its exercise. Small improvements in Church-state relations occurred in the late 1980s and early 1990s. In December 1997, just before Pope John Paul II's historic visit, the government allowed public celebration of Christmas, banned for 30 years. Although the pope's January 1998 visit was seen as a new dawn for the Church on the islands, Cuban Catholics said change has come slowly.

Cyprus*

Archd., 1 (Maronite); abp., 1; parishes, 13; priests, 17 (6 dioc., 11 rel.); bros., 7; srs., 43; bap., 79; Caths., 17,000 (2.2%); tot. pop., 770,000.

Republic in the eastern Mediterranean; capital, Nicosia. Christianity was preached on the island in apostolic times and has a continuous history from the fourth century. Latin and Eastern rites were established but the latter prevailed and became Orthodox after the schism of 1054. Christians have suffered under many governments, particularly during the period of Turkish dominion from late in the 16th to late in the 19th centuries, and from differences between the 80 percent Greek majority and the Turkish minority. About 80 percent of the population are Orthodox. Catholics are under the jurisdiction of the Maronite Archdiocese of Cipro, based in Nicosia.

Czech Republic*

Archd., 2; dioc., 6; ap. ex., 1; card., 1; abp., 2; bp., 12; parishes, 3,152; priests, 1,856 (1,301 dioc., 555 rel.); p.d., 137; sem., 410; bros., 110; srs., 2,484; catechists, 1,303; bap., 28,067; Caths., 4,107,000 (40%); tot. pop., 10,300,000.

Independent state (Jan. 1, 1993); formerly part of Czechoslovakia; capital, Prague. The martyrdom of Prince Wenceslaus in 929 triggered the spread of Christianity. Prague has had a continuous history as a diocese since 973. A parish system was organized about the 13th century in Bohemia and Moravia. Mendicant orders strengthened relations with the Latin rite in the 13th century. In the next century the teachings of John Hus in Bohemia brought trouble to the Church in the forms of schism and heresy and initiated a series of religious wars that continued for decades following his death at the stake in 1415. So many of the faithful joined the Bohemian Brethren that Catholics became a minority.

In the 1560s, a Counter-Reformation got under way and led to a gradual restoration through the thickets of Josephinism, the Enlightenment, liberalism and troubled politics. St. Jan Sarkander, a priest killed by Protestants in 1620, was accused by Protestants of helping an invading Polish army. (His 1995 canonization caused strains with the Protestant community.)

In 1920, two years after the establishment of the Republic of Czechoslovakia, the schismatic Czechoslovak Church was proclaimed at Prague, resulting in numerous defections from the Catholic Church in the Czech region. Following the accession of the Gottwald regime to power early in 1948, persecution began in the Czech part of Czechoslovakia. Hospitals, schools and property were nationalized and Catholic organizations were liquidated. A puppet organization was formed in 1949 to infiltrate the Church and implement an unsuccessful plan for establishing a schismatic church. In the same year Archbishop Josef Beran of Prague was placed under house arrest. A number of theatrical trials of bishops and priests were staged in 1950. Pressure was applied on Eastern Catholics in Slovakia to join the Orthodox Church. Diplomatic relations with the Holy See were terminated in 1950. In the following decade, thousands of priests were arrested and hundreds were deported, and attempts were made to force government-approved "peace priests" on the people. Pope Pius XII granted the Czech Church emergency powers to appoint clergy during the communist persecution.

From January to October 1968, Church-state relations improved to some extent under the Dubcek regime: A number of bishops were reinstated; some 3,000 priests were engaged in the pastoral ministry, although 1,500 were still barred from priestly work; the "peace priests" organization was disbanded. The Eastern Catholic Church, with 147 parishes, was re-established. In 1969, rehabilitation trials for priests and religious ended, but there was no wholesale restoration of priests and religious to their proper ways of life and work. Government restrictions continued to hamper the work of priests and nuns. Signatories of the human rights declaration Charter 77 were particular objects of government repression and retribution. In December 1983, the Czechoslovakian foreign minister met with the pope at Vatican City; it was the first meeting of a high Czech official with a pope since the country had been under communist rule. In 1984, two Vatican officials visited Czechoslovakia. In 1988, three new bishops were ordained in Czechoslovakia, the first since 1973. More episcopal appointments were made in 1989. The communist government fell in late 1989. In 1990, bishops were appointed to fill vacant sees; diplomatic relations between the Holy See and Czechoslovakia were re-established, and Pope John Paul II visited the country. In 1997 the issue of married Czech priests secretly ordained under communist rule was resolved when they began work in the country's new Eastern Catholic jurisdiction. Under a 1949 communist decree declaring priests Culture Ministry employees, Czech priest were still paid by the state in 1999. A Church spokesman said confiscation of Church property under communist rule left priests still financially dependent on the state.

Denmark*
Dioc., 1; abp., 1; bp., 2; parishes, 50; priests, 99 (46 dioc., 53 rel.); p.d., 2; sem., 5; bros., 4; srs., 240; bap., 660; Caths., 35,000 (.6%); tot. pop., 5,280,000.

Includes the Faroe Islands and Greenland. Constitutional monarchy in northwestern Europe; capital, Copenhagen. Christianity was introduced in the ninth century and the first diocese for the area was established in 831. Intensive evangelization and full-scale organization of the Church occurred from the second half of the 10th century and ushered in a period of great development and influence in the 12th and 13th centuries. Decline followed, resulting in almost total loss to the Church during the Reformation, when Lutheranism became the national religion. A few Catholic families practiced the faith secretly until religious freedom was legally assured in the mid-1800s. Since then, immigration has increased the number of Catholics. About 95 percent of the population are Evangelical Lutherans.

Catholicism was introduced in Greenland, a Danish island province northeast of North America, about 1000. The first diocese was established in 1124 and a line of bishops dated from then until 1537. The first known Churches in the Western Hemisphere, dating from about the 11th century, were on Greenland; the remains of 19 have been unearthed. The departure of Scandinavians and spread of the Reformation reduced the Church to nothing. The Moravian Brethren evangelized the Inuit from the 1720s to 1901. By 1930 the Danish Church — Evangelical Lutheran — was in full possession. Since 1930, priests have been in Greenland, which is part of the Copenhagen Diocese.

Djibouti
Dioc., 1; bp., 1; parishes, 5; priests, 7 (1 dioc., 6 rel.); sem., 1; bros., 7; srs., 19; catechists, 16; bap., 11; Caths., 7,000 (1.1%); tot. pop., 630,000. (AD)

Formerly French Territory of Afars and Issas. Independent (1977) republic in East Africa; capital, Djibouti. Christianity in the area, formerly part of Ethiopia, antedated but was overcome by the Arab invasion of 1200. Modern evangelization, begun in the latter part of the 19th century, had meager results. The hierarchy was established in 1955.

Dominica*
Dioc., 1; bp., 2; parishes, 16; priests, 39 (6 dioc., 33 rel.); bros., 6; srs., 27; catechists, 488; bap., 968; Caths., 60,000 (79%); tot. pop., 75,000.

Independent (Nov. 3, 1978) state in Caribbean; capital, Roseau. Evangelization began in 1642.

Dominican Republic*
Archd., 2; dioc., 9; mil. ord.; card., 1; abp., 2; bp., 15; parishes, 410; priests, 694 (300 dioc., 394 rel.); p.d., 184; sem., 575; bros., 79; srs., 1,492; catechists, 17,676; bap., 95,566; Caths., 7,240,000 (89.3%); tot. pop., 8,100,000.

Caribbean republic on the eastern two-thirds of the island of Hispaniola, bordering on Haiti; capital, Santo Domingo. Evangelization began shortly after discovery by Columbus in 1492 and Church organization, the first in America, was established by 1510. Catholicism is the state religion. Pope John Paul II visited the country in 1992 to mark the quincentennial celebrations of Columbus' discovery. The pope also opened the Fourth General conference of the Latin American Episcopate there.

Ecuador*
Archd., 4; dioc., 11; v.a., 7; p.a.; mil. ord.; card., 1; abp., 5; bp., 30; parishes, 1,109; priests, 1,795 (975 dioc., 820 rel.); p.d., 49; sem., 787; bros., 317; srs., 4,838; catechists, 20,489; bap., 248,333; Caths., 11,203,000 (93.8%); tot. pop., 11,940,000.

Republic on the west coast of South America, includes Galápogos Islands; capital, Quito. Evangelization began in the 1530s. The first diocese was established in 1545. Multiphased missionary work, spreading from the coastal and mountain regions into the Amazon, made the Church highly influential during the colonial period. The Church was practically enslaved by the constitution enacted in 1824, two years after Ecuador, as part of Colombia, gained independence from Spain. Some change for the better took place later in the century, but from 1891 until the 1930s the Church labored under serious liabilities imposed by liberal governments. Foreign missionaries were barred from the country for some time; the property of religious orders was confiscated; education was taken over by the state; traditional state support was refused; legal standing was denied; attempts to control Church offices were made through insistence on rights of patronage. A period of harmony and independence for the Church began after agreement was reached on Church-state relations in 1937. The Church was actively involved in peace talks that in 1998 ended a border dispute of some 170 years with Peru. As the 20th century came to a close, Ecuador's bishops were working to fight social turmoil and the results of severe economic austerity measures.

Egypt*

Patriarchates, 2 (Alexandria for the Copts and for the Melkites); dioc., 10; v.a.; ex.; patriarch, 1; abp., 2; bp., 13; parishes, 215; priests, 410 (204 dioc., 206 rel.); p.d., 1; sem., 137; bros., 52; srs., 1,310; catechists, 1,305; bap., 2,414; Caths., 218,000 (.35%); tot. pop., 62,010,000.

Arab Republic in northeastern Africa; capital, Cairo. Alexandria was the influential hub of a Christian community established by the end of the second century; it became a patriarchate and the center of the Coptic Church and had great influence on the spread of Christianity in various parts of Africa. Monasticism developed from desert communities of hermits in the third and fourth centuries. Arianism was first preached in Egypt in the 320s. In the fifth century, the Coptic Church went Monophysite through failure to accept doctrine formulated by the Council of Chalcedon in 451 with respect to the two natures of Christ. The country was thoroughly Arabized after 640 and was under the rule of Ottoman Turks from 1517 to 1798. English influence was strong during the 19th century. A monarchy established in 1922 lasted about 30 years, ending with the proclamation of a republic in 1953-54. By that time Egypt had become the leader of pan-Arabism against Israel. It waged two unsuccessful wars against Israel in 1948-49 and 1967. In 1979, following negotiations initiated by President Anwar Sadat, Egypt and Israel signed a peace agreement. Islam, the religion of some 90 percent of the population, is the state religion. The tiny Catholic minority is treated with respect and has a dialogue with Muslims.

El Salvador*

Archd.; dioc., 7; mil. ord.; abp., 2; bp., 10; parishes, 315; priests, 592 (379 dioc., 213 rel.); p.d., 3; sem., 335; bros., 199; srs., 1,295; catechists, 4,002; bap., 83,135; Cath., 5,530,000 (93.5%); tot. pop., 5,910,000.

Republic in Central America; capital, San Salvador. Evangelization affecting the whole territory followed Spanish occupation in the 1520s. The country was administered by the captaincy general of Guatemala until 1821, when independence from Spain was declared and it was annexed to Mexico. El Salvador joined the Central American Federation in 1825, declared independence in 1841 and became a republic formally in 1856.

During the country's 1980-92 civil war, Church leaders worked to achieve social justice. The San Salvador Archdiocese's human rights office, *Tutela Legal*, documented abuses and political killings and offered legal support to victims, despite Church persecution. Archbishop Oscar Romero of San Salvador, peace advocate and outspoken champion of human rights, was murdered on Mar. 24, 1980, while celebrating Mass. Four U.S. Church women were murdered the same year. Six Jesuits and two lay women were assassinated Nov. 16, 1989, at Central American University in El Salvador. Church leaders, particularly Archbishop Romero's successor, Archbishop Arturo Rivera Damas, were active in the peace process. In the 1990s, Church-government relations cooled. Church leaders often urged the U.S. government not to deport the hundreds of thousands of Salvadoran refugees who lived, often illegally, in the United States, sending money to their families in El Salvador. The situation worsened after the destruction of Hurricane Mitch in 1999.

England

Archd., 4; dioc., 15; ap. ex., 1; mil. ord. (Great Britain), 1; abp., 4; bp., 38; parishes, 2,495; priests, 5,365 (3,672 dioc., 1,693 rel.); p.d., 392; sem., 260; bros., 2,415; srs., 8,014; bap., 69,712; Caths., 4,776,639 (9%); tot. pop., 52,503,244. (Figures from 1999 Annuario Pontificio) Note: England and Wales share a joint Episcopal Conference; see also Wales.

Center of the United Kingdom of Great Britain (England, Scotland, Wales) and Northern Ireland, off the northwestern coast of Europe; capital, London. The arrival of St. Augustine of Canterbury and a band of monks in 597 marked the beginning of evangelization. Real organization of the Church took place some years after the Synod of Whitby, held in 663. Heavy losses were sustained in the wake of the Danish invasion in the 780s, but recovery starting from the time of Alfred the Great and dating especially from the middle of the 10th century led to Christianization of the whole country and close Church-state relations. The Norman Conquest of 1066 opened the Church in England to European influence. The Church began to decline in numbers in the 13th century. In the 14th century, John Wycliff presaged the Protestant Reformation.

Henry VIII, failing in 1529 to gain annulment of his marriage to Catherine of Aragon, refused to acknowledge papal authority over the Church in England, had himself proclaimed its head, suppressed all houses of religious, and persecuted people — Sts. Thomas More and John Fisher, among others — for not subscribing to the Oath of Supremacy and Act of Succession. He held the line on other-than-papal doctrine, however, until his death in 1547. Doctrinal aberrations were introduced during the reign of Edward VI (1547-53), through the Order of Communion, two books of Common Prayer, and the Articles of the Established Church. Mary Tudor's attempted Catholic restoration (1553-58) was a disaster, resulting in the deaths of more than 300 Protestants. Elizabeth (1558-1603) firmed up the established Church with the aid of Matthew Parker, archbishop of Canterbury, with formation of a hierarchy, legal enactments and multi-phased persecution. More than 100 priests and 62 lay persons were among the casualties of persecution during the underground Catholic revival that followed the return to England of missionary priests from France and The Lowlands.

Several periods of comparative tolerance ensued after Elizabeth's death. The first of several apostolic vicariates was established in 1685; this form of Church government was maintained until the restoration of the hierarchy and diocesan organization in 1850. The revolution of 1688 and subsequent developments to about 1781 subjected Catholics to a wide variety of penal laws and disabilities in religious, civic and social life. The situation began to improve in 1791, and from 1801 Parliament frequently considered proposals for the repeal of penal laws against Catholics. The Act of Emancipation restored citizenship rights to Catholics in 1829. Restrictions remained in force for some time afterward, however, on public religious worship and activity. The hierarchy was restored in 1850. Since then the Catholic Church, existing side by side with the established Churches of England and Scotland, has followed a general pattern of growth and development. After the Church of England began ordaining women priests in 1994, more than 200 Anglican priests and four Anglican bishops were received into the Catholic Church, although many said ordination of women was not their primary reason for leaving. (See also Ireland, Northern)

Equatorial Guinea*

Archd., 1; dioc., 2; abp., 1; bp., 2; parishes, 53; priests, 95 (43 dioc., 52 rel.); p.d. 1; sem., 63; bros., 36; srs., 222; catechists, 1,956; bap., 10,503; Caths., 374,000 (89%); tot. pop., 420,000.

Republic on the west coast of Africa, consisting of Rio Muni on the mainland and the islands of Bioko (formerly Fernando Po) and Annobon in the Gulf of Guinea: capital, Malabo (Santa Isabel). Evangelization began in 1841. The country became independent of Spain in 1968. The Church was severely repressed during the 11-year rule of President Macias Nguema. Developments since his overthrow in 1979 indicated some measure of improvement. An ecclesiastical province was established in October 1982.

In the 1990s, bishops worked to educate Catholics about the need for social justice and respect for human rights. In mid-1998, the government expelled three foreign missionaries involved in development programs partially funded by the United States.

Eritrea*

Dioc., 3; bp., 2; parishes, 93; priests, 289 (72 dioc., 217 rel.); p.d., 9; sem., 84; bros., 81; srs., 341; catechists, 154; bap., 4,187; Caths., 131,000 (3.2%); tot. pop., 4,102,000.

Independent state (May 24, 1993) in northeast Africa; formerly a province of Ethiopia. Christianity was introduced in the fourth century. Population is evenly divided between Christians and Muslims. Catholics form a small minority; most of the population is Orthodox or Muslim. In 1995, two new dioceses were established, but because of three decades of civil war, the dioceses had no facilities and little staffing. In 1998 the government announced plans to take over private schools and health clinics, most of which were run by the Church. Eritrean bishops form an episcopal conference with Ethiopia.

Estonia*

A.a.; abp., 1 (nuncio is apostolic administrator); parishes, 8; priests, 13 (8 dioc., 5 rel); sem., 4; bros., 1; srs., 15; bap., 61; Caths., 4,000 (.27%); tot. pop., 1,460,000.

Independent (1991) Baltic republic; capital, Tallinn. (Forcibly absorbed by the USSR in 1940; it regained independence in 1991.) Catholicism was introduced in the 11th and 12th centuries. Jurisdiction over the area was made directly subject to the Holy See in 1215. Lutheran penetration was general in the Reformation period, and Russian Orthodox influence was strong from early in the 18th century until 1917, when independence was attained. The first of several apostolic administrators were appointed in 1924. The small Catholic community was hard-hit during the 1940-91 Soviet occupation (not recognized by the Holy See or the United States). Since its independence, the small Catholic community in Estonia has worked to re-establish Catholic theology and education. In 1999 the Holy See and government of Estonia reached agreement on a number of issues, including guarantees that the Church could name its own bishops and that priests from abroad would be able to continue to work in the country.

Ethiopia*

Archd., 1; dioc., 1; v.a., 5; p.a., 1; card., 1; abp., 1; bp., 9; parishes, 192; priests, 413 (142 dioc., 271 rel.); p.d., 1; sem., 325; bros., 68; srs., 719; catechists, 1,626; bap., 17,516; Caths., 390,000 (.7%); tot. pop., 55,475,000.

People's republic in northeast Africa; capital, Addis Ababa. The country was evangelized by missionaries from Egypt in the fourth century and had a bishop by about 340. Following the lead of its parent body, the Egyptian (Coptic) Church, the Church in the area succumbed to the Monophysite heresy in the sixth century. An apostolic delegation was set up in Addis Ababa in 1937 and several jurisdictions were organized, some under Vatican congregations. The northern Church jurisdictions follow the Alexandrian rite, while the southern part of the country is Latin rite. The first Ethiopian cardinal, Archbishop Paulos Tzadua of Addis Ababa, was named in 1985. The small Church has good relations with Orthodox and Protestant Churches, all of which face the task of helping people move from a rural society to a more modern society without losing Christian identity. Although the constitution calls for religious freedom, treatment of the churches can vary in different localities. The bishops share an episcopal conference with the Eritrean bishops.

Falkland Islands

P.a., 1; parish, 1; priests, 2 (rel.); srs., 2; bap., 7; Caths., 1,000 (approx.) (25%); tot. pop., 4,000 (approx).

British colony off the southern tip of South America; capital, Port Stanley. The islands are called Islas Malvinas by Argentina, which also claims sovereignty.

Fiji*

Archd., 1; abp., 1; parishes, 34; priests, 113 (23 dioc., 90 rel.); sem., 48; bros., 43; srs., 176; bap., 1,912; Caths., 82,000 (9.9%); tot. pop., 810,000.

Independent island group (100 inhabited) in the southwest Pacific; capital, Suva. Marist missionaries began work in 1844 after Methodism had been firmly established. An apostolic prefecture was organized in 1863. The hierarchy was established in 1966.

Finland*

Dioc., 1; bp., 1; parishes, 7; priests, 20 (5 dioc., 15 rel.); p.d., 2; sem., 2; srs., 36; bap., 187; Caths., 7,000 (.1%); tot. pop., 5,140,000.

Republic in northern Europe; capital, Helsinki. Swedes evangelized the country in the 12th century. The Reformation swept the country, resulting in the prohibition of Catholicism in 1595, general reorganization of ecclesiastical life and affairs, and dominance of the Evangelical Lutheran Church. Catholics were given religious liberty in 1781 but missionaries and conversions were forbidden by law. The first Finnish priest since the Reformation was ordained in 1903 in Paris. An apostolic vicariate for Finland was erected in 1920 (made a diocese in 1955). A law on religious liberty, enacted in 1923, banned the foundation of monasteries.

France*

Archd., 19; dioc., 75; prel., 1; ap. ex., 2; mil. ord., 1; card., 5; abp., 31; bp., 141; parishes, 27,862; priests, 27,200 (20,913 dioc., 6,287 rel.); p.d., 1,326; sem., 1,603; bros., 3,985; srs., 52,872; catechists, 71,895; bap., 415,873; Caths., 47,420,000 (81%); tot. pop., 58,610,000.

Republic in western Europe; capital, Paris. Christianity was known around Lyons by the middle of the second century. By 250 there were 30 dioceses. The hierarchy reached a fair degree of organization by the end of the fourth century. Vandals and Franks subsequently invaded the territory and caused barbarian turmoil and doctrinal problems because of their Arianism. The Frankish nation was converted following the baptism of Clovis about 496. Christianization was complete by some time in the seventh century. From then on the Church, its leaders and people, figured in virtually every important development — religious, cultural, political and social — through the periods of the Carolingians, feudalism, the Middle Ages and monarchies to the end of the 18th century. The University of Paris became one of the intellectual centers of the 13th century. Churchmen and secular rulers were involved with developments surrounding the Avignon residence of the popes and curia from 1309 until near the end of the 14th century and with the disastrous Western Schism that followed.

Strong currents of Gallicanism and conciliarism ran through ecclesiastical and secular circles in France; the former was an ideology and movement to restrict papal control of the Church in the country, the latter sought to make the pope subservient to a general council. Calvinism entered the country about the middle of the 16th century and won a strong body of converts. Jansenism appeared in the next century, to be followed by the highly influential Enlightenment. The Revolution, which started in 1789 and was succeeded by the Napoleonic period, completely changed the status of the Church, taking a toll of numbers by persecution and defection and disenfranchising the Church in practically every way. Throughout the 19th century the Church was caught up in the whirl of imperial and republican developments and was made the victim of official hostility, popular indifference and liberal opposition.

In the 20th century, the Church has struggled with problems involving the heritage of the Revolution and its aftermath, the alienation of intellectuals, liberalism, the estrangement of the working classes because of the Church's former identification with the ruling class, and the massive needs of contemporary society. In the 1990s, French bishops fought a racist backlash that resulted from large-scale immigration from Africa.

French Guiana

Dioc., 1; bp., 1; parishes, 27; priests, 39 (6 dioc., 33 rel.); p.d., 6; bros., 2; srs., 85; bap., 2,053; catechists, 365; 128,000 (80%); tot. pop., 160,000. (AD)

French overseas department on the northeast coast of South America; capital, Cayenne. Catholicism was introduced in the 17th century. The Cayenne Diocese was established in 1956. In 1998 the bishops joined their counterparts in Martinique, Guadeloupe and Réunion to call slavery "an immense collective sin."

French Polynesia

Archd., 1; dioc., 1; abp., 2; bp., 2; parishes, 85; priests, 36 (14 dioc., 22 rel.); p.d., 20; sem., 8; bros., 39; srs., 70; bap., 1,370; Caths., 89,000 (40%); tot. pop., 228,000. (AD)

French overseas territory in the South Pacific, including Tahiti and the Marquesas Islands; capital, Papeete. The first phase of evangelization in the Marquesas Islands, begun in 1838, resulted in 216 baptisms in 10 years. A vicariate was organized in 1848 but real progress was not made until after the baptism of native rulers in 1853. Persecution caused missionaries to leave the islands several times. Isolated attempts to evangelize Tahiti were made in the 17th and 18th centuries. Two Picpus Fathers began missionary work in 1831. A vicariate was organized in 1848. By 1908, despite the hindrances of Protestant opposition, disease and other factors, the Church had firm roots. By the 1960s, more than 95 percent of the population was Catholic. The Church spoke out against French nuclear testing in the territory in the mid-1990s, but said the protests against France should be broadened to support all forms of peace.

Gabon*

Archd., 1; dioc., 3; abp., 1; bp., 4; parishes, 65; priests, 106 (36 dioc., 70 rel.); p.d., 1; sem., 55; bros., 23; srs., 167; catechists, 1,405; bap., 7,075; Caths., 650,000 (57%); tot. pop., 1,140,000.

Republic on the west coast of central Africa; capital Libreville. Sporadic missionary effort took place before 1881 when effective evangelization began. The hierarchy was established in 1955. In 1993, Gabon's president defeated a Catholic priest in presidential elections. In the late 1990s, the government and the Holy See signed an agreement setting out the rights of the Church in society.

Gambia*

Dioc., 1; bp., 1; parishes, 52; priests, 23 (11 dioc., 12 rel.); sem., 9; bros., 13; srs., 65; bap., 2,148; Caths., 33,000 (3%); tot. pop., 1,170,000.

Republic (1970) on the northwestern coast of Africa, capital, Banjui. Christianity was introduced by

Portuguese explorers in the 15th century; effective evangelization began in 1822. The country was under the jurisdiction of an apostolic vicariate until 1931. The hierarchy was established in 1957. Pope John Paul II has encouraged Catholics to dialogue with the majority Muslims.

Georgia*

A.a., 1; parishes, 27; priests, 10 (2 dioc., 8 rel); sem., 5; srs., 22; bap, 190; Caths., 100,000 (1.8%); tot. pop., 5,430,000

Independent (1991) state in the Caucasus; former Soviet republic; capital, Tbilisi. Christianity came to the area under Roman influence and, according to tradition, was spread through the efforts of St. Nino (or Christiana), a maiden who was brought as a captive to the country and is venerated as its apostle. The apostolic administration of the Caucasus (with seat in Georgia) was established in December 1993 for Latin-rite Catholics of Armenia, Azerbaijan and Georgia. Chaldean- and Armenian-rite Catholics also are present. Differences between Catholicism and Orthodoxy often are blurred on the parish level. The Catholic Church and the Armenian Orthodox Church have been unable to secure the return of Churches closed during the Soviet period, many of which were later given to the Georgian Orthodox Church.

Germany*

Archd., 7; dioc., 20; ap. ex., 1; mil. ord., 1; card., 5; abp., 8; bp., 93; parishes, 12,621; priests, 20,251 (15,518 dioc., 4,733 rel.); p.d., 2,016; sem., 1,601; bros., 1,901; srs., 42,033; catechists, 24,427; bap., 262,633; Caths., 28,220,000 (34.8%); tot. pop., 82,070,000.

Country in northern Europe; capital, Berlin. From 1949-90 it was partitioned into the Communist German Democratic Republic in the East (capital, East Berlin) and the German Federal Republic in the West (capital, Bonn). Christianity was introduced in the third century, if not earlier. Trier, which became a center for missionary activity, had a bishop by 400. Visigoth invaders introduced Arianism in the fifth century but were converted in the seventh century by the East Franks, Celtic and other missionaries. St. Boniface, the apostle of Germany, established real ecclesiastical organization in the eighth century.

Beginning in the Carolingian period, bishops began to act in dual roles as pastors and rulers, a state of affairs that inevitably led to confusion and conflict in Church-state relations and perplexing problems of investiture. The Church developed strength and vitality through the Middle Ages but succumbed to abuses that antedated and prepared the ground for the Reformation. Martin Luther's actions from 1517 made Germany a confessional battleground. Religious strife continued until conclusion of the Peace of Westphalia at the end of the Thirty Years' War in 1648. Nearly a century earlier the Peace of Augsburg (1555) had been designed, without success, to assure a degree of tranquillity by recognizing the legitimacy of different religious confessions in different states, depending on the decisions of princes. The implicit principle that princes should control the churches emerged in practice into the absolutism and Josephinism of subsequent years. St. Peter Canisius and his fellow Jesuits spearheaded a Counter Refor-

mation in the second half of the 16th century. Before the end of the century, however, 70 percent of the population of north and central Germany were Lutheran. Calvinism also had established a strong presence.

The Church suffered some impoverishment as a result of shifting boundaries and the secularization of property shortly after 1800. It came under direct attack in the Kulturkampf of the 1870s but helped to generate the opposition that resulted in a dampening of the campaign of Bismarck against it. Despite action by Catholics on the social front and other developments, discrimination against the Church spilled over into the 20th century and lasted beyond World War I. Catholics in politics struggled with others to pull the country through numerous postwar crises. The dissolution of the Center Party, agreed to by the bishops in 1933 without awareness of the ultimate consequences, contributed negatively to the rise of Hitler to supreme power. Church officials protested the Nazi anti-Church and anti-Semitic actions, but to no avail.

After World War II East Germany, compelled to communism under Soviet domination, initiated a program of control and repression of the Church. The regime eliminated religious schools, curtailed freedom for religious instruction and formation, and restricted the religious press. Beginning in the mid-1950s, the communists substituted youth initiation and Communist ceremonies for many sacraments. Bishops were generally forbidden to travel outside the Republic. The number of priests decreased, partly because of reduced seminary enrollments ordered by the East German government.

The official reunification of Germany took place Oct. 3, 1990. The separate episcopal conferences for East and West Germany were merged to form one conference in November 1990. During the 1990s, the united German bishops fought against introduction of the former East Germany's more liberal abortion law. After a series of political compromises and court challenges, a high-court decision allowed a woman to obtain abortions after visiting a state-approved counseling center and obtaining proof she had been counseled. This left German Church leaders searching for a compromise position, since they ran more than 250 such counseling centers but did not wish to advocate abortion. As the 20th century neared an end, German Church leaders also spoke on behalf of immigrants, refugees and asylum seekers and against a surge in racist and anti-Semitic attacks.

Ghana*

Archd., 3; dioc., 13; abp., 5; bp., 15; parishes, 289; priests, 853 (684 dioc., 169 rel.); p.d., 2; sem., 574; bros., 172; srs., 767; catechists, 5,982; bap., 50,591; Caths., 2,341,000 (13%); tot. pop., 18,340,000.

Republic on the western coast of Africa; capital, Accra. Priests visited the country in 1482, 11 years after discovery by the Portuguese, but missionary effort, hindered by the slave trade and other factors, was slight until 1880 when systematic evangelization began. An apostolic prefecture was set up in 1879. The hierarchy was established in 1950.

In 1985, the government shut down the Church's newspaper, *The Catholic Standard*, for criticizing the government; in 1989 the government ordered religious bodies to register. However, in 1992 the paper resumed publication, and five new diocese were established in 1995. In 1997 the bishops issued a pastoral letter urging an end to political corruption and ethnic tension.

Gibraltar

Dioc., 1; bp., 1; parishes, 5; priests, 13 (dioc.); sem., 2; srs., 5; bap., 339; Caths., 23,000 (85%); tot. pop., 27,000.

British dependency on the tip of the Spanish Peninsula on the Mediterranean. Evangelization took place after the Moors were driven out near the end of the 15th century. The Church was hindered by the British, who acquired the colony in 1713. Most of the Catholics were, and are, Spanish and Italian immigrants and their descendants. An apostolic vicariate was organized in 1817. The diocese was erected in 1910.

Great Britain (see separate entries for England, Scotland, Wales, Northern Ireland.)

Greece*

Archd., 4; dioc., 4; v.a., 1; ap. ex., 2; abp., 6; bp., 3; parishes, 64; priests, 95 (50 dioc., 45 rel.); p.d., 2; sem., 10; bros., 36; srs., 127; bap., 663; Caths., 63,000 (.6%); tot. pop., 10,520,000.

Republic in southeastern Europe on the Balkan Peninsula; capital, Athens. St. Paul preached the Gospel at Athens and Corinth on his second missionary journey and visited the country again on his third tour. Other Apostles may have passed through. Two bishops from Greece attended the First Council of Nicaea. After the division of the Roman Empire, the Church remained Eastern in rite and later broke ties with Rome as a result of the schism of 1054. A Latin-rite jurisdiction was set up during the period of the Latin Empire of Constantinople, 1204-1261, but crumbled afterward. Unity efforts of the Council of Florence had poor results and failed to save the Byzantine Empire from conquest by the Ottoman Empire in 1453. The country now has Latin, Byzantine and Armenian rites. The Greek Orthodox Church is predominant. The Catholic Church continues to work to obtain full legal rights.

Greenland (Numbers for Greenland are included in Denmark)

Grenada*

Dioc., 1; bp., 1; parishes, 20; priests, 20 (4 dioc., 16 rel.); p.d., 4; sem., 4; bros., 3; srs., 31; catechists, 125; bap., 806; Caths., 54,000 (59%); tot. pop., 91,000.

Independent island state in the West Indies; capital, St. George's.

Guam

Archd., 1; abp., 1; parishes, 23; priests, 40 (25 dioc., 15 rel.); p.d., 9; sem., 7; bro., 2; srs., 120; bap., 2,682; Caths., 120,000 (80%); tot. pop., 142,000.

Outlying area of U.S. in the southwest Pacific; capital, Agana. The first Mass was offered in the Mariana Islands in 1521. The islands were evangelized by the Jesuits, from 1668, and other missionaries. The first native Micronesian bishop was ordained in 1970. The

Agana Diocese, which had been a suffragan of San Francisco, was made a metropolitan see in 1984.

Guatemala*

Archd., 2; dioc., 10; prel., 1; v.a., 2; abp., 3; bp., 18; parishes, 412; priests, 916 (340 dioc., 576 rel.); p.d., 9; sem., 476; bros., 448; srs., 1,627; catechists, 30,054; bap., 348,384; Caths. 8,960,000 (85%); tot. pop. 10,520,000.

Republic in Central America; capital, Guatemala City. Evangelization dates from the beginning of Spanish occupation in 1524. The first diocese, for all Central American territories administered by the captaincy general of Guatemala, was established in 1534. The country became independent in 1839, following annexation to Mexico in 1821, secession in 1823 and membership in the Central American Federation from 1825. In 1870, a government installed by a liberal revolution repudiated the concordat of 1853 and took active measures against the Church. Separation of Church and state was decreed; religious orders were suppressed and their property seized; priests and religious were exiled; schools were secularized. Full freedom was subsequently granted.

During the nation's 36-year civil war, which ended in 1996, Church officials spoke out against atrocities and illegal drafting of youths and often were persecuted. The Guatemala City archbishop's human rights office, established after decades of war, was one of the few agencies able to document abuses. Bishops participated in the country's peace process, at times withdrawing in an effort to force government and guerrilla leaders back to the table.

After the war, the archbishop's human rights office began an extensive project to help document abuses during the war. Two days after the report was released in April 1998, Auxiliary Bishop Juan Gerardi Conedera of Guatemala City, who headed the project, was murdered. The bishop's murder was widely believed to have been in retribution for the report, but the case remained unsolved in 1999.

Guadeloupe

Dioc., 1; bp., 2; parishes, 45; priests, 58 (42 dioc., 16 rel.); p.d., 4; sem., 6; bros., 1; srs., 173; catechists, 2,930; bap., 5,133; Caths., 400,000 (95%); tot. pop., 422,000 (AD).

French overseas department in the Leeward Islands of the West Indies; capital, Basse-Terre. Catholicism was introduced in the islands in the 16th century. In 1998 the bishops of Guadaloupe joined their counterparts in Martinique, French Guiana and Réunion to call slavery "an immense collective sin."

Guinea*

Archd., 1; dioc., 2; abp., 1; bp., 3; parishes, 51; priests, 82 (63 dioc., 19 rel.); sem., 34; bros., 16; srs., 91; catechists, 264; bap., 2,831; Caths., 141,000 (2%); tot. pop., 7,610,000.

Republic on the west coast of Africa; capital, Conakry. Occasional missionary work followed exploration by the Portuguese about the middle of the 15th century; organized effort dates from 1877. The hierarchy was established in 1955. Following independence from France in 1958, Catholic schools were nationalized, youth organizations banned and missionaries restricted. Foreign missionaries were expelled in 1967. Archbishop Raymond-Marie Tchidimbo of Conakry, sentenced to life imprisonment in 1971 on a charge of conspiring to overthrow the government, was released in August 1979; he resigned his see. Private schools, suppressed by the government for more than 20 years, were again authorized in 1984.

Guinea-Bissau*

Dioc., 1; bp., 1; parishes, 29; priests, 64 (11 dioc., 54 rel.); sem., 17; bros., 15; srs., 132; bap., 2,100; Caths., 132,000 (12%); tot. pop., 1,110,000.

Formerly Portuguese Guinea. Independent state on the west coast of Africa; capital, Bissau. Catholicism was introduced in the second half of the 15th century but limited missionary work, hampered by the slave trade, had meager results. Missionary work in the 20th century began in 1933. An apostolic prefecture was made a diocese in 1977. In 1998, Bishop Settimio Ferrazzetta of Bissau worked to mediate a crisis between the government and military leaders.

Guyana

Dioc., 1; bp., 1; parishes, 24; priests, 51 (4 dioc., 47 rel.); sem., 3; bros., 4; srs., 48; catechists, 571; bap., 1,698; Caths., 87,000 (10.6%); tot. pop., 850,000.

Republic on the north coast of South America; capital, Georgetown. In 1899 the Catholic Church and other churches were given equal status with the Church of England and the Church of Scotland, which had sole rights up to that time. Most of the Catholics are Portuguese. The Georgetown Diocese was established in 1956, 10 years before Guyana became independent of England. The first native bishop was appointed in 1976. Schools were nationalized in 1976. In the late 1970s and in the 1980s, *The Catholic Standard* newspaper was cited by the Inter-American Press Association as the "sole independent voice" in Guyana.

Haiti*

Archd., 2; dioc., 7; abp., 3; bp., 10; parishes, 244; priests, 593 (336 dioc., 257 rel.); p.d., 3; sem., 336; bros., 323; srs., 1,034; catechists, 2,278; bap., 121,473; Caths., 6,509,000 (87%); tot. pop., 7,490,000.

Caribbean republic on the western third of Hispaniola adjacent to the Dominican Republic; capital, Port-au-Prince. Evangelization followed discovery by Columbus in 1492. Capuchins and Jesuits did most of the missionary work in the 18th century. From 1804, when independence was declared, until 1860, the country was in schism. Relations were regularized by a concordat concluded in 1860, when an archdiocese and four dioceses were established.

In the second half of the 20th century, the Church worked to develop the small nation, considered among the poorest in the Western Hemisphere. In the 1980s and 1990s, priests and religious often were targets of political violence, which resulted in a series of coups. The Church was sometimes seen as the lone voice for the people and, at times, was seen as backing the government. A Salesian priest, Father Jean-Bertrand Aristide, known for his fiery, anti-government sermons, won the December 1990 president election, considered the first genuinely democratic vote in Haitian history. A 1991 military coup forced him into exile for three years and resulted in an international trade embargo against Haiti. Aristide was laicized by the Vatican and married in January 1996. In the late 1990s, the Church continued its service in the social field through programs in basic literacy and operation of schools and health facilities.

Honduras*

Archd., 1; dioc., 6; abp., 3; bp., 6; parishes, 153; priests, 327 (154 dioc., 173 rel.); p.d., 2; sem., 119; bros., 29; srs., 505; catechists, 8,689; bap., 72,139; Caths., 5,822,000 (92.7%); tot. pop., 6,340,000.

Republic in Central America; capital, Tegucigalpa. Evangelization preceded establishment of the first diocese in the 16th century. Under Spanish rule and after independence from 1823, the Church held a favored position until 1880, when equal legal status was given to all religions. Harassment of priests and nuns working among indigenous peasants and Salvadoran refugees was reported during the years of Central American civil unrest in the late 20th century. In 1998 Hurricane Mitch killed more than 6,000 Hondurans and forced more than 2 million in the country to evacuate their homes. The Church took a lead role in post-hurricane relief and development efforts.

Hungary*

Archd., 4; dioc., 9; abb., 1; ap. ex., 1; mil. ord. 1; card., 1; abp., 6; bp., 18; parishes, 2,214; priests, 2,502 (1,999 dioc., 503 rel.); p.d., 36; sem., 476; bros., 153; srs., 1,659; catechists, 3,594; bap., 56,190; Caths., 6,557,000 (64.6%); tot. pop., 10,150,000.

Republic in east central Europe; capital, Budapest. The early origins of Christianity in the country, whose territory was subject to a great deal of change, is not known. Magyars accepted Christianity about the end of the 10th century. St. Stephen I promoted its spread and helped to organize some of its historical dioceses. Bishops became influential in politics as well as in the Church.

For centuries the country served as a buffer for the Christian West against barbarians from the East, notably the Mongols in the 13th century. Hussites and Waldensians prepared the way for the Reformation, which struck at almost the same time as the Turks. The Reformation made considerable progress after 1526, resulting in the conversion of large numbers to Lutheranism and Calvinism by the end of the century. Most of them or their descendants returned to the Church later, but many Magyars remained staunch Calvinists. Turks repressed the Churches, Protestant as well as Catholic, during a reign of 150 years, but they managed to survive. Domination of the Church was one of the objectives of government policy during the reigns of Maria Theresa and Joseph II in the second half of the 18th century; their Josephinism affected Church-state relations until World War I.

Secularization increased in the second half of the 19th century, which also witnessed the birth of many new Catholic organizations and movements. Catholics were involved in the social chaos and anti-religious atmosphere of the years following World War I, struggling with their compatriots for religious as well as political survival.

After World War II, the communist campaign against the Church started with the disbanding of Catholic organizations in 1946. In 1948, Caritas, the

Catholic charitable organization, was taken over, and all Catholic institutions were suppressed. Interference in Church administration and attempts to split the bishops preceded the arrest of Cardinal Jozsef Mindszenty Dec. 26, 1948, and his sentence to life imprisonment in 1949. (He was free for a few days during the unsuccessful uprising of 1956. He then took up residence at the U.S. Embassy in Budapest, where he remained until September 1971, when he was permitted to leave the country. He died in 1975 in Vienna.)

In 1950, religious orders and congregations were suppressed and 10,000 religious were interned. Several dozen priests and monks were assassinated, jailed or deported. About 4,000 priests and religious were confined in jail or concentration camps. The government sponsored a national "Progressive Catholic" Church and captive organizations for priests. Despite a 1964 agreement with the Holy See regarding episcopal appointments, bishops remained subject to government surveillance and harassment.

On Feb. 9, 1990, an accord was signed between the Holy See and Hungary re-establishing diplomatic relations. Pope John Paul II reorganized the ecclesiastical structure of the country in May 1993. In 1997, the Vatican and Hungary signed an agreement that restored some Church property confiscated under communism and provided some sources of funding for Church activities. Hungary's bishops have said social conflicts, political changes and economic strains have put new pressures on the Church.

Iceland*

Dioc., 1; bp., 1; parishes, 4; priests, 11 (5 dioc., 6 rel.); sem., 1; srs., 50; bap., 63; Caths., 3,000 (1%); tot. pop., 270,000.

Island republic between Norway and Greenland; capital, Rekjavik. Irish hermits were there in the eighth century. Missionaries subsequently evangelized the island and Christianity was officially accepted about 1000. The first bishop was ordained in 1056. The Black Death had dire effects, and spiritual decline set in during the 15th century. Lutheranism was introduced from Denmark between 1537 and 1552 and made the official religion. Some Catholic missionary work was done in the 19th century. Religious freedom was granted to the few Catholics in 1874. A vicariate was erected in 1929 and was made a diocese in 1968.

India*

Patriarchate, 1 (titular of East Indies); major archbishopric (Syro-Malabar), 1; archd., 22; dioc., 116; card., 3; patr., 1; abp., 29; bp., 139; parishes, 7,745; priests, 17,653 (10,176 dioc., 7,477 rel.); p.d., 33; sem., 9,828; bros., 2,718; srs., 76,542; catechists, 46,113; bap., 373,827; Caths., 17,211,000 (1.7%); tot. pop. 955,220,000.

Republic on the subcontinent of south central Asia; capital, New Delhi. Long-standing tradition credits the Apostle Thomas with the introduction of Christianity in the Kerala area. Evangelization followed the establishment of Portuguese posts and the conquest of Goa in 1510. Jesuits, Franciscans, Dominicans, Augustinians and members of other religious orders figured in the early missionary history. An archdiocese for Goa, with two suffragan sees, was

set up in 1558. Five provincial councils were held between 1567 and 1606.

Missionaries had some difficulties with the British East India Co., which exercised virtual government control from 1757 to 1858. They also had trouble because of a conflict that developed between policies of the Portuguese government, which pressed its rights of patronage in episcopal and clerical appointments, and the Vatican Congregation for the Propagation of the Faith, which sought greater freedom of action in the same appointments. This struggle resulted in the schism of Goa between 1838 and 1857. In 1886, when the number of Catholics was estimated to be 1 million, the hierarchy for India and Ceylon was restored.

Jesuits contributed greatly to the development of Catholic education from the second half of the 19th century. A large percentage of the Catholic population is located around Goa and Kerala and farther south. The country is predominantly Hindu. Anti-conversion laws in effect in several states have had a restrictive effect on pastoral ministry and social service.

Recent years have seen tensions within the Syro-Malabar rite over liturgy and tradition. In addition, there have been tensions between the Latin-rite and Eastern-rite Catholic churches in India over the care of Catholics outside the traditional boundaries of their rites. The Vatican has investigated several Jesuits in India for teaching relativism, which refrains from proclaiming Christ as the world's savior out of respect for other religions. In 1998, the number of cases of violence against Christians increased, as convents and schools were vandalized; five nuns were raped and nine were murdered. An independent commission probing the violence in western Indian said rightwing Hindus were responsible. The pro-Hindu government fell in mid-April 1999.

Indonesia*

Archd., 8; dioc., 26; mil. ord. 1; card., 1; abp., 9; bps., 33; parishes, 1,071; priests, 2,678 (930 dioc., 1,748 rel.); p.d., 19; sem., 2,730; bros., 1,145; srs., 6,691; catechists, 24,334; bap., 1,988,306; Caths., 5,686,000 (2.8%); tot. pop, 201,390,000.

East Timor (former Portuguese Timor annexed by Indonesia in 1976): Dioc., 2; bp., 2; parishes; 31; priests, 112 (40 dioc., 72 rel.); sem., 138; bros., 18; srs., 202; catechists, 1,030; bap., 19,906; Caths., 764,000 (86%); tot. pop., 891,000 An autonomy vote took place in August 1999.

Republic in the Malay Archipelago, consisting of some 3,000 islands; capital, Jakarta. Evangelization by the Portuguese began about 1511. St. Francis Xavier spent some 14 months in the area. Christianity was strongly rooted in some parts of the islands by 1600. Islam's rise to dominance began at this time. The Dutch East Indies Co., which gained effective control in the 17th century, banned evangelization by Catholic missionaries for some time, but Dutch secular and religious priests managed to resume the work. A vicariate of Batavia for all the Dutch East Indies was set up in 1841. About 90 percent of the population is Muslim. The hierarchy was established in 1961.

From 1981 to about 1996, Catholics and Protestants clashed more than 40 times over what Catholics perceived as Communion host desecration. At least three

Protestants died from beatings by Catholics after the incidents.

In the late-1990s, as the Indonesian economy took a nose-dive, Muslim-Christian violence increased, with hundreds of people, including Catholics, killed. Some characterized the violence as less sectarian and more incidents of religious differences exploited for political gain.

East Timor: Predominantly Catholic former Portuguese colony invaded by Indonesia in 1975 and annexed the following year. Most countries did not recognize the annexation. The Catholic Church worked to bring peace between the Indonesian government and guerrilla forces seeking independence. Bishop Carlos Filipe Ximenes Belo, apostolic administration of Dili, was a cowinner of the 1996 Nobel Peace Prize for his peace efforts. In 1999, dozens of civilians were killed — including more than two dozen at a Catholic church — during a terror campaign waged by pro-Indonesia paramilitaries in the run-up to an August vote on autonomy for East Timor.

Iran*

Archd., 4; dioc., 2; abp., 4; bp., 2; parishes, 19; priests, 14 (5 dioc., 9 rel.); p.d., 10; sem., 1; bro., 1; srs., 21; bap., 87; Caths., 12,000 (.02%); tot. pop., 60,690,000.

Islamic republic (Persia until 1935) in southwestern Asia; capital, Teheran. Some of the earliest Christian communities were established in this area outside the Roman Empire. They suffered persecution in the fourth century and were then cut off from the outside world. Nestorianism was generally professed in the late fifth century. Islam became dominant after 640. Some later missionary work was attempted but without success. Religious liberty was granted in 1834, but Catholics were the victims of a massacre in 1918. Islam is the religion of perhaps 98 percent of the population. Catholics belong to the Latin, Armenian and Chaldean rites.

After Iran nationalized many Church-run social institutions in 1980, about 75 Catholic missionaries left the country, by force or by choice. In recent years, however, Iranian authorities have shown more cooperation regarding entry visas for Church personnel. Although freedom of worship is guaranteed in Iran, Church sources said Catholic activities are monitored carefully by authorities. In March 1999, Pope John Paul II met with Iranian President Mohammed Khatami at the Vatican and discussed how to improve Christian-Muslim relations worldwide.

Iraq*

Patriarchate, 1; archd., 9; dioc., 5; ap. ex., 2; patriarch, 1; abp., 11; bp., 3; parishes, 82; priests, 130 (104 dioc., 26 rel.); p.d.,7; sem., 74; bros., 15; srs., 353; catechists, 813; bap., 4,011; Caths., 275,000 (1%); tot. pop., 21,180,000.

Republic in southwestern Asia; capital, Baghdad. Some of the earliest Christian communities were established in the area, whose history resembles that of Iran. Catholics belong to the Armenian, Chaldean, Latin and Syrian rites; Chaldeans are most numerous. Islam is the religion of some 90 percent of the population. Iraq's Chaldean Catholic patriarch has been outspoken against the international embargo against Iraq, saying it especially hurts children and the sick.

Ireland*

Archd., 4; dioc., 22; card., 1; abp., 9; bp., 40; parishes, 1,297; priests, 5,881 (3,473 dioc., 2,408 rel.); p.d., 4; sem., 386; bros., 1,054; srs., 9,656; bap., 66,096 (preceding figures include Northern Ireland); Caths., 4,541,000 (75%); tot. 6,049,000 (population numbers include Northern Ireland; in Republic of Ireland, Catholics comprise 95% of the population).

Republic in the British Isles; capital, Dublin. St. Patrick, who is venerated as the apostle of Ireland, evangelized parts of the island for some years after the middle of the fifth century. Conversion of the island was not accomplished, however, until the seventh century or later. Celtic monks were the principal missionaries. The Church was organized along monastic lines at first, but a movement developed in the 11th century for the establishment of jurisdiction along episcopal lines. By that time many Roman usages had been adopted. The Church gathered strength during the period from the Norman Conquest of England to the reign of Henry VIII despite a wide variety of rivalries, wars, and other disturbances.

Henry introduced an age of repression of the faith, which continued for many years under several of his successors. The Irish suffered from proscription of the Catholic faith, economic and social disabilities, subjection to absentee landlords and a plantation system designed to keep them from owning property, and actual persecution which took an uncertain toll of lives up until about 1714. Some penal laws remained in force until emancipation in 1829. Nearly 100 years later Ireland was divided by two, making Northern Ireland, consisting of six counties, part of the United Kingdom (1920) and giving dominion status to the Irish Free State, made up of the other 26 counties (1922). This state (Eire, in Gaelic) was proclaimed the Republic of Ireland in 1949. The Catholic Church predominates but religious freedom is guaranteed for all. The Irish Republic and Northern Ireland share a bishops' conference, which has worked for peace in Northern Ireland. Recent years have witnessed a decrease in vocations and growing turmoil over issues such as priestly pedophilia, divorce, and abortion.

Ireland, Northern

Tot. pop., 1,610,000; Catholics comprise more than one third. (Other statistics are included in Ireland).

Part of the United Kingdom, it consists of six of the nine counties of Ulster in the northeast corner of Ireland; capital, Belfast. Early history is given under Ireland.

Nationalist-unionist tensions fall primarily along Catholic-Protestant lines, with nationalists, mainly Catholics, advocating an end to British rule. Violence and terrorism began in the late 1960s and, by the late 1990s, more than 3,000 people had been killed. Catholic-Protestant tensions are highlighted each year during the Protestant marching season, when members of the Protestant Orange Order parade through Catholic neighborhoods to commemorate the 1690 Battle of the Boyne, when Protestant King William of Orange defeated Catholic King James II.

On Apr. 10, 1998, the governments of the Irish Republic and Great Britain and the political parties of Northern Ireland reached an agreement known as the Good Friday agreement. Irish archbishops supported it, and it was endorsed by the voters in Ireland and Northern Ireland. However, decommissioning of weapons for the outlawed, primarily Catholic Irish Republican Army remained a stumbling block to peace.

Catholics have claimed discrimination in the workplace and harassment from the Royal Ulster Constabulary, Northern Ireland's police force. Although Catholics make up about 47 percent of Northern Ireland's population, they make up only 7 percent of the force. Former Hong Kong Gov. Chris Patten was to head independent review of the constabulary.

Israel*

Patriarchates, 2 (Jerusalem for Latins; patriarchal vicariate for Greek-Melkites); archd., 2; ap.ex., 5; patriarch, 1; abp., 4; bp., 4; parishes, 97; priests, 384 (76 dioc., 308 rel.); p.d., 4; sem., 115; bros., 165; srs., 1,045; bap., 1,778; Caths., 106,000; tot. pop., 5,830,000.

Parliamentary democracy in the Middle East; capitals, Jerusalem and Tel Aviv (diplomatic). Israel was the birthplace of Christianity, the site of the first Christian communities. Some persecution was suffered in the early Christian era and again during the several hundred years of Roman control. Muslims conquered the territory in the seventh century and, except for the period of the Kingdom of Jerusalem established by Crusaders, remained in control most of the time up until World War I. The Church survived in the area, sometimes just barely, but it did not prosper greatly or show any notable increase in numbers. The British took over the protectorate of the area after World War I.

Partition into Israel for the Jews and Palestine for the Arabs was approved by the United Nations in 1947. War broke out a year later with the proclamation of the Republic of Israel. The Israelis won the war and 50 percent more territory than they had originally been ceded. War broke out again for six days in June 1967, and in October 1973, resulting in a Middle East crisis.

Judaism is the faith professed by about 85 percent of the inhabitants; approximately one-third of them are considered observant. Israeli-Holy See relations improved in 1994 with the implementation of full diplomatic relations, and the Church gained legal status in 1997. However, Palestinians Catholics have suffered with repeated border closings and persecution.

The Holy See repeatedly has asked for an internationally guaranteed statute to protect the sacred nature of Jerusalem, which is holy to Christians, Muslims and Jews. It has underlined that this means more than access to specific holy places and that the political and religious dimensions of Jerusalem are interrelated.

Italy*

Patriarchate, 1 (Venice); archd. 58 (37 are metropolitan sees); dioc., 158; prel., 3; abb., 7; mil. ord. 1; pat., 1 (Venice); card., 38; abp., 168; bps., 276 (hierarchy includes 214 residential, 30 coadjutors or auxiliaries, 108 in Curia offices, remainder in other offices or retired); parishes, 25,806; priests, 55,499 (36,566 dioc., 18,933 rel.); p.d., 1,966; sem., 6,337; bros., 4,193; srs., 114,775; catechists, 102,739; bap.,

477,662; Caths., 55,916,000 (97%); tot. pop., 57,520,000.

Republic in southern Europe; capital, Rome. A Christian community was formed early in Rome, probably by the middle of the first century. St. Peter established his see there. He and St. Paul suffered death for the faith there in the 60s. The early Christians were persecuted at various times there, as in other parts of the empire, but the Church developed in numbers and influence, gradually spreading out from towns and cities in the center and south to rural areas and the north.

Church organization, in the process of formation in the second century, developed greatly between the fifth and eighth centuries. By the latter date the Church had already come to grips with serious problems, including doctrinal and disciplinary disputes that threatened the unity of faith, barbarian invasions, and the need for the pope and bishops to take over civil responsibilities because of imperial default. The Church has been at the center of life on the peninsula throughout the centuries. It emerged from underground in 313, with the Edict of Milan, and rose to a position of prestige and lasting influence. It educated and converted the barbarians, preserved culture through the early Middle Ages and passed it on to later times, suffered periods of decline and gained strength through recurring reforms, engaged in military combat for political reasons and intellectual combat for the preservation and development of doctrine, saw and patronized the development of the arts, experienced all human strengths and weaknesses in its members.

From the fourth to the 19th centuries, the Church was a temporal as well as spiritual power. In the 1870s, the Papal States were annexed by the Kingdom of Italy. The 1929 Lateran Pacts included a treaty recognizing the Vatican as an independent state, a financial agreement by which Italy agreed to compensate the Vatican for loss of the papal states, and a concordat regulating Church-state relations. In 1984 the Vatican and Italy signed a revised concordat, reducing some of the Church's privileges and removing Catholicism as the state religion.

The Church strongly opposed Italy's abortion law in 1978 and forced a 1981 referendum on the issue. Abortion remained legal, and the Italian Church has taken a more low-profile stance. The Church has been active in social issues, including helping unprecedented numbers of illegal immigrants in the late 1990s. Church leaders have expressed concern about Italy's low birth rate. In 1997, a double earthquake destroyed a large section of the ceiling of the Basilica of St. Francis in Assisi, killing four people. Restoration experts began work almost immediately on the basilica, one of the Italian Church's largest tourism sites. The upper basilica was expected to be opened by Christmas 1999.

Jamaica*

Archd., 1; dioc., 2; abp., 2; bp., 2; parishes, 79; priests, 100 (55 dioc., 45 rel.); p.d., 29; sem., 19; bros., 12; srs., 188; catechists, 475; bap., 1,239; Caths., 109,000 (4.3%); tot. pop., 2,550,000.

Republic in the West Indies; capital, Kingston. Franciscans and Dominicans evangelized the island from about 1512 until 1655. Missionary work was interrupted after the English took possession but was resumed by Jesuits about the turn of the 19th century. An apostolic vicariate was organized in 1837. The hierarchy was established in 1967. In the late 1990s, Church leaders spoke out against violence; more than 800 people were murdered in Jamaica in 1997 alone.

Japan*

Archd., 3; dioc., 13; p.a., 1; card., 1; abp., 4; bp., 20; parishes, 876; priests, 1,806 (540 dioc., 1,266 rel.); p.d., 6; sem., 239; bros., 260; srs., 6,635; catechists, 1,742; bap., 8,970; Caths., 502,000 (.39%); tot. pop., 125,640,000.

Archipelago in the northwest Pacific; capital, Tokyo. Jesuits began evangelization in the middle of the 16th century and about 300,000 converts, most of them in Kyushu, were reported at the end of the century. The Nagasaki Martyrs were victims of persecution in 1597. Another persecution took some 4,000 lives between 1614 and 1651. Missionaries, banned for two centuries, returned about the middle of the 19th century and found Christian communities still surviving in Nagasaki and other places in Kyushu. A vicariate was organized in 1866. Religious freedom was guaranteed in 1889. The hierarchy was established in 1891. Several Japanese bishops at the 1998 Synod of Bishops for Asia said Catholicism has grown slowly in the region because the Church is too Western.

Since the 1980s, on several occasion Church leaders have apologized and asked forgiveness for the Church's complicity in the nation's aggression during the 1930s and 1940s. At the end of the 20th century, bishops and religious superiors suggested that during the 21st century the Japanese Church focus on pastoral care for migrant workers, concern for the environment and interreligious dialogue.

Jordan*

Archd., l; abp., 1; bp., 1; parishes, 64; priests, 80 (58 dioc., 22 rel.); sem., 8; bros., 9; srs., 250; bap., 925; Caths., 71,000 (1.2%); tot. pop., 5,770,000.

Constitutional monarchy in the Middle East; capital, Amman. Christianity there dates from apostolic times. Survival of the faith was threatened many times under the rule of Muslims from 636 and Ottoman Turks from 1517 to 1918, and in the Islamic Emirate of Trans-Jordan from 1918 to 1949. In the years following the creation of Israel, some 500,000 Palestinian refugees, including Christians, moved to Jordan. In the 1990s, Jordan cared for some 130,000 Iraqi refugees, including some 30,000 Chaldean Catholics. Islam is the state religion, but religious freedom is guaranteed for all. The Greek Melkite Archdiocese of Petra and Filadelfia is located in Jordan. Latin-rite Catholics are under the jurisdiction of the Latin Patriarchate of Jerusalem. Jordan established diplomatic relations with the Holy See in 1994.

Kazakhstan*

A.a., 1; bp., 1; parishes, 30; priests, 43 (26 dioc., 17 rel.); sem., 27; bros., 1; srs., 47; bap., 1,166; Caths., 300,000 (1.8%); tot. pop., 16,830,000.

Independent republic (1991); formerly part of USSR; capital, Astana. About 47 percent of the population is Muslim, and about 44 percent is Orthodox.

The Catholic population is mainly of German, Polish and Ukrainian origin, descendants of those deported during the Stalin regime. A Latin-rite apostolic administration was established in 1991. In 1998, the Vatican and the Kazakh government signed an agreement guaranteeing the Church legal rights.

Kenya*

Archd. 4; dioc., 17; v.a., 1; mil. ord., 1; card., 1; abp. 5; bp. 17; parishes, 607; priests, 1,737 (860 dioc., 877 rel.); p.d., 2; sem., 1,711; bros., 609; srs., 3,773; catechists, 8,103; bap., 221,301; Caths., 6,639,000 (20%); tot. pop., 33,140,000.

Republic in East Africa on the Indian Ocean; capital, Nairobi. Systematic evangelization by the Holy Ghost Missionaries began in 1889, nearly 40 years after the start of work by Protestant missionaries. The hierarchy was established in 1953. Three metropolitan sees were established in 1990. Kenyan Catholics were in the forefront of ministering to victims of the 1998 explosion at the U.S. Embassy in Nairobi. The Kenyan bishops have been very outspoken against ethnic violence, poverty, and government corruption and mismanagement.

Kiribati*

Dioc., 1; bp., 1; parishes, 23; priests, 18 (7 dioc., 11 rel.); sem., 13; bros., 20; srs., 82; catechists, 210; bap., 1,893; Caths., 43,000 (55.1%); tot. pop., 79,000.

Former British colony (Gilbert Islands) in Oceania; became independent July 12, 1979; capital, Bairiki on Tarawa. French Missionaries of the Sacred Heart began work in the islands in 1888. A vicariate for the islands was organized in 1897. The hierarchy was established in 1966.

Korea, North

Dioc., 2; abb., 1; bp., 1 (exiled); tot. pop., 22,470,000. No recent Catholic statistics available; there were an estimated 100,000 Catholics reported in 1969.

Northern part of peninsula in eastern Asia; formal name Democratic People's Republic of Korea (May 1, 1948); capital, Pyongyang. See South Korea for history before country was divided. After liberation from Japan in 1945, the Soviet regime in the North systematically punished all religions. After the 1950-53 Korean war, Christian worship was not allowed outside of homes until 1988, when the country's one Catholic Church was built in Pyongyang. A 1999 South Korean government report said North Korea clearly restricts religious practices, and churches in the North exist only for "show."

Korea, South*

Archd., 3; dioc., 11; mil. ord. 1; card., 1; abp., 3; bp., 19; parishes, 1,099; priests, 2,368 (1,980 dioc., 388 rel.); sem., 1,634; bros., 553; srs., 7,421; catechists, 11,706; bap., 148,082; Caths., 3,631,000 (7.8%); tot. pop., 45,990,000.

Southern part of peninsula in eastern Asia; formal name, Republic of Korea (1948); capital, Seoul. Some Catholics may have been in Korea before it became a "hermit kingdom" toward the end of the 16th century and closed its borders to foreigners. The modern introduction to Catholicism came in 1784 through lay converts. A priest arriving in the country in 1794 found 4,000 Catholics there who had never seen a priest. A vicariate was erected in 1831 but was not manned for several years thereafter. There were 15,000 Catholics by 1857. Four persecutions in the 19th century took a terrible toll; several thousand died in the last one, 1866-69. (Pope John Paul II canonized 103 martyrs of this period during his 1984 visit to South Korea.) Freedom of religion was granted in 1883, when Korea opened its borders. During World War II, most foreign priests were arrested and expelled, seminaries were closed and churches were taken over. After liberation from Japan in 1945, the Church in the South had religious freedom. Since the 1950-53 Korean war, the Church in South Korea has flourished. Church leaders in the South have worked at reconciliation with the North and to alleviate famine in the North.

Kuwait*

V.a., 1; pat. ex.; bp., 1; parishes, 4; priests, 9 (3 dioc., 6 rel.); p.d., 1; bros., 10; srs., 12; bap., 595; Caths., 156,000 (.9%); tot. pop., 1,810,000.

Constitutional monarchy (sultanate or sheikdom) in southwest Asia bordering on the Persian Gulf. Remote Christian origins probably date to apostolic times. Islam is the predominant and official religion. Catholics are mostly foreign workers; the Church enjoys religious freedom.

Kyrgyzstan*

Parishes, 3; Priests, 4 (4 rel.); bros., 1; Caths., 27,000; tot. pop., 4,640,000.

Independent republic bordering China; former Soviet republic; capital, Bishkek (former name, Frunze). Most of the people are Sunni Muslim. Established diplomatic relations with the Holy See in August 1992.

Laos

V.a., 4; bp., 4; parishes, 29; priests, 189 (18 dioc.); p.d., 1; sem., 8; bros., 1; srs., 79; catechists, 161; bap., 906; Caths., 36,000 (.6%); tot. pop., 5,190,000. (AD)

People's republic in southeast Asia; capital, Vientiane. Systematic evangelization by French missionaries started about 1881; earlier efforts ended in 1688. The first mission was established in 1885 by Father Xavier Guégo. An apostolic vicariate was organized in 1899. Most of the foreign missionaries were expelled following the communist takeover in 1975. Catholic schools remain banned, and the government lets foreign missionaries into the country only as "social workers." A Laotian bishop at the 1998 Synod of Bishops for Asia said religious practice was nearly normal in two of the country's four apostolic vicariates, but elsewhere was more controlled and sometimes difficult. Buddhism is the state religion.

Latvia*

Archd., 1; dioc., 3; abp., 1; bp., 4; parishes, 214; priests, 109 (88 dioc., 21 rel.); p.d., 1; sem., 50; srs., 80; catechist, 332; bap., 6,323; Caths., 410,000 (19.9%); tot. pop., 2,470,000.

Independent (1991) Baltic republic; capital, Riga. (Forcibly absorbed by the USSR in 1940; it regained independence in 1991). Catholicism was introduced late in the 12th century. Lutheranism became the dominant religion after 1530. Catholics were free to practice their faith during the long period of Russian control and during independence from 1918 to 1940. The relatively small Catholic community in Latvia was repressed during the 1940-91 Soviet takeover, which was not recognized by the Holy See or the United States. After Latvia declared its independence, the Church began to flourish, including among people who described themselves as nonreligious. In the late 1990s, one archbishop urged the Russian government not to interfere in disputes over citizenship for the country's ethnic Russians, who make up about one-third of the country's population.

Lebanon*

Patriarchates, 3; achd., 12 (1 Armenian, 4 Maronite, 7 Greek Melkite); dioc., 8 (1 Chaldean, 6 Maronite); v.a., 1 (Latin); card., 1 (patriarch of the Maronites); patriarchs, 2 (patriarchs of Antioch of the Maronites, Antioch of the Syrians and Cilicia of the Armenians who reside in Lebanon); abp., 22; bp., 17; parishes, 993; priests, 1,362 (740 dioc., 622 rel.); p.d., 2; sem., 428; bros., 84; srs., 2,918; bap., 15,775; Caths., 1,967,000 (62.6%); tot. pop., 3,140,000.

Republic in the Middle East; capital, Beirut. Christianity, introduced in apostolic times, was firmly established by the end of the fourth century and has remained so despite heavy Muslim influence since early in the seventh century. The country is the center of the Maronite rite. In the 1980s, the country was torn by violence and often heavy fighting among rival political-religious factions drawn along Christian-Muslim lines. Pope John Paul II convened a synod of bishops for Lebanon in 1995 to urge Lebanese to forgive and forget the wounds of the war. Synod members provoked controversy by directly criticizing Israeli occupation of southern Lebanon and Syria's continued deployment of troops in the area. In 1999, Lebanon was the site of a historic meeting of Mideast and North African Church leaders, who discussed the future of the Catholic Church in the Arab world.

Lesotho*

Archd., 1; dioc., 3; abp., 1; bp., 3; parishes, 78; priests, 134 (51 dioc., 83 rel.); sem., 87; bros., 48; srs., 600; catechists, 3,498; bap., 28,147; Caths., 774,000 (36%); tot. pop., 2,130,000.

Constitutional monarchy, an enclave in the southeastern part of South Africa; capital, Maseru. Oblates of Mary Immaculate, the first Catholic missionaries in the area, started evangelization in 1862. Father Joseph Gerard, whom Pope John Paul II beatified in 1988, worked 10 years before he made his first conversion. An apostolic prefecture was organized in 1894. The hierarchy was established in 1951. Under the military government of the late 1980s, Lesotho's Catholics pressed for democratic reforms. In the 1990s, they gave special pastoral care to families whose breadwinners had to travel to South Africa to work, often for weeks at a time.

Liberia*

Archd., 1; dioc., 2; abp., 1; bp., 1; parishes, 51; priests, 52 (26 dioc., 26 rel.); p.d., 4; sem., 47; bros., 17; srs., 42; bap. 3,593; Caths., 99,000 (3.4%); tot. pop., 2,880,000.

Republic in West Africa; capital, Monrovia. Missionary work and influence, dating intermittently from the 16th century, were slight before the Society of African Missions undertook evangelization in 1906. The hierarchy was established in 1982. Fighting within the country, which began in 1989, culminated in 1996 and resulted in the evacuation of most Church workers and the archbishop of Monrovia. The war claimed the lives of 150,000 and made refugees or displaced of another million. Most Church institutions in Monrovia were destroyed.

Libya*

V.a., 3; p.a., 1; bp., 2; parishes, 2; priests, 15 (4 dioc., 11 rel.); sem. 2; srs., 78; bap., 120; Caths., 50,000 (.8%); tot. pop., 5,780,000.

Arab state in North Africa; capital, Tripoli. Christianity was probably preached in the area at an early date but was overcome by the spread of Islam from the 630s. Islamization was complete by 1067, and there has been no Christian influence since then. Almost all Catholics are foreign workers. Islam is the state religion. After implementation of a U.N. embargo against the country in 1992, the government removed most limitations on entry of Catholic religious orders, especially health care workers. Libya established diplomatic relations with the Holy See in 1997.

Liechtenstein*

Archd. 1; abp., 1; parishes, 10; priests, 36 (16 dioc., 10 rel); bros., 3; srs., 62; bap., 316; Caths., 25,000 (80%); tot. pop., 31,000.

Constitutional monarchy in central Europe; capital, Vaduz. Christianity in the country dates from the fourth century; the area has been under the jurisdiction of Chur, Switzerland, since about that time. The Reformation had hardly any influence in the country. Catholicism is the state religion, but religious freedom for all is guaranteed by law.

Lithuania*

Archd., 2; dioc. , 5; card., 1; abp., 3; bp., 101; parishes, 69; priests, 753 (658 dioc., 951 rel.); p.d., 2; sem., 338; bros., 109; srs., 998; catechists, 1,501; bap., 35,470; Caths., 3,279,000 (84%); tot. pop., 3,800,000.

Baltic republic forcibly absorbed and under Soviet domination from 1940; regained independence, 1991; capital, Vilnius. Catholicism was introduced in 1251 and a short-lived diocese was established by 1260. Effective evangelization took place between 1387 and 1417, when Catholicism became the state religion. Losses to Lutheranism in the 16th century were overcome. Efforts of czars to "russify" the Church between 1795 and 1918 were strongly resisted. Concordat relations with the Vatican were established in 1927, nine years after independence from Russia and 13 years before Russia annexed Lithuania. The Russians closed convents and seminaries; in Kaunas, men needed government approval to attend the seminary. Priests were restricted in pastoral ministry and subject to appointment by government officials; no religious services were allowed outside churches; religious press and instruction were banned. Two bishops — Vincentas Sladkevicius and Julijonas Steponavicius — were forbidden to act as bishops and relegated to remote parishes in 1957 and 1961,

respectively. Some bishops and hundreds of priests and laity were imprisoned or detained in Siberia between 1945 and 1955. Despite such conditions, a vigorous underground Church flourished in Lithuania.

In the 1980s, government pressure eased, and some bishops were allowed to return to their dioceses. In 1989 Pope John Paul II appointed bishops in all six Lithuanian dioceses. The Church strongly supported the 1990 independence movement, and Lithuanian independence leaders urged young men to desert the Russian army and seek sanctuary in churches. However, communist rule nearly destroyed the Church's infrastructure, and in the late 1990s the Church was still seeking return of properties confiscated in 1940.

Luxembourg*

Archd., 1; abp., 2; parishes, 275; priests, 295 (215 dioc., 80 rel.); p.d., 5; sem., 13; bros., 17; srs., 734; catechism, 800; bap., 3,665; Caths. 368,000 (96%); tot. pop., 420,000.

Constitutional monarchy in western Europe; capital, Luxembourg. Christianity, introduced in the fifth and sixth centuries, was firmly established by the end of the eighth century. A full-scale parish system was in existence in the ninth century. Monastic influence was strong until the Reformation, which had minimal influence in the country. The Church experienced some adverse influence from the currents of the French Revolution. In recent years, the Church has restructured its adult formation program to involve more lay workers.

Macau

Dioc., 1; bp., 1; parishes, 10; priests, 70 (30 dioc., 40 rel.); sem., 2; bros., 13; srs., 173; bap., 394; Caths., 20,000; tot. pop., 420,000.

Former Portuguese-administered territory in southeast Asia across the Pearl River estuary from Hong Kong; to revert to Chinese control on Dec. 20, 1999. Christianity was introduced by the Jesuits in 1557. Diocese was established in 1576. Macau served as a base for missionary work in Japan and China. Portuguese and Chinese Catholics remained somewhat segregated throughout the more than 400 years of Portuguese rule. Bishop Domingos Lam Ka Tseung became the first Chinese bishop of Macau in 1988 and launched a lay formation plan that included Chinese and Portuguese language training. The Church has been prominent in education. A Catholic priest was among three religious leaders named to the committee to prepare for the enclave's return to Chinese rule.

Macedonia*

Dioc., 1; bp., 2; parishes, 30; priests, 60 (58 dioc., 2 rel.); sem., 18; srs., 122; bap., 767; Caths., 85,000 (3.9%); tot. pop., 2,190,000.

Former Yugoslav Republic of Macedonia; declared independence in 1992; capital, Skopje. The Diocese of Skopje-Prizren includes the Yugoslav province of Kosovo, so the Macedonian Church was intimately involved with ethnic Albanians during the period of ethnic cleansing by Serb forces and the retaliatory NATO air strikes.

Madagascar*

Archd., 3; dioc., 15; card., 1; abp., 4; bp., 16; parishes, 291; priests, 957 (376 dioc., 581 rel.); sem.,

799; bros., 500; srs., 3,144; catechists, 13,340; bap., 117,809; Caths., 3,351,000 (21%); tot. pop. 15,850,000.

Republic (Malagasy Republic) off the eastern coast of Africa; capital, Antananarivo. Missionary efforts were generally fruitless from early in the 16th century until the Jesuits were permitted to start open evangelization about 1845. An apostolic prefecture was set up in 1850 and an apostolic vicariate in the North was placed in charge of the Holy Ghost Fathers in 1898. There were 100,000 Catholics by 1900. The first native bishop was ordained in 1936. The hierarchy was established in 1955. In the late 1980s and early 1990s, the Church joined opposition calls for renewal of social institutions. Today, the Church in Madagascar runs hundreds of schools and dozens of orphanages; some consider it the largest landowner, after the government.

Malawi*
Archd., 1; dioc., 6; abp., 1; bp., 7; parishes, 162; priests, 430 (272 dioc., 158 rel.); sem., 277; bros., 93; srs., 717; catechists, 6,338; bap., 98,074; Caths., 2,352,000 (22%); tot. pop., 10,440,000.

Republic in the interior of East Africa; capital, Lilongwe. Missionary work, begun by Jesuits in the late 16th and early 17th centuries, was generally ineffective until the end of the 19th century. The Missionaries of Africa (White Fathers) arrived in 1889 and later were joined by others. A vicariate was set up in 1897. The hierarchy was established in 1959. In the late 1980s, the Church in Malawi helped hundreds of thousands of refugees from the war in Mozambique. Malawi's churches, especially the Catholic Church, were instrumental in bringing about the downfall of President Hastings Kamuzu Banda, who ruled for 30 years. A 1992 bishops' pastoral letter criticized Banda's rule and the nation's poverty and galvanized Malawians into pro-democracy protests. Banda responded by summoning the country's bishops, seizing copies of the letter and expelling an Irish member of the Malawi hierarchy. Western donors called off aid, and in 1994 Banda was forced to call multi-party elections, which he lost.

Malaysia
Archd., 2; dioc., 6; abp., 3; bp., 7; parishes, 143; priests, 219 (173 dioc., 46 rel.); p.d., 2; sem., 71; bros., 71; srs., 562; catechists, 2,235; bap., 21,660; Caths., 691,000 (3%); tot. pop., 21,724,000. (AD)

Parliamentary democracy in southeast Asia; capital, Kuala Lumpur. Christianity, introduced by Portuguese colonists about 1511, was confined almost exclusively to Malacca until late in the 18th century. The effectiveness of evangelization increased from then on because of the recruitment and training of native clergy. Singapore (see separate entry), founded in 1819, became a center for missionary work. Effective evangelization in Sabah and Sarawak began in the second half of the 19th century. The hierarchy was established in 1973. In accordance with government wishes for Bahasa Malaysia to be the national language, the Church has tried to introduce it into its liturgies. For more than a decade, Church leaders have campaigned against the Internal Security Act, which allows renewable 30-day detentions without trial. Prosely-

tizing Muslims is illegal, but the government allows conversions from other religions.

Maldives
Republic, an archipelago 400 miles southwest of India and Ceylon; capital, Male. No serious attempt was ever made to evangelize the area, which is completely Muslim. Population, 260,000.

Mali*
Archd., 1; dioc., 5; abp., 1; bp., 4; parishes, 42; priests, 154 (71 dioc., 83 rel.); sem., 34; bros., 22; srs., 206; catechists, 1,033; bap., 2,827; Caths., 110,000 (.1%); tot. pop., 11,480,000.

Republic, inland in western Africa; capital, Bamako. Catholicism was introduced late in the second half of the 19th century. Missionary work made little progress in the midst of the predominantly Muslim population. A vicariate was set up in 1921. The hierarchy was established in 1955. In recent years, the Church has promoted the role of women in society. Catholics have cordial relations with Muslims.

Malta*
Archd., 1; dioc., 1; abp., 3; bp., 1; parishes, 80; priests, 942 (491 dioc., 451 rel.); sem., 80; bros., 89; srs., 1,318; bap., 4,744; Caths., 368,000 (92%); tot. pop., 398,000.

Republic south of Sicily; capital, Valletta. Early catacombs and inscriptions are evidence of the early introduction of Christianity. St. Paul was shipwrecked on Malta in 60. Saracens controlled the islands from 870 to 1090, a period of difficulty for the Church. The line of bishops extends from 1090 to the present. Church-state conflict developed in recent years over passage of government-sponsored legislation affecting Catholic schools and Church-owned property. An agreement reached in 1985 ended the dispute and established a joint commission to study other Church-state problems.

Marshall Islands*
P.a., 1; parishes, 4; priests, 6 (rel.); p.d., 1; sem., 1; bros., 2; srs., 19; bap., 137; Caths., 4,000 (12.5%); tot. pop., 50,000.

Island republic in central Pacific Ocean; capital, Majura. Formerly administered by U.S. as part of U.N. Trust Territory of the Pacific; independent nation, 1991. An apostolic prefecture was erected May 25, 1993 (formerly part of Carolines-Marshall Diocese), with U.S. Jesuit Rev. James Gould as first apostolic prefect.

Martinique
Archd., 1; abp., 1; parishes, 47; priests, 64 (37 dioc., 27 rel.); p.d., 1; sem., 12; bros., 10; srs., 218; catechists, 2,007; bap., 4,122 Caths., 367,000 (87%); tot. pop., 409,000.

French overseas department in the West Indies; capital, Fort-de-France. Catholicism was introduced in the 16th century. The hierarchy was established in 1967. In 1998 the bishops joined their counterparts in Guadeloupe, French Guiana and Réunion to call slavery "an immense collective sin."

Mauritania*
Dioc., 1; bp.,1; parishes, 6; priests, 12 (2 dioc., 10 rel.); p.d., 1; srs., 37; bap., 18; Caths., 5,000 (.2%); tot. pop., 2,390,000. (AD)

Islamic republic on the northwest coast of Africa; capital, Nouakchott. With few exceptions, the Catholics in the country are foreign workers. At the 1994 Synod of Bishops for Africa, a bishop from Mauritania reported increasing problems with fundamentalist Muslims, but cautioned Church leaders against generalizing about Muslims.

Mauritius*

Dioc., 1; card., 1; bp., 1; parishes, 49; priests, 90 (57 dioc., 30 rel.); sem., 9; bros., 29; srs., 273; catechists, 807; bap., 6,285; Caths., 299,000 (26%); tot. pop., 1,150,000.

Island republic in the Indian Ocean; capital, Port Louis. Catholicism was introduced by Vincentians in 1722. Port Louis, made a vicariate in 1819 and a diocese in 1847, was a jumping-off point for missionaries to Australia, Madagascar and South Africa. During a 1989 visit to Mauritius, Pope John Paul II warned against sins that accompany its rapid economic development and booming tourism industry.

Mexico* (See Catholic Church in Mexico; see also Statistics of the Church in Mexico.)

Micronesia*

Dioc., 1; bp., 2; parishes, 20; priests, 41 (10 dioc., 31 rel.); p.d., 38; sem., 13; bros., 1; srs., 57; catechists, 572; bap., 1,835; Caths., 57,000 (52%); tot. pop., 111,000.

Federated States of Micronesia (Caroline archipelago) in southwest Pacific; capital, Palikir; former U.N. trust territory under U.S. administration; became independent nation September 1991. Effective evangelization began in the late 1880s. The government established diplomatic relations with the Holy See in 1994.

Moldova*

Dioc., 1; a.a., 1; parishes, 9; priests, 13 (6 dioc., 7 rel.); sem., 6; srs., 20; bap., 130; Caths., 20,000 (.34%); tot. pop., 4,310,000.

Independent republic, former constituent republic of the USSR; capital, Kishinev. The majority of people belong to the Orthodox Church. Catholics are mostly of Polish or German descent.

Monaco*

Archd., 1; abp., 1; parishes, 6; priests, 21 (13 dioc., 8 rel.); p.d., 1; sem., 6; bros., 1; srs., 22; bap., 280; Caths., 27,000 (90%); tot. pop., 30,000.

Constitutional monarchy, an enclave on the Mediterranean coast of France; capital, Monaco-Ville. Christianity was introduced before 1000. Catholicism is the official religion but freedom is guaranteed for all.

Mongolia*

Mission, 1; priests, 3 (rel.); sem., 3; bros., 1; srs., 11; bap., 22; Caths., 3,000 (.08%); tot. pop., 2,390,000.

Republic in north central Asia; formerly under communist control; capital Ulan Bator. Christianity was introduced by Oriental Orthodox. Some Franciscans were in the country in the 13th and 14th centuries, en route to China. Freedom of worship is guaranteed

under the new constitution, which went into effect in 1992. The government established relations with the Holy See in 1992 and indicated that missionaries would be welcome to help rebuild the country. The first Catholic parish was established in 1994, and by 1997 the Church had extended its work beyond the capital.

Morocco*

Archd., 2; abp., 3; parishes, 49; priests, 60 (15 dioc., 45 rel.); sem., 1; bros., 13; srs., 272; bap., 69; Caths., 25,000 (.09%); tot. pop., 27,310,000.

Constitutional monarchy in North Africa; capital, Rabat. Christianity was known in the area by the end of the third century. Bishops from Morocco attended a council at Carthage in 484. Catholic life survived under Visigoth and, from 700, Arab rule; later it became subject to influence from the Spanish, Portuguese and French. Islam is the state religion. The hierarchy was established in 1955. Pope John Paul II visited in 1985.

Mozambique

Archd., 3; dioc., 9; card., 1; abp. 3; bp., 11; parishes, 277; priests, 416 (88 dioc., 328 rel.); p.d., 1; sem., 281; bros., 90; srs., 881; catechists, 36,086; bap., 93,235; Caths., 3,087,000 (16.8%); tot. pop., 18,270,000. (AD)

Republic in southeast Africa; former Portuguese territory (independent, 1975); capital, Maputo (formerly Lourenco Marques). Christianity was introduced by Portuguese Jesuits about the middle of the 16th century. Evangelization continued from then until the 18th century, when it went into decline largely because of the Portuguese government's expulsion of the Jesuits. Conditions worsened in the 1830s, improved after 1881, but deteriorated again during the anticlerical period from 1910 to 1925. Conditions improved in 1940, the year Portugal concluded a new concordat with the Holy See and the hierarchy was established. Missionaries' outspoken criticism of Portuguese policies in Mozambique resulted in Church-state tensions in the years immediately preceding independence. The first two native bishops were ordained Mar. 9, 1975. Two ecclesiastical provinces were established in 1984. Mozambican bishops and members of the Rome-based Sant' Egidio Community were official mediators in the talks that ended 16 years of civil war in 1992. Since then, Church participation has flourished, with high attendance at Mass, a boom in vocations and active catechists at the parish level.

Myanmar

Archd., 3; dioc., 9; abp., 2; bp., 14; parishes, 263; priests, 476 (446 dioc., 30 rel.); sem., 254; bros., 76; srs., 1,116; catechists, 2,538; bap., 28,296; Caths., 559,000 (1.2%); tot. pop., 46,400,000. (AD)

Socialist republic in southeast Asia, formerly Burma; name changed to Myanmar in 1989; capital, Yangon (Rangoon). Christianity was introduced about 1500. Small-scale evangelization had limited results from the middle of the 16th century until the 1850s, when effective organization of the Church began. The hierarchy was established in 1955. Buddhism was declared the state religion in 1961, but the state is now officially secular. In 1965, Church schools and hospitals were nationalized. In 1966, all foreign missionaries who had entered the country for the first time after 1948 were forced to leave when the government refused to renew their work permits. The Church is involved primarily in pastoral and social activities.

Namibia* (South West Africa)

Archd., 1; dioc., 1; v.a., 1; abp., 1; bp., 2; parishes, 66; priests, 71 (13 dioc., 58 rel.); p.d., 41; sem., 28; bros., 36; srs., 288; catechists, 1,135; bap., 6,122; Caths., 275,000 (17%); tot. pop., 1,610,000. (AD)

Independent (Mar. 21, 1990) state in southern Africa; capital, Windhoek. The area shares the history of South Africa. The hierarchy was established in 1994. The Church is hindered by a lack of priests.

Nauru*

Parish, 1; priest, 1 (rel); p.d., 2; bros., 5; bap., 107; Caths., 4,000 (45%); tot. pop., 9,000.

Independent republic in western Pacific; capital, Yaren. Forms part of the Tarawa and Nauru Diocese (Kiribati). Established diplomatic relations with the Holy See in 1992.

Nepal*

P.a., 1; parishes, 21; priests, 42 (5 dioc.; 37 rel.); sem., 23; bros., 2; srs., 89; bap., 304; Caths., 6,000 (2.7%); tot. pop., 22,590,000.

Constitutional monarchy, the only Hindu kingdom in the world, in central Asia; capital, Katmandu. Little is known of the country before the 15th century. Some Jesuits passed through from 1628 and some sections were evangelized in the 18th century, with minimal results, before the country was closed to foreigners. Conversions from Hinduism, the state religion, are not recognized in law and are punishable by imprisonment.

Netherlands*

Archd., 1; dioc., 6; mil ord., 1; card., 2; abp., 2; bp., 20; parishes, 1,683; priests 4,263 (1,664 dioc., 2,599 rel.); p.d., 242; sem., 214; bros., 1,712; srs., 13,216; bap., 46,124; Caths., 5,590,000 (36.9%); tot. pop., 15,600,000.

Constitutional monarchy in northwestern Europe; capital, Amsterdam (seat of the government, The Hague). Evangelization, begun about the turn of the sixth century by Irish, Anglo-Saxon and Frankish missionaries, resulted in Christianization of the country by 800 and subsequent strong influence on The Lowlands. Invasion by French Calvinists in 572 brought serious losses to the Catholic Church and made the Reformed Church dominant. Catholics suffered a practical persecution of official repression and social handicap in the 17th century. The schism of Utrecht occurred in 1724. Only one-third of the population was Catholic in 1726. The Church had only a skeletal organization from 1702 to 1853, when the hierarchy was reestablished.

Despite this upturn, cultural isolation was the experience of Catholics until about 1914. From then on new vigor came into the life of the Church, and a whole new climate of interfaith relations began to develop. Before and for some years following the Second Vatican Council, the thrust and variety of thought and practice in the Dutch Church moved it to the vanguard position of "progressive" renewal. A synod of Dutch bishops held at the Vatican in January 1980 discussed ideological differences among Catholics with the aim of fostering unity and restoring some discipline within the nation's Church. However, even into the 1990s Church leaders spoke of a polarization among Catholics over issues such as sexual morality, ministries for women and priestly celibacy. The bishops also spoke out against permissive laws on euthanasia and assisted suicide.

Netherlands Antilles

Dioc., 1; bp., 1; parishes, 28; priests, 29 (13 dioc., 16 rel.); p.d., 1; sem., 6; bros., 7; srs., 60; bap., 2,736; Caths., 190,000 (82%); tot. pop., 230,000. (AD)

Autonomous part of The Netherlands. Consists of two groups of islands in the Caribbean; capital, Willemstad on Curacao. Christianity was introduced in the 16th century.

New Caledonia

Archd., 1; abp., 1; parishes, 28; priests, 44 (9 dioc., 35 rel.); p.d., 3; sem., 3; bros., 30; srs., 136; bap., 2,051; Caths., 110,000 (57.8%); tot. pop., 200,000.

French territory consisting of several islands in Oceania east of Queensland, Australia; capital, Noumea. Catholicism was introduced in 1843, nine years after Protestant missionaries began evangelization. A vicariate was organized in 1847. The hierarchy was established in 1966.

New Zealand*

Archd., 1; dioc., 5; mil. ord.; card., 1; abp., 1; bp., 10; parishes, 279; priests, 619 (369 dioc., 250 rel.); p.d., 1; sem., 34; bros., 180; srs., 1,183; bap., 8,217; Caths. 466,000 (14.1%); tot. pop., 3,760,000.

Parliamentary democracy in southwestern Pacific Ocean; capital, Wellington. Protestant missionaries were the first evangelizers. On North Island, Catholic missionaries started work before the establishment of two dioceses in 1848; their work among the Maoris was not organized until about 1881. On South Island, whose first resident priest arrived in 1840, a diocese was established in 1869. These three jurisdictions were joined in a province in 1896. The Marists were the predominant Catholic missionaries in the area. The first Maori bishop was named in 1988. In 1998, Pope John Paul II urged New Zealand's bishops not to allow the Church to fall prey to the practices and values of prevailing culture. However, the president of the bishops' conference used the same occasion to express the bishops' concern to the pope about inconsistency in the way the Vatican exercises its authority.

Nicaragua*

Archd., 1; dioc., 6; v.a., 1; card., 1; abp., 1; bp., 9; parishes, 223; priests, 411 (235 dioc., 176 rel.); p.d., 46; sem., 242; bros., 93; srs., 922; catechists, 6,491; bap., 66,944; Caths., 3,877,000 (89%); tot. pop., 4,350,000.

Republic in Central America: capital, Managua. Evangelization began shortly after the Spanish conquest, about 1524, and eight years later the first bishop took over jurisdiction of the Church in the country. Jesuits were leaders in missionary work during the colonial period, which lasted until the 1820s. Evangelization endeavor increased after establishment of the republic in 1838. In this century it was extended to the Atlantic coastal area, where Protestant missionaries began work about the middle of the 1900s.

Many Church leaders, clerical and lay, supported the aims but not necessarily all the methods of the revolution, which forced the resignation and flight July 17, 1979, of Anastasio Somoza, whose family had controlled the government since the early 1930s. During the Sandinista period that followed, four priests accepted government posts. Some Nicaraguan Catholics threw their energies behind the Sandinista program of land reform and socialism, forming what some called a "popular church'" based on liberation theology, whiles other strongly opposed the government. Managua Cardinal Miguel Obando Bravo helped mediate cease-fire talks during the war between the Sandinistas and U.S.-backed guerrillas. Land distribution, exacerbated by a wide gap in incomes, continued to be an issue, and in the late 1990s the Nicaraguan bishops continued to call for compromise between the government and former government officials. Despite an influx of aid after Hurricane Mitch killed more than 2,500 Nicaraguans and forced 900,000 to evacuate, Church leaders predicted an increase in poverty for the nation.

Niger*
Dioc., 1; bp., 1; parishes, 21; priests, 41 (4 dioc., 37 rel.); sem., 8; bros., 9; srs., 90; bap., 520; Caths., 19,000 (.2%); tot. pop., 9,790,000.

Republic in west central Africa; capital, Niamey. The first mission was set up in 1831. An apostolic prefecture was organized in 1942, and the first diocese was established in 1961. The country is predominantly Muslim. The Church is active in the fields of health and education.

Nigeria*
Archd., 9; dioc., 32; v.a., 3; p.a., 1; card., 1; abp., 10; bp., 41; parishes, 1,528; priests, 3,134 (2,494 dioc., 640 rel.); p.d., 6; sem., 3,888; bros., 428; srs., 2,968; catechists, 21,906; bap., 515,603; Caths., 13,483,000 (11%); tot. pop., 118,370,000.

Republic in West Africa; capital, Lagos. The Portuguese introduced Catholicism in the coastal region in the 15th century. Capuchins did some evangelization in the 17th century but systematic missionary work did not get under way along the coast until about 1840. A vicariate for this area was organized in 1870. A prefecture was set up in 1911 for missions in the northern part of the country, where Islam was strongly entrenched. From 1967, when Biafra seceded, until early in 1970 the country was torn by civil war. The hierarchy was established in 1950. Six dioceses were made metropolitan sees in 1994; four new dioceses were established as in 1995. Under the 1993-99 rule of Gen. Sani Abacha, Church leaders spoke out on behalf of human rights and democracy. After Abacha announced elections, the bishops said the country needed "new leading actors and fresh vision."

Northern Mariana Islands
Dioc., 1; bp., 1; parishes, 10; priests, 42 (14 dioc., 28 rel.); p.d., 2; sem., 5; bros., 5; srs., 29; bap., 1,018; Caths., 56,000 (88.8%); tot. pop., 63,000.

Commonwealth of Northern Mariana Islands, under U.S. sovereignty; formerly part of Trust Territory of Pacific Islands assigned to the U.S. in 1947. The Chalan Kanoa Diocese was established in 1984.

Norway*
Dioc., 1; prel., 2; bp., 4; parishes, 32; priests, 63 (23 dioc., 40 rel.); p.d., 3; sem., 11; bros., 4; srs., 214; bap., 682; Caths., 43,000 (.9%); tot. pop., 4,410,000.

Constitutional monarchy in northern Europe; capital, Oslo. Evangelization begun in the ninth century by missionaries from England and Ireland put the Church on a firm footing about the turn of the 11th century. The first diocese was set up in 1153 and development of the Church progressed until the Black Death in 1349 inflicted losses from which it never recovered. Lutheranism, introduced from outside in 1537 and furthered cautiously, gained general acceptance by about 1600 and was made the state religion. Legal and other measures crippled the Church, forcing priests to flee the country and completely disrupting normal activity. Changes for the better came in the 19th century, with the granting of religious liberty in 1845 and the repeal of many legal disabilities in 1897. Norway was administered as a single apostolic vicariate from 1892 to 1932, when it was divided into three jurisdictions.

Oman
Parishes, 4; priests, 7 (1 dioc., 6 rel.); bap., 220; Caths., 52,000 (24.6%); tot. pop., 2,400,000.

Independent monarchy in eastern corner of Arabian Peninsula; capital, Muscat. Under ecclesiastical jurisdiction of Arabia apostolic vicariate.

Pakistan*
Archd., 2; dioc., 4; abp., 3; bp., 5; parishes, 117; priests, 307 (151 dioc., 156 rel.); sem., 144; bros., 54; srs., 745; catechists, 498; bap., 18,984; Caths., 1,062,000 (.8%); tot. pop., 138,160,000.

Islamic republic in southwest Asia; capital, Islamabad. (Formerly included East Pakistan, which became the independent nation of Bangladesh in 1971.) Islam, firmly established in the eighth century, is the state religion. Christian evangelization of the native population began about the middle of the 19th century, years after earlier scattered attempts. The hierarchy was established in 1950. A series of death sentences against Christians accused of blasphemy resulted in acquittals during appeal processes, but in 1998 Bishop John Joseph of Faisalabad committed suicide to protest the strict blasphemy laws. Pakistani laws give more weight to Muslim witnesses than to non-Muslims and regulate interfaith marriages. In January 1999, Pakistan's upper house of parliament missed the deadline to act on a bill adopting Islamic law as Pakistan's legal code.

Palau*
Parishes, 1; priests 4 (2 dioc., 2 rel.); bro., 1; srs., 7; bap., 189; Caths., 8,000 (46%); tot. pop., 17,000.

Independent (1994) nation in western Pacific; capital, Koror; part of Caroline chain of Islands. Under ecclesiastical jurisdiction of diocese of Caroline Islands, Federated States of Micronesia.

Panama*

Archd., 1; dioc., 5; prel., 1; v.a., 1; abp., 3; bp., 11; parishes, 161; priests, 396 (166 dioc., 230 rel.); p.d., 55; sem., 125; bros., 52; srs., 559; catechists, 3,354; bap., 37,766; Caths., 2,349,000 (86.5%); tot. pop., 2,720,000.

Republic in Central America; capital, Panama City. Catholicism was introduced by Franciscan missionaries and evangelization started in 1514. The Panama Diocese, oldest in the Americas, was set up at the same time. The Catholic Church has favored status and state aid for missions, charities and parochial schools, but religious freedom is guaranteed to all religions. In May 1989, Panama's bishops accused the government of thwarting the presidential elections and of attempting to intimidate the Church. The elections' legitimate leader, Guillermo Endara, temporarily sought refuge at the Vatican embassy in Panama City. After increasing unrest and violence, on Dec. 24, 1989, the country's dictator, Gen. Manuel Noriega, sought refuge at the Vatican Embassy. Ten days later, after U.S. troops spent days blasting the embassy with loud rock music and after meetings with Church diplomatic officials, Noriega surrendered.

Papua New Guinea*

Archd., 4; dioc., 14; abp., 6; bp., 15; parishes, 374; priests, 518 (136 dioc., 382 rel.); p.d., 9; sem., 312; bros., 300; srs., 842; catechists, 2,515; bap., 43,193; Caths., 1,474,000 (35%); tot. pop., 4,210,000.

Independent (Sept. 16, 1975) republic (formerly under Australian administration) in southwest Pacific; capital, Port Moresby. Marists began evangelization about 1844 but were handicapped by many factors, including "spheres of influence" laid out for Catholic and Protestant missionaries. An apostolic prefecture was set up in 1896 and placed in charge of the Divine Word Missionaries. The territory suffered greatly during World War II. Hierarchy was established for New Guinea and adjacent islands in 1966. A decade-long war that began in the Bougainville area in the late 1980s left many churches, schools and health centers destroyed. At the end of the century, the Church fought social disintegration marked by violence, poverty and corruption.

Paraguay*

Archd., 1; dioc., 10; v.a., 2; mil. ord. 1; abp., 3; bp., 17; parishes, 323; priests, 659 (248 dioc., 411 rel.); p.d., 91; sem., 290; bros., 117; srs., 1,262; bap., 100,908; catechists, 21,600; Caths., 4,432,000 (87%); tot. pop., 5,090,000.

Republic in central South America; capital, Asunción. Catholicism was introduced in 1542, evangelization began almost immediately. A diocese erected in 1547 was occupied for the first time in 1556. On many occasions thereafter, dioceses in the country were left unoccupied because of political and other reasons. Jesuits who came into the country after 1609 devised the reductions system for evangelizing the Indians, teaching them agriculture, husbandry, trades and other arts, and giving them experience in property use and community life. The reductions were communes of Indians only, an average population of 3,000-4,000, under the direction of the missionaries. At their peak, some 30 reductions had a population of 100,000. Political officials regarded

the reductions with disfavor because they did not control them and feared that the Indians trained in them might foment revolt and upset the established colonial system under Spanish control. The reductions lasted until about 1768, when the Jesuits were expelled from Latin America.

Church-state relations following independence from Spain in 1811 were often tense because of government efforts to control the Church through continued exercise of Spanish patronage rights and by other means. The Church as well as the whole country suffered during the War of the Triple Alliance from 1865-70. After that time, the Church had the same kind of experience in Paraguay as in the rest of Latin America, with forces of liberalism, anticlericalism, massive educational needs, poverty, a shortage of priests and other personnel.

In the 1980s, Church-state tensions increased as Catholic leaders spoke out against President Alfredo Stroessner's decades of one-man rule. A 1988 papal visit seemed to increase the Church's confidence, as bishops repeatedly spoke out against him. The army general who overthrew Stroessner in 1989 said he did so in part to defend the Catholic Church.

Peru*

Archd., 7; dioc., 18; prel., 11; v.a., 8; mil. ord. 1; card., 1; abp., 12; bp., 48; parishes, 1,401; priests, 2,505 (1,302 dioc., 1,203 rel.); p.d., 69; sem., 2,056; bros., 550; srs., 5,390; catechists, 38,897; bap., 368,684; Caths., 22,043,000 (90.4%); tot. pop., 24,370,000.

Republic on the west coast of South America; capital, Lima. An effective diocese became operational in 1537, five years after the Spanish conquest. Evangelization, already under way, developed for some time after 1570 but deteriorated before the end of the colonial period in the 1820s. The first native-born saint of the new world was a Peruvian, Rose of Lima, a Dominican tertiary who died in 1617 and was canonized in 1671.

In the new republic founded after the wars of independence the Church experienced problems of adjustment, government efforts to control it through continuation of the patronage rights of the Spanish crown; suppression of houses of religious and expropriation of Church property; religious indifference and outright hostility. In the 20th century, liberation theology was born in Peru under the leadership of Father Gustavo Gutierrez. In the 1980s and early 1990s, the Maoist Sendero Luminoso guerrillas often targeted Church workers, who also found themselves prone to false charges of terrorism. A Peruvian cardinal was credited with much of the success of an early 1990s government effort to win the surrender of the rebels. When the government initiated a drastic economic program in 1990, Peruvian Church leaders worked to help feed and clothe the poor. In the late '90s, the Church successfully fought a government program of sterilization.

Philippines*

Archd., 16; dioc., 50; prel., 6; v.a., 7; mil. ord. 1; card., 3; abp., 18; bp., 93; parishes, 2,664; priests, 6,997 (4,664 dioc., 2,333 rel.); p.d., 6; sem., 7,618; bros., 625; srs., 9,676; catechists, 76,227; bap.,

1,712,736; Caths., 61,109,000 (83.1%); tot. pop., 73,530,000.

Republic, an archipelago of 7,000 islands off the southeast coast of Asia; capital, Manila. Systematic evangelization was begun in 1564 and resulted in firm establishment of the Church by the 19th century.

During the period of Spanish rule, which lasted from the discovery of the islands by Magellan in 1521 to 1898, the Church experienced difficulties with the patronage system under which the Spanish crown tried to control ecclesiastical affairs through episcopal and other appointments. This system ended in 1898 when the United States gained possession of the islands and instituted a policy of separation of Church and state. Anticlericalism flared late in the 19th century. The Aglipayan schism, an attempt to set up a nationalist Church, occurred in 1902.

Church leaders and human rights groups constantly criticized abuses under former president and dictator Ferdinand Marcos. Church newspapers were among those censored or closed after he declared martial law, and religious and lay people were arrested and held without formal charges for long periods of time. After Marcos declared himself the victor in the 1986 elections and international observers declared his win a fraud, the Philippine bishops' call for a nonviolent struggle for justice was seen as the catalyst for the nation's "people power" revolution. Corazon Aquino, Marcos' successor, took refuge with Carmelite nuns during the revolution. In the late 20th century, Church workers often found themselves unintentional victims in violence spurred by Muslim separatists' fight for autonomy in the southern Philippines. Church social action focused on the poor, overseas workers, ecology and a fight against the death penalty.

Poland*

Archd., 15; dioc., 26; mil. ord., 1; ordinariate, 1; cards., 5; abps., 16; bps., 96; parishes, 9,723; priests, 26,435 (20,485 dioc., 5,950 rel.); p.d., 32; sem., 6,762; bros., 1,409; srs., 25,554; catechists, 11,413; bap., 410,749; Caths., 36,874,000 (95.5%); tot. pop., 38,650,000.

Republic in eastern Europe; capital, Warsaw. The first traces of Christianity date from the second half of the ninth century. Its spread was accelerated by the union of the Slavs in the 10th century. The first diocese was set up in 968. Some tensions with the Orthodox were experienced. The Reformation, supported mainly by city dwellers and the upper classes, peaked from about the middle of the 16th century, resulting in numerous conversions to Lutheranism, the Reformed Church and the Bohemian Brethren. A successful Counter-Reformation, with the Jesuits in a position of leadership, was completed by about 1632. The movement served a nationalist as well as religious purpose; in restoring religious unity to a large degree, it united the country against potential invaders, the Swedes, Russians and Turks. The Counter-Reformation had bad side effects, leading to the repression of Protestants long after it was over and to prejudice against Orthodox who returned to allegiance with Rome in 1596 and later. The Church, in the same manner as the entire country, was adversely affected by the partitions of the 18th and 19th centuries. Russification hurt the Eastern- and Latin-rite Catholics.

In the republic established after World War I the Church reorganized itself, continued to serve as a vital force in national life, and enjoyed generally harmonious relations with the state. Progressive growth was strong until 1939, when German and Russian forces invaded and World War II began. In 1945, seven years before the adoption of a Soviet-type of constitution, the communist-controlled government initiated a policy that included a constant program of atheistic propaganda; a strong campaign against the hierarchy and clergy; the imprisonment in 1948 of 700 priests and even more religious; rigid limitation on the activities of the Catholic press and religious movements.

Regular contacts on a working level were initiated by the Vatican and Poland in 1974; regular diplomatic relations were established in 1989. Cardinal Karol Wojtyla of Cracow was elected to the papacy in 1978. Church and papal support was strong for the independent labor movement, Solidarity, which was recognized by the government in August 1980, but outlawed in December 1981, when martial law was imposed (martial law was suspended in 1982). In May 1989, following recognition of Solidarity and a series of political changes, the Catholic Church was given legal status for the first time since the communists took control of the government in 1944. In 1990, a new constitution was adopted declaring Poland a democratic state. In 1992, the pope restructured the Church in Poland, adding 13 new dioceses. A new concordat between the Polish government and the Holy See was signed in 1993.

Since the end of communist rule, Poland's Church has struggled with anti-Semitism among some clergy. A dispute over a Carmelite convent outside the former Nazi death camp at Auschwitz resulted in the convent's removal, but several years later the Church was forced to speak against Catholic protesters who posted hundreds of crosses outside the camp. A nearly eight-year national synod process concluded in 1999 with calls for priests to live less luxurious lifestyles and to keep parishes finances open. The Polish Church continued to be a source of missionary priests in more than 90 countries.

Portugal*

Patriarchate (Lisbon), 1; archd., 2; dioc., 17; mil. ord., 1; abp., 7; bp., 38; parishes, 4,359; priests, 4,249 (3,273 dioc., 976 rel.); p.d., 197; sem., 617; bros., 344; srs., 6,943; catechists, 57,968; bap., 102,518; Caths., 9,026,000 (92%); tot. pop., 9,800,000.

Republic in the western part of the Iberian peninsula; capital, Lisbon. Christianity was introduced before the fourth century. From the fifth century to early in the eighth century the Church experienced difficulties from the physical invasion of barbarians and the intellectual invasion of doctrinal errors in the forms of Arianism, Priscillianism and Pelagianism. The Church survived under the rule of Arabs from about 711 and of the Moors until 1249. Ecclesiastical life was fairly vigorous from 1080 to 1185, and monastic influence became strong. A decline set in about 1450. Several decades later Portugal became the jumping-off place for many missionaries to newly discovered colonies. The Reformation had little effect in the country.

In the early 1700s, King John V broke relations with

Rome and required royal approval of papal acts. His successor, Joseph I, expelled the Jesuits from Portugal and the colonies. Liberal revolutionaries with anti-Church policies made the 19th century a difficult one for the Church. Similar policies prevailed in Church-state relations in the 20th century until the accession of Premier Antonio de Oliveira Salazar to power in 1928; the hierarchy was seen as closely aligned with him. In 1940 Salazar concluded a concordat with the Holy See that regularized Church-state relations but still left the Church in a subservient condition.

In 1930, after lengthy investigation, the Church authorized devotion to Our Lady of Fátima, who appeared to three Portuguese children in 1917. In 1971 several priests were tried for subversion for speaking out against colonialism and for taking part in guerrilla activities in Angola. A military coup of Apr. 25, 1974, ended the dictatorship and led to democratic socialism. Pope John Paul II, who credited Our Lady of Fátima with saving his life during a 1981 assassination attempt on her feast day, visited Portugal several times. In the early 1980s, he urged Portuguese priests and laity to heal their growing split.

Puerto Rico
Archd., 1; dioc., 4; card., 1; bp., 9; parishes, 324; priests, 786 (396 dioc., 390 rel.); p.d., 390; sem., 95; bros., 77; srs., 1,167; catechists, 7,242; bap., 40,412; Caths., 3,091,000 (82.6%); tot. pop., 3,740,000. (AD)

A U.S. commonwealth, the smallest of the Greater Antilles, 885 miles southeast of the southern coast of Florida; capital, San Juan. Following its discovery by Columbus in 1493, the island was evangelized by Spanish missionaries and remained under Spanish ecclesiastical as well as political control until 1898, when it became a possession of the United States. The original diocese, San Juan, was erected in 1511. The present hierarchy was established in 1960.

Qatar
Parish, 1; priest, 1 (dioc.); p.d., 1; bap., 89; Caths., 60,000 (10.5%); tot. pop., 570,000.

Independent state in the Persian Gulf; capital, Doha. Under ecclesiastical jurisdiction of Arabia apostolic vicariate.

Réunion
Dioc., 1; bp., 1; parishes, 76; priests, 103 (57 dioc., 46 rel.); p.d., 6; sem., 24; bros., 33; srs., 377; catechists, 550; bap., 10,984; Caths., 560,000 (83.5%); tot. pop., 670,000. (AD)

French overseas department, 450 miles east of Madagascar; capital, Saint-Denis. Catholicism was introduced in 1667 and some intermittent missionary work was done through the rest of the century. An apostolic prefecture was organized in 1712. Vincentians began work there in 1817 and were joined later by Holy Ghost Fathers. In 1998 the bishops joined their counterparts in Guadeloupe, French Guiana and Martinique to call slavery "an immense collective sin."

Romania*
Archd., 3; dioc., 8; ord., 1; card., 1; abp., 8; bp., 9; parishes, 1,628; priests, 1,590 (1,425 dioc., 165 rel.); p.d., 3; sem., 911; bros., 180; srs., 1,196; bap., 10,671; Caths., 2,572,000 (11.7%); tot. pop., 22,570,000.

Republic in southeastern Europe; capital, Bucharest. Latin Christianity, introduced in the third century, all but disappeared during the barbarian invasions. The Byzantine rite was introduced by the Bulgars about the beginning of the eighth century and established firm roots. It eventually became Orthodox, but a large number of its adherents returned later to union with Rome.

Communists took over the government following World War II, forced the abdication of Michael I in 1947, and enacted a Soviet type of constitution in 1952. By that time a campaign against religion was already in progress. In 1948 the government denounced a concordat concluded in 1929, nationalized all schools and passed a law on religions that resulted in the disorganization of Church administration. The 1.5 million-member Romanian Byzantine-rite Church, by government decree, was incorporated into the Romanian Orthodox Church, and Catholic properties were given to the Orthodox. Five of the six Latin-rite bishops were immediately disposed of by the government, and the last was sentenced to 18 years' imprisonment in 1951. Religious orders were suppressed in 1949.

Some change for the better in Church-state relations was reported after the middle of the summer of 1964, although restrictions were still in effect. The Eastern Church regained liberty in 1990 with the change of government. The hierarchy was restored and diplomatic relations with the Holy See were re-established. Today, most Latin-rite Catholics are ethnic Hungarians residing in Transylvania.

Pope John Paul II visited Romania May 7-9, 1999, but remained in Bucharest; he split time between visits with Catholics and Orthodox and did not visit Transylvania, despite an invitation from the region's bishops. To facilitate the visit, Eastern Catholics gave up their demands for the return of all former Church properties and agreed to work on committees with Orthodox to discuss each case individually.

Russia*
A.a., 2 (1 for European Russia, 2 for Siberia); ap. ex., 1; abp., 2; bp., 1; parish, 276; priests, 225 (83 dioc., 142 rel.); p.d., 1; sem., 103; bros., 5; srs 287; bap., 1,364; Caths., 351,000; tot. pop., 147,100,000.

Federation in Europe and Asia; capital, Moscow. The Orthodox Church has been predominant in Russian history. It developed from the Byzantine Church before 1064. Some of its members subsequently established communion with Rome as the result of reunion movements, but most remained Orthodox. The government has always retained some kind of general or particular control of this Church.

From the beginning of the Communist government in 1917, all churches of whatever kind became the targets of official campaigns designed to negate their influence on society and/or to eliminate them entirely. An accurate assessment of the situation of the Catholic Church in Russia was difficult to make. Research by a Polish priest, reported in 1998, documented the arrests , trials and fabricated confessions of priests in the 1920s and 1930s. A team of research specialists made public by the Judiciary Committee of the U.S. House of Representatives in 1964 said: "The fate of the Catholic Church in the USSR and countries occupied by the

Russians from 1917 to 1959 shows the following: (a) the number killed: 55 bishops; 12,800 priests and monks; 2.5 million Catholic believers; (b) imprisoned or deported: 199 bishops; 32,000 priests and 10 million believers; (c) 15,700 priests were forced to abandon their priesthood and accept other jobs; and (d) a large number of seminaries and religious communities were dissolved; 1,600 monasteries were nationalized, 31,779 churches were closed. 400 newspapers were prohibited, and all Catholic organizations were dissolved." Several Latin-rite churches were open in places like Moscow, Leningrad, Odessa and Tiflis. Despite repression, Lithuania and Ukraine remained strongholds of Catholicism.

During his 1985-91 presidency, Soviet President Mikhail Gorbachev met twice with Pope John Paul II — meetings later credited with the return of religious freedom in the Soviet Union. In 1991, the pope established two Latin-rite apostolic administrations in the Russian Republic: one in Moscow and one based in Novosibirsk, Siberia. Siberia was split again in 1999, with the new administration based in Irkutsk.

Catholic communities in Europe and the United States have been instrumental in helping to rebuild the Church in Russia. Under a 1997 religion law, every religious organization in Russia had to register on a national level, then re-register each parish by the end of 1999 to enjoy full legal benefits such as owning property and publishing religious literature. The apostolic administrations registered with no problems, but in 1999 the Russian government rejected a registration application by the Jesuits.

Rwanda*

Archd., 1; dioc., 8; abp., 2; bp., 10; parishes, 132; priests, 415 (284 dioc., 131 rel.); p.d., 1; sem., 230; bros., 165; srs., 1,084; catechists, 3,303; bap., 105,317; Caths., 3,322,000 (56%); tot. pop., 5,880,000.

Republic in east central Africa; capital, Kigali. Catholicism was introduced about the turn of the 20th century. The hierarchy was established in 1959. Intertribal warfare between the ruling Hutus (90 percent of the population) and the Tutsis (formerly the ruling aristocracy) plagued the country for a number of years. In April 1994, the deaths of the presidents of Rwanda and Burundi in a suspicious plane crash sparked the outbreak of a ferocious civil war. Among the thousands of victims — mostly Tutsis — were three bishops and about 25 percent of the clergy. Many more thousands fled the country.

Although in 1996 Pope John Paul II said that all members of the Church who participated in the genocide must face the consequences, in 1997 the Vatican donated $50,000 to help ensure certain people — including priests and religious — received fair trials. In 1999, after the arrest of a bishop, the Vatican accused Rwanda of "a real and true defamatory campaign against the Catholic Church."

Saint Lucia*

Archd., 1; abp., 1; parishes, 23; priests, 31 (17 dioc., 14 rel.); p.d., 8; bros., 4; srs., 50; catechists, 344; bap., 2,336; Caths., 115,000 (78%); tot. pop., 147,000.

Independent (Feb. 22, 1979) island state in West Indies; capital, Castries.

Saint Vincent and the Grenadines*

Dioc., 1; bp., 1; parishes, 6; priests, 9 (5 dioc., 4 rel.); bros., 2; srs., 12; catechists, 62; bap., 168; Caths., 10,000 (9%); tot. pop., 106,000.

Independent state (1979) in West Indies; capital, Kingstown. The Kingstown diocese (St. Vincent) was established in 1989; it was formerly part of Bridgetown-Kingstown Diocese with see in Barbados. The Vatican established diplomatic relations with St. Vincent and the Grenadines in 1990. The Church is recognized for its role in education and health care.

Samoa, American

Dioc., 1; bp., 1; parishes, 10; priests, 10 (9 dioc., 1 rel.); p.d., 19; sem., 11; srs., 14; bap., 386; Caths., 10,000 (16%); tot. pop., 56,000.

Unincorporated U.S. territory in southwestern Pacific, consisting of six small islands; seat of government, Pago Pago on the Island of Tutuila. Samoa-Pago Pago Diocese established in 1982.

Samoa, Western*

Archd., 1; card., 1; parishes, 28; priests, 40 (24 dioc., 16 rel.); p.d., 15; sem., 13; bros., 19; srs., 76; catechists, 765; bap., 1,519; Caths., 37,000 (18.5%); tot. pop., 170,000.

Independent state in the southwestern Pacific; capital, Apia. Catholic missionary work began in 1845. Most of the missions now in operation were established by 1870 when the Catholic population numbered about 5,000. Additional progress was made in missionary work from 1896. The first Samoan priest was ordained in 1892. A diocese was established in 1966; elevated to a metropolitan see in 1982.

San Marino

Parishes, 13; priests, 28 (9 dioc., 19 rel.); p.d. 1; bro. 2; srs 23; bap, 270; Caths., 26,000 (96%); tot, pop., 26,000.

Republic, a 24-square-mile enclave in northeastern Italy; capital, San Marino. The date of initial evangelization is not known, but a diocese was established by the end of the third century. Ecclesiastically, it forms part of the Diocese of San Marino-Montefeltro in Italy.

São Tome and Principe*

Dioc., 1; bp., 1; parishes, 12; priests, 12 (rel.); sem. 8; bros., 3; srs., 39; catechists, 376; bap., 2,738; Caths., 104,000 (83%); tot. pop., 126,000.

Independent republic (July 12, 1975), consisting of two islands off the western coast of Africa in the Gulf of Guinea; former Portuguese territory; capital, São Tome. Evangelization was begun by the Portuguese who discovered the islands in 1471-72. The São Tome Diocese was established in 1534. In a 1992 visit to São Tome, a major transport center for slaves until the mid-1800s, Pope John Paul II condemned slavery as "a cruel offense" to African dignity.

Saudi Arabia

Priests, 6 (1 dioc., 5 rel.); srs. 16.; bap., 514.

Monarchy occupying four-fifths of Arabian peninsula; capital, Riyadh. Population is Muslim; all other religions are banned. Christians in the area are workers from other countries. The Church falls under the ecclesiastical jurisdiction of Arabia apostolic vicariate. In May 1999, Pope John Paul II met with the crown prince of Saudi Arabia at the Vatican

Scotland

Archd., 2; dioc., 6; card., 1; abp., 1; bp., 6; parishes, 459; priests, 847 (677 dioc., 170 rel.); p.d., 17; sem., 56; bros., 272; srs., 756; bap., 10,733; Caths., 700,075 (15%); tot. pop., 4,662,900. (Figures from 1999 Annuario Pontificio.)

Part of the United Kingdom, in the northern British Isles; capital, Edinburgh. Christianity was introduced by the early years of the fifth century. St. Ninian's arrival in 397 marked the beginning of Christianity in Scotland. The arrival of St. Columba and his monks in 563 inaugurated a new era of evangelization that reached into remote areas by the end of the sixth century. He was extremely influential in determining the character of the Church, which was tribal, monastic, and in union with Rome. Considerable disruption of Church activity resulted from Scandinavian invasions in the late eighth and ninth centuries. By 1153 the Scottish Church took a turn away from its insularity and was drawn into closer contact with the European community. Anglo-Saxon religious and political relations, complicated by rivalries between princes and ecclesiastical superiors, were not always the happiest.

From shortly after the Norman Conquest of England to 1560 the Church suffered adverse effects from the Hundred Years' War, the Black Death, the Western Schism and other developments. In 1560 Parliament abrogated papal supremacy over the Church in Scotland and committed the country to Protestantism in 1567. The Catholic Church was proscribed, to remain that way for more than 200 years, and the hierarchy was disbanded. Defections made the Church a minority religion from that time on. Presbyterian Church government was ratified in 1690. Priests launched the Scottish Mission in 1653, incorporating themselves as a mission body under an apostolic prefecture and working underground to serve the faithful in much the same way their confreres did in England. About 100 native priests, trained in clandestine places in the heather country, were ordained by the early 19th century. Catholics got some relief from legal disabilities in 1793 and more relief later. Many left the country about that time. Some of their numbers were filled subsequently by immigrants from Ireland. The hierarchy was restored in 1878. Scotland, though predominantly Protestant, has a better record for tolerance than Northern Ireland. In a 1997 message to celebrations marking 1,600 years of Christianity in Scotland, Pope John Paul II urged Catholics to make new efforts at evangelization and ecumenism.

Senegal*

Archd., 1; dioc., 5; card., 1; arbp., 1; bp., 6; parishes, 86; priests, 348 (200 dioc., 148 rel.); sem., 188; bros., 151; srs., 657; catechists, 1,856; bap., 14,317; Caths., 593,000 (6.7%); tot. pop., 8,800,000.

Republic in West Africa; capital, Dakar. The country had its first contact with Catholicism through the Portuguese some time after 1460. Some incidental missionary work was done by Jesuits and Capuchins in the 16th and 17th centuries. A vicariate for the area was placed in charge of the Holy Ghost Fathers in 1779. More effective evangelization efforts were accomplished after the Senegambia vicariate was erected in 1863; the hierarchy was established in 1955. During a 1992 trip to the predominantly Muslim country, Pope John Paul II praised the small Catholic community for its contributions, especially in the areas of health care and education.

Seychelles*

Dioc., 1; bp., 2; parishes, 17; priests, 15 (11 dioc., 4 rel.); sem., 1; bros., 3; srs., 59; catechists, 367; bap., 1,290; Caths., 70,000 (89%); tot. pop., 78,000.

Independent (1976) group of 92 islands in the Indian Ocean; capital, Victoria. Catholicism was introduced in the 18th century. An apostolic vicariate was organized in 1852. All education in the islands was conducted under Catholic auspices until 1954. In 1991, Bishop Felix Paul of Port Victoria said the country's one-party socialist government was an affront to the rights and dignity of its people, but President France-Albert René continued to lead the government into the 21st century. Pope John Paul II has warned Seychelles to beware of the dark side of tourism, a main industry in the country.

Sierra Leone*

Archd., 1; dioc., 2; abp., 2; bp., 2; parishes, 37; priests, 122 (52 dioc., 70 rel.); sem., 73; bros., 38; srs., 62; bap., 2,477; Caths., 138,000 (3%); tot. pop., 4,430,000.

Republic on the west coast of Africa; capital, Freetown. Catholicism was introduced in 1858. Members of the African Missions Society, the first Catholic missionaries in the area, were joined by Holy Ghost Fathers in 1864. Protestant missionaries were active in the area before their Catholic counterparts. Educational work had a major part in Catholic endeavor. The hierarchy was established in 1950. Most of the inhabitants are followers of traditional African religions.

Church leaders suffered at the hands of rebel soldiers in the late 1990s, when a military coup ousted the country's democratically elected government. Although some Church workers fled to neighboring Guinea, some remained. Rebels kidnapped several foreign missionaries and, shortly before West African intervention forces ousted them from power in 1998, they forced the archbishop of Freetown to strip naked while they plundered his office. After the war, at a grass-roots level, the Church began working toward reconciliation.

Singapore*

Archd., 1; abp., 1; parishes, 30; priests, 132 (77 dioc., 55 rel.); sem., 30; bros., 52; srs., 233; catechists, 1,247; bap., 3,760; Caths., 140,000 (3.7%); tot. pop., 3,740,000.

Independent island republic off the southern tip of the Malay Peninsula; capital, Singapore. Christianity was introduced in the area by Portuguese colonists about 1511. Singapore was founded in 1819; the first parish Church was built in 1846. Freedom of religion is generally respected, although in the late 1980s, nearly a dozen people involved in Catholic social work were arrested and detained without trial under the Internal Security Act.

Slovakia*

Archd., 2; dioc., 5; ap. ex., 1; card., 2; abp., 2; bp., 12; parishes, 1,440; priests, 2,255 (1,752 dioc., 503 rel.); p.d., 7; sem., 1,126; bros., 202; srs., 3,101; catechists, 2,185; bap., 50,375; Caths., 3,571,000 (66.3%); tot. pop., 5,380,000.

Independent state (Jan. 1, 1993); formerly part of Czechoslovakia; capital, Bratislava. Christianity was introduced in Slovakia in the eighth century by Irish and German missionaries, and the area was under the jurisdiction of German bishops. In 863, Sts. Cyril and Methodius began pastoral and missionary work in the region, ministering to the people in their own language. A diocese established at Nitra in 880 had a continuous history except for a century ending in 1024. The Church in Slovakia was severely tested by the Reformation and political upheavals. After World War I, when it became part of the Republic of Czechoslovakia, it was 75 percent Catholic.

Vigorous persecution of the Church began in Slovakia in 1944, when communists mounted an offensive against bishops, priests and religious. In 1945, Church schools were nationalized, youth organizations were disbanded, the Catholic press was curtailed, the training of seminarians was seriously impeded. Msgr. Josef Tiso, a Catholic priest who served as president of the Slovak Republic from 1939-45, was tried for "treason" in December 1946 and was executed the following April.

In 1972, the government ordered the removal of nuns from visible but limited apostolates to farms and mental hospitals. In 1973, the government allowed the ordination of three bishops in the Slovak region. Reports from Slovakia late in the same year stated that authorities there had placed severe restrictions on the education of seminarians and the work of priests.

When Slovakia split from Czechoslovakia in 1993, the country slid into economic difficulties. Church-state tensions increased, and the Slovakian government eventually apologized to Bishop Rudolf Balaz of Banska Bystrica, whose house had been raided in a government investigation of stolen art. In an attempt to fight the effects of decades of communism, in 1996 the bishops said all adult Catholics who had not received confirmation must undergo a special two-year catechism course. In 1998 Pope John Paul II encouraged the bishops to continue their efforts at adult formation in the faith.

Slovenia*

Archd., 1; dioc., 2; abp., 3; bp., 6; parishes, 801; priests, 1,137 (836 dioc., 301 rel.); p.d., 7; sem., 177; bros., 45; srs., 805; bap., 15,758; Caths., 1,629,000 (81.7%); tot. pop., 1,990,000.

Independent republic (1991) in southeastern Europe; formerly part of Yugoslavia; capital, Ljubljana. Established diplomatic relations with the Holy See in 1992. After independence, Church leaders found themselves in repeated skirmishes with Slovenia's governing coalition over religious education, restitution of Church property and the Church's proper social role.

Solomon Islands*

Archd., 1; dioc., 2; abp., 1; bp., 3; parishes, 29; priests, 51 (19 dioc., 32 rel.); sem., 37; bros., 14; srs., 111; catechists, 1,047; bap., 2,568; Caths., 78,000 (19.2%); tot. pop., 400,000.

Independent (July 7, 1978) island group in Oceania; capital, Honiara, on Guadalcanal. After violence interrupted the Marists' evangelization of the Southern Solomons, they resumed their work in 1898. An apostolic vicariate was organized in 1912. A similar jurisdiction was set up for the Western Solomons in 1959. World War II caused a great deal of damage to mission installations.

Somalia

Dioc., 1; parish, 1; priests, 5 (1 dioc., 4 rel.); bro., 1; srs., 4; Caths., 200; tot. pop., 10,220,000. (AD)

Republic on the eastern coast of Africa; capital, Mogadishu. The country has been Muslim for centuries. Pastoral activity has been confined to immigrants. Schools and hospitals were nationalized in 1972, resulting in the departure of some foreign missionaries.

South Africa*

Archd., 4; dioc., 21; v.a., 1; mil. ord., 1; abp., 4; bp., 28; parishes, 746; priests, 1,147 (398 dioc., 749 rel.); p.d., 187; sem., 419; bros., 215; srs., 2,964; catechists, 11,210; bap., 53,525; Caths., 3,104,000 (7.1%); tot. pop., 43,340,000.

Republic in the southern part of Africa; capitals, Cape Town (legislative), Pretoria (administrative) and Bloemfontein (judicial). Christianity was introduced by the Portuguese who discovered the Cape of Good Hope in 1488. Boers, who founded Cape Town in 1652, expelled Catholics from the region. There was no Catholic missionary activity from that time until the 19th century. After a period of British opposition, a bishop established residence in 1837, and evangelization got under way thereafter among the Bantus and white immigrants. The hierarchy was established in 1951.

Under South Africa's apartheid regime, the Church found itself the victim of attacks, from the parish level to the headquarters of the bishops' conference in Pretoria. Some Church leaders were detained, tortured and deported, particularly in the 1970s and 1980s. However, in a 1997 statement to South Africa's Truth Commission, the Catholic Church said its complicity with apartheid was in "acts of omission rather than commission. "Since the end of apartheid, Catholic leaders have spoken out against an increase in violence and anti-Muslim sentiment.

Spain*

Archd., 14; dioc., 53; mil. ord., 1; card., 6; abp., 21; bp., 92; parishes, 22,102; priests, 28,237 (18,976 dioc., 9,261 rel.); p.d., 210; sem., 2,861; bros., 5,369; srs., 63,139; catechists, 78,368; bap., 295,119; Caths., 36,790,000 (93.5%); tot. pop., 39,320,000.

Constitutional monarchy on the Iberian peninsula in southwestern Europe; capital, Madrid. Christians were on the peninsula by 200; some of them suffered martyrdom during persecutions of the third century. A council held in Elvira about 305 enacted the first legislation on clerical celibacy in the West. Vandals invaded the peninsula in the fifth century, bringing with them an Arian brand of Christianity that they retained until their conversion following the baptism of their king, Reccared, in 589.

In the seventh century, Toledo was the established as the primatial see. The Visigoth kingdom lasted to the time of the Arab invasion, 711-14. The Church survived under Muslim rule but experienced some doctrinal and disciplinary irregularities as well as harassment. Reconquest of most of the peninsula was accomplished by 1248; unification was achieved during the reign of Ferdinand and Isabella. The discoveries of Columbus and other explorers ushered in an era of colonial expansion in which Spain became one of the greatest mission-sending countries in history. In 1492, in repetition of anti-Semitic actions of 694, the expulsion of unbaptized Jews was decreed, leading to mass baptisms but a questionable number of real conversions in 1502. Activity by the Inquisition followed. Spain was not seriously affected by the Reformation. Ecclesiastical decline set in about 1650.

Anti-Church actions authorized by a constitution enacted in 1812 resulted in the suppression of religious and other encroachments on the leaders, people and goods of the Church. Political, religious and cultural turmoil recurred during the 19th century and into the 20th. A revolutionary republic was proclaimed in 1931, triggering a series of developments that led to civil war from 1936 to 1939. During the conflict, which pitted leftist Loyalists against the forces of Francisco Franco, more than 6,600 priests and religious and an unknown number of lay people were massacred. One-man, one-party rule, established after the civil war and with rigid control policies with respect to personal liberties and social and economic issues, continued for more than 35 years before giving way after the death of Franco to democratic reforms. Since the 1970s, the Catholic Church has not been the established religion; the constitution guarantees freedom for other religions as well. In the late 20th century, Spanish Church leaders fought a growing feeling of indifference among many Catholics.

Sri Lanka*

Archd., 1; dioc., 10; abp., 2; bp., 13; parishes, 384; priests, 876 (568 dioc., 308 rel.); sem., 394; bros., 246; srs., 2,237; catechists, 9,240; bap., 26,052; Caths., 1,238,000 (6.6%); tot. pop., 18,550,000.

Independent socialist republic, island southeast of India (formerly Ceylon); capital, Colombo. The Portuguese began evangelizing in the 16th century. In 1638, the Dutch began forcing Portuguese from the coastal areas. The Dutch outlawed Catholicism, banished priests and confiscated buildings, forcing people to become Calvinists. Blessed Joseph Vaz, an Oratorian priest, is credited with almost single-handedly reviving the Catholic Church toward the end of the 17th century.

Anti-Catholic laws were repealed by the British in 1806. The hierarchy was established in 1886; the country gained independence in 1948. Sri Lankan bishops repeatedly have called for reconciliation in the nearly two-decade war between the Liberation Tigers of Tamil Eelam and the Sinhalese-dominated government. In an unusual move in January 1998, Archbishop Nicholas M. Fernando of Colombo, authorized by the Vatican Congregation for the Doctrine of the Faith, lifted the excommunication of a prominent Sri Lankan theologian, Oblate Father Tissa Balasuriya.

Sudan*

Archd., 2; dioc., 7; abp., 3; bp., 9; parishes, 104; priests, 311 (188 dioc., 123 rel.); p.d., 4; sem., 240; bros., 76; srs., 283; catechists, 3,290; bap., 40,158; Caths., 2,347,000 (8.2%); tot. pop., 27,900,000.

Republic in northeastern Africa, the largest country on the continent; capital Khartoum. Christianity was introduced from Egypt and gained acceptance in the sixth century. Under Arab rule, it was eliminated in the northern region. No Christians were in the country in 1600.

Evangelization attempts begun in the 19th century in the south yielded hard-won results. By 1931 there were nearly 40,000 Catholics there, and considerable progress was made by missionaries after that time. In 1957, a year after the republic was established, Catholic schools were nationalized. An act restrictive of religious freedom went into effect in 1962, resulting in the harassment and expulsion of foreign missionaries. By 1964 all but a few Sudanese missionaries had been forced out of the southern region. The northern area, where Islam predominates, is impervious to Christian influence.

Late in 1971 some missionaries were allowed to return to work in the South. The hierarchy was established in 1974. The most recent fighting, which began in 1983, pits the mostly Arab and Muslim North against the mostly black African Christian and animist South. The imposition of Islamic penal codes in 1984 was a cause of concern to all Christian Churches. Recent government policies have denied Christians the right to places of worship and authorization to gather for prayer. Bishops from the South have condemned human rights violations — aggravated by famine and war — in their area. They have said they want peace but cannot accept an Islamic state.

Surinam*

Dioc., 1; bp., 1; parishes, 27; priests, 20 (5 dioc., 15 rel.); sem., 1; bros., 18; srs., 23; bap., 1,689; Caths., 92,000 (21%); tot. pop., 440,000.

Independent (Nov. 25, 1975) state in northern South America (formerly Dutch Guiana); capital, Paramaribo, Catholicism was introduced in 1683. Evangelization began in 1817.

Swaziland*

Dioc., 1; bp., 1; parishes, 15; priests, 40 (8 dioc., 32 rel.); sem., 13; bros., 9; srs., 58; bap., 730; Caths., 50,000 (5.2%); tot. pop., 910,000.

Monarchy in southern Africa; almost totally surrounded by South Africa; capital, Mbabane. Missionary work was entrusted to the Servites in 1913. An apostolic prefecture was organized in 1923. The hierarchy was established in 1951. Swaziland established diplomatic relations with the Holy See in 1992. In the 1990s, Swazi Catholics worked to help transform the country to a democracy but to retain the traditions of the people.

Sweden*

Dioc., 1; bp., 2; parishes, 38; priests, 131 (60 dioc., 71 rel.); p.d., 15; sem., 16; bros., 13; srs., 247; cat-

echists, 453; bap., 1,145; Caths., 166,000 (1.8%); tot. pop., 8,850,000.
Constitutional monarchy in northwestern Europe; capital, Stockholm. Christianity was introduced by St. Ansgar, a Frankish monk, in 829-830. The Church became well-established in the 12th century and was a major influence at the end of the Middle Ages. Political and other factors favored the introduction and spread of the Lutheran Church, which became the state religion in 1560. The Augsburg Confession of 1530 was accepted by the government; all relations with Rome were severed; monasteries were suppressed; the very presence of Catholics in the country was forbidden in 1617. A decree of tolerance for foreign Catholics was issued about 1781. Two years later an apostolic vicariate was organized for the country. In 1873 Swedes were given the legal right to leave the Lutheran Church and join another Christian Church. Membership in the Lutheran Church is presumed by law unless notice is given of membership in another church.

Since 1952 Catholics have enjoyed almost complete religious freedom. The hierarchy was re-established in 1953. Hindrances to growth of the Church are the strongly entrenched established church, limited resources, a clergy shortage and the size of the country. In the 1960s, an influx of guest workers increased the number of Catholics, and in the 1970s and 1980s, refugees helped increase Church numbers. In 1998, the pope named the first Swedish bishop in more than 400 years. Reforms due to be implemented by the year 2004 will give the Church and other minority faiths the right to operate as legal entities, including owning property.

Switzerland*
Dioc., 6; abb., 2; card., 2; abp., 5; bp., 17; parishes, 1,691; priests, 3,341 (1,949 dioc., 1,392 rel.); p.d., 95; sem., 188; bros., 398; srs., 6,978; catechists, 1,949; bap., 32,892; Caths., 3,289,000 (46.3%); tot. pop., 7,090,000.
Confederation in central Europe; capital, Bern. Christianity was introduced in the fourth century or earlier and was established on a firm footing before the barbarian invasions of the sixth century. Constance, established as a diocese in the seventh century, was a stronghold of the faith against the pagan Alamanni, in particular, who were not converted until some time in the ninth century. During this period of struggle with the barbarians, a number of monasteries of great influence were established. The Reformation in Switzerland was triggered by Zwingli in 1519 and furthered by him at Zurich until his death in battle against the Catholic cantons in 1531. Calvin set in motion the forces that made Geneva the international capital of the Reformation and transformed it into a theocracy. Catholics mobilized a Counter-Reformation in 1570, six years after Calvin's death. Struggle between Protestant and Catholic cantons was a fact of Swiss life for several hundred years. The Helvetic Constitution enacted at the turn of the 19th century embodied anti-Catholic measures and consequences, among them the dissolution of 130 monasteries. The Church was reorganized later in the century to meet the threats of liberalism, radicalism and the *Kulturkampf.* In the pro-

cess, the Church, even though on the defensive, gained the strength and cohesion that characterizes it to the present time. In 1973, constitutional articles banning Jesuits from the country and prohibiting the establishment of convents and monasteries were repealed. In the 1990s, Swiss bishops battled internal divisions that resulted in the transfer of a bishop to a new diocese in Liechtenstein.

Syria*
Patriarchates, 3 (Antioch of Maronites, Greek Melkites and Syrians; patriarchs of Maronites and Syrians reside in Lebanon); archd., 12 (1 Armenian, 2 Maronite, 5 Greek Melkite, 4 Syrian); dioc., 3 (Armenian, Chaldean, Maronite); v.a., 1 (Latin); ap.ex., 1; patriarch, 1; abp., 18; bp., 4; parishes, 204; priests, 248 (174 dioc., 74 rel.); p.d., 11; sem., 95; bros., 11; srs., 395; catechists, 1,486; bap., 2,562; Caths., 309,000 (2%); tot. pop., 14,950,000.
Arab socialist republic in southwest Asia; capital, Damascus. Christian communities were formed in apostolic times. It is believed that St. Peter established a see at Antioch before going to Rome. Damascus became a center of influence. The area was the place of great men and great events in the early history of the Church. Monasticism developed there in the fourth century; so did the Monophysite and Monothelite heresies to which a portion of the Church succumbed. Byzantine Syrians who remained in communion with Rome were given the name Melkites. Christians of various persuasions — Jacobites, Orthodox and Melkites — were subject to various degrees of harassment from the Arabs who took over in 638 and from the Ottoman Turks who isolated the country and remained in control from 1516 to the end of World War II.

Syrian Catholics are members of the Armenian, Chaldean, Greek-Melkite, Latin, Maronite and Syrian rites.

Taiwan
Archd., 1; dioc., 7; card., 1; abp., 3; bp., 9; parishes, 447; priests, 655 (215 dioc., 440 rel.); sem., 148; bros., 101; srs., 1,095; catechists, 602; bap., 3,729; Caths., 307,000 (1.3%); tot. pop., 22,620,000.
Democratic island state (also known as Formosa) 100 miles off the southern coast of mainland China; capital, Taipei. Attempts to introduce Christianity in the 17th century were unsuccessful. Evangelization in the 19th century resulted in some 1,300 converts in 1895. Missionary endeavor was hampered by the Japanese, who occupied the island following the Sino-Japanese war of 1894-95. Great progress was made in missionary endeavor among the Chinese who emigrated to the island (seat of the Nationalist Government of the Republic of China) following the Communist takeover of the mainland in 1949. The hierarchy was established in 1952. Many Taiwanese Catholics have worked to form a bridge to Catholics in mainland China. China has said the Vatican's diplomatic relations with Taiwan form the biggest stumbling block to Sino-Vatican relations.

Tajikistan*
Parishes, 2; priests, 3 (rel.); srs., 5; sem., 1; bap., 15; Cath., 2000; tot. pop. 6,050,000.
Independent republic (1992) in Asia; formerly part of the USSR; capital, Dushanbe. The majority of the

population is Sunni Muslim. When the Vatican established diplomatic relations in 1996, Church officials estimated most of the country's Catholics had fled. In 1997, the Vatican decided to establish a mission in the country.

Tanzania*

Archd., 4; dioc., 25; card., 1; abp., 5; bp., 30; parishes, 769; priests, 2,093 (1,379 dioc., 714 rel.); p.d. 1; sem., 838; bros., 611; srs., 6,720; catechists, 12,008; bap., 218,308; Caths., 7,924,000 (25.1%); tot. pop., 31,510,000.

Republic on and off the eastern coast of Africa; capital, Dar es Salaam. The first Catholic mission in the former Tanganyikan portion of the republic was manned by Holy Ghost Fathers in 1868. The hierarchy was established there in 1953. Zanzibar was the landing place of Augustinians with the Portuguese in 1499. Some evangelization was attempted between then and 1698 when the Arabs expelled all priests from the territory. There was no Catholic missionary activity from then until the 1860s. The Holy Ghost Fathers arrived in 1863 and were entrusted with the mission in 1872. Zanzibar was important as a point of departure for missionaries to Tanganyika, Kenya and other places in East Africa. A vicariate for Zanzibar was set up in 1906.

In the late 20th century the Church in Tanzania saw an increase in vocations and an active Church life. The bishops assisted hundreds of thousands of refugees from Rwanda, Burundi and Mozambique.

Thailand*

Archd., 2; dioc., 8; card., 1; abp., 4; bp., 11; parishes, 331; priests, 598 (362 dioc., 236 rel.); p.d., 1; sem., 252; bros., 120; srs., 1,453; catechists, 1,728; bap., 6,796; Caths., 260,000 (.4%); tot. pop., 60,600,000.

Constitutional monarchy in southeast Asia (formerly Siam); capital, Bangkok. The first Christians in the region were Portuguese traders who arrived early in the 16th century. A number of missionaries began arriving in the mid-1500s, but pastoral care was confined mostly to the Portuguese until the 1660s, when evangelization began. A seminary was organized in 1665, a vicariate was set up four years later, and a point of departure was established for China. Persecution and death for some of the missionaries ended evangelization efforts in 1688. It was resumed, however, and made progress from 1824 onward. In 1881 missionaries were sent from Siam to neighboring Laos. The hierarchy was established in 1965. Archbishop Michael Michai Kitbunchu was named the first Thai cardinal in 1983. The Church is recognized for its social justice efforts, including work with refugees.

Togo*

Archd., 1; dioc., 6; abp., 1; bp., 6; parishes, 121; priests, 343 (234 dioc., 109 rel.); sem., 254; bros., 177; srs., 591; catechists, 4,120; bap., 42,057; Caths., 1,055,000 (24.4%); tot. pop., 4,320,000.

Republic on the west coast of Africa; capital, Lome. The first Catholic missionaries in the area, where slave raiders operated for nearly 200 years, were members of the African Missions Society who arrived in 1563. They were followed by Divine Word Missionaries in 1914, when an apostolic prefecture was organized. At that time the Catholic population numbered about 19,000. The African Missionaries returned after their German predecessors were deported following World War I. The first native priest was ordained in 1922. The hierarchy was established in 1955. In the early 1990s, Archbishop Philippe Fanoko Kossi Kpodzro of Lome served as president of the transitional legislative assembly.

Tonga*

Dioc., 1; bp., 1; parishes, 12; priests, 18 (9 dioc., 9 rel.); sem., 26; bros., 9; srs., 67; bap., 526; Caths., 15,000 (14.5%); tot. pop., 95,000.

Polynesian monarchy in the southwestern Pacific, consisting of about 150 islands; capital Nuku'alofa. Marists started missionary work in 1842, some years after Protestants had begun evangelization. By 1880 the Catholic population numbered about 1,700. A vicariate was organized in 1937. The hierarchy was established in 1966. Tonga established diplomatic relations with the Holy See in 1994.

Trinidad and Tobago*

Archd., 1; abp., 2; bp., 1; parishes, 62; priests, 114 (42 dioc., 72 rel.); sem., 18; bros., 17; srs., 182; bap., 4,975; Caths., 413,000 (31.6%); tot. pop., 1,310,000.

Independent nation, consisting of two islands in the Caribbean; capital, Port-of-Spain. The first Catholic Church in Trinidad was built in 1591, years after several missionary ventures had been launched and a number of missionaries killed. Capuchins were there from 1618 until about 1802. Missionary work continued after the British gained control early in the 19th century. Cordial relations have existed between the Church and state, both of which have manifested their desire for the development of native clergy. In 1999, Church leaders protested reinstatement of the death penalty.

Tunisia*

Dioc., 1; abp., 1; parishes, 13; priests, 38 (17 dioc., 21 rel.); bros., 9; sem., 2; srs., 173; bap., 17; Caths., 22,000 (.2%); tot. pop., 9,220,000.

Republic on the northern coast of Africa; capital, Tunis. Ancient Carthage, now a site outside the capital city of Tunis, hosted early Church councils and was home to Church fathers like St. Augustine. Carthage was devastated by Vandals in the 5th century and invaded by Muslims in the seventh century, after which it had few Christians until the 19th century. An apostolic vicariate was organized in 1843, and the Carthage Archdiocese was established in 1884. The Catholic population in 1892 consisted of most of the approximately 50,000 Europeans in the country. When Tunis became a republic in 1956, most of the Europeans left the country. A 1964 agreement with the Vatican and Holy See suppressed the Archdiocese of Carthage and replaced it with the Territorial Prelature of Tunis. In 1995 the prelature was made a diocese.

Today Tunisia's Catholics are predominantly foreign nationals. The Church's social presence is seen in schools, hospitals and institutions for the disabled.

Turkey*

Patriarchate, 1 (Cilicia for the Armenians; the patriarch resides in Lebanon); archd., 3; v.a., 2; ord.,

1; ap. ex., 1; abp., 4; bp., 2; parishes, 52; priests, 64 (15 dioc., 49 rel.); p.d., 5; sem., 13; bros., 12; srs., 115; bap., 148; Caths., 32,000 (.05%); tot. pop., 63,750,000.

Republic in Asia Minor and southeastern Europe, capital, Ankara. Christian communities were established in apostolic times, as attested in the Acts of the Apostles, some of the Letters of St. Paul and Revelation. The territory was the scene of heresies and ecumenical councils, the place of residence of Fathers of the Church, the area in which ecclesiastical organization reached the dimensions of more than 450 sees in the middle of the seventh century. The region remained generally Byzantine except for the period of the Latin occupation of Constantinople from 1204 to 1261, but was conquered by the Ottoman Turks in 1453 and remained under their domination until establishment of the republic in 1923. Christians, always a minority, numbered more Orthodox than Catholics; they were all under some restrictions during the Ottoman period. They suffered persecution in the 19th and 20th centuries, the Armenians being the most numerous victims. Turkey is overwhelmingly Muslim. Catholics are tolerated to a degree.

Turkmenistan*

Mission, 1; priests, 2 (rel.); Caths., 5,000; tot. pop., 4,240,000.

Former constituent republic of USSR; independent, 1991; capital, Ashgabat. Almost all the population is Sunni Muslim. The Vatican established diplomatic relations with the country in 1996 and set up a mission in 1997.

Tuvalu

Independent mission, 1; priest, 1 (rel.); bap., 4; Caths., 100; tot. pop., 9,000.

Independent state (1978) in Oceania, consisting of 9 islands (formerly Ellice Islands); capital, Funafuti.

Uganda*

Archd., 1; dioc., 18; mil. ord.; card., 1; abp., 1; bp., 23; parishes, 384; priests, 1,446 (1,111 dioc., 335 rel.); p.d., 1; sem., 694; bros., 457; srs., 2,796; catechists, 11,078; bap., 284,770; Caths., 8,793,000 (42.9%); tot. pop., 20,440,000.

Republic in East Africa; capital, Kampala. The Missionaries of Africa (White Fathers) were the first Catholic missionaries, starting in 1879. Persecution broke out from 1885 to 1887, taking a toll of 22 Catholic martyrs, who were canonized in 1964, and a number of Anglican victims. (Pope Paul honored all those who died for the faith during a visit to Kampala in 1969.) By 1888, there were more than 8,000 Catholics. Evangelization was resumed in 1894, after being interrupted by war, and proceeded thereafter. The first native African bishop was ordained in 1939. The hierarchy was established in 1953.

The Church was suppressed during the erratic regime of President Idi Amin, who was deposed in the spring of 1979. Guerrilla activity in northern and southwestern Uganda has hampered Church workers, and Church leaders have called for peace so the country can develop. The Church has devoted much of its resources to caring for the many victims of HIV/AIDS in the country.

Ukraine*

Major archbishopric, 1 (Ukrainian); archd., 2 (1 Armenian and 1 Latin rite); dioc., 9 (6 Byzantine rite, 3 Latin); a.a., 1; pat. ex., 1; card., 1 (Ukrainian Major Archbishop Lubachivsky); abp., 2; bp., 19; parishes, 3,126; priests, 2,294 (1,889 dioc., 405 rel.); p.d., 5; sem., 1,392; bros., 293; srs., 910; bap., 27,476; Caths., 5,635,000 (11%); tot. pop., 50,640,000.

Independent republic bordering on the Black Sea; former USSR republic; capital, Kiev. The baptism of Vladimir and his people in 988 marked the beginning of Christianity in the territory of Kievan Rus, which is included in today's Ukraine. The 1596 Union of Brest brought the Ukrainian Byzantine-rite community back into communion with Rome. The Eastern Catholic Church was officially suppressed and underground in the USSR from the late 1940s; all of its bishops were killed or imprisoned and its property seized by the government and given to the Orthodox. Some Catholic priests continued to minister clandestinely under communist rule.

As the Eastern Church regained its legal status under Soviet President Mikhail Gorbachev, serious tensions arose with the Orthodox over ownership of property and the allegiance of priests and lay people. Latin-rite dioceses were re-established in 1991. In the late 1990s, rising inflation and weakening currency, aggravated by the government's and some companies' failure to pay wages, led Ukrainian Church leaders to fight homelessness and hunger.

United Arab Emirates

V.a, 1; bp., 1; parishes, 5; priests, 19 (3 dioc., 16 rel.); srs., 40; bap., 959; Caths., 155,000; tot. pop., 2,580,000.

Independent state along Persian Gulf; capital, Abu Dhabi. The apostolic vicariate of Arabia has its seat in Abu Dhabi. It includes the states of Bahrain, Oman, Qatar, Saudi Arabia and Yemen (see separate entries) as well as United Arab Emirates.

United States* (See Catholic Church in the United States; see also Catholic History in the United States and Statistics of the Church in the United States.)

Uruguay*

Archd., 1; dioc., 9; abp., 3; bp., 13; parishes, 229; priests, 536 (248 dioc., 288 rel.); p.d., 63; sem., 81; bros., 109; srs., 1,513; catechists, 4,987; bap., 37,459; catechists, 4,617; Caths., 2,548,000 (77.6%); tot. pop., 3,280,000.

Republic on the southeast coast of South America; capital, Montevideo. The Spanish established a settlement in 1624 and evangelization followed. Missionaries followed the reduction pattern to reach the Indians, form them in the faith and train them in agriculture, husbandry, other arts, and the experience of managing property and living in community. Montevideo was made a diocese in 1878. The constitution of 1830 made Catholicism the religion of the state and subsidized some of its activities, principally the missions to the Indians. Separation of Church and state was provided for in the constitution of 1917. In 1997, despite a court decision halting further investigations, the Church pledged to make one last effort to help search for people who remained missing from the 1973-85 military dictatorship.

Uzbekistan*

Mission, 1; parishes, 3; priests, 4 (4 rel.); p.d. 1; srs., 4; bap., 5; Caths. 4,000; tot. pop. 23,440,000.

Former republic of USSR; independent, 1991; capital, Tashkent. The majority of the population is Sunni Muslim. A small number of Catholics live in Tashkent. The Vatican established a mission in 1997.

Vanuatu*

Dioc., 1; bp., 1; parishes, 16; priests, 27 (13 dioc., 14 rel.); p.d., 1; sem., 9; bros., 16; srs., 66; bap., 564; Caths., 26,000 (16%); tot. pop., 180,000.

Independent (July 29, 1980) island group in the southwest Pacific (formerly New Hebrides); capital, Vila. Effective, though slow, evangelization by Catholic missionaries began about 1887. An apostolic vicariate was set up in 1904. The hierarchy was established in 1966.

Vatican City State (See separate entry).

Venezuela*

Archd., 9; dioc., 21; v.a., 4; ap. ex., 1; mil. ord. 1; card., 2; abp., 12; bp., 45; parishes, 1,149; priests, 2,419 (1,308 dioc., 1,111 rel.); p.d., 71; sem., 1,018; bros., 324; srs., 4,346; catechists, 30,922; bap., 417,045; Caths., 21,241,000 (91%); tot. pop., 23,210,000.

Republic in northern South America; capital, Caracas. Evangelization began in 1513-14 and involved members of a number of religious orders who worked in assigned territories, developing missions into pueblos or towns and villages of Indian converts. Nearly 350 towns originated as missions. The first diocese was established in 1531.

Fifty-four missionaries met death by violence from the start of missionary work until 1817. Missionary work was seriously hindered during the wars of independence in the second decade of the 19th century and continued in decline through the rest of the century as dictator followed dictator in a period of political turbulence. Restoration of the missions got under way in 1922. In the 1990s, the Church worked at reconciliation in the country but condemned government corruption and violent crime. Church leaders also called for respect for human rights.

Vietnam

Archd., 3; dioc., 22; card., 1; abp., 1; bp., 31; parishes, 2,141; priests, 2,294 (1,948 dioc., 346 rel.); p.d., 17; sem., 1,400; bros., 759; srs., 6,009; catechists, 4,409; bap., 141,360; Caths., 6,080,000 (7.9%); tot. pop., 76,550,000.

Country in southeast Asia, reunited officially July 2, 1976, as the Socialist Republic of Vietnam; capital, Hanoi.

Catholicism was introduced in 1533, but missionary work was intermittent until 1615, when Jesuits arrived to stay. Two vicariates were organized in 1659. A seminary was set up in 1666, and two native priests were ordained two years later. A congregation of native women religious formed in 1670 is still active. Severe persecution broke out in 1698, three times in the 18th century, and again in the 19th. Up to 300,000

people suffered in some way from persecution during the 50 years before 1883, when the French moved in to secure religious liberty for the Catholics. Most of the 117 beatified Martyrs of Vietnam were killed during this 50-year period. After the French were forced out of Vietnam in 1954, the country was partitioned at the 17th parallel. The North went Communist and the Viet Cong, joined by North Vietnamese regular army troops in 1964, fought to gain control of the South. In 1954 there were approximately 1.1 million Catholics in the North and 480,000 in the South. More than 650,000 fled to the South to avoid the government repression. In South Vietnam, the Church continued to develop during the war years.

After the end of the war in 1975, the government exercised control over virtually all aspects of Church life. In the late 1980s, bishops noted some softening of the government's hard line. In the 1990s, the Vatican and Vietnam held intermittent talks on Church-state issues, with sporadic progress reported. In 1997, the government censored the section of the "Catechism of the Catholic Church" that dealt with human rights. In March 1999, a Vatican envoy said progress toward diplomatic relations had been made.

Virgin Islands (U.S.)

Dioc., 1 (St. Thomas, suffragan of Washington, D.C.); bp., 1; parishes, 8; priests, 16 (11 dioc., 5 rel.); p.d., 22; sem., 3; bros., 13; srs., 14; bap., 437; Caths., 30,000 (29%); tot. pop., 102,000.

Organized unincorporated U.S. territory in Atlantic Ocean; capital, Charlotte Amalie on St. Thomas (one of the three principal islands). The islands were discovered by Columbus in 1493 and named for St. Ursula and her virgin companions. Missionaries began evangelization in the 16th century. A church on St. Croix dates from about 1660; another, on St. Thomas, from 1774. The Baltimore Archdiocese had jurisdiction over the islands from 1804 to 1820, when it was passed on to the first of several places in the Caribbean area. Some trouble arose over a pastoral appointment in the 19th century, resulting in a small schism. The Redemptorists took over pastoral care in 1858; normal conditions have prevailed since.

Wales

Wales: Archd., 1; dioc., 2; abp., 1; bp., 2; parishes, 187; priests, 258 (155 dioc., 103 rel.); p.d., 92; sem., 18; bros., 115; srs., 481; bap, 2,624; Caths., 147,318 (5%); tot. pop., 3,065,733 (Figures from 1999 Annuario Pontificio).

Part of the United Kingdom, on the western part of the island of Great Britain. Celtic missionaries completed evangelization by the end of the sixth century, the climax of what has been called the age of saints. Welsh Christianity received its distinctive Celtic character at this time. Some conflict developed when attempts were made — and proved successful later — to place the Welsh Church under the jurisdiction of Canterbury; the Welsh opted for direct contact with Rome.

The Church made progress despite the depredations of Norsemen in the eighth and ninth centuries. Norman infiltration occurred near the middle of the 12th century, resulting in a century-long effort to establish territorial dioceses and parishes to replace the Celtic organizational plan of monastic centers and satellite churches. The Western Schism produced split views and allegiances. Actions of Henry VIII in breaking away from Rome had serious repercussions. Proscription and penal laws crippled the Church, resulted in heavy defections and touched off a 150-year period of repression. Methodism prevailed by 1750. Modern Catholicism came to Wales with Irish immigrants in the 19th century, when the number of Welsh Catholics was negligible. Catholic emancipation was granted in 1829. The hierarchy was restored in 1850. Wales shares a bishops' conference with England.

Wallis and Futuna Islands

Dioc., 1; bp., 1; parishes, 5; priests, 9 (6 dioc., 3 rel.); sem., 8; bros., 4; srs., 46; bap., 296; Caths., 14,000; tot. pop., 14,000.

French overseas territory in the southwestern Pacific; capital Mata-Utu. Marists, who began evangelizing the islands in 1836-7, were the first Catholic missionaries. The entire populations of the two islands were baptized by the end of 1842 (Wallis) and 1843 (Futuna). The first missionary to the latter island was killed in 1841. Most of the priests on the islands are native Polynesians. The hierarchy was established in 1966.

Western Sahara

P.a., 1; parishes, 2; priests, 3 (rel.); Caths., 200; tot. pop., 350,000.

Former Spanish overseas province (Spanish Sahara) on the northwestern coast of Africa. Territory is under control of Morocco. Islam is the religion of non-Europeans. An apostolic prefecture was established in 1954 for the European Catholics there.

Yemen*

Parishes, 4; priests, 4 (rel.); bap., 4; Caths., 3,000; tot. pop., 16,480,000.

Republic on southern coast of Arabian peninsula; capital, San'a. Formerly North Yemen (Arab Republic of Yemen) and South Yemen (People's Republic of Yemen); formally reunited in 1990. Christians perished in the first quarter of the sixth century. Muslims have been in control since the seventh century. The state religion is Islam; the Church is under the ecclesiastical jurisdiction of Arabia apostolic vicariate. In the early 1990s, Salesians reported some harassment of Church workers in the South. In early 1998, three Missionaries of Charity nuns were murdered. The Vatican established diplomatic relations with Yemen in October 1998.

Yugoslavia*

Archd., 2; dioc., 3; abp., 3; bp., 4; parishes, 238; priests, 194 (157 dioc., 37 rel.); p.d., 1; sem., 37; bros., 7; srs., 330; bap., 3,796; Caths., 475,000 (6%); tot. pop., 7,968,000.

Republic in southeastern Europe formed in 1992, consisting of Serbia and Montenegro; capital, Belgrade. The four other republics (Croatia, Slovenia, Bosnia-Herzegovina, and Macedonia) which made up the federation of Yugoslavia created after World War II, proclaimed their independence in 1991-92; see separate entries.

Christianity was introduced from the seventh to ninth centuries in the regions combined to form the nation after World War I. Since these regions straddled the original line of demarcation for the Western and Eastern Empires (and churches), and since the Reformation had little lasting effect, the Christians are nearly all either Latin- or Eastern-rite Catholics or Orthodox. Yugoslavia was proclaimed a Socialist republic in 1945, the year in which began years of the harshest kind of total persecution of the Church. In an agreement signed June 25, 1966, the government recognized the Holy See's spiritual jurisdiction over the Church in the country and guaranteed to bishops the possibility of maintaining contact with Rome in ecclesiastical and religious matters. During the split of the Yugoslav republic, Catholic leaders joined Orthodox and, in some cases, Muslim leaders in calling for peace.

Zambia*

Archd., 2; dioc., 8; abp., 5; bp., 8; parishes, 238; priests, 593 (217 dioc., 376 rel.); p.d., 1; sem., 377; bros., 160; srs., 1,322; catechists, 9,133; bap., 54,934; Caths., 2,358,000 (28%); tot. pop., 8,480,000.

Republic in central Africa; capital, Lusaka. Portuguese priests did some evangelizing in the 16th and 17th centuries but no results of their work remained in the 19th century. Jesuits began work in the South in the 1880s and White Fathers in the North and East in 1895. Evangelization of the western region began for the first time in 1931. The number of Catholics doubled in the 20 years following World War II.

Zambian Catholics have welcomed tens of thousands of refugees from the region. During a 1989 visit, Pope John Paul II praised Zambians for their generosity and offered encouragement as they faced poverty. Zambian Catholics told the pope about fundamentalist sects and why Vatican teaching on marriage faced problems in a polygamous culture. In the 1990s, Zambian Church leaders worked caring for victims of HIV/AIDS and spoke out against foreign debt.

Zimbabwe*

Archd., 2; dioc., 5; abp., 4; bp., 6; parishes, 142; priests, 418 (148 dioc., 270 rel.); p.d., 13; sem., 355; bros., 98; srs., 1,096; catechists, 4,528; bap., 37,204; Caths., 1,099,000 (8.7%); tot. pop., 12,290,000.

Independent republic (1980) in south central Africa (formerly Rhodesia); capital, Harare (Salisbury). Earlier unsuccessful missionary ventures preceded the introduction of Catholicism in 1879. Missionaries began to make progress after 1893. The hierarchy was established in 1955; the first black bishop was ordained in 1973.

In 1969, four years after the government of Ian Smith made a unilateral declaration of independence from England, a new constitution was enacted for the purpose of assuring continued white supremacy over the black majority. Catholic and Protestant prelates in the country protested vigorously against the constitution and related enactments as opposed to human rights of the blacks and restrictive of the Church's freedom to carry out its pastoral, educational and social service functions. The Smith regime was ousted in 1979 after seven years of civil war in which at least 25,000 people were killed.

In 1997, the bishops published a report detailing more than 7,000 cases of killings, torture and human rights abuses by government troops in western Zimbabwe from 1981-87. As the Church entered the

(continued on page 346)

CATHOLIC WORLD STATISTICS

(Principal sources: *Statistical Yearbook of the Church,* 1997, the latest edition; figures are as of Dec. 31, 1997 unless indicated otherwise.)

	Africa	North America[1]	South America	Asia	Europe	Oceania	WORLD TOTALS
Patriarchates[2]	2	-	-	8	2	-	12
Archdioceses	78	85	95	113	166	18	555
Dioceses	367	352	393	310	502	54	1,978
Prelatures	-	8	32	6	6	-	52
Abbacies	-	-	2	-	11	-	13
Exarchates/Ords.	-	1	4	2	14	-	21
Military Ords.	3	4	9	3	12	2	33
Vicariates Apostolic	16	5	36	18	1	-	76
Prefectures	4	-	7	5	-	1	17
Apostolic Admin.	1	-	-	3	5	-	9
Independent Missions	1	1	-	5	-	2	9
Cardinals[3]	14	24	16	15	81	4	154
Patriarchs[2]	1	-	-	6	1	-	8
Archbishops	107	128	141	150	339	24	889[4]
Bishops	443	665	691	450	1,037	91	3,377[4]
Priests	25,279	79,893	40,120	40,441	213,398	5,077	404,208
Diocesan	14,873	51,154	22,341	23,789	148,595	2,769	263,521
Religious	10,406	28,739	17,779	16,652	64,803	2,308	140,687
Perm.Deacons	308	14,002	2,265	129	7,536	167	24,407
Brothers	7,083	11,388	6,038	7,274	24,460	1,967	58,210
Sisters	49,854	150,970	89,888	127,969	388,693	11,904	819,279
Maj. Seminarians	19,078	15,538	19,409	25,842	27,853	797	108,517
Sec. Inst. Mbrs. (Men)	27	49	95	69	422	1	663
Sec. Inst. Mbrs. (Women)	353	1,643	3,808	1,103	23,577	50	30,534
Lay Missionaries	1,248	3,631	18,309	1,520	1,124	236	26,068
Catechists	329,775	517,497	554,210	188,985	399,485	29,069	2,019,021
Parishes	10,497	33,352	19,903	19,395	133,811	2,411	219,369[5]
Kindergartens	9,867	8,181	6,605	9,700	23,283	588	58,224
Students	781,536	414,159	703,795	1,373,087	1,810,755	29,238	5,112,570
Elem./Primary Schools	29,543	13,160	9,251	13,622	18,363	2,566	86,505
Students	9,285,102	3,718,060	3,603,345	4,866,292	3,416,138	552,900	5,441,837
Secondary Schools	6,265	3,483	6,010	7,931	10,425	735	34,849
Students	2,050,080	1,448,702	2,228,192	4,199,371	3,614,826	340,738	3,881,909
Students in Higher Insts.[6]	24,093	340,452	117,779	725,905	196,918	6,542	1,411,689
Social Service Facilities	14,611	16,150	26,095	21,601	34,397	1,429	114,283
Hospitals	808	947	917	1,027	1,362	127	5,188
Dispensaries	4,191	5,676	3,507	3,198	3,917	175	17,157
Leprosariums	372	14	70	361	6	2	825
Homes for Aged/Handi.	455	1,569	1,597	1,222	7,092	274	12,209
Orphanages	729	866	1,414	2,968	2,043	226	8,246
Nurseries	1,645	1,241	4,056	2,485	2,402	82	11,911
Matrimonial Advice Ctrs.	1,429	2,262	1,833	1,031	3,866	202	10,618
Social Educ.Ctrs.	906	2,374	1,902	2,741	2,709	94	10,726
Other Institutions	4,081	4,708	10,799	6,568	10,000	247	37,403
Baptisms	3,130,227	4,317,125	5,053,743	2,756,252	2,666,690	141,054	8,065,091
Under Age 7	2,057,176	4,048,269	4,587,538	2,368,239	2,588,296	126,088	5,775,605
Over Age 7	1,073,051s	268,857	466,205	388,013	78,394	14,966	2,289,486
Marriages	272,781	856,745	805,755	521,788	1,049,133	28,051	3,534,253
Between Catholics	239,775	757,400	789,228	461,287	970,665	16,221	3,234,567
Mixed Marriages	33,006	99,345	16,527	60,501	78,468	11,839	299,686
Catholic Pop.[7]	112,871,000	213,490,000	282,266,000	105,294,000	283,313,000	8,020,000	9,005,254,000
World Population	756,896,000	464,709,000	323,444,000	3,562,142,000	684,421,000	29,155,000	5,820,767,000

1:Includes Central America. 2:For listing and description, see Index. 3:As of Aug. 15, 1999. 4:Figures for the hierarchy (cardinals, archbishops and bishops) included 2,603 ordinaries, 591 coadjutors or auxiliaries, 236 with offices in the Roman Curia, 32 in other offices, 958 retired. 5:160,399 have parish priests; 53,426 are administered by other priests; 477 are entrusted to permanent deacons; 187 to brothers; 1,011 to women Religious; 1,506 to lay people; 2,363 vacant. 6:There are also approximately 190,604 in universities for ecclesiastical studies and 2,033,318 other university students. 7:Percentages of Catholics in world population: Africa, 14.9; North America (Catholics 71,282,000; tot. pop., 296,310,000), 23.9; Central America (Catholics, 142,208,000; tot. pop., 166,399,000), 85.4; South America, 87.2; Asia, 2.9; Europe, 41.3; Oceania, 27.5; World, 17. (Catholic totals do not include those in areas that could not be surveyed, estimated to be approx. 5 million.)

(*continued from page 344*)
21st century, it was devoting tremendous resources toward palliative care of AIDS victims and work with AIDS orphans. However, the Church

was sometimes criticized for not doing enough to prevent the spread of AIDS, which Church and health-care workers said was exacerbated by poverty and cultural beliefs.

EPISCOPAL CONFERENCES

(Principal sources: *Annuario Pontificio* and Almanac survey.)

Episcopal conferences, organized and operating under general norms and particular statutes approved by the Holy See, are official bodies in and through which the bishops of a given country or territory act together as pastors of the Church.

Listed below according to countries or regions are titles and addresses of conferences and names and sees of presidents.

Africa, Northern: *Conference Episcopale Regionale du Nord de l'Afrique* (CERNA), 13 rue Khelifa-Boukhalfa, 16000 Algiers, Algeria. Abp. Henri Teissier (Algiers).

Africa, Southern: Southern African Catholic Bishops' Conference (SACBC), 140 Visagie St., P.O. Box 941, Pretoria 0001, S. Africa. Bp. Louis Ncarmiso Ndlovu, O.S.M. (Manzini, Swaziland).

Albania: *Conferenza Episcopale dell'Albania*, Sheshi Gijon Pali II, Kryeipeshkëvi, Shkodrë, Abp. Rrok Mirdita (Durrës-Tirana).

Angola and São Tome: *Conferencia Episcopal de Angola e HR Tome* (CEAST), C.P. 87 Luanda, Angola. Archbishop Zacarias Kamwenho (Lubango).

Antilles: Antilles Episcopal Conference (AEC), P.O. Box 3086, St. James (Trinidad and Tobago), W.I. Abp. Edgerton Roland Clarke (Kingston).

Arab Countries: *Conférence des Evêques Latins dans les Régions Arabes* (CELRA), Latin Patriarchate, P.O. Box 14152, Jerusalem (Old City). Patriarch Michel Sabbah (Jerusalem).

Argentina: *Conferencia Episcopal Argentina* (CEA), Calle Suipacha 1034, 1008 Buenos Aires. Abp. Estanislao Esteban Karlic (Paraná).

Australia: Australian Catholic Bishops' Conference, 63 Currong St., Braddon, A.C.T. 2601. Card. Edward Bede Clancy (Sydney).

Austria: *Österreichische Bischofskonferenz*, Wollzeile 2, A-1010 Vienna. Bp. Johann Weber (Graz-Seckau).

Bangladesh: Catholic Bishops' Conference of Bangladesh (CBCB), P.O. Box 3, Dhaka-1000. Abp. Michael Rozario (Dhaka).

Belgium: *Bisschoppenconferentie van België — Conférence Episcopale de Belgique*, Rue Guimard 1, B-1040 Brussel. Card. Godfried Danneels (Mechelen-Brussel).

Benin: *Conférence Episcopale du Bénin*, B.P. 491, Cotonou. Bp. Lucien Monsi-Agboka (Abomey).

Bolivia: *Conferencia Episcopal Boliviana* (CEB), Casilla 2309, Calle Potosi 814, La Paz. Abp. Julio Terrazas Sandoval, C.SS.R. (Santa Cruz de la Sierra).

Bosnia and Herzegovina: *Biskupska Konferencija Bosne i Hercegovine* (B.K. B.i.H.), *Nadbiskupski Ordinariat*, Kaptol 7, 71000 Sarajevo. Card. Vinko Puljic (Vrhbosna, Sarajevo).

Brazil: *Conferência Nacional dos Bispos do Brasil* (CNBB), C.P. 02067, SE/Sul Quadra 801, Conjunto "B," 70259-970 Brasilia, D.F. Card. Lucas Moreira Neves, O.P. (São Salvador da Bahia).

Bulgaria: *Mejduritual Episcopska Konferenzia vâv Bâlgaria*, Ul. Liulin Planina 5, 1606 Sofia. Bp. Christo Proykov (Briula, titular see).

Burkina Faso and Niger: *Conférence des Evêques de Burkina Faso et du Niger*, B.P. 1195, Ouagadougou, Burkina Faso. Bp. Jean-Baptiste Somé (Diebougou).

Burma: See Myanmar.

Burundi: *Conférence des Evêques catholiques du Burundi* (C.E.CA.B.), B. P. 1390, 5 Blvd. de l'Uprona, Bujumbura. Archbishop Simon Ntamwana (Gitega).

Cameroon: *Conférence Episcopale Nationale du Cameroun* (CENC), BP 807, Yaoundé. Bp. André Wouking (Bafoussam).

Canada: See Canadian Conference of Catholic Bishops.

Central African Republic: *Conférence Episcopale Centrafricaine* (CECA), B.P. 1518, Bangui. Bp. Paulin Pomodimo (Bossangoa).

Chad: *Conférence Episcopale du Tchad*, B.P. 456, N'Djaména. Abp. Charles Vandame, S.J. (N'Djamena).

Chile: *Conferencia Episcopal de Chile* (CECH), Casilla 517-V, Correo 21, Cienfuegas 47, Santiago. Card. Carlos Oviedo Cavada, O. de M. (Santiago de Chile).

China: Chinese Regional Episcopal Conference, 34 Lane 32, Kuang-Fu South Rd., Taipeh 10552, Taiwan. Bp. Paul Shan Kuo-hsi, S.J. (Kaohsiung).

Colombia: *Conferencia Episcopal de Colombia*, Apartado 7448, Carrera 8ª 47, N. 84-85, Santafé de Bogotá D.E. Abp. Alberto Giraldo Jaramillo, P.S.S. (Popayan).

Congo: *Conférence Episcopale du Congo*, B.P. 200, Brazzaville. Bp. Anatole Milandou (Kinkala).

Congo, Democratic Republic (formerly Zaire): *Conférence Episcopale du Zaïre* (CEZ), B.P. 3258, Kinshasa-Gombe. Bp. Faustin Ngabu (Goma).

Costa Rica: *Conferencia Episcopal de Costa Rica* (CECOR), Apartado 497, 1000 San Jose. Abp. Román Arrieta Villalobos (San Jose de Costa Rica).

Côte d'Ivoire: *Conference Episcopale de la Côte d'Ivoire*, B.P. 1287, Abidjan 01. Abp. Auguste Nobou (Korhogo).

Croatia: *Hrvatska Biskupska Konferencija*, Kaptol 22, HR-41000 Zagreb. Bp. Josip Bozanic (Zagreb).

Cuba: *Conferencia de Obispos Católicos de Cuba* (COCC), Apartado 594, Calle 26 n. 314 Miramar, 10100 Havana 1. Card. Jaime Lucas Ortega y Alamino (Havana).

Czech Republic: *Ceská Biskupská Konference*, Sekretariat, Thakurova 3, 160 00 Praha (Prague) 6. Card. Miloslav Vlk (Prague).

Dominican Republic: *Conferencia del Episcopado Dominicano* (CED), Apartado 186, Santo Domingo. Card. Nicolás de Jesús López Rodriguez (Santo Domingo).

Ecuador: *Conferencia Episcopal Ecuatoriana*, Apartado 1081, Avenida América 1805 y Lagasca, Quito. Abp. José Mario Ruiz Navas (Portoviejo).

El Salvador: *Conferencia Episcopal de El Salva-*

dor (CEDES). 15 Av. Norte 1420, Col. Layco, Apartado 1310, San Salvador. Bp. Marco Ren Revelo Contreras (Santa Ana).

Equatorial Guinea: *Conferencia Episcopal de Guinea Ecuatorial*, Apartado 106, Malabo. Bp. Anacleto Sima Ngua (Bata).

Ethiopia: Ethiopian Episcopal Conference, P.O. Box 2454, Addis Ababa. Card. Paulos Tzadua (Addis Ababa).

France: *Conférence des Evêques de France*, 106 rue du Bac, 75341 Paris CEDEX 07. Abp. Louis-Marie Billé (Aix).

Gabon: *Conférence Episcopale du Gabon*, B.P. 209, Oyem. Bp. Basile Mvé Engone, S.D.B. (Oyem).

Gambia, Liberia and Sierra Leone: Inter-Territorial Catholic Bishops' Conference of the Gambia, Liberia and Sierra Leone (ITCABIC), Santanno House, P.O. Box 893, Freetown, Sierra Leone. Bp. Benedict Dotu Sekey (Gbarnga, Liberia).

Germany: *Deutsche Bischofskonferenz*, Postfach 2962, Kaiserstrasse 163, D-53019 Bonn. Bp. Karl Lehmann (Mainz). Statutes approved Nov. 14, 1992.

Ghana: Ghana Bishops' Conference, National Catholic Secretariat, P.O. Box 9712 Airport, Accra. Bp. Peter Kodwo Appiah Turkson (Cape Coast).

Great Britain: Bishops' Conference of England and Wales, General Secretariat, 39 Eccleston Square, London, SWIV IBX. Vacant (Westminster). Bishops' Conference of Scotland, Archbishop's House, 196 Clyde St., Glasgow GI 4JY. Card. Thomas Winning (Glasgow).

Greece: *Conferentia Episcopalis Graeciae*, Odos Homirou 9, 106 72 Athens. Abp. Nikolaos Fóscolos (Athens).

Guatemala: *Conferencia Episcopal de Guatemala* (CEG), Apartado 1698, 01901 Ciudad de Guatemala. Bp. Jorge Mario Avila del Aguila, C.M. (Jalapa).

Guinea: *Conférence Episcopale de la Guinée*, B.P. 1006 Bis, Conakry. Abp. Robert Sarah (Conakry).

Guinea-Bissau: See Senegal.

Haiti: *Conférence Episcopale de Haïti* (CEH). B.P. 1572, Angle rues Piquant et Lammarre, Port-au-Prince. Abp. François Gayot, S.M.M. (Cap Haïtien).

Honduras: *Conferencia Episcopal de Honduras* (CEH), Apartado 847, Blvd. Suyapa, Tegucigalpa. Abp. Oscar Andrés Rodríguez Maradiaga (Tegucigalpa).

Hungary: *Magyar Katolikus Püspöki Konferencia*, PF 79, H-1406 Budapest. Abp. István Seregély (Eger).

India: Catholic Bishops' Conference of India (CBCI), CBCI Centre, Ashok Place, Goldakkhana, New Delhi-110001. Abp. Joseph Powathil (Changanacherry of the Syro-Malabars); Conference of Catholic Bishops of India - Latin Rite (CCBI - L.R.), Divya Deepti Sadan, Second Floor, P.B. 680, 9-10 Bhai Vir Singh Marg. Abp. Marianus Arokiasamy (Madurai). Statutes approved experimentally Jan. 13, 1994 .

Indian Ocean: *Conférence Episcopale de l'Océan Indien* (CEDOI) (includes Islands of Mauritius, Seychelles, Comore and La Réunion), 13 rue Msgr. Gonin, Port Louis, Mauritius. Bp. Maurice Piat, C.S.Sp. (Port Louis) .

Indonesia: *Konperensi Waligereja Indonesia* (KWI), Jl. Cut Mutiah 10, Tromolpos 3044, Jakarta 10002. Abp. Joseph Suwatan, M.S.C. (Manado).

Ireland: Irish Episcopal Conference, *"Ara Coeli,"* Armagh BT61 7QY. Abp. Sean B. Brady (Armagh).

Italy: *Conferenza Episcopale Italiana* (CEI), Circonvallazione Aurelia, 50, 00165 Rome. Card. Camillo Ruini (Vicar General, Rome).

Ivory Coast: See Côte d'Ivoire.

Japan: Catholic Bishops' Conference of Japan, Shiomi 2-10-10, Koto-Ku, Tokyo, 135. Bp. Stephen Fumio Hamao (Yokohama).

Kenya: Kenya Episcopal Conference (KEC), The Kenya Catholic Secretariat, P.O. Box 13475, Nairobi. Bp. John Njue (Embu).

Korea: Catholic Bishops' Conference of Korea, Box 16, Seoul 100-600. Bp. Nicholas Cheong Jin-suk (Cheong Ju).

Laos and Cambodia: *Conférence Episcopale du Laos et du Cambodge*, c/o Msgr. Pierre Bach, Paris Foreign Missions, 254 Silom Rd., Bangkok 10500. Bp. Yves-Georges Ramousse, M.E.P. (vicar apostolic, Phnom Penh, Cambodia).

Latvia: *Conferentia Episcopalis Lettoniae*, Mazâ Pils, 2, Riga 226050. Vacant.

Lesotho: Lesotho Catholic Bishops' Conference, Catholic Secretariat, P.O. Box 200, Maseru 100. Abp. Bernard Mohlalisi, O.M.I. (Maseru).

Liberia: See **Gambia, Liberia and Sierra Leone.**

Lithuania: *Conferentia Episcopalis Lituaniae*, Sventaragio, 4, 2001 Vilnius. Abp. Audrys Juozas Baèkis (Vilnius).

Madagascar: *Conférence Episcopale de Madagascar*, 102 bis Av. Maréchal Joffre, Antanimena, B. P 667, Antananarivo. Card. Armand Gaétan Razafindratandra (Antananarivo).

Malawi: Episcopal Conference of Malawi, Catholic Secretariat of Malawi, P.O. Box 30384, Lilongwe 3. Bp. Felix Eugenio Mkhori (Chikwawa).

Malaysia-Singapore-Brunei: Catholic Bishops' Conference of Malaysia, Singapore and Brunei (BCMSB), Xavier Selangor Darul Ehsan, 46000 Petaling Jaya, Malaysia. Abp. Peter Chung Hoan Ting (Kuching, Malaysia).

Mali: *Conférence Episcopale du Mali*, B.P. 298, Bamako. Bp. Jean-Gabriel Diarra.

Malta: *Konferenza Episkopali Maltija*, Archbishop's Curia, Floriana. Abp. Joseph Mercieca (Malta).

Mexico: *Conferencia del Episcopado Mexicano* (CEM), Prolongación Rio Acatlán, Lago de Guadalupe, 54760 Cuautitlán Izcalli, Mex. Bp. Luis Morales Reyes (Torreón).

Mozambique: *Conferência Episcopal de Moçambique* (CEM), Av. Paulo Samuel Kankhomba 188/RC, C.P. 286. Bp. Francisco João Silota, M.Afr. (Chimoio).

Myanmar: Myanmar Catholic Bishops' Conference (MCBC), 292 Pyi Rd., P.O. Box 1080, Yangon. Bp. Matthias U. Shwe (Taunggyi).

Namibia: Namibian Catholic Bishops' Conference (NCBC). P.O. Box 11525, Windhoek 9000. Abp. Bonifatius Haushiku (Windhoek).

Netherlands: *Nederlandse Bisschoppenconferentie*, Postbus 13049, NL-3507 LA, Utrecht. Card. Adrianus J. Simonis (Utrecht).

New Zealand: New Zealand Episcopal Conference, Private Bag 1937, Wellington 1. Bp. Peter James Cullinane (Palmerston North).

Nicaragua: *Conferencia Episcopal de Nicaragua* (CEN), Apartado Postal 2407, de Ferretería Lang 1 cuadro al Norte y 1 cuadro al Este, Managua. Bp. Bosco Vivas Robelo (Léon).

Niger: See **Burkina Faso.**

Nigeria: Catholic Bishops Conference of Nigeria, P.O. Box 951, 6 Force Rd., Lagos. Abp. Albert K. Obiefuna (Onitsha).

Pacific: *Conferentia Episcopalis Pacifici* (CE PAC), P.O. Box 289, Suva (Fiji). Abp. Michel Marie Bernard Calvet, S.M. (Noumea, New Caledonia).

Pakistan: Pakistan Episcopal Conference, P.O. Box 909, Lahore 54000. Abp. Armando Trindade (Lahore).

Panama: *Conferencia Episcopal de Panamá* (CEP), Apartado 870033, Panama 7. Abp. José Dimas Cedeño Delgado (Panama).

Papua New Guinea and Solomon Islands: Catholic Bishops' Conference of Papua New Guinea and Solomon Islands, P.O. Box 398, Waigani, N.C.D., Papua New Guinea. Bp. Raymond Philip Kalisz, S.V.D. (Wewak).

Paraguay: *Conferencia Episcopal Paraguaya* (CEP), Alberdi 782, Casilla Correo 1436, Asunción. Bp. Oscar Páez Garcete (Alto Parana).

Peru: *Conferencia Episcopal Peruana*, Apartado 310, Rio de Janeiro 488, Lima 100. Card. Augusto Vargas Alzamora, S.J. (Lima).

Philippines: Catholic Bishops' Conference of the Philippines (CBCP), P.O. Box 3601, 470 General Luna St., 1099 Manila. Abp. Oscar V. Cruz (Lingayen-Dagupan).

Poland: *Konferencja Episkopatu Polski*, Skwer Kardynala Stefana Wyszynskiego 6, 01-015 Warsaw. Card. Józef Glemp (Warsaw).

Portugal: *Conferência Episcopal Portuguesa*, Campo dos Mártires da Pátria, 43-1 Esq., 1100 Lisbon. Bp. João Alves (Coimbra).

Puerto Rico: *Conferencia Episcopal Puertorriqueña* (CEP), P.O. Box 40682, Estacion Minillas, San Juan 00940-0682. Bp. Ulises Aurelio Casiano Vargas (Mayagüez).

Romania: *Conferinte Episcopala România*, Via Popa Tatu 58, Bucharest. Abp. Ioan Robu (Bucharest).

Rwanda: *Conférence Episcopale du Rwanda* (C.Ep.R.), B.P. 357, Kigali. Vacant.

Scandinavia: *Conferentia Episcopalis Scandiae*, Trollbärsvägen 16, SE-426 55 Västra Frölunda (Sweden). Bp. Paul Verschuren, S.C.I. (Helsinki, Finland).

Senegal, Mauritania, Cape Verde and Guinea Bissau: *Conférence des Evêques du Sénégal, de la Mauritanie, du Cap-Vert et de Guinée-Bissau*, B.P. 941, Dakar, Senegal. Bp. Théodore Adrien Sarr (Kaolack; Senegal).

Sierra Leone: See **Gambia, Liberia and Sierra Leone.**

Slovakia: *Biskupská Konferencia Slovenska*, Kapitulská 11, 81521 Bratislava. Abp. Rudolf Baláz (Banska Bystrica).

Slovenia: *Slovenska Skofovska Konferenca*, Ciril-Metodov trg 4, p.p.121/III, 1001 Ljubljana. Abp. Franc Rodé, C.M. (Ljubljana).

Spain: *Conferencia Episcopal Española*, Apartado 29075, Calle Añastro 1, 28033 Madrid. Abp. Elías Yanes Alvarez (Zaragoza).

Sri Lanka: Catholic Bishops' Conference of Sri Lanka, 19 Balcombe Place, Cotta Rd., Borella, Colombo 8. Bp. Joseph Vianney Fernando (Kandy).

Sudan: Sudan Catholic Bishops' Conference

(SCBC), P.O. Box 6011, Khartoum. Abp. Gabriel Zubeir Wako (Khartoum).

Switzerland: *Conférence des Evêques Suisses*, Secretariat, C.P. 22, av. Moléson 21, CH-1706 Fribourg. Bp. Amédée Grab, O.S.B. (Lausanne, Genéve, and Fribourg).

Tanzania: Tanzania Episcopal Conference (TEC), P.O. Box 2133, Mansfield St., Dar-es-Salaam. Bp. Justin Tetemu Samba (Musoma).

Thailand: Bishops' Conference of Thailand, 122/6-7 Soi Naaksuwan, Nonsi Road, Yannawa, Bangkok 10120. Bp. George Yod Phimphisan, C.SS.R. (Udon Thani).

Togo: *Conférence Episcopale du Togo*, B.P. 348, Lomé. Abp. Philippe Fanoko Kossi Kpodzro (Lomé).

Uganda: Uganda Episcopal Conference, P.O. Box 2886, Kampala. Bp. Paul L. Kalanda (Fort Portal).

Ukraine: Ukraine Episcopal Conference, Obrzadku Laciñskiego, pl. Katedralna 1, 290008 Lviv. Abp. Marian Jaworski (Lviv of Latins).

United States: See **National Conference of Catholic Bishops.**

Uruguay: *Conferencia Episcopal Uruguaya* (CEU), Avenida Uruguay 1319, 11100 Montevideo. Bp. Raúl Horacio Scarrone Carrero (Florida).

Venezuela: *Conferencia Episcopal de Venezuela* (CEV), Apartado 4897, Torre a Madrices, Edificio Juan XXIII, Piso 4, Caracas 1010-A. Abp. Tulio Manuel Chirivella Varela (Barquisimeto).

Vietnam: *Conferenza Episcopale del Viêt Nam*, 40 Phô Nhâ Chung, Ha Noi. Card. Paul Joseph Pham Dinh Tung (Hâ Nôi).

Yugoslavia: Biskupska Konferencija Savezne Republike Jugoslavije, 11000 Beograd, Visegradska 23. Bp. Franc Perko (Beograd).

Zambia: Zambia Epscopal Conference, P.O. Box 31965, 10101 Lusaka. Bp. Telesphore George Mpundu (Mbala-Mpika).

Zimbabwe: Zimbabwe Catholic Bishops' Conference (ZCBC), Causeway, P.O. Box 8135, Harare. Bp. Francis Xavier Mugadzi (Gweru).

Regional Conferences

(Sources: Almanac survey; *Annuario Pontificio*.)

Africa: Symposium of Episcopal Conferences of Africa and Madagascar (SECAM) (*Symposium des Conférences Episcopales d'Afrique et de Madagascar*, SCEAM): Most Rev. Laurent Monsengwo Pasinya, archbishop of Kisangani (Democratic Republic of Congo), president. Address: Secretariat, P.O. Box 9156 Airport, Accra, Ghana.

Association of Episcopal Conferences of Central Africa (*Association des Conférences Episcopales de l'Afrique Centrale*, ACEAC): Comprises Burundi, Rwanda and Zaire. Bp. Evariste Ngoyagoye, Bubanza, Burundi, president. Address: B.P. 20511, Kinshasa, Democratic Republic of Congo.

Association of Episcopal Conferences of the Region of Central Africa (*Association des Conférences Episcopales de la Région de l'Afrique Central*, ACERAC): Comprises Cameroon, Chad, Congo, Equatorial Guinea, Central African Republic and Gabon. Bp. Anatole Milandou (Kinkala), president. Address: Secretariat, B.P. 200, Brazzaville, Republic of the Congo.

Association of Episcopal Conferences of Anglophone West Africa (AECAWA): Comprises Gambia, Ghana, Liberia, Nigeria and Sierra Leone.

Bp. Peter Kwasi Sarpong, Kumasi, Ghana, president. Address: P.O. Box 10-502, 1000 Monrovia, Liberia.

Association of Member Episcopal Conferences in Eastern Africa (AMECEA): Represents Eritrea, Ethiopia, Kenya, Malawi, Sudan, Tanzania, Uganda and Zambia. Affiliate members: Seychelles (1979), Somalia (1994). Bp. Josaphat L. Lebule, Same, Tanzania, president. Address: P.O. Box 21191, Nairobi, Kenya.

Regional Episcopal Conference of French-Speaking West Africa (Conférence Episcopale Régionale de l'Afrique de l'Ouest Francophone, CERAO): Comprises Benin, Burkina Faso, Cape Verde, Côte d'Ivoire, Guinea, Guinea-Bissau, Mali, Mauritania, Niger, Senegal and Togo. Bp. Anselme Titianma Sanon, Bobo-Dioulasso, president. Address: Secretariat General, B.P.470 CIDEX 1, Abidjan — Côte d'Ivoire.

Inter-Regional Meeting of Bishops of Southern Africa (IMBISA): Bishops of Angola, Botswana, Lesotho, Mozambique, Namibia, São Tome e Principe, South Africa, Swaziland and Zimbabwe. Bp. Francisco João Silota, M. Afr. (Chimoio, Mozambique), president. Address: 4 Bayswater Rd., Highlands, Harare, Zimbabwe.

Asia: Federation of Asian Bishops' Conferences (FABC): Represents 14 Asian episcopal conferences and four independent jurisdictions (Hong Kong, Macau, Nepal, Mongolia) as regular members (excluding the Middle East). Established in 1970; statutes approved experimentally Dec. 6, 1972. Abp. Oscar Cruz, Lingayen-Dagupan, Philippines (elected 1993), secretary general. Address: 16 Caine Road, Hong Kong.

Oceania: Federation of Catholic Bishops' Conferences of Oceania (FCBCO). Statutes approved December 25, 1997. Card. Thomas Stafford Williams, archbishop of Wellington, New Zealand, president. Address: P.O. Box 1937, Wellington, New Zealand.

Europe: Council of European Bishops' Conferences (Consilium Conferentiarum Episcoporum Europae, CCEE): Card. Miloslav Vlk, Prague, Czech Republic, president. Address of secretariat: Gallusstrasse 24, CH-9000 Sankt Gallen, Switzerland. Reorganized in 1993 in accordance with suggestions made during the 1991 Synod of Bishops on Europe.

Commission of the Episcopates of the European Community (Commissio Episcopatuum Communitatis Europaeae, COMECE): Established in 1980; represents episcopates of states which belong to European Community. Bp. Josef Homeyer, Hildesheim, Germany, president. Address of secretariat: 42, Rue Stévin, B-1000 Brussels, Belgium.

Central and South America: Latin American Bishops' Conference (Consejo Episcopal Latino-Americano, CELAM): Established in 1956; statutes approved Nov. 9, 1974. Represents 22 Latin American national bishops' conferences. Abp. Oscar Andrés Rodriguez Maradiaga, S.D.B., Tegucigalpa, Honduras, president. Address of the secretariat: Carrera 5 No. 118-31, Usaquén, Bogotá, Colombia.

Episcopal Secretariat of Central America and Panama (Secretariado Episcopal de America Central y Panama, SEDAC): Statutes approved experimentally Sept. 26, 1970. Bp. Raul Corriveau, P.M.E., Choluteca, Honduras, president. Address of secretary general: Calle 20 y Av Nexuci 124-25, Apartado 6386, Panama 5, Panama.

INTERNATIONAL CATHOLIC ORGANIZATIONS

(Principal sources: Br. Marcel Furic, Executive Secretary-General, Conference of International Catholic Organizations; Pontifical Council for the Laity; Almanac survey.)

Guidelines

International organizations wanting to call themselves "Catholic" are required to meet standards set by the Vatican's Council for the Laity and to register with and get the approval of the Papal Secretariat of State, according to guidelines dated Dec. 3 and published in Acta Apostolicae Sedis under date of Dec. 23, 1971.

Among conditions for the right of organizations to "bear the name Catholic" are:
• leaders "will always be Catholics," and candidates for office will be approved by the Secretariat of State;
• adherence by the organization to the Catholic Church, its teaching authority and teachings of the Gospel;
• evidence that the organization is really international with a universal outlook and that it fulfills its mission through its own management, meetings and accomplishments.

The guidelines also stated that leaders of the organizations "will take care to maintain necessary reserve as regards taking a stand or engaging in public activity in the field of politics or trade unionism. Abstention in these fields will normally be the best attitude for them to adopt during their term of office."

The guidelines were in line with a provision stated by the Second Vatican Council: "No project may claim the name 'Catholic' unless it has obtained the consent of the lawful Church authority."

They made it clear that all organizations are not obliged to apply for recognition, but that the Church "reserves the right to recognize as linked with her mission and her aims those organizations or movements which see fit to ask for such recognition."

Conference of International Catholic Organizations

A permanent body for collaboration among various organizations the conference seeks to promote the development of international life along the lines of Christian principles. Eleven international Catholic organizations participated in its foundation and first meeting in 1927 at Fribourg, Switzerland. In 1951, the conference established its general secretariat and adopted governing statutes which were approved by the Vatican Secretariat of State in 1953.

The permanent secretariat is located at 37-39 rue de Vermont, CH-1202 Geneva, Switzerland. Other office addresses are: 1 rue Varembe, CH-1211 Geneva 20, Switzerland (International Catholic Center of Geneva); 9, rue Cler, F-75007 Paris, France (International Catholic Center for UNESCO); ICO Information Center, 323 East 47th St., New York, N.Y. 10017.

Charter

According to its charter (adopted in November 1997), the conference "responds to the challenge of *Christifideles Laici: Open to the saving power of Christ the frontiers of States, economic and political systems, the vast domains of culture, civilization and development (no. 34)."*

In a universal vision of those problems, these organizations have the following responsibilities to their members:

• to make them increasingly aware of the compexities of the situations in which they live and work;

• to help them to grow in discernment and critical analysis;

• to facilitate the search for solutions to concrete difficulties.

The Conference is open to any organization which is acting and is involved recognizably Catholic in its work in the international world, which accepts the present Charter, respects its principles in practice and adheres to its Statutes. The Conference witnesses to the organized presence of Catholics in the international world.

Fundamental convictions

• their desire to announce Jesus Christ to the women and men of our time, and their vocation to serve the world, are indivisible; faith calls for action;

• their wish to contribute to the building of the Kingdom of God is demonstrated by solidarity with all women and men of good will;

• their desire for participation in decision-making in the Church in areas which concern their competence and in which they are involved.

A unique spirituality

In its desire to live fully its faith in Jesus Christ, the Conference stresses:

• the need to be rooted in reality, through a relationship with God lived out in the world;

• an experience of community nourished by group sharing and exchange;

• openness to the international dimension, validated by experiences at local level to which it gives meaning;

• adaptation to different human groups and to different sensibilities;

• the witness of Christian freedom to initiate, as well as willingness to live in *"solid and strong communion"* with the Church;

• desire to serve the universal Church through insertion in the local Churches by respecting diverse pastoral programmes, but also to participate in major events in the life of the universal Church.

Members

Members of the Conference of International Catholic Organizations are listed below. Information includes name, date and place of establishment (when available), address of general secretariat. Approximately 30 of the organizations have consultative status with other international or regional non-governmental agencies.

Caritas Internationalis (1951, Rome, Italy): Piazza San Calisto 16, I-00153, Rome, Italy. Coordinates and represents its 146 national member organizations (in 194 countries) operating in the fields of development, emergency aid, social action.

Catholic International Education Office (1952): 60, rue des Eburons, B-1000 Brussels, Belgium.

Catholic International Union for Social Service (1925, Milan, Italy): rue de la Poste 111, B-1210 Brussels, Belgium (general secretariat).

Christian Life Community (CVX) (1953): Borgo Santo Spirito 8, C.P. 6139, I-00195 Rome, Italy. First Sodality of Our Lady founded in 1563.

International Ascent, The: 84, rue Charles Michels, F-93206 Saint Denis Cedex, France. Member of ICO.

International Association of Charities (1617, Chatillon les Dombes, France): Rue Joseph Brand, 118, B-1030 Brussels, Belgium.

International Catholic Child Bureau (1948, in Paris): 63, rue de Lausanne, CH-1202 Geneva, Switzerland.

International Catholic Committee of Nurses and Medico-Social Assistants (ICCN) (1933): Square Vergote, 43, B-1040 Brussels, Belgium.

International Catholic Conference of Scouting (1948): Piazza Pasquale Paoli, 18, I-00186 Rome, Italy.

International Catholic Migration Commission (1951): 37-39 rue de Vermont, C.P. 96, CH-1211 Geneva 20, Switzerland. Coordinates activities worldwide on behalf of refugees and migrants, both administering programs directly and supporting the efforts of national affiliated agencies.

International Catholic Organization for Cinema and Audiovisual (1928, The Hague, The Netherlands): Rue du Saphir, 15, B-1040 Brussels, Belgium (general secretariat). Federation of National Catholic film offices.

International Catholic Society for Girls (1897): 37-39, rue de Vermont, CH-1202 Geneva, Switzerland.

International Catholic Union of the Press: 37-39 rue de Vermont, Case Postale 197, CH-1211 Geneva 20 CIC, Switzerland. Coordinates and represents at the international level the activities of Catholics and Catholic federations or associations in the field of press and information. Has seven specialized branches: International Federation of Catholic Journalists; International Federation of Dailies; International Federation of Periodicals; International Federation of Catholic News Agencies; International Catholic Federation of Teachers and Researchers in the Science and Techniques of Information; International Federation of Church Press Associations and International Federation of Book Publishers.

International Conference of Catholic Guiding (1965): c/o Mlle Francoise Parmentier, rue de la Tour 64, 75016 Paris. Founded by member bodies of interdenominational World Association of Guides and Girl Scouts.

International Coordination of Young Christian Workers (YCYCW): via dei Barbieri 22, I00186 Rome, Italy.

International Council of Catholic Men (ICCM) (Unum Omnes) (1948): Wahringer Str. 2-4, A.1090 Vienna IX, Austria.

International Federation of Catholic Medical Associations (1954): Palazzo San Calisto, I-00120 Vatican City.

International Federation of Catholic Parochial

Youth Communities (1962, Rome, Italy): St. Kariliquai 12, 6000 Lucerne 5, Switzerland.

International Federation of Catholic Pharmacists (1954): Bosdorf 180, 9190 Stekene, Belgium.

International Federation of Rural Adult Catholic Movements (1964, Lisbon, Portugal): Rue Jaumain 15, B-5330 Assesse, Belgium.

International Federation of Catholic Universities (1949): 21, rue d'Assas, F-75270 Paris Cedex 06, France.

International Federation of the Catholic Associations of the Blind: Avenue Dailly 90, B-1030 Brussels, Belgium. Coordinates actions of Catholic groups and associations for the blind and develops their apostolate.

International Independent Christian Youth (**IICY**): 11, rue Martin Bernard, F-75013 Paris, France.

International Military Apostolate (1967): Breite Strasse 25. D-53111 Bonn, Germany. Comprised of organizations of military men.

International Movement of Apostolate of Children (1929, France): 24, rue Paul Rivet, F-92350 Le Plessis Robinson, France.

International Movement of Apostolate in the Independent Social Milieux (MIAMSI) (1963): Piazza San Calisto 16, 00153 Rome, Italy.

International Movement of Catholic Agricultural and Rural Youth (1954, Annevoie, Belgium): 53, rue J. Coosemans, B-1030 Brussels, Belgium (permanent secretariat).

International Young Catholic Students (1946, Fribourg, Switzerland; present name, 1954): 171 rue de Rennes, F-75006 Paris, France.

Pax Romana (1921, Fribourg, Switzerland, divided into two branches, 1947): **Pax Romana - IMCS (International Movement of Catholic Students)** (1921): 171, rue de Rennes, F-75006, Paris, France, or undergraduates; **Pax Romana - ICMICA (International Catholic Movement for Intellectual and Cultural Affairs)** (1947): rue du Grand Bureau 15, CH-1227 Geneva, Switzerland. For Catholic intellectuals and professionals.

Society of St. Vincent de Paul (1833, Paris): 5, rue du Pré-aux-Clercs, F-75007 Paris, France.

Unda: International Catholic Association for Radio and Television (1928, Cologne, Germany): rue de l'Orme, 12, B-1040 Brussels, Belgium.

World Movement of Christian Workers (1961): Blvd. du Jubilé 124, 1080 Brussels, Belgium.

World Organization of Former Pupils of Catholic Education (1967, Rome): 48, rue de Richelieu, F-75001 Paris, France.

World Union of Catholic Teachers (1951): Piazza San Calisto 16, 00153 Rome, Italy.

World Union of Catholic Women's Organizations (1910): 18, rue Notre Dame des Champs, F-75006 Paris, France.

Other Catholic Organizations

Apostleship of Prayer (1849): Borgo Santo Spirito 5, I-00193 Rome, Italy. National secretariat in most countries.

Apostolatus Maris (Apostleship of the Sea) (1922, Glasgow, Scotland): Pontifical Council for Migrants and Itinerant People, Piazza San Calisto 16, 00153 Rome, Italy. (See Index.)

L'Arche Communities: B.P. 35, 60350 Cuise Lamotte, France.

Associationes Juventutis Salesianae (Associations of Salesian Youth) (1847): Via della Pisana, 1111, 00163 Rome, Italy.

Blue Army of Our Lady of Fatima: P.O. Box 976, Washington, NJ, 07882.

Catholic International Federation for Physical and Sports Education (1911; present name, 1957): 5, rue Cernuschi, F-75017 Paris, France.

Christian Fraternity of the Sick and Handicapped: 9, Avenue de la Gare, CH-1630, Bulle, Switzerland.

"Communione e Liberazione" Fraternity (1955, Milan, Italy): Via Marcello Malpighi 2, 00161 Rome, Italy. Catholic renewal movement.

"Focolare Movement" or "Work of Mary" (1943, Trent, Italy): Via di Frascati, 306, I-00040 Rocca di Papa (Rome), Italy.

Foi et Lumiere: 8 rue Serret, 75015 Paris, France.

Franciscans International: 345 E. 47th St., New York, NY 10017. A non-governmental organization at the UN.

Inter Cultural Association (ICA, 1937, Belgium) and Association Fraternelle Internationale (AFI): 91, rue de la Servette, CH-1202 Geneva, Switzerland.

International Association of Children of Mary (1847): 67 rue de Sèvres, F-75006 Paris, France.

International Catholic Rural Association (1962, Rome): Piazza San Calisto, 00153 Rome, Italy. International body for agricultural and rural organizations. Invited member of ICO.

International Catholic Union of Esperanto: Via Berni 9, 00185 Rome, Italy.

International Centre for Studies in Religious Education LUMEN VITAE (1934-35, Louvain, Belgium, under name Catechetical Documentary Centre; present name, 1956): 184, rue Washington, B-1050 Brussels, Belgium. Also referred to as Lumen Vitae Centre; concerned with all aspects of religious formation.

International Young Christian Workers (1925, Belgium): 11, rue Plantin, B-1070 Brussels, Belgium. Associate member of ICO.

Legion of Mary (1921, Dublin, Ireland): De Montfort House, North Brunswick St., Dublin, Ireland. (See Index.)

Medicus Mundi Internationalis (1964, Bensberg, Germany FR): P.O. Box 1547, 6501 BM Nijmegen, Netherlands. Promote health and medico-social services, particularly in developing countries; recruit essential health and medical personnel for developing countries; contribute to training of medical and auxiliary personnel; undertake research in the field of health.

NOVALIS, Marriage Preparation Center: University of St. Paul, 1 rue Stewart, Ottawa 2, Ont. Canada.

Our Lady's Teams (Equipes Notre-Dame) (1937, France): 49, rue de la Glacière, F-75013 Paris, France. Movement for spiritual formation of couples.

Pax Christi International (1950): rue du Vieux Marché aux grains 21, B-1000 Brussels, Belgium. International Catholic peace movement. Originated in Lourdes, France in 1948 by French and German Catholics to reconcile enemies from World War II; spread to Italy and Poland and acquired its international ctitle when it merged with the English organization Pax. Associate member of ICO.

Pro Sanctity Movement: Piazza S. Andrea della Valle 3, 00166 Rome, Italy.

St. Joan's International Alliance (1911, in England, as Catholic Women's Suffrage Society): Quai Churchill 19 - Boite 061, B-4020 Liège, Belgium. Associate member of ICO.

Salesian Cooperators (1876): Don Bosco College, Newton, N.J. 07860. Third Salesian family founded by St. John Bosco. Members commit themselves to an apostolate at the service of the Church, giving particular attention to youth in the Salesian spirit and style.

Secular Franciscan Order (1221, first Rule approved): Via Piemonte, 70, 00187, Rome, Italy.

Secular Fraternity of Charles de Foucauld: Katharinenweg 4, B4700 Eupen, Belgium.

Serra International (1953, in U.S.): 65 E. Wacker Pl. Suite 1210, Chicago, IL 60601.

Unio Internationalis Laicorum in Servitio Ecclesiae (1965, Aachen, Germany): Postfach 990125, Am Kielshof 2, 5000 Cologne, Germany 91. Consists of national and diocesan associations of persons who give professional services to the Church.

Union of Adorers of the Blessed Sacrament (1937): Largo dei Monti Parioli 3, I-00197, Rome, Italy.

World Catholic Federation for the Biblical Apostolate (1969, Rome): Mittelstrasse, 12, P.O. Box 601, D-7000, Stuttgart 1, Germany.

Regional Organizations

European Federation for Catholic Adult Education (1963, Lucerne, Switzerland): Hirschengraben 13, P.B. 2069, CH-6002 Lucerne, Switzerland.

European Forum of National Committees of the Laity (1968): 169, Booterstown Av., Blackrock, Co. Dublin, Ireland.

Movimiento Familiar Cristiano (1949-50, Montevideo and Buenos Aires): Carrera 17 n. 4671, Bogotá, D.E., Colombia. Christian Family Movement of Latin America.

MESSAGE OF POPE JOHN PAUL II
FOR THE CELEBRATION OF THE WORLD DAY OF PEACE

(Courtesy L'Osservatore Romano.) On Dec. 8, 1999, Pope John Paul II issued a message calling for "Respect for Human Rights: The Secret of True Peace." Following are excerpts:

Looking towards the World Day of Peace, let me state the conviction which I very much want to share with you: when the promotion of the dignity of the person is the guiding principle, and when the search for the common good is the overriding commitment, then solid and lasting foundations for building peace are laid.

Respect for Human Dignity, the Heritage of Humanity
2. The dignity of the human person is a transcendent value, always recognized as such by those who sincerely search for the truth. Indeed, the whole of human history should be interpreted in the light of this certainty. Every person, created in the image and likeness of God (cf. *Gen* 1:26-28) and therefore radically oriented towards the Creator, is constantly in relationship with those possessed of the same dignity.

Religious Freedom, the Heart of Human Rights
5. Religion expresses the deepest aspirations of the human person, shapes people's vision of the world and affects their relationships with others: basically it offers the answer to the question of the true meaning of life, both personal and communal. Religious freedom therefore constitutes the very heart of human rights.

The Right to Participate
6. All citizens have the right to participate in the life of their community: this is a conviction which is generally shared today. But this right means nothing when the democratic process breaks down because of corruption and favoritism, which not only obstruct legitimate sharing in the exercise of power but also prevent people from benefiting equally from community assets and services, to which everyone has a right....

The Right to Self-Fulfilment
8. Every human being has innate abilities waiting to be developed. At stake here is the full actualiza-

tion of one's own person and the appropriate insertion into one's social environment. In order that this may take place, it is necessary above all to provide adequate education to those who are just beginning their lives: their future success depends on this.

Global Progress in Solidarity
9. The rapid advance towards the globalization of economic and financial systems also illustrates the urgent need to establish who is responsible for guaranteeing the global common good and the exercise of economic and social rights.

Responsibility for the Environment
10. The promotion of human dignity is linked to the right to a healthy environment, since this right highlights the dynamics of the relationship between the individual and society. A body of international, regional and national norms on the environment is gradually giving juridic form to this right.

The Right to Peace
11. In a sense, promoting the right to peace ensures respect for all other rights, since it encourages the building of a society in which structures of power give way to structures of cooperation, with a view to the common good.

A Time of Decision, a Time of Hope
13. The new millennium is close at hand, and its approach has filled the hearts of many with hope for a more just and fraternal world. This is an aspiration which can, and indeed must, become a reality!

Jesus taught us to call God "Father," *Abba*, thus revealing to us the depth of our relationship with him. Infinite and eternal is his love for every person and for all humanity. Eloquent in this regard are God's words found in the book of the Prophet Isaiah:

Let us accept the invitation to share this love! In it is found the secret of respect for the rights of every woman and every man. The dawn of the new millennium will thus find us more ready to build peace together.

(Sources: Rev. Ronald Roberson, C.S.P., Associate Director, Ecumenical and Interreligious Affairs, NCCB.; Annuario Pontificio; Official Catholic Directory.*)*

The Second Vatican Council, in its Decree on Eastern Catholic Churches (*Orientalium Ecclesiarum*), stated the following points regarding Eastern heritage, patriarchs, sacraments and worship.

Venerable Churches: The Catholic Church holds in high esteem the institutions of the Eastern Churches, their liturgical rites, ecclesiastical traditions, and Christian way of life. For, distinguished as they are by their venerable antiquity, they are bright with that tradition which was handed down from the Apostles through the Fathers, and which forms part of the divinely revealed and undivided heritage of the universal Church (No. 1). That Church, Holy and Catholic, which is the Mystical Body of Christ, is made up of the faithful who are organically united in the Holy Spirit through the same faith, the same sacraments, and the same government and who, combining into various groups held together by a hierarchy, form separate Churches or rites. It is the mind of the Catholic Church that each individual Church or rite retain its traditions whole and entire, while adjusting its way of life to the various needs of time and place (No. 2).

Such individual Churches, whether of the East or of the West, although they differ somewhat among themselves in what are called rites (that is, in liturgy, ecclesiastical discipline, and spiritual heritage) are, nevertheless, equally entrusted to the pastoral guidance of the Roman Pontiff, the divinely appointed successor of St. Peter in supreme government over the universal Church. They are consequently of equal dignity, so that none of them is superior to the others by reason of rite (No. 3).

Eastern Heritage: Each and every Catholic, as also the baptized of every non-Catholic Church or community who enters into the fullness of Catholic communion, should everywhere retain his proper rite, cherish it, and observe it to the best of his ability (No. 4). The Churches of the East, as much as those of the West, fully enjoy the right, and are in duty bound, to rule themselves. Each should do so according to its proper and individual procedures (No. 5). All Eastern rite members should know and be convinced that they can and should always preserve their lawful liturgical rites and their established way of life, and that these should not be altered except by way of an appropriate and organic development (No. 6)

Patriarchs: The institution of the patriarchate has existed in the Church from the earliest times and was recognized by the first ecumenical Synods. By the name Eastern Patriarch is meant the bishop who has jurisdiction over all bishops (including metropolitans), clergy, and people of his own territory or rite, in accordance with the norms of law and without prejudice to the primacy of the Roman Pontiff (No. 7). Though some of the patriarchates of the Eastern Churches are of later origin than others, all are equal in patriarchal dignity. Still the honorary and lawfully established order of precedence among them is to be preserved (No. 8). In keeping with the most ancient tradition of the Church, the Patriarchs of the Eastern Churches are to be accorded exceptional respect, since each presides over his patriarchate as father and head.

EASTERN CATHOLIC CHURCHES

This sacred Synod, therefore, decrees that their rights and privileges should be re-established in accord with the ancient traditions of each Church and the decrees of the ecumenical Synods. The rights and privileges in question are those which flourished when East and West were in union, though they should be somewhat adapted to modern conditions.

The Patriarchs with their synods constitute the superior authority for all affairs of the patriarchate, including the right to establish new eparchies and to nominate bishops of their rite within the territorial bounds of the patriarchate, without prejudice to the inalienable right of the Roman Pontiff to intervene in individual cases (No. 9).

What has been said of Patriarchs applies as well, under the norm of law, to major archbishops, who preside over the whole of some individual Church or rite (No. 10).

Sacraments: This sacred Ecumenical Synod endorses and lauds the ancient discipline of the sacraments existing in the Eastern Churches, as also the practices connected with their celebration and administration (No. 12).

With respect to the minister of holy chrism (confirmation), let that practice be fully restored which existed among Easterners in most ancient times. Priests, therefore, can validly confer this sacrament, provided they use chrism blessed by a Patriarch or bishop (No. 13).

In conjunction with baptism or otherwise, all Eastern-Rite priests can confer this sacrament validly on all the faithful of any rite, including the Latin; licitly, however, only if the regulations of both common and particular law are observed. Priests of the Latin rite, to the extent of the faculties they enjoy for administering this sacrament, can confer it also on the faithful of Eastern Churches, without prejudice to rite. They do so licitly if the regulations of both common and particular law are observed (No. 14).

The faithful are bound on Sundays and feast days to attend the divine liturgy or, according to the regulations or custom of their own rite, the celebration of the Divine Praises. That the faithful may be able to satisfy their obligation more easily, it is decreed that this obligation can be fulfilled from the Vespers of the vigil to the end of the Sunday or the feast day (No. 15). Because of the everyday intermingling of the communicants of diverse Eastern Churches in the same Eastern region or territory, the faculty for hearing confession, duly and unrestrictedly granted by his proper bishop to a priest of any rite, is applicable to the entire territory of the grantor, also to the places and the faithful belonging to any other rite in the same territory, unless an Ordinary of the place explicitly decides otherwise with respect to the places pertaining to his rite (No. 16).

This sacred Synod ardently desires that where it has fallen into disuse the office of the permanent diaconate be restored. The legislative authority of each individual church should decide about the subdiaconate and the minor orders (No. 17).

By way of preventing invalid marriages between Eastern Catholics and baptized Eastern non-Catholics, and in the interests of the permanence and sanctity of marriage and of domestic harmony, this sacred Synod decrees that the canonical 'form' for the celebration of such marriages obliges only for lawfulness. For their validity, the presence of a sacred minister suffices, as long as the other requirements of law are honored (No. 18).

Worship: Henceforth, it will be the exclusive right of an ecumenical Synod or the Apostolic See to establish, transfer, or suppress feast days common to all the Eastern Churches. To establish, transfer, or suppress feast days for any of the individual Churches is within the competence not only of the Apostolic See but also of a patriarchal or archiepiscopal synod, provided due consideration is given to the entire region and to other individual Churches (No. 19). Until such time as all Christians desirably concur on a fixed day for the celebration of Easter, and with a view meantime to promoting unity among the Christians of a given area or nation, it is left to the Patriarchs or supreme authorities of a place to reach a unanimous agreement, after ascertaining the views of all concerned, on a single Sunday for the observance of Easter (No. 20). With respect to rules concerning sacred seasons, individual faithful dwelling outside the area or territory of their own rite may conform completely to the established custom of the place where they live. When members of a family belong to different rites, they are all permitted to observe sacred seasons according to the rules of any one of these rites (No. 21). From ancient times the Divine Praises have been held in high esteem among all Eastern Churches. Eastern clerics and religious should celebrate these Praises as the laws and customs of their own traditions require. To the extent they can, the faithful too should follow the example of their forebears by assisting devoutly at the Divine Praises (No. 22).

Restoration of Ancient Practices

An "Instruction for the Application of the Liturgical Prescriptions of the Code of Canons of the Eastern Churches" was published in Italian by the Congregation for Eastern-Rite Churches in January, 1996. Msgr. Alan Detscher, executive director of the U.S. bishops' Secretariat for the Liturgy, said it was the first instruction on liturgical renewal of the Eastern Catholic Churches since the Second Vatican Council (1962-65).

JURISDICTIONS AND FAITHFUL OF THE EASTERN CATHOLIC CHURCHES

Introduction

The Church originated in Palestine, whence it spread to other regions of the world where certain places became key centers of Christian life with great influence on the local churches in their respective areas. These centers developed into the ancient patriarchates of Constantinople, Alexandria, Antioch and Jerusalem in the East, and Rome in the West. The main lines of Eastern Church patriarchal organization and usages were drawn before the Roman Empire became two empires, East (Byzantine) and West (Roman), in 292. Other churches with distinctive traditions grew up beyond the boundaries of the Roman Empire in Persia, Armenia, Syria, Egypt, Ethiopia, and India. The "nestorian" church in Persia, known today as the Assyrian Church of the East, broke communion with the rest of the church in the wake of the Council of Ephesus (431) whose teachings it did not accept. The "monophysite" churches of Armenia, Syria, Egypt, Ethiopia, Eritrea and India (known today as the Oriental Orthodox Churches) did not accept the christological teachings of the Council of Chalcedon (451) and so broke away from the church within the Roman Empire. And finally, in the wake of the mutual excommunications of 1054 between the Patriarch of Constantinople and the papal legate, the church within the empire divided into what would become the Catholic Church in the West and the Orthodox Church in the East. This was a lengthy process of estrangement that culminated only in 1204 and the sack of Constantinople by the Latin Crusaders.

In the following centuries, attempts to overcome these divisions took place, most notably at the Second Council of Lyons in 1274 and the Council of Ferrara-Florence in 1438-39. Both failed. Subsequently, the Catholic Church began to send missionaries to work with separated Eastern Christians, and some groups within those churches spontaneously asked to enter into full communion with Rome. Thus began the formation of the Eastern Catholic Churches, which retained most of the liturgical, canonical, spiritual and theological patrimony of their non-Catholic counterparts.

The Code of Canons of the Eastern Churches groups these churches today into four categories: patriarchal, major archepiscopal, metropolitan, and other churches *sui iuris*.

STATISTICS

(Principal source: Annuario Pontificio.)
The following statistics are the sum of those reported for Eastern Catholic jurisdictions only, and do not include Eastern Catholics under the jurisdiction of Latin bishops. Some of the figures reported are only approximate. The churches are grouped according to their liturgical traditions.

ALEXANDRIAN

The liturgical tradition of Egypt, in particular that of the early Greek Patriarchate of Alexandria. In the Egyptian desert monasteries the rite evolved in a distinctive way and eventually became that of the Coptic Orthodox Church. The Greek Patriarchate of Alexandria adopted the Byzantine rite by the 12th century. The Coptic rite, with its Alexandrian origins, spread to Ethiopia in the 4th century where it underwent substantial modifications under strong Syrian influence. The Catholic Churches in this group are:

The Coptic Catholic Church (Patriarchate): Six dioceses in Egypt, 196,248.
Catholic missionaries were present since the 17th century. The Patriarchate was established first in 1824 and renewed in 1895. Liturgical languages are Coptic and Arabic.

The Ethiopian Catholic Church (Metropolitanate): Two dioceses in Ethiopia and three in Eritrea; 202,043. Catholic missionary activity began in the 19th century, and the present ecclesiastical structure dates from 1961. The liturgical languages are Ge'ez and Amharic.

ANTIOCHENE

The liturgical tradition of Antioch, one of the great centers of the early Christian world, also known as West Syrian. In Syria it developed under strong influence of Jerusalem, especially the Liturgy of St James, into the form used by today's Syrian Orthodox and Catholics in the Middle East and India. The Maronites of Lebanon developed their own liturgical traditions under the influence of both the Antiochene and Chaldean rites.
The Catholic Churches of this group are:

The Syro-Malankara Catholic Church (Metropolitanate): Four diocese in India; 326,654. Began in 1930 when two bishops, a priest, a deacon and a layman of the Malankara Orthodox Church were received into full communion with Rome. The liturgical language is Malayalam.

The Maronite Catholic Church (Patriarchate): Ten dioceses in Lebanon, three in Syria, two in the United States, and one each in Cyprus, Egypt, Argentina, Brazil, Australia, Canada, and Mexico, plus patriarchal exarchates in Jordan and Jerusalem; 3,221,939.
Founded by St. Maron in the 4th century, the Maronites claim to have always been in communion with Rome. They have no counterpart among the separated Eastern churches. The patriarchate dates to the 8th century, and was confirmed by Pope Innocent III in 1216. Liturgical language is Arabic.

The Syrian Catholic Church (Patriarchate): Four dioceses in Syria, two in Iraq, and one each in Lebanon, Egypt, and North America, and patriarchal exarchates in Turkey and Iraq/Kuwait;; 128,931.
Catholic missionary activity among the Syrian Orthodox began in the 17th century, and there has been an uninterrupted series of Catholic patriarchs since 1783. The liturgical languages are Syriac/Aramaic and Arabic.

ARMENIAN

The liturgical tradition of the Armenian Apostolic and Catholic Churches. It contains elements of the Syriac, Jerusalem, and Byzantine rites. From the 5th to the 7th centuries there was strong influence from Syria and Jerusalem. More Byzantine usages were adopted later, and in the Middle Ages elements of the Latin tradition were added.

The Armenian Catholic Church (Patriarchate): Two dioceses in Syria, one each in Lebanon, Iran, Iraq, Egypt, Turkey, Ukraine, France and Argentina. Apostolic Exarchate for the United States, and Ordinariates in Greece, Romania, and Eastern Europe (Armenia); 343,198.
Catholic missionaries had been working among the Armenians since the 14th century, and an Armenian Catholic patriarchate was established in Lebanon in 1742. The liturgical language is classical Armenian.

BYZANTINE

The tradition of the Eastern Orthodox and Byzantine Catholic Churches which originated in the Orthodox Patriarchate of Constantinople (Byzantium). Its present form is a synthesis of Constantinopolitan and Palestinian elements that took place in the monasteries between the 9th and 14th centuries. It is by far the most widely used Eastern liturgical tradition. The Catholic Churches of this group are:

Albanians: One apostolic administration in southern Albania; 2,164. Very small groups of Albanian Orthodox became Catholic in 1628 and again in 1900; liturgical language is Albanian.

Belarussians (formerly Byelorussian, also known as White Russian): No hierarchy. Most Belarusan Orthodox became Catholic with the Union of Brest in 1595-6, but this union was short lived. A modest revival has taken place since the end of communism. The liturgical language is Belarusan.

The Bulgarian Catholic Church: One apostolic exarchate in Bulgaria; 15,000. Originated with a group of Bulgarian Orthodox who became Catholic in 1861; liturgical language is Old Slavonic.

Eparchy of Krizevci: One diocese located in Croatia with jurisdiction over all of former Yugoslavia; 48,920.

A bishop for former Serbian Orthodox living in Catholic Croatia was first appointed in 1611; liturgical languages are Old Slavonic and Croatian.

The Greek Catholic Church: Apostolic exarchates in Greece and Turkey; 2,345. Catholic missionaries in Constantinople formed a small group of Byzantine Catholics there in the mid-19th century. Most of them moved to Greece in the 1920s. The liturgical language is Greek.

The Hungarian Catholic Church: One diocese and one apostolic exarchate in Hungary; 281,998.

Descendants of groups of Orthodox in Hungary who became Catholic in the 17th century and after. The liturgical language is Hungarian.

The Italo-Albanian Catholic Church: Two dioceses, one territorial abbey in Italy; 63,596.

Descended mostly from Albanian Orthodox who came to southern Italy and Sicily in the 15th century and eventually became Catholic; liturgical languages are Greek and Italian.

The Melkite Greek Catholic Church (Patriarchate): Five dioceses in Syria, seven in Lebanon, one each in Jordan, Israel, Brazil, US, Canada, Mexico, and Australia. Apostolic Exarchate in Venezuela, and patriarchal exarchates in Iraq and Kuwait; 1,189,557.

Catholic missionaries began work within the Greek Orthodox Patriarchate of Antioch in the mid-17th century. In 1724 it split into Catholic and Orthodox counterparts, the Catholics becoming known popularly as Melkites. Liturgical languages are Greek and Arabic.

The Romanian Greek Catholic Church (Metropolitanate): Five dioceses in Romania and one in the US; 1,118,823.

Romanian Orthodox in Transylvania formally entered into union with Rome in 1700; the liturgical language is Romanian.

Russians: No hierarchy. An apostoic exarchate was established for Russia in 1917 and for Russians in China in 1928, but neither is functioning today. Five parishes exist in the diaspora.

The Ruthenian Catholic Church (Metropolitanate in the United States): One diocese in Ukraine, four in the United States, and an apostolic exarchate in the Czech Republic. Originated with the reception of 63 Orthodox priests into the Catholic Church at the Union of Uzhhorod in 1646. Liturgical languages are Old Slavonic and English.

The Slovak Catholic Church: One diocese and one apostolic exarchate in Slovakia, and one diocese in Canada; 221,757.

Also originated with the Union of Uzhhorod in 1646; diocese of Presov was established for them in 1818. Liturgical languages are Old Slavonic and Slovak.

The Ukrainian Greek Catholic Church (Major Archbishopric): Six dioceses and one archepiscopal exarchate in Ukraine, two dioceses in Poland, five dioceses in Canada, four in the United States, one each in Australia, Brazil and Argentina, apostolic exarchates in Great Britain, Germany, and France; 5,181,759.

Originated with the Union of Brest between the Orthodox Metropolitanate of Kiev and the Catholic Church in 1595-6. Liturgical languages are Old Slavonic and Ukrainian.

CHALDEAN

Also called East Syrian, the liturgical tradition of the Chaldean Catholic and Syro-Malabar Catholic Churches as well as the Assyrian Church of the East. Descends from the ancient rite of the church of Mesopotamia in the Persian Empire. It is celebrated in the eastern dialect of classical Syriac. The Catholic Churches of this tradition are:

The Chaldean Catholic Church (Patriarchate): Ten dioceses in Iraq, three in Iran, one each in Lebanon, Egypt, Syria, Turkey, and the US; 303,096.

A group of disaffected members of the ("nestorian") Assyrian Church of the East asked for union with Rome in 1553. In that year Pope Julius III ordained their leader a bishop and named him Patriarch; liturgical languages are Syriac, Arabic.

The Syro-Malabar Catholic Church (Major Archbishopric): 22 dioceses in India; 3,885,388.

Descended from Thomas Christians of India who became Catholic in the wake of Portuguese colonization; the diocese of Ernakulam-Angamaly was raised to Major Archepiscopal status in 1993; the liturgical language is Malayalam.

EASTERN JURISDICTIONS

For centuries Eastern Churches were identifiable with a limited number of nationality and language groups in certain countries of the Middle East, Eastern Europe, Asia and Africa. The persecution of religion in the former Soviet Union since 1917 and in communist-controlled countries for more than 40 years following World War II — in addition to decimating and destroying the Church in those places — resulted in the emigration of many Eastern Catholics from their homelands. This forced emigration, together with voluntary emigration, has led to the spread of Eastern Churches to many other countries.

Europe

(Bishop Krikor Ghabroyan, of the Armenian Eparchy of Sainte-Croix-de-Paris, France, is apostolic visitator for Armenian Catholics in Western Europe who do not have their own bishop. Bishop Youssef Ibrahim Sarraf of Cairo of the Chaldeans is apostolic visitator for Chaldeans in Europe. Bishop Samis Mazloum is apostolic visitator for Maronites in Western and Northern Europe.)

Albania: Byzantine apostolic administration.

Austria: Byzantine ordinariate.

Bulgaria: Bulgarian apostolic exarchate
Croatia: Eparchy of Krizevci.
Czech Republic: Ruthenian apostolic exarchate.
France: Ukrainian apostolic exarchate. Armenian eparchy (1986). Ordinariate for all other Eastern Catholics.
Germany: Ukrainian apostolic exarchate.
Great Britain: Ukrainian apostolic exarchate.
Greece: Byzantine apostolic exarchate. Armenian ordinariate.
Hungary: Hungarian Byzantine eparchy, apostolic exarchate
Italy: Two Italo-Albanian eparchies, one abbacy.
Poland: Ukrainian metropolitan see (1996), one eparchy. Ordinariate for all other Eastern Catholics.
Romania: Romanian Byzantine metropolitan, four eparchies; Armenian ordinariate.
Russia: Russian apostolic exarchate (for Byzantine Catholics in Moscow).
Slovakia: Slovak Byzantine eparchy, one apostolic exarchate.
Ukraine: Armenian archeparchy; Ruthenian eparchy; Ukrainian major archbishopric, five eparchies.

Asia
Armenia: Armenian ordinariate (for Armenians of Eastern Europe).
China: Russian Byzantine apostolic exarchate.
Cyprus: Maronite archeparchy.
India: Syro-Malankara metropolitan see, three eparchies.
Syro-Malabar major archbishopric (1993), three metropolitan sees (1995), 18 eparchies.
Iran: Two Chaldean metropolitan sees, one archeparchy, one eparchy; Armenian eparchy.
Iraq: Two Syrian archeparchies; Melkite patriarchal exarchate; Chaldean patriarchate, two metropolitan sees, three archeparchies and five eparchies; Armenian archeparchy.
Israel (including Jerusalem): Syrians patriarchal exarchate; Maronite archeparchy; Melkite archeparchy, patriarchal exarchate; Chaldean patriarchal exarchate; Armenian patriarchal exarchate.
Jordan: Melkite archeparchy.
Kuwait: Melkite patriarchal exarchate; Lebanon Maronite patriarchate, four archeparchies and six eparchies; Syrian patriarchate, patriarchal exarchate; two Melkite metropolitan and five archeparchial sees; Chaldean eparchy; Armenian patriarchate, metropolitan see.
Syria: Two Maronite archeparchies, one eparchy; two Syrian metropolitan and two archeparchal sees; Melkite patriarchate, four metropolitan sees, one archeparchy; Chaldean eparchy; Armenian archeparchy, one eparchy .
Turkey: Syrian patriarchal exarchate; Greek apostolic exarchate; Chaldean archeparchy; Armenian archeparchy.
Oceania
Australia: Ukrainian eparchy; Melkite eparchy (1987); Maronite eparchy.

Africa
Egypt: Coptic patriarchate, five eparchies; Maronite eparchy; Syrian eparchy; Melkite patriarchal dependency; Chaldean eparchy; Armenian eparchy.

Eritrea: Three Ethiopian eparchies.
Ethiopia: Ethiopian metropolitan see, one eparchy.
Sudan: Melkite patriarchal dependency.

North America
Canada: One Ukrainian metropolitan, four eparchies; Slovak eparchy; Melkite eparchy; Armenian apostolic exarchate for Canada and the U.S. (New York is see city); Maronite eparchy.
United States: Two Maronite eparchies; Syrian eparchy (1995); one Ukrainian metropolitan see, three eparchies; one Ruthenian metropolitan see, three eparchies; Melkite eparchy; Romanian eparchy; Belarusan apostolic visitator; Armenian apostolic exarchate for Canada and U.S. (New York is see city); Chaldean eparchy; other Eastern Catholics are under the jurisdiction of local Latin bishops. (See Eastern Catholics in the United States.)
Mexico: Melkite eparchy; Maronite eparchy (1995).

South America
Armenian Catholics in Latin America (including Mexico and excluding Argentina) are under the jurisdiction of an apostolic exarchate (see city, Buenos Aires, Argentina).
Argentina: Ukrainian eparchy; Maronite eparchy; Armenian eparchy; ordinariate for all other Eastern Catholics.
Brazil: Maronite eparchy; Melkite eparchy; Ukrainian eparchy; ordinariate for all other Eastern Catholics.
Venezuela: Melkite apostolic exarchate.

Synods, Assemblies
These assemblies are collegial bodies which have pastoral authority over members of the Eastern Catholic Churches. (Canons 102-113, 152-153, 322 of Oriental Code of Canon Law.)
Patriarchal Synods: Synod of the Catholic Coptic Church: Stéphanos II Ghattas, C.M., patriarch of Alexandria of the Copts.
Synod of the Greek-Melkite Catholic Church: Maximos V Hakim, patriarch of Antioch of the Greek Catholics-Melkites.
Synod of the Syrian Catholic Church: Ignace Antoine II Hayek, patriarch of Antioch of the Syrians.
Synod of the Maronite Church: Cardinal Nasrallah Pierre Sfeir, patriarch of Antioch of the Maronites.
Synod of the Chaldean Church: Raphaël I Bidawid, patriarch of Babylonia of the Chaldeans.
Synod of the Armenian Catholic Church: Jean Pierre XVIII Kasparian, patriarch of Cilicia of the Armenians.

Major Archiepiscopal Synods:
The Synod of the Ukrainian Catholic Church (raised to major archiepiscopal status Dec. 23, 1963): Cardinal Myroslav Ivan Lubachivsky, major archbishop of Lviv of the Ukrainians, president.
The Synod of the Syro-Malabar Church (raised to major archiepiscopal status, Jan. 29, 1993): Most Rev. Varkey Vithayathil, C.SS.R., apostolic administrator of Ernakulam-Angamaly of the Syro-Malabars, president.

Councils, Assemblies, Conferences

Council of Ethiopian Churches: Cardinal Paul Tzadua, president.

Council of Romanian Churches: Abp. Lucian Muresan of Fagaras and Alba Julia, president.

Council of Ruthenian Churches, U.S.A.: Abp. Judson Michael Procyk of Pittsburgh of the Byzantines, president.

Council of Syro-Malankarese Churches: Abp. Cyril Baselios Malancharuvil, O.I.C., of Trivandrum of the Syro-Malankarese, president.

Assembly of the Catholic Hierarchy of Egypt (Dec. 5, 1983): Stéphanos II Ghattas, C.M., patriarch of Alexandria of the Copts, president.

Assembly of Catholic Patriarchs and Bishops of Lebanon: Cardinal Nasrallah Pierre Sfeir, patriarch of Antioch of the Maronites, president.

Assembly of Ordinaries of the Syrian Arab Republic: Maximos V Hakim, patriarch of Antioch of the Greek Catholics-Melkites, president.

Assembly of Catholic Ordinaries of the Holy Land (Jan. 27, 1992): Michel Sabbah, patriarch of Jerusalem of the Latins, president.

Interritual Union of the Bishops of Iraq: Raphael I Bidawid, patriarch of Babylonia of the Chaldeans, president.

Iranian Episcopal Conference (Aug. 11, 1977): Most Rev. Vartan Tékéyan, bishop of Ispahan of the Armenians, president.

Episcopal Conference of Turkey (Nov. 30, 1987): Most Rev. Louis A. Pelâtre, A.A., vicar apostolic of Istanbul, president.

EASTERN CATHOLIC CHURCHES IN U.S.

(Statistics, from the Annuario Pontificio *unless noted otherwise, are membership figures reported by Eastern jurisdictions. Additional Eastern Catholics are included in statistics for Latin dioceses.)*

Byzantine Tradition

Ukrainians: There were 120,925 reported in four jurisdictions in the U.S.: the metropolitan see of Philadelphia (1924, metropolitan 1958) and the suffragan sees of Stamford, Conn. (1956), St. Nicholas of Chicago (1961) and St. Josaphat in Parma (1983).

Ruthenians: There were 168,420 reported in four jurisdictions in the U.S.: the metropolitan see of Pittsburgh (est. 1924 at Pittsburgh; metropolitan and transferred to Munhall, 1969; transferred to Pittsburgh, 1977) and the suffragan sees of Passaic, N.J. (1963), Parma, Ohio (1969) and Van Nuys, Calif. (1981). Hungarian and Croatian Byzantine Catholics in the U.S. are also under the jurisdiction of Ruthenian bishops.

Melkites: There were 27,729 reported under the jurisdiction of the Melkite eparchy of Newton, Mass. (established as an exarchate, 1965; eparchy, 1976).

Romanians: There were 5,300 reported in 15 Romanian Catholic Byzantine Rite parishes in the U.S., under the jurisdiction of the Romanian eparchy of St. George Martyr, Canton, Ohio (established as an exarchate, 1982; eparchy, 1987).

Belarusans: Have one parish in the U.S. — Christ the Redeemer, Chicago, Ill.

Russians: Have parishes in California (St. Andrew, El Segundo, and Our Lady of Fatima Center, San Francisco); New York (St. Michael's Chapel of St. Patrick's Old Cathedral). They are under the jurisdiction of local Latin bishops.

Alexandrian Tradition

Copts: Have a Catholic Chapel—Resurrection, in Brooklyn, N.Y.

Antiochene Tradition

Maronites: There were 53,000 reported in two jurisdictions in the U.S.: the eparchy of St. Maron, Brooklyn (established at Detroit as an exarchate, 1966; eparchy, 1972; transferred to Brooklyn, 1977) and the eparchy of Our Lady of Lebanon of Los Angeles (established Mar. 1, 1994).

Syrians: The eparchy of Our Lady of the Deliverance of Newark with 11,200 faithful (see city, Newark, N.J.) was established in 1995 for Syrian Catholics of the U.S. and Canada.

Malankarese: Have a mission in Chicago.

Armenian Tradition

An apostolic exarchate for Canada and the United States (see city, New York) was established July 3, 1981; 35,000 in the two countries.

Chaldean Tradition

Chaldeans: There were 65,000 reported under the jurisdiction of the eparchy of St. Thomas Apostle of Detroit (established as an exarchate, 1982; eparchy, 1986).

Syro-Malabarese (Malabar): Have mission churches in Chicago and several other cities. Estimated 200,000 faithful with 50 priests.

Eastern Catholic Associates

Eastern Catholic Associates is the association of all Eastern Catholic bishops and their equivalents in law in the United States, representing the Armenian, Chaldean, Maronite, Melkite, Syriac, Romanian, Ruthenian and Ukrainian churches. The Syro-Malabar and Russian churches are also represented even though they do not have bishops in the U.S. President: Melkite Auxiliary Bishop Nicholas J. Samra of Newton, Mass. Address: 8525 Cole St., Warren, MI 48093.

The association meets at the same time as the National Conference of Catholic Bishops in the fall of each year.

BYZANTINE DIVINE LITURGY

The Divine Liturgy in all rites is based on the consecration of bread and wine by the narration-reactualization of the actions of Christ at the Last Supper, and the calling down of the Holy Spirit. Aside from this fundamental usage, there are differences between the Roman (Latin) Rite and Eastern Rites, and among the Eastern Rites themselves. Following is a general description of the Byzantine Divine Liturgy which is in widest use in the Eastern Churches.

In the Byzantine, as in all Eastern Rites, the bread and wine are prepared at the start of the Liturgy. The priest does this in a little niche or at a table in the sanctuary. Taking a round loaf of leavened bread stamped with religious symbols, he cuts out a square host and other particles while reciting verses expressing the symbolism of the action. When the bread and wine are ready, he says a prayer of offering and incenses the oblations, the altar, the icons and the people.

Liturgy of the Catechumens: At the altar a litany for all classes of people is sung by the priest. The congregation answers, "Lord, have mercy." The Little Entrance comes next. In procession, the priest leaves the sanctuary carrying the Book of the Gospels, and then returns. He sings prayers especially selected for the day and the feast. These are followed by the solemn singing of the prayer, "Holy God, Holy Mighty One, Holy Immortal One." The Epistle follows. The Gospel is sung or read by the priest facing the people at the middle door of the sanctuary.

An interruption after the Liturgy of the Catechumens, formerly an instructional period for those learning the faith, is clearly marked. Catechumens, if present, are dismissed with a prayer. Following this are a prayer and litany for the faithful.

Great Entrance: The Great Entrance or solemn Offertory Procession then takes place. The priest first says a long silent prayer for himself, in preparation for the great act to come. Again he incenses the oblations, the altar, the icons and people. He goes to the table on the Gospel side for the veil-covered paten and chalice. When he arrives back at the sanctuary door, he announces the intention of the Mass in the prayer: "May the Lord God remember all of you in his kingdom, now and forever." After another litany, the congregation recites the Nicene Creed.

Consecration: The most solemn portion of the sacrifice is introduced by the preface, which is very much like the preface of the Roman Rite. At the beginning of the last phrase, the priest raises his voice to introduce the singing of the Sanctus. During the singing he reads the introduction to the words of consecration. The words of consecration are sung aloud, and the people sing "Amen" to both consecrations. As the priest raises the Sacred Species in solemn offering, he sings: "Thine of Thine Own we offer unto Thee in behalf of all and for all." A prayer to the Holy Spirit is followed by the commemorations, in which special mention is made of the all-holy, most blessed and glorious Lady, the Mother of God and ever-Virgin Mary. The dead are remembered and then the living.

Holy Communion: A final litany for spiritual gifts precedes the Our Father. The Sacred Body and Blood are elevated with the words, "Holy Things for the Holy." The Host is then broken and commingled with the Precious Blood. The priest recites preparatory prayers for Holy Communion, consumes the Sacred Species, and distributes Holy Communion to the people under the forms of both bread and wine. During this time a communion verse is sung by the choir or congregation.

The Liturgy closes quickly after this. The consecrated Species of bread and wine are removed to the side table to be consumed later by the priest. A prayer of thanksgiving is recited, a prayer for all the people is said in front of the icon of Christ, a blessing is invoked upon all, and the people are dismissed.

BYZANTINE CALENDAR

The Byzantine calendar has many distinctive features of its own, although it shares common elements with the Roman calendar — e.g., general purpose, commemoration of the mysteries of faith and of the saints, identical dates for some feasts. Among the distinctive things are the following. The liturgical year begins on Sept. 1, the Day of Indiction, in contrast with the Latin or Roman start on the First Sunday of Advent late in November or early in December. The Advent season begins on Dec. 10.

Cycles of the Year

As in the Roman usage, the dating of feasts follows the Gregorian Calendar. Formerly, until well into this century, the Julian Calendar was used. (The Julian Calendar, which is now about 13 days late, is still used by some Eastern Churches.) The year has several cycles, which include proper seasons, the feasts of saints, and series of New Testament readings. All of these elements of worship are contained in liturgical books of the rite. The ecclesiastical calendar, called the *Menologion,* explains the nature of feasts, other observances and matters pertaining to the liturgy for each day of the year. In some cases, its contents include the lives of saints and the history and meaning of feasts.

The Divine Liturgy (Mass) and Divine Office for the proper of the saints, fixed feasts, and the Christmas season are contained in the *Menaion.* The *Triodion* covers the pre-Lenten season of preparation for Easter; Lent begins two days before the Ash Wednesday observance of the Roman Rite. The *Pentecostarion* contains the liturgical services from Easter to the Sunday of All Saints, the first after Pentecost. The *Evangelion* and *Apostolos* are books in which the Gospels, and Acts of the Apostles and the Epistles, respectively, are arranged according to the order of their reading in the Divine Liturgy and Divine Office throughout the year.

The cyclic progression of liturgical music throughout the year, in successive and repetitive periods of eight weeks, is governed by the *Oktoechos,* the *Book of Eight Tones.*

Sunday Names

Many Sundays are named after the subject of the Gospel read in the Mass of the day or after the name of a feast falling on the day — e.g., Sunday of the Publican and Pharisee, of the Prodigal Son, of the Samaritan Woman, of St. Thomas the Apostle, of the Fore-Fathers (Old Testament Patriarchs).

Other Sundays are named in the same manner as in the Roman calendar e.g., numbered Sundays of Lent and after Pentecost.

Holy Days

The calendar lists about 28 holy days. Many of the major holy days coincide with those of the Roman calendar, but the feast of the Immaculate Conception is observed on Dec. 9 instead of Dec. 8, and the feast of All Saints falls on the Sunday after Pentecost rather than on Nov. 1. Instead of a single All Souls' Day, there are five All Souls' Saturdays. According to regulations in effect in the Byzantine (Ruthenian) Archeparchy of Pittsburgh and its suffragan sees of Passaic, Parma and Van Nuys, holy days are obligatory, solemn and simple, and attendance at the Divine Liturgy is required on five obligatory days — the feasts of the Epiphany, the Ascension, Sts. Peter and Paul, the Assumption of the Blessed Virgin Mary, and Christmas. Although attendance at the liturgy is not obligatory on 15 solemn and seven simple holy days, it is recommended. In the Byzantine (Ukrainian) Archeparchy of Philadelphia and its suffragan sees of St. Josaphat in Parma, St. Nicholas (Chicago) and Stamford, the obligatory feasts are the Circumcision, Epiphany, Annunciation, Easter, Ascension, Pentecost, Dormition (Assumption of Mary), Immaculate Conception and Christmas.

Lent

The first day of Lent — the Monday before Ash Wednesday of the Roman Rite — and Good Friday are days of strict abstinence for persons in the age bracket of obligation. No meat, eggs, or dairy products may be eaten on these days. All persons over the age of 14 must abstain from meat on Fridays during Lent, Holy Saturday, and the vigils of the feasts of Christmas and Epiphany; abstinence is urged, but is not obligatory, on Wednesdays of Lent. The abstinence obligation is not in force on certain "free" or "privileged" Fridays.

Synaxis

An observance without a counterpart in the Roman calendar is the synaxis. This is a commemoration, on the day following a feast, of persons involved with the occasion for the feast — e.g., Sept. 9, the day following the feast of the Nativity of the Blessed Virgin Mary, is the Synaxis of Joachim and Anna, her parents.

Holy Week

In the Byzantine Rite, Lent is liturgically concluded with the Saturday of Lazarus, the day before Palm Sunday, which commemorates the raising of Lazarus from the dead. On the following Monday, Tuesday and Wednesday, the Liturgy of the Presanctified is prescribed.

On Holy Thursday, the Liturgy of St. Basil the Great is celebrated together with Vespers.

The Divine Liturgy is not celebrated on Good Friday. On Holy Saturday, the Liturgy of St. Basil the Great is celebrated along with Vespers.

BYZANTINE FEATURES

Art: Named for the empire in which it developed, Byzantine art is a unique blend of imperial Roman and classic Hellenic culture with Christian inspiration. The art of the Greek Middle Ages, it reached a peak of development in the 10th or 11th century. Characteristic of its products, particularly in mosaic and painting, are majesty, dignity, refinement and grace. Its sacred paintings, called icons, are reverenced highly in all the Eastern Churches of the Byzantine tradition.

Church Building: The classical model of Byzantine church architecture is the Church of the Holy Wisdom (*Hagia Sophia*), built in Constantinople in the first half of the sixth century and still standing. The square structure, extended in some cases in the form of a cross, is topped by a distinctive onion-shaped dome and surmounted by a triple-bar cross. The altar is at the eastern end of building, where the wall bellies out to form an apse. The altar and sanctuary are separated from the body of the church by a fixed or movable screen, the iconostas, to which icons or sacred pictures are attached (see below).

Clergy: The Byzantine Churches have married as well as celibate priests. In places other than the U.S., where married candidates have not been accepted for ordination since about 1929, men already married can be ordained to the diaconate and priesthood and can continue in marriage after ordination. Celibate deacons and priests cannot marry after ordination; neither can a married priest remarry after the death of his wife. Bishops must be unmarried.

Iconostas: A large screen decorated with sacred pictures or icons which separates the sanctuary from the nave of a church; its equivalent in the Roman Rite, for thus separating the sanctuary from the nave, is an altar rail. An iconostas has three doors through which the sacred ministers enter the sanctuary during the Divine Liturgy: smaller (north and south) Deacons' Doors and a large central Royal Door. The Deacons' Doors usually feature the icons of Sts. Gabriel and Michael; the Royal Door, the icons of the Evangelists—Matthew, Mark, Luke and John. To the right and left of the Royal Door are the icons of Christ the Teacher and of the Blessed Virgin Mary with the Infant Jesus. To the extreme right and left are the icons of the patron of the church and St. John the Baptist (or St. Nicholas of Myra). Immediately above the Royal Door is a picture of the Last Supper. To the right are six icons depicting the major feasts of Christ, and to the left are six icons portraying the major feasts of the Blessed Virgin Mary. Above the picture of the Last Supper is a large icon of Christ the King. Some icon screens also have pictures of the 12 Apostles and the major Old Testament prophets surmounted by a crucifixion scene.

Liturgical Language: In line with Eastern tradition, Byzantine practice has favored the use of the language of the people in the liturgy. Two great advocates of the practice were Sts. Cyril and Methodius, apostles of the Slavs, who devised the Cyrillic alphabet and pioneered the adoption of Slavonic in the liturgy.

Sacraments: Baptism is administered by immersion, and confirmation (Chrismation) is conferred at the same time. The Eucharist is administered by intinction, i.e., by giving the communicant a piece of consecrated leavened bread which has been dipped into the consecrated wine. When giving absolution in the sacrament of penance, the priest holds his stole over the head of the penitent. Distinctive marriage ceremonies include the crowning of the bride and groom. Ceremonies for anointing the sick closely resemble those of the Roman Rite. Holy orders are conferred by a bishop.

Sign of the Cross: The sign of the cross in conjunction with a deep bow expresses reverence for the presence of Christ in the Blessed Sacrament. (See also entry in Glossary.)

VESTMENTS, APPURTENANCES

Antimension: A silk or linen cloth laid on the altar for the Liturgy; it may be decorated with a picture of the burial of Christ and the instruments of his passion; the relics of martyrs are sewn into the front border.

Asteriskos: Made of two curved bands of gold or silver which cross each other to form a double arch; a star depends from the junction, which forms a cross; it is placed over the *diskos* holding the consecrated bread and is covered with a veil.

Diskos: A shallow plate, which may be elevated on a small stand, corresponding to the Roman-Rite paten.

Eileton: A linen cloth which corresponds to the Roman-Rite corporal.

Epimanikia: Ornamental cuffs; the right cuff symbolizing strength, the left, patience and good will.

Epitrachelion: A stole with ends sewn together, having a loop through which the head is passed; its several crosses symbolize priestly duties.

Lance: A metal knife used for cutting up the bread to be consecrated during the Liturgy.

Phelonion: An ample cape, long in the back and sides and cut away in front; symbolic of the higher gifts of the Holy Spirit.

Poterion: A chalice or cup which holds the wine and Precious Blood.

Spoon: Used in administering Holy Communion by intinction; consecrated leavened bread is dipped into consecrated wine and spooned onto the tongue of the communicant.

Sticharion: A long white garment of linen or silk with wide sleeves and decorated with embroidery; formerly the vestment for clerics in minor orders, acolytes, lectors, chanters, and subdeacons; symbolic of purity.

Veils: Three are used, one to cover the *poterion*, the second to cover the *diskos*, and the third to cover both.

Zone: A narrow clasped belt made of the same material as the *epitrachelion*; symbolic of the wisdom of the priest, his strength against enemies of the Church and his willingness to perform holy duties.

POPE JOHN PAUL II'S HOMILY FOR GREEK CATHOLICS

On May 8, 1999 during his trip to Romania, Pope John Paul II delivered a homily addressed to the Greek Catholics living in Romania. The occasion of the homily was the Byzantine-Romanian-rite eucharistic celebration at St. Joseph's Cathedral in Bucharest. The homily was delivered in Romanian. Following are excerpts from the Holy Father's address:

"Beloved brothers and sisters, your chains and the chains of your people are the glory and pride of the Church: The truth has set you free! They tried to silence your freedom, to suppress it, but they did not succeed. Inwardly you remained free, even though in chains; free, even though in tears and privation; free, even though your communities were attacked and violated; but "earnest prayer was made to God by the Church" (Acts 12:5) for you, for them, for all believers in Christ whom deceit sought to destroy. There is no son of darkness who can tolerate the hymn of freedom, since it reproaches him for his error and sin.

I have come in these days to pay homage to the Romanian people, who historically are a sign of the extension of Roman civilization into this part of Europe, where its memory, language and culture have been perpetuated. I have come to pay homage to the brothers and sisters who hallowed this land by the witness of their faith, producing a flourishing civilization inspired by the Gospel of Christ; to a Christian people proud of their identity, often defended at a high price in the sufferings and vicissitudes that have marked its life.

Today, I am here to pay homage to you, sons and daughters of the Greek Catholic Church, who for three centuries have borne witness to your faith in unity, sometimes with unprecedented sacrifices. I come to you to express the Catholic Church's gratitude, and not only hers: You have offered a witness of liberating truth to the entire Christian world, to all people of good will ... An exhilarating task awaits you: to rekindle hope in the hearts of the faithful belonging to your resurgent Church. Devote time and attention to the laity, particularly to the young, who are the Church's future: Teach them to meet Christ in liturgical prayer, restored to its beauty and solemnity after the constraints of secrecy, in diligent meditation on Sacred Scripture, in assimilation of the fathers, theologians and mystics. Teach young people to strive for difficult goals as befits the children of martyrs.

For Christians, these are days of forgiveness and reconciliation. Without this witness, the world will not believe: How can we credibly speak of God, who is love, if there is no repsite from conflict? Heal the wounds of the past with love. May your shared suffering not lead to separation but accomplish the miracle of reconciliation. Is this not the marvel that the world expects from believers? You too, dear brothers and sisters, are called to make your valuable contribution to the ecumenical dialogue in truth and in charity, according to the directives of the Second Vatican Council and the Church's magisterium.

On your journey to Christ, the source of true freedom, may they accompany you with Mary, the holy mother of God. I commend you to her in the words you sang to her with trusting abandonment at the time of persecution: "Do not desert us, O Mother, exhausted on the way, because we are the children of your tears.""

U.S. CATHOLIC HISTORY

(Update courtesy Rev. Clyde Crews, Ph.D.)

The starting point of the mainstream of Catholic history in the United States was Baltimore at the end of the Revolutionary War. Long before that time, however, Catholic explorers had traversed much of the country and missionaries had done considerable work among Indians in the Southeast, Northeast and Southwest. (See also Index: Chronology of Church in U.S.)

Spanish and French Missions

Missionaries from Spain evangelized Indians in Florida (which included a large area of the Southeast), New Mexico, Texas and California. Franciscan Juan de Padilla, killed in 1542 in what is now central Kansas, was the first of numerous martyrs among the early missionaries. The city of St. Augustine, settled by the Spanish in 1565, was the first permanent settlement in the United States and also the site of the first parish, established the same year with secular Father Martin Francisco Lopez de Mendoza Grajales as pastor. Italian Jesuit Eusebio Kino (1645-1711) established Spanish missions in lower California and southern Arizona, where he founded San Xavier del Bac mission in 1700. Bl. Junípero Serra (1713-84), who established nine of the famous chain of 21 Franciscan missions in California, was perhaps the most noted of the Spanish missionaries. He was beatified in 1988.

French missionary efforts originated in Canada and extended to parts of Maine, New York and areas around the Great Lakes and along the Mississippi River as far south as Louisiana. Sts. Isaac Jogues, René Goupil and John de Brébeuf, three of eight Jesuit missionaries of New France martyred between 1642 and 1649 (canonized in 1930), met their deaths near Auriesville, New York. Jesuit explorer Jacques Marquette (1637-75), who founded St. Ignace Mission at the Straits of Mackinac in 1671, left maps and a diary of his exploratory trip down the Mississippi River with Louis Joliet in 1673. Claude Allouez (1622-89), another French Jesuit, worked for 32 years among Indians in the Midwest, baptizing an estimated 10,000. French Catholics founded the colony in Louisiana in 1699. In 1727, Ursuline nuns from France founded a convent in New Orleans, the oldest in the United States.

English Settlements

Catholics were excluded by penal law from English settlements along the Atlantic coast.

The only colony established under Catholic leadership was Maryland, granted to George Calvert (Lord Baltimore) as a proprietary colony in 1632; its first settlement at St. Mary's City was established in 1634 by a contingent of Catholic and Protestant colonists who had arrived from England on the Ark and the Dove. Jesuits Andrew White and John Altham, who later evangelized Indians of the area, accompanied the settlers. The principle of religious freedom on which the colony was founded was enacted into law in 1649 as the Act of Toleration. It was the first such measure passed in the colonies and, except for a four-year period of Puritan control, remained in effect until 1688, when Maryland became a royal colony, and the Anglican Church was made the official religion in 1692. Catholics were disenfranchised and persecuted until 1776.

The only other colony where Catholics were assured some degree of freedom was Pennsylvania, founded by the Quaker William Penn in 1681.

One of the earliest permanent Catholic establishments in the English colonies was St. Francis Xavier Mission, Old Bohemia, in northern Maryland, founded by the Jesuits in 1704 to serve Catholics of Delaware, Maryland and southeastern Pennsylvania. Its Bohemia Academy, established in the 1740s, was attended by sons of prominent Catholic families in the area.

Catholics and the Revolution

Despite their small number, which accounted for about one percent of the population, Catholics made significant contributions to the cause for independence from England.

Father John Carroll (1735-1815), who would later become the first bishop of the American hierarchy, and his cousin, Charles Carroll (1737-1832), a signer of the Declaration of Independence, were chosen by the Continental Congress to accompany Benjamin Franklin and Samuel Chase to Canada to try to secure that country's neutrality. Father Pierre Gibault (1737-1804) gave important aid in preserving the Northwest Territory for the revolutionaries. Thomas FitzSimons (1741-1811) of Philadelphia gave financial support to the Continental Army, served in a number of campaigns and later, with Daniel Carroll of Maryland, became one of the two Catholic signers of the Constitution. John Barry (1745-1803), commander of the Lexington, the first ship commissioned by Congress, served valiantly and is considered a founder of the U.S. Navy. There is no record of the number of Catholics who served in Washington's armies, although 38 to 50 percent had Irish surnames.

Casimir Pulaski (1748-79) and Thaddeus Kosciusko (1746-1817) of Poland served the cause of the Revolution. Assisting also were the Catholic nations of France, with a military and naval force, and Spain with money and the neutrality of its colonies.

Acknowledgment of Catholic aid in the war and the founding of the Republic was made by General Washington in his reply to a letter from prominent Catholics seeking justice and equal rights: "I presume your fellow citizens of all denominations will not forget the patriotic part which you took in the accomplishment of our Revolution and the establishment of our government or the important assistance which they received from a nation [France] in which the Roman Catholic faith is professed."

In 1789, religious freedom was guaranteed under the First Amendment to the Constitution. Discriminatory laws against Catholics remained in force in many of the states, however, until well into the 19th century.

Beginning of Organization

Father John Carroll's appointment as superior of the American missions on June 9, 1784, was the first step toward organization of the Church in this country. According to a report he made to Rome the following year, there were 24 priests and approximately 25,000 Catholics, mostly in Maryland and Pennsylvania, in a general population of four million. Many of them had been in the Colonies for several generations. For the most part, however, they were an unknown minority laboring under legal and social handicaps.

Establishment of the Hierarchy

Father Carroll was named the first American bishop in 1789 and placed in charge of the Diocese of Baltimore, whose boundaries were coextensive with those of the United States. He was ordained in England Aug. 15, 1790, and installed in his see the following Dec. 12.

Ten years later, Father Leonard Neale became his coadjutor and the first bishop ordained in the United States. Bishop Carroll became an archbishop. in 1808 when Baltimore was designated a metropolitan see and the new dioceses of Boston, New York, Philadelphia and Bardstown (now Louisville) were established. These jurisdictions were later subdivided, and by 1840 there were, in addition to Baltimore, 15 dioceses, 500 priests and 663,000 Catholics in the general population of 17 million.

Priests and First Seminaries

The original number of 24 priests noted in Bishop Carroll's 1785 report was gradually augmented with the arrival of others from France and other countries. Among arrivals from France after the Civil Constitution of the Clergy went into effect in 1790, were Jean Louis Lefebvre de Cheverus and Sulpicians Ambrose Maréchal, Benedict Flaget and William Dubourg, who later became bishops.

The first seminary in the country was St. Mary's, established in 1791 in Baltimore, and placed under the direction of the Sulpicians. French seminarian Stephen T. Badin (1768-1853), who fled to the U.S. in 1792 and became a pioneer missionary in Kentucky, Ohio and Michigan, was the first priest ordained (1793) in the U.S. Demetrius Gallitzin (1770-1840), a Russian prince and convert to Catholicism who did pioneer missionary work in western Pennsylvania, was ordained to the priesthood in 1795; he was the first to receive all his orders in the U.S. By 1815, St. Mary's Seminary had 30 ordained alumni.

Two additional seminaries — Mt. St. Mary's at Emmitsburg, Md., and St. Thomas at Bardstown, Ky. — were established in 1809 and 1811, respectively. These and similar institutions founded later played key roles in the development and growth of the American clergy.

Early Schools

Early educational enterprises included the establishment in 1791 of a school at Georgetown which later became the first Catholic university in the U.S.; the opening of a secondary school for girls, conducted by Visitation Nuns, in 1799 at Georgetown; and the start of a similar school in the first decade of the 19th century at Emmitsburg, Md., by S .Elizabeth Ann Seton.

By the 1840s, which saw the beginnings of the present public school system, more than 200 Catholic elementary schools, half of them west of the Alleghenies, were in operation. From this start, the Church subsequently built the greatest private system of education in the world.

Sisterhoods

Institutes of women Religious were largely responsible for the development of educational and charitable institutions. Among them were Ursuline Nuns in Louisiana from 1727 and Visitation Nuns at Georgetown in the 1790s.

The first contemplative foundation in the country was established in 1790 at Fort Tobacco, Md., by three American-born Carmelites trained at an English convent in Belgium.

The first community of American origin was that of the Sisters of Charity of St. Joseph, founded in 1808 at Emmitsburg, Md., by Mother Elizabeth Ann Bayley Seton (canonized in 1975). Other early American communities were the Sisters of Loretto and Sisters of Charity of Nazareth, both founded in 1812 in Kentucky, and the Oblate Sisters of Providence, a black community founded in 1829 in Baltimore by Mother Mary Elizabeth Lange.

Among pioneer U.S. foundresses of European communities were Mother Rose Philippine Duchesne (canonized in 1980), who established the Religious of the Sacred Heart in Missouri in 1818, and Mother Theodore Guérin, who founded the Sisters of Providence of St.-Mary-of-the-Woods in Indiana in 1840.

The number of sisters' communities, most of them branches of European institutes, increased apace with needs for their missions in education, charitable service and spiritual life.

Trusteeism

The initial lack of organization in ecclesiastical affairs, nationalistic feeling among Catholics and the independent action of some priests were factors involved in several early crises.

In Philadelphia, some German Catholics, with the reluctant consent of Bishop Carroll, founded Holy Trinity, the first national parish in the U.S. They refused to accept the pastor appointed by the bishop and elected their own. This and other abuses led to formal schism in 1796, a condition which existed until 1802 when they returned to canonical jurisdiction. Philadelphia was also the scene of the Hogan Schism, which developed in the 1820s when Father William Hogan, with the aid of lay trustees, seized control of St. Mary's Cathedral. His movement, for churches and parishes controlled by other than canonical procedures and run in extralegal ways, was nullified by a decision of the Pennsylvania Supreme Court in 1822.

Similar troubles seriously disturbed the peace of the Church in other places, principally New York, Baltimore, Buffalo, Charleston and New Orleans.

Dangers arising from the exploitation of lay control were gradually diminished with the extension and enforcement of canonical procedures and with changes in civil law about the middle of the century.

Anti-Catholicism

Bigotry against Catholics waxed and waned during the 19th century and into the 20th. The first major campaign of this kind, which developed in the wake of the panic of 1819 and lasted for about 25 years, was mounted in 1830 when the number of Catholic immigrants began to increase to a noticeable degree. Nativist anti-Catholicism generated a great deal of violence, represented by climaxes in loss of life and property in Charlestown, Mass., in 1834, and in Philadelphia 10 years later. Later bigotry was fomented by the Know-Nothings, in the 1850s; the Ku Klux Klan, from 1866; the American Protective Association, from 1887, and the Guardians of Liberty. Perhaps the last eruption of virulently overt anti-Catholicism occurred during the campaign of Alfred E. Smith for the presidency in 1928. Observers feel the issue was muted to a considerable extent in the political area with the election of John F. Kennedy to the presidency in 1960.

The Catholic periodical press had its beginnings in response to the attacks of bigots. The *U.S. Catholic Miscellany* (1822-61), the first Catholic newspaper in the U.S., was founded by Bishop John England of Charleston to answer critics of the Church. This remained the character of most of the periodicals of the 19th and into the 20th century.

Growth and Immigration

Between 1830 and 1900, the combined factors of natural increase, immigration and conversion raised the Catholic population to 12 million. A large percentage of the growth figure represented immigrants: some 2.7 million, largely from Ireland, Germany and France, between 1830 and 1880; and another 1.25 million during the 1880s when Eastern and Southern Europeans came in increasing numbers. By the 1860s the Catholic Church, with most of its members concentrated in urban areas, was probably the largest religious body in the country.

The efforts of progressive bishops to hasten the acculturation of Catholic immigrants occasioned a number of controversies, which generally centered around questions concerning national or foreign-language parishes. One of them, called Cahenslyism, arose from complaints that German Catholic immigrants were not being given adequate pastoral care.

Eastern-Rite Catholics

The immigration of the 1890s included large numbers of Eastern-Rite Catholics with their own liturgies and tradition of a married clergy, but without their own bishops. The treatment of their clergy and people by some of the U.S. (Latin-Rite) hierarchy and the prejudices they encountered resulted in the defection of thousands from the Catholic Church.

In 1907, Basilian monk Stephen Ortynsky was ordained the first bishop of Byzantine-rite Catholics in the U.S. Eventually jurisdictions were established for most Byzantine- and other Eastern-rite Catholics in the country.

Councils of Baltimore

The bishops of the growing U.S. dioceses met at Baltimore for seven provincial councils between 1829 and 1849.

In 1846, they proclaimed the Blessed Virgin Mary patroness of the United States under the title of the Immaculate Conception, eight years before the dogma was proclaimed in Rome.

After the establishment of the Archdiocese of Oregon City in 1846 and the elevation to metropolitan status of St. Louis, New Orleans, Cincinnati and New York, the first of the three plenary councils of Baltimore was held.

The first plenary assembly was convoked on May 9, 1852, with Abp. Francis P. Kenrick of Baltimore as papal legate. The bishops drew up regulations concerning parochial life, matters of church ritual and ceremonies, the administration of church funds and the teaching of Christian doctrine.

The second plenary council, meeting from Oct. 7 to 21, 1866, under the presidency of Abp. Martin J. Spalding, formulated a condemnation of several current doctrinal errors and established norms affecting the organization of dioceses, the education and conduct of the clergy, the management of ecclesiastical property, parochial duties and general education.

Abp. (later Cardinal) James Gibbons called into session the third plenary council which lasted from Nov. 9 to Dec. 7, 1884. Among highly significant results of actions taken by this assembly were the preparation of the line of Baltimore catechisms which became a basic means of religious instruction in this country; legislation which fixed the pattern of Catholic education by requiring the building of elementary schools in all parishes; the establishment of the Catholic University of America in Washington, D.C., in 1889; and the determination of six holy days of obligation for observance in this country.

The enactments of the three plenary councils have had the force of particular law for the Church in the United States.

The Holy See established the Apostolic Delegation in Washington, D.C., on Jan. 24, 1893.

Slavery

In the Civil War period, as before, Catholics reflected attitudes of the general population with respect to the issue of slavery. Some supported it, some opposed it, but none were prominent in the Abolition Movement. Gregory XVI had condemned the slave trade in 1839, but no contemporary pope or American bishop published an official document on slavery itself. The issue did not split Catholics in schism as it did Baptists, Methodists and Presbyterians.

Catholics fought on both sides in the Civil War. Five hundred members of 20 or more sisterhoods served the wounded of both sides.

One hundred thousand of the four million slaves emancipated in 1863 were Catholics; the highest concentrations were in Louisiana, about 60,000, and Maryland, 16,000. Three years later, their pastoral care was one of the subjects covered in nine decrees issued by the Second Plenary Council of Baltimore. The measures had little practical effect with respect to integration of the total Catholic community, predicated as they were on the proposition that individual bishops should handle questions regarding segregation in churches and related matters as best they could in the pattern of local customs.

Long entrenched segregation practices continued in force through the rest of the 19th century and well into the 20th. The first effective efforts to alter them were initiated by Cardinal Joseph Ritter of St. Louis in 1947, Cardinal (then Abp.) Patrick O'Boyle of Washington in 1948, and Bishop Vincent Waters of Raleigh in 1953.

Friend of Labor

The Church became known during the 19th century as a friend and ally of labor in seeking justice for the working man. Cardinal Gibbons journeyed to Rome in 1887, for example, to defend and prevent a condemnation of the Knights of Labor by Leo XIII. The encyclical *Rerum Novarum* (1891) was hailed by many American bishops as a confirmation, if not vindication, of their own theories. Catholics have always formed a large percentage of union membership, and some have served unions in positions of leadership.

Americanism

Near the end of the century some controversy developed over what was characterized as Americanism or the phantom heresy. It was alleged that Americans were discounting the importance of contemplative virtues, exalting the practical virtues, and watering down the purity of Catholic doctrine for the sake of facilitating convert work.

The French translation of Father Walter Elliott's *Life of Isaac Hecker*, which fired the controversy, was one of many factors that led to the issuance of Leo XIII's *Testem Benevolentiae* in January 1899, in an attempt to end the matter. It was the first time the orthodoxy of the Church in the U.S. was called into question.

Schism

In the 1890s, serious friction developed between Poles and Irish in Scranton, Buffalo and Chicago, resulting in schism and the establishment of the Polish National Catholic Church. A central figure in the affair was Father Francis Hodur, who was excommunicated by Bishop William O'Hara of Scranton in 1898. Nine years later, his ordination by an Old Catholic Abp. of Utrecht gave the new church its first bishop.

Another schism of the period led to formation of the American Carpatho-Russian Orthodox Greek Catholic Church.

Coming of Age

In 1900, there were 12 million Catholics in the total U.S. population of 76 million, 82 dioceses in 14 provinces, and 12,000 priests and members of about 40 communities of men Religious. Many sisterhoods, most of them of European origin and some of American foundation, were engaged in Catholic educational and hospital work, two of their traditional apostolates.

The Church in the United States was removed from mission status with promulgation of the apostolic constitution *Sapienti Consilio* by Pope St. Pius X on June 29, 1908.

Before that time, and even into the early 1920s, the Church in this country received financial assistance from mission-aid societies in France, Bavaria and Austria. Already, however, it was making increasing contributions of its own. At the present time, it is one of the major national contributors to the worldwide Society for the Propagation of the Faith.

American foreign missionary personnel increased from 14 or less in 1906 to an all-time high in 1968 of 9,655 priests, brothers, sisters, seminarians, and lay persons. The first missionary seminary in the U.S. was in operation at Techny, Ill., in 1909, under the auspices of the Society of the Divine Word. Maryknoll, the first American missionary society, was established in 1911 and sent its first priests to China in 1918. Despite these contributions, the Church in the U.S. has not matched the missionary commitment of some other nations.

Bishops' Conference

A highly important apparatus for mobilizing the Church's resources was established in 1917 under the title of the National Catholic War Council. Its name was changed to National Catholic Welfare Conference several years later, but its objectives remained the same: to serve as an advisory and coordinating agency of the American bishops for advancing works of the Church in fields of social significance and impact — education, communications, immigration, social action, legislation, youth and lay organizations.

The forward thrust of the bishops' social thinking was evidenced in a program of social reconstruction they recommended in 1919. By 1945, all but one of their 12 points had been enacted into legislation — including many later social security programs.

The NCWC was renamed the United States Catholic Conference (USCC) in November 1966, when the hierarchy also organized itself as a territorial conference with pastoral-juridical authority under the title, National Conference of Catholic Bishops. The USCC is carrying on the functions of the former NCWC.

Catholic Press

The establishment of the National Catholic News Service (NC) — now the Catholic News Service (CNS) — in 1920 was an important event in the development of the Catholic press, which had its beginnings about a hundred years earlier. Early in the 20th century there were 63 weekly newspapers. The 1997 Catholic Press Directory reported 185 newspapers with a circulation in excess of 5.8 million and 250 magazines with a circulation of over 14.5 million.

Lay Organizations

A burst of lay organizational growth occurred from the 1930s onwards with the appearance of Catholic Action types of movements and other groups and associations devoted to special causes, social service and assistance for the poor and needy. Several special apostolates developed under the aegis of the National Catholic Welfare Conference (now the United States Catholic Conference); the outstanding one was the Confraternity of Christian Doctrine.

Nineteenth-century organizations of great influence included: The St. Vincent de Paul Society, whose first U.S. office was set up in 1845 in St. Louis; the Catholic Central Union (*Verein*), dating from 1855; the Knights of Columbus, founded in 1882; the Holy Name Society, organized in the U.S. in 1870; the Rosary Society (1891) and scores of chapters of the Sodality of the Blessed Virgin Mary.

Pastoral Concerns

The potential for growth of the Church in this country by immigration was sharply reduced but not entirely curtailed after 1921 with the passage of restrictive federal legislation. As a result, the Catholic population became more stabilized and, to a certain extent and for many reasons, began to acquire an identity of its own.

Some increase from outside has taken place in the past 50 years, however; from Canada, from Central and Eastern European countries, and from Puerto Rico and Latin American countries since World War II. This influx, while not as great as that of the 19th

century and early 20th, has enriched the Church here with a sizable body of Eastern-Rite Catholics for whom 12 ecclesiastical jurisdictions have been established. It has also created a challenge for pastoral care of millions of Hispanics in urban centers and in agricultural areas where migrant workers are employed.

The Church continues to grapple with serious pastoral problems in rural areas, where about 600 counties are no-priest land. The National Catholic Rural Life Conference was established in 1922 in an attempt to make the Catholic presence felt on the land, and the Glenmary Society since its foundation in 1939 has devoted itself to this single apostolate. Religious communities and diocesan priests are similarly engaged.

Other challenges lie in the cities and suburbs where 75 percent of the Catholic population lives. Conditions peculiar to each segment of the metropolitan area have developed in recent years as the flight to the suburbs has not only altered some traditional aspects of parish life but has also, in combination with many other factors, left behind a complex of special problems in inner city areas.

A Post-War World

In the year after the Second World War, Catholics increasingly assumed a mainline role in American life. This was evidenced especially in the 1960 election of John F. Kennedy as the nation's first Catholic president. Catholic writers and thinkers were making a greater impact in the nation's life. One example of this was Trappist Thomas Merton's runaway best-selling book of 1948, *The Seven Storey Mountain*; another was the early television success of Bishop Fulton Sheen's "Life is Worth Living" series, begun in 1952. Meanwhile, lay leader Dorothy Day, founder of the Catholic Worker movement, continued to challenge American society with her views on pacifism and evangelical poverty.

A Post-Conciliar World

Catholic life in the United States was profoundly affected by the Second Vatican Council (1962-65). In the post-conciliar generation, American Catholicism grew both in numbers and complexity. Lay ministry and participation expanded; extensive liturgical changes (including the use of English) were implemented; and the numbers of priests, vowed religious and seminarians declined.

The Church has taken a high profile in many social issues. This has ranged from opposition to abortion, capital punishments and euthanasia to support for civil rights, economic justice and international peace and cooperation. Meanwhile Catholics have been deeply involved in inter-faith and ecumenical relationships. And the bishops have issued landmark pastoral statements, including "The Challenge of Peace" (1983) and "Economic Justice for All" (1986).

In these years after the Council, the Catholics in America have known something of alienation, dissent and polarity. They also found new intensity and maturity. New U.S. saints have been declared by the universal church, such as Elizabeth Ann Seton (1975), John Nepomucene Neumann (1977), and Rose Philippine Duchesne (1988). Especially at the time of visits to America by Pope John Paul II (e.g., in 1979,

1987, 1993, and 1999), U.S. Catholics have given evidence – in their personal and corporate lives – of the ongoing power of faith, liturgy and the primal call of the Gospel in its many dimensions.

EARLY KEY DATES IN U.S. CATHOLIC CHRONOLOGY

Dates here refer mostly to earlier "firsts" and developments in the of Catholic history in the United States until the promulgation of the apostolic constitution Sapienti Consilio by Pope St. Pius X (June 29, 1908) by which the Church in the United States was removed from mission status. For other dates, see various sections of the Almanac.

Alabama

1540: Priests crossed the territory with De Soto's expedition.

1560: Five Dominicans in charge of mission at Santa Cruz des Nanipacna.

1682: La Salle claimed territory for France.

1704: First parish church established at Fort Louis de la Mobile under the care of diocesan priests.

1829: Mobile diocese established (redesignated Mobile-Birmingham, 1954-69).

1830: Spring Hill College, Mobile, established.

1834: Visitation Nuns established an academy at Summerville.

Alaska

1779: Mass celebrated for first time on shore of Port Santa Cruz on lower Bucareli Bay on May 13 by Franciscan Juan Riobo.

1868: Alaska placed under jurisdiction of Vancouver Island.

1879: Father John Althoff became first resident missionary.

1886: Abp. Charles J. Seghers, "Apostle of Alaska," murdered by a guide; had surveyed southern and northwest Alaska in 1873 and 1877. Sisters of St. Ann, first nuns in Alaska.

1887: Jesuits enter Alaska territory.

1894: Alaska made prefecture apostolic.

1902: Sisters of Providence opened hospital at Nome.

Arizona

1539: Franciscan Marcos de Niza explored the state.

1540: Franciscans Juan de Padilla and Marcos de Niza accompanied Coronado expedition through the territory.

1629: Spanish Franciscans began work among Moqui Indians.

1632: Franciscan Martin de Arvide killed by Indians.

1680: Franciscans José de Espeleta, Augustin de Santa Maria, José de Figueroa and José de Trujillo killed in Pueblo Revolt.

1700: Jesuit Eusebio Kino, who first visited the area in 1692, established mission at San Xavier del Bac, near Tucson. In 1783, under Franciscan administration, construction was begun of the Mission Church of San Xavier del Bac near the site of the original mission; it is still in use as a parish church.

1767: Jesuits expelled; Franciscans took over 10 missions.

1828: Spanish missionaries expelled by Mexican government.

1863: Jesuits returned to San Xavier del Bac briefly.

1869: Sisters of Loretto arrived to conduct schools at Bisbee and Douglas.

1897: Tucson diocese established.

Arkansas

1541: Priests accompanied De Soto expedition through the territory.

1673: Marquette visited Indians in east.

1686: Henri de Tonti established trading post, first white settlement in territory.

1700-1702: Fr. Nicholas Foucault working among Indians.

1805: Bishop Carroll of Baltimore appointed Administrator Apostolic of Arkansas.

1838: Sisters of Loretto opened first Catholic school.

1843: Little Rock diocese established. There were about 700 Catholics in state, two churches, one priest.

1851: Sisters of Mercy founded St. Mary's Convent in Little Rock.

California

1542: Cabrillo discovered Upper (Alta) California; name of priest accompanying expedition unknown.

1602: On Nov. 12 Carmelite Anthony of the Ascension offered first recorded Mass in California on shore of San Diego Bay.

1697: Missionary work in Lower and Upper Californias entrusted to Jesuits.

1767: Jesuits expelled from territory. Spanish Crown confiscated their property, including the Pious Fund for Missions. Upper California missions entrusted to Franciscans.

1769: Franciscan Junípero Serra, missionary in Mexico for 20 years, began establishment of Franciscan missions in California, in present San Diego. He was beatified in 1988.

1775: Franciscan Luis Jayme killed by Indians at San Diego Mission.

1779: Diocese of Sonora, Mexico, which included Upper California, established.

1781: On Sept. 4 an expedition from San Gabriel Mission founded present city of Los Angeles — Pueblo "de Nuestra Senora de los Angeles."

Franciscans Francisco Hermenegildo Garces, Juan Antonio Barreneche, Juan Marcello Diaz and José Matias Moreno killed by Indians.

1812: Franciscan Andres Quintana killed at Santa Cruz Mission.

1822: Dedication on Dec. 8 of Old Plaza Church, "Assistant Mission of Our Lady of the Angels."

1833: Missions secularized, finally confiscated.

1840: Pope Gregory XVI established Diocese of Both Californias.

1846: Peter H. Burnett, who became first governor of California in 1849, received into Catholic Church.

1848: Mexico ceded California to the United States.

1850: Monterey diocese erected; title changed to Monterey-Los Angeles, 1859; and to Los Angeles-San Diego, 1922.

1851: University of Santa Clara chartered.
Sisters of Notre Dame de Namur opened women's College of Notre Dame at San José; chartered in 1868; moved to Belmont, 1923.

1852: Baja California detached from Monterey diocese.

1853: San Francisco archdiocese established.

1855: Negotiations inaugurated to restore confiscated California missions to Church.

1868: Grass Valley diocese established; transferred to Sacramento in 1886. (Grass Valley was reestablished as a titular see in 1995.)

Colorado

1858: First parish in Colorado established.

1864: Sisters of Loretto at the Foot of the Cross, first nuns in the state, established academy at Denver.

1868: Vicariate Apostolic of Colorado and Utah established.

1887: Denver diocese established.

1888: Regis College (now University) founded.

Connecticut

1651: Probably first priest to enter state was Jesuit Gabriel Druillettes; ambassador of Governor of Canada, he participated in a New England Colonial Council at New Haven.

1756: Catholic Acadians, expelled from Nova Scotia, settled in the state.

1791: Rev. John Thayer, first native New England priest, offered Mass at the Hartford home of Noah Webster, his Yale classmate.

1808: Connecticut became part of Boston diocese.

1818: Religious freedom established by new constitution, although the Congregational Church remained, in practice, the state church.

1829: Father Bernard O'Cavanaugh became first resident priest in state.
Catholic Press of Hartford established.

1830: First Catholic church in state dedicated at Hartford.
Father James Fitton (1805-81), New England missionary, was assigned to Hartford for six years. He ministered to Catholics throughout the state.

1843: Hartford diocese established

1882: Knights of Columbus founded by Father Michael J. McGivney.

Delaware

1730: Mount Cuba, New Castle County, the scene of Catholic services.

1750: Jesuit mission at Apoquiniminck administered from Maryland.

1772: First permanent parish established at Coffee Run.

1792: French Catholics from Santo Domingo settled near Wilmington.

1816: St. Peter's Church, later the cathedral of the diocese, erected at Wilmington.

1830: Daughters of Charity opened school and orphanage at Wilmington.

1868: Wilmington diocese established.

1869: Visitation Nuns established residence in Wilmington.

District of Columbia

1641: Jesuit Andrew White evangelized Anacosta Indians.

1774: Father John Carroll ministered to Catholics.

1789: Georgetown, first Catholic college in U.S., established.

1791: Pierre Charles L'Enfant designed the Federal City of Washington. His plans were not fully implemented until the early 1900s.

1792: James Hoban designed the White House.

1794: Father Anthony Caffrey began St. Patrick's Church, first parish church in the new Federal City.

1801: Poor Clares opened school for girls in Georgetown.

1802: First mayor of Washington, appointed by President Jefferson, was Judge Robert Brent.

1889: Catholic University of America founded.

1893: Apostolic Delegation established; became an Apostolic Nunciature in 1984 with the establishment of full diplomatic relations between the U.S. and the Holy See.

Florida

1513: Ponce de León discovered Florida.

1521: Missionaries accompanying Ponce de León and other explorers probably said first Masses within present limits of U.S.

1528: Franciscans landed on western shore.

1539: Twelve missionaries landed with De Soto at Tampa Bay.

1549: Dominican Luis Cancer de Barbastro and two companions slain by Indians near Tampa Bay.

1565: City of St. Augustine, oldest in U.S., founded by Pedro Menendez de Aviles, who was accompanied by four secular priests.
America's oldest mission, Nombre de Dios, was established.
Father Martin Francisco Lopez de Mendoza Grajales became the first parish priest of St. Augustine, where first parish in the U.S. was established.

1572: St. Francis Borgia, general of the Society, withdrew Jesuits from Florida.

1606: Bishop Juan de las Cabeyas de Altamirano, O.P., conducted the first episcopal visitation in the U.S.

1620: The chapel of Nombre de Dios was dedicated to Nuestra Senora de la Leche y Buen Parto (Our Nursing Mother of the Happy Delivery); oldest shrine to the Blessed Mother in the U.S.

1704: Destruction of Florida's northern missions by English and Indian troops led by Governor James Moore of South Carolina. Franciscans Juan de Parga, Dominic Criodo, Tiburcio de Osorio, Augustine Ponze de León, Marcos Delgado and two Indians, Anthony Enixa and Amador Cuipa Feliciano, were slain by the invaders.

1735: Bishop Francis Martinez de Tejadu Diaz de Velasco, auxiliary of Santiago, was the first bishop to take up residence in U.S., at St. Augustine.

1793: Florida and Louisiana were included in Diocese of New Orleans.

1857: Eastern Florida made a vicariate apostolic.

1870: St. Augustine diocese established.

Georgia

1540: First priests to enter were chaplains with De Soto. They celebrated first Mass within territory of 13 original colonies.

1566: Pedro Martinez, first Jesuit martyr of the New World, was slain by Indians on Cumberland Island.

1569: Jesuit mission was opened at Guale Island by Father Antonio Sedeno.

1572: Jesuits withdrawn from area.

1595: Five Franciscans assigned to Province of Guale.

1597: Five Franciscan missionaries (Fathers Pedro de Corpa, Blas de Rodriguez, Miguel de Anon, Francisco de Berascolo and Brother Antonio de Badajoz) killed in coastal missions. Their cause for beatification was formally opened in 1984.

1606: Bishop Altamirano, O.P., conducted visitation of the Georgia area.

1612: First Franciscan province in U.S. erected under title of Santa Elena; it included Georgia, South Carolina and Florida.

1655: Franciscans had nine flourishing missions among Indians.

1742: Spanish missions ended as result of English conquest at Battle of Bloody Marsh.

1796: Augustinian Father Le Mercier was first post-colonial missionary to Georgia.

1798: Catholics granted right of refuge.

1800: First church erected in Savannah on lot given by city council.

1810: First church erected in Augusta on lot given by State Legislature.

1850: Savannah diocese established; became Savannah-Atlanta, 1937; divided into two separate sees, 1956.

1864: Father Emmeran Bliemel, of the Benedictine community of Latrobe, Pa., was killed at the battle of Jonesboro while serving as chaplain of the Confederate 10th Tennessee Artillery.

Hawaii

1825: Pope Leo XII entrusted missionary efforts in Islands to Sacred Hearts Fathers.

1827: The first Catholic missionaries arrived _ Fathers Alexis Bachelot, Abraham Armand and Patrick Short, along with three lay brothers. After three years of persecution, the priests were forcibly exiled.

1836: Father Arsenius Walsh, SS. CC., a British subject, was allowed to remain in Islands but was not permitted to proselytize or conduct missions.

1839: Hawaiian government signed treaty with France granting Catholics freedom of worship and same privileges as Protestants.

1844: Vicariate Apostolic of Sandwich Islands (Hawaii) erected.

1873: Father Damien de Veuster of the Sacred Hearts Fathers arrived in Molokai and spent the remainder of his life working among lepers. He was beatified in 1995.

Idaho

1840: Jesuit Pierre de Smet preached to the Flathead and Pend d'Oreille Indians; probably offered first Mass in state.

1842: Jesuit Nicholas Point opened a mission among Coeur d'Alene Indians near St. Maries.

1863: Secular priests sent from Oregon City to administer to incoming miners.

1867: Sisters of Holy Names of Jesus and Mary opened first Catholic school at Idaho City.

1868: Idaho made a vicariate apostolic.

1870: First church in Boise established.

Church lost most of missions among Indians of Northwest Territory when Commission on Indian Affairs appointed Protestant missionaries to take over.

1893: Boise diocese established.

Illinois

1673: Jesuit Jacques Marquette, accompanying Joliet, preached to Indians.

1674: Father Marquette set up a cabin for saying Mass in what later became City of Chicago.

1675: Father Marquette established Mission of the Immaculate Conception among Kaskaskia Indians, near present site of Utica; transferred to Kaskaskia, 1703.

1679: La Salle brought with him Franciscans Louis Hennepin, Gabriel de la Ribourde, and Zenobius Membre.

1680: Father Ribourde was killed by Kickapoo Indians.

1689: Jesuit Claude Allouez died after 32 years of missionary activity among Indians of Midwest; he had evangelized Indians of 20 different tribes. Jesuit Jacques Gravier succeeded Allouez as vicar general of Illinois.

1699: Mission established at Cahokia, first permanent settlement in state.

1730: Father Gaston, a diocesan priest, was killed at the Cahokia Mission.

1763: Jesuits were banished from the territory.

1778: Father Pierre Gibault championed Colonial cause in the Revolution and aided greatly in securing states of Ohio, Indiana, Illinois, Michigan and Wisconsin for Americans.

1827: The present St. Patrick's Parish at Ruma, oldest English-speaking Catholic congregation in state, was founded.

1833: Visitation Nuns established residence in Kaskaskia.

1843: Chicago diocese established.

1853: Quincy diocese established; transferred to Alton, 1857; Springfield, 1923. (Quincy and Alton were reestablished as titular sees in 1995.)

1860: Quincy College founded.

1877: Peoria diocese established.

1880: Chicago made archdiocese.

1887: Belleville diocese established.

1894: Franciscan Sisters of Bl. Kunegunda (now the Franciscan Sisters of Chicago) founded by Mother Marie Therese (Josephine Dudzik).

1908: Rockford diocese established.

First American Missionary Congress held in Chicago.

Indiana

1679: Recollects Louis Hennepin and Gabriel de la Ribourde passed through state.

1686: Land near present Notre Dame University at South Bend given by French government to Jesuits for mission.

1749: Beginning of the records of St. Francis Xavier Church, Vincennes. These records continue with minor interruptions to the present.

1778: Father Gibault aided George Rogers Clark in campaign against British in conquest of Northwest Territory.

1824: Sisters of Charity of Nazareth, Ky., opened St. Clare's Academy in Vincennes.

1825: Laying of cornerstone of third church of St. Francis Xavier, which later (from 1834-98) was the cathedral of the Vincennes diocese. The church was designated a minor basilica in 1970 and is still in use as a parish church.

1834: Vincennes diocese established with Simon Gabriel Bruté as bishop; title transferred to Indianapolis, 1898. (Vincennes was reestablished as a titular see in 1995.)

1840: Sisters of Providence founded St. Mary-of-the-Woods College for women.

1842: University of Notre Dame founded by Holy Cross Father Edward Sorin and Brothers of St. Joseph on land given the diocese of Vincennes by Father Stephen Badin.

1854: First Benedictine community established in state at St. Meinrad. It became an abbey in 1870 and an archabbey in 1954.

1857: Fort Wayne diocese established; changed to Fort Wayne-South Bend, 1960.

Iowa

1673: A Peoria village on Mississippi was visited by Father Marquette.

1679: Fathers Louis Hennepin and Gabriel de la Ribourde visited Indian villages.

1836: First permanent church, St. Raphael's, founded at Dubuque by Dominican Samuel Mazzuchelli.

1837: Dubuque diocese established.

1838: St. Joseph's Mission founded at Council Bluffs by Jesuit Father De Smet.

1843: Sisters of Charity of the Blessed Virgin Mary was first sisterhood in state.

Sisters of Charity opened Clarke College, Dubuque.

1850: First Trappist Monastery in state, Our Lady of New Melleray, was begun.

1881: Davenport diocese established.

1882: St. Ambrose College (now University), Davenport, established.

1893: Dubuque made archdiocese.

1902: Sioux City diocese established.

Kansas

1542: Franciscan Juan de Padilla, first martyr of the United States, was killed in central Kansas.

1858: St. Benedict's College (now Benedictine College) founded.

1863: Sisters of Charity opened orphanage at Leavenworth, and St. John's Hospital in following year.

1877: Leavenworth diocese established; transferred to Kansas City in 1947. (Leavenworth was reestablished as a titular see in 1995.)

1887: Dioceses of Wichita and Concordia established. Concordia was transferred to Salina in 1944, but reestablished as a titular see in 1995.)

1888: Oblate Sisters of Providence opened an orphanage for African-American boys at Leavenworth, first west of Mississippi.

Kentucky

1775: First Catholic settlers came to Kentucky.

1787: Father Charles Maurice Whelan, first resident priest, ministered to settlers in the Bardstown district.

1793: Father Stephen T. Badin began missionary work in Kentucky.

1806: Dominican Fathers built Priory at St. Rose of Lima.

1808: Bardstown diocese established with Benedict Flaget as its first bishop; see transferred to Louisville, 1841. (Bardstown was reestablished as a titular see in 1995.)

1811: Rev. Guy I. Chabrat first priest ordained west of the Allegheny Mountains.

St. Thomas Seminary founded.

1812: Sisters of Loretto founded by Rev. Charles Nerinckx; first religious community in the United States without foreign affiliation.

Sisters of Charity of Nazareth founded, the second native community of women founded in the West.

1814: Nazareth College for women established.

1816: Cornerstone of St. Joseph's Cathedral, Bardstown, laid.

1822: First foundation of Dominican Sisters in the U.S. established near Springfield.

1836: Hon. Benedict J. Webb founded Catholic Advocate, first Catholic weekly newspaper in Kentucky.

1848: Trappist monks took up residence in Gethsemani.

1849: Cornerstone of Cathedral of the Assumption laid at Louisville.

1853: Covington diocese established.

1855: Know-Nothing troubles in state.

Louisiana

1682: La Salle's expedition, accompanied by two priests, completed discoveries of De Soto at mouth of Mississippi. LaSalle named territory Louisiana.

1699: French Catholics founded colony of Louisiana. First recorded Mass offered Mar. 3, by Franciscan Father Anastase Douay.

1706: Father John Francis Buisson de St. Cosmé was killed near Donaldsonville.

1717: Franciscan Anthony Margil established first Spanish mission in north central Louisiana.

1718: City of New Orleans founded by Jean Baptiste Le Moyne de Bienville.

1720: First resident priest in New Orleans was the French Recollect Prothais Boyer.

1725: Capuchin Fathers opened school for boys.

1727: Ursuline Nuns founded convent in New Orleans, oldest convent in what is now U.S.; they conducted a school, hospital and orphan asylum.

1793: New Orleans diocese established.

1842: Sisters of Holy Family, a black congregation, founded at New Orleans by Henriette Delille and Juliette Gaudin.

1850: New Orleans made archdiocese.

1853: Natchitoches diocese established; transferred to Alexandria in 1910; became Alexandria-Shreveport in 1977; redesignated Alexandria, 1986. (Natchitoches diocese reestablished as a titular see in 1995.)

Maine

1604: First Mass in territory celebrated by Father Nicholas Aubry, accompanying De Monts' expedition which was authorized by King of France to begin colonizing region.

1605: Colony founded on St. Croix Island; two secular priests served as chaplains.

1613: Four Jesuits attempted to establish permanent French settlement near mouth of Kennebec River.

1619: French Franciscans began work among settlers and Indians; driven out by English in 1628.

1630: New England made a prefecture apostolic in charge of French Capuchins.

1633: Capuchin Fathers founded missions on Penobscot River.

1646: Jesuits established Assumption Mission on Kennebec River.

1688: Church of St. Anne, oldest in New England, built at Oldtown.

1704: English soldiers destroyed French missions.

1724: English forces again attacked French settlements, killed Jesuit Sebastian Rale.

1853: Portland diocese established.

1854: Know-Nothing uprising resulted in burning of church in Bath.

1856: Anti-Catholic feeling continued; church at Ellsworth burned.

1864: Sisters of Congregation of Notre Dame from Montréal opened academy at Portland.

1875: James A. Healy, first bishop of Negro blood consecrated in U.S., became second Bishop of Portland.

Maryland

1634: Maryland established by Lord Calvert. Two Jesuits among first colonists.

First Mass offered on Island of St. Clement in Lower Potomac by Jesuit Father Andrew White. St. Mary's City founded by English and Irish Catholics.

1641: St. Ignatius Parish founded by English Jesuits at Chapel Point, near Port Tobacco.

1649: Religious Toleration Act passed by Maryland Assembly. It was repealed in 1654 by Puritan-controlled government.

1651: Cecil Calvert, second Lord Baltimore, gave Jesuits 10,000 acres for use as Indian mission.

1658: Lord Baltimore restored Toleration Act.

1672: Franciscans came to Maryland under leadership of Father Massius Massey.

1688: Maryland became royal colony as a result of the Revolution in England; Anglican Church became the official religion (1692); Toleration Act repealed; Catholics disenfranchised and persecuted until 1776.

1704: Jesuits founded St. Francis Xavier Mission, Old Bohemia, to serve Catholics of Delaware, Maryland and southeastern Pennsylvania; its Bohemia Academy established in the 1740s was attended by sons of prominent Catholics in the area.

1784: Father John Carroll appointed prefect apostolic for the territory embraced by new Republic.

1789: Baltimore became first diocese established in U.S., with John Carroll as first bishop.

1790: Carmelite Nuns founded convent at Port Tobacco, the first in the English-speaking Colonies.

1791: First Synod of Baltimore held.

St. Mary's Seminary, first seminary in U.S., established.

1793: Rev. Stephen T. Badin first priest ordained by Bishop Carroll.

1800: Jesuit Leonard Neale became first bishop consecrated in present limits of U.S.

1806: Cornerstone of Assumption Cathedral, Baltimore, was laid.

1808: Baltimore made archdiocese.

1809: St. Joseph's College, Emmitsburg, founded (closed in 1973).

Sisters of Charity of St. Joseph founded by St. Elizabeth Ann Seton; first native American sisterhood.

1821: Assumption Cathedral, Baltimore, formally opened.

1829: Oblate Sisters of Providence, first congregation of black sisters, established at Baltimore by Mother Mary Elizabeth Lange.

First Provincial Council of Baltimore held; six others followed, in 1833, 1837, 1840, 1843, 1846 and 1849.

1836: Roger B. Taney appointed Chief Justice of Supreme Court by President Jackson.

1852: First of the three Plenary Councils of Baltimore convened. Subsequent councils were held in 1866 and 1884.

1855: German Catholic Central Verein founded.

1886: Abp. James Gibbons of Baltimore made cardinal by Pope Leo XIII.

Massachusetts

1630: New England made a prefecture apostolic in charge of French Capuchins.

1647: Massachusetts Bay Company enacted an anti-priest law.

1688: Hanging of Ann Glover, an elderly Irish Catholic widow, who refused to renounce her Catholic religion.

1732: Although Catholics were not legally admitted to colony, a few Irish families were in Boston; a priest was reported working among them.

1755-56: Acadians landing in Boston were denied services of a Catholic priest.

1775: General Washington discouraged Guy Fawkes Day procession in which pope was carried in effigy, and expressed surprise that there were men in his army "so void of common sense as to insult the religious feelings of the Canadians with whom friendship and an alliance are being sought."

1780: The Massachusetts State Constitution granted religious liberty, but required a religious test to hold public office and provided for tax to support Protestant teachers of piety, religion and morality.

1788: First public Mass said in Boston on Nov. 2 by Abbe de la Poterie, first resident priest.

1803: Church of Holy Cross erected in Boston with financial aid given by Protestants headed by John Adams.

1808: Boston diocese established.

1831: Irish Catholic immigration increased.

1832: St. Vincent's Orphan Asylum, oldest charitable institution in Boston, opened by Sisters of Mercy.

1834: Ursuline Convent in Charlestown burned by a Nativist mob.

1843: Holy Cross College founded.

1855: Catholic militia companies disbanded; nunneries' inspection bill passed.

1859: St. Mary's, first parochial school in Boston, opened.

1860: Portuguese Catholics from Azores settled in New Bedford.

1870: Springfield diocese established.

1875: Boston made archdiocese.

1904: Fall River diocese established.

Michigan

1641: Jesuits Isaac Jogues and Charles Raymbaut preached to Chippewas; named the rapids Sault Sainte Marie.

1660: Jesuit René Menard opened first regular mission in Lake Superior region.

1668: Father Marquette founded Sainte Marie Mission at Sault Sainte Marie.

1671: Father Marquette founded St. Ignace Mission on north shore of Straits of Mackinac.

1701: Fort Pontchartrain founded on present site of Detroit and placed in command of Antoine de la Mothe Cadillac. The Chapel of Sainte-Anne-de-Detroit founded.

1706: Franciscan Father Delhalle killed by Indians at Detroit.

1823: Father Gabriel Richard elected delegate to Congress from Michigan territory; he was the first priest chosen for the House of Representatives.

1833: Father Frederic Baraga celebrated first Mass in present Grand Rapids.

Detroit diocese established, embracing whole Northwest Territory.

1843: *Western Catholic Register* founded at Detroit.

1845: St. Vincent's Hospital, Detroit, opened by Sisters of Charity.

1848: Cathedral of Sts. Peter and Paul, Detroit, consecrated.

1853: Vicariate Apostolic of Upper Michigan established.

1857: Sault Ste. Marie diocese established; later transferred to Marquette. (Sault Ste. Marie reestablished as a titular see in 1995.)

1877: University of Detroit founded.

1882: Grand Rapids diocese established.

1897: Nazareth College for women founded.

Minnesota

1680: Falls of St. Anthony discovered by Franciscan Louis Hennepin.

1727: First chapel, St. Michael the Archangel, erected near town of Frontenac and placed in charge of French Jesuits.

1732: Fort St. Charles built; Jesuits ministered to settlers.

1736: Jesuit Jean Pierre Aulneau killed by Indians.

1839: Swiss Catholics from Canada settled near Fort Snelling; Bishop Loras of Dubuque, accompanied by Father Pellamourgues, visited the Fort and administered sacraments.

1841: Father Lucian Galtier built Church of St. Paul, thus forming nucleus of modern city of same name.

1850: St. Paul diocese established.

1851: Sisters of St. Joseph arrived in state.

1857: St. John's University founded.

1888: St. Paul made archdiocese; name changed to St. Paul and Minneapolis in 1966.

1889: Duluth, St. Cloud and Winona dioceses established.

Mississippi

1540: Chaplains with De Soto expedition entered territory.

1682: Franciscans Zenobius Membre and Anastase Douay preached to Taensa and Natchez Indians. Father Membre offered first recorded Mass in the state on Mar. 29, Easter Sunday.

1698: Priests of Québec Seminary founded missions near Natchez and Fort Adams.

1702: Father Nicholas Foucault murdered by Indians near Fort Adams.

1721: Missions practically abandoned, with only Father Juif working among Yazoos.

1725: Jesuit Mathurin de Petit carried on mission work in northern Mississippi.

1729: Indians tomahawked Jesuit Paul du Poisson near Fort Rosalie; Father Jean Souel shot by Yazoos.

1736: Jesuit Antoine Senat and seven French officers burned at stake by Chickasaws.

1822: Vicariate Apostolic of Mississippi and Alabama established.

1825: Mississippi made a separate vicariate apostolic.

1837: Natchez diocese established; became Natchez-Jackson in 1956; transferred to Jackson in 1977. (Natchez was established as a titular see.)

1848: Sisters of Charity opened orphan asylum and school in Natchez.

Missouri

1700: Jesuit Gabriel Marest established a mission among Kaskaskia Indians near St. Louis.

1734: French Catholic miners and traders settled Old Mines and Sainte Genevieve.

1750: Jesuits visited French settlers.

1762: Mission established at St. Charles.

1767: Carondelet mission established.

1770: First church founded at St. Louis.

1811: Jesuits established Indian mission school at Florissant.

1818: Bishop Dubourg arrived at St. Louis, with Vincentians Joseph Rosati and Felix de Andreis.

St. Louis University, the diocesan (Kenrick) seminary and the Vincentian Seminary in Perryville trace their origins to them.

Rose Philippine Duchesne arrived at St. Charles; founded first American convent of the Society of the Sacred Heart; missionary; beatified 1940; canonized 1988.

1826: St. Louis diocese established.

1828: Sisters of Charity opened first hospital west of the Mississippi, at St. Louis.

1832: The Shepherd of the Valley, first Catholic paper west of the Mississippi.

1845: First conference of Society of St. Vincent de Paul in U.S. founded at St. Louis.

1847: St. Louis made archdiocese.

1865: A Test Oath Law passed by State Legislature (called Drake Convention) to crush Catholicism in Missouri. Law declared unconstitutional by Supreme Court in 1866.

1867: College of St. Teresa for women founded at Kansas City.

1868: St. Joseph diocese established.

1880: Kansas City diocese established.

Montana

1743: Pierre and Francois Verendrye, accompanied by Jesuit Father Coquart, may have explored territory.

1833: Indian missions handed over to care of Jesuits by Second Provincial Council of Baltimore.

1840: Jesuit Pierre De Smet began missionary work among Flathead and Pend d'Oreille Indians.

1841: St. Mary's Mission established by Father De

Smet and two companions on the Bitter Root River in present Stevensville.

1845: Jesuit Antonio Ravalli arrived at St. Mary's Mission; Ravalli County named in his honor.

1859: Fathers Point and Hoecken established St. Peter's Mission near the Great Falls.

1869: Sisters of Charity founded a hospital and school in Helena.

1884: Helena diocese established.

1904: Great Falls diocese established; redesignated Great Falls-Billings in 1980.

Nebraska

1541: Coronado expedition, accompanied by Franciscan Juan de Padilla, reached the Platte River.

1673: Father Marquette visited Nebraska Indians.

1720: Franciscan Juan Miguel killed by Indians near Columbus.

1855: Father J. F. Tracy administered to Catholic settlement of St. Patrick and to Catholics in Omaha.

1856: Land was donated by Governor Alfred Cumming for a church in Omaha.

1857: Nebraska vicariate apostolic established.

1878: Creighton University established.

1881: Poor Clares, first contemplative group in state, arrived in Omaha.
Duchesne College established.

1885: Omaha diocese established.

1887: Lincoln diocese established.

Nevada

1774: Franciscan missionaries passed through Nevada on way to California missions.

1860: First parish, serving Genoa, Carson City and Virginia City, established.

1862: Rev. Patrick Manogue appointed pastor of Virginia City. He established a school for boys and girls, an orphanage and hospital.

1871: Church erected at Reno.

New Hampshire

1630: Territory made part of a prefecture apostolic embracing all of New England.

1784: State Constitution included a religious test which barred Catholics from public office; local support was provided for public Protestant teachers of religion.

1818: The Barber family of Claremont was visited by their son Virgil (converted to Catholicism in 1816) accompanied by Father Charles French, O.P. The visit led to the conversion of the entire Barber family.

1823: Father Virgil Barber, minister who became a Jesuit priest, built first Catholic church and school at Claremont.

1830: Church of St. Aloysius dedicated at Dover.

1853: New Hampshire made part of the Portland diocese.

1858: Sisters of Mercy began to teach school at St. Anne's, Manchester.

1877: Catholics obtained full civil liberty and rights.

1884: Manchester diocese established.

1893: St. Anselm's College opened; St. Anselm's Abbey canonically erected.

New Jersey

1668: William Douglass of Bergen was refused a seat in General Assembly because he was a Catholic.

1672: Fathers Harvey and Gage visited Catholics in Woodbridge and Elizabethtown.

1701: Tolerance granted to all but "papists."

1744: Jesuit Theodore Schneider of Pennsylvania visited German Catholics of New Jersey.

1762: Fathers Ferdinand Farmer and Robert Harding working among Catholics in state.

1765: First Catholic community organized in New Jersey at Macopin in Passaic County.

1776: State Constitution tacitly excluded Catholics from office.

1799: Foundation of first Catholic school in state, St. John's at Trenton.

1814: First church in Trenton erected.

1820: Father Richard Bulger, of St. John's, Paterson, first resident pastor in state.

1844: Catholics obtained full civil liberty and rights.

1853: Newark diocese established.

1856: Seton Hall University established.

1878: John P. Holland, teacher at St. John's School, Paterson, invented first workable submarine.

1881: Trenton diocese established.

New Mexico

1539: Territory explored by Franciscan Marcos de Niza.

1581: Franciscans Agustin Rodriguez, Juan de Santa Maria and Francisco Lopez named the region "New Mexico"; they later died at hands of Indians.

1598: Juan de Onate founded a colony at Chamita, where first chapel in state was built.

1609-10: Santa Fe founded.

1631: Franciscan Pedro de Miranda was killed by Indians.

1632: Franciscan Francisco Letrado was killed by Indians.

1672: Franciscan Pedro de Avila y Ayala was killed by Indians.

1675: Franciscan Alonso Gil de Avila was killed by Indians.

1680: Pueblo Indian revolt; 21 Franciscan missionaries massacred; missions destroyed.

1692: Franciscan missions refounded and expanded.

1696: Indians rebelled, five more Franciscan missionaries killed.

1850: Jean Baptiste Lamy appointed head of newly established Vicariate Apostolic of New Mexico.

1852: Sisters of Loretto arrived in Santa Fe.

1853: Santa Fe diocese established.

1859: Christian Brothers arrived, established first school for boys in New Mexico (later St. Michael's College).

1865: Sisters of Charity started first orphanage and hospital in Santa Fe. It was closed in 1966.

1875: Santa Fe made archdiocese.

New York

1524: Giovanni da Verrazano was first white man to enter New York Bay.

1642: Jesuits Isaac Jogues and Rene Goupil were mutilated by Mohawks; Rene Goupil was killed by them shortly afterwards. Dutch Calvinists rescued Father Jogues.

1646: Jesuit Isaac Jogues and John Lalande were martyred by Iroquois at Ossernenon, now Auriesville.

1654: The Onondagas were visited by Jesuits from Canada.

1655: First permanent mission established near Syracuse.

1656: Church of St. Mary erected on Onondaga Lake, in first French settlement within state. Kateri Tekakwitha, "Lily of the Mohawks," was born at Ossernenon, now Auriesville (d. in Canada, 1680). She was beatified in 1980.

1658: Indian uprisings destroyed missions among Cayugas, Senecas and Oneidas.

1664: English took New Amsterdam. Freedom of conscience allowed by the Duke of York, the new Lord Proprietor.

1667: Missions were restored under protection of Garaconthie, Onondaga chief.

1678: Franciscan Louis Hennepin, first white man to describe Niagara Falls, celebrated Mass there.

1682: Thomas Dongan appointed governor by Duke of York.

1683: English Jesuits came to New York, later opened a school.

1700: Although Assembly enacted a bill calling for religious toleration of all Christians in 1683, other penal laws were now enforced against Catholics; all priests were ordered out of the province.

1709: French Jesuit missionaries obliged to give up their central New York missions.

1741: Because of an alleged popish plot to burn city of New York, four whites were hanged and 11 blacks burned at stake.

1774: Elizabeth Bayley Seton, foundress of the American Sisters of Charity, was born in New York City on Aug. 28. She was canonized in 1975.

1777: State Constitution gave religious liberty, but the naturalization law required an oath to renounce allegiance to any foreign ruler, ecclesiastical as well as civil.

1785: Cornerstone was laid for St. Peter's Church, New York City, first permanent structure of Catholic worship in state.

Trusteeism began to cause trouble at New York.

1806: Anti-Catholic 1777 Test Oath for naturalization repealed.

1808: New York diocese established.

1823: Father Felix Varela of Cuba, educator, theologian and social reformer, arrived in New York; established churches and charitable organizations; published journals and philosophical works.

1828: New York State Legislature enacted a law upholding sanctity of seal of confession.

1834: First native New Yorker to become a secular priest, Rev. John McCloskey, was ordained.

1836: John Nepomucene Neumann arrived from Bohemia and was ordained a priest in Old St. Patrick's Cathedral, New York City. He was canonized in 1977.

1841: Fordham University and Manhattanville College established.

1847: Albany and Buffalo dioceses established.

1850: New York made archdiocese.

1853: Brooklyn diocese established.

1856: Present St. Bonaventure University and Christ the King Seminary founded at Allegany.

1858: Cornerstone was laid of second (present) St. Patrick's Cathedral, New York City. The cathedral was completed in 1879.

1868: Rochester diocese established.

1872: Ogdensburg diocese established.

1875: Abp. John McCloskey of New York made first American cardinal by Pope Pius IX.

1878: Franciscan Sisters of Allegany were first native American community to send members to foreign missions.

1880: William R. Grace was first Catholic mayor of New York City.

1886: Syracuse diocese established.

1889: Mother Frances Xavier Cabrini arrived in New York City to begin work among Italian immigrants. She was canonized in 1946.

North Carolina

1526: The Ayllon expedition attempted to establish a settlement on Carolina coast.

1540: De Soto expedition, accompanied by chaplains, entered state.

1776: State Constitution denied office to "those who denied the truths of the Protestant religion."

1805: The few Catholics in state were served by visiting missionaries.

1821: Bishop John England of Charleston celebrated Mass in the ballroom of the home of William Gaston at New Bern, marking the start of organization of the first parish, St. Paul's, in the state.

1835: William Gaston, State Supreme Court Justice, succeeded in having the article denying religious freedom repealed.

1852: First Catholic church erected in Charlotte.

1868: North Carolina vicariate apostolic established. Catholics obtained full civil liberty and rights.

1874: Sisters of Mercy arrived, opened an academy, several schools, hospitals and an orphanage.

1876: Benedictine priory and school (later Belmont Abbey College) founded at Belmont; priory designated an abbey in 1884.

North Dakota

1742: Pierre and Francois Verendrye, accompanied by Jesuit Father Coquart, explored territory.

1818: Canadian priests ministered to Catholics in area.

1840: Jesuit Father De Smet made first of several trips among Mandan and Gros Ventre Indians.

1848: Father George Belcourt, first American resident priest in territory, reestablished Pembina Mission.

1874: Grey Nuns arrived at Fort Totten to conduct a school.

1889: Jamestown diocese established; transferred to Fargo in 1897. (Jamestown was reestablished as a titular see in 1995.)

1893: Benedictines founded St. Gall Monastery at Devil's Lake. (It was moved to Richardton in 1899 and became an abbey in 1903.)

Ohio

1749: Jesuits in expedition of Céleron de Blainville preached to Indians.

First religious services were held within present limits of Ohio. Jesuit Joseph de Bonnecamps celebrated Mass at mouth of Little Miami River and in other places.

1751: First Catholic settlement founded among Huron Indians near Sandusky by Jesuit Father de la Richardie.

1790: Benedictine Pierre Didier ministered to French immigrants.

1812: Bishop Flaget of Bardstown visited and baptized Catholics of Lancaster and Somerset Counties.

1818: Dominican Father Edward Fenwick (later first bishop of Cincinnati) built St. Joseph's Church.

1821: Cincinnati diocese established.

1830: At request of Bishop Fenwick Dominican Sisters from Kentucky established second Dominican foundation in U.S. at Somerset (transferred to Columbus in 1868).

1831: Xavier University founded.

1843: Members of Congregation of Most Precious Blood arrived in Cincinnati from Switzerland.

1845: Cornerstone laid for St. Peter's Cathedral, Cincinnati.

1847: Cleveland diocese established.

1850: Cincinnati made archdiocese.

Marianists opened St. Mary's Institute, now University of Dayton.

1865: Sisters of Charity opened hospital in Cleveland, first institution of its kind in city.

1868: Columbus diocese established.

1871: Ursuline College for women opened at Cleveland.

Oklahoma

1540: De Soto expedition, accompanied by chaplains, explored territory.

1541: Coronado expedition, accompanied by Franciscan Juan de Padilla, explored state.

1630: Spanish Franciscan Juan de Salas labored among Indians.

1700: Scattered Catholic families were visited by priests from Kansas and Arkansas.

1874: First Catholic church built by Father Smyth at Atoka.

1876: Prefecture Apostolic of Indian Territory established with Benedictine Isidore Robot as its head.

1886: First Catholic day school for Choctaw and white children opened by Sisters of Mercy at Krebs.

1891: Vicariate Apostolic of Oklahoma and Indian Territory established.

1905: Oklahoma diocese established; title changed to Oklahoma City and Tulsa, 1930.

Oregon

1603: Vizcaino explored northern Oregon coast.

1774: Franciscan missionaries accompanied Juan Perez on his expedition to coast, and Heceta a year later.

1811: Catholic Canadian trappers and traders with John J. Astor expedition founded first American settlement - Astoria.

1834: Indian missions in Northwest entrusted to Jesuits by Holy See.

1838: Abbe Blanchet appointed vicar general to Bishop of Québec with jurisdiction over area which included Oregon Territory.

1839: First Mass celebrated at present site of St. Paul.

1843: Oregon vicariate apostolic established.

St. Joseph's College for boys opened.

1844: Jesuit Pierre de Smet established Mission of St. Francis Xavier near St. Paul.

Sisters of Notre Dame de Namur, first to enter Oregon, opened an academy for girls.

1846: Vicariate made an ecclesiastical province with Bishop Blanchet as first Abp. of Oregon City (now Portland).

1847: First priest was ordained in Oregon.

1848: First Provincial Council of Oregon.

1857: Death of Dr. John McLoughlin, "Father of Oregon."

1865: Rev. H. H. Spalding, a Protestant missionary, published the Whitman Myth to hinder work of Catholic missionaries.

1874: Catholic Indian Mission Bureau established.

1875: St. Vincent's Hospital, first in state, opened at Portland.

1903: Baker diocese established.

Pennsylvania

1673: Priests from Maryland ministered to Catholics in the Colony.

1682: Religious toleration was extended to members of all faiths.

1729: Jesuit Joseph Greaton became first resident missionary of Philadelphia.

1734: St. Joseph's Church, first Catholic church in Philadelphia, was opened by Father Greaton.

1741: Jesuit Fathers Schneider and Wappeler ministered to German immigrants.

Conewego Chapel, a combination chapel and dwelling, was built by Father William Wappeler, S.J., a priest sent to minister to the German Catholic immigrants who settled in the area in the 1730s.

1782: St. Mary's Parochial School opened at Philadelphia.

1788: Holy Trinity Church, Philadelphia, was incorporated; first exclusively national church organized in U.S.

1797: Augustinian Matthew Carr founded St. Augustine parish, Philadelphia.

1799: Prince Demetrius Gallitzin (Father Augustine Smith) built church in western Pennsylvania, at Loretto.

1808: Philadelphia diocese established.

1814: St. Joseph's Orphanage was opened at Philadelphia; first Catholic institution for children in U.S.

1842: University of Villanova founded by Augustinians.

1843: Pittsburgh diocese established.

1844: Thirteen persons killed, two churches and a school burned in Know-Nothing riots at Philadelphia.

1846: First Benedictine Abbey in New World founded near Latrobe by Father Boniface Wimmer.

1852: Redemptorist John Nepomucene Neumann became fourth bishop of Philadelphia. He was beatified in 1963 and canonized in 1977.

1853: Erie diocese established.

1868: Scranton and Harrisburg dioceses established.

1871: Chestnut Hill College, first for women in state, founded.

1875: Philadelphia made archdiocese.

1876: Allegheny diocese established by division of Pittsburgh diocese; reunited to Pittsburgh 1877, with resignation of its first and only bishop; suppressed in 1889. (It was later reestablished as a titular see.)

1891: Katharine Drexel founded Sisters of Blessed Sacrament for Indians and Colored Peoples. She was beatified in 1988.

1901: Altoona-Johnstown diocese established.

Rhode Island

1663: Colonial Charter granted freedom of conscience.

1719: Laws denied Catholics the right to hold public office.

1829: St. Mary's Church, Pawtucket, was first Catholic church in state.

1837: Parochial schools inaugurated in state. First Catholic church in Providence was built.

1851: Sisters of Mercy began work in Rhode Island.

1872: Providence diocese established.

1900: Trappists took up residence in state.

South Carolina

1569: Jesuit Juan Rogel was the first resident priest in the territory.

1573: First Franciscans arrived in southeastern section.

1606: Bishop Altamirano conducted visitation of area.

1655: Franciscans had two missions among Indians; later destroyed by English.

1697: Religious liberty granted to all except "papists."

1790: Catholics given right to vote.

1820: Charleston diocese established.

1822: Bishop England founded U.S. Catholic Miscellany, first Catholic paper of a strictly religious nature in U.S.

1830: Sisters of Our Lady of Mercy, first in state, took up residence at Charleston.

1847: Cornerstone of Cathedral of St. John the Baptist, Charleston, was laid.

1861: Cathedral and many institutions destroyed in Charleston fire.

South Dakota

1842: Father Augustine Ravoux began ministrations to French and Indians at Fort Pierre, Vermilion and Prairie du Chien; printed devotional book in Sioux language the following year.

1867: Parish organized among the French at Jefferson.

1878: Benedictines opened school for Sioux children at Fort Yates.

1889: Sioux Falls diocese established.

1902: Lead diocese established; transferred to Rapid City, 1930. (Lead was reestablished as a titular see in 1995.)

Tennessee

1541: Cross planted on shore of Mississippi by De Soto; accompanying the expedition were Fathers John de Gallegos and Louis De Soto.

1682: Franciscan Fathers Membre and Douay accompanied La Salle to present site of Memphis; may have offered the first Masses in the territory.

1800: Catholics were served by priests from Bardstown, Ky.

1822: Non-Catholics assisted in building church in Nashville.

1837: Nashville diocese established.

1843: Sisters of Charity opened a school for girls in Nashville.

1860: Sisters of St. Dominic from Somerset, Ohio, arrived in Nashville to open a school for girls.

1871: Christian Brothers opened a school for boys in Memphis; it later became Christian Brothers College (now University).

Texas

1541: Missionaries with Coronado expedition probably entered territory.

1553: Dominicans Diego de la Cruz, Hernando Mendez, Juan Ferrer, Brother Juan de Mina killed by Indians.

1675: Bosque-Larios missionary expedition entered region; Father Juan Larios offered first recorded high Mass.

1682: Mission Corpus Christi de Isleta (Ysleta) founded by Franciscans near El Paso, first mission in present-day Texas.

1690: Mission San Francisco de los Tejas founded in east Texas.

1703: Mission San Francisco de Solano founded on Rio Grande; rebuilt in 1718 as San Antonio de Valero or the Alamo.

1717: Franciscan Antonio Margil founded six missions in northeast.

1720: San José y San Miguel de Aguayo Mission founded by Fray Antonio Margil de Jesus.

1721: Franciscan Brother José Pita killed by Indians at Carnezeria.

1728: Site of San Antonio settled.

1738: Construction of San Fernando Cathedral at San Antonio.

1744: Mission church of the Alamo built.

1750: Franciscan Francisco Xavier was killed by Indians; so were José Ganzabal in 1752, and Alonzo Ferrares and José San Esteban in 1758.

1793: Mexico secularized missions.

1825: Governments of Cohuila and Texas secularized all Indian missions.

1838-39: Irish priests ministered to settlements of Refugio and San Patricio.

1841: Vicariate of Texas established.

1847: Ursuline Sisters established their first academy in territory at Galveston. Galveston diocese established.

1852: Oblate Fathers and Franciscans arrived in Galveston to care for new influx of German Catholics.
St. Mary's College (now University) founded at San Antonio.

1854: Know-Nothing Party began to stir up hatred against Catholics.
Oldest Polish settlement in Texas established Dec. 24; settlers named the area Panna Maria (Virgin Mary in Polish).

1858: Texas Legislature passed law entitling all schools granting free scholarships and meeting state requirements to share in school fund.

1874: San Antonio diocese established. Vicariate of Brownsville established.

1881: St. Edward's College founded: became first chartered college in state in 1889.
Sisters of Charity founded Incarnate Word College at San Antonio.

1890: Dallas diocese established; changed to Dallas-Ft. Worth, 1953; made two separate dioceses, 1969.

Utah

1776: Franciscans Silvestre de Escalante and Atanasio Dominguez reached Utah (Salt) Lake; first white men known to enter the territory.

1858: Jesuit Father De Smet accompanied General

Harney as chaplain on expedition sent to settle troubles between Mormons and U.S. Government.
1866: On June 29 Father Edward Kelly offered first Mass in Salt Lake City in Mormon Assembly Hall.
1886: Utah vicariate apostolic established.
1891: Salt Lake City diocese established.

Vermont
1609: Champlain expedition passed through territory.
1666: Captain La Motte built fort and shrine of St. Anne on Isle La Motte; Sulpician Father Dollier de Casson celebrated first Mass.
1668: Bishop Laval of Québec (beatified in 1980), administered confirmation in region; this was the first area in northeastern U.S. to receive an episcopal visit.
1710: Jesuits ministered to Indians near Lake Champlain.
1793: Discriminatory measures against Catholics were repealed.
1830: Father Jeremiah O'Callaghan became first resident priest in state.
1853: Burlington diocese established.
1854: Sisters of Charity of Providence arrived to conduct St. Joseph's Orphanage at Burlington.
1904: St. Michael's College founded.

Virginia
1526: Dominican Antonio de Montesinos offered first Mass on Virginia soil.
1561: Dominicans visited the coast.
1571: Father John Baptist de Segura and seven Jesuit companions killed by Indians.
1642: Priests outlawed and Catholics denied right to vote.
1689: Capuchin Christopher Plunket was captured and exiled to a coastal island where he died in 1697.
1776: Religious freedom granted.
1791: Father Jean Dubois arrived at Richmond with letters from Lafayette. The House of Delegates was placed at his disposal for celebration of Mass. A church was built in Norfolk (St. Mary of the Immaculate Conception). It was designated a minor basilica in 1991.
1796: A church was built at Alexandria.
1820: Richmond diocese established.
1822: Trusteeism created serious problems in diocese; Bishop Patrick Kelly resigned the see.
1848: Sisters of Charity opened an orphan asylum at Norfolk.
1866: School Sisters of Notre Dame and Sisters of Charity opened academies for girls at Richmond.

Washington
1774: Spaniards explored the region.
1838: Fathers Blanchet and Demers, "Apostles of the Northwest," were sent to territory by Abp. of Québec.
1840: Cross erected on Whidby Island, Puget Sound.
1843: Vicariate Apostolic of Oregon, including Washington, was established.
1844: Mission of St. Paul founded at Colville. Six Sisters of Notre Dame de Namur began work in area.
1846: Walla Walla diocese established; suppressed in 1850 (reestablished later as a titular see).
1850: Nesqually diocese established; transferred to

Seattle, 1907. (Nesqually reestablished as a titular see in 1995.)
1856: Providence Academy, the first permanent Catholic school in the Northwest, was built at Fort Vancouver by Mother Joseph Pariseau of the Sisters of Charity of Providence.
1887: Gonzaga University founded.

West Virginia
1749: Father Joseph de Bonnecamps, accompanying the Bienville expedition, may have offered first Mass in the territory.
1821: First Catholic church in Wheeling.
1838: Sisters of Charity founded school at Martinsburg.
1848: Visitation Nuns established academy for girls in Wheeling.
1850: Wheeling diocese established; name changed to Wheeling-Charleston, 1974. Wheeling Hospital incorporated, the oldest Catholic charitable institution in territory.
1955: Wheeling College established.

Wisconsin
1661: Jesuit René Menard, first known missionary in the territory, was killed or lost in the Black River district.
1665: Jesuit Claude Allouez founded Mission of the Holy Ghost at La Pointe Chegoimegon, now Bayfield; was the first permanent mission in region.
1673: Father Marquette and Louis Joliet traveled from Green Bay down the Wisconsin and Mississippi rivers.
1762: Suppression of Jesuits in French Colonies closed many missions for 30 years.
1843: Milwaukee diocese established.
1853: St. John's Cathedral, Milwaukee, was built.
1864: State charter granted for establishment of Marquette University. First students admitted, 1881.
1868: Green Bay and La Crosse dioceses established.
1875: Milwaukee made archdiocese.
1905: Superior diocese established.

Wyoming
1840: Jesuit Pierre De Smet offered first Mass near Green River.
1851: Father De Smet held peace conference with Indians near Fort Laramie.
1867: Father William Kelly, first resident priest, arrived in Cheyenne and built first church a year later.
1873: Father Eugene Cusson became first resident pastor in Laramie.
1875: Sisters of Charity of Leavenworth opened school and orphanage at Laramie.
1884: Jesuits took over pastoral care of Shoshone and Arapaho Indians.
1887: Cheyenne diocese established.

Puerto Rico
1493: Island discovered by Columbus on his second voyage; he named it San Juan de Borinquen (the Indian name for Puerto Rico).
1509: Juan Ponce de León, searching for gold, colonized the island and became its first governor; present population descended mainly from early Spanish settlers.

1511: Diocese of Puerto Rico established as suffragan of Seville, Spain; Bishop Alonso Manso, sailing from Spain in 1512, became first bishop to take up residence in New World.

1645: Synod held in Puerto Rico to regulate frequency of Masses according to distances people had to walk.

1898: Puerto Rico ceded to U.S. (became self-governing Commonwealth in 1952); inhabitants granted U.S. citizenship in 1917.

MISSIONARIES TO THE AMERICAS

An asterisk with a feast date indicates that the saint or blessed is listed in the General Roman Calendar or the proper calendar for U.S. dioceses.

Allouez, Claude Jean (1622-1689): French Jesuit; missionary in Canada and midwestern U.S.; preached to 20 different tribes of Indians and baptized over 10,000; vicar general of Northwest.

Altham, John (1589-1640): English Jesuit; missionary among Indians in Maryland.

Anchieta, José de, Bl. (1534-1597): Portuguese Jesuit, b. Canary Islands; missionary in Brazil; writer; beatified 1980; feast, June 9.

Andreis, Felix de (1778-1820): Italian Vincentian; missionary and educator in western U.S.

Aparicio, Sebastian, Bl. (1502-1600): Franciscan brother, born Spain; settled in Mexico, c. 1533; worked as road builder and farmer before becoming Franciscan at about the age of 70; beatified, 1787; feast, Feb. 25.

Badin, Stephen T. (1768-1853): French missioner; came to U.S., 1792, when Sulpician seminary in Paris was closed; ordained, 1793, Baltimore, the first priest ordained in U.S.; missionary in Kentucky, Ohio and Michigan; bought land on which Notre Dame University now stands; buried on its campus.

Baraga, Frederic (1797-1868): Slovenian missionary bishop in U.S.; studied at Ljubljana and Vienna, ordained, 1823; came to U.S., 1830; missionary to Indians of Upper Michigan; first bishop of Marquette, 1857-1868; wrote Chippewa grammar, dictionary, prayer book and other works.

Bertran, Louis, St. (1526-1581): Spanish Dominican; missionary in Colombia and Caribbean, 1562-69; canonized, 1671; feast, Oct. 9.

Betancur, Pedro de San José, Bl. (1626-1667): Secular Franciscan, b. Canary Islands; arrived in Guatemala, 1651; established hospital, school and homes for poor; beatified 1980; feast, Apr. 25.

Bourgeoys, Marguerite, St. (1620-1700): French foundress, missionary; settled in Canada, 1653; founded Congregation of Notre Dame, 1658; beatified, 1950; canonized 1982; feast, Jan. 12.

Brébeuf, Jean de, St. (1593-1649): French Jesuit; missionary among Huron Indians in Canada; martyred by Iroquois, Mar. 16, 1649; canonized, 1930; one of Jesuit North American martyrs; feast, Oct. 19* (U.S.).

Cancer de Barbastro, Louis (1500-1549): Spanish Dominican; began missionary work in Middle America, 1533; killed at Tampa Bay, Fla.

Castillo, John de, St. (1596-1628): Spanish Jesuit; worked in Paraguay Indian mission settlements (reductions); martyred; beatified, 1934; canonized, 1988; feast, Nov. 16.

Catala, Magin (1761-1830): Spanish Franciscan; worked in California mission of Santa Clara for 36 years.

Chabanel, Noel, St. (1613-1649): French Jesuit;

missionary among Huron Indians in Canada; murdered by renegade Huron, Dec. 8, 1649; canonized, 1930; one of Jesuit North American martyrs; feast, Oct. 19* (U.S.).

Chaumonot, Pierre Joseph (1611-1693): French Jesuit; missionary among Indians in Canada.

Claver, Peter, St. (1581-1654): Spanish Jesuit; missionary among Negroes of South America and West Indies; canonized, 1888; patron of Catholic missions among black people; feast, Sept. 9*.

Daniel, Anthony, St. (1601-1648): French Jesuit; missionary among Huron Indians in Canada; martyred by Iroquois, July 4, 1648; canonized, 1930; one of Jesuit North American martyrs; feast, Oct. 19* (U.S.).

De Smet, Pierre Jean (1801-1873): Belgian-born Jesuit; missionary among Indians of northwestern U.S.; served as intermediary between Indians and U.S. government; wrote on Indian culture.

Duchesne, Rose Philippine, St. (1769-1852): French nun; educator and missionary in the U.S.; established first convent of the Society of the Sacred Heart in the U.S., at St. Charles, Mo.; founded schools for girls; did missionary work among Indians; beatified, 1940; canonized, 1988; feast, Nov. 18* (U.S.).

Farmer, Ferdinand (family name, Steinmeyer) (1720-1786): German Jesuit; missionary in Philadelphia, where he died; one of the first missionaries in New Jersey.

Flaget, Benedict J. (1763-1850): French Sulpician bishop; came to U.S., 1792; missionary and educator in U.S.; first bishop of Bardstown, Ky. (now Louisville), 1810-32; 1833-50.

Gallitzin, Demetrius (1770-1840): Russian prince, born The Hague; convert, 1787; ordained priest at Baltimore, 1795; frontier missionary, known as Father Smith; Gallitzin, Pa., named for him.

Garnier, Charles, St. (c. 1606-1649): French Jesuit; missionary among Hurons in Canada; martyred by Iroquois, Dec. 7, 1649; canonized, 1930; one of Jesuit North American martyrs; feast, Oct. 19* (U.S.).

Gibault, Pierre (1737-1804): Canadian missionary in Illinois and Indiana; aided in securing states of Ohio, Indiana, Illinois, Michigan and Wisconsin for the Americans during Revolution.

Gonzalez, Roch, St. (1576-1628): Paraguayan Jesuit; worked in Paraguay Indian mission settlements (reductions); martyred; beatified, 1934; canonized, 1988; feast, Nov. 16.

Goupil, René, St. (1607-1642): French lay missionary; had studied surgery at Orleans, France; missionary companion of St. Isaac Jogues among the Hurons; martyred, Sept. 29, 1642; canonized, 1930; one of Jesuit North American martyrs; feast, Oct. 19* (U.S.).

Gravier, Jacques (1651-1708): French Jesuit; missionary among Indians of Canada and midwestern U.S.

Hennepin, Louis (d. c. 1701): Belgian-born Franciscan missionary and explorer of Great Lakes region and Upper Mississippi, 1675-81, when he returned to Europe.

Jesuit North American Martyrs: Isaac Jogues, Anthony Daniel, John de Brébeuf, Gabriel Lalemant, Charles Garnier, Noel Chabanel (Jesuit priests), and René Goupil and John Lalande (lay missionaries) who were martyred between Sept. 29, 1642, and Dec. 9, 1649, in the missions of New France; canonized June 29, 1930; feast, Oct. 19* (U.S.). See separate entries.

Jogues, Isaac, St. (1607-1646): French Jesuit; missionary among Indians in Canada; martyred near present site of Auriesville, N.Y., by Mohawks, Oct. 18, 1646; canonized, 1930; one of Jesuit North American martyrs; feast, Oct. 19* (U.S.).

Kino, Eusebio (1645-1711): Italian Jesuit; missionary and explorer in U.S.; arrived Southwest, 1681; established 25 Indian missions, took part in 14 exploring expeditions in northern Mexico, Arizona and southern California; helped develop livestock raising and farming in the area. He was selected in 1965 to represent Arizona in Statuary Hall.

Lalande, John, St. (d. 1646): French lay missionary, companion of Isaac Jogues; martyred by Mohawks at Auriesville, N.Y., Oct. 19, 1646; canonized, 1930; one of Jesuit North American martyrs; feast, Oct. 19* (U.S.).

Lalemant, Gabriel, St. (1610-1649): French Jesuit; missionary among the Hurons in Canada; martyred by the Iroquois, Mar. 17, 1649; canonized, 1930; one of Jesuit North American martyrs; feast, Oct. 19* (U.S.).

Lamy, Jean Baptiste (1814-1888): French prelate; came to U.S., 1839; missionary in Ohio and Kentucky; bishop in Southwest from 1850; first bishop (later Abp.) of Santa Fe, 1850-1885. He was nominated in 1951 to represent New Mexico in Statuary Hall.

Las Casas, Bartolome (1474-1566): Spanish Dominican; missionary in Haiti, Jamaica and Venezuela; reformer of abuses against Indians and black people; bishop of Chalapas, Mexico, 1544-47; historian.

Laval, Françoise de Montmorency, Bl. (1623-1708): French-born missionary bishop in Canada; named vicar apostolic of Canada, 1658; first bishop of Québec, 1674; jurisdiction extended over all French-claimed territory in New World; beatified 1980; feast, May 6.

Manogue, Patrick (1831-1895): Missionary bishop in U.S., b. Ireland; migrated to U.S.; miner in California; studied for priesthood at St. Mary's of the Lake, Chicago, and St. Sulpice, Paris; ordained, 1861; missionary among Indians of California and Nevada; coadj. bishop, 1881-84, and bishop, 1884-86, of Grass Valley; first bishop of Sacramento, 1886-1895, when see was transferred there.

Margil, Antonio, Ven. (1657-1726): Spanish Franciscan; missionary in Middle America; apostle of Guatemala; established missions in Texas.

Marie of the Incarnation, St. (Marie Guyard Martin) (1599-1672): French widow; joined Ursuline Nuns; arrived in Canada, 1639; first superior of Ursulines in Québec; missionary to Indians; writer; beatified 1980; feast, Apr. 30.

Marquette, Jacques (1637-1675): French Jesuit; missionary and explorer in America; sent to New France, 1666; began missionary work among Ottawa Indians on Lake Superior, 1668; accompanied Joliet down the Mississippi to mouth of the Arkansas, 1673, and returned to Lake Michigan by way of Illinois River; made a second trip over the same route; his diary and map are of historical significance. He was selected in 1895 to represent Wisconsin in Statuary Hall.

Massias (Macias), John de, St. (1585-1645): Dominican brother, a native of Spain; entered Dominican Friary at Lima, Peru, 1622; served as doorkeeper until his death; beatified, 1837; canonized 1975; feast, Sept. 16.

Mazzuchelli, Samuel C. (1806-1864): Italian Dominican; missionary in midwestern U.S.; called builder of the West; writer. A decree advancing his beatification cause was promulgated July 6, 1993.

Membre, Zenobius (1645-1687): French Franciscan; missionary among Indians of Illinois; accompanied LaSalle expedition down the Mississippi (1681-1682) and Louisiana colonizing expedition (1684) which landed in Texas; murdered by Indians.

Nerinckx, Charles (1761-1824): Belgian priest; missionary in Kentucky; founded Sisters of Loretto at the Foot of the Cross.

Nobrega, Manoel (1517-1570): Portuguese Jesuit; leader of first Jesuit missionaries to Brazil, 1549.

Padilla, Juan de (d. 1542): Spanish Franciscan; missionary among Indians of Mexico and southwestern U.S.; killed by Indians in Kansas; protomartyr of the U.S.

Palou, Francisco (c. 1722-1789): Spanish Franciscan; accompanied Junípero Serra to Mexico, 1749; founded Mission Dolores in San Francisco; wrote history of the Franciscans in California.

Pariseau, Mother Mary Joseph (1833-1902): Canadian Sister of Charity of Providence; missionary in state of Washington from 1856; founded first hospitals in northwest territory; artisan and architect. Represents Washington in National Statuary Hall.

Peter of Ghent (d. 1572): Belgian Franciscan brother; missionary in Mexico for 49 years.

Porres, Martin de, St. (1579-1639): Peruvian Dominican oblate; his father was a Spanish soldier and his mother a black freedwoman from Panama; called wonder worker of Peru; beatified, 1837; canonized, 1962; feast, Nov. 3*.

Quiroga, Vasco de (1470-1565): Spanish missionary in Mexico; founded hospitals; bishop of Michoacan, 1537.

Ravalli, Antonio (1811-1884): Italian Jesuit; missionary in far-western United States, mostly Montana, for 40 years.

Raymbaut, Charles (1602-1643): French Jesuit; missionary among Indians of Canada and northern U.S.

Richard, Gabriel (1767-1832): French Sulpician; missionary in Illinois and Michigan; a founder of University of Michigan; elected delegate to Congress from Michigan, 1823; first priest to hold seat in the House of Representatives.

Rodriguez, Alfonso, St. (1598-1628): Spanish Jesuit; missionary in Paraguay; martyred; beatified, 1934; canonized, 1988; feast, Nov. 16.

Rosati, Joseph (1789-1843): Italian Vincentian; missionary bishop in U.S. (vicar apostolic of Mississippi and Alabama, 1822; coadj. of Louisiana and the

Two Floridas, 1823-26; administrator of New Orleans, 1826-29; first bishop of St. Louis, 1826-1843).

Sahagun, Bernardino de (c. 1500-1590): Spanish Franciscan; missionary in Mexico for over 60 years; expert on Aztec archaeology.

Seelos, Francis X. (1819-1867): Redemptorist missionary, born Bavaria; ordained, 1844, at Baltimore; missionary in Pittsburgh and New Orleans.

Seghers, Charles J. (1839-1886): Belgian missionary bishop in North America; Apostle of Alaska; Abp. of Oregon City (now Portland), 1880-1884; murdered by berserk companion while on missionary journey.

Serra, Junípero, Bl. (1713-1784): Spanish Franciscan, b. Majorca; missionary in America; arrived Mexico, 1749, where he did missionary work for 20 years; began work in Upper California in 1769 and established nine of the 21 Franciscan missions along the Pacific coast; baptized some 6,000 Indians and confirmed almost 5,000; a cultural pioneer of California. Represents California in Statuary Hall. He was declared venerable May 9, 1985, and was beatified Sept. 25, 1988; feast, July 1* (U.S.).

Solanus, Francis, St. (1549-1610): Spanish Franciscan; missionary in Paraguay, Argentina and Peru; wonder worker of the New World; canonized, 1726; feast, July 14.

Sorin, Edward F. (1814-1893): French priest; member of Congregation of Holy Cross; sent to U.S. in 1841; founder and first president of the University of Notre Dame; missionary in Indiana and Michigan.

Todadilla, Anthony de (1704-1746): Spanish Capuchin; missionary to Indians of Venezuela; killed by Motilones.

Turibius de Mogrovejo, St. (1538-1606): Spanish Abp. of Lima, Peru, c. 1580-1606; canonized 1726; feast, Mar. 23*.

Twelve Apostles of Mexico (early 16th century): Franciscan priests; arrived in Mexico, 1524: Fathers Martin de Valencia (leader), Francisco de Soto, Martin de la Coruna, Juan Suares, Antonio de Ciudad Rodrigo, Toribio de Benevente, Garcia de Cisneros, Luis de Fuensalida, Juan de Ribas, Francisco Ximenes; Brothers Andres de Coroboda, Juan de Palos.

Valdivia, Luis de (1561-1641): Spanish Jesuit; defender of Indians in Peru and Chile.

Vasques de Espiñosa, Antonio (early 17th century): Spanish Carmelite; missionary and explorer in Mexico, Panama and western coast of South America.

Vieira, Antonio (1608-1687): Portuguese Jesuit; preacher; missionary in Peru and Chile; protector of Indians against exploitation by slave owners and traders; considered foremost prose writer of 17th-century Portugal.

White, Andrew (1579-1656): English Jesuit; missionary among Indians in Maryland.

Wimmer, Boniface (1809-1887): German Benedictine; missionary among German immigrants in the U.S.

Youville, Marie Marguerite d', St. (1701-1771): Canadian widow; foundress of Sisters of Charity (Grey Nuns), 1737, at Montréal: beatified, 1959; canonized 1990, first native Canadian saint; feast, Dec. 23.

Zumarraga, Juan de (1468-1548): Spanish Franciscan; missionary; first bishop of Mexico; introduced first printing press in New World, published first book in America, a catechism for Aztec Indians; extended missions in Mexico and Central America; vigorous opponent of exploitation of Indians; approved of devotions at Guadalupe; leading figure in early church history in Mexico.

FRANCISCAN MISSIONS

The 21 Franciscan missions of Upper California were established during the 54-year period from 1769 to 1822. Located along the old El Camino Real, or King's Highway, they extended from San Diego to San Francisco and were the centers of Indian civilization, Christianity and industry in the early history of the state.

Junípero Serra (beatified 1988) was the great pioneer of the missions of Upper California. He and his successor as superior of the work, Fermin Lasuen, each directed the establishment of nine missions. One hundred and 46 priests of the Order of Friars Minor, most of them Spaniards, labored in the region from 1769 to 1845; 67 of them died at their posts, two as martyrs. The regular time of mission service was 10 years.

The missions were secularized by the Mexican gov-

ernment in the 1830s but were subsequently restored to the Church by the U.S. government. They are now variously used as the sites of parish churches, a university, houses of study and museums.

The names of the missions and the order of their establishment were as follows:

San Diego de Alcala, San Carlos Borromeo (El Carmelo), San Antonio de Padua, San Gabriel Arcangel, San Luis Obispo de Tolosa, San Francisco de Asis (Dolores), San Juan Capistrano; Santa Clara de Asis, San Buenaventura, Santa Barbara, La Purisima Concepcion de Maria Santisima, Santa Cruz, Nuestra Señora de la Soledad, San José de Guadalupe; San Juan Bautista, San Miguel Arcangel, San Fernando Rey de España, San Luis Rey de Francia, Santa Iñes, San Rafael Arcangel, San Francisco Solano de Sonoma (Sonoma).

AMERICAN CATHOLICS OF THE PAST

A

Abbelin, Peter (1843-1917): Priest, monsignor, and vicar general of the Milwaukee archdiocese; adherent of the German language and culture and the separateness of German Catholics.

Alemany, Joseph Sadoc, O.P. (1814-88): Bishop of Monterey, 1850-53 and first abp. of San Francisco (1853-84); labored in American missions in Ohio, Kentucky, and Tennessee; attended Vatican Council I and the Third Plenary Council of Baltimore.

Allen, Fred (1894-1956): Entertainer; after a successful stage career, moved to radio in 1932 and became best known for *The Fred Allen Show* and the *Texaco Star Theater.*

Allen, Gracie (d. 1964): Entertainer and wife of George Burns, with whom she had a long and successful career; enjoyed success on stage, radio, and in films; one of the most popular entertainers of her generation.

Allouez, Claude Jean: See under Missionaries to the Americas.

Altham, John: See under Missionaries to the Americas.

Amat, Thaddeus, C.M. (1811-78): Missionary bishop; born in Spain; bp. of Monterey, California, 1854-59 and bp. of Monterey-Los Angeles, 1859-78; founded the cathedral of St. Vibiana and directed the expansion of the Church in California.

Andreis, Felix de: See under Missionaries to the Americas.

Anchieta, José de, Bl.: See under Missionaries to the Americas.

Aparicio, Sebastian, Bl.: See under Missionaries to the Americas.

Avery, Martha (1851-1929): Catholic lay writer and lecturer; one-time Socialist, convert to Catholicism in 1904; supported social reform and papal encyclical *Rerum Novarum;* founder of the Catholic Truth Guild.

B

Badin, Stephen T.: See under Missionaries to the Americas.

Baraga, Frederic: See under Missionaries to the Americas.

Baker, Josephine (1906-75): African-American dancer and entertainer; worked her way out of poverty as a dancer in Philadelphia, Boston, and Harlem; moved to Paris in the 1920s; success allowed her to open *Chez Josephine,* her own nightclub, in 1926; French citizen in 1937; worked with the Red Cross and the French Resistance during World War II; granted the *Croix de Guerre* and *Legion d'Honneur* with the rosette of the Resistance; took part in the Civil Rights Movement in the 1960s.

Baraga, Frederic: See under Missionaries to the Americas.

Barry, John (1745-1803): Father of the U.S. Navy; born in Ireland; went to sea at a young age and eventually became a wealthy shipowner in the American colonies; supported the American Revolution and was made captain of the brig *Lexington;* the first American naval officer to engage the vaunted British Navy at sea; assisted the new republic in building a fleet.

Barry, Leonora (1849-1930): Lay leader of the Knights of Labor; helped pass the Pennsylvania Factory Inspection Act in 1889; supporter of the suffrage movement and prohibition.

Bauer, Mother Benedicta (1803-65): German-born Dominican missionary sister; founded convents in Brooklyn, Ohio, Tennessee, and Green Bay, and began the Dominican motherhouse in Racine, Wisconsin.

Barrymore, Ethel (1879-1959): Actress and member of the famed Barrymore family; educated by the Sisters of Notre Dame de Namur; enjoyed a brilliant career on stage and screen; won Academy Award for best Supporting Actress in 1944 for *None But the Lonely Heart.*

Benson, William (1891-1957): Admiral; graduated Naval Academy, 1877; served on various assignments and taught at the Academy, 1890-93; appointed commandant of the Philadelphia Naval Yard, 1913-15; first chief of naval operations, 1915; admiral, 1916; first president of the National Council of Catholic men, 1921-25; devout Catholic.

Bernardin, Joseph L. (1928-96): Archbishop of Chicago, 1982-96 and Cardinal from 1983; auxiliary bp. of Atlanta, 1966-72 and abp. of Cincinnati, 1972-82; became renowned for the grace with which he bore a scurrilous accusation of sexual misconduct and his suffering from terminal cancer; authored a bestselling book on dying in Christ.

Bertran, Louis, St.: See under Missionaries to the Americas.

Betancur, Pedro de San José, Bl.: See under Missionaries to the Americas.

Beauregard, Pierre (1818-93) Confederate general in the Civil War; directed the bombardment of Fort Sumter in 1861; participated in the battles of First Manassas (Bull Run) and Shiloh; defended Charleston in 1863.

Bishop, William (1885-1953): Priest and founder of the Glenmary Home Missioners.

Black Elk (1866-1950): Native American, called the Holy Man of the Oglala; as a young man, he lived with his tribe in Montana at the time of Custer's death at Little Big Horn and took part in the tragic Wounded Knee Massacre of 1890; converted in 1904 and known as a zealous catechist.

Blanc, Anthony (1792-1860): The first archbishop of New Orleans, 1850-60; bp. of New Orleans in 1835.

Blanchet, Francis N. (1795-1883): First archbishop of Oregon City (now Portland); his brother, Augustin Blanchet (1797-1887), was first bp. of Nesqually (now Seattle) from 1850-79.

Bohachevsky, Constantine (1884-1961): First metropolitan of the Byzantine Rite archeparchy of Philadelphia.

Bonaparte, Charles Joseph (1851-1921): Secretary of the Navy and U.S. Attorney General; the grandson of Jerome Bonaparte (brother to Napoleon Bonaparte); supporter and friend of Theodore Roosevelt; aggressively pursued Roosevelt's antitrust policy.

Bourgeoys, Marguerite, St.: See under Missionaries to the Americas.

Brady, Matthew (c.1823-96) Photographer; photographed Pres. Lincoln; best known for his photographic record of the Civil War, now in the Library of Congress.

Brébeuf, Jean de, St.: See under Missionaries to the Americas.

Brennan, Francis J. (1894-1968): Cardinal and American prelate who served for many years in Rome; judge, 1940-59, and dean, 1959-67, of the Roman Rota in Rome; bp. in 1967; cardinal in 1967.

Brennan, William (1906-98): Associate justice of the U.S. Supreme Court, 1956-90; justice on the New Jersey supreme court, 1952-56; the most influential liberal during the 1980s and a supporter of abortion.

Brent, Margaret (1601-c.1671): The first woman in Maryland to own land; migrated to Maryland in 1638 and granted land by Lord Baltimore; named executrix for Governor Leonard Calvert.

Brown, Fr. Raymond, S.S. (d. 1998): Scripture scholar and professor of biblical studies at Union Theological Seminary in New York; author of over 37 books on Scripture and co-editor of two editions of *The Jerome Biblical Commentary*.

Brownson, Orestes (1803-76): Journalist and author and one of the leading lay theologians of the 19th century.

Burke, John (1875-1936): Paulist priest, social reformer, and editor of *Catholic World* (1903-22); coordinated the National Catholic War Council to advance Catholic perspectives during World War I; general secretary of the National Catholic Welfare Conference (NCWC); worked to promote a settlement of the Church-State conflict in Mexico.

Byrne, Andrew (1802-62): First bishop of Little Rock, Arkansas; worked to establish the new diocese in the face of numerous obstacles, including a chronic shortage of priests; avoided involvement in assorted controversies, especially slavery.

C

Cabot, John (c. 1450-98): Explorer; born in Italy; won the support of King Henry VII of England to find an all-water route to the East; set out to find the "Northwest Passage" but reached only Newfoundland; later made a voyage along the eastern coast of North America in the search for Japan; gave to England much of its claim to North America.

Cabrini, Frances Xavier: See under Saints of the Church.

Calvert, Cecil (1606-75): Second Lord Baltimore and a major figure in early Maryland; eldest son of Lord George Calvert, first Lord of Baltimore; inherited his father's control of Maryland in 1632; strove to make the colony a model for religious toleration and protected Catholics from Puritan persecution through "The Act of Concerning Religion" following the execution of King Charles I in 1649.

Calvert, Charles (1628-1714): Third Lord Baltimore and second Lord Proprietary of Maryland; his period as Lord Baltimore marked the decline in the fortunes of the Calverts in Maryland; his eldest son, Benedict Calvert, abjured Catholicism in 1713.

Calvert, George (1580-1632): Founder of the Maryland colony and first Lord Baltimore; petitioned for a charter to found a colony in Maryland; his son, Cecil, inherited the title of Lord Baltimore.

Cancer de Barbastro, Louis: See under Missionaries to the Americas.

Capra, Frank (1897–1991): Academy Award winning film director best known for such classics as *It Happened One Night* (1934), *Mr. Deeds Goes to Town*

(1936), and *You Can't Take It with You* (1938), and *It's a Wonderful Life* (1946).

Carberry, John J. (1904-98): Archbishop of St, Louis, 1968-79 and Cardinal from 1969.

Carey, Mathew (1760-1839): American publisher and banker; co-founder of *Columbian Magazine* (1786) and *American Museum* (1787), the first nationally read American literary journal; launched the country's largest publishing house, served on the board of the bank of Pennsylvania, helped establish the Hibernian Society (for Irish immigrants).

Carroll, Austin (1835-1909): Sister of Mercy and caretaker of the poor.

Carroll, Charles (1737-1834): Called "First Citizen," one of the most prominent Catholic leaders in the cause of American independence; U.S. Senator, 1789-92; last surviving signer of the Declaration of Independence.

Carroll, Daniel (1733-96): Elder brother of Abp. John Carroll and a Catholic leader during the American Revolution and the creation of the Constitution; supported the ratification of the Constitution; one of four Catholics chosen to represent American Catholics in congratulating George Washington on his election as president.

Carroll, John (1735-1815): First bishop and archbishop of Baltimore and the architect of the Church in the United States; a member of the Carroll family of Maryland; entered the Jesuits in Europe but returned to America after the suppression of the order; missionary priest in Maryland from 1774-83; named Superior of American missions in 1784; appointed bp. of Baltimore in 1789 with his diocese extending across the whole of the United States; promoted in 1808 to abp. of Baltimore; supported religious liberty and tolerance and established the Church on a firm administrative and spiritual footing in the new country.

Carson, Christopher "Kit" (1809-68): Trapper, guide, and frontiersman; convert to Catholicism under the influence of Padre Antonio José Martinez; active as a soldier in California against the Mexican army in 1846-47; served as Indian agent to the Utes and helped negotiate peace with the Cheyenne, Arapaho, and Navaho; later waged several campaigns against the Apaches and Navahos.

Cartier, Jacques (1491-1557): French explorer; sailed up the St. Lawrence River in the hopes of finding a route to the East; entered the Gulf of St. Lawrence and encountered the native tribes; his explorations opened up the wilderness of North America to further French exploration.

Casey, Solanus, O.F.M., Cap. (1870-1957): Capuchin friar and noted healer; after failing academically in the seminary of St. Francis de Sales, entered the Capuchins and was finally ordained as a priest simplex, in which he was not given faculties to hear confessions or to preach; acquired a reputation for holiness and miracles, with a special devotion to the Eucharist and the BVM; his cause was opened in 1982 and given formal recognition in 1992.

Castillo, John de, St.: See under Missionaries to the Americas.

Catala, Magin: See under Missionaries to the Americas.

Chabanel, Noel, St.: See under Missionaries to the Americas.

Champlain, Samuel de (1567-1635): French explorer and governor; established a fort at Quebec and explored Lakes Huron and Ontario, making possible the further exploration of the Mississippi Valley; established French relations with the Huron.

Charlot, Chief (c. 1831-1910): Native American chief of the Kalispel in Idaho; known properly as Little-Claw-of-the-Grizzly-Bear; became chief in 1870 and attempted to negotiate with the Federal Government to adhere to the terms of earlier treaties; continued white violations of Indian territory brought gradual destitution of the tribe; moved in 1889 to the Flathead reservation in Montana.

Chaumonot, Pierre Joseph: See under Missionaries to the Americas.

Chavez, Cesar (1927-93): Founder of the United Farmworkers (UFW) and social activist; established the National Farmworkers Association (NFWA) for migrant farmworkers; joined with the Agricultural Workers Organizing Committee (AWOC) to form the United Farmworkers Organizing Committee (UFWOC), the foundation for the UFWA; led a famous strike against the agricultural industry in the 1960s.

Cheverus, Jean Lefebvre de (1768-1836): Missionary, cardinal and bishop of Boston from 1810-23; born and ordained in France, he left his native country in the face of the Revolution; served as a priest in Boston from 1796-1808; established the diocese on a firm footing before departing back to France in 1823; made a cardinal in 1836.

Cody, John P. (1907-82): Archbishop of Chicago, 1965-82 and Cardinal from 1967; headed the largest archdiocese in America during the turbulent postconciliar period; abp. of New Orleans, 1964-65; his time in Chicago was marked by numerous challenges to authority; also an advocate of civil rights.

Connolly, John, O.P. (1750-1825): Dominican friar and the second bp. of New York, 1814-25; born in Ireland; served in Rome during the turbulent days of the French occupation; became the second bp. of New York; worked to advance the cause of the Church in the city.

Conway, Katherine (1853-1927): Editor and novelist; trustee of the Boston Public Library; opposed extension of full suffrage to women.

Conwell, Bp. Henry (1748-1842): Bishop. of Philadelphia, 1820-42; his time was marked by the difficulties of the Hogan Schism and trusteeism; summoned to Rome over diocesan management; coadjutor bp., Francis Kenrick, was appointed in 1830, and Conwell held the see in name only until his death.

Cooke, Cardinal Terence J. (1921-83): Archbisop of New York, 1968-83 and Cardinal from 1969; work also included efforts to promote the Military Vicariate; his cause for canonization is currently being promoted.

Corcoran, James (1820-89): A priest and theologian; advised the Baltimore Provincial Councils and the Baltimore Plenary Councils; theological advisor to Vatican Council I (1869-70); a staunch supporter of antebellum Southern culture, separation of Church and State, and ultramontane Catholicism.

Corrigan, Michael A. (1839-1902): Archbishop of New York from 1885-1902; one of the most vocal leaders of conservative Catholicism and a vigorous opponent of Americanism; complained to Rome about

the Knights of Labor and supported Pope Leo XIII's encyclical *Testem Benevolentiae,* condemning the errors of Americanism.

Coughlin, Fr. Charles (1891-1979): Priest and famous radio preacher who enjoyed national prominence during the Great Depression; founded the National Union for Social Justice to promote social justice, but both his writings and radio program were increasingly anti-Semitic; forced from the air in 1942.

Crétin, Joseph (1799-1857): Missionary bishop; born in France; worked in the Dubuque missions; preached among the Winnebago Indians; appointed the first bp. of St. Paul, 1851-57; heavily promoted the Church in the region, founding 26 churches, 24 schools, and a hospital.

Crosby, "Bing" (1903-77): Singer and entertainer; called Bing after his fondness for "The Bingville Bungle" comic strip; became famous as a singer from 1932 and starred in over 70 films, including the popular "Road" series with Bob Hope; among his most beloved films was *Going My Way* (1944), in which he played a priest; two songs, "White Christmas" and "Silent Night," became all-time classics.

Crowley, Patrick (1911-74): Lawyer and cofounder of the Christian Family Movement in the 1940s with his wife Patricia; helped establish the International Confederation of the Christian Family Movement (ICCFM) in 1966 and served on the Papal Commission on Birth Control from 1964-67.

Curley, James (1796-1889): Massachusetts politician; the model for Edwin O'Connor's novel *The Last Hurrah;* served in the U.S. House of Representatives, 1910-14; elected mayor of Boston for the first of several times in 1914; elected governor of Massachusetts in 1934.

Curran, John (1859-1936): Labor priest and supporter of mine workers; a friend of Theodore Roosevelt and John Mitchell, head of the United Mine Workers; involved himself in a variety of labor disputes.

Cushing, Cardinal Richard J. (1895-1970): Archbishop of Boston, 1944-70 and Cardinal from 1958; auxiliary bp. of Boston, 1939-44; close friend of the Kennedy family and one of the most respected and beloved Catholic leaders in the United States; supported reforms of Vatican Council II.

D

Daley, Richard (1902-76): Mayor of Chicago, 1955-76; oversaw one of the most efficient political machines in American politics; campaigned vigorously for John F. Kennedy and proved essential in his victory in 1960; presided over the city during the 1968 Democratic National Convention; his son, Richard M. Daley, subsequently served as mayor of Chicago and Secretary of Commerce in the Clinton administration.

Damien de Veuster, S.S.C.C. (1840-89) "The Leper Priest of Molokai"; born in Belgium; entered the Sacred Hearts Fathers and replaced his brother Pamphile in the Hawaiian missions; after labors on the Big Island, went to Molokai to work among the lepers from 1873; established orphanages, hospitals, and houses for the lepers; diagnosed with leprosy in 1884; honored with the rank of Knight Commander of the Royal Order of Kalakaua, 1881; beatified by Pope John Paul II in 1995.

Daniel, Anthony, St.: See under Missionaries to the Americas.

David, Jean Baptiste, S.S. (1761-1841): Missionary, Sulpician, and coadj. bishop of Bardstown, 1819-41; the first bp. consecrated in the West (in 1819), he resisted appointment as bp. of Bardstown in 1832; assisted in the founding of the Sisters of Charity of Nazareth.

Davis, Thurston, S.J. (1913-86): Jesuit priest, professor, and editor; editor of *America* from 1953-68; founder of La Farge Institute to promote the study of religious traditions.

Day, Dorothy (1897-1980): Social activist and founder of the Catholic Worker movement; after a socialist youth marked by an abortion, she converted to Catholicism in 1927, following the birth and baptism of her daughter that same year; met Peter Maurin in 1932 and launched in 1933 *The Catholic Worker*, the foundation for the Catholic Worker movement; created the first of many houses of hospitality in New York, 1935; opposed World War II, the Korean War, and Vietnam; arrested in 1973 with Cesar Chavez during a farm workers' demonstration; one of the most influential lay Catholics of the 20th century.

Dearden, John F. (1907-88): Archbishop of Detroit, 1958-80 and Cardinal from 1969; bp. of Pittsburgh, 1950-58; president of the NCCB from 1966-71.

De Cheverus, John L.: See Cheverus, John

De Smet, Pierre Jean: See under Missionaries to the Americas.

Dietz, Peter (1878-1947): Labor priest and editor; editor of *Central Blatt* and *Social Justice* from 1909-10; secretary of Social Service Commission of American Federation of Catholic Societies, 1911-18; founder of American Academy for Christian Democracy for Women, 1915.

Dohen, Dorothy (1923-84): Writer and social worker; editor of *Integrity* from 1952-56; professor, Fordham University, 1960-84; author on Catholic lay spirituality.

Doherty, Catherine de Hueck (1896-1985): Social activist and spiritual writer; born in Russia and fled during the Bolshevik Revolution; established Friendship House to care for those in need of food, shelter, and clothing; subsequently established Madonna House to promote spirituality of a Western and Eastern inspiration.

Dooley, Thomas (1927-61): Physician, activist, and one of the most popular Catholics in the 1950s; enlisted in the U.S. Navy after graduating from medical school; worked to care for the North Vietnamese refugees who fled their homes following Dienbienphu; supported the South Vietnamese government; authored numerous popular books on his work; in 1959, he was one of the most admired men in America (the only other Catholic on the list was John F. Kennedy).

Dorsey, John (1874-1926): Missionary and the first African-American Josephite priest ordained in the United States; supporter of Catholic missions among African-Americans, including pastoral assignments in Nashville and Memphis; assaulted in 1924 and left paralyzed; endured humiliations, persecutions, and violence for the Catholic faith.

Dougherty, Dennis (1865-1951): Archbishop of Philadelphia, 1918-51 and cardinal from 1921; bp. of Nueva Segovia, P.I., from 1903-08; bp. of Jaro,

P.I., from 1908-15; bp. of Buffalo, from 1915-18; served as abp. in the long period of the Great Depression and World War II.

Drexel, Katharine: See under Saints of the Church.

Drossaerts, Arthur J. (1862-1940): The first Archbishop of San Antonio, 1926-40; native of Holland; ordained on June 15, 1889; bp. of San Antonio 1918-26.

Dubois, Jean, S.S. (1764-1842): Bishop of New York from 1826-42; born in France, journeyed to labor in the missions of the United States.

Dubourg, Louis William, S.S. (1766-1833): Bishop of Louisiana and the Two Floridas (now New Orleans), 1815-25; born in Santo Domingo; ordained in 1788; later returned to France, serving as bp. of Montauban,1826-33, and abp. of Besançon in 1833.

Duchesne, Rose Philippine, St.: See under Missionaries to the Americas.

Duffy, Fr. Francis (1871-1932): Chaplain and educator; served for 14 years as a teacher at Dunwoodie Seminary; served as a chaplain during World War I from 1917-20; promoted ecumenism and supported Alfred E. Smith.

Durante, Jimmy (1893-1980): Comedian best known for his hoarse voice, ample nose, and timeworn hat; starred in numerous films and Broadway shows, including *Red, Hot, and Blue* (1936).

E

Elliott, Walter (1842-1928): Priest, missionary, and editor; Civil War veteran; joined the Paulists in 1868 and ordained in 1872; labored among non-Catholics and established the Apostolic Mission House for home mission work; founding editor of the *Missionary*; author of famous biography on Isaac Hecker, 1891 that helped spark the Americanist controversy and the issue of the encyclical *Testem Benevolentiae*.

Ellis, John Tracy (1905-92): Historian and educator, for many years, the dean of Catholic Church historians in the U.S.; ordained in 1938; professor at Catholic University of America from 1938-64; earned praise for his many writings; president of the American Catholic Historical Society and American Society of Church History.

England, John (1786-1842): First Bishop of Charleston, 1820-42; born in Ireland; president of College of St. Mary, in Cork, Ireland, from 1812-17; ardent supporter of the compatibility between Catholicism and American democracy; founded the first national Catholic newspaper, the U.S. Catholic Miscellany; invited in 1926 to address the U.S. Congress, the first Catholic clergyman so honored; apostolic delegate to Haiti, 1833-37.

F

Farley, John (1842-1918): Archbishop of New York, 1902-18 and Cardinal from 1911; born in Ireland; auxiliary bp. of New York from 1895-1902; promoted education.

Farmer, Ferdinand: See under Missionaries to the Americas.

Feehan, Patrick (1829-1902): First Archbishop of Chicago, 1880-92; born in Ireland and ordained in St. Louis in 1852; bp. of Nashville from 1865-80; renowned preacher and promoter of education; later years troubled by poor relations with Polish Catholics and internal conflicts among the Irish priests.

Fenton, Joseph (1906-69): American theologian, priest, and supporter of neo-Scholasticism; professor and dean of theology at Catholic University of America; cofounder of Catholic Theological Society of America, 1946; cofounder of Mariological Society, 1949; *peritus* at Vatican Council II, 1962-65.

Fenwick, Edward D., O.P. (1768-1832): First Bishop of Cincinnati from 1822-32; founder of the *Catholic Telegraph-Register*, 1831; efforts at education and missions prompted a Protestant counter-reaction, including Lyman Beecher's *Plea for the West.*

Fink, Michael, O.S.B. (1834-1904): First Bishop of Leavenworth (now Kansas City), from 1877-1904; born in Germany; coadj. vicar apostolic from 1871-74, and vicar apostolic from 1874-77, of the Kansas and Indian Territory.

Fitzsimmons, Thomas (1741-1811): Signer of the U.S. Constitution; born in Ireland; founded the Friendly Sons of St. Patrick in America; assisted the cause of the American Revolution; was one of two Catholic delegates (with Daniel Carroll) to the Constitutional convention in 1787; served in the House of Representatives, 1788-95; grandfather of General Gordon B. Meade, victor of the Battle of Gettysburg in 1863.

Flaget, Benedict J.: See under Missionaries to the Americas.

Flanagan, Edward (1886-1948): Founder of Father Flanagan's Boys' Town; born in Ireland and ordained in 1912; served in Omaha, Nebraska, founded Boys' Town in 1917 to care for homeless boys; the home became internationally known.

Floersh, John (1886-1968): First Archbishop of Louisville from 1937-67; coadj. bp. of Louisville from 1923-24; bp. of Louisville from 1924-37.

Ford, John (1895-1973): Motion Picture Director and anticommunist; a director of some 130 films, he won five Academy Awards for Best Director, including *Stagecoach* (1939), *The Grapes of Wrath* (1940), *How Green Was My Valley* (1941), and *The Quiet Man* (1952); received the Presidential Medal of Freedom.

Friess, Mother Caroline (1824-92): Mother superior, School Sisters of Notre Dame in America from 1850-92; born in France; by 1892, her sisters had founded 265 parochial schools in 16 states and taught 70,000 pupils.

Furfrey, Paul (1897-1992): Priest, sociologist, and social justice reformer; professor and chairman of Sociology department, Catholic University of America, 1934-66; director, Juvenile Delinquency Evaluation Project, 1956-61; spokesperson for Christian personalism; supporter of Catholic Worker Movement, and anti-war activist during Vietnam.

G

Gallitzin, Demetrius: See under Missionaries to the Americas.

Garnier, Charles, St.: See under Missionaries to the Americas.

Gaston, William (1778-1844): Catholic layperson and prominent leader in North Carolina; first Catholic to serve in the North Carolina state legislature and supreme court; served in U.S. House of Representatives; although a slaveholder, advocated abolition.

Gibault, Pierre: See under Missionaries to the Americas.

Gibbons, James (1834-1921): Archbishop of Baltimore, 1877-1921, the second American cardinal from 1886, and one of the foremost American prelates of the 19th century; vicar apostolic for North Carolina, 1868-72; bp. of Richmond, 1872-77; coadj. bp. of Baltimore, May-Oct., 1877; defended the Knights of Labor and was a famed champion of the poor and working class; promoted the Americanization of the Church; immensely popular in the country among Catholics and non-Catholics.

Glennon, John J. (1862-1946): Archbishop of St. Louis, 1903-46 and Cardinal from 1946; born in Ireland; coadj. bp. of Kansas City, Mo. From 1896-1903; coadj. of St. Louis from Apr.-Oct., 1903; promoted Catholic social work; founded schools, hospitals, and a new seminary; first cardinal from the see of St. Louis.

Goldstein, David (1870-1958): Convert from Judaism and prominent Catholic layperson; born in England and raised in a Jewish family and as a Socialist; converted in 1905 and became opponent of Socialism; cofounder (with Martha Moore Avery) of the Catholic Truth Guild in 1917; founder, Catholic Campaigners for Christ, 1936.

Gonzalez, Roch, St.: See under Missionaries to the Americas.

Goupil, René, St.: See under Missionaries to the Americas.

Gravier, Jacques: See under Missionaries to the Americas.

Guérin, Mother Theodore (1798-1856): Beati and founding superior of the Sisters of Providence, St. Mary-of-the Woods, Indiana, 1840-56; beatified on Oct. 25, 1998 by Pope John Paul II.

Guiney, Louise (1861-1920): Essayist, poet, and scholar; a major figure in the literary revival in the United States of the late 19th century.

H

Haas, Francis (1899-1953): Priest, professor, sociologist, and editor; supporter of labor and social and racial justice; named to the Civil Rights Commission by President Harry Truman.

Hallinan, Paul (1911-68): Priest, chaplain, and Archbishop of Atlanta from 1962-68; served as army chaplain from 1942-45; president of National Association of Newman Club Chaplains from 1952-58; bp. of Charleston from 1958-62; as abp., he supported civil rights.

Hayes, Carlton (1882-1964): Diplomat and historian; earned a doctorate in history from Columbia University; noted historian; co-founded the National Association of Christians and Jews; ambassador to Spain from 1942-45.

Hayes, Helen (1900-93): Actress; enjoyed a career of 60 years, winner of two Academy Awards, as well as Emmy Awards and Tony Awards; beloved figure on the Broadway stage; authored autobiography, *My Life in Three Acts* (1990).

Hayes, Patrick J. (1867-1938): Archbishop of New York, 1919-38 and Cardinal from 1924; auxiliary bp. of New York, 1914-19; Military Ordinary for Catholic American chaplains during World War I; founded Catholic Charities of the Archdiocese of New York and did much to promote social welfare; wielded much influence in local politics (his private residence was termed "The Powerhouse").

Healy, James (1830-1900): Bishop of Portland from

1875-1900; son of an Irish father and an African-American mother; founded 60 parishes, 68 mission stations, and 18 schools and convents; also served as consultant to the U.S. Bureau of Indian Affairs.

Hecker, Isaac (1819-88): Priest, theologian and founder of the Paulists; convert in 1844; entered the Redemptorists; missionary in the U.S., 1851-57; founder and superior of the Congregation of Missionary Priests of St. Paul the Apostle (Paulists), 1858-88; developed an apologetic that stressed the benefits of American culture and political traditions; following his death, the story of his life by Walter Elliott was the cause of the Americanist controversy that sparked the papal encyclical *Testem Benevolentiae*, 1899, by Pope Leo XIII, condemning assorted ideas connected with Hecker.

Heeney, Cornelius (1754-1848): Philanthropist; born in Ireland and emigrated to New York; partner for a time to John Jacob Astor in fur trading; helped establish old St. Patrick's Cathedral; patron of John McCloskey, the future cardinal abp. of New York; devoted time and money to Catholic charities.

Hennepin, Louis (1626-after 1701): Missionary and member of the Recollet Order of Friars Minor; traveled to the Mississippi River and was captured by the Sioux; rescued by the French explorer Daniel Guysolon du Lhut.

Henni, John M. (1805-81): First Archbishop of Milwaukee from 1875-81; born in Switzerland; first bp. of Milwaukee from 1844-75.

Heuser, Herman (1852-1933): Priest, professor, and editor; born in Germany; founding editor of *American Ecclesiastical Review*, 1899-1914; founding editor of the *Dolphin*, 1900-08.

Hildebrand, Dietrich von (1889-1977): Philosopher; born in Florence; converted in 1914; fled Europe to escape the Nazis and joined Fordham University in 1942; distanced himself from Catholic teachings following Vatican Council II; ranked as one of the prominent philosophers of the second half of the 20th century.

Hitchcock, Alfred (1899–1980) Anglo-American film director; considered a true master of suspense films; directed such films as *The Lady Vanishes* (1938), *Notorious* (1946), *Strangers on a Train* (1951), *Psycho* (1960), and *Frenzy* (1972).

Hogan, John J. (1829-1913): First Bishop of Kansas City, 1880-1913; born in Ireland; first bp. of St. Joseph from 1868-80.

Hughes, John J. (1797-1864): First Archbishop of New York, 1850-64; born in Ireland and ordained in 1826 in New York; coadj. bp. of New York from 1837-42; bp. of New York from 1842-50; opposed anti-Catholic riots in 1844; one of the foremost Catholic leaders in the U.S.; addressed Congress in 1847; traveled to Europe to promote the Union cause during the Civil War; championed the cause of immigrants.

I

Ireland, John (1838-1918): First archbishop of St. Paul from 1888-1918; born in Ireland and ordained in 1861 in St. Paul; coadj. bp. of St. Paul from 1875-84; bp. of St. Paul from 1884-88; promoted the Catholic University of America and was an ardent support of Americanizing the Church in the U.S.,

Knights of Labor and a controversial school plan; leading figure in the Americanist controversy.

Ireland, Mother Seraphine (1842-1930): Mother Superior of the Sisters of St. Joseph, province of St. Paul, 1882-1921; sister of Abp. John Ireland; helped to promote the Sisters of St. Joseph Carondelet in the Midwest of the U.S.

Ives, Levi (1797-1867): Convert to Catholicism and raised as an Episcopalian, he became bp. of North Carolina in 1831; a member of the Tractarian movement, he entered the Catholic Church in 1852; worked as a promoter of Catholic Charities from 1854-67.

J

Jackson, Carol (1911-37): Catholic convert and editor; raised an atheist, she converted in 1941; influenced by Catholic Worker Movement; cofounder and coeditor of *Integrity* from 1946-52.

Jesuit North American Martyrs: See under Missionaries to the Americas.

Jogues, Isaac, St.: See under Missionaries to the Americas.

Jolliet, Louis (1645-1700): French explorer; after brief studies to be a priest, he became a fur trader; set out in 1673 with Fr. Jacques Marquette to explore the copper mines of Lake Superior; reached the Mississippi, Ohio, and Arkansas Rivers; had positive dealing with local native Americans.

Jones, Mother Mary (c.1830-1930): Irish-born labor union organizer and political activist; operated dressmaking business in 1861; founder of the Social Democratic Party in 1898; organizer of the United Mine Workers of America in 1900; a founder of the Industrial Workers of the World in 1905; known as "mother" among the male labor workers.

K

Keane, John J. (1839-1918): Archbishop of Dubuque from 1900-11 and a defender of the Americanist movement; born in Ireland; bp. of Richmond from 1878-88; rector of the Catholic University of America from 1888-97; consultor of Congregation for Propagation of the Faith, 1897-1900; opposed the condemnation of the Knights of Labor and was an ally of the work of John Ireland and John Gibbons.

Kelley, Francis (1870-1948): Priest and founder of the Catholic Church Extension Society; founder and editor of *Extension Magazine* from 1905-24; bp. of Oklahoma City-Tulsa from 1924-28.

Kelly, Grace (1929-82): Actress and Princess Consort of Monaco; after a start in television and on stage, she launched a major film career in *High Noon* (1951); won the Academy Award for *The Country Girl* (1954); met Prince Rainier III of Monaco at the Cannes Film Festival in 1954 and married him in 1956; died, after a car crash, on Sept. 14, 1982.

Kennedy, John F. (1917-63): President of the United States; born into the powerful Kennedy family of Massachusetts, he became a hero during World War II for his command of PT109; served in U.S. Congress and then U.S. Senate (1952-60); married Jacqueline Bouvier in 1953; elected the first Catholic president in 1960; domestic policy included largely failed programs of tax cuts, civil rights, and social security; foreign policy distinguished by the Bay of Pigs and the Cuban Missile Crisis; assassinated on Nov. 22, 1963.

Kennedy, Joseph (1888-1969): Diplomat, businessman, and patriarch of the Kennedy family; born into the family of a ward boss in Boston, he earned his first million by the age of 30; involved in banking, shipbuilding, and motion pictures, he also profited from bootlegging during Prohibition; named chairman of the Securities and Exchange Commission in 1934 by Franklin Roosevelt; ambassador to Great Britain from 1937-40; devoted his later years to pushing his children's political advancement.

Kennedy, Robert (1925-68): U.S. Senator and Attorney General; third son of Joseph Kennedy and brother of John F. Kennedy; managed his brother's successful presidential bid in 1960 and was named Attorney General; served as JFK's foremost advisor and was a strong force in the passing of the Civil Rights Act (1964); elected Senator from New York in 1964; launched campaign for president in 1968, during which he was assassinated.

Kenrick, Francis P. (1796-1863): Archbishop of Baltimore from 1851-63; born in Ireland and educated in Rome; labored in Bardstown, Kentucky and defended the Catholic faith; coadj. of Philadelphia from 1830-42, with the task of repairing diocesan unity after trustee crisis; bp. of Philadelphia from 1842-51; founded St. Charles Borromeo Seminary in 1832 and promoted education; organized and presided over the first Plenary Council of Baltimore in 1852; promoted the foundation of the North American College.

Kenrick, Peter (1806-96): Brother of Francis Kenrick and first archbishop of St. Louis from 1847-95; born in Ireland; after service in Ireland, invited by his brother to Philadelphia; rector of the cathedral and president of St. Charles Borromeo Seminary from 1833-41; coadj. bp. of St. Louis from 1841-43; bp. from 1843-47; took part in Vatican Council I and opposed the definition of papal infallibility.

Kerby, William (1870-1936): Priest and founder of the national Conference of Catholic Charities; founded and organized the national Conference of Catholic Charities in 1910; cofounder of the National Catholic School of Social Service in 1918; editor of *American Ecclesiastical Review* from 1927-36; promoted social justice.

Kilmer, Joyce (1886-1918): Poet; born Alfred Kilmer, he converted to Catholicism in 1913 with his wife; a popular poet in the United States and Europe; killed in World War I during the Second Battle of the Marne.

Kino, Eusebio: See under Missionaries to the Americas.

Kohlmann, Anthony (1771-1836): Jesuit and theologian; born in Alsace; joined the Russian Jesuit chapter in 1803; sent to the United States; pastor and administrator of the diocese of New York from 1808-15; won "The Catholic Question," a controversy over the seal of confession in 1812; consultor to Vatican congregations in Rome from 1824-36.

Kosciuszko, Thaddeus (1746-1817): Polish soldier; a member of the minor Polish aristocracy, he became a soldier and volunteered for the American Revolution in 1776; commissioned as a colonel, he designed West Point and helped in the victory at Saratoga and Ticonderoga; retired to Poland and fought against the Russians in a doomed effort to win Polish independence.

Kreisler, Fritz (1875-62): Composer and violinist; born in Austria, debuted in New York as a virtuoso violinist and toured from 1888-89; opposed the Nazis and was forced to leave Europe in 1939; American citizen in 1943.

Krol, John Joseph (1910-96): Archbishop of Philadelphia from 1961-88 and Cardinal from 1967; auxiliary bp. of Cleveland from 1953-61; one of the most devoted supporters of Pope John Paul II among the American hierarchy.

L

L'Enfant, Pierre (1754-1825): Architect; born in France; submitted plans in 1791 for the new capital city at Washington at Pres. Washington's request; eventually dismissed because of various personality differences; in 1889 the plans were recovered from the archives, and the capital was developed in 1901 along his vision.

La Farge, John (1880-1963): Priest, reformer, and editor; founder of the Cardinal Gibbons Institute in 1924, to educate African-Americans in Maryland; editor on the staff of *America* from 1926-63; founded the Laymen's union in 1934 to promote spiritual formation among African-Americans.

Lafayette, Marquis de (1757-1834): French soldier and statesman; a member of a French noble family, he joined the Continental Army in 1777 and received a position on George Washington's staff; instrumental in winning support for the American cause in Europe; a leading figure in the early days of the French Revolution, he was condemned by the Jacobins in 1792 and fled France; returned in 1797 and resumed a public life in 1814.

Lalemant, Gabriel, St.: See under Missionaries to the Americas.

Lamy, Jean Baptiste: See under Missionaries to the Americas.

Lange, Mary (1784-1882): Founding mother superior of the Oblate Sisters of Providence in Baltimore from 1829-32; born in the Santo Domingo, Haiti, her family emigrated to Cuba and then the U.S.; taught Haitian children in Baltimore; founded the Oblate Sisters of Providence to educate African-American children; served among the poor, the sick, and the dying, especially during the cholera epidemics in Baltimore.

Las Casas, Bartolome: See under Missionaries to the Americas.

Lathrop, Rose Hawthorne (1851-1926): Cofounder of the Dominican Congregation of St. Rose of Lima in 1900; the third daughter of Nathaniel Hawthorne; married George Parsons Lathrop with whom she entered the Church in 1891; separated from her husband because of his alcoholism (he died in 1898); established the Dominican Congregation of St. Rose of Lima (Servants of Relief for Incurable Cancer), to care for those dying and neglected; pioneered hospice work in the United States for the terminally ill.

Laval, Françoise de Montmorency, Bl.: See under Missionaries to the Americas.

Lewis, Edmonia (1845-after 1909): First African-American sculptress; daughter of an African-American father and an Ojibwe mother; studied at Oberlin College, Ohio, and Boston; emigrated to Rome where she remained for the rest of her life; Pope Pius XI visited her studio; her work was displayed in Europe and the United States, including the National Museum of American Art.

Ligutti, Luigi (1885-1983): Priest and leading figure in the Catholic rural life movement; born in Italy; after pastoral service became executive secretary and director of the National Catholic Rural Life Conference from 1938-58; editor of *Land and Home* from 1942-47; editor of *Christian Farmer News Letter* in 1947; director on international affairs for the NCRLC from 1958-70; founded the Agrimissio in Rome, to promote agriculture in the developing parts of the world.

Lombardi, Vince (1913–70): American football coach; born in New York City; head coach of the Green Bay Packers from 1959-69 and won five championships; head coach briefly of the Washington Redskins, from 1969-70.

Lombardo, Guy (1902-77): Canadian born band leader; led the band of the Royal Canadians, debuting in New York in 1929; was best known for his New Year's Eve performances in New York City.

Longstreet, James (1821-1904): Confederate general during the Civil War; graduated from West point in 1842 and fought in the Mexican War; one of the most competent corps commanders under Robert E. Lee; after the war, he joined the Republican Party and served in assorted posts; converted in 1877.

Loras, Matthias (1792-1858): First bishop of Dubuque from 1837-58; born in France, he was a friend and schoolmate of St. Jean Vianney; after a distinguished career in France, he went to America in 1828; as bp., he promoted a seminary, missionary activity on the Mississippi River, German and Irish immigration.

Lord, Daniel (1888-1955): Jesuit priest and writer; author of 30 books, 50 plays, 12 musicals, and six pageants; assisted Cecil B. DeMille on the film *King of Kings*; helped draft Motion Picture Production Code; director of the Sodality of the Blessed Virgin from 1948-55, the largest Catholic youth organization in the U.S.

Luce, Clare Boothe (1903-87): Author, playwright, ambassador, and politician; wife of Henry C. Luce (publisher of *Time*, *Fortune*, and *Sports Illustrated*); converted to Catholicism in 1946 under the influence of then Msgr. Fulton J. Sheen; keynote speaker at the 1944 Republican National Convention; leading woman Catholic politician, serving in the U.S. House from 1942-46; U.S. ambassador to Italy from 1953-57.

Lucey, Robert E. (1891-1977): Archbishop of San Antonio from 1941-69; pastoral work in Los Angeles, especially among the homeless from 1916-34; bp. of Amarillo from 1934-41; supported CCD programs and the policies of Lyndon Johnson concerning poverty and the Vietnam War.

Lynch, Patrick N. (1817-82): Bishop of Charleston from 1858-82 and a leading Catholic in the South during the Civil War; born in Ireland; sent twice to Europe to plead the Southern cause; returned to the U.S. after the war only following a presidential pardon; took part in Vatican Council I and was in favor of papal infallibility.

M

McCarthy, Joseph (1908-57): American politician; U.S. senator from Wisconsin (1947-57); rose to national prominence through the permanent subcommittee on investigations which looked into the threat of Communists against the country; held public hearings in which he accused army officials, members of the media, and public figures of being Communists; his charges were never proved, and he was censured by the Senate in 1954.

McCloskey, John (1810-85): Archbishop of New York from 1864-85 and the first U.S. Cardinal from 1875; coadj. bp. of New York from 1843-47; first bp. of Albany from 1847-64; attended Vatican Council I (1869-70); promoted harmony and growth of the Church in New York; completed St. Patrick's cathedral, an important symbol of Catholicism's progress in the city and the prosperity of its members; made cardinal in recognition of McCloskey's work and the prominence of the New York archdiocese.

McGinley, Phyllis (1905-78): Writer and poet; her first book of poetry was published in 1934; she won the Pulitzer Prize in 1961 for *Times Three*; won numerous other literary awards.

McIntyre, James F. (1886-1979): Archbishop of Los Angeles from 1948-70 and Cardinal from 1953; auxiliary bp. of New York from 1941-46; coadj. abp. of New York from 1946-48; oversaw the rapid and extensive expansion of the Church in Los Angeles; by 1970, there were 318 parishes and 350 schools; supported CCD programs and seminary education.

McKenzie, Fr. John (1910-91): Jesuit priest and biblical scholar; first Catholic president of the Society of Biblical Literature; eventually left the Jesuits.

McMaster, James (1820-86): Journalist; converted in 1845, he studied briefly with the Redemptorists; launched a career in journalism in 1846; editor of the *Freeman's Journal* which became a powerful voice in American Catholicism; imprisoned briefly in 1861-62 for his opposition to Lincoln and the civil war; inaugurated the first American pilgrimage to Rome.

McQuaid, Bernard (1823-1909): First bishop of Rochester from 1868-1909; promoted Americanization and education; predicted suffrage for women.

Mack, Connie (1862-1956): Baseball player and manager of the Philadelphia Athletics from 1901-51; he led to nine American League pennants and five World Series championships between 1902 and 1930.

Machebeuf, Joseph P. (1812-89): First bishop of Denver, 1887-89; born in France; vicar apostolic Colorado and Utah from 1868-87; established 102 churches and chapels, ten hospitals, nine academies, and a college.

Manning, Timothy (1909-89): Archbishop of Los Angeles, 1970-85 and Cardinal from 1973; born in Ireland; American citizen, 1944; auxiliary bp. of Los Angeles from 1946-67; first bp. of Fresno, 1967-69; coadj. archbishop of Los Angeles from 1969-70.

Manogue, Patrick: See under Missionaries to the Americas.

Marechal, Ambrose, S.S. (1766-1828): Archbishop of Baltimore from 1817-28; born in France; member of the Sulpicians, taught in French seminaries and St. Mary's Seminary, Baltimore; period as abp. was marked by a transition in the life of the Church as growth of the Irish influence was increasingly felt.

Margil, Antonio: See under Missionaries to the Americas.

Marie of the Incarnation, Bl.: See under Missionaries to the Americas.

Markoe, William (1892-1969): Jesuit priest and advocate of interracial justice; as a priest, authored articles in America promoting social justice for African-Americans; editor of *Chronicale/Interracial Review* from 1930-33; served as a missionary in the Jesuit mission band in Missouri province from 1948-51.

Marquette, Jacques: See under Missionaries to the Americas.

Marty, Martin (1834-96): Missionary, Benedictine, and bishop; born in Switzerland; arrived in St. Meinrad, Indiana in 1860; first abbot, 1870; chose himself as a missionary to the Dakota (Sioux) Indians, 1876 and encountered initial refusal from the local pastor as he did not bear a *celebret*; labored among the Native Americans; vicar apostolic of the Dakota Territory, 1880-89; first bishop of Sioux Falls, 1889-94; bishop of St. Cloud, 1894-96; called "Black Robe Lean Chief" among the Native Americans.

Massias (Macias), John de, St.: See under Missionaries to the Americas.

Maurin, Aristide Peter (1877-1949): Lay activist and cofounder with Dorothy Day of the Catholic Worker Movement; born in France; embraced a Franciscan spirit of poverty; met Day in 1932; founded with her *The Catholic Worker*, 1933 and hence the widely influential Catholic Worker movement; his obituary was reported in *The New York Times* and *L'Osservatore Romano*.

Mazzuchelli, Samuel C.: See under Missionaries to the Americas.

Meany, William George (1894-80): Labor leader and president of the American Federation of Labor and Congress of Industrial Organizations (1955–79); a plumber; secretary-treasurer of the AFL, 1939-52; president, AFL, 1952-55; head of the new federation after the merger of the AFL and CIO from 1955; denounced economic policies of Pres. Jimmy Carter.

Medeiros, Humberto S. (1915-83): Archbishop of Boston from 1970-83 and cardinal from 1973; born in the Azores and a U.S. citizen from 1940; bp. of Brownsville from 1966-70; abp. during a turbulent period in modern U.S. Catholic history; took part in the 1978 papal conclaves.

Membre, Zenobius: See under Missionaries to the Americas.

Merton, Thomas (1915-68): Trappist monk and influential spiritual writer; after a famed conversion entered the Trappists; authored *Seven Storey Mountain, Seeds of Contemplation, Mystics and Zen Masters, The New Man*.

Mestrovic, Ivan (1883-1962): Sculptor; born in Croatia; studied in Vienna; exhibited throughout Europe and inspired a nationalist movement among the Croats and Serbs; imprisoned by the Fascists, 1941 (released through Vatican intervention); emigrated to the U.S., 1947; citizen, 1953; taught at Syracuse University and Notre Dame; first sculptor to be honored with a one-man show at the Metropolitan Museum of Art.

Meyer, Albert (1903-65): Archbishop of Chicago, 1958-65 and Cardinal from 1959; bp. of Superior from 1946-53; abp. of Milwaukee, 1953-58; worked for civil rights and promoted ecumenism.

Michel, Virgil (1890-1938): Liturgist; considered the founder of the American Catholic liturgical movement.

Monaghan, John (1889-1961): Priest and social activist; born in Ireland; taught at cathedral College, New York, 1922-38; co-founder of the Association of Catholic Trade Unionist (ACTU) to inform Catholic trade unionists of Catholic social teaching; beloved pastor of St. Margaret Mary parish, 1939-54 and St. Michael's parish, 1954-61.

Mooney, Edward (1882-1958): First archbishop of Detroit, 1937-58 and Cardinal from 1946; apostolic delegate to India from 1926-31; apostolic delegate Japan from 1931-33; bp. of Rochester from 1933-37; brilliant diplomat; curtailed the activities of Fr. Charles Coughlin.

Moylan, Stephen (1737-1811): Revolutionary era general and businessman; born in Ireland; quartermaster general of the Continental Army and distinguished soldier during the war.

Mudd, Samuel (1833-83): Physician and supposed member of the conspiracy against Abraham Lincoln in 1865; imprisoned from 1865-69; pardoned by Andrew Johnson.

Muench, Aloysius (1889-1962): Cardinal from 1959 and the first American to hold office in the Curia; bp. of Fargo from 1935-59; apostolic visitator to Germany, 1946 and nuncio to Germany from 1951-59.

Mundelein, George (1872-1939): Archbishop of Chicago from 1915-39 and Cardinal from 1924; auxiliary bp. of Brooklyn from 1909-15; first cardinal in the Midwest; supporter of Franklin Roosevelt.

Murray, John Courtney (1904-67): Jesuit priest and influential theologian; professor of theology and philosophy, *peritus* at Vatican Council II, and editor of *Theological Studies* from 1941-67; studied the Church's relationship to society and state.

N

Nerinckx, Charles: See under Missionaries to the Americas.

Neumann, St. John: See under Saints of the Church.

Noll, John F. (1875-1956): Bishop of Fort Wayne, 1925-56, personal titular abp. in 1953, and publisher; established *Our Sunday Visitor* in 1912.

O

O'Boyle, Patrick A. (1896-1987): Archbishop of Washington, D.C., 1948-73 and Cardinal from 1967; director of the Catholic War Relief Services and War relief Services of the National Catholic Welfare Conference; champion of civil rights.

O'Connell, Denis (1849-1927): Bishop of Richmond, 1912-26; friend of Cardinal James Gibbons; rector of the North American College; rector of the Catholic University of America; opposed anti-Catholicism in Virginia.

O'Connell, William H. (1859-1944): Archbishop of Boston, 1907-44 and Cardinal from 1911; bp. of Portland, 1901-06; coad. bp. Boston (Constantia), 1906-07; prominent figure in American Catholic life and politics.

O'Connor, Edwin (1918-68): Author; columnist for the Boston Herald under the pseudonym "Roger Swift"; author of *The Oracle* (1951), *The Last Hurrah* (1958), *The Edge of Sadness* (1961), *I was Dancing* (1964), and *All in the Family* (1966).

O'Connor, Flannery (1925-64): Author; novels included *Wise Blood* (1952) and *The Violent Bear It*

Away (1960), and short stories, collected in such works as *A Good Man is Hard to Find* (1955).

O'Hara, Edwin (1881-1956): Bishop of Great Falls, 1930-56 and social activist; promoter of social justice, including workers' rights and rural life; named personal abp. in 1954.

O'Hara, John F., C.S.C. (1888-1960): Archbishop of Philadelphia, 1951-60 and Cardinal from 1958; delegate of U.S. military vicar, 1940-45; bp. Buffalo, 1945-51; promoted concern for Native Americans, Hispanics, and African-Americans and education.

O'Neill, Thomas (Tip) (1912-94): Speaker of the House of Representatives from 1977-87; first elected in 1952 to Congress, winning JFK's old seat; majority whip of House Democrats, 1971-73; majority leader, 1973-77; advanced liberal agenda throughout his career; followed the maxim "All politics is local."

O'Reilly, John (1844-90): Poet, author, and editor; editor of the *Pilot*, 1870, for Catholic and Irish interests; authored volumes of poetry and the novel *Moondyne* (1875).

O'Sullivan, Mary (1864-1943): Reformer and labor organizer; national organizer for women of the AFL, 1892; founded the National Women's Trade League.

P

Pace, Edward (1861-1938): Priest and scholar; founder and dean of Philosophy department of Catholic University of America; founding editor of Catholic Encyclopedia; early leader in experimental psychology.

Padilla, Juan de: See under Missionaries to the Americas.

Palladino, Laurence, S.J. (1837-1927): Jesuit missionary, the last pioneer missionary of the Northwest; born in Italy; sent to Montana Territory, 1867; built the first church in the Helena Mission (later the first cathedral); director of diocesan schools, 1889-92; president of Gonzaga College, 1894.

Palou, Francisco: See under Missionaries to the Americas.

Pariseau, Mother Mary Joseph: See under Missionaries to the Americas.

Percy, Walker (1916–90): Novelist; author of *The Moviegoer* (1961), *Love in the Ruins* (1971), and *The Second Coming* (1980); expressed a rich understanding of change in the South.

Peter, Carl J. (1932-91): Priest and theologian; chairman of Department of Theology, Catholic University of America, 1975-77; ranked as one of CUA's greatest scholars; served on International Theological Commission.

Peyton, Fr. Patrick (1909-92): Holy Cross priest and evangelist; established Family Rosary Crusade, 1947, to promote the rosary among families; coined the motto "The family that prays together, stays together."

Powderly, Terence (1849-1924): Labor leader and director of the Knights of Labor, a secret organization that repudiate strikes; reached his period of greatest influence from 1879-93; source of controversy in the Church.

Powers, J.F. (1917-99): Author and novelist; taught at Marquette University and University of Michigan; member of the American Academy and Institute of Arts and Letters; notable works included *Morte*

d'Urban (1962, winner of the National Book Award and Thormod Monsen award), *Wheat That Springeth Green* (1988, National Book Award and National Book Critics Circle finalist, Wethersfield Institute Award); considered one of the most prominent Catholic writers of the 1950s and 1960s.

Pulaski, Casimir (1748-79): Polish soldier during the American Revolution; joined staff of General Washington, 1777; fought in numerous battles and killed at Savannah.

Purcell, John B. (1783-1883): First archbishop of Cincinnati, 1850-83; born in Ireland; bp. of Cincinnati, 1833-50; supported the Union during the Civil War; last years marked by financial troubles.

Q

Quigley, Martin (1890-1964): Editor and publisher; founded motion picture trade magazines; devised the Motion Picture Production Code; helped found the Legion of Decency.

Quiroga, Vasco de: See under Missionaries to the Americas.

R

Rappe, Louis Amadeus (1801-77): First bishop of Cleveland, 1847-70; born in France; established parishes, missions, hospitals, and missions.

Ravalli, Antonio (1811-84): Italian Jesuit; missionary in far-western United States, mostly Montana, for 40 years.

Raymbaut, Charles (1602-43): French Jesuit; missionary among Indians of Canada and northern U.S.

Reedy, William (1925-83): Priest and editor; editor of *Ave Maria*, for Catholic families; columnist for *Our Sunday Visitor*.

Repplier, Agnes (1855-1950): Author of essays and biographies; wrote for *Atlantic Monthly*.

Résé, Frederic (1791-1871): First bishop of Detroit, 1833-71; born in Germany; inactive from 1841 because of ill health; remained in Europe from 1838.

Richard, Gabriel: See under Missionaries to the Americas.

Riepp, Benedicta (1825-62): Benedictine nun; born in Bavaria; established first monastery of women Benedictines in North America.

Ritter, Cardinal Joseph E. (1892-1967): Archbishop of St. Louis, 1946-67 and Cardinal from 1961; aux. bp. of Indianapolis, 1933-34; bp. of Indianapolis, 1934-44; first abp. Indianapolis, 1944-46; promoted national episcopal conference and Catholic charities; active at Vatican Council II.

Rockne, Knute (1888–1931): Football coach; born in Norway; head coach of Notre Dame (1918- 31); died in a plane crash.

Rosati, Joseph: See under Missionaries to the Americas.

Rosecrans, William (1819-98): Union general; campaigned in West Virginia and Mississippi; defeated at the battle of Chickamauga, Georgia (1863), and relieved of duties.

Rudd, Daniel (1854-1933): Journalist and civil rights leader; founded the *Ohio Star Tribune* (*American Catholic Tribune*), 1886 for African-American Catholics; founded African-American Catholic lay congress.

Russell, Mother Mary (1829-98): Superior of the Order of Sisters of Mercy; invited to San Francisco by Abp. Joseph Alemany; founded St. Mary's Hospital, first Catholic hospital on the west coast.

Ruth, Babe (1895-1948): Baseball player, known as "the Sultan of Swat"; pitcher for the Boston Red Sox (1915-19) and outfielder for the New York Yankees (1920-35); hit 714 home runs, played in 10 World Series, and held 54 major-league records; inducted into the Baseball Hall of Fame in 1936.

Ryan, James H. (1886-1947): First archbishop of Omaha, 1945-47; rector of the Catholic University of America, 1928-35; titular bp. of Modra, 1933-35; bp. of Omaha, 1935-45; promoter of education; supported the New Deal and policies of FDR.

Ryan, John (1869-1945): Priest, influential social reformer, and educator; the leading Catholic voice in the U.S. on social issues in the first half of the 20th century.

Ryan, Thomas (1851-1928): Financier and philanthropist; founder of the American Tobacco Company and National Bank of Commerce; donated over 20 million dollars to Catholic charities.

S

Sadlier, Mary (1820-1903): Novelist; born in Ireland; author of over 30 novels and books, focusing on contemporary issues; editor of *The Tablet*; noted Catholic philanthropist.

Seattle, Chief (1786-1866): Native American chief of the Suquamish of Puget Sound; baptized a Catholic at the age of 54; maintained excellent relations with the white settlers; his daughter, Princess Angeline, was also a Catholic.

Seelos, Francis X.: See under Missionaries to the Americas.

Seghers, Charles J.: See under Missionaries to the Americas.

Serra, Junípero, Bl.: See under Missionaries to the Americas.

Seton, Elizabeth: See under Saints of the Church.

Shea, John Gilmary (1826-92): Editor and the "Father of American Catholic historians"; editor and author of over 200 publications and supporter of the U.S. Bishops.

Sheed, Francis "Frank" (1897-1981): Author and apologist; cofounded the influential publisher Sheed and Ward, 1933; lectured and wrote in defense of the Catholic faith.

Sheen, Fulton J. (1895-1979): Archbishop, radio and television personality, and educator; internationally famous as a preacher on radio and television; aux. bp. of New York, 1951-66; bp. of Rochester, 1966-69; titular abp. of Newport; national director of the Society of the Propagation for the Faith; perhaps the most popular and socially influential American Catholic of the 20th century.

Shehan, Lawrence J. (1898-1984): Archbishop of Baltimore, 1961-74 and Cardinal from 1965; aux. bp. of Baltimore and Washington, 1945-53; first bp. of Bridgeport, 1953-61; coad. abp. of Baltimore, Sept.-Dec., 1961; supported the civil rights movement and took part in Martin Luther King's March on Washington, 1963; abp. during a time of deep social unrest.

Sheil, Bernard (1886-1969): Archbishop and social activist; aux. bp. of Chicago, 1928-69; titular abp. of Selge, 1959-69; formed the Catholic Youth Organization (CYO), 1931; supported organized Labor and FDR; opposed Fr. Coughlin and Sen. Joseph McCarthy.

Sheridan, Philip (1831-88) Union general; took part in the Chattanooga (1863) and Wilderness (1864) campaigns; defeated the Confederate forces at the Battle of Five Forks (1865); brilliant cavalry leader.

Shields, James (1806-79): Union general and U.S. Senator; member of the Illinois Supreme Court, 1843-45; brigadier general during Civil War; the only person to represent three states in the U.S. Senate (Illinois, Minnesota, Missouri).

Shields, Thomas (1862-1921): Priest, psychologist, and educator; professor at Catholic University of America; promoted dialogue between theology and modern science and philosophy.

Shuster, George (1894-1977): Author, editor, and educator; president of Hunter College, 1940-69.

Siuwheem, Louise (d. c. 1850): Native American, member of the Couer d'Alene tribe in Idaho; known for her zeal and care for the sick; a friend of Fr. Pierre de Smet.

Slattery, John (1851-1926): Priest and advocate for civil rights; member of the Mill Hill missions and sought to have a Mill Hill community for the U.S.; supported African American rights and vocations.

Smith, Alfred E. (1873-1944): Four-time governor of New York (1919-20, 1923-28) and presidential candidate in 1928; as governor, he was responsible for numerous reforms; the Democratic nominee for president, he was the first Roman Catholic candidate for president; defeated by Herbert Hoover, primarily because of the Catholic issue and Prohibition.

Solanus, Francis, St.: See under Missionaries to the Americas.

Sorin, Edward F.: See under Missionaries to the Americas.

Spalding, Catherine (d. 1858): Cofoundress of the Sisters of Charity of Nazareth, Kentucky; her sisters cared for orphans, educated the poor, and eventually expanded into health care.

Spalding, John (1840-1916): First bishop of Peoria from 1877-1908; supporter of separation of Church and State; authored numerous books and articles; helped found the Catholic University of America.

Spalding, Martin (1810-72): Archbishop of Baltimore, 1864-72; perhaps the most influential Catholic apologist of the 19th century; bp. of Louisville, 1850-64; supported the Confederacy during the Civil War; promoted evangelization among the former slaves; favored papal infallibility at Vatican Council I; ranked as one of the foremost prelates in the American Church, esp. for his work in shaping and directing the immigrant influx.

Spellman, Francis J. (1889-1967): Archbishop of New York, 1939-67 and Cardinal from 1946; studies in Rome led to appointment to the Vatican Secretariat of State; arranged for publication of the anti-fascist encyclical, *Non Abbiamo Bisogno*, 1931 in Paris; auxiliary bp. of Boston, 1932-39; good friend of Cardinal Eugenio Pacelli (the future Pope Pius XII); reorganized diocesan finances and centralized authority; Military Vicar for the Armed Forces, 1939-67; staunch anti-Communist and supporter of the Vietnam War; supported the Vatican II Declaration on Religious Liberty and modern biblical scholarship; the most influential American prelate from 1939-58.

Stritch, Samuel (1887-1958): Archbishop of Chicago, 1939-58 and Cardinal from 1946; bp. of Toledo,

1921-30; abp. of Milwaukee, 1930-39; active in the National Catholic Welfare Conference and Catholic Action; named proprefect of the Congregation for the Propagation of the Faith, 1958; died in Rome.

Sullivan, John L. (1858–1918) Boxer; won in 1882 the bare-knuckles heavyweight championship over Paddy Ryan; called the "Great John L."; won in 1889 the last bare-knuckles title bout over Jake Kilrain; defeated, using gloves, in 1892, by James J. Corbett.

T

Talbot, Francis X., S.J. (1889-1953): Editor and author; editor-in-chief of *America*, 1936-44; founded Catholic Poetry Society of America; author of numerous books; president of Loyola College, Baltimore, 1947-51.

Taney, Roger (1777-1864): Chief Justice of the U.S. Supreme Court, 1836-64; Attorney General of the U.S., 1831-34; participated in over 300 decisions, but is remembered for the Dred Scott decision, 1857, in which he ruled that slaves and their descendants had no rights as citizens; disagreed with Lincoln over several actions during the Civil War.

Tekakwitha, Kateri: See under Saints of the Church.

Timon, John, C.M. (1797-1867): First bishop of Buffalo, 1847-67; superior of the Vincential province of the U.S., 1835-39; prefect apostolic for the Republic of Texas, 1839-47.

Todadilla, Anthony de: See under Missionaries to the Americas.

Tolton, Augustus (1854-97): First African-American priest in the U.S.; escaped from slavery with his mother to Illinois and discerned a vocation; studied in Rome as no American seminary would take him; ordained, 1886; pastor in Quincy and Chicago, Illinois; encountered racism, esp. from fellow priests.

Toscanini, Arturo (1867–1957): Italian conductor; began his career as conductor of the Rio de Janeiro opera; returned to Italy and conducted the premieres of Leoncavallo's *Pagliacci* (1892) and Puccini's *La Bohème* (1896); later musical director at La Scala, Milan; in the U.S., conducted at the Metropolitan Opera, 1908–14, the New York Philharmonic, 1926–36, and the NBC Symphony, which was formed for him (1937–54).

Touissant, Pierre, Venerable (1766-1853): Former slave and businessman; born into slavery in Haiti; served as a domestic servant and permitted to learn French (studied Catholic books and sermons); given his freedom in 1807; became a successful hairdresser; devout Catholic; cause opened in 1990 by Cardinal John O'Connor, declared venerable in 1997 by Pope John Paul II.

Tracy, Spencer (1900-67) Film actor; won Academy Awards as best Actor for *Captains Courageous* (1937) and *Boys' Town* (1938); other films include *Adam's Rib* (1949), *The Last Hurrah* (1958), and *Guess Who's Coming to Dinner* (1967).

Tunney, Gene (1898-1978): Boxer; won, 1922, the light-heavyweight title over Battling Levinsky, but lost it that same year (to Harry Greb) in his only defeat as a professional; defeated Jack Dempsey In 1926 for the heavyweight championship; retired as champion in 1928.

Turibius de Mongrovejo, St. : See under Missionaries to the Americas.

Turner, Thomas (1877-1978): Educator and civil rights leader; professor of biology at Howard University, 1913; acting dean of the School of Education at Howard University, 1914-20; worked against discrimination, esp. in the Church, through the Federated Colored Catholics (FCC).

Twelve Apostles of Mexico: See under Missionaries to the Americas.

U-V

Valdivia, Luis de: See under Missionaries to the Americas.

Varela, Féliz (1788-1853): Cuban patriot and scholar; promoter of Thomistic philosophy, the abolition of slavery in Cuba, and education; founded in 1825 in Philadelphia the newspaper *El Habanero*, the first Spanish Catholic magazine in the U.S.; vicar general of the diocese of New York from 1829; founder of *The Protestant's Abrider and Annotator*, 1830, and *Catholic Expositor and Literary Magazine*, 1841-43, the first pastoral magazine and the first literary magazine for Catholics respectively in the U.S.

Vasques de Espiñosa, Antonio: See under Missionaries to the Americas.

Verot, Augustin, S.S. (1805-76): Bishop and vocal participant at Vatican Council I; vicar apostolic of Florida, 1856-61; bp. of Savannah, 1861-70; bp. of St. Augustine, 1870-76; known as the "rebel bishop" during the Civil War for his support of the Confederacy; spoke frequently and loudly at the Vatican Council, calling for recognition of those of African descent, vindication of Galileo, and ecumenical dialogue; opposed papal infallibility, but signed the conciliar document.

Verrazano, Giovanni da (1484-1528): Explorer and navigator; searched for a westward route to Cathay and reached the coast of North America; explored Newfoundland and the east coast; killed by Caribbean Indians.

Vespucci, Amerigo (1451-1512): Explorer; journeyed with European explorers between 1497-1502; coined the phrase, "New World"; his name was used by the German cartographer Martin Waldseemüller, in a 1507 map designating the area called "South America."

Vieira, Antonio: See under Missionaries to the Americas.

W

Wagner, Robert (d. 1953): U.S. Senator from New York, 1926-49; born in Germany; elected to state senate, 1911; member of the commission that investigated the notorious Triangle Shirtwaist Co. (in which 147 women died); elected to the N.Y. Supreme Court, 1918; converted to Catholicism in 1946.

Walker, James (Jimmy) (1881-1946): Flamboyant New York City Mayor, 1926-32; rose through New York City's political world, the son of a state legislator; also dabbled in the theater and song writing; after initial success as mayor, suffered severe scandals and resigned in 1932; reconciled to the Church before his death.

Walsh, James A., M.M. (1867-1936): Cofounder (with Thomas F. Price) of Maryknoll, the first U.S. established foreign mission society and first sponsor of a U.S. foreign mission seminary; superior of Maryknoll, 1911-36; titular bp., 1933-36.

Walsh, James E., M.M. (1891-1981): Bishop, religious superior, and missionary; after ordination in 1915 was sent as one of four Maryknoll missionaries to China; vicar apostolic of Kongmoon, China, 1927-36; superior of Maryknoll, 1936-46; general secretary, Catholic Central Bureau, Shanghai, China, 1948; imprisoned by Chinese communists, 1958-70.

Walsh, Robert (1784-1859): Journalist and author; founded The American Review of History and Politics, 1811, American Register, 1817, and, with William Frye, the National Gazette and Literary Register; dedicated Federalist and patriot.

Walworth, Clarence (1820-1900): Priest and social activist; converted in 1845 and entered the Redemptorists; worked with Isaac Hecker and served for a time as a Paulist (he left in 1865 over disagreements with Hecker); promoted social justice and the temperance movement; authored numerous books and articles.

Ward, Maisie (1889-1975): Publisher, street preacher, and activist; wife of Francis Sheed, with whom she cofounded the publishing firm of Sheed and Ward; author of 27 books; supported numerous social reform organizations, including the Catholic Worker, Friendship House, and land reform in India.

Warde, Mary (1810-84): Mercy Sister; born in Ireland; entered the Sisters of Mercy and was sent to Pittsburgh; opened houses, boarding schools for girls, and eventually cared for the sick and orphans in New England, encountering much resistance from the Know-Nothings.

Weigel, Gustave, S.J. (1906-64): Jesuit priest and ecumenist; professor of theology at the Catholic University of Chile, 1937-48; professor at Woodstock College, 1949-64; lecturer and supporter of the ecumenical movement.

White, Andrew: See under Missionaries to the Americas.

Whitfield, James (1770-1834): Archbishop of Baltimore, 1828-34; born in England; coadj. bishop of Baltimore, 1828.

Williams, John J. (1822-1907): First archbishop of Boston, 1875-1907; bp. of Boston, 1866-75; worked to accommodate the waves of Catholic immigrants into the archdiocese; established many new parishes and found priests to speak in a host of different languages.

Williams, Mary Lou (d. 1981): Jazz musician and composer; taught herself music and the piano; worked with many other famous Jazz musicians, including Dizzy Gillespie, Benny Goodman, and Duke Ellington; composed Jazz for sacred music; founded the Pittsburgh Jazz Festival; a devout Catholic and one of the foremost Jazz artists in the U.S,

Williams, Michael (1877-1950): Author, editor, and leading lay Catholic during and after World War I; belonged briefly to the utopian colony of Upton Sinclair; assistant director of the National Catholic War Council during WWI; founder and editor of *Commonweal*, a journal by and for lay Catholics, 1924-37.

Wimmer, Boniface: See under Missionaries to the Americas.

Wolff, Madeleva (1877-1964): Educator, author, poet, religious, and the first woman religious to receive a doctorate from the University of California at Berkeley; president of St. Mary's College, Notre Dame, Indiana, 1934-61, she was responsible for numerous innovations and the rise of the school to national prominence.

Wood, Abp. James F. (1813-83): First Archbishop of Philadelphia, 1875-83; convert in 1836; coadj. bp. of Philadelphia, 1857-60; bp. of Philadelphia, 1860-75.

Wright, John J. (1909-79): Cardinal from 1969 and prefect of the Congregation of the Clergy, 1969-79; auxiliary bp. of Boston, 1947-50; first bp. of Worcester, 1950-59; bp. of Pittsburgh, 1959-69; the first American to head a congregation in Rome with global duties.

Wynne, John, S.J. (1859-1925): Jesuit priest and author; editor of *Messenger of the Sacred Heart*, 1892-1909; founder of *America*, 1909, the foremost Jesuit journal of opinion in the U.S.; vice-postulator of the causes of the Jesuit North American Martyrs (beatified in 1925 and canonized in 1930).

X, Y, Z

Yorke, Peter (1864-1925): Priest, editor, and social activist; born in Ireland; chancellor of the archdiocese of San Francisco and editor of the archdiocesan newspaper; opposed anti-Catholicism in San Francisco; supported the Teamsters in the Strike of 1901; founded the Irish newspaper, *The Leader*, 1902; a well-known spiritual figure in the Bay Area.

Youville, Marie Marguerite d', St.: See under Missionaries to the Americas.

Zahm, John (1851-1921): Holy Cross priest, theologian, and scientist; professor of physics at Notre Dame, 1875-92; sought to reconcile modern science and the Catholic faith; American provincial for the Congregation of the Holy Cross; traveled with Theodore Roosevelt to South America.

Zumarraga, Juan de: See under Missionaries to the Americas.

CATHOLICS IN THE U.S. GOVERNMENT

CATHOLICS IN PRESIDENTS' CABINETS

From 1789 to 1940, nine Catholics were appointed to cabinet posts by six of 32 presidents. The first was Roger Brooke Taney (later named first Catholic Supreme Court Justice) who was appointed in 1831 by Pres. Andrew Jackson. Catholics have been appointed to cabinet posts from the time of Pres. Franklin D. Roosevelt to the present.

Listed below in chronological order are presidents, Catholic cabinet officials, posts held, dates.

Andrew Jackson — Roger B. Taney, Attorney General, 1831-33, Secretary of Treasury, 1833-34.

Franklin Pierce — James Campbell, Postmaster General, 1853-57.

James Buchanan — John B. Floyd, Secretary of War, 1857-61.

William McKinley — Joseph McKenna, Attorney General, 1897-98.

Theodore Roosevelt — Robert J. Wynne, Postmaster General, 1904-05; Charles Bonaparte, Secretary of Navy, 1905-06, Attorney General, 1906-09.

Franklin D. Roosevelt — James A. Farley, Postmaster General, 1933-40; Frank Murphy, Attorney General, 1939-40; Frank C. Walker, Postmaster General, 1940-45.

Harry S. Truman — Robert E. Hannegan, Postmaster General, 1945-47; J. Howard McGrath, Attorney General, 1949-52; Maurice J. Tobin, Secretary of Labor, 1948-53; James P. McGranery, Attorney General, 1952-53.

Dwight D. Eisenhower — Martin P. Durkin, Secretary of Labor, 1953; James P. Mitchell, Secretary of Labor, 1953-61.

John F. Kennedy — Robert F. Kennedy, Attorney General, 1961-63; Anthony Celebrezze, Secretary of Health, Education and Welfare, 1962-63; John S. Gronouski, Postmaster General, 1963.

Lyndon B. Johnson — (Robert F. Kennedy, 1963-64, Anthony Celebrezze, 1963-65, and John S. Gronouski, 1963-65, reappointed to posts held in Kennedy Cabinet, see above.) John T. Connor, Secretary of Commerce, 1965-67; Lawrence O'Brien, Postmaster General, 1965-68.

Richard M. Nixon — Walter J. Hickel, Secretary of Interior, 1969-71; John A. Volpe, Secretary of Transportation, 1969-72; Maurice H. Stans, Secretary of Commerce, 1969-72; Peter J. Brennan, Secretary of Labor, 1973-74; William E. Simon, Secretary of Treasury, 1974.

Gerald R. Ford — (Peter J. Brennan, 1974-75, and William E. Simon, 1974-76, reappointed to posts held above.)

Jimmy Carter — Joseph Califano, Jr., Secretary of Health, Education and Welfare, 1977-79; Benjamin Civiletti, Attorney General, 1979-81; Moon Landrieu, Secretary of Housing and Urban Development, 1979-81; Edmund S. Muskie, Secretary of State, 1980-81.

Ronald Reagan — Alexander M. Haig, Secretary of State, 1981-82; Raymond J. Donovan, Secretary of Labor, 1981-84; Margaret M. Heckler, Secretary of Health and Human Services, 1983-85; William J. Bennett, Secretary of Education, 1985-88; Ann Dore McLaughlin, Secretary of Labor, 1988-89; Lauro F. Cavazos, Secretary of Education, 1988-89; Nicholas F. Brady, Secretary of Treasury, 1988-89.

George Bush — Lauro F. Cavazos (reappointed), Secretary of Education, 1989-90; Nicholas F. Brady (reappointed), Secretary of Treasury, 1989-93 ; James D. Watkins, Secretary of Energy, 1989-93; Manuel Lujan, Jr., Secretary of Interior, 1989-93 ; Edward J. Derwinski, Secretary of Veteran Affairs, 1989-92; Lynn Martin, Secretary of Labor, 1990-93; Edward Madigan, Secretary of Agriculture, 1991-93; William P. Barr, Attorney General, 1991-93.

Bill Clinton -- Henry G. Cisneros, Secretary of Housing and Urban Development, 1993-97; Federico F. Peña, Secretary of Transportation, 1993-97 ; Donna Shalala, Secretary of Health and Human Services, 1993- ; William M. Daley, Secretary of Commerce, 1997- ; Andrew Cuomo, Secretary of Housing and

Urban Development, 1997- ; Alexis H. Herman, Secretary of Labor, 1997- .

Cabinet members who became Catholics after leaving their posts were: Thomas Ewing, Secretary of Treasury under William A. Harrison, and Secretary of Interior under Zachary Taylor; Luke E. Wright, Secretary of War under Theodore Roosevelt; Albert B. Fall, Secretary of Interior under Warren G. Harding.

CATHOLIC SUPREME COURT JUSTICES

Roger B. Taney, Chief Justice 1836-64; app. by Andrew Jackson.

Edward D. White, Associate Justice 1894-1910, app. by Grover Cleveland; Chief Justice 1910-21, app. by William H. Taft.

Joseph McKenna, Associate Justice 1898-1925; app. by William McKinley.

Pierce Butler, Associate Justice 1923-39; app. by Warren G. Harding.

Frank Murphy, Associate Justice 1940-49; app. by Franklin D. Roosevelt.

William Brennan, Associate Justice 1956-90; app. by Dwight D. Eisenhower.

Antonin Scalia, Associate Justice 1986-; app. by Ronald Reagan.

Anthony M. Kennedy, Associate Justice 1988-; app. by Ronald Reagan.

Clarence Thomas, Associate Justice 1991- ; app. by George Bush.

Sherman Minton, Associate Justice from 1949 to 1956, became a Catholic several years before his death in 1965.

CATHOLICS IN STATUARY HALL

Statues of 13 Catholics deemed worthy of national commemoration by the donating states are among those enshrined in National Statuary Hall and other places in the U.S. Capitol. The Hall, formerly the chamber of the House of Representatives, was erected by Act of Congress July 2, 1864.

Donating states, names and years of placement are listed.

Arizona: Rev. Eusebio Kino, S. J., missionary, 1965.

California: Rev. Junípero Serra, O. F. M. missionary, 1931. (Beatified 1988.)

Hawaii: Father Damien, missionary, 1969.(Beatified 1995.)

Illinois: Gen. James Shields, statesman, 1893.

Louisiana: Edward D. White, Justice of the U.S. Supreme Court (1894-1921), 1955.

Maryland: Charles Carroll, statesman, 1901.

Nevada: Patrick A. McCarran, statesman, 1960.

New Mexico: Dennis Chavez, statesman, 1966. (Abp. Jean B. Lamy, pioneer prelate of Santa Fe, was nominated for Hall honor in 1951.)

North Dakota: John Burke, U.S. treasurer, 1963.

Oregon: Dr. John McLoughlin, pioneer, 1953.

Washington: Mother Mary Joseph Pariseau, pioneer missionary and humanitarian.

West Virginia: John E. Kenna, statesman, 1901.

Wisconsin: Rev. Jacques Marquette, S.J., missionary, explorer, 1895.

CHURCH-STATE RELATIONS IN THE UNITED STATES

CHURCH-STATE DECISIONS OF THE SUPREME COURT

(Among sources of this selected listing of U.S. Supreme Court decisions was *The Supreme Court on Church and State*, Joseph Tussman, editor; Oxford University Press, New York, 1962.)

Watson v. Jones, 13 Wallace 679 (1872): The Court declared that a member of a religious organization may not appeal to secular courts against a decision made by a church tribunal within the area of its competence.

Reynolds v. United States, 98 US 145 (1879); **Davis v. Beason, 133 US 333** (1890); **Church of Latter-Day Saints v. United States, 136 US 1** (1890): The Mormon practice of polygamy was at issue in three decisions and was declared unconstitutional:.

Bradfield v. Roberts, 175 US 291 (1899): The Court denied that an appropriation of government funds for an institution (Providence Hospital, Washington, D.C.) run by Roman Catholic sisters violated the No Establishment Clause of the First Amendment.

Pierce v. Society of Sisters, 268 US 510 (1925): The Court denied that a state can require children to attend public schools only. The Court held that the liberty of the Constitution forbids standardization by such compulsion, and that the parochial schools involved had claims to protection under the Fourteenth Amendment.

Cochran v. Board of Education, 281 US 370 (1930): The Court upheld a Louisiana statute providing textbooks at public expense for children attending public or parochial schools. The Court held that the children and state were beneficiaries of the appropriations, with incidental secondary benefit going to the schools.

United States v. MacIntosh, 283 US 605 (1931): The Court denied that anyone can place allegiance to the will of God above his allegiance to the government since such a person could make his own interpretation of God's will the decisive test as to whether he would or would not obey the nation's law. The Court stated that the nation, which has a duty to survive, can require citizens to bear arms in its defense.

Everson v. Board of Education, 330 US 1 (1947): The Court upheld the constitutionality of a New Jersey statute authorizing free school bus transportation for parochial as well as public school students. The Court expressed the opinion that the benefits of public welfare legislation, included under such bus transportation, do not run contrary to the concept of separation of Church and State.

McCollum v. Board of Education, 333 US 203 (1948): The Court declared unconstitutional a program for releasing children, with parental consent, from public school classes so they could receive religious instruction on public school premises from representatives of their own faiths.

Zorach v. Clauson, 343 US 306 (1952): The Court upheld the constitutionality of a New York statute permitting, on a voluntary basis, the release during school time of students from public school classes for religious instruction given off public school premises.

Torcaso v. Watkins, 367 US 488 (1961): The Court declared unconstitutional a Maryland requirement that one must make a declaration of belief in the existence of God as part of the oath of office for notaries public.

McGowan v. Maryland, 81 Sp Ct 1101; Two Guys from Harrison v. McGinley, 81 Sp Ct 1135; Gallagher v. Crown Kosher Super Market, 81 Sp Ct 1128; Braunfield v. Brown, 81 Sp Ct 1144 (1961): The Court ruled that Sunday closing laws do not violate the No Establishment of Religion Clause of the First Amendment, even though the laws were religious in their inception and still have some religious overtones. The Court held that, "as presently written and administered, most of them, at least, are of a secular rather than of a religious character, and that presently they bear no relationship to establishment of religion as those words are used in the Constitution of the United States."

Engel v. Vitale, 370 US 42 (1962): The Court declared that the voluntary recitation in public schools of a prayer composed by the New York State Board of Regents is unconstitutional on the ground that it violates the No Establishment of Religion Clause of the First Amendment.

Abington Township School District v. Schempp and Murray v. Curlett, 83 Sp Ct 1560 (1963): The Court ruled that Bible reading and recitation of the Lord's Prayer in public schools, with voluntary participation by students, are unconstitutional on the ground that they violate the No Establishment of Religion Clause of the First Amendment.

Chamberlin v. Dade County, 83 Sp Ct 1864 (1964): The Court reversed a decision of the Florida Supreme Court concerning the constitutionality of prayer and devotional Bible reading in public schools during the school day, as sanctioned by a state statute which specifically related the practices to a sound public purpose.

Board of Education v. Allen, No. 660 (1968): The Court declared constitutional the New York school book loan law which requires local school boards to purchase books with state funds and lend them to parochial and private school students.

Walz v. Tax Commission of New York (1970): The Court upheld the constitutionality of a New York statute exempting church-owned property from taxation.

Earle v. DiCenso, Robinson v. DiCenso, Lemon v. Kurtzman, Tilton v. Richardson (1971): In Earle v. DiCenso and Robinson v. DiCenso, the Court ruled unconstitutional a 1969 Rhode Island statute which provided salary supplements to teachers of secular subjects in parochial schools; in Lemon v. Kurtzman, the Court ruled unconstitutional a 1968 Pennsylvania statute which authorized the state to purchase services for the teaching of secular subjects in nonpublic schools. The principal argument against constitutionality in these cases was that the statutes and programs at issue entailed excessive entanglement of government with religion. In Tilton v. Richardson, the Court held that this argument did not apply to a prohibitive degree with respect to federal grants, under the Higher Education Facilities Act of 1963, for the construction of facilities for nonreligious purposes by four church-related institutions of higher learning, three of which were Catholic, in Connecticut.

Yoder, Miller and Yutzy (1972): In a case appealed

on behalf of Yoder, Miller and Yutzy, the Court ruled that Amish parents were exempt from a Wisconsin statute requiring them to send their children to school until the age of 16. The Court said in its decision that secondary schooling exposed Amish children to attitudes, goals and values contrary to their beliefs, and substantially hindered "the religious development of the Amish child and his integration into the way of life of the Amish faith-community at the crucial adolescent state of development."

Committee for Public Education and Religious Liberty, et al., v. Nyquist, et al., No. 72-694 (1973): The Court ruled that provisions of a 1972 New York statute were unconstitutional on the grounds that they were violative of the No Establishment Clause of the First Amendment and had the "impermissible effect" of advancing the sectarian activities of church-affiliated schools. The programs ruled unconstitutional concerned: (1) maintenance and repair grants, for facilities and equipment, to ensure the health, welfare and safety of students in nonpublic, non-profit elementary and secondary schools serving a high concentration of students from low income families; (2) tuition reimbursement ($50 per grade school child, $100 per high school student) for parents (with income less than $5,000) of children attending nonpublic elementary or secondary schools; tax deduction from adjusted gross income for parents failing to qualify under the above reimbursement plan, for each child attending a nonpublic school.

Sloan, Treasurer of Pennsylvania, et al., v. Lemon, et al., No. 72-459 (1973): The Court ruled unconstitutional a Pennsylvania Parent Reimbursement Act for Nonpublic Education which provided funds to reimburse parents (to a maximum of $150) for a portion of tuition expenses incurred in sending their children to nonpublic schools. The Court held that there was no significant difference between this and the New York tuition reimbursement program (above), and declared that the Equal Protection Clause of the Fourteenth Amendment cannot be relied upon to sustain a program held to be violative of the No Establishment Clause.

Levitt, et al., v. Committee for Public Education and Religious Liberty, et al., No. 72-269 (1973): The Court ruled unconstitutional the Mandated Services Act of 1970 under which New York provided $28 million ($27 per pupil from first to seventh grade, $45 per pupil from seventh to 12th grade) to reimburse nonpublic schools for testing, recording and reporting services required by the state. The Court declared that the act provided "impermissible aid" to religion in contravention of the No Establishment Clause.

In related decisions handed down June 25, 1973, the Court: (1) affirmed a lower court decision against the constitutionality of an Ohio tax credit law benefiting parents with children in nonpublic schools; (2) reinstated an injunction against a parent reimbursement program in New Jersey; (3) affirmed South Carolina's right to grant construction loans to church-affiliated colleges, and dismissed an appeal contesting its right to provide loans to students attending church-affiliated colleges (Hunt v. McNair, Durham v. McLeod).

Wheeler v. Barrera (1974): The Court ruled that nonpublic school students in Missouri must share in federal funds for educationally deprived students on a comparable basis with public school students under Title I of the Elementary and Secondary Education Act of 1965.

Norwood v. Harrison (93 S. Ct. 2804): The Court ruled that public assistance which avoids the prohibitions of the "effect" and "entanglement" tests (and which therefore does not substantially promote the religious mission of sectarian schools) may be confined to the secular functions of such schools.

Wiest v. Mt. Lebanon School District (1974): The Court upheld a lower court ruling that invocation and benediction prayers at public high school commencement ceremonies do not violate the principle of separation of Church and state.

Meek v. Pittenger (1975): The Court ruled unconstitutional portions of a Pennsylvania law providing auxiliary services for students of nonpublic schools; at the same time, it ruled in favor of provisions of the law permitting textbook loans to students of such schools. In denying the constitutionality of auxiliary services, the Court held that they had the "primary effect of establishing religion" and involved "excessive entanglement" of Church and state officials with respect to supervision; objection was also made against providing such services only on the premises of non-public schools and only at the request of such schools.

TWA, Inc., v. Hardison, 75-1126; International Association of Machinists and Aero Space Workers v. Hardison, 75-1385 (1977): The Court ruled that federal civil rights legislation does not require employers to make more than minimal efforts to accommodate employees who want a particular working day off as their religion's Sabbath Day, and that an employer cannot accommodate such an employee by violating seniority systems determined by a union collective bargaining agreement. The Court noted that its ruling was not a constitutional judgment but an interpretation of existing law.

Wolman v. Walter (1977): The Court ruled constitutional portions of an Ohio statute providing tax-paid textbook loans and some auxiliary services (standardized and diagnostic testing, therapeutic and remedial services, off school premises) for nonpublic school students. It decided that other portions of the law, providing state funds for nonpublic school field trips and instructional materials (audio-visual equipment, maps, tape recorders), were unconstitutional.

Byrne v. Public Funds for Public Schools (1979): The Court decided against the constitutionality of a 1976 New Jersey law providing state income tax deductions for tuition paid by parents of children attending parochial and other private schools.

Student Bus Transportation (1979): The Court upheld a Pennsylvania law providing bus transportation at public expense for students to non-public schools up to 10 miles away from the boundaries of the public school districts in which they lived.

Reimbursement (1980): The Court upheld the constitutionality of a 1974 New York law providing direct cash payment to non-public schools for the costs of state-mandated testing and record-keeping.

Ten Commandments (1980): The Court struck down a 1978 Kentucky law requiring the posting of the Ten Commandments in public school classrooms in the state.

Widmar v. Vincent (1981): The Court ruled that

the University of Missouri at Kansas City could not deny student religious groups the use of campus facilities for worship services. The Court also, in Brandon v. Board of Education of Guilderland Schools, declined without comment to hear an appeal for reversal of lower court decisions denying a group of New York high school students the right to meet for prayer on public school property before the beginning of the school day.

Lubbock v. Lubbock Civil Liberties Union (1983): By refusing to hear an appeal in this case, the Court upheld a lower court ruling against a public policy of permitting student religious groups to meet on public school property before and after school hours.

Mueller v. Allen (1983): The Court upheld a Minnesota law allowing parents of students in public and non-public (including parochial) schools to take a tax deduction for the expenses of tuition, textbooks and transportation. Maximum allowable deductions were $500 per child in elementary school and $700 per child in grades seven through 12.

Lynch v. Donnelly (1984): The Court ruled 5-to-4 that the First Amendment does not mandate "complete separation of church and state," and that, therefore, the sponsorship of a Christmas nativity scene by the City of Pawtucket, R.I., was not unconstitutional. The case involved a scene included in a display of Christmas symbols sponsored by the city in a park owned by a non-profit group. The majority opinion said "the Constitution (does not) require complete separation of church and state; it affirmatively mandates accommodation, not merely tolerance, of all religions and forbids hostility toward any. Anything less" would entail callous indifference not intended by the Constitution. Moreover, "such hostility would bring us into 'war with our national tradition as embodied in the First Amendment's guaranty of the free exercise of religion.' " (The additional quotation was from the 1948 decision in McCollum v. Board of Education.)

Christmas Nativity Scene (1985): The Court upheld a lower court ruling that the Village of Scarsdale, N.Y., must make public space available for the display of privately sponsored nativity scenes.

Wallace v. Jaffree, No. 83-812 (1985): The Court ruled against the constitutionality of a 1981 Alabama law calling for a public-school moment of silence that specifically included optional prayer.

Grand Rapids v. Ball, No. 83-990, and Aguilar v. Felton, No. 84-237 (1985): The Court ruled against the constitutionality of programs in Grand Rapids and New York City allowing public school teachers to teach remedial entitlement subjects (under the Elementary and Secondary Education Act of 1965) in private schools, many of which were Catholic.

Bender v. Williamsport Area School District (1986): The Court let stand a lower federal court decision allowing a public high school Bible study group the same "equal access" to school facilities as that enjoyed by other extracurricular clubs. A similar decision was handed down in 1990 in Board of Education v. Mergens, involving Westside High School in Omaha.

County of Allegheny v. American Civil Liberties Union (1989): The Court ruled (1) The display of a Christmas nativity scene in the Allegheny County Courthouse in Pittsburgh, Pa., violated the principle of separation of church and state because it appeared to be a government-sponsored endorsement of Christian belief. (2) The display of a Hanukkah menorah outside the Pittsburgh-Allegheny city-county building was constitutional because of its "particular physical setting" with secular symbols.

Unemployment Division v. Smith (1990): The Court ruled that religious use of the hallucinogenic cactus peyote is not covered by the First Amendment protection of religious freedom.

Lee v. Weisman (1992): In the Court banned officially organized prayer at public school graduation ceremonies.

Lamb's Chapel v. Center Moriches Union School District (1993): The Court reversed a ruling by the 3rd U.S. Circuit Court of Appeals, declaring that the school district was wrong in prohibiting the congregation of Lamb's Chapel from using public school meeting space after hours to show a film series addressing family problems from a religious perspective. In view of the variety of organizations permitted to use school property after school hours, said the Court's opinion: "There would have been no realistic danger that the community would think that the district was endorsing religion or any particular creed, and any benefit to religion or to the church would have been no more than incidental."

5th U.S. Circuit Court of Appeals (1993): The Court let stand a ruling by the 5th U.S. Circuit Court of Appeals, permitting students in Texas, Mississippi and Louisiana to include student-organized and student-led prayers in graduation exercises.

Church of Lukumi Babalu Aye v. City of Hialeah (1993): The Court ruled that municipal laws that effectively prohibit a single church from performing its religious rituals are unconstitutional. The ordinances at issue singled out one religion, Santeria, for the purpose of restricting its members from the practice of ritual animal sacrifices.

Zobrest v. Catalina Foothills School District (1993): The Court ruled that a public school district may provide a sign-language interpreter for a deaf student attending a Catholic school without violating constitutional separation of church and state. The majority opinion said: "Handicapped children, not sectarian schools are the primary beneficiaries of the Disabilities Education Act; to the extent sectarian schools benefit at all from (the act), they are only incidental beneficiaries."

Fairfax County, Va., school district (1994): The Court upheld lower court rulings against a Fairfax County, Va., school district's practice of charging churches more rent than other entities for the use of school buildings.

Board of Education of Kiryas Joel Village School District v. Grumet (1994): In, the Court ruled in 1994 that a school district created to meet the special education needs of an Hasidic Jewish community violated the Establishment Clause of the Constitution. The Court said the New York Legislature effectively endorsed a particular religion when it established a public school district for the Satmar Hasidic Village of Kiryas Joel.

Agostino v. Felton (1997): The court reversed, 5 to 4, its 1985 Aguilar v. Felton ruling, which had declared it unconstitutional for teachers employed by public school districts to hold Title I remedial programs for low-income students on the property of church-related schools.

Boerne v. Flores (1997): The court ruled, 6 to 3, that the Religious Freedom Restoration Act (1993) was unconstitutional because Congress overstepped its constitutional authority in enacting the law. Congress "has been given the power to 'enforce,' not the power to determine what constitutes a constitutional violation," said the majority opinion.

RELIGION IN PUBLIC SCHOOLS
(Based on a Catholic News Service article by Carol Zimmermann.)

A diverse group of religious and civil rights organizations issued a joint statement Apr. 13, 1995, in an effort to clarify the confusing issue of prayer and religious observances or discussions in public schools. Their six-page statement outlines what is and what is not currently permissible in expressing religious beliefs in public schools.

The statement says, for example: "Students have the right to pray individually or in groups, or to discuss their religious views with their peers so long as they are not disruptive." But, the statement specifies that such prayers or discussions do not include "the right to have a captive audience listen or to compel other students to participate."

Prayer at Graduations
Regarding prayer at graduation ceremonies, the document says school officials may not mandate or organize prayer, but hardly sets the record straight about student-led prayer at these services.

"The courts have reached conflicting conclusions under the federal Constitution" in this area, says the statement, recommending that schools consult their lawyers for the rules that apply to them, "until the issue is authoritatively resolved."

Since the Supreme Court's 1992 Lee v. Weisman opinion prohibited school authorities from even arranging for a speaker to present a prayer, lower courts in different states have made various rulings about student-led prayer at commencement exercises.

In Virginia, the state's Attorney General and the Board of Education proposed guidelines in mid-April to allow student-led prayer at graduations, despite a 1994 ruling by a U.S. district judge banning all prayer at graduations.

Religion in the Classroom
"It is permissible and desirable to teach objectively about the role of religion in the history of the United States and other countries," but public school teachers may not specifically teach religion.

The same rules apply to the recurring controversy surrounding theories of evolution. Teachers may discuss explanations of the beginnings of life, but only within the confines of classes on religion or social studies. Public school teachers are required, according to the statement, to teach only scientific explanations of life's beginnings in science classes. And, just as teachers may not advance a religious view, they should not ridicule a student's religious belief.

Constitutional Protection
The statement says that students' expressions of religious beliefs in reports, homework or artwork are constitutionally protected. Likewise, students have the right to speak to and attempt to persuade their peers on religious topics. "But school officials should intercede to stop student religious speech if it turns into religious harassment aimed at a student or a small group of students."

The statement also says:

• Students have the right to distribute religious literature to their schoolmates, subject to reasonable restrictions for any non-school literature.

• Student religious clubs in secondary schools "must be permitted to meet and to have equal access" to school media for announcing their events.

• Religious messages on T-shirts and the like cannot be singled out for suppression.

• Schools can use discretion about dismissing students for off-site religious instruction.

The 35 organizations that endorsed the statement included the National Association of Evangelicals, the American Jewish Congress, the Christian Legal Society, the National Council of Churches, the Baptist Joint Committee on Public Affairs, the American Muslim Council, the Presbyterian Church (USA) and the American Civil Liberties Union.

Purpose of the Statement
"By making this document available," said Phil Baum, executive director of the American Jewish Congress, "the organizations are attempting to clarify what has become one of the most divisive issues of our time: religion in the public schools."

He said the document attempts to "ensure that the rights of all students are respected in the public schools."

Baum noted that the American Jewish Congress, which initiated the effort to draft the statement, had a long-standing commitment to ensuring that public schools are themselves religiously neutral.

"We believe, however, that it is inconsistent with that historic commitment to ask the public schools to root out private expressions of religious faith."

CHURCH TAX EXEMPTION
The exemption of church-owned property was ruled constitutional by the U.S. Supreme Court May 4, 1970, in the case of Walz v. The Tax Commission of New York.

Suit in the case was brought by Frederick Walz, who purchased in June 1967, a 22-by-29-foot plot of ground in Staten Island valued at $100 and taxable at $5.24 a year. Shortly after making the purchase, Walz instituted a suit in New York State, contending that the exemption of church property from taxation authorized by state law increased his own tax rate and forced him indirectly to support churches in violation of his constitutional right to freedom of religion under the First Amendment. Three New York courts dismissed the suit, which had been instituted by mail. The Supreme Court, judging that it had probable jurisdiction, then took the case.

In a 7-1 decision affecting Church-state relations in every state in the nation, the Court upheld the New York law under challenge.

For and Against
Chief Justice Warren E. Burger, who wrote the majority opinion, said that Congress from its earliest days

had viewed the religion clauses of the Constitution as authorizing statutory real estate tax exemption to religious bodies. He declared: "Nothing in this national attitude toward religious tolerance and two centuries of uninterrupted freedom from taxation has given the remotest sign of leading to an established church or religion, and on the contrary it has operated affirmatively to help guarantee the free exercise of all forms of religious beliefs."

Justice William O. Douglas wrote in dissent that the involvement of government in religion as typified in tax exemption may seem inconsequential but: "It is, I fear, a long step down the establishment path. Perhaps I have been misinformed. But, as I read the Constitution and the philosophy, I gathered that independence was the price of liberty."

Burger rejected Douglas' "establishment" fears. If tax exemption is the first step toward establishment, he said, "the second step has been long in coming."

The basic issue centered on the following question: Is there a contradiction between federal constitutional provisions against the establishment of religion, or the use of public funds for religious purposes, and state statutes exempting church property from taxation? In the Walz decision, the Supreme Court ruled that there is no contradiction.

Legal Background

The U.S. Constitution makes no reference to tax exemption. There was no discussion of the issue in the Constitutional Convention nor in debates on the Bill of Rights.

In the Colonial and post-Revolutionary years, some churches had established status and were state-supported. This changed with enactment of the First Amendment, which laid down no-establishment as the federal norm. This norm was adopted by the states which, however, exempted churches from tax liabilities.

No establishment, no hindrance, was the early American view of Church-state relationships. This view, reflected in custom law, was not generally formulated in statute law until the second half of the 19th century, although specific tax exemption was provided for churches in Maryland in 1798, in Virginia in 1800, and in North Carolina in 1806.

The first major challenge to church property exemption was initiated by the Liberal League in the 1870s. It reached the point that President Grant included the recommendation in a State of the Union address in 1875, stating that church property should bear its own proportion of taxes. The plea fell on deaf ears in Congress, but there was some support for the idea at state levels. The exemption, however, continued to survive various challenges.

About 36 state constitutions contain either mandatory or permissive provisions for exemption. Statutes provide for exemption in all other states.

There has been considerable litigation challenging this exemption, but most of it focused on whether a particular property satisfied statutory requirements. Few cases before Walz focused on the strictly constitutional question, whether directly under the First Amendment or indirectly under the Fourteenth.

Objections

Objectors to the tax exempt status of churches feel that churches should share, through taxation, in the cost of the ordinary benefits of public services they enjoy, and/or that the amount of "aid" enjoyed through exemption should be proportionate to the amount of social good they do.

According to one opinion, exemption is said to weaken the independence of churches from the political system which benefits them by exemption.

In another view, exemption is said to involve the government in decisions regarding what is and what is not religion.

The Wall of Separation

Thomas Jefferson, in a letter written to the Danbury (Conn.) Baptist Association Jan. 1, 1802, coined the metaphor, "a wall of separation between Church and State," to express a theory concerning interpretation of the religion clauses of the First Amendment: "Congress shall make no law respecting an establishment of religion or prohibiting the free exercise thereof."

The metaphor was cited for the first time in judicial proceedings in 1879, in the opinion by Chief Justice Waite in Reynolds v. United States. It did not, however, figure substantially in the decision.

Accepted as Rule

In 1947 the wall of separation gained acceptance as a constitutional rule, in the decision handed down in Everson v. Board of Education. Associate Justice Black, in describing the principles involved in the No Establishment Clause, wrote:

"Neither a state nor the Federal Government can set up a church. Neither can pass laws which aid one religion, aid all religions, or prefer one religion over another. Neither can force nor influence a person to go to or to remain away from church against his will or force him to profess a belief or disbelief in any religion. No person can be punished for entertaining or professing religious beliefs or disbeliefs, for church attendance or non-attendance. No tax in any amount, large or small, can be levied to support any religious activities or institutions, whatever they may be called, or whatever form they may adopt to teach or practice religion. Neither a state nor the Federal Government can, openly or secretly, participate in the affairs of any religious organizations or groups and vice versa. In the words of Jefferson, the clause against establishment of religion by law was intended to erect 'a wall of separation between Church and State.' "

Mr. Black's associates agreed with his statement of principles, which were framed without reference to the Freedom of Exercise Clause. They disagreed, however, with respect to application of the principles, as the split decision in the case indicated. Five members of the Court held that the benefits of public welfare legislation — in this case, free bus transportation to school for parochial as well as public school students — did not run contrary to the concept of separation of Church and state embodied in the First Amendment.

U.S. CATHOLIC JURISDICTIONS, HIERARCHY, STATISTICS

The organizational structure of the Catholic Church in the United States consists of 33 provinces with as many archdioceses (metropolitan sees); 151 suffragan sees (dioceses); five Eastern Church jurisdictions immediately subject to the Holy See — the eparchies of St. Maron and Our Lady of Lebanon of Los Angeles (Maronites), Newton (Melkites), St. Thomas Apostle of Detroit (Chaldeans) and St. George Martyr of Canton, Ohio (Romanians); and the Military Services Archdiocese. The eparchy of Our Lady of Deliverance of Newark for Syrian-rite Catholics in the U.S. and Canada has its seat in Newark, N.J. An Armenian apostolic exarchate for the United States and Canada has its seat in New York. Each of these jurisdictions is under the direction of an archbishop or bishop, called an ordinary, who has apostolic responsibility and authority for the pastoral service of the people in his care.

The structure includes the territorial episcopal conference known as the National Conference of Catholic Bishops. In and through this body, which is strictly ecclesiastical and has defined juridical authority, the bishops exercise their collegiate pastorate over the Church in the entire country (see Index).

Related to the NCCB is the United States Catholic Conference (USCC), a civil corporation and operational secretariat through which the bishops, in cooperation with other members of the Church, act on a wider-than-ecclesiastical scale for the good of the Church and society in the United States (see Index).

The representative of the Holy See to the Church in the United States is an Apostolic Pro-Nuncio (presently Archbishop Gabriel Montalvo).

ECCLESIASTICAL PROVINCES

(Sources: The Official Catholic Directory, Catholic News Service.)

The 33 ecclesiastical provinces bear the names of archdioceses, i.e., of metropolitan sees.

Anchorage: Archdiocese of Anchorage and suffragan sees of Fairbanks, Juneau. Geographical area: Alaska.

Atlanta: Archdiocese of Atlanta (Ga.) and suffragan sees of Savannah (Ga.); Charlotte and Raleigh (N.C.), Charleston (S.C.). Geographical area: Georgia, North Carolina, South Carolina.

Baltimore: Archdiocese of Baltimore (Md.) and suffragan sees of Wilmington (Del.); Arlington and Richmond (Va.); Wheeling-Charleston (W. Va.). Geographical area: Maryland (except five counties), Delaware, Virginia, West Virginia.

Boston: Archdiocese of Boston (Mass.) and suffragan sees of Fall River, Springfield and Worcester (Mass.); Portland (Me.); Manchester (N.H.); Burlington (Vt.). Geographical area: Massachusetts, Maine, New Hampshire, Vermont.

Chicago: Archdiocese of Chicago and suffragan sees of Belleville, Joliet, Peoria, Rockford, Springfield. Geographical area: Illinois.

Cincinnati: Archdiocese of Cincinnati and suffragan sees of Cleveland, Columbus, Steubenville, Toledo, Youngstown. Geographical area: Ohio.

Denver: Archdiocese of Denver (Colo.) and

suffragan sees of Colorado Springs and Pueblo (Colo.); Cheyenne (Wyo.). Geographical area: Colorado, Wyoming.

Detroit: Archdiocese of Detroit and suffragan sees of Gaylord, Grand Rapids, Kalamazoo, Lansing, Marquette, Saginaw. Geographical area: Michigan.

Dubuque: Archdiocese of Dubuque and suffragan sees of Davenport, Des Moines, Sioux City. Geographical area: Iowa.

Hartford: Archdiocese of Hartford (Conn.) and suffragan sees of Bridgeport and Norwich (Conn.); Providence (R.I.). Geographical area: Connecticut, Rhode Island.

Indianapolis: Archdiocese of Indianapolis and suffragan sees of Evansville, Fort Wayne-South Bend, Gary, Lafayette. Geographical area: Indiana.

Kansas City (Kans.): Archdiocese of Kansas City and suffragan sees of Dodge City, Salina, Wichita. Geographical area: Kansas.

Los Angeles: Archdiocese of Los Angeles and suffragan sees of Fresno, Monterey, Orange, San Bernardino, San Diego. Geographical area: Southern and Central California.

Louisville: Archdiocese of Louisville (Ky.) and suffragan sees of Covington, Lexington and Owensboro (Ky.); Knoxville, Memphis and Nashville (Tenn.). Geographical area: Kentucky, Tennessee.

Miami: Archdiocese of Miami and suffragan sees of Orlando, Palm Beach, Pensacola-Tallahassee, St. Augustine, St. Petersburg, Venice. Geographical area: Florida.

Milwaukee: Archdiocese of Milwaukee and suffragan sees of Green Bay, La Crosse, Madison, Superior. Geographical area: Wisconsin.

Mobile: Archdiocese of Mobile, Ala., and suffragan sees of Birmingham (Ala.); Biloxi and Jackson (Miss.). Geographical area: Alabama, Mississippi.

Newark: Archdiocese of Newark and suffragan sees of Camden, Metuchen, Paterson, Trenton. Geographical area: New Jersey.

New Orleans: Archdiocese of New Orleans and suffragan sees of Alexandria, Baton Rouge, Houma-Thibodaux, Lafayette, Lake Charles and Shreveport. Geographical area: Louisiana.

New York: Archdiocese of New York and suffragan sees of Albany, Brooklyn, Buffalo, Ogdensburg, Rochester, Rockville Centre, Syracuse. Geographical area: New York.

Oklahoma City: Archdiocese of Oklahoma City (Okla.) and suffragan sees of Tulsa (Okla.) and Little Rock (Ark.). Geographical area: Oklahoma, Arkansas.

Omaha: Archdiocese of Omaha and suffragan sees of Grand Island, Lincoln. Geographical area: Nebraska.

Philadelphia: Archdiocese of Philadelphia and suffragan sees of Allentown, Altoona-Johnstown, Erie, Greensburg, Harrisburg, Pittsburgh, Scranton. Geographical area: Pennsylvania.

Philadelphia (Byzantine, Ukrainians): Metropolitan See of Philadelphia (Byzantine) and Eparchies of St. Josaphat in Parma (Ohio), St. Nicholas of the Ukrainians in Chicago and Stamford, Conn. The jurisdiction extends to all Ukrainian Catholics in the U.S. from the ecclesiastical province of Galicia in the Ukraine.

Pittsburgh (Byzantine, Ruthenians): Metropolitan See of Pittsburgh, Pa. and Eparchies of Passaic (N.J.), Parma (Ohio), Van Nuys (Calif.).

Portland: Archdiocese of Portland (Ore.) and suffragan sees of Baker (Ore.); Boise (Ida.); Great Falls-Billings and Helena (Mont.). Geographical area: Oregon, Idaho, Montana.

St. Louis: Archdiocese of St. Louis and suffragan sees of Jefferson City, Kansas City-St. Joseph, Springfield-Cape Girardeau. Geographical area: Missouri.

St. Paul and Minneapolis: Archdiocese of St. Paul and Minneapolis (Minn.) and suffragan sees of Crookston, Duluth, New Ulm, St. Cloud and Winona (Minn.); Bismarck and Fargo (N.D.); Rapid City and Sioux Falls (S.D.). Geographical area: Minnesota, North Dakota, South Dakota.

San Antonio: Archdiocese of San Antonio (Tex.) and suffragan sees of Amarillo, Austin, Beaumont, Brownsville, Corpus Christi, Dallas, El Paso, Fort Worth, Galveston-Houston, Lubbock, San Angelo, Tyler and Victoria (Tex.). Geographical area: Texas.

San Francisco: Archdiocese of San Francisco (Calif.) and suffragan sees of Oakland, Sacramento, San Jose, Santa Rosa and Stockton (Calif.); Honolulu (Hawaii); Reno (Nev.); Las Vegas (Nev.); Salt Lake City (Utah). Geographical area: Northern California, Nevada, Utah, Hawaii.

Santa Fe: Archdiocese of Santa Fe (N.M.) and suffragan sees of Gallup and Las Cruces (N.M.); Phoenix and Tucson (Ariz.). Geographical area: New Mexico, Arizona.

Seattle: Archdiocese of Seattle and suffragan sees of Spokane, Yakima. Geographical area: Washington.

Washington: Archdiocese of Washington, D.C., and suffragan see of St. Thomas (Virgin Islands). Geographical area: District of Columbia, five counties of Maryland, Virgin Islands.

ARCHDIOCESES, DIOCESES, ARCHBISHOPS, BISHOPS

(Sources: *Official Catholic Directory*; Catholic News Service; *L'Osservatore Romano*. As of Aug. 20, 1999.)

Information includes name of diocese, year of foundation (as it appears on the official document erecting the see), present ordinaries (year of installation), auxiliaries and former ordinaries (for biographies, see Index).

Archdioceses are indicated by an asterisk.

Albany, N.Y. (1847): Howard J. Hubbard, bishop, 1977.

Former bishops: John McCloskey, 1847-64; John J. Conroy, 1865-77; Francis McNeirny, 1877-94; Thomas M. Burke, 1894-1915; Thomas F. Cusack, 1915-18; Edmund F. Gibbons, 1919-54; William A. Scully, 1954-69; Edwin B. Broderick, 1969-76.

Alexandria, La. (1853): Sam G. Jacobs, bishop, 1989. Established at Natchitoches, transferred to Alexandria 1910; title changed to Alexandria-Shreveport, 1977; redesignated Alexandria, 1986, when Shreveport was made a diocese.

Former bishops: Augustus M. Martin, 1853-75; Francis X. Leray, 1877-79, administrator, 1879-83; Anthony Durier, 1885-1904; Cornelius Van de Ven, 1904-32; Daniel F. Desmond, 1933-45; Charles P. Greco, 1946-73; Lawrence P. Graves, 1973-82; William B. Friend, 1983-86; John C. Favalora, 1986-89.

Allentown, Pa. (1961): Edward P. Cullen, 1997.

Former bishop: Joseph McShea, 1961-83; Thomas J. Welsh, 1983-97.

Altoona-Johnstown, Pa. (1901): Joseph V. Adamec, bishop, 1987.

Established as Altoona, name changed, 1957.

Former bishops: Eugene A. Garvey, 1901-20; John J. McCort, 1920-36; Richard T. Guilfoyle, 1936-57; Howard J. Carroll, 1958-60; J. Carroll McCormick, 1960-66; James J. Hogan, 1966-86.

Amarillo, Tex. (1926): John W. Yanta, bishop, 1997.

Former bishops; Rudolph A. Gerken, 1927-33; Robert E. Lucey, 1934-41; Laurence J. Fitzsimon, 1941-58; John L. Morkovsky, 1958-63; Lawrence M. De Falco, 1963-79; Leroy T. Matthiesen, 1980-97.

Anchorage,* Alaska (1966): Francis T. Hurley, archbishop, 1976.

Former archbishop: Joseph T. Ryan, 1966-75.

Arlington, Va. (1974): Paul S. Loverde, bishop, 1999.

Former bishop: Thomas J. Welsh, 1974-83, John R. Keating, 1983-98.

Atlanta,* Ga. (1956; archdiocese, 1962): John F. Donoghue, archbishop, 1993.

Former ordinaries: Francis E. Hyland, 1956-61; Paul J. Hallinan, first archbishop, 1962-68; Thomas A. Donnellan, 1968-87; Eugene A. Marino, S.S.J., 1988-90; James P. Lyke, 1991-92.

Austin, Tex. (1947): John E. McCarthy, bishop, 1986.

Former bishops: Louis J. Reicher, 1947-71; Vincent M. Harris, 1971-86.

Baker, Ore. (1903): Thomas J. Connolly, bishop, 1971.

Established as Baker City, name changed, 1952.

Former bishops: Charles J. O'Reilly, 1903-18; Joseph F. McGrath, 1919-50; Francis P. Leipzig, 1950-71.

Baltimore,* Md. (1789; archdiocese, 1808): Cardinal William H. Keeler, archbishop, 1989. Gordon D. Bennett, S.J., P. Francis Murphy, William C. Newman, auxiliaries.

Former ordinaries: John Carroll, 1789-1815, first archbishop; Leonard Neale, 1815-17; Ambrose Marechal, S.S., 1817-28; James Whitfield, 1828-34; Samuel Eccleston, S.S., 1834-51; Francis P. Kenrick, 1851-63; Martin J. Spalding, 1864-72; James R. Bayley, 1872-77; Cardinal James Gibbons, 1877-1921; Michael J. Curley, 1921-47; Francis P. Keough, 1947-61; Cardinal Lawrence J. Shehan, 1961-74; William D. Borders, 1974-89.

Baton Rouge, La. (1961): Alfred C. Hughes, bishop, 1993.

Former bishops: Robert E. Tracy, 1961-74; Joseph V. Sullivan, 1974-82; Stanley J. Ott, 1983-93.

Beaumont, Tex. (1966): Joseph A. Galante, bishop, 1994.

Former bishops: Vincent M. Harris, 1966-71; Warren L. Boudreaux, 1971-77; Bernard J. Ganter, 1977-93.

Belleville, Ill. (1887): Wilton D. Gregory, bishop, 1994.

Former bishops: John Janssen, 1888-1913; Henry Althoff, 1914-47; Albert R. Zuroweste, 1948-76; William M. Cosgrove, 1976-81; John N. Wurm, 1981-84; James P. Keleher, 1984-93.

Biloxi, Miss. (1977): Joseph Lawson Howze, bishop, 1977.

Birmingham, Ala. (1969): David E. Foley, bishop, 1994.

Former bishops: Joseph G. Vath, 1969-87; Raymond J. Boland, 1988-93.

Bismarck, N. Dak. (1909): Paul A. Zipfel, bishop, 1996.

Former bishops: Vincent Wehrle, O.S.B., 1910-39; Vincent J. Ryan, 1940-51; Lambert A. Hoch, 1952-56; Hilary B. Hacker, 1957-82; John F. Kinney, 1982-95.

Boise, Ida. (1893): Michael P. Driscoll, 1999.

Former bishops: Alphonse J. Glorieux, 1893-1917; Daniel M. Gorman, 1918-27; Edward J. Kelly, 1928-56; James J. Byrne, 1956-62; Sylvester Treinen, 1962-88; Tod David Brown, 1989-98.

Boston,* Mass. (1808; archdiocese, 1875): Cardinal Bernard F. Law, archbishop, 1984. John R. McNamara, John P. Boles, William F. Murphy, John B. McCormack, Francis Xavier Irwin, Emilio Allué, S.D.B., auxiliaries.

Former ordinaries: John L. de Cheverus, 1810-23; Benedict J. Fenwick, S.J., 1825-46; John B. Fitzpatrick, 1846-66; John J. Williams, 1866-1907, first archbishop; Cardinal William O'Connell, 1907-44; Cardinal Richard Cushing, 1944-70; Cardinal Humberto Medeiros, 1970-83.

Bridgeport, Conn. (1953): Edward M. Egan, bishop, 1988.

Former bishops: Lawrence J. Shehan, 1953-61; Walter W. Curtis, 1961-88.

Brooklyn, N.Y. (1853): Thomas V. Daily, bishop, 1990. Joseph M. Sullivan, Rene A. Valero, Ignatius Catanello, Gerald Barbarito, auxiliaries.

Former bishops: John Loughlin, 1853-91; Charles E. McDonnell, 1892-1921; Thomas E. Molloy, 1921-56; Bryan J. McEntegart, 1957-68; Francis J. Mugavero, 1968-90.

Brownsville, Tex. (1965): Raymundo J. Pena, bishop, 1995.

Former bishops: Adolph Marx, 1965; Humberto S. Medeiros, 1966-70; John J. Fitzpatrick, 1971-91; Enrique San Pedro, S.J., 1991-94.

Buffalo, N.Y. (1847): Henry J. Mansell, bishop, 1995. Edward M. Grosz, auxiliary.

Former bishops: John Timon, C.M., 1847-67; Stephen V. Ryan, C.M., 1868-96; James E. Quigley, 1897-1903; Charles H. Colton, 1903-15; Dennis J. Dougherty, 1915-18; William Turner, 1919-36; John A. Duffy, 1937-44; John F. O'Hara, C.S.C., 1945-51; Joseph A. Burke, 1952-62; James McNulty, 1963-72; Edward D. Head, 1973-95.

Burlington, Vt. (1853): Kenneth A. Angell, bishop, 1992.

Former bishops: Louis De Goesbriand, 1853-99; John S. Michaud, 1899-1908; Joseph J. Rice, 1910-38; Matthew F. Brady, 1938-44; Edward F. Ryan, 1945-56; Robert F. Joyce, 1957-71; John A. Marshall, 1972-91.

Camden, N.J. (1937): Nicholas A. Di Marzio, 1999.

Former bishops: Bartholomew J. Eustace, 1938-56; Justin J. McCarthy, 1957-59; Celestine J. Damiano,

1960-67; George H. Guilfoyle, 1968-89, James T. McHugh, 1989-98.

Charleston, S.C. (1820): Robert J. Baker, bishop, 1999.

Former bishops: John England, 1820-42; Ignatius W. Reynolds, 1844-55; Patrick N. Lynch, 1858-82; Henry P. Northrop, 1883-1916; William T. Russell, 1917-27; Emmet M. Walsh, 1927-49; John J. Russell, 1950-58; Paul J. Hallinan, 1958-62; Francis F. Reh, 1962-64; Ernest L. Unterkoefler, 1964-90; David B. Thompson, 1990-99.

Charlotte, N.C. (1971): William G. Curlin, bishop, 1994.

Former bishops: Michael J. Begley, 1972-84; John F. Donoghue, 1984-93.

Cheyenne, Wyo. (1887): Joseph Hart, bishop, 1978. Former bishops: Maurice F. Burke, 1887-93; Thomas M. Lenihan, 1897-1901; James J. Keane, 1902-11; Patrick A. McGovern, 1912-51; Hubert M. Newell, 1951-78.

Chicago,* Ill. (1843; archdiocese, 1880): Cardinal Francis E. George, archbishop, 1997. Thad J. Jakubowski, John R. Gorman, Raymond E. Goedert, Edwin M. Conway, Gerald F. Kicanas, John R. Manz, Joseph N. Perry, auxiliaries.

Former ordinaries: William Quarter, 1844-48; James O. Van de Velde, S.J., 1849-53; Anthony O'Regan, 1854-58; James Duggan, 1859-70; Thomas P. Foley, administrator, 1870-79; Patrick A. Feehan, 1880-1902, first archbishop; James E. Quigley, 1903-15; Cardinal George Mundelein, 1915-39; Cardinal Samuel Stritch, 1939-58; Cardinal Albert Meyer, 1958-65; Cardinal John Cody, 1965-82; Cardinal Joseph L. Bernardin, 1982-96.

Cincinnati,* Ohio (1821; archdiocese, 1850): Daniel E. Pilarczyk, archbishop, 1982. Carl K. Moeddel, auxiliary.

Former ordinaries: Edward D. Fenwick, O.P., 1822-32; John B. Purcell, 1833-83, first archbishop; William H. Elder, 1883-1904; Henry Moeller, 1904-1925; John T. McNicholas, O.P., 1925-50; Karl J. Alter, 1950-69; Paul F. Leibold, 1969-72; Joseph L. Bernardin, 1972-82.

Cleveland, Ohio (1847): Anthony M. Pilla, bishop, 1980. A. Edward Pevec, A. James Quinn, auxiliaries.

Former bishops: L. Amadeus Rappe, 1847-70; Richard Gilmour, 1872-91; Ignatius F. Horstmann, 1892-1908; John P. Farrelly, 1909-21; Joseph Schrembs, 1921-45; Edward F. Hoban, 1945-66; Clarence G. Issenmann, 1966-74; James A. Hickey, 1974-80.

Colorado Springs, Colo. (1983): Richard C. Hanifen, bishop, 1984.

Columbus, Ohio (1868): James A. Griffin, bishop, 1983.

Former bishops: Sylvester H. Rosecrans, 1868-78; John A. Watterson, 1880-99; Henry Moeller, 1900-03; James J. Hartley, 1904-44; Michael J. Ready, 1944-57; Clarence Issenmann, 1957-64; John J. Carberry, 1965-68; Clarence E. Elwell, 1968-73; Edward J. Herrmann, 1973-82.

Corpus Christi, Tex. (1912): vacant.

Former bishops: Paul J. Nussbaum, C.P., 1913-20; Emmanuel B. Ledvina, 1921-49; Mariano S. Garriga, 1949-65; Thomas J. Drury, 1965-83; Rene H. Gracida, 1983-97. Roberto O. Gonzalez, O.F.M., 1997-99.

Covington, Ky. (1853): Robert W. Muench, bishop, 1996.

Former bishops: George A. Carrell, S.J., 1853-68; Augustus M. Toebbe, 1870-84; Camillus P. Maes, 1885-1914; Ferdinand Brossart, 1916-23; Francis W. Howard, 1923-44; William T. Mulloy, 1945-59; Richard Ackerman, C.S.Sp., 1960-78; William A. Hughes, 1979-95.

Crookston, Minn. (1909): Victor H. Balke, bishop, 1976.

Former bishops: Timothy Corbett, 1910-38; John H. Peschges, 1938-44; Francis J. Schenk, 1945-60; Laurence A. Glenn, 1960-70; Kenneth J. Povish, 1970-75.

Dallas, Tex. (1890): Charles V. Grahmann, bishop, 1990.

Established 1890, as Dallas, title changed to Dallas-Ft. Worth 1953; redesignated Dallas, 1969, when Ft. Worth was made diocese.

Former bishops: Thomas F. Brennan, 1891-92; Edward J. Dunne, 1893-1910; Joseph P. Lynch, 1911-54; Thomas K. Gorman, 1954-69; Thomas Tschoepe, 1969-90.

Davenport, Ia. (1881): William E. Franklin, bishop, 1993.

Former bishops: John McMullen, 1881-83; Henry Cosgrove, 1884-1906; James Davis, 1906-26; Henry P. Rohlman, 1927-44; Ralph L. Hayes, 1944-66; Gerald F. O'Keefe, 1966-93.

Denver,* Colo. (1887; archdiocese, 1941): Charles J. Chaput, O.F.M. Cap., archbishop, 1997.

Former ordinaries: Joseph P. Machebeuf, 1887-89; Nicholas C. Matz, 1889-1917; J. Henry Tihen, 1917-31; Urban J. Vehr, 1931-67, first archbishop; James V. Casey, 1967-86; J. Francis Stafford, 1986-96.

Des Moines, Ia. (1911): Joseph L. Charron, C.PP.S., bishop, 1993.

Former bishops: Austin Dowling, 1912-19; Thomas W. Drumm, 1919-33; Gerald T. Bergan, 1934-48; Edward C. Daly, O.P., 1948-64; George J. Biskup, 1965-67; Maurice J. Dingman, 1968-86; William H. Bullock, 1987-93.

Detroit,* Mich. (1833; archdiocese, 1937): Cardinal Adam J. Maida, archbishop, 1990. Thomas J. Gumbleton, Moses B. Anderson, S.S.E., Kevin M. Britt, John C. Nienstedt, Allen H. Vigneron, Leonard P. Blair, auxiliaries.

Former ordinaries: Frederic Rese, 1833-71; Peter P. Lefevere, administrator, 1841-69; Caspar H. Borgess, 1871-88; John S. Foley, 1888-1918; Michael J. Gallagher, 1918-37; Cardinal Edward Mooney, 1937-58, first archbishop; Cardinal John F. Dearden, 1958-80; Cardinal Edmund C. Szoka, 1981-90.

Dodge City, Kans. (1951): Ronald M. Gilmore, bishop, 1998.

Former bishops: John B. Franz, 1951-59; Marion F. Forst, 1960-76; Eugene J. Gerber, 1976-82; Stanley G. Schlarman, bishop, 1983-98.

Dubuque,* Iowa (1837; archdiocese, 1893): Jerome Hanus, O.S.B., archbishop, 1995.

Former ordinaries: Mathias Loras, 1837-58; Clement Smyth, O.C.S.O., 1858-65; John Hennessy, 1866-1900, first archbishop; John J. Keane, 1900-11; James J. Keane, 1911-29; Francis J. Beckman, 1930-46; Henry P. Rohlman, 1946-54; Leo Binz, 1954-61; James J. Byrne, 1962-83; Daniel W. Kucera, O.S.B., 1984-95.

Duluth, Minn. (1889): Roger L. Schwietz, O.M.I., bishop, 1990.

Former bishops: James McGolrick, 1889-1918; John T. McNicholas, O.P., 1918-25; Thomas A. Welch, 1926-59; Francis J. Schenk, 1960-69; Paul F. Anderson, 1969-82; Robert H. Brom, 1983-89.

El Paso, Tex. (1914): Armando X. Ochoa, bishop, 1996.
Former bishops: Anthony J. Schuler, S.J., 1915-42; Sidney M. Metzger, 1942-78. Patrick F. Flores, 1978-79; Raymundo J. Pena, 1980-95.

Erie, Pa. (1853): Donald W. Trautman, bishop, 1990.
Former bishops: Michael O'Connor, 1853-54; Josue M. Young, 1854-66; Tobias Mullen, 1868-99; John E. Fitzmaurice, 1899-1920; John M. Gannon, 1920-66; John F. Whealon, 1966-69; Alfred M. Watson, 1969-82; Michael J. Murphy, 1982-90.

Evansville, Ind. (1944): Gerald A. Gettelfinger, bishop, 1989.
Former bishops: Henry J. Grimmelsman, 1944-65; Paul F. Leibold, 1966-69; Francis R. Shea, 1970-89.

Fairbanks, Alaska (1962): Michael J. Kaniecki, S.J., bishop, 1985.
Former bishops: Francis D. Gleeson, S.J., 1962-68; Robert L. Whelan, S.J., 1968-85.

Fall River, Mass. (1904): Sean O'Malley, O.F.M. Cap., bishop, 1992.
Former bishops: William Stang, 1904-07; Daniel F. Feehan, 1907-34; James E. Cassidy, 1934-51; James L. Connolly, 1951-70; Daniel A. Cronin, 1970-91.

Fargo, N. Dak. (1889): James S. Sullivan, bishop, 1985.
Established at Jamestown, transferred, 1897.
Former bishops: John Shanley, 1889-1909; James O'Reilly, 1910-34; Aloysius J. Muench, 1935-59; Leo F. Dworschak, 1960-70; Justin A. Driscoll, 1970-84.

Fort Wayne-South Bend, Ind. (1857): John M. D'Arcy, bishop, 1985. Daniel R. Jenky, C.S.C., auxiliary.
Established as Fort Wayne, name changed, 1960.
Former bishops: John H. Luers, 1858-71; Joseph Dwenger, C.Pp. S., 1872-93; Joseph Rademacher, 1893-1900; Herman J. Alerding, 1900-24; John F. Noll, 1925-56; Leo A. Pursley, 1957-76; William E. McManus, 1976-85.

Fort Worth, Tex. (1969): Joseph P. Delaney, bishop, 1981.
Former bishop: John J. Cassata, 1969-80.

Fresno, Calif. (1967): John T. Steinbock, bishop, 1991.
Formerly Monterey-Fresno, 1922.
Former bishops (Monterey-Fresno): John J. Cantwell, administrator, 1922-24; John B. MacGinley, first bishop, 1924-32; Philip G. Sher, 1933-53; Aloysius J. Willinger, 1953-67.
Former bishops (Fresno): Timothy Manning, 1967-69; Hugh A. Donohoe, 1969-80; Joseph J. Madera, M.Pp.S., 1980-91.

Gallup, N. Mex. (1939): Donald Pelotte, S.S.S., bishop, 1990.
Former bishops: Bernard T. Espelage, O.F.M., 1940-69; Jerome J. Hastrich, 1969-90.

Galveston-Houston, Tex. (1847): Joseph A. Fiorenza, bishop, 1985. Curtis J. Guillory, S.V.D.; James A. Tamayo, auxiliaries.
Established as Galveston, name changed, 1959.
Former bishops: John M. Odin, C.M., 1847-61; Claude M. Dubuis, 1862-92; Nicholas A. Gallagher,

1892-1918; Christopher E. Byrne, 1918-50; Wendelin J. Nold, 1950-75; John L. Morkovsky, 1975-84.

Gary, Ind. (1956): Dale J. Melczek, bishop, 1996.
Former bishops: Andrew G. Grutka, 1957-84; Norbert F. Gaughan, 1984-96.

Gaylord, Mich. (1971): Patrick R. Cooney, bishop, 1989, installed 1990.
Former bishops: Edmund C. Szoka, 1971-81; Robert J. Rose, 1981-89.

Grand Island, Neb. (1912): Lawrence J. McNamara, bishop, 1978.
Established at Kearney, transferred, 1917.
Former bishops: James A. Duffy, 1913-31; Stanislaus V. Bona, 1932-44; Edward J. Hunkeler, 1945-51; John L. Paschang, 1951-72; John J. Sullivan, 1972-77.

Grand Rapids, Mich. (1882): Robert J. Rose, bishop, 1989. Joseph C. McKinney, auxiliary.
Former bishops: Henry J. Richter, 1883-1916; Michael J. Gallagher, 1916-18; Edward D. Kelly, 1919-26; Joseph G. Pinten, 1926-40; Joseph C. Plagens, 1941-43; Francis J. Haas, 1943-53; Allen J. Babcock, 1954-69; Joseph M. Breitenbeck, 1969-89.

Great Falls-Billings, Mont. (1904): Anthony M. Milone, bishop, 1988.
Established as Great Falls; name changed, 1980.
Former bishops: Mathias C. Lenihan, 1904-30; Edwin V. O'Hara, 1930-39; William J. Condon, 1939-67; Eldon B. Schuster, 1968-77; Thomas J. Murphy, 1978-87.

Green Bay, Wis. (1868): Robert J. Banks, bishop, 1990. Robert F. Morneau, auxiliary.
Former bishops: Joseph Melcher, 1868-73; Francis X. Krautbauer, 1875-85; Frederick X. Katzer, 1886-91; Sebastian G. Messmer, 1892-1903; Joseph J. Fox, 1904-14; Paul P. Rhode, 1915-45; Stanislaus V. Bona, 1945-67; Aloysius J. Wycislo, 1968-83; Adam J. Maida, 1984-90.

Greensburg, Pa. (1951): Anthony G. Bosco, bishop, 1987.
Former bishops: Hugh L. Lamb, 1951-59; Willam G. Connare, 1960-87.

Harrisburg, Pa. (1868): Nicholas C. Dattilo, bishop, 1990.
Former bishops: Jeremiah F. Shanahan, 1868-86; Thomas McGovern, 1888-98; John W. Shanahan, 1899-1916; Philip R. McDevitt, 1916-35; George L. Leech, 1935-71; Joseph T. Daley, 1971-83; William H. Keeler, 1984-89.

Hartford,* Conn. (1843; archdiocese, 1953): Daniel A. Cronin, archbishop, 1991, installed, 1992. Peter A. Rosazza, Christie A. Macaluso, auxiliaries.
Former ordinaries: William Tyler, 1844-49; Bernard O'Reilly, 1850-56; F. P. MacFarland, 1858-74; Thomas Galberry, O.S.A., 1876-78; Lawrence S. McMahon, 1879-93; Michael Tierney, 1894-1908; John J. Nilan, 1910-34; Maurice F. McAuliffe, 1934-44; Henry J. O'Brien, 1945-68, first archbishop; John F. Whealon, 1969-91.

Helena, Mont. (1884): Robert C. Morlino, 1999.
Former bishops: John B. Brondel, 1884-1903; John P. Carroll, 1904-25; George J. Finnigan, C.S.C., 1927-32; Ralph L. Hayes, 1933-35; Joseph M. Gilmore, 1936-62; Raymond Hunthausen, 1962-75; Elden F. Curtiss, 1976-93; Alexander J. Brunett, 1994-97.

Honolulu, Hawaii (1941): Francis X. DiLorenzo (apostolic administrator, 1993), bishop, 1994.

Former bishops: James J. Sweeney, 1941-68; John J. Scanlan, 1968-81; Joseph A. Ferrario, 1982-93.
Houma-Thibodaux, La. (1977): C. Michael Jarrell, bishop, 1993.
Former bishop: Warren L. Boudreaux, 1977-92.
Indianapolis,* Ind. (1834; archdiocese, 1944): Daniel M. Buechlein, O.S.B., archbishop, 1992.
Established at Vincennes, transferred, 1898.
Former ordinaries: Simon G. Bruté, 1834-39; Celestine de la Hailandiere, 1839-47; John S. Bazin, 1847-48; Maurice de St. Palais, 1849-77; Francis S. Chatard, 1878-1918; Joseph Chartrand, 1918-33; Joseph E. Ritter, 1934-46, first archbishop; Paul C. Schulte, 1946-70; George J. Biskup, 1970-79; Edward T. O'Meara, 1980-92.
Jackson, Miss. (1837): William R. Houck, bishop, 1984.
Established at Natchez; title changed to Natchez-Jackson, 1956; transferred to Jackson, 1977 (Natchez made titular see).
Former bishops: John J. Chanche, S.S., 1841-52; James Van de Velde, S.J., 1853-55; William H. Elder, 1857-80; Francis A. Janssens, 1881-88; Thomas Heslin, 1889-1911; John E. Gunn, S.M., 1911-24; Richard O. Gerow, 1924-67; Joseph B. Brunini, 1968-84.
Jefferson City, Mo. (1956): John R. Gaydos, bishop, 1997.
Former bishops: Joseph Marling, C.Pp.S., 1956-69; Michael F. McAuliffe, 1969-97.
Joliet, Ill. (1948): Joseph L. Imesch, bishop, 1979. Roger L. Kaffer, auxiliary.
Former bishops: Martin D. McNamara, 1949-66; Romeo Blanchette, 1966-79.
Juneau, Alaska (1951): Michael W. Warfel, bishop, 1996.
Former bishops: Dermot O'Flanagan, 1951-68; Joseph T. Ryan, administrator, 1968-71; Francis T. Hurley, 1971-76, administrator, 1976-79; Michael H. Kenny, 1979-95.
Kalamazoo, Mich. (1971): James A. Murray, bishop, 1997.
Former bishop: Paul V. Donovan, 1971-94; Alfred J. Markiewicz, 1995-97.
Kansas City,* Kans. (1877; archdiocese, 1952): James P. Keleher, archbishop, 1993.
Established as vicariate apostolic, 1850, became Diocese of Leavenworth, 1877, transferred to Kansas City 1947.
Former ordinaries: J. B. Miege, vicar apostolic, 1851-74; Louis M. Fink, O.S.B., vicar apostolic, 1874-77, first bishop, 1877-1904; Thomas F. Lillis, 1904-10; John Ward, 1910-29; Francis Johannes, 1929-37; Paul C. Schulte, 1937-46; George J. Donnelly, 1946-50; Edward Hunkeler, 1951-69, first archbishop; Ignatius J. Strecker, 1969-93.
Kansas City-St. Joseph, Mo. (Kansas City, 1880; St. Joseph, 1868; united 1956): Raymond J. Boland, bishop, 1993.
Former bishops: John J. Hogan, 1880-1913; Thomas F. Lillis, 1913-38; Edwin V. O'Hara, 1939-56; John P. Cody, 1956-61; Charles H. Helmsing, 1962-77; John J. Sullivan, 1977-93.
Former bishops (St. Joseph): John J. Hogan, 1868-80, administrator, 1880-93; Maurice F. Burke, 1893-1923; Francis Gilfillan, 1923-33; Charles H. Le Blond, 1933-56.

Knoxville, Tenn. (1988): vacant
Former bishops: Anthony J. O'Connell, bishop, 1988-98.
La Crosse, Wis. (1868): Raymond L. Burke, bishop, 1995.
Former bishops: Michael Heiss, 1868-80; Kilian C. Flasch, 1881-91; James Schwebach, 1892-1921; Alexander J. McGavick, 1921-48; John P. Treacy, 1948-64; Frederick W. Freking, 1965-83; John J. Paul, 1983-94.
Lafayette, Ind. (1944): William L. Higi, bishop, 1984.
Former bishops: John G. Bennett, 1944-57; John J. Carberry, 1957-65; Raymond J. Gallagher, 1965-82; George A. Fulcher, 1983-84.
Lafayette, La. (1918): Edward J. O'Donnell, bishop, 1994.
Former bishops: Jules B. Jeanmard, 1918-56; Maurice Schexnayder, 1956-72; Gerard L. Frey, 1973-89; Harry J. Flynn, 1989-94.
Lake Charles, La. (1980): Jude Speyrer, bishop, 1980.
Lansing, Mich. (1937): Carl F. Mengeling, bishop, 1995; installed 1996.
Former bishops: Joseph H. Albers, 1937-65; Alexander Zaleski, 1965-75; Kenneth J. Povish, 1975-95.
Las Cruces, N. Mex. (1982): Ricardo Ramirez, C.S.B., bishop, 1982.
Las Vegas, Nev. (1995): Daniel F. Walsh, bishop, 1995.
Formerly Reno-Las Vegas, 1976; made separate diocese 1995.
Lexington, Ky. (1988): James Kendrick Williams, bishop, 1988.
Lincoln, Neb. (1887): Fabian W. Bruskewitz, bishop, 1992.
Former bishops: Thomas Bonacum, 1887-1911; J. Henry Tihen, 1911-17; Charles J. O'Reilly, 1918-23; Francis J. Beckman, 1924-30; Louis B. Kucera, 1930-57; James V. Casey, 1957-67; Glennon P. Flavin, 1967-92.
Little Rock, Ark. (1843): Andrew J. McDonald, bishop, 1972.
Former bishops: Andrew Byrne, 1844-62; Edward Fitzgerald, 1867-1907; John Morris, 1907-46; Albert L. Fletcher, 1946-72.
Los Angeles,* Calif. (1840; archdiocese, 1936): Cardinal Roger M. Mahony, archbishop, 1985. Thomas J. Curry, Joseph M. Sartoris, Gerald E. Wilkerson, Gabino Zavala, auxiliaries.
Founded as diocese of Two Californias, 1840; became Monterey diocese, 1850; Baja California detached from Monterey diocese, 1852; title changed to Monterey-Los Angeles, 1859; Los Angeles-San Diego, 1922; became archdiocese under present title, 1936 (San Diego became separate see).
Former ordinaries: Francisco Garcia Diego y Moreno, O.F.M., 1840-46; Joseph S. Alemany, O.P., 1850-53; Thaddeus Amat, C.M., 1854-78; Francis Mora, 1878-96; George T. Montgomery, 1896-1903; Thomas J. Conaty, 1903-15; John J. Cantwell, 1917-47, first archbishop; Cardinal James McIntyre, 1948-70; Cardinal Timothy Manning, 1970-85.
Louisville,* Ky. (1808; archdiocese, 1937): Thomas C. Kelly, O.P., archbishop, 1982.
Established at Bardstown, transferred, 1841.

Former ordinaries: Benedict J. Flaget, S.S., 1810-32; John B. David, S.S., 1832-33; Benedict J. Flaget, S.S., 1833-50; Martin J. Spalding, 1850-64; Peter J. Lavialle, 1865-67; William G. McCloskey, 1868-1909; Denis O'Donaghue, 1910-24; John A. Floersh, 1924-67, first archbishop; Thomas J. McDonough, 1967-81.

Lubbock, Tex. (1983): Placido Rodriguez, C.M.F., bishop, 1994.

Former bishop: Michael J. Sheehan, 1983-93.

Madison, Wis. (1946): William H. Bullock, bishop, 1993. George O. Wirz, auxiliary.

Former bishops: William P. O'Connor, 1946-67; Cletus F. O'Donnell, 1967-92.

Manchester, N.H. (1884): John B. McCormack, bishop, 1998; Francis J. Christian, auxiliary.

Former bishops: Denis M. Bradley, 1884-1903; John B. Delany, 1904-06; George A. Guertin, 1907-32; John B. Peterson, 1932-44; Matthew F. Brady, 1944-59; Ernest J. Primeau, 1960-74; Odore J. Gendron, 1975-90; Leo E. O'Neil, 1990-97.

Marquette, Mich. (1857): James H. Garland, bishop, 1992.

Founded as Sault Ste. Marie and Marquette; changed to Marquette, 1937.

Former bishops: Frederic Baraga, 1857-68; Ignatius Mrak, 1869-78; John Vertin, 1879-99; Frederick Eis, 1899-1922; Paul J. Nussbaum, C.P., 1922-35; Joseph C. Plagens, 1935-40; Francis Magner, 1941-47; Thomas L. Noa, 1947-68; Charles A. Salatka, 1968-77; Mark F. Schmitt, 1978-92.

Memphis, Tenn. (1970): J. Terry Steib, S.V.D., bishop, 1993.

Former bishops: Carroll T. Dozier, 1971-82; J. Francis Stafford, 1982-86; Daniel M. Buechlein, O.S.B.,1987-92.

Metuchen, N.J. (1981): Vincent DePaul Breen, bishop, 1997.

Former bishops: Theodore E. McCarrick, 1981-86; Edward T. Hughes, 1987-97.

Miami,* Fla. (1958; archdiocese, 1968): John C. Favalora, archbishop, 1994. Agustin A. Roman, Gilberto Fernandez, Thomas G. Wenski, auxiliaries.

Former ordinaries: Coleman F. Carroll, 1958-77, first archbishop; Edward A. McCarthy, 1977-94.

Milwaukee,* Wis. (1843; archdiocese, 1875): Rembert G. Weakland, O.S.B., archbishop, 1977. Richard J. Sklba, auxiliary.

Former ordinaries: John M. Henni, 1844-81, first archbishop; Michael Heiss, 1881-90; Frederick X. Katzer, 1891-1903; Sebastian G. Messmer, 1903-30; Samuel A. Stritch, 1930-39; Moses E. Kiley, 1940-53; Albert G. Meyer, 1953-58; William E. Cousins, 1959-77.

Mobile,* Ala. (1829; archdiocese, 1980): Oscar H. Lipscomb, first archbishop, 1980.

Founded as Mobile, 1829; title changed to Mobile-Birmingham, 1954; redesignated Mobile, 1969.

Former bishops: Michael Portier, 1829-59; John Quinlan, 1859-83; Dominic Manucy, 1884; Jeremiah O'Sullivan, 1885-96; Edward P. Allen, 1897-1926; Thomas J. Toolen, 1927-69; John L. May, 1969-80.

Monterey in California (1967): Sylvester D. Ryan, bishop, 1992.

Formerly Monterey-Fresno, 1922. (Originally established in 1850, see Los Angeles listing.)

Former bishops (Monterey-Fresno): John J.

Cantwell, administrator, 1922-24; John B. MacGinley, first bishop, 1924-32; Philip G. Sher, 1933-53; Aloysius J. Willinger, 1953-67.

Former bishops (Monterey): Harry A. Clinch, 1967-82; Thaddeus A. Shubsda, 1982-91.

Nashville, Tenn. (1837): Edward U. Kmiec, bishop, 1992.

Former bishops: Richard P. Miles, O.P., 1838-60; James Whelan, O.P., 1860-64; Patrick A. Feehan, 1865-80; Joseph Rademacher, 1883-93; Thomas S. Byrne, 1894-1923; Alphonse J. Smith, 1924-35; William L. Adrian, 1936-69; Joseph A. Durick, 1969-75; James D. Niedergeses, 1975-92.

Newark,* N.J. (1853; archdiocese, 1937): Theodore E. McCarrick, archbishop, 1986. Dominic A. Marconi, David Arias, O.A.R., Charles J. McDonnell, Paul G. Bootkoski, auxiliaries.

Former ordinaries: James R. Bayley, 1853-72; Michael A. Corrigan, 1873-80; Winand M. Wigger, 1881-1901; John J. O'Connor, 1901-27; Thomas J. Walsh, 1928-52, first archbishop; Thomas A. Boland, 1953-74; Peter L. Gerety, 1974-86.

New Orleans,* La. (1793; archdiocese, 1850): Francis B. Schulte, archbishop, 1988; installed, 1989. Dominic Carmon, S.V.D., Gregory M. Aymond, auxiliaries.

Former ordinaries: Luis Penalver y Cardenas, 1793-1801; John Carroll, administrator, 1805-15; W. Louis Dubourg, S.S., 1815-25; Joseph Rosati, C.M., administrator, 1826-29; Leo De Neckere, C.M., 1829-33; Anthony Blanc, 1835-60, first archbishop; Jean Marie Odin, C.M., 1861-70; Napoleon J. Perche, 1870-83; Francis X. Leray, 1883-87; Francis A. Janssens, 1888-97; Placide L. Chapelle, 1897-1905; James H. Blenk, S.M., 1906-17; John W. Shaw, 1918-34; Joseph F. Rummel, 1935-64; John P. Cody, 1964-65; Philip M. Hannan, 1965-88.

Newton, Mass. (Melkite) (1966; eparchy, 1976): John A. Elya, B.S.O., eparch, 1993; installed, 1994. Nicholas Samra, auxiliary.

Former ordinaries: Justin Najmy, exarch, 1966-68; Joseph Tawil, exarch, 1969-76, first eparch, 1976-89; Ignatius Ghattas, B.S.O., 1990-92.

New Ulm, Minn. (1957): Raymond A. Lucker, bishop, 1975; installed, 1976.

Former bishop: Alphonse J. Schladweiler, 1958-75.

New York,* N.Y. (1808; archdiocese, 1850): Cardinal John J. O'Connor, archbishop, 1984. Anthony F. Mestice, Austin B. Vaughan, Francisco Garmendia, William J. McCormack, Patrick J. Sheridan, Robert A. Brucato, Jame F. McCarthy, auxiliaries.

Former ordinaries: Richard L. Concanen, O.P., 1808-10; John Connolly, O.P., 1814-25; John Dubois, S.S., 1826-42; John J. Hughes, 1842-64, first archbishop; Cardinal John McCloskey, 1864-85; Michael A. Corrigan, 1885-1902; Cardinal John Farley, 1902-18; Cardinal Patrick Hayes, 1919-38; Cardinal Francis Spellman, 1939-67; Cardinal Terence J. Cooke, 1968-83.

Norwich, Conn. (1953): Daniel A. Hart, bishop, 1995.

Former bishops: Bernard J. Flanagan, 1953-59; Vincent J. Hines, 1960-75; Daniel P. Reilly, 1975-94.

Oakland, Calif. (1962): John S. Cummins, bishop, 1977.

Former bishop: Floyd L. Begin, 1962-77.

Ogdensburg, N.Y. (1872): vacant.

Former bishops: Edgar P. Wadhams, 1872-91; Henry Gabriels, 1892-1921; Joseph H. Conroy, 1921-39; Francis J. Monaghan, 1939-42; Bryan J. McEntegart, 1943-53; Walter P. Kellenberg, 1954-57; James J. Navagh, 1957-63; Leo R. Smith, 1963; Thomas A. Donnellan, 1964-68; Stanislaus J. Brzana, 1968-93; Paul S. Loverde, 1993-99.

Oklahoma City,* Okla. (1905; archdiocese, 1972): Eusebius J. Beltran, archbishop, 1993.

Former ordinaries: Theophile Meerschaert, 1905-24; Francis C. Kelley, 1924-48; Eugene J. McGuinness, 1948-57; Victor J. Reed, 1958-71; John R. Quinn, 1971-77, first archbishop; Charles A. Salatka, 1977-92.

Omaha,* Nebr. (1885; archdiocese, 1945): Elden F. Curtiss, archbishop, 1993.

Former ordinaries: James O'Gorman, O.C.S.O., 1859-74, vicar apostolic; James O'Connor, vicar apostolic, 1876-85, first bishop, 1885-90; Richard Scannell, 1891-1916; Jeremiah J. Harty, 1916-27; Francis Beckman, administrator, 1926-28; Joseph F. Rummel, 1928-35; James H. Ryan, 1935-47, first archbishop; Gerald T. Bergan, 1948-69; Daniel E. Sheehan, 1969-93.

Orange, Calif. (1976): Tod D. Brown, bishop, 1998. Former bishop: William R. Johnson, 1976-86. Norman F. McFarland, 1986-98.

Orlando, Fla. (1968): Norbert M. Dorsey, C.P., bishop, 1990.

Former bishops: William Borders, 1968-74; Thomas J. Grady, 1974-89.

Our Lady of Deliverance of Newark (for Syrian-rite Catholics of the U.S. and Canada) (1995): Joseph Younan, bishop, 1996.

Our Lady of Lebanon of Los Angeles, Calif. (Maronite) (1994): John G. Chedid, eparch, 1994.

Owensboro, Ky. (1937): John J. McRaith, bishop, 1982.

Former bishops: Francis R. Cotton, 1938-60, Henry J. Soenneker, 1961-82.

Palm Beach, Fla. (1984): Anthony J. O'Connell, bishop, 1998.

Former bishop: Thomas V. Daily, 1984-90; J. Keith Symons, 1990-98.

Parma, Ohio (Byzantine, Ruthenian) (1969): Basil Schott, O.F.M., bishop, 1996.

Former bishops: Emil Mihalik, 1969-84; Andrew Pataki, 1984-95.

Passaic, N.J. (Byzantine, Ruthenian) (1963): Andrew Pataki, eparch, 1996.

Former bishops: Stephen Kocisko, 1963-68; Michael J. Dudick, 1968-95.

Paterson, N.J. (1937): Frank J. Rodimer, bishop, 1978.

Former bishops: Thomas H. McLaughlin, 1937-47; Thomas A. Boland, 1947-52; James A. McNulty, 1953-63; James J. Navagh, 1963-65; Lawrence B. Casey, 1966-77.

Pensacola-Tallahassee, Fla. (1975): John H. Ricard, S.S.J., bishop, 1997.

Former bishops: Rene H. Gracida, 1975-83; J. Keith Symons, 1983-90; John M. Smith, 1991-95.

Peoria, Ill. (1877): John J. Myers, bishop, 1990.

Former bishops: John L. Spalding, 1877-1908; Edmund M. Dunne, 1909-29; Joseph H. Schlarman, 1930-51; William E. Cousins, 1952-58; John B. Franz, 1959-71; Edward W. O'Rourke, 1971- 90.

Philadelphia,* Pa. (1808; archdiocese, 1875): Cardinal Anthony J. Bevilacqua, archbishop, 1988. Edward P. Cullen, Robert P. Maginnis, Joseph F. Martino, auxiliaries.

Former ordinaries: Michael Egan, O.F.M., 1810-14; Henry Conwell, 1820-42; Francis P. Kenrick, 1842-51; John N. Neumann, C.SS.R., 1852-60; James F. Wood, 1860-83, first archbishop; Patrick J. Ryan, 1884-1911; Edmond F. Prendergast, 1911-18; Cardinal Dennis Dougherty, 1918-51; Cardinal John O'Hara, C.S.C., 1951-60; Cardinal John Krol, 1961-88.

Philadelphia,* Pa. (Byzantine, Ukrainian) (1924; metropolitan, 1958): Stephen Sulyk, archbishop, 1981. Walter Paska, auxiliary.

Former ordinaries: Stephen Ortynsky, O.S.B.M., 1907-16; Constantine Bohachevsky, 1924-61; Ambrose Senyshyn, O.S.B.M., 1961-76; Joseph Schmondiuk, 1977-78; Myroslav J. Lubachivsky, 1979-80, apostolic administrator, 1980-81.

Phoenix, Ariz. (1969): Thomas J. O'Brien, bishop, 1982.

Former bishops: Edward A. McCarthy, 1969-76; James S. Rausch, 1977-81.

Pittsburgh,* Pa. (Byzantine, Ruthenian) (1924; metropolitan, 1969): Judson M. Procyk, archbishop, 1995.

Former ordinaries: Basil Takach 1924-48; Daniel Ivancho, 1948-54; Nicholas T. Elko, 1955-67; Stephen J. Kocisko, 1968-91, first metropolitan; Thomas V. Dolinay, 1991-93.

Pittsburgh, Pa. (1843): Donald W. Wuerl, bishop, 1988. William J. Winter, David A. Zubic, auxiliaries.

Former bishops: Michael O'Connor, 1843-53, 1854-60; Michael Domenec, C.M., 1860-76; J. Tuigg, 1876-89; Richard Phelan, 1889-1904; J.F. Regis Canevin, 1904-20; Hugh C. Boyle, 1921-50; John F. Dearden, 1950-58; John J. Wright, 1959-69; Vincent M. Leonard, 1969-83; Anthony J. Bevilacqua, 1983-88.

Portland, Me. (1853): Joseph J. Gerry, O.S.B., bishop, 1989. Michael R. Cote, auxiliary.

Former bishops: David W. Bacon, 1855-74; James A. Healy, 1875-1900; William H. O'Connell, 1901-06; Louis S. Walsh, 1906-24; John G. Murray, 1925-31; Joseph E. McCarthy, 1932-55; Daniel J. Feeney, 1955-69; Peter L. Gerety, 1969-74; Edward C. O'Leary, 1974-88.

Portland,* Ore. (1846): John G. Vlazny, archbishop, 1997. Kenneth D. Steiner, auxiliary.

Established as Oregon City, name changed, 1928.

Former ordinaries: Francis N. Blanchet, 1846-80 vicar apostolic, first archbishop; Charles J. Seghers, 1880-84; William H. Gross, C.SS.R., 1885-98; Alexander Christie, 1899-1925; Edward D. Howard, 1926-66; Robert J. Dwyer, 1966-74; Cornelius M. Power, 1974-86; William J. Levada, 1986-95; Francis E. George, 1996-97.

Providence, R.I. (1872): Robert E. Mulvee, bishop, 1997. Robert McManus, auxiliary.

Former bishops: Thomas F. Hendricken, 1872-86; Matthew Harkins, 1887-1921; William A. Hickey, 1921-33; Francis P. Keough, 1934-47; Russell J. McVinney, 1948-71; Louis E. Gelineau, 1972-97.

Pueblo, Colo. (1941): Arthur N. Tafoya, bishop, 1980.

Former bishops: Joseph C. Willging, 1942-59; Charles A. Buswell, 1959-79.

Raleigh, N.C. (1924): F. Joseph Gossman, bishop, 1975.

Former bishops: William J. Hafey, 1925-37; Eugene J. McGuinness, 1937-44; Vincent S. Waters, 1945-75.

Rapid City, S. Dak. (1902): Blase Cupich, bishop, 1998.

Established at Lead, transferred, 1930.

Former bishops: John Stariha, 1902-09; Joseph F. Busch, 1910-15; John J. Lawler, 1916-48; William T. McCarty, C.SS.R., 1948-69; Harold J. Dimmerling, 1969-87; Charles J. Chaput, O.F.M. Cap., 1988-97.

Reno, Nev. (1931): Phillip F. Straling, bishop, 1995.

Established at Reno, 1931; title changed to Reno-Las Vegas, 1976; redesignated Reno, 1995, when Las Vegas was made a separate diocese.

Former bishops (Reno/Reno-Las Vegas): Thomas K. Gorman, 1931-52; Robert J. Dwyer, 1952-66; Joseph Green, 1967-74; Norman F. McFarland, 1976-86; Daniel F. Walsh, 1987-95.

Richmond, Va. (1820): Walter F. Sullivan, bishop, 1974.

Former bishops: Patrick Kelly, 1820-22; Ambrose Marechal, S.S., administrator, 1822-28; James Whitfield, administrator, 1828-34; Samuel Eccleston, S.S., administrator, 1834-40; Richard V. Whelan, 1841-50; John McGill, 1850-72; James Gibbons, 1872-77; John J. Keane, 1878-88; Augustine Van de Vyver, 1889-1911; Denis J. O'Connell, 1912-26; Andrew J. Brennan, 1926-45; Peter L. Ireton, 1945-58; John J. Russell, 1958-73.

Rochester, N.Y. (1868): Matthew H. Clark, bishop, 1979.

Former bishops: Bernard J. McQuaid, 1868-1909; Thomas F. Hickey, 1909-28; John F. O'Hern, 1929-33; Edward F. Mooney, 1933-37; James E. Kearney, 1937-66; Fulton J. Sheen, 1966-69; Joseph L. Hogan, 1969-78.

Rockford, Ill. (1908): Thomas G. Doran, bishop, 1994.

Former bishops: Peter J. Muldoon, 1908-27; Edward F. Hoban, 1928-42; John J. Boylan, 1943-53; Raymond P. Hillinger, 1953-56; Loras T. Lane, 1956-68; Arthur J. O'Neill, 1968-94.

Rockville Centre, N.Y. (1957): John R. McGann, bishop, 1976. James McHugh, coadjutor. John C. Dunne, Emil A. Wcela, auxiliaries.

Former bishop: Walter P. Kellenberg, 1957-76.

Sacramento, Calif. (1886): William K. Weigand, bishop, 1993; installed, 1994. Richard J. Garcia, auxiliary.

Former bishops: Patrick Manogue, 1886-95; Thomas Grace, 1896-1921; Patrick J. Keane, 1922-28; Robert J. Armstrong, 1929-57; Joseph T. McGucken, 1957-62; Alden J. Bell, 1962-79; Francis A. Quinn, 1979-93.

Saginaw, Mich. (1938): Kenneth E. Untener, bishop, 1980.

Former bishops: William F. Murphy, 1938-50; Stephen S. Woznicki, 1950-68; Francis F. Reh, 1969-80.

St. Augustine, Fla. (1870): John J. Snyder, bishop, 1979.

Former bishops: Augustin Verot, S.S., 1870-76; John Moore, 1877-1901; William J. Kenny, 1902-13; Michael J. Curley, 1914-21; Patrick J. Barry, 1922-40; Joseph P. Hurley, 1940-67; Paul F. Tanner, 1968-79.

St. Cloud, Minn. (1889): John F. Kinney, bishop, 1995.

Former bishops: Otto Zardetti, 1889-94; Martin Marty, O.S.B., 1895-96; James Trobec, 1897-1914; Joseph F. Busch, 1915-53; Peter Bartholome, 1953-68; George H. Speltz, 1968-87; Jerome Hanus, O.S.B.,1987-94.

St. George's in Canton, Ohio (Byzantine, Romanian) (1982; eparchy, 1987): John Michael Botean, bishop, 1996.

Former bishop: Vasile Louis Puscas, 1983-93.

St. Josaphat in Parma, Ohio (Byzantine, Ukrainians) (1983): Robert M. Moskal, bishop, 1984.

St. Louis,* Mo. (1826; archdiocese, 1847): Justin F. Rigali, archbishop, 1994. Edward K. Braxton, Joseph F. Naumann, Michael J. Sheridan, auxiliaries.

Former ordinaries: Joseph Rosati, C.M., 1827-43; Peter R. Kenrick, 1843-95, first archbishop; John J. Kain, 1895-1903; Cardinal John Glennon, 1903-46; Cardinal Joseph Ritter, 1946-67; Cardinal John J. Carberry, 1968-79; John L. May, 1980-92.

St. Maron, Brooklyn, N.Y. (Maronite) (1966; diocese, 1971): Hector Y. Doueihi, eparch, 1997.

Established at Detroit; transferred to Brooklyn, 1977.

Former eparch: Francis Zayek, exarch 1966-72, first eparch 1972-97

St. Nicholas in Chicago (Byzantine Eparchy of St. Nicholas of the Ukrainians) (1961): Michael Wiwchar, C.SS.R., bishop, 1993.

Former bishops: Jaroslav Gabro, 1961-80; Innocent H. Lotocky, O.S.B.M., 1981-93.

St. Paul and Minneapolis,* Minn. (1850; archdiocese, 1888): Harry J. Flynn, archbishop, 1995. Frederick F. Campbell, auxiliary.

Former ordinaries: Joseph Cretin, 1851-57; Thomas L. Grace, O.P., 1859-84; John Ireland, 1884-1918, first archbishop; Austin Dowling, 1919-30; John G. Murray, 1931-56; William O. Brady, 1956-61; Leo Binz, 1962-75; John R. Roach, 1975-95.

St. Petersburg, Fla. (1968): Robert N. Lynch, bishop, 1996.

Former bishops: Charles McLaughlin, 1968-78; W. Thomas Larkin, 1979-88; John C. Favalora, 1989-94.

St. Thomas the Apostle of Detroit (Chaldean) (1982; eparchy, 1985): Ibrahim N. Ibrahim, exarch, 1982; first eparch, 1985.

Salina, Kans. (1887): George K. Fitzsimons, bishop, 1984.

Established at Concordia, transferred, 1944.

Former bishops: Richard Scannell, 1887-91; John F. J. Hennessy, administrator, 1891-98; John F. Cunningham, 1898-1919; Francis J. Tief, 1921-38; Frank A. Thill, 1938-57; Frederick W. Freking, 1957-64; Cyril J. Vogel, 1965-79; Daniel W. Kucera, O.S.B., 1980-84.

Salt Lake City, Utah (1891): George H. Niederauer, bishop, 1995.

Former bishops: Lawrence Scanlan, 1891-1915; Joseph S. Glass, C.M., 1915-26; John J. Mitty, 1926-32; James E. Kearney, 1932-37; Duane G. Hunt, 1937-60; J. Lennox Federal, 1960-80; William K. Weigand, 1980-93.

San Angelo, Tex. (1961): Michael D. Pfeifer, O.M.I., bishop, 1985.

Former bishops: Thomas J. Drury, 1962-65; Thomas Tschoepe, 1966-69; Stephen A. Leven, 1969-79; Joseph A. Fiorenza, 1979-84.

San Antonio,* Tex. (1874; archdiocese, 1926): Patrick F. Flores, archbishop, 1979. Thomas J. Flanagan, Patrick J. Zurek, auxiliaries.

Former ordinaries: Anthony D. Pellicer, 1874-80; John C. Neraz, 1881-94; John A. Forest, 1895-1911; John W. Shaw, 1911-18; Arthur Jerome Drossaerts, 1918-40, first archbishop; Robert E. Lucey, 1941-69; Francis Furey, 1969-79.

San Bernardino, Calif. (1978): Gerald R. Barnes, bishop, 1995.

Former bishop: Phillip F. Straling, 1978-95.

San Diego, Calif. (1936): Robert H. Brom, bishop, 1990. Gilbert Espinoza Chavez, auxiliary.

Former bishops: Charles F. Buddy, 1936-66; Francis J. Furey, 1966-69; Leo T. Maher, 1969-90.

San Francisco,* Calif. (1853): William J. Levada, archbishop, 1995. John C. Wester, auxiliary.

Former ordinaries: Joseph S. Alemany, O.P., 1853-84; Patrick W. Riordan, 1884-1914; Edward J. Hanna, 1915-35; John Mitty, 1935-61; Joseph T. McGucken, 1962-77; John R. Quinn, 1977-95.

San Jose, Calif. (1981): R. Pierre DuMaine, first bishop, 1981-98. Patrick J. McGrath, co-adjutor.

Santa Fe*, N. Mex. (1850; archdiocese, 1875): Michael J. Sheehan, archbishop, 1993.

Former ordinaries: John B. Lamy, 1850-85; first archbishop; John B. Salpointe, 1885-94; Placide L. Chapelle, 1894-97; Peter Bourgade, 1899-1908; John B. Pitaval, 1909-18; Albert T. Daeger, O.F.M., 1919-32; Rudolph A. Gerken, 1933-43; Edwin V. Byrne, 1943-63; James P. Davis, 1964-74; Robert F. Sanchez, 1974-93.

Santa Rosa, Calif. (1962): vacant.

Former bishops: Leo T. Maher, 1962-69; Mark J. Hurley, 1969-86; John T. Steinbock, 1987-91; G. Patrick Ziemann, 1992-99.

Savannah, Ga. (1850): John Kevin Boland, bishop, 1995.

Former bishops: Francis X. Gartland, 1850-54; John Barry, 1857-59; Augustin Verot, S.S., 1861-70; Ignatius Persico, O.F.M. Cap., 1870-72; William H. Gross, C.SS.R., 1873-85; Thomas A. Becker, 1886-99; Benjamin J. Keiley, 1900-22; Michael Keyes, S.M., 1922-35; Gerard P. O'Hara, 1935-59; Thomas J. McDonough, 1960-67; Gerard L. Frey, 1967-72; Raymond W. Lessard, 1973-95.

Scranton, Pa. (1868): James C. Timlin, bishop, 1984. John M. Dougherty, auxiliary.

Former bishops: William O'Hara, 1868-99; Michael J. Hoban, 1899-1926; Thomas C. O'Reilly, 1928-38; William J. Hafey, 1938-54; Jerome D. Hannan, 1954-65; J. Carroll McCormick, 1966-83; John J. O'Connor, 1983-84.

Seattle,* Wash. (1850; archdiocese, 1951): Alexander J. Brunett, archbishop, 1997.

Established as Nesqually, name changed, 1907.

Former ordinaries: Augustin M. Blanchet, 1850-79; Aegidius Junger, 1879-95; Edward J. O'Dea, 1896-1932; Gerald Shaughnessy, S.M., 1933-50; Thomas A. Connolly, first archbishop, 1950-75; Raymond G. Hunthausen, 1975-91; Thomas J. Murphy, 1991-97.

Shreveport, La. (1986): William B. Friend, bishop, 1986.

Sioux City, Ia. (1902): Daniel N. DiNardo, bishop, 1998.

Former bishops: Philip J. Garrigan, 1902-19; Edmond Heelan, 1919-48; Joseph M. Mueller, 1948-70; Frank H. Greteman, 1970-83; Lawrence D. Soens, 1983-98.

Sioux Falls, S. Dak. (1889): Robert J. Carlson, bishop, 1995.

Former bishops: Martin Marty, O.S.B., 1889-94; Thomas O'Gorman, 1896-1921; Bernard J. Mahoney, 1922-39; William O. Brady, 1939-56; Lambert A. Hoch, 1956-78; Paul V. Dudley, 1978-95.

Spokane, Wash. (1913): William S. Skylstad, bishop, 1990.

Former bishops: Augustine F. Schinner, 1914-25; Charles D. White, 1927-55; Bernard J. Topel, 1955-78; Lawrence H. Welsh, 1978-90.

Springfield, Ill. (1853): Daniel L. Ryan, bishop, 1984.

Established at Quincy, transferred to Alton 1857; transferred to Springfield 1923.

Former bishops: Henry D. Juncker, 1857-68; Peter J. Baltes, 1870-86; James Ryan, 1888-1923; James A. Griffin, 1924-48; William A. O'Connor, 1949-75; Joseph A. McNicholas, 1975-83.

Springfield, Mass. (1870): Thomas L. Dupre, bishop, 1995.

Former bishops: Patrick T. O'Reilly, 1870-92; Thomas D. Beaven, 1892-1920; Thomas M. O'Leary, 1921-49; Christopher J. Weldon, 1950-77; Joseph F. Maguire, 1977-91; John A. Marshall, 1991-94.

Springfield-Cape Girardeau, Mo. (1956): John J. Leibrecht, bishop, 1984.

Former bishops: Charles Helmsing, 1956-62; Ignatius J. Strecker, 1962-69; William Baum, 1970-73; Bernard F. Law, 1973-84.

Stamford, Conn. (Byzantine, Ukrainian) (1956): Basil Losten, eparch, 1977.

Former eparchs: Ambrose Senyshyn, O.S.B.M., 1956-61; Joseph Schmondiuk, 1961-77.

Steubenville, Ohio (1944): Gilbert I. Sheldon, bishop, 1992.

Former bishops: John K. Mussio, 1945-77; Albert H. Ottenweller, 1977-92.

Stockton, Calif. (1962): Stephen E. Blaire, bishop, 1999.

Former bishops: Hugh A. Donohoe, 1962-69; Merlin J. Guilfoyle, 1969-79; Roger M. Mahony, 1980-85; Donald W. Montrose, 1986-99.

Superior, Wis. (1905): Raphael M. Fliss, bishop, 1985.

Former bishops: Augustine F. Schinner, 1905-13; Joseph M. Koudelka, 1913-21; Joseph G. Pinten, 1922-26; Theodore M. Reverman, 1926-41; William P. O'Connor, 1942-46; Albert G. Meyer, 1946-53; Joseph Annabring, 1954-59; George A. Hammes, 1960-85.

Syracuse, N.Y. (1886): James M. Moynihan, bishop, 1995. Thomas J. Costello, auxiliary.

Former bishops: Patrick A. Ludden, 1887-1912; John Grimes, 1912-22; Daniel J. Curley, 1923-32; John A. Duffy, 1933-37; Walter A. Foery, 1937-70; David F. Cunningham, 1970-76; Frank J. Harrison, 1976-87; Joseph T. O'Keefe, 1987-95.

Toledo, Ohio (1910): James R. Hoffman, bishop, 1980. Robert W. Donnelly, auxiliary.

Former bishops: Joseph Schrembs, 1911-21; Samuel A. Stritch, 1921-30; Karl J. Alter, 1931-50; George J. Rehring, 1950-67; John A. Donovan, 1967-80.

Trenton, N.J. (1881): John M. Smith, bishop, 1997.
Former bishops: Michael J. O'Farrell, 1881-94; James A. McFaul, 1894-1917; Thomas J. Walsh, 1918-28; John J. McMahon, 1928-32; Moses E. Kiley, 1934-40; William A. Griffin, 1940-50; George W. Ahr, 1950-79; John C. Reiss, 1980 -97.

Tucson, Ariz. (1897): Manuel D. Moreno, bishop, 1982.
Former bishops: Peter Bourgade, 1897-99; Henry Granjon, 1900-22; Daniel J. Gercke, 1923-60; Francis J. Green, 1960-81.

Tulsa, Okla. (1972): Edward J. Slattery, bishop, 1993.
Former bishops: Bernard J. Ganter, 1973-77; Eusebius J. Beltran, 1978-92.

Tyler, Tex. (1986): Edmond Carmody, bishop, 1992.
Former bishop: Charles E. Herzig, 1987-91.

Van Nuys, Calif. (Byzantine, Ruthenian) (1981): George M. Kuzma, eparch, 1991.
Former bishop: Thomas V. Dolinay, 1982-90.

Venice, Fla. (1984): John J. Nevins, bishop, 1984.

Victoria, Tex. (1982): David E. Fellhauer, bishop, 1990.
Former bishop: Charles V. Grahmann, 1982-89.

Washington,* D.C. (1939): Cardinal James A. Hickey, archbishop, 1980. Alvaro Corrada del Rio, S.J., Leonard Olivier, S.V.D., William E. Lori, auxiliaries.
Former ordinaries: Michael J. Curley, 1939-47; Cardinal Patrick O'Boyle, 1948-73; Cardinal William Baum, 1973-80.

Wheeling-Charleston, W. Va. (1850): Bernard W. Schmitt, bishop, 1989.
Established as Wheeling; name changed, 1974.
Former bishops: Richard V. Whelan, 1850-74; John J. Kain, 1875-93; Patrick J. Donahue, 1894-1922; John J. Swint, 1922-62; Joseph H. Hodges, 1962-85; Francis B. Schulte, 1985-88.

Wichita, Kans. (1887): Eugene J. Gerber, bishop, 1982, installed, 1983; Thomas J. Olmsted, coadjutor bishop, 1999.
Former bishops: John J. Hennessy, 1888-1920; Augustus J. Schwertner, 1921-39; Christian H. Winkelmann, 1940-46; Mark K. Carroll, 1947-67; David M. Maloney, 1967-82.

Wilmington, Del. (1868): Michael A. Saltarelli, bishop, 1995.

Former bishops: Thomas A. Becker, 1868-86; Alfred A. Curtis, 1886-96; John J. Monaghan, 1897-1925; Edmond Fitzmaurice, 1925-60; Michael Hyle, 1960-67; Thomas J. Mardaga, 1968-84; Robert E. Mulvee, 1985-95.

Winona, Minn. (1889): Bernard J. Harrington, 1998.
Former bishops: Joseph B. Cotter, 1889-1909; Patrick R. Heffron, 1910-27; Francis M. Kelly, 1928-49; Edward A. Fitzgerald, 1949-69; Loras J. Watters, 1969-86; John G. Vlazny, 1987-97.

Worcester, Mass. (1950): Daniel P. Reilly, bishop, 1994.George E. Rueger, auxiliary.
Former bishops: John J. Wright, 1950-59; Bernard J. Flanagan, 1959-83; Timothy J. Harrington, 1983-94.

Yakima, Wash. (1951):Carlos A. Sevilla, S.J., bishop, 1996
Former bishops: Joseph P. Dougherty, 1951-69; Cornelius M. Power, 1969-74; Nicolas E. Walsh, 1974-76; William S. Skylstad, 1977-90; Francis E. George, O.M.I., 1990-96.

Youngstown, Ohio (1943): Thomas J. Tobin, bishop, 1995; installed 1996.Former bishops: James A. McFadden, 1943-52; Emmet M. Walsh, 1952-68; James W. Malone, 1968-95.

Apostolic Exarchate for Armenian Catholics in the United States and Canada, New York, N.Y. (1981): Hovhannes Tertzakian, O.M. Ven., exarch, 1995.
Former exarch: Nerses Mikael Setian, 1981-93.

Archdiocese for the Military Services, U.S.A., Washington, D.C. (1957; restructured, 1985): Archbishop Edwin F. O'Brien, military ordinary, 1997. Francis X. Roque, Joseph J. Madera, M.Pp.S., John J. Glynn, auxiliaries.
Military vicar appointed, 1917; canonically established, 1957, as U.S. Military Vicariate under jurisdiction of New York archbishop; name changed, restructured as independent jurisdiction, 1985.
Former military vicars: Cardinal Patrick Hayes, 1917-38; Cardinal Francis Spellman, 1939-67; Cardinal Terence J. Cooke, 1968-83; Cardinal John J. O'Connor, apostolic administrator, 1984-85.
Former military ordinaries: Archbishop Joseph T. Ryan, 1985-91; Joseph T. Dimino, 1991-97.
(Note: For coverage of Missionary Bishops, see under Missionary Activity of the Church of the U.S.)

CHANCERY OFFICES OF U.S. ARCHDIOCESES AND DIOCESES

A chancery office, under this or another title, is the central administrative office of an archdiocese or diocese. (Archdioceses are indicated by asterisk.)

Albany, NY: Pastoral Center, 40 N. Main Ave. 12203.

Alexandria, LA: The Chancery Office, P.O. Box 7417. 71306.

Allentown, PA: The Chancery Office, 202 N. 17th St., P.O. Box F. 18105-1538.

Altoona-Johnstown, PA: The Chancery, 126 Logan Blvd., Hollidaysburg. 16648.

Amarillo, TX: Paastoral Center, P.O. Box 5644. 79117-5644.

Anchorage,* AK: The Chancery Office, 225 Cordova St., Anchorage 99501.

Arlington, VA: The Chancery Office, Suite 704, 200 N. Glebe Rd. 22203-3728.

Atlanta,* GA: Catholic Center, 680 W. Peachtree St. N.W. 30308.

Austin, TX: The Chancery Office, 1600 N. Congress Ave., P.O. Box 13327. 78711.

Baker, OR: Diocesan Pastoral Office, P.O. Box 5999, Bend. 97708.

Baltimore,* MD: The Chancery Office, 320 Cathedral St. 21201.

Baton Rouge, LA: Catholic Life Center, P.O. Box 2028. 70821-2028.

Beaumont, TX: Diocesan Pastoral Office, 703 Archie St., P.O. Box 3948. 77704-3948.

Belleville, IL: The Chancery, 222 S. Third St., 62220.

Biloxi, MS: The Chancery Office, P.O. Box 1189. 39533.

Birmingham, AL: St. Thomas Catholic Life Center, P.O. Box 12047. 35202-2047.

Bismarck, ND: The Chancery Office, 420 Raymond St., Box 1575. 58502-1575.

Boise, ID: The Chancery Office, 303 Federal Way. 83705-5925.

Boston,* MA: The Chancery Office, 2121 Commonwealth Ave., Brighton. 02135.

Bridgeport, CT: The Catholic Center, 238 Jewett Ave. 06606.

Brooklyn, NY: The Chancery Office, 75 Greene Ave., P.O. Box C. 11202.

Brownsville, TX: The Catholic Pastoral Center, P.O. Box 2279, 1910 E. Elizabeth St. 78522.

Buffalo, NY: The Chancery Office, 795 Main St. 14203.

Burlington, VT: The Chancery Office, 351 North Ave., P.O. Box 526. 05401-0526.

Camden, NJ: Camden Diocesan Center, 1845 Haddon Ave., P.O. Box 709, 08101.

Charleston, SC: The Chancery Office, 119 Broad St., P.O. Box 818. 29402.

Charlotte, NC: The Pastoral Center, P.O. Box 36776. 28236.

Cheyenne, WY: The Chancery Office, Box 426. 82003-0426.

Chicago,* IL: Pastoral Center, P.O. Box 1979. 60690.

Cincinnati,* OH: The Chancery Office, 100 E. 8th St. 45202.

Cleveland, OH: The Chancery Office, 1027 Superior Ave. 44114.

Colorado Springs, CO: The Chancery Office, 29 W. Kiowa. 80903.

Columbus, OH: The Chancery Office, 198 E. Broad St. 43215-3766.

Corpus Christi, TX: The Chancery Office, 620 Lipan St. P.O. Box 2620. 78403-2620.

Covington, KY: The Catholic Center, P.O. Box 18548, Erlanger 41018-0548.

Crookston, MN: The Chancery Office, 1200 Memorial Dr., P.O. Box 610. 56716.

Dallas, TX: The Chancery Office, 3725 Blackburn, P.O. Box 190507. 75219.

Davenport, IA: The Chancery Office, St. Vincent Center, 2706 N. Gaines St. 52804-1998.

Denver,* CO: Catholic Pastoral Center, 1300 South Steele St. 80210

Des Moines, IA: The Chancery Office, P.O. Box 1816. 50306.

Detroit,* MI: The Chancery Office, 1234 Washington Blvd. 48226.

Dodge City, KS: The Chancery Office, 910 Central Ave., P.O. Box 137. 67801.

Dubuque,* IA: The Chancery Office, P.O.Box 479. 52004-0479.

Duluth, MN: Pastoral Center, 2830 E. 4th St. 55812.

El Paso, TX: The Chancery Office, 499 St. Matthews St. 79907.

Erie, PA: St. Mark Cahtolic Center, P.O. Box 10397. 16514-0297.

Evansville, IN: The Chancery Office, P.O. Box 4169. 47724-0169.

Fairbanks, AK: The Chancery Office, 1316 Peger Rd. 99709.

Fall River, MA: The Chancery Office, Box 2577. 02722.

Fargo, ND: The Chancery Office, 1310 Broadway, Box 1750. 58107.

Fort Wayne-South Bend, IN: The Chancery Office, P.O. Box 390, Fort Wayne. 46801.

Fort Worth, TX: Catholic Center, 800 W. Loop 820 South. 76108.

Fresno, CA: The Chancery Office, 1550 N. Fresno St. 93703-3788.

Gallup, NM: The Chancery Office, 711 S. Puerco Dr., P.O. Box 1338. 87305.

Galveston-Houston, TX: The Chancery Office, P.O. Box 907. 77001.

Gary, IN: The Chancery Office, 9292 Broadway, Merrillville. 46410.

Gaylord, MI: Diocesan Pastoral Center, 1665 W. M-32. 49735.

Grand Island, NE: The Chancery Office, 311 W. 17th St., P.O. Box 996. 68802.

Grand Rapids, MI: The Chancery Office, 660 Burton St., S.E. 49507.

Great Falls-Billings, MT: The Chancery Office, P.O. Box 1399, Great Falls. 59403-1399.

Green Bay, WI: The Chancery Office, P.O. Box 23825. 54305-3825.

Greensburg, PA: The Chancery Office, 723 E. Pittsburgh St. 15601.

Harrisburg, PA: The Chancery Office, P.O. Box 2153. 17105.

Hartford,* CT: The Chancery Office, 134 Farmington Ave. 06105.

Helena, MT: The Chancery Office, 515 North Ewing, P.O. Box 1729. 59624-1729.

Honolulu, HI: The Chancery Office, 1184 Bishop St. 96813.

Houma-Thibodaux, LA: The Chancery Office, P.O. Box 9077, Houma, La. 70361.

Indianapolis,* IN: The Archbishop Edward T. O'Meara Catholic Center, 1400 N. Meridian St., P.O. Box 1410. 46206-1410.

Jackson, MS: The Chancery Office, 237 E. Amite St., P.O. Box 2248. 39225-2248.

Jefferson City, MO: Chancery Office, 605 Clark Ave., P.O. Box 417. 65102-0417.

Joliet, IL: The Chancery Office, 425 Summit St. 60435.

Juneau, AK: The Chancery Office, 419 6th St., No. 200. 99801.

Kalamazoo, MI: The Chancery Office, 215 N. Westnedge Ave. 49007.

Kansas City,* KS: The Chancery Office, 12615 Parallel Pkwy. 66109.

Kansas City-St. Joseph, MO: The Chancery Office, P.O. Box 419037, Kansas City. 64141-6037.

Knoxville, TN: The Chancery Office, 805 Northshore Dr., P.O. Box 11127. 37939-1127.

La Crosse, WI: The Chancery Office, 3710 East Ave. S., Box 4004. 54602-4004.

Lafayette in Indiana: The Bishop's Office, P.O. Box 260. 47902-0260.

Lafayette, LA: The Chancery Office, 1408 Carmel Ave. 70501.

Lake Charles, LA: The Chancery Office, P.O. Box 3223. 70602.

Lansing, MI: The Chancery Office, 300 W. Ottawa St. 48933-1577.

Las Cruces, NM: The Chancery Office, 1280 Med Park Dr., 88005.

Las Vegas, NV: Chancery Office, P.O. Box 18316. 89114-8316.

Lexington, KY: Catholic Center, P.O. Box 12350. 40582.

Lincoln, NE: The Chancery Office, P.O. Box 80328. 68501.

Little Rock, AR: The Chancery Office, 2415 N. Tyler St. P.O. Box 7239. 72217.

Los Angeles,* CA: Archdiocesan Catholic Center, 3424 Wilshire Blvd. 90010-2241.

Louisville,* Ky.: Chancery Office, 212 E. College St., P.O. Box 1073. 40201-1073.

Lubbock, TX: The Chancery Office, P.O. Box 98700. 79499.

Madison, WI: Bishop O'Connor Catholic Pastoral Center, P.O. Box 44983, 3577 High Point Road. 53744-4983.

Manchester, NH: The Chancery Office, 153 Ash St., P.O. Box 310. 03105.

Marquette, MI: The Chancery Office, 444 S. Fourth St., P.O. Box 550. 49855.

Memphis, TN: The Catholic Center, 5825 Shelby Oaks Dr., P.O. Box 341669. 38184-1669.

Metuchen, NJ: The Chancery Office, P.O. Box 191. 08840.

Miami,* FL: The Chancery Office, 9401 Biscayne Blvd., Miami Shores. 33138.

Milwaukee,* WI: The Chancery Office, P.O. Box 07912. 53207.

Mobile,* AL: The Chancery Office, 400 Government St., P.O. Box 1966. 36633.

Monterey, CA: The Chancery Office, P.O. Box 2048. 93942.

Nashville, TN: The Chancery Office, 2400 21st Ave. S. 37212-5387.

Newark,* NJ: Chancery Office, P.O. Box 9500. 07104-0500.

New Orleans,* LA: The Chancery Office, 7887 Walmsley Ave. 70125.

Newton, MA (Melkite): The Chancery Office, 19 Dartmouth St., W. Newton. 02165.

New Ulm, MN: Catholic Pastoral Center, 1400 Sixth St. N., 56073-2099.

New York,* NY: The Chancery Office, 1011 First Ave. 10022.

Norwich, CT: The Chancery Office, 201 Broadway, P.O. Box 587. 06360-0587.

Oakland, CA: The Chancery Office, 2900 Lakeshore Ave. 94610.

Ogdensburg, NY: The Chancery Office, 622 Washington St., P.O. Box 369. 13669.

Oklahoma City,* OK: The Chancery Office, P.O. Box 32180. 73123.

Omaha,* NE: The Chancery Office, 100 N. 62nd St. 68132.

Orange, CA: The Chancery Office, 2811 E. Villa Real Dr., P.O. Box 14195. 92613.

Orlando, FL: The Chancery Office, P.O. Box 1800. 32802-1800.

Our Lady of Deliverance of Newark, for Syrian rite Catholics of the U.S. and Canada: P.O. Box 8366, Union City, NJ 07087.

Our Lady of Lebanon of Los Angeles, CA (Maronite): The Chancery Office, P.O. Box 16397, Beverly Hills 90209.

Owensboro, KY: The Catholic Pastoral Center, 600 Locust St. 42301-2130.

Palm Beach, FL: The Chancery Office, P.O. Box 109650, Palm Beach Gardens 33410.

Parma, OH (Byzantine): The Chancery Office, 1900 Carlton Rd. 44134-3129.

Passaic, NJ (Byzantine): The Chancery Office, 445 Lackawanna Ave., W. Paterson. 07424.

Paterson, NJ: Diocesan Pastoral Center, 777 Valley Rd., Clifton. 07013.

Pensacola-Tallahassee, FL: Pastoral Center, P.O. Drawer 17329, Pensacola. 32522.

Peoria, IL: The Chancery Office, 607 N.E. Madison Ave., P.O. Box 1406. 61655.

Philadelphia,* PA: The Chancery Office, 222 N. 17th St. 19103.

Philadelphia,* PA (Byzantine): The Chancery Office, 827 N. Franklin St. 19123-2097.

Phoenix, AZ: The Chancery Office, 400 E. Monroe St. 85004.

Pittsburgh,* PA (Byzantine): The Chancery Office, 66 Riverview Ave. 15214.

Pittsburgh, PA: Pastoral Center, 111 Blvd. of the Allies. 15222-1618.

Portland, ME: The Chancery Office, 510 Ocean Ave., P.O. Box 11559. 04104.

Portland, OR*: Pastoral Center, 2838 E. Burnside St., Portland, OR 97214.

Providence, RI: The Chancery Office, One Cathedral Sq. 02903.

Pueblo, CO: Catholic Pastoral Center, 1001 N. Grand Ave. 81003.

Raleigh, NC: Catholic Center, 715 Nazareth St. 27606-2187.

Rapid City, SD: The Chancery Office, 606 Cathedral Dr., P.O. Box 678. 57709.

Reno, NV: Pastoral Center, 515 Court St., P.O. Box 1211. 89504-1211.

Richmond, VA: The Chancery Office, 811 Cathedral Pl., 23220.

Rochester, NY: The Pastoral Center, 1150 Buffalo Rd. 14624-1890.

Rockford, IL: The Chancery Office, 1245 N. Court St., P.O. Box 7044. 61126.

Rockville Centre, NY: The Chancery Office, 50 N. Park Ave. 11570.

Sacramento, CA: Pastoral Center, 2110 Broadway. 95818.

Saginaw, MI: The Chancery Office, 5800 Weiss St. 48603.

St. Augustine, FL: Catholic Center, P.O. Box 24000, Jacksonville, FL 32241-4000.

St. Cloud, MN: The Chancery Office, P.O. Box 1248. 56302.

St. George's in Canton, OH (Byzantine, Romanian): The Chancery Office, 1121 44th St. N.E., Canton. 44714.

St. Josaphat in Parma, OH (Byzantine): The Chancery Office, P.O. Box 347180, Parma. 44134.

St. Louis,* MO: The Catholic Center, 4445 Lindell Blvd. 63108.

St. Maron of Brooklyn (Maronite): The Chancery Office, 294 Howard Ave., Staten Island, NY 10301.

St. Nicholas in Chicago (Byzantine): The Chancery Office, 2245 W. Rice St. 60622.

St. Paul and Minneapolis,* MN: The Chancery Office, 226 Summit Ave., St. Paul. 55102.

St. Petersburg, FL: The Chancery Office, P.O. Box 40200. 33743.

St. Thomas the Apostle of Detroit (Chaldean Catholic Diocese – USA): The Chancery Office, 25603 Berg Rd., Southfield, MI 48034.

Salina, KS: The Chancery Office, P.O. Box 980. 67402.

Salt Lake City, UT: The Chancery Office, 27 C St. 84103.

San Angelo, TX: The Chancery Office, P.O. Box 1829. 76902.

San Antonio,* TX: The Chancery Office, P.O. 2718 W. Woodlawn Ave. 78228.

San Bernardino, CA: The Chancery Office, 1201 E. Highland Ave. 92404.

San Diego, CA: Pastoral Center, P.O. Box 85728. 92186.

San Francisco,* CA: The Chancery Office, 445 Church St. 94114.

San Jose, CA: The Chancery Office, 900 Lafayette St., Suite 301, Santa Clara 95050-4966.

Santa Fe,* NM: Catholic Center, 4000 St. Joseph's Pl. N.W., Albuquerque. 87120.

Santa Rosa, CA: The Chancery Office, P.O. Box 1297. 95402.

Savannah, GA: Catholic Pastoral Center, 601 E. Liberty St. 31401.

Scranton, PA: The Chancery Office, 300 Wyoming Ave. 18503.

Seattle,* WA: The Chancery Office, 910 Marion St. 98104-1299.

Shreveport, LA: Catholic Center, 2500 Line Ave. 71104.

Sioux City, IA: The Chancery Office, P.O. Box 3379. 51102.

Sioux Falls, SD: Catholic Pastoral Center, 3100 W. 41st St. 57105.

Spokane, WA: Catholic Pastoral Center, Catholic Diocese of Spokane, P.O. Box 1453. 99210.

Springfield, IL: Catholic Pastoral Center, 1615 West Washington, P.O. Box 3187. 62708-3187.

Springfield, MA: The Chancery Office, P.O. Box 1730. 01101.

Springfield-Cape Girardeau, MO: The Catholic Center, 601 S. Jefferson Ave., Springfield. 65806.

Stamford, CT (Byzantine): The Chancery Office, 14 Peveril Rd. 06902.

Steubenville, OH: The Chancery Office, P.O. Box 969. 43952.

Stockton, CA: The Chancery Office, P.O. Box 4237. 95204.

Superior, WI: The Chancery Office, 1201 Hughitt Ave., Box 969. 54880.

Syracuse, NY: The Chancery Office, P.O. Box 511. 13201.

Toledo, OH: The Chancery Office, P.O. Box 985. 43697-0985.

Trenton, NJ: Pastoral Center, 701 Lawrenceville Rd., P.O. Box 5147. 08648.

Tucson, AZ: The Chancery Office, 192 S. Stone Ave., Box 31. 85702.

Tulsa, OK: The Chancery Office, P.O. Box 2009. 74101.

Tyler, TX: The Chancery Office, 1015 E.S.E. Loop 323. 75701.

Van Nuys, CA (Byzantine): The Chancery Office, 8131 N. 16th St., Phoenix, AZ 85020.

Venice, FL: The Catholic Center, 1000 Pinebrook Rd. 34292.

Victoria, TX: The Chancery Office, P.O. Box 4070. 77903.

Washington,* DC: Archdiocesan Pastoral Center, P.O. Box 29260. 20017.

Wheeling-Charleston, WV: The Chancery Office, 1300 Byron St., P.O. Box 230, Wheeling. 26003.

Wichita, KS: The Chancery Office, 424 N. Broadway. 67202.

Wilmington, DE: The Chancery Office, P.O. Box 2030, 1925 Delaware Ave., Suite 1-A. 19899.

Winona, MN: The Chancery Office, P.O. Box 588. 55987.

Worcester, MA: The Chancery Office, 49 Elm St. 01609.

Yakima, WA: The Chancery Office, 5301-A Tieton Dr. 98908.

Youngstown, OH: The Chancery Office, 144 W. Wood St. 44503.

Military Archdiocese: 962 Wayne Ave., Silver Spring, MD 20910.

Armenian Apostolic Exarchate for the United States and Canada: 110 E. 12th St., New York, NY 10003.

(Sources: Catholic Almanac *survey*, The Official Catholic Directory, Annuario Pontificio, *Catholic News Service. As of Aug. 20, 1999. For notable former bishops of the U.S., see under "American Catholics of the Past," elsewhere in the U.S. Church section.*)

Information includes: date and place of birth; educational institutions attended; date of ordination to the priesthood with, where applicable, name of archdiocese (*) or diocese in parentheses; date of episcopal ordination; episcopal appointments; date of resignation/retirement.

A

Abramowicz, Alfred L.: b. Jan. 27, 1919, Chicago, Ill.; educ. St. Mary of the Lake Seminary (Mundelein, Ill.), Gregorian Univ. (Rome); ord. priest (Chicago*) May 1, 1943; ord. titular bp. of Paestum and aux. bp. of Chicago, June 13, 1968; retired Jan. 24, 1995.

Adamec, Joseph V.: b. Aug. 13, 1935, Bannister, Mich.; educ. Michigan State Univ. (East Lansing), Nepomucene College and Lateran Univ. (Rome); ord. priest (for Nitra diocese, Slovakia), July 3, 1960; incardinated in Saginaw diocese; ord. bp. of Altoona-Johnstown, May 20, 1987.

Adams, Edward J.: b. Aug. 24, 1944. Philadelphia, Pa.; educ. St. Charles Borromeo Seminary (Philadelphia), Pontifical Ecclesiastical Academy (Rome); ord. priest (Philadelphia*), May 16, 1970; in Vatican diplomatic service from 1976; ord. titular abp. of Scala Oct. 23, 1996; papal nuncio to Bangladesh

Ahern, Patrick V.: b. Mar. 8, 1919, New York, N.Y.; educ. Manhattan College and Cathedral College (New York City), St. Joseph's Seminary (Yonkers, N.Y.), St. Louis Univ. (St. Louis, Mo.), Notre Dame Univ. (Notre Dame, Ind.); ord. priest (New York*) Jan. 27, 1945; ord. titular bp. of Naiera and aux. bp. of New York, Mar. 19, 1970; retired Apr. 26, 1994.

Allué, Emilio S., S.D.B.: b. Feb. 18, 1935, Huesca, Spain; educ. Salesain schools (Huesca, Spain) Don Bosco College/Seminary (Newton, N.J.); Salesian Pontifical Univ. (Rome), Fordham Univ. (New York); ord. priest Dec. 22, 1966, in Rome; ord. titular bp. of Croe and aux. bp. of Boston, Sept. 17, 1996.

Anderson, Moses B., S.S.E.: b. Sept. 9, 1928, Selma, Ala.; educ. St. Michael's College (Winooski, Vt.), St. Edmund Seminary (Burlington, Vt.), Univ. of Legon (Ghana); ord. priest May 30, 1958; ord. titular bp. of Vatarba and aux. bp. of Detroit, Jan. 27, 1983.

Angell, Kenneth A.: b. Aug. 3, 1930, Providence, R.I.; educ. St. Mary's Seminary (Baltimore, Md.); ord. priest (Providence) May 26, 1956; ord. titular bp. of Septimunicia and aux. bp. of Providence, R.I., Oct. 7, 1974; bp. of Burlington, Oct. 6, 1992; installed Nov. 9, 1992.

Apuron, Anthony Sablan, O.F.M. Cap.: b. Nov. 1, 1945, Agana, Guam; educ. St. Anthony College and Capuchin Seminary (Hudson, N.H.), Capuchin Seminary (Garrison, N.Y.), Maryknoll Seminary (New York), Notre Dame Univ. (Notre Dame, Ind.); ord. priest Aug. 26, 1972, in Guam; ord. titular bp. of Muzuca in Proconsulari and aux. bp. of Agana, Guam (unicorporated U.S. territory), Feb. 19, 1984; abp. of Agana, Mar. 10, 1986.

Arias, David, O.A.R.: b. July 22, 1929, Leon, Spain; educ. St. Rita's College (San Sebastian, Spain), Our Lady of Good Counsel Theologate (Granada, Spain),

Teresianum Institute (Rome, Italy); ord. priest May 31, 1952; ord. titular bp. of Badie and aux. bp. of Newark, Apr. 7, 1983; episcopal vicar for Hispanic affairs.

Arkfeld, Leo, S.V.D.: b. Feb. 4, 1912, Butte, Nebr.; educ. Divine Word Seminary (Techny, Ill.), Sacred Heart College (Girard, Pa.); ord. priest Aug. 15, 1943; ord. titular bp. of Bucellus and vicar apostolic of Central New Guinea, Nov. 30, 1948; name of vicariate changed to Wewak, May 15, 1952; first bp. of Wewak, Nov. 15, 1966; app. abp. of Madang, Papua New Guinea, Dec. 19, 1975; resigned Dec. 31, 1987.

Arzube, Juan A.: b. June 1, 1918, Guayaquil, Ecuador; educ. Rensselaer Polytechnic Institute (Troy, N.Y.), St. John's Seminary (Camarillo, Calif.); ord. priest (Los Angeles*) May 5, 1954; ord. titular bp. of Civitate and aux. bp. of Los Angeles, Mar. 25, 1971; retired Sept 7, 1993.

Aymond, Gregory M.: b. Nov. 12, 1949, New Orleans, La.; educ. St. Joseph Seminary College, Notre Dame Seminary (New Orleans, La.); ord. priest (New Orleans*) May 10, 1975; ord. titular bp. of Acolla and aux. bp. of New Orleans, Jan. 10, 1997.

B

Baker, Robert J.: b. June 4, 1944, Fostoria, Ohio; educ. Pontifical College Josephinum, Columbus, Ohio, Gregorian Univ., Rome; ordained (St. Augustine) March 21, 1970; app. bp of Charleston, July 13, 1999; ord. Sept. 29, 1999.

Balke, Victor H.: b. Sept. 29, 1931, Meppen, Ill.; educ. St. Mary of the Lake Seminary (Mundelein, Ill.), St. Louis Univ. (St. Louis, Mo.); ord. priest (Springfield, Ill.) May 24, 1958; ord. bp. of Crookston, Sept. 2, 1976.

Baltakis, Paul Antanas, O.F.M.: b. Jan. 1, 1925, Troskunai, Lithuania; educ. seminaries of the Franciscan Province of St. Joseph (Belgium); ord. priest Aug. 24, 1952, in Belgium; served in U.S. as director of Lithuanian Cultural Center, New York, and among Lithuanian youth; head of U.S. Lithuanian Franciscan Vicariate, Kennebunkport, Maine, from 1979; ord. titular bp. of Egara, Sept. 24, 1984; assigned to pastoral assistance to Lithuanian Catholics living outside Lithuania (resides in Brooklyn).

Banks, Robert J.: b. Feb. 26, 1928, Winthrop, Mass.; educ. St. John's Seminary (Brighton, Mass.), Gregorian Univ., Lateran Univ. (Rome); ord. priest (Boston*) Dec. 20, 1952, in Rome; rector of St. John's Seminary, Brighton, Mass., 1971-81; vicar general of Boston archdiocese, 1984; ord. titular bp. of Taraqua and aux. bp. of Boston, Sept. 19, 1985; bp. of Green Bay, Oct. 16, 1990, installed Dec. 5, 1990.

Barbarito, Gerald M.: b. Jan. 4, 1950, Brooklyn, N.Y.; educ. Cathedral College (Douglaston, N.Y.), Immaculate Conception Seminary (Huntington, N.Y.), Catholic University (Washington, D.C.); ord. priest (Brooklyn) Jan. 31, 1976; ord. titular bp. of Gisipa and aux. bp. of Brooklyn, Aug. 22, 1994.

Barnes, Gerald R.: b. June 22, 1945, Phoenix, Ariz., of Mexican descent; educ. St. Leonard Seminary (Dayton, O.), Assumption-St. John's Seminary (San Antonio, Tex.); ord. priest (San Antonio*) Dec. 20, 1975; ord. titular bp. of Montefiascone and aux. bp. of San Bernardino, Mar. 18, 1992; bp. of San Bernardino, Dec. 28, 1995.

Baum, William W.: (See Cardinals, Biographies.)

Begley, Michael J.: b. Mar. 12, 1909, Mattineague, Mass.; educ. Mt. St. Mary Seminary (Emmitsburg, Md.); ord. priest (Raleigh) May 26, 1934; ord. first bp. of Charlotte, N.C., Jan. 12, 1972; retired May 29, 1984.

Beltran, Eusebius J.: b. Aug. 31, 1934, Ashley, Pa.; educ. St. Charles Seminary (Philadelphia, Pa.); ord. priest (Atlanta*) May 14, 1960; ord. bp. of Tulsa, Apr. 20, 1978; app. abp. of Oklahoma City, Nov. 24, 1992; installed Jan 22, 1993.

Bennett, Gordon D., S.J.: b. October 21, 1946, Denver; educ. Mount St. Michael's, Spokane, Wash., Jesuit School of Theology, Berkeley, Calif., Fordham Univ., NY; entered Society of Jesus, 1966; ord priest June 14, 1975; app. Titular Bp. of Nesqually and Aux. Bp. of Baltimore, Dec. 23, 1997, ord. Mar 3, 1998.

Bevilacqua, Anthony J.: (See Cardinals, Biographies.)

Blair, Leonard P.: b. Dec. 12, 1949, Detroit; educ. Sacred Heart Seminary, Detroit, Pontifical North American College, Gregorian University, and the Angelicum, Rome; ord. priest (Detroit*) June 26, 1976; at Vatican Secretariat of State, 1986-1991, Secretary to the President of the Prefecture for the Economic Affairs of the Holy See, 1994-1997; app. aux. of Detroit, July 9, 1999, ord. Aug. 24, 1999.

Blaire, Stephen E.: b. Dec. 22, 1941, Los Angeles, Calif; educ. St. John's Seminary (Camarillo, Calif.); ord. priest (Los Angeles*) Apr. 29, 1967; ord. titular bp. of Lamzella and aux. of Los Angeles, May 31, 1990; app. bp. of Stockton, Jan. 19, 1999, ins. March 16, 1999.

Boland, Ernest B., O.P.: b. July 10, 1925, Providence, R.I.; educ. Providence College (Rhode Island), Dominican Houses of Study (Somerset, Ohio; Washington, D.C.); ord. priest June 9, 1955; ord. bp. of Multan, Pakistan, July 25, 1966; resigned Oct. 20, 1984.

Boland, J.(John) Kevin: b. Apr. 25, 1935, Cork, Ireland (brother of Bp. Raymond J. Boland); educ. Christian Brothers School (Cork, Ire.), All Hallows Seminary (Dublin); ord. priest (Savannah), June 14, 1959; ord. bp. of Savannah, Apr. 18, 1995.

Boland, Raymond J.: b. Feb. 8, 1932, Tipperary, Ireland; educ. National Univ. of Ireland and All Hallows Seminary (Dublin); ord. priest (Washington*) June 16, 1957, in Dublin; vicar general and chancellor of Washington archdiocese; ord. bp. of Birmingham, Ala., Mar. 25, 1988; app. bp. of Kansas City-St. Joseph, Mo., June 22, 1993.

Boles, John P.: b. Jan. 21, 1930, Boston, Mass.; educ. St. John Seminary, Boston College (Boston, Mass.); ord. priest (Boston*) Feb. 2, 1955; ord. titular bp. of Nova Sparsa and aux. bp. of Boston, May 21, 1992.

Bootkoski, Paul G: b. July 4, 1940, Newark, N.J.; educ. Seton Hall Univ. (South Orange, N.J.), Immaculate Conception Seminary (Darlington, N.J.); ord. priest (Newark*) May 29, 1966; ord. titular bp. of Zarna and aux. bp. of Newark, Sept. 5, 1997.

Borders, William D.: b. Oct. 9, 1913, Washington, Ind.; educ. St. Meinrad Seminary (St. Meinrad, Ind.), Notre Dame Seminary (New Orleans, La.), Notre Dame Univ. (Notre Dame, Ind.); ord. priest (New Orleans*) May 18, 1940; ord. first bp. of Orlando, June 14, 1968; app. abp. of Baltimore, Apr. 2, 1974, installed June 26, 1974; retired Apr. 11, 1989.

Bosco, Anthony G.: b. Aug. 1, 1927, New Castle, Pa.; educ. St. Vincent Seminary (Latrobe, Pa.), Lateran Univ. (Rome); ord. priest (Pittsburgh) June 7, 1952; ord. titular bp. of Labicum and aux. of Pittsburgh, June 30, 1970; app. bp. of Greensburg, Apr. 14, 1987, installed June 30, 1987.

Botean, John Michael: b. July 9, 1955, Canton, Ohio; educ. St. Fidelis Seminary (Herman, Pa.), Catholic University of America (Washington, DC), St. Gregory Melkite Seminary (Newton Centre, Mass), Catholic Theological Union (Chicago, Ill.); ord. priest (Romanian rite St. George's in Canton), May 18, 1986; ord. bp. of Saint George's in Canton for Romanians Aug. 24, 1996.

Boyle, Paul M., C.P.: b. May 28, 1926, Detroit, Mich.; educ. Passionist houses of study, Lateran Univ. (Rome); professed in Congregation of the Passion July 9, 1946; ord. priest May 30, 1953; president of Conference of Major Superiors of Men, 1969-74; superior general of Passionists, 1976-88; ord. titular bp. of Canapium and first vicar apostolic of Mandeville, Jamaica, July 9, 1991.

Braxton, Edward K.: b. June 28, 1944, Chicago, Ill.; educ. Loyola Univ. of Chicago, Univ. of St. Mary of the Lake and Mundelein Seminary (Chicago), Louvain Univ. (Belgium); ord. priest (Chicago*) May 13, 1970; ord. titular bp. of Macomades rusticiana and aux. bp. of St. Louis, May 17, 1995.

Breen, Vincent DePaul: b. Dec. 24, 1936, Brooklyn, N.Y.; educ. Cathedral College of Immaculate Conception (Brooklyn, N.Y.), North American College, Gregorian Univ. (Rome); ord. priest (Brooklyn) July 15, 1962, in Rome; vicar of education for diocese of Brooklyn; app. bp. of Metuchen, July 8, 1997.

Breitenbeck, Joseph M.: b. Aug. 3, 1914, Detroit, Mich.; educ. University of Detroit, Sacred Heart Seminary (Detroit, Mich.), North American College and Lateran Univ. (Rome), Catholic Univ. (Washington, D.C.); ord. priest (Detroit*) May 30, 1942; ord. titular bp. of Tepelta and aux. bp. of Detroit, Dec. 20, 1965; app. bp. of Grand Rapids, Oct. 15, 1969, installed Dec. 2, 1969; retired July 11, 1989.

Britt, Kevin Michael: b. Nov. 19, 1944, Detroit, Mich.; educ. Sacred Heart Seminary, St. John Provincial Seminary, Universtiy of Detroit Mercy (Detroit, Mich.), Lateran Univ. (Rome); ord. priest (Detroit*) June 28, 1970; ord. titular bp. of Esco and aux. of Detroit, Jan. 6, 1994.

Broderick, Edwin B.: b. Jan. 16, 1917, New York, N.Y.; educ. Cathedral College (New York City), St. Joseph's Seminary (Yonkers, N.Y.), Fordham Univ. (New York City); ord. priest (New York*) May 30, 1942; ord. titular bp. of Tizica and aux. of New York, Apr. 21, 1967; bp. of Albany, 1969-76; executive director of Catholic Relief Services, 1976-82. Bp. emeritus of Albany.

Brom, Robert H.: b. Sept. 18, 1938, Arcadia, Wis.; educ. St. Mary's College (Winona, Minn.), Gregorian Univ. (Rome); ord. priest (Winona) Dec. 18, 1963, in Rome; ord. bp. of Duluth, May 23, 1983; coadjutor bp. of San Diego, May, 1989; bp. of San Diego, July 10, 1990.

Brown, Tod D.: b. Nov. 15, 1936, San Francisco, Calif.; educ. St. John's Seminary (Camarillo, Calif.), North American College (Rome); ord. priest (Monterey-Fresno) May 1, 1963; ord. bp. of Boise, Apr. 3, 1989; app. bp. of Orange, June 30, 1998.

Brucato, Robert A.: b. Aug. 14, 1931, New York, N.Y. educ. Cathedral College (New York), St. Joseph's Seminary (Dunwoodie, N.Y.), Univ. of Our Lady of the Lake (San Antonio, Tex.); ord. priest (New York*) June 1, 1957; air force chaplain for 22 years; ord. titular bp. of Temuniana and aux. of New York, Aug. 25, 1997.

Brunett, Alexander J.: b. Jan. 17, 1934, Detroit, Mich; educ. Gregorian Univ. (Rome), Sacred Heart Seminary, University of Detroit (Detroit, Mich.), Marquette Univ. (Milwaukee, Wis.); ord. priest (Detroit*), July 13, 1958; ord. bp. of Helena, July 6, 1994; app.Abp. of Seattle Oct. 28, 1997, installed Dec. 18, 1997.

Bruskewitz, Fabian W.: b. Sept. 6, 1935, Milwaukee, Wis.; educ. North American College, Gregorian Univ. (Rome); ord. priest (Milwaukee*) July 17, 1960; ord. bp. of Lincoln, May 13, 1992.

Buechlein, Daniel M., O.S.B.: b. Apr. 20, 1938; educ. St. Meinrad College and Seminary (St. Meinrad, Ind.), St. Anselm Univ. (Rome); solemn profession as Benedictine monk, Aug. 15, 1963; ord. priest (St. Meinrad Archabbey) May 3, 1964; ord. bp. of Memphis, Mar. 2, 1987; app. abp. of Indianapolis, July 14, 1992; installed Sept. 9, 1992.

Bukovsky, John, S.V.D.: b. Jan. 18, 1924, Cerova, Slovakia; educ. Slovakia, Divine Word Seminary (Techny, Ill.), Catholic Univ. (Washington, D.C.), Univ. of Chicago, Gregorian Univ. (Rome); ord. priest Dec. 3, 1950; became U.S. citizen 1958; worked at East European desk of Secretariat of State; ord. titular abp. of Tabalta, Oct. 13, 1990; nuncio to Romania, 1990-94; app. papal representative to Russia, Dec. 20, 1994.

Bullock, William H.: b. Apr. 13, 1927, Maple Lake, Minn.; educ. St. Thomas College and St. Paul Seminary (St. Paul, Minn.), Notre Dame Univ. (Notre Dame, Ind.); ord. priest (St. Paul-Minneapolis*) June 7, 1952; ord. titular bp. of Natchez and aux. bp. of St. Paul and Minneapolis, Aug. 12, 1980; app. bp. of Des Moines, Feb. 10, 1987; app. bp. of Madison, Wis., Apr. 13, 1993.

Burke, John J., O.F.M.: b. Mar. 16, 1935, River Edge, N.J.; educ. St. Joseph Seminary (Callicoon, N.Y.), St. Bonaventure Univ. (St. Bonaventure, N.Y.), Holy Name College (Washington, D.C.); solemnly professed in Franciscan Order, Aug. 20, 1958; ord. priest Feb. 25, 1961; missionary in Brazil from 1964; ord. coadjutor bp. of Miracema do Tocantins, Brazil, Mar. 25, 1995; bp. of Miracema do Tocantins, Feb. 14, 1996.

Burke, Raymond L.: b. June 30, 1948, Richland Center, Wis.; educ. Holy Cross Seminary (La Crosse, Wis.), Catholic Univ. (Washington, D.C.), North American College and Gregorian Univ. (Rome); ord. priest (La Crosse) June 29, 1975; ord. bp. of La Crosse Jan. 6, 1995, installed Feb. 22, 1995.

Buswell, Charles A.: b. Oct. 15, 1913, Homestead, Okla.; educ. St. Louis Preparatory Seminary (St. Louis, Mo.), Kenrick Seminary (Webster Groves, Mo.), American College, Univ. of Louvain (Belgium); ord. priest (Oklahoma City*) July 9, 1939; ord. bp. of Pueblo, Sept. 30, 1959; resigned Sept. 18, 1979.

C

Camacho, Tomas Aguon: b. Sept. 18, 1933, Chalon Kanoa, Saipan; educ. St. Patrick's Seminary (Menlo

Park, Calif.); ord. priest June 14, 1961; ord. first bp. of Chalan Kanoa, Northern Marianas (U.S. Commonwealth), Jan. 13, 1985.

Campbell, Frederick F.: b. Aug. 5, 1943, Elmira, N.Y.; educ. Ohio State Univ., St. Paul Seminary, St. Paul, Minn.; ord. priest (St. Paul and Minneapolis*) May 31, 1980; app. titular bp. of Afufenia and aux. bp. of St. Paul and Minneapolis, March 2, 1999, ord. May 14, 1999.

Carlson, Robert J.: b. June 30, 1944, Minneapolis, Minn.; educ. Nazareth Hall and St. Paul Seminary (St. Paul, Minn.), Catholic Univ. (Washington, D.C.): ord. priest (St. Paul-Minneapolis*) May 23, 1970; ord. titular bp. of Avioccala and aux. bp. of St. Paul and Minneapolis, Jan. 11, 1984; app. coadjutor bp. of Sioux Falls, Jan. 13, 1994; succeeded as bp. of Sioux Falls, Mar. 21, 1995.

Carmody, Edmond: b. Jan. 12, 1934, Ahalena, Kerry, Ireland; educ. St. Brendan's College (Killarney), St. Patrick Seminary (Carlow, Ire.); ord. priest (San Antonio*) June 8, 1957; missionary in Peru 1984-89; ord. titular bp. of Mortlach and aux. bp. of San Antonio, Dec. 15, 1988; app. bp. of Tyler, Mar. 24, 1992.

Carmon, Dominic, S.V.D.: b. Dec. 13, 1930, Opelousas, La.; entered Society of Divine Word, 1946; ord. priest Feb. 2, 1960; missionary in Papua-New Guinea, 1961-68; ord. titular bp. of Rusicade and aux. bp. of New Orleans, Feb. 11, 1993.

Casey, Luis Morgan: b. June 23, 1935, Portageville, Mo.; ord. priest (St. Louis*) Apr. 7, 1962; missionary in Bolivia from 1965; ord. titular bp. of Mibiarca and aux. of La Paz, Jan. 28, 1984; vicar apostolic of Pando, Bolivia, Jan. 18, 1988 and apostolic administrator (1995) of La Paz.

Catanello, Ignatius A.: b. July 23, 1938, Brooklyn, N.Y.; educ. Cathedral Preparatory Seminary and St. Francis College (Brooklyn, N.Y.), Catholic Univ. (Washington, D.C.); St. John's University (Jamaica, N.Y.), New York University; ord. priest (Brooklyn) May 28, 1966; ord. titular bp. of Deulto and aux. bp. of Brooklyn, Aug. 22, 1994.

Chaput, Charles J., O.F.M. Cap.: b. Sept. 26, 1944, Concordia, Kans.; educ. St. Fidelis College (Herman, Pa.), Capuchin College and Catholic Univ. (Washington, D.C.), Univ. of San Francisco; solemn vows as Capuchin, July 14, 1968; ord. priest Aug. 29, 1970; ord. bp. of Rapid City, S.D., July 26, 1988, the second priest of Native American ancestry (member of Prairie Band Potawatomi Tribe) ordained a bp. in the U.S.; app bp. of Denver, installed Apr. 7, 1997.

Charron, Joseph L., C.PP.S.: b. Dec. 30, 1939, Redfield, S.D.; educ. St. John's Seminary (Collegeville, Minn.); ord. priest June 3, 1967; ord. titular bp. of Bencenna and aux. bp. of St. Paul and Minneapolis, Jan. 25, 1990; app. bp. of Des Moines, Nov. 12, 1993.

Chavez, Gilbert Espinoza: b. May 9, 1932, Ontario, Calif.; educ. St. Francis Seminary (El Cajon, Calif.), Immaculate Heart Seminary (San Diego), Univ. of Calif.; ord. priest (San Diego) Mar. 19, 1960; ord. titular bp. of Magarmel and aux. of San Diego, June 21, 1974.

Chedid, John: b. July 4, 1923, Eddid, Lebanon; educ. seminaries in Lebanon and Pontifical Urban College (Rome); ord. priest Dec. 21, 1951, in Rome; ord. titular bp. of Callinico and aux. bp. of St. Maron of Brooklyn for the Maronites, Jan. 25, 1981; app. first bp. of Eparchy of Our Lady of Lebanon of Los Angeles for the Maronites, Mar. 1, 1994.

Christian, Francis J.: b. Oct. 8, 1942, Peterborough, N.H.; educ. St. Anselm College (Manchester, N.H.), St. Paul Seminary (Ottawa), American College in Louvain (Belgium); ord. priest (Manchester) June 29, 1968; ord titular bp. of Quincy and aux. of Manchester May 14, 1996.

Clark, Matthew H.: b. July 15, 1937, Troy, N.Y.; educ. St. Bernard's Seminary (Rochester, N.Y.), Gregorian Univ. (Rome); ord. priest (Albany) Dec. 19, 1962; ord. bp. of Rochester, May 27, 1979; installed June 26, 1979.

Clinch, Harry A.: b. Oct. 27, 1908, San Anselmo, Calif.; educ. St. Joseph's College (Mountain View, Calif.), St. Patrick's Seminary (Menlo Park, Calif.); ord. priest (Monterey-Fresno) June 6, 1936; ord. titular bp. of Badiae and aux. bp. of Monterey-Fresno, Feb. 27, 1957; app. first bp. of Monterey in Calif., Oct. 16, 1967; resigned Jan. 19, 1982.

Coggin, Walter A., O.S.B.: b. Feb. 10, 1916, Richmond, Va.; ord. priest June 19, 1943; app. abbot ordinary of abbacy nullius of Mary Help of Christians, Belmont N.C., 1959; blessed Mar. 28, 1960; resigned 1970.

Connolly, Thomas J.: b. July 18, 1922, Tonopah, Nev.; educ. St. Patrick's Seminary (Menlo Park, Calif.), Catholic Univ. (Washington, D.C.), Lateran Univ. (Rome); ord. priest (Reno-Las Vegas) Apr. 8, 1947; ord. bp. of Baker, June 30, 1971.

Connors, Ronald G., C.SS.R.: b. Nov. 1, 1915, Brooklyn, N.Y.; ord. priest June 22, 1941; ord. titular bp. of Equizetum and coadjutor bp. of San Juan de la Maguana, Dominican Republic, July 20, 1976; succeeded as bp. of San Juan de la Maguana, July 20, 1977; retired Feb. 20, 1991.

Conway, Edwin M.: b. Mar. 6, 1934, Chicago, Ill.; educ. St. Mary of the Lake Seminary (Chicago), Loyola in Chicago; ord. priest (Chicago*) May 3, 1960; ord. titular bp. of Auguro and aux. of Chicago, Mar. 20, 1995.

Cooney, Patrick R.: b. Mar. 10, 1934, Detroit, Mich.; educ. Sacred Heart Seminary (Detroit), Gregorian Univ. (Rome), Notre Dame Univ. (Notre Dame, Ind.); ord. priest (Detroit*) Dec. 20, 1959; ord. titular bp. of Hodelm and aux. bp. of Detroit, Jan. 27, 1983; app. bp. of Gaylord, Nov. 6, 1989; installed Jan. 28, 1990.

Corrada del Rio, Alvaro, S.J.: b. May 13, 1942, Santurce, Puerto Rico; entered Society of Jesus, 1960, at novitiate of St. Andrew-on-Hudson (Poughkeepsie, N.Y.); educ. Jesuit seminaries, Fordham Univ. (New York), Institut Catholique (Paris); ord. priest July 6, 1974, in Puerto Rico; pastoral coordinator of Northeast Catholic Hispanic Center, New York, 1982-85; ord. titular bp. of Rusticana and aux. bp. of Washington, D.C., Aug. 4, 1985; app. apostolic administrator of Caguas, Puerto Rico, Aug. 5, 1997 (retains his title as aux. bp. of Washington.)

Coscia, Benedict Dominic, O.F.M.: b. Aug. 10, 1922, Brooklyn, N.Y.; educ. St. Francis College (Brooklyn, N.Y.), Holy Name College (Washington, D.C.); ord. priest June 11, 1949; ord. bp. of Jatai, Brazil, Sept. 21, 1961.

Costello, Thomas J.: b. Feb. 23, 1929, Camden, N.Y.; educ. Niagara Univ. (Niagara Falls, N.Y.), St.

Bernard's Seminary (Rochester, N.Y.), Catholic Univ. (Washington, D.C.); ord. priest (Syracuse) June 5, 1954; ord. titular bp. of Perdices and aux. bp. of Syracuse Mar. 13, 1978.

Cote, Michael R.: b. June 19, 1949, Sanford, Me.; educ. Our Lady of Lourdes Seminary (Cassadaga, N.Y.), St. Mary's Seminary College (Baltimore, Md.); Gregorian Univ. (Rome), Catholic Univ. (Washington, D.C.); ord. priest (Portland, Me.) June 29, 1975 by Pope Paul VI in Rome; secretary, 1989-94 at apostolic nunciature, Washington; ord. titular bp. of Cebarades and aux. of Portland, Me., July 27, 1995.

Cotey, Arnold R., S.D.S.: b. June 15, 1921, Milwaukee, Wis.; educ. Divine Savior Seminary (Lanham, Md.), Marquette Univ. (Milwaukee, Wis.); ord. priest June 7, 1949; ord. first bp. of Nachingwea (now Lindi), Tanzania, Oct. 20, 1963; retired Nov. 11, 1983.

Cronin, Daniel A.: b. Nov. 14, 1927, Newton, Mass.; educ. St. John's Seminary (Boston, Mass.), North American College and Gregorian Univ. (Rome); ord. priest (Boston*) Dec. 20, 1952; attaché apostolic nunciature (Addis Ababa), 1957-61; served in papal Secretariat of State, 1961-68; ord. titular bp. of Egnatia and aux. bp. of Boston, Sept. 12, 1968; bp. of Fall River, Dec. 16, 1970; abp. of Hartford, Dec. 10, 1991.

Crowley, Joseph R.: b. Jan. 12, 1915, Fort Wayne, Ind.; educ. St. Mary's College (St. Mary, Ky.), St. Meinrad Seminary (St. Meinrad, Ind.); served in US Air Force, 1942-46; ord. priest (Ft. Wayne-S. Bend) May 1, 1953; editor of Our Sunday Visitor 1958-67; ord. titular bp. of Maraguis and aux. bshop of Fort Wayne-South Bend, Aug. 24, 1971; retired May 8, 1990.

Cullen, Edward P.: b. Mar. 15, 1933, Philadelphia, Pa.; educ. St. Charles Borromeo Seminary (Overbrook, Pa.), Univ. of Pennsylvania and LaSalle Univ. (Philadelphia), Harvard Graduate School of Business; ord. priest (Philadelphia*) May 19, 1962; ord. titular bp. of Paria in Proconsolare and aux. of Philadelphia, Feb. 8, 1994; app. bp. of Allentown, Dec. 16, 1997, ord. Feb. 9, 1998.

Cummins, John S.: b. Mar. 3, 1928, Oakland, Calif.; educ. St. Patrick's Seminary (Menlo Park, Calif.), Catholic Univ. (Washington, D.C.), Univ. of Calif.; ord. priest (San Francisco*) Jan. 24, 1953; executive director of the Calif. Catholic Conference 1971-76; ord. titular bp. of Lambaesis and aux. bp. of Sacramento, May 16, 1974; app. bp. of Oakland, installed June 30, 1977.

Cupich, Blase: b. Mar. 19, 1949, Omaha, Neb.; educ. College of St. Thomas (St. Paul, Minn.), Gregorian Univ. (Rome), Catholic University of America (Washington, D.C.); ord. priest (Omaha*), Aug. 16, 1975; service at the apostolic nunciature, Washington, D.C., 1981-87; rector, Pontifical College Josephinum (Columbus, Ohio) 1989-97; app. bp. of Rapid City, S.D., July 7, 1998; installed Sept. 21, 1998.

Curlin, William G.: b. Aug. 30, 1927, Portsmouth, Va.; educ. Georgetown Univ. (Washington, D.C.), St. Mary's Seminary (Baltimore, Md.); ord. priest (Washington*), May 25, 1957; ord. titular bp. of Rosemarkie and aux. bp. of Washington, Dec. 20, 1988; app. bp. of Charlotte, Feb. 22, 1994.

Curry, Thomas J.: b. Jan. 17, 1943, Drumgoon,

Ireland; educ. Patrician College (Ballyfin, Ire.), All Hallows Seminary (Dublin, Ire.); ord. priest (Los Angeles*) June 17, 1967; ord. titular bp. of Ceanannus Mór and aux. of Los Angeles, Mar. 19, 1994.

Curtiss, Elden F.: b. June 16, 1932, Baker, Ore.; educ. St. Edward Seminary College and St. Thomas Seminary (Kenmore, Wash.); ord. priest (Baker) May 24, 1958; ord. bp. of Helena, Mont., Apr. 28, 1976; app. abp. of Omaha, Nebr., May 4, 1993.

D

Daily, Thomas V.: b. Sept. 23, 1927, Belmont, Mass.; educ. Boston College, St. John's Seminary (Brighton, Mass.); ord. priest (Boston*) Jan. 10, 1952; missionary in Peru for five years as a member of the Society of St. James the Apostle; ord. titular bp. of Bladia and aux. bp. of Boston, Feb. 11, 1975; app. first bp. of Palm Beach, Fla., July 17, 1984; app. bp. of Brooklyn, Feb. 20, 1990; installed Apr. 18, 1990.

Daly, James: b. Aug. 14, 1921, New York, N.Y.; educ. Cathedral College (Brooklyn, N.Y.), Immaculate Conception Seminary (Huntington, L.I.); ord. priest (Brooklyn) May 22, 1948; ord. titular bp. of Castra Nova and aux. bp. of Rockville Centre, May 9, 1977; retired July 1, 1996.

D'Antonio, Nicholas, O.F.M.: b. July 10, 1916, Rochester, N.Y.; educ. St. Anthony's Friary (Catskill, N.Y.); ord. priest June 7, 1942; ord. titular bp. of Giufi Salaria and prelate of Olancho, Honduras, July 25, 1966; resigned 1977; vicar general of New Orleans archdiocese and episcopal vicar for Spanish Speaking, 1977-91.

D'Arcy, John M.: b. Aug. 18, 1932, Brighton, Mass.; educ. St. John's Seminary (Brighton, Mass.), Angelicum Univ. (Rome); ord. priest (Boston*) Feb. 2, 1957; spiritual director of St. John's Seminary; ord. titular bp. of Mediana and aux. bp. of Boston, Feb. 11, 1975; app. bp. of Fort Wayne-South Bend, Feb. 26, 1985, installed May 1, 1985.

Dattilo, Nicholas C.: b. Mar. 8, 1932, Mahoningtown, Pa.; educ. St. Vincent Seminary (Latrobe, Pa.), St. Charles Borromeo Seminary (Philadelphia, Pa.); ord. priest (Pittsburgh) May 31, 1958; ord. bp. of Harrisburg, Jan. 26, 1990.

Delaney, Joseph P.: b. Aug. 29, 1934, Fall River, Mass.; educ. Cardinal O'Connell Seminary (Boston, Mass.), Theological College (Washington, D.C.), North American College (Rome), Rhode Island College (Providence, R.I.); ord. priest (Fall River) Dec. 18, 1960; ord. bp. of Fort Worth, Tex., Sept. 13, 1981.

De Palma, Joseph A., S.C.J.: b. Sept. 4, 1913, Walton, N.Y.; ord. priest May 20, 1944; superior general of Congregation of Priests of the Sacred Heart, 1959-67; ord. first bp. of De Aar, South Africa, July 19, 1967; retired Nov. 18, 1987.

De Paoli, Ambrose: b. Aug. 19, 1934, Jeannette, Pa., moved to Miami at age of nine; educ. St. Joseph Seminary (Bloomfield, Conn.), St. Mary of the West Seminary (Cincinnati, O.), North American College and Lateran Univ. (Rome); ord. priest (Miami*) Dec. 18, 1960, in Rome; served in diplomatic posts in Canada, Turkey, Africa and Venezuela; ord. titular abp. of Lares, Nov. 20, 1983, in Miami; apostolic pro-nuncio to Sri Lanka, 1983-88; apostolic delegate in southern Africa and pro-nuncio to Lesotho, 1988; first apostolic nuncio to South Africa, 1994.

De Simone, Louis A.: b. Feb. 21, 1922, Philadelphia, Pa.; educ. Villanova Univ. (Villanova, Pa.), St. Charles Borromeo Seminary (Overbrook, Pa.); ord. priest (Philadelphia*) May 10, 1952; ord. titular bp. of Cillium and aux. bp. of Philadelphia, Aug. 12, 1981; retired Apr. 5, 1997.

Di Lorenzo, Francis X.: b. Apr. 15, 1942, Philadelphia, Pa.; educ. St. Charles Borromeo Seminary (Philadelphia), Univ. of St. Thomas (Rome); ord. priest (Philadelphia*) May 18, 1968; ord. titular bp. of Tigia and aux. bp. of Scranton, Mar. 8, 1988; app. apostolic administrator of Honolulu, Oct. 12, 1993; bp. of Honolulu, Nov. 29, 1994.

DiMarzio, Nicholas: b. June 16, 1944, Newark, N.J.; educ. Seton Hall University (South Orange, N.J.), Immaculate Conception Seminary (Darlington, N.J.), Catholic Univ. (Washington, D.C.), Fordham Univ. (New York), Rutgers Univ. (New Brunswick, N.J.); ord. priest (Newark*) May 30, 1970; ord. titular bp. of Mauriana and aux. bp. of Newark, Oct. 31, 1996, app. Bishop of Camden, June 8, 1999, installed July 22, 1999.

Dimino, Joseph T.: b. Jan. 7, 1923, New York, N.Y.; educ. Cathedral College (New York, N.Y.), St. Joseph's Seminary (Yonkers, N.Y.), Catholic Univ. (Washington, D.C.); ord. priest (New York*) June 4, 1949; ord. titular bp. of Carini and aux. bp. of the Military Services archdiocese, May 10, 1983; app. ordinary of Military Services archdiocese, May 14, 1991; retired Aug. 12, 1997.

DiNardo, Daniel N.: b. May 23, 1949, Steubenville, OH; educ. Catholic Univ. of America (Washington, DC) North American College, (Rome), Gregorian Univ. (Rome); ord. priest (Pittsburgh) July 16, 1977; app. Coadjutor Bp. of Sioux City Aug. 19, 1997, ord. Oct. 7, 1997, Bp. of Sioux City Nov. 28, 1998.

Dion, George E., O.M.I.: b. Sept. 25, 1911, Central Falls, R.I.; educ. Holy Cross College (Worcester, Mass.), Oblate Juniorate (Colebrook, N.H.), Oblate Scholasticates (Natick, Mass., and Ottawa, Ont.); ord. priest June 24, 1936; ord. titular bp. of Arpaia and vicar apostolic of Jolo, Philippines Apr. 23, 1980; retired Oct. 11, 1991; titular bp. of Arpaia.

Donnelly, Robert William: b. Mar. 22, 1931, Toledo, O.; educ. St. Meinrad Seminary College (St. Meinrad, Ind.), Mount St. Mary's in the West Seminary (Norwood, O.); ord. priest (Toledo) May 25, 1957; ord. titular bp. of Garba and aux. bp. of Toledo, May 3, 1984.

Donoghue, John F.: b. Aug. 9, 1928, Washington, D.C.; educ. St. Mary's Seminary (Baltimore, Md.); Catholic Univ. (Washington, D.C.); ord. priest (Washington*) June 4, 1955; chancellor and vicar general of Washington archdiocese, 1973-84; ord. bp. of Charlotte, N.C., Dec. 18, 1984; app. abp. of Atlanta, June 22, 1993; installed Aug. 19, 1993.

Donovan, Paul V.: b. Sept. 1, 1924, Bernard, Iowa; educ. St. Gregory's Seminary (Cincinnati, Ohio), Mt. St. Mary's Seminary (Norwood, Ohio), Lateran Univ. (Rome); ord. priest (Lansing) May 20, 1950; ord. first bp. of Kalamazoo, Mich., July 21, 1971; retired Nov. 22, 1994.

Doran, Thomas George: b. Feb. 20, 1936, Rockford, Ill.; educ. Loras College (Dubuque, Ia.), Gregorian Univ. (Rome), Rockford College (Rockford, Ill.); ord. priest (Rockford) Dec. 20, 1961; ord. bp. of Rockford, June 24, 1994.

Dorsey, Norbert M., C.P.: b. Dec. 14, 1929, Spring-field, Mass.; educ. Passionist seminaries (eastern U.S. province), Pontifical Institute of Sacred Music and Gregorian Univ. (Rome, Italy); professed in Passionists, Aug. 15, 1949; ord. priest Apr. 28, 1956; assistant general of Passionists, 1976-86; ord. titular bp. of Mactaris and aux. bp. of Miami, Mar. 19, 1986; app. bp. of Orlando, Mar. 20, 1990, installed May 25, 1990.

Doueihi, Stephen Hector: b. June 25, 1927, Zghorta, Lebanon; educ. University of St. Joseph (Beirut, Lebanon), Propaganda Fide, Gregorian Univ. and Institute of Oriental Study (Rome); ord. priest Aug. 14, 1955; came to U.S. in 1973; ord. eparch of Eparchy of St. Maron of Brooklyn, Jan 11, 1997

Dougherty, John Martin: b. Apr. 29, 1932, Scranton, Pa.; educ. St. Charles College (Catonsville, Md.), St. Mary's Seminary (Baltimore), Univ. of Notre Dame (South Bend); ord. priest (Scranton) June 15, 1957; ord. titular bp. of Sufetula and aux. bp. of Scranton, Mar. 7, 1995.

Driscoll, Michael P.: b. Aug. 8, 1939, Long Beach, Calif.; educ. St. John Seminary (Camarillo, Calif), Univ. of Southern Calif.; ord. priest (Los Angeles*) May 1, 1965; ord. titular bp. of Massita and aux. bp. of Orange, Mar. 6, 1990; app. bp. of Boise, Jan. 19, 1999, ins. Mar. 18, 1999.

Dudick, Michael J.: b. Feb. 24, 1916, St. Clair, Pa.; educ. St. Procopius College and Seminary (Lisle, Ill.); ord. priest (Passaic, Byzantine Rite) Nov. 13, 1945; ord. bp. of Byzantine Eparchy of Passaic, Oct. 24, 1968; retired Nov. 6, 1995.

Dudley, Paul V.: b. Nov. 27, 1926, Northfield, Minn.; educ. Nazareth College and St. Paul Seminary (St. Paul, Minn.); ord. priest (St. Paul-Minneapolis*) June 2, 1951; ord. titular bp. of Ursona and aux. bp. of St. Paul and Minneapolis, Jan. 25, 1977; app. bp. of Sioux Falls, installed Dec. 13, 1978; retired Mar. 21, 1995.

Duffy, Paul, O.M.I.: b. July 25, 1932, Norwood, Mass; educ Oblate houses of study in Canada and Washington, D.C.; ord. priest 1962; missionary in Zambia from 1984; app. first bp. of Mongu, Zambia, July 1, 1997.

Duhart, Clarence James, C.SS.R.: b. Mar. 23, 1912, New Orleans, La.; ord. priest June 29, 1937; ord. bp. of Udon Thani, Thailand, Apr. 21, 1966; resigned Oct. 2, 1975.

DuMaine, (Roland) Pierre: b. Aug. 2, 1931, Paducah, Ky.; educ. St. Joseph's College (Mountain View, Calif.), St. Patrick's College and Seminary (Menlo Park, Calif.), Univ. of Calif. (Berkeley), Catholic Univ. (Washington, D.C.); ord. priest (San Francisco) June 15, 1957; ord. titular bp. of Sarda and aux. bp. of San Francisco, June 29, 1978; app. first bp. of San Jose, Jan. 27, 1981; installed Mar. 18, 1981.

Dunne, John C.: b. Oct. 30, 1937, Brooklyn, N.Y.; educ. Cathedral College (Brooklyn, N.Y.). Immaculate Conception Seminary (Huntington, N.Y.), Manhattan College (New York); ord. priest (Rockville Centre) June 1, 1963; ord. titular bp. of Abercorn and aux. bp. of Rockville Centre, Dec. 13, 1988. Vicar for Central Vicariate.

Dupre, Thomas L.: b. Nov. 10, 1933, South Hadley Falls, Mass.; educ. College de Montreal, Assumption College (Worcester, Mass.), Catholic Univ. (Washington, D.C.), ord. priest (Springfield, Mass.) May 23, 1959; ord. titular bp. of Hodelm and aux. bp. of

Springfield, Mass. May 31, 1990; bp. of Springfield, Mar. 14, 1995.

Durning, Dennis V., C.S.Sp.: b. May 18, 1923, Germantown, Pa.; educ. St. Mary's Seminary (Ferndale, Conn.); ord. priest June 3, 1949; ord. first bp. of Arusha, Tanzania, May 28, 1963; resigned Mar. 6, 1989.

E

Egan, Edward M.: b. Apr. 2, 1932, Oak Park, Ill.; educ. Quigley Preparatory Seminary (Chicago, Ill.), St. Mary of the Lake Seminary (Mundelein, Ill.), Gregorian Univ. (Rome); ord. priest (Chicago*) Dec. 15, 1957, in Rome; judge of Roman Rota, 1972-85; ord. titular bp. of Allegheny and aux. bp. of New York, May 22, 1985; bp. of Bridgeport, Nov. 5, 1988.

Elya, John A., B.S.O.: b. Sept. 16, 1928, Maghdouche, Lebanon; educ. diocesan monastery (Sidon, Lebanon), Gregorian Univ. (Rome, Italy); professed as member of Basilian Salvatorian Order, 1949; ord. priest Feb. 17, 1952, in Rome; came to U.S., 1958; ord. titular bp. of Abilene of Syria and aux. bp. of Melkite diocese of Newton, Mass., June 29, 1986; app. bp. of Newton (Melkites), Nov. 25, 1993.

F

Favalora, John C.: b. Dec. 5, 1935, New Orleans, La.; educ. St. Joseph Seminary (St. Benedict, La.), Notre Dame Seminary (New Orleans, La.), Gregorian Univ. (Rome), Catholic Univ. of America (Washington, D.C.), Xavier Univ. and Tulane Univ. (New Orleans); ord. priest (New Orleans*) Dec. 20, 1961; ord. bp. of Alexandria, La., July 29, 1986; bp. of St. Petersburg, Mar. 14, 1989; app. abp. of Miami, installed Dec. 20, 1994.

Federal, Joseph Lennox: b. Jan. 13, 1910, Greensboro, N.C.; educ. Belmont Abbey College (Belmont Abbey, N.C.), Niagara Univ. (Niagara Falls, N.Y.), Univ. of Fribourg (Switzerland), North American College and Gregorian Univ. (Rome); ord. priest (Raleigh) Dec. 8, 1934; ord. titular bp. of Appiaria and aux. bp. of Salt Lake City, Apr. 11, 1951; app. coadjutor with right of succession, May, 1958; bp. of Salt Lake City, Mar. 31, 1960; retired Apr. 22, 1980.

Fellhauer, David E.: b. Aug. 19, 1939, Kansas City, Mo.; educ. Pontifical College Josephinum (Worthington, O.), St. Paul Univ. (Ottawa, Ont.); ord. priest (Dallas), May 29, 1965; ord. bp. of Victoria, May 28, 1990.

Fernandez, Gilberto: b. Feb. 13, 1935, Havana, Cuba; educ. El Buen Pastor Seminary (Havana); ord. priest (Havana*), May 15, 1959; came to U.S. 1967; app. titular bp. of Irina and aux. of Miami, June 24, 1997.

Ferrario, Joseph A.: b. Mar. 3, 1926, Scranton, Pa.; educ. St. Charles College (Catonsville, Md.), St. Mary's Seminary (Baltimore, Md.), Catholic Univ. (Washington, D.C.); Univ. of Scranton; ord. priest (Honolulu) May 19, 1951; ord. titular bp. of Cuse and aux. bp. of Honolulu, Jan. 13, 1978; bp. of Honolulu, May 13, 1982; retired Oct. 12, 1993.

Fiorenza, Joseph A.: b. Jan. 25, 1931, Beaumont, Tex.; educ. St. Mary's Seminary (LaPorte, Tex.); ord. priest (Galveston-Houston) May 29, 1954; ord. bp. of San Angelo, Oct. 25, 1979; app. bp. of Galveston-Houston, Dec. 18, 1984, installed Feb. 18,

1985 vice president, NCCB/USCC, 1995-1998, President, 1998-.

Fitzpatrick, John J.: b. Oct. 12, 1918, Trenton, Ont., Canada; educ. Urban Univ. (Rome), Our Lady of the Angels Seminary (Niagara Falls, N.Y.); ord. priest (Buffalo) Dec. 13, 1942; ord. titular bp. of Cenae and aux. bp. of Miami, Aug. 28, 1968; bp. of Brownsville, Tex., May 28, 1971; retired Nov. 30, 1991.

Fitzsimons, George K.: b. Sept. 4, 1928, Kansas City, Mo.; educ. Rockhurst College (Kansas City, Mo.), Immaculate Conception Seminary (Conception, Mo.); ord. priest (Kansas City-St. Joseph) Mar. 18, 1961; ord. titular bp. of Pertusa and aux. bp. of Kansas City-St. Joseph, July 3, 1975; app. bp. of Salina, Mar. 28, 1984, installed May 29, 1984.

Flanagan, Thomas Joseph: b: Oct. 23, 1930, Rathmore, Ireland; educ. St. Patrick's College, Thurles, Ireland; ord priest (San Antonio*) June 10, 1956; app. titular bp. of Bavagaliana and aux. bp. of San Antonio, Jan. 5, 1998, ord. Feb. 16, 1998.

Fliss, Raphael M.: b. Oct. 25, 1930, Milwaukee, Wis.; educ. St. Francis Seminary (Milwaukee, Wis.), Catholic University (Washington, D.C.), Pontifical Lateran Univ. (Rome); ord. priest (Milwaukee*) May 26, 1956; ord. coadjutor bp. of Superior with right of succession, Dec. 20, 1979; bp. of Superior, June 27, 1985.

Flores, Patrick F.: b. July 26, 1929, Ganado, Tex.; educ. St. Mary's Seminary (Houston, Tex.); ord. priest (Galveston-Houston) May 26, 1956; ord. titular bp. of Itolica and aux. bp. of San Antonio, May 5, 1970 (first Mexican-American bp.); app. bp. of El Paso, Apr..4, 1978, installed May 29, 1978; app. abp. of San Antonio 1979; installed Oct. 13, 1979.

Flynn, Harry J.: b. May 2, 1933, Schenectady, N.Y.; educ. Siena College (Loudonville, N.Y.), Mt. St. Mary's College (Emmitsburg, Md.); ord. priest (Albany) May 28, 1960; ord. coadjutor bp. of Lafayette, La., June 24, 1986; bp. of Lafayette, La., May 15, 1989; app. coadjutor abp. of St. Paul and Minneapolis, Feb. 24, 1994, installed Apr. 27, 1994; abp. of St. Paul and Minneapolis, Sept. 8, 1995.

Foley, David E.: b. Feb. 3, 1930, Worcester, Mass.; educ. St. Charles College (Catonsville, Md.), St. Mary's Seminary (Baltimore, Md.); ord. priest (Washington*) May 26, 1952; ord. titular bp. of Octaba and aux. bp. of Richmond, June 27, 1986; app. bp. of Birmingham, Mar. 22, 1994.

Foley, John Patrick: b. Nov. 11, 1935, Sharon Hill, Pa.; educ. St. Joseph's Preparatory School (Philadelphia, Pa.), St. Joseph's College (now University) (Philadelphia, Pa.), St. Charles Borromeo Seminary (Overbrook, Pa.), St. Thomas Univ. (Rome), Columbia School of Journalism (New York); ord. priest (Philadelphia*) May 19, 1962; assistant editor (1967-70) and editor (1970-84) of *The Catholic Standard and Times*, Philadelphia archdiocesan paper; ord. titular abp. of Neapolis in Proconsulari, May 8, 1984, in Philadelphia; app. president of the Pontifical Council for Social Communications, Apr. 5, 1984.

Forst, Marion F.: b. Sept. 3, 1910, St. Louis, Mo.; educ. St. Louis Preparatory Seminary (St. Louis, Mo.), Kenrick Seminary (Webster Groves, Mo.); ord. priest (St. Louis*) June 10, 1934; ord. bp. of Dodge City, Mar. 24, 1960; app. titular bp. of Scala and aux.

bp. of Kansas City, Kans., Oct. 16, 1976; retired Dec. 23, 1986. Titular bp. of Leavenworth.

Franklin, William Edwin: b. May 3, 1930, Parnell, Iowa; educ. Loras College and Mt. St. Bernard Seminry (Dubuque, Iowa); ord. priest (Dubuque*) Feb. 4, 1956; ord. titular bp. of Surista and aux. bp. of Dubuque, Apr. 1, 1987; app. bp. of Davenport, Nov. 12, 1993, installed Jan. 20, 1994.

Franzetta, Benedict C.: b. Aug. 1, 1921, East Liverpool, O.; educ. St. Charles College (Catonsville, Md.), St. Mary Seminary (Cleveland, O.); ord. priest (Youngstown) Apr. 29, 1950; ord. titular bp. of Oderzo and aux. bp. of Youngstown, Sept. 4, 1980; retired Sept. 4, 1996.

Frey, Gerard L.: b. May 10, 1914, New Orleans, La.; educ. Notre Dame Seminary (New Orleans, La.); ord. priest (New Orleans*) Apr. 2, 1938; ord. bp. of Savannah, Aug. 8, 1967; app. bp. of Lafayette, La., Nov. 7, 1972, installed Jan, 7, 1973; retired May 15, 1989.

Friend, William B.: b. Oct. 22, 1931, Miami, Fla.; educ. St. Mary's College (St. Mary, Ky.), Mt. St. Mary Seminary (Emmitsburg, Md.), Catholic Univ. (Washington, D.C.), Notre Dame Univ. (Notre Dame, Ind.); ord. priest (Mobile*) May 7, 1959; ord. titular bp. of Pomaria and aux. bp. of Alexandria-Shreveport, La., Oct. 30, 1979; app. bp. of Alexandria-Shreveport, Nov. 17, 1982, installed Jan 11, 1983; app. first bp. of Shreveport, June, 1986; installed July 30, 1986.

G

Galante, Joseph A.: b. July 2, 1938, Philadelphia, Pa.; educ. St. Joseph Preparatory School, St. Charles Seminary (Philadelphia, Pa.); Lateran Univ., Angelicum, North American College (Rome); ord. priest (Philadelphia*) May 16, 1964; on loan to diocese of Brownsville, Tex., 1968-72, where he served in various diocesan posts; returned to Philadelphia, 1972; assistant vicar (1972-79) and vicar (1979-87) for religious; undersecretary of Congregation for Institutes of Consecrated Life and Societies of Apostolic Life (Rome), 1987-92; ord. titular bp. of Equilium and aux. bp. of San Antonio, Dec. 11, 1992; app. bp. of Beaumont, Apr. 5, 1994.

Garcia, Richard J.: b. Apr. 24, 1947, San Francisco; educ. St. Patrick's Seminary (Menlo Park, Calif.); ord priest (San Francisco*) May 13, 1973; app. Titular bp. of Bapara and aux. bp. of Sacramento, Nov. 25, 1997, ord. Jan. 28, 1998.

Garland, James H.: b. Dec. 13, 1931, Wilmington, Ohio; educ. Wilmington College (Ohio), Ohio State Univ. (Columbus, O.); Mt. St. Mary's Seminary (Cincinnati, O.), Catholic Univ. (Washington, D.C.); ord. priest (Cincinnati*) Aug. 15, 1959; ord. titular bp. of Garriana and aux. bp. of Cincinnati, July 25, 1984; app. bp. of Marquette, Oct. 6, 1992; installed Nov. 11, 1992.

Garmendia, Francisco: b. Nov. 6, 1924, Lozcano, Spain; ord. priest June 29, 1947, in Spain; came to New York in 1964; became naturalized citizen; ord. titular bp. of Limisa and aux. bp. of New York, June 29, 1977. Vicar for Spanish pastoral development in New York archdiocese.

Garmo, George: b. Dec. 8, 1921, Telkaif, Iraq; educ. St. Peter Chaldean Patriarchal Seminary (Mossul, Iraq), Pontifical Urban Univ. (Rome); ord. priest Dec. 8, 1945; pastor of Chaldean parish in Detroit arch-

diocese, 1960-64, 1966-80; ord. abp. of Chaldean archdiocese of Mossul Iraq, Sept. 14, 1980.

Garner, Robert F.: b. Apr. 27, 1920, Jersey City, N.J.; educ. Seton Hall Univ. (S. Orange, N.J.), Immaculate Conception Seminary (Darlington, N.J.); ord. priest (Newark*) June 15, 1946; ord. titular bp. of Blera and aux. bp. of Newark, June 25, 1976. Retired July 11, 1995.

Gaughan, Norbert F.: b. May 30, 1921, Pittsburgh, Pa.; educ. St. Vincent College (Latrobe, Pa.), Univ. of Pittsburgh; ord. priest (Pittsburgh) Nov. 4, 1945; ord. titular bp. of Taraqua and aux. bp. of Greensburg, June 26, 1975; app. bp. of Gary, July 24, 1984, installed Oct. 2, 1984. Retired June 1, 1996.

Gaydos, John R.: b. Aug. 14, 1943, St. Louis, Mo.; educ Cardinal Glennon College (St. Louis, Mo.), North Americsan College, Gregorian Univ. (Rome); ord. priest (St. Louis*) Dec. 20, 1968; ord. bp. of Jefferson City, Aug. 27, 1997.

Gelineau, Louis E.: b. May 3, 1928, Burlington, Vt.; educ. St. Michael's College (Winooski, Vt.), St. Paul's Univ. Seminary (Ottawa, Ont.), Catholic Univ. (Washington, D.C.); ord. priest (Burlington) June 5, 1954; ord. bp. of Providence, R.I., Jan. 26, 1972; retired June 11, 1997.

Gendron, Odore J.: b. Sept. 13, 1921, Manchester, N.H.; educ. St. Charles Borromeo Seminary (Sherbrooke, Que., Canada), Univ. of Ottawa, St. Paul Univ. Seminary (Ottawa, Ont., Canada); ord. priest (Manchester) May 31, 1947; ord. bp. of Manchester, Feb. 3, 1975; resigned June 12, 1990.

George, Cardinal Francis E., O.M.I.: (See Cardinals, Biographies).

Gerber, Eugene J.: b. Apr. 30, 1931, Kingman, Kans.; educ. St. Thomas Seminary (Denver, Colo.), Wichita State Univ.; Catholic Univ. (Washington, D.C.), Angelicum (Rome); ord. priest (Wichita) May 19, 1959; ord. bp. of Dodge City, Dec. 14, 1976; app. bp. of Wichita, Nov. 17, 1982, installed Feb. 9, 1983.

Gerety, Peter L.: b. July 19, 1912, Shelton, Conn.; educ. Sulpician Seminary (Paris, France); ord. priest (Hartford*) June 29, 1939; ord. titular bp. of Crepedula and coadjutor bp. of Portland, Me., with right of succession, June 1, 1966; app. apostolic administrator of Portland, 1967; bp. of Portland, Me., Sept. 15, 1969; ord. abp. of Newark, Apr. 2, 1974; installed June 28, 1974; retired June 3, 1986.

Gerry, Joseph J., O.S.B.: b. Sept. 12, 1928, Millinocket, Me.; educ. St. Anselm Abbey Seminary (Manchester, N.H.), Univ. of Toronto (Canada), Fordham Univ. (New York); ord. priest June 12, 1954; abbot of St. Anselm Abbey, Manchester, N.H., 1972; ord. titular bp. of Praecausa and aux. of Manchester, Apr. 21, 1986; bp. of Portland, Me., Dec. 27, 1988, installed Feb. 21, 1989.

Gettelfinger, Gerald A.: b. Oct. 20, 1935, Ramsey, Ind.; educ. St. Meinrad Seminary (St. Meinrad, Ind.), Butler Univ. (Indianapolis, Ind.); ord. priest (Indianapolis*) May 7, 1961; ord. bp. of Evansville, Apr. 11, 1989.

Gilbert, Edward J., C.SS.R.: b. Dec. 26, 1936, Brooklyn, N.Y.; educ. Mt. St. Alphonsus Seminary (Esopus, New York), Catholic Univ. (Washington, D.C.); ord. priest (Redemptorists, Baltimore Province) June 21, 1964; ord. bp. of Roseau, Dominica, Sept. 7, 1994.

Gilmore, Ronald W.: b. Apr. 23, 1942, Wichita, KS.;

educ. University Seminary (Ottawa), St. Paul University (Ottawa); ord. priest (Wichita), June 7, 1969; app. Bp. of Dodge City, May 11, 1998, ord. July 16, 1998.

Glynn, John J.: b. Aug. 6, 1926, Boston, Mass.; educ. St. John's Seminary (Brighton, Mass.); ord. priest (Boston*), Apr. 11, 1951; Navy chaplain, 1960-85; ord. titular bp. of Monteverde and aux. bp. of Military Services archdiocese, Jan. 6, 1992.

Goedert, Raymond E.: b. Oct. 15, 1927, Oak Park, Ill.; educ. Quigley Preparatory Seminary (Chicago, Ill.), St. Mary of the Lake Seminary and Loyola Univ. (Chicago, Ill.), Gregorian Univ. (Rome); ord. priest (Chicago*), May 1, 1952; ord. titular bp. of Tamazeni and aux. bp. of Chicago, Aug. 29, 1991.

Gonzalez, Roberto O., O.F.M., b. June 2, 1950, Elizabeth, N.J.; educ. St. Joseph Seminary (Callicoon, N.Y.), Siena College, (Loudonville, N.Y.), Washington Theological Union (Silver Spring, Md.), Fordham Univ. (New York, N.Y.); solemnly professed in Franciscan Order, 1976; ord. priest May 8, 1977; ord. titular bp. of Ursona and aux. bp. of Boston, Oct. 3, 1988; app. coadjutor bp. of Corpus Christi, May 16, 1995; bishop of Corpus Christi, Apr. 1, 1997; app. abp. of San Juan de Puerto Rico, Mar. 26, 1999, ord. May 8, 1999.

Gorman, John R.: b. Dec. 11, 1925, Chicago, Ill.; educ, St. Mary of the Lake Seminary (Mundelein, Ill.), Loyola Univ. (Chicago, Ill.); ord. priest (Chicago*) May 1, 1956; ord. titular bp. of Catula and aux. bp. of Chicago, Apr. 11, 1988.

Gossman, F. Joseph: b. Apr. 1, 1930, Baltimore, Md.; educ. St. Charles College (Catonsville, Md.), St. Mary's Seminary (Baltimore, Md.), North American College (Rome), Catholic Univ. (Washington, D.C.); ord. priest (Baltimore*) Dec. 17, 1955; ord. titular bp. of Agunto and aux. bp. of Baltimore, Sept. 11, 1968; app. bp. of Raleigh Apr. 8, 1975.

Gottwald, George J.: b. May 12, 1914, St. Louis, Mo.; educ. Kenrick Seminary (Webster Groves, Mo.); ord. priest (St. Louis*) June 9, 1940; ord. titular bp. of Cedamusa and aux. bp. of St. Louis, Aug. 8, 1961; resigned Aug. 2, 1988.

Gracida, Rene H.: b. June 9, 1923, New Orleans, La.; educ. Rice Univ. and Univ. of Houston (Houston, Tex.), Univ. of Fribourg (Switzerland); ord. priest (Miami*) May 23, 1959; ord. titular bp. of Masuccaba and aux. bp. of Miami, Jan. 25, 1972; app. first bp. of Pensacola-Tallahassee, Oct. 1, 1975, installed Nov. 6, 1975; app. bp. of Corpus Christi, May 24, 1983, installed July 11, 1983; retired Apr. 1, 1997.

Grady, Thomas J.: b. Oct. 9, 1914, Chicago, Ill.; educ. St. Mary of the Lake Seminary (Mundelein, Ill.), Gregorian Univ. (Rome), Loyola Univ. (Chicago, Ill.); ord. priest (Chicago*) Apr. 23, 1938; ord. titular bp. of Vamalla and aux. bp. of Chicago, Aug. 24, 1967; app. bp. of Orlando, Fla., Nov. 11, 1974, installed Dec. 16, 1974; resigned Dec. 12, 1989.

Graham, John J.: b. Sept. 11, 1913, Philadelphia, Pa.; educ. St. Charles Borromeo Seminary (Philadelphia, Pa.), Pontifical Roman Seminary (Rome, Italy); ord. priest (Philadelphia*) Feb. 26, 1938; ord. titular bp. of Sabrata and aux. bp. of Philadelphia, Jan. 7, 1964; retired Nov. 8, 1988.

Grahmann, Charles V.: b. July 15, 1931, Halletsville, Tex.; educ. The Assumption-St. John's Seminary (San Antonio, Tex.); ord. priest (San Anto-

nio*) Mar. 17, 1956; ord. titular bp. of Equilium and aux. bp. of San Antonio, Aug. 20, 1981; app. first bp. of Victoria, Tex., Apr. 13, 1982; app. coadjutor bp. of Dallas, Dec. 9, 1989; bp. of Dallas, July 14, 1990.

Gregory, Wilton D.: b. Dec. 7, 1947, Chicago, Ill.; educ. Quigley Preparatory Seminary South, Niles College of Loyola Univ. (Chicago, Ill.), St. Mary of the Lake Seminary (Mundelein, Ill.), Pontifical Liturgical Institute, Sant'Anselmo (Rome); ord. priest (Chicago*) May 9, 1973; ord. titular bp. of Oliva and aux. bp. of Chicago, Dec. 13, 1983; app. bp. of Belleville, Dec. 29, 1993; installed Feb. 10, 1994 vice president, NCCB/USCC, 1998-.

Griffin, James A.: b. June 13, 1934, Fairview Park, O.; educ. St. Charles College (Baltimore, Md.), Borromeo College (Wicklife, O.); St Mary Seminary (Cleveland, O.); Lateran Univ. (Rome); Cleveland State Univ.; ord. priest (Cleveland) May 28, 1960; ord. titular bp. of Holar and aux. bp. of Cleveland, Aug. 1, 1979; app. bp. of Columbus, Feb. 8, 1983.

Grosz, Edward M.: b. Feb. 16, 1945, Buffalo, N.Y.; educ. St. John Vianney Seminary (East Aurora, N.Y.), Notre Dame Univ. (Notre Dame, Ind.); ord. priest (Buffalo) May 29, 1971; ord. titular bp. of Morosbisdus and aux. bp. of Buffalo, Feb. 2, 1990.

Guillory, Curtis J., S.V.D.: b. Sept. 1, 1943, Mallet, La.; educ. Divine Word College (Epworth, Iowa), Chicago Theological Union (Chicago), Creighton Univ. (Omaha, Neb.); ord. priest Dec. 16, 1972; ord. titular bp. of Stagno and aux. bp. of Galveston-Houston, Feb. 19, 1988.

Gumbleton, Thomas J.: b. Jan. 26, 1930, Detroit, Mich.; educ. St. John Provincial Seminary (Detroit, Mich.), Pontifical Lateran Univ. (Rome); ord. priest (Detroit*) June 2, 1956; ord. titular bp. of Ululi and aux. bp. of Detroit, May 1, 1968.

H

Ham, J. Richard, M.M.: b. July 11, 1921, Chicago, Ill.; educ. Maryknoll Seminary (New York); ord. priest June 12, 1948; missionary to Guatemala, 1958; ord. titular bp. of Puzia di Numidia and aux. bp. of Guatemala, Jan. 6, 1968; resigned see 1979; aux. bp. of St. Paul and Minneapolis, October, 1980; retired Oct. 29, 1990.

Hanifen, Richard C.: b. June 15, 1931, Denver, Colo,; educ. Regis College and St. Thomas Seminary (Denver, Colo.), Catholic Univ. (Washington, D.C.), Lateran Univ. (Rome); ord. priest (Denver*) June 6, 1959; ord. titular bp. of Abercorn and aux. bp. of Denver, Sept. 20, 1974; app. first bp. of Colorado Springs, Nov. 10, 1983; installed Jan. 30, 1984.

Hannan, Philip M.: b. May 20, 1913, Washington, D.C.; educ. St. Charles College (Catonsville, Md.), Catholic Univ. (Washington, D.C.), North American College (Rome); ord. priest (Washington*) Dec. 8, 1939; ord. titular bp. of Hieropolis and aux. bp. of Washington, D.C., Aug. 28, 1956; app. abp. of New Orleans, installed Oct. 13, 1965; retired Dec. 6, 1988.

Hanus, Jerome George, O.S.B.: b. May 25, 1940, Brainard, Nebr.; educ. Conception Seminary (Conception, Mo.), St. Anselm Univ. (Rome), Princeton Theological Seminary (Princeton, N.J.); ord. priest (Conception Abbey, Mo.) July 30, 1966; abbot of Conception Abbey, 1977-87; president of Swiss American Benedictine Congregation, 1984-87; ord. bp. of St. Cloud, Aug. 24, 1987; app. coadjutor abp.

of Dubuque, Aug. 23, 1994; abp. of Dubuque, Oct. 16, 1995.

Harrington, Bernard J.: b. Sept. 6, 1933, Detroit; educ. Sacred Heart Seminary (Detroit), St. John's Provincial Seminary (Plymouth, Mich.), Catholic Univ. of America (Washington, D.C.), University of Detroit; ord. priest (Detroit*) June 6, 1959; ord. titular bp. of Uzali and aux. bp. of Detroit, Jan. 6, 1994; app. Bp. of Winona, Nov. 5, 1998, ordained Jan. 6, 1999.

Harrison, Frank J.: b. Aug. 12, 1912; Syracuse, N.Y.; educ. Notre Dame Univ. (Notre Dame, Ind.), St. Bernard's Seminary (Rochester, N.Y.), ord. priest (Syracuse) June 4, 1937; ord. titular bp. of Aquae in Numidia and aux. of Syracuse, Apr. 22, 1971; app. bp. of Syracuse, Nov. 9, 1976, installed Feb. 6, 1977; retired June 16, 1987.

Hart, Daniel A.: b. Aug. 24, 1927, Lawrence, Mass.; educ. St. John's Seminary (Brighton, Mass.); ord. priest (Boston*) Feb. 2, 1953; ord. titular bp. of Tepelta and aux. bp. of Boston, Oct. 18, 1976; bp. of Norwich Sept. 12, 1995.

Hart, Joseph: b. Sept. 26, 1931, Kansas City, Missouri; educ. St. John Seminary (Kansas City, Mo.), St. Meinrad Seminary (Indianapolis, Ind.); ord. priest (Kansas City-St. Joseph) May 1, 1956; ord. titular bp. of Thimida Regia and aux. bp. of Cheyenne, Wyo., Aug. 31, 1976; app. bp. of Cheyenne, installed June 12, 1978.

Harvey, James M.: b. Oct. 20, 1949, Milwaukee, Wis.; educ. De Sales Preparatory Seminary and St. Francis De Sales College, Milwaukee, North American College and Gregorian Univ. (Rome); ord. priest (Milwaukee*) June 29, 1975; entered Vatican diplomatic service, 1980; Apostolic Nunciature, Dominican Republic, 1980-82; transferred to the Vatican Secretariat of State, 1982; named assessor of the Secretariat, 1997; named titular bp. of Memphis and prefect of the papal household, Feb. 7, 1998; ordained bp. Mar. 19, 1998.

Head, Edward D.: b. Aug. 5, 1919, White Plains, N.Y.; educ. Cathedral College, St. Joseph's Seminary, Columbia Univ. (New York City); ord. priest (New York*) Jan. 27, 1945; director of New York Catholic Charities; ord. titular bp. of Ardsratha and aux. bp. of New York, Mar. 19, 1970; app. bp. of Buffalo, Jan. 23, 1973, installed Mar. 19, 1973; retired Apr. 18, 1995.

Heim, Capistran F., O.F.M.: b. Jan. 21, 1934, Catskill, N.Y.; educ. Franciscan Houses of Study; ord. priest Dec. 18, 1965; missionary in Brazil; ord. first bp. of prelature of Itaituba, Brazil, Sept. 17, 1988; installed Oct. 2, 1988.

Hermes, Herbert, O.S.B.: b. May 25, 1933, Scott City, Kans.; ord. priest (St. Benedict Abbey, Atchison, Kans.), May 26, 1960; missionary in Brazil; ord. bp. of territorial prelature of Cristalandia, Brazil, Sept. 2, 1990.

Herrmann, Edward J.: b. Nov. 6, 1913, Baltimore, Md.; educ. Mt. St. Mary's Seminary (Emmitsburg, Md.), Catholic Univ. (Washington, D.C.); ord. priest (Washington*) June 12, 1947; ord. titular bp. of Lamzella and aux. bp. of Washington, D.C., Apr. 26, 1966; app. bp. of Columbus, June 26, 1973; resigned Sept. 18, 1982.

Hickey, Dennis W.: b. Oct. 28, 1914, Dansville, N.Y.; educ. Colgate Univ. and St. Bernard's Seminary (Rochester, N.Y.); ord. priest (Rochester) June 7, 1941; ord. titular bp. of Rusuccuru and aux. bp. of Rochester, N.Y., Mar. 14, 1968; retired Jan. 16, 1990.

Hickey, James A.: (See Cardinals, Biographies.)

Higi, William L.: b. Aug. 29, 1933, Anderson, Ind.; educ. Our Lady of the Lakes Preparatory Seminary (Wawasee, Ind.), Mt. St. Mary of the West Seminary and Xavier Univ. (Cincinnati, O.); ord. priest (Lafayette, Ind.) May 30, 1959; ord. bp. of Lafayette, Ind., June 6, 1984.

Hoffman, James R.: b. June 12, 1932, Fremont, O.; educ. Our Lady of the Lake Minor Seminary (Wawasee, Ind.), St. Meinrad College (St. Meinrad, Ind.), Mt. St. Mary Seminary (Norwood, O.), Catholic Univ. (Washington, D.C.); ord. priest (Toledo) July 28, 1957; ord. titular bp. of Italica and aux. bp. of Toledo, June 23, 1978; bp. of Toledo, Dec. 16, 1980.

Hogan, James J.: b. Oct. 17, 1911, Philadelphia, Pa.; educ. St. Charles College (Catonsville, Md.), St. Mary's Seminary (Baltimore), Gregorian Univ. (Rome), Catholic Univ. (Washington, D.C.); ord. priest (Trenton) Dec. 8, 1937; ord. titular bp. of Philomelium and aux. bp. of Trenton, Feb. 25, 1960; app. bp. of Altoona-Johnstown, installed July 6, 1966; retired Nov. 4, 1986.

Hogan, Joseph L.: b. Mar. 11, 1916, Lima, N.Y.; educ. St. Bernard's Seminary (Rochester, N.Y.), Canisius College (Buffalo, N.Y.), Angelicum (Rome); ord. priest (Rochester) June 6, 1942; ord. bp. of Rochester, Nov. 28, 1969; resigned Nov. 28, 1978.

Houck, William Russell: b. June 26, 1926, Mobile, Ala.; educ. St. Bernard Junior College (Cullman, Ala.), St. Mary's Seminary College and St. Mary's Seminary (Baltimore, Md.), Catholic Univ. (Washington, D.C.); ord. priest (Mobile*) May 19, 1951; ord. titular bp. of Alessano and aux. bp. of Jackson, Miss., May 27, 1979, by Pope John Paul II; app. bp. of Jackson, Apr. 11, 1984, installed June 5, 1984.

Howze, Joseph Lawson: b. Aug. 30, 1923, Daphne, Ala.; convert to Catholicism, 1948; educ. St. Bonaventure Univ. (St. Bonaventure, N.Y.); ord. priest (Raleigh) May 7, 1959; ord. titular bp. of Massita and aux. bp. of Natchez-Jackson, Jan. 28, 1973; app. first bp. of Biloxi, Miss., Mar. 8, 1977; installed June 6, 1977.

Hubbard, Howard J.: b. Oct. 31, 1938, Troy, N.Y.; educ. St. Joseph's Seminary (Dunwoodie, N.Y.); North American College and Gregorian Univ. (Rome), Catholic Univ. (Washington, D.C.); ord. priest (Albany) Dec. 18, 1963; ord. bp. of Albany, Mar. 27, 1977.

Hughes, Alfred C.: b. Dec. 2, 1932, Boston, Mass.; educ. St. John Seminary (Brighton, Mass.), Gregorian Univ. (Rome); ord. priest (Boston*) Dec. 15, 1957, in Rome; ord. titular bp. of Maximiana in Byzacena and aux. bp. of Boston, Sept. 14, 1981; app. bp. of Baton Rouge, Sept. 7, 1993.

Hughes, Edward T.: b. Nov. 13, 1920, Lansdowne, Pa.; educ. St. Charles Seminary, Univ. of Pennsylvania (Philadelphia); ord. priest (Philadelphia*) May 31, 1947; ord. titular bp. of Segia and aux. bp. of Philadelphia, July 21, 1976; app. bp. of Metuchen, Dec. 11, 1986, installed Feb. 5, 1987; retired July 8, 1997.

Hughes, William A.: b. Sept. 23, 1921, Youngstown, O.; educ. St. Charles College (Catonsville, Md.), St. Mary's Seminary (Cleveland, O.), Notre Dame Univ. (Notre Dame, Ind.); ord. priest (Youngstown) Apr. 6,

1946; ord. titular bp. of Inis Cathaig and aux. bp. of Youngstown, Sept. 12, 1974; app. bp. of Covington, installed May 8, 1979. Retired July 4, 1995.

Hunthausen, Raymond G.: b. Aug. 21, 1921, Anaconda, Mont.; educ. Carroll College (Helena, Mont.), St. Edward's Seminary (Kenmore, Wash.), St. Louis Univ. (St. Louis, Mo.), Catholic Univ. (Washington, D.C.), Fordham Univ. (New York City), Notre Dame Univ. (Notre Dame, Ind.); ord. priest (Helena) June 1, 1946; ord. bp. of Helena, Aug. 30, 1962; app. abp. of Seattle, Feb. 25, 1975; retired Aug. 21, 1991.

Hurley, Francis T.: b. Jan. 12, 1927, San Francisco, Calif.; educ. St. Patrick's Seminary (Menlo Park, Calif.), Catholic Univ. (Washington, D.C.); ord. priest (San Francisco*) June 16, 1951; assigned to NCWC in Washington, D.C., 1957; assistant (1958) and later (1968) associate secretary of NCCB and USCC; ord. titular bp. of Daimlaig and aux. bp. of Juneau, Alaska, Mar. 19, 1970; app. bp. of Juneau, July 20, 1971, installed Sept. 8, 1971; app. abp. of Anchorage, May 4, 1976, installed July 8, 1976.

Hurley, Mark J.: b. Dec. 13, 1919, San Francisco, Calif.; educ. St. Patrick's Seminary (Menlo Park, Calif.), Univ. of Calif. (Berkeley), Catholic Univ. (Washington, D.C.), Lateran Univ. (Rome), Univ. of Portland (Portland, Ore.); ord. priest (San Francisco*) Sept. 23, 1944; ord. titular bp. of Thunusuda and aux. bp. of San Francisco, Jan. 4, 1968; app. bp. of Santa Rosa, Nov. 19, 1969; resigned Apr. 15, 1986.

I-J

Ibrahim, Ibrahim N.: b. Oct. 1, 1937, Telkaif, Mosul, Iraq.; educ. Patriarchal Seminary (Mosul, Iraq), St. Sulpice Seminary (Paris, France); ord. priest Dec. 30, 1962, in Baghdad, Iraq; ord. titular bp. of Anbar and apostolic exarch for Chaldean Catholics in the United States, Mar. 8, 1982, in Baghdad; installed in Detroit, Apr. 18, 1982; app. first eparch, Aug. 3, 1985, when exarchate was raised to eparchy of St. Thomas Apostle of Detroit.

Imesch, Joseph L.: b. June 21, 1931, Detroit, Mich.; educ. Sacred Heart Seminary (Detroit, Mich.), North American College, Gregorian Univ. (Rome); ord. priest (Detroit*) Dec. 16, 1956; ord. titular bp. of Pomaria and aux. bp. of Detroit, Apr. 3, 1973; app. bp. of Joliet, June 30, 1979.

Irwin, Francis X.: b. Jan 9, 1934, Medford, Mass.; educ. Boston College High School, Boston College, St. John's Seminary (Brighton, Mass.), Boston College School of Social Service; ord. priest (Boston*) Feb. 2, 1960; ord. titular bp. of Ubaza and aux. bp. of Boston, Sept. 17, 1996.

Jacobs, Sam Galip: b. Mar. 4, 1938, Greenwood, Miss.; educ. Immaculata Seminary (Lafayette, La.), Catholic Univ. (Washington, D.C.); ord. priest (Lafayette) June 6, 1964; became priest of Lake Charles diocese, 1980, when that see was established; ord. bp. of Alexandria, La., Aug. 24, 1989.

Jakubowski, Thad J.: b. Apr. 5, 1924, Chicago, Ill.; educ. Mundelein Seminary, St. Mary of the Lake Univ., Loyola Univ. (Chicago); ord priest (Chicago*) May 3, 1950; ord. titular bp. of Plestia and aux. bp. of Chicago, Apr. 11, 1988.

Jarrell, C. Michael: b. May 15, 1940, Opelousas, La.; educ. Immaculata Minor Seminary (Lafayette, La.); Catholic Univ. (Washington, D.C.); ord. priest

(Lafayette, La.) June 3, 1967; ord. bp. of Houma-Thibodaux, Mar. 4, 1993.

Jenky, Daniel R.: b. Mar. 3, 1947, Chicago; educ. University of Notre Dame; ord. priest April 6, 1974; Religious Superior of the Holy Cross religious at Notre Dame, 1985-1990; app.Titular Bp. of Amanzia and Aux. of Fort Wayne-South Bend, Oct. 21, 1997, ord. Dec. 16, 1997.

K

Kaffer, Roger L.: b. Aug. 14, 1927, Joliet, Ill.; educ. Quigley Preparatory Seminary (Chicago, Ill.), St. Mary of the Lake Seminary (Mundelein, Ill.), Gregorian Univ. (Rome); ord. priest (Joliet) May 1, 1954; ord. titular bp. of Dusa and aux. bp. of Joliet, June 26, 1985.

Kalisz, Raymond P., S.V.D.: b. Sept. 25, 1927, Melvindale, Mich.; educ. St. Mary's Seminary (Techny, Ill.); ord. priest Aug. 15, 1954; ord. bp. of Wewak, Papua New Guinea, August 15, 1980.

Kaniecki, Michael Joseph, S.J.: b. Apr. 13, 1935, Detroit Mich.; joined Jesuits 1953; educ. Xavier Univ. (Milford, O.), Mt. St. Michael's Seminary (Spokane, Wash.), Regis College (Willowdale, Ont.); ord. priest June 5, 1965; ord. coadjutor bp. of Fairbanks, May 1, 1984; bp. of Fairbanks, June 1, 1985.

Keeler, Cardinal William Henry: (See Cardinals, Biographies.)

Keleher, James P.: b. July 31, 1931, Chicago, Ill.; educ. Quigley Preparatory Seminary (Chicago, Ill.), St. Mary of the Lake Seminary (Mundelein, Ill.); ord. priest (Chicago*) Apr. 12, 1958; ord. bp. of Belleville, Dec. 11, 1984; app. abp. of Kansas City, Kans., June 28, 1993.

Kelly, Thomas C., O.P.: b. July 14, 1931, Rochester, N.Y.; educ. Providence College (Providence, R.I.), Immaculate Conception College (Washington, D.C.), Angelicum (Rome); professed in Dominicans, Aug. 26, 1952; secretary, apostolic delegation, Washington, D.C., 1965-71; associate general secretary, 1971-77, and general secretary, 1977-81, NCCB/USCC; ord. titular bp. of Tusurus and aux. bp. of Washington, D.C., Aug. 15, 1977; app. abp. of Louisville, Dec. 28, 1981, installed Feb. 18, 1982.

Kicanas, Gerald F.: b. Aug. 18, 1941, Chicago, Ill.; educ. Quigley Preparatory Seminary, St. Mary of the Lake Seminary and Loyola University in Chicago; ord. priest (Chicago*) Apr. 27, 1967; ord. titular bp. of Bela and aux. of Chicago, Mar. 20, 1995.

Kinney, John F.: b. June 11, 1937, Oelwein, Iowa; educ. Nazareth Hall and St. Paul Seminaries (St. Paul, Minn.); Pontifical Lateran University (Rome); ord. priest (St. Paul-Minneapolis*) Feb. 2, 1963; ord. titular bp. of Caorle and aux. bp. of St. Paul and Minneapolis, Jan. 25, 1977; app. bp. of Bismarck June 30, 1982; app. bp. of St. Cloud, May 9, 1995.

Kmiec, Edward U.: b. June 4, 1936, Trenton, N.J.; educ. St. Charles College (Catonsville, Md.), St. Mary's Seminary (Baltimore, Md.), Gregorian Univ. (Rome); ord. priest (Trenton) Dec. 20, 1961; ord. titular bp. of Simidicca and aux. bp. of Trenton, Nov. 3, 1982; app. bp. of Nashville, Oct. 13, 1992; installed Dec. 3, 1992.

Krawczak, Arthur H.: b. Feb. 2, 1913, Detroit, Mich.; educ. Sacred Heart Seminary, Sts. Cyril and Methodius Seminary (Orchard Lake, Mich.), Catholic Univ. (Washington, D.C.); ord. priest (Detroit*)

May 18, 1940; ord. titular bp. of Subbar and aux. bp. of Detroit, Apr. 3, 1973; retired Aug. 17, 1982.

Kucera, Daniel W., O.S.B.: b. May 7, 1923, Chicago, Ill.; educ. St. Procopius College (Lisle, Ill.), Catholic Univ. (Washington, D.C.); professed in Order of St. Benedict, June 16, 1944; ord. priest May 26, 1949; abbot, St. Procopius Abbey, 1964-71; pres. Illinois Benedictine College, 1959-65 and 1971-76; ord. titular bp. of Natchez and aux. bp. of Joliet, July 21, 1977; app. bp. of Salina, Mar. 5, 1980; app. abp. of Dubuque, installed Feb. 23, 1984; retired Oct. 16, 1995.

Kuchmiak, Michael, C.SsR.: b. Feb. 5, 1923, Obertyn, Horodenka, Western Ukraine; left during World War II; educ. St. Josaphat Ukrainian Seminary (Rome, Italy), St. Mary's Seminary (Meadowvale, Ont., Canada); ord. priest May 13, 1956; in the U.S. from 1967; ord. titular bp. of Agathonis and aux. bp. of Ukrainian metropolitan of Philadelphia, Apr. 27, 1988; exarch of apostolic exarchate for Ukrainian Catholics in Great Britain, June 24, 1989.

Kupfer, William F., M.M.: b. Jan. 28, 1909, Brooklyn, N.Y.; educ. Cathedral College (Brooklyn, N.Y.), Maryknoll Seminary (Maryknoll, N.Y.); ord. priest June 11, 1933; missionary in China; app. prefect apostolic of Taichung, Taiwan, 1951; ord. first bp. of Taichung, July 25, 1962; retired Sept. 3, 1986.

Kurtz, Robert, C.R.: b. July 25, 1939, Chicago, Ill.; ord. priest Mar. 11, 1967; ord. bp. of Hamilton, Bermuda, Sept. 15, 1995.

Kuzma, George M.: b. July 24, 1925, Windber, Pa.; educ. St. Francis Seminary (Loretto, Pa.), St. Procopius College (Lisle, Ill.), Sts. Cyril and Methodius Byzantine Catholic Seminary, Duquesne Univ. (Pittsburgh, Pa.); ord. priest (Pittsburgh*, Byzantine Rite), May 5, 1955; ord. titular bp. of Telmisso and aux. bp. of Byzantine eparchy of Passaic, 1987; app. bp. of Byzantine diocese of Van Nuys, Calif., Oct. 23, 1990, installed Jan. 15, 1991.

L

Lambert, Francis, S.M.: b. Feb. 7, 1921, Lawrence, Mass.; educ. Marist Seminary (Framingham, Mass.); ord. priest, June 29, 1946; served in Marist missions in Oceania; provincial of Marist Oceania province, 1971; ord. bp. of Port Vila, Vanuatu (New Hebrides), Mar. 20, 1977; retired Nov. 30, 1996..

Larkin, W. Thomas: b. Mar. 31, 1923, Mt. Morris, N.Y.; educ. St. Andrew Seminary and St. Bernard Seminary (Rochester, N.Y.); Angelicum Univ. (Rome); ord. priest (St. Augustine) May 15, 1947; ord. bp. of St. Petersburg, May 27, 1979; retired Nov. 29, 1988.

Law, Bernard F.: (See Cardinals, Biographies.)

Leibrecht, John J.: b. Aug. 30, 1930, Overland, Mo.; educ. Catholic Univ. (Washington, D.C.); ord. priest (St. Louis*) Mar. 17, 1956; superintendent of schools of St. Louis archdiocese, 1962-1981; ord. bp. of Springfield-Cape Girardeau, Mo., Dec. 12, 1984.

Lessard, Raymond W.: b. Dec. 21, 1930, Grafton, N.D.; educ. St. Paul Seminary (St. Paul, Minn.), North American College (Rome); ord. priest (Fargo) Dec. 16, 1956; served on staff of the Congregation for Bp.s in the Roman Curia, 1964-73; ord. bp. of Savannah, Apr. 27, 1973; retired Feb. 7, 1995.

Levada, William J.: b. June 15, 1936, Long Beach, Calif.; educ. St. John's College (Camarillo, Calif.),

Gregorian Univ. (Rome); ord. priest (Los Angeles*) Dec. 20, 1961; ord. titular bp. of Capri and aux. bp. of Los Angeles, May 12, 1983; app. abp. of Portland, Ore., July 3, 1986; coadjutor abp. of San Francisco, Aug. 17, 1995; abp. of San Francisco Dec. 27, 1995.

Lipscomb, Oscar H.: b. Sept. 21, 1931, Mobile, Ala.; educ. McGill Institute, St. Bernard College (Cullman, Ala.), North American College and Gregorian Univ. (Rome), Catholic Univ. (Washington, D.C.); ord. priest (Mobile*) July 15, 1956; ord. first abp. of Mobile, Nov. 16, 1980.

Lohmuller, Martin N.: b. Aug. 21, 1919, Philadelphia, Pa.; educ. St. Charles Borromeo Seminary (Philadelphia, Pa.), Catholic Univ. (Washington, D.C.); ord. priest (Philadelphia*) June 3, 1944; ord. titular bp. of Ramsbury and aux. bp. of Philadelphia, Apr. 2, 1970; retired Oct. 11, 1994.

Lori, William E.: b. May 6, 1951, Louisville, Ky.; educ. St. Pius X College (Covington, Ky.), Mount St. Mary's Seminary (Emmitsburg, Md.), Catholic Univ. (Washington, D.C.); ord. priest (Washington*) May 14, 1977; ord. titular bp. of Bulla and aux. bp. of Washington, D.C., Apr. 20, 1995.

Losten, Basil: b. May 11, 1930, Chesapeake City, Md.; educ. St. Basil's College (Stamford, Conn.), Catholic University (Washington, D.C.); ord. priest (Philadelphia*, Ukrainian Byzantine) June 10, 1957; ord. titular bp. of Arcadiopolis in Asia and aux. bp. of Ukrainian archeparchy of Philadelphia, May 25, 1971; app. apostolic administrator of archeparchy, 1976; app. bp. of Ukrainian eparchy of Stamford, Sept. 20, 1977.

Lotocky, Innocent Hilarius, O.S.B.M.: b. Nov. 3, 1915, Petlykiwci, Ukraine; educ. seminaries in Ukraine, Czechoslovakia and Austria; ord. priest Nov. 24, 1940; ord. bp. of St. Nicholas of Chicago for the Ukrainians, Mar. 1, 1981; retired July 15, 1993.

Loverde, Paul S.: b. Sept. 3, 1940, Framingham, Mass.; educ. St. Thomas Seminary (Bloomfield, Conn.), St. Bernard Seminary (Rochester, N.Y.), Gregorian Univ. (Rome), Catholic Univ. (Washington, D.C.); ord. priest (Norwich), Dec. 18, 1965; ord. titular bp. of Ottabia and aux. bp. of Hartford, Apr. 12, 1988; app. bp. of Ogdensburg, Nov. 11, 1993; installed Jan. 17, 1994; app. bp. of Arlington, Jan. 25, 1999, ins. Mar. 25, 1999.

Lubachivsky, Myroslav I.: (See Cardinals, Biographies.)

Lucker, Raymond A.: b. Feb. 24, 1927, St. Paul, Minn.; educ. St. Paul Seminary (St. Paul, Minn.); University of Minnesota (Minneapolis), Angelicum (Rome); ord. priest (St. Paul and Minneapolis*) June 7, 1952; director of USCC department of education, 1968-71; ord. titular bp. of Meta and aux. bp. of St. Paul and Minneapolis, Sept. 8, 1971; app. bp. of New Ulm, Dec. 23, 1975, installed Feb. 19, 1976.

Lynch, George E.: b. Mar. 4, 1917, New York, N.Y.; educ. Fordham Univ. (New York), Mt. St. Mary's Seminary (Emmitsburg, Md.), Catholic Univ. (Washington, D.C.); ord. priest (Raleigh) May 29, 1943; ord. titular bp. of Satafi and aux. bp. of Raleigh Jan. 6, 1970; retired Apr. 16, 1985.

Lynch, Robert N.: b. May 27, 1941, Charleston, W. Va.; educ. Pontifical College Josephinism (Columbus, Ohio); John XXIII National Seminary (Weston, Mass.); ord. priest (Miami*) May 13, 1978; associate general secretary (1984-89) and general secretary (1989-95) of the NCCB/USCC; app. bp. of St. Petersburg, Dec. 5, 1995; ord. and installed Jan. 26, 1996; app. apostolic administrator of Palm Beach (while continuing as bp. of St. Petersburg), June 2, 1998.

Lyne, Timothy J.: b. Mar. 21, 1919, Chicago, Ill.; educ. Quigley Preparatory Seminary, St. Mary of the Lake Seminary (Mundelein, Ill.); ord. priest (Chicago*) May 1, 1943; ord. titular bp. of Vamalla and aux. bp. of Chicago, Dec. 13, 1983; retired Jan. 24, 1995.

M

Macaluso, Christie Albert: b. June 12, 1945, Hartford, Conn.; educ. St. Thomas Seminary (Bloomfield, Conn.), St. Mary's Seminary (Baltimore, Md), Trinity College (Hartford, Conn.), New York University; ord. priest (Hartford*) May 21, 1971; ord. titular bp. of Grass Valley and aux. bp. of Hartford, June 10, 1997.

McAuliffe, Michael F.: b. Nov. 22, 1920, Kansas City, Mo.; educ. St. Louis Preparatory Seminary (St. Louis, Mo.), Catholic Univ. (Washington, D.C.): ord. priest (Kansas City-St. Joseph) May 31, 1945; ord. bp. of Jefferson City, Aug. 18, 1969; retired .June, 1997.

McCarrick, Theodore E.: b. July 7, 1930, New York, N.Y.; educ. Fordham Univ. (Bronx, N.Y.), St. Joseph's Seminary (Dunwoodie, N.Y.), Catholic Univ. (Washington, D.C.); ord. priest (New York*) May 31, 1958; dean of students Catholic Univ. of America, 1961-63; pres., Catholic Univ. of Puerto Rico, 1965-69; secretary to Cardinal Cooke, 1970; ord. titular bp. of Rusubisir and aux. bp. of New York, June 29, 1977; app. first bp. of Metuchen, N.J., Nov. 19, 1981, installed Jan. 31, 1982; app. abp. of Newark, June 3, 1986, installed July 25, 1986.

McCarthy, Edward A.: b. Apr. 10, 1918, Cincinnati, O.; educ. Mt. St. Mary Seminary (Norwood, O.), Catholic Univ. (Washington, D.C.), Lateran and Angelicum (Rome); ord. priest (Cincinnati*) May 29, 1943; ord. titular bp. of Tamascani and aux. bp. of Cincinnati, June 15, 1965; first bp. of Phoenix, Ariz., Dec. 2, 1969; app. coadjutor abp. of Miami, Fla., July 7, 1976; succeeded as abp. of Miami, July 26, 1977; retired Nov. 3, 1994.

McCarthy, James F.: b. July 9, 1942, Mount Kisco, N.Y.; educ. Cathedral College and St. Joseph's Seminary, New York; ord. priest (New York*) June 1, 1968; app. titular bp. of Veronna and aux. bp. of New York, May 11, 1999, ins. June 29, 1999.

McCarthy, John E.: b. June 21, 1930, Houston, Tex.; educ. Univ. of St. Thomas (Houston, Tex.); ord. priest (Galveston-Houston) May 26, 1956; assistant director Social Action Dept. USCC, 1967-69; executive director Texas Catholic Conference; ord. titular bp. of Pedena and aux. bp. of Galveston-Houston, Mar. 14, 1979; app. bp. of Austin, Dec. 19, 1985, installed Feb. 25, 1986.

McCormack, John B.: b Aug. 12, 1935, Winthrop, Mass; educ. St. John Seminary College and St. John Seminary Theologate (Boston, Mass.); ord. priest (Boston*) Feb. 2, 1960; ord. titular bp. of Cerbali and aux. bp. of Boston, Dec. 27, 1995; app. bp. of Manchester, N.H., July 21, 1998, installed Sept. 22, 1998.

McCormack, William J.: b. Jan. 24, 1924, New York, N.Y.; educ. Christ the King Seminary, St. Bonaventure Univ. (St. Bonaventure, N.Y.); ord. priest (New York*) Feb. 21, 1959; national director of Society for the Propagation of the Faith, 1980; ord. titular bp. of Nicives and aux. bp. of New York, Jan. 6, 1987.

McDonald, Andrew J.: b. Oct. 24, 1923, Savannah, Ga.; educ. St. Mary's Seminary (Baltimore, Md.), Catholic Univ. (Washington, D.C.), Lateran Univ. (Rome); ord. priest (Savannah) May 8, 1948; ord. bp. of Little Rock, Sept. 5, 1972.

McDonnell, Charles J.: b. July 7, 1928, Brooklyn, N.Y.; educ. Seton Hall Univ. (South Orange, N.J.), Immaculate Conception Seminary (Darlington, N.J.), Long Island Univ. (Brooklyn, N.Y.); ord. priest (Newark*) May 29, 1954; U.S. Army Chaplain, 1965-89; retired from active duty with rank of Brigadier General; ord. titular bp. of Pocofelto and aux. bp. of Newark, May 12, 1994.

McDonough, Thomas J.: b. Dec. 5, 1911, Philadelphia, Pa.; educ. St. Charles Seminary (Overbrook, Pa.), Catholic Univ. (Washington, D.C.); ord. priest (Philadelphia*) May 26, 1938; ord. titular bp. of Thenae and aux. bp. of St. Augustine, Apr. 30, 1947; app. aux. bp. of Savannah, Jan. 2, 1957; named bp. of Savannah, installed Apr. 27, 1960; app. abp. of Louisville, installed May 2, 1967; resigned Sept. 29, 1981. Died Aug. 4, 1998.

McDowell, John B.: b. July 17, 1921, New Castle, Pa.; educ. St. Vincent College, St. Vincent Theological Seminary (Latrobe, Pa.), Catholic Univ. (Washington, D.C.); ord. priest (Pittsburgh) Nov. 4, 1945; superintendent of schools, Pittsburgh diocese, 1955-70; ord. titular bp. of Tamazuca, and aux. bp. of Pittsburgh, Sept. 8, 1966; retired Sept. 9, 1996.

McFarland, Norman F.: b. Feb. 21, 1922, Martinez, Calif.; educ. St. Patrick's Seminary (Menlo Park, Calif.), Catholic Univ. (Washington, D.C.); ord. priest (San Francisco*) June 15, 1946; ord. titular bp. of Bida and aux. bp. of San Francisco, Sept. 8, 1970; apostolic adminstrator of Reno, 1974; app. bp. of Reno, Feb. 10, 1976, installed Mar. 31, 1976; title of see changed to Reno-Las Vegas; app. bp. of Orange, Calif., Dec. 29, 1986; installed Mar. 31, 1976; resigned June 30, 1998.

McGann, John R.: b. Dec. 2, 1924, Brooklyn, N.Y.; educ. Cathedral College (Brooklyn, N.Y.), Immaculate Conception Seminary (Huntington, L.I.); ord. priest (Brooklyn) June 3, 1950; ord. titular bp. of Morosbisdus and aux. bp. of Rockville Centre, Jan. 7, 1971; vicar general and episcopal vicar; app. bp. of Rockville Centre May 3, 1976, installed June 24, 1976.

McGarry, Urban, T.O.R.: b. Nov. 11, 1911, Warren, Pa.; ord. priest Oct. 3, 1942; in India; prefect apostolic of Bhagalpur, Aug. 7, 1956; ord. first bp. of Bhagalpur, India, May 10, 1965; resigned Nov. 30, 1987.

McGrath, Patrick J.: b. July 11, 1945, Dublin, Ire.; educ. St. John's College Seminary (Waterford, Ire.), Lateran Univ. (Rome, Italy); ord. priest in Ireland June 7, 1970; came to U.S. same year and became San Francisco archdiocesan priest; ord. titular bp. of Allegheny and aux. bp. of San Francisco, Jan. 25, 1989; app. coadjutor bp. of San Jose, June 30, 1998.

McHugh, James T.: b. Jan. 3, 1932, Orange, N.J. educ. Seton Hall Univ. (S. Orange, N.J.), Immaculate

Conception Seminary (Darlington, N.J.), Fordham Univ. (New York, N.Y.), Catholic Univ. (Washington, D.C.), Angelicum (Rome, Italy); ord. priest (Newark*) May 25, 1957; assistant director, 1965-67, and director, 1967-75, of Family Life Division, USCC; director, 1972-78, of NCCB Office for Pro-Life Activities; special advisor to Mission of Permanent Observer of Holy See to UN; ord. titular bp. of Morosbisdo and aux. of Newark, Jan. 25, 1988; bp. of Camden, May 13, 1989, ins. June 20, 1989; app. coadjutor bp. of Rockville Center, Dec. 7, 1998, ins. Feb. 22, 1999.

McKinney, Joseph C.: b. Sept. 10, 1928, Grand Rapids, Mich.: educ. St. Joseph's Seminary (Grand Rapids, Mich.), Seminaire de Philosophie (Montreal, Canada), Urban Univ. (Rome, Italy); ord. priest (Grand Rapids) Dec. 20, 1953; ord. titular bp. of Lentini and aux. bp. of Grand Rapids, Sept. 26, 1968.

McLaughlin, Bernard J.: b. Nov. 19, 1912, Buffalo, N.Y.; educ. Urban Univ. (Rome, Italy); ord. priest (Buffalo) Dec. 21, 1935, at Rome; ord. titular bp. of Mottola and aux. bp. of Buffalo, Jan. 6, 1969; resigned Jan. 5, 1988.

McManus, Robert J.: b. July 5, 1951, Warwick, RI; educ. Our Lady of Providence Seminary, Catholic Univ. (Washington, DC), Seminary of Toronto, Canada, Pontifical Gregorian Univ. (Rome); ord. priest (Providence) May 27, 1978; diocesan Vicar for Education and Rector of Our Lady of Providence; app. titular bp. of Allegheny and aux. of Providence, Dec. 1, 1998, ord. Feb. 22, 1999.

McNabb, John C., O.S.A.: b. Dec. 11, 1925, Beloit, Wis.; educ. Villanova Univ. (Villanova, Pa.), Augustinian College and Catholic Univ. (Washington, D.C.), De Paul Univ. (Chicago, Ill.); ord. priest May 24, 1952; ord. titular bp. of Saia Maggiore, June 17, 1967 (resigned titular see, Dec. 27, 1977); prelate of Chulucanas, Peru, 1967; first bp. of Chulucanas, Dec. 12, 1988.

McNamara, John R.: b. Sept. 4, 1927, Worcester, Mass.; educ. Holy Cross College (Worcester, Mass.), St. John's Seminary (Boston, Mass.); ord. priest (Boston*) Jan. 10, 1952; served as chaplain in the U.S. Navy 1962-88; attained the rank of Rear Admiral and was Chief of Naval Chaplains; ord. titular bp. of Risinium and aux. bp. of Boston, May 21, 1992.

McNamara, Lawrence J.: b. Aug. 5, 1928, Chicago, Ill.; educ. St. Paul Seminary (St. Paul, Minn.), Catholic Univ. (Washington, D.C.); ord. priest (Kansas City-St. Joseph) May 30, 1953; executive director of Campaign for Human Development 1973-77; ord. bp. of Grand Island, Nebr., Mar. 28, 1978.

McNaughton, William J., M.M.: b. Dec. 7, 1926, Lawrence, Mass.; educ. Maryknoll Seminary (Maryknoll, N.Y.); ord. priest June 13, 1953; ord. titular bp. of Thuburbo Minus and vicar apostolic of Inchon, Korea, Aug. 24, 1961; first bp. of Inchon, Mar. 10, 1962, when vicariate was raised to diocese.

McRaith, John Jeremiah: b. Dec. 6, 1934, Hutchinson, Minn.; educ. St. John Preparatory School (Collegeville, Minn.), Loras College, St. Bernard Seminary (Dubuque, Ia); ord. priest (New Ulm) Feb. 21, 1960; exec. dir. of Catholic Rural Life Conference, 1971-78; ord. bp. of Owensboro, Ky., Dec. 15, 1982.

Madera, Joseph J., M.Sp.S.: b. Nov. 27, 1927, San Francisco, Calif.; educ. Domus Studiorum of the Missionaries of the Holy Spirit (Coyoacan, D.F. Mexico); ord. priest June 15, 1957; ord. coadjutor bp. of Fresno, Mar. 4, 1980; bp. of Fresno, July 1, 1980; app. titular bp. of Orte and aux. of Military Services archdiocese, June 30, 1991.

Maginnis, Robert P.: b. Dec. 22, 1933, Philadelphia, Pa.; educ. St. Charles Borromeo Seminary (Overbrook, Pa.); ord. priest (Philadelphia*) May 13, 1961; ord. titular bp. of Siminina and aux. bp. of Philadelphia, Mar. 11, 1996.

Maguire, Joseph F.: b. Sept. 4, 1919, Boston, Mass.; educ. Boston College, St. John's Seminary (Boston, Mass.); ord. priest (Boston*) June 29, 1945; ord. titular bp. of Macteris and aux. bp. of Boston, Feb. 2, 1972; app. coadjutor bp. of Springfield, Mass., Apr. 13, 1976; succeeded as bp. of Springfield, Mass., Oct. 15, 1977; retired Dec. 27, 1991.

Mahoney, James P.: b. Aug. 16, 1925, Kingston, N.Y.; educ. St. Joseph's Seminary (Dunwoodie, N.Y.); ord. priest (New York*) May 19, 1951; ord. titular bp. of Ipagro and aux. bp. of New York, Sept. 15, 1972; retired May 10, 1997.

Mahony, Roger M.: (See Cardinals, Biographies.)

Maida, Adam J.: (See Cardinals, Biographies.)

Malone, James W.: b. Mar. 8, 1920, Youngstown, O.; educ. St. Charles Preparatory Seminary (Catonsville, Md.), St. Mary's Seminary (Cleveland, O.), Catholic Univ. (Washington, D.C.); ord. priest (Youngstown) May 26, 1945; ord. titular bp. of Alabanda and aux. bp. of Youngstown, Mar. 24, 1960; apostolic administrator, 1966; bp. of Youngstown, installed June 20, 1968; president of NCCB/USCC, 1983-86; retired Dec. 5, 1995.

Maloney, Charles G.: b. Sept. 9, 1912, Louisville, Ky.; educ. St. Joseph's College (Rensselaer, Ind.), North American College (Rome); ord. priest (Louisville*) Dec. 8, 1937; ord. titular bp. of Capsa and aux. bp. of Louisville, Feb. 2, 1955; resigned Jan. 8, 1988; transferred to Bardstown, 1995, when it was reestablished as a titular see.

Manning, Elias (James), O.F.M. Conv.: b. Apr. 14, 1938, Troy, N.Y.; educ. Sao José Seminary (Rio de Janeiro, Brazil); ord. priest Oct. 30, 1965, in New York; ord. bp. of Valenca, Brazil, May 13, 1990.

Manning, Thomas R., O.F.M.: b. Aug. 29, 1922, Baltimore, Md.; educ. Duns Scotus College (Southfield, Mich.), Holy Name College (Washington, D.C.); ord. priest June 5, 1948; ord. titular bp. of Arsamosata, July 14, 1959 (resigned titular see Dec. 30, 1977); prelate of Coroico, Bolivia, July 14, 1959; became first bp., 1983, when prelature was raised to diocese; retired Oct. 9, 1996.

Mansell, Henry J.: b. Oct. 10, 1937, New York, N.Y.; educ. Cathedral College, St. Joseph's Seminary and College (New York); North American College, Gregorian Univ. (Rome); ord. priest (New York*) Dec. 19, 1962; ord. titular bp. of Marazane and aux. bp. of New York, Jan. 6, 1993, by John Paul II in Vatican City; app. bp. of Buffalo, Apr. 18, 1995; installed June 12, 1995.

Manz, John R.: b. Nov. 14, 1945, Chicago, Ill; educ. Niles College Seminary (Niles, Ill), Univ. of St. Mary of the Lake-Mundelein Seminary (Chicago); ord. priest (Chicago*) May 12, 1971; ord. titular bp. of Mulia and aux. bp. of Chicago, Mar. 5, 1996.

Marcinkus, Paul C.: b. Jan. 15, 1922, Cicero, Ill.; ord. priest (Chicago*) May 3, 1947; served in Vatican secretariat from 1952; ord. titular bp. of Orta, Jan. 6, 1969; secretary (1968-71) and president (1971-89) of Institute for Works of Religion (Vatican Bank); titular abp., Sept. 26, 1981; former pro-president of Pontifical Commission for the State of Vatican City (resigned in 1990).

Marconi, Dominic A.: b. Mar. 13, 1927, Newark, N.J.; educ. Seton Hall Univ. (S. Orange, N.J.), Immaculate Conception Seminary (Darlington, N.J.), Catholic Univ. (Washington, D.C.); ord. priest (Newark*) May 30, 1953; ord. titular bp. of Bure and aux. bp. of Newark, June 25, 1976.

Marino, Eugene A., S.S.J.: b. May 29, 1934, Biloxi, Miss.; educ. Epiphany Apostolic College and Mary Immaculate Novitiate (Newburgh, N.Y.), St. Joseph's Seminary (Washington, D.C.), Catholic Univ. (Washington, D.C.), Loyola Univ. (New Orleans, La.), Fordham Univ. (New York City); ord. priest June 9, 1962; ord. titular bp. of Walla Walla and aux. bp. of Washington, D.C., Sept. 12, 1974; abp. of Atlanta, installed May 5, 1988; resigned July 10, 1990.

Martino, Joseph F.: b. May 1, 1946, Philadelphia, Pa.; educ. St. Charles Borromeo Seminary (Overbrook, Pa.), Gregorian Univ. (Rome); ord. priest (Philadelphia*) Dec. 18, 1970; ord. titular bp. of Cellae in Mauretania and aux. bp. of Philadelphia, Mar. 11, 1996.

Matthiesen, Leroy Theodore: b. June 11, 1921, Olfen, Tex.; educ. Josephinum College (Columbus, O.), Catholic Univ. (Washington, D.C.), Register School of Journalism; ord. priest (Amarillo) Mar. 10, 1946; ord. bp. of Amarillo, May 30, 1980; retired Jan. 21, 1997.

Melczek, Dale J.: b. Nov. 9, 1938, Detroit, Mich.; educ. St. Mary's College (Orchard Lake, Mich.), St. John's Provincial Seminary (Plymouth, Mich.), Univ. of Detroit; ord. priest (Detroit*) June 6, 1964; ord. titular bp. of Trau and aux. bp. of Detroit, Jan. 27, 1983; apostolic administrator of Gary, Aug. 19, 1992; coadjutor bp. of Gary, Oct. 28, 1995; bp. of Gary, June 1, 1996.

Mengeling, Carl F.: b. Oct. 22, 1930, Hammond, Ind.; educ. St. Meinrad College and Seminary (St. Meinrad, Ind.), Alphonsianum Univ. (Rome); ord. priest (Gary) May 25, 1957; ord. bp. of Lansing Jan. 25, 1996.

Mestice, Anthony F.: b. Dec. 6, 1923, New York, N.Y.; educ. St. Joseph Seminary (Yonkers, N.Y.); ord. priest (New York*) June 4, 1949; ord. titular bp. of Villa Nova and aux. bp. of New York, Apr. 27, 1973.

Michaels, James E., S.S.C.: b. May 30, 1926, Chicago, Ill.; educ. Columban Seminary (St. Columban, Neb.), Gregorian Univ. (Rome); ord. priest Dec. 21, 1951; ord. titular bp. of Verbe and aux. bp. of Kwang Ju, Korea, Apr. 14, 1966; app. aux. bp. of Wheeling, Apr. 3, 1973 (title of see changed to Wheeling-Charleston, 1974); resigned Sept. 22, 1987.

Milone, Anthony M.: b. Sept. 24, 1932, Omaha, Nebr.; educ. North American College (Rome); ord. priest (Omaha*) Dec. 15, 1957, in Rome; ord. titular bp. of Plestia and aux. bp. of Omaha, Jan. 6, 1982; app. bp. of Great Falls-Billings, Dec. 14, 1987, installed Feb. 23, 1988.

Minder, John, O.S.F.S.: b. Nov. 1, 1923, Philadelphia, Pa.; educ. Catholic Univ. (Washington, D.C.); ord. priest June 3, 1950; ord. bp. of Keimos (renamed Keimos-Upington, 1985), South Africa, Jan. 10, 1968.

Moeddel, Carl K.: b. Dec. 28, 1937, Cincinnati, Ohio; educ. Athenaeum of Ohio, Mt. St. Mary's Seminary (Cincinnati); ord. priest (Cincinnati*) Aug. 15, 1962; ord. titular bp. of Bistue and aux. bp. of Cincinnati, Aug. 24, 1993.

Montrose, Donald W.: b. May 13, 1923, Denver, Colo.; educ. St. John's Seminary (Camarillo, Calif.); ord. priest (Los Angeles*) May 7, 1949; ord. titular bp. of Forum Novum and aux. bp. of Los Angeles, May 12, 1983; app. bp. of Stockton, Dec. 17, 1985, installed Feb. 20, 1986; res. Jan. 19, 1999.

Moreno, Manuel D.: b. Nov. 27, 1930, Placentia, Calif.; educ. Univ. of Calif. (Los Angeles), Our Lady Queen of Angels (San Fernando, Calif.), St. John's Seminary (Camarillo, Calif.); ord. priest (Los Angeles*) Apr. 25, 1961; ord. titular bp. of Tanagra and aux. bp. of Los Angeles, Feb. 19, 1977; bp. of Tucson, Jan. 12, 1982, installed Mar. 11, 1982.

Morlino, Robert C.: b. Dec. 31, 1946, Scranton, Pa.; educ. Fordham Univ., University of Notre Dame, Weston School of Theology, Cambridge, Mass., Gregorian University, Rome; ord. priest for the Society of Jesus, Maryland Province, June 1, 1974; incardinated into the Diocese of Kalamazoo, Mich., Oct. 26, 1983, app. bp. of Helena, July 6, 1999, ins. Sept. 21, 1999.

Morneau, Robert F.: b. Sept. 10, 1938, New London, Wis.; educ. St. Norbert's College (De Pere, Wis.), Sacred Heart Seminary (Oneida, Wis.), Catholic Univ. (Washington, D.C.); ord. priest (Green Bay) May 28, 1966; ord. titular bp. of Massa Lubrense and aux. bp. of Green Bay, Feb. 22, 1979.

Moskal, Robert M.: b. Oct. 24, 1937, Carnegie, Pa.; educ. St. Basil Minor Seminary (Stamford, Conn.), St. Josaphat Seminary and Catholic Univ. (Washington, D.C.); ord. priest (Philadelphia*, Byzantine Ukrainian) Mar. 25, 1963; ord. titular bp. of Agatopoli and aux. bp. of the Ukrainian archeparchy of Philadelphia, Oct. 13, 1981; app. first bp. of St. Josaphat in Parma, Dec. 5, 1983.

Moynihan, James M.: b. July 16, 1932, Rochester, N.Y.; educ. St. Bernard's Seminary (Rochester, N.Y.), North American College and Gregorian Univ. (Rome); ord. priest (Rochester) Dec. 15, 1957, in Rome; ord. bp. of Syracuse May 29, 1995.

Muench Robert W.: b. Dec. 28, 1942, Louisville, Ky.; educ. St. Joseph Seminary and Notre Dame Seminary (New Orleans, La.), Catholic Univ. (Washington, D.C.); ord. priest (New Orleans*) June 18, 1968; ord. titular bp. of Mactaris and aux. bp. of New Orleans, June 29, 1990; app. bp. of Covington Jan., 1996; installed Mar. 19, 1996.

Mulvee, Robert E.: b. Feb. 15, 1930, Boston, Mass.; educ. St. Thomas Seminary (Bloomfield, Conn.), University Seminary (Ottawa, Ont., Canada), American College (Louvain, Belgium), Lateran Univ. (Rome); ord. priest (Manchester) June 30, 1957; ord. titular bp. of Summa and aux. bp. of Manchester, N.H., Apr. 14, 1977; app. bp. of Wilmington, Del., Feb. 19, 1985; app. coadjutor bp. of Providence, Feb. 9, 1995; bp. of Providence, June 11, 1997.

Mundo, Miguel P.: b. July 25, 1937, New York, N.Y.; educ. Fordham Univ. (Bronx, N.Y.), St. Jerome's College (Kitchener, Ont., Canada), St Francis Seminary (Loretto, Pa.); ord. priest (Camden) May 19, 1962; missionary in Brazil from 1963; ord. titular bp. of Blanda Julia and aux. bp. of Jatai, Brazil, June 2, 1978.

Murphy, Michael J.: b. July 1, 1915, Cleveland, O.; educ. Niagara Univ. (Niagara Falls, N.Y.); North American College (Rome), Catholic Univ. (Washington, D.C.); ord. priest (Cleveland) Feb. 28, 1942; ord. titular bp. of Ariendela and aux. bp. of Cleveland, June 11, 1976; app. coadjutor bp. of Erie, Nov. 20, 1978; bp. of Erie, July 16, 1982; retired June 12, 1990.

Murphy, Philip Francis: b. Mar. 25, 1933, Cumberland, Md.; educ. St. Mary Seminary (Baltimore, Md.), North American College (Rome); ord. priest (Baltimore*) Dec. 20, 1958; ord. titular bp. of Tacarata and aux. bp. of Baltimore, Feb. 29, 1976.

Murphy, William F.: b. May 14, 1940, Boston Mass.; educ. Boston Latin School (Boston), Harvard College, St. John's Seminary (Boston), Gregorian Univ. (Rome); ord. priest (Boston*) Dec. 16, 1964; ord. titular bp. of Saia Maggiore and aux. bp. of Boston, Dec. 27, 1995.

Murray, James A.: b. July 5, 1932, Jackson, Mich.; educ. Sacred Heart Seminary Detroit, St. John Provincial Seminary (Plymouth, Mich.), Catholic Univ. of America; ord. priest (Lansing) June 7, 1958; app. bp. of Kalamazoo, Nov. 18, 1997, ord. Jan. 27, 1998.

Murry, George V., S.J.: b. Dec. 28, 1948, Camden, N.J.; educ. St. Joseph's College (Philadelphia, Pa.), St. Thomas Seminary (Bloomfield, Conn.), St. Mary Seminary (Baltimore, Md.), Jesuit School of Theology (Berkeley, Calif), George Washington Univ. (Washington, D.C.); entered Jesuits 1972; ord. priest June 9, 1979; ord. titular bp. of Fuerteventura and aux. bp. of Chicago, Mar. 20, 1995; app. co-adjutor of St. Thomas in the Virgin Islands, May 5, 1998; bp. of St. Thomas in the Virgin Islands, June 30, 1999.

Myers, John Joseph: b. July 26, 1941, Ottawa, Ill.; educ. Loras College (Dubuque, Ia.), North American College and Gregorian Univ. (Rome), Catholic Univ. of America (Washington, D.C.); ord. priest (Peoria) Dec. 17, 1966, in Rome; ord. coadjutor bp. of Peoria, Sept. 3, 1987; bp. of Peoria, Jan. 23, 1990.

N

Naumann, Joseph F.: b. June 4, 1949, St. Louis, Mo.; educ. Cardinal Glennon Seminary College and Kenrick Seminary (St. Louis, Mo.); ord. priest (St. Louis*) 1975; app. titular bp. of Caput Cilla and aux. bp. of St. Louis, July 9, 1997.

Nevins, John J.: b. Jan. 19, 1932, New Rochelle, N.Y.; educ. Iona College (New Rochelle, N.Y.), Catholic Univ. (Washington, D.C.); ord. priest (Miami*) June 6, 1959; ord. titular bp. of Rusticana and aux. bp. of Miami, Mar. 24, 1979; app. first bp. of Venice, Fla., July 17, 1984; installed Oct. 25, 1984.

Newman, William C.: b. Aug. 16, 1928, Baltimore, Md.; educ. St. Mary Seminary (Baltimore, Md.), Catholic Univ. (Washington, D.C.), Loyola College (Baltimore, Md.); ord. priest (Baltimore*) May 29, 1954; ord. titular bp. of Numluli and aux. bp. of Baltimore, July 2, 1984.

Neylon, Martin J., S.J.: b. Feb. 13, 1920, Buffalo, N.Y.; ord. priest June 18, 1950; ord. titular bp. of Libertina and coadjutor vicar apostolic of the Caroline and Marshall Islands, Feb. 2, 1970; vicar apostolic of Caroline and Marshall Is., Sept. 20, 1971; first bp. of Carolines-Marshalls when vicariate apostolic was raised to diocese, 1979; title of see changed to Caroline Islands, Apr. 23, 1993; retired Mar. 25, 1995.

Niederauer, George H.: b. June 14, 1936, Los An-geles, Calif.; educ. St. John's Seminary (Camarillo, Calif.), Catholic Univ. (Washington, D.C.), Loyola Univ. of Los Angeles, Univ. of Southern Calif., Loretto Heights College (Denver, Colo.); ord. priest (Los Angeles*) Apr. 30, 1962; app. bp. of Salt Lake City, Nov. 3, 1994, ord. Jan. 25, 1995.

Niedergeses, James D.: b. Feb. 2, 1917, Lawrenceburg, Tenn.; educ. St. Bernard College (St. Bernard, Ala.), St. Ambrose College (Davenport, Ia.), Mt. St. Mary Seminary of the West and Athenaeum (Cincinnati, Ohio); ord. priest (Nashville) May 20, 1944; ord. bp. of Nashville, May 20, 1975; retired Oct. 13, 1992.

Nienstedt, John C.: b. Mar. 18, 1947, Detroit, Mich.; educ. Sacred Heart Seminary (Detroit), North American College, Gregorian Univ., Alphonsianum (Rome); ord. priest (Detroit*) July 27, 1974; served in Vatican Secretariat of State, 1980-86; rector of Sacred Heart Seminary (Detroit), 1988-94; pastor of the Shrine of the Little Flower (Royal Oak, Mich.), 1994; ord. titular bp. of Alton and aux. bp. of Detroit, July 9, 1996.

Nolker, Bernard, C.SS.R.: b. Sept. 25, 1912, Baltimore, Md.; educ. St. Mary's College (North East, Pa.), St. Mary's College (Ilchester, Md.), Mt. St. Alphonsus Seminary (Esopus, N.Y.); ord. priest June 18, 1939; ord. first bp. of Paranagua, Brazil, Apr. 25, 1963; retired Mar. 14, 1989.

Novak, Alfred, C.SS.R.: b. June 2, 1930, Dwight, Nebr.; educ. Immaculate Conception Seminary (Oconomowoc, Wis.); ord. priest July 2, 1956; ord. titular bp. of Vardimissa and aux. bp. of Sao Paulo, Brazil, May 25, 1979; bp. of Paranagua, Brazil, Mar. 14, 1989.

O

O'Brien, Edwin F.: b. Apr. 8, 1939, Bronx, N.Y.; educ. St. Joseph's Seminary (Yonkers, N.Y.), Angelicum (Rome); ord. priest (New York*) May 29, 1965; ord. titular bp. of Tizica and aux. bp. of New York, Mar. 25, 1996; app. coadjutor abp. for Military Services Archdiocese, Apr. 8, 1997; abp. of Military Services Archdiocese, Aug. 12, 1997.

O'Brien, Thomas Joseph: b. Nov. 29, 1935, Indianapolis, Ind.; educ. St. Meinrad High School Seminary, St. Meinrad College Seminary (St. Meinrad, Ind.); ord. priest (Tucson) May 7, 1961; ord. bp. of Phoenix, Jan. 6, 1982.

Ochoa, Armando: b. Apr. 3, 1943, Oxnard, Calif.; educ. Ventura College (Ventura, Calif.), St. John's College and St. John's Seminary (Camarillo, Calif.); ord. priest (Los Angeles*) May 23, 1970; ord. titular bp. of Sitifi and aux. bp. of Los Angeles, Feb. 23, 1987; app. bp. of El Paso, Apr. 1, 1996; installed June 26, 1996.

O'Connell, Anthony J.: b. May 10, 1938, Lisheen, Co. Clare, Ireland; came to U.S. at age 20; educ. Mt. St. Joseph College (Cork), Mungret College (Limerick), Kenrick Seminary (St. Louis); ord. priest (Jefferson City) Mar. 30, 1963; ord. First Bp. of Knoxville, Tenn., Sept. 8, 1988; app. Bp. of Palm Beach, Nov. 12, 1998, ord. Jan. 14, 1999.

O'Connor, John J.: (See Cardinals, Biographies.)

O'Donnell, Edward J.: b. July 4, 1931, St. Louis, Mo.; educ. St. Louis Preparatory Seminary and Kenrick Seminary (St. Louis, Mo.); ord. priest (St. Louis*) Apr. 6, 1957; ord. titular bp. of Britania and aux. bp. of St. Louis Feb. 10, 1984; app. bp. of Lafayette, La., installed Dec. 16, 1994.

O'Keefe, Gerald F.: b. Mar. 30, 1918, St. Paul, Minn.; educ. College of St. Thomas, St. Paul Seminary (St. Paul, Minn.); ord. priest (St. Paul-Minneapolis*) Jan. 29, 1944; ord. titular bp. of Candyba and aux. bp. of St. Paul, July 2, 1961; bp. of Davenport, Oct. 20, 1966, installed Jan. 4, 1967; retired Nov. 12, 1993.

O'Leary, Edward C.: b. Aug. 21, 1920, Bangor, Me.; educ. Holy Cross College (Worcester, Mass.), St. Paul's Seminary (Ottawa, Canada); ord. priest (Portland, Me.) June 15, 1946; ord. titular bp. of Moglena and aux. bp. of Portland, Me., Jan. 25, 1971; app. bp. of Portland, installed Dec. 18, 1974; retired Sept. 27, 1988.

Olivier, Leonard J., S.V.D.: b. Oct. 12, 1923, Lake Charles, La.; educ. St. Augustine Major Seminary (Bay St. Louis, Miss.), Catholic Univ. (Washington, D.C.), Loyola Univ. (New Orleans, La.); ord. priest June 29, 1951; ord. titular bp. of Leges in Numidia and aux. bp. of Washington, Dec. 20, 1988.

Olmsted, Thomas J.: b. Jan. 21, 1947, Oketo, Kansas; educ. St. Thomas Seminary (Denver), North American College and Pontifical Gregorian University (Rome); ord. priest (Lincoln) July 2, 1973; served in Vatican Secretariat of State, 1979-1988; Dean of Formation, Pontifical College Josephinum, Columbus, O., 1993, President and Rector, Pontifical College, Josephinum, 1997; app. coadjutor bp. of Wichita, Feb. 16, 1999, ord. April 20, 1999.

O'Malley, Sean, O.F.M.Cap.: b. June 29, 1944, Lakewood, O.; educ. St. Fidelis Seminary (Herman, Pa.), Capuchin College and Catholic Univ. (Washington, D.C.); ord. priest Aug. 29, 1970; episcopal vicar of priests serving Spanish speaking in Washington archdiocese, 1974-84; executive director of Spanish Catholic Center, Washington, from 1973; ord. coadjutor bp. of St. Thomas, Virgin Islands, Aug. 2, 1984; bp. of St. Thomas, Oct. 16, 1985; app. bp. of Fall River, June 16, 1992.

O'Neill, Arthur J.: b. Dec. 14, 1917, East Dubuque, Ill.; educ. Loras Collge (Dubuque, Ia.), St. Mary's Seminary (Baltimore, Md.); ord. priest (Rockford) Mar. 27, 1943; ord. bp. of Rockford, Oct. 11, 1968; retired Apr. 19, 1994.

O'Rourke, Edward W.: b. Oct. 31, 1917, Downs, Ill.; educ. St. Mary's Seminary (Mundelein, Ill.), Aquinas Institute of Philosophy and Theology (River Forest, Ill.); ord. priest (Peoria) May 28, 1944; executive director of National Catholic Rural Life Conference, 1960-71; ord. bp. of Peoria, July 15, 1971; retired Jan. 22, 1990.

Ottenweller, Albert H.: b. Apr. 5, 1916, Stanford, Mont.; educ. St. Joseph's Seminary (Rensselaer, Ind.), Catholic Univ. (Washington, D.C.); ord. priest (Toledo) June 19, 1943; ord. titular bp. of Perdices and aux. bp. of Toledo, May 29, 1974; app. bp. of Steubenville, Oct. 11, 1977, installed Nov. 22, 1977; retired Jan. 28, 1992.

P

Paska, Walter: b. Nov. 29, 1923, Elizabeth, N.J.; educ. St. Charles Seminary (Catonsville, Md.), Catholic Univ. (Washington, D.C.), Fordham Univ. (New York); ord. priest (Philadelphia of Ukrainians*) June 2, 1947; ord. titular bp. of Tigilava and aux. of Ukrai-

nian archdiocese of Philadelphia, Mar. 19, 1992.

Pataki, Andrew: b. Aug. 30, 1927, Palmerton,Pa.; educ. St. Vincent College (Latrobe, Pa.), St. Procopius College, St. Procopius Seminary (Lisle, Ill.), Sts. Cyril and Methodius Byzantine Catholic Seminary (Pittsburgh, Pa.), Gregorian Univ. and Oriental Pontifical Institute (Rome, Italy); ord. priest (Pittsburgh,* Ruthenian Byzantine) Feb. 24, 1952; ord. titular bp. of Telmisso and aux. bp. of Byzantine diocese of Passaic, Aug. 23, 1983; app. bp. of Ruthenian Byzantine diocese of Parma, July 3, 1984; app. bp. of Ruthenian Byzantine diocese of Passaic, Nov. 6, 1995; installed Feb. 8, 1996.

Paul, John J.: b. Aug. 17, 1918, La Crosse, Wis.; educ. Loras College (Dubuque, Iowa), St. Mary's Seminary (Baltimore, Md.), Marquette Univ. (Milwaukee, Wis.), ord. priest (Lincoln) Jan. 24, 1943; ord. titular bp. of Lambaesis and aux. bp. of La Crosse, Aug. 4, 1977; app. bp. of La Crosse, Oct. 18, 1983, installed Dec. 5, 1983; retired Dec. 10, 1994.

Pearce, George H., S.M.: b. Jan. 9, 1921, Brighton, Mass.; educ. Marist College and Seminary (Framington, Mass.); ord. priest Feb. 2, 1947; ord. titular bp. of Attalea in Pamphylia and vicar apostolic of the Samoa and Tokelau Islands, June 29, 1956; title changed to bp. of Apia, June 21, 1966; app. abp. of Suva, Fiji Islands, June 22, 1967; resigned Apr. 10, 1976.

Pelotte, Donald E., S.S.S.: b. Apr. 13, 1945, Waterville, Me.; educ. Eymard Seminary and Junior College (Hyde Park, N.Y.), John Carroll Univ. (Cleveland, O.), Fordham Univ. (Bronx, N.Y.); ord. priest Sept. 2, 1972; ord. coadjutor bp. of Gallup, May 6, 1986 (first priest of Native American ancestry to be named U.S. bp.); bp. of Gallup, Mar. 20, 1990.

Peña, Raymundo J.: b. Feb. 19, 1934, Robstown, Tex.; educ. Assumption Seminary (San Antonio, Tex.); ord. priest (Corpus Christi) May 25, 1957; ord. titular bp. of Trisipa and aux. bp. of San Antonio, Dec. 13, 1976; app. bp. of El Paso, Apr. 29, 1980; app. bp. of Brownsville, May 23, 1995.

Pevec, A. Edward: b. Apr. 16, 1925, Cleveland, O.; educ. St. Mary's Seminary, John Carroll Univ. (Cleveland, O.); ord. priest (Cleveland) Apr. 29, 1950; ord. titular bp. of Mercia and aux. bp. of Cleveland, July 2, 1982.

Perry, Joseph N.: b. Apr. 18, 1948, Chicago, Ill.; educ. Capuchin Seminary of St. Lawrence, (Milwaukee), St. Mary Capuchin Seminary, Crown Point, (Indiana), St. Francis Seminary (Milwaukee), Catholic Univ.of America (Washington, D.C.); ord. priest (Milwaukee*), May 24, 1975; app. titular bp. of Lead and aux. bp. of Chicago, May 5, 1998; ord. June 29, 1998.

Pfeifer, Michael, O.M.I.: b. May 18, 1937, Alamo, Tex.; educ. Oblate school of theology (San Antonio, Tex.); ord. priest Dec. 21, 1964; provincial of southern province of Oblates of Mary Immaculate, 1981; ord. bp. of San Angelo, July 26, 1985.

Pilarczyk, Daniel E.: b. Aug. 12, 1934, Dayton, Ohio; educ. St. Gregory's Seminary (Cincinnati, O.), Urban Univ. (Rome), Xavier Univ. and Univ. of Cincinnati (Cincinnati, O.); ord. priest (Cincinnati*) Dec. 20, 1959; ord. titular bp. of Hodelm and aux. bp. of Cincinnati, Dec. 20, 1974; app. abp. of Cincinnati, Oct. 30, 1982; installed Dec. 20, 1982. President of NCCB/USCC, 1989-92.

Pilla, Anthony M.: b. Nov. 12, 1932, Cleveland, O.;

educ. St. Gregory College Seminary (Cincinnati, O.), Borromeo College Seminary (Wickliffe, O.), St. Mary Seminary and John Carroll Univ. (Cleveland, O.); ord. priest (Cleveland) May 23, 1959; ord. titular bp. of Scardona and aux. bp. of Cleveland, Aug. 1, 1979; app. apostolic administrator of Cleveland, 1980; bp. of Cleveland, Nov. 13, 1980. President of NCCB/USCC, 1995-98.

Popp, Bernard F.: b. Dec. 6, 1917, Nada, Tex.; educ. St. John's Seminary and St. Mary's Univ. (San Antonio, Tex.); ord. priest (San Antonio*) Feb. 24, 1943; ord. titular bp. of Capsus and aux. bp. of San Antonio, July 25, 1983; retired Mar. 23, 1993.

Potocnak, Joseph J., S.C.J.: b. May 13, 1933, Berwick, Pa.; educ. Dehon Seminary (Great Barrington, Mass.), Kilroe Seminary (Honesdale, Pa.), Sacred Heart (Hales Corners, Wis.); ord. priest Sept 21, 1966; missionary in South Africa from 1973; ord. bp. of De Aar, South Africa, May 1, 1992.

Povish, Kenneth J.: b. Apr. 19, 1924, Alpena, Mich.; educ. St. Joseph's Seminary (Grand Rapids, Mich.), Sacred Heart Seminary (Detroit, Mich.), Cathoic Univ. (Washington, D.C.); ord. priest (Saginaw) June 3, 1950; ord. bp. of Crookston, Sept. 29, 1970; app. bp. of Lansing, Oct. 8, 1975, installed Dec. 11, 1975; retired Nov. 7, 1995.

Procyk, Judson M.: b. Apr. 9, 1931, Greensburg, Pa.; educ. St. Procopius College (Lisle, Ill.), Duquesne University and Byzantine Seminary of Sts. Cyril and Methodius (Pittsburgh, Pa.), Casa Santa Maria (Rome); ord. priest (Pittsburgh*, Byzantine Ruthenian) May 19, 1957; ord. metropolitan abp. of Byzantine archdiocese of Pittsburgh, Feb. 7, 1995.

Puscas, Vasile Louis: b. Sept. 13, 1915, Aurora, Ill.; educ. Quigley Preparatory Seminary (Chicago, Ill.), seminary in Oradea-Mare (Romania), Propaganda Fide Seminary (Rome), Illinois Benedictine College (Lisle, Ill.); ord. priest (Erie) May 14, 1942; ord. titular bp. of Leuce and first exarch of apostolic exarchate for Byzantine Romanians in the U.S., June 26, 1983 (seat of the exarchate, Canton, Ohio); app. first eparch, Apr. 11, 1987, when exarchate was raised to eparchy of St. George's in Canton; retired July 15, 1993.

Q

Quinn, Alexander James: b. Apr. 8, 1932, Cleveland, O.; educ. St. Charles College (Catonsville, Md.), St. Mary Seminary (Cleveland, O.), Lateran Univ. (Rome), Cleveland State Univ.; ord. priest (Cleveland) May 24, 1958; ord. titular bp. of Socia and aux. bp. of Cleveland, Dec. 5, 1983.

Quinn, Francis A.: b. Sept. 11, 1921, Los Angeles, Calif.; educ. St. Joseph's College (Mountain View, Calif.), St. Patrick's Seminary (Menlo Park, Calif.), Catholic Univ. (Washington, D.C.); Univ. of Calif. (Berkeley); ord. priest (San Francisco*) June 15, 1946; ord. titular bp. of Numana and aux. bp. of San Francisco, June 29, 1978; app. bp. of Sacramento Dec. 18, 1979; retired Nov. 30, 1993.

Quinn, John R.: b. Mar. 28, 1929, Riverside, Calif.; educ. St. Francis Seminary (El Cajon, Calif.), North American College (Rome); ord. priest (San Diego) July 19, 1953; ord. titular bp. of Thisiduo and aux. bp. of San Diego, Dec. 12, 1967; bp. of Oklahoma City and Tulsa, Nov. 30, 1971; first abp. of Oklahoma City, Dec. 19, 1972; app. abp. of San Fran-

cisco Feb. 22, 1977, installed Apr. 26, 1977; president NCCB/USCC, 1977-80; resigned see Dec. 27, 1995.

R

Ramirez, Ricardo, C.S.B.: b. Sept. 12, 1936, Bay City, Tex.; educ. Univ. of St. Thomas (Houston, Tex.), Univ. of Detroit (Detroit, Mich.), St. Basil's Seminary (Toronto, Ont.), Seminario Concilium (Mexico City, Mexico), East Asian Pastoral Institute (Manila, Philippines); ord. priest Dec. 10, 1966; ord titular bp. of Vatarba and aux. of San Antonio, Dec. 6, 1981; app. first bp. of Las Cruces, N. Mex., Aug. 17, 1982; installed Oct. 18, 1982.

Raya, Joseph M.: b. July 20, 1917, Zahle, Lebanon; educ. St. Louis College (Paris, France), St. Anne's Seminary (Jerusalem); ord. priest July 20, 1941; came to U.S., 1949, became U.S. citizen; ord. abp. of Acre, Israel, of the Melkites, Oct. 20, 1968; resigned Aug. 20, 1974; assigned titular metropolitan see of Scytopolis (resides in Canada).

Reichert, Stephen J., O.F.M. Cap.: b. May 14, 1943, Leoville, Kans.; educ. Capuchin minor seminary (Victoria, Kans.), St. Fidelis College (Hermann, Pa.), Capuchin College (Washington, D.C.); ord. priest Sept. 27, 1969; missionary in Papua New Guinea since 1970; ord. bp. of Mendi, Papua New Guinea, May 7, 1995.

Reilly, Daniel P.: b. May 12, 1928, Providence, R.I.; educ. Our Lady of Providence Seminary (Warwick, R.I.), St. Brieuc Major Seminary (Cotes du Nord, France); ord. priest (Providence) May 30, 1953; ord. bp. of Norwich, Aug. 6, 1975; app. bp. of Worcester, Oct. 27, 1994, installed Nov. 8, 1994.

Reiss, John C.: b. May 13, 1922, Red Bank, N.J.; educ. Catholic Univ. (Washington, D.C.), Immaculate Conception Seminary (Darlington, N.J.); ord. priest (Trenton) May 31, 1947; ord. titular bp. of Simdicca and aux. bp. of Trenton, Dec. 12, 1967; app. bp. of Trenton, Mar. 11, 1980; retired July 1, 1997.

Riashi, Georges, B.C.O.: b. Nov. 25, 1933, Kaa-el-Rim, Lebanon; ord. priest Apr. 4, 1965; parish priest of Our Lady of Redemption Parish, Warren, Mich. (Newton Greek-Catholic Melkite eparchy); U.S. citizen; ord. first bp. of eparchy of St. Michael's of Sydney (Australia) for Greek-Catholic Melkites, July 19, 1987; app. abp. of archeparchy of Tripoli of Lebanon for Greek-Melkites, Aug. 5, 1995.

Ricard, John H., S.S.J.: b. Feb. 29, 1940, Baton Rouge, La.; educ. St. Joseph's Seminary (Washington, D.C.), Tulane Univ. (New Orleans, La.); ord. priest May 25, 1968; ord. titular bp. of Rucuma and aux. of Baltimore, July 2, 1984; urban vicar, Baltimore; app. bp. of Pensacola-Tallahassee, Jan 21, 1997.

Rigali, Justin F.: b. Apr. 19, 1935, Los Angeles, Calif.; educ. St. John's Seminary (Camarillo, Calif.); ord. priest (Los Angeles*) Apr. 25, 1961; in Vatican diplomatic service from 1964; ord. titular abp. of Bolsena, Sept. 14, 1985, by Pope John Paul II; president of the Pontifical Ecclesiastical Academy, 1985-89; secretary of Congregation for Bp.s, 1989-94, and the College of Cardinals, 1990-94; app. abp. of St. Louis, Jan. 25, 1994, installed Mar. 16, 1994.

Riley, Lawrence J.: b. Sept. 6, 1914; Boston, Mass.; educ. Boston College and St. John's Seminary (Boston, Mass.), North American College and Gregorian Univ. (Rome), Catholic Univ. (Washington, D.C.); ord. priest (Boston*) Sept. 21, 1940; ord. titular bp. of Daimlaig and aux. bp. of Boston, Feb. 2, 1972; retired Jan. 22, 1990.

Roach, John R.: b. July 31, 1921, Prior Lake, Minn.; educ. St. Paul Seminary (St. Paul, Minn.), Univ. of Minnesota (Minneapolis); ord. priest (St. Paul and Minneapolis*) June 18, 1946; ord. titular bp. of Cenae and aux. bp. of St. Paul and Minneapolis, Sept. 8, 1971; app. abp. of St. Paul and Minneapolis, May 28, 1975; president of NCCB/USCC, 1980-83; retired Sept 8, 1995.

Rodimer, Frank J.: b. Oct. 25, 1927, Rockaway, N.J.; educ. Seton Hall Prep (South Orange, N.J.), St. Charles College (Catonsville, Md.), St. Mary's Seminary (Baltimore, Md.), Immaculate Conception Seminary (Darlington, N.J.), Catholic Univ. (Washington, D.C.); ord. priest (Paterson) May 19, 1951; ord. bp. of Paterson, Feb. 28, 1978.

Rodriguez, Migúel, C.SS.R.: b. Apr. 18, 1931, Mayaguez, P.R.; educ. St. Mary's Minor Seminary (North East, Pa.), Mt. St. Alphonsus Major Seminary (Esopus, N.Y.); ord. priest June 22, 1958; ord. bp. of Arecibo, P.R., Mar. 23, 1974; resigned Mar. 20, 1990.

Rodriguez, Placido, C.M.F.: b. Oct. 11, 1940, Celaya, Guanajuato, Mexico; educ. Claretian Novitate (Los Angeles, Calif.), Claretville Seminary College (Calabasas, Calif.), Catholic Univ. (Washington, D.C.), Loyola Univ. (Chicago, Ill.); ord. priest May 23, 1968; ord. titular bp. of Fuerteventura and aux. bp. of Chicago, Dec. 13, 1983; app. bp. of Lubbock, Tex., Apr. 5, 1994.

Roman, Agustin A.: b. May 5, 1928, San Antonio de los Banos, Havana, Cuba; educ. San Alberto Magno Seminary (Matanzas, Cuba), Missions Etrangeres (Montreal, Canada), Barry College (Miami, Fla.); ord. priest July 5, 1959, Cuba; vicar for Spanish speaking in Miami archdiocese, 1976; ord. titular bp. of Sertei and aux. bp. of Miami, Mar. 24, 1979.

Roque, Francis X.: b. Oct. 9, 1928, Providence R.I.; educ. St. John's Seminary (Brighton, Mass.); ord. priest (Providence) Sept. 19, 1953; became chaplain in U.S. Army 1961; ord. titular bp. of Bagai and aux. bp. of Military Services archdiocese, May 10, 1983.

Rosazza, Peter Anthony: b. Feb. 13, 1935, New Haven, Conn.; educ. St. Thomas Seminary (Bloomfield, Conn.), Dartmouth College (Hanover, N.H.), St. Bernard's Seminary (Rochester, N.Y.), St. Sulpice (Issy, France); ord. priest (Hartford*) June 29, 1961; ord. titular bp. of Oppido Nuovo and aux. bp. of Hartford, June 24, 1978.

Rose, Robert John: b. Feb. 28, 1930, Grand Rapids, Mich.; educ. St. Joseph's Seminary (Grand Rapids, Mich.), Seminaire de Philosophie (Montreal, Canada), Urban University (Rome), Univ. of Michigan (Ann Arbor); ord. priest (Grand Rapids) Dec. 21, 1955; ord. bp. of Gaylord, Dec. 6, 1981; app. bp. of Grand Rapids, installed Aug. 30, 1989.

Rueger, George E.: b. Sept. 3, 1933, Framingham, Mass; educ. Holy Cross College (Worcester, Mass.), St. John's Seminary (Brighton), Harvard University (Cambridge, Mass.); ord. priest (Worcester), Jan. 6, 1958; ord. titular bp. of Maronana and aux. bp. of Worcester, Feb. 25, 1987.

Ryan, Daniel L.: b. Sept. 28, 1930, Mankato, Minn.;

educ. St. Procopius Seminary (Lisle, Ill.), Lateran Univ. (Rome); ord. priest (Joliet) May 3, 1956; ord. titular bp. of Surista and aux. bp. of Joliet, Sept. 30, 1981; app. bp. of Springfield, Ill., Nov. 22, 1983, installed Jan. 18, 1984.

Ryan, James C., O.F.M.: b. Nov. 17, 1912, Chicago, Ill.; educ. St. Joseph's Seraphic Seminary (Westmont, Ill.), Our Lady of the Angels Seminary (Cleveland, O.); ord. priest June 24, 1938; ord. titular bp. of Margo and prelate of Santarem, Brazil, April 9, 1958; first bp. of Santarem, Dec. 4, 1979; retired Nov. 27, 1985.

Ryan, Joseph T.: b. Nov. 1, 1913, Albany, N.Y.; educ. Manhattan College (New York City); ord. priest (Albany) June 3, 1939; national secretary of Catholic Near East Welfare Assn. 1960-65; ord. first abp. of Anchorage, Alaska, Mar. 25, 1966; app. titular abp. of Gabi and coadjutor abp. of the military ordinariate, Oct. 24, 1975; app. military vicar of U.S. military archdiocese, Mar. 16, 1985; resigned May 14, 1991.

Ryan, Sylvester D.: b. Mar. 3, 1930, Catalina Is. Calif.; educ. St. John's Seminary (Camarillo, Calif.); ord. priest (Los Angeles*) May 3, 1957; ord. titular bp. of Remesiana and aux. bp. of Los Angeles, May 31, 1990; app. bp. of Monterey, Jan. 28, 1992.

S

Salatka, Charles A.: b. Feb. 26, 1918, Grand Rapids, Mich.; educ. St. Joseph's Seminary (Grand Rapids, Mich.), Catholic Univ. (Washington, D.C.), Lateran Univ. (Rome); ord. priest (Grand Rapids) Feb. 24, 1945; ord. titular bp. of Cariana and aux. bp. of Grand Rapids, Mich., Mar. 6, 1962; app. bp. of Marquette, installed Mar. 25, 1968; app. abp. of Oklahoma City, Sept. 27, 1977; retired Nov. 24, 1992.

Saltarelli, Michael A.: b. Jan. 17, 1932, Jersey City, N.J.; educ. Seton Hall College and Immaculate Conception Seminary (S. Orange, N.J.); ord. priest (Newark*), May 28, 1960; ord. titular bp. of Mesarfelta and aux. bp. of Newark, July 30, 1990; app. Bp. of Wilmington, Nov. 21, 1995; installed Jan. 23, 1996.

Samra, Nicholas J.: b. Aug. 15, 1944, Paterson, N.J.; educ. St. Anselm College (Manchester, N.H.), St. Basil Seminary (Methuen, Mass.), St. John Seminary (Brighton, Mass.); ord. priest (Newton) May 10, 1970; ord. titular bp. of Gerasa and aux. bp. of Melkite diocese of Newton, July 6, 1989.

Sanchez, Robert F.: b. Mar. 20, 1934, Socorro, N.M.; educ. Immaculate Heart Seminary (Santa Fe, N.M.), Gregorian Univ. (Rome), Catholic Univ. (Washington, D.C.); ord. priest (Santa Fe*) Dec. 20, 1959; ord. abp. of Santa Fe, N.M., July 25, 1974; resigned Apr. 6, 1993.

Sartoris, Joseph M.: b. July 1, 1927, Los Angeles, Calif.; educ. St. John's Seminary (Camarillo, Calif.); ord. priest (Los Angeles*) May 30, 1953; ord. titular bp. of Oliva and aux. bp. of Los Angeles, Mar. 19, 1994. San Pedro regional bp..

Scarpone Caporale, Gerald, O.F.M.: b. Oct. 1, 1928, Watertown, Mass.; ord. priest June 24, 1956; ord. coadjutor bp. of Comayagua, Honduras, Feb. 21, 1979; succeeded as bp. of Comayagua, May 30, 1979.

Schad, James L.: b. July 20, 1917, Philadelphia, Pa.; educ. St. Mary's Seminary (Baltimore, Md.); ord. priest (Camden) Apr. 10, 1943; ord. titular bp. of Panatoria and aux. bp. of Camden, Dec. 8, 1966; retired Jan 26, 1993.

Schlarman, Stanley Gerard: b. July 27, 1933, Belleville, Ill.; educ. St. Henry Prep Seminary (Belleville, Ill.), Gregorian Univ. (Rome), St. Louis Univ. (St. Louis, Mo.); ord. priest (Belleville) July 13, 1958, Rome; ord. titular bp. of Capri and aux. bp. of Belleville, May 14, 1979; app. bp. of Dodge City, Mar. 1, 1983; resigned May 12, 1998.

Schleck, Charles A., C.S.C.: b. July 5, 1925, Milwaukee, Wis.; educ. Univ. of Notre Dame (Indiana), Univ. of St. Thomas (Rome); ord. priest Dec. 22, 1951; ord. titular abp. of Africa (Mehdia), Apr. 1, 1995; adjunct secretary of Congregation for Evangelization of Peoples; president of the superior council of the Pontifical Mission Societies.

Schmidt, Firmin M., O.F.M. Cap.: b. Oct. 12, 1918, Catherine, Kans.; educ. Catholic Univ. (Washington, D.C.); ord. priest June 2, 1946; app. prefect apostolic of Mendi, Papua New Guinea, Apr. 3, 1959; ord. titular bp. of Conana and first vicar apostolic of Mendi, Dec.15, 1965; became first bp. of Mendi when vicariate apostolic was raised to a diocese, Nov. 15, 1966; retired Feb. 22, 1995.

Schmitt, Bernard W.: b. Aug. 17, 1928, Wheeling, W. Va.; educ. St. Joseph College (Catonsville, Md.), St. Mary's Seminary (Baltimore), Ohio Univ. (Athens, O.); ord. priest (Wheeling-Charleston) May 28, 1955; ord. titular bp. of Walla Walla and bp. of Wheeling-Charleston, Aug. 1, 1988; bp. of Wheeling-Charleston, Mar. 29, 1989.

Schmitt, Mark F.: b. Feb. 14, 1923, Algoma, Wis.; educ. Salvatorian Seminary (St. Nazianz, Wis.), St. John's Seminary (Collegeville, Minn.); ord. priest (Green Bay) May 22, 1948; ord. titular bp. of Ceanannus Mor and aux. bp. of Green Bay, June 24, 1970; app. bp. of Marquette, Mar. 21, 1978, installed May 8, 1978; retired Oct. 6, 1992.

Schmitz Simon, Paul, O.F.M. Cap.: b. Dec. 4, 1943, Fond du Lac, Wis.; ord. priest Sept. 3, 1970; missionary in Nicaragua from 1970; superior of vice province of Capuchins in Central America (headquartered in Managua), 1982-84; ord. titular bp. of Elepla and aux. of the vicariate apostolic of Bluefields, Nicaragua, Sept. 17, 1984; app. bp. of vicariate apostolic of Bluefields, Aug. 17, 1994.

Schoenherr, Walter J.: b. Feb. 28, 1920, Detroit, Mich.; educ. Sacred Heart Seminary (Detroit, Mich.), Mt. St. Mary Seminary (Norwood, O.); ord. priest (Detroit*) Oct. 27, 1945; ord. titular bp. of Timidana and aux. bp. of Detroit, May 1, 1968; retired Mar. 7, 1995.

Schott, Basil, O.F.M.: b. July 21, 1939, Freeland, Pa.; entered Byzantine Franciscans, professed Aug. 4, 1959; educ. Immaculate Conception College (Troy, N.Y.), St. Mary's Seminary (Norwalk, Conn.) and Post Graduate Center (New York, N.Y.); ord. priest Aug. 29, 1965; ord. bp. of Byzantine eparchy of Parma, July 11, 1996.

Schulte, Francis B.: b. Dec. 23, 1926, Philadelphia, Pa.; educ. St. Charles Borromeo Seminary (Overbrook, Pa.); ord. priest (Philadelphia*) May 10, 1952; ord. titular bp. of Afufenia and aux. bp. of Philadelphia, Aug. 12, 1981; app. bp. of Wheeling-Charleston, June 4, 1985; abp. of New Orleans, Dec. 6, 1988, installed Feb. 14, 1989.

Schwietz, Roger L., O.M.I.: b. July 3, 1940, St. Paul, Minn.; educ. Univ. of Ottawa (Canada), Gregorian Univ. (Rome); ord. priest Dec. 20, 1967; ord. bp. of Duluth Feb. 2, 1990.

Setian, Nerses Mikail: b. Oct. 18,1918, Sebaste, Turkey; educ. Armenian Pontifical College and Gregorian Univ. (Rome); ord. priest Apr. 13, 1941, in Rome; ord. titular bp. of Ancira of the Armenians and first exarch of the apostolic exarchate for Armenian Catholics in Canada and the United States (see city New York), Dec. 5, 1981; retired Nov. 24, 1993.

Sevilla, Carlos A., S.J.: b. Aug. 9, 1935, San Francisco, Calif.; entered Jesuits Aug. 14, 1953; educ. Gonzaga Univ. (Spokane, Wash.), Santa Clara Uiv. (Santa Clara, Calif.), Jesuitenkolleg (Innsbruck, Austria), Catholic Institute of Paris (France); ord. priest June 3, 1966; ord. titular bp. of Mina and aux. bp. of San Francisco, Jan. 25, 1989; bp. of Yakima, Dec. 31, 1996.

Sheehan, Daniel E.: b. May 14, 1917, Emerson, Nebr.; educ. Creighton Univ. (Omaha, Nebr.), Kenrick Seminary (Webster Groves, Mo.), Catholic Univ. (Washington, D.C.); ord. priest (Omaha*) May 23, 1942; ord. titular bp. of Capsus and aux. bp. of Omaha, Mar. 19, 1964; app. abp. of Omaha, installed Aug. 11, 1969; retired May 4, 1993.

Sheehan, Michael J.: b. July 9, 1939, Wichita, Kans.; educ. Assumption Seminary (San Antonio, Tex.), Gregorian Univ. and Lateran Univ. (Rome); ord. priest (Dallas) July 12, 1964; ord. first bp. of Lubbock, Tex., June 17, 1983; apostolic administrator of Santa Fe, Apr. 6, 1993; app. abp. of Santa Fe, Aug. 17, 1993.

Sheets, John R., S.J.: b. Sept. 21, 1922, Omaha, Neb.; joined Jesuits, 1940; educ. St. Louis Univ. (St. Louis, Mo.), St. Mary's College (St. Mary's, Kans.), Univ. of Innsbruck (Austria); ord. priest June 17, 1953; final profession of vows as Jesuit, Aug. 15, 1957; ord. titular bp. of Murcona and aux. bp. of Fort Wayne-South Bend, Ind., June 25, 1991. Retired: September 23, 1997.

Sheldon, Gilbert I.: b. Sept. 20, 1926, Cleveland, O.; educ. John Carroll Univ. and St. Mary Seminary (Cleveland, O.); ord. priest (Cleveland) Feb. 28, 1953; ord. titular bp. of Taparura and aux. bp. of Cleveland, June 11, 1976; app. bp. of Steubenville, Jan. 28, 1992.

Sheridan, Michael J.: b. Mar. 4, 1945, St. Louis, Mo.; educ. Glennon College, Kenrick Seminary (St. Louis, Mo.), Angelicum (Rome); ord. priest (St. Louis*) 1971; app. titular bp. of Thibiuca and aux. bp. of St. Louis, July 9, 1997.

Sheridan, Patrick J.: b. Mar. 10, 1922, New York, N.Y.; educ. St. Joseph's Seminary (Yonkers, N.Y.), University of Chicago; ord. priest (New York*) Mar. 1, 1947; ord. titular bp. of Curzola and aux. bp. of New York, Dec. 12, 1990.

Sklba, Richard J.: b. Sept. 11, 1935, Racine, Wis.; educ. Old St. Francis Minor Seminary (Milwaukee, Wis.), North American College, Gregorian Univ., Pontifical Biblical Institute, Angelicum (Rome); ord. priest (Milwaukee*) Dec. 20, 1959; ord. titular bp. of Castra and aux. bp. of Milwaukee, Dec. 19, 1979.

Skylstad, William S.: b. Mar. 2, 1934, Omak, Wash.; educ. Pontifical College Josephinum (Worthington, Ohio), Washington State Univ. (Pullman, Wash.), Gonzaga Univ. (Spokane, Wash.); ord. priest (Spokane) May 21, 1960; ord. bp. of Yakima, May 12, 1977; app. bp. of Spokane, Apr. 17, 1990.

Slattery, Edward J.: b. Aug. 11, 1940, Chicago, Ill.; educ. Quigley Preparatory, St. Mary of the Lake Seminary (Mundelein, Ill.), Loyola Univ. (Chicago);

ord. priest (Chicago*) Apr. 26, 1966; vice president, 1971-76, and president, 1976-94, of the Catholic Church Extension Society; ord. bp. of Tulsa, Jan. 6, 1994.

Smith, John M.: b. June 23, 1935, Orange, N.J.; educ. Immaculate Conception Seminary (Darlington, N.J.), Seton Hall Univ. (South Orange, N.J.), Catholic Univ. (Washington, D.C.); ord. priest (Newark*) May 27, 1961; ord. titular bp. of Tre Taverne and aux. bp. of Newark, Jan. 25, 1988; app. bp. of Pensacola-Tallahassee, Fla., June 25, 1991; app. coadjutor bp. of Trenton, Nov. 21, 1995; bp. of Trenton, July 1, 1997.

Smith, Philip F., O.M.I.: b. Oct. 16, 1924, Lowell, Mass.; ord. priest Oct. 29, 1950; ord. titular bp. of Lamfua and vicar apostolic of Jolo, Philippine Islands, Sept. 8, 1972; app. coadjutor abp. of Cotabato, Philippines, Apr. 11, 1979; abp. of Cotabato, Mar. 14, 1980.

Snyder, John J.: b. Oct. 25, 1925, New York, N.Y.; educ. Cathedral College (Brooklyn, N.Y.), Immaculate Conception Seminary (Huntington, N.Y.); ord. priest (Brooklyn) June 9, 1951; ord. titular bp. of Forlimpopli and aux. bp. of Brooklyn, Feb. 2, 1973; app. bp. of St. Augustine, installed Dec. 5, 1979.

Soens, Lawrence D.: b. Aug. 26, 1926, Iowa City, Ia.; educ. Loras College (Dubuque, Ia.), St. Ambrose College (Davenport, Ia.), Kenrick Seminary (St. Louis, Mo.), Univ. of Iowa; ord. priest (Davenport) May 6, 1950; ord. bp. of Sioux City, Aug. 17, 1983, resigned Nov. 28, 1998.

Sowada, Alphonse A., O.S.C.: b. June 23, 1933, Avon, Minn.; educ. Holy Cross Scholasticate (Fort Wayne, Ind.), Catholic Univ. (Washington, D.C.), ord. priest May 31, 1958; missionary in Indonesia from 1958; ord. bp. of Agats, Indonesia, Nov. 23, 1969.

Speltz, George H.: b. May 29, 1912, Altura, Minn.; educ. St. Mary's College, St. Paul's Seminary (St. Paul, Minn.), Catholic Univ. (Washington, D.C.); ord. priest (St. Cloud) June 2, 1940; ord. titular bp. of Claneus and aux. bp. of Winona, Mar. 25, 1963; app. coadjutor bp. of St. Cloud, Apr. 4, 1966; bp. of St. Cloud, Jan. 31, 1968; retired Jan. 13, 1987.

Speyrer, Jude: b. Apr. 14, 1929, Leonville, La.; educ. St. Joseph Seminary (Covington, La.), Notre Dame Seminary (New Orleans, La.), Gregorian Univ. (Rome), Univ. of Fribourg (Switzerland); ord. priest (Lafayette, La.) July 25, 1953; ord. first bp. of Lake Charles, La., Apr. 25, 1980.

Stafford, James Francis: (See Cardinals, Biographies).

Steib, J. (James) Terry, S.V.D.: b. May 17, 1940, Vacherie, La.; educ. Divine Word seminaries (Bay St. Louis, Miss., Conesus, N.Y., Techny, Ill.), Xavier Univ. (New Orleans, La.); ord. priest Jan. 6, 1967; ord. titular bp. of Fallaba and aux. bp. of St. Louis, Feb. 10, 1984; app. bp. of Memphis, Mar. 24, 1993.

Steinbock, John T.: b. July 16, 1937, Los Angeles, Calif.; educ. Los Angeles archdiocesan seminaries; ord. priest (Los Angeles*) May 1, 1963; ord. titular bp. of Midila and aux. bp. of Orange, Calif., July 14, 1984; app. bp. of Santa Rosa, Jan. 27, 1987; app. bp. of Fresno, Oct. 15, 1991.

Steiner, Kenneth Donald: b. Nov. 25, 1936, David City, Nebr.; educ. Mt. Angel Seminary (St. Benedict, Ore.), St. Thomas Seminary (Seattle, Wash); ord. priest (Portland,* Ore.) May 19, 1962; ord. titular bp.

of Avensa and aux. bp. of Portland, Ore., Mar. 2, 1978.

Straling, Phillip F.: b. Apr. 25, 1933, San Bernardino, Calif.; educ. Immaculate Heart Seminary, St. Francis Seminary, Univ. of San Diego and San Diego State University (San Diego, Calif.), North American College (Rome); ord. priest (San Diego) Mar. 19, 1959; ord. first bp. of San Bernardino, Nov. 6, 1978; app. first bp. of Reno, Mar. 21, 1995, when Reno-Las Vegas diocese was made two separate dioceses.

Strecker, Ignatius J.: b. Nov. 23, 1917, Spearville, Kans.; educ. St. Benedict's College (Atchison, Kans.), Kenrick Seminary (Webster Groves, Mo.), Catholic Univ. (Washington, D.C.); ord. priest (Wichita) Dec. 19, 1942; ord. bp. of Springfield-Cape Girardeau, Mo., June 20, 1962; abp. of Kansas City, Kans., Oct. 28, 1969; retired June 28, 1993.

Sullivan, James S.: b. July 23, 1929, Kalamazoo, Mich.; educ. Sacred Heart Seminary (Detroit, Mich.), St. John Provincial Seminary (Plymouth, Mich.); ord. priest (Lansing) June 4, 1955; ord. titular bp. of Siccessi and aux. bp. of Lansing, Sept. 21, 1972; app. bp. of Fargo, Apr. 2, 1985; installed May 30, 1985.

Sullivan, John J.: b. July 5, 1920, Horton, Kans.; educ. Kenrick Seminary (St. Louis, Mo.); ord. priest (Oklahoma City*) Sept. 23, 1944; vice-president of Catholic Church Extension Society and national director of Extension Lay Volunteers, 1961-68; ord. bp. of Grand Island, Sept. 19, 1972; app. bp. of Kansas City-St. Joseph, June 27, 1977, installed Aug. 17, 1977; retired June 22, 1993.

Sullivan, Joseph M.: b. Mar. 23, 1930, Brooklyn, N.Y.; educ. Immaculate Conception Seminary (Huntington, N.Y.), Fordham Univ. (New York); ord. priest (Brooklyn) June 2, 1956; ord. titular bp. of Suliana and aux. bp. of Brooklyn, Nov. 24, 1980.

Sullivan, Walter F.: b. June 10, 1928, Washington, D.C.; educ. St. Mary's Seminary (Baltimore, Md.), Catholic Univ. (Washington, D.C.); ord. priest (Richmond) May 9, 1953; ord. titular bp. of Selsea and aux. bp. of Richmond, Va., Dec. 1, 1970; app. bp. of Richmond, June 4, 1974.

Sulyk, Stephen: b. Oct. 2, 1924, Balnycia, Western Ukraine; migrated to U.S. 1948; educ. Ukrainian Catholic Seminary of the Holy Spirit (Hirschberg, Germany), St. Josaphat's Seminary and Catholic Univ. (Washington, D.C.); ord. priest (Philadelphia,* Byzantine) June 14, 1952; ord. abp. of the Ukrainian archeparchy of Philadelphia, Mar. 1, 1981.

Symons, J. Keith: b. Oct. 14, 1932, Champion, Mich.; educ. St. Thomas Seminary (Bloomfield, Conn.), St. Mary Seminary (Baltimore, Md.); ord. priest (St. Augustine) May 18, 1958; ord. titular bp. of Siguitanus and aux. bp. of St. Petersburg, Mar. 19, 1981; app. bp. of Pensacola-Tallahassee, Oct. 4, 1983, installed Nov. 8, 1983; app. bp. of Palm Beach, June 12, 1990; resigned, June 2, 1998.

Szoka, Edmund C.: (See Cardinals, Biographies.)

T

Tafoya, Arthur N.: b. Mar. 2, 1933, Alameda, N.M.; educ. St. Thomas Seminary (Denver, Colo.), Conception Seminary (Conception, Mo.); ord. priest (Santa Fe*) May 12, 1962; ord. bp. of Pueblo, Sept. 10, 1980.

Tamayo, James A.: b. Oct. 23, 1949, Brownsville, Tex.; educ. Del Mar College (Corpus Christi, Tex.), Univ. of St. Thomas and Univ. of St. Thomas School of Theology (Houston); ord. priest (Corpus Christi)

June 11, 1976; ord. titular bp. of Ita and aux. bp. of Galveston-Houston, Mar. 10, 1993. Episcopal vicar for Hispanics.

Tertzakian, Hovhannes, O.M.Ven.: b. Jan. 3, 1924, Aleppo, Syria; educ. Mekhitarist Monastery of St. Lazarus (Venice, Italy); Gregorian Univ. (Rome); entered Mekhitarist Order of Venice, 1938, final vows Oct. 24, 1945; ord. priest Sept. 8, 1948; came to U.S., 1984; ord. titular bp. of Trebizond for Armenians and apostolic exarch for Armenian Catholics in the United States and Canada, Apr. 29, 1995.

Thomas, Elliott G.: b. July 15, 1926, Pittsburgh, Pa.; educ. Howard Univ. (Washington, D.C.), Gannon Univ. (Erie, Pa.), St. Vincent de Paul Seminary (Boynton Beach, Fla.); ord. priest (St. Thomas, Virgin Islands) June 6, 1986; ord. bp. of St. Thomas in the Virgin Islands, Dec. 12, 1993; resigned June 30, 1999.

Thompson, David B.: b. May 29, 1923, Philadelphia, Pa.; educ. St. Charles Seminary (Overbrook, Pa.), Catholic Univ. (Washington, D.C.); ord. priest (Philadelphia*) May 27, 1950; ord. coadjutor bp. of Charleston, May 24, 1989; bp. of Charleston, Feb. 22, 1990; res. July 13, 1999

Timlin, James C.: b. Aug. 5, 1927, Scranton, Pa.; educ. St. Charles College (Catonville, Md.), St. Mary's Seminary (Baltimore, Md.), North American College (Rome); ord. priest (Scranton) July 16, 1951; ord. titular bp. of Gunugo and aux. bp. of Scranton, Sept. 21, 1976; app. bp. of Scranton, Apr. 24, 1984.

Tobin, Thomas J.: b. Apr. 1, 1948, Pittsburgh, Pa.; educ. St. Mark Seminary High School, Gannon Univ. (Erie, Pa.), St. Francis College (Loretto, Pa.), North American College (Rome); ord. priest (Pittsburgh) July 21, 1973; ord. titular bp. of Novica and aux. bp. of Pittsburgh, Dec. 27, 1992; app. bp. of Youngstown Dec. 5, 1995; installed Feb. 2, 1996.

Trautman, Donald W.: b. June 24, 1936, Buffalo, N.Y.; educ. Our Lady of Angels Seminary (Niagara Falls, N.Y.), Theology Faculty (Innsbruck, Austria), Pontifical Biblical Institute (Rome), Catholic Univ. (Washington, D.C.); ord. priest (Buffalo) Apr. 7, 1962, in Innsbruck; ord. titular bp. of Sassura and aux. of Buffalo, Apr. 16, 1985; app. bp. of Erie, June 12, 1990.

Tschoepe, Thomas: b. Dec. 17, 1915, Pilot Point, Tex.; educ. Pontifical College Josephinum (Worthington, O.); ord. priest (Dallas) May 30, 1943; ord. bp. of San Angelo, Tex., Mar. 9, 1966; app. bp. of Dallas, Tex., Aug. 27, 1969; retired July 14, 1990.

Turley Murphy, Daniel T. , O.S.A.: b. Jan. 25, 1943, Chicago, Ill.; ord. priest Dec. 21, 1961; ord. coadjutor bp. of Chulucanas, Peru, Aug. 17, 1996.

U-V

Untener, Kenneth E.: b. Aug. 3, 1937, Detroit, Mich.; educ. Sacred Heart Seminary (Detroit, Mich.), St. John's Provincial Seminary (Plymouth, Mich.), Gregorian Univ. (Rome); ord. priest (Detroit*) June 1, 1963; ord. bp. of Saginaw, Nov. 24, 1980.

Valero, René A.: b. Aug. 15, 1930, New York, N.Y.; educ. Cathedral College, Immaculate Conception Seminary (Huntington, N.Y.), Fordham Univ. (New York); ord. priest (Brooklyn) June 2, 1956; ord. titular bp. of Turris Vicus and aux. bp. of Brooklyn, Nov. 24, 1980.

Vaughan, Austin B.: b. Sept. 27, 1927, New York, N.Y.; educ. North American College and Gregorian

Univ. (Rome), ord. priest (New York*) Dec. 8, 1951; pres. Catholic Theological Society of America, 1967; rector of St. Joseph's Seminary (Dunwoodie, N.Y.), 1973; ord. titular bp. of Cluain Iraird and aux. bp. of New York, June 29, 1977.

Veigle, Adrian J.M., T.O.R.: b. Sept. 15, 1912, Lilly, Pa.; educ. St. Francis College (Loretto, Pa.), Pennsylvania State College; ord. priest May 22, 1937; ord. titular bp. of Gigthi June 9, 1966 (resigned titular see May 26, 1978); prelate of Borba, Brazil, 1966; retired July 6, 1988.

Vigernon, Allen H.: b. Oct. 21, 1948, Detroit, Mich.; educ. Sacred Heart Seminary (Detroit, Mich.), North American College, Gregorian Univ. (Rome) Catholic Univ.(Washington, DC); ord. priest (Detroit*) July 26, 1975; served in Vatican Secretariat of State, 1991-94; rector of Sacred Heart Seminary (Detroit), 1994; ord. titular bp. of Sault Sainte Marie and aux. bp. of Detroit, July 9, 1996.

Vlazny, John G.: b. Feb. 22, 1937, Chicago, Ill.; educ. Quigley Preparatory Seminary (Chicago, Ill.), St. Mary of the Lake Seminary (Mundelein, Ill.), Gregorian Univ. (Rome), Univ. of Michigan, Loyola Univ. (Chicago, Ill.); ord. priest (Chicago*) Dec. 20, 1961; ord. titular bp. of Stagno and aux. bp. of Chicago, Dec. 13, 1983; app. bp. of Winona, Minn., May 19, 1987; app. abp. of Portland in Oregon, Oct. 28, 1997, installed Dec. 19, 1997.

W

Walsh, Daniel Francis: b. Oct. 2, 1937, San Francisco, Calif.; educ. St. Joseph Seminary (Mountain View, Calif.), St. Patrick Seminary (Menlo Park, Calif.) Catholic Univ. (Washington, D.C.); ord. priest (San Francisco*) Mar. 30, 1963; ord. titular bp. of Tigia and aux. bp. of San Francisco, Sept. 24, 1981; app. bp. of Reno-Las Vegas, June 9, 1987; app. first bp. of Las Vegas Mar. 21, 1995, when the Reno-Las Vegas diocese was made two separate dioceses.

Ward, John J.: b. Sept. 28, 1920, Los Angeles, Calif.; educ. St. John's Seminary (Camarillo, Calif.), Catholic Univ. (Washington, D.C.); ord. priest (Los Angeles*) May 4, 1946; ord. titular bp. of Bria and aux. of Los Angeles, Dec. 12, 1963; retired May 7, 1996; titular bp. of Calif..

Warfel, Michael William: b. Sept 16, 1948, Elkhart, Ind.; educ. Indiana Univ, St. Gregory's College Seminary, Mt. St. Mary's Seminary of the West (Cincinnati, Ohio); ord. priest Apr. 26, 1980; ord. bp. of Juneau, Dec. 17, 1996.

Watters, Loras J.: b. Oct. 14, 1915, Dubuque, Ia.; educ. Loras College (Dubuque, Ia.), Gregorian Univ. (Rome), Catholic Univ. (Washington, D.C.); ord. priest (Dubuque*) June 7, 1941; ord. titular bp. of Fidoloma and aux. bp. of Dubuque, Aug. 26, 1965; bp. of Winona, installed Mar. 13, 1969; retired Oct. 14, 1986.

Watty Urquidi, Ricardo, M.Sp.S.: b. July 16, 1938, San Diego, Calif.; ord. priest June 8, 1968; ord. titular bp. of Macomedes and aux. bp. of Mexico City, July 19, 1980; app. first bp. of Nuevo Laredo, Mexico, Nov. 6, 1989.

Wcela, Emil A.: b. May 1, 1931, Bohemia, N.Y.; educ. St. Francis College (Brooklyn, N.Y.), Immaculate Conception Seminary (Huntington, N.Y.), Catholic Univ. (Washington, D.C.), Pontifical Biblical Institute (Rome, Italy); ord. priest (Brooklyn) June 2,

1956; ord. titular bp. of Filaca and aux. bp. of Rockville Centre, Dec. 13, 1988.

Weakland, Rembert G., O.S.B.: b. Apr. 2, 1927, Patton, Pa.; joined Benedictines, 1945; ord. priest June 24, 1951; abbot-primate of Benedictine Confederation, 1967-77; ord. abp. of Milwaukee, Nov. 8, 1977.

Weigand, William K.: b. May 23, 1937, Bend, Ore.; educ. Mt. Angel Seminary (St. Benedict, Ore.), St. Edward's Seminary and St. Thomas Seminary (Kenmore, Wash.); ord. priest (Boise) May 25, 1963; ord. bp. of Salt Lake City, Nov. 17, 1980; app. bp. of Sacramento, Nov. 30, 1993, installed Jan. 27, 1994.

Weitzel, John Quinn, M.M.: b. May 10, 1928, Chicago, Ill.; educ. Maryknoll Seminary (Maryknoll, N.Y.); ord. priest Nov. 5, 1955; missionary to Samoa, 1979; ord. bp. of Samoa-Pago Pago, American Samoa, Oct. 29, 1986.

Welsh, Thomas J.: b. Dec. 20, 1921, Weatherly, Pa.; educ. St. Charles Borromeo Seminary (Philadelphia, Pa.), Catholic Univ. (Washington, D.C.); ord. priest (Philadelphia*) May 30, 1946; ord. titular bp. of Scattery Island and aux. bp. of Philadelphia, Apr. 2, 1970; app. first bp. of Arlington, Va., June 4, 1974; app. bp. of Allentown, Feb. 8, 1983, installed Mar. 21, 1983. Retired: December 16, 1997.

Wenski, Thomas G.: b. Oct. 18, 1950, West Palm Beach, Fla.; educ. St. John Vianney College Seminary, St. Vincent de Paul Regional Seminary, Fordham Univ.; ord. priest (Miami*) May 15, 1976; director of Miami Haitian Apostolate; app..titular bp. of Kearney and aux. of Miami, June 24, 1997.

Wester, John Charles: b. Nov. 5, 1950, San Francisco; educ.St. John's Seminary, Camarillo, Calif., St. Patrick's Seminary, Menlo Park, Calif., univ of San Francisco; ord. priest (San Francisco*) May 15, 1976; app. titular bp. of Lamiggiga and aux. bp. of San Francisco, June 30, 1998.

Whelan, Robert L., S.J.: b. Apr. 16, 1912, Wallace, Ida.; educ. St. Michael's College (Spokane, Wash.), Alma College (Alma, Calif.); ord. priest June 17, 1944; ord. titular bp. of Sicilibba and coadjutor bp. of Fairbanks, Alaska, with right of succession, Feb. 22, 1968; bp. of Fairbanks, Nov. 30, 1968; retired June 1, 1985.

Wilkerson, Gerald E.: b. Oct. 21, 1939, Des Moines, Iowa; educ. St. John's Seminary (Camarillo, Calif.); ord. priest (Los Angeles*) Jan. 5, 1965; app. Titular Bp. of Vincennes and aux. bp. of Los Angeles, Nov. 5, 1997, ord. Jan. 21, 1998.

Williams, James Kendrick: b. Sept. 5, 1936, Athertonville, Ky.; educ. St. Mary's College (St. Mary's, Ky.), St. Maur's School of Theology (South Union, Ky.); ord. priest (Louisville*) May 25, 1963; ord. titular bp. of Catula and aux. bp. of Covington, June 19, 1984; first bp. of Lexington, Ky., installed Mar. 2, 1988.

Winter, William J.: b. May 20, 1930, Pittsburgh, Pa.; educ. St. Vincent College and Seminary (Latrobe, Pa.), Gregorian Univ. (Rome, Italy); ord. priest (Pittsburgh), Dec. 17, 1955; ord. titular bp. of Uthina and aux. bp. of Pittsburgh, Feb. 13, 1989.

Wirz, George O.: b. Jan. 17, 1929, Monroe, Wis.; educ. St. Francis Seminary and Marquette Univ. (Milwaukee, Wis.); Cath. Univ. (Washington, D.C.); ord. priest (Madison) May 31, 1952; ord. titular bp. of Municipa and aux. bp. of Madison, Mar. 9, 1978.

Wiwchar, Michael, C.SS.R.: b. May 9, 1932,

Komarno, Manitoba, Canada; educ. Redemptorist Seminary (Windsor, Ontario); made solemn vows as Redemptorist, 1956; ord. priest, June 28, 1959; pastor St. John the Baptist Parish, Newark, N.J., 1990-93; ord. bp. of St. Nicholas of Chicago for the Ukrainians, Sept. 28, 1993.

Wuerl, Donald W.: b. Nov. 12, 1940, Pittsburgh, Pa.; educ. Catholic Univ. (Washington, D.C.), North American College, Angelicum (Rome); ord. priest (Pittsburgh) Dec. 17, 1966, in Rome; ord. titular bp. of Rosemarkie Jan. 6, 1986, in Rome; aux. bp. of Seattle, 1986-87; app. bp. of Pittsburgh Feb. 11, 1988, installed Mar. 25, 1988.

Wycislo, Aloysius John: b. June 17, 1908, Chicago, Ill.; educ. St. Mary's Seminary (Mundelein, Ill.), Catholic Univ. (Washington, D.C.); ord. priest (Chicago*) Apr. 4, 1934; ord. titular bp. of Stadia and aux. bp. of Chicago, Dec. 21, 1960; app. bp. of Green Bay, installed Apr. 16, 1968; resigned May 10, 1983.

Y-Z

Yanta, John W.: b. Oct. 2, 1931, Runge, Tex.; educ. St. John's Preparatory Seminary and Assumption Seminary (San Antonio); ord. priest (San Antonio*) Mar. 17, 1956; ord. titular bp. of Naratcata and aux. bp. of San Antonio Dec. 30, 1994; app. bp. of Amarillo, Jan. 21,1997, installed Mar. 17, 1997.

Younan, Joseph: b. Nov. 15, 1944, Hassakeh, Syria; educ. Our Lady of Deliverance Seminary (Charfet, Lebanon), Pontifical College of the Propagation of the Faith (Rome); ord. priest Sept. 12, 1971; came to U.S., 1986; served Syrian Catholics in U.S.; ord. first bp. Our Lady of Deliverance of Newark for Syrian Catholics in the U.S. and Canada, Jan. 7, 1996, in Kamisly, Syria.

Zavala, Gabino: b. Sept. 7, 1951, Guerrero, Mexico; became U.S. citizen, 1976; educ. St. John's Seminary (Los Angeles), Catholic Univ. (Washington, D.C.); ord. priest (Los Angeles*) May 28, 1977; ord. titular bp. of Tamascani and aux. bp. of Los Angeles, Mar. 19, 1994.

Zayek, Francis: b. Oct. 18, 1920, Manzanillo, Cuba; ord. priest Mar. 17, 1946; ord. titular bp. of Callinicum and aux. bp. for Maronites in Brazil, Aug. 5, 1962; named apostolic exarch for Maronites in U.S., with headquarters in Detroit; installed June 11. 1966; first eparch of St. Maron of Detroit, Mar. 25, 1972; see transferred to Brooklyn, June 27, 1977; given personal title of abp., Dec. 22, 1982; retired Nov. 23, 1996.

Ziemann, Patrick G.: b. Sept. 13, 1941, Pasadena, Calif.; educ. St. John's College Seminary and St. John's Seminary (Camarillo, Calif.), Mt. St. Mary's College (Los Angeles, Calif.); ord. priest (Los Angeles*) Apr. 29, 1967; ord. titular bp. of Obba and aux. bp. of Los Angeles, Feb. 23, 1987; app. bp. of Santa Rosa, July 14, 1992; resigned, July 22, 1999.

Zipfel, Paul A.: b. Sept. 22, 1935, St. Louis, Mo.; educ. Cardinal Glennon College, Kenrick Seminary (St. Louis, Mo.), Catholic Univ. (Washington, D.C.), St. Louis Univ. (St. Louis, Mo.); ord. priest (St. Louis*) Mar. 18, 1961; ord. titular bp. of Walla Walla and aux. bp. of St. Louis, June 29, 1989; app. bp. of Bismarck, Dec. 31, 1996.

Zubic, David A.: b. Sept. 4, 1949, Sewickley, Pa.; educ. St. Paul Seminary-Duquesne Univ. (Pittsburgh), St. Mary's Seminary (Baltimore), Duquesne Univ.

(Pittsburgh); ord. priest (Pittsburgh) May 3, 1975; ord. titular bp. of Jamestown and aux. of Pittsburgh, Apr. 6, 1997.

Zurek, Patrick J.: b. Aug. 17, 1948, Wallis, Tex.; educ. Univ.of St. Thomas (Houston), Angelicum and Alphonsian Academy (Rome); ord priest (Austin) June 29, 1975; app. titular bp. of Tamugadi and aux. bp. of San Antonio, Jan. 5, 1998, ord. Feb. 16, 1998.

BISHOP-BROTHERS

(The asterisk indicates brothers who were bishops at the same time.)

There have been 10 pairs of brother-bishops in the history of the U.S. hierarchy.

Living: Francis T. Hurley,* abp. of Anchorage and Mark J. Hurley,* bp. emeritus of Santa Rosa. Raymond J. Boland,* bp. of Kansas City-St. Joseph, Mo. and John Kevin Boland,* bp. of Savannah.

Deceased: Francis Blanchet* of Oregon City (Portland) and Augustin Blanchet* of Walla Walla; John S. Foley of Detroit and Thomas P. Foley of Chicago; Francis P. Kenrick,* apostolic administrator of Philadelphia, bp. of Philadelphia and Baltimore, and Peter R. Kenrick* of St. Louis; Matthias C. Lenihan of Great Falls and Thomas M. Lenihan of Cheyenne; James O'Connor, vicar apostolic of Nebraska and bp. of Omaha, and Michael O'Connor of Pittsburgh and Erie; Jeremiah F. and John W. Shanahan, both of Harrisburg; Sylvester J. Espelage, O.F.M.* of Wuchang, China, who died 10 days after the ordination of his brother, Bernard T. Espelage, O.F.M.* of Gallup; Coleman F. Carroll* of Miami and Howard Carroll* of Altoona-Johnstown.

U.S. BISHOPS OVERSEAS

Cardinal William W. Baum, major penitentiary; Cardinal Edmund C. Szoka, president of Prefecture for Economic Affairs of the Holy See; Cardinal James Francis Stafford, president of the Pontifical Council for the Laity; Abp. John P. Foley, president of Pontifical Commission for Social Communications; Abp. Ambrose de Paoli, first apostolic nuncio to South Africa, pro-nuncio to Lesotho and apostolic delegate to several other countries in southern Africa; Abp. Charles A. Schleck, C.S.C., adjunct secretary of the Congregation for the Evangelization of Peoples; Abp. Edward Joseph Adams, nuncio in Bangladesh; Abp. George Riashi, B.C.O., abp. of archeparchy of Tripoli of Lebanon (Lebanon) for Greek-Catholic Melkites; Bp. James M. Harvey, prefect of the Papal Household; Bp. Michael R. Kuchmiak, exarch of apostolic exarchate of Great Britain for Ukrainian Catholics; Abp. John Bukovsky, S.V.D. (naturalized U.S. citizen), papal representative to Russia. Cardinal Myroslav Ivan Lubachivsky, major abp. of Lviv of the Ukrainians (Ukraine), became a U.S. citizen in 1952 and was abp. of Philadelphia Ukrainian Archeparchy, 1979-80. (See also Missionary Bishops.)

RETIRED/RESIGNED U.S. PRELATES

Information, as of Aug. 20, 1998, includes name of the prelate and see held at the time of retirement or resignation; abp.s are indicated by an asterisk. Most of the prelates listed below resigned their sees because of age in accordance with church law. See Index: Biographies, U.S. Bishops.

Forms of address of retired residential prelates (unless they have a titular see): Abp. or Bp. Emeritus of (last see held); Former Abp. or Bp. of (last see held).

Alfred L. Abramowicz (Chicago, aux.), Patrick V. Ahern (New York, aux.), Leo Arkfeld, S.V.D.* (Madang, Papua New Guinea), Juan Arzube (Los Angeles, aux.), Michael J. Begley (Charlotte), Ernest B. Boland, O.P. (Multan, Pakistan), William D. Borders* (Baltimore), Joseph M. Breitenbeck (Grand Rapids), Edwin B. Broderick (Albany), Charles A. Buswell (Pueblo).

Harry A. Clinch (Monterey), John W. Comber, M.M. (Foratiano, titular see), Ronald G. Connors, C.SS.R. (San Juan de la Maguana, Dominican Republic), Arnold R. Cotey, S.D.S. (Nachingwea, now Lindi, Tanzania), Joseph R. Crowley (Ft. Wayne-S. Bend, aux.), James J. Daly (Rockville Centre, aux.), Nicholas D'Antonio, O.F.M. (Olancho, Honduras).

Joseph A. DePalma, S.C.J. (DeAar, South Africa), Louis A. DeSimone (Philadelphia, aux.), Joseph T. Dimino* (Military Services archdiocese), George Dion, O.M.I. (titular see, Arpaia), Paul V. Donovan (Kalamazoo), Michael J. Dudick (Passaic, Byzantine rite), Paul V. Dudley (Sioux Falls), Dennis V. Durning, C.S.Sp. (Arusha, Tanzania), J. Lennox Federal (Salt Lake City), Joseph A. Ferrario (Honolulu), John J. Fitzpatrick (Brownsville), Marion F. Forst (Dodge City), Benedict C. Franzetta (Youngstown, aux.), Gerard L. Frey (Lafayette, La.).

Robert F. Garner (Newark, aux.), Norbert F. Gaughan (Gary), Louis E. Gelineau (Providence), Odore Gendron (Manchester), Peter L. Gerety* (Newark), George J. Gottwald (St. Louis, aux.), Rene H. Gracida (Corpus Christi), Thomas J. Grady (Orlando), John J. Graham (Philadelphia, aux.), J. Richard Ham, M.M. (St. Paul and Minneapolis, aux.), Philip M. Hannan* (New Orleans), Frank J. Harrison (Syracuse), Edward D. Head (Buffalo).

Edward J. Herrmann (Columbus), Dennis W. Hickey (Rochester, aux.), James J. Hogan (Altoona-Johnstown), Joseph L. Hogan (Rochester), Edward T. Hughes (Metuchen), William A. Hughes (Covington), Raymond G. Hunthausen* (Seattle), Mark J. Hurley (Santa Rosa), Arthur H. Krawczak (Detroit, aux.), Daniel W. Kucera, O.S.B.* (Dubuque), William F. Kupfer, M.M. (Taichung, Taiwan), Francis Lambert, S.M. (Port Vila, Vanuatu), W. Thomas Larkin (St. Petersburg) Raymond W. Lessard (Savannah), Martin N. Lohmuller (Philadelphia, aux.), Innocent Hilarius Lotocky, O.S.B.M. (St. Nicholas of Chicago for Ukrainians), George E. Lynch (Raleigh, aux.), Timothy J. Lyne (Chicago, aux.).

Michael F. McAuliffe (Jefferson City), Edward A. McCarthy* (Miami), Thomas J. McDonough* (Louisville), John B. McDowell (Pittsburgh, aux.), Norman McFarland (Orange, Calif.), Urban McGarry, T.O.R. (Bhagalpur, India), Bernard J. McLaughlin (Buffalo, aux.), Joseph F. Maguire (Springfield, Mass.), James P. Mahoney (New York, aux.), James W. Malone (Youngstown), Charles G. Maloney (Louisville, aux.), Thomas R. Manning, O.F.M. (Coroico, Bolivia), Paul C. Marcinkus* (titular see of Orta), Eugene A. Marino, S.S.J.* (Atlanta), Leroy T. Matthiesen (Amarillo), James E. Michaels (Wheeling-Charleston, aux.), Donald W. Montrose (Stockton), Michael J. Murphy (Erie), Martin J. Neylon, S.J. (Caroline Islands), James D. Niedergeses (Nashville), Bernard

Nolker, C.SS.R. (Parangua, Brazil), Gerald F. O'Keefe (Davenport), Joseph T. O'Keefe (Syracuse), Edward C. O'Leary (Portland, Me.), Arthur J. O'Neill (Rockford). Edward W. O'Rourke (Peoria), Albert H. Ottenweller (Steubenville), John J. Paul (La Crosse), George H. Pearce, S.M.* (Suva, Fiji Islands), Bernard F. Popp (San Antonio, aux.), Kenneth J. Povish (Lansing),Vasile Louis Puscas (St. George's in Canton of the Romanians), Francis A. Quinn (Sacramento), John R. Quinn* (San Francisco), Joseph M. Raya* (Acre), John C. Reiss (Trenton), Lawrence J. Riley (Boston, aux.), John R. Roach* (St. Paul and Minneapolis), Miguel Rodriguez, C.SS.R. (Arecibo, P.R.), James C. Ryan, O.F.M. (Santarem, Brazil), Joseph T. Ryan* (Military Services archdiocese).

Charles A. Salatka* (Oklahoma City), Robert F. Sanchez* (Santa Fe), James L. Schad (Camden, aux.), Stanley G. Schlarman (Dodge City), Firmin M. Schmidt, O.F.M. Cap. (Mendi, Papua New Guinea), Mark Schmitt (Marquette), Walter J. Schoenherr (Detroit, aux.), Nerses Mikail Setian (Armenian Exarchate), Daniel E. Sheehan* (Omaha), John R. Sheets, SJ (Fort Wayne-South Bend, aux.), George H. Speltz (St. Cloud), Ignatius J. Strecker* (Kansas City, Kans.), John J. Sullivan (Kansas City-St. Joseph, Mo.).

Elliott Thomas (Virgin Islands), David B. Thompson (Charleston), Thomas Tschoepe (Dallas), Adrian Veigle, T.O.R. (Borba, Brazil, Prelate), John J. Ward (Los Angeles, aux.), Loras J. Watters (Winona), Thomas J. Welsh (Allentown), Robert L. Whelan (Fairbanks), Aloysius J. Wycislo (Green Bay), Francis Zayek (St. Maron of Brooklyn); Patrick Ziemann (Santa Rosa).

CATHEDRALS, BASILICAS, AND SHRINES IN THE U.S.

CATHEDRALS IN THE UNITED STATES

A cathedral is the principal church in a diocese, the one in which the bishop has his seat (cathedra). He is the actual pastor, although many functions of the church, which usually serves a parish, are the responsibility of a priest serving as the rector. Because of the dignity of a cathedral, the dates of its dedication and its patronal feast are observed throughout a diocese.

The pope's cathedral, the Basilica of St. John Lateran, is the highest-ranking church in the world.

(Archdioceses are indicated by asterisk.)

Albany, N.Y.: Immaculate Conception.
Alexandria, La.: St. Francis Xavier.
Allentown, Pa.: St. Catherine of Siena.
Altoona-Johnstown, Pa.: Blessed Sacrament (Altoona); St. John Gualbert (Johnstown).
Amarillo, Tex.: St. Laurence.
Anchorage,* Alaska: Holy Family.
Arlington, Va: St. Thomas More.
Atlanta,* Ga.: Christ the King.
Austin, Tex.: St. Mary (Immaculate Conception).
Baker, Ore.: St. Francis de Sales.
Baltimore,* Md.: Mary Our Queen; Basilica of the National Shrine of the Assumption of the Blessed Virgin Mary (Co-Cathedral).
Baton Rouge, La.: St. Joseph.
Beaumont, Tex.: St. Anthony (of Padua).
Belleville, Ill.: St. Peter.
Biloxi, Miss.: Nativity of the Blessed Virgin Mary.
Birmingham, Ala.: St. Paul.
Bismarck, N.D.: Holy Spirit.
Boise, Id.: St. John the Evangelist.
Boston,* Mass.: Holy Cross.
Bridgeport, Conn.: St. Augustine.
Brooklyn, N.Y.: St. James (Minor Basilica).
Brownsville, Tex.: Immaculate Conception.
Buffalo, N.Y.: St. Joseph.
Burlington, Vt.: Immaculate Conception.
Camden, N.J.: Immaculate Conception.
Charleston, S.C.: St. John the Baptist.
Charlotte, N.C.: St. Patrick.
Cheyenne, Wyo.: St. Mary.
Chicago,* Ill.: Holy Name (of Jesus).

Cincinnati,* Ohio: St. Peter in Chains.
Cleveland, Ohio: St. John the Evangelist.
Colorado Springs, Colo: St. Mary.
Columbus, Ohio: St. Joseph.
Corpus Christi, Tex.: Corpus Christi.
Covington, Ky.: Basilica of the Assumption.
Crookston, Minn.: Immaculate Conception.
Dallas, Tex.: Cathedral-Santuario de Guadalupe.
Davenport, Ia.: Sacred Heart.
Denver,* Colo.: Immaculate Conception (Minor Basilica).
Des Moines, Ia.: St. Ambrose.
Detroit,* Mich.: Most Blessed Sacrament.
Dodge City, Kans.: Sacred Heart.
Dubuque,* Ia.: St. Raphael.
Duluth, Minn.: Our Lady of the Rosary.
El Paso, Tex.: St. Patrick.
Erie, Pa.: St. Peter.
Evansville, Ind.: Most Holy Trinity (Pro-Cathedral).
Fairbanks, Alaska: Sacred Heart.
Fall River, Mass.: St. Mary of the Assumption.
Fargo, N.D.: St. Mary.
Fort Wayne-S. Bend, Ind.: Immaculate Conception (Fort Wayne); St. Matthew (South Bend).
Fort Worth, Tex.: St. Patrick.
Fresno, Calif.: St. John (the Baptist).
Gallup, N.M.: Sacred Heart.
Galveston-Houston, Tex.: St. Mary (Minor Basilica, Galveston); Sacred Heart Co-Cathedral (Houston).
Gary, Ind.: Holy Angels.
Gaylord, Mich.: St. Mary, Our Lady of Mt. Carmel.
Grand Island, Nebr.: Nativity of Blessed Virgin Mary.
Grand Rapids, Mich.: St. Andrew.
Great Falls-Billings, Mont.: St. Ann (Great Falls); St. Patrick Co-Cathedral (Billings).
Green Bay, Wis.: St. Francis Xavier.
Greensburg, Pa.: Blessed Sacrament.
Harrisburg, Pa.: St. Patrick.
Hartford,* Conn.: St. Joseph.
Helena, Mont.: St. Helena.
Honolulu, Hawaii: Our Lady of Peace; St. Theresa of the Child Jesus (Co-Cathedral).
Houma-Thibodaux, La.: St. Francis de Sales (Houma); St. Joseph Co-Cathedral (Thibodaux).

Indianapolis,* Ind.: Sts. Peter and Paul.
Jackson, Miss.: St. Peter.
Jefferson City, Mo.: St. Joseph.
Joliet, Ill.: St. Raymond Nonnatus.
Juneau, Alaska: Nativity of the Blessed Virgin Mary.
Kalamazoo, Mich.: St. Augustine.
Kansas City,* Kans.: St. Peter the Apostle.
Kansas City-St. Joseph, Mo.: Immaculate Conception (Kansas City); St. Joseph Co-Cathedral (St. Joseph).
Knoxville, Tenn.: Sacred Heart of Jesus.
La Crosse, Wis.: St. Joseph the Workman.
Lafayette, Ind.: St. Mary.
Lafayette, La.: St. John the Evangelist.
Lake Charles, La.: Immaculate Conception.
Lansing, Mich.: St. Mary.
Las Cruces, N. Mex.: Immaculate Heart of Mary.
Las Vegas, Nev.: Guardian Angel.
Lexington, Ky.: Christ the King.
Lincoln, Nebr.: Cathedral of the Risen Christ.
Little Rock, Ark.: St. Andrew.
Los Angeles,* Calif.: St. Vibiana (closed May 22, 1995, because of earthquake-related damage). Ground was broken in 1997 for new Cathedral of Our Lady of the Angels of Los Angeles.
Louisville,* Ky.: Assumption.
Lubbock, Tex.: Christ the King.
Madison, Wis.: St. Raphael.
Manchester, N.H.: St. Joseph.
Marquette, Mich.: St. Peter.
Memphis, Tenn.: Immaculate Conception.
Metuchen, N.J.: St. Francis (of Assisi).
Miami,* Fla.: St. Mary (Immaculate Conception).
Milwaukee,* Wis.: St. John.
Mobile,* Ala.: Immaculate Conception (Minor Basilica).
Monterey, Calif.: San Carlos Borromeo.
Nashville, Tenn.: Incarnation.
Newark,* N.J.: Sacred Heart (Minor Basilica).
New Orleans,* La.: St. Louis. (Minor Basilica)
Newton, Mass. (Melkite): Our Lady of the Annunciation (Boston).
New Ulm, Minn.: Holy Trinity.
New York,* N.Y.: St. Patrick.
Norwich, Conn.: St. Patrick.
Oakland, Calif.: St. Francis de Sales.
Ogdensburg, N.Y.: St. Mary (Immaculate Conception).
Oklahoma City,* Okla.: Our Lady of Perpetual Help.
Omaha,* Nebr.: St. Cecilia.
Orange, Calif.: Holy Family.
Orlando, Fla.: St. James.
Our Lady of Deliverance of Newark, New Jersey for Syrian Rite Catholics in the U.S. and Canada: Our Lady of Deliverance.
Our Lady of Lebanon of Los Angeles, Calif. (Maronite): Our Lady of Mt. Lebanon-St. Peter.
Owensboro, Ky.: St. Stephen.
Palm Beach, Fla.: St. Ignatius Loyola, Palm Beach Gardens.
Parma, Ohio (Byzantine): St. John the Baptist.
Passaic, N.J. (Byzantine): St. Michael.
Paterson, N.J.: St. John the Baptist.
Pensacola-Tallahassee, Fla.: Sacred Heart (Pensacola); Co-Cathedral of St. Thomas More (Tallahassee).

Peoria, Ill.: St. Mary.
Philadelphia,* Pa.: Sts. Peter and Paul (Minor Basilica).
Philadelphia,* Pa. (Byzantine): Immaculate Conception of Blessed Virgin Mary.
Phoenix, Ariz.: Sts. Simon and Jude.
Pittsburgh,* Pa. (Byzantine): St. John the Baptist, Munhall.
Pittsburgh, Pa.: St. Paul.
Portland, Me.: Immaculate Conception.
Portland,* Ore.: Immaculate Conception.
Providence, R.I.: Sts. Peter and Paul.
Pueblo, Colo.: Sacred Heart.
Raleigh, N.C.: Sacred Heart.
Rapid City, S.D.: Our Lady of Perpetual Help.
Reno, Nev.: St. Thomas Aquinas.
Richmond, Va.: Sacred Heart.
Rochester, N.Y.: Sacred Heart.
Rockford, Ill.: St. Peter.
Rockville Centre, N.Y.: St. Agnes.
Sacramento, Calif.: Blessed Sacrament.
Saginaw, Mich.: St. Mary.
St. Augustine, Fla.: St. Augustine (Minor Basilica).
St. Cloud, Minn.: St. Mary.
St. George's in Canton, Ohio (Byzantine, Romanian): St. George.
St. Josaphat in Parma, Oh. (Byzantine): St. Josaphat.
St. Louis,* Mo.: St. Louis.
St. Maron, Brooklyn, N.Y. (Maronite): Our Lady of Lebanon.
St. Nicholas in Chicago (Byzantine): St. Nicholas.
St. Paul and Minneapolis,* Minn.: St. Paul (St. Paul); Basilica of St. Mary Co-Cathedral (Minneapolis).
St. Petersburg, Fla.: St. Jude the Apostle.
St. Thomas the Apostle of Detroit (Chaldean): Our Lady of Chaldeans Cathedral (Mother of God Church), Southfield, Mich.
Salina, Kans.: Sacred Heart.
Salt Lake City, Utah: The Madeleine.
San Angelo, Tex.: Sacred Heart.
San Antonio,* Tex.: San Fernando.
San Bernardino, Calif: Our Lady of the Rosary.
San Diego, Calif.: St. Joseph.
San Francisco,* Calif.: St. Mary (Assumption).
San Jose, Calif.: St. Joseph (Minor Basilica); St. Patrick, Proto-Cathedral.
Santa Fe,* N.M.: San Francisco de Asis.
Santa Rosa, Calif.: St. Eugene.
Savannah, Ga.: St. John the Baptist.
Scranton, Pa.: St. Peter.
Seattle,* Wash.: St. James.
Shreveport, La.: St. John Berchmans.
Sioux City, Ia.: Epiphany.
Sioux Falls, S.D.: St. Joseph.
Spokane, Wash.: Our Lady of Lourdes.
Springfield, Ill.: Immaculate Conception.
Springfield, Mass.: St. Michael.
Springfield-Cape Girardeau, Mo.: St. Agnes (Springfield): St. Mary (Cape Girardeau).
Stamford, Conn. (Byzantine): St. Vladimir.
Steubenville, Ohio: Holy Name.
Stockton, Calif: Annunciation.
Superior, Wis.: Christ the King.
Syracuse, N.Y.: Immaculate Conception.
Toledo, Ohio: Queen of the Most Holy Rosary.
Trenton, N.J.: St. Mary (Assumption).

Tucson, Ariz.: St. Augustine.
Tulsa, Okla.: Holy Family.
Tyler, Tex.: Immaculate Conception.
Van Nuys, Calif. (Byzantine): St. Mary (Patronage of the Mother of God), Van Nuys; St. Stephen's (Pro-Cathedral), Phoenix, Ariz.
Venice, Fla: Epiphany.
Victoria, Tex.: Our Lady of Victory.
Washington,* D.C.: St. Matthew.
Wheeling-Charleston, W. Va.: St. Joseph (Wheel-

ing); Sacred Heart (Charleston).
Wichita, Kans.: Immaculate Conception.
Wilmington, Del.: St. Peter.
Winona, Minn.: Sacred Heart.
Worcester, Mass.: St. Paul.
Yakima, Wash.: St. Paul.
Youngstown, Ohio: St. Columba.
Apostolic Exarchate for Armenian Catholics in the U.S. and Canada: St. Ann (110 E. 12th St., New York, N.Y. 10003).

BASILICAS IN THE UNITED STATES

Basilica is a title assigned to certain churches because of their antiquity, dignity, historical importance or significance as centers of worship. Major basilicas have the papal altar and holy door, which is opened at the beginning of a Jubilee Year; minor basilicas enjoy certain ceremonial privileges.

Among the major basilicas are the patriarchal basilicas of St. John Lateran, St. Peter, St. Paul Outside the Walls and St. Mary Major in Rome; St. Francis and St. Mary of the Angels in Assisi, Italy.

The patriarchal basilica of St. Lawrence, Rome, is a minor basilica.

The dates in the listings below indicate when the churches were designated as basilicas.

Minor Basilicas in U.S., Puerto Rico, Guam

Alabama: Mobile, Cathedral of the Immaculate Conception (Mar. 10, 1962).
Arizona: Phoenix, St. Mary's (Immaculate Conception) (Sept. 11, 1985).
California: San Francisco, Mission Dolores (Feb. 8, 1952); Carmel, Old Mission of San Carlos (Feb. 5, 1960); Alameda, St. Joseph (Jan. 21, 1972); San Diego, Mission San Diego de Alcala (Nov. 17, 1975); San Jose, St. Joseph (Jan. 28, 1997).
Colorado: Denver, Cathedral of the Immaculate Conception (Nov. 3, 1979).
District of Columbia: National Shrine of the Immaculate Conception (Oct. 12, 1990).
Florida: St. Augustine, Cathedral of St. Augustine (Dec. 4, 1976).
Illinois: Chicago, Our Lady of Sorrows (May 4, 1956), Queen of All Saints (Mar. 26, 1962).
Indiana: Vincennes, Old Cathedral (Mar. 14, 1970). Notre Dame, Parish Church of Most Sacred Heart, Univ. of Notre Dame (Nov. 23, 1991).
Iowa: Dyersville, St. Francis Xavier (May 11, 1956); Des Moines, St. John the Apostle (Oct. 4, 1989).
Kentucky: Trappist, Our Lady of Gethsemani (May 3, 1949); Covington, Cathedral of Assumption (Dec. 8, 1953).
Louisiana: New Orleans, St. Louis King of France (Dec. 9, 1964).
Maryland: Baltimore, Assumption of the Blessed Virgin Mary (Sept. 1, 1937; designated national shrine, 1993); Emmitsburg, Shrine of St. Elizabeth Ann Seton (Feb. 13, 1991).
Massachusetts: Roxbury, Perpetual Help ("Mission Church") (Sept. 8, 1954); Chicopee, St. Stanislaus (June 25, 1991).
Michigan: Grand Rapids, St. Adalbert (Aug. 22, 1979).

Minnesota: Minneapolis. St. Mary (Feb. 1, 1926).
Missouri: Conception, Basilica of Immaculate Conception (Sept. 14, 1940); St. Louis, St. Louis King of France (Jan. 27, 1961).
New Jersey: Newark, Cathedral Basilica of the Sacred Heart (Dec. 22, 1995).
New York: Brooklyn, Our Lady of Perpetual Help (Sept. 5, 1969), Cathedral-Basilica of St. James (June 22, 1982); Lackawanna, Our Lady of Victory (1926); Youngstown, Blessed Virgin Mary of the Rosary of Fatima (Oct. 7, 1975).
North Carolina: Asheville, St. Lawrence (Apr. 6, 1993; ceremonies, Sept. 5, 1993); Belmont, Our Lady Help of Christians (July 27, 1998)..
North Dakota: Jamestown, St. James (Oct. 26, 1988).
Ohio: Carey, Shrine of Our Lady of Consolation (Oct. 21, 1971).
Pennsylvania: Latrobe, St. Vincent Basilica, Benedictine Archabbey (Aug. 22, 1955); Conewago, Basilica of the Sacred Heart (June 30, 1962); Philadelphia, Sts. Peter and Paul (Sept. 27, 1976); Danville, Sts. Cyril and Methodius (chapel at the motherhouse of the Sisters of Sts. Cyril and Methodius) (June 30, 1989); Loretto, St. Michael the Archangel (September 9, 1996); Scranton, National Shrine of St. Ann (Oct. 18, 1997).
Texas: Galveston, St. Mary Cathedral (Aug. 11, 1979).
Virginia: Norfolk, St. Mary of the Immaculate Conception (July 9, 1991).
Wisconsin: Milwaukee, St. Josaphat (Mar. 10, 1929).
Puerto Rico: San Juan, Cathedral of San Juan (Jan. 25, 1978).
Guam: Agana, Cathedral of Dulce Nombre de Maria (Sweet Name of Mary) (1985).

BASILICA OF THE NATIONAL SHRINE OF THE IMMACULATE CONCEPTION

The Basilica of the National Shrine of the Immaculate Conception is dedicated to the honor of the Blessed Virgin Mary, declared patroness of the United States under this title in 1846, eight years before the proclamation of the dogma of the Immaculate Conception. The church was designated a minor basilica by Pope John Paul II Oct. 12, 1990. The church is the eighth largest religious building in the world and the largest Catholic church in the Western Hemisphere, with numerous special chapels and with normal seating and standing accommodations for 6,000 people. Open daily, it is adjacent to The Catholic University of America, at Michigan Ave. and Fourth St. N.E., Washington, D.C. 20017. Msgr. Michael J. Bransfield is the rector.

SHRINES AND PLACES OF HISTORIC INTEREST IN THE U.S.

(Principal source: Catholic Almanac *survey.)*

Listed below, according to state, are shrines, other centers of devotion and some places of historic interest with special significance for Catholics. The list is necessarily incomplete because of space limitations. Information includes: name and location of shrine or place of interest, date of foundation, sponsoring agency or group, and address for more information.

Alabama: St. Jude Church of the City of St. Jude, Montgomery (1934; dedicated, 1938); Mobile Archdiocese. Address: 2048 W. Fairview Ave., Montgomery 36108.

• Shrine of the Most Blessed Trinity, Holy Trinity (1924); Missionary Servants of the Most Blessed Trinity. Address: Holy Trinity 36859.

Arizona: Chapel of the Holy Cross, Sedona (1956); Phoenix Diocese: P.O. Box 1043, W. Sedona 86339.

• Mission San Xavier del Bac, near Tucson (1692); National Historic Landmark; Franciscan Friars and Tucson Diocese; Address: 1950 W. San Xavier Rd., Tucson 85746-7409.

• Shrine of St. Joseph of the Mountains, Yarnell (1939); erected by Catholic Action League; currently maintained by Board of Directors. Address: P.O. Box 267, Yarnell 85362.

California: Mission San Diego de Alcala (July 16, 1769); first of the 21 Franciscan missions of Upper California; Minor Basilica; National Historic Landmark; San Diego Diocese. Address: 10818 San Diego Mission Rd., San Diego 92108.

• Carmel Mission Basilica (Mission San Carlos Borromeo del Rio Carmelo), Carmel by the Sea (June 3, 1770); Monterey Diocese. Address: 3080 Rio Rd., Carmel 93923.

• Old Mission San Luis Obispo de Tolosa, San Luis Obispo (Sept. 1, 1772); Monterey Diocese (Parish Church). Address: Old Mission Church, 751 Palm St., San Luis Obispo 93401.

• San Gabriel Mission, San Gabriel (Sept. 8, 1771); Los Angeles Archdiocese (Parish Church, staffed by Claretians). Address: 537 W. Mission, San Gabriel 91776.

• Mission San Francisco de Asis (Oct. 9, 1776) and Mission Dolores Basilica (1860s); San Francisco Archdiocese. Address: 3321 Sixteenth St., San Francisco 94114.

• Old Mission San Juan Capistrano, San Juan Capistrano (Nov. 1, 1776); Orange Diocese. Address: P.O. Box 697, San Juan Capistrano 92693.

• Old Mission Santa Barbara, Santa Barbara (Dec. 4, 1786); National Historic Landmark; Parish Church, staffed by Franciscan Friars. Address: 2201 Laguna St., Santa Barbara 93105.

• Old Mission San Juan Bautista, San Juan Bautista (June 24, 1797); National Historic Landmark; Monterey Diocese (Parish Church). Address: P.O. Box 400, San Juan Bautista 95045.

• Mission San Miguel, San Miguel (July 25, 1797); Parish Church, Monterey diocese; Franciscan Friars. Address: P.O. Box 69, San Miguel 93451-0069.

• Old Mission Santa Inés, Solvang (1804); Historic Landmark; Los Angeles Archdiocese (Parish Church, staffed by Capuchin Franciscan Friars). Address: P.O. Box 408, Solvang 93464.

Franciscan Friars founded 21 missions in California. (See Index: Franciscan Missions.)

• Shrine of Our Lady of Sorrows, Sycamore (1883); Sacramento Diocese. Address: c/o Our Lady of Lourdes Church, 745 Ware Ave., Colusa 95932.

Colorado: Mother Cabrini Shrine, Golden; Missionary Sisters of the Sacred Heart. Address: 20189 Cabrini Blvd., Golden 80401.

Connecticut: Shrine of Our Lady of Lourdes, Litchfield (1958); Montfort Missionaries. Address: P.O. Box 667, Litchfield 06759.

• Shrine of the Infant of Prague, New Haven (1945); Dominican Friars. Address: P.O. Box 1202, 5 Hillhouse Ave., New Haven 06505.

District of Columbia: Mount St. Sepulchre, Franciscan Monastery of the Holy Land (1897; church dedicated, 1899); Order of Friars Minor. Address: 1400 Quincy St. N.E., Washington, D.C. 20017.

• Basilica of the National Shrine of the Immaculate Conception. See Index for separate entry.

Florida: Mary, Queen of the Universe Shrine, Orlando (1986, temporary facilities; new shrine dedicated, 1993); Orlando diocese. Address: 8300 Vineland Ave., Orlando, 32821.

• Our Lady of La Leche Shrine (Patroness of Mothers and Mothers-to-be) and Mission of Nombre de Dios, Saint Augustine (1565); Angelus Crusade Headquarters. St. Augustine Diocese. Address: 30 Ocean Ave., St. Augustine 32084.

Illinois: Holy Family Log Church, Cahokia (1799; original log church erected 1699); Belleville Diocese (Parish Church). Address: 116 Church St., Cahokia 62206.

• Marytown/Shrine of St. Maximilian Kolbe and Retreat Center, Libertyville; Our Lady of the Blessed Sacrament Sanctuary of Perpetual Eucharistic Adoration (1930 and Archdiocesan Shrine to St. Maximilian Kolbe (1989), conducted by Conventual Franciscan Friars, 1600 West Park Ave., Libertyville 60048.

• National Shrine of Our Lady of the Snows, Belleville (1958); Missionary Oblates of Mary Immaculate. Address: 442 S. De Mazenod Dr., Belleville 62223.

• National Shrine of St. Jude, Chicago (1929); located in Our Lady of Guadalupe Church, founded and staffed by Claretians. Address: 3200 E. 91st St., Chicago 60617.

• National Shrine of St. Therese and Museum, Darien (1930, at St. Clara's Church, Chicago; new shrine, 1987, after original destroyed by fire); Carmelites of Most Pure Heart of Mary Province. Address: Carmelite Visitor Center, 8501 Bailey Rd., Darien 60561.

• Shrine of St. Jude Thaddeus, Chicago (1929) located in St. Pius V Church, staffed by Dominicans, Central Province. Address: 1909 S. Ashland Ave., Chicago 60608.

Indiana: Our Lady of Monte Cassino Shrine, St. Meinrad (1870); Benedictines. Address: Saint Meinrad Archabbey, Indiana StateHighway 62, St. Meinrad 47577.

• Old Cathedral (Basilica of St. Francis Xavier), Vincennes (1826, parish records go back to 1749); Evansville Diocese. Minor Basilica, 1970. Address: 205 Church St., Vincennes 47591.

Iowa: Grotto of the Redemption, West Bend (1912); Sioux City Diocese. Life of Christ in stone. Mailing address: P.O. Box 376, West Bend 50597.

Louisiana: National Votive Shrine of Our Lady of Prompt Succor, New Orleans (1810); located in the Chapel of the Ursuline Convent (a National Historic Landmark). Address: 2635 State St., New Orleans 70118.

• Shrine of St. Ann. Mailing address: 4920 Loveland St., Metaire 70006.

• Shrine of St. Roch, New Orleans (1876); located in St. Roch's Campo Santo (Cemetery); New Orleans Archdiocese. Address: 1725 St. Roch Ave., New Orleans 70117.

Maryland: Basilica of the National Shrine of the Assumption of the Blessed Virgin Mary, Baltimore (1806). Mother Church of Roman Catholicism in the U.S. and the first metropolitan cathedral. Designed by Benjamin Henry Latrobe (architect of the Capitol) it is considered one of the finest examples of neoclassical architecture in the world. The church hosted many of the events and personalities central to the growth of Roman Catholicism in the U.S. Address: Cathedral and Mulberry Sts., Baltimore, MD 21201.

• National Shrine Grotto of Our Lady of Lourdes, Emmitsburg (1809, Grotto of Our Lady; 1875, National Shrine Grotto of Lourdes); Public oratory, Archdiocese of Baltimore. Address: Mount St. Mary's College and Seminary, Emmitsburg 21727.

• National Shrine of St. Elizabeth Ann Seton, Emmitsburg. Religious/Historical. Foundation of Sisters of Charity (1809); first parochial school in America (1810); dedicated as Minor Basilica (1991); Address: 333 South Seton Ave., Emmitsburg 21727.

• St. Francis Xavier Shrine, "Old Bohemia", near Warwick (1704), located in Wilmington, Del., Diocese; restoration under aupices of Old Bohemia Historical Society, Inc. Address: P.O. Box 61, Warwick 21912.

Massachusetts: National Shrine of Our Lady of La Salette, Ipswich (1945); Missionaries of Our Lady of La Salette. Address: 251 Topsfield Rd., Ipswich 01938.

• Our Lady of Fatima Shrine, Holliston (1950); Xaverian Missionaries. Address: 101 Summer St., Holliston 01746.

• St. Anthony Shrine, Boston (1947); downtown Service Church with shrine; Boston Archdiocese and Franciscans of Holy Name Province. Address: 100 Arch St., Boston 02107.

• Saint Clement's Eucharistic Shrine, Boston (1945); Boston Archdiocese, staffed by Oblates of the Virgin Mary. Address: 1105 Boylston St., Boston 02215.

• National Shrine of The Divine Mercy, Stockbridge (1960); Congregation of Marians. Address: National Shrine of The Divine Mercy, Eden Hill, Stockbridge 01262.

Michigan: Cross in the Woods-Parish, Indian River (1947); Gaylord diocese; staffed by Franciscan Friars of Sacred Heart Province, St. Louis. Address: 7078 M-68, Indian River 49749.

• Shrine of the Little Flower, Royal Oak (c. 1929, by Father Coughlin); Detroit archdiocese. Address: 2123 Roseland, Royal Oak 48073.

Missouri: Memorial Shrine of St. Rose Philippine Duchesne, St. Charles; Religious of the Sacred Heart of Jesus. Address: 619 N. Second St., St. Charles 63301.

• National Shrine of Our Lady of the Miraculous Medal, Perryville; located in St. Mary of the Barrens Church (1837); Vincentians. Address: 1811 W. St. Joseph St., Perryville 63775.

• Old St. Ferdinand's Shrine, Florissant (1819, Sacred Heart Convent; 1821, St. Ferdinand's Church); Friends of Old St. Ferdinand's, Inc. Address: No. 1 Rue St. Francois, Florissant 63031.

• Shrine of Our Lady of Sorrows, Starkenburg (1888; shrine building, 1910); Jefferson City Diocese. Address: c/o Church of the Risen Savior, 605 Bluff St., Rhineland 65069.

Nebraska: The Eucharistic Shrine of Christ the King (1973); Lincoln diocese and Holy Spirit Adoration Sisters. Address: 1040 South Cotner Blvd., Lincoln 68510.

New Hampshire: Shrine of Our Lady of Grace, Colebrook (1948); Missionary Oblates of Mary Immaculate. Address: R.R. 1, Box 521, Colebrook 03576-9535.

• Shrine of Our Lady of La Salette, Enfield (1951); Missionaries of Our Lady of La Salette. Address: Rt. 4A, P.O. Box 420, Enfield 03748.

New Jersey: Blue Army Shrine of the Immaculate Heart of Mary (1978); National Center of the Blue Army of Our Lady of Fatima, USA, Inc. Address: Mountain View Rd. (P.O. Box 976), Washington 07882.

• Shrine of St. Joseph, Stirling (1924); Missionary Servants of the Most Holy Trinity. Address: 1050 Long Hill Rd., Stirling 07980.

New Mexico: St. Augustine Mission, Isleta (1613); Santa Fe Archdiocese. Address: P.O. Box 463, Isleta, Pueblo 87022.

• Santuario de Nuestro Senor de Esquipulas, Chimayo (1816); Santa Fe archdiocese, Sons of the Holy Family; national historic landmark, 1970. Address: Santuario de Chimayo, P.O. Box 235; Chimayo 87522.

New York: National Shrine of Bl. Kateri Tekakwitha, Fonda (1938); Order of Friars Minor Conventual. Address: P.O. Box 627, Fonda 12068.

• Marian Shrine (National Shrine of Mary Help of Christians), West Haverstraw (1953); Salesians of St. John Bosco. Address: Filors Lane, W. Haverstraw 10993.

• National Shrine Basilica of Our Lady of Fatima, Youngstown (1954); Barnabite Fathers. Address: 1023 Swann Rd., Youngstown 14174. Designated a national shrine in 1994.

• Original Shrine of St. Ann in New York City (1892); located in St. Jean Baptiste Church; Blessed Sacrament Fathers. Address: 184 E. 76th St., New York 10021.

• Our Lady of Victory National Shrine, Lackawanna (1926); Minor Basilica. Address: 767 Ridge Rd., Lackawanna 14218.

• Shrine Church of Our Lady of Mt. Carmel, Brooklyn (1887); Brooklyn Diocese (Parish Church). Address: 275 N. 8th St., Brooklyn 11211.

• Shrine of Our Lady of Martyrs, Auriesville (1885); Society of Jesus. Address: Auriesville 12016.

• Shrine of Our Lady of the Island, Eastport (1975); Montfort Missionaries. Address: Box 26, Eastport, N.Y., 11941.

• Shrine of St. Elizabeth Ann Seton, New York City (1975); located in Our Lady of the Rosary Church.

Address: 7 State St., New York 10004.

• Shrine of St. Frances Xavier Cabrini, New York (1938; new shrine dedicated 1960); Missionary Sisters of the Sacred Heart. Address: 701 Fort Washington Ave., New York 10040.

Ohio: Basilica and National Shrine of Our Lady of Consolation, Carey (1867); Minor Basilica; Toledo Diocese; staffed by Conventual Franciscan Friars. Address: 315 Clay St., Carey 43316.

• National Shrine of Our Lady of Lebanon, North Jackson (1965); Eparchy of Our Lady of Lebanon of Los Angeles. Address: 2759 N. Lipkey Rd., N. Jackson 44451.

• Our Lady of Czestochowa Shrine, Garfield Heights (1939); Sisters of St. Joseph, Third Order of St. Francis. Address: 12215 Granger Rd., Garfield Hts. 44125.

• Our Lady of Fatima, Ironton (1954); Old Rt. 52, Haverhill, Ohio. Mailing address: St. Joseph Church, P.O. Box 499, Ironton 45638-0499.

• St. Anthony Shrine, Cincinnati (1888); Franciscan Friars, St. John Baptist Province. Address: 5000 Colerain Ave., Cincinnati 45223.

• Shrine and Oratory of the Weeping Madonna of Mariapoch, Burton (1956); Social Mission Sisters. Parma Diocese (Byzantine). Address: 17486 Mumford Rd., Burton 44021.

• Shrine of the Holy Relics (1892); Sisters of the Precious Blood. Address: 2291 St. Johns Rd., Maria Stein 45860.

• Sorrowful Mother Shrine, Bellevue (1850); Society of the Precious Blood. Address: 4106 State Rt. 269, Bellevue 44811.

Oklahoma: National Shrine of the Infant Jesus of Prague, Prague (1949); Oklahoma City Archdiocese. Address: P.O. Box 488, Prague 74864.

Oregon: The Grotto (National Sanctuary of Our Sorrowful Mother), Portland (1924); Servite Friars. Address: P.O. Box 20008, Portland 97294.

Pennsylvania: Basilica of the Sacred Heart of Jesus, Conewago Township (1741; present church, 1787); Minor Basilica; Harrisburg Diocese. Address: 30 Basilica Dr., Hanover 17331.

• National Shrine Center of Our Lady of Guadalupe, Allentown (1974); located in Immaculate Conception Church; Allentown Diocese. Address: 501 Ridge Ave., Allentown 18102.

• National Shrine of Our Lady of Czestochowa (1955); Order of St. Paul the Hermit (Pauline Fathers). Address: P.O. Box 2049, Doylestown 18901.

• National Shrine of St. John Neumann, Philadelphia (1860); Redemptorist Fathers, St. Peter's Church. Address: 1019 N. 5th St., Philadelphia 19123.

• National Shrine of the Sacred Heart, Harleigh (1975); Scranton Diocese. Address: P.O. Box 500, Harleigh (Hazleton) 18225.

• Old St. Joseph's National Shrine, Philadelphia (1733); Philadelphia Archdiocese (Parish Church). Address: 321 Willings Alley, Philadelphia 19106.

• St. Ann's Basilica Shrine, Scranton (1902); Passionist Community. Designated a minor basilica Aug. 29, 1996. Address: 1230 St. Ann's St., Scranton 18504.

• St. Anthony's Chapel, Pittsburgh (1883); Pittsburgh Diocese. Address: 1700 Harpster St., Pittsburgh 15212.

• Shrine of St. Walburga, Greensburg (1974); Sisters of St. Benedict. Address: 1001 Harvey Ave., Greensburg 15601.

Texas: National Shrine of Our Lady of San Juan Del Valle, San Juan (1949); Brownsville Diocese; staffed by Oblates of Mary Immaculate. Mailing address: P.O. Box 747, San Juan 78589.

Vermont: St. Anne's Shrine, Isle La Motte (1666); Burlington Diocese, conducted by Edmundites. Address: West Shore Rd., Isle La Motte 05463.

Wisconsin: Holy Hill - National Shrine of Mary, Help of Christians (1857); Discalced Carmelite Friars. Address: 1525 Carmel Rd., Hubertus 53033.

• National Shrine of St. Joseph, De Pere (1889); Norbertine Fathers. Address: 1016 N. Broadway, De Pere 54115.

• Shrine of Mary, Mother Thrice Admirable Queen and Victress of Schoenstatt (1965), Address: W284 N698 Cherry Lane, Waukesha 53188-9402.

The two conferences described below are related in membership and directive control but distinct in nature, purpose and function.

The National Conference of Catholic Bishops (NCCB) is a strictly ecclesiastical body in and through which the bishops of the United States act together, officially and with authority as pastors of the Church. It is the sponsoring organization of the United States Catholic Conference.

The United States Catholic Conference (USCC) is a civil corporation and operational secretariat in and through which the bishops, together with other members of the Church, act on a wider scale for the good of the Church and society. It is sponsored by the National Conference of Catholic Bishops.

The principal officers of both conferences are: Bishop Joseph A. Fiorenza, president; Bishop Wilton D. Gregory, vice president; Bishop Robert J. Banks, treasurer; Archbishop Harry J. Flynn, secretary.

The membership of the Administrative Committee of the NCCB and the Administrative Board of the USCC is identical.

Headquarters of both conferences are located at 3211 Fourth St. N.E., Washington, D.C. 20017.

NCCB-USCC REGIONS

I. Maine, Vermont, New Hampshire, Massachusetts, Rhode Island, Connecticut. II. New York. III. New Jersey, Pennsylvania. IV. Delaware, District of Columbia, Florida, Georgia, Maryland, North Carolina, South Carolina, Virgin Islands, Virginia, West Virginia. V. Alabama, Kentucky, Louisiana, Mississippi, Tennessee. VI. Michigan, Ohio. VII. Illinois, Indiana, Wisconsin,. VIII. Minnesota, North Dakota, South Dakota. IX. Iowa, Kansas, Missouri, Nebraska,. X. Arkansas, Oklahoma, Texas. XI. California, Hawaii, Nevada. XII. Idaho, Montana, Alaska, Washington, Oregon. XIII. Utah, Arizona, New Mexico, Colorado, Wyoming.

NATIONAL CONFERENCE OF CATHOLIC BISHOPS

The National Conference of Catholic Bishops (NCCB), established by action of the U.S. hierarchy Nov. 14, 1966, is a strictly ecclesiastical body with defined juridical authority over the Church in this country. It was set up with the approval of the Holy See and in line with directives from the Second Vatican Council. Its constitution was formally ratified during the November, 1967, meeting of the U.S. hierarchy.

The NCCB is a development from the Annual Meeting of the Bishops of the United States, whose pastoral character was originally approved by Pope Benedict XV Apr. 10, 1919. The address of the Conference is 3211 Fourth St. N.E., Washington, D.C. 20017. Rev. Msgr. Dennis M. Schnurr, J.C.D., is general secretary.

Pastoral Council

The conference, one of many similar territorial conferences envisioned in the conciliar Decree on the Pastoral Office of Bishops in the Church (No. 38), is "a council in which the bishops of a given nation or territory (in this case, the United States) jointly exercise their pastoral office to promote the greater good which the Church offers mankind, especially through

NATIONAL CATHOLIC CONFERENCES

the forms and methods of the apostolate fittingly adapted to the circumstances of the age."

Its decisions, "provided they have been approved legitimately and by the votes of at least two-thirds of the prelates who have a deliberative vote in the conference, and have been recognized by the Apostolic See, are to have juridically binding force only in those cases prescribed by the common law or determined by a special mandate of the Apostolic See, given either spontaneously or in response to a petition of the conference itself."

All bishops who serve the Church in the U.S., its territories and possessions, have membership and voting rights in the NCCB. Retired bishops cannot be elected to conference offices nor can they vote on matters which by law are binding by two-thirds of the membership. Only diocesan bishops can vote on diocesan quotas, assessments or special collections.

Officers, Committees

The conference operates through a number of bishops' committees with functions in specific areas of work and concern. Their basic assignments are to prepare materials on the basis of which the bishops, assembled as a conference, make decisions, and to put suitable action plans into effect.

The principal officers are: Bishop Joseph A. Fiorenza, president; Bishop Wilton D. Gregory, vice president; Bishop Robert J. Banks, treasurer; Archbishop Harry J. Flynn, secretary.

These officers, with several other bishops, hold positions on executive-level committees — Executive Committee, the Committee on Budget and Finance, the Committee on Personnel, and the Committee on Priorities and Plans. They also, with other bishops, serve on the NCCB Administrative Committee.

The standing committees and their chairmen (Archbishops and Bishops) are as follows.

African American Catholics, George V. Murry, S.J.
American College, Louvain, Edward K. Braxton.
Bishops' Welfare Emergency Relief, Joseph Fiorenza.
Boundaries of Dioceses and Provinces, Joseph Fiorenza.
Canonical Affairs, David E. Fellhauer.
Consecrated Life, Joseph J. Gerry, O.S.B.
Diaconate: Gerald F. Kicanas.
Doctrine, Daniel E. Pilarczyk.
Ecumenical and Interreligious Affairs: Alexander Brunett.
Evangelization, Michael J. Sheehan.
Hispanic Affairs: Gerald R. Barnes.
Home Missions: Edward J. Slattery.
Laity: G. Patrick Ziemann.
Latin America: Roberto O. González, O.F.M.
Lay Ministry, Subcommittee: Phillip Straling.
Lay Ministry, SubCommittee on Youth, Roger L. Schwietz, O.M.I.
Liturgy: Jerome G. Hanus, O.S.B.
Marriage and Family Life: Thomas J. O'Brien.
Migration: Nicholas A. DiMarzio.
North American College, Rome: Donald Wuerl.
Pastoral Practices: Stephen E. Blaire.
Priestly Formation: John C. Favalora.
Priestly Life and Ministry: Richard C. Hanifen.
Pro-Life Activities: William Cardinal Keeler.
Relationship between Eastern and Latin Catholic Churches: Andrew Pataki.

Science and Human Values: Edward M. Egan.
Selection of Bishops, Joseph A. Fiorenza.
Vocations: Roger L. Schwietz, O.M.I.
Women in Society and in the Church: John Z. Vlazny.
World Missions: Curtis J. Guillory, S.V.D.

Ad hoc committees and their chairmen are as follows:

1999 Special Assembly, Robert N. Lynch.
Aid to the Church in Central and Eastern Europe, Cardinal Adam Maida.
Bishops Life and Ministry, William S. Skylstad.
Catechism, Oversee the Use of the, Daniel M. Buechlein, O.S.B.
Catholic Charismatic Renewal, Sam G. Jacobs.
Economic Concerns of the Holy See, James P. Keleher.
Forum on the Principles of Translation, Jerome G. Hanus, O.S.B.
Health Care Issues and the Church, Donald W. Wuerl.
Implementation of Ex Corde Ecclesiae, Rev. Thomas T. Toale, Ph.D.
Native American Catholics, Donald E. Pelotte, S.S.S.
Nomination of Conference Officers, James P. Keleher.
Review of Scripture Translations, Richard J. Sklba.
Review of Statutes and Bylaws, Daniel Pilarczyk.
Sexual Abuse, John F. Kinney.
Shrines, James P. Keleher.
Stewardship, Sylvester Ryan.
Subcommittee for Implementation of *Ex Corde Ecclesiae*, Cardinal Anthony Bevilacqua.

UNITED STATES CATHOLIC CONFERENCE

The United States Catholic Conference, Inc. (USCC), is the operational secretariat and service agency of the National Conference of Catholic Bishops for carrying out the civic-religious work of the Church in this country. It is a civil corporation related to the NCCB in membership and directive control but distinct from it in purpose and function.

The address of the Conference is 3211 Fourth St. N.E., Washington, D.C. 20017. Rev. Msgr. Dennis M. Schnurr, J.C.D., is general secretary.

Service Secretariat

The USCC, as of Jan. 1, 1967, took over the general organization and operations of the former National Catholic Welfare Conference, Inc., whose origins dated back to the National Catholic War Council of 1917. The council underwent some change after World War I and was established on a permanent basis Sept. 24, 1919, as the National Catholic Welfare Council to serve as a central agency for organizing and coordinating the efforts of U.S. Catholics in carrying out the social mission of the Church in this country. In 1923, its name was changed to National Catholic Welfare Conference, Inc., and clarification was made of its nature as a service agency of the bishops and the Church rather than as a conference of bishops with real juridical authority in ecclesiastical affairs.

The Official Catholic Directory states that the USCC assists "the bishops in their service to the Church in this country by uniting the people of God where voluntary collective action on a broad interdiocesan level is needed. The USCC provides an organizational structure and the resources needed to insure coordination, cooperation, and assistance in the public, educational and social concerns of the Church at the national, regional, state and, as appropriate, diocesan levels."

Officers, Departments

The principal officers of the USCC are: Bishop Joseph A. Fiorenza, president; Bishop Wilton Gregory, vice president; Bishop Robert J. Banks, treasurer; Archbishop Harry J. Flynn, secretary. These officers, with several other bishops, hold positions on executive-level committees — the Executive Committee; the Committee on Priorities and Plans; the Committee on Budget and Finance; the Committee on Personnel. They also serve on the Administrative Board.

The Executive Committee, organized in 1969, is authorized to handle matters of urgency between meetings of the Administrative Board and the general conference, to coordinate items for the agenda of general meetings, and to speak in the name of the USCC.

The major departments are: Catholic Campaign for Human Development; Communications; Domestic Policy; Education; Sapientia Christiana; International Policy; Subcommittee on Catechesis. A National Advisory Council of bishops, priests, men and women religious, lay men and women advises the Administrative Board on overall plans and operations of the USCC.

The administrative general secretariat, in addition to other duties, supervises staff-service offices of Finance, General Counsel, Government Liaison, Priorities and Plans, Management Information Services, Human Resources, General Services, Research.

Most of the organizations and associations affiliated with the USCC are covered in separate Almanac entries.

STATE CATHOLIC CONFERENCES

These conferences are agencies of bishops and dioceses in the various states. Their general purposes are to develop and sponsor cooperative programs designed to cope with pastoral and common-welfare needs, and to represent the dioceses before governmental bodies, the public, and in private sectors. Their membership consists of representatives from the dioceses in the states— bishops, clergy and lay persons in various capacities.

The National Association of State Catholic Conference Directors maintains liaison with the general secretariat of the United States Catholic Conference. President: Robert J. Castagna, executive director of Oregon Catholic Conference.

Arizona Catholic Conference, 400 E. Monroe St., Phoenix, AZ 85004; Exec. Dir., Rev. Msgr. Edward J. Ryle.

California Catholic Conference, 1010 11th St., Suite 200, Sacramento, CA 95814; Exec. Dir., Edward Dolejsi.

Colorado Catholic Conference, 1300 S. Steele St., Denver, CO, 80210-2599; Exec. Dir., James P. Tatten.

Connecticut Catholic Conference, 134 Farmington Ave., Hartford, CT 06105; Exec. Dir., Marie T. Hilliard.

District of Columbia Catholic Conference, P.O. Box 29260, Washington, DC 20017; Exec. Dir., Ronald G. Jackson.

Florida Catholic Conference, P.O. Box 1638, Tallahassee, FL 32302; Exec. Dir., D. Michael McCarron, Ph.D.

Georgia Catholic Conference, Office Bldg., 3200 Deans Bridge Rd., Augusta, GA 30906; Exec. Dir., Cheatham E. Hodges, Jr.

Hawaii Catholic Conference, St. Stephen Diocesan Center, 6301 Pali Hwy., Kaneohe, Hawaii 96744; Exec. Dir., Rev. Marc R. Alexander, S.T.D.

Illinois, Catholic Conference of, 500 North Clark St., Chicago, IL 60610; 200 Broadway, Springfield, Ill. 62701; Exec. Dir., Doug Delaney.

Indiana Catholic Conference, 1400 N. Meridian St., P.O. Box 1410, Indianapolis, IN 46206; Exec. Dir., M. Desmond Ryan, Ph.D.

Iowa Catholic Conference, 505 Fifth Ave., Suite No. 818, Des Moines, IA 50309-2393; Exec. Dir., Timothy McCarthy.

Kansas Catholic Conference, 6301 Antioch, Merriam, KS 66202; Exec. Dir., Robert Runnels, Jr.

Kentucky, Catholic Conference of, 1042 Burlington Lane, Frankfort, KY 40601; Exec. Dir., Jane J. Chiles.

Louisiana Catholic Conference, 3423 Hundred Oaks Ave., Baton Rouge, LA 70808; Exec. Dir., Kirby J. Ducote.

Maryland Catholic Conference, 188 Duke of Gloucester St., Annapolis, MD 21401; Exec. Dir., Richard J. Dowling, Esq..

Massachusetts Catholic Conference, 55 Franklin St., Boston, MA 02110; Exec. Dir., Gerald D. D'Avolio, Esq.

Michigan Catholic Conference, 505 N. Capitol Ave., Lansing, MI 48933; president and CEO, Sr. Monica Kostielney, R.S.M.

Minnesota Catholic Conference, 475 University Ave. W., St. Paul, MN 55103; Exec. Dir., Rev. David F. McCauley.

Missouri Catholic Conference, P.O. Box 1022, 600 Clark Ave., Jefferson City, MO 65102; Exec. Dir., Louis C. DeFeo, Jr.

Montana Catholic Conference, P.O. Box 1708, Helena, MT 59624; Exec. Dir., Sharon Hoff.

Nebraska Catholic Conference, 215 Centennial Mall South, Suite 410, Lincoln, NE 68508; Exec. Dir., James R. Cunningham.

New Jersey Catholic Conference, 211 N. Warren St., Trenton, NJ 08618; Exec. Dir., William F. Bolan, Jr., J.D.

New Mexico Catholic Conference, 514 Marble Ave. N.W., Albuquerque, NM 87107; Dir., Juan B. Montoya.

New York State Catholic Conference, 465 State St., Albany, NY 12203; Exec. Dir., John M. Kerry.

North Dakota Catholic Conference, 227 West Broadway Suite No. 2, Bismarck, ND 58501; Exec. Dir., Christopher T. Dodson.

Ohio, Catholic Conference of, 9 E. Long St., Suite 201, Columbus, OH 43215; Exec. Dir., Timothy V. Luckhaupt.

Oregon Catholic Conference, 2838 E. Burnside, Portland, OR 97214; general counsel and Exec. Dir., Robert J. Castagna.

Pennsylvania Catholic Conference, 223 North St., Box 2835, Harrisburg, PA 17105.; Exec. Dir., Robert J. O'Hara, Jr.

Texas Catholic Conference, 1625 Rutherford Lane,

Bldg. D, Austin, TX 78754; Exec. Dir., Bro. Richard Daly, C.S.C.

Washington State Catholic Conference, 508 2nd Ave. West, Seattle, WA 98119-3928; Exec. Dir., Sr. Sharon Park, O.P.

West Virginia State Catholic Conference, P.O. Box 230, Wheeling, WV 26003; Dir., Rev. John R. Gallagher.

Wisconsin Catholic Conference, 30 W. Mifflin St., Suite 302, Madison, WI 53703; Exec. Dir., John A. Huebscher.

CATHOLIC RELIEF SERVICES

Catholic Relief Services is the official overseas aid and development agency of U.S. Catholics; it is a separately incorporated organization of the U.S. Catholic Conference.

Long-term Development Projects

CRS was founded in 1943 by the bishops of the United States to help civilians in Europe and North Africa caught in the disruption and devastation of World War II. As conditions in Europe improved in the late 1940s and early 1950s, the works conducted by CRS spread to other continents and areas — Asia, Africa and Latin America.

Although best known for its record of disaster response, compassionate aid to refugees and commitment to reconstruction and rehabilitation, CRS places primary focus on long-term development projects designed to help people to help themselves and to determine their own future. Administrative funding for CRS comes largely from the Catholic Relief Services Annual Appeal. Major support is derived from private, individual donors and through a program of sacrificial giving called Operation Rice Bowl.

Kenneth F. Hackett is executive director. CRS headquarters are located at 209 W. Fayette St., Baltimore, Md. 21201.

CATHOLIC CAMPAIGN FOR HUMAN DEVELOPMENT

The Catholic Campaign for Human Development was inaugurated by the U.S. Catholic Conference in November, 1969, to combat injustice, oppression, alienation and poverty in this country by funding self-help programs begun and carried out by the poor or by the poor and non-poor working together, and by seeking a re-evaluation of the priorities of individuals, families, the Church and the civic community with respect to the stewardship of God-given goods. The campaign got underway with a collection taken up in all parishes throughout the country on Nov. 22, 1970. Seventy-five percent of the money contributed in this and subsequent annual collections was placed in a national fund principally for funding self-help projects and also for educational purposes; 25 percent remained in the dioceses where it was collected. From 1970, the campaign has distributed approximately $200 million to more than 3,000 self-help projects. National Office: 3211 Fourth St., N.E., Washington, D.C. 20017.

NCCB 1999 LABOR DAY STATEMENT

Social Security and Solidarity

Cardinal Roger Mahony, Archbishop of Los Angeles and Chairman, Domestic Policy Committee of the United States Catholic Conference issued on Sept. 6, 1999 the annual Labor Statement by the NCCB. Under the title, "Social Security and Solidarity," the statement declares:

The nation is having a national dialogue on how to reform Social Security. The U.S. Bishops offered their reflections in a recent statement, *A Commitment to all Generations: Social Security and the Common Good.* The bishops believe that Social Security reflects our commitment as a society to ensure a minimum level of security for all workers, their families, and persons with disabilities. It provides an effective and dignified way for Americans to honor their responsibility to provide basic income security and medical insurance (through Medicare) for the elderly, persons with disabilities, and their dependents. Social Security has helped reduce poverty rates for the elderly; The disability benefits of Social Security assist low- and average-wage workers often as much as, or more than, the retirement part; Social Security benefits lift over a million children out of poverty each year through the survivors' benefits due them upon the death of a parent.

With the support of organized labor, other laws have been enacted to further protect all workers and their families: The minimum wage act seeks to protect workers and their families from economic exploitation by requiring a common wage floor; The Earned Income Credit (EITC) allows low-income families to augment their income through the income tax system; The Family and Medical Leave Act permits workers to take time off from work to care for themselves or their families.

... Here are themes drawn from Catholic teaching that are relevant to the choices we face on the future of Social Security:

Human Dignity — We must recognize our responsibilities to the elderly and persons with disabilities to insure their dignity and worth so that they can enjoy their God-given rights.

Common Good — Because we live in community, our human rights are realized as part of that community. We must all work together, across generations and economic lines, for the sake of the common good, for the general welfare of the entire human family.

Option for the Poor and Solidarity — The Biblical mandate requires us to care for the widow, the orphan, and the stranger. Today there are still widows and orphans needing assistance. There are also "strangers" to our community or to us, such as persons with disabilities, older Americans and immigrants, who need the support of their families and the community to continue to live productive and dignified lives.

Subsidiarity — Individuals, employers, and employees, often cannot achieve security for themselves and their families without some form of support offered by the entire nation. This concept of social insurance is a necessary complement to achieving that security for average and low wage earning families. Government should participate in creating a comprehensive program for insurance against illness, disability, unemployment, and old age.

U.S. STATISTICAL SUMMARY

(Principal sources: The Official Catholic Directory, *1999; Bill Ryan, USCC Dept. of Communications. Comparisons, where given, are with figures reported in the previous edition of the* Directory. *Totals below do not include statistics for Outlying Areas of U.S. These are given in tables on the preceding pages and elsewhere in the* Almanac; *see Index.)*

Catholic Population: 62,018,436; increase, 454,667.
Percent of total population: 22.7%.
Jurisdictions: 34 archdioceses (includes 33 metropolitan sees and the Military Archdiocese), 157 dioceses (includes St. Thomas, Virgin Islands, and the eparchy of Our Lady of Deliverance of Newark for Syrians of the U.S. and Canada), 1 apostolic exarchate (New York-based Armenian exarchate for U.S. and Canada). **Vacant jurisdictions (as of August 10, 1999),** :.
Cardinals: 12 (9 head archiepiscopal sees in U.S. and Puerto Rico; 3 are Roman Curia officials). As of July 10, 1999.
Archbishops: 48. Diocesan, in U.S., 33 (includes 9 cardinals and military archbishop); retired, 20; outside U.S., 9. As of July 10, 1999.
Bishops: 410. Diocesan, in U.S. (and Virgin Islands), 188; auxiliaries, 91; retired, 10; serving outside U.S., 25. As of July 10, 1999.
Priests: 47,199; decrease, 364. Diocesan, 31,370 (decrease, 287); religious order priests (does not include those assigned overseas), 15,829 (decrease, 96). There were 478 newly ordained priests, a decrease of 31.
Permanent Deacons: 12,675; increase, 428.
Brothers: 5,970; decrease, 145.
Sisters: 85,034; decrease, 1,378.
Seminarians: 4,826. Diocesan seminarians, 3,302; religious order seminarians, 1,524.
Receptions into Church: 1,184,828. Includes 1,040,837 infant baptisms; 73,426 adult baptisms and 88,161 already baptized persons received into full communion with the Church.
First Communions: 878,431.
Confirmations: 626,570.
Marriages: 273,700
Deaths: 469,483.
Parishes: 19,584.
Seminaries, Diocesan: 74.
Religious Seminaries: 118.
Colleges and Universities: 238. Students, 698,855
High Schools: 1,358. Students, 653,701.
Elementary Schools: 6,745. Students 1,963,587.
Non-Residential Schools for Handicapped: 84. Students, 18,030.
Teachers: 167,687 (priests, 1,998; brothers, 1,149; scholastics, 51; sisters, 9,549; laity, 154,940).
Public School students in Religious Instruction Programs: 4,448,509. High school students, 808,017; elementary school students, 3,675,492.
Hospitals: 586; patients treated, 72,010,150.
Health Care Centers: 529; patients treated, 5,198,665.
Specialized Homes: 1,375; patients assisted, 538,996.
Residential Care of Children (Orphanages): 150; total assisted, 84,662.
Day Care and Extended Day Care Centers: 1,378; total assisted, 133,928.
Special Centers for Social Services: 2,260; assisted annually, 19,536,360.

PERCENTAGE OF CATHOLICS IN TOTAL POPULATION IN U.S.

(Source: The Official Catholic Directory, 1999; figures are as of Jan. 1, 1999. Total general population figures at the end of the table are U.S. Census Bureau estimates for Jan. 1 of the respective years. Archdioceses are indicated by an asterisk; for dioceses marked +, see Dioceses with Interstate Lines.)

State Diocese	Catholic Pop.	Total Pop.	Cath. Pct.	State Diocese	Catholic Pop.	Total Pop.	Cath. Pct.
Alabama	137,971	4,097,150	3.3	Illinois continued			
*Mobile	66,013	1,452,506	4.5	Rockford	323,109	1,228,630	26.2
Birmingham	71,958	2,644,644	2.7	Springfield	163,713	1,106,124	14.8
Alaska	52,196	605,445	8.6	Indiana	746,572	5,714,908	13.0
*Anchorage	29,307	389,401	7.5	*Indianapolis	217,886	2,201,503	9.8
Fairbanks	16,846	141,759	11.8	Evansville	89,973	482,447	18.6
Juneau	6,043	74,285	8.1	Ft.Wayne-S.Bend	156,621	1,156,129	13.5
Arizona	759,045	4,421,187	17.1	Gary	184,430	759,673	24.2
Phoenix	423,525	3,113,775	13.6	Lafayette	97,662	1,115,156	8.7
Tucson	335,520	1,307,412	25.6	Iowa	507,571	2,793,694	18.1
Arkansas				*Dubuque	218,108	923,000	23.6
Little Rock	89,091	2,522,813	3.5	Davenport	106,460	726,646	14.6
California	8,907,905	32,646,734	27.8	Des Moines	99,224	671,091	14.7
*Los Angeles	4,080,793	10,652,600	38.0	Sioux City	83,779	472,957	17.7
*San Francisco	422,000	1,700,000	24.8	Kansas	394,622	2,401,471	16.4
Fresno	349,633	2,263,150	15.4	*Kansas City	190,418	952,000	20.0
Monterey	179,110	895,550	20.0	Dodge City	42,566	212,332	20.0
Oakland	496,122	2,255,100	22.0	Salina	51,779	321,132	16.1
Orange	615,041	2,674,091	23.0	Wichita	109,859	916,007	11.9
Sacramento	454,000	2,873,646	15.7	Kentucky	357,301	3,762,532	9.4
San Bernardino	821,443	3,042,385	26.9	*Louisville	178,420	1,139,022	15.6
San Diego	776,093	2,866,727	27.0	Covington	85,202	401,127	21.2
San Jose	400,226	1,609,037	24.8	Lexington	41,997	1,444,148	2.9
Santa Rosa	141,792	745,138	19.0	Owensboro	51,702	778,235	6.6
Stockton	171,622	1,069,310	16.0	Louisiana	1,327,739	4,333,656	30.6
Colorado	535,382	3,946,812	13.5	*New Orleans	482,373	1,332,771	36.1
*Denver	346,144	2,644,004	13.0	Alexandria	48,050	401,211	11.9
Colorado Springs	81,515	702,808	11.5	Baton Rouge	207,511	809,065	25.6
Pueblo	107,723	600,000	17.9	Houma-			
Connecticut	1,342,970	3,278,264	40.9	Thibodaux	130,274	202,000	64.4
*Hartford	757,793	1,806,705	41.9	Lafayette	336,746	559,055	60.2
Bridgeport	360,918	833,315	43.3	Lake Charles	84,908	259,425	32.7
Norwich+	224,259	638,244	35.1	Shreveport	37,8777	70,129	4.9
Delaware				Maine			
Wilimington	173,702	1,108,890	15.6	Portland	227,183	1,227,927	18.5
District of Columbia				Maryland			
*Washington+	510,000	2,413,700	21.1	*Baltimore	484,287	2,849,409	16.9
Florida	2,067,351	14,797,241	13.9	Massachusetts	2,975,137	6,074,105	48.9
*Miami	787,672	3,597,277	21.8	*Boston	2,042,688	3,761,400	54.3
Orlando	323,766	3,094,540	10.4	Fall River	341,482	721,500	47.3
Palm Beach	224,364	1,445,543	15.5	Springfield	288,967	800,500	36.0
Pensacola-				Worcester	302,000	790,705	38.1
Tallahassee	65,904	1,274,850	5.1	Michigan	2,227,369	9,505,935	23.4
St. Augustine	131,478	1,570,181	8.3	*Detroit	1,453,756	4,266,650	34.0
St. Petersburg	358,951	2,393,006	15.0	Gaylord	82,074	458,130	17.9
Venice	175,216	1,421,844	12.3	Grand Rapids	153,601	1,167,900	13.1
Georgia	385,800	7,410,632	5.2	Kalamazoo	114,632	912,044	12.5
*Atlanta	311,000	4,945,355	6.2	Lansing	210,878	1,695,979	12.4
Savannah	74,800	2,465,277	3.0	Marquette	72,552	319,700	22.6
Hawaii				Saginaw	139,876	685,532	20.4
Honolulu	236,688	1,186,602	19.9	Minnesota	1,242,535	4,692,843	26.4
Idaho				*St. Paul and			
Boise	122,640	1,250,000	9.8	Minneapolis	752,325	2,757,989	27.2
Illinois	3,724,499	11,812,795	31.5	Crookston	42,122	236,100	17.8
*Chicago	2,358,000	5,682,000	42.0	Duluth	81,560	417,125	19.5
Belleville	109,233	853,645	12.7	New Ulm	69,840	278,780	25.0
Joliet	538,078	1,494,978	35.9	St. Cloud	148,243	474,546	31.2
Peoria	232,366	1,447,418	16.0	Winona	148,445	528,303	28.0

State Diocese	Catholic Pop.	Total Pop.	Cath. Pct.	State Diocese	Catholic Pop.	Total Pop.	Cath. Pct.
Mississippi	111,915	2,706,501	4.1	Pennsylvania continued			
Biloxi	66,507	726,476	9.1	Erie	229,659	874,900	26.2
Jackson	45,408	1,980,025	2.2	Greensburg	187,166	679,421	27.5
Missouri	859,039	5,318,969	16.1	Harrisburg	234,831	1,940,954	12.0
*St. Louis	555,000	2,064,548	26.8	Pittsburgh	755,459	1,995,320	37.8
Jefferson City	89,730	799,266	11.2	Scranton	362,546	1,054,814	34.3
Kansas City-				Rhode Island			
St. Joseph	156,870	1,299,555	12.0	Providence	629,891	987,429	63.7
Springfield-				South Carolina			
Cape Girardeau	57,439	1,155,600	4.9	Charleston	121,637	3,760,000	3.2
Montana	121,617	817,272	14.8	South Dakota	158,555	714,591	22.1
Great Falls-				Rapid City	35,605	211,591	16.8
Billings	55,117	392,900	14.0	Sioux Falls	122,950	503,000	24.4
Helena	66,500	424,372	15.6	Tennessee	167,932	5,275,784	3.1
Nebraska	356,597	1,629,983	21.8	Knoxville	43,765	2,012,885	2.1
*Omaha	214,574	822,892	26.0	Memphis	60,804	1,438,524	4.2
Grand Island	53,967	290,429	18.5	Nashville	63,363	1,824,375	3.4
Lincoln	88,056	516,662	17.0	Texas	4,859,022	19,666,286	24.7
Nevada	454,870	1,827,778	24.8	*San Antonio	673,026	1,890,760	35.5
Las Vegas	390,000	1,300,000	30.0	Amarillo	46,356	393,822	11.7
Reno	64,870	527,778	12.2	Austin	350,000	1,915,392	18.2
New Hampshire				Beaumont	87,604	577,664	15.0
Manchester	330,513	1,173,000	28.1	Brownsville	774,056	906,945	85.3
New Jersey	3,340,331	7,980,990	41.8	Corpus Christi	363,000	863,242	42.0
*Newark	1,319,558	2,651,785	49.7	Dallas	555,172	2,971,699	18.6
Camden	418,713	1,291,117	32.4	El Paso+	597,275	784,511	76.1
Metuchen	495,322	1,194,578	41.4	Fort Worth	207,490	2,372,666	8.7
Paterson	403,207	1,080,261	37.3	Galveston			
Trenton	703,531	1,763,249	39.8	-Houston	906,330	4,396,876	20.6
New Mexico	438,237	1,898,430	23.0	Lubbock	55,781	410,180	13.5
*Santa Fe	257,258	1,044,376	24.6	San Angelo	82,008	715,375	11.4
Gallup	44,480	379,555	11.7	Tyler	52,362	1,211,878	4.3
Las Cruces	136,499	474,499	28.7	Victoria	108,562	255,276	42.5
New York	7,347,611	18,440,251	39.8	Utah			
*New York	2,371,355	5,254,300	45.1	Salt Lake City	98,800	2,591,045	3.8
Albany	403,403	1,340,388	30.0	Vermont			
Brooklyn	1,625,547	4,216,060	38.5	Burlington	147,840	589,000	25.1
Buffalo	741,506	1,587,808	46.6	Virginia	527,174	6,736,394	7.8
Ogdensburg	136,090	430,422	31.6	Arlington	336,123	2,228,575	15.0
Rochester	337,613	1,479,727	22.8	Richmond	191,051	4,507,819	4.2
Rockville Centre	1,359,432	2,907,955	46.7	Washington	654,151	5,608,346	11.6
Syracuse	372,665	1,223,591	30.4	*Seattle	508,900	4,425,100	11.4
North Carolina	260,675	7,528,791	3.4	Spokane	78,432	721,646	10.8
Charlotte	119,160	3,882,756	3.0	Yakima	66,819	461,600	14.4
Raleigh	141,515	3,646,035	3.8	West Virginia			
North Dakota	165,678	644,552	25.7	Wheeling-			
Bismarck	66,76325	3,552	26.3	Charleston	97,232	1,815,787	5.3
Fargo	98,915	391,000	25.2	Wisconsin	1,652,547	5,200,717	31.7
Ohio	2,190,118	11,112,137	19.7	*Milwaukee	695,934	2,197,939	31.6
*Cincinnati	547,000	2,901,082	18.8	Green Bay	388,150	898,050	43.2
Cleveland	827,971	2,822,180	29.3	La Crosse	219,358	824,206	26.6
Columbus	193,955	2,243,099	8.6	Madison	260,817	885,562	29.4
Steubenville	41,452	520,177	7.9	Superior	88,288	394,960	22.3
Toledo	322,938	1,402,733	23.0	Wyoming			
Youngstown	256,802	1,222,866	21.0	Cheyenne	49,800	484,010	10.2
Oklahoma	150,191	3,687,642	4.0				
*Oklahoma City	92,391	2,029,100	4.5	Eastern Churches	443,195	-	-
Tulsa	57,800	1,478,542	3.9	Military			
Oregon	325,539	3,217,000	10.1	Archdiocese	1,194,000	-	-
*Portland	289,951	2,799,200	10.3	Outlying Areas	2,866,199	-	-
Baker	35,588	417,800	8.5				
Pennsylvania	3,555,974	11,982,977	29.6	Grand Totals '99	62,018,436	272,282,718	22.7
*Philadelphia	1,411,256	3,217,000	43.8				
Allentown	259,847	1,084,189	23.9	Grand Totals '98	61,563,769	270,536,283	22.7
Altoona-Johnstown	115,210	647,357	17.7	Grand Totals '89	54,918,989	244,258,663	22.4

CATHOLIC POPULATION OF THE UNITED STATES

(Source: The *Official Catholic Directory*, 1999; figures as of Jan. 1, 1999. Archdioceses are indicated by an asterisk; for dioceses marked +, see Dioceses with Interstate Lines.)

State Diocese	Cath. Pop.	Dioc. Priests	Rel. Priests	Total Priests	Perm. Deac.	Bros.	Sisters	Parishes
Alabama	137,971	176	85	261	69	50	371	130
*Mobile	66,013	107	40	147	41	16	201	76
Birmingham	71,958	69	45	114	28	34	170	54
Alaska	52,196	38	37	75	57	5	63	70
*Anchorage	29,307	19	9	28	12	1	41	19
Fairbanks	16,846	5	24	29	40	4	16	41
Juneau	6,043	14	4	18	5	-	6	10
Arizona	759,045	253	173	426	299	19	510	150
Phoenix	423,525	140	104	244	172	11	234	86
Tucson	335,520	113	69	182	127	8	276	64
Arkansas, Little Rock	89,091	83	65	148	77	41	314	90
California	8,907,905	2,150	1,552	3,702	671	489	4,966	1,069
*Los Angeles	4,080,793	604	594	1,198	161	177	1,926	287
*San Francisco	422,000	227	206	433	52	47	825	93
Fresno	349,663	108	32	140	5	4	123	84
Monterey	179,110	81	17	98	3	52	117	46
Oakland	496,122	167	100	267	76	20	320	89
Orange	615,041	185	99	284	48	5	367	54
Sacramento	454,000	165	71	236	102	29	191	98
San Bernardino	821,443	142	94	236	79	21	155	97
San Diego	776,093	208	95	303	82	22	354	98
San Jose	400,226	110	203	313	10	69	431	48
Santa Rosa	141,792	85	20	105	18	39	91	43
Stockton	171,622	68	21	89	35	4	66	32
Colorado	535,382	265	176	461	164	35	678	196
*Denver	346,144	159	126	305	134	22	436	112
Colorado Spr.	81,515	34	21	55	18	3	140	31
Pueblo	107,723	72	29	101	12	10	102	53
Connecticut	1,342,970	813	267	1,080	676	66	1,775	386
*Hartford	757,793	411	133	544	544	40	1,001	220
Bridgeport	360,918	259	70	329	83	-	487	88
Norwich+	224,259	143	64	207	49	26	287	78
Delaware, Wilmington+	173,702	126	94	220	48	33	271	55
D.C.,*Washington+	510,000	333	541	874	232	152	827	139
Florida	2,067,351	874	473	1,347	444	147	1,321	451
*Miami	787,672	264	115	379	122	56	345	108
Orlando	323,766	121	59	180	125	13	136	70
Palm Beach	224,364	99	40	139	35	3	182	46
Pensacola-Tallahassee	65,904	71	9	80	40	4	56	54
St. Augustine	131,478	91	27	118	26	3	108	50
St. Petersburg	358,951	134	146	280	81	47	355	73
Venice	175,216	94	77	171	15	21	139	50
Georgia	385,800	186	127	313	173	15	251	122
*Atlanta	311,000	121	99	220	136	1	121	69
Savannah	74,800	65	28	93	37	14	130	53
Hawaii, Honolulu	236,688	69	78	147	26	48	180	66
Idaho, Boise	120,640	90	15	105	34	6	103	58
Illinois	3,724,499	1,823	1,118	2,941	990	508	5,564	1,060
*Chicago	2,358,000	928	799	1,727	612	366	3,176	378
Belleville	109,233	142	41	183	36	10	265	127
Joliet	538,078	197	106	303	140	90	765	120
Peoria	232,366	252	50	302	96	8	335	165
Rockford	323,109	159	60	219	104	15	323	105
Springfield	163,713	145	62	207	2	19	700	165
Indiana	746,572	617	366	983	86	183	1,999	434
*Indianapolis	217,886	167	113	280	-	58	784	138
Evansville	89,973	104	9	113	22	2	324	70
Ft. Wayne-South Bend	156,621	101	175	276	32	105	682	87

State Diocese	Cath. Pop.	Dioc. Priests	Rel. Priests	Total Priests	Perm. Deac.	Bros.	Sisters	Par- ishes
Indiana continued								
Gary	184,430	125	50	175	28	16	128	77
Lafayette	97,662	120	19	139	4	2	81	62
Iowa	507,571	687	49	736	213	32	1,457	503
*Dubuque	218,108	260	36	296	66	27	998	211
Davenport	106,460	142	3	145	50	1	243	89
Des Moines	99,224	114	10	124	61	4	113	87
Sioux City	83,779	171	-	171	36	-	103	116
Kansas	394,622	337	100	437	6	25	1,535	354
*Kansas City	190,418	97	75	172	-	23	810	119
Dodge City	42,566	48	2	50	4	-	128	51
Salina	51,779	70	15	85	-	1	221	92
Wichita	109,859	122	8	130	2	1	376	92
Kentucky	357,301	431	95	526	144	100	1,861	300
*Louisville	178,420	185	59	244	96	83	1,026	113
Covington	85,202	113	2	115	18	9	430	48
Lexington	41,977	50	21	71	30	3	176	60
Owensboro	51,702	83	13	96	-	5	229	79
Louisiana	1,327,739	705	345	1,050	320	189	1,288	492
*New Orleans	482,373	229	202	431	186	129	831	146
Alexandria	48,050	66	16	82	6	3	64	48
Baton Rouge	207,511	88	38	126	25	13	109	70
Houma-Thibodaux	130,274	75	3	78	25	10	31	40
Lafayette	363,746	158	55	213	47	31	173	121
Lake Charles	84,908	48	17	65	25	2	27	36
Shreveport	37,877	41	14	55	6	1	53	31
Maine, Portland	227,183	180	53	233	18	26	457	138
Maryland, *Baltimore	484,287	304	291	595	187	80	1,212	155
Massachusetts	2,975,137	1,583	1,008	2,591	319	254	4,148	749
*Boston	2,042,688	958	707	1,665	212	110	2,646	382
Fall River	341,482	180	135	315	56	27	366	111
Springfield	288,967	203	49	252	51	10	645	130
Worcester	302,000	242	117	359	-	107	491	126
Michigan	2,227,369	1,118	416	1,533	289	129	3,075	802
*Detroit	1,453,756	495	308	803	147	107	1,890	306
Gaylord	82,074	72	16	88	12	1	59	81
Grand Rapids	153,601	123	21	144	20	1	296	90
Kalamazoo	114,632	55	14	69	17	7	217	46
Lansing	210,878	156	31	186	56	13	410	95
Marquette	72,552	103	12	115	21	-	64	74
Saginaw	139,876	114	14	128	16	-	139	110
Minnesota	1,242,535	834	324	1,158	248	148	2,692	726
*St.Paul & Minneapolis	752,325	345	155	500	174	53	1,090	222
Crookston	42,122	49	4	53	8	2	177	71
Duluth	81,560	83	14	97	24	1	175	94
New Ulm	69,840	89	1	90	2	-	86	81
St. Cloud	148,243	138	139	277	37	69	674	140
Winona	148,445	130	11	141	3	23	490	118
Mississippi	111,915	123	60	183	27	44	344	118
Biloxi	66,507	56	28	84	20	32	55	44
Jackson	45,408	67	32	99	7	12	289	74
Missouri	859,039	792	590	1,382	335	298	2,707	470
*St. Louis	555,000	471	412	883	213	175	2,161	227
Jefferson City	89,730	114	8	122	56	8	92	95
Kansas City-St. Joseph	156,870	131	106	237	59	38	329	84
Springfield-Cape Girardeau	57,439	76	64	140	7	77	125	64
Montana	121,617	161	25	186	29	1	139	110
Great Falls-Billings	55,117	75	14	89	3	-	78	52
Helena	66,500	86	11	97	26	1	61	58
Nebraska	356,597	452	132	584	145	31	563	316
*Omaha	214,574	229	120	349	143	22	340	139
Grand Island	53,967	80	-	80	-	-	98	43
Lincoln	88,056	143	12	155	2	9	125	134
Nevada	454,870	57	28	85	15	8	78	52

State Diocese	Cath. Pop.	Dioc. Priests	Rel. Priests	Total Priests	Perm. Deac.	Bros.	Sisters	Par- ishes
Nevada continued								
Las Vegas	390,000	32	17	49	7	5	42	24
Reno	64,870	25	11	36	8	3	36	28
New Hampshire								
Manchester	330,513	243	77	320	25	42	742	131
New Jersey	3,340,331	1,790	582	2,364	878	255	3,744	708
*Newark	1,319,558	757	244	993	230	116	1,505	236
Camden	418,713	320	49	369	126	14	366	126
Metuchen	495,322	210	30	240	128	23	423	108
Paterson	403,207	266	196	462	150	42	941	111
Trenton	703,531	237	63	300	244	60	509	127
New Mexico	438,237	196	164	360	192	108	487	193
*Santa Fe	257,258	106	89	195	136	91	273	91
Gallup	44,480	64	27	91	33	13	141	58
Las Cruces	136,499	26	48	74	23	4	73	44
New York	7,347,611	3,480	1,756	5,236	1,119	898	10,296	1,669
*New York	2,371,355	882	1,010	1,892	320	419	3,707	413
Albany	403,403	306	118	424	93	86	1,001	186
Brooklyn	1,625,547	685	220	905	174	182	1,273	218
Buffalo	741,506	435	198	633	92	46	1,446	265
Ogdensburg	136,090	167	15	182	58	9	203	120
Rochester	337,613	277	62	339	121	39	681	161
Rockville Centre	1,359,432	441	76	517	194	99	1,488	134
Syracuse	372,665	287	57	344	67	18	497	172
North Carolina	260,675	170	125	295	87	11	225	137
Charlotte	119,160	88	67	155	65	5	135	67
Raleigh	141,515	82	58	140	22	6	90	70
North Dakota	165,678	220	37	257	88	29	306	221
Bismarck	66,763	67	28	95	56	21	153	62
Fargo	98,915	153	9	162	32	8	153	159
Ohio	2,190,118	1,567	547	2,114	642	295	4,430	929
*Cincinnati	547,000	349	260	609	137	177	1,340	235
Cleveland	827,971	499	143	642	168	75	1,598	235
Columbus	193,955	194	40	234	64	5	388	107
Steubenville	41,452	116	19	135	6	8	78	73
Toledo	322,938	213	53	266	207	7	764	163
Youngstown	256,802	196	32	228	60	23	262	116
Oklahoma	150,191	169	53	222	110	15	276	153
*Oklahoma City	92,391	96	31	127	60	10	153	72
Tulsa	57,800	73	22	95	50	5	123	81
Oregon	325,539	187	187	374	35	76	567	160
*Portland	289,951	147	179	326	29	76	539	125
Baker	35,588	40	8	48	6	-	28	35
Pennsylvania	3,555,974	2,615	929	3,544	374	255	8,485	1,293
*Philadelphia	1,411,256	796	419	1,215	157	141	3,873	287
Allentown	259,847	244	74	318	77	10	590	153
Altoona-Johnstown	115,210	156	61	217	19	10	106	112
Erie	229,659	244	15	259	11	2	518	127
Greensburg	187,166	155	82	237	-	41	286	107
Harrisburg	234,831	162	38	200	60	1	529	89
Pittsburgh	755,459	500	125	625	18	47	1,764	218
Scranton	362,546	358	115	473	32	4	819	200
Rhode Island								
Providence	629,891	308	150	458	92	124	769	158
South Carolina								
Charleston	121,637	92	34	126	63	28	137	85
South Dakota	158,555	162	67	229	51	20	507	251
Rapid City	35,605	42	27	69	29	8	77	95
Sioux Falls	122,950	120	40	160	22	12	430	156
Tennessee	167,932	163	49	212	76	67	288	135
Knoxville	43,765	45	18	63	24	15	51	43
Memphis	60,804	65	10	75	25	48	84	42
Nashville	63,363	53	21	74	27	4	153	50
Texas	4,859,022	1,149	851	2,000	1,247	241	2,940	996
*San Antonio	673,026	151	222	373	254	91	939	144

State Diocese	Cath. Pop.	Dioc. Priests	Rel. Priests	Total Priests	Perm. Deac.	Bros.	Sisters	Par- ishes
Texas continued	4,859,022	1,149	851	2,000	1,247	241	2,940	996
Amarillo	46,356	61	2	63	44	-	148	35
Austin	350,000	117	51	168	149	38	118	95
Beaumont	87,604	50	22	72	31	3	53	44
Brownsville	774,056	50	46	96	83	13	117	63
Corpus Christi	363,000	105	60	165	74	36	273	84
Dallas	555,172	100	84	184	139	6	158	65
El Paso	597,275	92	40	132	14	16	247	58
Fort Worth	207,490	60	49	109	64	11	108	87
Galveston-Houston	906,330	195	218	413	256	18	508	151
Lubbock	55,781	33	9	42	48	-	38	36
San Angelo	82,008	48	18	66	36	-	36	49
Tyler	52,362	31	20	51	35	8	59	35
Victoria	108,562	56	10	66	20	1	138	50
Utah, Salt Lake City	98,800	54	32	86	40	12	60	43
Vermont, Burlington	147,840	137	51	188	38	2	239	94
Virginia	527,174	309	118	427	70	23	402	205
Arlington	336,123	145	77	222	46	17	192	63
Richmond	191,051	164	41	205	24	6	210	142
Washington	654,151	350	247	597	155	50	1,031	257
*Seattle	508,900	199	135	334	86	33	650	138
Spokane	78,432	88	101	189	44	14	326	78
Yakima	66,819	63	11	74	25	3	55	41
West Virginia								
Wheeling-Charleston	97,232	122	42	164	30	14	304	113
Wisconsin	1,652,547	1,127	552	1,679	321	141	5,351	877
*Milwaukee	695,934	465	344	809	171	81	3,670	254
Green Bay	388,150	235	143	378	81	44	672	199
La Crosse	219,358	197	32	229	24	6	499	173
Madison	260,817	151	19	170	1	8	396	137
Superior	88,288	79	14	93	44	2	114	114
Wyoming, Cheyenne+	49,800	51	9	60	7	1	29	36
EASTERN CHURCHES	443,195	558	114	672	101	36	313	576
*Philadelphia	68,103	59	6	65	4	5	80	78
St. Nicholas	9,500	28	15	43	11	-	4	36
Stamford	16,684	34	16	50	3	5	44	50
St. Josaphat (Parma)	11,522	42	1	43	6	10	11	38
*Pittsburgh	75,261	64	9	73	-	5	105	85
Parma	12,680	38	1	39	3	-	12	38
Passaic	51,771	91	13	104	19	4	21	97
Van Nuys	3,063	20	5	25	5	7	4	16
St. Maron (Maronites)	30,000	59	10	69	12	-	7	34
Our Lady of Lebanon (Maronites)	23,711	30	9	39	7	-	8	27
Newton (Melkites)	27,500	43	19	62	30	-	3	35
St. Thomas Apostle of Detroit (Chaldean)	70,000	21	-	21	-	-	-	12
St. George Martyr (Romanian)	5,300	15	2	17	1	-	-	15
Our Lady of Deliverance (Syrians, U.S.-Canada)	12,100	9	-	9	-	-	- 8	
Armenian Ex.(U.S.-Canada)	26,000	5	8	13	-	-	14	7
MILITARY ARCHDIOCESE	1,194,000	-	-	-	-	-	-	-
OUTLYING AREAS								
Puerto Rico	2,587,012	420	330	750	401	58	1,124	323
Samoa-Pago Pago	12,160	9	-	9	19	-	14	11
Caroline Islands	64,881	12	12	24	39	3	32	21
Chalan Kanoa (North. Mariana Islands)	53,066	13	1	14	2	-	37	12
Guam, *Agana	115,080	27	19	46	9	1	120	24
Marshall Islands	4,000	1	5	6	2	-	16	4
Virgin Islands, St. Thomas	30,000	9	6	15	21	3	14	8
GRAND TOTALS '99	62,018,436	31,370	15,829	47,210	12,675	5,970	84,034	19,584
Grand Totals 1998	61,563,769	31,657	15,925	47,563	12,247	6,115	85,412	19,628
Grand Totals 1989	54,918,989	34,390	18,558	52,948	9,065	6,977	104,419	19,705

[1]Priest chaplains are on loan from their dioceses or religious community. The 1999 *Annuario Pontificio* reported 384 diocesan and 70 religious order chaplains in the United States.

RECEPTIONS INTO THE CHURCH IN THE UNITED STATES

(Source: The Official Catholic Directory, 1999; figures as of Jan. 1, 1999. Archdioceses are indicated by an asterisk; for dioceses marked +, see Dioceses with Interstate Lines. Information includes infant and adult baptisms and those received into full communion.)

State Diocese	Infant Baptisms	Adult Bapts.	Rec'd into Full Comm.
Alabama	2,641	432	889
*Mobile	1,158	193	363
Birmingham	1,483	239	526
Alaska	1,020	173	110
*Anchorage	549	138	68
Fairbanks	363	22	27
Juneau	108	13	15
Arizona	17,774	992	1,405
Phoenix	10,767	636	849
Tucson	7,007	356	556
Arkansas, Little Rock	1,917	306	524
California	193,433	9,138	8,891
*Los Angeles	91,140	2,108	2,038
*San Francisco	7,078	464	262
Fresno	17,748	558	1,043
Monterey	4,979	172	431
Oakland	8,885	568	710
Orange	16,713	830	562
Sacramento	7,967	739	858
San Bernardino	11,806	1,601	1,050
San Diego	11,154	1,165	625
San Jose	8,023	521	411
Santa Rosa	3,134	198	140
Stockton	4,806	214	761
Colorado	13,327	1,180	1,352
*Denver	10,086	810	884
Colorado Springs	1,427	196	235
Pueblo	1,814	174	233
Connecticut	19,780	608	807
*Hartford	10,964	254	371
Bridgeport	5,871	208	139
Norwich+	2,945	146	297
Delaware, Wilmington+	2,988	256	319
District of Columbia			
*Washington+	7,701	627	676
Florida	37,375	3,158	4,241
*Miami	16,091	945	1,261
Orlando	6,016	532	918
Palm Beach	4,179	287	357
Pensacola-Tallahassee	1,210	152	195
St. Augustine	2,162	261	423
St. Petersburg	4,654	727	588
Venice	3,063	254	499
Georgia	8,129	778	1,589
*Atlanta	6,522	513	1,160
Savannah	1,607	265	429
Hawaii, Honolulu	3,288	356	401
Idaho, Boise	2,458	212	126
Illinois	63,444	3,733	4,374
*Chicago	39,150	1,979	1,532
Belleville	1,619	306	315
Joliet	11,002	391	678
Peoria	3,053	451	513
Rockford	6,074	266	784
Springfield	2,546	340	552
Indiana	12,391	1,868	2,314
*Indianapolis	4,284	864	953
Evansville	1,462	107	203

State Diocese	Infant Baptisms	Adult Bapts.	Rec'd into Full Comm.
Indiana con.			
Ft.Wayne-S. Bend	2,704	422	425
Gary	2,154	179	232
Lafayette	1,787	296	501
Iowa	8,493	730	1,382
*Dubuque	3,482	162	443
Davenport	1,490	235	228
Des Moines	1,929	231	334
Sioux City	1,592	102	377
Kansas	8,222	1,025	1,510
*Kansas City	3,833	416	798
Dodge City	1,028	93	98
Salina	924	107	201
Wichita	2,437	409	413
Kentucky	6,070	1,084	1,468
*Louisville	3,041	339	639
Covington	1,320	419	155
Lexington	732	137	308
Owensboro	977	189	366
Louisiana	19,791	1,419	2,096
*New Orleans	7,059	649	480
Alexandria	668	110	130
Baton Rouge	2,678	216	364
Houma-Thibodaux	1,854	54	159
Lafayette	5,497	148	556
Lake Charles	1,528	129	173
Shreveport	507	113	234
Maine, Portland	2,923	282	334
Maryland,*Baltimore	8,059	660	1,344
Massachusetts	39,337	918	1,348
*Boston	25,355	515	356
Fall River	5,368	122	222
Springfield	4,028	137	496
Worcester	4,586	144	274
Michigan	29,256	3,340	4,237
*Detroit	16,268	1,394	2,257
Gaylord	1,132	182	280
Grand Rapids	2,976	413	
Kalamazoo	1,631	225	331
Lansing	4,049	763	927
Marquette	1,109	97	118
Saginaw	2,091	266	324
Minnesota	18,258	865	2,464
*St. Paul and Minneapolis	11,051	497	1,638
Crookston	719	22	105
Duluth	1,179	93	124
New Ulm	1,092	68	127
St. Cloud	2,400	87	228
Winona	1,817	98	242
Mississippi	1,574	643	574
Biloxi	815	438	242
Jackson	759	205	332
Missouri	13,082	1,686	1,636
*St. Louis	8,494	512	722
Jefferson City	1,377	221	335
Kansas City-St. Jos.	2,506	470	319
Springfield-Cape Girardeau	705	483	260

State / Diocese	Infant Baptisms	Adult Bapts.	Rec'd into Full Comm.
Montana	1,730	517	217
Great Falls-Billings	1,001	105	125
Helena	729	412	92
Nebraska	6,786	752	985
*Omaha	4,339	510	685
Grand Island	1,098	91	140
Lincoln	1,349	151	160
Nevada	5,794	475	532
Las Vegas	4,137	315	391
Reno	1,657	160	141
New Hampshire			
Manchester	5,215	181	176
New Jersey	49,811	2,100	2,277
*Newark	16,547	474	716
Camden	6,822	814	421
Metuchen	7,015	179	263
Paterson	8,724	171	324
Trenton	10,703	462	553
New Mexico	9,903	649	752
*Santa Fe	6,006	294	550
Gallup	986	264	112
Las Cruces	2,911	91	90
New York	103,409	4,155	4,317
*New York	34,776	1,012	684
Albany	4,983	299	350
Brooklyn	21,953	805	864
Buffalo	7,910	217	449
Ogdensburg	1,911	477	110
Rochester	5,225	294	706
Rockville Centre	20,952	626	542
Syracuse	5,699	425	612
North Carolina	6,315	589	942
Charlotte	3,098	323	488
Raleigh	3,217	266	454
North Dakota	2,511	193	339
Bismarck	1,204	114	135
Fargo	1,307	79	204
Ohio	32,012	4,137	5,067
*Cincinnati	8,369	1,187	1,016
Cleveland	10,901	1,033	1,024
Columbus	3,785	536	651
Steubenville	681	410	1,091
Toledo	4,773	573	722
Youngstown	3,503	398	563
Oklahoma	3,066	682	856
*Oklahoma City	1,924	455	565
Tulsa	1,142	227	291
Oregon	5,586	824	877
*Portland	4,800	699	716
Baker	786	125	161
Pennsylvania	44,692	3,479	3,876
*Philadelphia	18,101	1,216	823
Allentown	3,979	184	400
Altoona-Johnstown	1,560	112	246
Erie	2,354	585	288
Greensburg	2,060	146	335
Harrisburg	3,477	279	575
Pittsburgh	8,801	532	870
Scranton	4,360	425	339
Rhode Island			
Providence	6,179	171	477
South Carolina			
Charleston	2,008	289	470
South Dakota	2,802	117	459
Rapid City	969	41	118
South Dakota continued			
Sioux Falls	1,833	76	341
Tennessee	3,436	660	939
Knoxville	715	142	248
Memphis	1,110	248	309
Nashville	1,611	270	382
Texas	81,976	9,388	6,455
*San Antonio	14,044	649	618
Amarillo	1,095	74	192
Austin	6,820	603	914
Beaumont	1,263	176	405
Brownsville	4,564	3,990	595
Corpus Christi	5,621	180	617
Dallas	10,888	906	653
El Paso	8,556	129	259
Fort Worth	4,917	529	604
Galveston-Houston	17,429	1,601	919
Lubbock	1,684	77	114
San Angelo	2,192	163	172
Tyler	1,337	216	255
Victoria	1,566	95	138
Utah, Salt Lake City	2,619	482	581
Vermont, Burlington	1,773	98	177
Virginia	10,188	1,433	1,159
Arlington	6,654	784	514
Richmond	3,534	649	645
Washington	11,172	1,869	1,100
*Seattle	6,773	1,323	741
Spokane	1,321	374	211
Yakima	3,078	172	148
West Virginia			
Wheeling-Charleston	1,277	322	320
Wisconsin	21,553	1,673	1,738
*Milwaukee	9,350	625	881
Green Bay	4,653	228	313
La Crosse	3,007	154	369
Madison	3,456	444	-
Superior	1,087	222	175
Wyoming, Cheyenne+	1,097	315	177
Eastern Churches	4,602	199	431
*Philadelphia	330	17	64
St. Nicholas	56	12	2
Stamford	163	9	12
St. Josaphat (Parma)	135	4	4
*Pittsburgh	305	37	60
Parma	129	18	36
Passaic	362	11	33
Van Nuys	66	12	78
St. Maron (Maronites)	409	16	38
Our Lady of Lebanon (Maronites)	438	24	20
Newton (Melkites)	401	17	9
St. Thomas Apostle of Detroit (Chaldeans)	1,654	20	-
St. George Martyr (Romanian)	36	-	5
Our Lady of Deliverance (Syrians, U.S.-Can.)	66	2	18
Armenian Ex. (U.S.-Can.)	52	-	52
Military Archdiocese	5,073	973	418
Outlying Areas	38,121	6,485	9,190
Grand Totals '98	1,044,837	73,426	88,161
Grand Totals '89	946,303	82,409	N/A

HISPANIC CATHOLICS IN THE UNITED STATES

The nation's Hispanic population totaled 22.4 million, according to figures reported by the U.S. Census Bureau in 1990. It was estimated that 80 percent of the Hispanics were baptized Catholics.

Pastoral Patterns

Pastoral ministry to Hispanics varies, depending on differences among the people and the availability of personnel to carry it out.

The pattern in cities with large numbers of Spanish-speaking is built around special and bilingual churches, centers or other agencies where pastoral and additional forms of service are provided in a manner suited to the needs, language and culture of the people. Services in some places are extensive and include legal advice, job placement, language instruction, recreational and social assistance, specialized counseling, replacement services. In many places, however, even where there are special ministries, the needs are generally greater than the means required to meet them.

Some urban dwellers have been absorbed into established parishes and routines of church life and activity. Many Spanish-speaking communities remain in need of special ministries. An itinerant form of ministry best meets the needs of the thousands of migrant workers who follow the crops.

Demographic and ministerial data were the subjects of a national survey commissioned by the Bishops' Committee for Hispanic Affairs and carried out by its secretariat. It was reported in November, 1990, that responses were received from 152 archdioceses and dioceses. Twelve or more dioceses and archdioceses had Hispanic populations of more than 50 percent; 27 others were a quarter or more Hispanic. Fifty-five percent of the reporting jurisdictions had Hispanic apostolates. Overall, ministerial emphasis was reported in six areas: youth, small Christian communities, the Cursillo movement, Catholic Charities and social ministry, lay leadership formation, and charismatic renewal. Other sources reported that well over 80 percent of Hispanics were located in urban areas, and that 54 percent were 25 years of age or younger. It was estimated that perhaps 100,000 Catholic Hispanics a year were being lost, principally to fundamentalist and pentecostal sects.

Pastoral ministry to Hispanics was the central concern of three national meetings, Encuentros, held in 1972, 1977 and 1985.

The third National Encuentro in 1985 produced a master pastoral plan for ministry which the National Conference of Catholic Bishops approved in 1987. Its four keys are collaborative ministry; evangelization; a missionary option regarding the poor, the marginalized, the family, women and youth; the formation of lay leadership.

The U.S. bishops, at their annual meeting in November, 1983, approved and subsequently published a pastoral letter on Hispanic Ministry under the title, "The Hispanic Presence: Challenge and Commitment." (For text, see pp. 46-49 of the 1985 *Catholic Almanac*.)

Bishops

As of Aug. 1, 1999, there were 23 (20 active) bishops of Hispanic origin in the United States; all were

HISPANIC, BLACK, AND NATIVE-AMERICAN CATHOLICS

named since 1970 (for biographies, see Index). Ten were heads of archdioceses or dioceses: Archbishop Patrick F. Flores (San Antonio); Bishops Raymundo J. Peña (Brownsville), Ricardo Ramirez, C.S.B. (Las Cruces), Arthur N. Tafoya (Pueblo), Manuel D. Moreno (Tucson), Placido Rodriguez, C.M.F. (Lubbock), Gerald R. Barnes (San Bernardino), Armando Ochoa (El Paso), and Carlos A. Sevilla, S.J. (Yakima). Eleven were auxiliary bishops: Gabino Zavala (Los Angeles), Gilbert Espinoza Chavez (San Diego), Joseph J. Madera (Military Services), Francisco Garmendia (New York), Agustin Roman (Miami), Rene Valero (Brooklyn), David Arias, O.A.R. (Newark), Alvaro Corrada del Rio, S.J. (Washington, D.C.), James A. Tamayo (Galveston-Houston), Emilio Simeon Allué (Boston) and Gilberto Fernanadez (Miami). Resigned/retired prelates: Archbishop Robert F. Sanchez (Santa Fe), Bishop Juan Arzube (Los Angeles, auxiliary), Bishop Rene H. Gracida (Corpus Christi). Bishop Roberto O. Gonzalez, O.F.M. (Corpus Christi), was appointed archbishop of San Juan de Puerto Rico on Mar. 26, 1999 by Pope John Paul II.

Hispanic priests and nuns in the U.S. number about 1,600 and 2,000, respectively, according to an estimate made in June, 1988, by Father Gary Riebe Estrella, S.V.D., director of a Hispanic vocational recruitment program.

Secretariat for Hispanic Affairs

The national secretariat was established by the U.S. Catholic Conference for service in promoting and coordinating pastoral ministry to the Spanish-speaking. Its basic orientation is toward integral evangelization, combining religious ministry with development efforts in programs geared to the culture and needs of Hispanics. Its concerns are urban and migrant Spanish-speaking people; communications and publications in line with secretariat purposes and the service of people; bilingual and bicultural religious and general education; liaison for and representation of Hispanics with church, civic and governmental agencies.

The secretariat publishes a newsletter, *En Marcha*, available to interested parties.

Ronaldo M. Cruz is executive director of the national office at 3211 Fourth St. N.E., Washington, D.C. 20017.

The secretariat works in collaboration with regional and diocesan offices and pastoral institutes throughout the country.

The Northeast Regional Office, officially the Northeast Hispanic Catholic Center, was established in 1976 under the auspices of the bishops in 12 states from Maine to Virginia. It has established the Conference of Diocesan Directors of the Hispanic Apostolate, the Association of Hispanic Deacons, a Regional Youth Task Force and a Regional Committee of Diocesan Coordinators of Religious Educators for the Hispanics. The office is the official publishing house for the Hispanic Lectionary approved by the National Conference of Catholic Bishops for the United States. The center has liturgical, evangelization and youth ministry departments and an office of cultural affairs. Mario J. Paredes is executive director. The center is located at 1011 First Ave., New York, NY 10022.

The Southeast Regional Office serves 26 dioceses

in Tennessee, North and South Carolina, Florida, Georgia, Mississippi, Alabama and Louisiana. Father Mario Vizcaino, Sch. P., is director of the region and institute. The office is located at 7700 S.W. 56 St., Miami, FL 33155. The Southeast Pastoral Institute serves as the educational arm of the regional office by providing formation programs for the development of leadership skills focused on ministry among Hispanics, at the Miami site and in the various dioceses of the region.

In the Southwest, the Mexican American Cultural Center serves as convener of diocesan directors and representatives of Hispanic ministry in Arkansas, Oklahoma and Texas.

A regional office serving the Mountain States (Arizona, New Mexico, Utah, Colorado and Wyoming) is under the coordination of Deacon Germán Toro, 27 C St., Salt Lake City, UT 84103.

The Northwest Regional Office for Hispanic Affairs serves 11 dioceses in Alaska, Montana, Washington, Oregon and Idaho. Father Heliodoro Lucatero is president. The office is located at 2838 Burnside, Portland, OR 97214. It serves as convener for regional workshops, retreats, formation programs and social advocacy.

National Hispanic Priests Association

The National Association of Hispanic Priests of the USA (ANSH - *La Asociación Nacional de Sacerdotes Hispanos*, EE. UU.) was established in September, 1989, with a representation of about 2,400 Hispanic priests residing and ministering in the United States. The association came into its present form after a 20 year process of organization by different groups of Hispanic priests around the country. By 1985, the first National Convention of Hispanic Priests was organized in New York City, and in 1989 the Association was established in Miami, Florida as a non-profit Corporation for priestly fraternity and support for Hispanic Priests in the United States. Among the multiple objectives are: to help members develop their priestly identity in the United States and encourage a genuine spirituality; to provide a national forum of Hispanic Priests to help solve the problems that arise in the Hispanic community; to promote vocations to the priesthood among the Hispanics; to pray and ask for more Hispanic bishops in the U.S., for the growing needs of the Catholic Hispanic community; and to cooperate with the Bishops and the laity in implementing the National Pastoral Plan for Hispanic Ministry. The Association publishes a quarterly Newsletter and holds an annual national convention. The president is Rev. José H. Gomez, S.T.D. 2472 Bolsover, Suite 442, Houston, TX 77005.

National Catholic Council for Hispanic Ministry (NCCHM)

The council is a volunteer federation of Roman Catholic organizations, agencies and movements committed to the development of Hispanics/Latinos in Church and society. It was established June 17, 1990, at a gathering at Mundelein College, Chicago; its by-laws were adopted in January, 1991, at Mercy Center, Burlingame, Calif. The council convokes a national gathering every three years called *Raices y Alas* (Roots and Wings). With funding from foundations NCCHM has designed and piloted a leadership development program that links contemporary understandings of leadership with experiences and insights from faith and Hispanic cultures. NCCHM has 53 member organizations. It publishes *Puentes*, a newsletter. Exec. Dir., Rosa Maria Sanchez, 2025 Chickasau Ave., Los Angeles, CA 90041.

Mexican American Cultural Center

This national center, specializing in pastoral studies and language education, was founded in 1972 to provide programs focused on ministry among Hispanics and personnel working with Hispanics in the U.S. Courses — developed according to the see-judge-act methodology — include culture, faith development, Scripture, theology, and praxis; some are offered in Spanish, others in English. Intensive language classes are offered in Spanish, with emphasis on pastoral usage.

The center also conducts workshops for the development of leadership skills and for a better understanding of Hispanic communities. Faculty members serve as resource personnel for pastoral centers, dioceses and parishes throughout the U.S. The center offers master-degree programs in pastoral ministry in cooperation with Incarnate Word College, Boston College, the Oblate School of Theology, St. Mary's University and Loyola University, New Orleans and other educational institutions.

The center is a distribution agency for the circulation of bilingual pastoral materials in the U.S. and Latin America. Sister Maria Elena Gonzalez, R.S.M., is president of the center which is located at 3019 W. French Place, San Antonio, TX 78228.

Institute of Hispanic Liturgy

Spanish-speaking communities in the U.S. are served by the Institute of Hispanic Liturgy, a national organization of liturgists, musicians, artists and pastoral agents, funded in part by the U.S. Bishops. The institute promotes the study of liturgical texts, art, music and popular religiosity in an effort to develop liturgical spirituality among Hispanics. It works closely with the U.S. Bishops' Committee on the Liturgy, and has published liturgical materials. Rev. Heliodoro Lucatero, is the president; Sr. Doris Mary Turek, S.S.N.D., is executive director. Address: P.O. Box 29387, Washington, D.C. 20017.

BLACK CATHOLICS IN THE UNITED STATES

National Office

The National Office for Black Catholics, organized in July, 1970, is a central agency with the general purposes of promoting active and full participation by black Catholics in the Church and of making more effective the presence and ministry of the Church in the black community.

Its operations are in support of the aspirations and calls of black Catholics for a number of objectives, including the following:

• representation and voice for blacks among bishops and others with leadership and decision-making positions in the Church;

• promoting vocations to the priesthood and religious life;

• sponsoring programs of evangelization, pastoral ministry, education and liturgy on a national level;

• recognition of the black heritage in liturgy, community life, theology and education.

Walter T. Hubbard is executive director of the NOBC. The NOBC office is located at 3025 Fourth St. N.E., Washington, D.C. 20017.

National Black Catholic Clergy Caucus

The National Black Catholic Clergy Caucus, founded in 1968 in Detroit, is a fraternity of several hundred black priests, permanent deacons and brothers pledged to mutual support in their vocations and ministries.

The Caucus develops programs of spiritual, theological, educational and ministerial growth for its members, to counteract the effects of institutionalized racism within the Church and American society. A bimonthly newsletter is published.

The NBCCC office is located at 343 N. Walnut St., P.O. Box 1088, Opelousas, LA 70571.

Other peer and support groups are the National Black Sisters' Conference and the National Black Catholic Seminarians Association.

National Black Catholic Congress

The National Black Catholic Congress, Inc., was formed in 1985 exclusively to assist in the development of the Roman Catholic Church in the African American community and to devise more effective means of evangelization of African American peoples in the United States. Its fundamental purpose is the formation and development of concrete approaches toward the evangelization of African Americans through revitalization of African American Catholic life.

The Congress is under the sponsorship of the African American Roman Catholic bishops of the United States, the National Black Catholic Clergy Caucus, the National Black Sisters' Conference, the National Association of Black Catholic Administrators and the Knights of Peter Claver and the Ladies Auxiliary Knights of Peter Claver. The Congress is also in consultation with African American clergy and vowed religious women communities. The Congress sponsors Pastoring in African American Parishes, an annual workshop first held in 1988 and An African American Catholic Ministries Program, a week-long curriculum presented twice a year, usually in January and June.

The National Black Catholic Congress sponsored the seventh assembly of African-American Catholics and those serving in African American communities, July 9 to 12, 1992, in New Orleans. The most recent National Congress convened in Baltimore, Aug. 27 to 31, 1997.

The Congress is sponsoring construction of "Our Mother of Africa Chapel" at the Basilica of the National Shrine of the Immaculate Conception in Washington, D.C.

The office of the Congress is located at The Archdiocese of Baltimore Catholic Center, 320 Cathedral St., Room 712, Baltimore, MD 21201. The executive director is Dr. Hilbert D. Stanley.

Committee and Secretariat

The Committee on African American Catholics, established by the National Conference of Catholic Bishops in 1987, is chaired by Bishop George V. Murry, S.J., auxiliary of Chicago. The purpose of the committee is to assist the bishops in their evangelization efforts to the African American community by initiating, encouraging and supporting programs which recognize and respect African American genius and values. Priorities of the Committee include implementation of the National Black Catholic Pastoral Plan of 1987, inculturation of liturgy and ministry, and increasing lay leadership and vocations.

Also established as a service agency to the committee was a Secretariat for African American Catholics under the executive direction of Beverly Carroll. The secretariat is the officially recognized voice of the African American community as it articulates its gifts and aspirations regarding ministry, evangelization and worship. It also serves as a liaison to the National Black Catholic Clergy Caucus, the National Black Catholic Seminarians Association, the National Black Sisters' Conference, National Black Catholic Administrators, Knights of St. Peter Claver and Ladies Auxiliary, the National Black Catholic Congress, and the National Black Catholic Theological Society. The committee and secretariat have offices at 3211 Fourth St. N.E., Washington, D.C. 20017.

Bishops

There were 13 (12 active) black bishops, as of Sept. 1, 1999: Five were heads of dioceses: Bishops Joseph L. Howze (Biloxi), J. Terry Steib, S.V.D. (Memphis), Wilton D. Gregory (Belleville, Vice-President of the NCCB), Elliott G. Thomas (St. Thomas, Virgin Islands) and John H. Ricard, S.S.J. (Pensacola-Tallahassee). Seven were auxiliary bishops: Moses Anderson, S.S.E. (Detroit), Curtis J. Guillory, S.V.D. (Galveston-Houston), Leonard J. Olivier, S.V.D. (Washington), Dominic Carmon, S.V.D. (New Orleans), George V. Murry, S.J. (Chicago), Edward K. Braxton (St. Louis), and Gordon D. Bennett, S.J. (Baltimore). Archbishop Eugene A. Marino, S.S.J., of Atlanta, resigned in July, 1990. Bishop Wilton Gregory was elected Vice-President of the NCCB in November, 1998.

Josephite Pastoral Center

The Josephite Pastoral Center was established in September, 1968, as an educational and pastoral service agency for the Josephites in their mission work, specifically in the black community, subsequently to all those who minister in the African-American community. St. Joseph's Society of the Sacred Heart, the sponsoring body has about 134 priests and 11 brothers in 64 mostly southern parishes in 17 dioceses. The staff of the center includes Father John G. Harfmann, S.S.J., director, and Maria M. Lannon, administrator. Address: St. Joseph Seminary 1200 Varnum St. N.E., Washington, D.C. 20017

African-American Evangelization

The National Black Catholic Pastoral Plan adopted by the National Black Catholic Congress in May, 1987, was approved and recommended for implementation by the National Conference of Catholic Bishops in November, 1989.

Following is an account of several points in the bishops' statement, based on coverage by the CNS Documentary Service, *Origins*, Dec. 28, 1989 (Vol. 19, No. 30).

"Evangelization," wrote the bishops, "would not be complete if it did not take account of the unceasing interplay of the Gospel and of man's concrete life, both personal and social. Evangelization involves an explicit message, adapted to the different situations constantly being realized, about the rights and duties of every human being, about family life, without which personal growth and development are hardly possible, about life in society, about international life, peace, justice and development — a message especially energetic today about liberation."

Three Areas

The pastoral plan "embraces three broad areas: 1) the Catholic identity of African-American Catholics; 2) ministry and leadership within the African-American community; and 3) the responsibility of this community to reach out to the broader society. Within these areas are such issues as culture, family, youth, spirituality, liturgy, ministry, lay leadership, parishes, education, social action and community development."

Reflecting a recommendation of the pastoral plan, the bishops encourage African-American Catholics to "discover their past" since "the possession of one's history is the first step in an appreciation of one's culture."

NATIVE-AMERICAN CATHOLICS IN THE UNITED STATES

The Kateri Tekakwitha Conference is so named in honor of Blessed Kateri Tekakwitha, "Lily of the Mohawks," who was born in 1656 at Ossernenon (Auriesville), N.Y., in 1656, baptized in 1676, lived near Montreal, died in 1680, and beatified in 1980.

The conference was established in 1939 as a missionary-priest advisory group in the Diocese of Fargo. It was a missionary-priest support group from 1946 to 1977. Since 1977 it has been a gathering of Catholic Native peoples together with men and women — clerical, religious and lay persons — who minister with Native Catholic communities.

The primary focus of conference concern and activity is evangelization, with specific emphasis on development of Native ministry and leadership. Other priorities include catechesis, liturgy, family life, social justice ministry, chemical dependency, youth ministry, spirituality and native Catholic dialogue. Conferences and local Kateri Circles serve as occasions for the exchange of ideas, prayer and mutual support. Since 1980, the national center has promoted and registered 130 Kateri Circles in the U.S. and Canada. Publications include a quarterly newsletter.

The conference has a board of 12 directors, the majority of whom are Native people. Archbishop Charles Chaput, O.F.M. Cap., is the episcopal moderator. Address: Tekakwitha Conference National Center, P.O. Box 6768, Great Falls, Mont. 59406.

MISSIONARY ACTIVITY OF THE U.S. CHURCH

OVERSEAS MISSIONS

From the U.S. Catholic Mission Handbook: Mission Inventory 1996-1997 *(the most recent issue), reproduced with permission of the United States Catholic Mission Council, 3029 Fourth St. N.E., Washington, D.C.*

Field Distribution, 1997

Africa: 799 (449 men; 350 women). Largest numbers in Kenya, 194; Tanzania, 102; Ghana, 79; Uganda, 68; Zambia, 60; Nigeria, 52; South Africa, 50.

Asia: 892 (612 men; 280 women). Largest numbers in Philippines, 212; Japan, 174; Taiwan, 105; China PRC-Hong Kong SAR, 88; India,72; Korea,64. (Those present in China were there for professional services.)

Caribbean: 360 (209 men; 151 women). Largest numbers in Puerto Rico, 76; Jamaica, 63; Haiti, 55; Dominican Republic and Belize, 47 each.

Eurasia (Kazakhstan, Russia, Siberia): 12 (8 men; 4 women). Largest group 10, Russia.

Europe: 172 (85 men; 87 women). Largest numbers in Italy, 50; Ireland, 21; England, 15; Germany, 13.

Latin America: 1,573 (858 men; 715 women). Largest numbers in Brazil, 303; Peru, 282; Mexico, 243; Bolivia, 155; Guatemala, 143.

Middle East: 61 (45 men; 16 women); Largest numbers in Israel, 29; Sudan, 13.

North America (Canada and Greenland): 82 (38 men; 44 women). Largest number in Canada, 81.

Pacific: 213 (149 men; 64 women). Largest numbers in Papua New Guinea,89; Micronesia, 35; Australia, 22; Guam, 16.

TOTAL: 4,164 (2,453 men; 1,711 women).

Missionary Personnel, 1997

Bishops: See below.

Religious Priests: Sixty-five mission-sending groups had 1,736 priests in overseas assignments. Listed below are those with 15 or more members abroad.

Jesuits, 339; Maryknoll Fathers and Brothers, 311; Redemptorists, 111; Oblates of Mary Immaculate, 106; Society of Divine Word , 92; Franciscans (O.F.M.) 89; Franciscans (O.F.M. Cap), 77; Holy Cross Fathers, 48; Dominicans, 40; Columbans, 39; Vincentians, 31; Franciscans (O.F.M. Conv.), 24; Passionists, 23; Marianists, 20; Oblates of St. Francis de Sales, 19; Society of Precious Blood, 18; Xaverian Missionaries, 16; Congregstion of Sacred Heart, 16; Legionaries of Christ, 15; Salesians, 15; Spiritans, 15.

Diocesan Priests: There were 172 priests from 86 dioceses The majority were in Latin American countries.

Religious Brothers: Forty mission-sending groups had 347 brothers in overseas assignments. Those with 15 or more members:

Christian Brothers (Brothers of the Christian Schools), 54; Holy Cross Brothers, 40; Marianists, 36; Maryknoll Priests and Brothers, 35; Franciscans (O.F.M.), 26.

Religious Sisters: Two hundred and sixty-six mission-sending communities of women Religious

had 1,513 sisters in overseas missions. Those with 15 or more members:

Maryknoll Mission Sisters, 239; School Sisters of Notre Dame, 71; Dominicans, 48; Sisters of Mercy (various communities), 42; Daughters of Charity, 37; Sisters of Holy Cross (36); Immaculate Heart of Mary Sisters, 31; Sisters of Notre Dame de Namur, 29; Medical Mission Sisters, 27; Marist Missionary Sisters, 25; Franciscan Sisters of Philadelphia, 23; Ursulines, 21; Little Sisters of the Poor, 20; Franciscan Sisters of Allegany, 19; Missionaries of Charity, 20; Sisters of St. Joseph of Carondelet, 18; Society of the Sacred Heart, 16; Medical Missionaries of Mary, Missionary Sisters of Our Lady of Africa and Congregation of Sisters of St. Agnes, 15 each.

Lay Persons: Forty-five mission sending groups had 343 members in overseas missions.

Maryknoll Mission Associates, 101; Jesuit Volunteers International, 30; Salesian Lay Missionaries, 21; Religious of the Assumption, 15.

Seminarians: There were 18 from 5 groups. Legionaries of Christ, 10; Society of Our Lady of the Most Holy Trinity, 4; Franciscans, 2; Holy Cross Fathers, 1; Jesuits, 1.

MISSIONARY BISHOPS

Africa

South Africa: Keimoes-Upington (diocese), John B. Minder, O.S.F.S.; De Aar (diocese), Joseph J. Potocnak, S.C.J.

Zambia: Mongu (diocese), Paul Duffy, O.M.I.

Asia

Indonesia: Agats (diocese), Alphonse A. Sowada, O.S.C.

Iraq: Mossul (Chaldean-rite archdiocese), George Garmo.

Korea: Inchon (diocese), William J. McNaughton, M.M.

Philippines: Cotabato (archdiocese), Philip F. Smith, O.M.I. (emeritus; resigned, May 30, 1998).

Central America, West Indies

Dominica: Roseau (diocese), Edward J. Gilbert, C.SS.R.

Honduras: Comayagua (diocese), Gerald Scarpone Caporale, O.F.M.

Jamaica: Mandeville (diocese), Paul M. Boyle, C.P.

Nicaragua: Bluefields (vicariate apostolic), Paul Schmitz Simon, O.F.M. Cap.

Virgin Islands: St. Thomas (diocese), Elliott G. Thomas, bishop, 1993.

North America

Bermuda: Hamilton (diocese), Robert Kurtz, C.R.

Mexico: Nuevo Laredo (diocese), Ricardo Watty Urquidi, M.Sp.S., first bishop.

Oceania

American Samoa: Samoa-Pago Pago (diocese), John Quinn Weitzel, M.M.

Papua New Guinea: Mendi (diocese), Stephen J. Reichert, O.F.M.Cap.; Wewak (diocese), Raymond P. Kalisz, S.V.D.

South America

Bolivia: Pando (vicariate apostolic), Luis Morgan Casey.

Brazil: Cristalandia (prelacy), Herbert Hermes,

O.S.B.; Jatai (diocese), Benedito Domingos Coscia, O.F.M.; Itaituba (prelacy), Capistran Heim, O.F.M.; Jataí (diocese), Miguel P. Mundo aux. bishop; Miracema do Tocantins (diocese), John J. Burke, O.F.M.; Paranagua (diocese), Alfred Novak, C.Ss.R.;

Valença (diocese), Elias James Manning, O.F.M. Conv. **Peru**: Chulucanas (diocese), John C. McNabb, O.S.A.; Daniel Thomas Turley Murphy, O.S.A., coadjutor.

U.S. CATHOLIC MISSION ASSOCIATION

This is a voluntary association of individuals and organizations for whom the missionary presence of the universal Church is of central importance. It is a nonprofit religious, educational and charitable organization which exists to promote global missions. Its primary emphasis is on cross-cultural evangelization and the promotion of international justice and peace. The association is also responsible for gathering and publishing annual statistical data on U.S. missionary personnel overseas. President: William J. Morton, S.S.C.; Executive Director, Sister Rosanne Rustemeyer, S.S.N.D. Address: 3029 Fourth St. NE, Washington, D.C. 20017.

Mission Statement

In its 1996-97 handbook, the association included the following in a mission statement.

"In the Church, our understanding of the mission of evangelization is evolving to embrace dialogue, community building, struggles for justice, efforts to model justice and faith in our lifestyles, activities and structures, in addition to the teaching/preaching/witnessing role traditionally at the heart of the mission enterprise. Still, the contemporary 'identity-confusion' about 'mission' stands forth as a major challenge for USCMA as we move toward the 21st century.

"The larger context of mission is the Spirit moving in the Signs of our Times: the liberation movements, the women's movements, the economy movements, the rising awareness and celebration of cultural diversity, the search for ways to live peacefully and creatively with great pluralism, rapid technological change, the emergence of the global economy, the steady increase in poverty and injustice, the realigning of the global political order - and the many ripples radiating out from each of these."

Home Missions

The expression "home missions" is applied to places in the U.S. where the local church does not have its own resources, human and otherwise, which are needed to begin or, if begun, to survive and grow. These areas share the name "missions" with their counterparts in foreign lands because they too need outside help to provide the personnel and means for making the Church present and active there in carrying out its mission for the salvation of people.

Dioceses in the Southeast, the Southwest, and the Far West are most urgently in need of outside help to carry on the work of the Church. Millions of persons live in counties in which there are no resident priests. Many others live in rural areas beyond the reach and influence of a Catholic center. According to recent statistics compiled by the Glenmary Research Center, there are more than 500 priestless counties in the United States.

Mission Workers

A number of forces are at work to meet the pastoral needs of these missionary areas and to establish permanent churches and operating institutions where they are required. In many dioceses, one or more missions and stations are attended from established parishes and are gradually growing to independent status. Priests, brothers and sisters belonging to scores of religious institutes are engaged full-time in the home missions. Lay persons, some of them in affiliation with special groups and movements, are also involved.

The Society for the Propagation of the Faith, which conducts an annual collection for mission support in all parishes of the U.S., allocates 40 per cent of this sum for disbursement to home missions through the American Board of Catholic Missions.

Various mission-aid societies frequently undertake projects in behalf of the home missions.

The Glenmary Home Missioners, founded by Father W. Howard Bishop in 1939, is the only home mission society established for the sole purpose of carrying out the pastoral ministry in small towns and rural districts of the United States. Glenmary serves in many areas where at least 20 per cent of the people live in poverty and less than one per cent are Catholic. With 61 priests and 19 professed brothers as of January, 1998, the Glenmary Missioners had missions in the archdioceses of Atlanta and Cincinnati, and in the dioceses of Birmingham, Charlotte, Covington, Jackson, Lexington, Little Rock, Nashville, Owensboro, Richmond, Savannah, Tulsa, Tyler and Wheeling-Charleston. National headquarters are located at 4119 Glenmary Trace, Fairfield, Ohio. The mailing address is P.O. Box 465618, Cincinnati, Ohio 45246.

Organizations

Black and Indian Mission Office (The Commission for Catholic Missions among the Colored People and the Indians): Organized officially in 1885 by decree of the Third Plenary Council of Baltimore. Provides financial support for religious works among Blacks and Native Americans in 133 archdioceses and dioceses through funds raised by an annual collection in all parishes of the U.S. on the first Sunday of Lent, the designated Sunday. In 1997, $7,155,207 was raised; disbursements amounted to $4,566,000 for Black missions and $2,434,000 for Native American evangelization programs.

Bureau of Catholic Indian Missions (1874): Established as the representative of Catholic Indian missions before the federal government and the public; made permanent organization in 1884 by Third Plenary Council of Baltimore. After a remarkable history of rendering important services to the Indian people, the bureau continues to represent the Catholic Church in the U.S. in her apostolate to the American Indian. Concerns are evangelization, catechesis, liturgy, family life, education, advocacy.

Catholic Negro-American Mission Board (1907): Support priests and sisters in southern states and provide monthly support to sisters and lay teachers in the poorest Black schools.

Board of Directors of the three organizations above are: Cardinal John O'Connor, president; Cardinal Anthony Bevilacqua; Cardinal William Keeler; Msgr. Paul A. Lenz, secretary-treasurer; Patricia L. O'Rourke, D.St.G.G., assistant secretary/treasurer.

Address: 2021 H Street NW, Washington, DC 20006-4207.

The Catholic Church Extension Society (1905): Established with papal approval for the purpose of preserving and extending the Church in rural and isolated parts of the U.S. and its dependencies through the collection and disbursement of funds for home mission work. Since the time of its founding, more than $275 million have been received and distributed for this purpose. Disbursements, made at the requests

of bishops in 75 designated mission dioceses, exceeded $12 million for fiscal year 1997. The 10,500th church project built with the help of the society was dedicated in 1997. The society also distributes parish calendars. Works of the society are supervised by a 14-member board of governors: Cardinal Francis George of Chicago, chancellor; Rev. Msgr. Kenneth Velo, president; three archbishops, three bishops and six lay people. Headquarters: 150 S. Wacker Drive, 20th Floor, Chicago, IL 60601.

National Catholic Rural Life Conference: Founded in 1923 through the efforts of Bishop Edwin V. O'Hara. Applies the Gospel message to rural issues through focus on rural parishes and the provision of services including distribution of educational materials development of prayer and worship resources, advocacy for strong rural communities. Bishop Raymond L. Burke of LaCrosse, president; Brother David G. Andrews C.S.C., executive director. National headquarters: 4625 Beaver Ave., Des Moines, IA 50310.

POPE JOHN PAUL II'S MESSAGE FOR WORLD MISSION SUNDAY 1999

(Courtesy, Vatican Information Service.) On May 23, 1999, the Solemnity of Pentecost, Pope John Paul II issued his annual message for World Mission Sunday, Oct. 24, 1999. Following are excerpts:

In this last year of the century which prepares us for the Great Jubilee of 2000, we feel strongly the urge to lift up our eyes and hearts to the Father, in order to know him "as he is and as the Son has revealed him to us" (CCC 2779).

Our Father who art in heaven

2. The Church is missionary in order to proclaim untiringly that God is Father, filled with love for all mankind.

… It is the duty of believers to proclaim and testify that while he "dwells in unapproachable light" (1 *Tim* 6,16), the heavenly Father in his Son, who was born of the Virgin Mary, died and is risen, has made himself near to all human beings, and made them capable of "responding to him, knowing him and loving him" (cfr *CCC* 52).

Hallowed be thy name

3. The knowledge that the encounter with God promotes and exalts the dignity of the human person leads the Christian to pray….

So that God's name may be made holy among all nations, the Church works to draw humanity and creation into the plan of the Creator who in his love, destined us to be holy and blameless before him. (cfr *Eph* 1,9.4).

Thy kingdom come

4. With these words believers pray for the coming of the divine Kingdom and Christ's return in glory.

… Enlightened by the Spirit, the Church proclaims that this kingdom of justice, peace and love, already announced in the Gospel, is mysteriously brought about with the passing of time, thanks to individuals, families and communities who choose to live Christ's teaching in a radical way, in the spirit of the Beatitudes.

Give us this day our daily bread

5. In our day there is growing awareness that everyone has the right to their "daily bread," that is, to what is necessary for life.

… The Christian community is called to co-operate

with development and peace by means of work of human promotion, Institutes of education and formation at the service of the young, by constantly denouncing all forms of oppression and injustice.

Forgive us our trespasses

6. Missionary activity cannot fail to carry to individuals and to entire peoples the good news of the Lord's loving mercy. The Father who is in heaven, as is clearly seen in the parable of the Prodigal Son, is loving and he forgives the repentant sinner, forgetting his sins, restoring serenity and peace. This is the authentic face of God, the loving Father, who gives us the strength to conquer evil with good and enables those who respond to his love to share in the Redemption of the world.

As we forgive those who trespass against us

7. The Church is called, through her missionary activity, to make the reassuring reality of divine Fatherhood present, not only through words but above all through the holiness of missionaries and of the People of God.

Faced with the terrible and numerous consequences of sin, it is the duty of believers to offer signs of forgiveness and love.

Lead us not into temptation

8. With this last request, in the "Our Father" we ask God not to allow us to take the path of sin and to free us from evil, which is often inspired by a personal being, Satan, who desires to obstruct the plan of God and the salvation He works though Christ.

Final conclusions

9. Those who work at the outposts of the Church are like watchmen on the walls of God's City. We ask them: "Watchman, what of the night?" (*Is* 21,11), and we hear the answer: "Hark, your watchmen lift up their voice, together they sing for joy: for eye to eye they see the return of the Lord to Zion" (*Is* 52,8) Their generous witness in every corner of the earth proclaims "As the third millennium of the Redemption draws near, God is preparing a great springtime for Christianity and we can already see its first signs." (*Redemptoris Missio* 86).

THE CATHOLIC CHURCH IN CANADA

Background

The first date in the remote background of the Catholic history of Canada was July 7, 1534, when a priest in the exploration company of Jacques Cartier celebrated Mass on the Gaspe Peninsula.

Successful colonization and the significant beginnings of the Catholic history of the country date from the foundation of Québec in 1608 by Samuel de Champlain and French settlers. Montréal was established in 1642.

The earliest missionaries were Franciscan Récollets (Recollects) and Jesuits who arrived in 1615 and 1625, respectively. They provided some pastoral care for the settlers but worked mainly among the 100,000 Indians — Algonquins, Hurons and Iroquois — in the interior and in the Lake Ontario region. Eight of the Jesuit missionaries, killed in the 1640s, were canonized in 1930. (See Index: Jesuit North American Martyrs.) Sulpician Fathers, who arrived in Canada late in the 1640s, played a part in the great missionary period which ended about 1700.

Kateri Tekakwitha, "Lily of the Mohawks," who was baptized in 1676 and died in 1680, was declared "Blessed" June 22, 1980.

The communities of women religious with the longest histories in Canada are the Canonesses of St. Augustine and the Ursulines, since 1639; and the Hospitallers of St. Joseph, since 1642. Communities of Canadian origin are the Congregation of Notre Dame, founded by St. Marguerite Bourgeoys in 1658, and the Grey Nuns, formed by St. Marie Marguerite d'Youville in 1737.

Mother Marie (Guyard) of the Incarnation, an Ursuline nun, was one of the first three women missionaries to New France; called "Mother of the Church in Canada," she was declared "Blessed" June 22, 1980.

Start of Church Organization

Ecclesiastical organization began with the appointment in 1658 of François De Montmorency-Laval, "Father of the Church in Canada," as vicar apostolic of New France. He was the first bishop of Québec from 1674 to 1688, with jurisdiction over all French-claimed territory in North America. He was declared "Blessed" June 22, 1980.

In 1713, the French Canadian population numbered 18,000. In the same year, the Treaty of Utrecht ceded Acadia, Newfoundland and the Hudson Bay Territory to England. The Acadians were scattered among the American Colonies in 1755.

The English acquired possession of Canada and its 70,000 French-speaking inhabitants in virtue of the Treaty of Paris in 1763. Anglo-French and Anglican-Catholic differences and tensions developed. The pro-British government at first refused to recognize the titles of church officials, hindered the clergy in their work and tried to install a non-Catholic educational system. Laws were passed which guaranteed religious liberties to Catholics (Québec Act of 1774, Constitutional Act of 1791, legislation approved by Queen Victoria in 1851), but it took some time before actual respect for these liberties matched the legal enactments. The initial moderation of government antipathy toward the Church was caused partly by the loyalty of Catholics to the Crown during the American Revolution and the War of 1812.

Growth

The 15 years following the passage in 1840 of the Act of Union, which joined Upper and Lower Canada, were significant. New communities of men and women religious joined those already in the country. The Oblates of Mary Immaculate, missionaries par excellence in Canada, advanced the penetration of the West which had been started in 1818 by Abbé Provencher. New jurisdictions were established, and Québec became a metropolitan see in 1844. The first Council of Québec was held in 1851. The established Catholic school system enjoyed a period of growth. Laval University was inaugurated in 1854 and canonically established in 1876.

Archbishop Elzear-Alexandre Taschereau of Québec was named Canada's first cardinal in 1886. The apostolic delegation to Canada was set up in 1899. It became a nunciature October 16, 1969, with the establishment of diplomatic relations with the Vatican. The present Apostolic Nuncio is Archbishop Paolo Romeo, appointed on February 5, 1999.

Early in this century, Canada had eight ecclesiastical provinces, 23 dioceses, three vicariates apostolic, 3,500 priests, 2 million Catholics, about 30 communities of men religious, and 70 or more communities of women religious. The Church in Canada was phased out of mission status and removed from the jurisdiction of the Congregation for the Propagation of the Faith in 1908.

Diverse Population

The greatest concentration of Catholics is in the eastern portion of the country. In the northern and western portions, outside metropolitan centers, there are some of the most difficult parish and mission areas in the world. Bilingual (English-French) differences in the general population are reflected in the Church; for example, in the parallel structures of the Canadian Conference of Catholic Bishops, which was established in 1943. Québec is the center of French cultural influence. Many language groups are represented among Catholics, who include more than 257,000 members of Eastern Rites in one metropolitan see, seven eparchies and an apostolic exarchate.

Education, a past source of friction between the Church and the government, is administered by the civil provinces in a variety of arrangements authorized by the Canadian Constitution. Denominational schools have tax support in one way in Québec and Newfoundland, and in another way in Alberta, Ontario and Saskatchewan. Several provinces provide tax support only for public schools, making private financing necessary for separate church-related schools.

ECCLESIASTICAL JURISDICTIONS OF CANADA

Provinces

Names of ecclesiastical provinces and metropolitan sees in bold face: suffragan sees in parentheses.

Edmonton (Calgary, St. Paul).

Gatineau-Hull (Amos, Mont-Laurier, Rouyn Noranda).

Grouard-McLennan (Mackenzie-Ft. Smith, Prince George, Whitehorse).

Halifax (Antigonish, Charlottetown, Yarmouth).

Keewatin-LePas (Churchill-Hudson Bay, Labrador-Schefferville, Moosonee).

Kingston (Alexandria-Cornwall, Peterborough, Sault Ste. Marie).

Moncton (Bathurst, Edmundston, St. John).

Montréal (Joliette, St. Jean-Longueuil, St. Jerome, Valleyfield).

Ottawa (Hearst, Pembroke, Timmins).

Québec (Chicoutimi, Ste.-Anne-de-la-Pocatiere, Trois Rivieres).

Regina (Prince Albert, Saskatoon, Abbey of St. Peter).

Rimouski (Baie-Comeau, Gaspe).

St. Boniface (no suffragan).

St. John's (Grand Falls, St. George).

Sherbrooke (Nicolet, St. Hyacinthe).

Toronto (Hamilton, London, St. Catharines, Thunder Bay).

Vancouver (Kamloops, Nelson, Victoria).

Winnipeg—Ukrainian (Edmonton, New Westminster, Saskatoon, Toronto).

Jurisdictions immediately subject to the Holy See: Roman-Rite Archdiocese of Winnipeg, Byzantine Eparchy of Sts. Cyril and Methodius for Slovaks, Byzantine Eparchy of St. Sauveur de Montréal for Greek Melkites; Antiochene Eparchy of St. Maron of Montréal for Maronites.

JURISDICTIONS, HIERARCHY

(Principal sources: Information office, Canadian Conference of Catholic Bishops; Rev. Mr. William Kokesch, Dir., Communications Service, Canadian Conference of Catholic Bishops; Catholic Almanac survey; Annuario Pontificio; L'Osservatore Romano; Catholic News Service. As of June 1, 1999.)

Information includes names of archdioceses (indicated by asterisk) and dioceses, date of foundation, present ordinaries and auxiliaries; addresses of chancery office/bishop's residence; cathedral.

Alexandria-Cornwall, Ont. (1890 as Alexandria; name changed to Alexandria-Cornwall, 1976): Eugéne Philippe LaRocque, bishop, 1974.

Diocesan Center: 220, chemin Montréal, C.P. 1388, Cornwall, Ont. K6H 5V4. Cathedral: St. Finnans (Alexandria); Nativity Co-Cathedral (Cornwall).

Amos, Qué. (1938): Gérard Drainville, bishop, 1978.

Bishop's Residence: 450, rue Principale Nord, Amos, Qué. J9T 2M1. Cathedral: St. Teresa of Ávila.

Antigonish, N.S. (Arichat, 1844; transferred, 1886): Colin Campbell, bishop, 1987.

Chancery Office: 155 Main St., P.O. Box 1330, Antigonish, N.S., B2G 2L7. Cathedral: St. Ninian.

Baie-Comeau, Qué. (p.a., 1882; v.a., 1905; diocese Gulf of St. Lawrence, 1945; name changed, to Hauterive, 1960; present title, 1986): Pierre Morissette, bishop, 1990.

Bishop's Residence: 639, rue de Bretagne,

Baie-Comeau, Qué., G5C 1X2. Cathedral: Paroisse St. Jean-Eudes.
Bathurst, N.B. (Chatham, 1860; transferred, 1938): André Richard, C.S.C., bishop, 1989.
Bishop's Residence: 645, avenue Murray, C.P. 460, Bathurst, N.-B., E2A 3Z4. Cathedral: Sacred Heart of Jesus.
Calgary, Alberta. (1912): Frederick Henry, bishop, 1997.
Address: Room 290, Catholic Pastoral Center, 120 17 Ave. SW, Calgary, Alberta. T2S 2T2. Cathedral: St. Mary.
Charlottetown, P.E.I. (1829): Joseph Vernon Fougere, bishop, 1992.
Bishop's Residence: P.O. Box 907, Charlottetown, P.E.I., C1A 7L9. Cathedral: St. Dunstan's.
Chicoutimi, Qué. (1878): Jean-Guy Couture, bishop, 1979. Roch Pedneault, auxiliary.
Bishop's Residence: 602, Racine Est, Chicoutimi, Qué. G7H 6J6. Cathedral: St. Francois-Xavier.
Churchill-Hudson Bay, Man. (p.a., 1925; v.a. Hudson Bay, 1931; diocese of Churchill, 1967; present title, 1968): Reynald Rouleau, O.M.I., bishop, 1987.
Diocesan Office: P.O. Box 10, Churchill, Man. R0B 0E0. Cathedral: Holy Canadian Martyrs.
Edmonton,* Alberta. (St. Albert, 1871; archdiocese, transferred Edmonton, 1912): Joseph N. MacNeil, archbishop, 1973; Thomas C. Colins, coadjutor, 1999.
Archdiocesan Office: 8421-101 Avenue, Edmonton, Alberta. T6A 0L1. Cathedral: Basilica of St. Joseph.
Edmonton, Alberta. (Ukrainian Byzantine) (ap. ex. of western Canada, 1948; eparchy, 1956): Lawrence Daniel Huculak, O.S.B.M., eparch, 1997.
Eparch's Residence: 9645 - 108th Ave., Edmonton, Alta. T5H 1A3. Cathedral: St. Josaphat.
Edmundston, N.B. (1944): François Thibodeau, C.J.M., bishop, 1994.
Diocesan Center: 60, rue Bouchard, Edmundston, N.B. E3V 3K1. Cathedral: Immaculate Conception.
Gaspé, Qué. (1922): Raymond Dumais, bishop, 1994.
Bishop's House: 172, rue Jacques-Cartier, Gaspé, Qué. G4X 1M9. Cathedral: Christ the King.
Gatineau-Hull,* Qué. (1963, as Hull; name changed, 1982; archdiocese, 1990): Roger Ébacher, bishop, 1988; first archbishop, Oct. 31, 1990.
Diocesan Center: 180 Boul. Mont-Bleu, Hull, Qué. J8Z 3J5.
Grand Falls, Nfld. (Harbour Grace, 1856; present title, 1964): vacant.
Chancery Office: P.O. Box 397, Grand Falls, Windsor, Nfld. A2A 2J8. Cathedral: Immaculate Conception.
Grouard-McLennan,* Alberta (v.a. Athabaska-Mackenzie, 1862; Grouard, 1927; archdiocese Grouard-McLennan, 1967); vacant.
Archbishop's Residence: C.P. 388, McLennan, Alberta. T0H 2L0. Cathedral: St. Jean-Baptiste (McLennan).
Halifax,* N.É. (1842; archdiocese, 1852): Terrence Prendergast, S.J., archbishop, 1998.
Chancery Office: P.O. Box 1527, Halifax, N.É. B3J 2Y3.
Hamilton, Ont. (1856): Anthony Tonnos, bishop, 1984. Matthew Ustrzycki, auxiliary.
Chancery Office: 700 King St. West, Hamilton, Ont. L8P1C7. Cathedral: Christ the King.

Hearst, Ont. (p.a., 1918; v.a., 1920; diocese, 1938): André Vallée, P.M.É., bishop, 1996.
Bishop's Residence: 76 7e rue, C.P. 1330, Hearst, Ont. P0L 1N0. Cathedral: Notre Dame of the Assumption.
Joliette, Qué. (1904): Gilles Lussier, bishop, 1991.
Bishop's Residence: C.P. 470, 2 rue Saint-Charles-Borromée Nord, Joliette, Qué. J6E 6H6. Cathedral: St. Charles Borromeo.
Kamloops, B.C. (1945): Lawrence Sabatini, C.S., bishop, 1982.
Bishop's Residence: 635A Tranquille Rd., Kamloops, B.C. V2B 3H5. Cathedral: Sacred Heart.
Keewatin-Le Pas,* Man. (v.a., 1910; archdiocese, 1967): Peter-Alfred Sutton, O.M.I., archbishop, 1986.
Archbishop's Residence: P.O. Box 270, The Pas, Man. R9A 1K4. Cathedral: Our Lady of the Sacred Heart.
Kingston,* Ont. (1826; archdiocese, 1889): Francis J. Spence, archbishop, 1982.
Chancery Office: 390 Palace Rd., Kingston Ont. K7L 4T3. Cathedral: St. Mary of the Immaculate Conception.
Labrador City-Schefferville, Qué. (v.a. Labrador, 1946; diocese, 1967): Douglas Crosby, O.M.I., bishop, 1997.
Bishop's Residence: 320 avenue Elizabeth, C.P. 545, Labrador City, Labaador, Nfld. A2V 2K7. Cathedral: Our Lady of Perpetual Help.
London, Ont. (1855; transferred Sandwich, 1859; London, 1869): John M. Sherlock, bishop, 1978. Richard Grecco, auxiliary.
Bishop's Residence: 1070 Waterloo St., London, Ont. N6A 3Y2. Cathedral: St. Peter's Cathedral Basilica.
Mackenzie-Fort Smith, N.W.T. (v.a. Mackenzie, 1902; diocese Mackenzie-Fort Smith, 1967): Denis Croteau, O.M.I., bishop, 1986.
Diocesan Office: 5117-52nd St., Yellowknife, NWT X1A 1T7. Cathedral: St. Joseph (Ft. Smith).
Moncton,* N.B. (1936): Ernest Léger, archbishop, 1997.
Archbishop's Residence: 452, rue Amirault, Dieppe, N.B. E1A 1G3. Cathedral: Our Lady of the Assumption.
Mont-Laurier, Qué. (1913): Jean Gratton, bishop, 1978.
Bishop's Residence: 435, rue de la Madone, Mont-Laurier, Qué. J9L 1S1. Cathedral: Notre Dame de Fourvières.
Montréal,* Qué. (1836; archdiocese, 1886): Cardinal Jean-Claude Turcotte, archbishop, 1990. Anthony Mancini, Louis Dicaire, Jude Saint-Antoine, André Rivest, auxiliaries.
Archbishop's Residence: 2000, rue Sherbrooke Ouest, Montréal, Qué. H3H 1G4. Cathedral: Basilica of Mary Queen of the World and Saint James.
Montréal, Qué. (Sauveur de Montréal, Eparchy of Greek Melkites) (ap. ex. 1980; eparchy, 1984): Sleiman Hajjar, eparch, 1988.
Address: 34 Maplewood, Montréal, Qué. H2V 2MI.
Montréal, Que. (St. Maron of Montréal, Maronites) (1982): Joseph Khoury, eparch, 1996.
Chancery Office: 12475 rue Grenet, Montréal, Qué. H4J 2K4. Cathedral: St. Maron.
Moosonee, Ont. (v.a. James Bay, 1938; diocese Moosonee, 1967): Vincent Cadieux, O.M.I., bishop, 1992.

Bishop's Residence: C.P. 40, Moosonee, Ont. P0L IY0. Cathedral: Christ the King.

Nelson, B.C. (1936): Eugene J. Cooney, bishop, 1996.

Bishop's Residence: 402 West Richards St., Nelson, B.C. VIL 3K3. Cathedral: Mary Immaculate.

New Westminster, B.C. (Ukrainian Byzantine) (1974): Severian Stephen Yakymyshyn, O.S.B.M., eparch, 1995.

Eparch's address: 502 5th Ave., New Westminster, BC V3L 1S2.

Nicolet, Qué. (1885): Raymond Saint-Gelais, bishop, 1989.

Bishop's Residence: 49, rue Mgr Brunault, Nicolet, Qué. J3T 1X7. Cathedral: St.-Jean-Baptiste.

Ottawa,* Ont. (Bytown, 1847, name changed, 1854; archdiocese, 1886): Marcel Gervais, A.J., archbishop, 1989.

Archbishop's Residence: 1247 Place Kilborn, Ottawa, Ont. KIH 6K9. Cathedral: Basilica of Notre Dame-of-Ottawa.

Pembroke, Ont. (v.a. 1882; diocese, 1898): Brendan M. O'Brien, bishop, 1993.

Bishop's Residence: 188 Renfrew St., P.O. Box 7, Pembroke, Ont. K8A 6XI. Cathedral: St. Columbkille.

Peterborough, Ont. (1882): James L. Doyle, bishop, 1976.

Bishop's Residence: 350 Hunter St. West, PO Box 175, Peterborough, Ont. K9J 6Y8. Cathedral: St. Peter-in-Chains.

Prince Albert, Sask. (v.a., 1890; diocese, 1907): Blaise Morand, bishop, 1983.

Address: 1415-4th Ave. West, Prince-Albert, Sask. S6V 5H1. Cathedral: Sacred Heart.

Prince George, B.C. (p.a., 1908; v.a. Yukon and Prince Rupert, 1944; diocese Prince George, 1967): Gerald Wiesner, O.M.I., bishop, 1993.

Chancery Office: P.O. Box 7000, 2935 Highway 16 West, Prince George, B.C. V2N 3Z2. Cathedral: Sacred Heart.

Québec,* Qué. (v.a., 1658; diocese, 1674; archdiocese, 1819; metropolitan, 1844; primatial see, 1956): Maurice Couture, S.V., archbishop, 1990. Jean Pierre Blais, Eugène Tremblay, Jean Gagnon, auxiliaries.

Chancery Office: 1073, boul. René Lévesque Ouest, Québec, Qué. G1S 4R5. Cathedral: Notre-Dame-de-Québec (Basilica).

Regina,* Sask. (1910; archdiocese, 1915): Peter Mallon, archbishop, 1995.

Chancery Office: 445 Broad St. North, Regina, Sask. S4R 2X8. Cathedral: Our Lady of the Most Holy Rosary.

Rimouski,* Qué. (1867; archdiocese, 1946): Bertrand Blanchet, archbishop, 1992.

Archbishop's Residence: 34, rue de l'Évêché Ouest, C.P. 730, Rimouski, Qué. G5L 7C7.

Rouyn-Noranda, Qué. (1973): Jean-Guy Hamelin, bishop, 1974.

Bishop's Residence: 515, avenue Cuddihy, C.P. 1060, Rouyn-Noranda, Qué. J9X 4C5. Cathedral: St. Michael the Archangel.

Saint-Boniface,* Man. (1847; archdiocese, 1871): Antoine Hacault, archbishop, 1974.

Archbishop's Residence: 151, avenue de la Cathedrale, Saint-Boniface, Man. R2H OH6. Cathedral: Basilica of St. Boniface.

St. Catharines, Ont. (1958): John A. O'Mara, bishop, 1994.

Bishop's Residence: P.O. Box 875, St. Catharines, Ont. L2R 6Y3. Cathedral: St. Catherine of Alexandria.

St. George's, Nfld. (p.a., 1870; v.a., 1890; diocese, 1904): Raymond J. Lahey, bishop, 1986.

Bishop's Residence: 16 Hammond Dr., Corner Brook, Nfld. A2H 2W2. Cathedral: Most Holy Redeemer and Immaculate Conception.

Saint-Hyacinthe, Qué. (1852): François Lapierre, P.M.E., bishop, 1998.

Bishop's Residence: 1900, rue Girouard Ouest, C.P. 190, Saint-Hyacinthe, Qué. J2S 7B4. Cathedral: St. Hyacinthe the Confessor.

Saint-Jean-Longueuil, Qué. (1933 as St.-Jean-de-Québec; named changed, 1982): Jacques Berthelet, C.S.V., bishop, 1996.

Bishop's Residence: 740, boulevard Sainte-Foy, C.P. 40, Longueuil, Qué. J4K 4X8. Cathedral: St. John the Evangelist.

St. Jérôme, Qué. (1951): Gilles Cazabon, O.M.I., bishop, 1998; Vital Massé, auxiliary.

Bishop's Residence: 355, rue Saint-Georges, C.P. 580, Saint-Jerome, Qué. J7Z 5V3. Cathedral: St. Jerome.

Saint John, N.B. (1842): Joseph Faber MacDonald, bishop, 1998.

Chancery Office: 1 Bayard Dr., Saint John, N.B. E2L 3L5. Cathedral: Immaculate Conception.

St. John's,* Nfld. (p.a., 1784; v.a., 1796; diocese, 1847; archdiocese, 1904): James H. MacDonald, C.S.C., archbishop, 1991.

Chancery Office: P.O. Box 1363, St. John's, Nfld. A1C 5H5. Cathedral: St. John the Baptist.

St. Paul in Alberta (1948): vacant.

Bishop's Residence: 4410, 51e avenue, Saint Paul, Alta. T0A 3A2. Cathedral: St. Paul.

Sainte-Anne-de-la-Pocatière, Qué. (1951): Clément Fecteau, bishop, 1996.

Bishop's Residence: 1200, 4e avenue, C.P. 430, La Pocatière, Qué. G0R 1Z0. Cathedral: St. Anne.

Saskatoon, Sask. (1933): V. James Weisgerber, bishop, 1996.

Chancery Office: 100-5th Ave. North, Saskatoon, Sask. S7K 2N7. Cathedral: St. Paul.

Saskatoon, Sask. (Ukrainian Byzantine) (ap. ex., 1951; diocese, 1956): vacant.

Address: 866 Saskatchewan Crescent East, Saskatoon, Sask. S7N 0L4.

Sault Ste. Marie, Ont. (1904): Jean-Louis Plouffe, bishop, 1990. Paul-André Durocher, auxiliary.

Chancery Office: 387 Algonquin, P.O. Box 510, North Bay, Ont. P1B 8J1. Sudbury Office: 435, Avenue Notre Dame, Sudbury, Ont. B3C-5K6. Cathedral: Pro-Cathedral of the Assumption, North Bay.

Sherbrooke,* Qué. (1874; archdiocese, 1951); André Gaumond, archbishop, 1996.

Archbishop's Residence: 130, rue de la Cathedrale, C.P. 430, Sherbrooke, Qué. J1H 5K1. Cathedral: St. Michel.

Thunder Bay, Ont. (Ft. William, 1952; transferred, 1970): Frederick J. Colli, bishop, 1994.

Bishop's Residence: P.O. Box 10400, Thunder Bay, Ont. P4N 5W4. Cathedral: St. Patrick.

Timmins, Ont. (v.a. Temiskaming, 1908; diocese

Haileybury, 1915; present title, 1938): Paul Marchand, S.M.M., bishop, 1999.
Address: 65, Ave. Jubilee Est, Timmins, Ont. P4N 5W4. Cathedral: St. Anthony of Padua.
Toronto,* Ont. (1841; archdiocese, 1870): Cardinal Aloysius M. Ambrozic, archbishop, 1990. John Stephen Knight, Nicola De Angelis, C.F.I.C., Robert B. Clune, Anthony Meagher, auxiliaries.
Chancery Office: Catholic Pastoral Centre, 1155 Yonge St., Toronto, Ont. M4Y 1W2. Cathedral: St. Michael.
Toronto, Ont. (Eparchy for Slovakian Byzantine) (1980): vacant.
Eparch's Residence: 223 Carlton Rd., Unionville, Ont. L3R 3M2.
Toronto, Ont. (Eparchy for Ukrainian Byzantine) (ap. ex., 1948; eparchy, 1956): Isidore Borecky (exarch 1948-56), first eparch, 1956. Cornelius Pasichny, O.S.B.M., eparch, 1998.
Chancery Office: 139 Franklin Ave., Toronto, Ont. M6P 3Y9. Cathedral: St. Josaphat.
Trois-Rivières, Qué. (1852): Martin Veillette, bishop, 1996.
Bishop's Residence: 362, rue Bonaventure, C.P. 879, Trois-Rivieres, Qué. G9A 5J9. Cathedral: The Assumption.
Valleyfield, Qué. (1892): Robert Lebel, bishop, 1976.
Bishop's Residence: 11, rue de l'Eglise, Valleyfield, Qué. J6T 1J5. Cathedral: St. Cecilia.
Vancouver,* B. C. (v.a. British Columbia, 1863; diocese New Westminster, 1890; archdiocese Vancouver, 1908): Adam Exner, O.M.I., archbishop, 1991.
Chancery Office: 150 Robson St., Vancouver, B.C. V6B 2A7. Cathedral: Holy Rosary.
Victoria, B.C. (diocese Vancouver Is., 1846; archdiocese, 1903; diocese Victoria, 1908): Raymond Roussin, SM, bishop, 1999.
Chancery Office: Diocesan Pastoral Centre, #1-4044 Nelthorpe St., Victoria, B.C. V8X 2A1. Cathedral: St. Andrew.
Whitehorse, Y.T. (v.a., 1944; diocese 1967): Thomas Lobsinger, O.M.I., bishop, 1987.
Chancery Office: 406 Steele St., Whitehorse, Yukon Y1A 2C8. Cathedral: Sacred Heart.
Winnipeg,* Man. (1915): Leonard J. Wall, archbishop, 1992.
Chancery Office: Catholic Centre, 1495 Pembina Highway, Winnipeg, Man., R3T 2C6. Cathedral: St. Mary.
Winnipeg,* Man. (Ukrainian Byzantine)

(Ordinariate of Canada, 1912; ap. ex. Central Canada, 1948; ap. ex. Manitoba, 1951; archeparchy Winnipeg, 1956): Michael Bzdel, C.Ss.R., archeparch, 1993. Stefan Soroka, auxiliary.
Archeparchy Office: 235 Scotia St., Winnipeg, Man., R2V 1V7. Cathedral: Sts. Vladimir and Olga.
Yarmouth, N.É. (1953): James M. Wingle, bishop, 1993.
Address: C.P. 278, 53 rue Park, Yarmouth, N.É. B5A 4B2. Cathedral: St. Ambrose.
Military Ordinariate of Canada (1951):Donald J. Thériault, bishop, 1998.
Address: Canadian Forces Support Unit (Ottawa), Uplands Site – Bldg. 469, Ottawa, Ont. K1A 0K2.
An Apostolic Exarchate for Armenian-Rite Catholics in Canada and the United States was established in July, 1981, with headquarters in New York City (110 E. 12th St., New York, NY 10003). Hovhannes Tertzakian, O.M., exarch, 1995.
The eparchy of Our Lady of Deliverance of Newark for Syrian-rite Catholics in the United States and Canada was established Nov. 6, 1995. Address: 502 Palisade Ave., Union City, NJ 07087. Most Rev. Joseph Younan, bishop.
Hungarian Emigrants throughout the world, resides in Canada: Most Rev. Attila Mikloshazy, S.J., titular bishop of Castel Minore. Address: 2661 Kingston Rd., Scarborough, Ont. M1M 1M3.
Note: The diocese of Gravelbourg, in Saskatchewan, was dissolved in September, 1998, as part of a reorganization of Canadian dioceses. The regions under the jurisdiction of Gravelbourg were integrated into the neighboring dioceses of Regina and Saskatoon. The Territorial Abbacy of St. Peter, Muenster, Sask., was also dissolved.

Dioceses with Interprovincial Lines

The following dioceses, indicated by + in the table, have interprovincial lines.
Churchill-Hudson Bay includes part of Northwest Territories.
Keewatin-LePas includes part of Manitoba and Saskatchewan provinces.
Labrador City-Schefferville includes the Labrador region of Newfoundland and the northern part of Québec province.
Mackenzie-Fort Smith, Northwest Territories, includes part of Alberta and Saskatchewan provinces.
Moosonee, Ont., includes part of Québec province.
Pembroke, Ont., includes one county of Québec province.
Whitehorse, Y.T., includes part of British Columbia.

CANADIAN CONFERENCE OF CATHOLIC BISHOPS

The Canadian Conference of Catholic Bishops was established Oct. 12, 1943, as a permanent voluntary association of the bishops of Canada, was given official approval by the Holy See in 1948, and acquired the status of an episcopal conference after the Second Vatican Council.

The CCCB acts in two ways: (1) as a strictly ecclesiastical body through which the bishops act together with pastoral authority and responsibility for the Church throughout the country; (2) as an operational secretariat through which the bishops act on a wider

scale for the good of the Church and society.
At the top of the CCCB organizational table are the president, an executive committee, a permanent council and a plenary assembly. The membership consists of all the bishops of Canada.

Departments and Offices

The CCCB's work is planned and co-ordinated by the Programmes and Priorities Committee composed of the six chairmen of the national episcopal commissions and the two general secretaries.

It is chaired by the vice-president of the CCCB. The CCCB's twelve episcopal commissions undertake study and projects in special areas of pastoral work. Six serve nationally (social affairs; canon law/inter-rite; relations with associations of clergy, consecrated life and laity; evangelization of peoples; ecumenism; and theology); three relate to French sectors (*communications sociale, éducation Chrétienne, liturgie*) and three relate to corresponding English sectors (social communications, Christian education, liturgy).

The general secretariat consists of a French and an English general secretary and their assistants and directors of public relations. Current general secretaries are: Rev. Emilius Goulet, P.S.S. (French speaking) and Msgr. Peter Schonenbach (English speaking).

Administrative services for purchasing, archives and library, accounting, personnel, publications, printing and distribution are supervised by directors who relate to the general secretaries.

Various advisory councils and committees with mixed memberships of lay persons, religious, priests and bishops also serve the CCCB on a variety of topics.

Operations

Meetings for the transaction of business are held at least once a year by the plenary assembly, six times a year by the executive committee, and four times a year by the permanent council.

Cardinal Jean-Claude Turcotte, of Montréal, Qué., is president of the CCCB and Bishop Gerald Wiesner, O.M.I., of Prince George, is vice president for the 1995-97 term.

Secretariat is located at 90 Parent Ave., Ottawa, K1N 7B1, Canada.

CANADIAN SHRINES

Our Lady of the Cape (Cap de la Madeleine), Queen of the Most Holy Rosary: The Three Rivers, Québec, parish church, built of fieldstone in 1714 and considered the oldest stone church on the North American continent preserved in its original state, was rededicated June 22, 1888, as a shrine of the Queen of the Most Holy Rosary. Thereafter, the site increased in importance as a pilgrimage and devotional center, and in 1904 St. Pius X decreed the crowning of a statue of the Blessed Virgin which had been donated 50 years earlier to commemorate the dogma of the Immaculate Conception. In 1909, the First Plenary Council of Québec declared the church a shrine of national pilgrimage. In 1964, the church at the shrine was given the status and title of minor basilica.

St. Anne de Beaupre: The devotional history of this shrine in Québec, began with the reported cure of a cripple, Louis Guimont, on Mar. 16, 1658, the starting date of construction work on a small chapel of St. Anne. The original building was successively enlarged and replaced by a stone church which was given the rank of minor basilica in 1888. The present structure, a Romanesque-Gothic basilica, houses the shrine proper in its north transept. The centers of attraction are an eight-foot-high oaken statue and the great relic of St. Anne, a portion of her forearm.

St. Joseph's Oratory: The massive oratory basilica standing on the western side of Mount Royal and overlooking the city of Montréal had its origin in a primitive chapel erected there by Blessed Andre Bessette, C.S.C., in 1904. Eleven years later, a large crypt was built to accommodate an increasing number of pilgrims, and in 1924 construction work was begun on the large church. A belfry, housing a 60-bell carillon and standing on the site of the original chapel, was dedicated May 15, 1955, as the first major event of the jubilee year observed after the oratory was given the rank of minor basilica.

Martyrs' Shrine: A shrine commemorating several of the Jesuit Martyrs of North America who were killed between 1642 and 1649 in the Ontario and northern New York area is located on the former site of old Fort Sainte Marie. Before its location was fixed near Midland, Ont., in 1925, a small chapel had been erected in 1907 at old Mission St. Ignace to mark the martyrdom of Fathers Jean de Brebeuf and Gabriel Lalemant. This sanctuary has a U.S. counterpart in the Shrine of the North American Martyrs near Auriesville, N.Y., under the care of the Jesuits.

Others

Other shrines and historic churches in Canada include the following.

In Québec City: the Basilica of Notre Dame, dating from 1650, once the cathedral of a diocese stretching from Canada to Mexico; Notre Dame des Victoires, on the waterfront, dedicated in 1690; the Ursuline Convent, built in 1720, on du Parloir St.

In Montréal: Notre Dame Basilica, patterned after the famous basilica of the same name in Paris, constructed in 1829; the Shrine of Mary, Queen of All Hearts.

Near Montréal: the Chapel of St. Marie Marguerite d'Youville, foundress of the Grey Nuns; Notre Dame de Lourdes, at Rigaud.

STATISTICAL SUMMARY OF THE CATHOLIC CHURCH IN CANADA

(Principal source: 1999 *Directory of the Canadian Conference of Catholic Bishops*; figures as of January, 1999); Catholic population statistics are those reported in the 1991 Canadian Census. Archdioceses are indicated by an asterisk. For dioceses marked +, see Canadian dioceses with interprovincial lines.

Canada's 10 civil provinces and two territories are divided into 18 ecclesiastical provinces consisting of 18 metropolitan sees (archdioceses) and 45 suffragan sees; there are also eight Oriental Rite dioceses, one archdiocese and three eparchies immediately subject to the Holy See, and the Military Ordinariate.

This table presents a regional breakdown of Catholic statistics. In some cases, the totals are approximate because diocesan boundaries fall within several civil provinces.

Civil Province Diocese	Cath. Pop.	Dioc. Priests	Rel. Priests	Total Priests	Perm. Deacs.	Bro- thers	Sis- ters	Lay Assts.	Par- ishes[1]
Newfoundland	213,055	96	24	120	-	15	371	3	211
*St. John's	119,260	42	15	57	-	12	281	-	92
Grand Falls	37,940	31	-	31	-	-	33	-	73
Labrador-Schefferville+	13,550	-	8	8	-	3	24	2	25
St. George's	42,305	23	1	24	-	-	33	1	21
Prince Edward Island									
Charlottetown	60,625	59	2	61	1	-	175	3	59
Nova Scotia	450,270	228	29	257	28	6	726	23	221
*Halifax	152,515	60	16	76	26	1	317	20	53
Antigonish	138,990	144	10	154	1	4	380	1	128
Yarmouth	39,505	24	3	27	1	1	29	2	40
New Brunswick	386,480	233	62	295	3	31	839	59	256
*Moncton	105,775	66	30	96	1	23	295	5	61
Bathurst	115,560	60	13	73	-	6	242	24	63
Edmundston	52,435	43	9	52	-	1	130	20	32
St. John	112,710	64	10	74	2	1	172	10	100
Québec	6,057,315	3,010	1,952	4,962	364	2,023	16,311	1,733	1,883
*Gatineau-Hull	216,725	63	35	98	2	8	274	105	60
*Montréal	1,656,297	605	870	1,475	100	587	5,576	53	282
*Québec	902,545	562	346	908	79	432	3,664	167	258
*Rimouski	152,565	136	24	160	4	44	747	18	118
*Sherbrooke	235,145	227	113	340	19	91	1,130	86	135
Amos	103,890	33	19	52	1	14	137	155	66
Baie Comeau	93,715	45	19	64	8	9	93	28	49
Chicoutimi	275,580	208	49	257	33	59	667	133	97
Gaspé	94,645	66	15	81	3	4	186	18	65
Joliette	177,138	77	61	138	5	122	314	95	57
Mont Laurier	72,755	40	25	65	-	21	110	57	59
Montréal, St. Maron (Maronites)	80,000	10	6	16	1	-	5	-	13
Montréal, St. Sauveur (Greek-Melkites)	38,000	4	8	12	1	-	-	-	6
Nicolet	177,620	168	25	193	21	90	642	24	85
Rouyn-Noranda	56,475	29	11	40	-	5	92	37	41
Ste-Anne-de-la-Pocatière	87,865	129	1	130	6	-	198	63	54
St.-Hyacinthe	330,515	171	86	257	29	189	994	171	113
St.-Jean-Longueuil	524,150	124	54	178	2	88	390	231	91
St. Jérôme	353,310	98	75	178	15	114	267	168	79
Trois Rivières	243,085	133	79	212	26	96	723	40	91
Valleyfield	185,295	82	31	123	9	50	102	84	64
Ontario	3,575,065	1,584	988	2,572	356	189	3,596	309	1,273
*Kingston	102,650	77	5	83	7	-	186	-	72
*Ottawa	364,285	157	177	334	38	55	867	22	113
*Toronto	1,420,395	399	486	885	117	78	859	85	222
Alexandria-Cornwall	56,020	41	4	45	16	4	77	8	34
Hamilton	480,695	145	101	246	1	20	345	46	151
Hearst	34,840	32	-	32	-	2	17	18	28

Civil Province Diocese	Cath. Pop.	Dioc. Priests	Rel. Priests	Total Priests	Perm. Deacs.	Bro- thers	Sis- ters	Lay Assts.	Par- ishes[1]
Ontario *continued*									
London	414,285	230	99	329	2	6	478	75	172
Moosonee+	3,905	1	5	6	1	3	10	3	16
Pembroke+	64,925	74	3	77	8	4	202	1	67
Peterborough	83,680	111	6	117	8	-	120	4	74
St. Catharine's	145,850	61	35	96	1	4	61	5	48
Sault Ste. Marie	218,850	102	30	132	111	4	258	24	118
Thunder Bay	78,480	33	19	52	20	2	50	3	42
Timmins	55,195	28	5	33	7	5	39	14	33
Toronto (Ukrainians)	41,010	89	9	98	19	2	27	1	75
Toronto (Slovaks, Sts. Cyril and Methodius)	10,000	4	4	8	-	-	-	-	8
Manitoba	346,180	191	125	316	57	27	649	21	404
*Keewatin-LePas+	35,195	4	16	20	-	2	17	3	52
*St. Boniface	101,920	91	66	157	17	19	417	16	105
*Winnipeg	170,590	62	27	89	19	4	173	-	102
*Winnipeg (Ukrainians)	33,490	33	10	43	21	1	34	-	128
Churchill-Hudson Bay+	4,985	1	6	7	-	1	8	3	17
Saskatchewan+	301,335	184	89	273	8	11	535	25	399
*Regina#	124,190	89	24	113	-	5	170	10	169
Prince-Albert	57,580	33	12	55	2	2	101	11	87
Saskatoon#	75,140	39	39	78	-	2	242	4	11
Saskatoon (Ukrainians)	20,080	23	14	37	6	2	22	-	132
Alberta	665,870	234	195	429	11	42	677	73	525
*Edmonton	294,935	80	115	195	-	33	437	38	180
*Grouard-McLennan	40,715	5	17	23	1	-	31	17	70
Calgary	250,605	95	47	143	1	9	151	-	118
Edmonton (Ukrainians)	26,250	29	13	42	8	-	39	-	87
St. Paul	53,365	25	3	28	1	-	19	18	70
British Columbia	600,175	175	151	326	5	40	351	28	300
*Vancouver	340,775	84	93	177	-	30	180	-	74
Kamloops	47,010	12	11	23	-	4	18	-	79
Nelson	63,570	25	16	41	-	-	27	7	53
New Westminster (Ukrainians)	7,555	14	3	17	3	-	2	-	18
Prince George	51,200	8	12	20	1	2	30	16	45
Victoria	90,065	32	16	48	-	4	94	5	31
Yukon Territory									
Whitehorse+	8,235	3	10	13	2	2	9	10	22
Northwest Territories									
MacKenzie-Ft. Smith+	19,745	2	4	6	1	-	16	-	41
Military Ordinariate	75,183	32*	5**	37	2	-	-	22	22 **
TOTALS	12,498,605[2]	6,031	3,632	9,663	838	2,386	24,255	2,309	5,6716

[1]Denotes both parishes and missions.
[2]Catholics comprise about 44% of the total population.
*The Canadian Military Ordinariate does not incardinate clerics.
**Not included in the total.
Figures for the archdiocese of Regina and the diocese of Saskatoon (Saskatchewan province) reflect the dissolution of the diocese of Gravelbourg in 1998 and the distribution of its jurisdictions.

472

THE CATHOLIC CHURCH IN MEXICO

BACKGROUND

Start of Church Organization

The history of the Catholic Church in Mexico began in 1519 with the capture of Mexico's native civilization, the Aztec Empire, by the Spanish *conquistadores* under Hernándo Cortés. The Spanish army besieged the Aztec capital of Tenochtitlan, massacred most of the inhabitants, strangled the Aztec emperor Montezuma, and crushed the rest of the empire. Mexico City became the chief city of New Spain and the cultural and religious center of colonial Mexico; it was declared a diocese in 1530.

The record of Colonial Spanish treatment of the native peoples of Mexico is a grim one. The Indians suffered exploitation, slavery, and rapid depletion of their population from disease; they were forced to labor in inhuman conditions in mines and endured servitude in the *encomienda* system.

In sharp contrast to the treatment of the natives by the government was the effort to evangelize Mexico by the religious orders who followed the command of Pope Alexander VI in the 1494 Treaty of Tordesillas to convert all peoples who should be encountered in the coming age of exploration. A papal bull, dated Apr. 25, 1521, gave to the Franciscans the permission of the Holy See to preach in New Spain. They were joined by the Dominicans and, later, by the Jesuits. The missionary orders soon distinguished themselves by their resistance to the brutal enslavement of the Indians, their mastery of native languages, and their willingness to endure enormous hardships in bringing the faith to the distant corners of Mexico.

As the Church became more established, however, the missionary priests and friars came increasingly into conflict with the secular clergy, who desired full control over the ecclesiastical affairs, resented the extensive powers of the religious orders, and normally identified closely with the interests of the crown. The government thus decreed that the missionaries were to have ten years in which to convert the Indians after which control should pass to the diocesan clergy. This was protested by the missionary orders, and the conflict was resolved in favor of the diocesan priests finally in 1640 thanks to the efforts of Bishop Juan de Palafox de Mendoza of Puebla.

The alliance of the secular clergy with the government was a reflection of the control enjoyed by Spanish crown over the Church in Mexico. The Holy See had granted to the kings of Spain royal patronage over the Church in Mexico, and the practice of the *Patronato Real*, meant that the king nominated all Church officials in New Spain and held authority over the Church's temporal concerns. A major element in this policy was the forced conversion of the local peoples. Coerced into adopting the faith, many Indians were insincere or hesitant to embrace a faith that was forced upon them. To insure the full embrace of the faith, Spanish authorities received permission from King Philip II in 1569 to introduce the Inquisition to Mexico. Indians who had survived the mines, diseases, and brutality of the colonial rulers were now subjected to tribunals to test their faith. This practice was eventually ended when authorities decided that the natives were not culpable because of limited intelligence. Nevertheless, the close identification of the diocesan clergy with the interests and policies of the Spanish crown created a hostility toward the Church in Mexico by the lower classes that endures even today.

On the positive side, the Church did much through its missionaries to save many Indians from death and enslavement and to preserve vital portions of Mesoamerican culture, art, and history. Equally, friars traveled to northern Mexico and beyond, bringing the faith into California, Texas, and New Mexico.

The native peoples were given a profound encouragement to embrace the Catholic faith in 1531 by the appearance of Our Lady of Guadalupe to the farmer Juan Diego (beatified in 1990 by Pope John Paul II) on the Tepeyac hill just outside of Mexico City. The shrine built in her honor remains the most important religious site in Mexico. Enshrined within it is the mantle brought by Juan Diego to Bishop Zumaragga to convince him of the genuine nature of the apparition. Miraculously emblazoned upon it is the life-size image of the Virgin Mary.

MEXICAN INDEPENDENCE

The Spanish domination of Mexico endured for nearly three centuries, deteriorating gradually throughout the 1700s as the gulf widened between the Spanish ruling class and the native classes that were joined by the *mestizos* and *creoles* (descendants of Native Americans and Europeans). Unrest broke out into a full-scale rebellion in 1810 with the uprising of many priests led by Father Miguel Hidalgo y Costilla and, after his execution, by Father José Maria Morelos y Pavón. While suppressed in 1816 by the colonial regime, with the support of the upper classes and most of the diocesan clergy, it proved only the first of several revolts, culminating in the 1821 declaration of Mexican independence. By the terms of the independence, the Church received a special status and had enormous sway in political life.

A republic was proclaimed in 1834 and various liberal regimes came to power. Anticlericalism became commonplace, made even more strident by the lingering hostility over the Church's activities with Spanish colonial government. Much influenced by the ideals of the European revolutions then taking place, the Mexican republican movements were strongly anti-Catholic. For more than a decade, power was in the hands of Antonio López de Santa Anna (of the Alamo fame) and Valentin Gómez Farías. After the Mexican-American War (1846-1848), the political instability led to the dictatorship of Santa Anna.

Santa Anna was toppled in 1855 by a liberal regime whose anti-Church legislation sparked an armed struggle called the War of the Reform (1858-1861). The laws issued by the government included the *Ley Juárez*, abolishing all ecclesiastical courts, and the *Ley Lerdo*, forcing the Church to sell all of its lands. Deprived of its properties, the Church lost control of education and schools, and Mexico's educational system became often bitterly anti-Catholic.

While the liberal forces won the War of the Reform, the conflict had so debilitated Mexico that the French were able to intervene in 1861 and install their puppet, the Austrian duke Maximilian, on the Mexican throne. As the United States was embroiled in its own civil war from 1861-1865, it was unable to respond to French imperialist ambitions in Mexico. Maximilian initially enjoyed the support of the conservative elements and the Church, but his liberal reforms alienated the mistrustful conservatives and he soon clung to power only with French support. When France finally withdrew its troops in 1867, Maximilian was deposed by republican forces and executed.

MODERN MEXICO

The fall of Emperor Maximilian signaled a restoration of the anticlerical constitution of 1857 and the elevation of Benito Juárez – the republican leader long recognized by the United States – as president. His successor, Sebastián Lerdo de Tijada, was toppled in 1876 by Porfirio Diáz who remained dictator for thirty-four years. A civil war ended his regime, and more bloodshed ensued. Finally, a constitution was issued in 1917 that placed severe restrictions on the Church: there could be no criticism of the government, only Mexicans could be clergy, the Church was not permitted to own property, and any privileges were stripped away.

The situation became worse from 1923 when the papal legate was expelled. The administration of Plutarco Calles (1924-1928) launched a wave of persecution that sparked a popular but ultimately unsuccessful uprising called the Cristero Rebellion. Coupled with the repressive measures of local governments, the Calles regime and its successors forced the Church into very difficult circumstances, with only a few priests remaining in the country. The tragedy was deepened by the execution of dozens of priests and nuns by republican forces for assorted and imaginary crimes or for speaking out on behalf of the poor or oppressed Catholics. A number of the executed clergy have been beatified and canonized since the tragedy, most so during the pontificate of Pope John Paul II. The persecution prompted Pope Pius XI to issue the encyclicals *Iniquis afflictisque* (1926) and *Acerba animi* (1932).

An easing of the situation began in 1940 as the rigid anticlerical laws ceased to be enforced with enthusiasm. A rapprochement was visible in the 1958 elections, when the Church received conciliatory gestures from the ruling Revolutionary Party and its presidential candidate Adolfo López Mateos. The Church continued to exist under numerous legal disabilities and was oppressed in a number of the Mexican states.

Gradual improvement in relations between Mexico and the Holy See led to the exchange in 1990 of personal representatives between the Mexican president and Pope John Paul II. The Holy Father's efforts to build a further diplomatic bridge culminated in the establishment of full diplomatic ties in 1992. This was followed by the final easing of many of the handicaps under which the Church had long suffered.

The faith of the Mexican people is profoundly deep, as was seen in the nearly frenzied greeting given to Pope John Paul II in 1979, 1990, 1993, and 1999. However, social unrest, poverty, economic challenges, the violence of drug cartels, and corruption still plague the country. Church leaders – especially religious orders – have been outspoken in their criticism against government human rights abuses and corruption. During the mid-1990s, the Jesuits said they were the target of a "campaign of intimidation" because of their human rights work.

On May 24, 1993, Cardinal Juan Jesus Posadas

Ocampo of Guadalajara was killed during a supposed shoot-out among rival drug cartels. The murder remained unsolved, although Cardinal Posadas' successor, Cardinal Juan Sandoval Íñiguez, continued to claim that high-ranking officials, including the Mexican attorney general at the time, lied to protect others involved in a plot.

In the 1970s and 1980s, one of Mexico's most prominent proponents of liberation theology was Bishop Samuel Ruiz Garcia of San Cristobal de las Casas. In the early 1990s the Vatican began investigating his views, but because he had the trust of indigenous

peasants, in 1994 he was thrown into the role of mediator between the government and the mostly native Zapatista National Liberation Army in Chiapas. He continued that role until 1998, when he resigned after accusing the government of "dismantling any possible means or effort to solve the crisis in Chiapas." Mexico's bishops said at that time that they would provide support to the peace process but would not seek to mediate the conflict. Currently, the Church in Mexico faces threats of defections among Catholics to Evangelical Protestant sects and religious indifference.

ORGANIZATION

Presently, the Church in Mexico is organized into 14 provinces. There are 14 archdioceses, 56 dioceses, 7 prelacies, and 1 vicariate apostolic. As of August 15, 1999, there were four Mexican members of the College of Cardinals: Ernesto Corripio Ahumada, Norberto Rivera Carrera, Juan Sandoval Íñiguez, and Adolfo Antonio Suárez Rivera. (For statistical information on the Church in Mexico, see below.)

The current apostolic delegation to Mexico was set up in 1992 as a nunciature with the establishment of renewed formal diplomatic relations with the Vatican. The present Apostolic Nuncio is Archbishop Justo Mullor Garcia, appointed on Apr. 2, 1997.

ECCLESIASTICAL JURISDICTIONS OF MEXICO
Provinces
Names of ecclesiastical provinces and metropolitan sees in bold face: suffragan sees in parentheses.

Acapulco (Ciudad Lázaro Cárdenas, Chilpancingo-Chilapa, Ciudad Altamirano, Tlapa).

Chihuahua (Ciudad Juárez, Cuauhtémoc-Madera, Parral, Tarahumara).

Durango (Culiacán, Mazatlán, Torreón, El Salto).

Guadalajara (Aquascalientes, Autlán, Ciudad Guzmán, Colima, San Juan de los Lagos, Tepic, Zacatecas; Prelature of Jesús Maria del Nayar).

Hermosillo (Ciudad Obregón, La Paz, Mexicali, Tijuana).

México (Atlacomulco, Cuernavaca, Toluca, Tula, Tulancingo).

Monterrey (Ciudad Valles, Ciudad Victoria, Linares, Matamoros, Nuevo Laredo, Saltillo, Tampico, Nuevao Casas Grandes).

Morelia (Apatzingán, Tacámbaro, Zamora).

Oaxaca (San Cristóbal de las Casas, Tapachula, Tehuantepec, Tuxtla Gutiérrez, Tuxtepec; Prelacies of Mixes and Huautla).

Puebla de los Angeles (Huajuapan de León, Huejutla, Tehuacán, Tlaxcala).

San Luis Potosi (Celaya, León, Querétaro, Matehuala).

Tlalnepantla (Texcoco, Cuautitlán, Netzahualcóyotl, Ecatepec).

Xalapa (Papantla, San Andrés Tuxtla, Coatzacoalcos, Tuxpan, Veracruz).

Yucatán (Campeche, Tabasco, Prelacy of Cancún-Chetumal; Eparchy of Nuestra Señora del Paraiso).

Jurisdictions, Hierarchy
(Principal sources: Information office, Mexican Conference of Catholic Bishops; *Catholic Almanac*

survey; *Annuario Pontificio*; *L'Osservatore Romano*; Catholic News Service. As of June 1, 1999.)

Information includes names of archdioceses (indicated by asterisk) and dioceses, date of foundation, present ordinaries and auxiliaries; addresses of chancery office/bishop's residence.

Acapulco* (1958; promoted to archdiocese, 1983): Rafael Bello Ruiz, archbishop, 1976.

Diocesan Address: Apartado Postal 201, Quebrada 16, 39300 Acapulco, Guerrero.

Aquascalientes (1899): Rafael Muñoz Núñez, bishop, 1984.

Diocesan Address: Apartado 167, Galeana 105 Norte, 20000 Aquascalientes, Aquascalientes, Mexico.

Apatzingán (1962): Miguel Patiño Velázquez, M.S.F., bishop, 1981.

Diocesan Address: Apartado 100, Calle Esteban Baca Calderón 1, 60600 Apatzingán, Mich.

Atlacomulco (1984): vacant.

Diocesan Address: Hidalgo 1, Apartado 22, 50450 Atlacomulco, Méx.

Autlán (1961): Lázaro Pérez Jiménez, bishop, 1991.

Diocesan Address: Apartado 8, Hidalgo 74, 48900 Autlán, Jal., Mexico.

Campeche (1895): José Luis Amezcua Melgoza, bishop, 1995.

Diocesan Address: Calle 55, n. 5, Apartado 127, 24000 Campeche, Camp.

Cancún-Chetumal, Prelacy of (1970, as Chetumal; name changed to Cancún-Chetumal, 1996): Jorge Bernal Vargas, bishop, 1978.

Diocesan Address: Apartado Postal 165, Othón P. Blanco 150, 77000 Chetumal, Quintana Roo, Mexico.

Celaya (1973): Jesús Humberto Velázquez Garay, bishop, 1988.

Diocesan Address: Curia Diocesana, Apartado 207, Manuel Doblado 110, 38000 Celaya, Gto.

Chihuahua* (1891; promoted to archdiocese, 1958): José Fernández Arteaga, archbishop, 1991.

Diocesan Address: Apartado Postal 7, 31000 Chihuahua, Chihuahua.

Chilpancingo-Chilapa (1863): Efren Ramos Salazar, 1990.

Diocesan Address: Av. Revolución 500-A, 41100 Chilapa, Gro.

Ciudad Altamirano (1964): Carlos Garfias Merlos, bishop, 1996.

Diocesan Address: Juárez 18 Oriente, Apdo 17, 40660 Ciudad Altamirano, Gro.

Ciudad Guzmán (1972): Serafín Vásquez Elizalde, bishop, 1977.
Diocesan Address: Ramón Corona 26, Apartado 86, 49000 Ciudad Guzman, Jal.
Ciudad Juárez (1957): Renato Ascencio León, bishop, 1994.
Diocesan Address: Apartado Postal 188, 32000 Cd. Juárez, Chih., Mexico.
Ciudad Lázaro Cárdenas (1985): Salvador Flores Huerta, bishop, 1993.
Diocesan Address: Apartado 500, Av. Tamarindos 17 y Ciudad del Carmen, 60950 Ciudad Lázaro Cardenas, Mich.
Ciudad Obregón (1959): Vicente Garcia Bernal, bishop, 1988.
Diocesan Address: Apartado 402, Sonora 161 Norte, 85000 Ciudad Obregón, Son.
Ciudad Valles (1960): José Guadalupe Galván Galindo, bishop, 1994.
Diocesan Address: Calle 16 de Septiembre 726, Apartado 170, 79000 Ciudad Valles, S.L.P.
Ciudad Victoria (1964): Antonio González Sánchez, bishop, 1995.
Diocesan Address: Morelos 1046 entre 7 y 88, 87000 Ciudad Victoria, Tamps.
Coatzacoalcos (1984): Carlos Talavera Ramírez, bishop, 1984.
Diocesan Address: Apartado 513, Aldama 502, 96400 Coatzacoalcos, Ver.
Colima (1881): Gilberto Valbuena Sánchez, bishop, 1989.
Diocesan Address: Palacio Episcopal, Hidalgo 135, Apartado 1, 28000 Colima, Colima, Mexico.
Cuauhtémoc-Madera (1966): Juan Guillermo López Soto, bishop, 1995.
Diocesan Address: Apartado Postal 209, 31500 Cuauhtemoc, Chihuahua, Mexico.
Cuautitlán (1979): Manuel Samaniego Barriga, bishop, 1979.
Diocesan Address: Apartado 21, Sor Juana Inés de la Cruz 208, 54800 Cuautitlán de Romero Rubio, Méx.
Culiacán (1883 as Sinaloa; name changed to Culiacán, 1959): Benjamin Jiménez Hernández, bishop, 1993.
Diocesan Address: Apartado Postal 666, 80220 Culiacán, Sinaloa, Mexico.
Cuernavaca (1891): Luis Reynoso Cervantes, bishop, 1987.
Diocesan Address: Apartado 13, calles Hidalgo y Morelos, Anexo Catedral, 62000 Curenavaca, Mor.
Durango* (1620, promoted to archdiocese, 1891): José Trinidad Medel Pérez, archbishop, 1993.
Diocesan Address: Apartado Postal 116, 34000 Durango, Durango, Mexico.
Ecatepec (1993): Onésimo Cepeda Silva, bishop, 1995.
Diocesan Address: Plaza Principal s/n, San Cristóbal Centro, Apartado Postal 95, 55000 Ecatepec de Morelos, Méx.
El Salto, Prelacy of (1968): Manuel Mireles Vaquera, bishop, 1988.
Prelature Address: Apartado Postal 58, Col. Alvaro Obregón 382, 34950 El Salto, Durango, Mexico.
Guadalajara* (1548; promoted to archdiocese, 1863): Cardinal Juan Sandoval Íñiguez, archbishop, 1994.
Diocesan Address: Arzobispado, Apartado Postal 1-331, Calle Liceo 17, 44100 Guadalajara, Jal.

Hermosillo* (1779, as Sonora, promoted to an archdiocese, 1963): José Ulises Macias Salcedo, archbishop, 1996.
Diocesan Address: Apartado 1, Dr. Paliza 81, 83260 Hermosillo, Son.
Huajuapan de Leon (1903): bishop, vacant.
Diocesan Address: Apartado 43, Madero 8, 69000 Huajuapan de León, Oax.
Huautla, Prelacy of (1972): Hermengildo Ramirez Sánchez, M.J., bishop, 1978.
Diocesan Address: Casa Prelaticia, Apartado 2, 68500 Huautla de Jiménez, Oaxaca.
Huejutla (1922): Salvador Martínez Pérez, bishop, 1994.
Diocesan Address: Obispado, Apartado 8, Ave. Corona del Rosal s/n, 43000 Huejutla, Hgo.
Jesús María of Nayar, Prelature of (1962): José Antonio Pérez Sánchez, O.F.M., bishop, 1992.
Diocesan Address: Curia Prelaticia de Jesús María, Apartado 33-B, 63150 Tepic, Nayar.
La Paz (1988): BraulioRafael León Villegas, bishop, 1990.
Diocesan Address: Apartado 25, Revolución y 5 de Mayo, 23000 La Paz, Baja California Sur.
León (1863): José Guadalupe Martin Rábago, bishop, 1995.
Diocesan Address: Pedro Moreno 312, 37000 León, Gto.
Linares (1925): Ramón Calderón Batres, bishop, 1988.
Diocesan Address: Morelos y Antonio de Jesús Sacedón, Apartado 70, 67700 Linares, N.L.
Matamoros (1958): Francisco Javier Chavolla Ramos, bishop, 1991.
Diocesan Address: Apartado 70, Calle 5 Entre Morelos y González, 87351 Matamoros, Tamps.
Matehuala (1997): Rodrigo Aguilar Martínez, bishop, 1997.
Diocesan Address: Júarez 512 Sur, Apartado 40, 78700 Matehuala, S.L.P.
Mazatlán (1958): Rafael Barraza Sánchez, bishop, 1981.
Diocesan Address: Apartado Postal 1, Canizales y Benito Juárez, 82000 Mazatlán. Sin., Mexico.
Mexicali (1966): José Isidro Guerrero Macias, bishop, 1997.
Diocesan Address: Av. Morelos 192, Apartado 3-547, 21100 Mexicali B.C. Norte.
México* (1530, promoted to an archdiocese, 1546): Cardinal Norberto Rivera Carrera, archbishop, 1995.
Diocesan Address: Curia Arzobispal, Apartado Postal 24-433, Durango 90, Col. Roma, 06700 México D.F.
Mixes, Prelacy of (1964): Braulio Sánchez Fuentes, S.D.B., bishop, 1978.
Diocesan Address: Casa Prelaticia, C.P. 70283, Ayutla, Mixes, Oaxaca, Mexico.
Monterrey* (1777, as Linares o Nuevo León, promoted to an archdiocese, 1891): Cardinal Adolfo Antonio Suárez Rivera, archbishop, 1983.
Diocesan Address: Apartado 7, Zuazua 1100, 64000 Monterrey, N.L.
Morelia* (1536, as Michoacan, promoted to an archdiocese 1863, renamed Morelia, 1924): Alberto Suárez Inda, archbishop, 1995.
Diocesan Address: Apartado 17, 58000 Morelia, Mich.

Netzahualcóyotl (1979): José María Hernández González, bishop, 1989.

Diocesan Address: Apartado 89 4 Avenida con Bellas Artes, Col. Evolución, 57700 Cuidad Netzahualcóyotl, Méx.

Nuestra Señora del Paraiso, Eparchy of (Greek Melkites, 1988): Antonio Mouhanna, eparch, 1998.

Diocesan Address: Matías Romero 1014, Dpto. 601, Col. Del Valle, 3100 Mexico, D.F.

Nuevo Casas Grandes, Prelacy of (1977): Hilario Chávez Joya, bishop, 1977.

Diocesan Address: Apartado Postal 198, 31700 Nuevo Casas Grandes, Chihuahua.

Nuevo Laredo (1989): Ricardo Watty Urquidi, M.Sp.S., bishop, 1989.

Diocesan Address: Saltillo 206, Col. México, 88280 Nuevo Laredo, Tamps.

Oaxaca* (Also Antequera, 1535, promoted to archdiocese, 1891): Hector González Martínez, archbishop, 1993.

Diocesan Address: Independencia 700, Apartado Postal n. 31, 68000 Oaxaca, Oax.

Papantla (1922): Lorenzo Cárdenas Aregullin, bishop, 1980.

Diocesan Address: Apartado 27, Juárez 1102, 73800 Tezutlán, Pue.

Parral (1992): José Andrés Corrál Arredondo, bishop, 1992.

Diocesan Address: Apartado Postal 313, 33800 H. del Parral, Chihuahua.

Puebla de los Angeles* (1525, as Tlaxcala, renamed Puebla de los Angeles, 1903): Rosendo Huesca Pacheco, archbishop, 1977.

Diocesan Address: Apartado 235, Av. 2, Sur N. 305, 72000 Puebla, Pue.

Querétaro (1863): Mario de Gasperín Gasperín, bishop, 1989.

Diocesan Address: Apartado Postal 49, 76000 Querétaro, Qro.

Saltillo (1891): Francisco Raúl Villalobos Padilla, bishop, 1975.

Diocesan Address: Hidalgo Sur 166, Apartado 25, 25000 Saltillo, Coah.

San Andrés Tuxtla (1959): Guillermo Ranzahuer González, 1959.

Diocesan Address: Constitución y Morelos, 95700 San Andrés Tuxtla, Ver.

San Cristóbal de las Casas (1539, as Chiapas, renamed San Cristóbal de las Casas, 1964): Samuel Ruiz Garcia, bishop, 1960.

Diocesan Address: Calle 20 de Noviembre n. 1, 29000 San Cristóbal de las Casas, Chiapas.

San Juan de los Lagos (1972): Javier Navarro Rodríguez, bishop, 1999.

Diocesan Address: Morelos 30, Apartado N. 1, 47000 San Juan de los Lagos, Jal.

San Luis Potosí* (1854, promoted to an archdiocese, 1988): Luis Morales Reyes, archbishop, 1999.

Diocesan Address: Calle Francisco Madero N. 300, Apartado N. 1, 17800 San Luis Potosí, S.L.P.

Tabasco (1880): Florencio Olvera Ochoa, 1992.

Diocesan Address: Apartado Postal 97, Fidencia 502, 86000 Villahermosa, Tab.

Tacámbaro (1913): Rogelio Cabrera López, bishop, 1996.

Diocesan Address: Apartado 4, Profesor Enrique Aguilar 49, 61650 Tacámbaro, Mich.

Tampico (1870, as Ciudad Victoria o Tamaulipas, renamed as Tampico, 1958): Rafael Gallardo Garcia, bishop, 1987.

Diocesan Address: Apartado 545, Calle Altamira 116 Oriente, 89000 Tampico, Tamps.

Tapachula (1957): Felipe Arizmendi Esquivel, bishop, 1991.

Diocesan Address: Apartado 70, Av. Primera Sur 1, 30700 Tapachula, Chiapas.

Tarahumara (1957, as a vicariate apostolic, promoted to diocese, 1993): José Luis Dibildox Martinez, bishop, 1994.

Diocesan Address: Apartado Postal 11, 33190 Guachochi, Chihuahua.

Tehuacán (1962): Mario Espinosa Contreras, bishop, 1996.

Diocesan Address: Apartado Postal 137, Agustin A. Cacho 113, 75700 Tehuacán, Pue.

Tehuantepec (1891): Arturo Lona Reyes, bishop, 1971.

Diocesan Address: Apartado Postal 93, Av. Hidalgo 36, 70760 Tehuantepec, Oax.

Tepic (1891): Alfonso Humberto Robles Cota, bishop, 1981.

Diocesan Address: Apartado 15, Av. De las Flores 10, Fracción residencial La Loma, 63137 Tepic, Nay.

Texcoco (1960): Carlos Aguiar Retes, bishop, 1997.

Diocesan Address: Apartado Postal 35, Pedro de Gante 2, 56100 Texcoco, Méx.

Tijuana (1963): Rafael Romo Muñoz, bishop, 1996.

Diocesan Address: Apartado 226, Calle Décima y Av. Ocampo 8585, 22000 Tijuana, B.C.N.

Tlalnepantla* (1777, promoted to archdiocese, 1898): Ricardo Guizar Díaz, archbishop, 1996.

Diocesan Address: Apartado 268, Av. Juárez 42, 54000, Tlalnepantla, Méx.

Tlapa (1992): Alejo Zavala Castro, bishop, 1992.

Diocesan Address: Anexo Catedral, Centro, 41300 Tlapa de Comonfort, Gro.

Tlaxcala (1959): Luis Munive Escobar, bishop, 1959; Jacinto Guerrero Torres, coadjutor bishop, 1991.

Diocesan Address: Apartado 84, Lardizábal 45, 90000 Tlaxcala, Tlax.

Toluca (1950): Francisco Robles Ortega, bishop, 1996.

Diocesan Address: Apartado 82, Portal Reforma 104 Norte, 50000 Toluca, Méx.

Torreón (1958): bishop, vacant.

Diocesan Address: Apartado Postal 430, Av. Morelos 46 Poniente, 27000 Torreón, Coah.

Tula (1961): Octavio Villegas Aguilar, bishop, 1994.

Diocesan Address: 5 de Mayo, n. 5, Apartado 31, 42800 Tula de Allende, Hgo.

Tulancingo (1863): Pedro Aranda Díaz-Muñoz, bishop, 1975.

Diocesan Address: Apartado 14, Plaza de la Constitución, 43600 Tulancingo, Hgo.

Tuxpan (1962): Luis Gabriel Cuara Méndez, bishop, 1989.

Diocesan Address: Avda. Independencia 56, 92800 Tuxpan, Ver.

Tuxtepec (1979): José de Jesús Castillo Rentería, M.N.M., bishop, 1979.

Diocesan Address: Apartado Postal 9, Guerrero s/n, 68300 Tuxtepec, Oax.

Tuxtla Gutiérrez (1964): Felipe Aguirre Franco, bishop, 1988.

Diocesan Address: Templo de Santo Domingo de Guzman 1/a Poniente Norte 236, 29000 Tuxtla Gutiérrez, Chis.

Veracruz (1962): José Guadalupe Padilla Lozano, bishop, 1963.

Diocesan Address: Insurgentes Veracruzanos 470, 91700 Veracruz, Ver.

Xalapa* (1863, as Veracruz and Xalapa, promoted to archdiocese, 1951): Sergio Obeso Rivera, archbishop, 1979.

Diocesan Address: Apartado 359, Av. Manuel Avila Camacho 73, 91000 Xalapa, Ver.

Yucatán* (1561, promoted to archdiocese, 1906): Emilio Carlos Berlie Belaunzarán, archbishop, 1995.

Diocesan Address: Calle 58 N. 501, 97000 Mérida, Yuc.

Zacatecas (1863): Fernando Chávez Ruvalcaba, bishop, 1999.

Diocesan Address: Apartado 1, Miguel Auza 219, 98000 Zacatecas, Zacatecas, Mexico.

Zamora (1863): Carlos Suárez Cázares, bishop, 1994.

Diocesan Address: Apartado 18, Hidalgo 69 Sur, 59600 Zamora, Mich.

MEXICAN CONFERENCE OF CATHOLIC BISHOPS

(Sources: Annuario Pontificio*; Rev. Luis Barrera Flores, Adjunct Secretary,* Conferencia del Episcopado Mexicano*;* Conferencia del Episcopado Mexicano, Directorio, 1998-2000*; translation courtesy Suzanne Lea.)*

STRUCTURE

The Mexican Conference of Bishops (CEM) is the permanent body of Mexican bishops. The bishops adhere to the guidelines of the conference in specific fulfillment of their pastoral labors. They do this in order to obtain the greatest good for the people that the church can achieve.

The conference proposes:

1) To study the problems that occur in pastoral work, and to seek solutions.

2) To initiate, with a common end in mind and a common course of action, the forms and methods of preaching that best suit the needs of the country.

3) In regard to the collective salvific mission of the church: To look for and to teach the best way in which the respective activities of the deacons, priests, religious, and lay person will be most efficient.

4) To facilitate relations with the civil authority and with other organizations in specific cases.

5) To write to the Episcopal commission regarding patrimonial and proprietary matters, and give counsel on determined financial or labor related points.

All those elected to the body of the CEM will have three years of service and will not be reelected to the same position after two three year sessions have been completed consecutively.

Permanent Assembly

The Permanent Assembly is the representative arm of the bishops belonging to the CEM. Its function is to ensure the continuation of the works of the conference and the fulfillment of its accords.

The Permanent Assembly is comprised of the Presidential Assembly and the Assembly of Pastoral Regions.

The Permanent Assembly meets four times per year in ordinary session. It meets in extraordinary sessions whenever the majority of its members or those of the Presidential Assembly determine them to be necessary.

A session is valid if two-thirds of its members are present.

Officers

President: Bishop Luis Morales Reyes, of San Luis Potosí.

Vice-President: Bishop José Guadalupe Martin Rábago, of Léon.

Secretary General: Bishop Abelardo Alvarado Alcantara, Aux. of Mexico.

General Treasurer: Bishop José Guadalupe Galván Galindo, of Ciudad Valles.

Vocals: Archbishop Alberto Suárez Inda, of Morelia; Mario de Gasperín Gasperín, of Querataro.

Commissions

Section One:

Biblical Studies: Bishop Rogelio Cabrera López.

Doctrine: Bishop Lázaro Pérez Jiménez.

Education and Culture: Bishop Francisco Robles Ortega.

Evangelization: Bishop José Luis Chavez Botello.

Liturgy: Bishop Mario de Gasperín Gasperín.

Missions: Archbishop Ricardo Guizar Díaz.

Pastoral Sanctuaries: Bishop Efren Ramos Salazar.

Preaching: Bishop José Lizares Estrada.

Social Communications: Bishop Onésimo Cepeda Silva.

Social Justice: Bishop Jacinto Guerrero Torres.

Section Two:

Clergy: Archbishop Alberto Suárez Inda.

Consecrated Life: Bishop Ricardo Watty Urquidi, M.Sp.S.

Lay Apostolates: Bishop Carlos Talavera Ramírez.

Lay Ministry and Diaconate: Bishop José de Jesus Martinez Zepeda.

Priestly Formation: Bishop Benjamin Jiménez Hernández.

Seminaries and Vocations: Bishop Carlos Suárez Cázares.

STATISTICAL SUMMARY OF THE CATHOLIC CHURCH IN MEXICO

(*Principal sources:* Annuario Pontificio,*1999;* Conferencia del Epsicopado Mexicano, Directorio, 1998-2000; *figures as of January, 1999; Catholic population statistics are those reported in the most recent* Annuario *population estimates. Archdioceses are indicated by an asterisk.*)
Current ecclesiastical organization includes 14 provinces: 14 archdioceses, 56 dioceses, 7 prelacies, and 1 vicariate apostolic. The Catholic population of Mexico comprises approximately 90% of the overall Mexican population of 136,237,505. This table presents a provincial breakdown of Catholic statistics. In some cases, the totals are approximate because diocesan estimates are often considered unreliable owing to difficulties in adequate assessment of demographics and population distribution.

Province Diocese	Cath. Pop.	Dioc. Priests	Rel. Priests	Total Priests	Perm. Deacs.	Bro- thers	Sis- ters	Par- ishes[1]
Acapulco	5,242,869	276	43	319	16	62	400	234
Acapulco*	2,730,000	85	15	100	15	27	195	80
Ciudad Lázaro Cardenas	540,000	25	11	36	1	18	64	22
Chilpancingo-Chilapa	872,869	96	14	110	-	14	28	87
Ciudad Altamirano	650,000	49	3	52	-	3	91	25
Tlapa	450,000	21	-	21	-	-	22	20
Chihuahua	3,787,745	228	104	332	16	139	537	178
Chihuahua*	917,354	76	26	102	8	34	76	53
Ciudad Juárez	1,650,000	63	27	90	-	35	178	50
Cuauhtémoc -Madera	293,899	25	13	38	-	13	82	24
Nuevo Casas Grandes	207,000	19	9	28	-	13	31	21
Parral	476,280	31	8	39	8	10	57	16
Tarahumara	243,212	14	21	35	-	34	113	14
Durango	5,294,208	478	75	553	-	109	1073	267
Durango*	1,401,208	202	18	220	-	41	440	105
Culiacán	1,859,000	121	6	127	-	12	344	68
El Salto	280,000	12	-	12	-	-	22	14
Mazatlán	658,000	68	10	78	-	11	116	38
Torreón	1,096,000	75	41	116	-	45	151	42
Guadalajara	10,738,438	2,013	384	2,397	4	866	5,424	788
Guadalajara*	4,899,000	878	296	1,174	2	664	3,161	334
Aquascalientes	1,400,000	199	29	228	-	66	610	77
Autlán	296,434	103	-	103	1	-	166	39
Ciudad Guzmán	470,000	109	11	120	-	59	180	54
Colima	549,534	124	9	133	-	15	232	51
San Juan de los Lagos	991,391	239	16	255	-	27	437	57
Tepic	919,296	183	6	189	-	13	215	64
Zacatecas	1,040,783	169	5	174	-	7	399	97
Jesús Maria of Nayar, Prelature of	172,000	9	12	21	1	15	24	15
Hermosillo	6,666,963	429	156	585	5	278	1,075	253
Hermosillo*	1,034,000	119	3	122	1	8	107	58
Ciudad Obregón	1,552,000 76	26	102	1	36	105	50	
La Paz	359,000	32	28	60	1	31	189	22
Mexicali	1,589,963	74	32	106	-	53	140	41
Tijuana	2,132,000	128	67	195	2	150	534	82
México	26,456,654	1,305	1,094	2,399	55	2,496	5,107	693
Mexico*	19,678,000	718	972	1,690	51	2,348	4,558	406
Atlacomulco	784,110	57	5	62	2	6	85	40
Cuernavaca	1,776,000	112	53	165	1	71	14	98
Toluca	1,936,000	220	51	271	-	45	151	42
Tula	1,164,430	66	10	76	1	14	109	35
Tulancingo	1,118,114	132	3	135	-	12	190	72
Monterrey	10,110,347	712	217	929	9	392	1,846	433
Monterrey*	4,185,000	281	114	395	6	252	774	147
Ciudad Valles	800,000	49	14	63	-	14	130	35

Province Diocese	Cath. Pop.	Dioc. Priests	Rel. Priests	Total Priests	Perm. Deacs.	Bro- thers	Sis- sters	Par- ishes[1]
Monterey continued								
Ciudad Victoria	395,800	30	12	42	-	16	123	31
Linares	202,210	34	2	36	-	2	42	21
Matamoros	1,352,647	74	8	82	-	8	88	48
Nuevo Laredo	806,000	38	16	54	1	23	97	31
Saltillo	1,400,490	119	32	151	2	52	427	67
Tampico	968,200	87	19	106	-	25	165	53
Morelia	5,276,975	831	140	971	6	402	2,357	385
Morelia*	2,637,000	445	110	555	6	252	774	147
Apatzingán	646,000	50	3	53	-	66	610	77
Tacámbaro	375,129	75	2	77	-	2	129	40
Zamora	1,618,846	261	25	286	-	82	844	121
Oaxaca	6,693,524	369	139	508	361	171	1,001	316
Oaxaca*	1,472,100	144	40	184	14	51	276	126
San Cristobal de las Casas	974,336	24	30	54	311	37	157	38
Tapachula	1,027,616	53	9	62	-	9	143	37
Tehuantepec	1,286,000	44	8	52	-	9	120	33
Tuxtla Gutiérrez	1,000,000	69	14	83	-	19	239	36
Tuxtepec	639,000	22	12	34	17	13	25	22
Huautla, Prelacy of	104,972	8	4	12	-	7	5	7
Mixes, Prelacy of	189,500	5	22	27	19	26	36	17
Puebla de los Angeles	7,303,760	764	139	903	2	368	1,658	452
Puebla de los Angeles*	4,213,370	389	100	489	1	312	1,004	229
Huajuapan de León	597,000	98	-	98	-	-	135	68
Huejutla	480,383	77	9	86	-	9	68	38
Tehuacán	878,007	76	10	86	-	20	144	53
Tlaxcala	1,135,000	124	20	144	1	27	307	64
San Luis Potosi	6,812,911	753	314	1,067	9	550	3,410	324
San Luis Potosi*	1,643,694	178	46	224	9	95	740	72
Celaya	1,030,708	145	53	198	-	67	520	61
Leon	2,675,000	239	115	354	-	180	1,005	90
Matehuala	325,509	27	-	27	-	-	35	15
Querétaro	1,138,000	164	100	264	-	208	1,110	86
Tlalnepantla	14,538,840	694	185	879	51	464	1,001	462
Tlalnepantla*	3,057,840	212	80	292	7	133	284	120
Texcoco	2,550,000	124	12	136	24	22	268	70
Cuautitlan	1,536,000	128	46	174	-	195	249	73
Ecatepec	3,235,000	91	12	103	20	31	126	79
Netzahualcoyotl	4,160,000	139	35	174	-	83	74	120
Xalapa	9,259,650	553	50	603	27	62	1,084	334
Xalapa*	1,933,983	232	11	243	-	17	464	128
Coatzacoalcos	1,242,000	38	9	47	4	12	84	24
Papantla	1,752,667	92	2	94	-	5	155	41
San Andrés Tuxtla	841,000	49	2	51	20	2	97	35
Tuxpan	1,250,000	71	-	71	3	-	61	46
Veracruz	2,240,000	71	26	97	-	26	223	60
Yucatán	4,160,234	279	105	388	13	169	700	199
Yucatán*	1,390,625	152	39	191	11	55	311	88
Campeche	517,109	51	16	67	1	55	123	32
Tabasco	1,500,000	72	13	85	1	16	185	53
Cancún-Chetumal, Prelacy of	750,000	3	38	41	-	43	81	25
Nuestra Señora del Paraiso, Eparchy of	2,500	1	0	1	-	-	-	1
Totals:	122,343,118	9,684	3,145	12,829	574	6,528	26,673	5,318

CONSECRATED LIFE

INSTITUTES OF CONSECRATED LIFE

Religious institutes and congregations are special societies in the Church — institutes of consecrated life — whose members, called Religious, commit themselves, by public vows to observance of the evangelical counsels of poverty, chastity and obedience in a community kind of life in accordance with rules and constitutions approved by church authority.

Secular institutes (covered in its own Almanac entry) are also institutes of consecrated life.

The particular goal of each institute and the means of realizing it in practice are stated in the rule and constitutions proper to the institute. Local bishops can give approval for rules and constitutions of institutes of diocesan rank. Pontifical rank belongs to institutes approved by the Holy See. General jurisdiction over all Religious is exercised by the Congregation for Institutes of Consecrated Life and Societies of Apostolic Life. General legislation concerning Religious is contained in Canons 573 to 709 in Book II, Part III, of the Code of Canon Law.

All institutes of consecrated life are commonly called religious orders, despite the fact that there are differences between orders and congregations. The best known orders include the Benedictines, Trappists, Franciscans, Dominicans, Carmelites and Augustinians, for men; and the Carmelites, Benedictines, Poor Clares, Dominicans of the Second Order and Visitation Nuns, for women. The orders are older than the congregations, which did not appear until the 16th century.

Contemplative institutes are oriented to divine worship and service within the confines of their communities, by prayer, penitential practices, other spiritual activities and self-supporting work. Examples are the Trappists and Carthusians, the Carmelite and Poor Clare nuns. Active institutes are geared for pastoral ministry and various kinds of apostolic work. Mixed institutes combine elements of the contemplative and active ways of life. While most institutes of men and women can be classified as active, all of them have contemplative aspects.

Clerical communities of men are those whose membership is predominantly composed of priests.

Non-clerical or lay institutes of men are the various brotherhoods.

"The Consecrated Life and Its Role in the Church and in the World," was the topic of the ninth general assembly of the Synod of Bishops held Oct. 2 to 29, 1994.

Societies of Apostolic Life

Some of the institutes listed below have a special kind of status because their members, while living a common life like that which is characteristic of Religious, do not profess the vows of Religious. Examples are the Maryknoll Fathers, the Oratorians of St. Philip Neri, the Paulists and Sulpicians. They are called societies of apostolic life and are the subject of Canons 731 to 746 in the Code of Canon Law.

RELIGIOUS INSTITUTES OF MEN IN THE UNITED STATES

(Sources: *The Official Catholic Directory*; Catholic *Almanac* survey.)

Africa, Missionaries of, M. Afr.: Founded 1868 at Algiers by Cardinal Charles M. Lavigerie; known as White Fathers until 1984. Generalate, Rome Italy; U.S. headquarters, 1624 21st St. N.W., Washington, DC 20009. Missionary work in Africa.

African Missions, Society of, S.M.A.: Founded 1856, at Lyons, France, by Bishop Melchior de Marion Brésillac. Generalate, Rome, Italy; American province (1941), 23 Bliss Ave., Tenafly, NJ 07670. Missionary work.

Alexian Brothers, C.F.A.: Founded 14th century in western Germany and Belgium during the Black Plague. Motherhouse, Aachen, Germany; generalate, 198 James Blvd., Signal Mountain, TN 37377. Hospital and general health work.

Assumptionists (Augustinians of the Assumption), A.A.: Founded 1845, at Nimes, France, by Rev. Emmanuel d'Alzon; in U.S., 1946. General house, Rome, Italy; U.S. province, 330 Market St., Brighton, MA 02135. Educational, parochial, ecumenical, retreat, foreign mission work.

Atonement, Franciscan Friars of the, S.A.: Founded as an Anglican Franciscan community in 1898 at Garrison, N.Y., by Rev. Paul Wattson. Community corporately received into the Catholic Church in 1909. Generalate, St. James Friary, P.O. Box 5, Graymoor, Garrison NY 10524. Ecumenical, mission, retreat and charitable works.

Augustinian Recollects, O.A.R.: Founded 1588: in U.S., 1944. General motherhouse, Rome, Italy. Missionary, parochial, education work.

St. Augustine Province (1944), 29 Ridgeway Ave., W. Orange, NJ 07052.

St. Ezekiel House: U.S. Delegates, 2800 Schurz Ave., Bronx, NY 10465 (New York); P.O. Box 310, Mesilla, NM 88044 (South).

Augustinians (Order of St. Augustine), O.S.A.: Established canonically in 1256 by Pope Alexander IV; in U.S., 1796. General motherhouse, Rome, Italy.

St. Thomas of Villanova Province (1796), P.O. Box 340, Villanova, PA 19085-0340.

Our Mother of Good Counsel Province (1941), Tolentine Center, 20300 Governors Hwy., Olympia Fields, IL 60461.

St. Augustine, Province of (1969), 1605 28th St., San Diego, CA 92102.

U.S. Address of King City, Ont., Canada, Province: Mother of Consolation Monastery.

U.S. Region of Castile, Spain, Province (1963), Vicar, 3648 61st St., Port Arthur, TX 77642.

Barnabites (Clerics Regular of St. Paul), C.R.S.P.: Founded 1530, in Milan, Italy, by St. Anthony M. Zaccaria; approved 1533; in U.S., 1952. Historical motherhouse, Church of St. Barnabas (Milan). Generalate, Rome, Italy; North American province, P.O. Box 167, Youngstown, NY 14174. Parochial, educational, mission work.

Basil the Great, Order of St. (Basilian Order of St. Josaphat), O.S.B.M.: General motherhouse, Rome, Italy; U.S. province, 31-12 30th St., Long Island City, NY 11106. Parochial work among Byzantine Ukrainian Rite Catholics.

Basilian Fathers (Congregation of the Priests of St. Basil), C.S.B.: Founded 1822, at Annonay, France. General motherhouse, Toronto, Ont., Canada. U.S. addresses: 445 King's Hwy., Rochester, NY 14617 (East); 4500 Memorial Dr., Houston, TX 77007 (West). Educational, parochial work.

Basilian Salvatorian Fathers, B.S.O.: Founded 1684, at Saida, Lebanon, by Eftimios Saifi; in U.S., 1953. General motherhouse, Saida, Lebanon; American headquarters, 30 East St., Methuen, MA 01844. Educational, parochial work among Eastern Rite peoples.

Benedictine Monks (Order of St. Benedict), O.S.B.: Founded 529, in Italy, by St. Benedict of Nursia; in U.S., 1846.

• **American Cassinese Congregation** (1855). Pres., Rt. Rev. Melvin J. Valvano, O.S.B., Newark Abbey, 528 Dr. Martin Luther King Blvd., Newark, NJ 07102. Abbeys and Priories belonging to the congregation: St. Vincent Archabbey, 300 Fraser Purchase Rd., Latrobe, PA 15650; St. John's Abbey, P.O. Box 2015, Collegeville, MN 56321; St. Benedict's Abbey, Atchison, KS 66002; St. Mary's Abbey, Delbarton, Morristown, NJ 07960; Newark Abbey, 528 Dr. Martin Luther King, Jr., Blvd., Newark, NJ 07102; Belmont Abbey, 100 Belmont - Mt. Holly Rd., Belmont, NC 28012; St. Bernard Abbey, Cullman, AL 35055; St. Procopius Abbey, 5601 College Rd., Lisle, IL 60532; St. Gregory's Abbey, Shawnee, OK 74801; St. Leo Abbey, St. Leo, FL 33574; Assumption Abbey, P.O. Box A, Richardton, ND 58652;

St. Bede Abbey, Peru, IL 61354; St. Martin's Abbey, 5300 Pacific Ave. S.E., Lacey, WA 98503-1297; Holy Cross Abbey, P.O. Box 1510, Canon City, CO 81215; St. Anselm's Abbey, 100 St. Anselm Dr., Manchester, NH 03102; St. Andrew Abbey, 10510 Buckeye Rd., Cleveland, OH 44104-3725; Holy Trinity Priory, P.O. Box 990, Butler, PA 16003; St. Maur Priory, 4615 N. Michigan Rd., Indianapolis, IN 46208; Benedictine Priory, 6502 Seawright Dr., Savannah, GA 31406; Woodside Priory, 302 Portola Rd., Portola Valley, CA 94028; Mary Mother of the Church Abbey, 12617 River Rd., Richmond, VA 23233; Abadia de San Antonio Abad, P.O. Box 729, Humacao, PR 00792.

• **Swiss-American Congregation** (1870). Abbeys and priory belonging to the congregation: St. Meinrad Archabbey, St. Meinrad, IN 47577; Conception Abbey, P.O. Box 501, Conception, MO 64433-0501; Mt. Michael Abbey, 22520 Mt. Michael Rd., Elkhorn, NE 68022; Subiaco Abbey, Subiaco, AR 72865; St. Joseph's Abbey, St. Benedict, LA 70457; Mt. Angel Abbey, St. Benedict, OR 97373; Marmion Abbey, Butterfield Rd., Aurora, IL 60504;

St. Benedict's Abbey, Benet Lake, WI 53102; Glastonbury Abbey, 16 Hull St., Hingham, MA 02043; Blue Cloud Abbey, Marvin, SD 57251-0098; Corpus Christi Abbey, HCR2, Box 6300, Sandia, TX 78383; Prince of Peace Abbey, 650 Benet Hill Rd., Oceanside, CA 92054; St. Benedict Abbey, 252 Still River Rd., PO Box 67, Still River (Harvard), MA 01467.

• **Congregation of St. Ottilien for Foreign Missions:** St. Paul's Abbey, Newton, NJ 07860; Christ the King Priory, P.O. Box 528, Schuyler, NE 68661.

• **Congregation of the Annunciation**, St. Andrew Abbey, P.O. Box 40, Valyermo, CA 93563-0042.

• **English Benedictine Congregation:** St. Anselm's Abbey, 4501 S. Dakota Ave. N.E., Washington, DC 20017; Abbey of St. Gregory the Great, Cory's Lane, Portsmouth, RI 02871-1352; Abbey of St. Mary and St. Louis, 500 S. Mason Rd., St. Louis, MO 63141.
• **Houses not in Congregations:** Mount Saviour Monastery, 231 Monastery Rd., Pine City, NY 14871-9787; Conventual Priory of St. Gabriel the Archangel, 58 Priory Hill Rd., Weston, VT 05161-6400.

Benedictines, Camaldolese Congregation, O.S.B. Cam.: Founded 1012, at Camaldoli, near Arezzo, Italy, by St. Romuald; in U.S. 1958. General motherhouse, Arezzo, Italy; U.S. foundation, New Camaldoli Hermitage, Big Sur, CA 93920.

Benedictines, Olivetan, O.S.B.: General motherhouse, Siena, Italy. U.S. monasteries, Our Lady of Guadalupe Abbey, Pecos, NM 87552; Holy Trinity Monastery, P.O. Box 298, St. David, AZ 85630-0298; Monastery of the Risen Christ, P.O. Box 3931, San Luis Obispo, CA 93403; Benedictine Monastery of Hawaii, P.O. Box 490, Waialua, Hawaii 96791.

Benedictines, Subiaco Congregation, O.S.B.: Independent priory, 1983. Monastery of Christ in the Desert, Abiquiu, NM 87510; St, Mary's Monastery, P.O. Box 345, Petersham, MA 01366.

Benedictines, Sylvestrine, O.S.B.: Founded 1231, in Italy by Sylvester Gozzolini. General motherhouse, Rome, Italy; U.S. foundations; 17320 Rosemont Rd., Detroit, MI 48219; 2711 E. Drahner Rd., Oxford, MI 48051; 1697 State Highway 3, Clifton, NJ 07012.

Blessed Sacrament, Congregation of the, S.S.S.: Founded 1856, at Paris, France, by St. Pierre Julien Eymard; in U.S., 1900. General motherhouse, Rome, Italy; U.S. province, 5384 Wilson Mills Rd., Cleveland, OH 44143. Eucharistic apostolate.

Brigittine Monks (Order of the Most Holy Savior), O.Ss.S.: Monastery of Our Lady of Consolation, 23300 Walker Lane, Amity, OR 97101.

Camaldolese Hermits of the Congregation of Monte Corona, Er. Cam.: Founded 1520, from Camaldoli, Italy, by Bl. Paul Giustiniani. General motherhouse, Frascati (Rome), Italy; U.S. foundation, Holy Family Hermitage, 1501 Fairplay Rd., Bloomingdale, OH 43910-7971.

Camillian Fathers and Brothers (Order of St. Camillus; Order of Servants of the Sick), O.S.Cam.: Founded 1582, at Rome, by St. Camillus de Lellis; in U.S., 1923. General motherhouse, Rome, Italy; North American province, 10101 W. Wisconsin Ave., Wauwatosa, WI 53226.

Carmelites (Order of Our Lady of Mt. Carmel), O. Carm.: General motherhouse, Rome, Italy. Educational, charitable work.

Most Pure Heart of Mary Province (1864), 1317 Frontage Rd., Darien, IL 60559.

North American Province of St. Elias (1931), P.O. Box 3079, Middletown, NY 10940-0890.

Mt. Carmel Hermitage, Pineland, R.D. 3, Box 36, New Florence, PA 15944.

Carmelites, Order of Discalced, O.C.D.: Established 1562, a Reform Order of Our Lady of Mt. Carmel; in U.S., 1924. Generalate, Rome, Italy. Spiritual direction, retreat, parochial work.

California-Arizona Province, Central Office (1983), 926 E. Highland Ave., P.O. Box 2178, Redlands, CA 92373.

Province of St. Thérèse (Oklahoma,1935), 515 Marylake Dr., Little Rock AR 72206.

Immaculate Heart of Mary Province (1947), 1233 S. 45th St., Milwaukee, WI 53214.

Polish Province of the Holy Spirit (1949), 1628 Ridge Rd., Munster, IN 46321.

Carmelites of Mary Immaculate, C.M.I.: Founded 1831, in India, by Bl. Kuriakose Elias Chavara and two other Syro-Malabar priests; canonically established, 1855. Generalate, Kerala, India; North American headquarters, Holy Family Church, 21 Nassau Ave., Brooklyn, NY 11222.

Carthusians, Order of, O. Cart.: Founded 1084, in France, by St. Bruno; in U.S., 1951. General motherhouse, St. Pierre de Chartreuse, France; U.S. charterhouse of the Transfiguration, R.R. 2, Box 2411, Arlington, VT 05250. Cloistered contemplatives; semi-eremitic.

Charity, Brothers of, F.C.: Founded 1807, in Belgium, by Canon Peter J. Triest. General motherhouse, Rome, Italy: American District (1963), 7720 Doe Lane, Laverock, PA 19038.

Charity, Servants of (Guanellians), S.C.: Founded 1908, in Italy, by Bl. Luigi Guanella. General motherhouse, Rome, Italy; U.S. headquarters, St. Louis School, 16195 Old U.S. 12, Chelsea, MI 48118.

Christ, Society of, S.Ch.: Founded 1932, General Motherhouse, Poznan, Poland; U.S.-Canadian Province, 3000 Eighteen Mile Rd., Sterling Heights, MI 48311.

Christian Brothers, Congregation of, C.F.C. (formerly Christian Brothers of Ireland): Founded 1802 at Waterford, Ireland, by Bl. Edmund Ignatius Rice; in U.S., 1906. General motherhouse, Rome, Italy. Educational work.

American Province, Eastern U.S. (1916), 21 Pryer Terr., New Rochelle, NY 10804.

Brother Rice Province, Western U.S. (1966), 958 Western Ave., Joliet, IL 60435.

Christian Instruction, Brothers of (La Mennais Brothers), F.I.C.: Founded 1817, at Ploermel, France, by Abbe Jean Marie de la Mennais and Abbe Gabriel Deshayes. General motherhouse, Rome, Italy; American province, Notre Dame Institute, P.O. Box 159, Alfred, ME 04002.

Christian Schools, Brothers of the (Christian Brothers), F.S.C.: Founded 1680, at Reims, France, by St. Jean Baptiste de la Salle. General motherhouse, Rome, Italy; U.S. Conference, 4351 Garden City Dr., Suite 200, Landover, MD 20785. Educational, charitable work.

Baltimore Province (1845), Box 29, Adamstown, MD 21710.

Brothers of the Christian Schools (Midwest Province) (1995), 7650 S. County Line Rd., Burr Ridge, IL 60521-6950.

New York Province (1848), 800 Newman Springs Rd., Lincroft, NJ 07738.

Long Island-New England Province (1957), Christian Brothers Center, 635 Ocean Rd., Narragansett, RI 02882-1314.

San Francisco Province (1868), P.O. Box 3720, Napa, CA 94558.

New Orleans-Santa Fe Province (1921), De La Salle Christian Brothers, 1522 Carmel Dr., Lafayette, LA 70501.

Cistercians, Order of, O.Cist.: Founded 1098, by St. Robert. Headquarters, Rome, Italy.
Our Lady of Spring Bank Abbey, 17304 Havenwood Rd., Sparta, WI 54656-8177.
Our Lady of Dallas Monastery, 1 Cistercian Rd., Irving, TX 75039.
Cistercian Monastery, 564 Walton Ave., Mt. Laurel, NJ 08054.
Cistercian Conventual Priory, St. Mary's Priory, R.D. 1, Box 206, New Ringgold, PA 17960.
Cistercians of the Strict Observance, Order of (Trappists), O.C.S.O.: Founded 1098, in France, by St. Robert; in U.S., 1848. Generalate, Rome, Italy.
Our Lady of Gethsemani Abbey (1848), Trappist, KY 40051.
Our Lady of New Melleray Abbey (1849), 6500 Melleray Circle, Peosta, IA 52068.
St. Joseph's Abbey (1825), Spencer, MA 01562.
Holy Spirit Monastery (1944), 2625 Hwy. 212 S.W., Conyers, GA 30208.
Our Lady of Guadalupe Abbey (1947), P.O. Box 97, Lafayette, OR 97127.
Our Lady of the Holy Trinity Abbey (1947), 1250 South 9500 East, Huntsville, UT 84317.
Abbey of the Genesee (1951), P.O. Box 900, Piffard, NY 14533.
Mepkin Abbey (1949), 1098 Mepkin Abbey Rd., Moncks Corner, SC 29461-4796.
Our Lady of the Holy Cross Abbey (1950), 901 Cool Spring Lane, Berryville, VA 22611.
Assumption Abbey (1950), Rt. 5, Box 1056, Ava, MO 65608.
Abbey of New Clairvaux (1955), Vina, CA 96092.
St. Benedict's Monastery (1956), 1012 Monastery Rd., Snowmass, CO 81654.
Claretians (Missionary Sons of the Immaculate Heart of Mary), C.M.F.: Founded 1849, at Vich, Spain, by St. Anthony Mary Claret. General headquarters, Rome, Italy. Missionary, parochial, educational, retreat work.
Western Province, 1119 Westchester Pl., Los Angeles, CA 90019-3523.
Eastern Province, 400 N. Euclid Ave. Oak Park, IL 60302.
Clerics Regular Minor (Adorno Fathers) C.R.M.: Founded 1588, at Naples, Italy, by Ven. Augustine Adorno and St. Francis Caracciolo. General motherhouse, Rome, Italy; U.S. address, 575 Darlington Ave., Ramsey, NJ 07446.
Columban, Society of St. (St. Columban Foreign Mission Society), S.S.C.: Founded 1918. General headquarters, Dublin, Ireland. U.S. headquarters., P.O. Box 10, St. Columbans, NE 68056. Foreign mission work.
Comboni Missionaries of the Heart of Jesus (Verona Fathers), M.C.C.J.: Founded 1867, in Italy by Bl. Daniel Comboni; in U.S., 1939. General motherhouse, Rome, Italy; North American headquarters, Comboni Mission Center, 8108 Beechmont Ave., Cincinnati, OH 45255. Mission work in Africa and the Americas.
Consolata Missionaries, I.M.C.: Founded 1901, at Turin, Italy, by Bl. Joseph Allamano. General motherhouse, Rome, Italy; U.S. headquarters, P.O. Box 5550, 2301 Rt. 27, Somerset, NJ 08875.
Crosier Fathers (Canons Regular of the Order of the Holy Cross), O.S.C.: Founded 1210, in Bel-

gium by Bl. Theodore De Celles. Generalate, Rome, Italy; U.S. Province of St. Odilia, 3510 Vivian Ave., Shoreview, MN 55126-3852. Mission, retreat, educational work.
Cross, Brothers of the Congregation of Holy, C.S.C.: Founded 1837, in France, by Rev. Basil Moreau; U.S. province, 1841. Generalate, Rome, Italy. Educational, social work; missions.
Midwest Province (1841), Box 460, Notre Dame, IN 46556.
Southwest Province (1956), St. Edward's University, 1101 St. Edward's Dr., Austin, TX 78704-6512.
Eastern Province (1956), 85 Overlook Circle, New Rochelle, NY 10804.
Cross, Congregation of Holy, C.S.C.: Founded 1837, in France; in U.S., 1841. Generalate, Rome, Italy. Educational and pastoral work; home missions and retreats; foreign missions; social services and apostolate of the press.
Indiana Province (1841), 1304 E. Jefferson Blvd., South Bend, IN 46617.
Eastern Province (1952), 835 Clinton Ave., Bridgeport, CT 06604-2393.
Southern Province (1968), 2111 Brackenridge St., Austin, TX 78704.
Divine Word, Society of the, S.V.D.: Founded 1875, in Holland, by Bl. Arnold Janssen. North American Province founded 1897 with headquarters in Techny, IL General motherhouse, Rome, Italy.
Province of Bl. Joseph Freinademetz (Chicago Province) (1985, from merger of Eastern and Northern provinces), 1985 Waukegan Rd., Techny, IL 60082.
St. Augustine (Southern Province) (1940), 201 Ruella Ave., Bay St. Louis, MS 39520.
St. Therese of the Child Jesus (Western Province) (1964), 2737 Pleasant St., Riverside, CA 92507.
Dominicans (Order of Friars Preachers), O.P.: Founded early 13th century by St. Dominic de Guzman. General headquarters, Santa Sabina, Rome, Italy. Preaching, teaching, missions, research, parishes.
Eastern Province of St. Joseph (1805), 869 Lexington Ave., New York, NY 10021-6680.
Most Holy Name of Jesus (Western) Province (1912), 5877 Birch Ct., Oakland, CA 94618.
St. Albert the Great (Central) Province (1939), 1909 S. Ashland Ave., Chicago, IL 60608.
Southern Dominican Province (1979), 1421 N. Causeway Blvd., Suite 200, Metairie, LA 70001-4144.
Spanish Province, U.S. foundation (1926), P.O. Box 279, San Diego, TX 78384.
Edmund, Society of St., S.S.E.: Founded 1843, in France, by Fr. Jean Baptiste Muard. General motherhouse, Edmundite Generalate, 270 Winooski Park, Colchester, VT 05439-0270. Educational, missionary work.
Eudists (Congregation of Jesus and Mary), C.J.M.: Founded 1643, in France, by St. John Eudes. General motherhouse, Rome, Italy; North American province, 6125 Premiere Ave., Charlesbourg, Que. G1H 2V9, Canada; U.S. community, 36 Flohr Ave., Seneca, N.Y. 14224. Parochial, educational, pastoral, missionary work.
Francis, Brothers of Poor of St., C.F.P.: Founded 1857. Motherhouse, Aachen, Germany; U.S. province, P.O. Box 187, Burlington, IA 52601. Educational work, especially with poor and neglected youth.

Francis, Third Order Regular of St., T.O.R.:
Founded 1221, in Italy; in U.S., 1910. General
motherhouse, Rome, Italy. Educational, parochial,
missionary work.

Most Sacred Heart of Jesus Province (1910), 215
57th St., Pittsburgh, PA 15201.

Immaculate Conception Province (1925), 2400 Dike
Rd., Winter Park, FL 32792.

St. Francis on the Brazos Parish (former Commissariat of the Spanish Province, 1924), 301 Jefferson
Ave., Waco, TX 76701-1419.

Francis de Sales, Oblates of St., O.S.F.S.: Founded
1871, by Fr. Louis Brisson. General motherhouse,
Rome, Italy. Educational, missionary, parochial work.

Wilmington-Philadelphia Province (1906), 2200
Kentmere Parkway, Box 1452, Wilmington, DE
19899.

Toledo-Detroit Province (1966), 2056 Parkwood
Ave., Toledo, OH 43620.

**Francis Xavier, Brothers of St. (Xaverian Broth-
ers),** C.F.X.: Founded 1839, in Belgium, by Theodore
J. Ryken. Generalate, Twickenham, Middlesex, England. Educational work.

Sacred Heart Province, 10318-B Baltimore National
Pike, Ellicott City, MD 21043.

St. Joseph Province, 704 Brush Hill Rd., Milton,
MA 02186.

Franciscan Brothers of Brooklyn, O.S.F.: Founded
in Ireland; established at Brooklyn, 1858. Generalate,
135 Remsen St., Brooklyn, NY 11201. Educational
work.

Franciscan Brothers of Christ the King, O.S.F.:
Founded 1961. General motherhouse, 2707 N. U.S.
Hwy 35, LaPorte, IN 46350.

Franciscan Brothers of the Holy Cross, F.F.S.C.:
Founded 1862, in Germany. Generalate, Hausen, Linz
Rhein, Germany; U.S. region, 2500 St. James Rd.,
Springfield, IL 62707. Educational work.

**Franciscan Brothers of the Third Order Regu-
lar, O.S.F.:** Generalate, Mountbellew, Ireland; U.S.
region, 2117 Spyglass Trail W., Oxnard, CA 93030.
(Mailing address: 4522 Gainsborough Ave., Los Angeles, CA 90029.)

Franciscan Friars of the Immaculate, F.F.I:
Founded 1990, Italy. General motherhouse,
Benevento, Italy. U.S. addresses, 600 Pleasant St.,
New Bedford, MA. 02740; 22 School Hill Rd., Bal-
tic, CT 06330.

Franciscan Friars of the Renewal, C.F.R.: Community established under jurisdiction of the archbishop of New York. Central House, St. Crispin Friary, 420 E. 156th St., Bronx, NY 10455.

**Franciscan Missionary Brothers of the Sacred
Heart of Jesus, O.S.F.:** Founded 1927, in the St.
Louis archdiocese. Motherhouse, St. Joseph Rd.,
Eureka, MO 63025. Care of aged, infirm, homeless
men and boys.

Franciscans (Order of Friars Minor), O.F.M.: A
family of the First Order of St. Francis (of Assisi)
founded in 1209 and established as a separate jurisdiction in 1517; in U.S., 1844. General headquarters,
Rome, Italy. English-speaking conference:, 3140
Meramec St., St. Louis, MO 63118. Preaching, missionary, educational, parochial, charitable work.

Immaculate Conception Province (1855), 125 Thompson St., New York, NY 10012.

Sacred Heart Province, Franciscan Missionary

Union (1858), 3140 Meramec St., St. Louis, MO
63118.

Assumption of the Blessed Virgin Mary Province
(1887), Pulaski, WI 54162.

Most Holy Name of Jesus Province (1901), 126 W.
32nd St., New York, NY 10001.

St. Barbara Province (1915), 1500 34th Ave., Oakland, CA 94601.

Our Lady of Guadalupe Province (1985), 1350
Lakeview Rd. S.W., Albuquerque, NM 87105.

Holy Cross Custody (1912), 14246 Main St., P.O.
Box 608, Lemont, IL 60439.

Most Holy Savior Vice-Province, 232 S. Home Ave.,
Pittsburgh, PA 15202.

Mt. Alverna Friary, 517 S. Belle Vista Ave., Youngstown, OH 44509.

Holy Family Croatian Custody (1926), 4848 S. Ellis
Ave., Chicago, IL 60615.

St. Casimir Lithuanian Vice-Province, P.O. Box 980,
Kennebunkport, ME 04046.

Holy Gospel Province (Mexico), U.S. foundation,
2400 Marr St., El Paso, TX 79903.

Commissariat of the Holy Land, Mt. St. Sepulchre,
1400 Quincy St. N.E., Washington, DC 20017.

Holy Dormition Friary, Byzantine Slavonic Rite,
P.O. Box 270, Sybertsville, PA 18251.

Academy of American Franciscan History, 1712
Euclid Ave., Berkeley, CA 94709.

Franciscans (Order of Friars Minor Capuchin),
O.F.M. Cap.: A family of the First Order of St. Francis
(of Assisi) founded in 1209 and established as a separate jurisdiction in 1528. General motherhouse, Rome,
Italy. Missionary, parochial work, chaplaincies.

St. Joseph Province (1857), 1740 Mt. Elliott Ave.,
Detroit, MI 48207.

St. Augustine Province (1873), 220 37th St., Pittsburgh, PA 15201.

St. Mary Province (1952), 30 Gedney Park Dr.,
White Plains, NY 10605.

Province of the Stigmata (1918), P.O. Box 809,
Union City, NJ 07087.

Western American Capuchin Province, Our Lady
of the Angels, 1345 Cortez Ave., Burlingame, CA
94010.

St. Stanislaus Friary (1948), 2 Manor Dr., Oak
Ridge, NJ 07438.

Province of Mid-America (1977), 3553 Wyandot St.,
Denver, CO 80211.

Vice-Province of Texas, 2601 Singleton Blvd., Dallas, TX 75212.

St. John the Baptist Vice-Province, 216 Arzuaga St.,
P.O. Box 21350, Rio Piedras, Puerto Rico 00928.

Franciscans (Order of Friars Minor Conventual),
O.F.M. Conv.: A family of the First Order of St.
Francis (of Assisi) founded in 1209 and established
as a separate jurisdiction in 1517; first U.S. foundation, 1852. General curia, Rome, Italy. Missionary,
educational, parochial work.

Immaculate Conception Province (1852), Immaculate Conception Friary, P.O. Box 629, Rensselaer, NY
12144.

St. Anthony of Padua Province (1906), 12300 Folly
Quarter Rd., Ellicott City, MD 21042.

St. Bonaventure Province (1939), 6107 Kenmore
Ave., Chicago, IL 60660.

Our Lady of Consolation Province (1926), 101 Anthony Dr., Mt. St. Francis, IN 47146.

St. Joseph of Cupertino Province (1981), P.O. Box 820, Arroyo Grande, CA 93421.

Glenmary Missioners (The Home Missioners of America): Founded 1939, in U.S. General headquarters, P.O. Box 465618, Cincinnati, OH 45246. Home mission work.

Good Shepherd, Little Brothers of the, B.G.S.: Founded 1951, by Bro. Mathias Barrett. Foundation House, P.O. Box 389, Albuquerque, NM 87103. General headquarters, Hamilton, Ont., Canada. Operate shelters and refuges for aged and homeless; homes for handicapped men and boys, alcoholic rehabilitation center.

Holy Eucharist, Brothers of the, F.S.E.: Founded in U.S., 1957. Generalate, P.O. Box 25, Plaucheville, LA 71362. Teaching, social, clerical, nursing work.

Holy Family, Congregation of the Missionaries of the, M.S.F.: Founded 1895, in Holland, by Rev. John P. Berthier. General motherhouse, Rome, Italy; U.S. provincialate, 10415 Midland Blvd., St. Louis, MO 63114. Belated vocations for the missions.

Holy Family, Sons of the, S.F.: Founded 1864, at Barcelona, Spain, by Bl. Jose Mañanet y Vives; in U.S., 1920. General motherhouse, Barcelona, Spain; U.S. address, 401 Randolph Rd., P.O. Box 4138, Silver Spring, MD 20904.

Holy Ghost Fathers, C.S.Sp.: Founded 1703, in Paris, by Claude Francois Poullart des Places; in U.S., 1872. Generalate, Rome, Italy. Missions, education.

Eastern Province (1872), 6230 Brush Run Rd., Bethel Park, PA 15102. Western Province (1964), 1700 W. Alabama St., Houston, TX 77098.

Holy Ghost Fathers of Ireland (1971), U.S. delegates: 4849 37th St., Long Island City, NY 11101 (East); St. Dunstan's Church, 1133 Broadway, Mill Brae, CA 94030 (West); St. John Baptist Church, 1139 Dryades St., New Orleans, LA 70113.

Holy Spirit, Missionaries of the, M.Sp.S.: Founded 1914, at Mexico City, Mexico, by Felix Rougier. General motherhouse, Mexico City; U.S. headquarters, Our Lady of Guadalupe, 500 N. Juanita Ave., P.O. Box 1091, Oxnard, CA 93030. Missionary work.

Immaculate Heart of Mary, Brothers of the, I.H.M.: Founded 1948, at Steubenville, Ohio, by Bishop John K. Mussio. Motherhouse, 609 N. 7th St., Steubenville, OH 43952. Educational, charitable work.

Jesuits (Society of Jesus), S.J.: Founded 1534, in France, by St. Ignatius of Loyola; received papal approval, 1540; suppressed in 1773 and revived in 1814 by Pope Pius VII; first U.S. province, 1833. The Jesuits remain the largest single order in the Church. Generalate, Rome, Italy; U.S. national office, Jesuit Conference, 1616 P Street, Suite 400, Washington, DC 20036. Missionary, educational, literary work.

Maryland Province (1833), 5704 Roland Ave., Baltimore, MD 21210.

New York Province (1943), 39 East 83rd St., New York, NY 10028.

Missouri Province (1863), 4511 W. Pine Blvd., St. Louis, MO 63108-2191.

New Orleans Province (1907), 500 S. Jefferson Davis Pkwy., New Orleans, LA 70119.

California Province (1909), 300 College Ave., P.O. Box 519, Los Gatos, CA 95031.

New England Province (1926), 771 Harrison Ave., Boston, MA 02118.

Chicago Province (1928), 2050 N. Clark St., Chicago, IL 60614.

Oregon Province (1932), 2222 N.W. Hoyt, Portland, OR 97210.

Detroit Province (1955), 7303 W. Seven Mile Rd., Detroit, MI 48221.

Wisconsin Province (1955), PO Box 080288, Milwaukee, WI 53208-0288.

Province of the Antilles (1947), U.S. address, 13339 S.W. 9 Terrace, Miami, FL 33184.

John of God, Brothers of the Hospitaller Order of St., O.H.: Founded 1537, in Spain. General motherhouse, Rome, Italy; American province, 2425 S. Western Ave., Los Angeles, CA 90018. Nursing work and related fields.

Joseph, Congregation of St., C.S.J.: General motherhouse, Rome, Italy; U.S. vice province, 338 North Grand Ave., San Pedro, CA 90731-2006. Parochial, missionary, educational work.

Joseph, Oblates of St., O.S.J.: Founded 1878, in Italy, by Bl. Joseph Marello; in U.S., 1929. General motherhouse, Rome, Italy. Párochial, educational work.

Eastern Province, Route 315, R.R. 4, Box 14, Pittston, PA 18640.

California Province, 544 W. Cliff Dr., Santa Cruz, CA 95060.

Josephite Fathers, C.J.: General motherhouse, Ghent, Belgium; U.S. foundation, 180 Patterson Rd., Santa Maria, CA 93455.

Josephites (St. Joseph's Society of the Sacred Heart), S.S.J.: Established 1893, in U.S. as American congregation (originally established in U.S. in 1871 by Mill Hill Josephites from England). General motherhouse, 1130 N. Calvert St., Baltimore, MD 21202. Evangelization in African American community.

LaSalette, Missionaries of Our Lady of, M.S.: Founded 1852, by Msgr. de Bruillard; in U.S., 1892. Motherhouse, Rome, Italy.

Our Lady of Seven Dolors Province (1934), 915 Maple Ave., Hartford, CT 06114.

Immaculate Heart of Mary Province (1945), 947 Park St., Attleboro, MA 02703.

Mary Queen Province (1958), 4650 S. Broadway, St. Louis, MO 63111.

Mary Queen of Peace Province (1967), P.O. Box 250, Twin Lakes, WI 53181.

Lateran, Canons Regular of the, C.R.L.: General house, Rome, Italy; U.S. address: 2317 Washington Ave., Bronx, NY 10458.

Legionaries of Christ, L.C.: Founded 1941, in Mexico, by Rev. Marcial Maciel; in U.S., 1965. General headquarters, Rome, Italy; U.S. headquarters, 393 Derby Ave., Orange, CT 06477; novitiate, 475 Oak Ave., Cheshire, CT 06410.

Little Brothers of St. Francis, L.B.S.F.: Founded 1970 in Archdiocese of Boston by Bro. James Curran. General fraternity, 785-789 Parker St., Roxbury (Boston), MA 02120-3021. Combine contemplative life with evangelical street ministry.

Mariannhill, Congregation of the Missionaries of, C.M.M.: Trappist monastery, begun in 1882 by Abbot Francis Pfanner in Natal, South Africa, became an independent modern congregation in 1909; in U.S., 1920. Generalate, Rome, Italy; U.S.-Canadian province (1938), Our Lady of Grace Monastery, 23715

Ann Arbor Trail, Dearborn Hts., MI 48127-1449. Foreign mission work.

Marians of the Immaculate Conception, Congregation of, M.I.C.: Founded 1673; U.S. foundation, 1913. General motherhouse, Rome, Italy. Educational, parochial, mission, publication work.

St. Casimir Province (1913), 6336 S. Kilbourn Ave., Chicago, IL 60629.

St. Stanislaus Kostka Province (1948), Eden Hill, Stockbridge, MA 01262.

Marist Brothers, F.M.S.: Founded 1817, in France, by Bl. Marcellin Champagnat. General motherhouse, Rome, Italy. Educational, social, catechetical work.

Esopus Province, 1241 Kennedy Blvd., Bayonne, NJ 07002 (office).

Poughkeepsie Province, 26 First Ave., Pelham, NY 10803.

Marist Fathers (Society of Mary), S.M.: Founded 1816, at Lyons, France, by Jean Claude Colin; in U.S., 1863. General motherhouse, Rome, Italy. Educational, foreign mission, pastoral work.

Washington Province (1924), 815 Varnum St., N.E., Washington, DC 20017.

Boston Province (1924), 27 Isabella St., Boston, MA 02116.

San Francisco Western Province (1962), 625 Pine St., San Francisco, CA 94108.

Maronite Monks, Congregation of (Cloistered Penitents of St. Francis), O. Mar.: Most Holy Trinity Monastery, 67 Dugway Rd., Petersham, MA 01366; Holy Nativity Monastery, Bethlehem, S.D. 57708.

Maronite Lebanese Missionaries, Congregation of, C.M.L.M.: Founded in Lebanon 1865; established in the U.S., 1991. U.S. foundation, Our Lady of the Cedars Maronite Mission, 11935 Bellfort Village, Houston, TX 77031.

Mary, Society of (Marianist Fathers and Brothers; Brothers of Mary), S.M.: Founded 1817, at Bordeaux, France, by Rev. William-Joseph Chaminade; in U.S., 1849. General motherhouse, Rome, Italy. Educational work.

Cincinnati Province (1849), 4435 E. Patterson Rd., Dayton, OH 45430-1095.

St. Louis Province (1908), PO Box 23130, St. Louis, MO 63156.

Pacific Province (1948), PO Box 1775, Cupertino, CA 95015.

New York Province (1961), 4301 Roland Ave., Baltimore, MD 21210.

Province of Meribah (1976), 240 Emory Rd., Mineola, NY 11501.

Mary Immaculate, Missionary Oblates of, O.M.I.: Founded 1816, in France, by Bl. Charles Joseph Eugene de Mazenod; in U.S., 1849. General house, Rome, Italy. U.S. Province: 391 Michigan Ave., N.E., Washington, D.C., 20017. Parochial, foreign mission, educational work; ministry to marginal.

Maryknoll (Catholic Foreign Mission Society of America), M.M.: Founded 1911, in U.S., by Frs. Thomas F. Price and James A. Walsh. General Center, Maryknoll, NY 10545.

Mekhitarist Order of Venice, O.M.Ven.: Founded 1701; transferred to Venice, 1717. U.S. address: 110 E. 12th, New York, N.Y. 10003. Promote ecclesia community among Armenians.

Mekhitarist Order of Vienna, C.M.Vd.: Estab-

lished 1773. General headquarters, Vienna, Austria. U.S. address, 4900 Maryland Ave., La Crescenta, CA 91214. Work among Armenians in U.S.

Mercedarians (Order of Our Lady of Mercy), O. de M.: Founded 1218, in Spain, by St. Peter Nolasco. General motherhouse, Rome, Italy; U.S. headquarters, 3205 Fulton Rd., Cleveland, OH 44109.

Mercy, Brothers of, F.M.M.: Founded 1856, in Germany. General motherhouse, Montabaur, Germany. American headquarters, 4520 Ransom Rd., Clarence, NY 14031. Hospital work.

Mercy, Brothers of Our Lady, Mother of, C.F.M.M.: Founded 1844, in The Netherlands by Abp. Jan Zwijsen. Generalate, Tilburg, The Netherlands; U.S. region, 2336 S. C St., Oxnard, CA 93033-3501.

Mercy, Congregation of Priests of (Fathers of Mercy), C.P.M.: Founded 1808, in France, by Rev. Jean Baptiste Rauzan; in U.S., 1839. General mission house, 806 Shaker Musuem Rd., South Union, KY 42283. Mission work.

Mill Hill Missionaries (St. Joseph's Society for Foreign Missions), M.H.M.: Founded 1866, in England, by Cardinal Vaughan; in U.S., 1951. International headquarters, London, England; American headquarters, 222 W. Hartsdale Ave., Hartsdale, N.Y. 10530.

Minim Fathers, O.M.: General motherhouse, Rome, Italy. North American delegation (1970), 3431 Portola Ave., Los Angeles, CA 90032.

Missionaries of St. Charles, Congregation of the (Scalabrinians), C.S.: Founded 1887, at Piacenza, Italy, by Bl. John Baptist Scalabrini. General motherhouse, Rome, Italy.

St. Charles Borromeo Province (1888), 27 Carmine St., New York, NY 10014.

St. John Baptist Province (1903), 546 N. East Ave., Oak Park, IL 60302.

Missionaries of the Blessed Sacrament, M.S.S.: Regional headquarters, P.O. Box 4337, Corpus Christi, TX 78469. Promotion of Perpetual Eucharistic adoration.

Missionaries of the Holy Apostles, M.Ss.A.: Founded 1962, Washington, D.C., by Very Rev. Eusebe M. Menard. North American headquarters, 33 Prospect Hill Rd., Cromwell, CT 06416.

Missionary Fraternity of Mary, F.M.M.: General headquarters, Guatemala; U.S. foundation 340 Pine St., Seaford, DE 19973.

Missionary Servants of Christ, M.S.C.: Founded 1979 in U.S. by Bro. Edwin Baker. Headquarters, 1534 Newton St., N.E., Washington, D.C. 20017-3011.

Missionary Society of St. Paul of Nigeria: Generalate Abuja, Nigeria; U.S. Region, 12686 Crosby-Lynchburg Rd., P.O. Box 3200, Barrette Station, TX 77532.

Missionhurst - CICM (Congregation of the Immaculate Heart of Mary): Founded 1862, at Scheut, Brussels, Belgium, by Very Rev. Theophile Verbist. General motherhouse, Rome, Italy; U.S. province, 4651 N. 25th St., Arlington, VA 22207. Home and foreign mission work.

Montfort Missionaries (Missionaries of the Company of Mary), S.M.M.: Founded 1715, by St. Louis Marie Grignon de Montfort; in U.S., 1948. General motherhouse, Rome, Italy; U.S. province, 101-18

104th St., Ozone Park, NY 11416. Mission work.
Mother Co-Redemptrix, Congregation of, C.M.C.: Founded 1953 at Lein-Thuy, Vietnam (North), by Fr. Dominic Mary Tran Dinh Thu; in U.S., 1975. General house, Hochiminhville, Vietnam; U.S. provincial house, 1900 Grand Ave., Carthage, MO 64836. Work among Vietnamese Catholics in U.S.
Oblates of the Virgin Mary, O.M.V.: Founded 1815, in Italy; in U.S., 1976; Generalate, Rome, Italy; U.S. provincialate: Two Ipswich St., Boston, MA 02215.
Oratorians (Congregation of the Oratory of St. Philip Neri), C.O.: Founded 1575, at Rome, by St. Philip Neri. A confederation of autonomous houses. U.S. addresses: P.O. Box 11586, Rock Hill, SC 29731; P.O. Box 1688, Monterey, CA 93940; 4450 Bayard St., Pittsburgh, PA 15213; P.O. Drawer II, Pharr, TX 78577; 109 Willoughby St., Brooklyn, NY 11201.
Pallottines (Society of the Catholic Apostolate), S.A.C.: Founded 1835, at Rome, by St. Vincent Pallotti. Generalate, Rome, Italy. Charitable, educational, parochial, mission work.
Immaculate Conception Province (1953), P.O. Box 979, South Orange, NJ 07079.
Mother of God Province (1946), 5424 W. Blue Mound Rd., Milwaukee, WI 53208.
Irish Province (1909), U.S. address: 3352 4th St., Wyandotte, MI 48192.
Queen of Apostles Province (1909), 448 E. 116th St., New York, NY 10029.
Christ the King Province, 3452 Niagara Falls, Blvd., N. Tonawanda, NY 14120.
Paraclete, Servants of the, s.P.: Founded 1947, Santa Fe, N.M., archdiocese. Generalate and U.S. motherhouse, 18161 State Hwy. 4, Jemez Springs, NM 87025-0010. Devoted to care of priests.
Paris Foreign Missions Society, M.E.P.: Founded 1662, at Paris, France. Headquarters, Paris, France; U.S. establishment, 930 Ashbury St., San Francisco, CA 94117. Mission work and training of native clergy.
Passionists (Congregation of the Passion), C.P.: Founded 1720, in Italy, by St. Paul of the Cross. General motherhouse, Rome, Italy.
St. Paul of the Cross Province (Eastern Province) (1852), 80 David St., South River, NJ 08882.
Holy Cross Province (Western Province), 5700 N. Harlem Ave., Chicago, IL 60631.
Patrician Brothers (Brothers of St. Patrick), F.S.P.: Founded 1808, in Ireland, by Bishop Daniel Delaney; U.S. novitiate, 7820 Bolsa Ave., Midway City, CA 92655. Educational work.
Patrick's Missionary Society, St., S.P.S.: Founded 1932, at Wicklow, Ireland, by Msgr. Patrick Whitney; in U.S., 1953. International headquarters, Kiltegan Co., Wicklow, Ireland. U.S. foundations: 70 Edgewater Rd., Cliffside Park, NJ 07010; 19536 Eric Dr., Saratoga, CA 95070; 1347 W. Granville Ave., Chicago, IL 60660.
Pauline Fathers (Order of St. Paul the First Hermit), O.S.P.P.E.: Founded 1215; established in U.S., 1955. General motherhouse, Czestochowa, Jasna Gora, Poland; U.S. province, P.O. Box 2049, Doylestown, PA 18901.
Pauline Fathers and Brothers (Society of St. Paul for the Apostolate of Communications), S.S.P.: Founded 1914, by Very Rev. James Alberione; in U.S., 1932. Motherhouse, Rome, Italy; New York province

(1932), 6746 Lake Shore Rd., Derby, NY 14047; Los Angeles province, 112 S. Herbert Ave., Los Angeles, CA 90063. Social communications work.
Paulists (Missionary Society of St. Paul the Apostle), C.S.P.: Founded 1858, in New York, by Fr. Isaac Thomas Hecker. Motherhouse: 86-11 Midland Pkwy, Jamaica Estates, N.Y. 11432. Missionary, ecumenical, pastoral work.
Piarists (Order of the Pious Schools), Sch.P.: Founded 1617, at Rome, Italy, by St. Joseph Calasanctius. General motherhouse, Rome, Italy. U.S. province, 363 Valley Forge Rd., Devon, PA 19333.
New York-Puerto Rico vice-province (Calasanzian Fathers), P.O. Box 118, Playa Sta., Ponce, PR 00734.
California vice province, 3951 Rogers St., Los Angeles, CA 90063. Educational work.
Pius X, Brothers of St.: Founded 1952, at La Crosse, Wis., by Bishop John P. Treacy. Motherhouse, P.O. Box 217, De Soto, WI 54624. Education.
Pontifical Institute for Foreign Missions, P.I.M.E.: Founded 1850, in Italy, at request of Pope Pius IX. General motherhouse, Rome, Italy; U.S. province, 17330 Quincy Ave., Detroit, MI 48221. Foreign mission work.
Precious Blood, Society of, C.Pp.S.: Founded 1815, in Italy, by St. Gaspar del Bufalo. General motherhouse, Rome, Italy.
Cincinnati Province, 431 E. Second St., Dayton, OH 45402.
Kansas City Province, P.O. Box 339, Liberty, MO 64068.
Pacific Province, 2337 134th Ave. W., San Leandro, CA 94577.
Atlantic Province, 540 St. Clair Ave. West, Toronto M6C 14A, Canada.
Premonstratensians (Order of the Canons Regular of Premontre; Norbertines), O. Praem.: Founded 1120, at Premontre, France, by St. Norbert; in U.S., 1893. Generalate, Rome, Italy. Educational, parish work.
St. Norbert Abbey, 1016 N. Broadway, DePere, WI 54115.
Daylesford Abbey, 220 S. Valley Rd., Paoli, PA 19301.
St. Michael's Abbey, 19292 El Toro Rd., Silverado, CA 92676.
Priestly Fraternity of St. Peter, F.S.S.P.: Founded and approved Oct. 18, 1988; first foundation in U.S., 1991. U.S. headquarters, Our Lady of Guadalupe Seminary, Griffin Rd., P.O. Box 196, Elmhurst, PA 18416.
Providence, Sons of Divine, F.D.P.: Founded 1893, at Tortona, Italy, by Bl. Luigi Orione; in U.S., 1933. General motherhouse, Rome, Italy; U.S. address, 111 Orient Ave., E. Boston, MA 02128.
Redemptorist Fathers and Brothers (Congregation of the Most Holy Redeemer), C.SS.R.: Founded 1732, in Italy, by St. Alphonsus Mary Liguori. Generalate, Rome, Italy. Mission work.
Baltimore Province (1850), 7509 Shore Rd., Brooklyn, NY 11209.
Redemptorist-Denver Province (1875), Box 300399, Denver, CO 80203-0399.
New Orleans Vice-Province, 5354 Plank Rd., P.O. Box 53900, Baton Rouge, LA 70892.
Richmond Vice-Province (1942), 313 Hillman St., P.O. Box 1529, New Smyrna Beach, FL 32170.

Resurrectionists (Congregation of the Resurrection), C.R.: Founded 1836, in France, under direction of Bogdan Janski. Motherhouse, Rome, Italy. U.S. Province, 2250 N. Latrobe Ave., Chicago, IL 60639-3018.

Ontario Kentucky Province, U.S. address, 338 N. 25th St., Louisville, KY 40212.

Rogationist Fathers, R.C.J.: Founded by Bl. Annibale (Hannibal) di Francia, 1887. General motherhouse, Rome, Italy. U.S. delegation: 2688 S. Newmark Ave., Sanger, CA 91343. Charitable work.

Rosary, Brothers of Our Lady of the Holy, F.S.R.: Founded 1956, in U.S., Motherhouse and novitiate, 232 Sunnyside Dr., Reno, NV 89503-3510.

Rosminians (Institute of Charity), I.C.: Founded 1828, in Italy, by Antonio Rosmini-Serbati. General motherhouse, Rome, Italy; U.S. address, 2327 W. Heading Ave., Peoria, IL 61604. Charitable work.

Sacred Heart, Brothers of the, S.C.: Founded 1821, in France, by Rev. Andre Coindre. General motherhouse, Rome, Italy, Educational work.

New Orleans Province (1847), 4540 Elysian Fields Ave., New Orleans, LA 70122.

New England Province (1945), 685 Steere Farm Rd., Pascoag, RI 02859.

New York Province (1960), P.O. Box 68, Belvidere, NJ 07823.

Sacred Heart, Missionaries of the, M.S.C.: Founded 1854, by Rev. Jules Chevelier. General motherhouse, Rome, Italy; U.S. province, 305 S. Lake St., Aurora, IL 60507-0271.

Sacred Heart of Jesus, Congregation of the (Sacred Heart Fathers and Brothers), S.C.J.: Founded 1877, in France. General motherhouse, Rome, Italy; U.S. provincial office: P.O. Box 289, Hales Corners, WI 53110. Educational, preaching, mission work.

Sacred Hearts of Jesus and Mary, Congregation of (Picpus Fathers), SS.CC.: Founded 1805, in France, by Fr. Coudrin. General motherhouse, Rome, Italy. Mission, educational work.

Eastern Province (1946), 77 Adams St. (Box 111), Fairhaven, MA 02719.

Western Province (1970), 724 E. Bonita Ave., San Dimas, CA 91773.

Hawaii Province, Box 797, Kaneohe, Oahu, Hawaii 96744.

Sacred Hearts of Jesus and Mary, Missionaries of the, M.SS.CC.: Founded 1833, in Naples, Italy, by Cajetan Errico. General motherhouse, Rome, Italy; U.S. headquarters, 2249 Shore Rd., Linwood, NJ 08221.

Salesians of St. John Bosco (Society of St. Francis de Sales), S.D.B.: Founded 1859, by St. John (Don) Bosco. Generalate, Rome, Italy.

St. Philip the Apostle Province (1902), 148 Main St., P.O. Box 639, New Rochelle, NY 10802-0639.

San Francisco Province (1926), 1100 Franklin St., San Francisco, CA 94109.

Salvatorians (Society of the Divine Savior), S.D.S.: Founded 1881, in Rome, by Fr. Francis Jordan; in U.S., 1896. General headquarters, Rome, Italy; U.S. province, 1735 Hi-Mount Blvd., Milwaukee, WI 53208-1720. Educational, parochial, mission work; campus ministries, chaplaincies.

Scalabrinians: See Missionaries of St. Charles.

Servites (Order of Friar Servants of Mary), O.S.M.: Founded 1233, at Florence, Italy, by Seven Holy Founders. Generalate, Rome, Italy. General apostolic ministry.

Eastern Province (1967), 3121 W. Jackson Blvd., Chicago, IL 60612.

Western Province (1967), 5210 Somerset St., Buena Park, CA 90621.

Somascan Fathers, C.R.S.: Founded 1534, at Somasca, Italy, by St. Jerome Emiliani. General motherhouse, Rome, Italy; U.S. address, Pine Haven Boys Center, River Rd., P.O. Box 162, Suncook, NH 03275.

Society of Our Lady of the Most Holy Trinity, S.O.L.T.: Headquarters, Casa San Jose, 109 W. Avenue F, PO Box 152, Robstown, TX 78380.

Sons of Mary Missionary Society (Sons of Mary, Health of the Sick), F.M.S.I.: Founded 1952, in the Boston archdiocese, by Rev. Edward F. Garesche, S.J. Headquarters, 567 Salem End Rd., Framingham, MA 01702.

Stigmatine Fathers and Brothers (Congregation of the Sacred Stigmata), C.S.S.: Founded 1816, by St. Gaspar Bertoni. General motherhouse, Rome, Italy; North American Province, 554 Lexington St., Waltham, MA 02154. Parish work.

Sulpicians (Society of Priests of St. Sulpice), S.S.: Founded 1641, at Paris, by Rev. Jean Jacques Olier. General motherhouse, Paris, France; U.S. province, 5408 Roland Ave., Baltimore, MD 21210. Education of seminarians and priests.

Theatines (Congregation of Clerics Regular), C.R.: Founded 1524, at Rome, by St. Cajetan. General motherhouse, Rome, Italy; U.S. headquarters, 1050 S. Birch St., Denver, CO 80246.

Trappists: See Cistercians of the Strict Observance.

Trinitarians (Order of the Most Holy Trinity), O.SS.T.: Founded 1198, by St. John of Matha; in U.S., 1911. General motherhouse, Rome, Italy; U.S. headquarters, P.O. Box 5719, Baltimore, MD 21208.

Trinity Missions (Missionary Servants of the Most Holy Trinity), S.T.: Founded 1929, by Fr. Thomas Augustine Judge. Generalate, 1215 N. Scott St., Arlington, VA 22209-3097. Home mission work.

Viatorian Fathers (Clerics of St. Viator), C.S.V.: Founded 1831, in France, by Fr. Louis Joseph Querbes. General motherhouse, Rome, Italy. Province of Chicago (1882), 1212 E. Euclid St., Arlington Hts., IL 60004. Educational work.

Vincentians (Congregation of the Mission; Lazarists), C.M.: Founded 1625, in Paris, by St. Vincent de Paul; in U.S., 1818. General motherhouse, Rome, Italy. Educational work.

Eastern Province (1867), 500 E. Chelten Ave., Philadelphia, PA 19144.

Midwest Province (1888), 13663 Rider Trail North, Earth City, MO 63045.

New England Province (1975), 234 Keeney St., Manchester, CT 06040-7048.

American Italian Branch, Our Lady of Pompei Church, 3600 Claremont St., Baltimore, MD 21224.

American Spanish Branch (Barcelona, Spain), 234 Congress St., Brooklyn, NY 11201.

American Spanish Branch (Zaragoza, Spain), Holy Agony Church, 1834 3rd Ave., New York, NY 10029.

Western Province (1975), 650 W. 23rd St., Los Angeles, CA 90007.

Southern Province (1975), 3826 Gilbert Ave., Dallas, TX 75219.
Vocationist Fathers (Society of Divine Vocations), S.D.V.: Founded 1920, in Italy; in U.S., 1962. Generalate, Rome, Italy; U.S. headquarters,

90 Brooklake Rd., Florham Park, NJ 07932.
Xaverian Missionary Fathers, S.X.: Founded 1895, by Bl. Guido Conforti, at Parma, Italy. General motherhouse, Rome, Italy; U.S. province, 12 Helene Ct., Wayne, NJ 07470. Foreign mission work.

MEMBERSHIP OF RELIGIOUS INSTITUTES OF MEN

(Principal source: *Annuario Pontificio*. Statistics as of Jan. 1, 1999 unless indicated otherwise.) Listed below are world membership statistics of institutes of men of pontifical right with 500 or more members; the number of priests is in parentheses. Also listed are institutes with less than 500 members with houses in the United States.

Jesuits (15,418) 21,955
Franciscans (Friars Minor) (11,760) 17,760
Salesians (11,243) 17,464
Franciscans (Capuchins) (7,352) 11,323
Benedictines (4,820) 8,281
Brothers of Christian Schools 6,995
Dominicans (4,824) 6,530
Society of the Divine Word (3,661) 5,972
Redemptorists (4,317) 5,817
Marist Brothers 5,107
Oblates of Mary Immaculate (3,619) 4,941
Franciscans (Conventuals) (2,746) 4,574
Vincentians (3,206) 4,046
Discalced Carmelites (O.C.D.) (2,461) 3,872
Holy Spirit (Holy Ghost),
  Congregation (2,388) 3,092
Claretians (1,972) 2,926
Augustinians (2,216) 2,895
Passionists (1,810) 2,442
Priests of the Sacred Heart (1,676) 2,386
Trappists (1,080) 2,383
Missionaries of the Sacred
  Heart of Jesus (1,576) 2,308
Pallottines (1,559) 2,279
Carmelites (O.Carm.) (1,475) 2,405
Combonian Missionaries of the
  Heart of Jesus (1,321) 2,259
Missionaries of Africa (1,871) 2,223
Carmelites of BVM (1,180) 1,956
Christian Brothers 1,774
Holy Cross, Congregation (793) 1,722
Marianists (509) 1,633
Legionaries of Christ (363) 1,499
Hospitallers of St. John of God (142) 1,478
Piarists (1,108) 1,453
Marists (1,187) 1,430
Brothers of the Sacred Heart (50) 1,402
Congregation of the Immaculate Heart of
  Mary (Missionhurst; Scheut Missionaries)
  (1,006) 1,343
Premonstratensians (958) 1,326
Cistercians (Common Observance) (739) . 1,277
Augustinians (Recollects) (987) 1,273
Sacred Hearts, Congregation
  (Picpus) (885) 1,258
Brothers of Christian Instruction
  of St. Gabriel (31) 1,249
Salvatorians (797) 1,239
Brothers of Christian Instruction
  of Ploërmel (7) 1,211
Society of St. Paul (567) 1,152
Montfort Missionaries (771) 1,070
Little Workers of Divine Providence (737)1,068

Society of African Missions (881) 1,042
Ministers of Sick (Camillians) (674) 1,037
Consolata Missionaries (756) 1,007
Servants of Mary (761) 995
Blessed Sacrament, Congregation of (687) 986
Assumptionists (672) 980
Missionaries of Holy Family (674) 955
LaSalette Missionaries (669) 940
Missionaries of St. Francis de Sales
  of Annecy (470) 916
Xaverian Missionaries (693) 904
Franciscans (Third Order Regular) (558) 845
Viatorians (324) 802
Canons Regular of St. Augustine (637) 797
Maryknollers (567) 777
Mercedarians (525) 743
Scalabrinians (619) 741
Columbans (660) 739
Oblates of St. Francis de Sales (550) 714
Mill Hill Missionaries (553) 707
Order of St. Basil the Great (Basilians of St.
  Josaphat) (305) 684
Congregation of St. Joseph (529) 668
Missionaries of the
  Most Precious Blood (466) 663
Brothers of Charity (Ghent) 604
Oratorians (397) 599
Society of Christ (395) 594
Pontifical Institute for
  Foreign Missions (505) 583
Trinitarians (378) 578
Marian Fathers and Brothers (350) 544
Eudists (403) 535
Somascans (346) 517
Brothers of the Immaculate Conception (5)500
Crosiers (Order of Holy Cross) (323) 482
Oblates of St. Joseph (311) 461
Servants of Charity(335) 457
Order of St. Paul the First Hermit (256) 432
Resurrection, Congregation of (345) 428
Stigmatine Fathers and Brothers (323) 425
Mariannhill Missionaries (203) 388
Barnabites (312) 387
Paris Foreign Mission Society (385) 385
Missionaries of the Holy Spirit (255) 377
St. Patrick's Mission Society (346) 366
Sulpicians (365) 365
Rogationists (211) 362
Rosminians (264) 361
Maronite Order of Lebanon (261) 357
Carthusians (176) 351
Xaverian Brothers (as of 1995) 291
Little Brothers of Jesus (69) 252

RELIGIOUS INSTITUTES OF WOMEN IN THE UNITED STATES

(Sources: *The Official Catholic Directory*; *Catholic Almanac* survey.)

Adorers of the Blood of Christ, A.S.C.: Founded 1834, in Italy; in U.S., 1870. General motherhouse, Rome, Italy U.S. provinces: 2 Pioneer Lane, Red Bud, IL 62278; 1400 South Sheridan, Wichita, KS 67213; 3950 Columbia Ave., Columbia, PA 17512. Education, retreats, social services, pastoral ministry.

Africa, Missionary Sisters of Our Lady of (Sisters of Africa), M.S.O.L.A.: Founded 1869, at Algiers, Algeria, by Cardinal Lavigerie; in U.S., 1929. General motherhouse, Rome, Italy; U.S. headquarters, 49 W. Spring St., Winooski, VT 05404-1397. Medical, educational, catechetical and social work in Africa.

Agnes, Sisters of St., C.S.A.: Founded 1858, in U.S., by Rev. Caspar Rehrl. General motherhouse, 475 Gillett St., Fond du Lac, WI 54935. Education, health care, social services.

Ann, Sisters of St., S.S.A.: Founded 1834, in Italy; in U.S., 1952. General motherhouse, Rome, Italy; U.S. headquarters, Mount St. Ann, Ebensburg, PA 15931.

Anne, Sisters of St., S.S.A.: Founded 1850, at Vaudreuil, Que., Canada; in U.S., 1866. General motherhouse, Lachine, Que., Canada; U.S. address, 720 Boston Post Rd., Marlboro, MA 01752. Retreat work, pastoral ministry, religious education.

Anthony, Missionary Servants of St., M.S.S.A.: Founded 1929, in U.S., by Rev. Peter Baque. General motherhouse, 100 Peter Baque Rd., San Antonio, TX 78209. Social work.

Antonine Maronite Sisters: Established in U.S., 1966. U.S. address, 2691 N. Lipkey Rd., North Jackson, OH 44451.

Armenian Sisters of the Immaculate Conception: U.S. address, 6 Eliot Rd., Lexington, MA 02173.

Assumption, Little Sisters of the, L.S.A.: Founded 1865, in France; in U.S., 1891. General motherhouse, Paris, France; U.S. provincialate, 214 E. 30th St., New York, NY 10016. Social work, nursing, family life education.

Assumption, Religious of the, R.A.: Founded 1839, in France; in U.S., 1919. Generalate, Paris, France; North American province, 227 N. Bowman Ave., Merion Sta., PA 19066.

Assumption of the Blessed Virgin, Sisters of the, S.A.S.V.: Founded 1853, in Canada; in U.S., 1891. General motherhouse, Nicolet, Que., Canada; U.S. province, 316 Lincoln St., Worcester, MA 01605. Education, mission, pastoral ministry.

Augustinian Nuns of Contemplative Life, O.S.A.: Established in Spain in 13th century; U.S. foundation, Convent of Our Mother of Good Counsel, 4328 W. Westminster Pl., St. Louis, MO 63108.

Augustinian Sisters, Servants of Jesus and Mary, Congregation of, O.S.A.: Generalate, Rome, Italy; U.S. foundation. St. John School, 513 E. Broadway, Brandenburg, KY 40108.

Basil the Great, Sisters of the Order of St. (Byzantine Rite), O.S.B.M.: Founded fourth century, in Cappadocia, by St. Basil the Great and his sister St. Macrina; in U.S., 1911. Generalate, Rome, Italy; U.S. motherhouses: Philadelphia Ukrainian Byzantine Rite, 710 Fox Chase Rd., Philadelphia, PA 19111; Pittsburgh Ruthenian Byzantine Rite, Mount St. Macrina P.O. Box 878, Uniontown, PA 15401. Education, health care.

Benedict, Sisters of the Order of St., O.S.B.: Our Lady of Mount Caritas Monastery (founded 1979, Ashford, Conn.), 54 Seckar Rd., Ashford, CT 06278. Contemplative.

Benedictine Nuns, O.S.B.: St. Scholastica Priory, Box 606, Petersham, MA 01366. Cloistered.

Benedictine Nuns of the Congregation of Solesmes, O.S.B.: U.S. establishment, 1981, in Burlington diocese. Monastery of the Immaculate Heart of Mary, 4103 Vt. Rte 100, Westfield, VT 05874. Cloistered, papal enclosure.

Benedictine Nuns of the Primitive Observance, O.S.B.: Founded c. 529, in Italy; in U.S., 1948. Abbey of Regina Laudis, Flanders Rd., Bethlehem, CT 06751. Cloistered.

Benedictine Sisters, O.S.B.: Founded c. 529, in Italy; in U.S., 1852. General motherhouse, Eichstatt, Bavaria, Germany. U.S. addresses: St. Emma Monastery, Motherhouse and Novitiate, 1001 Harvey Ave., Greensburg, PA 15601; Abbey of St. Walburga, 6717 S. Boulder Rd., Boulder, CO 80303.

Benedictine Sisters (*Regina Pacis*), O.S.B.:

Founded 1627, in Lithuania as cloistered community; reformed 1918 as active community; established in U.S. 1957, by Mother M. Raphaela Simonis. Regina Pacis, 333 Wallace Rd., Bedford, NH 03102.

Benedictine Sisters, Missionary, O.S.B.: Founded 1885. Generalate, Rome, Italy; U.S. motherhouse, 300 N. 18th St., Norfolk, NE 68701.

Benedictine Sisters, Olivetan, O.S.B.: Founded 1887, in U.S. General motherhouse, Holy Angels Convent, P.O. Drawer 130, Jonesboro, AR 72403. Educational, hospital work.

Benedictine Sisters of Perpetual Adoration of Pontifical Jurisdiction, Congregation of the, O.S.B.: Founded in U.S., 1874, from Maria Rickenbach, Switzerland. General motherhouse, 8300 Morganford Rd., St. Louis, MO 63123.

Benedictine Sisters of Pontifical Jurisdiction, O.S.B.: Founded c. 529, in Italy. No general motherhouse in U.S. Three federations:

• **Federation of St. Scholastica** (1922). Pres., Sister Regina Crowley, O.S.B., 5807 N. Kolmar Ave., Chicago, IL 60646. Motherhouses belonging to the federation:

Mount St. Scholastica, 801 S. 8th St., Atchison, Kans. 66002; Benedictine Sisters of Elk Co., St. Joseph's Monastery, St. Mary's, PA 15857; Benedictine Sisters of Erie, 6101 E. Lake Rd., Erie, PA 16511; Benedictine Sisters of Chicago, St. Scholastica Priory, 7430 Ridge Blvd., Chicago, IL 60645; Benedictine Sisters of the Sacred Heart, 1910 Maple Ave., Lisle, IL 60532-2164; Benedictine Sisters of Elizabeth, St. Walburga Monastery, 851 N. Broad St., Elizabeth, NJ 07208-2593; Benedictine Sisters of Pittsburgh, 4530 Perrysville Ave., Pittsburgh, PA 15229;

Red Plains Monastery, 728 Richland Rd. S.W., Piedmont, OK 73078., St. Joseph's Monastery, 2200 S. Lewis, Tulsa, OK 74114; St. Gertrude's Monastery, 14259 Benedictine Lane, Ridgely, MD 21660; St. Walburga Monastery, 2500 Amsterdam Rd., Covington, KY 41016; Sacred Heart Monastery, Cullman, AL 35056; Benedictine Sisters of Virginia, Bristow, VA 22013; St. Scholastica Convent, 416 W. Highland Dr., Boerne, TX 78006; St. Lucy's Priory, 19045 E. Sierra Madre Ave., Glendora, CA 91741; Benedictine Sisters of Florida, Holy Name Monastery, P.O. Box 2450, St. Leo, FL 33574-2450; Benet Hill Monastery, 2555 N. Chelton Rd., Colorado Springs, CO 80909; Queen of Heaven Monastery (Byzantine Rite), 8640 Squires Lane N.E., Warren, OH 44484; Benedictine Sisters of Baltimore, Emmanuel Monastery, 2229 W. Joppa Rd., Lutherville, MD 21093; Queen of Angels Monastery, 717 King's Hwy, Liberty, MO 64068.

• **Federation of St. Gertrude the Great** (1937). Office: Sacred Heart Monastery, P.O. Box 364, Richardton, ND 58652. Pres., Sister Ruth Fox, O.S.B. Motherhouses belonging to the federation:

Mother of God Monastery, 110 28th Ave., S.E., Watertown, SD 57201; Sacred Heart Monastery, 1005 W. 8th St., Yankton, SD 57078; Mt. St. Benedict Monastery, 620 E. Summit Ave., Crookston, MN 56716; Sacred Heart Monastery, P.O. Box 364, Richardton, ND 58652; Convent of St. Martin, 2110-C St. Martin's Dr., Rapid City, SD 57702; Monastery of Immaculate Conception, 802 E. 10th St., Ferdinand, IN 47532; Monastery

of St. Gertrude, HC3, Box 121, Cottonwood, ID 83522;

Monastery of St. Benedict Center, Box 5070, Madison, WI 53705; Queen of Angels Monastery, 840 S. Main St., Mt. Angel, OR 97362; St. Scholastica Monastery, P.O. Box 3489, Fort Smith, AR 72913; Our Lady of Peace Monastery, 3710 W. Broadway, Columbia, MO 65203; Queen of Peace Monastery, Box 370, Belcourt, ND 58316; Our Lady of Grace Monastery, 1402 Southern Ave., Beech Grove, IN 46107; Holy Spirit Monastery, 22791 Pico St., Grand Terrace, CA 92324; Spirit of Life Monastery, 10760 W. Glennon Dr., Lakewood, CO 80226. St. Benedict's Monastery 225 Masters Ave., Winnipeg, MB, R4A 2A1, Canada; The Dwelling Place Monastery, 150 Mt. Tabor Rd., Martin, KY 41649.

• **Federation of St. Benedict** (1947). Pres., Sister Colleen Haggerty, O.S.B., St. Benedict Convent, 104 Chapel Lane, St. Joseph, MN 56374-0220. Motherhouses in U.S. belonging to the federation:

St. Benedict's Convent, St. Joseph, MN 56374; St. Scholastica Monasstery, 1001 Kenwood Ave., Duluth, MN 55811-2300; St. Bede Monastery, 1190 Priory Rd., Eau Claire, WI 54702; St. Mary Monastery, Nauvoo, IL 62354; Annunciation Monastery, 7520 University Dr., Bismarck, ND 58504; St. Paul's Priory, 2675 Larpenteur Ave., E., St. Paul, MN 55109; St. Placid Priory, 500 College St. N.E., Lacey, WA 98516; Mt. Benedict Monastery, 309 E. 5450 South, Ogden, UT 84405.

Bethany, Sisters of, C.V.D.: Founded 1928, in El Salvador; in U.S. 1949. General motherhouse, Santa Tecla, El Salvador. U.S. address: 850 N. Hobart Blvd., Los Angeles, CA 90029.

Bethlemita Sisters, Daughters of the Sacred Heart of Jesus: Founded 1861, in Guatemala. Motherhouse, Bogota, Colombia; U.S. address, St. Joseph Residence, 330 W. Pembroke St., Dallas, TX 75208.

Blessed Virgin Mary, Institute of the (Loreto Sisters), I.B.V.M.: Founded 17th century in Belgium; in U.S., 1954. Motherhouse, Rathfarnham, Dublin, Ireland; U.S. address: 2521 W. Maryland Ave., Phoenix, AZ 85017.

Blessed Virgin Mary, Institute of the (Loretto Sisters), I.B.V.M.: Founded 1609, in Belgium; in U.S., 1880. U.S. address, Loretto Convent, Box 508, Wheaton, IL 60189. Educational work.

Bon Secours, Congregation of, C.B.S.: Founded 1824, in France; in U.S. 1881. Generalate, Rome, Italy; U.S. provincial house, 1525 Marriottsville Rd., Marriottsville, MD 21104. Hospital work.

Brigid, Congregation of St., C.S.B.: Founded 1807, in Ireland; in U.S. 1953. U.S. regional house, 5118 Loma Linda Dr., San Antonio, TX 78201.

Brigittine Sisters (Order of the Most Holy Savior), O.SS.S.: Founded 1344, at Vadstena, Sweden, by St. Bridget; in U.S., 1957. General motherhouse, Rome, Italy; U.S. address, Vikingsborg, 4 Runkenhage Rd., Darien, CT 06820.

Canossian Daughters of Charity (Canossian Sisters): Founded 1808 in Verona, Italy, by St. Magdalen of Canossa. General motherhouse, Rome, Italy; U.S. provincial house, 5625 Isleta Blvd. S.W., Albuquerque, NM 87105.

Carmel, Congregation of Our Lady of Mount, O. Carm.: Founded 1825, in France; in U.S. 1833.

Generalate, P.O. Box 476, Lacombe, LA 70445. Education, social services, pastoral ministry, retreat work. **Carmel, Institute of Our Lady of Mount, O. Carm.:** Founded 1854, in Italy; in U.S., 1947. General motherhouse, Rome, Italy; U.S. novitiate, 5 Wheatland St., Peabody, MA 01960. Apostolic work. **Carmelite Community of the Word, C.C.W.:** Motherhouse and Novitiate, 394 Bem Rd., Gallitzin, PA 16641.

Carmelite Nuns, Discalced, O.C.D.: Founded 1562, Spain. First foundation in U.S. in 1790, at Charles County, Md.; this monastery was moved to Baltimore. Monasteries in U.S. are listed below, according to states.

Alabama: 716 Dauphin Island Pkwy., Mobile 36606. Arkansas: 7201 W. 32nd St., Little Rock 72204. California: 215 E. Alhambra Rd., Alhambra 91801; 27601 Highway 1, Carmel 93923; 68 Rincon Rd., Kensington 94707; 1883 Ringsted Dr., P.O. Box 379, Solvang 93463; 6981 Teresian Way, Georgetown 95634; 5158 Hawley Blvd., San Diego 92116; 721 Parker Ave., San Francisco 94118; 530 Blackstone Dr., San Rafael 94903; 1000 Lincoln St., Santa Clara 9550.

Colorado: 6138 S. Gallup St., Littleton 80120. Georgia: Coffee Bluff, 11 W. Back St., Savannah 31419. Hawaii: 6301 Pali Hwy., Kaneohe, HI 96744; Illinois: 310 N. River Rd., Des Plaines 60016. Indiana: 2500 Cold Spring Rd., Indianapolis 46222; 59 Allendale Pl., Terre Haute 47802. Iowa: 17937 250th St., Eldridge 52748; 2901 S. Cecilia St., Sioux City 51106. Kentucky: 1740 Newburg Rd., Louisville 40205. Louisiana: 1250 Carmel Ave., Lafayette 70507; 73530 River Rd., Covington 70430.

Maryland: 1318 Dulaney Valley Rd., Towson, Baltimore 21204; 5678 Mt. Carmel Rd., La Plata, 20646. Massachusetts: 61 Mt. Pleasant Ave., Roxbury, Boston 02119; 15 Mt. Carmel Rd., Danvers 01923. Michigan: 4300 Mt. Carmel Dr. NE, Ada 49301; 35750 Moravian Dr., Clinton Township 48035; U.S. 2 Highway, P.O. Box 397, Iron Mountain 49801; 3501 Silver Lake Rd., Traverse City 49684. Minnesota: 8251 De Montreville Trail N., Lake Elmo 55042-9547. Mississippi: 2155 Terry Rd., Jackson 39204.

Missouri: 2201 W. Main St., Jefferson City 65101; 9150 Clayton Rd., Ladue, St. Louis Co. 63124; 424 E. Monastery Rd., Springfield 65807. Nevada: 1950 La Fond Dr., Reno 89509-3099. New Hampshire: 275 Pleasant St., Concord, 03301. New Jersey: P.O. Box 785, Flemington 08822; 189 Madison Ave., Morristown 07960. New Mexico: 49 Mt. Carmel Rd., Santa Fe 87501-4552. New York: c/o Chancery Office, Diocese of Brooklyn, 75 Greene Ave., Brooklyn 11238; 139 De Puyster Ave., Beacon 12508; 75 Carmel Rd., Buffalo 14214; 1931 W. Jefferson Rd., Pittsford 14534; 428 Duane Ave., Schenectady 12304.

OH: 3176 Fairmount Blvd., Cleveland Heights 44118. Oklahoma: 20,000 N. County Line Rd., Piedmont 73078. Oregon: 87609 Green Hill Rd., Eugene 97402. Pennsylvania: 70 Monastery Rd., Elysburg 17824-9697; 510 E. Gore Rd., Erie 16509; R.D. 6, Box 28, Center Dr., Latrobe 15650; P.O. Box 57, Loretto 15940; Byzantine Rite, R.R. No. 1, Box 1336, Sugarloaf 18249; 66th and Old York Rd., Philadelphia 19126. Rhode Island: Watson Ave. at Nayatt Rd., Barrington 02806.

Texas: 600 Flowers Ave., Dallas 75211; 5801 Mt.

Carmel Dr., Arlington 76017; 1100 Parthenon Pl., Roman Forest, New Caney 77357-3039; 6301 Culebra and St. Joseph Way, San Antonio 78238. Utah: 5714 Holladay Blvd., Salt Lake City 84121. Vermont: RR 2, Box 4784, Barre, 05641. Washington: 2215 N.E. 147th St., Shoreline 98155. Wisconsin: W267 N2517 Meadowbrook Rd., Pewaukee 53072.

Carmelite Nuns of the Ancient Observance (Calced Carmelites), O. Carm.: Founded 1452, in The Netherlands; in U.S., 1930, from Naples, Italy, convent (founded 1856). U.S. monasteries: Carmelite Monastery of St. Therese, 3551 Lanark Rd., Lanark, PA 18036; Carmel of Mary, Wahpeton, ND 58075; Our Lady of Grace Monastery, 1 St. Joseph Pl., San Angelo, TX 76905; Carmel of the Sacred Heart, 430 Laurel Ave., Hudson, WI 54016. Papal enclosure.

Carmelite Sisters (Corpus Christi), O. Carm.: Founded 1908, in England; in U.S., 1920. General motherhouse, Tunapuna, Trinidad, W.I. U.S. address: Mt. Carmel Home, 412 W. 18th St., Kearney, NE 68847. Home and foreign mission work.

Carmelite Sisters for the Aged and Infirm, O. Carm.: Founded 1929, at New York, by Mother M. Angeline Teresa, O. Carm. Motherhouse, 600 Woods Rd., Avila-on-Hudson, Germantown, NY 12526. Social work, nursing and educating in the field of gerontology.

Carmelite Sisters of Charity, C.a.Ch.: Founded 1826 at Vich, Spain, by St. Joaquina de Vedruna. Generalate, Rome, Italy; U.S. address, 701 Beacon Rd., Silver Spring, MD 20903.

Carmelite Sisters of St. Therese of the Infant Jesus, C.S.T.: Founded 1917, in U.S. General motherhouse, 1300 Classen Dr., Oklahoma City, OK 73103. Educational work.

Carmelite Sisters of the Divine Heart of Jesus, Carmel D.C.J.: Founded 1891, in Germany; in U.S., 1912. General motherhouse, Sittard Netherlands. U.S. provincial houses: 1230 Kavanaugh Pl., Milwaukee, WI 52313 (Northern Province); 10341 Manchester Rd., St. Louis, MO 63122 (Central Province); 8585 La Mesa Blvd., La Mesa, CA 92041 (South Western Province). Social services, mission work.

Carmelite Sisters of the Most Sacred Heart of Los Angeles, O.C.D.: Founded 1904, in Mexico. General motherhouse and novitiate, 920 E. Alhambra Rd., Alhambra, CA 91801. Social services, retreat and educational work.

Carmelites, Calced (O. Carm.): Founded 1856 in Naples, Italy. U.S. address: Carmelite Monastery of St Therese, 3551 Lanark Rd., Coopersburg, PA 18036.

Carmelites of St. Theresa, Congregation of Missionary, C.M.S.T.: Founded 1903, in Mexico. General motherhouse, Mexico City, Mexico; U.S. foundation, 9548 Deer Trail Dr., Houston, TX 77038.

Casimir, Sisters of St., S.S.C.: Founded 1907, in U.S. by Mother Maria Kaupas. General motherhouse, 2601 W. Marquette Rd., Chicago, IL 60629. Education, missions, social services.

Cenacle, Congregation of Our Lady of the Retreat in the, R.C.: Founded 1826, in France; in U.S., 1892. Generalate, Rome, Italy. Eastern Province: Cenacle Rd., Lake Ronkonkoma, L.I., NY 11779; Midwestern Province, 513 Fullerton Pkwy., Chicago, IL 60614.

Charity, Daughters of Divine, F.D.C.: Founded 1868, at Vienna, Austria; in U.S., 1913. General motherhouse, Rome, Italy. U.S. province: 205 Major Ave., Staten Island, NY 10305. Education, social services.

Charity, Little Missionary Sisters of, L.M.S.C.: Founded 1915, in Italy by Bl. Luigi Orione; in U.S., 1949. General motherhouse, Rome, Italy; U.S. address, 120 Orient Ave., East Boston, MA 02128.

Charity, Missionaries of, M.C.: Founded 1950, in Calcutta, India, by Mother Teresa; first U.S. foundation 1971. General motherhouse, 54A Lower Circular Road, Calcutta 700016, India. U.S. address, 335 E. 145th St., Bronx, NY 10451. Service of the poor.

Charity, Religious Sisters of, R.S.C.: Founded 1815, in Ireland; in U.S., 1953. Motherhouse, Dublin, Ireland; U.S. headquarters, 206 N. Edgemont St., Los Angeles, CA 90029.

Charity, Sisters of (of Seton Hill), S.C.: Founded 1870, at Altoona, Penn., from Cincinnati foundation. Generalate, Mt. Thor Rd., Greensburg, PA 15601. Educational, hospital, social, foreign mission work.

Charity, Sisters of (Grey Nuns of Montréal), S.G.M.: Founded 1737, in Canada by St. Marie Marguerite d'Youville; in U.S., 1855. General administration, Montréal, Que. H2Y 2L7, Canada; U.S. provincial house, 10 Pelham Rd., Lexington, MA 02173.

Charity, Sisters of (of Leavenworth), S.C.L.: Founded 1858, in U.S. Motherhouse, 4200 S. 4th St., Leavenworth, KS 66048.

Charity, Sisters of (of Nazareth), S.C.N.: Founded 1812, in U.S. General motherhouse, SCN Center, P.O. Box 172, Nazareth, KY 40048. Education, health services.

Charity, Sisters of (of St. Augustine), C.S.A.: Founded 1851, at Cleveland, Ohio. Motherhouse, 5232 Broadview Rd., Richfield, OH 44286.

Charity, Sisters of Christian, S.C.C.: Founded 1849, in Paderborn, Germany, by Bl. Pauline von Mallinckrodt; in U.S., 1873. Generalate, Rome, Italy. U.S. provinces: Mallinckrodt Convent, 350 Bernardsville Rd., Mendham, NJ 07945; 2041 Elmwood Ave., Wilmette, IL 60091, Education, health services, other apostolic work.

Charity, Vincentian Sisters of, V.S.C.: Founded 1835, in Austria; in U.S., 1902. General motherhouse, 8200 McKnight Rd., Pittsburgh, PA 15237.

Charity, Vincentian Sisters of, V.S.C.: Founded 1928, at Bedford, Ohio. General motherhouse, 1160 Broadway, Bedford, OH 44146.

Charity of Cincinnati, Ohio, Sisters of, S.C.: Founded 1809; became independent community, 1852. General motherhouse, 5900 Delhi Rd., Mt. St. Joseph, OH 45051. Educational, hospital, social work.

Charity of Ottawa, Sisters of (Grey Nuns of the Cross), S.C.O.: Founded 1845, at Ottawa, Canada; in U.S., 1857. General motherhouse, Ottawa, Canada; U.S. provincial house, 975 Varnum Ave., Lowell, MA 01854. Educational, hospital work, extended health care.

Charity of Our Lady, Mother of Mercy, Sisters of, S.C.M.M.: Founded 1832, in Holland; in U.S., 1874. General motherhouse, Den Bosch, Netherlands; U.S. provincialate, 520 Thompson Ave., East Haven, CT 06512.

Charity of Our Lady, Mother of the Church,

S.C.M.C.: U.S. foundation, 1970. General motherhouse, Baltic, CT 06330.

Charity of Our Lady of Mercy, Sisters of, O.L.M.: Founded 1829, in Charleston, S.C. Generalate and motherhouse, 424 Fort Johnson Rd., P. O. Box 12410, Charleston, SC 29422. Education, campus ministry, social services.

Charity of Quebec, Sisters of (Grey Nuns), S.C.Q.: Founded 1849, at Quebec; in U.S., 1890. General motherhouse, 2655 Le Pelletier St., Beauport, Que. GIC 3X7, Canada; U.S. address, 359 Summer St., New Bedford, MA 02740. Social work.

Charity of St. Elizabeth, Sisters of (Convent Station, N.J.), S.C.: Founded 1859, at Newark, N. J. General motherhouse, P.O. Box 476, Convent Station, NJ 07961-0476. Education, pastoral ministry, social services.

Charity of St. Hyacinthe, Sisters of (Grey Nuns), S.C.S.H.: Founded 1840, at St. Hyacinthe, Canada; in U.S., 1878. General motherhouse, 16470 Avenue Bourdages, SUD, St. Hyacinthe, Que. J2T 4J8, Canada; U.S. regional house, 98 Campus Ave., Lewiston, ME 04240.

Charity of St. Joan Antida, Sisters of, S.C.S.J.A.: Founded 1799, in France; in U.S., 1932. General motherhouse, Rome, Italy; U.S. provincial house, 8560 N. 76th Pl., Milwaukee, WI 53223.

Charity of St. Louis, Sisters of, S.C.S.L.: Founded 1803, in France; in U.S., 1910. Generalate, Rome, Italy; U.S. provincialate, 4907 S. Catherine St., Plattsburgh, NY 12901.

Charity of St. Vincent de Paul, Daughters of, D.C.: Founded 1633, in France; in U.S. 1809, at Emmitsburg, Md., by St. Elizabeth Ann Seton. General motherhouse, Paris, France. U.S. provinces: Emmitsburg, MD 21727; 7800 Natural Bridge Rd., St. Louis, MO 63121; 9400 New Harmony Rd., Evansville, IN 47720; 96 Menands Rd., Albany, NY 12204; 26000 Altamont Rd., Los Altos Hills, CA 94022.

Charity of St. Vincent de Paul, Sisters of, V.Z.: Founded 1845, in Croatia; in U.S., 1955. General motherhouse, Zagreb, Croatia; U.S. foundation, 171 Knox Ave., West Seneca, NY 14224.

Charity of St. Vincent de Paul, Sisters of, Halifax, S.C.: Founded 1856, at Halifax, N. S., from Emmitsburg foundation. Generalate, Mt. St. Vincent, Halifax, N. S., Canada. U.S. addresses: Commonwealth of Massachusetts, 125 Oakland St., Wellesley Hills, MA 02481; Boston Province, 26 Phipps St., Quincy, MA 02169; New York Province, 84-32 63rd Ave., Middle Village, NY 11379. Educational, hospital, social work.

Charity of St. Vincent de Paul, Sisters of, New York, S.C.: Founded 1817, from Emmitsburg foundation. General motherhouse, Mt. St. Vincent on Hudson, 6301 Riverdale Ave., Bronx, NY 10471. Educational, hospital work.

Charity of the Blessed Virgin Mary, Sisters of, B.V.M.: Founded 1833, in U.S. by Mary Frances Clarke. General motherhouse, BVM Center, 1100 Carmel Dr., Dubuque, IA 52001. Education, pastoral ministry, social services.

Charity of the Immaculate Conception of Ivrea, Sisters of, S.C.I.C.: Founded 18th century, in Italy; in U.S., 1961. General motherhouse, Rome, Italy; U.S. address, Immaculate Virgin of Miracles Convent, Box 348, Mt. Pleasant, PA 15666.

Charity of the Incarnate Word, Congregation of the Sisters of, C.C.V.I.: Founded 1869, at San Antonio, Tex., by Bishop C. M. Dubuis. Generalate, 4709 Broadway, San Antonio, TX 78209.

Charity of the Incarnate Word,Congregation of the Sisters of (Houston, Tex.), C.C.V.I.: Founded 1866, in U.S., by Bishop C. M. Dubuis. General motherhouse, P.O. Box 230969, Houston, TX 77223. Educational, hospital, social work.

Charity of the Sacred Heart, Daughters of, F.C.S.C.J.: Founded 1823, at La Salle de Vihiers, France; in U.S., 1905. General motherhouse, La Salle de Vihiers, France; U.S. address, Sacred Heart Province, Grove St., P.O. Box 642, Littleton, NH 03561.

Charles Borromeo, Missionary Sisters of St. (Scalabrini Srs.): Founded 1895, in Italy; in U.S., 1941. American novitiate, 1414 N. 37th Ave., Melrose Park, IL 60601.

Child Jesus, Sisters of the Poor, P.C.J.: Founded 1844, at Aix-la-Chapelle, Germany; in U.S., 1924. General motherhouse, Simpelveld, Netherlands, American provincialate, 4567 Olentangy River Rd., Columbus, OH 43214.

Chretienne, Sisters of Ste., S.S.CH.: Founded 1807, in France; in U.S., 1903. General motherhouse, Metz, France; U.S. provincial house, 297 Arnold St., Wrentham, MA 02093. Educational, hospital, mission work.

Christ the King, Missionary Sisters of, M.S.C.K.: Founded 1959 in Poland; in U.S., 1978. General motherhouse, Poznan, Poland; U.S. address, 3000 18 Mile Rd., Sterling Heights, MI 48314.

Christ the King, Sister Servants of, S.S.C.K.: Founded 1936, in U.S. General motherhouse, Loretto Convent, Mt. Calvary, WI 53057. Social services.

Christ the King, Sisters of, S.C.K.: Hermitage of Christ the King, 6501 Orchard Station Rd., Sebastopol, CA 95472.

Christian Doctrine, Sisters of Our Lady of, R.C.D.: Founded 1910, in New York. Central office, 23 Haskell Ave., Suffern, NY 10901.

Christian Education, Religious of, R.C.E.: Founded 1817, in France; in U.S., 1905. General motherhouse, France; U.S. provincial residence, 55 Parkwood Dr., Milton, MA 02186.

Cistercian Nuns, O. Cist.: Headquarters, Rome, Italy; U.S. address, Valley of Our Lady Monastery, E. 11096 Yanke Dr., Prairie du Sac, WI 53578.

Cistercian Nuns of the Strict Observance, Order of, O.C.S.O.: Founded 1125, in France, by St. Stephen Harding; in U.S., 1949. U.S. addresses: Mt. St. Mary's Abbey, 300 Arnold St., Wrentham, MA 02093; Santa Rita Abbey, HC1, Box 929, Sonoita, AZ 85637; Our Lady of the Redwoods Abbey, Whitethorn, CA 95589. Our Lady of the Mississippi Abbey, 8400 Abbey Hill Rd., Dubuque, IA 52001; Our Lady of the Angels Monastery, 3365 Monastery Dr., Crozet, VA 22932.

Clare, Sisters of St., O.S.C.: General motherhouse, Dublin, Ireland; U.S. foundation, St. Francis Convent, 226 Santa Clara Dr.,Vista, CA 92083.

Claretian Missionary Sisters (Religious of Mary Immaculate), R.M.I.: Founded 1855, in Cuba; in U.S., 1956. Generalate, Rome, Italy; U.S. address, 9600 W. Atlantic Ave., Delray Beach, FL 33446.

Clergy, Congregation of Our Lady, Help of the, C.L.H.C.: Founded 1961, in U.S. Motherhouse,

Maryvale Convent, 2522 June Bug Rd., Vale, NC 28168.

Clergy, Servants of Our Lady Queen of the, S.R.C.: Founded 1929, in Canada; in U.S., 1934. General motherhouse, 57 Jules A. Brillant, Rimouski, Que. G5L 1X1 Canada. Domestic work.

Colettines: See Franciscan Poor Clare Nuns.

Columban, Missionary Sisters of St., S.S.C.: Founded 1922, in Ireland; in U.S., 1930. General motherhouse, Wicklow, Ireland; U.S. region, 73 Mapleton St., Brighton, MA 02135.

Comboni Missionary Sisters (Missionary Sisters of Verona), C.M.S.: Founded 1872, in Italy; in U.S., 1950. U.S. address, 1307 Lakeside Ave., Richmond, VA 23228.

Consolata Missionary Sisters, M.C.: Founded 1910, in Italy, by Bl. Giuseppe Allamano; in U.S., 1954. General motherhouse, Turin, Italy; U.S. headquarters, 6801 Belmont Rd., Belmont, MI 49306.

Cordi-Marian Missionary Sisters, M.C.M.: Founded 1921, Mexico City; U.S. foundation, 1926. General motherhouse, Mexico. U.S. address, 11624 FM 471, Apt. 402, San Antonio, TX 78253.

Cross, Daughters of the, D.C.: Founded 1640, in France; in U.S., 1855. General motherhouse, 1000 Fairview St., Shreveport, LA 71104. Educational work.

Cross, Daughters of, of Liege, F.C.: Founded 1833, in Liege, Belgium; in U.S., 1958. U.S. address, 165 W. Eaton Ave., Tracy, CA 95376.

Cross, Sisters of the Holy, C.S.C.: Founded 1841, at Le Mans, France, established 1847, in Canada; in U.S., 1881. General motherhouse, St. Laurent, Montreal, Que., Canada; U.S. regional office, 377 Island Pond Rd., Manchester, NH 03109. Educational work.

Cross, Sisters of the Holy, Congregation of, C.S.C.: Founded 1841, at Le Mans, France; in U.S., 1843. General motherhouse, Saint Mary's, Notre Dame, IN 46556. Education, health care, social services, pastoral ministry.

Cross and Passion, Sisters of the (Passionist Sisters), C.P.: Founded 1852; in U.S., 1924. Generalate, Northampton, England; U.S. address: Holy Family Convent, One Wright Lane, N. Kingstown, RI 02852.

Cyril and Methodius, Sisters of Sts., SS.C.M.: Founded 1909, in U.S., by Rev. Matthew Jankola. General motherhouse, Villa Sacred Heart, Danville, PA 17821. Education, care of aged.

Disciples of the Lord Jesus Christ, D.L.J.C.: Founded 1972; canonically erected 1991. Address, P.O. Box 17, Channing, TX 79018.

Divine Compassion, Sisters of, R.D.C.: Founded 1886, in U.S. General motherhouse, 52 N. Broadway, White Plains, NY 10603. Education, other ministries.

Divine Love, Daughters of, D.D.L.: Founded 1969, in Nigeria; in U.S., 1990. General house, Enugu, Nigeria; U.S. regional house, 140 North Ave., Highwood, IL 60040.

Divine Spirit, Congregation of the, C.D.S.: Founded 1956, in U.S., by Archbishop John M. Gannon. Motherhouse, 409 W. 6th St., Erie, PA 16507. Education, social services.

Divine Zeal, Daughters of, F.D.Z.: Founded 1887 in Italy by Bl. Hannibal Maria DiFrancia; in U.S., 1951. Generalate, Rome; U.S. headquarters, Hannibal House Spiritual Center, 1526 Hill Rd., Reading, PA 19602.

DOMINICANS

Nuns of the Order of Preachers (Dominican Nuns), O.P.: Founded 1206 by St. Dominic at Prouille, France. Cloistered, contemplative. Two branches in the United States:

•**Dominican Nuns having perpetual adoration.** First monastery established 1880, in Newark, N.J., from Oullins, France, foundation (1868). Autonomous monasteries:

Monastery of St. Dominic, 375 13th Ave., Newark, NJ 07103-2124; Corpus Christi Monastery, 1230 Lafayette Ave., Bronx, NY 10474; Blessed Sacrament, 29575 Middlebelt Rd., Farmington Hills, MI 48334-2311; Monastery of the Angels, 1977 Carmen Ave., Los Angeles, CA 90068; Corpus Christi, 215 Oak Grove Ave., Menlo Park, CA 94025; Infant Jesus, 1501 Lotus Lane, Lufkin, TX 75904-2699.

• **Dominican Nuns devoted to the perpetual Rosary.** First monastery established 1891, in Union City, N.J., from Calais, France, foundation (1880). Autonomous monasteries (some also observe perpetual adoration):

Dominican Nuns of Perpetual Rosary, 14th and West Sts., Union City, NJ 07087; 217 N. 68th St., Milwaukee, WI 53213; Perpetual Rosary, 1500 Haddon Ave., Camden, NJ 08103; Our Lady of the Rosary, 335 Doat St., Buffalo, NY 14211; Our Lady of the Rosary, 543 Spingfield Ave., Summit, NJ 07901; Monastery of the Mother of God, 1430 Riverdale St., W. Springfield, MA 01089-4698; Perpetual Rosary, 802 Court St., Syracuse, NY 13208; Immaculate Heart of Mary, 1834 Litziz Pike, Lancaster, PA 17601-6585; Mary the Queen, 1310 W. Church St., Elmira, NY 14905; St. Jude, Marbury, AL 36051; Our Lady of Grace Monastery, 11 Race Hill Rd., North Guilford, CT 06437; St. Dominic's Monastery, 4901 16th St. N.W., Washington, DC 20011.

Dominican Sisters of Charity of the Presentation, O.P.: Founded 1696, in France; in U.S., 1906. General motherhouse, Tours, France; U.S. headquarters, 3012 Elm St., Dighton, MA 02715. Hospital work.

Dominican Sisters of Hope (O.P.): Formed 1995 through merger of Dominican Sisters of the Most Holy Rosary, Newburgh, NY; Dominican Sisters of the Sick Poor, Ossining, NY and Dominican Sisters of St. Catherine of Siena, Fall River, MA. General Offices: 229 N. Highland Ave., Ossining, NY 10562.

Dominican Sisters of Our Lady of the Rosary and of St. Catherine of Siena (Cabra): Founded 1644 in Ireland. General motherhouse, Cabra, Dublin, Ireland. U.S. regional house, 1930 Robert E. Lee Rd., New Orleans, LA 70122.

Dominican Sisters of the Perpetual Rosary (O.P.): 217 N. 68th St., Milwaukee, WI 53213. Cloistered, contemplative.

Dominican Sisters of the Roman Congregation of St. Dominic, O.P.: Founded 1621, in France; in U.S., 1904. General motherhouse, Rome, Italy; U.S. province, 305 Oberlin St., Iowa City, IA 52245. Educational work.

Eucharistic Missionaries of St. Dominic, O.P.: Founded 1927, in Louisiana. General motherhouse, 3801 Canal St., Suite 400, New Orleans, LA 70119. Parish work, social services.

Religious Missionaries of St. Dominic, O.P.: General motherhouse, Rome, Italy. U.S. address (Spanish province), 2237 Waldron Rd., Corpus Christi, TX 78418.

Sisters of St. Dominic, O.P.: Names of congregations are given below, followed by the date of foundation, and location of motherhouse.

St. Catherine of Siena, 1822. 2645 Bardstown Rd., St. Catharine, KY 40061.

St. Mary of the Springs, 1830. 2320 Airport Dr., Columbus, OH 43219.

Most Holy Rosary, 1847. Sinsinawa, WI 53824.

Most Holy Name of Jesus, 1850. 1520 Grand Ave., San Rafael, CA 94901.

Holy Cross, 1853. Albany Ave., Amityville, NY 11701.

St. Cecilia, 1860. 801 Dominican Dr., Nashville, TN 37228.

St. Mary, 1860. 7300 St. Charles Ave., New Orleans, LA 70118.

St. Catherine of Siena, 1862. 5635 Erie St., Racine, WI 53402.

Sacred Heart Convent, 1873. 1237 W. Monroe St., Springfield, IL 62704.

Our Lady of the Rosary, 1876. Sparkill, NY 10976.

Queen of the Holy Rosary, 1876. P.O. Box 3908, Mission San Jose, CA 94539.

Most Holy Rosary, 1892. 1257 Siena Heights Dr., Adrian, MI 49221.

Our Lady of the Sacred Heart, 1877. 2025 E. Fulton St., Grand Rapids, MI 49503.

St. Dominic, 1878. 496 Western Hwy., Blauvelt, NY 10913.

St. Catherine de Ricci, 1880. 750 Ashbourne Rd., Elkins Park, PA 19117.

Sisters of St. Dominic, 1881. 1 Ryerson Ave., Caldwell, NJ 07006.

Dominican Sisters of Houston, 1882. 6501 Almeda Rd., Houston, TX 77021-2095.

Tacoma Dominican Center, 1888. 935 Fawcett Ave., Tacoma, WA 98402.

Holy Cross, 1890. P.O. Box 280, Edmonds, WA 98020.

St. Rose of Lima (Servants of Relief for Incurable Cancer) 1896. Hawthorne, NY 10532.

Dominican Sisters of Great Bend, 1902. 3600 Broadway, Great Bend, KS 67530.

Mission Center, 1911. Box 1288, Kenosha, WI 53141.

St. Rose of Lima, 1923. 775 Drahner Rd., Oxford, MI 48371.

Immaculate Conception, 1929. 9000 W. 81st St., Justice, IL 60458.

Immaculate Heart of Mary, 1929. 1230 W. Market St., Akron, OH 44313.

Dominican Sisters of Oakford (St. Catherine of Siena), 1889. Motherhouse, Oakford, Natal, South Africa. U.S. regional house, 1965. 1855 Miramonte Ave., Mountain View, CA 94040.

(END OF LISTING FOR DOMINICANS)

Dorothy, Institute of the Sisters of St., S.S.D.: Founded 1834, in Italy; by St. Paola Frassinetti; in U.S., 1911. General motherhouse, Rome, Italy; U.S. provincialate, Mt. St. Joseph, 13 Monkeywrench Lane, Bristol, RI 02809.

Eucharist, Religious of the, R.E.: Founded 1857, in Belgium; in U.S., 1900. General motherhouse,

Belgium; U.S. foundation, 2907 Ellicott Terr., N.W., Washington, DC 20008.

Family, Congregation of the Sisters of the Holy, S.S.F.: Founded 1842, in Louisiana, by Henriette Delille and Juliette Gaudin. General motherhouse, 6901 Chef Menteur Hwy., New Orleans, LA 70126. Educational, hospital work.

Family, Little Sisters of the Holy, P.S.S.F.: Founded 1880, in Canada; in U.S., 1900. General motherhouse, Sherbrooke, Quebec, Canada. U.S. novitiate, 285 Andover St., Lowell, MA 01852.

Family, Sisters of the Holy, S.H.F.: Founded 1872, in U.S. General motherhouse, P.O. Box 3248, Mission San Jose, CA 94539. Educational, social work.

Family of Nazareth, Sisters of the Holy, C.S.F.N.: Founded 1875, in Italy; in U.S., 1885. General motherhouse, Rome, Italy. U.S. provinces: Sacred Heart, 310 N. River Rd., Des Plaines, IL 60016; Immaculate Conception BVM, 4001 Grant Ave., Torresdale, Philadelphia, PA 19114; St. Joseph, 285 Bellevue Rd., Pittsburgh, PA 15229; Immaculate Heart of Mary, Marian Heights, 1428 Monroe Turnpike, Monroe, CT 06468; Bl. Frances Siedliska Provincialate, 1814 Egyptian Way, Box 530959, Grand Prairie, TX 75053.

Filippini, Religious Teachers, M.P.F.: Founded 1692, in Italy; in U.S., 1910. General motherhouse, Rome, Italy; U.S. provinces: St. Lucy Filippini Province, Villa Walsh, Morristown, NJ 07960; Queen of Apostles Province, 474 East Rd., Bristol, CT 06010. Educational work.

Francis de Sales, Oblate Sisters of St., O.S.F.S.: Founded 1866, in France; in U.S., 1951. General motherhouse, Troyes, France; U.S. headquarters, Villa Aviat Convent, 399 Childs Rd., MD 21916. Educational, social work.

FRANCISCANS

Bernardine Sisters of the Third Order of St. Francis, O.S.F.: Founded 1457, at Cracow, Poland; in U.S., 1894. Generalate, 403 Allendale Rd., King of Prussia, PA 19406. Educational, hospital, social work.

Capuchin Poor Clares (Madres Clarisas Capuchinas): U.S. establishment, 1981, Amarillo diocese. Convent of the Blessed Sacrament and Our Lady of Guadalupe, 4201 N.E. 18th St., Amarillo, TX 79107. Cloistered.

Congregation of the Servants of the Holy Child Jesus of the Third Order Regular of St. Francis, O.S.F.: Founded 1855, in Germany; in U.S., 1929. General motherhouse, Würzburg, Germany; American motherhouse, Villa Maria, 641 Somerset St., North Plainfield, NJ 07060-4909.

Congregation of the Third Order of St. Francis of Mary Immaculate, O.S.F.: Founded 1865, in U.S., by Fr. Pamphilus da Magliano, O.F.M. General motherhouse, 520 Plainfield Ave., Joliet, IL 60435. Educational and pastoral work.

Daughters of St. Francis of Assisi, D.S.F.: Founded 1894, in Hungary; in U.S., 1946. Provincial motherhouse, 507 N. Prairie St., Lacon, IL 61540. Nursing, CCD work.

Eucharistic Franciscan Missionary Sisters, E.F.M.S.: Founded 1943, in Mexico. Motherhouse, 943 S. Soto St., Los Angeles, CA 90023.

Felician Sisters (Congregation of the Sisters of St. Felix), C.S.S.F.: Founded 1855, in Poland by Bl. Mary Angela Truszkowska; in U.S., 1874. General motherhouse, Rome, Italy. U.S. provinces: 36800 Schoolcraft Rd., Livonia, MI 48150; 600 Doat St., Buffalo, NY 14211; 3800 W. Peterson Ave., Chicago, IL 60659; 260 South Main St., Lodi, NJ 07644; 1500 Woodcrest Ave., Coraopolis, PA 15108; 1315 Enfield St., Enfield, CT 06082; 4210 Meadowlark Lane, S.E., Rio Rancho, NM 87124-1021.

Franciscan Handmaids of the Most Pure Heart of Mary, F.H.M.: Founded 1916, in U.S. General motherhouse, 15 W. 124th St., New York, NY 10027. Educational, social work.

Franciscan Hospitaller Sisters of the Immaculate Conception, F.H.I.C.: Founded 1876, in Portugal; in U.S., 1960. General motherhouse, Lisbon, Portugal; U.S. novitiate, 300 S. 17th St., San Jose, CA 95112.

Franciscan Missionaries of Mary, F.M.M.: Founded 1877, in India; in U.S., 1904. General motherhouse, Rome, Italy; U.S. provincialate, 3305 Wallace Ave., Bronx, NY 10467. Mission work.

Franciscan Missionaries of Our Lady, O.S.F.: Founded 1854, at Calais, France; in U.S., 1913. General motherhouse, Desvres, France; U.S. provincial house, 4200 Essen Lane, Baton Rouge, LA 70809. Hospital work.

Franciscan Missionaries of St. Joseph (Mill Hill Sisters), F.M.S.J.: Founded 1883, at Rochdale, Lancashire, England; in U.S., 1952. Generalate, Manchester, England; U.S. headquarters, Franciscan House, 1006 Madison Ave., Albany, NY 12208.

Franciscan Missionary Sisters for Africa, O.S.F.: American foundation, 1953. Generalate, Ireland; U.S. headquarters, 172 Foster St., Brighton, MA 02135.

Franciscan Missionary Sisters of Assisi, F.M.S.A.: First foundation in U.S., 1961. General motherhouse, Assisi, Italy; U.S. address, St. Francis Convent, 1039 Northampton St., Holyoke, MA 01040.

Franciscan Missionary Sisters of Our Lady of Sorrows, O.S.F.: Founded 1939, in China, by Bishop Rafael Palazzi, O.F.M.; in U.S., 1949. U.S. address, 3600 S.W. 170th Ave., Beaverton, OR 97006-5099. Educational, social, domestic, retreat and foreign mission work.

Franciscan Missionary Sisters of the Divine Child, F.M.D.C.: Founded 1927, at Buffalo, NY, by Bishop William Turner. General motherhouse, 6380 Main St., Williamsville, NY 14221. Educational, social work.

Franciscan Missionary Sisters of the Infant Jesus, F.M.I.J.: Founded 1879, in Italy; in U.S., 1961. Generalate, Rome, Italy. U.S. provincialate, 1215 Kresson Rd., Cherry Hill, NJ 08003.

Franciscan Missionary Sisters of the Sacred Heart, F.M.S.C.: Founded 1860, in Italy; in U.S., 1865. Generalate, Rome, Italy; U.S. provincialate, 250 South St., Peekskill, NY 10566. Educational and social welfare apostolates.

Franciscan Poor Clare Nuns (Poor Clares, Order of St. Clare, Poor Clares of St. Colette), P.C., O.S.C., P.C.C.: Founded 1212, at Assisi, Italy, by St. Francis of Assisi; in U.S., 1875. Proto-monastery, Assisi, Italy. Addresses of autonomous motherhouses in U.S. are listed below.
3626 N. 65th Ave., Omaha, NE 68104-3299; 720 Henry Clay Ave., New Orleans, LA 70118-5891; 6825

Nurrenbern Rd., Evansville, IN 47712-8518; 1310 Dellwood Ave., Memphis, TN 38127; 920 Centre St., Jamaica Plain, MA 02130; 201 Crosswicks St., Bordentown, NJ 08505; 1271 Langhorne-Newtown Rd., Langhorne, PA 19047; 4419 N. Hawthorne St., Spokane, WA 99205; 86 Mayflower Ave., New Rochelle, NY, 10801-1615; 421 S. 4th St., Sauk Rapids, MN 56379-1898; 8650 Russell Ave. S., Minneapolis, MN 55431; 3501 Rocky River Dr., Cleveland, OH 44111; 1671 Pleasant Valley Rd., Aptos, CA 95001; 2111 S. Main St., Rockford, IL 61102; 215 E. Los Olivos St., Santa Barbara, CA 93105; 460 River Rd., Andover, MA 01810; 809 E. 19th St., Roswell, NM 88201; 28210 Natoma Rd., Los Altos Hills, CA 94022; 1916 N. Pleasantburg Dr., Greenville, SC 29609-4080; 28 Harpersville Rd., Newport News, VA 23601; 1175 N. 300 W., Kokomo, IN 46901-1799; 3900 Sherwood Blvd., Delray Beach, FL 33445; 200 Marycrest Dr., St. Louis, MO 63129; 6029 Estero Blvd., Fort Myers Beach, FL 33931; 9300 Hwy 105, Brenham, TX 77833.

Franciscan Sisters, Daughters of the Sacred Hearts of Jesus and Mary, O.S.F.: Founded 1860, in Germany; in U.S., 1872. Generalate, Rome, Italy; U.S. motherhouse, P.O. Box 667, Wheaton, IL 60189. Educational, hospital, foreign mission, social work.

Franciscan Sisters Daughters of Mercy, F.H.M.: Founded 1856, in Spain; in U.S., 1962. General motherhouse, Palma de Mallorca, Spain; U.S. address, 612 N. 3rd St., Waco, TX 76701.

Franciscan Sisters of Allegany, O.S.F.: Founded 1859, at Allegany, N.Y., by Fr. Pamphilus da Magliano, O.F.M. General motherhouse Allegany, 115 East Main St., Allegany, NY 14706. Educational, hospital, foreign mission work.

Franciscan Sisters of Baltimore, O.S.F.: Founded 1868, in England; in U.S., 1881. General motherhouse, 3725 Ellerslie Ave., Baltimore, MD 21218. Educational work; social services.

Franciscan Sisters of Chicago, O.S.F.: Founded 1894, in U.S., by Mother Mary Therese (Josephine Dudzik). General motherhouse, 14700 Main St., Lemont, IL 60439. Educational work, social services.

Franciscan Sisters of Christian Charity, O.S.F.: Founded 1869, in U.S. Motherhouse, Holy Family Convent, 2409 S. Alverno Rd., Manitowoc, WI 54220. Educational, hospital work.

Franciscan Sisters of Little Falls, Minn., O.S.F.: Founded 1891, in U.S. General motherhouse, Little Falls, MN 56345. Health, education, social services, pastoral ministry, mission work.

Franciscan Sisters of Mary, F.S.M.: Established, 1987, through unification of the Sisters of St. Mary of the Third Order of St. Francis (founded 1872, St. Louis) and the Sisters of St. Francis of Maryville, Mo. (founded 1894). Address of general superior: 1100 Bellevue Ave., St. Louis, MO 63117-1883. Health care, social services.

Franciscan Sisters of Mary Immaculate of the Third Order of St. Francis of Assisi, F.M.I.: Founded 16th century, in Switzerland; in U.S., 1932. General motherhouse, Bogota, Colombia; U.S. provincial house, 4301 N.E. 18th Ave., Amarillo, TX 79107-7220. Education.

Franciscan Sisters of Our Lady of Perpetual Help, O.S.F.: Founded 1901, in U.S., from Joliet, Ill.,

foundation. General motherhouse, 335 South Kirkwood Rd., St. Louis, MO 63122. Educational, hospital work.

Franciscan Sisters of Peace, F.S.P.: Established 1986, in U.S., as archdiocesan community, from Franciscan Missionary Sisters of the Sacred Heart. Congregation Center, 20 Ridge St., Haverstraw, NY 10927.

Franciscan Sisters of Ringwood, F.S.R.: Founded 1927, at Passaic, New Jersey. General motherhouse, Mt. St. Francis, 474 Sloatsburg Rd., Ringwood, NJ 07456. Educational work.

Franciscan Sisters of St. Elizabeth, F.S.S.E.: Founded 1866, at Naples, Italy, by Bl. Ludovico of Casorio; in U.S., 1919. General motherhouse, Rome; U.S. delegate house, 499 Park Rd., Parsippany, NJ 07054. Educational work, social services.

Franciscan Sisters of St. Joseph, F.S.S.J.: Founded 1897, in U.S. General motherhouse, 5286 S. Park Ave., Hamburg, NY 14075. Educational, hospital work.

Franciscan Sisters of St. Joseph (of Mexico): U.S. foundation, St. Paul College, 3015 4th St. N.E., Washington, DC 20017.

Franciscan Sisters of the Atonement (Graymoor Sisters), S.A.: Founded 1898, in U.S., as Anglican community; entered Church, 1909. General motherhouse, St. Francis Convent – Graymoor, 41 Old Highland Turnpike, Garrison, NY 10524. Mission work.

Franciscan Sisters of St. Paul, Minn., O.S.F.: Founded 1863, at Neuwied, Germany (Franciscan Sisters of the Blessed Virgin Mary of the Holy Angels); in U.S., 1923. General motherhouse, Rhine, Germany; U.S. motherhouse, 1388 Prior Ave. S., St. Paul, MN 55116. Educational, hospital, social work.

Franciscan Sisters of the Immaculate Conception, O.S.F.: Founded in Germany; in U.S., 1928. General motherhouse, Kloster, Bonlanden, Germany; U.S. province, 291 W. North St., Buffalo, NY 14201.

Franciscan Sisters of the Immaculate Conception, O.S.F.: Founded 1874, in Mexico; in U.S., 1926. U.S. provincial house, 11306 Laurel Canyon Blvd., San Fernando, CA 91340.

Franciscan Sisters of the Immaculate Conception, Missionary, M.F.I.C.: Founded 1873, in U.S. General motherhouse, Rome, Italy; U.S. address, 790 Centre St., Newton, MA 02158. Educational work.

Franciscan Sisters of the Immaculate Conception and St. Joseph for the Dying, O.S.F.: Founded 1919, in U.S. General motherhouse, 1249 Joselyn Canyon Rd., Monterey, CA 93940.

Franciscan Sisters of the Poor, S.F.P.: Founded 1845, at Aachen, Germany, by Bl. Frances Schervier; in U.S., 1858. Congregational office, 133 Remsen St., Brooklyn, NY 11201. Hospital, social work and foreign missions.

Franciscan Sisters of the Sacred Heart, O.S.F.: Founded 1866, in Germany; in U.S., 1876. General motherhouse, St. Francis Woods, 9201 W. St. Francis Rd., Frankfort, IL 60423. Education, health care, other service ministries.

Hospital Sisters of the Third Order of St. Francis, O.S.F.: Founded 1844, in Germany; in U.S., 1875. General motherhouse, Muenster, Germany; U.S. motherhouse, Box 19431, Springfield, IL 62794. Hospital work.

Institute of the Franciscan Sisters of the Eucha-

rist, F.S.E.: Founded 1973. Motherhouse, 405 Allen Ave., Meriden, CT 06450.

Little Franciscans of Mary, P.F.M.: Founded 1889, in U.S. General motherhouse, Baie St. Paul, Quebec, Canada. U.S. region, 2 Dupont St., Worcester, MA 01604. Educational, hospital, social work.

Missionary Sisters of the Immaculate Conception of the Mother of God, S.M.I.C.: Founded 1910, in Brazil; in U.S., 1922, U.S. provincialate, P.O. Box 3026, Paterson, NJ 07509. Mission, educational, health work, social services.

Mothers of the Helpless, M.D.: Founded 1873, in Spain; in U.S., 1916. General motherhouse, Valencia, Spain; U.S. address, Sacred Heart Residence, 432 W. 20th St., New York, NY 10011.

Poor Clares of Perpetual Adoration, P.C.P.A.: Founded 1854, at Paris, France; in U.S., 1921, at Cleveland, Ohio. U.S. monasteries: 4200 N. Market Ave., Canton, OH 44714; 2311 Stockham Lane, Portsmouth, OH 45662-3049; 4108 Euclid Ave., Cleveland, OH 44103; 3900 13th St. N.E., Washington, DC 20017; 5817 Old Leeds Rd., Birmingham, AL 35210. Contemplative, cloistered, perpetual adoration.

St. Francis Mission Community, O.S.F.: Autonomous province of Franciscan Sisters of Mary Immaculate. Address: 4305 54th St., Lubbock, TX 79413.

School Sisters of St. Francis, O.S.F.: Founded 1874, in U.S. General motherhouse, 1501 S. Layton Blvd., Milwaukee, WI 53215.

School Sisters of St. Francis, (Pittsburgh, Pa.), O.S.F.: Established 1913, in U.S. Motherhouse, Mt. Assisi Convent, 934 Forest Ave., Pittsburgh, PA 15202. Education, health care services and related ministries.

School Sisters of the Third Order of St. Francis (Bethlehem, Pa.), O.S.F.: Founded in Austria, 1843; in U.S., 1913. General motherhouse, Rome, Italy; U.S. province, 395 Bridle Path Rd., Bethlehem, PA 18017. Educational, mission work.

School Sisters of the Third Order of St. Francis (Panhandle, Tex.), O.S.F.: Established 1931, in U.S., from Vienna, Austria, foundation (1845). General motherhouse, Vienna, Austria; U.S. center and novitiate, P.O. Box 906, Panhandle, TX 79068. Educational, social work.

Sisters of Mercy of the Holy Cross, S.C.S.C.: Founded 1856, in Switzerland; in U.S. 1912. General motherhouse, Ingenbohl, Switzerland; U.S. provincial residence, 501 S. Center Ave., Merrill, WI 54452.

Sisters of Our Lady of Mercy (Mercedarians), S.O.L.M.: General motherhouse, Rome, Italy; U.S. addresses: Most Precious Blood, 133 27th Ave., Brooklyn, NY 11214; St. Edward School, Pine Hill, NJ 08021.

Sisters of St. Elizabeth, S.S.E.: Founded 1931, at Milwaukee, Wis. Address, 2005 Division St., Manitowoc, WI 53005.

Sisters of St. Francis (Clinton, Iowa), O.S.F.: Founded 1868, in U.S. General motherhouse, 588 N. Bluff Blvd., Clinton, IA 57232-3953. Educational, hospital, social work.

Sisters of St. Francis (Millvale, Pa.), O.S.F.: Founded 1865, Pittsburgh. General motherhouse, 146 Hawthorne Rd., Millvale P.O., Pittsburgh, PA 15209. Educational, hospital work.

Sisters of St. Francis (Hastings-on-Hudson), O.S.F.: Founded 1893, in New York. General motherhouse, 49 Jackson Ave., Hastings-on-Hudson, NY 10706-3217. Education, parish ministry, social services.

Sisters of St. Francis of Assisi, O.S.F.: Founded 1849, in U.S. General motherhouse, 3221 S. Lake Dr., St. Francis, WI, 53235-3799. Education, other ministries.

Sisters of St. Francis of Christ the King, O.S.F.: Founded 1864, in Austria; in U.S., 1909. General motherhouse, Rome, Italy; U.S. provincial house, 13900 Main St., Lemont, IL 60439. Educational work, home for aged.

Sisters of St. Francis of Penance and Christian Charity, O.S.F.: Founded 1835, in Holland; in U.S., 1874. General motherhouse, Rome, Italy. U.S. provinces: 4421 Lower River Rd., Stella Niagara, NY 14144; 2851 W. 52nd Ave., Denver, CO 80221; 3910 Bret Harte Dr., P.O. Box 1028, Redwood City, CA 94064.

Sisters of St. Francis of Philadelphia, O.S.F.: Founded 1855, at Philadelphia, by Mother Mary Francis Bachmann and St. John N. Neumann. General motherhouse, Convent of Our Lady of the Angels, Aston, PA 19014. Education, health care, social services.

Sisters of St. Francis of Savannah, Mo., O.S.F.: Founded 1850, in Austria; in U.S., 1922. Provincial house, La Verna Heights, Box 488, 104 E. Park, Savannah, MO 64485-0488. Educational, hospital work.

Sisters of St. Francis of the Congregation of Our Lady of Lourdes, O.S.F.: Founded 1916, in U.S. General motherhouse, 6832 Convent Blvd., Sylvania, OH 43560-2897. Education, health care, social services, pastoral ministry.

Sisters of St. Francis of the Holy Cross, O.S.F.: Founded 1881, in U.S., by Rev. Edward Daems, O.S.C. General motherhouse, 3025 Bay Settlement Rd., Green Bay, WI 54311. Educational, nursing work, pastoral ministry, foreign missions.

Sisters of St. Francis of the Holy Eucharist, O.S.F.: Founded 1378, in Switzerland; in U.S., 1893. General motherhouse, 2100 N. Noland Rd., Independence, MO 64050. Education, health care, social services, foreign missions.

Sisters of St. Francis of the Holy Family, O.S.F.: U.S. foundation, 1875. Motherhouse, Mt. St. Francis, 3390 Windsor Ave., Dubuque, IA 52001. Varied apostolates.

Sisters of St. Francis of the Immaculate Conception, O.S.F.: Founded 1890, in U.S. General motherhouse, 2408 W. Heading Ave., West Peoria, IL 61604-5096. Education, care of aging, pastoral ministry.

Sisters of St. Francis of the Immaculate Heart of Mary, O.S.F.: Founded 1241, in Bavaria; in U.S., 1913. General motherhouse, Rome, Italy; U.S. motherhouse, Hankinson, ND 58041. Education, social services.

Sisters of St. Francis of the Martyr St. George, O.S.F.: Founded 1859, in Germany; in U.S., 1923. General motherhouse, Thuine, Germany; U.S. provincial house, St. Francis Convent, 2120 Central Ave., Alton, IL 62002. Education, social services, foreign mission work.

Sisters of St. Francis of the Perpetual Adoration, O.S.F.: Founded 1863, in Germany; in U.S., 1875. General motherhouse, Olpe, Germany. U.S. provinces:

Box 766, Mishawaka, IN 46544; 7665 Assisi Heights, Colorado Springs, CO 80919.

Sisters of St. Francis of the Providence of God, O.S.F.: Founded 1922, in U.S., by Msgr. M. L. Krusas. General motherhouse, 3603 McRoberts Rd., Pittsburgh, PA 15234. Education, varied apostolates.

Sisters of St. Francis of the Third Order Regular, O.S.F.: Founded 1861, at Buffalo, N.Y., from Philadelphia foundation. General motherhouse, P.O. Box 275, Williamsville, NY 14231-0275. Educational, hospital work.

Sisters of St. Joseph of the Third Order of St. Francis, S.S.J.: Founded 1901, in U.S. Administrative office, 1300 Maria Dr., Stevens Pt., WI 54481-0305. Education, health care, social services.

Sisters of the Infant Jesus, I.J.: Founded 1662, at Rouen, France; in U.S., 1950. Motherhouse, Paris, France. Generalate, Rome, Italy. U.S. address: 20 Reiner St., Colma, CA 94014.

Sisters of the Sorrowful Mother (Third Order of St. Francis), S.S.M.: Founded 1883, in Italy; in U.S., 1889. General motherhouse, Rome, Italy. U.S. address: 17600 E. 51st St., Broken Arrow, OK 74012. Educational, hospital work.

Sisters of the Third Franciscan Order, O.S.F.: Founded 1860, at Syracuse, N.Y. Generalate offices, 2500 Grant Blvd., Syracuse, NY 13208.

Sisters of the Third Order of St. Francis, O.S.F.: Founded 1877, in U.S., by Bishop John L. Spalding. Motherhouse, 1175 St. Francis Lane, E. Peoria, IL 61611-1299. Hospital work.

Sisters of the Third Order of St. Francis (Oldenburg, Ind.), O.S.F.: Founded 1851, in U.S. General motherhouse, Convent of the Immaculate Conception, Oldenburg, IN 47036. Education, social services, pastoral ministry, foreign missions.

Sisters of the Third Order of St. Francis of Penance and Charity, O.S.F.: Founded 1869, in U.S., by Rev. Joseph Bihn. Motherhouse, St. Francis Ave., Tiffin, OH 44883. Education, social services.

Sisters of the Third Order of St. Francis of the Perpetual Adoration, F.S.P.A.: Founded 1849, in U.S. Generalate, 912 Market St., La Crosse, WI 54601. Education, health care.

Sisters of the Third Order Regular of St. Francis of the Congregation of Our Lady of Lourdes, O.S.F.: Founded 1877, in U.S. General motherhouse, Assisi Heights, Rochester, MN 55901. Education, health care, social services.

(END OF LISTING FOR FRANCISCANS)

Good Shepherd Sisters (Servants of the Immaculate Heart of Mary), S.C.I.M.: Founded 1850, in Canada; in U.S., 1882. General motherhouse, Quebec, Canada; Provincial House, Bay View, 313 Seaside Ave., Saco, Maine 04072. Educational, social work.

Good Shepherd, Sisters of Our Lady of Charity of the, R.G.S.: Founded 1835, in France by St. Mary Euphrasia Pelletier; in U.S., 1843. Generalate, Rome, Italy. U.S. provinces: 2849 Fischer Pl., Cincinnati, OH 45211; 82-31 Doncaster Pl., Jamaica, NY 11432; 504 Hexton Hill Rd., Silver Spring, MD 20904; 7654 Natural Bridge Rd., St. Louis, MO 63121; 5100 Hodgson Rd., St. Paul, MN 55112. Active and contemplative (Contemplative Sisters of the Good Shepherd, C.G.S.).

Graymoor Sisters: See **Franciscan Sisters of the Atonement.**

Grey Nuns of the Sacred Heart, G.N.S.H.: Founded 1921, in U.S. General motherhouse, 1750 Quarry Rd., Yardley, PA 19067.

Guadalupan Missionaries of the Holy Spirit, M.G.Sp.S.: Founded 1930 in Mexico by Rev. Felix de Jesus Rougier, M.Sp.S. General motherhouse, Mexico; U.S. delegation: 2483 S.W. 4th St. Miami, FL 33135.

Guardian Angel, Sisters of the, S.A.C.: Founded 1839, in France. General motherhouse, Madrid, Spain; U.S. foundation, 4529 New York St., Los Angeles, CA 90022.

Handmaids of Mary Immaculate, A.M.I.: Founded 1952 in Helena, Mont. Address: Mountain View Rd., Washington, NJ 07882.

Handmaids of the Holy Child Jesus, Congregation of, H.H.C.J.: Founded 1931 in Nigeria. General motherhouse, Nigeria. U.S. headquarters, 1707 Bryant Ave. N., Minneapolis, MN 55411.

Handmaids of the Precious Blood, Congregation of, H.P.B.: Founded 1947, at Jemez Springs, N. Mex. Motherhouse and novitiate, Cor Jesu Monastery, P.O. Box 90, Jemez Springs, NM 87025.

Helpers, Society of, H.H.S.: Founded 1856, in France; in U.S., 1892. General motherhouse, Paris, France; American province, 303 W. Barry Ave., Chicago, IL 60657.

Hermanas Catequistas Guadalupanas, H.C.G.: Founded 1923, in Mexico; in U.S., 1950. General motherhouse, Mexico; U.S. addresses: 4110 S. Flores, San Antonio, TX 78214; 115 Arlington Ct., San Antonio, TX 78210.

Hermanas Josefinas, H.J.: General motherhouse, Mexico; U.S. foundation, Assumption Seminary, 2600 W. Woodlawn Ave., P.O. Box 28240, San Antonio, TX 78284. Domestic work.

Holy Child Jesus, Society of the, S.H.C.J.: Founded 1846, in England; in U.S., 1862. General motherhouse, Rome, Italy. U.S. province: 460 Shadeland Ave., Drexel Hill, PA 19026.

Holy Faith, Congregation of the Sisters of the, C.H.F.: Founded 1856, in Ireland; in U.S., 1953. General motherhouse, Dublin, Ireland; U.S. province, 12322 S. Paramount Blvd., P.O. Box 2085, Downey, CA 90242.

Holy Heart of Mary, Servants of the, S.S.C.M.: Founded 1860, in France; in U.S., 1889. General motherhouse, Montreal, Quebec, Canada; U.S. province, 145 S. 4th Ave., Kankakee, IL 60901. Educational, hospital, social work.

Holy Names of Jesus and Mary, Sisters of the, S.N.J.M.: Founded 1843, in Canada by Bl. Marie Rose Durocher; in U.S., 1859. Generalate, Longueuil, Quebec, Canada. U.S. addresses: Oregon Province, Box 25, Marylhurst, OR 97036; California Province, P.O. Box 907, Los Gatos, CA 95033; New York Province, 1061 New Scotland Rd., Albany, NY 12208; Washington Province, 2911 W. Ft. Wright Dr., Spokane, WA 99204.

Holy Spirit, Community of the, C.H.S.: Founded 1970 in San Diego, Calif. Address: 6151 Rancho Mission Rd., No. 205, San Diego, CA 95108.

Holy Spirit, Daughters of the, D.H.S.: Founded 1706, in France; in U.S., 1902. Generalate, Bretagne, France; U.S. motherhouse, 72 Church St., Putnam, CT 06260. Educational work, district nursing; pastoral ministry.

Holy Spirit, Mission Sisters of the, M.S.Sp.: Founded 1932, at Cleveland, Ohio. Motherhouse, 1030 N. River Rd., Saginaw, MI 48603.

Holy Spirit, Missionary Sisters, Servants of the: Founded 1889, in Holland; in U.S., 1901. Generalate, Rome, Italy; U.S. motherhouse, Convent of the Holy Spirit, Techny, IL 60082.

Holy Spirit, Sisters of the, C.S.Sp.: Founded 1890, in Rome, Italy; in U.S. as independent diocesan community, 1929. General motherhouse, 10102 Granger Rd., Garfield Hts., OH 44125. Educational, social, nursing work.

Holy Spirit, Sisters of the, S.H.S.: Founded 1913, in U.S., by Most Rev. J. F. Regis Canevin. General motherhouse, 5246 Clarwin Ave., Ross Township, Pittsburgh, PA 15229-2208. Educational, nursing work; care of aged.

Holy Spirit and Mary Immaculate, Sisters of, S.H.Sp.: Founded 1893, in U.S. Motherhouse, 301 Yucca St., San Antonio, TX 78203. Education, hospital work.

Holy Spirit of Perpetual Adoration, Sister Servants of the: Founded 1896, in Holland; in U.S., 1915. Generalate, Bad Driburg, Germany; U.S. novitiate, 2212 Green St., Philadelphia, PA 19130.

Holy Union Sisters, S.U.S.C.: Founded 1826, in France; in U.S., 1886. Generalate, Rome, Italy. U.S. provinces: 550 Rock St., Fall River, MA 02720-3426; Box 993, Main St., Groton, MA 01450. Varied ministries.

Home Mission Sisters of America (Glenmary Sisters): Founded 1952, in U.S. Glenmary Center, P.O. Box 22264, Owensboro, KY 42302-2264.

Home Visitors of Mary, Sisters, H.V.M.: Founded 1949, in Detroit, Mich. Motherhouse, 121 E. Boston Blvd., Detroit, MI 48202.

Humility of Mary, Congregation of, C.H.M.: Founded 1854, in France; in U.S., 1864. U.S. address, Humility of Mary Center, 820 West Central Park Ave., Davenport, IA 52804.

Humility of Mary, Sisters of the, H.M.: Founded 1854, in France; in U.S., 1864. U.S. address, Villa Maria Community Center, Villa Maria, PA 16155.

Immaculate Conception, Little Servant Sisters of the: Founded 1850, in Poland; in U.S., 1926. General motherhouse, Poland; U.S. provincial house, 1000 Cropwell Rd., Cherry Hill, NJ 08003. Education, social services, African missions.

Immaculate Conception, Sisters of the, R.C.M.: Founded 1892, in Spain; in U.S., 1962. General motherhouse, Madrid, Spain; U.S. address, 2230 Franklin, San Francisco, CA 94109.

Immaculate Conception, Sisters of the, C.I.C.: Founded 1874, in U.S. General motherhouse, P.O. Box 50426, New Orleans, LA 70185.

Immaculate Conception of the Blessed Virgin Mary, Sisters of the (Lithuanian): Founded 1918, at Mariampole, Lithuania; in U.S., 1936. U.S. headquarters, Immaculate Conception Convent, 600 Liberty Hwy., Putnam, CT 06260.

Immaculate Heart of Mary, Missionary Sisters, I.C.M.: Founded 1897, in India; in U.S., 1919. Generalate, Rome, Italy; U.S. province, 283 E. 15th St., New York, NY 10003. Educational social, foreign mission work.

Immaculate Heart of Mary, Sisters of the: Founded 1848, in Spain; in U.S., 1878. General

motherhouse, Rome, Italy. U.S. province, 4100 Sabino Canyon Rd., Tucson, AZ 85715. Educational work.

Immaculate Heart of Mary, Sisters of the (California Institute of the Most Holy and Immaculate Heart of the B.V.M.), I.H.M.: Founded 1848, in Spain; in U.S., 1871. Generalate, 3431 Waverly Dr., Los Angeles, CA 90027.

Immaculate Heart of Mary, Sisters, Servants of the, I.H.M.: Founded 1845, at Monroe, Mich., by Rev. Louis Florent Gillet. Generalate, 610 W. Elm St., Monroe, MI 48161.

Immaculate Heart of Mary, Sisters, Servants of the, I.H.M.: Founded 1845; established in Scranton, Penn., 1871. General motherhouse, 2300 Adams Ave., Scranton, PA 18509.

Immaculate Heart of Mary, Sisters Servants of the, I.H.M.: Founded 1845; established in West Chester, Penn., 1872. General motherhouse, Villa Maria, Immaculata, PA 19345.

Immaculate Heart of Mary of Wichita, Sisters of, I.H.M.: Established at Wichita, 1979. Address: 605 N. Woodchuck, Wichita, KS 67212.

Incarnate Word, Religious of, C.V.I.: General motherhouse, Mexico City, Mexico. U.S. address, 153 Rainier Ct., Chula Vista, CA 92011.

Incarnate Word and Blessed Sacrament, Congregation of, C.V.I.: Founded 1625, in France; in U.S., 1853. Incarnate Word Convent, 3400 Bradford Pl., Houston, TX 77028.

Incarnate Word and Blessed Sacrament, Congregation of the, I.W.B.S.: Motherhouse, 1101 Northeast Water St., Victoria, TX 77901.

Incarnate Word and Blessed Sacrament, Congregation of the, I.W.B.S.: Motherhouse, 2930 S. Alameda, Corpus Christi, TX 78404.

Incarnate Word and Blessed Sacrament, Sisters of the, S.I.W.: Founded 1625, in France; in U.S. 1853. Motherhouse, 6618 Pearl Rd., Parma Heights, Cleveland, OH 44130.

Infant Jesus, Congregation of the (Nursing Sisters of the Sick Poor), C.I.J.: Founded 1835, in France; in U.S., 1905. General motherhouse, 310 Prospect Park W., Brooklyn, NY 11215.

Jesus, Daughters of, F.I.: Founded 1871, in Spain; in U.S., 1950. General motherhouse, Rome, Italy; U.S. address, 2021 Stuart Ave., Baton Rouge, LA 70808.

Jesus, Daughters of (*Filles de Jesus*), F.J.: Founded 1834, in France; in U.S., 1904. General motherhouse, Kermaria, Locmine, France; U.S. address, 4209 3rd Ave. S., Great Falls, Mont. 59405. Educational, hospital, parish and social work.

Jesus, Little Sisters of: Founded 1939, in Sahara; in U.S., 1952. General motherhouse, Rome, Italy; U.S. headquarters, 400 N. Streeper St., Baltimore, MD 21224.

Jesus, Servants of, S.J.: Founded 1974, in U.S. Central Office, 9075 Big Lake Rd., P.O. Box 128, Clarkston, MI 48016.

Jesus, Society of the Sisters, Faithful Companions of, F.C.J.: Founded 1820, in France; in U.S., 1896. General motherhouse, Kent, England. U.S. province: St. Philomena Convent, Cory's Lane, Portsmouth, RI 02871.

Jesus and Mary, Little Sisters of, L.S.J.M.: Founded 1974 in U.S. Address: Joseph House, P.O. Box 1755, Salisbury, MD 21802.

Jesus and Mary, Religious of, R.J.M.: Founded

1818, at Lyons, France; in U.S., 1877. General motherhouse, Rome, Italy; U.S. province, 3706 Rhode Island Ave., Mt. Ranier, MD 20712. Educational work.

Jesus Crucified, Congregation of: Founded 1930, in France; in U.S., 1955. General motherhouse, Brou, France; U.S. foundations: Regina Mundi Priory, 550 South Waterloo Rd., Devon, PA 19333-1798; St. Paul's Priory, 61 Narragansett, Newport, RI 02840-4099.

Jesus Crucified and the Sorrowful Mother, Poor Sisters of, C.J.C.: Founded 1924, in U.S., by Rev. Alphonsus Maria, C.P. Motherhouse, 261 Thatcher St., Brockton, MA 02402. Education, nursing homes, catechetical centers.

Jesus, Mary and Joseph, Missionaries of, M.J.M.J.: Founded 1942, in Spain; in U.S., 1956. General motherhouse, Madrid, Spain; U.S. regional house, 12940 Up River Rd., Corpus Christi, TX 78410.

Joan of Arc, Sisters of St., S.J.A.: Founded 1914, in U.S., by Rev. Marie Clement Staub, A.A. General motherhouse, 1505, rue de l'Assomption Sillery, Que. G1S 4T3, Canada. U.S. novitiate, 529 Eastern Ave., Fall River, MA 02723. Spiritual and temporal service of priests.

John the Baptist, Sisters of St., C.S.J.B.: Founded 1878, in Italy; in U.S., 1906. General motherhouse, Rome, Italy; U.S. provincialate, 3308 Campbell Dr., Bronx, N.Y. 10465. Education, parish and retreat work; social services.

Joseph, Poor Sisters of St.: Founded 1880, in Argentina. General motherhouse, Muniz, Buenos Aires, Argentina; U.S. addresses, Casa Belen, 305 E. 4th St., Bethlehem, PA 78015; Casa Nazareth, 5321 Spruce St., Reading, PA 19602; St. Gabriel Convent, 4319 Sano St., Alexandria, VA 22312.

Joseph, Religious Daughters of St., F.S.J.: Founded 1875, in Spain. General motherhouse, Spain; U.S. foundation, 319 N. Humphreys Ave., Los Angeles, CA 90022.

Joseph, Religious Hospitallers of St., R.H.S.J.: Founded 1636, in France; in U.S., 1894. Generalate, Montréal, Qué., Canada; U.S. address, Holy Family Convent, 100 Mansfield Ave., P.O. Box 176, Burlington, VT 05401. Hospital work.

Joseph, Servants of St., S.S.J.: Founded 1874, in Spain; in U.S., 1957. General motherhouse, Salamanca, Spain; U.S. address, 203 N. Spring St., Falls Church, VA 22046.

Joseph, Sisters of St., C.S.J. or S.S.J.: Founded 1650, in France; in U.S., 1836, at St. Louis. Independent motherhouses in U.S.:

637 Cambridge St., Brighton, MA 02135; 1515 W. Ogden Ave., La Grange Park, IL, 60525; 480 S. Batavia St., Orange, CA 92668.

St. Joseph Convent, 1725 Brentwood Rd., Brentwood, NY 11717-5587; 23 Agassiz Circle, Buffalo, NY 14214; 129 Convent Ave., Rutland, VT 05701; 3430 Rocky River Dr., Cleveland, OH 44111; 1440 W. Division Rd., Tipton, IN 46072-8584herhouse and Novitiate, P.O. Box 34, Nazareth, MI 49074; 1425 Washington St., Watertown, NY 13601; Mt. Gallitzin Academy, 1016 State St., Baden, PA 15005-1399; 5031 W. Ridge Rd., Erie, PA 16506.

4095 East Ave., Rochester, NY 14610; 215 Court St., Concordia, KS 66901; Mont Marie, Holyoke, MA

01040; Pogue Run Rd., Wheeling, WV 26003; 3700 E. Lincoln St., Wichita, KS 67218.

Joseph, Sisters of St. (Lyons, France), C.S.J.: Founded 1650, in France; in U.S., 1906. General motherhouse, Lyons, France; U.S. provincialate, 93 Halifax St., Winslow, ME 04901. Educational, hospital work.

Joseph, Sisters of St., of Peace, C.S.J.P.: Founded 1884, in England; in U.S. 1885. Generalate, 1225 Newton St. N.E., Washington, DC 20017. Educational, hospital, social service work.

Joseph of Carondelet, Sisters of St., C.S.J.: Founded 1650, in France; in U.S., 1836, at St. Louis, Mo. U.S. headquarters, 2307 S. Lindbergh Blvd., St. Louis, MO 63131.

Joseph of Chambery, Sisters of St.: Founded 1650, in France; in U.S., 1885. Generalate, Rome, Italy; U.S. provincial house, 27 Park Rd., West Hartford, CT 06119. Educational, hospital, social work.

Joseph of Chestnut Hill, Sisters of St., S.S.J.: Founded 1650; Philadelphia foundation, 1847. Motherhouse, Mt. St. Joseph Convent, Chestnut Hill, PA 19118.

Joseph of Cluny, Sisters of St., S.S.J.C.: Founded 1807, in France. Generalate, Paris, France; U.S. provincial house, Brenton St., Newport, RI 02840.

Joseph of Medaille, Sisters of, C.S.J.: Founded 1650, in France; in U.S., 1855. Became an American congregation Nov. 30, 1977. Central office, 1821 Summit Rd., Suite 210, Cincinnati, OH 45237.

Joseph of St. Augustine, Florida, Sisters of St., S.S.J.: General motherhouse, 241 St. George St., P.O. Box 3506, St. Augustine, FL 32085. Educational, hospital, pastoral, social work.

Joseph of St. Mark, Sisters of St., S.J.S.M.: Founded 1845, in France; in U.S., 1937. General motherhouse, 21800 Chardon Rd., Euclid, Cleveland, OH 44117. Nursing homes.

Joseph the Worker, Sisters of St., S.J.W.: General motherhouse, St. William Convent, 1 St. Joseph Lane, Walton, KY 41094.

Lamb of God, Sisters of the, A.D.: Founded 1945, in France; in U.S., 1958. General motherhouse, France; U.S. address, 2068 Wyandotte Ave., Owensboro KY 42301.

Life, Sisters of, S.V. (Sorer Vitae): Founded by Cardinal John J. O'Connor, 1991, to protect life. Address: St. Frances de Chantal Convent, 198 Hollywood Ave., Bronx, NY 10465.

Little Sisters of the Gospel, L.S.G.: Founded 1963 in France by Rev. Rene Voillaume; in U.S., 1972. U.S. address, Box 305, Mott Haven Sta., Bronx, NY 10454.

Little Workers of the Sacred Hearts, P.O.S.C.: Founded 1892, in Italy; in U.S., 1948. General house, Rome, Italy; U.S. address, Our Lady of Grace Convent, 635 Glenbrook Rd., Stamford, CT 06906.

Living Word, Sisters of the, S.L.W.: Founded 1975, in U.S. Motherhouse, Living Word Center, 800 N. Fernandez Ave. B, Arlington Heights, IL 60004-5316. Education, hospital, parish ministry work.

Loretto at the Foot of the Cross, Sisters of, S.L.: Founded 1812 in U.S., by Rev. Charles Nerinckx. General motherhouse, Nerinx, KY 40049. Educational work.

Louis, Congregation of Sisters of St., S.S.L.: Founded 1842, in France; in U.S., 1949. General motherhouse, Monaghan, Ireland; U.S. regional house, 22300 Mulholland Dr., Woodland Hills, CA 91364. Educational, medical, parish, foreign mission work.

Lovers of the Holy Cross Sisters (Phat Diem): Founded 1670, in Vietnam; in U.S. 1976. U.S. address, Holy Cross Convent, 14700 South Van Ness Ave., Gardena, CA 90249.

Mantellate Sisters, Servants of Mary, of Blue Island, O.S.M.: Founded 1861, in Italy; in U.S., 1916. Generalate, Rome, Italy; U.S. motherhouse, 13811 S. Western Ave., Blue Island, IL 60406. Educational work.

Mantellate Sisters, Servants of Mary, of Plainfield, O.S.M.: Founded 1861 in Italy; in U.S., 1916. Address:16949 S. Drauden Rd., Plainfield, IL 60544.

Marian Sisters of the Diocese of Lincoln: Founded 1954. Motherhouse, Marian Center, R.R. 1, Box 108, Waverly, NE 68462.

Marianites of Holy Cross, Congregation of the Sisters, M.S.C.: Founded 1841, in France; in U.S., 1843. Motherhouse, Le Mans, Sarthe, France. North American headquarters, 1011 Gallier St., New Orleans, LA 70117.

Marist Sisters, Congregation of Mary, S.M.: Founded 1824, in France. General motherhouse, Rome, Italy; U.S. convents: St. Albert the Great, 4855 Parker, Dearborn Hts., MI 48125; St. Barnabas, 24262 Johnston, E. Detroit, MI 48021; Our Lady of the Snows, 4810 S. Leamington, Chicago, IL 60638; Marie, Madre de la Iglesia, 4419 St. James, Detroit, MI 48210.

Mary, Company of, O.D.N.: Founded 1607, in France; in U.S., 1926. General motherhouse, Rome, Italy; U.S. motherhouse, 16791 E. Main St., Tustin, CA 92680-4034.

Mary, Daughters of the Heart of, D.H.M.: Founded 1790, in France; in U.S., 1851. Generalate, Paris, France; U.S. provincialate, 1339 Northampton St., Holyoke, MA 01040. Education, retreat work.

Mary, Missionary Sisters of the Society of (Marist Sisters), S.M.S.M.: Founded 1845, at St. Brieuc, France; in U.S., 1922. General motherhouse, Rome, Italy; U.S. provincial house, 349 Grove St., Waltham, MA 02154. Foreign missions.

Mary, Servants of, O.S.M.: Founded 13th century, in Italy; in U.S., 1893. General motherhouse, England; U.S. provincial motherhouse, 7400 Military Ave., Omaha, NE 68134.

Mary, Servants of (Servite Sisters), O.S.M.: Founded 13th century, in Italy; in U.S., 1912. General motherhouse, Servants of Mary Convent, 1000 College Ave., Ladysmith, WI 54848.

Mary, Sisters of St., of Oregon, S.S.M.O.: Founded 1886, in Oregon, by Bishop William H. Gross, C.Ss.R. General motherhouse, 4440 S.W. 148th Ave., Beaverton, OR 97007. Educational, nursing work.

Mary, Sisters of the Little Company of, L.C.M.: Founded 1877, in England; in U.S., 1893. Generalate, London, England; U.S. provincial house, 9350 S. California Ave., Evergreen Park, IL 60805.

Mary, Sisters Servants of (Trained Nurses), S.M.: Founded 1851, at Madrid, Spain; in U.S., 1914.General motherhouse, Rome, Italy; U.S. motherhouse, 800 N. 18th St., Kansas City, KS 66102. Home nursing.

Mary and Joseph, Daughters of, D.M.J.: Founded 1817, in Belgium; in U.S., 1926. Generalate, Rome,

Italy; American provincialate, 5300 Crest Rd., Rancho Palos Verdes, CA 90274.

Mary Help of Christians, Daughters of (Salesian Sisters of St. John Bosco), F.M.A.: Founded 1872, in Italy, by St. John Bosco and St. Mary Dominic Mazzarello; in U.S., 1908. General motherhouse, Rome, Italy; U.S. provinces, 655 Belmont Ave., Haledon, NJ 07508; 6019 Buena Vista St., San Antonio, TX 78237. Education, youth work.

Mary Immaculate, Daughters of (Marianist Sisters), F.M.I.: Founded 1816, in France, by Very Rev. William-Joseph Chaminade. General motherhouse, Rome, Italy; U.S. foundation, 251 W. Ligustrum Dr., San Antonio, TX 78228. Educational work.

Mary Immaculate, Religious of, R.M.I.: Founded 1876, in Spain; in U.S., 1954. Generalate, Rome, Italy: U.S. foundation, 719 Augusta St., San Antonio, TX 78215.

Mary Immaculate, Sisters Minor of, S.M.M.I.: Established in U.S., 1989. Address: 138 Brushy Hill Rd., Danbury, CT 06818.

Mary Immaculate, Sisters of, S.M.I.: Founded 1948, in India, by Bishop Louis LaRavoire Morrow; in U.S., 1981. General motherhouse, Bengal, India; U.S. address, R.D. 5, Box 1231, Leechburg, PA 15656.

Mary Immaculate, Sisters Servants of, S.S.M.I.: Founded 1878 in Poland. General motherhouse, Mariowka-Opoczynska, Poland; American provincialate, 1220 Tugwell Dr., Catonsville, MD 21228.

Mary Immaculate, Sisters Servants of, S.S.M.I: Founded 1892, in Ukraine; in U.S., 1935. General motherhouse, Rome, Italy; U.S. address, 9 Emmanuel Dr., P.O. Box 6, Sloatsburg, NY 10974. Educational, hospital work.

Mary of Namur, Sisters of St., S.S.M.N.: Founded 1819, at Namur, Belgium; in U.S., 1863. General motherhouse, Namur, Belgium. U.S. provinces: 250 Bryant, Buffalo, NY 14222; 909 West Shaw St., Ft. Worth, TX 76110.

Mary of Providence, Daughters of St., D.S.M.P.: Founded 1872, at Como, Italy; in U.S., 1913. General motherhouse, Rome, Italy; U.S. provincial house, 4200 N. Austin Ave., Chicago, IL 60634. Special education for mentally handicapped.

Mary of the Immaculate Conception, Daughters of, D.M.: Founded 1904, in U.S., by Msgr. Lucian Bojnowski. General motherhouse, 314 Osgood Ave., New Britain, CT 06053. Educational, hospital work.

Mary Queen, Congregation of, C.M.R.: Founded in Vietnam; established in U.S., 1979. U.S. region, 625 S. Jefferson, Springfield, MO 65806.

Mary Reparatrix, Society of, S.M.R.: Founded 1857, in France; in U.S., 1908. Generalate, Rome, Italy. U.S. province, 225 E. 234th St., Bronx, NY 10470.

Medical Mission Sisters (Society of Catholic Medical Missionaries, Inc.), M.M.S.: Founded 1925, in U.S., by Mother Anna Dengel. Generalate, London, Eng.; U.S. headquarters, 8400 Pine Rd., Philadelphia, PA 19111. Medical work, health education, especially in mission areas.

Medical Missionaries of Mary, M.M.M.: Founded 1937, in Ireland, by Mother Mary Martin; in U.S., 1950. General motherhouse, Dublin, Ireland; U.S. headquarters, 563 Minneford Ave., City Island, Bronx, NY 10464. Medical aid in missions.

Medical Sisters of St. Joseph, M.S.J.: Founded 1946, in India; first U.S. foundation, 1985. General motherhouse, Kerala, S. India; U.S. address, 3435 E. Funston, Wichita, KS 67218. Health care apostolate.

Mercedarian Missionaries of Berriz, M.M.B.: Founded 1930, in Spain; in U.S., 1946. General motherhouse, Rome, Italy. U.S. headquarters, 1400 N.E. 42nd Terr., Kansas City, MO 64106.

Mercy, Daughters of Our Lady of, D.M.: Founded 1837, in Italy, by St. Mary Joseph Rossello; in U.S., 1919. General motherhouse, Savona, Italy; U.S. motherhouse, Villa Rossello, 1009 Main Rd., Newfield, NJ 08344. Educational, hospital work.

Mercy, Missionary Sisters of Our Lady of, M.O.M.: Founded 1938, in Brazil; in U.S., 1955. General motherhouse, Brazil; U.S. address, 388 Franklin St., Buffalo, NY 14202.

Mercy, Religious Sisters of, R.S.M.: Founded 1973 in U.S. Motherhouse, 1835 Michigan Ave., Alma, MI 48801.

Mercy, Sisters of, Daughters of Christian Charity of St. Vincent de Paul, S.M.D.C.: Founded 1842, in Hungary; U.S. foundation, Rt. 1, Box 353A, 240 Longhouse Dr., Hewitt, NJ 07421.

Mercy, Sisters of, of the Americas: Formed in July, 1991, through union of 25 regional communities of Sisters of Mercy which previously were independent motherhouses or houses which formed the Sisters of Mercy of the Union. Mother Mary Catherine McAuley founded the Sisters of Mercy in Dublin, Ireland, in 1831; the first establishment in the U.S., 1843, in Pittsburgh. Address of administrative office: 8300 Colesville Rd., No. 300, Silver Spring, MD 20910. Pres., Sr. Doris Gottemoeller. Total in congregation 6,367.

Mercy of the Blessed Sacrament, Sisters of, H.M.S.S.: Founded 1910 in Mexico; in U.S., 1926. General motherhouse, Mexico. U.S. regional house, 222 W. Cevallos St., San Antonio, TX 78204.

Mill Hill Sisters: See Franciscan Missionaries of St. Joseph.

Minim Daughters of Mary Immaculate, C.F.M.M.: Founded 1886, in Mexico; in U.S., 1926. General motherhouse, Leon, Guanajuato, Mexico; U.S. address, Our Lady of Lourdes High School, Box 1865, Nogales, AZ 85621.

Misericordia Sisters, S.M.: Founded 1848, in Canada; in U.S., 1887. General motherhouse, 12435 Ave. Misericorde, Montreal H4J 2G3, Canada; U.S. address, 820 Jungles Ave., Aurora, IL 60505. Social work with unwed mothers and their children; hospital work.

Mission Helpers of the Sacred Heart, M.H.S.H.: Founded 1890, in U.S. General motherhouse, 1001 W. Joppa Rd., Baltimore, MD 21204. Religious education, evangelization.

Missionary Catechists of the Sacred Hearts of Jesus and Mary (Violetas), M.C.: Founded 1918, in Mexico; in U.S., 1943. Motherhouse, Tlalpan, Mexico; U.S. address, 805 Liberty St., Victoria, TX 77901.

Missionary Daughters of the Most Pure Virgin Mary, M.D.P.V.M.: Founded in Mexico; in U.S., 1916. Address: 919 N. 9th St., Kingsville, TX 78363.

Mother of God, Missionary Sisters of the, M.S.M.G.: Byzantine, Ukrainian Rite, Stamford.

Motherhouse, 711 N. Franklin St., Philadelphia, PA 19123.

Mother of God, Sisters Poor Servants of the, S.M.G.: Founded 1869, in London, England; in U.S., 1947. General motherhouse, Maryfield, Roehampton, London. U.S. address: Maryfield Nursing Home, Greensboro Rd., High Point, NC 27260. Hospital, educational work.

Nazareth, Poor Sisters of: Founded in England; U.S. foundation, 1924. General motherhouse, Hammersmith, London, England; U.S. novitiate, 3333 Manning Ave., Los Angeles, CA 90064. Social services, education.

Notre Dame, School Sisters of, S.S.N.D.: Founded 1833, in Germany; in U.S., 1847. General motherhouse, Rome, Italy. U.S. provinces: 13105 Watertown Plank Rd., Elm Grove, WI 53122-2291; 6401 N. Charles St., Baltimore, MD 21212; 320 E. Ripa Ave., St. Louis, MO 63125; 170 Good Counsel Dr., Mankato, MN 56001-3138; Wilton, CT 06897; P.O. Box 227275, Dallas, TX 75222-7275; 1431 Euclid Ave., Berwyn, IL 60402.

Notre Dame, Sisters of, S.N.D.: Founded 1850, at Coesfeld, Germany; in U.S., 1874. General motherhouse, Rome, Italy. U.S. provinces: 13000 Auburn Rd., Chardon, OH 44024; 1601 Dixie Highway, Covington, KY 41011; 3837 Secor Rd., Toledo, OH 43623; 1776 Hendrix Ave., Thousand Oaks, CA 91360.

Notre Dame, Sisters of the Congregation of, C.N.D.: Founded 1658, in Canada by St. Marguerite Bourgeoys; in U.S., 1860. General motherhouse, Montréal, Qué., Canada; U.S. province, 223 West Mountain Rd., Ridgefield, CT 06877. Education.

Notre Dame de Namur, Sisters of, S.N.D.: Founded 1803, in France; in U.S., 1840. General motherhouse, Rome, Italy. U.S. provinces: 351 Broadway, Everett, MA 02149; 30 Jeffrey's Neck Rd., Ipswich, MA 01938; 468 Poquonock Ave., Windsor, CT 06095-2473; 1531 Greenspring Valley Rd., Stevenson, MD 21153; 305 Cable St., Baltimore, MD 21210; 701 E. Columbia Ave., Cincinnati, OH 45215; 14800 Bohlman Rd., Saratoga, CA 95070; SND Base Communities, 3037 Fourth St. N.E., Washington, DC 20017-1102. Educational work.

Notre Dame de Sion, Congregation of, N.D.S.: Founded 1843, in France; in U.S., 1892. Generalate, Rome, Italy; U.S. province, 349 Westminster Rd., Brooklyn, NY 11218. Creation of better understanding and relations between Christians and Jews.

Notre Dame Sisters: Founded 1853, in Czechoslovakia; in U.S., 1910. General motherhouse, Javornik, Czech Republic; U.S. motherhouse, 3501 State St., Omaha, NE 68112. Educational work.

Oblates of the Mother of Orphans, O.M.O: Founded 1945, in Italy. General motherhouse, Milan, Italy. U.S. address, 20 E. 72nd St., New York, NY 10021.

Our Lady of Charity, North American Union of Sisters of, Eudist Sisters (Sisters of Our Lady of Charity of the Refuge), N.A.U.-O.L.C.: Founded 1641, in Caen, France, by St. John Eudes; in U.S., 1855. Autonomous houses were federated in 1944 and in May, 1978, the North American Union of the Sisters of Our Lady of Charity was established. General motherhouse and administrative center, Box 327, Wisconsin Dells, WI 53965. Primarily devoted to

re-education and rehabilitation of women and girls in residential and non-residential settings.
Independent houses: 1125 Malvern Ave., Hot Springs, AR 71901; 620 Roswell Rd. N.W., Carrollton, OH 44615; 4500 W. Davis St., Dallas, TX 75211.

Our Lady of Sorrows, Sisters of, O.L.S.: Founded 1839, in Italy; in U.S., 1947. General motherhouse, Rome, Italy; U.S. headquarters, 9894 Norris Ferry Rd., Shreveport, LA 71106.

Our Lady of the Garden, Sisters of, O.L.G.: Founded 1829, in Italy, by St. Anthony Mary Gianelli. Motherhouse, Rome, Italy; U.S. address, 67 Round Hill Rd., Middletown, CT 06457.

Our Lady of Victory Missionary Sisters, O.L.V.M.: Founded 1922, in U.S. Motherhouse, Victory Noll, Box 109, Huntington, IN 46750. Educational, social work.

Pallottine Missionary Sisters (Missionary Sisters of the Catholic Apostolate), S.A.C.: Founded in Rome, 1838; in U.S., 1912. Generalate, Rome, Italy; U.S. provincialate, 15270 Old Halls Ferry Rd., Florissant, MO 63034.

Pallottine Sisters of the Catholic Apostolate, C.S.A.C.: Founded 1843, at Rome, Italy; in U.S., 1889. General motherhouse, Rome; U.S. motherhouse, St. Patrick's Villa, Harriman Heights, Harriman, NY 10926. Educational work.

Parish Visitors of Mary Immaculate, P.V.M.I.: Founded 1920, in New York. General motherhouse, Box 658, Monroe, NY 10950. Mission work.

Passion of Jesus Christ, Religious of (Passionist Nuns), C.P.: Founded 1771, in Italy, by St. Paul of the Cross; in U.S., 1910. U.S. convents: 2715 Churchview Ave., Pittsburgh, PA 15227; 631 Griffin Pond Rd., Clarks Summit, PA 18411; 8564 Crisp Rd., Whitesville, KY 42378; 1151 Donaldson Hwy., Erlanger, KY 41018; 15700 Clayton Rd., Ellisville, MO 63011.Contemplatives.

Passionist Sisters: See **Cross and Passion, Sisters of the.**

Paul, Daughters of St. (Missionary Sisters of the Media of Communication), D.S.P.: Founded 1915, at Alba, Piedmont, Italy; in U.S., 1932. General motherhouse, Rome, Italy; U.S. provincial house, 50 St. Paul's Ave., Boston, MA 02130. Apostolate of the communications arts.

Paul of Chartres, Sisters of St., S.P.C.: Founded 1696, in France. General house, Rome, Italy; U.S. address, 1300 County Rd. 492, Marquette, MI 49855.

Perpetual Adoration of Guadalupe, Sisters of, A.P.G.: U.S. foundation, 2403 W. Travis, San Antonio, TX 78207.

Peter Claver, Missionary Sisters of St., S.S.P.C.: Founded 1894 in Austria by Bl. Maria Teresa Ledochowska; in U.S., 1914. General motherhouse, Rome, Italy; U.S. address, 667 Woods Mill Rd. S., Chesterfield, MO 63017.

Pious Disciples of the Divine Master, P.D.D.M.: Founded 1924 in Italy; in U.S., 1948. General motherhouse, Rome, Italy; U.S. headquarters, 60 Sunset Ave., Staten Island, NY 10314.

Pious Schools, Sisters of, Sch. P.: Founded 1829 in Spain; in U.S., 1954. General motherhouse, Rome, Italy; U.S. headquarters, 17601 Nordhoff St., Northridge, CA 91325.

Poor, Little Sisters of the, L.S.P.: Founded 1839, in France by Bl. Jeanne Jugan; in U.S., 1868. General

motherhouse, St. Pern, France. U.S. provinces: 110-30 221st St., Queens Village, NY 11429; 601 Maiden Choice Lane, Baltimore, MD 21228; 80 W. Northwest Hwy., Palatine, IL 60067. Care of aged.

Poor Clare Missionary Sisters (Misioneras Clarisas), M.C.: Founded Mexico. General motherhouse, Rome, Italy; U.S. novitiate, 1019 N. Newhope, Santa Ana, CA 92703.

Poor Clare Nuns: See **Franciscan Poor Clare Nuns.**

Poor Handmaids of Jesus Christ (Ancilla Domini Sisters), P.H.J.C.: Founded 1851, in Germany by Bl. Mary Kasper; in U.S., 1868. General motherhouse, Dernbach, Westerwald, Germany; U.S. motherhouse, Ancilla Domini Convent, Donaldson, IN 46513. Educational, hospital work, social services.

Precious Blood, Daughters of Charity of the Most: Founded 1872, at Pagani, Italy; in U.S., 1908. General motherhouse, Rome, Italy; U.S. convent, 1482 North Ave., Bridgeport, CT 06604.

Precious Blood, Missionary Sisters of the, C.P.S.: Founded 1885, at Mariannhill, South Africa; in U.S., 1925. Generalate, Rome, Italy: U.S. novitiate, P.O. Box 97, Reading, PA 19607. Home and foreign mission work.

Precious Blood, Sisters Adorers of the, A.P.B.: Founded 1861, in Canada; in U.S., 1890. General motherhouse, Canada. U.S. autonomous monasteries: 54th St. and Fort Hamilton Pkwy., Brooklyn, NY 11219; 700 Bridge St., Manchester, NH 03104; 7408 S.E. Alder St., Portland, OR 97215; 166 State St., Portland, ME 04101; 1106 State St., Lafayette, IN 47905-1219; 400 Pratt St., Watertown, NY 13601. Cloistered, contemplative.

Precious Blood, Sisters of the, C.Pp.S.: Founded 1834, in Switzerland; in U.S., 1844. Generalate, 4000 Denlinger Rd., Dayton, OH 45426. Education, health care, other ministries.

Precious Blood, Sisters of the Most, C.Pp.S.: Founded 1845, in Steinerberg, Switzerland; in U.S., 1870. General motherhouse, 204 N. Main St., O'Fallon, MO 63366. Education, other ministries.

Presentation, Sisters of Mary of the, S.M.P.: Founded 1829, in France; in U.S., 1903. General motherhouse, Broons, Côtes-du-Nord, France. U.S. address, Maryvale Novitiate, 11550 River Rd., Valley City, ND 58072. Educational, hospital work.

Presentation of Mary, Sisters of the, P.M.: Founded 1796, in France by Bl. Marie Rivier; in U.S., 1873. General motherhouse, Castel Gandolfo, Italy. U.S. provincial houses: 495 Mammoth Rd., Manchester, NH 03104; 209 Lawrence St., Methuen, MA 01844.

Presentation of the B.V.M., Sisters of the, P.B.V.M.: Founded 1775, in Ireland; in U.S., 1854, in San Francisco. U.S. motherhouses: 2360 Carter Rd., Dubuque, IA 52001; 880 Jackson Ave., New Windsor, NY 12553; 2340 Turk Blvd., San Francisco, CA 94118; St. Colman's Convent, Watervliet, NY 12189;
1101 32nd Ave., S., Fargo ND 58103; Presentation Convent, Aberdeen, SD 57401; 99 Church St., Leominster, MA 01453; 419 Woodrow Rd., Staten Island, NY 10312.

Presentation of the Blessed Virgin Mary, Sisters of, of Union: Founded in Ireland, 1775; union established in Ireland, 1976; first U.S. vice province, 1979.

Generalate, Kildare, Ireland. U.S. provincialate, 729 W. Wilshire Dr., Phoenix, AZ 85007.

Providence, Daughters of Divine, F.D.P.: Founded 1832, Italy; in U.S., 1964. General motherhouse, Rome, Italy; U.S. address, 3100 Mumphrey Rd., Chalmette, LA 70043.

Providence, Missionary Catechists of Divine, M.C.D.P.: Administrative house, 2318 Castroville Rd., San Antonio, TX 78237.

Providence, Oblate Sisters of, O.S.P.: Founded 1829, in U.S., by Mother Mary Elizabeth Lange and Father James Joubert, S.S. First order of black nuns in U.S. General motherhouse, 701 Gun Rd., Baltimore, MD 21227. Educational work.

Providence, Sisters of, S.P.: Founded 1861, in Canada; in U.S., 1873. General motherhouse, Our Lady of Victory Convent, Gamelin St., Holyoke, MA 01040.

Providence, Sisters of, S.P.: Founded 1843, in Canada; in U.S., 1854. General motherhouse, Montreal, Canada. U.S. provinces: P.O. Box 11038, Seattle, WA 98111; 9 E. 9th Ave., Spokane, WA 99202; 353 N. River Rd., Des Plaines, IL 60616.

Providence, Sisters of (of St. Mary-of-the-Woods), S.P.: Founded 1806, in France; in U.S., 1840. Generalate, St. Mary-of-the-Woods, IN 47876.

Providence, Sisters of Divine, C.D.P.: Founded 1762, in France; in U.S., 1866. Generalate, Box 197, Helotes, TX 78023. Educational, hospital work.

Providence, Sisters of Divine, C.D.P.: Founded 1851, in Germany; in U.S., 1876. Generalate, Rome, Italy. U.S. provinces: 9000 Babcock Blvd., Allison Park, PA 15101; 8351 Florissant Rd., St. Louis, MO 63121; 363 Bishops Hwy., Kingston, MA 02364. Educational, hospital work.

Providence, Sisters of Divine (of Kentucky), C.D.P.: Founded 1762, in France; in U.S., 1889. General motherhouse, Fenetrange, France; U.S. province, 1000 St. Anne Dr., Melbourne, KY 41059. Education, social services, other ministries.

Redeemer, Oblates of the Most Holy, O.SS.R.: Founded 1864, in Spain. General motherhouse, Spain; U.S. foundation, 60-80 Pond St., Jamaica Plain, MA 02130.

Redeemer, Order of the Most Holy, O.SS.R.: Founded 1731, by St. Alphonsus Liguori; in U.S., 1957. U.S. addresses: Mother of Perpetual Help Monastery, P.O. Box 220, Esopus, NY 12429; St. Alphonsus Monastery, Liguori, MO 63057.

Redeemer, Sisters of the Divine, S.D.R.: Founded 1849, in Niederbronn, France; in U.S., 1912. General motherhouse, Rome, Italy; U.S. province, 999 Rock Run Road, Elizabeth, PA 15037. Educational, hospital work; care of the aged.

Redeemer, Sisters of the Holy, C.S.R.: Founded 1849, in Alsace; in U.S., 1924. General motherhouse, Wuerzburg, Germany; U.S. provincial house, 521 Moredon Rd., Huntingdon Valley, PA 19006. Personalized medical care in hospitals, homes for aged, private homes; retreat work.

Reparation of the Congregation of Mary, Sisters of, S.R.C.M.: Founded 1903, in U.S. Motherhouse, St. Zita's Villa, Monsey, NY 10952.

Reparation of the Sacred Wounds of Jesus, Sisters of, S.R.: Founded 1959 in U.S. General motherhouse, 2120 S.E. 24th Ave., Portland, OR 97214.

Resurrection, Sisters of the, C.R.: Founded 1891, in Italy; in U.S., 1900. General motherhouse, Rome, Italy. U.S. provinces: 7432 Talcott Ave., Chicago, IL 60631; Mt. St. Joseph, 35 Boltwood Ave., Castleton-on-Hudson, NY 12033. Education, nursing.

Rita, Sisters of St., O.S.A.: General motherhouse, Wurzburg, Germany. U.S. foundation, St. Monica's Convent, 3920 Green Bay Rd., Racine, WI 53404.

Rosary, Congregation of Our Lady of the Holy, R.S.R.: Founded 1874, in Canada; in U.S., 1899. General motherhouse, Rimouski, Que., Canada. U.S. regional house, 20 Thomas St., Portland, ME 04102-3638. Educational work.

Rosary, Missionary Sisters of the Holy, M.S.H.R.: Founded 1924, in Ireland; in U.S., 1954. Motherhouse, Dublin, Ireland. U.S. regional 741 Polo Rd., Bryn Mawr, PA 19010. African missions.

Sacrament, Missionary Sisters of the Most Blessed, M.SS.S.: General motherhouse, Madrid, Spain; U.S. foundation: 1111 Wordin Ave., Bridgeport, CT 06605.

Sacrament, Nuns of the Perpetual Adoration of the Blessed, A.P.: Founded 1807 in Rome, Italy; in U.S., 1925. U.S. monasteries: 145 N. Cotton Ave., El Paso, TX 79901; 771 Ashbury St., San Francisco, CA 94117.

Sacrament, Oblate Sisters of the Blessed, O.S.B.S.: Founded 1935, in U.S.; motherhouse, St. Sylvester Convent, P.O. Box 217, Marty, SD 57361. Care of American Indians.

Sacrament, Servants of the Blessed, S.S.S.: Founded 1858, in France, by St. Pierre Julien Eymard; in U.S., 1947. General motherhouse, Rome, Italy; American provincial house, St. Charles Borromeo Parish, 1818 Coal Pl. SE, Albuquerque, NM 87106. Contemplative.

Sacrament, Sisters of the Blessed, for Indians and Colored People, S.B.S.: Founded 1891, in U.S., by Bl. Katharine Drexel. General motherhouse, St. Elizabeth's Convent, Bensalem, PA 19020.

Sacrament, Sisters of the Most Holy, M.H.S.: Founded 1851, in France; in U.S., 1872. Generalate, 313 Corona Dr. (P.O. Box 30727), Lafayette, LA 70593.

Sacrament, Sisters Servants of the Blessed, S.J.S.: Founded 1904, in Mexico; in U.S., 1926. General motherhouse, Mexico; U.S. address, 215 Lomita St., El Segundo, CA 90245.

Sacramentine Nuns (Religious of the Order of the Blessed Sacrament and Our Lady), O.S.S.: Founded 1639, in France; in U.S., 1912. U.S. monasteries: 235 Bellvale Lakes Rd., Warwick,, NY 10990; US 31, Conway, MI 49722. Perpetual adoration of the Holy Eucharist.

Sacred Heart, Daughters of Our Lady of the: Founded 1882, in France; in U.S., 1955. General motherhouse, Rome, Italy; U.S. address, 424 E. Browning Rd., Bellmawr, NJ 08031. Educational work.

Sacred Heart, Missionary Sisters of the (Cabrini Sisters), M.S.C.: Founded 1880, in Italy, by St. Frances Xavier Cabrini; in U.S., 1889. General motherhouse, Rome, Italy; U.S. provincial office: 222 E. 19th St., 5B, New York, NY 10003. Educational, health, social and catechetical work.

Sacred Heart, Religious of the Apostolate of the,

R.A.: General motherhouse, Madrid, Spain; U.S. address, 1310 W. 42nd Pl., Hialiah, FL 33012.

Sacred Heart, Society Devoted to the, S.D.S.H.: Founded 1940, in Hungary; in U.S., 1956. U.S. motherhouse, 9814 Sylvia Ave., Northridge, CA 91324. Educational work.

Sacred Heart, Society of the, R.S.C.J.: Founded 1800, in France; in U.S., 1818. Generalate, Rome, Italy. U.S. provincial house, 4389 W. Pine Blvd., St. Louis, MO 63108. Educational work.

Sacred Heart of Jesus, Apostles of, A.S.C.J.: Founded 1894, in Italy; in U.S., 1902. General motherhouse, Rome, Italy; U.S. motherhouse, 265 Benham St., Hamden, CT 06514. Educational, social work.

Sacred Heart of Jesus, Handmaids of the, A.C.J.: Founded 1877, in Spain. General motherhouse, Rome, Italy; U.S. province, 616 Coopertown Rd., Haverford, PA 19041. Educational, retreat work.

Sacred Heart of Jesus, Missionary Sisters of the Most (Hiltrup), M.S.C.: Founded 1899, in Germany; in U.S., 1908. General motherhouse, Rome, Italy; U.S. province, 51 Seminary Ave., Reading, PA 19605. Education, health care, pastoral ministry.

Sacred Heart of Jesus, Oblate Sisters of the, O.S.H.J.: Founded 1894; in U.S., 1949. General motherhouse, Rome, Italy; U.S. headquarters, 50 Warner Rd., Hubbard, OH 44425. Educational, social work.

Sacred Heart of Jesus, Servants of the Most, S.S.C.J.: Founded 1894, in Poland; in U.S., 1959. General motherhouse, Cracow, Poland; U.S. address, 866 Cambria St., Cresson, PA 16630. Education, health care, social services.

Sacred Heart of Jesus, Sisters of the, S.S.C.J.: Founded 1816, in France; in U.S., 1903. General motherhouse, St. Jacut, Brittany, France; U.S. provincial house, 5922 Blanco Rd., San Antonio, TX 78216-6679. Educational, hospital, domestic work.

Sacred Heart of Jesus and of the Poor, Servants of the (Mexican), S.S.H.J.P.: Founded 1885, in Mexico; in U.S., 1907. General motherhouse, Apartado 92, Puebla, Pue., Mexico; U.S. address, 3310 S. Zapata Hwy, Laredo, TX 78043.

Sacred Heart of Jesus and Our Lady of Guadalupe, Missionaries of the: U.S. address, 1212 E. Euclid Ave., Arlington Heights, IL 60660.

Sacred Heart of Jesus for Reparation, Congregation of the Handmaids of the, A.R.: Founded 1918, in Italy; in U.S., 1958. U.S. address, Sunshine Park, R.D. 3, Steubenville, OH 43952.

Sacred Heart of Mary, Religious of the, R.S.H.M.: Founded 1848, in France; in U.S., 1877. Generalate, Rome, Italy. U.S. provinces; 50 Wilson Park Dr., Tarrytown, NY 10591; 441 N. Garfield Ave., Montebello, CA 90640-2901.

Sacred Hearts and of Perpetual Adoration, Sisters of the, SS.CC.: Founded 1797, in France; in U.S., 1908. General motherhouse, Rome, Italy; U.S. provinces: 1120 Fifth Ave., Honolulu, Hawaii 96816 (Pacific); 419 Hood St., Fall River, MA 02720 (East Coast). Varied ministries.

Sacred Hearts of Jesus and Mary, Sisters of the, S.H.J.M.: Established 1953, in U.S. General motherhouse, Essex, England; U.S. address, 844 Don Carlo Dr., El Cerrito, CA 94530.

Savior, Company of the, C.S.: Founded 1952, in Spain; in U.S., 1962. General motherhouse, Madrid, Spain; U.S. foundation, 820 Clinton Ave., Bridgeport, CT 06604.

Savior, Sisters of the Divine, S.D.S.: Founded 1888, in Italy; in U.S., 1895. General motherhouse, Rome, Italy; U.S. province, 4311 N. 100th St., Milwaukee, WI 53222. Educational, hospital work.

Sisters of St. Benedict Center, Slaves of Mary Immaculate, M.I.C.M.: Founded in U.S. Address: 254 Still River Rd., P.O. Box 22, Still River, MA 01467.

Social Service, Sisters of, S.S.S.: Founded in Hungary, 1923, by Sr. Margaret Slachta. U.S. generalate, 440 Linwood Ave., Buffalo, NY 14209. Social work.

Social Service, Sisters of, of Los Angeles, S.S.S.: Founded 1908, in Hungary; in U.S., 1926. General motherhouse, 2303 S. Figueroa Way, Los Angeles, CA 90007-2504.

Teresa of Jesus, Society of St., S.T.J.: Founded 1876, in Spain; in U.S., 1910. General motherhouse, Rome, Italy; U.S. provincial house, 18080 St. Joseph's Way, Covington, LA 70433.

Thomas of Villanova, Congregation of Sisters of St., S.S.T.V.: Founded 1661, in France; in U.S., 1948. General motherhouse, Neuilly-sur-Seine, France; U.S. foundation W. Rocks Rd., Norwalk, CT 06851.

Trinity, Missionary Servants of the Most Blessed, M.S.B.T.: Founded 1912, in U.S., by Very Rev. Thomas A. Judge. General motherhouse, 3501 Solly Ave., Philadelphia, PA 19136. Educational, social work; health services.

Trinity, Sisters Oblates to the Blessed, O.B.T.: Founded 1923, in Italy. U.S. novitiate, Beekman Rd., P.O. Box 98, Hopewell Junction, NY 12533.

Trinity, Sisters of the Most Holy, O.Ss.T.: Founded 1198, in Rome; in U.S., 1920. General motherhouse, Rome, Italy; U.S. address, Immaculate Conception Province, 21281 Chardon Rd., Euclid, OH 44117. Educational work.

Trinity, Society of Our Lady of the Most Holy, S.O.L.T.: Motherhouse, P.O. Box 189 Skidmore, TX 78389.

Ursula of the Blessed Virgin, Society of the Sisters of St., S.U.: Founded 1606, in France; in U.S., 1902. General motherhouse, France; U.S. novitiate, 139 S. Mill Rd., Rhinebeck, NY 12572. Educational work.

Ursuline Nuns (Roman Union), O.S.U.: Founded 1535, in Italy; in U.S., 1727. Generalate, Rome, Italy. U.S. provinces: 323 E. 198th St., Bronx, NY 10458; 210 Glennon Heights Rd., Crystal City, MO 63019; 639 Angela Dr., Santa Rosa, CA 95401; 45 Lowder St., Dedham, MA 02026.

Ursuline Nuns of the Congregation of Paris, O.S.U.: Founded 1535, in Italy; in U.S., 1727, in New Orleans. U.S. motherhouses: 20860 St, Rte. 251, St. Martin, OH 45118-9705; 901 E. Miami St., Paola, KS 66071; 3115 Lexington Rd., Louisville, KY 40206; 2600 Lander Rd., Cleveland, OH. 44124; 8001 Cummings Rd., Maple Mount, KY 42356; 4045 Indian Rd., Toledo, OH 43606; 4250 Shields Rd., Canfield, OH 44406; 1339 E. McMillan St., Cincinnati, OH 45206.

Ursuline Sisters of the Congregation of Tildonk, Belgium, O.S.U.: Founded 1535, in Italy; Tildonk congregation, 1832; in U.S., 1924. Generalate, Brussels, Belgium; U.S. address, 81-15 Utopia Parkway, Jamaica, NY 11432. Educational, foreign mission work.

Ursuline Sisters of Belleville, O.S.U.: Founded 1535, in Italy; in U.S., 1910; established as diocesan community, 1983. Central house, 1026 N. Douglas Ave., Belleville, IL 62221. Educational work.

Ursuline Sisters (Irish Ursuline Union), O.S.U.: Generalate, Dublin, Ireland; U.S. address, 1973 Torch Hill Rd., Columbus, GA 31903.

Venerini Sisters, Religious, M.P.V.: Founded 1685, in Italy; in U.S., 1909. General motherhouse, Rome, Italy; U.S. provincialate; 23 Edward St., Worcester, MA 01605.

Vietnamese Adorers of the Holy Cross, M.T.G.: Founded 1670 in Vietnam; in U.S. 1976. General motherhouse 7408 S.E. Adler, Portland, OR 97215.

Vincent de Paul, Sisters: See **Charity of St. Vincent de Paul, Sisters of.**

Visitation Nuns, V.H.M.: Founded 1610, in France; in U.S. (Georgetown, DC), 1799. Contemplative, educational work. Two federations in U.S.

First Federation of North America. Major pontifical enclosure. Pres., Mother Mary Jozefa Kowalewski, Monastery of the Visitation, Snellville, GA 30278. Addresses of monasteries belonging to the federation: 2300 Springhill Ave., Mobile, AL 36607; Beach Rd., Tyringham, MA 01264; 12221 Bievenue Rd, Rockville, VA 23146; 5820 City Ave., Philadelphia, PA 19131; 1745 Parkside Blvd., Toledo, OH 43607; 2055 Ridgedale Dr., Snellville, GA 30278.

Second Federation of North America. Constitutional enclosure. Pres., Sr. Anne Madeleine Godefroy, Monastery of the Visitation, St. Louis, MO 63131. Addresses of monasteries belonging to the federation: 1500 35th St., Washington, DC 20007; 3020 N. Ballas Rd., St. Louis, MO 63131-2316; 200 E. Second St., Frederick, MD 21701; Mt. de Chantal Monastery of the Visitation, 410 Washington Ave., Wheeling, WV 26003; 8902 Ridge Blvd., Brooklyn, NY 11209; 2936 36th St., Rock Island, IL 61201; 2455 Visitation Dr., Mendota Heights, St. Paul, MN 55120.

Visitation of the Congregation of the Immaculate Heart of Mary, Sisters of the, S.V.M.: Founded 1952, in U.S. Motherhouse, 2950 Kaufmann Ave., Dubuque, IA 52001. Educational work, parish ministry.

Vocationist Sisters (Sisters of the Divine Vocations): Founded 1921, in Italy; in U.S., 1967 General motherhouse, Naples, Italy; U.S. foundation, Perpetual Help Nursery, 172 Broad St., Newark, NJ 07104.

Wisdom, Daughters of, D.W.: Founded 1703, in France, by St. Louis Marie Grignion de Montfort; in U.S., 1904. General motherhouse, Vendee, France; U.S. province, 385 Ocean Ave., Islip, NY 11751-4600. Education, health care, parish ministry, social services.

Xaverian Missionary Society of Mary, Inc., X.M.M.: Founded 1945, in Italy; in U.S., 1954. General motherhouse, Parma, Italy; U.S. address, 242 Salisbury St., Worcester, MA 01609.

ORGANIZATIONS OF RELIGIOUS

Conferences

Conferences of major superiors of religious institutes, dating from the 1950s, are encouraged by the Code of Canon Law (Code 708) "so that joining forces they can work toward the achievement of the purpose of their individual institutes more fully, transact common business and foster suitable coordination and cooperation with conferences of bishops and also with individual bishops." Statutes of the conferences must be approved by the Holy See "by which alone they are erected" (Canon 709). Conferences have been established in 24 countries of Europe, 14 in North and Central America, 10 in South America, 35 in Africa and 19 in Asia and Oceania.

Listed below are U.S. and international conferences.

Conference of Major Superiors of Men: Founded in 1956; canonically established Sept. 12, 1957. Membership, 269 major superiors representing institutes with a combined membership of approximately 24,000. President, Bro. Joseph Klein, F.M.S.; executive director, Rev. Stephen Henrich, O.S.C. National office: 8808 Cameron St., Silver Spring, MD 20910.

Leadership Conference of Women Religious: Founded in 1956; canonically established Dec. 12, 1959. Membership, nearly 1,000 (Dec. 31, 1996), representing approximately 400 religious institutes. President, Sister Mary Waskowiak, R.S.M.; executive director, Sister Mary Christine Fellerhoff, C.S.A. National office: 8808 Cameron St., Silver Spring, MD 20910.

Council of Major Superiors of Women Religious: Canonically erected June 13, 1992. Membership, 141 superiors of 103 religious congregations. Chairperson, Mother Mary Bernard Nettle, I.S.P. National office: P.O. Box 4467, Washington, DC 20017-0467.

International Union of Superiors General (Women): Established Dec. 8, 1965; approved, 1967. General secretary, Sister Marguerite Letourneau, S.G.M. Address: Piazza di Ponte S. Angelo, 28, 00186, Rome, Italy.

Union of Superiors General (Men): Established in 1957. President, Father Camillo Maccise, O.C.D; general secretary, Bro. Lino Da Campo, F.S.F. Address: Via dei Penitenzieri 19, 00193 Rome, Italy.

Latin American Confederation of Religious (Confederacion Latinoamericana de Religiosos - CLAR): Established in 1959; statutes reformed in 1984. President, Fr. Guido Zegarra, O.F.M.; secretary general, Pedro Acevedo, F.S.C. Address: Calle 64 No 10-45, Piso 5°. Apartado Aéreo 56804, Santafé de Bogotá, D.C., Colombia.

Union of European Conferences of Major Superiors (UCESM): Established Dec. 25, 1983. President, Bro. Jacques Scholte; permanent secretary, Françoise Pecqueraux, Rue Joseph II 174, B1000 Bruxelles, Belgium.

Other Organizations

Institute on Religious Life (1974). To foster more effective understanding and implementation of teachings of the Church on religious life, promote vocations to religious life and the priesthood, and promote growth in sanctity of all the faithful according to their state in life. Executive director, Rev. James Downey.

National office, P.O. Box 41007, Chicago, IL 60641.

National Association of Religious Brothers (1972): To publicize the unique vocations of brothers, to further communication among brothers and provide liaison with various organizations of the Church. Executive secretary, Kenneth Pfister, F.S.C. National office, 1337 West Ohio, Chicago, IL 60622.

National Black Sisters' Conference (1968): Black Catholic women religious and associates networking to provide support through prayer, study, solidarity and programs. President, Sr. Patricia J. Chappell, S.N.D.de N. Address: 3027 4th St. NE, Washington, DC 20017.

National Conference of Vicars for Religious (1967): National organization of diocesan officials concerned with relations between their respective dioceses and religious communities engaged therein. President, Sr. Therese Sullivan, S.P., 9292 Broadway,

Merrillville, IN 46410; secretary, Eymard Flood, O.S.C., 2811 East Villareal Dr., P.O. Box 14195, Orange, CA, 92863-159.

National Religious Vocation Conference (NRVC) (1988, with merger of National Sisters Vocation Conference and National Conference of Religious Vocation Directors): Service organization of men and women committed to the fostering and discernment of vocations. Executive director, Sr. Catherine Bertrand, S.S.N.D. Address: 1603 S. Michigan Ave., No. 400, Chicago, IL 60616.

Religious Formation Conference (1953): Originally the Sister Formation Conference; membership includes women and men Religious and non-canonical groups. Facilitates the ministry of formation, both initial and ongoing, in religious communities. Executive director, Sister Jane Finnerty, O.S.U. National office: 8820 Cameron St., Silver Spring, MD 20910.

SECULAR INSTITUTES

(Sources: *Catholic Almanac* survey; United States Conference of Secular Institutes; *Annuario Pontificio*.)

Secular institutes are societies of men and women living in the world who dedicate themselves to observe the evangelical counsels and to carry on apostolic works suitable to their talents and opportunities in the areas of their everyday life.

"Secular institutes are not religious communities but they carry with them in the world a profession of evangelical counsels which is genuine and complete, and recognized as such by the Church. This profession confers a consecration on men and women, laity and clergy, who reside in the world. For this reason they should chiefly strive for total self-dedication to God, one inspired by perfect charity. These institutes should preserve their proper and particular character, a secular one, so that they may everywhere measure up successfully to that apostolate which they were designed to exercise, and which is both in the world and, in a sense, of the world" (Decree on the Appropriate Renewal of Religious Life, No. 11; Second Vatican Council).

Secular institutes are under the jurisdiction of the Congregation for Institutes of Consecrated Life and Societies of Apostolic Life. General legislation concerning them is contained in Canons 710 to 730 of the Code of Canon Law.

A secular institute reaches maturity in several stages. It begins as an association of the faithful, technically called a pious union, with the approval of a local bishop. Once it has proved its viability, he can give it the status of an institute of diocesan right, in accordance with norms and permission emanating from the Congregation for Institutes of Consecrated Life and Societies of Apostolic Life. On issuance of a separate decree from this congregation, an institute of diocesan right becomes an institute of pontifical right.

Secular institutes, which originated in the latter part of the 18th century, were given full recognition and approval by Pius XII Feb. 2, 1947, in the apostolic constitution *Provida Mater Ecclesia*. On Mar. 25 of the same year a special commission for secular institutes was set up within the Congregation for Religious. Institutes were commended and confirmed by

Pius XII in a *motu proprio* of Mar. 12, 1948, and were the subject of a special instruction issued a week later, Mar. 19, 1948.

The World Conference of Secular Institutes (CMIS) was approved by the Vatican May 23, 1974. Address: Via Tullio Levi-Civita 5, 00146 Rome, Italy.

The United States Conference of Secular Institutes (USCSI) was established following the organization of the World Conference of Secular Institutes in Rome. Its membership is open to all canonically erected secular institutes with members living in the United States. The conference was organized to offer secular institutes an opportunity to exchange experiences, to do research in order to help the Church carry out its mission, and to search for ways and means to make known the existence of secular institutes in the U.S. Address: P.O. Box 4556, 12th St. NE, Washington, DC 20017.

Institutes in the U.S.

Apostolic Oblates: Founded in Rome, Italy, 1947; established in the U.S., 1962; for women. Approved as a secular institute of pontifical right Dec. 8, 1994. Addresses: 2125 W. Walnut Ave., Fullerton, CA 92633; 6762 Western Ave., Omaha, NE 68132; 730 E. 87th St., Brooklyn, NY 11236.

Caritas Christi: Originated in Marseilles, 1937; for women. Established as a secular institute of pontifical right Mar. 19, 1955. Address: P.O. Box 5162, River Forest, IL 60305. International membership.

Company of St. Paul: Originated in Milan, Italy, 1920; for lay people and priests. Approved as a secular institute of pontifical right June 30, 1950. Address: Rev. Stuart Sandberg, 52 Davis Ave., White Plains, NY 10605.

Crusaders of St. Mary: Founded 1947 in Madrid, Spain; approved as a secular institute of diocesan right, 1988; for men. Address: 2001 Great Falls St., McLean, VA 22101

Diocesan Laborer Priests: Founded in Spain 1885; approved as a secular institute of pontifical right, 1952. The specific aim of the institute is the promotion, sustenance and cultivation of apostolic, religious and priestly vocations. Address: Rev. Rutilio J. del Riego, 3706 15th St. N.E., Washington, DC 20017.

Don Bosco Volunteers: Founded 1917 by Bl. Philip Rinaldi; for women. Approved as a secular institute of pontifical right Aug. 5, 1978. Follow spirituality and charism of St. John Bosco. Address: Rev. Paul P. Avallone, S.D.B., Don Bosco Volunteers, 202 Union Ave., Paterson, NJ 07502.

Don Bosco Secular Institute (for men): Same address as above.

Fr. Kolbe Missionaries of the Immaculata: Founded in Bologna, Italy, in 1954, by Fr. Luigi Faccenda, O.F.M. Conv.; for women. Approved as a secular institute of pontifical right Mar. 25, 1992. Live the fullness of baptismal consecration, strive for perfect charity and promote the knowledge and veneration of Mary. Address: 531 E. Merced Ave., West Covina, CA 91790.

Handmaids of Divine Mercy: Founded in Bari, Italy, 1951; for women. Approved as an institute of pontifical right 1972. Address: Elisabeth Gagliano, 2943 Philip Ave., Bronx, NY 10465.

Institute of Secular Missionaries: Founded in Vitoria, Spain, 1939; for women. Approved as a secular institute, 1955. Address: 2710 Ruberg Ave., Cincinnati, OH 45211, Att. E. Dilger.

Institute of the Heart of Jesus: Originated in France Feb. 2, 1791; restored Oct. 29, 1918; for diocesan priests and laity. Received final approval from the Holy See as a secular institute of pontifical right Feb. 2, 1952. U.S. address, Rev. Francis X. Mawn, St. Rose Rectory, 601 Broadway, Chelsea, MA 02150.

Lay Missionaries of the Passion: Founded in Catania, Sicily; for women. Approved as a secular institute of diocesan right July 1, 1980. Address: Dorothy Armstrong, 633 Main St., Dicksen City, PA 18519.

Little Franciscan Family: Founded in Italy, 1929, by Father Ireneo Mazzotti, O.F.M.; for women. Approved as a secular institute of pontifical right, 1983. Address: Julie Curley, 319 Main St., Cromwell, CT 06416.

Mission of Our Lady of Bethany: Founded in France, 1948; for women. Approved as a secular institute of diocesan right, 1965. Address: Estelle Nichols, 7 Locksley St., Jamaica Plain, MA 02130.

Missionaries of the Kingship of Christ the King: Under this title are included three distinct and juridically separate institutes founded by Agostino Gemelli, O.F.M. (1878-1959) and Armida Barelli (1882-1952). Two are active in the U.S.

(1) Women Missionaries of the Kingship of Christ — Founded in 1919, in Italy; definitively approved as an institute of pontifical right 1953. U.S. branch established 1950.

(2) Men Missionaries of the Kingship of Christ — Founded 1928, in Italy, as an institute of diocesan right. U.S. branch established 1962.

Addresses: Rev. Damien Dougherty, O.F.M., P.O. Box 278, Eime Rd., Dittmer, MO 63023 (for Men Missionaries); Rev. Dominic Monti, O.F.M., 10400 Lorain Ave., Silver Spring, MD 20901 (for Women Missionaries).

Nuestra Señora de la Altagracia: Founded in Dominican Republic, 1956; approved as a secular institute of diocesan right, 1964; for women. Address: Ms. Christiana Perez, 129 Van Siclen Ave., Brooklyn, NY 11207.

Oblate Missionaries of Mary Immaculate: Founded, 1952; approved as a secular institute of pontifical right 1984; for women. Address: Oblate Missionaries of Mary Immaculate, P.O. Box 303, Manville, RI 02838. International membership.

Opus Spiritus Sancti: Originated in West Germany, 1952; for diocesan priests and unmarried permanent deacons. Formally acknowledged by Rome as a secular institute of diocesan right, 1977. Address: Rev. James D. McCormick, 421 E. Bluff, Carroll, IA 51401.

St. Francis de Sales Secular Institute: Founded in Vienna, Austria, 1940; for women. Pontifical right, 1964. Addresses: Rev. John J. Conmy, 1120 Blue Bell Rd., Childs, MD 21916; Joan Bereswill, 3503 Jean St., Fairfax, VA 22030.

Schoenstatt Sisters of Mary: Originated in Schoenstatt, Germany, 1926; for women. Established as a secular institute of diocesan right May 20, 1948; of pontifical right Oct. 18, 1948. Addresses: W. 284 N. 404 Cherry Lane, Waukesha, WI 53188; House Schoenstatt, HCO 1, Box 100, Rockport, TX 78382.

Secular Institute of Pius X: Originated in Manchester, N.H., 1940; for priests and laymen. Approved as a secular institute, 1959. Also admits married couples and unmarried men as associate members. Addresses: C.P. 7731, Charlesbourg, Qué. G1G 5W6, Canada; Roger Duchesneu, 27 Cove St., Goffstown, NH 03345.

Secular Institute of Schoenstatt Fathers: Founded in Germany by Fr. Joseph Kentenich in 1965; for priests serving the International Schoenstatt Movement in over 20 countries. Approved as a secular institute of pontifical right, June 24, 1988. Address: W. 284 N. 746 Cherry Lane, Waukesha, WI 53188.

Servitium Christi Secular Institute of the Blessed Sacrament: Founded in Holland, 1952; for women. Approved as a secular institute of diocesan right May 8, 1963. Address: Miss Elaine Kozlowski, 1215 Greenwood Ave., #2, Pueblo, CO 81003.

Society of Our Lady of the Way: Originated, 1936; for women. Approved as a secular institute of pontifical right Jan. 3, 1953. Addresses: 2339 N. Catalina, Los Angeles, CA 90027; 80 Manhattan Ave., Jersey City, NJ 07307.

Voluntas Dei Institute: Originated in Canada, 1958 by Father L. M. Parent; for secular priests and laymen (with married couples as associates). Approved as a secular institute of pontifical right, July 12, 1987. Established in 21 countries. Address: Rev. Michael Craig, 4257 Tazewell Terr., Burtonsville, MD 20866.

The *Annuario Pontificio* lists the following secular institutes of pontifical right which are not established in the U.S.:

For men: Christ the King; Institute of Our Lady of Life; Institute of Prado; Priests of the Sacred Heart of Jesus.

For women: Alliance in Jesus through Mary; Apostles of the Sacred Heart; Catechists of Mary, Virgin and Mother; Catechists of the Sacred Heart of Jesus (Ukrainian); Company of St. Ursula; Cordimarian Filiation; Daughters of the Nativity of Mary; Daughters of the Queen of the Apostles; Daughters of the Sacred Heart; Evangelical Crusade; Faithful Servants of Jesus; Handmaids of Our Mother of Mercy; Institute of Notre Dame du Travail; Institute of Our Lady of Life; Institute of St. Boniface; Little Apostles of Charity.

Life and Peace in Christ Jesus; Missionaries of Royal Priesthood; Missionaries of the Sick; Oblates of Christ the King; Oblates of the Sacred Heart of Jesus; Servants of Jesus the Priest; Servite Secular Institute; Union of the Daughters of God; Workers of Divine Love; Workers of the Cross; Handmaids of Holy Church; Augustinian Auxiliary Missionaries; Heart of Jesus; Apostolic Missionaries of Charity; Combonian Secular Missionaries; Missionaries of the Gospel; Secular Servants of Jesus Christ Priest; Women of Schoenstatt; Missionaries of Infinite Love.

Associations

Caritas: Originated in New Orleans, 1950; for women. Follow guidelines of secular institutes. Small self-supporting groups who live and work among the poor and oppressed; work in Louisiana and Guatemala. Address: Box 308, Abita Springs, LA 70420.

Daughters of Our Lady of Fatima: Originated in Lansdowne, Pa., 1949; for women. Received diocesan approval, Jan., 1952. Address: Fatima House, Rolling Hills Rd., Ottsville, PA 18942.

Focolare Movement: Founded in Trent, Italy, in 1943, by Chiara Lubich; for men and women. Approved as an association of the faithful, 1962. It is not a secular institute by statute; however, vows are observed by its totally dedicated core membership of 4,000 who live in small communities called Focolare (Italian word for "hearth") centers. There are 17 resident centers in the U.S. and four in Canada. GEN (New Generation) is the youth organization of the movement. An estimated 75,000 are affiliated with the movement in the U.S. and Canada; 2,000,000, worldwide. Publications include Living City, monthly; GEN II and GEN III for young people and children. Five week-long summer conventions, called "Mariapolis" ("City of Mary"), are held annually. Address for information: P.O. Box 496, New York, NY 10021 (indicate men's or women's branch).

Jesus-Caritas Fraternity of Priests: An international association of diocesan priests who strive to combine an active life with a contemplative calling by their membership in small fraternities. U.S. address for information: Rev. Paul M. Esser, St. Paul the Apostle Parish, 5700 Washington Ave., Racine, WI 53406.

Franciscan Missionaries of Jesus Crucified: Founded in New York in 1987; separate communities for women and men. Approved as an association of the faithful Jan. 7, 1992. To provide an opportunity for persons with disabilities to live a life of total consecration in the pursuit of holiness in the apostolate of service to the Church and to those who suffer in any way. Address: Louise D. Principe, F.M.J.C., 400 Central Ave., Apt. 3D, Albany, NY 12206.

Madonna House Apostolate: Originated in Toronto, Canada, 1930; for priests and lay persons. Public association of the Christian faithful. Address: Madonna House, Combermere, Ontario, Canada K0J ILO - Jean Fox (women), Albert Osterberger (men), Rev. Robert Pelton (priests). International membership and missions.

Opus Spiritus Sancti: Originated in Germany; for women. An association of the faithful. Address: Theresa Berger, 415 E. Oak St., Algona, IA 50511.

Pax Christi: Lay institute of men and women dedicated to witnessing to Christ, with special emphasis on service to the poor in Mississippi. Addresses: St. Francis Center, 708 Ave. I, Greenwood, MS 38930; LaVerna House, 2108 Altawoods Blvd., Jackson, MS 39204.

Rural Parish Workers of Christ the King: Founded in 1942; for women. A secular institute of the Archdiocese of St. Louis. Dedicated to the glory of God in service of neighbor, especially in rural areas. Address: Rt. 1, Box 1667, Cadet, MO 63630.

Teresian Institute: Founded in Spain 1911 by Pedro Poveda. Approved as an association of the faithful of pontifical right Jan. 11, 1924. Mailing Address: 3400 S. W. 99th Ave., Miami, FL 33165.

Holy Family Institute (aggregated to the Society of St. Paul): Founded by Fr. James Alberione in 1963 for married couples who wish to commit themselves to seeking evangelical perfection in marriage; definitively approved by the Holy See, 1993. First Americans professed, 1988. Address: 9531 Akron-Canfield Rd., Box 498, Canfield, OH 44406.

THIRD ORDERS

Third orders (commonly called secular orders) are societies of the faithful living in the world who seek to deepen their Christian life and apostolic commitment in association with and according to the spirit of various religious orders. The orders are called "third" because their foundation usually followed the establishment of the first and second religious orders with which they are associated.

In addition to the recognized third orders, there are other groups of lay persons with strong ties to religious orders. Relationships of this kind serve the spiritual good of the faithful and also enrich the religious orders in a complementary fashion, with the mutual vitality of prayer in the cloister or convent and action in the marketplace.

Augustine, Third Order Secular of St.: Founded, 13th century; approved Nov. 7, 1400.

Carmelites, Lay (Third Order of Our Lady of Mt. Carmel): Rule for laity approved by Pope Nicholas V, Oct. 7, 1452; new statutes, January, 1991. Addresses (Lay Carmelite Office): 8501 Bailey Rd., Darien, IL 60561; P.O. Box 613, Williamston, MA 01267; P.O. Box 27, Tappan, NY 10983-0027. Approximately 270 communities and 10,000 members in the U.S. and Canada.

Carmelites, The Secular Order of Discalced (formerly the Third Order Secular of the Blessed Virgin Mary of Mt Carmel and of St. Teresa of Jesus): Rule based on the Carmelite reform established by St. Teresa and St. John of the Cross, 16th century; approved Mar. 23, 1594. Revised rule approved May 10, 1979. Office of National Secretariat, U.S.A.; P.O. Box 3079, San Jose, CA 95156-3079. Approximately 24,445 members throughout the world; 130 groups/communities and 5,200 members in the U.S. and Canada.

Dominican Laity: Founded in the 13th century. Addresses of provincial promoters in the United States: Central Province, 1909 South Ashland Ave., Chicago, IL 60608-2994; Eastern Province, 141 E.

65th St., New York, NY 10021-6607; Southern Province, P.O. Box 12927, Raleigh, NC 27605-2927; Western Province, 5877 Birch Ct., Oakland, CA 94618-1626.

Franciscan Order, Secular (SFO): Founded, 1209 by St. Francis of Assisi; approved Aug. 30, 1221. National Minister, William Wicks, SFO, 3307 Quail Meadows Dr., Santa Maria, CA 93455; International Secretariate, Via Pomponia Grecina, 31, 00145 Rome. *Tau USA*, quarterly. Approximately 780,000 throughout the world; 18,000 in U.S.

Mary, Third Order of: Founded, Dec. 8, 1850; rule approved by the Holy See, 1857. Addresses of provincial directors: Marist Provincial House, 815 Varnum St. N.E., Washington, DC 20017; Marist Fathers, 518 Pleasant St., Framingham, MA 01701; Marist Fathers, 2335 Warring St., Berkeley, CA

94704. Approximately 14,000 in the world, 5,600 in U.S.

Mary, Secular Order of Servants of (Servite): Founded, 1233; approved, 1304. Revised rule approved 1995. Address: National Assistant for the Secular Order, 3121 W. Jackson Blvd., Chicago, IL 60612.

Mercy, Secular Third Order of Our Lady of (Mercedarian): Founded, 1219 by St. Peter Nolasco; approved the same year.

Norbert, Third Order of St.: Founded, 1122 by St. Norbert; approved by Pope Honorius II, 1126.

Oblates of St. Benedict: Lay persons affiliated with a Benedictine abbey or monastery who strive to direct their lives, as circumstances permit, according to the spirit and Rule of St. Benedict.

Trinity, Third Order Secular of the Most: Founded 1198; approved, 1219.

PRIESTLY ORDINATIONS IN 1999

The Life Cycle Institute, Catholic University of America, issued the report Class of 1999: Priests for the Third Millennium, *a survey of priestly ordinations.*

Age Distribution: Ages Under 30, 25%; Ages Under 40, 73%; Ages 50, 92%; median age: 37.

Racial/Ethnic Distribution: Caucasian/European American, 75%; Hispanic/Latino, 10%; Asian or Pacific Islander, 9%; African-American, 2%; Native American, 2%; European, 1%; African, 1%; Mixed descent, 1%.

Place of Birth: United States, 75%; Vietnam, 5%; Mexico, 3%; Western Europe, 2%; Colombia, 2%.

Previous Catholic Education: Elementary School, 63%; High School, 51%; College or University, 61%.

COMPARATIVE STATISTICS FOR RELIGIOUS

The Center for Applied Research in the Apostolate (CARA) at Georgetown University assembled comparative data on numbers of vocations, seminary enrollments, ordinations, and religious covering the years 1965-99. *The sources used included CARA research and records,* The Official Catholic Directory, *and the* Annuarium Statisticum Ecclesiae, *published annually by the Holy See.*

Year	1965	1975	1985	1995	1999
Priests	58,632	58,909	57,317	49,052	46,352
Diocesan priests	35,925	36,005	35,052	32,349	30,880
Religious priests	22,707	22,904	22,265	16,705	15,461
Priestly ordinations	994	771	533	511	460
Graduate level seminarians	8,325	5,279	4,063	3,172	3,386
Permanent deacons	0	898	7,204	10,932	12,184
Religious brothers	12,271	8,625	7,544	6,535	5,725
Religious sisters	179,954	135,225	115,386	90,809	82,693
Total parishes	17,637	18,515	19,244	19,331	19,185
Parishes with no resident priest	549	702	1,051	2,161	2,617

DEMOGRAPHIC DIFFERENCES AMONG THE CLERGY

(Courtesy, Center for Applied Research in the Apostolate (CARA), Georgetown University.) Dr. John H. Moragan, John Henry Cardinal Newman Fellow at the Graduate Theological Foundation in Indiana, published Scholar, Priest and Pastor, a study of 1,000 clergy of each of the four U.S. religious denominations – Methodist, Lutheran, Episcopal, and Catholic. The survey includes the following demographic information:

Denomination	Catholic	Methodist	Lutheran	Episcopalian
Average age	56	46	48	53
Gender (male)	100%	80%	98%	94%
Ethnicity	94% white	96% white	96% white	100% white
Advanced degrees	58%	32%	38%	22%
Hours worked	64	52	48	52

APOSTOLATES AND MINISTRIES

RIGHTS AND OBLIGATIONS OF ALL THE FAITHFUL

The following rights are listed in Canons 208-223 of the revised Code of Canon Law; additional rights are specified in other canons.

They are all equal in dignity because of their baptism and regeneration in Christ.

They are bound always to preserve communion with the Church.

According to their condition and circumstances, they should strive to lead a holy life and promote the growth and holiness of the Church.

They have the right and duty to work for the spread of the divine message of salvation to all peoples of all times and places.

They are bound to obey declarations and orders given by their pastors in their capacity as representatives of Christ, teachers of the faith and rectors of the Church.

They have the right to make known their needs, especially their spiritual needs, to pastors of the Church.

They have the right, and sometimes the duty, of making known to pastors and others of the faithful their opinions about things pertaining to the good of the Church.

They have the right to receive help from their pastors, from the spiritual goods of the Church and especially from the word of God and the sacraments.

They have the right to divine worship performed according to prescribed rules of their rite, and to follow their own form of spiritual life in line with the doctrine of the Church.

They have the right to freely establish and control associations for good and charitable purposes, to foster the Christian vocation in the world, and to hold meetings related to the accomplishment of these purposes.

They have the right to promote and support apostolic action but may not call it "Catholic" unless they have the consent of competent authority.

They have a right to a Christian education.

They have a right to freedom of inquiry in sacred studies, in accordance with the teaching authority of the Church.

They have a right to freedom in the choice of their state of life.

No one has the right to harm the good name of another person or to violate his or her right to maintain personal privacy.

They have the right to vindicate the rights they enjoy in the Church, and to defend themselves in a competent ecclesiastical forum.

They have the obligation to provide for the needs of the Church, with respect to things pertaining to divine worship, apostolic and charitable works, and the reasonable support of ministers of the Church.

They have the obligation to promote social justice and to help the poor from their own resources.

In exercising their rights, the faithful should have regard for the common good of the Church and for the rights and duties of others.

Church authority has the right to monitor the exercise of rights proper to the faithful, with the common good in view.

RIGHTS AND OBLIGATIONS OF LAY PERSONS

In addition to rights and obligations common to all the faithful and those stated in other canons, lay persons are bound by the obligations and enjoy the rights specified in these canons (224-231).

Lay persons, like all the faithful, are called by God to the apostolate in virtue of their baptism and confirmation. They have the obligation and right, individually or together in associations, to work for the spread and acceptance of the divine message of salvation among people everywhere; this obligation is more urgent in those circumstances in which people can hear the Gospel and get to know Christ only through them (lay persons).

They are bound to bring an evangelical spirit to bear on the order of temporal things and to give Christian witness in carrying out their secular pursuits.

Married couples are obliged to work for the building up of the people of God through their marital and family life.

Parents have the most serious obligation to provide for the Christian education of their children according to the doctrine handed down by the Church.

Lay persons have the same civil liberty as other citizens. In the use of this liberty, they should take care that their actions be imbued with an evangelical spirit. They should attend to the doctrine proposed by the magisterium of the Church but should take care that, in questions of opinion, they do not propose their own opinion as the doctrine of the Church.

Qualified lay persons are eligible to hold and perform the duties of ecclesiastical offices open to them in accord with the provisions of law.

Properly qualified lay persons can assist pastors of the Church as experts and counselors.

Lay persons have the obligation and enjoy the right to acquire knowledge of doctrine commensurate with their capacity and condition.

They have the right to pursue studies in the sacred sciences in pontifical universities or facilities and in institutes of religious sciences, and to obtain academic degrees.

If qualified, they are eligible to receive from ecclesiastical authority a mandate to teach sacred sciences.

Laymen can be invested by liturgical rite and in a stable manner in the ministries of lector and acolyte.

Lay persons, by temporary assignment, can fulfill the office of lector in liturgical actions; likewise, all lay persons can perform the duties of commentator or cantor.

In cases of necessity and in the absence of the usual ministers, lay persons — even if not lectors or acolytes — can exercise the ministry of the word, lead liturgical prayers, confer baptism and distribute Communion, according to the prescripts of law.

Lay persons who devote themselves permanently or temporarily to the service of the Church are obliged to acquire the formation necessary for carrying out their duties in a proper manner.

They have a right to remuneration for their service which is just and adequate to provide for their own needs and those of their families; they also have a right to insurance, social security and health insurance.

SPECIAL APOSTOLATES AND GROUPS

Apostleship of the Sea (1920, Glasgow, Scotland; 1947 in U.S.): 3211 Fourth St. NE, Washington, DC 20017 (national office). An international Catholic organization for the moral, social and spiritual welfare of seafarers and those involved in the maritime industry. Formally instituted by the Holy See in 1952 (apostolic constitution *Exul Familia*), it is a sector of the Pontifical Council for Migrants and Itinerant Peoples. Its norms were updated by Pope John Paul II in a *motu proprio* dated Jan. 31, 1997. The U.S. unit, an affiliate of the NCCB-USCC, serves port chaplains in 63 U.S. ports. Nat. Dir., Robert Mario Balderas, a permanent deacon.

Auxiliaries of Our Lady of the Cenacle (1878, France): 22 Bedford Court, Amherst, MA 01002. An association of consecrated Catholic laywomen, under the direction of the Congregation of Our Lady of the Cenacle. They profess annually the evangelical counsels of celibacy, poverty and obedience and serve God through their own professions and life styles and pursue individual apostolates. Reg. Dir., Dr. Carolyn Jacobs.

Catholic Central Union of America (1855): 3835 Westminster Pl., St. Louis, MO 63108; membership, 2,000; *Social Justice Review*, bimonthly. One of the oldest Catholic lay organizations in the U.S. and the first given an official mandate for Catholic Action by a committee of the American bishops (1936).

Catholic Medical Mission Board (1928): 10 W. 17th Street, New York, NY 10011. A charitable, non-profit organization dedicated to providing health care supplies and support for the medically disadvantaged in developing and transitional countries. CMMB depends upon the financial generosity of over 25,000 individual donors and through product contributions by major pharmaceutical corporations. In 1996, CMMB provided medical assistance totaling $49,712,669 to Central America (13 countries); Eastern Europe (12 countries); Asia (5 countries); South America (5 countries) and Africa (6 countries). For each single dollar CMMB received in fiscal year 1996, it was able to provide thirteen and a half dollars worth of actual benefit to the missions it serves. CMMB's medical program includes a placement service for health care specialists who volunteer at Catholic medical facilities in developing countries. Pres., Terry Kirch.

Catholic Movement for Intellectual and Cultural Affairs of Pax Romana: 31 Chesterfield Rd., Stamford, CT 06902. The U.S. affiliate of *Pax Romana - ICMICA* (see International Catholic Organizations); *The Notebook*, quarterly. Pres., Joseph Kirchner.

Catholic Network of Volunteer Service (1963; formerly, International Liaison of Lay Volunteers in Mission): 4121 Harewood Rd. N.E., Washington, DC 20017. Network for lay mission programs, coordinating and facilitating efforts of volunteer mission organizations. The Response, annual directory. Exec. Dir., Jim Lindsay.

Catholic Volunteers in Florida (1983): P.O. Box 702, Goldenrod, FL 32733. Co-sponsored by the bishops of Florida to promote values of social justice by direct service to farm workers, homeless, hungry, low-income people, single mothers and others in need. Volunteers, 20 years of age and older, serve for a one-year period in urban and rural settings.

Center for Applied Research in the Apostolate (CARA): Georgetown University, Washington, DC 20057. A non-profit research center serving the planning needs of the Catholic Church. CARA gathers empirical data for use by bishops, diocesan agencies, parishes, congregations of men and women religious and Catholic organizations. The CARA Report, quarterly; CARA Catholic Ministry Formation Directory, annually.

Christian Family Movement (CFM) (1947): National office, Box 272, Ames, IA 50010. Originated in Chicago to Christianize family life and create communities conducive to Christian family life. Since 1968, CFM in the U.S. has included couples from all Christian churches.

Christian Life Communities (1971, promulgation of revised norms by Pope Paul VI; originated, 1563, as Sodalities of Our Lady, at the Jesuit College in Rome): 3601 Lindell Blvd., Room 202, St. Louis, MO 63108 (national office); the world CLC office is in Rome. Small communities of primarily lay persons who come together to form committed individuals for service to the world and the Church.

Cursillo Movement (1949, in Spain; in U.S., 1957): National Cursillo Center, P.O. Box 210226, Dallas, TX 75211. An instrument of Christian renewal designed to form and stimulate persons to engage in evangelizing their everyday environments.

Franciscan Mission Service of North America, an Overseas Lay Ministry Program (1990): P.O. Box 29034, Washington, DC 20017. Lay missioners work with Franciscan sisters, brothers and priests for a minimum of three years in underdeveloped countries. Exec. Dir. Joseph Nangle, O.F.M.

Grail, The (1921, in The Netherlands, by Rev. Jacques van Ginneken, S.J.; 1940, in U.S.): Grailville, 932 O'Bannonville Rd., Loveland, Ohio 45140 (U. S. headquarters); Duisburger Strasse 442, 45478 Mulheim, Germany (international secretariat). An international movement of women concerned about the full development of all peoples, working in education, religious, social, cultural and ecological areas.

International Catholic Charismatic Renewal Services: Palazzo della Cancelleria, 00120 Vatican City. The mailing address of the U.S. National Service Committee is P.O. Box 628, Locust Grove, VA 22508. *(See also Charismatic Renewal in the Glossary.)*

Jesuit Volunteer Corps (1956): 18th and Thompson Sts., Philadelphia, PA 19121 (address for information). Sponsored by the Society of Jesus in the U.S. Men and women volunteers work throughout the U.S. serving the poor directly and working for structural change.

LAMP Ministries (Lay Apostolic Ministries with the Poor): 2704 Schurz Ave., Bronx, NY 10465. Missionary service of evangelization with the materially poor and homeless in the larger metropolitan New York-New Jersey area. Newsletter, two times a year. Directors, Drs. Tom and Lyn Scheuring.

Lay Mission-Helpers Association (1955): 3424 Wilshire Blvd., Los Angeles, CA 90010. Trains and assigns men and women for work in overseas apostolates for periods of two to three years. Approximately 700 members of the association have served in overseas assignments since its founding. Director, Msgr. Michael Meyers. **The Mission Doctors Association** (same address) recruits, trains and sends Catholic physicians and their families to mission hospitals and clinics throughout the world for tours of two to three years. Additionally, MDA has a short-term program for volunteer physicians with a term of service of 1-2 months. Pres., Dr. Timothy Lefevre.

Legion of Mary (1921, in Dublin, Ireland, by Frank Duff): P.O. Box 1313, St. Louis, MO 63188 (U.S. address); De Montfort House, Dublin 7, Ireland (headquarters). Membership: active Catholics of all ages, under the direction of local bishops and priests, for the work of conversion, conservation and consolation.

Movimiento Familiar Cristiano - USA (MFC) (1969): Movement of Catholic Hispanic families united in their efforts to promote the human and Christian virtues of the family so that it may bécome a force that forms persons, transmits the faith and contributes to the total development of the community. Rev. Clemente Barron, C.P., national spiritual director. Address: 700 Waverly, San Antonio, TX 78201.

National Catholic Conference for Seafarers (affiliated with the Apostleship of the Sea in the U.S.): Seaman's Center, 221-20th St., Galveston, TX 77550. Pres., Mrs. Karen Lai.

Pax Christi USA (1972): 532 W. 8th St., Erie, PA 16503. U.S. section of Pax Christi (see International Catholic Organizations). Founded to establish peacemaking as a priority for the American Catholic Church. *Pax Christi USA*, quarterly; membership, 11,500.

Volunteer Missionary Movement (1969): 5980 W. Loomis Rd., Milwaukee, WI 53129. Independent lay international mission organization with origins in the Catholic tradition but ecumenical and open to all Christian denominations. *Bridges*, quarterly.

Volunteers for Educational and Social Services (VESS): 1625 Rutherford Lane, Bldg. D, Austin, TX. 78754. A program of the Texas Catholic Conference. Volunteers offer their services for a year at mission-sites throughout Texas as teachers, social workers, counselors, ESL instructors, immigration and refugee assistants, parish, youth and campus ministers, health care workers and nurses. The experience offers individuals with the opportunity to acquire professional experience by ministering to the needs of parishes, agencies and schools that are economically disadvataged. Dir., Michael G. Guerra.

CATHOLIC YOUTH ORGANIZATIONS

Camp Fire Boys and Girls: 4601 Madison Ave., Kansas City, MO 64112. The National Catholic Committee for Girl Scouts and Camp Fire, a standing committee of the National Federation for Catholic Youth Ministry, cooperates with Camp Fire Boys and Girls.

Catholic Forester Youth Program, Catholic Or-

der of Foresters: Naperville, IL 60566. To develop Christian leadership and promote the moral, intellectual, social and physical growth of its youth members. Catholic Forester. Membership: youth up to 16 years of age — over 19,046 in 610 local courts in U.S. High Chief Ranger-Pres., Robert Ciesla.

Catholic Youth Organization (CYO): Name of parish-centered diocesan Catholic youth programs throughout the country. CYO promotes a program of spiritual, social and physical activities. The original CYO was organized in 1930 by Archbishop Bernard Sheil, auxiliary bishop of Chicago.

Columbian Squires (1925): 1 Columbus Plaza, New Haven, CT 06510-3326. The official youth organization of the Knights of Columbus. To train and develop leadership through active participation in a well-organized program of spiritual, service, social, cultural and athletic activities. Membership: Catholic young men, 12-18 years old. More than 25,000 in over 1,000 circles (local units) active in the U.S., Canada, Puerto Rico, Philippines, Mexico, the Bahamas, Virgin Islands and Guam. Squires Newsletter, monthly.

Girl Scouts: 830 Third Ave., New York, NY 10022. Girls from archdioceses and dioceses in the U.S. and its possessions participate in Girl Scouting through the collaboration of Girl Scouts of the U.S.A., with the National Catholic Committee for Girl Scouts and Camp Fire, a standing committee of the National Federation for Catholic Youth Ministry.

Holy Childhood Association (Pontifical Association of the Holy Childhood) (1843): 1720 Massachusetts Ave. N.W., Washington, DC 20036. The official children's mission-awareness society of the Church. Provides mission awareness for elementary-grade students in parochial schools and religious education programs and financial assistance to children in more than 100 developing countries. Publishes *It's Our World*, three times a year, in two grade levels. Nat. Dir., Rev. Francis W. Wright, C.S.Sp.

The National Catholic Committee on Scouting: P.O. Box 152079, Irving, TX 75015-2079. Works with the Boy Scouts of America in developing the character and spiritual life of members in units chartered to Catholic and non-Catholic organizations. National Committee Chairman, Robert Runnels of Leawood, Kans. Admin. Sec., Eleanore Starr,

National Catholic Forensic League (1952): 21 Nancy Rd., Milford, MA 01757. To develop articulate Catholic leaders through an inter-diocesan program of speech and debate activities. Newsletter, quarterly. Membership: 925 schools; membership open to Catholic, private and public schools through the local diocesan league. Exec. Sec.-Treas., Richard Gaudette.

National Catholic Young Adult Ministry Association (1982): 3700-A Oakview Terr. N.E., Washington, DC 20017. A response to the needs of young adults, an invitation to share their gifts with the larger community and a challenge to live gospel values in the world. A national network for single and married young adults. Pres., Lori Spanbauer.

National Federation for Catholic Youth Ministry, Inc. (1981): 3700-A Oakview Terr. NE, Washington, DC 20017. To foster the development of youth ministry in the United States. Exec. Dir., Robert McCarty.

Young Christian Students: 19646 W. Dunlap Rd., Dennison, IL 62423. A student movement for Christian personal and social change.

CAMPUS MINISTRY

Campus ministry is an expression of the Church's special desire to be present to all who are involved in higher education and to further dialogue between the Church and the academic community. In the words of the U.S. bishops' 1985 pastoral letter entitled "Empowered by the Spirit," this ministry is "the public presence and service through which properly prepared baptized persons are empowered by the Spirit to use their talents and gifts on behalf of the Church in order to be sign and instrument of the Kingdom in the academic world."

Campus ministry, carried on by lay, Religious and ordained ministers, gathers members of the Church on campus to form the faith community, appropriate the faith, form Christian consciences, educate for justice and facilitate religious development.

The dimensions and challenge of this ministry are evident from, among other things, the numbers involved: approximately 550,000 Catholics on more than 230 Catholic college and university campuses; about four million in several thousand non-Catholic private and public institutions; 1,200 or more campus ministers. In many dioceses, the activities of ministers are coordinated by a local diocesan director. Two professional organizations serve the ministry on the national level:

The National Association of Diocesan Directors of Campus Ministry, Mr. Joseph J. Kiesel-Nield, pres., 706 N. Sprague, Ellensburg, WA 98926.

The Catholic Campus Ministry Association, with a membership of 1,200, 300 College Park Ave., Dayton, OH 45469. Exec. Dir., Donald R. McCrabb.

COLLEGE SOCIETIES

Alpha Sigma Nu (1915): Marquette Univ., Brooks 201, P.O. Box 1881, Milwaukee, WI 53201-1881 (national headquarters). National honor society of the 30 Jesuit institutions of higher education in the U.S. and a chapter at Sogany University in Korea; members chosen on the basis of scholarship, loyalty and service; 1,575 student and 38,000 alumni members. Member, Association of College Honor Societies. Gamma Pi Epsilon (1925) merged with Alpha Sigma Nu in 1973 to form society for men and women. Exec. Dir., Peg Fennig.

Delta Epsilon Sigma (1939): Barry University, Miami Shores, FL 33161. National scholastic honor society for students, faculty and alumni of colleges and universities with a Catholic tradition. *Delta Epsilon Sigma Journal*, three times a year. Membership: 60,000 in 116 chapters. Sec., Dr. J. Patrick Lee.

Kappa Gamma Pi (1926): KGP National Office,

10215 Chardon Rd., Chardon, OH, 44024-9700. A national Catholic college honor society for graduates who, in addition to academic excellence, have shown outstanding leadership in extra-curricular activities. *Kappa Gamma Pi News*, five times a year. Membership: more than 37,000 in 139 colleges; 20 alumnae chapters in metropolitan areas. Nat. Exec. Sec., Christine Walick.

Phi Kappa Theta: 3901 W. 86th St., Suite 425, Indianapolis, IN 46268. National social fraternity with a Catholic heritage. Merger (1959) of Phi Kappa Fraternity, founded at Brown Univ. in 1889, and Theta Kappa Phi Fraternity, founded at Lehigh Univ. in 1919. *The Temple Magazine*, semi-annually, and news-

letters. Membership: 2,800 undergraduate and 50,500 alumni in 63 collegiate and 40 alumni chapters. Exec. Dir., Mark T. McSweeney.

National Catholic Student Coalition (1982): 300 College Park Ave., Dayton, OH 45469. National coalition of Catholic campus ministry groups at public and private institutions of higher education. Formed after National Newman Club Federation and the National Federation of Catholic College Students dissolved in the 1960s. The U.S. affiliate of Pax Romana - IMCS (see International Catholic Organizations). Publishes *The Catholic Collegian*, four times a year. Membership: 200 campus groups. Exec. Dir., Jamie Williams.

ASSOCIATIONS, MOVEMENTS, SOCIETIES IN THE U.S.

(Principal source: *Catholic Almanac* survey.)

Academy of American Franciscan History (1944): 1712 Euclid Ave., Berkeley, CA 94709. To encourage the study of the Franciscan Order in the New World. Dir., Dr. John F. Schwaller.

Aid to the Church in Need (1947): U.S. office, P.O. Box 576, Deer Park, NY 11729. Assists the pastoral activities of the church in Third World countries, Eastern Europe and the former Soviet Union. *Mirror* (newsletter), 9 times a year.

Albanian Catholic Institute "Daniel Dajani, S.J." (1992): Xavier Hall, University of San Francisco, San Francisco, CA 94117. To assist the rebuilding of the Catholic Church in Albania and to promote the dissemination of knowledge of Albania's national, religious and cultural heritage. Founder, Gjon Sinishta (1930-95) in memory of the martyr Daniel Dajani (d. 1946). Exec. Dir., Raymond Frost; Jesuit Community Liaison, Paul Bernardicou, S.J.

American Benedictine Academy (1947): Saint Meinrad Archabbey, 1 Hill Dr. Saint Meinrad, IN, 47577. To promote Benedictine values in contemporary culture. Pres., Eugene Hensell, O.S.B.

American Catholic Correctional Chaplains Association (1952): Office of Detention Ministry, c/o Archdiocese of Los Angeles, 3424 Wilshire Blvd., Los Angeles, CA 90010-2241. 220 in 300 institutions. Pres., Bro. Peter Donohue, C.F.X.

American Catholic Historical Association (1919): The Catholic University of America, Washington, DC 20064. *The Catholic Historical Review*, quarterly. Sec.-Treas., Rev. Msgr. Robert Trisco.

American Catholic Philosophical Association (1926): The Catholic University of America, Washington, DC 20064. *American Catholic Philosophical Quarterly*; *Proceedings*, annually.

American Committee on Italian Migration (1952): 352 W. 44th St., New York, NY 10036; 6,000. *ACIM Newsletter* and *ACIM Nuova Via*, 6 times a year.

American Friends of the Vatican Library (1981): 157 Lakeshore Rd., Grosse Point Farms, MI 48236. Sponsored by the Catholic Library Association. To assist in supporting the Vatican Library: *AMICI*, newsletter.

Ancient Order of Hibernians in America, Inc. (1836): 31 Logan St., Auburn, NY 13021; 120,000. *National Hibernian Digest*, bimonthly. Nat. Sec., Thomas McNabb.

Apostleship of Prayer (1844-France; 1861-U.S.):

3 Stephen Ave., New Hyde Park, NY 11040. Promotes Daily Offering and Sacred Heart devotion. Nat. Dir., Rev. John H. Rainaldo, S.J.

Apostolate for Family Consecration (1975): 3375 County Rd. 36, Bloomingdale, OH 43910. Pope John Paul II Holy Family Center, known as Catholic Familyland, Pres., Jerome F. Coniker. To transform families and parishes and nourish families through the Catholic faith.

Archconfraternity of Christian Mothers (Christian Mothers) (1881): 220 37th St., Pittsburgh, PA 15201; over 3,500 branches. Dir., Rev. Bertin Roll, O.F.M. Cap.

Archconfraternity of the Holy Ghost (1912): Holy Ghost Fathers, 2401 Bristol Pike, Bensalem, PA 19020 (U.S. headquarters).

Archdiocese for the Military Services Seminary Education Fund (1988): 3311 Toledo Terrace, Hyattsville, MD 20782.

Association for Spiritual, Ethical, and Religious Values in Counseling (ASERVIC): Dept. of Educational Psychology and Special Education, Southern Illinois Univ. at Carbondale, Carbondale, IL 62901. Division of the American Counseling Association. *Counseling and Values*, 3 times a year.

Association for Social Economics (formerly the Catholic Economic Association) (1941): Marquette University, Milwaukee, WI 53233; 1,300. *Review of Social Economy*, quarterly.

Association of Catholic Diocesan Archivists (1979): 100 Chartres St., New Orleans, LA, 7-116-2596. To work for establishment of an archival program in every American diocese. *ACDA Bulletin*, quarterly. Pres., Charles Nolan.

Association of Marian Helpers (1944): Eden Hill, 2 Prospect Rd., Stockbridge, MA 01263; 900,000, mostly in U.S. *Marian Helpers Bulletin*, quarterly. To promote vocations to Church service and support worldwide apostolates of Marians of the Immaculate Conception. Exec. Dir., Rev. Joseph, M.I.C.

Beginning Experience (1974): 1209 Washington Blvd., Detroit, MI 48226; 150 teams throughout the world. Adult and youth programs to help divorced, widowed and separated start a new beginning in their lives. Exec. Dir., Emilia Alberico.

The Blue Army USA (1947): P.O. Box 976, Washington, NJ 07882. U.S. branch of the World Apostolate of Fatima. Promote call to Holiness,

Fatima Message. Fatima shrine; *Soul*, bimonthly; *Hearts Aflame*, quarterly. Nat. Pres., Most Rev. James S. Sullivan.

Calix Society (1947): 7601 Wayzata Blvd., Minneapolis, MN 55426; Association of Catholic alcoholics maintaining their sobriety through 12-step program. Sec.-Treas., Bill Fox.

Canon Law Society of America (1939): Catholic University, Washington, DC 20064. To further research and study in canon law; 1,600. Exec. Coord., Rev. Patrick Cogan, S.A.

Cardinal Mindszenty Foundation (CMF) (1958): P.O. Box 11321, St. Louis, MO 63105. To uphold and defend the Catholic Church, family life and freedom for all under God. Publishes *The Mindszenty Report*, monthly. Pres., Eleanor Schlafly.

Catholic Aid Association (1878): 3499 N. Lexington Ave., St. Paul, MN 55126; 80,000. *Catholic Aid News*, monthly. Fraternal life insurance society. Pres. F. L. Spanier.

Catholic Alumni Clubs International (1957): 215 W. Wood St., Lowellville, OH 44436. To advance social, cultural and spiritual well-being of members. Membership limited to single Catholics with professional education; 7,500 in 48 clubs in U.S. Pres., Guy A. DiMarino.

Catholic Answers (1982): P.O. Box 17490, San Diego, CA 92177. *This Rock*, monthly. Apologetics and evangelization organization. Founder and dir., Karl Keating.

Catholic Biblical Association of America (1936): The Catholic University of America, Washington, DC 20064; 1,350. *The Catholic Biblical Quarterly*; *Old Testament Abstracts*, *CBQ* monograph series. Exec. Sec., Joseph Jensen, O.S.B.

Catholic Book Publishers Association, Inc. (1987): 2 Park Ave., Manhasset, NY 11030. Exec. Dir., Charles A. Roth.

Catholic Coalition on Preaching: Madonna University, 36600 Schoolcraft Rd. Livonia, MI 48150-1173. Pres., Rev. Francis Tebbe, O.F.M.

Catholic Commission on Intellectual and Cultural Affairs (CCICA) (1946): LaSalle University, Philadelphia, PA 19141; 350. Exec. Dir., Bro. Daniel Burke, F.S.C.

Catholic Committee of Appalachia (1970): P.O. Box 662, Wheeling, WV 26288. Exec. Coord., Todd Garland.

Catholic Daughters of the Americas (1903): 10 W. 71st St., New York, NY 10023; 125,000. Share Magazine. Nat. Regent, Grace M. Rinaldi.

Catholic Familyland (1975): 3375 County Rd. 36, Bloomingdale, OH, 43910. Canonically named the John Paul II Holy Family Center; functions under the auspices of the Apostolate for Family Consecration. Pres., Jerome F. Coniker.

Catholic Golden Age (1975): P.O. Box 3658, Scranton, PA 18505-0658; CGA World, quarterly. For Catholics over 50 years of age.

Catholic Guardian Society (1913): 1011 First Ave., New York, NY 10022. Exec. Dir., John J. Frein.

Catholic Home Bureau (1899): 1011 First Ave., New York, NY 10022. Exec. Dir., Sr. Una McCormack, O.P.

Catholic Home Study Service (1936): P.O. Box 363, Perryville, MO 63775. Provides instruction in the Catholic faith by mail free of charge. Dir., Rev. Oscar Lukefahr, C.M.

Catholic Interracial Council of New York, Inc. (1934): 899 Tenth Ave., New York, NY 10019. To promote racial and social justice.

Catholic Knights of America (1877): Publication Office, 1850 Dalton St., Cincinnati, OH 45214; 7,800. *C K of A Journal*, monthly. Fraternal insurance society.

Catholic Knights of Ohio (1891): 22005 Mastick Rd., Fairview Park, OH 44126; 8,000 in Ohio and Kentucky. *The Messenger*, monthly. Fraternal insurance society. Pres., Victor D. Huss.

Catholic Kolping Society of America (1923): P.O. Box 46252, Chicago, IL 60646. *Kolping Banner*, monthly. International society concerned with spiritual and educational development of members.

Catholic Lawyers' Guild: Organization usually on a diocesan basis, under different titles.

Catholic League for Religious Assistance to Poland (1943): 984 N. Milwaukee Ave., Chicago, IL 60622-4199. Exec. Dir., Most Rev. Thad Jakubowski.

Catholic League for Religious and Civil Rights (1973): 1011 First Ave., New York, NY 10022; local chapters throughout U.S. *Catalyst*, league journal. Serves Catholic community as an anti-defamation and civil rights agency. Pres., William A. Donohue.

Catholic Library Association (1921): 100 North St., Suite 224, Suite 224, Pittsfield, MA 01201-5109. *Catholic Library World, Catholic Periodical and Literature Index*, quarterlies. Exec.Dir., Jean R. Bostley, S.S.J.

Catholic Marketing Network (1955): 6000 Campus Circle Dr. #110, Irving, TX 75063. A trade associaton founded to encourage the most effective production and distribution of Catholic goods and provide a common forum for mutual interchange of ideas .*Catholic Marketing Network*, quarterly.

Catholic Medical Association (formerly National Federation of Catholic Physicians' Guilds) (1927): 850 Elm Grove Rd., Elm Grove, WI 53122; Linacre Quarterly. Exec. Dir., Robert H. Herzog.

Catholic Near East Welfare Association (1926): 1011 First Ave., Suite 1552, New York, NY 10022. A papal agency for humanitarian and pastoral support serving the churches and peoples of the Middle East, Northeast Africa, India and Eastern Europe, with offices in New York, Vatican City, Addis Ababa, Amman, Jordan, Jerusalem and Beirut, Lebanon. Pres., Cardinal John O'Connor; Sec. Gen., Msgr. Robert L. Stern.

Catholic Order of Foresters (1883): 355 Shuman Blvd., P.O. Box 3012, Naperville, IL 60566; 136,685. *The Catholic Forester*, bimonthly. Fraternal insurance society. High Chief Ranger, Robert Ciesla.

Catholic Press Association of the U.S. and Canada, Inc. (1911): 3555 Veterans Memorial Highway, Unit O, Ronkonkoma, NY 11779. *The Catholic Journalist*, monthly; *Catholic Press Directory*, annually. Pres., Christopher J. Gunty; Exec. Dir., Owen P. McGovern.

Catholic Theological Society of America (1946), Ursuline College, 2550 Lander Rd., Pepper Pike, OH 44124. *Proceedings*, annually.

Catholic Union of Texas, The K.J.T. (1889): 214 E. Colorado St., La Grange, TX 78945; 18,226. *Nasinec*, weekly, and *K. J. T. News*, monthly. Fraternal and insurance society. Pres., Elo J. Goerig.

Catholic War Veterans (1935): 441 N. Lee St., Alexandria, VA 22314; 500 posts, Catholic War Veteran, bimonthly.

Catholic Worker Movement (1933): 36 E. First St., New York, NY 10003. *The Catholic Worker*, 8 times a year. Lay apostolate founded by Peter Maurin and Dorothy Day; has Houses of Hospitality in over 60 U.S. cities and several communal farms in various parts of the country. Promotes the practice of the works of mercy, nonviolence, personalism, voluntary poverty.

Catholic Workman (*Katolicky Delnik*) (1891): 111 West Main St., New Prague, MN 56071; 16,405. *Catholic Workman*, monthly. Fraternal and insurance society.

Catholics Against Capital Punishment (1992), P.O. Box 3125, Arlington, VA 22203. Promoes greater awareness of papal and episcopal statements against the death penalty. *CACP News Notes*, bimonthly. Nat. Coord., Frank McNeirney.

Catholics United for Spiritual Action, Inc. (CUSA) (1947): 63 Wall St., New York, NY 10005. A group-correspondence apostolate for the disabled.

Catholics United for the Faith (1968): 827 N. Fourth St., Steubenville, OH 43952; 23,000 worldwide, *Lay Witness*, monthly. Lay apostolic group concerned with spiritual and doctrinal formation of members. Pres., Curtis Martin.

Center of Concern (1971): 1225 Otis St., Washington, DC 20017. Exec. Dir., James E. Hugis.

Central Association of the Miraculous Medal (1915): 475 E. Chelten Ave., Philadelphia, PA 19144. *Miraculous Medal*, quarterly. Dir., Rev. William J. O'Brien, C.M.

Chaplains' Aid Association, Inc. (1917): 3311 Toledo Terrace, Hyattsville, MD 20780. To receive and administer funds toward education of seminarians to become priest-chaplains in military services. Pres., Most Rev. Joseph T. Dimino.

Christian Foundation for Children and Aging: One Elmwood Ave., Kansas City, KS 66103. Grassroots movement dedicated to improving through sponsorship the lives of children and aging at Catholic mission sites around the world. Exec. Dir., Louis Finocchario.

Christophers, Inc., The (1945): 12 E. 48th St., New York, NY 10017. Founded by Rev. James Keller, M.M. The Christophers stimulate personal initiative and responsible action in line with Judeo-Christian principles through broadcast of Christopher radio and TV programs; free distribution of *Christopher News Notes*, ten times a year; publication of a weekly Christopher column in over 200 newspapers; Spanish literature; annual media awards; youth outreach. Dir., Rev. Thomas J. McSweeney.

Citizens for Educational Freedom (1959): 921 S. Walter Reed Dr., Suite 1, Arlington, VA 22204. Nonsectarian group concerned with parents' right to educational choice by means of tuition tax credits and vouchers. Exec. Dir., Patrick J. Reilly.

Confraternity of Bl. Junipero Serra (1989): P.O. Box 7125, Mission Hills, CA 91346; 3,500 in U.S. and foreign countries. Founded in Monterey (Calif.) diocese to help promote process of canonization of Bl. Junipero Serra and increase spiritual development of members. Dir., Rev. Thomas L. Davis, Jr.; Spiritual Dir., Rev. Noel F. Moholy, O.F.M.

Confraternity of Catholic Clergy (1976): 4445 W. 64th St., Chicago, IL 60629. Association of priests pledged to pursuit of personal holiness, loyalty to the Pope, theological study and adherence to authentic teachings of the Catholic faith. Sec., Rev. L. Dudley Day, O.S.A.

Confraternity of Christian Doctrine, Inc.: 3211 Fourth St., N.E., Washington, DC 20017. A distinct entity, separately incorporated and directed by a Board of Trustees from the United States Catholic Conference of Bishops. Its purpose is to foster and promote the teaching of Christ as understood and handed down by the Roman Catholic Church. To this end it licenses use of the Lectionary for Mass and the New American Bible (NAB), the Revised Psalms of the NAB and the Revised New Testament of the NAB, translations made from the original languages in accordance with the papal encyclical *Divino Afflante Spiritu* (1943) of Pope Pius XII.

Confraternity of the Immaculate Conception of Our Lady of Lourdes (1874): Box 561, Notre Dame, IN 46556. Distributors of Lourdes water.

Confraternity of the Most Holy Rosary: See **Dominican Rosary Apostolate.**

Couple to Couple League (1971), P.O. Box 111184, Cincinnati, OH 45211. Founded to teach and promote marital chastity through Natural Family Planning. Pres., John F. Kippley.

Courage (1980): c/o St. John the Baptist Church and Friary, 210 West 31st St., New York, NY 10001. To live chaste lives in accordance with the Church's teaching on homosexuality. Newsletter, 4 times a year. Nat. Dir., Rev. John F. Harvey, O.S.F.S.

Damien-Dutton Society for Leprosy Aid, Inc. (1944): 616 Bedford Ave., Bellmore, NY 11710; 25,000. *Damien Dutton Call*, quarterly. Provides medicine, rehabilitation and research for conquest of leprosy. Pres., Howard E. Crouch; Vice Pres., Elizabeth Campbell.

Daughters of Isabella (1897): P.O. Box 9585, New Haven, CT 06535; 100,000. To unite Catholic women into a fraternal order for spiritual benefits and to promote higher ideals within society.

Disaster Response Office (1990): Catholic Charities USA, 1731 King St., Suite 200, Alexandria, VA 22314. Promotes and facilitates Catholic disaster response in the U.S. Dir., Jane A. Gallagher.

Dominican Rosary Apostolate (1806): 141 E. 65th St., New York, NY 10021. Dir., Rev. Edward L. Martin, O.P.

Edith Stein Guild, Inc. (1955): Church of St. John the Baptist, 210 W. 31st St., New York, NY 10001. Assists and encourages Jewish Catholics; fosters among Catholics a better understanding of their Jewish heritage; promotes spread of knowledge of life and writings of Bl. Edith Stein; fosters better understanding between Jews and Christians and supports the Church's spirit of ecumenism. Pres., Mrs. Cabiria Nardiello; Liaison, Rev. Philip F. Romano, O.F.M. Cap.

Enthronement of the Sacred Heart in the Home (1907): P.O. Box 111, Fairhaven, MA 02719.

Family Rosary, Inc., The (1942): 4 Pine West Plaza, Albany, NY 12205. Founded by Father Patrick Peyton,

C.S.C. Encourages family prayer, especially the Rosary. Pres., Rev. John Phalen, C.S.C.

Federation of Diocesan Liturgical Commissions (FDLC) (1969): P.O. Box 29039, Washington, DC 20017. Voluntary association of personnel from diocesan liturgical commissions and worship offices. The main purpose is promotion of the liturgy as the heart of Christian life, especially in the parish community. Exec. Dir., Rev. Michael J. Spillane.

Federation of Seminary Spiritual Directors (1972): c/o Sacred Heart Major Seminary, 2701 Chicago Blvd., Detroit, MI, 48206. Responsible for priestly spiritual formation in high school and college seminaries, novitiates, theologates and houses of formation in the U.S. Pres., Dan Trapp.

Fellowship of Catholic Scholars (1977): 215 Law School, Notre Dame, IN 46556; 1,000 members. Interdisciplinary research and publications of Catholic scholars in accord with the magisterium of the Catholic Church. Pres., Prof. Gerard V. Bradley.

First Catholic Slovak Ladies' Association, USA (1892): 24950 Chagrin Blvd., Beachwood, OH 44122; 102,000. *Fraternally Yours*, monthly. Fraternal insurance society. Pres., Mary Ann Johanek.

First Catholic Slovak Union (Jednota) (1890): FCSU Corporate Center, 6611 Rockside Rd., Suite 300, Independence, OH 44131; 96,206. *Jednota*, biweekly. Nat. Pres., Thomas Hricik.

Foundation for the Family (1986): P.O. Box 111184, Cincinnati, OH 45211. Established by Couple to Couple League (see entry above) to provide materials for family not relating to Natural Family Planning.

Foundations and Donors Interested in Catholic Activities, Inc. (FADICA): 1350 Connecticut Ave. N.W., Suite 303, Washington, DC 20036. A consortium of private foundations providing continuing education and research to members to make church-related philanthropy more effective. Pres., Francis J. Butler.

Franciscan Apostolate of the Way of the Cross (1949): P.O. Box 23, Boston, MA 02112. Distributes religious materials to the sick and shut-in. Dir., Rev. Robert Lynch, O.F.M.

Franciscan Canticle, Inc. (1983): 370 W. Arenas Rd., Palm Springs, CA 92262. Community of men and women artists who use their gifts and talents to promote the work of God.

Free The Fathers (1983): 845 Oak St. Chattanooga, TN 37403. To work for the freedom of bishops and priests imprisoned in China. Pres., John M. Davies.

Friends of the Holy Land, Inc. (1974): 347 Mile Square Rd., Yonkers, NY 10701; 300 members. To provide spiritual and material support for the Christian communities in the Holy Land; *Friends of the Holy Land Newsletter*. Gen. Dir., Ernest F. Russo.

Gabriel Richard Institute (1949): 2820 West Maple Rd., Suite No. 101, Troy, MI 48084. Conducts Christopher Leadership Course. Dir., Rev. Thomas J. Bresnahan; Nat. Mgr., Dolores Ammar.

Guard of Honor of the Immaculate Heart of Mary (1932): 135 West 31st St., New York, NY 10001. An archconfraternity approved by the Holy See whose members cultivate devotion to the Blessed Virgin Mary, particularly through a daily Guard Hour of Prayer.

Holy Name Society: Founded in 1274 by Blessed John Vercelli, master general of the Dominicans, to promote reverence for the Holy Name of Jesus; this is still the principal purpose of the society, which also develops lay apostolic programs in line with directives of the Second Vatican Council. Introduced in the U.S. by Dominican Father Charles H. McKenna in 1870-71, the society has about 5 million members on diocesan and parochial levels. With approval of the local bishop and pastor, women as well as men may be members.

Holy Name Society, National Association (NAHNS) (1970): P.O. Box 12032, Baltimore, MD 21281. *Holy Name Newsletter*, monthly. Association of diocesan and parochial Holy Name Societies.

Hungarian Catholic League of America, Inc. (1945): One Cathedral Sq., Providence, RI 02903. Chair., Rev. Msgr. William I. Varsanyi.

International Institute of the Heart of Jesus (1972): 7236 Wellauer Rd., Milwaukee, WI 53213; Rev. Walter O. Kern, 5337 Genesee St., Bowmansville, NY 14026; *Delegacion Latino-americana*, IIHJ, Casilla 118, Correo 35, Las Condes, Santiago, Chile (president's office). Promote awareness and appreciation of the mystery of the Heart of Christ.

Italian Catholic Federation (1924): 675 Hegenberger Rd., #110, Oakland, CA 94621; 19,000. Fraternal organization of Italian-American Catholics.

John Carroll Society, The (1951): P.O. Box 29260, Washington, DC 20017. Chaplain, Rev. Peter Vaghi.

Judean Society, Inc., The (1966): 1075 Space Park Way No. 336, Mt. View, CA 94043.

Knights of Peter Claver (1909), and **Knights of Peter Claver, Ladies Auxiliary** (1926): 1825 Orleans Ave., New Orleans, LA 70116. 35,000. The Claverite, biannually. Fraternal and aid society. National Chaplain, Most Rev. Curtis J. Guillory, S.V.D.

Knights of St. John, International Supreme Commandery (1886): 89 So. Pine Ave., Albany, N.Y. 12208. Supreme Sec., Maj. Gen. Joseph Hauser, Jr.

Ladies of Charity of the United States of America (1960): P.O. Box 31697, St. Louis, MO 63131; 25,000 in U.S.; 250,000 worldwide. International Association founded by St. Vincent de Paul in 1617.

Latin Liturgy Association (1975): Office of the Chairman, 740 Carriage Way, Baton Rouge, LA 70808; 850. To promote the use of the Latin language and music in the approved rites of the Church. Quarterly journal. Chair., Dr. Robert J. Edgeworth.

Legatus (1987): 30 Frank Lloyd Wright Dr., P.O. Box 997, Ann Arbor, MI 48106. To apply Church's moral teaching in business and personal lives of members. *Legatus Newsletter*, monthly.

Lithuanian Groups: Ateitininkai, members of **Lithuanian Catholic Federation Ateitis** (1910), 1209 Country Lane, Lemont, IL 60439; *Ateitis*, bimonthly; Pres., Juozas Polikaitis. **Knights of Lithuania** (1913): Roman Catholic educational-fraternal organization; Vytis, monthly; Pres., Evelyn Ozelis, 2533 W. 45th St., Chicago, IL 60632. **Lithuanian Catholic Alliance** (1886), 71-73 S. Washington St., Wilkes-Barre, PA 18701; fraternal insurance organization; Pres., Thomas E. Mack.

Lithuanian Roman Catholic Federation of America (1906): 4545 W. 63rd St., Chicago, IL 60629. Umbrella organization for Lithuanian parishes and organizations; *The Observer*, bimonthly; Pres., Saulius Kuprys.

Lithuanian Roman Catholic Priests' League (1909): 50 Orton-Marotta Way, Boston, MA 02127. Religious-professional association. Pres., Rev. Albert Contons.

Lithuanian Catholic Religious Aid, Inc. (1961): 351 Highland Blvd., Brooklyn, NY 11207; to assist Catholics in Lithuania. Chairman and Pres., Most Rev. Paul Baltakis.

Little Flower Mission League (1957), P.O. Box 25, Plaucheville, LA 71362. Sponsored by the Brothers of the Holy Eucharist. Dir., Bro. André M. Lucia, F.S.E.

Little Flower Society (1923): 1313 Frontage Rd.; Darien, IL 60561; 200,000 Nat. Dir., Rev. Robert E. Colaresi, O. Carm.

Liturgical Conference, The: 8750 Georgia Ave., Suite 123, Silver Spring, MD 20910. Liturgy, Homily Service. Education, research and publication programs for renewing and enriching Christian liturgical life. Ecumenical.

Loyal Christian Benefit Association (1890): P.O. Box 13005, Erie, PA 16514. Fraternal benefit and insurance society. *The Fraternal Leader*, quarterly.

Marian Movement of Priests (1972): P.O. Box 8, St. Francis, ME 04774-0008 (U.S.); Via Mercalli, 23, 20122 Milan, Italy (internatl. headquarters); 4,000 clergy; 53,000 religious and laity (U.S.). Spiritual renewal through consecration to the Immaculate Heart of Mary. Nat. Dir., Rev. Albert G. Roux.

Mariological Society of America (1949): Marian Library, Box 1390, University of Dayton, Dayton, OH 45469. *Marian Studies*, annually. Founded by Rev. Juniper B. Carol, O.F.M., to promote greater appreciation of and scientific research in Marian theology. Sec., Rev. Thomas A. Thompson, S.M.

Marriage Encounter, National: 4704 Jamerson Pl., Orlando, FL 32807. Brings couples together for a weekend program of events directed by a team of several couples and a priest, to develop their abilities to communicate with each other as husband and wife. The national office of Worldwide Marriage Encounter is located at 2210 East Highland Ave., #106, San Bernardino, CA 92404.

Maryheart Crusaders, The (1964): 22 Button St., Meriden, CT 06450. Pres., Louise D'Angelo.

Men of the Sacred Heart (1964): National Shrine of the Sacred Heart, Harleigh, PA 18225. Promote enthronement of Sacred Heart.

Militia Immaculata National Center - Marytown (1917): 1600 W. Park Ave., Libertyville, IL 60048; canonically established with international headquarters in Rome. A pious association for evangelization and catechesis beginning with members' own total consecration to the Immaculate Virgin Mary.

Missionary Association of Catholic Women (1916): 3501 S. Lake Dr., P.O. Box 07212, Milwaukee, WI 53207-0912.

Missionary Vehicle Association, Inc. (MIVA America) (1971): 1400 Michigan Ave., N.E., Washington, DC 20017-7234. To raise funds and distribute them annually as vehicle grants to missionaries working with the poor in Third World countries. Nat. Dir., Rev. Philip De Rea, M.S.C.; Exec. Dir., Rev. Anthony F. Krisak.

Morality in Media, Inc. (1962): 475 Riverside Dr., New York, NY 10115. Interfaith national organization. Newsletter, bimonthly. Works by constitutional means to curb the explosive growth of hard-core pornography and to turn back the tide of grossly offensive, indecent media. A major project is the National Obscenity Law Center which provides legal information for prosecutors and other attorneys. Pres., Robert W. Peters.

National Assembly of Religious Women (NARW): 529 S. Wabash Ave., Suite 404, Chicago, IL 60605. Founded as the National Assembly of Women Religious, 1970; title changed, 1980. A movement of feminist women committed to prophetic tasks of giving witness, raising awareness and engaging in public action and advocacy for justice in church and society.

National Association for Lay Ministry (1977): 5420 S. Cornell Ave., Chicago, IL 60615. Acts as advocate and support for lay people who respond to a call to ministry in the Church.

National Association of Catholic Family Life Ministers: Univ. of Dayton, 300 College Park, Dayton, OH 45469. Strives to be a voice and advocate for families and family ministry in Church and society. Pres., Kay Ryan, C.S.J.

National Association of Catholic Home Educators (1993): 6102 Saints Hill Lane, Broad Run, VA 22014. Promotion of homeschooling. *The Catholic Home Educator*, quarterly.

National Association of Church Personnel Administrators (1971): 100 E. 8th St., Cincinnati, OH 45202. Association for human resource and personnel directors dedicated to promotion and development of just personnel practices for all church employees. Exec. Dir., Sr. Ellen Doyle, O.S.U.

National Association of Diocesan Ecumenical Officers: 7800 Kenrick Rd., St. Louis, MO 63119. Network of Catholics involved in ecumenical and interreligious work. Pres., Ms. Garland Pohl; Dir. Ecumenical Office, Rev. Vincent A. Heier.

National Association of Pastoral Musicians (1976): 225 Sheridan St., N.W., Washington, DC 20011; 9,000. Dedicated to fostering the art of musical liturgy. Pastoral Music, six times a year. Exec. Dir., Rev. Virgil C. Funk.

National Association of Priest Pilots (1964):, 660 Bush Ave., Garner, IA 50438-1513. Pres., Rev. John Hemann.

National Catholic AIDS Network: P.O. Box 422984, San Francisco, CA 94142. Exec. dir., Rev. Rodney DeMartini; Board Pres., Rev. Robert J. Vitillo.

National Catholic Band Association (1953): Box 1023, Notre Dame University, Notre Dame, IN 46556.

National Catholic Cemetery Conference (1949): 710 N. River Rd., Des Plaines, IL 60016. Exec. Dir., Irene K. Pesce.

National Catholic Conference for Interracial Justice (NCCIJ) (1960): 1200 Varnum St. N.E., Washington, DC 20017. Exec. Dir., Rev. Mr. Joseph M. Conrad, Jr.

National Catholic Conference of Airport Chaplains (1986): P.O. Box 2220, Newark, N.J., 07114.

Provides support and communication for Catholics performing pastoral ministry to airport and airline workers and Catholic travelers; affiliated with Bishops' Committee on Migration, NCCB. Episcopal liaison, Most Rev. James C. Timlin. Pres., Rev. David J. Baratelli, Ed.S.

National Catholic Council on Alcoholism and Related Drug Problems, Inc.: 1550 Hendrickson St., Brooklyn, NY 11234. An affiliate of the NCCB/USCC. Committed to assisting members in a greater awareness of alcoholism, other chemical addictions and prevention issues.

National Catholic Development Conference (1968): 86 Front St., Hempstead, NY 11550. Professional association of organizations and individuals engaged in raising funds for Catholic charitable activities. Pres., George T. Holloway.

National Catholic Ministry to the Bereaved (NCMB) (1990): 606 Middle Ave. Elyria, OH 44035. Offers ongoing education, resources and assistance to dioceses, parishes and caregivers in their ministry to the bereaved. Pres., Sr. Maureen O'Brien, O.P.

National Catholic Pharmacists Guild of the United States (1962): 1012 Surrey Hills Dr., St. Louis, MO 63117. Publishes *The Catholic Pharmacist*. Co-Pres. and Exec. Dir., John P. Winkelmann.

National Catholic Society of Foresters (1891): 320 S. School St., Mt. Prospect, IL 60056 52,000; *National Catholic Forester*, quarterly. A fraternal insurance society. Pres. and CEO, Sue Koleczek.

National Catholic Stewardship Council (1962): 1275 K St. N.W., Suite 980, Washington, DC 20005-4006. A professional association which fosters an environment in which stewardship is understood, accepted and practiced throughout the church. Nat. Dir., Matthew R. Paratore.

National Catholic Women's Union (1916): 3835 Westminster Pl., St. Louis, MO 63108; 7,000.

National Center for the Laity (1977): 10 E. Pearson St., No. 101, Chicago, IL 60611. *Initiatives*, six times a year. To promote and implement the vision of Vatican II: That the laity are the Church in the modern world as they attend to their occupational, family and neighborhood responsibilities.

National Center for Urban Ethnic Affairs (1971): P.O. Box 20, Cardinal Station, Washington, DC 20064. Research and action related to the Church's concern for cultural pluralism and urban neighborhoods. An affiliate of the USCC. Pres., Dr. John A. Kromkowski.

National Christ Child Society Inc. (1887): 5101 Wisconsin Ave. N.W., Suite 304, Washington, DC 20016. Founder, Mary V. Merrick. A non-profit Catholic association of volunteers of all denominations dedicated to the service of needy children and youth regardless of race or creed. Membership: approximately 7,000 adult members in 37 chapters in U.S. Exec. Dir., Margaret Saffell.

National Committee of Catholic Laymen, The (1977): 215 Lexington Ave., Fourth Floor, New York, NY 10016. Lobbying and publishing organization representing "orthodox" Catholics who strongly support Pope John Paul II; *Catholic Eye*, monthly. Pres., J.P. McFadden.

National Conference of Catechetical Leadership (formerly, National Conference of Diocesan Directors of Religious Education) (1936): 3021 4th St. N.E., Washington, DC 20017; 1,300. To promote catechetical ministry at the national diocesan and parish levels. Exec. Dir., Neil A. Parent.

National Conference of Diocesan Vocation Directors (NCDVD) (1961): P.O. Box 1570, Little River, SC 29566. Professional organization for diocesan vocation personnel providing resources and on-going education in their promoting, assessing and forming of candidates for the diocesan priesthood.

National Council for Catholic Evangelization (1983): 5998 Alcala Parkway, USD Campus, San Diego, CA 92110. To promote evangelization as the "primary and essential mission of the Church," in accordance with *Evangelii Nuntiandi*, the 1975 apostolic exhortation of Pope Paul VI. Pres., Sr. Priscilla Lemire, R.J.M.

National Council of Catholic Men: 4712 Randolph Dr., Annandale, VA 22003. A federation of Catholic organizations through which Catholic men may be heard nationally on matters of common interest. NCCM is a constituent of the National Council of Catholic Laity.

National Council of Catholic Women (1920): 1275 K St. N.W., Suite 975, Washington, DC 20005. A federation of some 7,000 organizations of Catholic women in the U.S. *Catholic Woman*, bimonthly. NCCW unites Catholic organizations and individual Catholic women of the U.S., develops their leadership potential, assists them to act upon current issues in the Church and society, provides a medium through which Catholic women may speak and act upon matters of common interest, and relates to other national and international organizations in the solution of present-day problems. It is an affiliate of the World Union of Catholic Women's Organizations. Exec. Dir., Annette P. Kane.

National Evangelization Teams (NET): 110 Crusader Ave., West St. Paul, MN 55118-4427. Trains Catholic young adults to be evangelists to peers and high school/junior high youth through traveling retreat teams.

National Federation of Priests' Councils (1968): 1337 West Ohio, Chicago, IL 60622-6490. To give priests' councils a representative voice in matters of presbyteral, pastoral and ministerial concern to the U.S. and the universal Church. Publishes *Touchstone*, quarterly, with a circulation of 25,000. Pres., Rev. Donald J. Wolf; Exec. Dir., Bro. Bernard Stratman, S.M.

National Institute for the Word of God (1972): 487 Michigan Ave. N.E., Washington, DC 20017. For renewed biblical preaching, Bible sharing and evangelization. Dir., Rev. John Burke, O.P.

National Life Center, Inc.: 686 N. Broad St., Woodbury, NJ 08096. Interdenominational guidance and referral service organization offering pregnant women alternatives to abortion. Pres., Denise F. Cocciolone.

National Organization for Continuing Education of Roman Catholic Clergy, Inc. (1973): Madonna University, 36600 Schoolcraft Rd., Livonia, MI, 48151-1173. Membership: 152 dioceses, 66 religious provinces, 46 institutions, 49 individuals in U.S., 18 associates outside U.S. Pres., Rev. Francis S. Tebbe, O.F.M.

National Pastoral Life Center: 18 Bleecker St., New York, NY 10012-2404. Services for parishes. *Church*, quarterly. Dir., Rev. Philip Murnion.

NETWORK, A Catholic Social Justice Lobby

(1971): 801 Pennsylvania Ave. S.E., Suite 460, Washington, DC 20003. *NETWORK Connection*, bimonthly. A national Catholic social justice lobby. Nat. Coord., Kathy Thornton, R.S.M.

Nocturnal Adoration Society of the United States (1882): 184 E. 76th St., New York, NY 10021. Nat. Dir., Rev. Bernard J. Camire, S.S.S.

North American Academy of Liturgy: c/o CSSR Executive Office, Valparaiso Univ., Valparaiso, IN 46383. *Proceedings*, annually. Foster ecumenical and interreligious liturgical research, publication and dialogue on a scholarly level. Pres., Alan Barthel.

North American Conference of Separated and Divorced Catholics (1972): P.O. Box 360, Richland, OR 97870. Pres., Irene Varley.

North American Forum on the Catechumenate: 3033 Fourth St. NE, Washington, DC 20017. An international network committed to the implementation of the Order of Christian Initiation of Adults. Exec. Dir., Vacant.

Order of the Alhambra (1904): 4200 Leeds Ave., Baltimore, MD 21229. 7,000 in U.S. and Canada. Fraternal society dedicated to assisting developmentally disabled and handicapped children. Supreme Commander, Angelo Miele.

Our Lady's Rosary Makers (1949): 4611 Poplar Level Rd., Louisville, KY 40233; 23,000 members. To supply missionaries with free rosaries for distribution throughout the world. *News Bulletin*, monthly. Pres., Barbara Williamson.

Paulist National Catholic Evangelization Association (1977): 3031 Fourth St., N.E., Washington, DC 20017-1102. *Share the Word*, bimonthly magazine; *Evangelization Update*, bimonthly newsletter. To work with unchurched and alienated Catholics; to develop, test and document contemporary ways in which Catholic parishes and dioceses can evangelize the unchurched and inactive Catholics. Dir., Rev. Kenneth Boyack, C.S.P.

Perpetual Eucharistic Adoration: 660 Club View Dr., Los Angeles, CA 90024. Promote programs of Perpetual Eucharistic adoration/exposition in parishes throughout the world.

Philangeli (Friends of the Angels) (1949 in England; 1956 in U.S.): Viatorian Fathers, 1115 E. Euclid St., Arlington Heights, IL 60004.

Pious Union of Prayer (1898): St. Joseph's Home, 541 Pavonia Ave., Jersey City, NJ 07306; 20,000. *St. Joseph's Messenger* and *Advocate of the Blind*, quarterly.

Polish Roman Catholic Union of America (1887): 984 N. Milwaukee Ave., Chicago, IL 60622. *Narod Polski*, bimonthly. Fraternal benefit society.

Pontifical Mission for Palestine (1949): 1011 First Ave., New York, NY 10022. A papal relief and development agency of the Holy See for the Middle East, with offices in New York, Vatican City, Amman, Beirut and Jerusalem.

Pontifical Missionary Union (1916): 366 Fifth Ave., New York, NY 10001. To promote mission awareness among clergy, religious, candidates to priestly and religious life, and others engaged in pastoral ministry of the Church. Nat. Dir., Most Rev. William J. McCormack; Nat. Sec., Rev. Eugene LaVerdiere, S.S.S.

Priests' Eucharistic League (1887): 5384 Wilson Mills Rd., Cleveland, OH 44143; 5,000. *Emmanuel*, 10 issues a year. Nat. Dir., Rev. Anthony Schueller, S.S.S.

Pro Ecclesia Foundation (1970): 350 5th Ave., New York, NY 10118. Publishes *Pro Ecclesia Magazine*. Pres., Dr. Timothy A. Mitchell.

Pro Maria Committee (1952): 22 Second Ave., Lowell, MA 01854-2808. Promote devotion to Our Lady of Beauraing (See Index).

Pro Sanctity Movement: Pro Sanctity Spirituality Center, 205 S. Pine Dr., Fullerton, CA 92833; 730 E. 87th St., Brooklyn, NY 11236; 6762 Western Ave., Omaha, NE 68132; 1102 N. 204 St. Elkhorn, NE 68022. A worldwide force of laity organized to spread God's call of all persons to holiness.

Project Children (1975): P.O. Box 933, Greenwood Lake, NY 10925. Nonsectarian volunteer group; provide children of Northern Ireland with a six-week summer vacation with host families in the U.S.

The Providence Association of the Ukrainian Catholics in America (Ukrainian Catholic Fraternal Benefit Society) (1912): 817 N. Franklin St., Philadelphia, PA 19123.

Queen of the Americas Guild, Inc. (1979): P.O. Box 851, St. Charles, IL 60174; 7,000 members. To build English information center and retreat center near Basilica in Mexico City and spread the message of Guadalupe. Pres., Frank E. Smoczynski.

Raskob Foundation for Catholic Activities, Inc. (1945): P.O. Box 4019, Wilmington, DE 19807-0019. Pres., Gerard S. Garey.

Reparation Society of the Immaculate Heart of Mary, Inc. (1946): 100 E. 20th St., Baltimore, MD 21218. *Fatima Findings*, monthly.

Retrouvaille: P.O.Box 25, Kelton, PA 19346. A ministry to hurting marriages. Retrouvaille consists of a weekend experience with follow-up sessions designed to provide couples with ways and means of healing and reconciling. Emphasis is placed on communication, enabling husband and wife to rediscover each other and to examine their lives in a new and positive way. The ministry is neither a retreat nor a sensitivity group, nor does it include group dynamics or discussions. The program is conducted by trained couples and priests, with programs offered under the auspices of diocesan family life agencies. International Coordinating Team: Bill and Peg Swaan.

Sacred Heart League: 6050 Hwy 61 N, P.O. Box 190, Walls, MS 38680. Pres., Rev. Robert Hess, S.C.J.

St. Ansgar's Scandinavian Catholic League (1910): 28 W. 25th St., New York, NY 10010-2705; 1,000. *St. Ansgar's Bulletin*, annually. Prayers and financial support for Church in Scandinavia. Pres., Astrid M. O'Brien.

St. Anthony's Guild (1924): Paterson, NJ 07509; Promotes devotion to St. Anthony of Padua and support for formation programs, infirm friars and ministries of the Franciscans of Holy Name Province. *The Anthonian*, quarterly. Dir., Rev. Joseph Hertel, O.F.M.

St. Bernadette Institute of Sacred Art (1993): P.O. Box 8249, Albuquerque, NM 87198-8249. To promote, initiate, encourage interest and sustain projects and persons engaged in sacred art.

St. Gregory Foundation for Latin Liturgy (1989): Newman House, 21 Fairview Ave., Mount Pocono, PA 18344. To promote within the Church in the U.S. the use of the Latin language in the Mass in accordance with the teachings of Vatican II. Founder and Pres., Very Rev. Peter M.J. Stravinskas, Ph.D., S.T.D.

St. Jude League (1929): 205 W. Monroe St., Chicago, IL 60606. Promotes devotion to St. Jude; supports work of Claretian Missionaries throughout the world. Dir., Rev. Mark J. Brummel, C.M.F.

St. Margaret of Scotland Guild, Inc. (1938): Graymoor, Garrison, NY 10524; 500. Moderator, Bro. Pius MacIsaac.

St. Martin de Porres Guild (1935): 141 E. 65th St., New York, NY 10021. Dir., Rev. Raymond F. Halligan, O.P.

Serra International (1934): 65 E. Wacker Pl., Suite 1210, Chicago, IL 60601; 21,000 members in 673 clubs in 35 countries. *Serran*, bimonthly. Fosters vocations to the priesthood, and religious life, trains Catholic lay leadership. Formally aggregated to the Pontifical Society for Priestly Vocations, 1951.

Slovak Catholic Federation (1911): 915 Cornell St., Youngstown, OH, 44502-2765. Founded by Rev. Joseph Murgas to promote and coordinate religious activities among Slovak Catholic fraternal societies, religious communities and Slovak ethnic parishes in their effort to address themselves to the special needs of Slovak Catholics in the U.S. and Canada. Pres., Rev. Msgr. Peter M. Polando.

Slovak Catholic Sokol (1905): 205 Madison St., Passaic, NJ 07055; 38,000. Slovak Catholic Falcon, weekly. Fraternal benefit society.

Society for the Propagation of the Faith (1822): 366 Fifth Ave., New York, NY 10001; established in all dioceses. Church's principal instrument for promoting mission awareness and generating financial support for the missions. General fund for ordinary and extraordinary subsidies for all mission dioceses. *Mission*, 4 times a year; *Director's Newsletter*, monthly. Is subject to Congregation for the Evangelization of Peoples. Nat. Dir., Most Rev. William J. McCormack.

Society of St. Monica (1986): 215 Falls Ave., Cuyahoga Falls, OH 44221; more than 10,000 members worldwide. Confident, daily prayer for the return of inactive Catholics and Catholics who have left the Church. Founder and Spir. Dir., Rev. Dennis M. McNeil.

Society of St. Peter Apostle (1889): 366 Fifth Ave., New York, NY 10001; all dioceses. Church's central fund for support of seminaries, seminarians and nov-ices in all mission dioceses. Nat. Dir., Most Rev. William J. McCormack.

Society of the Divine Attributes (1974): 2905 Castlegate Ave., Pittsburgh, PA 15226. Contemplative prayer society; 3,000 members worldwide (lay, clerical and religious). Spir. Dir. Rev. Ronald D. Lawler, O.F.M. Cap.

Spiritual Life Institute of America (1960): Box 219, Crestone, CO 81131. Forefront, seasonal. An eremetical movement to foster the contemplative spirit in America. Founder, Rev. William McNamara, O.C.D. Second foundation: Nova Nada, Primitive Wilderness Hermitage, Kemptville, Nova Scotia, Canada B0W 1Y0. Third foundation, Holy Hill Hermitage, Skreen, Co. Sligo, Ireland.

Support Our Aging Religious (SOAR) (1986): 1400 Spring St., Suite 320, Silver Spring, MD 20910. Laity-led campaign to raise funds for retired religious.

Theresians of the United States (1961): 2577 N. Chelton Rd., Suite 207, Colorado Springs, CO 80909. Spiritual, educational and ministerial organization of Christian women. Exec. Dir., Sr. Rose Ann Barmann, O.S.B. International division: Theresian World Ministry (1971), same address.

United Societies of U.S.A. (1903): 613 Sinclair St., McKeesport, PA 15132; 3,755 members. *Prosvita-Enlightenment*, bimonthly newspaper.

United States Catholic Historical Society (1884): The Catholic Center, 1011 First Ave., New York, NY 10022. Chairman, Brian Butler. Exec Dir., Edward J. Thompson.

Western Catholic Union (1877): 510 Maine St., Quincy, IL 62301; 19,000 members. *Western Catholic Union Record*, quarterly. A fraternal benefit society. Pres., Mark A. Wiewel.

Women for Faith and Family (1984): P.O. Box 8326, St. Louis, MO 63132. *Voices*, quarterly. An international movement to promote Catholic teachings especially on all issues involving the family and roles for women. Members sign an 8-point statement of fidelity to the Church; 60,000 signers worldwide. Dir., Helen Hull Hitchcock.

Young Ladies' Institute (1887): 1111 Gough St., San Francisco, CA 94109-6606; 13,000. *Voice of YLI*, bimonthly. Grand Sec., Frances Ridley.

Young Men's Institute (1883): 1625 "C" Palmetto Ave., Pacifica, CA 94044; 4,500. *Institute Journal*, bimonthly. Grand Sec., Clifford C. Smethurst.

PERSONAL PRELATURE OF THE HOLY SEE: OPUS DEI

Founded in Madrid in 1928 by Msgr. Josemaría Escrivá de Balaguer (beatified in 1992), Opus Dei has the aim of spreading throughout all sectors of society a profound awareness of the universal call to holiness and apostolate (of Christian witness and action) in the ordinary circumstances of life, and, more specifically, through one's professional work. On Nov. 28, 1982, Pope John Paul II established Opus Dei as a personal prelature with the full title, Prelature of the Holy Cross and Opus Dei. The 1998 edition of *Annuario Pontificio* reported that the prelature had 1,649 priests (49 newly ordained) and 363 major seminarians. Also, there were 80,074 lay persons – men and women, married and single, of every class and social condition – of about 80 nationalities, as well as 1,603 churches and pastoral centers.

Further, the prelature operates the Pontifical University of the Holy Cross in Rome; it was established in 1985 and received approval as a pontifical instutution in 1995. Courses of study include theology, philosophy, canon law, and the recently established School of Social Communications.

In the United States, members of Opus Dei, along with cooperators and friends, conduct apostolic works corporately in major cities in the East and Midwest, Texas and on the West Coast. Elsewhere, corporate works include universities, vocational institutes, train-ing schools for farmers and numerous other apostolic initiatives. Opus Dei information offices are located at: 524 North Avenue, Suite 200, New Rochelle, NY 10801 (Tel. 914-235-1201); and 655 Levering Ave., Los Angeles, CA 90024 (Tel. 310-208-0941).

KNIGHTS OF COLUMBUS

The Knights of Columbus, a fraternal benefit society of Catholic men, is a family service organization founded by Fr. Michael J. McGivney and chartered by the General Assembly of Connecticut on Mar. 29, 982.

Knights of Columbus membership totals 1,590,661 (as of June 30, 1998) in more than 10,800 councils in the U.S., Canada, the Philippines, Mexico, Puerto Rico, Panama, Guatemala, Guam, the Dominican Republic, the Virgil Islands, the Bahamas, and Saipan.

In keeping with their general purpose to be of service to the Church, the Knights and their families are active in many apostolic works and community programs.

The Knights cooperate with the U.S. bishops in Pro-Life activities and are engaged in other apostolic endeavors as well. According to the annual report of the Supreme Knight (August, 1998), charitable contributions in 1997 were $107,128,844 – an all-time high.

The programmatic activities of the Knights remain much the same from one year to the next. The K of C have announced in connection with the Jubilee the restoration of the *Maderno Atrium* of St. Peter's Basilica in Rome. It is named for the architect, Carlo Maderno (1556-1629). The atrium is the big "front porch" through which every visitor to St. Peter's passes. This is one of a series of projects for the restoration of St. Peter's funded by the Knights over the years: renovation of the roof of the Blessed Sacrament Chapel (1993); renovation of the Room of the Architects and Room of the Window Panes (1987-88); restoration of the facade (1985-86); construction of chapels in the grottoes (1981-82).

On October 15, 1998, Pope John Paul II received the Supreme Knight, Supreme Chaplain, and Board of Directors in audience. At that time the Knights presented the Pope with a check for $1.6 million representing annual earnings from the $20 million Vicarius Christi Fund. That brought to nearly $28 million the amount the K of C has given the Pope from this source since 1981. The Pope addressed the Knights and observed:

"Our meeting today gives me yet another opportunity to express my gratitude for the witness of Chris-tian faith, fraternal solidarity and firm commitment to the Church's apostolate which has always been the hallmark of your Order.

"An important aspect of this witness has been your desire, from your foundation, to support the pastoral ministry of the Bishop of Rome, who, by the will of Christ, "is the perpetual and visible source and foundation of the unity both of the Bishops and of the whole company of the faithful" (*Lumen Gentium*, 23; *Catechism of the Catholic Church*, 882). Rooted in a profound sense of Catholic unity with the Successor of Peter, this desire led to the establishment of the Vicarius Christi Fund as a means of assisting the Pope in a practical way in the fulfillment of his duties. In thanking you for your donation of the proceeds of the Fund for the past year, I ask you to convey to all the Knights my personal appreciation.

"In particular, I wish to say a warm word of gratitude for your Order's generous payment of the mortgage of the Holy See's Permanent Observer Mission to the United Nations Organization. Thanks to this notable gift, the Mission is better able to carry out its important activity in representing the Church's vision and concerns in the international community. As Christians throughout the world prepare to welcome the New Millennium as a time of hope and promise (cf. *Tertio Millennio Adveniente*, 46), I see in this gesture the readiness of the Knights of Columbus to be an effective part of the Church's joyful proclamation of the liberating power of the Gospel to shape a world of ever greater justice, solidarity and peace.

"Dear Friends, I encourage you to carry forward the fine tradition of the Knights of Columbus and, inspired by your Catholic faith, to continue your strenuous efforts for the pro-life cause. In a recent meeting with Bishops from the United States I urged Catholics to continue to make their voices heard in the formulation of cultural, economic, political and legislative projects which defend and enhance human life. A nation 'needs the wisdom and courage to overcome the moral ills and spiritual temptations inherent in its march through history.... Democracy stands or falls with the values which it embodies and promotes' May the efforts of the Knights of Columbus bear much fruit. "

Catholic Charities USA (formerly National Conference of Catholic Charities): 1731 King St., Suite 200, Alexandria, VA 22314. Founded in 1910 by Most Rev. Thomas J. Shahan and Rt. Rev. Msgr. William J. Kerby in cooperation with lay leaders of the Society of St. Vincent de Paul to help advance and promote the charitable programs and activities of Catholic community and social service agencies in the United States. As the central and national organization for this purpose, it services a network of more than 1,400 agencies and institutions by consultation, information and assistance in planning and evaluating social service programs under Catholic auspices.

Diocesan member agencies provide shelter, food, counseling, services to children, teen parents and the elderly, and a variety of other services to people in need — without regard to religion, gender, age or national origin. Each year millions of people receive help from Catholic Charities; in 1995 (latest statistics available), more than 10 million turned to Catholic Charities agencies for help. In addition, Catholic Charities is an advocate for persons and families in need.

Catholic Charities USA serves members through national and regional meetings, training programs, literature and social policy advocacy on the national level. It is charged by the U.S. bishops with responding to disasters in this country. Catholic Charities USA's president represents North America before Caritas Internationalis, the international conference of Catholic Charities, and thus maintains contact with the Catholic Charities movement throughout the world. Publications include *Charities USA*, a quarterly membership magazine, and a directory of U.S. Catholic Charities agencies and institutions. Pres. of Catholic Charities USA: Rev. Fred Kammer, S.J.

Society of St. Vincent de Paul, Council of the United States (originally called the Conference of Charity): National Council, 58 Progress Parkway, St. Louis, MO 63043. An association of Catholic lay men and women devoted to personal service to the poor through the spiritual and corporal works of mercy. The first conference was formed at Paris in 1833 by Bl. Frederic Ozanam and his associates.

The first conference in the U.S. was organized in 1845 at St. Louis. There are now approximately 4,400 units of the society in this country, with a membership of more than 60,000. The society operates world wide in more than 130 countries and has more than 800,000 members.

In the fiscal year 1994-95, members of the society in this country distributed among poor persons financial and other forms of assistance valued at approximately $165,000,000.

Besides person-to-person assistance, increasing emphasis is being given to stores and rehabilitation workshops of the society through which persons with marginal income can purchase refurbished goods at minimal cost. Handicapped persons are employed in renovating goods and store operations. The society also operates food centers, shelters, criminal justice and other programs. Publications include *The Ozanam News*, a biannual membership magazine, and *The United States Councilor*, a quarterly newsletter. Nat. Pres., Joseph H. Mueller; Exec. Dir., Rita W. Porter.

Catholic Health Association of the United States (CHA): National Headquarters, 4455 Woodson Road, St. Louis, MO 63134 (with an office at 1875 Eye

CATHOLIC SOCIAL SERVICES

Street N.W., Suite 1000, Washington, DC 20006). Represents more than 1,200 Catholic-sponsored facilities and organizations, works with its members to: promote justice and compassion in healthcare, influence public policy, shape a continuum of care through integraated delivery, and strengthen ministry presence and influence in the U.S. healthcare system. CHA supports and strengthens the Catholic health ministry by being a castalyst through research and development (leading edge tools for sustaining a faith-based ministry in price competitive markets), education and facilitation (annual assembly, conferences, and other methods for engaging the ministry), and advocacy (a united ministry voice for public policy). CHA members make up the nation's largest group of not-for-profit healthcare facilities under a single form of sponsorship.

National Association of Catholic Chaplains: 3501 S. Lake Dr., Milwaukee, WI 53207. Founded in 1965. membership is over 3,500.

SOCIAL SERVICE ORGANIZATIONS

(See separate article for a listing of facilities for the handicapped.)

The Carroll Center for the Blind (formerly the Catholic Guild for All the Blind): 770 Centre St., Newton, MA 02158, the center conducts diagnostic evaluation and rehabilitation programs for blind people over 16 years of age, and provides computer training and other services. Pres., Rachel Rosenbaum.

Xavier Society for the Blind: 154 E. 23rd St., New York, NY 10010. Founded in 1900 by Rev. Joseph Stadelman, S.J., it is a center for publications for the blind and partially sighted. Dir., Rev. Alfred E. Caruana, S.J.

International Catholic Deaf Association: 8002 S. Sawyer Rd., Darien, IL 60561. Established by deaf adults in Toronto, Canada, in 1949, the association has more than 8,000 members in 130 chapters, mostly in the U.S. It is the only international lay association founded and controlled by deaf Catholic adults. The ICDA publishes *The Deaf Catholic*, bimonthly, sponsors regional conferences, workshops and an annual convention. Pres., Kathleen Kush.

National Catholic Office for the Deaf: 7202 Buchanan St., Landover Hills, MD 20784. Formally established in 1971, at Washington, D.C., to provide pastoral service to those who teach deaf children and adults, to the parents of deaf children, to pastors of deaf persons, and to organizations of the deaf. Exec.Dir., Arvilla Rank.

National Apostolate with People with Mental Retardation: 4516 30th St. N.W., Washington, DC 20008. Established in 1968 to promote the full participation by persons with mental retardation in the life of the Church. It publishes the *NAPMR Quarterly* and a newsletter (four times a year). Provides consultation, information and referral services on Church-related questions about mental retardation. Exec. Dir., Dr. Michela M. Perrone.

National Catholic Office for Persons with Disabilities (NCPD): P.O. Box 29113, Washington, DC 20017. NCPD's mission is to provide resources and consultation to a national network of diocesan directors who oversee access and inclusion at the parish level; to collaborate with other national Catholic organizations, advocating for inclusion within all their programs and initiatives and to work with Catholic organizations addressing the concerns and needs of those with various disabilities. Established in 1982 as a result of the 1978 Pastoral Statement of the U.S. Catholic Bishops on People with Disabilities., the office continues to press for words and actions which promote meaningful participation and inclusion at all levels of the Church.

OTHER SOCIAL SERVICES

Cancer Hospitals or Homes: The following homes or hospitals specialize in the care of cancer patients. They are listed according to state.

Our Lady of Perpetual Help Home, Servants of Relief for Incurable Cancer, 760 Washington St., S.W., Atlanta, GA 30315 (48).

Rose Hawthorne Lathrop Home, Servants of Relief for Incurable Cancer, 1600 Bay St., Fall River, MA 02724 (35).

Our Lady of Good Counsel Home, Servants of Relief for Incurable Cancer, 2076 St. Anthony Ave., St. Paul, MN 55104 (40).

Calvary Hospital, Inc., 1740 Eastchester Rd., Bronx, NY 10461 (200). Operated in connection with Catholic Charities, Department of Health and Hospitals, Archdiocese of New York.

St. Rose's Home, Servants of Relief for Incurable Cancer, 71 Jackson St., New York, NY 10002 (60).

Rosary Hill Home, Servants of Relief for Incurable Cancer, 600 Linda Ave., Hawthorne, NY 10532 (72).

Holy Family Home, Servants of Relief for Incurable Cancer, 6707 State Rd., Parma, OH 44134 (50).

Sacred Heart Free Home for Incurable Cancer, Servants of Relief for Incurable Cancer, 1315 W. Hunting Park Ave., Philadelphia, PA 19140 (45).

Substance Abuse: Facilities for substance abuse (alcohol and other drugs) include:

Daytop Village, Inc., 54 W. 40th St., New York, NY 10018. Msgr. William B. O'Brien, president. Twenty-eight residential and ambulatory sites in New York, New Jersey, Pennsylvania, Florida, Texas and California.

Good Shepherd Gracenter, Convent of the Good Shepherd, 1310 Bacon St., San Francisco, CA 94134. Residential program for chemically dependent women.

New Hope Manor, 35 Hillside Rd., Barryville, NY 12719. Residential substance abuse treatment center for teen-age girls and women ages 13-40. Residential; half-way house and aftercare program totaling 6 months or more.

St. Joseph's Hospital, L.E. Phillips Libertas Center for the Chemically Dependent, 2661 County Road I, Chippewa Falls, WI 54729 (46). Residential and outpatient. Adult and adolescent programs. Hospital Sisters of the Third Order of St. Francis.

St. Joseph's Hospital (Chippewa Falls, WI) Libertas Center for the Treatment of Chemical Dependency, 1701 Dousman St., Green Bay, WI 54302 (23). Residental and outpatient adolescent programs. Hospital Sisters of the Third Order of St. Francis.

St. Luke's Addiction Recovery Services, 7707 NW 2nd Ave., Miami, FL 33150. A program of Catholic Community Services, Miami. Adult residential and family outpatient recovery services for drug, alcohol addiction and DUI.

Miami Substance Abuse Prevention Programs, 7707

N.W. Second Ave., Miami, FL 33150. Trains parents, youth, priests and teachers as prevention volunteers in the area of substance abuse.

Transitus House, 1830 Wheaton St., Chippewa Falls, WI 54729. Two programs for chenically dependent: adult intensive residential (15 beds, women); adolescent intensive residential (5 beds; girls 15-18 yrs.). Hospital Sisters of the Third Order of St. Francis.

Matt Talbot Inn, 2270 Professor Ave., Cleveland, OH 44113. Two programs: Chemical dependency Residential Treatment/Halfway House (capacity 27) and outpatient treatment/aftercare. Serves male clients 18 years and over.

Sacred Heart Rehabilitation Center, Inc., 2203 St. Antoine, Detroit, MI 48201 (admissions/assessment, outpatient); 400 Stoddard Rd., P.O. Box 41038, Memphis, MI 48041 (12 beds, detoxification; 70 beds residential treatment); 28573 Schoenherr, Warren, MI 48093 (outpatient). All facilities serve male and female clients 18 and over.

Straight and Narrow, Inc., 396 Straight St., Paterson, NJ 07501. Facilities and services include (at various locations): Straight and Narrow Hospital (Mount Carmel Guild), substance abuse, detoxification (20 beds); Alpha House for Drug and Alcohol Rehabilitation (women; 30 beds — 25 adults, 5 children), Dismas House for Drug and Alcohol Rehabilitation (men; 78 beds); The Guild for Drug and Alcohol Rehabilitation (men, 56 beds); juvenile residential units; outpatient services and facility; three halfway houses; counseling services; employment assistance; intoxicated driver's resource center; medical day care center (available to HIV infected persons and persons diagnosed with AIDS); methadone clinic.

The National Catholic Council on Alcoholism and Related Drug Problems, Inc., 1550 Hendrickson St., Brooklyn, NY 11234, offers educational material to those involved in pastoral ministry on ways of dealing with problems related to alcoholism and medication dependency.

Convicts: Priests serve as full- or part-time chaplains in penal and correctional institutions throughout the country. Limited efforts have been made to assist in the rehabilitation of released prisoners in Halfway House establishments.

Dining Rooms: Facilities for Homeless: Representative of places where meals are provided, and in some cases lodging and other services as well, are:

St. Anthony Foundation, 121 Golden Gate Ave., San Francisco, CA 94102. Founded in 1950 by the Franciscan Friars. Multi-program social service agency serving people who are poor and homeless. Dining room serves up to 2,100 meals daily; more than 25 million since its founding. Other services include free clothing and furniture; free medical clinic; residential drug and alcohol rehabilitation programs; employment program; emergency shelter, housing and daytime facility for homeless women; residence for low-income senior women; free hygiene services; case management for seniors; social services.

St. Vincent de Paul Free Dining Room, 675 23rd St., Oakland, CA 94612. Administered by Daughters of Charity of St. Vincent de Paul, under sponsorship of St. Vincent de Paul Society. Hot meals served at lunch time 7 days a week. Also provides counseling, referral/information services.

St. Vincent's Dining Room, 505 W. 3rd St., Reno, NV 89503.

St. Vincent Dining Room, 1501 Las Vegas Blvd., Las Vegas, NV 89101. Structured program for 275 men in which job development office works with homeless to enable them to find employment. For non-residents, there is a hot meal every day at noon. Emergency overnight shelter facility for families, women and men.

Good Shepherd Center, Little Brothers of the Good Shepherd, 218 Iron St. S.W., P.O. Box 749, Albuquerque, NM 87103.

Holy Name Centre for Homeless Men, Inc., 18 Bleeker St., New York, NY 10012. A shelter for alcoholic, homeless men. Provides social services and aid to transients and those in need. Affiliated with New York Catholic Charities.

St. Francis Inn, 2441 Kensington Ave., Philadelphia, PA 19125. Serves hot meals. Temporary shelter for men. Day center for women. Thrift shop.

St. John's Hospice for Men, staffed by Little Brothers of the Good Shepherd, 1221 Race St., Philadelphia, PA 19107. Hot meals served daily; 36-bed shelter; clothing distribution, showers, mail distribution, drug/alcohol rehabilitation and work programs. Good Shepherd Program of St. John's Hospice, 1225 Race St., Philadelphia, PA 19107. Ten-bed facility for homeless men with AIDS.

Camillus House, Little Brothers of the Good Shepherd, 726 N.E. First Ave., Miami, FL 33132. Free comprehensive services for the poor and homeless including daily dinner; night lodging for 70; clothing distribution; showers; mail distribution; drug/alcohol rehabilitation program. Forty-eight units of single-room occupancy housing for employed formerly homeless women and men who have completed drug and alcohol rehabilitation programs.

Camillus Health Concern, Little Brothers of the Good Shepherd, 708 N.E. First Ave., Miami, FL 33132. Free comprehensive medical and social services for the homeless.

Shelters: Facilities for runaways, the abused, exploited and homeless include:

Anthony House, supported by St. Anthony's Guild (see Index). Three locations: 38 E. Roosevelt Ave., Roosevelt, NY 11575 (with St. Vincent de Paul Society — for homeless men); 128 W. 112th St., New York, NY 10026 (emergency food and clothing); 6215 Holly St., P.O. Box 880, Zellwood, FL 32798 (for migrant workers and their families).

Good Shepherd Shelter-Convent of the Good Shepherd. Office, 2561 W. Venice Blvd., Los Angeles, CA 90019. Non-emergency long-term shelter for battered women and their children.

Covenant House, 346 W. 17th St., New York, NY 10011. President, Sister Mary Rose McGeady, D.C. Provides crisis care — food, shelter, clothing, medical treatment, job placement and counseling — for homeless youth without regard to race, creed, color and national origin. Locations: New York, New Jersey (Newark, Atlantic City), Houston, Ft. Lauderdale, New Orleans, Anchorage, Los Angeles, Detroit, Orlando, Washington, D.C.; Toronto (Canada), Tegucigalpa (Honduras), Guatemala City (Guatemala), Mexico City (Mexico).

Crescent House, 1000 Howard Ave., Suite 1200, New Orleans, LA 70113. Provides temporary shelter, counseling and advocacy for battered women and their children.

The Dwelling Place, 409 W. 40th St., New York, NY 10018. For homeless women 30 years of age and over.

Gift of Hope, Missionaries of Charity, 724 N.W. 17th St., Miami, FL 33136. Shelter for women and children; soup kitchen for men.

House of the Good Shepherd, 1114 W. Grace St., Chicago, IL 60613. For abused women with children.

Mercy Hospice, Sisters of Mercy, 334 S. 13th St., Philadelphia, PA 19107. Temporary shelter and relocation assistance for homeless women and children.

Mt. Carmel House, Carmelite Sisters, 471 G Pl., N.W., Washington, DC 20001. For homeless women.

Ozanam Inn, 843 Camp St., New Orleans, LA 70130. Under sponsorship of the St. Vincent de Paul Society. Hospice for homeless men.

St. Christopher Inn, P.O. Box 150, Graymoor, Garrison, NY 10524. Temporary shelter (21 days) for alcohol- and drug-free homeless and needy men.

Siena-Francis House, Inc., P.O. Box 217 D.T.S., Omaha, NE 68102. Two units, both at 1702 Nicholas St., Omaha, NE 68101: Siena House (for homeless and abused women or women with children; provides 24-hour assistance and advocacy services); Francis House (temporary shelter for homeless men). Also at this location: a 50-bed residential substance abuse program.

Unwed Mothers: Residential and care services for unwed mothers are available in many dioceses.

FACILITIES FOR RETIRED AND AGED PERSONS

(Sources: *Almanac* survey, *The Official Catholic Directory*.)

This list covers residence, health care and other facilities for the retired and aged under Catholic auspices. Information includes name, type of facility if not evident from the title, address, and total capacity (in parentheses); unless noted otherwise, facilities are for both men and women. Many facilities for the aged offer intermediate nursing care.

Alabama: Allen Memorial Home (Skilled Nursing), 735 S. Washington Ave., Mobile 36603 (94).

Cathedral Place Apartments (Retirement Complex), 351 Conti St., Mobile 36602 (192).

Mercy Medical (Acute Rehabilitation Hospital, Skilled and Post-Acute Nursing, Hospice, Home Health and Assisted and Independent Living), P.O. Box 1090, Daphne 36526 (157 beds; 120 assisted units; 32 independent apartments). Not restricted to elderly.

Sacred Heart Residence Little Sisters of the Poor, 1655 McGill Ave., Mobile 36604 (75).

Seton Haven (Retirement Complex), 3721 Wares Ferry Rd., Montgomery 36193 (104).

Arizona: Desert Crest Campus (Retirement Complex), 2101 E. Maryland Ave., Phoenix 85016 (114 apartments and cottages) and 2151 E. Maryland Ave., Phoenix 85016 (66).

California: Alexis Apartments of St. Patrick's Parish, 756 Mission St. 94103; 390 Clementina St., San Francisco 94103 (206).

Casa Manana Inn, 3700 N. Sutter St., Stockton 95204 (162). Non-profit housing for low-income elderly over 62.

Cathedral Plaza, 1551 Third Ave., San Diego 92101 (222 apartments).

Francis of Assisi Community, 145 Guerrero St., San Francisco 94103 (120). Low-income elderly.

Guadalupe Plaza, 4142 42nd St., San Diego 92105 (127 apartments).

Jeanne d'Arc Manor, 85 S. Fifth St., San Jose 95112 (121). For low income elderly and handicapped.

La Paz Villas, P.O. Box 1962, Palm Desert 92261 (24 units).

Little Flower Haven (Residential Care Facility for Retired), 8585 La Mesa Blvd., La Mesa 91941 (85).

Little Sisters of the Poor, St. Anne's Home, 300 Lake St., San Francisco 94118 (103).

Little Sisters of the Poor, Jeanne Jugan Residence, 2100 South Western Ave., San Pedro, Calif. 90732 (104).

Madonna Residence (Housing for low-income women over 60), 1055 Pine St., San Francisco 94109 (57).

Marian Residence (Retirement Home), 124 S. College Dr., Santa Maria 93454 (34).

Mercy McMahon Terrace (Residential Care Facility), 3865 J St., Sacramento 95816 (118 units).

Mercy Retirement and Care Center, 3431 Foothill Blvd., Oakland 94601 (135 residential; 59 skilled nursing).

Mother Gertrude Home for Senior Citizens, 11320 Laurel Canyon Blvd., San Fernando 91340 (114).

Nazareth House (Residential and Skilled Care), 2121 N. 1st St., Fresno 93703 (85 residential; 39 skilled nursing).

Nazareth House (Residential and Skilled Nursing), 3333 Manning Ave., Los Angeles 90064 (127 residential; 33 skilled nursing).

Nazareth House (Retirement Home), 245 Nova Albion Way, San Rafael 94903 (139).

Nazareth House Retirement Home, 6333 Rancho Mission Rd., San Diego 92108 (122).

O'Connor Woods (Retirement Community), 3400 Wagner Heights, Stockton 95209 (235 independent, 48 assisted living).

Our Lady of Fatima Villa (Skilled Nursing Facility), 20400 Saratoga-Los Gatos Rd., Saratoga 95070 (85).

St. Bernardine Plaza (Retirement Home), 550 W. 5th St., San Bernardino 92401 (150 units).

St. Francis Home, 1718 W. 6th St., Santa Ana 92703 (65).

St. John of God (Retirement and Care Center), 2035 W. Adams Blvd., Los Angeles 90018.

St. John's Plaza, 8150 Broadway, Lemon Grove 91945 (100).

Vigil Light Apartments, 1945 Long Dr., Santa Rosa 95405 (48).

Villa Scalabrini (Retirement Center and Skilled Nursing Care), 10631 Vinedale St., Sun Valley 91352 (130 residence; 58 skilled nursing).

Villa Siena (Residence and Skilled Nursing Care), 1855 Miramonte Ave., Mountain View 94040 (50, residence; 20, skilled nursing care).

Colorado: Francis Heights, Inc., 2626 Osceola St., Denver 80212 (384 units; 431 residents).

Gardens at St. Elizabeth (Congregate Housing and Assisted Living), 2835 W. 32nd Ave., Denver 80211 (209 congregate; 81 assisted living).

Little Sisters of the Poor, 3629 W. 29th Ave., Denver 80211 (78).

Connecticut: Augustana Homes (Residence), Simeon Rd., Bethel 06801.

Carmel Ridge, 6454 Main St., Trumbull 06611.

Holy Family Home and Shelter, Inc., 88 Jackson St., P.O. Box 884, Willimantic 06226.

Matulaitis Nursing Home, 10 Thurber Rd., Putnam 06260 (119).

Monsignor Bojnowski Manor, Inc. (Skilled Nursing Facility), 50 Pulaski St., New Britain 06053 (54).

Notre Dame Convalescent Home, 76 West Rocks Rd., Norwalk 06851 (60).

St. Joseph Living Center, 14 Club Rd., Windham 06280 (120).

St. Joseph's Manor (Health Care Facility; Home for Aged), Carmelite Srs. for Aged and Infirm, 6448 Main St., Trumbull 06611 (297).

St. Joseph's Residence, Little Sisters of the Poor, 1365 Enfield St., Enfield, Conn. 06082 (93).

St. Lucian's Home for the Aged, 532 Burritt St., New Britain 06053 (42).

St. Mary's Home (Residence and Health Care Facility) 2021 Albany Ave., W. Hartford 06117.

Delaware: The Antonian, 1701 W. 10th St., Wilmington 19805 (136 apartments).

Jeanne Jugan Residence, Little Sisters of the Poor, 185 Salem Church Rd., Newark 19713 (80).

Marydale Retirement Village, 135 Jeandell Dr., Newark 19713 (108 apartments).

St. Patrick's House, Inc., 115 E. 14th St., Wilmington 19801 (16).

District of Columbia: Jeanne Jugan Residence — St. Joseph Villa, Little Sisters of the Poor, 4200 Harewood Rd., N.E. Washington 20017 (87).

Florida: All Saints Home, 5888 Blanding Blvd., Jacksonville 32246 (60).

Archbishop McCarthy Residence (Retirement Apartments), 13201 N.W. 28th Avenue, Opa Locka 33054 (113 apartments).

Bon Secour-Maria Manor Nursing Care Center, 10300 4th St. N., St. Petersburg 33716 (274).

Carroll Manor (Retirement Apartments), 3667 S. Miami Ave., Miami 33133 (230 apartments).

Casa Calderon, Inc. (Retirement Apartments), 800 W. Virginia St., Tallahassee 32304.

Haven of Our Lady of Peace (Assisted Living and Nursing Home), 5203 N. 9th Ave., Pensacola 32504 (89).

Marian Towers, Inc. (Retirement Apartments), 17505 North Bay Rd., Miami Beach 33160.

Noreen McKeen Residence for Geriatric Care (Skilled and Intermediate Care), 315 Flagler Dr. S., W. Palm Beach 33401.

Palmer House, Inc., 1225 S.W. 107th Ave., Miami 33174 (120 apartments).

St. Andrew Towers (Retirement Apartments), 2700 N.W. 99th Ave., Coral Springs 33065 (432).

St. Catherine Laboure (Skilled and Intermediate Care), 1750 Stockton St., Jacksonville 32204 (232).

St. Dominic Gardens (Retirement Apartments), 5849 N.W. 7th St., Miami 33126 (149 apartments).

St. Elizabeth Gardens, Inc. (Retirement Apartments), 801 N.E. 33rd St., Pompano Beach 33064 (150).

St. John's Rehabilitation Hospital and Nursing Center, Inc., 3075 N.W. 35th Ave., Lauderdale Lakes 33311.

Stella Maris House, Inc., 8636 Harding Ave., Miami Beach 33141 (136 apartments).

Illinois: Addolorata Villa (Sheltered Intermediate, Skilled Care Facility; Apartments), 555 McHenry Rd., Wheeling 60090 (135 health care; 100 apartments).

Alvernia Manor (Sheltered Care), 13950 Main St., Lemont 60439 (50).

Carlyle Healthcare Center, 501 Clinton St., Carlyle 62231 (131).

Carmelite Carefree Village, 8419 Bailey Rd., Darien 60561 (105).

Cor Mariae Center (Assisted Living and Nursing Home), 3330 Maria Linden Dr., Rockford 61107 (90).

Cortland Manor Retirement Home, 1900 N. Karlov, Chicago 60639. (56).

Holy Family Health Center, 2380 Dempster, Des Plaines 60016 (362).

Holy Family Villa (Intermediate Care Facility), 12395 McCarthy Rd., Lemont 60439 (99).

Jugan Terrace, Little Sisters of the Poor, 2300 N. Racine, Chicago 60614 (50 apartments).

Little Sisters of the Poor, St. Joseph's Home for the Elderly, 80 W. Northwest Hwy., Palatine 60067 (67).

Little Sisters of the Poor Center for the Aging, 2325 N. Lakewood Ave., Chicago, Ill. 60614 (96).

Maria Care Center (Skilled Intermediary Facility), 350 W. S. First St., Red Bud 62278 (115).

Marian Heights Apartments (Elderly, Handicapped), 20 Marian Heights Dr., Alton 62002 (127).

Marian Park, Inc., 2126 W. Roosevelt Rd., Wheaton 60187 (117 apartments).

Maryhaven, Inc. (Skilled and Intermediate Care Facility), 1700 E. Lake Ave., Glenview 60025 (147).

Mayslake Village (Retirement Apartments), 1801 35th St., Oak Brook 60521 (630 apartments).

Mercy Residence at Tolentine Center, 20300 Governors Hwy., Olympia Fields 60461 (52).

Meredith Memorial Home, 16 S. Illinois St., Belleville 62220 (70).

Merkle-Knipprath (Apartments and Nursing Facility), Rt. 1, Franciscan Brothers. Clifton 60927 (130).

Mother Theresa Home (Skilled, Intermediate and Sheltered Care), 1270 Franciscan Dr., Lemont 60439 (150).

Nazarethville (Intermediate and Sheltered Care), 300 N. River Rd., Des Plaines 60016 (83).

Our Lady of Angels Retirement Home, 1201 Wyoming, Joliet 60435 (96).

Our Lady of the Snows, Apartment Community, 9500 West Illinois Highway 15, Belleville 62223. Retirement community (166 apartments); adjoining skilled-care facility (57 beds).

Our Lady of Victory Nursing Home (Intermediate and Skilled Care), 20 Briarcliff Lane, Bourbonnais 60914 (97).

Pope John Paul I Apartments (Elderly and Handicapped), 1 Pope John Paul Plaza, Springfield 62703 (150).

Queen of Peace Center, 1910 Maple Ave., Lisle 60532.

Resurrection Nursing Pavilion (Skilled Care), 1001 N. Greenwood, Park Ridge 60068 (295).

Resurrection Retirement Community, 7262 W. Peterson Ave., Chicago, 60631 (473 apartments).

Rosary Hill Home (Women), 9000 W. 81st St., Justice 60458 (50).

St. Andrew Home (Retirement Residence), 7000 N. Newark Ave., Niles 60648 (196).

St. Ann's Healthcare Center, 770 State St., Chester 62233 (119).

St. Anne Center (Nursing Home), 4405 Highcrest Rd., Rockford 61107 (179).

St. Anne Place (Retirement Apartments),4444 Brendenwood Rd., Rockford 61107 (106 apartments).

St. Benedict Home, 6930 W. Touhy Ave., Niles 60714 (130).

St. Elizabeth Home (Residence), 704 W. Marion St., Joliet 60436. Group living for Senior women.

St. James Manor, 1251 East Richton Rd., Crete 60417 (110).

St. Joseph's Home (Sheltered and Intermediate Care), 3306 S. 6th St. Rd., Springfield 62703 (112).

St. Joseph's Home (Sheltered and Intermediate Care), 2223 W. Heading Ave., Peoria 61604 (186).

St. Joseph's Home for the Aged, 659 E. Jefferson St., Freeport 61032 (120).

St. Joseph Home of Chicago, Inc. (Skilled Care), 2650 N. Ridgeway Ave., Chicago 60647 (173).

St. Patrick's Residence, 1400 Brookdale Rd., Naperville 60563 (210).

Villa Franciscan (Skilled Care), Franciscan Sisters Health Care Corporation, 210 N. Springfield, Joliet 60435 (176).

Villa Scalabrini (Sheltered, Intermediate and Skilled), 480 N. Wolf Rd., Northlake 60164 (265).

Indiana: Albertine Home, 1501 Hoffman St., Hammond 46327 (33).

Little Company of Mary Health Facility (Comprehensive Nursing), 7520 S. US Hwy 421, San Pierre 46374 (200).

Providence Retirement Home, 703 E. Spring St., New Albany 47150 (95).

Sacred Heart Home (Comprehensive Nursing), 515 N. Main St., Avilla 46710 (133). LaVerna Terrace, same address; independent living for senior citizens, handicapped and disabled (51 units).

St. Anne Home (Residential and Comprehensive Nursing), 1900 Randallia Dr., Ft. Wayne 46805 (205).

St. Anthony Home, Inc., 203 Franciscan Rd., Crown Point 46307 (219).

St. Augustine Home for the Aged, Little Sisters of the Poor, 2345 W. 86th St., Indianapolis 46260 (90).

St. John's Home for the Aged, Little Sisters of the Poor, 1236 Lincoln Ave., Evansville 47714 (71).

St. Mary's Regina Continuing Care Center (Intermediate Care Facility), 3900 Washington Ave., Evansville 47714 (128).

St. Paul Hermitage (Residential and Intermediate Care Nursing), 501 N. 17th Ave., Beech Grove 46107 (95).

Iowa: The Alverno Health Care Facility (Nursing Care), 849 13th Ave. N., Clinton 52732 (138).

Bishop Drumm Retirement Center, 5837 Winwood Dr., Johnston 50131 (nursing care, 150). McAuley Terrace Apartments (85 units).

Hallmar-Mercy Hospital, 701 Tenth St. S.E., Cedar Rapids 52403 (62).

Holy Spirit Retirement Home (Intermediate Care), 1701 W. 25th St., Sioux City 51103 (94).

Kahl Home for the Aged and Infirm (Skilled and Intermediate Care Facility), 1101 W. 9th St., Davenport 52804 (135).

The Marian Home, 2400 6th Ave. North, Fort Dodge 50501 (Intermediate Care, 97) and Marian Village (Apartments), 2320 6th Ave. North, Fort Dodge 50501.

Padre Pio Health Care Center, Stonehill Care Center (Residence, Nursing Home), 3485 Windsor, Dubuque 52001 (250). Stonehill Adult Center (Day Care), same address.

St. Anthony Nursing Home (Intermediate Care), 406 E. Anthony St., Carroll 51401 (80). Orchard View, same address (50 apartments).

St. Francis Continuation Care and Nursing Home Center, Burlington 52601 (19 skilled nursing; 69 intermediate care). Orchard City of St. Francis, same address (12 independent living apartment units).

Kansas: Catholic Care Center (Skilled and Intermediate Care Facility), 6700 E. 45th St, Wichita 67226 (178 beds — includes 16 Alzheimer and 6 AIDS).

Mt. Joseph Senior Community (Intermediate Care Facility), 1110 W. 11, Concordia 66901 (99 nursing and 20 personal care beds; 12 apartments).

St. Elizabeth Home Health Agency, 2225 Canterbury Rd., Hays 67601.

St. John Rest Home (Nursing Facility), 701 Seventh St., Victoria 67671 (90 nursing).

St. John's of Hays (Nursing Facility), 2010 E. 25th, Hays 67601 (60).

St. Joseph Care Center (Intermediate and Skilled Care Facility), 759 Vermont Ave., Kansas City 66101 (201 nursing).

Villa Maria, Inc. (Intermediate Care Facility), 116 S. Central, Mulvane 67110 (66).

Kentucky: Bishop Soenneker Personal Care Home, 9545 Ky. 144, Philpot 42366 (60).

Carmel Home (Residence, Adult Day Care, Respite Care and Nursing Care), 2501 Old Hartford Rd., Owensboro 42303 (115).

Carmel Manor (Skilled, Intermediate and Personal Care Home), 100 Carmel Manor Rd., Ft. Thomas, 41075 (145).

Madonna Manor Nursing Home, 2344 Amsterdam Rd., Villa Hills 41017 (60). Also has 49 senior citizen apartments.

Marian Home, 3105 Lexington Rd., Louisville 40206 (70).

Nazareth Home, 2000 Newburg Rd., Louisville 40205 (168).

St. Charles Care Center and Village, 500 Farrell Dr., Covington 41011 (147). Nursing home; adult day health program. Independent living cottages (35). Assisted living (60). Independent living apartments (12).

Louisiana: Annunciation Inn, 1220 Spain St., New Orleans 70117 (106 residential units).

Bethany M.H.S. Health Care Center (Women), P.O. Box 2308, Lafayette 70502 (42).

Château de Notre Dame (Residence and Nursing Home), 2832 Burdette St., New Orleans 70125 (106 residential units, 6 assisted living units, 180 nursing beds).

Christopher Inn Apartments, 2110 Royal St., New Orleans 70116 (144 residential units).

Consolata Home (Nursing Home), 2319 E. Main St., New Iberia 70560 (114).

Haydel Heights Apartments, 4402 Reynes St., New Orleans 70126 (65 units).

Lafon Nursing Home of the Holy Family, 6900 Chef Menteur Hwy., New Orleans 70126 (171).

Mary-Joseph Residence for the Elderly, 4201 Woodland Dr., New Orleans 70131 (122).

Metairie Manor, 4929 York St., Metairie 70001 (287 residential units).

Nazareth Inn, 9630 Haynes Blvd., New Orleans 70127 (270 apartments).

Ollie Steele Burden Manor (Nursing Home), 4250 Essen Lane, Baton Rouge 70809 (184).

Our Lady of Prompt Succor Home, 751 E. Prudhomme Lane, Opelousas 70570 (80).

Our Lady's Manor, Inc., 402 Monroe St., Alexandria 71301 (104 apartments).

Place Dubourg, 201 Rue Dubourg, LaPlace 70068 (115 residential units).

Rouquette Lodge, 4300 Hwy 22, Mandeville 70471 (119 residential units).

St. John Berchmans Manor, 3400 St. Anthony St., New Orleans 70122 (150 residential units).

St. Joseph's Home (Nursing Home), 2301 Sterlington Rd., Monroe 71211 (132).

St. Margaret's Daughters Home (Nursing Home), 6220 Chartres St., New Orleans 70117 (115).

St. Martin Manor, 1501 N. Johnson St., New Orleans 70116 (140 residential units).

Villa St. Maurice and Villa St. Maurice II, 500 St. Maurice Ave., New Orleans 70117 (185 residential units).

Village du Lac, Inc., 1404 Carmel Ave., Lafayette 70501 (200). For handicapped and elderly.

Wynhoven Apartments and Wynhoven II (Residence for Senior Citizens), 4600-10th St., Marrero 70072 (350).

Wynhoven II, 4606-10th St., Marrero 70072 (150).

Maine: Deering Pavilion (Apartments for Senior Citizens), 880 Forest Ave., Portland 04103 (200 units).

Mt. St. Joseph, Highwood St., Waterville 04901 (88).

St. Andre Health Care Facility, Inc. (Nursing Facility), 407 Pool St., Biddeford 04005 (96).

St. Joseph's Manor (Nursing Care Facility), 1133 Washington Ave., Portland 04103 (50 skilled nursing; 150 intermediate nursing). Adult and child day care centers, same address.

St. Marguerite D'Youville Pavilion, 102 Campus Ave., Lewiston 04240 (280). Maison Marcotte (Independent Living Community), 100 Campus Ave., Lewiston 04240 (128 apartments).

St. Xavier's Home (Apartments), 199 Somerset St., Bangor 04401 (19 units).

Seton Village, Inc., 1 Carver St., Waterville 04901 (140 housing units).

Maryland: Cardinal Shehan Center, Inc., 2300 Dulaney Valley Rd., Towson 21204 (438).

Little Sisters of the Poor, St. Martin's Home (for the Aged), 601 Maiden Choice Lane, Baltimore 21228 (106).

Sacred Heart Home, 5805 Queens Chapel Rd., Hyattsville 20782 (102).

St. Joseph Nursing Home, 1222 Tugwell Dr., Baltimore 21228 (40).

Villa Rosa Nursing Home, 3800 Lottsford Vista Rd., Mitchellville 20721 (101).

Massachusetts: Catholic Memorial Home (Nursing Home), 2446 Highland Ave., Fall River 02720 (300). Alzheimer unit (43).

Don Orione Nursing Home, 111 Orient Ave., East Boston 02128 (190). Adult day care center (30).

D'Youville Manor (Nursing Home), 981 Varnum Ave., Lowell 01854 (196). Day care program (20).

Jeanne Jugan Residence, Little Sisters of the Poor (Home for the Elderly), 186 Highland Ave., Somerville 02143 (84). Jeanne Jugan Pavilion, 190 Highland Ave., Somerville 02143 (apartments, 27; residents, 28).

Madonna Manor (Nursing Home), 85 N. Washington St., N. Attleboro 02760 (129).

Marian Manor, for the Aged and Infirm (Nursing Home), 130 Dorchester St., S. Boston, 02127 (363).

Marian Manor of Taunton (Nursing Home), 33 Summer St., Taunton 02780 (116).

Maristhill Nursing Home, 66 Newton St., Waltham 02154 (120).

MI Nursing/Restorative Center, Zero Bennington St., Lawrence 01841 (250). Alzheimer beds (42).

MI Residential Community, 189 Maple St., Lawrence 01841 (304 apartments). Adult Day Health Care Center (52).

Mt. St. Vincent Nursing Home, 35 Holy Family Rd., Holyoke 01040 (125).

Our Lady's Haven (Nursing Home), 71 Center St., Fairhaven 02719 (117).

Sacred Heart Home (Nursing Home), 359 Summer St., New Bedford 02740 (217).

St. Joseph Manor Nursing Home, 215 Thatcher St., Brockton 02402 (120).

St. Joseph's Nursing Care Center, 321 Centre St., Dorchester, Boston 02122 (123).

St. Patrick's Manor (Nursing Home), 863 Central St., Framingham 01701 (332).

Michigan: Bishop Noa Home for Senior Citizens (Nursing Home and Residence), 2900 3rd Ave. S., Escanaba 49829 (109).

Lourdes Nursing Home (Skilled Facility), 2300 Watkins Lake Rd., Waterford 48328 (108).

McFadden Home (Residence), 2150 Watkins Lake Rd., Waterford 48328 (6).

Marian Hall (Residence), 529 M.L. King Ave., Flint 48502 (97).

Marycrest Manor (Skilled Nursing Facility), 15475 Middlebelt Rd., Livonia 48154 (55).

Ryan Senior Residences of the Archdiocese of Detroit. Nine residences:

Casa Maria, 600 Maple Vista, Imlay City 48444 (87).

Kundig Center, 3300 Jeffries Freeway, Detroit 48208 (153).

Madonna Villa 17825 Fifteen Mile Rd., Clinton Twp. 48035 (89).

Marian-Oakland West, 29250 W. Ten Mile Rd., Farmington Hills 48336 (90).

Marian Place, 408 W. Front St., Monroe 48161 (51).

Marydale Center, 3147 Tenth Ave., Port Huron 48060 (57).

Maryhaven, 11350 Reeck Rd., Southgate 48195 (90).

Stapleton Center, 9341 Agnes St., Detroit 48214 (59).

Villa Marie, 15131 Newburgh Rd., Livonia 48154 (89).

St. Ann's Home, (Residence and Nursing Home), 2161 Leonard St. N.W., Grand Rapids 49504 (130).

St. Catherine House, 1641 Webb Ave., Detroit 48206 (12).

St. Elizabeth Briarbank (Women, Residence), 1315 N. Woodward Ave., Bloomfield Hills 48304 (54).

St. Francis Home (Nursing Home), 915 N. River Rd., Saginaw 48609 (100).

St. Joseph's Home, 4800 Cadieux Rd., Detroit 48224 (104).

St. Jude Home, Inc., (Residence), 2270 Marwood, Waterford 48328 (6).

Villa Elizabeth (Nursing Home), 2100 Leonard St. N.E., Grand Rapids 49505 (136). Country Villa (Assisted Living Apartments), 2110 Leonard N.E., Grand Rapids 49505 (48 units).

Villa Francesca (Residence, Women), 565 W. Long Lake Rd., Bloomfield Hills 48302 (18).

Minnesota: Alverna Apartments, 300 8th Ave. S.E., Little Falls 56345 (60). Retirement community.

Assumption Home, 715 North First St., Cold Spring 56320 (Skilled nursing beds, 95). Respite care. Adult day services; home delivered meals.

Benedictine Health Center, 935 Kenwood Ave., Duluth 55811 (Nursing home, 120; day care, 72). Respite care.

Divine Providence Community Home (Skilled Nursing Care), 700 Third Ave. N.W., Sleepy Eye 56085 (58). Lake Villa Maria Senior Housing (21 units).

Franciscan Health Community, 1925 Norfolk Ave., St. Paul 55116 (140).

John Paul Apartments, 200 8th Ave. N., Cold Spring 56320 (61).

Little Sisters of the Poor, Holy Family Residence (Skilled Nursing and Intermediate Care), 330 S. Exchange St., St. Paul 55102 (76). Independent living apartments (32).

Madonna Towers (Retirement Apartments and Nursing Home), 4001 19th Ave. N.W., Rochester 55901 (182).

Mary Rondorf Retirement Home of Sacred Heart Parish, Inc., 222 N.E. 5th St., Staples 56479 (45). Board and lodging with special services.

Mother of Mercy Nursing Home and Retirement Center, 230 Church Ave., Box 676, Albany 56307 (Skilled nursing home, 84; retirement housing, 33).

Regina Nursing Home and Retirement Residence, Hastings 55033. Nursing home (61); retirement home (42); boarding care (32).

Sacred Heart Hospice (Skilled Nursing Home, Adult Day Care, Home Health Care) 1200 Twelfth St. S.W., Austin 55912 (59).

St. Ann's Residence, 330 E. 3rd St., Duluth 55805 (193). Senior housing. Meals and lodging with supportive services.

St. Anne Hospice, Inc. (Skilled Nursing Home), 1347 W. Broadway, Winona 55987 (134). Adult day care.

St. Benedict's Center, 1810 Minnesota Blvd. S.E., St. Cloud 56304 (222 bed skilled nursing care; adult day care, respite care. Benedict Village (Retirement Apartments), 2000 15th Ave. S.E., St. Cloud 56304. Benedict Homes (Alzheimer Residential Care) and Benedict Court (Assisted Living), 1980 15th Ave. S.E., St. Cloud 56304.

St. Elizabeth's Hospital, Nursing Home and Health Care Center, 1200-5th Grant Blvd., Wabasha 55981 (157). Assisted living apartments (23).

St. Francis Home, 501 Oak St., Breckenridge 56520 (124).

St. Mary's Regional Health Center (Hospital and Nursing Center), 1027 Washington Ave., Detroit Lakes 56501 (100).

St. Mary's Villa (Nursing Home), Box 397, Pierz 56364 (101).

St. Otto's Care Center (Nursing Home), 920 S.E. 4th St., Little Falls 56345 (150).

St. William's Nursing Home, Parkers Prairie 56361 (90).

Villa of St. Francis Nursing Home, 1001 Scott Ave., Morris 56267 (140).

Villa St. Vincent (Skilled Nursing Home and Residence), 516 Walsh St., Crookston 56716. Skilled Nursing home (80);special care unit (24); apartments (27); board and care (34).

Mississippi: Notre Dame de la Mer Retirement Apartments, 292 Hwy. 90, Bay St. Louis 39520.

Santa Maria Retirement Apartments, 674 Beach Blvd., Biloxi, 39530.

Villa Maria Retirement Apartments, 921 Porter Ave., Ocean Springs 39564.

Missouri: Cathedral Square Towers, 444 W. 12th St., Kansas City 64105. Apartments for elderly and handicapped (156).

Chariton Apartments (Retirement Apartments), 4249 Michigan Ave., St. Louis 63111 (122 units; 143 residents).

DePaul Health Center - St. Anne's Division (Skilled Nursing), 12303 DePaul Dr., Bridgeton 63044 (96).

LaVerna Heights Retirement Home (Women), 104 E. Park Ave., Savannah 64485 (40). Nursing facility.

LaVerna Village Nursing Home, 904 Hall Ave., Savannah 64485 (120).

Little Sisters of the Poor (Home for Aged), 3225 N. Florissant Ave., St. Louis 63107 (120).

Mary, Queen and Mother Center (Nursing Care), 7601 Watson Rd., St. Louis 63119.

Mother of Good Counsel Home (Skilled Nursing, Women), 6825 Natural Bridge Rd., Northwoods, 63121 (114).

Our Lady of Mercy Country Home, 2205 Hughes Rd., Liberty 64068 (115).

Price Memorial Skilled Nursing Facility, Forby Rd., P.O. Box 476, Eureka 63025 (120).

St. Agnes Home for the Elderly, 10341 Manchester Rd., Kirkwood 63122 (122).

St. Joseph Hill Infirmary, Inc., (Nursing Care Facility, Men), St. Joseph Road, Eureka 63025 (127).

St. Joseph's Home (Residential and Intermediate Care), 723 First Capitol Dr., St. Charles 63301 (100).

St. Joseph's Home (Residential and Intermediate Care Facility), 1306 W. Main St., Jefferson City 65109 (100).

Nebraska: Bergan Mercy Medical Center, Mercy Care Center (Skilled Nursing Facility for Chronic, Complex and Subacute Levels of Care and Rehabilitation), 1870 S. 75th St., Omaha 68124 (250).

Madonna Rehabilitation Hospital, 5401 South St., Lincoln 68506.

Mercy Villa, 1845 S. 72nd St., Omaha 68124 (36).

Mt. Carmel Home, Keens Memorial (Nursing Home), 412 W. 18th St., Kearney 68847 (79).

New Cassel Retirement Center, 900 N. 90th St., Omaha 68114 (156).

St. Joseph's Nursing Home, 401 N. 18th St., Norfolk 68701 (83).

St. Joseph's Retirement Community, 320 E. Decatur St., West Point 68788 (70). Assisted living.

St. Joseph's Villa (Nursing Home), 927 7th St., David City 68632 (65).

New Hampshire: Mount Carmel Nursing Home, 235 Myrtle St., Manchester 03104 (120).

St. Ann Home (Nursing Home), 195 Dover Point Rd., Dover 03820 (54).

St. Francis Home (Nursing Home), 406 Court St., Laconia 03246 (51). Apartments (25).

St. Teresa Manor (Nursing Home), 519 Bridge St., Manchester 03104 (5). Bishop Primeau Apartments, same address (25).

St. Vincent de Paul Nursing Home, 29 Providence Ave., Berlin 03570 (80).

New Jersey: Holy Family Residence, 44 Rifle Camp Rd., P.O. Box 536, W. Paterson 07424 (64).

McCarrick Care Center, 15 Dellwood Lane, Somerset 08873 (120).

Mater Dei Nursing Home, 176 Rt. 40, Newfield 08344 (64).

Morris Hall (St. Joseph Skilled Nursing Center, St. Mary Residence), 2361 Lawrenceville Rd., Lawrenceville 08648 (220).

Mount St. Andrew Villa (Residence), 55 W. Midland Ave., Paramus 07652 (56).

Our Lady's Residence (Nursing Home), 1100 Clematis Ave., Pleasantville 08232 (214).

St. Ann's Home for the Aged (Skilled and Intermediate Nursing Care Home, Women), 198 Old Bergen Rd., Jersey City 07305 (106). Adult Medical Day Care (50).

St. Francis Health Resort (Residence), Denville 07834 (100), Apartments, 63.

St. Joseph's Home for the Elderly, Little Sisters of the Poor, 140 Shepherd Lane, Totowa 07512 (116; also, 18 independent living units).

St. Joseph's Rest Home for Aged Women, 46 Preakness Ave., Paterson 07522 (25).

St. Joseph's Senior Residence (Sheltered Care), 1 St. Joseph Terr., Woodbridge 07095 (60).

St. Mary's Catholic Home (Skilled Nursing Home), 1730 Kresson Rd., Cherry Hill 08003 (215). The Manor at St. Mary's, 1743 Kresson Rd., Cherry Hill 08003 (82).

St. Vincent's Nursing Home, 45 Elm St., Montclair 07042 (135).

Villa Maria (Residence and Infirmary, Women), 641 Somerset St., N. Plainfield 07061 (84).

New Mexico: Good Shepherd Manor (Residential Care for Aged Persons), Little Brothers of the Good Shepherd, P.O. Box 10248, Albuquerque 87184 (40).

New York: Bernardine Apartments, 417 Churchill Ave., Syracuse 13205.

Brothers of Mercy Sacred Heart Home (Residence) 4520 Ransom Rd., Clarence 14031 (82). Brothers of Mercy Nursing Home, 10570 Bergtold Rd., Clarence 14031 (240). Brothers of Mercy Housing Co., Inc. (Apartments), 10500 Bergtold Rd., Clarence 14031 (100 units).

Carmel Richmond Nursing Home, 88 Old Town Rd., Staten Island 10304 (300). Skilled Nursing, adult day health care.

Ferncliff Nursing Home, 52 River Rd., Rhinebeck 12572 (328).

Frances Schervier Home and Hospital, 2975 Independence Ave., Bronx 10463 (364). Frances Schervier Long Term Health Care Program, same address (310 slots). Frances Schervier Housing Development Fund Corporation, 2995 Independence Ave., Bronx 10463 (154 units).

Good Samaritan Nursing Home (Skilled Nursing), 101 Elm St., Sayville, N.Y. 11782 (100).

The Heritage (Apartments with Skilled Nursing Care), 1450 Portland Ave., Rochester 14621 (237).

Holy Family Home, 1740-84th St., Brooklyn 11214 (200).

Holy Family Home (Adult Home), 410 Mill St., Williamsville 14221 (85).

Kateri Residence (Skilled Nursing), 150 Riverside Dr., New York 10024 (520).

Little Sisters of the Poor, Jeanne Jugan Residence (Skilled Nursing and Health Related; Adult Care), 3200 Baychester Ave., Bronx 10475 (92).

Little Sisters of the Poor, Queen of Peace Residence, 110-30 221st St., Queens Village 11429 (130).

Mary Manning Walsh Home (Nursing Home), 1339 York Ave., New York 10021 (362).

Mercy Healthcare Center (Skilled Nursing Facility), Tupper Lake 12986 (54).

Mt. Loretto Nursing Home, (Skilled Nursing Home), Sisters of the Resurrection, 302 Swart Hill Rd., Amsterdam 12010 (120).

Nazareth Nursing Home (Women), 291 W. North St., Buffalo 14201 (125).

Our Lady of Consolation Geriatric Care Center (Skilled Nursing) 111 Beach Dr., West Islip 11795 (250). Also long term home health care program.

Our Lady of Hope Residence (Home for the Aged), Little Sisters of the Poor, 1 Jeanne Jugan Lane, Latham 12210 (100; also 16 apartments).

Ozanam Hall of Queens Nursing Home, Inc., 42-41 201st St., Bayside 11361 (432).

Providence Rest, 3304 Waterbury Ave., Bronx 10465 (200).

Resurrection Nursing Home (Skilled Nursing Facility), Castleton 12033 (80).

St. Ann's Home (Skilled Nursing Facility), 1500 Portland Ave., Rochester 14621 (354). Home Connection (Adult Day Health Care Program), same address (60).

St. Cabrini Nursing Home, 115 Broadway, Dobbs Ferry 10522 (304).

St. Clare Manor (Nursing Home), 543 Locust St., Lockport 14094 (28).

St. Columban's on the Lake (Retirement Home), 2546 Lake Rd., Silver Creek 14136 (50).

St. Elizabeth Home (Adult Home), 5539 Broadway, Lancaster 14086 (115).

St. Francis Home (Skilled Nursing Facility), 147 Reist St., Williamsville 14221 (142).

St. Joseph Manor (Nursing Home), W. State St., Olean 14760 (22).

St. Joseph Nursing Home, 2535 Genesee St., Utica 13501 (120).

St. Joseph's Guest Home, Missionary Sisters of St. Benedict, 350 Cuba Hill Rd., Huntington 11743 (48).

St. Joseph's Home (Nursing Home), 420 Lafayette St., Ogdensburg 13669 (82).

St. Joseph's Villa (Adult Home), 38 Prospect Ave., Catskill 12414 (60).

St. Luke Manor, 17 Wiard St., Batavia 14020 (20).

St. Mary's Manor, 515 Sixth St., Niagara Falls 14301 (119).

St. Patrick's Home for the Aged and Infirm, 66 Van Cortlandt Park S., Bronx 10463 (264).

St. Teresa Nursing Home, 120 Highland Ave., Middletown 10940 (92).

St. Vincent's Home for the Aged, 319 Washington Ave., Dunkirk 14048 (40).

Terence Cardinal Cooke Health Care Center (Skilled Nursing), 1249 Fifth Ave., New York 10029.

Teresian House, Washington Ave. Extension, Albany 12203 (300).

Uihlein Mercy Center (Nursing Home), 420 Old Military Rd., Lake Placid 12946 (155).

North Carolina: Maryfield Nursing Home, Greensboro Rd., High Point 27260 (115).

North Dakota: Carrington Health Center (Nursing Home), Carrington 58421 (40).

Manor St. Joseph (Basic Care Facility), Edgeley 58433 (40).

Marillac Manor Retirement Center, 1016 28th St., Bismarck 58501 (78 apartments).

St. Anne's Guest Home, 524 N. 17th St., Grand Forks 58203 (30) Apartments (56). Adult basic care facility.

St. Vincent's Care Center (Nursing Facility), 1021 N. 26th St., Bismarck 58501 (101).

Ohio: Archbishop Leibold Home for the Aged, Little Sisters of the Poor, 476 Riddle Rd., Cincinnati 45220 (115).

The Assumption Village, 9800 Market St., North Lima 44452 (150). Long term nursing facility.

Francesca Residence (Retirement), 39 N. Portage Path, Akron 44303 (40).

House of Loreto (Nursing Home), 2812 Harvard Ave. N.W., Canton 44709 (100).

Jennings Hall, Inc. (Nursing Care), 10204 Granger Rd., Cleveland 4125 (15000).

Little Sisters of the Poor, Sacred Heart Home, 4900 Navarre Ave., Oregon 43616 (126).

Little Sisters of the Poor, Sts. Mary and Joseph Home for Aged, 4291 Richmond Rd., Cleveland 44122 (124).

The Maria-Joseph Living Care Center, 4830 Salem Ave., Dayton 45416 (420).

Mercy St. Theresa Center, 7010 Rowan Hill Dr., Cincinnati 45227 (177).

Mercy Siena Woods (Nursing Home, Skilled and Intermediate Care, Alzheimer Center), 235 W. Orchard Spring Dr., Dayton 45415 (99).

Mount Alverna (Intermediate Care Nursing Facility), 6765 State Rd., Cleveland 44134 (203).

Mt. St. Joseph (Skilled Nursing Facility, Dual Certified), 21800 Chardon Rd., Cleveland 44117 (100).

Nazareth Towers, 300 E. Rich St., Columbus 43215. Hi-rise apartments for independent living for senior citizens (208).

St. Augustine Manor (Skilled Nursing Facility), 7801 Detroit Ave., Cleveland 44102 (248).

St. Clare Retirement Community (Skilled Nursing, Assisted Care, Apartments), Franciscan Sisters of the Poor, 100 Compton Rd., Cincinnati 45215 (171).

St. Francis Health Care Centre, 401 N. Broadway St., Green Springs 44836 (191).

St. Francis Home, Inc. (Residence and Nursing Care), 182 St. Francis Ave., Tiffin 44883 (116).

St. Joseph's Nursing Home and Assisted Living, 2308 Reno Dr., Louisville 44641 (100, nursing home; 40 assisted living).

St. Margaret Hall (Rest Home and Nursing Facility), Carmelite Sisters for the Aged and Infirm, 1960 Madison Rd., Cincinnati 45206 (135).

St. Raphael Home (Nursing Home), 1550 Roxbury Rd., Columbus 43212 (78).

St. Rita's Home (Skilled Nursing Home), 880 Greenlawn Ave., Columbus 43223 (100).

Schroder Manor Retirement Community (Residential Care, Skilled Nursing Care and Independent Living Units), Franciscan Sisters of the Poor, 1302 Millville Ave., Hamilton 45013 (173).

The Villa Sancta Anna Home for the Aged, Inc., 25000 Chagrin Blvd., Beachwood 44122 (68).

The Village at St. Edward (Apartments, Nursing Care and Assisted Living), 3131 Smith Rd., Fairlawn 44333 (290).

Oklahoma: Franciscan Villa, 17110 E. 51st St., Broken Arrow 74012. Intermediate nursing care (60); apartments (40 independent; 22 assisted living).

St. Ann's Home, 9400 St. Ann's Dr., Oklahoma City 73162 (102).

Westminster Village, Inc. (Residence), 1601 Academy, Ponca City 74604 (108).

Oregon: Benedictine Nursing Center, 540 S. Main St., Mt. Angel 97362 (130). Home Health Agency, Outpatient Therapies. Benedictine Institute for Long Term Care. Child Development Center.

Evergreen Court Retirement Apartments, 451 O'Connell St., North Bend 97459 (80).

Maryville Nursing Home, 14645 S.W. Farmington, Beaverton 97007 (147).

Mt. St. Joseph Residence and Extended Care Center, 3060 S.E. Stark St., Portland 97214 (298).

St. Catherine's Residence and Nursing Center, 3959 Sheridan Ave., North Bend 97459 (153).

St. Elizabeth Hospital and Health Care Center, 3985 Midway Lane, Baker City 97814 (120).

Pennsylvania: Antonian Towers, 2405 Hillside Ave., Easton 18042 (50 apartments).

Ascension Manor I (Senior Citizen Housing), 911 N. Franklin St., Philadelphia 19123 (140 units).

Ascension Manor II (Senior Citizen Housing), 970 N. 7th St., Philadelphia 19123 (140 units).

Benetwood Apartments, Benedictine Sisters of Erie, 641 Troupe Rd., Harborcreek 16421 (75). Subsidized housing for low income elderly and handicapped persons.

Bethlehem Retirement Village, 100 W. Wissahickon Ave., Flourtown 19031. Apartments for well elderly (100).

Christ the King Manor, 1100 W. Long Ave., Du Bois 15801 (160).

D'Youville Manor (Residential Care Facility), 1750 Quarry Rd., Yardley 19067 (50).

Garvey Manor (Nursing Home), Logan Blvd., Hollidaysburg 16648 (150).

Grace Mansion (Personal Care Facility), Holy Family Residential Services , 1200 Spring St., Bethlehem (28).

Holy Family Apartments (Low Income), Clay and Valley Sts., New Philadelphia 17959 (11).

Holy Family Apartments, 330-338 13th Ave., Bethlehem 18018 (50 apartments).

Holy Family Home, Little Sisters of the Poor, 5300 Chester Ave., Philadelphia 19143 (106).

Holy Family Manor (Skilled and Intermediate Nursing Facility), 1200 Spring St., Bethlehem 18018 (208).

Holy Family Residence (Personal Care Facility), 900 W. Market St., Orwigsburg 17961 (50).

Holy Redeemer Health System, Inc., Sisters of the Holy Redeemer: St. Joseph's Manor, 1616 Huntingdon Pike, Meadowbrook 19046 (262 bed personal assisted living; 24 bed cognitive impairment); Lafayette-Redeemer, 8580 Verree Rd., Philadelphia 19111 (295 independent-living apartments; 120 bed nursing; 5 bed assisted living); Redeemer Village, 1551 Huntingdon Pike, Huntingdon Valley 19006 (200 units low income subsidized housing for aged and disabled). Also sponsor a hospital, home-care, hospice and other related facilities.

Immaculate Mary Home (Nursing Care Facility), 2990 Holme Ave., Philadelphia 19136 (296).

John XXIII Home (Skilled, Intermediate and Personal Care), 2250 Shenango Freeway, Hermitage 16148 (142).

Little Flower Manor Nursing Home (Skilled Nursing), 1201 Springfield Rd., Darby 19023 (127).

Little Flower Manor of Diocese of Scranton, (Long-Term Skilled Nursing Care Facility), 200 S. Meade St., Wilkes-Barre 18702 (133).

Little Sisters of the Poor, 1028 Benton Ave., Pittsburgh 15212 (106).

Little Sisters of the Poor, Holy Family Residence, 2500 Adams Ave., Scranton 18509 (58).

Maria Joseph Manor (Skilled Nursing, Personal Care Facility and Independent Living Cottages), 875 Montour Blvd., Danville 17821 (96).

Marian Hall Home for the Aged (Women), 934 Forest Ave., Pittsburgh 15202 (25).

Marian Manor (Intermediate Care), 2695 Winchester Dr., Pittsburgh 15220 (170).

Mount Macrina Manor (Skilled Nursing Facility), 520 W. Main St., Uniontown 15401 (120).

Neumann Apartments (Low Income), 25 N. Nichols St., St. Clair 17970 (25).

Queen of Angels Apartments, 22 Rothermel St., Hyde Park, Reading 19605 (45 units).

Queen of Peace Apartments (Low Income), 777 Water St., Pottsville 17901 (65).

Sacred Heart Manor (Nursing Home and Independent Living), 6445 Germantown Ave., Philadelphia 19119 (171 nursing home; 24 personal care; 72 independent living).

St. Anne's Home and Village, 3952 Columbia Ave., Columbia 17512 (Nursing home, 121; personal care, 18; independent living, 36 cottages).

St. Anne Home (Nursing Facility), 685 Angela Dr., Greensburg 15601 (125).

St. Basil's Home (Personal Care Facility) 530 W. Main St., Box 878, Uniontown 15401 (11).

St. Ignatius Nursing Home, 4401 Haverford Ave., Philadelphia 19104 (176).

St. John Neumann Nursing Home, 10400 Roosevelt Blvd., Philadelphia 19116 (224).

St. Joseph Home for the Aged (Residential and Skilled Nursing Facility), 1182 Holland Rd., Holland 18966 (96).

St. Joseph Nursing and Health Care Center (Skilled Nursing Facility), 5324 Penn Ave., Pittsburgh 15224 (158).

St. Leonard's Home Inc. (Personal Care Facility), 601 N. Montgomery St., Hollidaysburg 16648 (21).

St. Mary of Providence Center, R.D. 2, Box 145, Elverson 19520 (Senior Citizen Housing, 39 units). Center is also a House of Spirituality.

St. Mary's Home of Erie, 607 E. 26th St., Erie 16504. Residential and personal care (131); skilled and intermediate nursing care (228, includes Alzheimer Center, 37); adult day care (49).

Saint Mary's Manor (Residential, Personal Care, Short-Term Rehabilitation and Nursing Care), 701 Lansdale Ave., Lansdale 19446 (160).

St. Mary's Villa Nursing Home, St. Mary's Villa Rd., Elmhurst 18416 (112).

Trexler Pavilion (Personal Care Facility), 1220 Prospect Ave., Bethlehem 18018 (25).

Villa de Marillac Nursing Home, 5300 Stanton Ave., Pittsburgh 15206 (52).

Villa St. Teresa (Residence, Women), 1215 Springfield Rd., Darby 19023 (53).

Villa Teresa (Nursing Home), 1051 Avila Rd., Harrisburg 17109 (184).

Vincentian Home (Nursing Facility), 111 Perrymont Rd., Pittsburgh 15237 (221).

Rhode Island: Jeanne Jugan Residence of the Little Sisters of the Poor, 964 Main St., Pawtucket 02860 (99).

Saint Antoine Residence (Skilled Nursing Facility), 400 Mendon Rd., North Smithfield 02896 (260).

St. Clare Home (Nursing Facility), 309 Spring St., Newport 02840 (46).

St. Francis House, 167 Blackstone St., Woonsocket 02895 (60). Residential, assisted living.

Scalabrini Villa (Convalescent, Rest - Nursing Home). 860 N. Quidnessett Rd., North Kingstown 02852 (70).

South Carolina: Carter-May Home, 1660 Ingram Rd., Charleston 29407 (15). Personal care home for elderly ladies.

South Dakota: Brady Memorial Home (Skilled

Nursing Facility), 500 S. Ohlman St., Mitchell 57301 (83). Independent living units (3); congregate apartments (6); adult day care.

Maryhouse, Inc. (Skilled Nursing Facility), 717 E. Dakota, Pierre 57501 (82 skilled nursing, 23 sub-acute care beds).

Mother Joseph Manor (Skilled Nursing Facility), 1002 North Jay St., Aberdeen 57401 (81). Apartment units (7). Adult day care program. Respite nursing care.

Prince of Peace Retirement Community, 4500 Prince of Peace Pl., Sioux Falls 57103. Skilled nursing home (90 beds); independent living apartments (74); assisted living aprartments (32); Alzheimer Special Care Unit (20).

St. William's Home for the Aged (Intermediate Care, 60), and Angela Hall (Assisted Living Center for Developmentally Handicapped Women, 22), 901 E. Virgil, Box 432, Milbank 57252. Adult day care program (10).

Tekakwitha Nursing Home (Skilled and Intermediate Care), Sisseton 57262 (101). Tekakwitha Housing Corp. (Independent Living), P.O. Box 208, Sisseton 57262 (24 units).

Tennessee: Alexian Village of Tennessee, 100 James Blvd., Signal Mountain 37377 (277 retirement apartments) and Health Care Center (114). Assisted living (33).

St. Mary Manor, 1771 Highway 45 Bypass, Jackson 38305 (149 retirement apartments).

St. Peter Manor (Retirement Community), 108 N. Auburndale, Memphis 38104.

St. Peter Villa (Intermediate and Skilled Care), 141 N. McLean, Memphis 38104 (180).

Villa Maria Manor, 32 White Bridge Rd., Nashville 37205 (214 apartments).

Texas: Casa, Inc., Housing for Elderly and Handicapped, 3201 Sondra Dr., Fort Worth 76107 (200 apartments).

Casa Brendan Housing for the Elderly and Handicapped (56 apartments) and Casa II, Inc. (30 apartments), 1300 Hyman St., Stephenville 76401 (86).

John Paul II Nursing Home (Intermediate Care and Personal Care), 215 Tilden St., Kenedy 78119.

Mother of Perpetual Help Home (Intermediate Care Facility), 519 E. Madison Ave., Brownsville 78520 (33).

Mt. Carmel Home (Personal Care Home), 4130 S. Alameda St., Corpus Christi 78411 (92).

Nuestro Hogar Housing for Elderly and Handicapped, 709 Magnolia St., Arlington 76012 (65 apartments).

The Regis Retirement Home and St. Elizabeth Nursing Home, 400 Austin Ave., Waco 76701 (291).

St. Ann's Nursing Home, P.O. Box 1179, Panhandle 79068 (56).

St. Dominic Nursing Home, 6502 Grand Ave., Houston 77021 (120).

St. Dominic Residence Hall, 2401 E. Holcombe Blvd., Houston 77021 (137).

St. Francis Nursing Home (Intermediate Care Facility), 630 W. Woodlawn, San Antonio 78212 (152).

St. Francis Village, Inc. (Retired and Elderly), 1 Chapel Plaza, Crowley 76036 (450).

St. Joseph Residence (Personal Care Home), 330 W. Pembroke St., Dallas 75208 (49).

San Juan Nursing Home, Inc. (Skilled and Intermediate Care Facility), P.O. Box 1238, San Juan 78589 (127).

Villa Maria (Home for Aged Women-Men), 920 S. Oregon St., El Paso 79901 (24 units).

Villa Maria, Inc. (Apartment Complex), 3146 Saratoga Blvd., Corpus Christi 78415 (48 units). Corpus Christi diocese.

Utah: St. Joseph Villa (Senior Care Complex), 451 Bishop Federal Lane, Salt Lake City 84115 (230).

Vermont: Loretto Home for Aged, 59 Meadow St., Rutland 05701 (57).

Michaud Memorial Manor (Residential Home for Elderly), Derby Line 05830 (24).

St. Joseph's Home for Aged, 243 N. Prospect St., Burlington 05401 (36).

Virginia: Madonna Home (Home for Aged), 814 W. 37th St., Norfolk 23508 (16).

Marian Manor (Assisted Living, Nursing Care), 5345 Marian Lane, Virginia Beach 23462 (100 units; 30 beds nursing care).

Marywood Apartments, 1261 Marywood Lane, Richmond 23229 (112 units).

McGurk House Apartments, 2425 Tate Springs Rd., Lynchburg 24501 (88 units).

Our Lady of the Valley Retirement Community, 650 N. Jefferson St., Roanoke 24016.

Russell House Apartments, 900 First Colonial Rd., Virginia Beach 23454 (127).

St. Francis Home, 2511 Wise St., Richmond 23225 (31).

St. Joseph's Home for the Aged, Little Sisters of the Poor, 1503 Michael Rd., Richmond 23229 (72).

St. Mary's Woods (Independent and Assisted Living Apartments), 1257 Marywood Lane, Richmond 23229 (118 apartments).

Seton Manor (Apartments), 215 Marcella Rd., Hampton 23666 (112).

Washington: Cathedral Plaza Apartments (Retirement Apartments), W. 1120 Sprague Ave., Spokane 99204 (150).

Chancery Place (Retirement Apartments), 910 Marion, Seattle 98104 (84 units; independent living).

The Delaney, W. 242 Riverside Ave., Spokane 99201 (84).

Elbert House, 16000 N.E. 8th St., Bellevue 98008.

Emma McRedmond Manor, 7960-169th N.E., Redmond 98052.

Fahy Garden Apartments, W. 1403-11 Dean Ave., Spokane 99201 (31).

Fahy West Apartments, W. 1523 Dean Ave., Spokane 99201 (55).

The Franciscan (Apartments), 15237-21stAve. S.W., Seattle 98166 (38).

Providence Mt. St. Vincent (Nursing Center and Retirement Apartments), 4831 35th Ave. S.W., Seattle 98126.

St. Brendan Continuing Care Center, E. 17 8th Ave., Spokane 99202.

St. Joseph Care Center, 20 West 9th Ave., Spokane 99204 (103).

Tumwater Apartments, 5701-6th Ave. S.W., Tumwater 98501 (50).

West Virginia: Welty Home for the Aged, 21 Washington Ave., Wheeling 26003 (45).

Wisconsin: Alexian Village of Milwaukee (Retirement Community/Skilled Nursing Home), 7979 W. Glenbrook Rd., Milwaukee 53223 (320 apartments; 87 skilled nursing; 30 assisted living; adult day care).

Bethany-St. Joseph Health Care Center, 2501 Shelby Rd., La Crosse 54601 (226).

Clement Manor (Retirement Community and Skilled Nursing), 3939 S. 92nd St., Greenfield 53228 (164 skilled nursing; 200 units independent and assisted living). Adult day care.

Divine Savior Nursing Home, 715 W. Pleasant St., Portage 53901 (111 skilled nursing; 14 self care).

Felician Village (Independent Living), 1700 S. 18th St., Manitowoc 54020 (134 apartments).

Franciscan Care Center, 2915 North Meade St., Appleton 54911 (235).

Franciscan Skemp Healthcare, Mayo Health System: Arcadia Campus Nursing Home, 464 S. St. Joseph Ave., Arcadia 54612 (75); LaCrosse Campus Nursing Home, 620 S. 11th St., La Crosse 54601 (95).

Franciscan Villa (Skilled Nursing Home), 3601 S. Chicago Ave., S. Milwaukee 53172 (150).

Hope Nursing Home, 438 Ashford Ave., Lomira 53048 (42).

McCormick Memorial Home, 212 Iroquois St., Green Bay 54301 (74).

Marian Catholic Home (Skilled Care Nursing Home), 3333 W. Highland Blvd., Milwaukee 53208 (360).

Marian Franciscan Center, 9632 W. Appleton Ave., Milwaukee 53225 (345).

Marian Housing Center (Independent Living), 4105 Spring St., Racine 53405 (40).

Maryhill Manor Nursing Home (Skilled Nursing Facility), 501 Madison Ave., Niagara 54151 (75).

Milwaukee Catholic Home (Continuing Care Retirement Community), 2462 N. Prospect Ave., Milwaukee 53211 (130 apartments; 56 skilled nursing).

Nazareth House (Skilled Nursing Facility), 814 Jackson St., Stoughton 53589 (99).

St. Ann Rest Home (Intermediate Care Facility, Women), 2020 S. Muskego Ave., Milwaukee 53204 (54).

St. Anne's Home for the Elderly, 3800 N. 92nd St., Milwaukee 53222 (106 skilled nursing beds, 16 independent apartments).

St. Camillus Campus (Continuing Care Retirement Community), 10100 West Blue Mound Road, Wauwatosa 53226 (297 independent apartments; 108 assisted living units; 192 skilled nursing beds). Also adult day care, licensed home health care, support home services; 24-bed subacute care unit.

St. Catherine Infirmary (Nursing Home), 5635 Erie St., Racine 53402 (41).

St. Elizabeth Nursing Home, 502 St. Lawrence Ave., Janesville 53545 (43).

St. Francis Home (Skilled Nursing Facility), 1800 New York Ave., Superior 54880 (192).

St. Francis Home (Skilled Nursing), 365 Gillett St., Fond du Lac 54935 (70).

St. Joan Antida Home (Skilled Nursing), 6700 W. Beloit Rd., W. Allis 53219 (73).

St. Joseph's Home, 705 Clyman St., Watertown 53094 (28).

St. Joseph's Home, 9244 29th Ave., Kenosha 53143 (93). Independent living apartments; skilled nursing home. St. Joseph Adult Day Care, same address.

St. Joseph's Home, 5301 W. Lincoln Ave., W. Allis 53219 (51 assisted living; 74 skilled care; adult day care).

St. Joseph's Nursing Home, 2902 East Ave. S., La Crosse 54601 (80).

St. Joseph's Nursing Home of St. Joseph Memorial Hospital, 400 Water Ave., Hillsboro 54634 (65).

St. Joseph Residence, Inc. (Nursing Home), 107 E. Beckert Rd., New London 54961 (107 skilled nursing; 27 apartments).

St. Mary's Home for the Aged (Skilled Nursing, Alzheimer's Unit, Respite Care), 2005 Division St., Manitowoc 54220 (297).

St. Mary's Nursing Home, 3516 W. Center St., Milwaukee 53210 (130).

St. Monica's Senior Citizens Home, 3920 N. Green Bay Rd., Racine 53404 (125).

St. Paul Home, Inc. (Intermediate and Skilled Nursing Home), 1211 Oakridge Ave., Kaukauna 54130 (129). Assisted living also.

Villa Clement (Health Center), 9047 W. Greenfield Ave., W. Allis 53214 (194).

Villa Loretto Nursing Home, Mount Calvary 53057 (52).

Villa St. Anna (Assisted Living Facility), 5737 Erie St., Racine 53402 (71 private units).

Villa St. Francis, Inc., 1910 W. Ohio Ave., Milwaukee 53215. Independent and assisted living (142 private units).

FACILITIES FOR CHILDREN AND ADULTS WITH DISABILITIES

(Sources: *Catholic Almanac* survey; *The Official Catholic Directory.*)

This listing covers facilities and programs with educational and training orientation. Information about other services for the handicapped can generally be obtained from the Catholic Charities Office or its equivalent (c/o Chancery Office) in any diocese. (See Index for listing of addresses of chancery offices in the U.S.)

Abbreviation code: b, boys; c, coeducational; d, day; g, girls; r, residential. Other information includes chronological age for admission. The number in parentheses at the end of an entry indicates total capacity or enrollment.

Deaf and Hearing Impaired

California: St. Joseph's Center for Deaf and Hard of Hearing, 3880 Smith St., Union City 94587.

Louisiana: Chinchuba Institute (d,c; birth through 18 yrs.), 1131 Barataria Blvd., Marrero 70072.

Missouri: St. Joseph Institute for the Deaf (r,d,c; birth to 14 years), 1483 82nd Blvd., University City, St. Louis 63132 (120).

St. Joseph Institute for the Deaf, 1809 Clarkson, Chesterfield, MO 63017.

New York: Cleary School for the Deaf (d,c; infancy through 21), 301 Smithtown Blvd., Nesconset, NY 11767-2077 (70).

St. Francis de Sales School for the Deaf (d,c; infant

through elementary grades), 260 Eastern Parkway, Brooklyn 11225 (220).

St. Joseph's School for the Deaf (d,c; parent-infant through 14 yrs.), 1000 Hutchinson River Pkwy, Bronx 10465 (160).

Ohio: St. Rita School for the Deaf (r,d,c; birth to 12th grade), 1720 Glendale-Milford Rd., Cincinnati 45215 (162).

Pennsylvania: Archbishop Ryan School for Hearing Impaired Children (d,c; parent-infant programs through 8th grade), 233 Mohawk Ave., Norwood, PA 19074 (49).

De Paul Institute (d,c; birth through 21 yrs.), 2904 Castlegate Ave., Pittsburgh 15226 (115).

Emotionally and/or Socially Maladjusted

This listing includes facilities for abused, abandoned and neglected as well as emotionally disturbed children and youth.

Alabama: St. Mary's Home for Children (r,c; referred from agencies), 4350 Moffat Rd., Mobile 36618 (44).

California: Hanna Boys Center (r,b; 10-15 yrs. at intake; school, 4th to 10th grade), Box 100, Sonoma 95476 (107). Treatment center and therapeutic special school for boys with emotional problems, behavior disorders, learning disabilities.

Rancho San Antonio (r,b; 13-17 yrs.), 21000 Plummer St., Chatsworth 91311 (102).

St. Vincent's (r,d,g; 12-17 yrs.), 4200 Calle Real, P.O. Box 669, Santa Barbara 93102 (14). Rehabilitation programs for girls on probation. Also offers affordable housing and therapy to adult mothers of young children (r,d,w; 18 yrs. and over) (21).

Colorado: Mt. St. Vincent Home (r,c; 5-13 yrs.), 4159 Lowell Blvd., Denver 80211 (45). Day treatment (5-13 yrs.), same address (16).

Connecticut: St. Francis Home for Children (r,d,c; 4-17 yrs.), 651 Prospect St., New Haven 06511 (70).

Mt. St. John (r,b; 11-16 yrs.), 135 Kirtland St., Deep River 06417 (77). Home and school for boys.

Delaware: Our Lady of Grace Home for Children (r,d,c; 6-12 yrs.), 487 E. Chestnut Hill Rd., Newark 19713 (14).

Seton Villa, Siena Hall and Children's Home (r,c; group home; 12-18 yrs,; mothers and their children), c/o 2307 Kentmere Pkwy, Wilmington 19806 (44).

Florida: Boystown of Florida (r,b; 12-16 yrs.; group home), 11400 S.W. 137th Ave., Miami 33186 (43).

Georgia: Village of St. Joseph (r,c; 6-16 yrs.), 2969 Butner Rd. S.W., Atlanta 30331. Residential care center for emotionally disturbed children.

Illinois: Guardian Angel Home (d,c; r,b), 1550 Plainfield Rd., Joliet 60435 (35).

Maryville Academy (r,c; 6-18 yrs.), 1150 North River Rd., Des Plaines 60016.

Mission of Our Lady of Mercy, Mercy Home for Boys and Girls (r,d,c; 15-18 yrs.), 1140 W. Jackson Blvd., Chicago 60607 (100).

St. Joseph's Carondelet Child Center (r,b, 5-21 yrs.; d.c.,5-18 yrs., 739 E. 35th St., Chicago 60616 (134).

Indiana: Gibault School for Boys (r; 10-18 yrs.), 6301 South U.S. Highway 41, P.O. Box 2316, Terre Haute 47802 (147).

Hoosier Boys Town (r; 10-18 yrs.), 7403 Cline Ave., Schererville 46375 (68).

Kentucky: Boys' Haven (r; 12-18 yrs.), 2301 Goldsmith Lane, Louisville 40218 (67).

Maryhurst School (r,g; 13-17 yrs.), 1015 Dorsey Lane, Louisville 40223 (55).

Louisiana: Hope Haven Center (r,c; 5-18 yrs.), 1101 Barataria Blvd., Marrero 70072 (150). Residential treatment center and school.

Maison Marie Group Home (r,g; 14-18 yrs.), 3020 Independence St., Metairie 70006.

Maryland: Good Shepherd Center (r,g; 13-18 yrs.), 4100 Maple Ave., Baltimore. 21227 (105).

Massachusetts: The Brightside for Families and Children (r,d,c; 6-16 yrs.), 2112 Riverdale St., W. Springfield 01089.

McAuley Nazareth Home for Boys (r; 6-13 yrs.), 77 Mulberry St., Leicester 01524 (16). Residential treatment center.

St. Vincent Home (r,c 5-22 yrs.), 2425 Highland Ave., Fall River 02720 (62). Residential treatment center.

Michigan: Boysville of Michigan, Inc. (r,d,c; 13-17 yrs.), Corporate offices, 8759 Clinton-Macon Rd., Clinton 49236 (650). Facilities located throughout the state and northern Ohio.

Don Bosco Hall (r,b; 13-17 years.), 10001 Petoskey Ave., Detroit 48204 (35).

Vista Maria (r,g; 11-18 yrs.), 20651 W. Warren Ave., Dearborn Heights 48127 (150).

Minnesota: St. Cloud Children's Home (r,c; 8-18 yrs.), 1726 7th Ave. S., St. Cloud 56301 (90). Day Treatment Program (d,c; 7-14 yrs.), same address (12). Intensive Care Unit (r,c; 13-17 yrs.), Box 1006, Fergus Falls 56538 (22).

St. Elizabeth Home (r,c; 18 yrs. and older), 306 15th Ave. N., St. Cloud 56301 (14). Primarily for mentally ill.

Missouri: Child Center of Our Lady (r,d,c; 5-14 yrs.), 7900 Natural Bridge Rd., St. Louis. 63121 (60).

Marygrove (r,d,c; 6-21 yrs.) (97); intense treatment unit (r,b; 13-18 yrs) (13); overnight crises care (r,d,c; birth to 18 yrs.) (8), 2705 Mullanphy Lane, Florissant. 63031. Sequoia Group Home (r,g; 17-21 yrs.) (10); Sycamore House, Foster Care (r,c, 6-21 yrs. (3).

St. Joseph's Home for Boys (r,d,b; 6-14 yrs.), 4753 S. Grand Blvd., St. Louis 63111 (50).

Montana: Big Sky Ranch (r,g; 12-18 yrs.), P.O. Box 1128, Glendive 59330 (8). Moderate level group home.

Nebraska: Father Flanagan's Boys' Home (r,c; 10-16 yrs.), 14100 Crawford St., Boys Town 68010 (556). Boys Town National Research Hospital (r,d,c; 1-18 yrs.), 555 N. 30th St., Omaha 68131. Center for Abused Handicapped Children; diagnosis of speech, language and hearing problems in children. Boys Town also has various facilities or programs in Brooklyn, N.Y.; Portsmouth, R.I.; Philadelphia, Pa.; Washington, D.C.; Tallahassee, Orlando and Delray Beach, Fla.; Atlanta, Ga.; New Orleans, La.; San Antonio, Tex., Las Vegas, Nev., and southern California.

New Jersey: Catholic Community Services/Mt. Carmel Guild, 1160 Raymond Blvd., Newark 07102.

Collier Group Home (r,g; 13-18 yrs.), 180 Spring St., Red Bank 07701 (10).

Collier High School (d,c; 13-18 yrs.), 160 Conover Rd., Wickatunk 07765 (140).

Mt. St. Joseph Children's Center (r,d,b; 6-14 yrs.), 124 Shepherd Lane, Totowa 07512 (32).

New York: The Astor Home for Children (r,d,c; 5-12 yrs.), 36 Mill St., P.O. Box 5005, Rhinebeck 12572 (75). Child Guidance Clinics/Day Treatment (Rhinebeck, Poughkeepsie, Beacon, Bronx). Head Start - Day Care (Poughkeepsie, Beacon, Red Hook, Dover, Millerton).

Baker Victory Services, 780 Ridge Rd. Lackawanna 14218.

Good Shepherd Services (r,d,c), 305 Seventh Ave. 10001. City-wide residential programs for adolescents (12-21 yrs.), foster care and adoption services (0-21 yrs.); training institute for human services workers; day treatment program (13-18 yrs.); community-based neighborhood family services in South Brooklyn Community (0-adult), LaSalle School (r,d,b; 12-18 yrs.), 391 Western Ave., Albany 12203 (145). Fully accredited Jr./Sr. High School with certified special education program. Juvenile sexual victim/offender treatment, drug and alcohol treatment; community services and preventive programs.

Madonna Heights Services (r,d,g; 12-18 yrs.), 151 Burrs Lane, Dix Hills 11746 (110). Also conducts group homes on Long Island and outpatient programs.

Saint Anne Institute (r,d,g; 12-18 yrs.), 160 N. Main Ave., Albany 12206 (124). Critical level, preventive services. Sex abuse prevention and juvenile sex offender programs, substance abuse program. Regents accredited school. Special education pre-school (3-4 yrs.).

St. Catherine's Center for Children (r,d,c; birth through 12 yrs.), 40 N. Main Ave., Albany 12203. Group homes, day treatment, prevention and therapeutic family programs.

St. John's of Rockaway Beach (r,b; 9-21 yrs.), 144 Beach 111th St., Rockaway Park 11694 (100). Programs include Diagnostic centers and independent living programs.

North Dakota: Home on the Range (r,c; 10-18 yrs.), 16351 I-94, Sentinel Butte 58654 (79). Residential and emergency shelter therapeutic programs.

Home on the Range — Red River Victory Ranch (r,b; 10-18 yrs.), P.O. Box 9615, Fargo 58106 (12). Residential chemical addictions program.

Ohio: Diocesan Child Guidance Center, Inc. (d,c; preschool) Outpatient counseling program (c; 2-18 yrs.), 840 W. State St., Columbus 43222.

Marycrest (r,g; 13-18 yrs.), 7800 Brookside Rd., Independence 44131 (70). Residential treatment and transitional living for adolescent girls and adolescent mothers.

Catholic Charities Services/Parmadale (r,c; 12-18 yrs.), 6753 State Rd., Parma 44134.

Rosemont (r,g;d,c; 11-18 yrs.), 2440 Dawnlight Ave., Columbus 43211 (150). Mental health and AOD services; outreach services include baby day care (birth-3 yrs.).

Oregon: St. Mary's Home for Boys (r; 10-18 yrs.), 16535 S.W. Tualatin Valley Highway, Beaverton 97006 (56). Day treatment (20).

Pennsylvania: Auberle (r,c; 7-18 yrs.), 1101 Hartman St., McKeesport 15132 (181). Residential treatment for boys; emergency shelter care, foster care, group home for girls and family preservation program.

De LaSalle in Towne (d,b; 14-17 yrs.), 25 S. Van Pelt St., Philadelphia 19103 (80).

De LaSalle Vocational Day Treatment (b; 15-18 yrs.), P.O. Box 344 - Street Rd. and Bristol Pike, Bensalem 19020 (120).

Gannondale (r,g; 12-17 yrs.), 4635 E. Lake Rd., Erie 16511 (45).

Harborcreek Youth Services (r,d,c; 10-17 yrs.), 5712 Iroquois Ave., Harborcreek 16421 (150). Also conducts group homes.

Holy Family Institute (r,d,c; 0-18 yrs.), 8235 Ohio River Blvd., Emsworth 15202 (125). Also conducts in-home services, foster care and group homes.

Lourdesmont Good Shepherd Youth and Family Services (r,g;d,c; 12-17 yrs.), 537 Venard Rd., Clarks Summit 18411 (100).

St. Gabriel's Hall (r,b; 10-18 yrs.), P.O. Box 7280, Audubon 19407 (220). Also conducts group homes.

St. Michael's School (r,b; d,c; 12-17 yrs.), Box 370, Tuckhannock 18657. Also conducts group homes, day treatment and educational programs.

Tennessee: DeNeuville Heights School for Girls (r; 12-17 yrs.), 3060 Baskin St., Memphis 38127 (52).

St. Peter Home (r,g; 13-18 yrs.), 1805 Poplar, Memphis 38104 (74).

Texas: St. Joseph Adolescent and Family Counseling Center (c; 13-17 yrs.), 325 W. 12th St., LB #3, Suite 103, Dallas 75208 (20).

Washington: Morning Star Boys Ranch (Spokane Boys' Ranch, Inc.), (r,b; 10-18 yrs.), Box 8087 Manito Station, Spokane 99203 (30).

Wisconsin: Our Lady of Charity Center (r,c; 10-17 yrs.), 2640 West Point Rd., P.O. Box 11737, Green Bay 54304.

St. Charles Youth and Family Services (r,d,b; 12-18 yrs.), 151 S. 84th St., Milwaukee 53214 (63).

Wyoming: St. Joseph's Children's Home (r,c; 6-18 yrs.), P.O. Box 1117, Torrington 82240 (50). Also conducts group home. Newell Children's Center (r,c; 6-18 years), same address (12).

Developmentally Challenged

This listing includes facilities for children, youth, and adults with learning disabilities.

Alabama: Father Purcell Memorial Exceptional Children's Center (r, c; birth to 10 yrs.), 2048 W. Fairview Ave., Montgomery 36108 (58). Skilled nursing facility.

Father Walter Memorial Child Care Center (r,c; birth-12 yrs.), 2815 Forbes Dr., Montgomery 36110 (44). Skilled nursing facility.

California: Child Study Center of St. John's Hospital (d,c; birth-18 yrs.), 1339 - 20th St., Santa Monica. 90404 (80).

St. Madeleine Sophie's Center (d,c; 18 yrs. and older), 2111 E. Madison Ave., El Cajon 92019 (142).

Tierra del Sol Foundation (d,c; 18 yrs. and older), 9919 Sunland Blvd., Sunland 91040 (200); 14547 Gilmore St., Van Nuys 91411 (50).

Connecticut: Gengras Center (d,c; 3-21 yrs.), St. Joseph College, 1678 Asylum Ave., W. Hartford 06117 (112).

Villa Maria Education Center (d,c; 6-14 yrs.), 161 Sky Meadow Dr., Stamford 06903 (60). For children with learning disabilities.

District of Columbia: Lt. Joseph P. Kennedy, Jr., Institute (d,c; 6 weeks to 5 yrs. for Kennedy Institute for Child Development Center; 6-21 yrs. for Kennedy School; 18 yrs. and older for training and employment, therapeutic and residential services). Founded in 1959 for people of all ages with developmental disabilities and their families in the Washington archdiocese. Heaquarters: 801 Buchanan St. N.E. Washington 20017. Other locations in District of Columbia and Maryland. No enrollment limit.

Florida: L'Arche Harbor House, (c; 20 yrs. and older; community home), 700 Arlington Rd., Jacksonville 32211.

Marian Center Services for Developmentally Handicapped and Mentally Retarded (r,d,c; 2-21 yrs.), 15701 Northwest 37th Ave., Opa Locka 33054. Pre-school, school, workshop residence services.

Morning Star School (d,c; 4-16 yrs.), 725 Mickler Rd., Jacksonville 32211 (110). For children with learning disabilities.

Morning Star School (d,c; school age), 954 Leigh Ave., Orlando 32804 (55).

Morning Star School (d,c; 6-14 yrs.), 4661-80th Ave. N., Pinellas Park 34665 (60). For children with learning disabilities and other learning handicaps.

Morning Star School (d,c; 6-16 yrs.), 210 E. Linebaugh Ave., Tampa 33612. (87). For children with learning disabilities.

Georgia: St. Mary's Home (r,c), 2170 E. Victory Dr., Savannah 31404.

Illinois: Bartlett Learning Center (r,d,c; 3-21 yrs.), 801 W. Bartlett Rd., Bartlett 60103 (121).

Brother James Court (r, men over 18 yrs.), 2500 St. James Rd., Springfield 62707 (96).

Good Shepherd Manor (men; 18 yrs. and older), Little Brothers of the Good Shepherd, P.O. Box 260, Momence. 60954 (120). Resident care for developmentally disabled men.

Misericordia Home South (r,c), 2916 W. 47th St., Chicago 60632 (130). For severely and profoundly impaired children.

Misericordia Home - Heart of Mercy Village (r,c; 6-45 yrs.), 6300 North Ridge, Chicago 60660 (400).

Mt. St. Joseph (developmentally disabled women; over age 21), 24955 N. Highway 12, Lake Zurich 60047 (160).

St. Coletta's of Illinois (r,d,; 6 to adult), 123rd and Wolf Rd., Palos Park 60464: St. Coletta's Residential Program (111 in 19 group homes and apartments); Lt. Joseph P. Kennedy, Jr., School (50d, 80r); Kennedy Job Training Center (100d, 40r).

St. Francis School for Exceptional Children (r,c; 6-12 yrs.), 1209 S. Walnut Ave., Freeport 61032 (44).

St. Mary of Providence (r,women; 18 yrs. and older), 4200 N. Austin Ave., Chicago 60634 (96). Day program (c; 6-21 yrs.).

St. Rose Center (d,c; 21 yrs. and older), 4911 S. Hoyne Ave., Chicago 60609 (60). For mentally handicapped adults.

St. Vincent Community Living Facility (r,c; adults, over 18 yrs.) (20), and St. Vincent Supported Living Arrangement (r,c; adults, over 18 yrs.) (20), 659 E. Jefferson St., Freeport 61032.

Springfield Developmental Center (m; 21 yrs. and over), 2500 St. James Rd., Springfield 62707.

Vocational Training

Indiana: Marian Day School (d,c; 6-16 yrs.), 700 Herndon Dr., Evansville 47711 (35). For learning disabled and mild mentally retarded.

Kansas: Lakemary Center, Inc. (r,d,c), 100

Lakemary Dr., Paola 66071 (200). Children and adults.

Kentucky: Pitt Academy (d,c), 4605 Poplar Level Rd., Louisville 40213 (75).

Louisiana: Department of Special Education, Archdiocese of New Orleans, St. Michael Special School (d,c; 6-21 yrs.), 1522 Chippewa St., New Orleans 70130.

Holy Angels Residential Facility (r,c; teen-age, 14 yrs. and older), 10450 Ellerbe Rd., Shreveport 71106 (180).

Ocean Avenue Community Home, 361 Ocean Ave., Gretna 70053. Group home (6).

Padua Community Services (r,c; birth-25 yrs.), 200 Beta St., Belle Chasse 70037 (32).

St. Jude the Apostle, 1430 Claire Ave., Gretna 70053. Group home, adults (6).

St. Mary's Residential Training School (r,c: 3-22 yrs.), P.O. Drawer 7768, Alexandria 71306 (152).

St. Peter the Fisherman, 62269 Airport Dr., Slidell 70458. Group home (6).

St. Rosalie (r; men 18 and up), 119 Kass St., Gretna 70056. Group home (6).

Sts. Mary and Elizabeth, 720 N. Elm St., Metairie 70003. Group home; men, ages 18-80 (6).

Maryland: The Benedictine School for Exceptional Children (r,c; 6-21 yrs.), 14299 Benedictine Lane, Ridgely 21660 (145). Also conducts Habilitation Center (r,c; 17 yrs. and older) (50) and 17 community-based homes (21 yrs. and older).

Francis X. Gallagher Services (r), 2520 Pot Spring Rd., Timonium 21093 (192). Adult vocational program (124); adult medical program (100).

St. Elizabeth School and Habilitation Center (d,c; 11-21 yrs.), 801 Argonne Dr., Baltimore 21218 (120).

Massachusetts: Cardinal Cushing School and Training Center (r,d,c; 16-22 yrs.), Hanover 02339 (116 r; 28d).

Mercy Centre (d,c; 3-22 yrs. and over), 25 West Chester St., Worcester 01605 (176).

St. Coletta Day School (d,c; 3-22 yrs.), 85 Washington St., Braintree 02184 (70).

Michigan: Our Lady of Providence Center (r,g; 11-30 yrs., d,c; 26 yrs. and older), 16115 Beck Rd., Northville. 48118 (100).

St. Louis Center and School (r,d,b; 6-18 yrs. child care; 18-36 yrs. adult foster care), 16195 Old U.S. 12, Chelsea 48118 (68).

Minnesota: Mother Teresa Home (r,c; 18 yrs. and older), 101-10th Ave. N., Cold Spring 56320 (14).

St. Francis Home (r,c; 18 yrs. and older), 25-2nd St. N., Waite Park 56387 (4).

St. Luke's Home (r,; 18 yrs. and older), 411 8th Ave. N., Cold Springs 56320.

Missouri: Department of Special Education, Archdiocese of St. Louis, 4472 Lindell Blvd., St. Louis. 63108. Serves children with developmental disabilities, mental retardation or learning disabilities; services include special ungraded day classes in 8 parish schools (280).

Good Shepherd Homes (residential for developmentally disabled men; 18 yrs. and up), The Community of the Good Shepherd, 10101 James A. Reed Rd., Kansas City 64134 (30).

St.Mary's Special School (r,c; 5-21 yrs.), 1724 Redman, St. Louis 63138 (24). St. Mary's Supported Living (r,c) (24); suprvised homes for adolescents or adults. St. Mary's Early Intervention (d,c) (30); early intervention for toddlers.

Nebraska: Madonna School for Exceptional Children (d,c; 5-21 yrs.), 2537 N. 62nd St., Omaha 68104 (65). Children with learning problems.

Villa Marie School and Home for Exceptional Children (r,d,c; 6-18 yrs.), P.O. Box 80328, Lincoln 68501 (18).

New Jersey: Archbishop Damiano School (d,c; 3-21 yrs.), 1145 Delsea Dr., Westville Grove 08093.

Catholic Community Services, Archdiocese of Newark, 1160 Raymond Blvd., Newark 07102. Services include: Mt. Carmel Guild, St. Anthony's and St. Patrick's Special Education Schools (see separate entries).

Department of Special Education, Diocese of Camden, 1845 Haddon Ave., Camden 08101. Services include: Archbishop Damiano School (above), and full time programs (d,c; 6-21 yrs.) at 4 elementary (96) and 2 high schools (60) and some religious education programs.

Department for Persons with Disabilities, Diocese of Paterson, 1049 Weldon Rd., Oak Ridge, N.J. 07438. Services include 8 residential programs for adults, one adult training center, family support services.

Felician School for Exceptional Children (d,c; 5-21 yrs.), 260 S. Main St., Lodi 07644 (145).

McAuley School for Exceptional Children (d,c; 5-21 yrs.), 1633 Rt. 22 at Terrill Rd., Watchung 07060 (48).

Mt. Carmel Guild Special Education School (d,c ; 6-21 yrs.), 60 Kingsland Ave., Kearny 07032.

St. Anthony's Special Education School (d,c), 25 N. 7th St., Belleville 07104.

Sister Georgine School (d,c; 6-17 yrs.), 544 Chestnut Ave., Trenton 08611 (30).

St. Patrick's Special Education School (d,c), 72 Central Ave., Newark 07102.

New York: Baker Victory Services (r), 780 Ridge Rd., Lackawanna, N.Y. 14218. Residential care for handicapped and retarded children; nursery school program for emotionally disturbed pre-school children.

Bishop Patrick V. Ahern High School (d,c; 15-21 yrs.), 100 Merrill Ave., Staten Island 10314 (45).

Cantalician Center for Learning (d,c; birth-21 yrs.), 3233 Main St., Buffalo 14214. Infant and pre-school; elementary and secondary; workshop (426). Three group homes. Rehabilitation, day treatment and senior rehabilitation programs.

Catholic Charities Residential Services, Rockville Center Diocese, 269 W. Main St., Bay Shore 11706. Conducts residences for developmentally disabled adults (88).

Cobb Memorial School (r,d,c; 5-21 yrs.), 100-300 Mt. Presentation Way, Altamont 12009 (32).

Joan Ann Kennedy memorial Preschool (d,c; 3-5 yrs.), 26 Sharpe Ave., Staten Island 10302 (32).

L'Arche (r, adults), 1232 Teall Ave., Syracuse 13206 (12). Homes where assistants and persons with developmental disabilities share life, following the philosophy of Jean Vanier. Member of International L'Arche Federation.

Maryhaven Center of Hope (r,d,c; school age to adult), Myrtle Ave., Port Jefferson 11777. Offers variety of services.

Mercy Home for Children (r,c), 310 Prospect Park West, Brooklyn 11215. Conducts six residences for adolescents and young adults who are developmentally disabled: Visitation, Warren, Vincent Haire, Santulli and Littlejohn residences (Brooklyn), Kevin Keating Residence (Queens) (72).

Office for Disabled Persons, Catholic Charities, Diocese of Brooklyn, 191 Joralemon St., Brooklyn 11201. Services include: adult day treatment center; community residences for mentally retarded adults; special events for disabled children (from age 3) and adults.

Office for Disabled Persons, Archdiocese of New York, 1011 First Ave., New York 10022. Services include consultation and referral, variety of services for deaf, blind, mentally retarded, mentally ill.

School of the Holy Childhood (d,c; 5-21 yrs.), 100 Groton Parkway, Rochester 14623 (115). Adult program, 18-50 yrs (80).

Seton Foundation for Learning (d,c; 5-15 yrs.), 104 Gordon St., Staten Is. 10304 (44).

North Carolina: Holy Angels (r,c; birth to adult), 6600 Wilkinson Blvd., P.O. Box 710, Belmont 28012 (65).

North Dakota: Friendship, Inc. (r,d,c; all ages), 3004 11th St. South, Fargo 58103 (305).

Ohio: Julie Billiart School (d,c; 6-12 yrs.), 4982 Clubside Rd., Cleveland 44124 (125). Non-graded school for children with learning problems.

Mary Immaculate School (d,c; 6-14 yrs.), 3837 Secor Rd., Toledo 43623 (80). For children with learning disabilities.

OLA/St. Joseph Center (d,c; 6-16 yrs.), 2346 W. 14th St., Cleveland 44113 (80).

Rose Mary, The Johanna Graselli Rehabilitation and Education Center (r,c; 5 yrs. and older), 19350 Euclid Ave., Cleveland 44117 (84).

St. John's Villa (r,c; continued care and training, 15 yrs. and over), P.O. Box 457, Carrollton 44615 (143).

Oregon: Providence Montessori School Early Intervention Program (d,c; 3-5 yrs.), 830 N.E. 47th Ave., Portland 97213 (12).

Pennsylvania: Clelian Heights School for Exceptional Children (r,d,c; 5-21 yrs.), R.D. 9, Box 607, Greensburg 15601 (95). Also conducts re-socialization program (r,d,c; young adults).

Divine Providence Village (adults), 686 Old Marple Rd., Springfield 19064 (96).

Don Guanella Village: Don Guanella School (r,d,b; 6-21 yrs.) and C.K. Center (r; adults, post-school age), 1797-1799 S. Sproul Rd., Springfield 19064.

John Paul II, Center for Special Learning (d,c; 3-21 yrs.), 450 S. 6th St., Reading 19602 (65).

McGuire Memorial (r,d,c; 18 mos. to adult.), 2119 Mercer Rd., New Brighton 15066 (99). Also provides respite cre and adult training day program

Mercy Special Learning Center (d,c; 3-21 yrs. and early intervention), 830 S. Woodward St., Allentown 18103 (90).

Our Lady of Confidence Day School (d,c; 4½-21 yrs.), 10th and Lycoming Sts., Philadelphia 19140 (140).

Queen of the Universe Day Center (d,c; 4½-16 yrs.), 2443 Trenton Rd., Levittown 19056 (48).

St. Anthony School Programs (d,c; 5-21 yrs.), 2718 Custer Ave., Pittsburgh 15227 (100). Inclusive education at 9 sites throughout Allegheny County.

St. Joseph Center for Special Learning (d,c; 4-21 yrs.), 2075 W. Norwegian St., Pottsville 17901 (50).

St. Joseph's Center (r,d,c; birth-10 yrs.), 2010 Adams Ave., Scranton 18509 (90).

St. Katherine Day School (d,c; 4½-21 yrs.), 930 Bowman Ave., Wynnewood 19096 (135).

Tennessee: Madonna Learning Center, Inc., for Retarded Children (d,c; 5-16 yrs.), 7007 Poplar Ave., Germantown 38138 (52).

Texas: Notre Dame of Dallas School (d,c; 3-21 yrs.), 2018 Allen St., Dallas, Tex. 75204. Academic and vocational training for developmentally handicapped.

Virginia: St. Coletta School (d,c; 5-22 yrs.), 3130 Lee Highway, Arlington 22201 (25). For developmentally disabled. Services include: occupational, physical and language therapy; vocational program with job search, placement, training and follow-up services.

St. Mary's Infant Home (r,c; birth to 14 yrs.), 317 Chapel St., Norfolk 23504 (88). For multiple handicapped.

Wisconsin: St Coletta School, W495 Hwy 18, Jefferson 53549. Year round special education programs for adolescents and adults; pre-vocational and vocational skills training; residential living alternatives. Young adult population. Employment opportunities for those who qualify (500).

St. Coletta Day School (c; 8-17 yrs.), 1740 N. 55th St., Milwaukee. 53208 (12).

Orthopedically/Physically Challenged

Pennsylvania: St. Edmond's Home for Children (r,c; 1-21 yrs.)., 320 S. Roberts Rd., Rosemont 19010 (40).

Virginia: St. Joseph Villa Housing Corp. (adults), 8000 Brook Rd., Richmond 23227 (60 apartments).

Visually Challenged

Maine: Educational Services for Blind and Visually Impaired Children (Catholic Charities, Maine), 1066 Kenduskeag Ave., Bangor 04401; 66 Western Ave., Fairfield 04937; 15 Westminster St., Lewiston 04240; 562 Congress St., Portland 04101. Itinerant teachers, instructional materials center.

New Jersey: St. Joseph's School for the Blind (r,d,c; 3-21 yrs.), 253 Baldwin Ave., Jersey City 07306 (60). For visually impaired, multiple handicapped.

New York: Lavelle School for the Blind (d,c; 3-21 yrs.), East 221st St. and Paulding Ave., Bronx 10469 (100). For visually impaired, multiple handicapped.

Pennsylvania: St. Lucy Day School (d,c; pre-K to 8th grade), 130 Hampden Rd., Upper Darby 19082. For children with visual impairments.

RETREATS, SPIRITUAL RENEWAL PROGRAMS

There is great variety in retreat and renewal programs, with orientations ranging from the traditional to teen encounters. Central to all of them are celebration of the liturgy and deepening of a person's commitment to faith and witness in life.

Features of many of the forms are as follows.

Traditional Retreats: Centered around conferences and the direction of a retreat master; oriented to the personal needs of the retreatants; including such standard practices as participation in Mass, reception of the sacraments, private and group prayer, silence and meditation, discussions.

Team Retreat: Conducted by a team of several leaders or directors (priests, religious, lay persons) with division of subject matter and activities according to their special skills and the nature and needs of the group.

Closed Retreat: Involving withdrawal for a period of time – overnight, several days, a weekend – from everyday occupations and activities.

Open Retreat: Made without total disengagement from everyday involvements, on a part-time basis.

Private Retreat: By one person, on a kind of do-it-yourself basis with the one-to-one assistance of a director.

Special Groups: With formats and activities geared to particular groups; e.g., members of Alcoholics Anonymous, vocational groups and apostolic groups.

Marriage Encounters: Usually weekend periods of husband-wife reflection and dialogue; introduced into the U.S. from Spain in 1967.

Charismatic Renewal: Featuring elements of the movement of the same name; "Spirit-oriented," communitarian and flexible, with spontaneous and shared prayer, personal testimonies of faith and witness.

Christian Community: Characterized by strong community thrust.

Teens Encounter Christ (TEC), SEARCH: Formats adapted to the mentality and needs of youth, involving experience of Christian faith and commitment in a community setting.

Christian Maturity Seminars: Similar to teen encounters in basic concept but different to suit persons of greater maturity.

Renew International: Spiritual renewal process involving the entire parish. Office, 1232 George St., Plainfield, NJ 07062. Director, Msgr. Thomas A. Kleissler.

Cursillo: see separate entry.

Conference

Retreats International Inc.: National Office, Box 1067, Notre Dame, IN 46556. The first organization for promoting retreats in the U.S. was started in 1904 in New York. Its initial efforts and the gradual growth of the movement led to the formation in 1927 of the National Catholic Laymen's Retreat Conference, the forerunner of the men's division of Retreats International. The women's division developed from the National Laywomen's Retreat Movement which was founded in Chicago in 1936. The men's and women's divisions merged July 9, 1977. The services of the organization include an annual summer institute for retreat and pastoral ministry, regional conferences for retreat center leadership and area meetings of directors and key leadership in the retreat movement. The officers are: Episcopal advisor, Auxiliary Bishop Robert Morneau of Green Bay; Pres., Larry Novakowski; Exec. Dir., Anne M. Luther.

HOUSES OF RETREAT AND RENEWAL

(Principal sources: *Catholic Almanac* survey; *The Official Catholic Directory*.)

Abbreviation code: m, men; w, women; mc, married couples; y, youth. Houses and centers without code generally offer facilities to most groups. An asterisk after an abbreviation indicates that the facility is primarily for the group designated but that special groups are also accommodated. Houses furnish information concerning the types of programs they offer.

Alabama: Blessed Trinity Shrine Retreat, 107 Holy Trinity Rd., Holy Trinity 36859; Visitation Sacred Heart Retreat House, 2300 Spring Hill Ave., Mobile 36607.

Alaska: Holy Spirit Retreat House, 10980 Hillside Dr., Anchorage 99516.

Arizona: Franciscan Renewal Center, 5802 E. Lincoln Dr., Scottsdale 85253; Holy Trinity Monastery, P.O. Box 298, St. David 85630, Benedictine community, self-directed/Spirit-directed monastic retreat; Mount Claret Retreat Center, 4633 N. 54th St., Phoenix 85018; Our Lady of Solitude House of Prayer, P.O. Box 1140, Black Canyon City 85324; Redemptorist Picture Rocks Retreat House, 7101 W. Picture Rocks Rd., Tucson 85743.

Arkansas: Brothers and Sisters of Charity, Little Portion Hermitage, 350 C R 048, Barryville, 72616-8505; Little Portion Retreat and Training Center, Rt. 4, Box 430, Eureka Springs 72632; St. Scholastica Retreat Center, P.O. Box 3489, Ft. Smith 72913.

California: Angela Center, 535 Angela Dr., Santa Rosa 95401; Christ the King Retreat Center, 6520 Van Maren Lane, Citrus Heights 95621; Claretian Retreat Center, 1119 Westchester Pl., Los Angeles 90019; De Paul Center, 1105 Bluff Rd., Montebello 90640; El Carmelo Retreat House, P.O. Box 446, Redlands 92373; Heart of Jesus Retreat Center, 2927 S. Greenville St., Santa Ana 92704; Holy Spirit Retreat Center, 4316 Lanai Rd., Encino 91436; Holy Transfiguration Monastery (m*), Monks of Mt. Tabor (Byzantine Ukrainian), 17001 Tomki Rd., P.O. Box 217, Redwood Valley, Calif. 95470; Jesuit Retreat House, 300 Manresa Way, Los Altos 94022; Madonna of Peace Renewal Center (y), P.O. Box 71, Copperopolis 95228; Mary and Joseph Retreat Center, 5300 Crest Rd., Rancho Palos Verdes 90275; Marywood Retreat Center, 2811 E. Villa Real Dr., Orange 92863-1595; Mater Dolorosa Retreat Center, 700 N. Sunnyside Ave., Sierra Madre 91024; Mercy Center, 2300 Adeline Dr., Burlingame 94010; Mission San Luis Rey Retreat, 4050 Mission Ave., Oceanside, 92057-6402; Mount Alverno Retreat and Conference Center, 3910 Bret Harte Dr., Redwood City 94061; New Camaldoli Hermitage, Big Sur 93920; Poverello of Assisi Retreat House, 1519 Woodworth St., San Fernando 91340; Presentation Education and Retreat Center, 19480 Bear Creek Rd., Los Gatos 95033; Prince of Peace Abbey, 650 Benet Hill Rd., Oceanside 92054; Pro Sanctity Spirituality Center, 205 S. Pine St., Fullerton 92633 (for day use); Sacred Heart Retreat House (w*), 920 E. Alhambra Rd., Alhambra 91801; St. Andrew's Abbey Retreat House, Valyermo 93563; St. Anthony's Retreat House, P.O. Box 249, Three Rivers 93271; St. Clare's Retreat, 2381 Laurel Glen Rd., Soquel 95073; St. Francis Retreat, P.O. Box 970, San Juan Bautista 95045; St. Francis Youth Center (y), 2400 E. Lake Ave., Watsonville 95076; St. Joseph's Salesian Youth Center, P.O. Box 1639, 8301 Arroyo Dr., Rosemead 91770; St. Mary's Seminary and Retreat House, 1964 Las Canoas Rd., Santa Barbara 93105; San Damiano Retreat, P.O. Box 767, Danville 94526; San Miguel Retreat House, P.O. Box 69, San Miguel 93451; Santa Sabina Center, 25 Magnolia Ave., San Rafael 94901; Serra Retreat, 3401 S. Serra Rd., Box 127, Malibu 90265; Starcross Community, 34500 Annapolis Rd., Annapolis 95412; Villa Maria del Mar, Santa Cruz, 2-1918 E. Cliff Dr., Santa Cruz 95062; Villa Maria — House of Prayer (w), 1252 N. Citrus Dr., La Habra 90631.

Colorado: Benet Hill Monastery, 2555 N. Chelton Rd., Colorado Springs 80909; Benet Pines Retreat Center, 15780 Highway 83, Colorado Springs 80921; Sacred Heart Retreat House, Box 185, Sedalia 80135; Spiritual Life Institute (individuals only), Nada Hermitage, P.O. Box 219, Crestone 81131. Private desert retreats with minimal direction.

Connecticut: Spiritual Life Center, Archdiocese of Hartford, 467 Bloomfield Ave., Bloomfield 06002; Edmundite Apostolate and Conference Center, Enders Island, Mystic 06355; Emmaus Spiritual Life Center, 24 Maple Ave., Uncasville 06382; Holy Family Retreat, 303 Tunxis Rd., West Hartford 06107; Immaculata Retreat House, P.O. Box 55, Willimantic 06226; Mercy Center at Madison, P.O. Box 191, 167 Neck Rd., Madison 06443; My Father's House, Box 22, North Moodus Rd., Moodus 06469; Our Lady of Calvary Retreat (w*), 31 Colton St., Farmington 06032; Trinita Retreat Center, 595 Town Hill Rd., Rt. 219, New Hartford 06057; Villa Maria Retreat House, 159 Sky Meadow Dr., Stamford 06903.

Delaware: St. Francis Renewal Center, 1901 Prior Rd., Wilmington 19809.

District of Columbia: Washington Retreat House, 4000 Harewood Rd. N.E., Washington 20017.

Florida: Cenacle Retreat House, 1400 S. Dixie Highway, Lantana 33462-5492; Dominican Retreat House, Inc., 7275 S.W. 124th St., Miami 33156; Franciscan Center, 3010 Perry Ave., Tampa 33603; John Paul II Retreat House, 720 N.E. 27th St., Miami 33137; Our Lady of Perpetual Help Retreat and Spirituality Center, 2989 S. Moon Dr., Venice 34292; Saint John Neumann Renewal Center, 685 Miccosukee Rd., Tallahassee 32308; St. Leo Abbey Retreat Center, P.O. Box 2350, St. Leo 33574.

Georgia: Ignatius House, 6700 Riverside Dr. N.W., Atlanta 30328.

Idaho: Nazareth Retreat Center, 4450 N. Five Mile Rd., Boise 83704.

Illinois: Bellarmine Jesuit Retreat House (ma), 175 W. County Line Rd, Barrington 60010; Bishop Lane Retreat House, 7708 E. McGregor Rd., Rockford 61102.; Cabrini Retreat Center, 9430 Golf Rd., Des Plaines 60016; Carmelite Spiritual Center, 8433 Bailey Rd., Darien 60561; Cenacle Retreat House, 513 Fullerton Parkway, Chicago 60614; Cenacle Retreat House, P.O. Box 797, Warrenville 60555.; King's House of Retreats, Henry 61537; La Salle Manor, Christian Brothers Retreat House, 12480 Galena Rd.,

Plano 60545; Retreat and Renewal Center, 700 N. 66th St., Belleville 62223; St. Mary's Retreat House, P.O. Box 608, 14230 Main St., Lemont 60439; Tolentine Center, 20300 Governors Highway, Olympia Fields 60461; Villa Redeemer Retreat Center, 1111 N. Milwaukee Ave., P.O. Box 6, Glenview 60025. **Indiana:** Archabbey Guest House, St. Meinrad Archabbey, St. Meinrad 47577; Benedict Inn Retreat and Conference Center, 1402 Southern Ave., Beech Grove 46107; Fatima Retreat House, 5353 E. 56th St., Indianapolis 46226-1486; John XXIII Center, 407 W. McDonald St., Hartford City 47348; Kordes Enrichment Center, 841 E. 14th St., Ferdinand 47532; Lindenwood, PHJC Ministry Center, P.O. Box 1, Donaldson 46513-0001; Mary's Solitude, St.Mary's, Notre Dame 46556; Mount Saint Francis Retreat Center and Friary, 101 St. Anthony Dr., Mount Saint Francis 47146; Our Lady of Fatima Retreat Center, P.O. Box 929, Notre Dame 46556; Sarto Retreat House, 4200 N. Kentucky Ave., Evansville 47711. **Iowa:** American Martyrs Retreat House, 2209 N. Union Rd., P.O. Box 605, Cedar Falls 50613; Emmanuel House of Prayer Country Retreat and Solitude Center, 4427 Kotts Rd. N.E., Iowa City 52240; New Melleray Guest House, 6500 Melleray Circle, Peosta 52068; Shalom Retreat Center, 1001 Davis Ave., Dubuque 52001. **Kansas:** Manna House of Prayer, 323 East 5th St., Box 675, Concordia 66901; Spiritual Life Center, 7100 E. 45th St., N. Wichita 67226. **Kentucky:** Catherine Spalding Center, P.O. Box 24, Nazareth 40048; Flaget Center, 1935 Lewiston Dr., Louisville 40216; Marydale Retreat Center, 945 Donaldson Hwy., Erlanger 41018; Mt. St. Joseph Retreat Center, 8001 Cummings Rd., Maple Mount 42356; Our Lady of Gethsemani (m, w, private), The Guestmaster, Abbey of Gethsemani, Trappist 40051. **Louisiana:** Abbey Christian Life Center, St. Joseph's Abbey, St. Benedict 70457; Ave Maria Retreat House, HC 62, Box 368 AB, Marrero 70072; Cenacle Retreat House (w*), 5500 St. Mary St., P.O. Box 8115, Metairie 70011; Jesuit Spirituality Center (m,w; directed), P.O. Box C, Grand Coteau 70541; Lumen Christi Retreat Center, 100 Lumen Christi Lane, Hwy. 311, Schriever 70395; Manresa House of Retreats (m), P.O. Box 89, Convent 70723; Maryhill Renewal Center, 600 Maryhill Rd., Pineville 71360; Our Lady of the Oaks Retreat House, P.O. Box D, 214 Church St., Grand Coteau 70541; Regina Coeli Retreat Center, 17225 Regina Coeli Rd., Covington 70433. **Maine:** Marie Joseph Spiritual Center, RFD 2, Biddeford 04005; St. Paul Retreat and Cursillo Center, 136 State St., Augusta 04330. **Maryland:** Bon Secours Spiritual Center, Marriottsville 21104; Christian Brothers Spiritual Center (m,w,y), P.O. Box 29, 2535 Buckeyestown Pike, Adamstown 21710; Loyola on the Potomac Retreat House, Faulkner 20632; Msgr. Clare J. O'Dwyer Retreat House (y*), 15523 York Rd., P.O. Box 310, Sparks 21152; Our Lady of Mattaponi Youth Retreat and Conference Center, 11000 Mattaponi Rd., Upper Marlboro 20772. **Massachusetts:** Boston Cenacle Society, 25 Avery St., Dedham 02026; Calvary Retreat Center, 59 South St., P.O. Box 219, Shrewsbury 01545; Campion Renewal Center, 319 Concord Rd., Weston 02193; Don Orione Center, P.O. Box 205, Old Groveland Rd.,

Bradford 01835; Eastern Point Retreat House, Gonzaga Hall, 37 Niles Pond Rd., Gloucester 01930; Espousal Center, 554 Lexington St., Waltham 02452; Esther House of Spiritual Renewal, Sisters of St. Anne, 1015 Pleasant St., Worcester 01602; Genesis Spiritual Life Center, 53 Mill St., Westfield 01085; Glastonbury Abbey (Benedictine Monks), 16 Hull St.,Hingham 02043; Holy Cross Fathers Retreat House, 490 Washington St., N. Easton 02356; La Salette Center for Christian Living, 947 Park St., Attleboro 02703; LaSalette Retreat House, 251 Topsfield Rd., Ipswich 01938; Marian Center, 1365 Northampton St., Holyoke 01040 (day and evening programs); Miramar Retreat Center, P.O. Box M, Duxbury, 02331; Mt. Carmel Christian Life Center, Oblong Rd., Box 613, Williamstown 01267; Sacred Heart Retreat Center, Salesians of St. John Bosco, P.O. Box 567, Ipswich 01938; St. Benedict Abbey (Benedictine Monks), 252 Still River Rd., P.O. Box 67, Still River 01467; St. Joseph Villa Retreat Center, Sisters of St. Joseph, 339 Jerusalem Rd., Cohasset 02025; St. Joseph's Abbey Retreat House (m) (Trappist Monks), North Spencer Rd., Spencer 01562; St. Stephen Priory Spiritual Life Center (Dominican), 20 Glen St., Box 370, Dover 02030. **Michigan:** Augustine Center, 2798 U.S. 31 North, Box 84, Conway 49722; Capuchin Retreat, 62460 Mt. Vernon, Box 188, Washington 48094; Colombiere Conference Center, Box 139, 9075 Big Lake Rd., Clarkston 48347; Manresa Jesuit Retreat House, 1390 Quarton Rd., Bloomfield Hills 48304; Queen of Angels Retreat, 3400 S. Washington Rd., P.O. Box 2026, Saginaw 48605; St. Francis Retreat Center, Diocese of Lansing, 703 E. Main St., De Witt 48820; St. Lazare Retreat House, 18600 W. Spring Lake Rd., P.O. Box 462, Spring Lake 49456; St. Mary's Retreat House (w*), 775 W. Drahner Rd., Oxford 48371; St. Paul of the Cross Retreat Center (m*), 23333 Schoolcraft, Detroit 48223. **Minnesota:** Benedictine Center, St. Paul's Monastery, 2675 E. Larpenteur Ave., St. Paul 55109; Catholic Youth Ministry Services (y*), 328 W. Kellogg Blvd., St. Paul 55102; The Cenacle, 1221 Wayzata Blvd., Wayzata 55391; Center for Spiritual Development, 211 Tenth St. S., P.O. Box 538, Bird Island 55310; Christ the King Retreat Center, 621 First Ave. S., Buffalo 55313; Christian Brothers' Retreat Center, 15525 St. Croix Trail North, Marine-on-St. Croix 55047; Franciscan Retreats, Conventual Franciscan Friars, 16385 St. Francis Lane, Prior Lake 55372; Jesuit Retreat House (m), 8243 DeMontreville Trail North, Lake Elmo 55042; Maryhill (m,w*), 1988 Summit Ave., St. Paul 55105; Villa Maria Center, Villa Maria Center, 29847 County 2 Blvd., Frontenac 55026. **Missouri:** The Cenacle, 7654 Natural Bridge Rd., St. Louis 63121; Il Ritiro - The Little Retreat, P.O. Box 38, Eime Rd., Dittmer 63023; Maria Fonte Solitude (private; individual hermitages), P.O. Box 322, High Ridge 63049; Marianist Retreat and Conference Center, P.O. Box 718, Eureka 63025-0718; Mercy Center, 2039 N. Geyer Rd., St. Louis 63131; Our Lady of Assumption Abbey (m,w), Trappists, Rt. 5, Box 1056, Ava 65608-9142; Pallottine Renewal Center, 15270 Old Halls Ferry Rd., Florissant 63034; Queen of Heaven Solitude (private, individual hermitages), Rt. 1, Box 107A, Marionville 65705; White House

Retreat, 7400 Christopher Dr., St. Louis 63129; Windridge Solitude, 1932 W. Linda Lane, Lonedell 63060.

Montana: Sacred Heart Retreat Center, 26 Wyoming Ave., P.O. Box 153, Billings 59103; Ursuline Retreat Centre, 2300 Central Ave., Great Falls 59401.

Nebraska: Crosier Renewal Center, 223 E. 14th St., P.O. Box 789, Hastings 68902; Our Lady of Good Counsel retreat House, R.R. 1, Box 110, 7303 N. 112th St., Waverly 68462-9646.

Nevada: Monastery of Christ in the Mountains, P.O.Box 708, Caliente 89008.

New Hampshire: Epiphany Monastery, 96 Scobie Rd., P.O. Box 60, New Boston 03070; La Salette Shrine (private and small groups), 410 NH, Route 4A, P.O. Box 420, Enfield 03748; Oblate Retreat House, Oblates of Mary Immaculate, 200 Lowell Rd., Hudson 03051.

New Jersey: Bethlehem Hermitage, 82 Pleasant Hill Rd., Chester 07930; Carmel Retreat House, 1071 Ramapo Valley Rd., Mahwah 07430; Cenacle Retreat House, 411 River Rd., Highland Park 08904; Father Judge Apostolic Center (young adults), 1292 Long Hill Rd., Stirling 07980; Felician Retreat House, 35 Windemere Ave., Mt. Arlington 07856; Loyola House of Retreats, 161 James St., Morristown 07960; Marianist Family Retreat Center (families*), 417 Yale Ave., Box 488, Cape May Point 08212-0488; Maris Stella (Vacation Home for Sisters*), 7201 Long Beach Blvd., Harvey Cedars 08008; Mt. St. Francis Retreat House, 474 Sloatsburg Rd., Ringwood 07456; Queen of Peace Retreat House, St. Paul's Abbey, P.O. Box 7, Newton 07860; Sacred Heart Retreat Center (y*, m,w), 20 Old Swartswood Rd., Newton 07860; St. Joseph by the Sea Retreat House, 400 Rte. 35 N., South Mantoloking 08738; St. Pius X Spiritual Life Center, P.O. Box 216, Blackwood 08012; San Alfonso Retreat House, P.O. Box 3098, 755 Ocean Ave., Long Beach 07740; Sanctuary of Mary, Pilgrimage Place, Branchville 07826; Stella Maris Retreat House, 981 Ocean Ave., Elberon 07740; Villa Pauline Retreat House, 350 Bernardsville Rd., Mendham 07945; Xavier Retreat and Conference Center, P.O. Box 211, Convent Station 07961.

New Mexico: Dominican Retreat House, 2348 Pajarito Rd. S.W., Albuquerque 87105; Holy Cross Retreat, Conventual Franciscan Friars, P.O. Box 158, Mesilla Park 88047; Pecos Benedictine Abbey, Pecos 87552; Sacred Heart Retreat, P.O. Box 1989, Gallup 87301.

New York: Bethany Retreat House, County Road 105, Box 1003, Highland Mills 10930; Bethlehem Retreat House, Abbey of the Genesee, Piffard 14533; Bishop Molloy Retreat House, 86-45 Edgerton Blvd., Jamaica, L.I. 11432; Blessed Kateri Retreat House, National Kateri Shrine, P.O. Box 627, Fonda, N.Y. 11432; Cardinal Spellman Retreat House, Passionist Community, 5801 Palisade Ave., Bronx (Riverdale) 10471; Cenacle Center for Spiritual Renewal, 310 Cenacle Rd., Lake Ronkonkoma 11779; Cenacle Retreat House, State Rd., P.O. Box 467, Bedford Village 10506; Christ the King Retreat and Conference Center, 500 Brookford Rd., Syracuse 13224; Cormaria Retreat House, Sag Harbor, L.I. 11963; Dominican Spiritual Life Center, 1945 Union St., Niskayuma 12309; Don Bosco Retreat Center, Box 9000, Filor's Lane, West Haverstraw 10993;

Graymoor Spiritual Life Center, Graymoor, Route 9, P.O. Box 300, Garrison 10524; Monastery of the Precious Blood (w), Ft. Hamilton Parkway and 54th St., Brooklyn 11219 (single day retreats); Mount Alvernia Retreat House, Box 858, Wappingers Falls 12590; Mount Irenaeus Franciscan Mountain Retreat, Holy Peace Friary, P.O. Box 100, West Clarksville, NY 14786; Mount Manresa Retreat House, 239 Fingerboard Rd., Staten Island 10305; Mt. St. Alphonsus Redemptorist Retreat Ministry, P.O. Box 219, Esopus 12429; Notre Dame Retreat House, Box 342, 5151 Foster Rd., Canandaigua 14424; Our Lady of Hope Center, 434 River Rd., Newburgh 12550; Regina Maria Retreat House, 77 Brinkerhoff St., Plattsburgh 12901-2701; St. Andrew's House, 257 St. Andrew's Rd., Walden 12586; St. Columban Center, Diocese of Buffalo, 6892 Lake Shore Rd., P.O. Box 816, Derby 14047; St. Gabriel Retreat House (y, mc), 64 Burns Rd., P.O. Box P, Shelter Island 11965; St. Ignatius Retreat House, P.O. Box 756, Searingtown Rd., Manhasset 11030; St. Josaphat's Retreat House, Basilian Monastery, East Beach Rd., Glen Cove 11542; St. Joseph Center (Spanish Center), 275 W. 230th St., Bronx 10463; St. Mary's Villa, 150 Sisters Servants Lane, Sloatsburg 10974; St. Paul Center, 21-35 Crescent St., Astoria 11105; St. Ursula Retreat Center, P.O. Box 86, Middle Rd. and Blue Point Ave., Blue Point 11715; Stella Maris Retreat Center, 130 E. Genesee St., Skaneateles 13152; Stella Niagara Center of Renewal, 4421 Lower River Rd., Stella Niagara 14144; Tagaste Monastery, 220 Lafayette Ave., Suffern 10901; Trinity Retreat, 1 Pryer Manor Rd., Larchmont 10538.

North Carolina: Avila Retreat Center, 711 Mason Rd., Durham 27712; Living Waters Catholic Reflection Center, 103 Living Waters Lane, Maggie Valley 28751.

North Dakota: Presentation Prayer Center, 1101 32nd Ave. S., Fargo 58103; Queen of Peace Retreat, 1310 Broadway, Fargo 58102.

Ohio: Bergamo Center for Lifelong Learning, 4400 Shakertown Rd., Dayton 45430; Franciscan Renewal Center, Pilgrim House, 321 Clay St., Carey 43316; Friarhurst Retreat House, 8136 Wooster Pike, Cincinnati 45227; Jesuit Retreat House, 5629 State Rd., Cleveland 44134; Loyola of the Lakes, 700 Killinger Rd., Clinton 44216; Maria Stein Center, 2365 St. Johns Rd., Maria Stein 45860; Milford Spiritual Center, 5361 S. Milford Rd., Milford 45150; Our Lady of the Pines, 1250 Tiffin St., Fremont 43420; Sacred Heart Retreat and Renewal Center, 3128 Logan Ave., P.O. Box 6074, Youngstown 44501; St. Joseph Christian Life Center, 18485 Lake Shore Blvd., Cleveland 44119; St. Joseph Renewal Center, 200 St. Francis Ave., Tiffin 44883; St. Therese Retreat Center, Diocese of Columbus, 5277 E. Broad St., Columbus 43213.

Oklahoma: St. Gregory's Abbey, 1900 W. MacArthut, Shawnee 74804.

Oregon: Franciscan Renewal Center, 0858 S.W. Palatine Hill Rd., Portland 97219; Loyola Renewal Center, 3220 S.E. 43rd St., Portland 97206; Mount Angel Abbey Retreat House, 1 Abbey Lane, St. Benedict 97373; Our Lady of Peace Retreat, 3600 S. W. 170th Ave., Beaverton 97006; Sita Retreat Center, P.O.Box 310, Gold Hill 97525; Shalom Prayer Center, Benedictine Sisters, 840 S. Main St., Mt.

Angel 97362-9527; Trappist Abbey Retreat (m,w), P.O. Box 97, Lafayette 97127.

Pennsylvania: Dominican Retreat House, 750 Ashbourne Rd., Elkins Park 19027; Doran Hall Retreat and Renewal Center, 443 Mt. Thor Rd., Greensburg 15601; Fatima House, 601 Rolling Hills Rd., Ottsville 18942; Fatima Renewal Center, 1000 Seminary Rd., Dalton 18414; Gilmary Diocesan Center, 601 Flaugherty Run Rd., Coraopolis 15108-3899; Jesuit Center for Spiritual Growth, Box 223, Church Rd., Wernersville 19565; Kearns Spirituality Center, 9000 Babcock Blvd., Allison Park 15101; Mariawald Renewal Center, P.O. Box 97 (Welch Rd.), Reading 19607; Mount St. Macrina Retreat Center, 510 W. Main St., Box 878, Uniontown 15401; Sisters of St. Benedict of Westmoreland County, St. Emma Retreat House, 1001 Harvey Ave., Greensburg 15601-1494; St. Francis Retreat Center (y*), c/o Dept. of Youth Ministry, 900 W. Market St., Orwigsburg 17961; St. Francis Center for Renewal, Monocacy Manor, 395 Bridle Path Rd., Bethlehem 18017; St. Francis Retreat House, 3918 Chipman Rd., Easton 18042; St. Gabriel's Retreat House, 631 Griffin Pond Rd., Clarks Summit 18411; St. Joseph's in the Hills, 315 S. Warren Ave., Malvern 19355; St. Paul of the Cross Retreat Center, 148 Monastery Ave., Pittsburgh 15203; Saint Raphaela Center, 616 Coopertown Rd., Haverford 19041; St. Vincent Retreat Program (m,w,mc; summers only), Latrobe 15650; Villa of Our Lady Retreat Center (w, mc, y), HCR No. 1, Box 41, Mt. Pocono 18344.

Rhode Island: Bethany Renewal Center, 397 Fruit Hill Ave., N. Providence 02911; Father Marot CYO Center (y), 53 Federal St., Woonsocket 02895; Our Lady of Peace Spiritual Life Center, 333 Ocean Rd., Box 507, Narragansett 02882-0507; St. Dominic Savio Youth Center (y*), Broad Rock Rd., Box 67, Peace Dale 02883.

South Carolina: Springbank Retreat Center, Rt. 2, Box 180, Kingstree 29556.

South Dakota: St. Martin's Community Center, 2110C St. Martin's Dr., Rapid City 57702; Sioux Spiritual Center (for Native Americans), Diocese of Rapid City, HC 77, Box 271, Howes 57748.

Tennessee: Carmelites of Mary Immaculate Center of Spirituality, 610 Bluff Rd., Liberty 37095.

Texas: Bishop DeFalco Retreat Center, 2100 N. Spring, Amarillo 79107; Bishop Rene H. Gracida Retreat Center, Diocese of Corpus Christi, 3036 Saratoga Blvd., Corpus Christi 78415; Bishop Thomas J. Drury Retreat Center, 1200 Lantana St., Corpus Christi 78407; Catholic Renewal Center of North Texas, 4503 Bridge St., Ft. Worth 76103; Cenacle Retreat House, 420 N. Kirkwood, Houston 77079; Christian Renewal Center (Centro de Renovacion Cristiana), Oblates of Mary Immaculate, P.O. Box 635, Dickinson 77539; Holy Family Retreat Center, 9920 N. Major Dr., Beaumont 77713-7618; Holy Name Retreat Center, 430 Bunker Hill Rd., Houston 77024; Holy Spirit Retreat and Conference Center, 501 Century Dr. S., Laredo 78040; Montserrat Retreat House, Lake Dallas 75065; Moye Center, 600 London, Castroville 78009; Oblate Renewal Center, 5700 Blanco Rd., San Antonio 78216; San Juan Retreat House (Nuestra Señora de San Juan Retreat Center), P.O. Box 747, San Juan 78589.

Utah: Abbey of Our Lady of the Holy Trinity (m), 1250 S 9500 E, Huntsville 84317; Our Lady of the Mountains, 1794 Lake St., Ogden 84401-3016.

Virginia: Dominican Retreat, 7103 Old Dominion Dr., McLean 22101-2799; Holy Family Retreat House, The Redemptorists, P.O. 3151, 1414 N. Mallory St., Hampton 23663; Missionhurst Mission Center, 4651 N. 25th St., Arlington 22207; Retreat House, Holy Cross Abbey, Rt. 2, Box 3870, Berryville 22611.

Washington: Immaculate Heart Retreat Center, 6910 S. Ben Burr Rd., Spokane 99223. Palisades Retreat House, P.O. Box 3739, Federal Way 98063; St. Peter the Apostle Retreat Center, 15880 Summitview Rd., Cowiche 98923.

West Virginia: Bishop Hodges Pastoral Center, Rt. 1, Box 9D, Huttonsville, 26273; Cenacle Retreat House, 1114 Virginia St. E., Charleston 25301; Good Counsel Friary, Rt. 7, Box 183, Morgantown 26505; John XXIII Pastoral Center, 100 Hodges Rd., Charleston, W. Va. 25314; Paul VI Pastoral Center, 667 Stone and Shannon Rd., Wheeling 26003; Priest Field Pastoral Center, Rt. 51, Box 133, Kearneysville 25430.

Wisconsin: Archdiocesan Retreat Center, 3501 S. Lake Dr., P.O. Box 07912, Milwaukee 53207; Cardoner Retreat Center, 1501 S. Layton Blvd., Milwaukee 53215; Holy Name Retreat House, Chambers Island; mailing address, 1825 Riverside Drive, P.O. Box 23825, Green Bay 54305; Jesuit Retreat House, 4800 Fahrnwald Rd., Oshkosh 54901; Monte Alverno Retreat Center, 1000 N. Ballard Rd., Appleton 54911; Redemptorist Retreat Center, 1800 N. Timber Trail Lane, Oconomowoc 53066-4897; St. Anthony Retreat Center, 300 E. 4th St., Marathon 54448; St. Bede Retreat and Conference Center, 1190 Priory Rd., P.O. Box 66, Eau Claire 54702; Saint Benedict Center (monastery and ecumenical retreat and conference center), P.O. Box 5070, Madison 53705-0070; St. Francis Retreat Center, 503 S. Browns Lake Dr., P.O. Box 368, Burlington 53105; St. Joseph's Retreat Center, 3035 O'Brien Rd., Bailey's Harbor 54202; St. Vincent Pallotti Center, N6409 Bowers Rd., Elkhorn 53121; Schoenstatt Center, W. 284 N. 698 Cherry Lane, Waukesha 53188.

LEGAL STATUS OF CATHOLIC EDUCATION

The right of private schools to exist and operate in the United States is recognized in law. It was confirmed by the U.S. Supreme Court in 1925 when the tribunal ruled (Pierce v. Society of Sisters, see Church-State Decisions of the Supreme Court) that an Oregon state law requiring all children to attend public schools was unconstitutional.

Private schools are obliged to comply with the education laws in force in the various states regarding such matters as required basic curricula, periods of attendance, and standards for proper accreditation.

The special curricula and standards of private schools are determined by the schools themselves. Thus, in Catholic schools, the curricula include not only the subject matter required by state educational laws but also other fields of study, principally, education in the Catholic faith.

The Supreme Court has ruled that the First Amendment to the U.S. Constitution, in accordance with the No Establishment of Religion Clause of the First Amendment, prohibits direct federal and state aid from public funds to church-affiliated schools. (See several cases in Church-State Decisions of the Supreme Court.)

Public Aid

This prohibition does not extend to all child-benefit and public-purpose programs of aid to students of non-public elementary and secondary schools.

Statutes authorizing such programs have been ruled constitutional on the grounds that they:
• have a "secular legislative purpose";
• neither inhibit nor advance religion as a "principal or primary effect";
• do not foster "excessive government entanglement with religion."

Aid programs considered constitutional have provided bus transportation, textbook loans, school lunches and health services, and "secular, neutral or non-ideological services, facilities and materials provided in common to all school children," public and non-public.

The first major aid to education program in U.S. history containing provisions benefiting nonpublic school students was enacted by the 89th Congress and signed into law by President Lyndon B. Johnson Apr. 11, 1965. The Elementary and Secondary Education Act was designed to avoid the separation of Church and state impasse which had blocked all earlier aid proposals pertaining to nonpublic, and especially church-affiliated, schools. The objective of the program, under public control, is to serve the public purpose by aiding disadvantaged pupils in nonpublic as well as public schools.

With respect to college and university education in church-affiliated institutions, the Supreme Court has upheld the constitutionality of statutes providing student loans and, under the Federal Higher Education Facilities Act of 1963, construction loans and grants for secular-purpose facilities.

Catholic schools are exempt from real estate taxation in all of the states. Since Jan. 1, 1959, nonprofit parochial and private schools have also been exempt from several federal excise taxes.

CATHOLIC EDUCATION

Shared and Released Time

In a shared time program of education, students enrolled in Catholic or other church-related schools take some courses (e.g., religion, social studies, fine arts) in their own schools and others (e.g., science, mathematics, industrial arts) in public schools. Such a program has been given serious consideration in recent years by Catholic and other educators. Its constitutionality has not been seriously challenged, but practical problems — relating to teacher and student schedules, transportation, adjustment to new programs, and other factors — are knotty.

Several million children of elementary and high school age of all denominations have the opportunity of receiving religious instruction on released time. Under released time programs they are permitted to leave their public schools during school hours to attend religious instruction classes held off the public school premises. They are released at the request of their parents. Public school authorities merely provide for their dismissal, and take no part in the program.

NCEA

The National Catholic Educational Association, founded in 1904, is a voluntary organization of educational institutions and individuals concerned with Catholic education in the U.S. Its objectives are to promote and encourage the principles and ideals of Christian education and formation by suitable service and other activities.

The NCEA serves approximately 200,000 Catholic educators at all levels from pre-K through university. Its official publication is *Momentum*. Numerous service publications are issued to members.

Bishop John J. Leibrecht of Springfield-Cape Girardeau, chairman of the Board of Directors; Leonard F. DeFiore, president. Address: 1077 30th St. N.W., Washington, D.C. 20007.

SUMMARY OF SCHOOL STATISTICS

The status of Catholic educational institutions and programs in the United States and outlying areas at the beginning of 1999 was reflected in figures (as of Jan. 1) reported by The Official Catholic Directory.

Colleges and Universities: 238 (U.S., 233; Outlying Areas, 5).

College and University Students: 698,855 (U.S., 676,646; Outlying Areas, 22,209).

High Schools: 1,358 (794 diocesan and parochial; 564 private). U.S., 1,246 (725 diocesan and parochial; 521 private). Outlying Areas, 112 (69 diocesan and parochial; 43 private).

High School Students: 653,701 (374,204 diocesan and parochial; 279,497 private). U.S., 628,615 (360,520 diocesan and parochial; 268,095 private). Outlying Areas, 25,086 (13,684 diocesan and parochial; 11,402 private).

Public High School Students Receiving Religious Instruction: 808,017 (U.S., 790,997; Outlying Areas, 17,020).

Elementary Schools: 7,086 (6,745 diocesan and parochial; 341 private). U.S., 6,926 (6,648 diocesan and parochial; 278 private). Outlying Areas, 160 (97 diocesan and parochial; 63 private).

Elementary School Students: 2,060,996 (1,963,587 diocesan and parochial; 97,409 private). U.S., 2,009,045 (1,932,556 diocesan and parochial; 76,489 private). Outlying Areas, 51,951 (31,031 diocesan and parochial; 20,920 private).

Public Elementary School Students Receiving Religious Instruction: 3,675,492 (U.S., 3,613,957; Outlying Areas, 61,535).

Non-Residential Schools for Handicapped: 84 (U.S.). Students: 18,030 (U.S.).

Teachers: 167,687 U.S., 162,196: Lay Persons 149,930; Sisters, 9,212; Priests, 1,898; Brothers, 1,114; Scholastics, 42. Outlying Areas, 5,491: Lay Persons, 5,010; Sisters, 337; Priests, 100; Brothers, 35; scholastics, 9.

Seminaries: 192 (74 diocesan; 118 religious). U.S.: 179 (69 diocesan; 110 religious). Outlying Areas: 13 (5 diocesan; 8 religious).

Seminarians: 4,826 (3,302 diocesan; 1,524 religious). U.S.: 4,747 (3,354 diocesan; 1,493 religious). Outlying Areas: 79 (48 diocesan; 31 religious).

TRENDS IN CATHOLIC EDUCATION

(Courtesy the Center for Applied Research in the Apostolate, CARA, Georgetown University and Official Catholic Directory. Analysing statistics from these sources, here are some trends in Catholic education.)

Catholic Colleges and Universities: The number of Catholic colleges and universities declined by two; the number of student enrollments increased by almost 6,000, to a new high.

Catholic High Schools: Enrollment declined by around 7,000.

Grade Schools: Enrollment increased by around 8,000.

Religious Education Programs: At the high school level, enrollment increased by around 3,500; at the elementary school level, enrollment increased by nearly 175,000.

Teachers: The number of lay teachers increased by over 4,000; the number of priests, scholastics, religious brothers, and sisters in teaching roles declined slightly.

CATHOLIC SCHOOLS AND STUDENTS IN THE UNITED STATES

(Source: *Official Catholic Directory*, 1998; figures as of Jan. 1, 1998. Archdioceses are indicated by an asterisk.)

State Diocese	Univs. Colleges	Students	High Schools	Students	Elem. Schools	Students
Alabama	1	1,781	8	3,196	41	11,258
*Mobile	1	1,781	3	1,595	21	5,976
Birmingham	-	-	5	1,601	20	5,282
Alaska	-	-	2	333	5	757
*Anchorage	-	-	1	112	3	417
Fairbanks	-	-	1	221	1	255
Juneau	-	-	-	-	1	85
Arizona	-	-	8	5,462	47	13,549
Phoenix	-	-	5	3,825	23	7,950
Tucson	-	-	3	1,637	24	5,599
Arkansas						
Little Rock	-	-	5	1,870	32	6,746
California	13	41,197	113	70,833	600	180,083
*Los Angeles	5	10,961	51	30,174	228	69,010
*San Francisco	3	11,036	13	7,977	65	20,927
Fresno	-	-	2	1,487	23	5,403
Monterey	-	-	4	1,562	14	3,862
Oakland	3	4,500	9	6,327	52	15,043
Orange	—	—	6	5,770	38	13,859
Sacramento	-	-	7	4,072	46	12,971
San Bernardino-	-	2	932	35	8,558	
San Diego	1	6,753	5	3,240	44	13,687
San Jose	1	7,947	6	5,841	29	10,397
Santa Rosa	-	-	6	2,064	14	3,005
Stockton	-	-	2	1,387	12	3,361
Colorado	1	11,240	7	2,774	45	14,060
*Denver	1	11,240	5	2,627	37	11,508
Colorado Springs	-	-	-	-	4	1,348
Pueblo	-	-	2	146	4	1,204
Connecticut	-	5	15,052	24	10,542	129	33,935
*Hartford	2	3,920	11	4,992	72	19,056
Bridgeport	3	11,132	8	3,513	35	10,318
Norwich	-	-	5	2,037	23	4,561
Delaware, Wilmington	-	-	8	4,587	29	10,771
District of Columbia						
*Washington, D.C.	3	15,514	17	8,676	87	29,514
Florida	3	17,715	32	22,174	187	66,326
*Miami	2	10,707	14	10,390	57	24,437
Orlando	-	-	4	2,376	31	12,474
Palm Beach	-	-	3	2,241	14	4,398
Pensacola-Tall.	-	-	1	625	9	2,527
St. Augustine	-	-	2	1,954	21	7,302
St. Petersburg	1	7,008	5	3,012	44	11,120
Venice	-	-	3	1,576	9	3,508
Georgia	-	-	7	3,792	28	9,581
*Atlanta	-	-	2	2,048	13	4,807
Savannah	-	-	5	1,744	15	4,774
Hawaii, Honolulu	1	2,114	8	3,404	26	8,003
Idaho, Boise	-	-	1	734	13	2,515
Illinois	12	54,735	78	48,806	508	162,542
*Chicago	6	41,047	46	31,945	272	98,525
Belleville	-	-	3	1,675	37	7,436
Joliet	3	12,019	8	5,679	56	19,740
Peoria	1	150	6	2,577	48	12,440
Rockford	-	-	8	4,241	41	12,257
Springfield	2	1,519	7	2,689	54	12,044
Indiana	11	23,435	22	12,572	178	48,671
*Indianapolis	2	2,613	9	5,308	62	19,581
Evansville	-	-	5	1,832	24	6,076

State Diocese	Univs. Colleges	Students	High Schools	Students	Elem. Schools	Students
Indiana continued						
Ft.Wayne-S. Bend	5	13,476	4	3,117	40	10,977
Gary	1	1,035	3	1,941	30	7,659
Lafayette	3	6,311	1	374	21	4,280
Iowa	7	9,006	24	8,875	115	27,154
*Dubuque	3	4,176	7	3,113	52	12,361
Davenport	2	3,450	7	1,614	20	4,178
Des Moines	1	369	2	1,490	15	4,674
Sioux City	1	1,011	8	2,658	28	5,941
Kansas	4	4,323	16	6,305	97	22,046
*Kansas City	3	2,420	7	3,616	43	11,463
Dodge City	-	-	-	-	10	1,150
Salina	-	-	5	691	12	1,951
Wichita	1	1,903	4	1,998	32	7,482
Kentucky	5	6,636	25	11,702	124	34,943
*Louisville	3	4,359	10	6,507	59	18,733
Covington	1	1,500	9	3,241	31	8,547
Lexington	-	-	3	895	15	3,463
Owensboro	1	777	3	1,059	19	4,200
Louisiana	4	11,117	50	27,966	174	70,853
*New Orleans	3	10,165	23	16,473	81	34,176
Alexandria	-	-	3	633	9	2,745
Baton Rouge	1	952	8	4,185	26	12,711
Houma-Thib.	-	-	3	1,502	10	4,829
Lafayette	-	-	10	3,849	31	11,135
Lake Charles	-	-	1	576	8	3,047
Shreveport	-	-	2	748	9	2,210
Maine, Portland	1	5,123	3	975	19	4,206
Maryland,*Baltimore	3	11,428	22	10,922	73	24,814
Massachusetts	14	33,306	51	23,265	211	60,277
*Boston	8	21,576	35	14,659	130	39,978
Fall River	1	2,882	4	2,601	24	5,920
Springfield	2	1,070	4	1,694	32	7,856
Worcester	3	7,778	8	4,311	24	6,369
Michigan	6	26,363	53	20,602	298	71,309
*Detroit	4	20,127	34	13,744	131	39,088
Gaylord	-	-	4	619	19	3,364
Grand Rapids	1	2,483	4	1,870	38	7,297
Kalamazoo	-	-	3	942	22	3,944
Lansing	1	3,750	4	2,375	39	10,229
Marquette	-	-	-	-	10	1,705
Saginaw	-	-	3	912	30	5,164
Minnesota	7	23,065	21	9,905	191	46,262
*St.Paul and Minn.	3	15,904	11	7,050	89	28,193
Crookston	-	-	1	161	9	1,214
Duluth	1	1,743	-	-	13	1,905
New Ulm	-	-	3	507	19	3,453
St. Cloud	2	3,831	2	818	33	6,212
Winona	1	1,587	4	1,369	28	5,285
Mississippi	1	21	9	2,602	30	6,636
Biloxi	-	-	5	1,810	14	3,405
Jackson	1	21	4	792	16	3,231
Missouri	4	16,913	41	20,469	250	66,775
*St.Louis	2	12,867	29	15,517	156	43,381
Jefferson City	-	-	2	908	37	6,261
Kansas City-St. Joseph	2	4,046	7	3,216	34	13,344
Springfield-Cape Girar.	-	-	3	828	23	3,789
Montana	2	2,390	4	914	16	3,222
Great Falls-Billings	1	1,190	2	529	12	2,422
Helena	1	1,200	2	385	4	780
Nebraska	2	7,295	28	10,307	93	21,339
*Omaha	2	7,295	18	6,983	62	15,211
Grand Island	-	-	4	1,147	7	728
Lincoln	-	-	6	2,177	24	5,400

State Diocese	Univs. Colleges	Students	High Schools	Students	Elem. Schools	Students
Nevada	-	-	2	1,677	10	3,449
Las Vegas	-	-	1	1,100	6	2,331
Reno	-	-	1	577	4	1,118
New Hampshire						
Manchester	6	6,135	4	2,420	37	7,884
New Jersey	7	20,994	75	36,625	360	113,420
*Newark	4	16,416	37	15,622	144	44,743
Camden	-	-	11	5,943	50	15,440
Metuchen	-	-	6	3,738	44	14,290
Paterson	2	2,228	10	3,954	61	17,012
Trenton	1	2,350	11	7,368	61	21,935
New Mexico	1	1,600	5	2,015	29	6,235
*Santa Fe	1	1,600	2	1,711	15	4,043
Gallup	-	-	3	304	10	1,650
Las Cruces	-	-	-	-	4	542
New York	30	109,605	128	65,146	714	228,945
*New York	12	63,735	55	21,323	238	82,064
Albany	4	4,000	7	2,897	40	9,234
Brooklyn	3	19,143	21	17,417	157	55,224
Buffalo	7	14,462	17	6,074	94	23,685
Ogdensburg	1	271	2	638	24	4,296
Rochester	-	-	8	3,542	55	13,716
Rockville Cen.	2	5,079	12	11,142	63	30,172
Syracuse	1	2,915	6	2,113	43	10,554
North Carolina	2	939	3	1,831	32	10,865
Charlotte	2	939	2	1,185	15	5,883
Raleigh	-	-	1	646	17	4,982
North Dakota	1	2,148	4	1,466	26	4,094
Bismarck	1	2,148	3	1,180	14	1,965
Fargo	-	-	1	286	12	2,129
Ohio	12	32,986	79	45,536	444	143,973
*Cincinnati	4	19,198	22	15,984	112	41,153
Cleveland	3	6,396	23	14,388	140	51,898
Columbus	1	1,977	11	4,785	45	14,166
Steubenville	1	2,022	3	715	15	2,832
Toledo	2	1,838	14	6,736	86	22,326
Youngstown	1	1,555	6	2,928	45	11,498
Oklahoma	1	650	4	2,393	33	7,373
*Oklahoma City	1	650	2	923	21	3,915
Tulsa	-	-	2	1,470	12	3,258
Oregon	2	4,201	9	4,867	45	10,057
*Portland	2	4,201	9	4,867	42	9,471
Baker	-	-	-	-	3	586
Pennsylvania	26	73,981	99	51,548	601	178,513
*Philadelphia	11	32,823	37	29,993	241	90,187
Allentown	2	3,436	9	4,302	56	14,281
Altoona-Johnstown	2	4,506	3	1,177	30	4,927
Erie	2	6,095	8	3,076	43	10,771
Greensburg	2	2,362	2	788	28	5,812
Harrisburg	-	-	8	3,736	43	11,691
Pittsburgh	3	13,219	11	4,241	110	28,380
Scranton	4	11,540	11	4,235	50	12,464
Rhode Island, Prov.	2	7,780	12	5,310	50	14,510
South Carolina						
Charleston	-	-	2	1,292	24	6,547
South Dakota	2	1,809	5	1,613	24	4,952
Rapid City	-	-	2	616	2	681
Sioux Falls	2	1,809	3	997	22	4,271
Tennessee	2	2,231	10	4,557	36	10,610
Knoxville	-	-	2	963	8	2,588
Memphis	1	1,869	6	2,399	13	3,895
Nashville	1	362	2	1,195	15	4,127
Texas	8	20,922	55	17,092	235	71,577

State Diocese	Univs. Colleges	Students	High Schools	Students	Elem. Schools	Students
Texas continued						
*San Antonio	4	11,702	10	3,764	41	13,489
Amarillo	-	-	1	120	8	966
Austin	1	3,422	4	679	16	3,490
Beaumont	-	-	1	627	6	1,839
Brownsville	-	-	1	700	8	2,711
Corpus Christi	1	10	2	920	23	4,541
Dallas	1	3,092	17	3,458	32	15,087
El Paso	-	-	3	1,010	12	4,374
Fort Worth	-	-	4	1,554	16	6,475
Galveston-Houston	1	2,696	8	3,537	51	13,831
Lubbock	-	-	-	-	2	429
San Angelo	-	-	-	-	3	850
Tyler	-	-	1	160	4	904
Victoria	-	-	3	563	13	2,591
Utah, Salt Lake City	-	-	2	1,142	10	3,046
Vermont, Burlington	3	4,005	2	734	11	2,376
Virginia	3	4,049	14	5,858	61	21,333
Arlington	3	4,049	5	3,831	35	12,996
Richmond	-	-	9	2,027	26	8,337
Washington	3	11,999	13	6,719	78	21,588
*Seattle	2	7,500	9	5,485	55	16,207
Spokane	1	4,499	3	1,179	16	3,416
Yakima	-	-	1	55	7	1,965
West Virginia, Wheeling-Charleston	1	1,532	8	1,673	27	5,502
Wisconsin	9	28,584	29	11,883	364	67,769
*Milwaukee	5	21,725	14	7,096	145	33,752
Green Bay	2	3,150	6	2,249	78	13,180
La Crosse	1	1,800	7	1,862	78	10,400
Madison	1	1,909	2	676	45	7,550
Superior	-	-	-	-	18	2,887
Wyoming, Cheyenne	-	-	1	54	6	1,074
EASTERN CHURCHES	2	757	3	565	27	4,931
*Philadelphia	1	685	1	330	7	1,410
St. Nicholas (Chicago)	-	1	90	2	450	
Stamford	-	-	1	145	4	476
St. Josaphat (Parma)	-	-	-	-	2	272
*Pittsburgh	-	-	-	-	3	533
Parma	-	-	-	-	2	325
Passaic	-	-	-	-	3	449
Van Nuys	-	-	-	-	-	-
St. Maron (Maronites)	-	-	-	-	-	-
Our Lady of Lebanon (Maronites)	-	-	-	-	-	-
Newton (Melkites)	-	-	-	-	-	-
St. Thomas Apostle of Detroit (Chaldeans)	-	-	-	-	-	-
St. George Martyr (Romanians)	-	-	-	-	-	-
Armenians (Ap. Ex.)	-	-	-	-	4	1,016
SCHOOLS AND STUDENTS IN OUTLYING AREAS						
American Samoa	-	-	2	262	2	406
Caroline Islands	-	-	5	798	5	1,732
Guam	-	-	3	1,080	7	2,182
Marshall Islands	-	-	2	310	6	1,225
Marianas	-	-	1	386	3	494
Puerto Rico	5	22,209	98	22,010	134	45,262
Virgin Islands	-	-	-	-	3	650
GRAND TOTALS 1999	238	698,855	1,358	653,701	7,086	2,060,996
Grand Totals 1998	240	692,951	1,347	660,583	7,151	2,052,948
Grand Totals, 1989	232	551,466	1,364	661,284	7,549	1,977,212

CATHOLIC UNIVERSITIES AND COLLEGES IN THE UNITED STATES

(Sources: Catholic Almanac *survey;* The Official Catholic Directory.*)*

Listed below are institutions of higher learning established under Catholic auspices. Some of them are now independent.

Information includes: name of each institution; indication of male (m), female (w), coeducational (c) student body; name of founding group or group with which the institution is affiliated; year of foundation; total number of students, in parentheses.

Albertus Magnus College (c): 700 Prospect St., New Haven, CT 06511. Dominican Sisters; 1925; independent (1,655).

Allentown College of St. Francis de Sales (c): 2755 Station Ave., Center Valley, PA 18034. Oblates of St. Francis de Sales; 1965 (1,693).

Alvernia College (c): Reading, PA 19607. Bernardine Sisters; 1958 (1,270).

Alverno College (w): 3401 S. 39th St., Milwaukee, WI 53215. School Sisters of St. Francis; 1887; independent (2,089).

Anna Maria College (c): 50 Sunset Lane, Paxton, MA 01612. Sisters of St. Anne;1946; independent (1,927).

Aquinas College (c): 1607 Robinson Rd. S.E., Grand Rapids, MI 49506. Sisters of St. Dominic; 1922; independent (2,483).

Aquinas College (c): 4210 Harding Rd., Nashville, TN 37205. Dominican Sisters; 1961 (385). Offers BA in Elementary Teacher Education, BSN, and ASN (362).

Aquinas Institute of Theology (c): 3642 Lindell Boulevard, St. Louis, Missouri 63108. Dominicans, 1961; graduate theology; offers distance learning program in pastoral studies and specializations in preaching (200).

Assumption College (c): 500 Salisbury St., Worcester, MA 01615-0005. Assumptionist Religious; 1904 (3,115).

Avila College (c): 11901 Wornall Rd., Kansas City, MO 64145-1698. Sisters of St. Joseph of Carondelet; 1916 (1,246).

Barat College (c): 700 Westleigh Rd., Lake Forest, IL 60045. Society of the Sacred Heart; 1919; independent (883).

Barry University (c): 11300 N.E. 2nd Ave., Miami Shores, FL 33161. Dominican Sisters (Adrian, Mich.); 1940 (7,418).

Bellarmine College (c): 2001 Newburg Rd., Louisville, KY 40205; Louisville archdiocese; independent (2,316).

Belmont Abbey College (c): 100 Belmont-Mt. Holly Rd., Belmont, NC 28012. Benedictine Fathers; 1876 (939).

Benedictine College (c): 1020 N. Second St., Atchison, KS 66002. Benedictines; 1859; independent (916).

Benedictine University (formerly Illinois Benedictine College) (c): 5700 College Rd., Lisle, IL 60532-0900. Benedictine Monks of St. Procopius Abbey; 1887 (2,828).

Boston College (University Status) (c): Chestnut Hill, MA 02167. Jesuit Fathers; 1863 (14,652).

Brescia University (c): 717 Frederica St., Owensboro, KY 42301. Ursuline Sisters; 1950 (777).

Briar Cliff College (c): 3303 Rebecca St., Sioux City, IA 51104. Sisters of St. Francis of the Holy Family; 1930 (1,003).

Cabrini College (c): 610 King of Prussia Rd., Radnor, PA 19087. Missionary Srs. of Sacred Heart; 1957; private (2,111).

Caldwell College (c): 9 Ryerson Ave., Caldwell, NJ 07006. Dominican Sisters; 1939 (1,978).

Calumet College of St. Joseph (c): 2400 New York Ave., Whiting, IN 46394. Society of the Precious Blood, 1951 (1,035).

Canisius College (c): 2001 Main St., Buffalo, NY 14208. Jesuit Fathers; 1870; independent (4,628).

Cardinal Stritch University (c): 6801 N. Yates Rd., Milwaukee, WI 53217. Sisters of St. Francis of Assisi; 1937 (5,516).

Carlow College (w): 3333 5th Ave., Pittsburgh, PA 15213. Sisters of Mercy; 1929 (2,377).

Carroll College (c): Helena, MT 59625. Diocesan; 1909 (1,200).

Catholic Distance University (c): 120 East Colonial Highway, Hamilto n, VA 20158-9012. Offers External Degree programs, including Masters degrees in Religious Studies (7,000).

Catholic University of America, The (c): Michigan Ave. & Fourth St., N.E., Washington, DC 20064. Hierarchy of the United States; 1887. Pontifical University (5,989).

Chaminade University of Honolulu (c): 3140 Waialae Ave., Honolulu, Hawaii 96816. Marianists; 1955 (2,592).

Chestnut Hill College (w): Philadelphia, PA 19118. Sisters of St. Joseph; 1924 (1,285).

Christendom College (c): 134 Christendom Dr., Front Royal, VA 22630; 1977 (214).

Christian Brothers University (c): 650 E. Parkway S., Memphis, TN 38104. Brothers of the Christian Schools; 1871 (1,869).

Clarke College (c): 1550 Clarke Dr., Dubuque, Iowa 52001. Sisters of Charity, BVM; 1843; independent (1,250).

Creighton University (c): 2500 California Plaza, Omaha, NE 68178. Jesuit Fathers; 1878; independent (6,226).

Dallas, University of (c): 1845 E. Northgate, Irving, TX 75062. Dallas diocese; 1956; independent (2,897).

Dayton, University of (c): 300 College Park, Dayton, Ohio 45469-1660. Marianists; 1850 (10,002).

DePaul University (c): One E. Jackson Blvd., Chicago, IL 60604. Vincentians; 1898 (17,769).

Detroit Mercy, University of (c): 4001 W. McNichols Rd., Detroit, MI, 48221; 8200 W. Outer Dr., Detroit MI 48219. Society of Jesus and Sisters of Mercy; 1877; independent (6,500).

Dominican College of Blauvelt (c):Orangeburg, NY 10962. Dominican Sisters; 1952; independent (1,712).

Dominican College of San Rafael (c): 50 Acacia Ave., San Rafael, CA 94901-2298. Dominican Sisters; 1890; independent (1,479).

Dominican University (formerly Rosary College) (c): 7900 W. Division St., River Forest, IL 60305. Sinsinawa Dominican Sisters; 1901 (1,800).

Duquesne University (c): 600 Forbes Ave., Pittsburgh, PA 15282. Congregation of the Holy Ghost; 1878 (9,285).

D'Youville College (c): 320 Porter Ave., Buffalo, NY 14201. Grey Nuns of the Sacred Heart; 1908; independent (1,875).

Edgewood College (c): 855 Woodrow St., Madison, WI 53711. Sinsinawa Dominican Sisters; 1927 (1,909).

Emmanuel College (w): 400 The Fenway, Boston, MA 02115. Sisters of Notre Dame de Namur; 1919; independent (1,560).

Fairfield University (c): 1073 North Benson Rd., Fairfield, CT 06430. Jesuits; 1942 (5,208).

Felician College (c): 262 S. Main St., Lodi, NJ 07644. Felician Sisters; 1942; independent (1,255).

Fontbonne College (c): 6800 Wydown Blvd., St. Louis, MO 63105. Sisters of St. Joseph of Carondelet; 1917; independent (1,984).

Fordham University (c): Fordham Rd. and Third Ave., New York, NY 10458. Society of Jesus (Jesuits); 1841; independent (13,688).

Franciscan University of Steubenville (c): 1235 University Blvd., Steubenville, Ohio 43952. Franciscan TOR Friars; 1946 (2,022). Also offers Distance Learning programs.

Gannon University (c): 109 University Square, Erie, PA 16541-0001. Diocese of Erie; 1933 (3,327).

Georgetown University (c): 37th and O Sts. N.W., Washington, DC 20057. Jesuit Fathers; 1789 (12,629).

Georgian Court College (w/c): 900 Lakewood Ave., Lakewood, NJ 08701. Sisters of Mercy; 1908 (2,422).

Gonzaga University (c): E. 502 Boone Ave., Spokane, WA 99258. Jesuit Fathers; 1887 (4,499).

Great Falls, University of (c): 1301 20th St. S., Great Falls, MT 59405. Sisters of Providence; 1932; independent (1,190).

Gwynedd-Mercy College (c): Gwynedd Valley, PA 19437. Sisters of Mercy; 1948; independent (2,520).

Hilbert College (c): 5200 S. Park Ave., Hamburg, NY 14075. Franciscan Sisters of St. Joseph; 1957; independent (865).

Holy Cross, College of the (c): Worcester, MA 01610. Jesuits; 1843 (2,736).

Holy Family College (c): Grant and Frankford Aves., Philadelphia, PA 19114 and One Campus Dr., Newtown, PA 18940. Sisters of Holy Family of Nazareth; 1954; independent (2,647).

Holy Names College (c): 3500 Mountain Blvd., Oakland, CA 94619. Sisters of the Holy Names of Jesus and Mary; 1868; independent (800).

Immaculata College (w): Immaculata, PA 19345. Sisters, Servants of the Immaculate Heart of Mary; 1920 (2,599).

Incarnate Word, University of the (c): 4301 Broadway, San Antonio, TX 78209. Sisters of Charity of the Incarnate Word; 1881 (3,583).

Iona College (c): 715 North Ave., New Rochelle, NY 10801. Congregation of Christian Brothers; 1940; independent (4,897).

John Carroll University (c): 20700 North Park Blvd., Cleveland, OH 44118. Jesuits; 1886 (4,473).

King's College (c): 133 North River St., Wilkes-Barre, PA 18711. Holy Cross Fathers; 1946 (2,237).

La Roche College (c): 9000 Babcock Blvd., Pittsburgh, PA 15237. Sisters of Divine Providence; 1963 (1,641).

La Salle University (c): 1900 W. Olney Ave., Philadelphia, PA 19141. Christian Brothers; 1863 (5,376).

Le Moyne College (c): Syracuse, NY 13214. Jesuit Fathers; 1946; independent (approx. 2,750, full-time, part-time, graduate)

Lewis University (c): Romeoville, IL 60446. Christian Brothers; 1932 (4,264).

Loras College (c): 1450 Alta Vista St., Dubuque, IA 52004. Archdiocese of Dubuque; 1839 (1,683).

Lourdes College (c): 6832 Convent Blvd., Sylvania, OH 43560. Sisters of St. Francis; 1958 (1,307).

Loyola College (c): 4501 N. Charles St., Baltimore, MD 21210. Jesuits; 1852; combined with Mt. St. Agnes College, 1971 (6,241).

Loyola Marymount University (c): 7900 Loyola Blvd., Los Angeles, CA 90045-2699. Society of Jesus; Religious of Sacred Heart of Mary, Sisters of St. Joseph of Orange; 1911.

Loyola University (c): 6363 St. Charles Ave., New Orleans, LA 70118. Jesuit Fathers; 1912 (5,232).

Loyola University Chicago (c): 820 N. Michigan Ave., Chicago, IL 60611. Society of Jesus; 1870 (approx. 15,000). Mallinckrodt College (Wilmette) and Mundelein College (Chicago) became part of Loyola University Chicago, in January and June, 1991, respectively.

Madonna University (c): 36600 Schoolcraft Rd., Livonia, MI 48150. Felician Sisters; 1947 (3,294).

Magdalen College (c): 511 Kearsarge Mountain Rd., Warner, NH 03278; Magdalen College Corporation; 1973 (70).

Manhattan College (c): 4513 Manhattan College Pkwy., Riverdale, NY 10471. De La Salle Christian Brothers; 1835; independent (2,963). Cooperative program with College of Mt. St. Vincent.

Marian College of Fond du Lac (c): 45 S. National Ave., Fond du Lac, WI 54935. Sisters of St. Agnes; 1936 (2,099).

Marian College (c): 3200 Cold Spring Rd., Indianapolis, IN 46222. Sisters of St. Francis (Oldenburg, Ind.); 1851; independent (1,339).

Marist College (c): Poughkeepsie, NY 12601. Marist Brothers of the Schools; 1946; independent (4,300).

Marquette University (c): P.O. Box 1881, Milwaukee, WI 53201-1881. Jesuit Fathers; 1881; independent (10,400).

Mary, University of (c): 7500 University Dr., Bismarck, ND 58504. Benedictine Sisters; 1959 (2,267).

Marygrove College (c): 8425 W. McNichols Rd., Detroit, MI 48221. Sisters, Servants of the Immaculate Heart of Mary; 1905; independent (4,506).

Marylhurst College (c): Marylhurst, OR 97036. Srs. of Holy Names of Jesus and Mary; 1893; independent (2,904).

Marymount College (w): 100 Marymount Ave., Tarrytown, NY 10591. Religious of the Sacred Heart of Mary; 1907; independent (842). Coed in weekend degree programs.

Marymount Manhattan College (w): 221 E. 71st St., New York, NY 10021. Religious of the Sacred Heart of Mary; 1936; independent (1,330).

Marymount University (c): 2807 N. Glebe Rd., Arlington, VA 22207. Religious of the Sacred Heart of Mary; 1950; independent (3,695).

Marywood College (c): Scranton, PA 18509. Sisters, Servants of the Immaculate Heart of Mary; 1915; independent (2,948).

Mater Dei College (c): 5428 State Hwy. 37, Ogdensburg, NY 13669. Sisters of St. Joseph; 1960; independent (508).

Mercyhurst College (c): 501 E. 38th St., Erie, PA 16546. Sisters of Mercy; 1926 (2,868).

Merrimack College (c): North Andover, MA 01845. Augustinians;1947 (2,100).

Misericordia (College Misericordia) (c): Dallas, PA 18612. Religious Sisters of Mercy of the Union; 1924 (1,644).

Molloy College (c): 1000 Hempstead Ave., P.O. Box 5002, Rockville Centre, NY 11570-5002. Dominican Sisters; 1955; independent (2,252).

Mount Aloysius College (c): 7373 Admiral Peary Hwy., Cresson, PA 16630. Sisters of Mercy; 1939 (2,601).

Mount Marty College (c): 1105 W. 8th St., Yankton, SD 57078. Benedictine Sisters; 1936 (1,003).

Mount Mary College (w): 2900 N. Menomonee River Pkwy., Milwaukee, WI 53222. School Sisters of Notre Dame; 1913 (1,326).

Mount Mercy College (c): 1330 Elmhurst Dr. N.E., Cedar Rapids, IA 52402. Sisters of Mercy; 1928; independent (1,200).

Mount St. Clare College (c): 400 N. Bluff Blvd., Clinton, IA 52732. Sisters of St. Francis of Clinton, Iowa; 1918 (631).

Mount St. Joseph, College of (c): 5701 Delhi Rd., Cincinnati, OH 45233-1670. Sisters of Charity; 1920 (2,242).

Mount Saint Mary College (c): Newburgh, NY 12550. Dominican Sisters; 1959; independent (2,011).

Mount St. Mary's College (c): Emmitsburg, MD 21727. Founded by Fr. John DuBois, 1808; independent (1,884).

Mount St. Mary's College (w/c): 12001 Chalon Rd., Los Angeles, CA 90049 and 10 Chester Pl., Los Angeles, CA 90007 (Doheny Campus); (2,022). Sisters of St. Joseph of Carondelet; 1925. Coed in music, nursing and graduate programs.

Mount Saint Vincent, College of (c): 6301 Riverdale Ave., Bronx, NY 10471. Sisters of Charity; 1847; independent (1,580). Cooperative program with Manhattan College.

Neumann College (c):One Neumann Dr., Aston, PA 19014. Sisters of St. Francis; 1965; independent (1,403).

Newman University (c): 3100 McCormick Ave., Wichita, KS 67213. Sisters Adorers of the Blood of Christ; 1933 (1,903).

New Rochelle, College of (w/c): 29 Castle Pl., New Rochelle, NY 10805 (main campus). Ursuline Order; 1904; independent (7,503). Coed in nursing, graduate, new resources divisions.

Niagara University (c): Lewiston Rd. Niagara Univ., NY 14109-2015. Vincentian Fathers and Brothers; 1856 (2,888).

Notre Dame, College of (c): 1500 Ralston Ave., Belmont, CA 94002. Sisters of Notre Dame de Namur; 1851; independent (1,754).

Notre Dame, University of (c): (Full title: University of Notre Dame du Lac) Notre Dame, IN 46556. Congregation of Holy Cross; 1842 (10,359).

Notre Dame College (c): 2321 Elm St., Manchester, NH 03104. Sisters of Holy Cross; 1950; independent (1,240).

Notre Dame College of Ohio (w): 4545 College Rd., Cleveland, OH 44121. Sisters of Notre Dame; 1922 (685).

Notre Dame of Maryland, College of (w): 4701 N. Charles St., Baltimore, MD 21210. School Sisters of Notre Dame; 1873 (3,180).

Oblate School of Theology (c): 285 Oblate Dr., San Antonio, TX 78216-6693. Oblates of Mary Immaculate; 1903 (241). Graduate theology programs.

Ohio Dominican College (c): Columbus, OH 43219. Dominican Sisters of St. Mary of the Springs; 1911 (1,977).

Our Lady of Corpus Christi (c): PO Box 9785, Corpus Christi TX 78496; independent; 1997.

Our Lady of Holy Cross College (c): 4123 Woodland Dr., New Orleans, LA 70131. Congregation of Sisters Marianites of Holy Cross; 1916 (1,278).

Our Lady of the Elms, College of (w): 291 Springfield St., Chicopee, MA 01013-2839. Sisters of St. Joseph; 1928 (1,016).

Our Lady of the Lake University (c): 411 S.W. 24th St., San Antonio, TX 78207. Sisters of Divine Providence; 1895 (3,689).

Parks College of Saint Louis University (c): Cahokia, IL 62206. Jesuits; 1927; independent (600).

Pontifical Catholic University of Puerto Rico (c): 2250 Avenida de las Americas, Ponce, PR 00731. Hierarchy of Puerto Rico; 1948; Pontifical University (10,801).

Portland, University of (c): 5000 N. Willamette Blvd., Portland, OR 97203. Holy Cross Fathers; 1901; independent (2,783).

Presentation College (c): Aberdeen, SD 7401. Sisters of the Presentation; 1951 (506).

Providence College (c): 549 River Ave., Providence, RI 02918. Dominican Friars; 1917 (5,673, day, evening, and graduate).

Quincy University (c): 1800 College Ave., Quincy, IL 62301. Franciscan Friars; 1860 (1,125).

Regis College (w): Weston, MA 02193-1671. Sisters of St. Joseph; 1927; independent (1,121).

Regis University (c): 3333 Regis Blvd. Denver, CO 80221. Jesuits; 1887 (11,240).

Rivier College (c): 420 Main St., Nashua, NH 03060-5086. Sisters of the Presentation of Mary; 1933; independent (2,716).

Rockhurst College (c): 1100 Rockhurst Rd., Kansas City, MO 64110. Jesuit Fathers; 1910 (2,800).

Rosemont College of the Holy Child Jesus (w): Rosemont, PA 19010-1699. Society of the Holy Child Jesus; 1921 (1,210).

Sacred Heart University (c): 5151 Park Ave., Fairfield, CT 06432. Diocese of Bridgeport; 1963; independent (5,715).

St. Ambrose University (c): Davenport, IA 52803. Diocese of Davenport; 1882 (2,819).

Saint Anselm College (c): Manchester NH 03102-1030. Benedictines; 1889 (1,984).

Saint Benedict, College of (w): 37 S. College Ave., St. Joseph, MN 56374. Benedictine Sisters; 1913 (1,929). Sister college of St. John's University, Collegeville (see below).

St. Bonaventure University (c): St. Bonaventure, NY 14778. Franciscan Friars; 1858; independent (2,857).

St. Catherine, College of (w): 2004 Randolph Ave., St. Paul, MN 55105. Sisters of St. Joseph of Carondelet; 1905 (4,114).

St. Edward's University (c): 3001 S. Congress Ave., Austin, TX 78704. Holy Cross Brothers; 1881; independent (3,422).

Saint Elizabeth, College of (w): 2 Convent Rd., Morristown, NJ 07960-6989. Sisters of Charity; 1899; independent (2,184). Coed in adult undergraduate and graduate programs.

St. Francis, College of (c): 500 N. Wilcox St., Joliet, IL 60435. Sisters of St. Francis of Mary Immaculate; 1920; independent (221).

St. Francis College (c): 180 Remsen St., Brooklyn Heights, NY 11201. Franciscan Brothers; 1884; private, independent in the Franciscan tradition (2,231).

St. Francis College (c): P.O. Box 600, Loretto, PA 15940. Franciscan Friars; 1847; independent (1,905).

St. Francis, University of (c): 2701 Spring St., Fort Wayne, IN 46808-3994. Sisters of St. Francis; 1890 (1,731).

St. Gregory's University (c): 1900 W. MacArthur, Shawnee, OK 74801. Benedictine Monks; 1876 (600).

St. John's University (c): 8000 Utopia Pkwy., Jamaica, NY 11439 (Queens Campus); 300 Howard Ave., Staten Island, NY 10301 (Staten Island Campus). Vincentians; 1870 (20,882).

St. John's University (m): Collegeville, MN 56321. Benedictines; 1857 (1,854). All classes and programs are coeducational with College of St. Benedict (see above).

St. Joseph, College of (c): 171 Clement Rd., Rutland, VT 05701. Sisters of St. Joseph; 1950; independent (538).

Saint Joseph College (w/c): 1678 Asylum Ave., West Hartford, CT 06117-2700. Sisters of Mercy; 1932 (1,943). Women's college in undergraduate liberal arts. Coed in graduate school and Weekend College.

Saint Joseph's College (c): 278 Whites Bridge Rd., Standish, ME 04084-5263. Sisters of Mercy; 1912 (2,232, residential graduate and undergraduate; 2,891 in distance education). Offers distance education program).

Saint Joseph's College (c): P.O. Box 909, Rensselaer, IN 47978. Society of the Precious Blood; 1891 (902).

St. Joseph's College (c): 245 Clinton Ave., Brooklyn, NY 11205 (1,319) and 155 W. Roe Blvd., Patchogue, N.Y. 11772 (2,951). Sisters of St. Joseph; 1916; independent.

St. Joseph's University (c): 5600 City Ave., Philadelphia, PA 19131. Jesuit Fathers; 1851 (2,830).

Saint Leo College (c): P.O. Box 6665, Saint Leo, FL 33574. Order of St. Benedict; 1889; independent.

Saint Louis University (c): 221 N. Grand Blvd., St. Louis, MO 63103. Society of Jesus; 1818; independent (10,883).

Saint Martin's College (c): 5300 Pacific Ave. SE, Lacey, WA 98503-1297. Benedictine Monks; 1895 (1,033 main campus; 496 extension campuses).

Saint Mary, College of (w): 1901 S. 72nd St., Omaha, NE 68124. Sisters of Mercy; 1923; independent.

Saint Mary College (c): Leavenworth, KS 66048. Sisters of Charity of Leavenworth; 1923 (561).

Saint Mary-of-the-Woods College (w): St. Mary-of-the-Woods, IN 47876. Sisters of Providence; 1840 (1,274).

Saint Mary's College (w): Notre Dame, IN 46556. Sisters of the Holy Cross; 1844 (1,361).

Saint Mary's College (c): 3535 Indian Trail, Orchard Lake, MI 48324. Secular Clergy; 1885 (326).

St. Mary's College (c): Moraga, CA 94575. Brothers of the Christian Schools; 1863 (4,318).

Saint Mary's University of Minnesota (c): 700 Terrace Heights, Winona, MN 55987-1399. Brothers of the Christian Schools; 1912 (1,587).

St. Mary's University of San Antonio (c): One Camino Santa Maria, San Antonio, TX 78228-8607. Society of Mary (Marianists); 1852 (4,189).

Saint Meinrad School of Theology (c): St. Meinrad, IN 47577. Benedictines. (60 full and part-time lay students.) Graduate-level theological studies.

St. Michael's College (c): Colchester, VT 05439. Society of St. Edmund; 1904 (2,658).

St. Norbert College (c): De Pere, WI 54115. Norbertine Fathers; 1898; independent (2,100).

Saint Peter's College (c): 2641 Kennedy Blvd., Jersey City, NJ 07306. Society of Jesus; 1872; independent (3,512).

Saint Rose, College of (c): 432 Western Ave., Albany, NY 12203. Sisters of St. Joseph of Carondelet; 1920; independent (4,031).

St. Scholastica, The College of (c): 1200 Kenwood Ave., Duluth, MN 55811. Benedictine Sisters; 1912; independent (1,743).

St. Thomas, University of (c): 2115 Summit Ave., St. Paul, MN 55105. Archdiocese of St. Paul and Minneapolis; 1885 (10,790).

St. Thomas, University of (c): 3800 Montrose Blvd., Houston, TX 77006-4696. Basilian Fathers; 1947 (2,696).

St. Thomas Aquinas College (c): Sparkill, NY 10976. Dominican Sisters of Sparkill; 1952; independent, corporate board of trustees (2,100).

St. Thomas University (c): 16400 N.W. 32nd Ave., Miami, FL 33054. Archdiocese of Miami; 1962 (3,289).

Saint Vincent College (c): 300 Fraser Purchase Rd., Latrobe, PA 15650-2690. Benedictine Fathers; 1846 (1,150).

St. Xavier University (c): 3700 W. 103rd St., Chicago, IL 60655. Sisters of Mercy; chartered 1847 (4,100).

Salve Regina University (c): Ochre Point Ave., Newport, RI 02840-4192. Sisters of Mercy; 1934 (2,108). Offers distance learning programs in graduate studies.

San Diego, University of (c): 5998 Alcala Park, San Diego, CA 92110. San Diego diocese and Religious of the Sacred Heart; 1949; independent (6,753).

San Francisco, University of (c): 2130 Fulton St., San Francisco, CA 94117. Jesuit Fathers; 1855 (7,803).

Santa Clara University (c): 500 El Camino Real, Santa Clara, CA 95053. Jesuit Fathers; 1851; independent (7,946).

Santa Fe, College of (c): 1600 St. Michael's Dr., Santa Fe, NM 87505. Brothers of the Christian Schools; 1947 (1,600).

Scranton, University of (c): Scranton, PA 18510. Society of Jesus; 1888; independent (4,711).

Seattle University (c): 900 Broadway, Seattle, WA 98122. Society of Jesus; 1891 (5,990).

Seton Hall University (c): South Orange Ave., South Orange, NJ 07079. Diocesan Clergy; 1856 (9,760).

Seton Hill College (w): Seton Hill Dr., Greensburg, PA 15601-1599. Sisters of Charity of Seton Hill; 1883 (1,030).

Siena College (c): 515 Loudon Rd., Loudonville, NY 12211. Franciscan Friars; 1937 (3,011).

Siena Heights College (c): 1247 E. Siena Heights Dr., Adrian, MI 49221. Adrian Dominican Sisters; 1919 (3,753).

Silver Lake College of the Holy Family (c): 2406 S. Alverno Rd., Manitowoc, WI 54220-9319. Franciscan Sisters of Christian Charity; 1935 (2,511).

Spalding University (c): 851 S. 4th Ave., Louisville, KY 40203. Sisters of Charity of Nazareth; 1814; independent (1,583).

Spring Hill College (c): 4000 Dauphin St., Mobile, AL 36608. Jesuit Fathers; 1830 (1003).

Stonehill College (c): 320 Washington St., Easton, MA 02357. Holy Cross Fathers; 1948; independent (2,882).

Thomas Aquinas College (c): 10000 N. Ojai Rd., Santa Paula, CA 93060. Founded 1971 (246).

Thomas More College (c): Crestview Hills, Covington, KY 41017. Diocese of Covington; 1921 (1,520).

Trinity College of Vermont (w): 208 Colchester Ave., Burlington, VT 05401. Sisters of Mercy; 1925 (779).

Trinity College (w): 125 Michigan Ave. N.E., Washington, DC 20017. Sisters of Notre Dame de Namur; 1897 (1,450). Coed in graduate school.

Ursuline College (w): 2550 Lander Rd., Cleveland, OH 44124. Ursuline Nuns; 1871 (1,233).

Villanova University (c): 800 Lancaster Ave., Villanova, PA 19085. Order of St. Augustine; 1842 (9,972).

Viterbo College (c): 815 S. 9th, La Crosse, WI 54601. Franciscan Sisters of Perpetual Adoration; 1890 (1,790).

Walsh University (c): 2020 Easton St. N.W., North Canton, Ohio 44720-3396. Brothers of Christian Instruction; 1958 (1,555).

Wheeling Jesuit University (c): 316 Washington Ave., Wheeling, WV 26003-6295. Jesuit Fathers; 1954 (1,532).

Xavier University (c): 3800 Victory Pkwy., Cincinnati, OH 45207. Jesuit Fathers; 1831 (6,504).

Xavier University of Louisiana (c): 7325 Palmetto St., New Orleans, LA 70125-1098. Sisters of Blessed Sacrament; 1925 (2,589).

Catholic Two-Year Colleges

Ancilla Domini College (c): P.O. Box 1, Donaldson, IN 46513. Ancilla Domini Sisters; 1937 (549).

Assumption College for Sisters: 350 Bernardsville Rd., Mendham, NJ 07945. Sisters of Christian Charity; 1953 (48).

Castle College: 23 Searles Rd., Windham, NH 03087. Sisters of Mercy; 1963; independent (100).

Chatfield College (c): St. Martin, OH 45118. Ursulines; 1971 (400).

The College of St. Catherine-Minneapolis (c): 601 25th Ave. S., Minneapolis, MN 55454. Sisters of St. Joseph of Carondelet (1,029).

Donnelly College (c): 608 N. 18th St., Kansas City, KS 66102. Archdiocesan College; 1949 (718).

Don Bosco Technical Institute (m): 1151 San Gabriel Blvd., Rosemead, CA 91770. Salesians; 1969 (784).

Holy Cross College (c): 1801 N. Michigan, P.O. Box 308, Notre Dame, IN 46556-0308. Brothers of Holy Cross; 1966 (484).

Manor Junior College (c): 700 Fox Chase Road, Jenkintown, PA 19046. Sisters of St. Basil the Great; 1947.

Maria College (c): 700 New Scotland Ave., Albany, NY 12208. Sisters of Mercy; 1963 (815).

Marymount College Palos Verdes (c): 30800 Palos Verdes Dr., E., Rancho Palos Verdes, CA 90275-6299. Religious of the Sacred Heart of Mary; independent (1,100).

St. Catharine College (c): 2735 Bardstown Rd., St. Catharine, KY 40061. Dominican Sisters; 1931 (460).

Springfield College in Illinois (c): 1500 N. Fifth St., Springfield, IL 62702. Ursuline Sisters; 1929 (394).

Trocaire College (c): 360 Choate Ave., Buffalo, NY 14220. Sisters of Mercy; 1958; independent (959).

Villa Maria College of Buffalo (c): 240 Pine Ridge Rd., Buffalo, NY 14225. Felician Sisters 1960; independent (410).

DIOCESAN AND INTERDIOCESAN SEMINARIES

(Sources: Catholic Almanac survey; The Official Catholic Directory; Catholic News Service.)

Information, according to states, includes names of archdioceses and dioceses, and names and addresses of seminaries. Types of seminaries, when not clear from titles, are indicated in most cases. Interdiocesan seminaries are generally conducted by religious orders for candidates for the priesthood from several dioceses. The list does not include houses of study reserved for members of religious communities. Archdioceses are indicated by an asterisk.

California: Los Angeles* — St. John's Seminary (major), 5012 Seminary Rd., Camarillo 93012-2599; St. John's Seminary College, 5118 Seminary Rd., Camarillo 93012-2599.

San Diego — St. Francis Seminary (college and pre-theology formation program), 1667 Santa Paula Dr., San Diego 92111.

San Francisco*— St. Patrick's Seminary (major), 320 Middlefield Rd., Menlo Park 94025.

Connecticut: Hartford* — St. Thomas Seminary (college formation program), 467 Bloomfield Ave., Bloomfield 06002-2999.

Norwich — Holy Apostles College and Seminary (adult vocations; minor and major), 33 Prospect Hill Rd., Cromwell 06416.

Stamford Byzantine Rite - Ukrainian Catholic Seminary: St. Basil College Seminary (minor), 195 Glenbrook Rd., Stamford 06902-3099.

District of Columbia: Washington, D.C.* — Theological College (national, major), The Catholic University of America, 401 Michigan Ave., N.E. 20017. St. Josaphat's Seminary, 201 Taylor St. N.E., Washington 20017. (Major house of formation serving the four Ukrainian Byzantine-rite dioceses in the U.S.)

Florida: Miami* — St. John Vianney College Seminary, 2900 S.W. 87th Ave., Miami 33165.

Palm Beach — St. Vincent de Paul Regional Seminary (major), 10701 S. Military Trail, Boynton Beach 33436.

Illinois: Chicago* — Archbishop Quigley Preparatory Seminary (high school), 103 East Chestnut St., Chicago 60611; St. Joseph Seminary (college), 6551 N. Sheridan Rd., Chicago 60626. University of St. Mary of the Lake Mundelein Seminary (School of Theology), 1000 E. Maple Ave., Mundelein 60060.

Indiana: Indianapolis* — Saint Meinrad Seminary, College and School of Theology (interdiocesan), St. Meinrad 47577.

Iowa: Davenport — St. Ambrose University Seminary (interdiocesn), 518 W. Locust St., Davenport 52803.

Dubuque* — Seminary of St. Pius X (interdiocesan), Loras College, Dubuque 52001.

Louisiana: New Orleans* - Notre Dame Seminary Graduate School of Theology, 2901 S. Carrollton Ave., New Orleans 70118; St. Joseph Seminary College (interdiocesan), St. Benedict 70457.

Maryland: Baltimore* — Mount St. Mary's Seminary and University, 5400 Roland Ave., Baltimore 21210; Mount St. Mary's Seminary, Emmitsburg 21727-7797.

Massachusetts: Boston* — St. John's Seminary, School of Theology, 127 Lake St., Brighton 02135; St. John's Seminary, College of Liberal Arts, 197 Foster St., Brighton 02135; Pope John XXIII National Seminary (for ages 30-60), 558 South Ave., Weston 02193.

Newton — Melkite Greek Catholic — St. Gregory the Theologian Seminary, 233 Grant Ave., Newton 02159.

Michigan: Detroit* — Sacred Heart Major Seminary (college/theologate and institute for ministry), 2701 Chicago Blvd., Detroit 48206; Sts. Cyril and Methodius Seminary, St. Mary's College (theologate and college) independent, primarily serving Polish-American community, 3535 Indian Trail, Orchard Lake 48324-1623.

Grand Rapids — Christopher House, 723 Rosewood Ave., S.E., East Grand Rapids 49506.

Minnesota: St. John's School of Theology and Seminary, St. John's University, P.O. Box 7288, Collegeville 56321-7288.

St. Paul and Minneapolis* — St. Paul Seminary School of Divinity, University of St. Thomas, St. Paul 55101; St. John Vianney Seminary (college residence), 2115 Summit Ave., St. Paul 55105.

Winona — Immaculate Heart of Mary Seminary, St. Mary's University, No. 43, 700 Terrace Heights, Winona 55987.

Missouri: Jefferson City — St. Thomas Aquinas Preparatory Seminary (High School Seminary), 245 N. Levering Ave., P.O. Box 858, Hannibal 63401.

St. Louis* — Kenrick-Glennon Seminary (St. Louis Roman Catholic Theological Seminary). Kenrick School of Theology and Cardinal Glennon College, 5200 Glennon Dr., St. Louis 63119.

Montana: Helena — Pre-Seminary Program, Carroll College, Helena 59625.

Nebraska: Seward – St. Gregory the Great Seminary, 1301 280th Rd., 68434 (pre-theology).

New Jersey: Newark* — Immaculate Conception Seminary — college seminary; major seminary; graduate school — Seton Hall University, 400 South Orange Ave., South Orange 07079.

New York: Brooklyn — Cathedral Seminary Residence of the Immaculate Conception (college and pre-theology), 7200 Douglaston Parkway, Douglaston 11362; Cathedral Preparatory Seminary, 56-25 92nd St., Elmhurst 11373.

Buffalo — Christ the King Seminary (interdiocesan theologate), P.O. Box 607, 711 Knox Rd., East Aurora 14052-0607.

New York* — St. Joseph's Seminary (major), 201 Seminary Ave., Dunwoodie, Yonkers 10704; St. John Neumann Residence (college and pre-theology), 5655 Arlington Ave., Riverdale 10471. Cathedral Preparatory Seminary, 946 Boston Post Rd., Rye 10580.

Ogdensburg — Wadhams Hall Seminary College (interdiocesan), 6866 State Hwy. 37, Ogdensburg 13669.

Rockville Centre — Seminary of the Immaculate Conception (major), Lloyd Harbor, Huntington, L.I. 11743.

St. Maron Eparchy, Brooklyn — Our Lady of Lebanon Maronite Seminary, 7164 Alaska Ave. N.W., Washington, DC 20012.

North Dakota: Fargo — Cardinal Muench Seminary (interdiocesan high school, college and pre-theology), 100 35th Ave. N.E., Fargo 58102.

Ohio: Cincinnati* — Mt. St. Mary's Seminary of the West, 6616 Beechmont Ave., Cincinnati 45230 (division of the Athenaeum of Ohio).

Cleveland — St. Mary Seminary and Graduate School of Theology, 28700 Euclid Ave. Wickliffe 44092.

Columbus — Pontifical College Josephinum (national), theologate and college, 7625 North High St., Columbus 43235-1498.

Oregon: Portland* — Mount Angel Seminary (interdiocesan, college, pre-theology program, graduate school of theology), 1 Abbey Dr., St. Benedict 97373.

Pennsylvania: Erie — St. Mark Seminary, P.O. Box 10397, Erie 16514.

Greensburg — St. Vincent Seminary (interdiocesan; pre-theology program; theologate; graduate programs in theology; religious education), 300 Fraser Purchase Rd., Latrobe 15650-2690.

Philadelphia* — Theological Seminary of St. Charles Borromeo, 100 East Wynnewood Rd., Wynnewood 19096. (College, pre-theology program, spirituality year pogram, theologate.)

Pittsburgh* (Byzantine-Ruthenian) — Byzantine Catholic Seminary of Sts. Cyril and Methodius (college, pre-theology program, theologate), 3605 Perrysville Ave., Pittsburgh 15214.

Pittsburgh — St. Paul Seminary (interdiocesan, college and pre-theology), 2900 Noblestown Rd., Pittsburgh 15205.

Scranton — St. Pius X Seminary (college and pre-theology formation; interdiocesan), Dalton 18414. Affiliated with the University of Scranton.

Rhode Island: Providence — Seminary of Our Lady of Providence (House of Formation; college students and pre-theology), 485 Mount Pleasant Ave., Providence 02908.

Texas: Dallas — Holy Trinity Seminary (college and pre-theology; English proficiency and academic

foundation programs), P.O. Box 140309, Irving 75014.
El Paso — St. Charles Seminary College, P.O. Box
17548, El Paso 79917.

Galveston-Houston — St. Mary's Seminary
(theologate), 9845 Memorial Dr., Houston 77024.

San Antonio* — Assumption Seminary (theologate
and pre-theology, Hispanic ministry emphasis), 2600
W. Woodlawn Ave., San Antonio 78228.

Washington: Spokane — Bishop White Seminary,
College Formation Program, E. 429 Sharp Ave., Spokane 99202.

Wisconsin: Milwaukee* — St. Francis Seminary,
3257 S. Lake Dr., St. Francis 53235; College Program, 2497 N. Murray Ave., Milwaukee, WI 53211.
Sacred Heart School of Theology (interdiocesan seminary for second-career vocations), P.O. Box 429,
Hales Corners, Wis. 53130.

North American College

Founded by the U.S. Bishops in 1859, the North
American College serves as a residence and house
of formation for U.S. seminarians and graduate students in Rome. The first ordination of an alumnus
took place June 14, 1862. Pontifical status was
granted the college by Pope Leo XIII Oct. 25, 1884.
Students pursue theological and related studies
principally at the Pontifical Gregorian University
and at the Pontifical University of Saint Thomas
Aquinas (the Angelicum). The current rector is Rev.
Msgr. Timothy Dolan, Ph.D. Address: 00120 Città
del Vaticano.

American College of Louvain

Founded by U.S. Bishops in 1857, the American
College of Louvain, in Belgium, is a seminary for
U.S. students. It also serves as a community for English-speaking graduate-student priests and religious
priests pursuing studies at the Catholic University of
Louvain (Université Catholique de Louvain, founded
1425). The college is administered by an American
rector and faculty, and operates under the auspices of
a committee of the national Conference of Catholic
Bishops. The current rector is Very Rev. David
Windsor, C.M. Address: The American College,
Catholic University of Louvain, Naamsestraat 100,
B-3000, Leuven, Belgium.

WORLD AND U.S. SEMINARY STATISTICS

The 1999 *Statistical Yearbook of the Church* reported the following comparative statistics for the years 1990
to 1997 of candidates in Philosophy and Theology (major seminarians). World totals are given first; U.S.
statistics are given in parentheses.

Year	Total Major Seminarians	Diocesan	Religious
1990	196,155 (5,552)	64,629 (3,676)	31,526 (1,876)
1991	199,668 (5,487)	66,305 (3,777)	33,363 (1,710)
1992	102,000 (5,380)	67,960 (3,645)	34,040 (1,735)
1993	103,709 (5,123)	68,829 (3,505)	34,880 (1,618)
1994	105,075 (5,100)	69,613 (3,526)	35,462 (1,574)
1995	106,346 (4,831)	69,777 (3,234)	36,569 (1,597)
1996	105,870 (4,785)	70,034 (3,268)	35,836 (1,517)
1997	108,517 (4,729)	70,534 (3,311)	37,983(1,418)

PONTIFICAL UNIVERSITIES

(Principal source: *Annuario Pontificio*.) These
universities, listed according to country of location, have been canonically erected and authorized
by the Congregation for Catholic Education to
award degrees in stated fields of study. New laws
and norms governing ecclesiastical universities
and faculties were promulgated in the apostolic
constitution *Sapientia Christiana*, issued Apr. 15,
1979.

Argentina: Pontifical Catholic University of S.
Maria of Buenos Aires (June 16, 1960): Av. Alicia
Moreau de Justo 1400, 1107 Buenos Aires.

Belgium: Catholic University of Louvain (founded
Dec. 9, 1425; canonically erected, 1834), with autonomous institutions for French- (Louvain) and
Flemish- (Leuven) speaking: Place de l'Universite I,
B-1348 Louvain-La-Neuve (French); Naamsestraat
22/b, B-3000 Leuven (Flemish).

Brazil: Pontifical Catholic University of Rio de
Janeiro (Jan. 20, 1947): Rua Marquês de São Vicente
225, 22451-000 Rio de Janeiro, RJ.

Pontifical Catholic University of Minas Gerais (June
5, 1983): Av. Dom José Gaspar 500, C.P. 2686, 30161-
000 Belo Horizonte, MG.

Pontifical Catholic University of Parana (Aug. 6,
1985): Rua Imaculada Conceição, 1155, Prado Velho,
C.P. 670, 80001 Curitiba, PR.

Pontifical Catholic University of Rio Grande do Sul
(Nov. 1, 1950): Av. Ipiranga 6681, C.P. 1429,
90001-000 Porto Alegre, RS.

Pontifical Catholic University of São Paulo (Jan.
25, 1947): Rua Monte Alegre 984, 05014-901 São
Paulo SP.

Pontifical University of Campinas (Sept. 8, 1956): Rua
Marechal Deodoro 1099, 13020-000 Campinas, SP.

Canada: Laval University (Mar. 15, 1876): Case
Postale 460, Québec G1K 7P4.

St. Paul University (formerly University of Ottawa)
(Feb. 5, 1889): 223 Rue Main, Ottawa, Ont. K1S 1C4.

University of Sherbrooke (Nov. 21, 1957): Chemin
Ste.-Catherine, 2500, boulevard de l'Université,
Sherbrooke, Qué. J1K 12R1.

Chile: Pontifical Catholic University of Chile (June
21, 1888): Avenida Bernardo O'Higgins, 340, Casilla
114D, Santiago.

Catholic University of Valparaíso (Nov. 1, 1961):
Avenida Brasil 2950, Casilla 4059, Valparaíso.

Colombia: Bolivarian Pontifical Catholic University (Aug. 16, 1945): Circular 1a, N.70-01, Apartado
56006, Medellín.

Pontifical Xaverian University (July 31, 1937): Carrera 7, N. 40-62, Apartado 56710, Santafé de Bogota D.C.; Apartado 26239, Calle 18, N. 118-250, Cali (Cali campus).

Cuba: Catholic University of St. Thomas of Villanueva (May 4, 1957): Avenida Quenta 16,660, Marianao.

Dominican Republic: Pontifical Catholic University "Mother and Teacher" (Sept. 9, 1987): Apartado 822, Santiago de Los Caballeros.

Ecuador: Pontifical Catholic University of Ecuador (July 16, 1954): Doce de Octubre, N. 1076, Apartado 17-01-2184, Quito.

France: Catholic University of Lille (Nov. 18, 1875): Boulevard Vauban 60, 59016 Lille Cedex.

Catholic Faculties of Lyon (Nov. 22, 1875): 25, Rue du Plat, 69288 Lyon Cedex 02.

Catholic Institute of Paris (Aug. 11, 1875): 21, Rue d'Assas, 75270 Paris Cedex 06.

Catholic Institute of Toulouse (Nov. 15, 1877): Rue de la Fonderie 31, 31068 Toulouse.

Catholic University of the West (Sept. 16, 1875): 3, Place André Leroy, B.P. 808, 49005 Angers.

Germany: Catholic University Eichstätt (Apr. 1, 1980): Ostenstrasse 26, D-85072, Eichstätt, Federal Republic of Germany.

Guatemala: Rafael Landívar University (Oct. 18, 1961): Vista Hermosa III, Zona 16, Guatemala.

Ireland: St. Patrick's College (Mar. 29, 1896): Maynooth, Co. Kildare.

Italy: Catholic University of the Sacred Heart (Dec. 25, 1920): Largo Gemelli 1, 20123 Milan.

Libera University Mary of the Assumption (Oct. 26, 1939): Via della Transpontina 21, 00193 Rome, Italy.

Japan: Jochi Daigaku (Sophia University) (Mar. 29, 1913): Chiyoda-Ku, Kioi-cho 7, Tokyo 102.

Lebanon: St. Joseph University of Beirut (Mar. 25, 1881): Rue de l'Université St.-Joseph, Boite Postale 293, Beyrouth (Beirut), Liban.

Netherlands: Catholic University of Nijmegen (June 29, 1923): P.B. 9102, Comeniuslaam 4, 6500 HC, Nijmegen.

Panama: University of S. Maria La Antigua (May 27, 1965): Apartado 6-1696, Panama 6.

Paraguay: Catholic University of Our Lady of the Assumption (Feb. 2, 1965): Independencia Nacional y Comuneros, Casilla 1718, Asunción.

Peru: Pontifical Catholic University of Peru (Sept. 30, 1942): Av. Universitaria, s/n. San Miguel, Apartado 1761, Lima 100.

Philippines: Pontifical University of Santo Tomás (Nov. 20, 1645): España Street, 1008 Manila.

Poland: Catholic University of Lublin (July 25, 1920): Aleje Racùawickie 14, Skr. Poczt. 129, 20-950, Lublin.

Catholic Theological Academy (June 29, 1989): Ul. Dewajtis 5, 01-815, Warsaw.

Pontifical Academy of Theology of Krakow (Dec. 8, 1981): Ul. Kanonicza, 25, 31-002 Kraków.

Portugal: Portuguese Catholic University (Nov. 1, 1967): Palma de Cima, 1 600 Lisbon.

Puerto Rico: Pontifical Catholic University of Puerto Rico (Aug. 15, 1972): 2250 Ave. Las Américas Suite 523, Ponce, Puerto Rico 00731-6382.

Spain: Catholic University of Navarra (Aug. 6, 1960): Campus Universitario, E-31080 Pamplona.

Pontifical University "Comillas" (Mar. 29, 1904): Campus de Cantoblanco, 28049 Madrid.

Pontifical University of Salamanca (Sept. 25, 1940): Compañía 5, 37002 Salamanca.

University of Deusto (Aug. 10, 1963): Avenida de las Universidades, 28, 48007 Bilbao o Apartado 1, 48080 Bilbao.

Taiwan (China): Fu Jen Catholic University (Nov. 15, 1923, at Peking; reconstituted at Taipeh, Sept. 8, 1961): Hsinchuang, Taipeh Hsien 24205.

United States: The Catholic University of America (Mar. 7, 1889): 620 Michigan Ave. N.E., Washington, D.C. 20064.

Georgetown University (Mar. 30, 1833): 37th and O Sts. N.W., Washington, D.C. 20057.

Niagara University (June 21, 1956): Lewiston Rd., Niagara Falls, N.Y. 14109.

Uruguay: Catholic University of Uruguay "Dámaso Antonio Larrañaga" (Jan. 25, 1985): Avda. 8 de Octubre 2738, 11.600 Montevideo.

Venezuela: Catholic University "Andrés Bello" (Sept. 29, 1963): Esquina Jesuitas, Apartado 29068, Caracas 1021.

ECCLESIASTICAL FACULTIES

(Principal source: *Annuario Pontificio*) These faculties in Catholic seminaries and universities, listed according to country of location, have been canonically erected and authorized by the Congregation for Catholic Education to award degrees in stated fields of study. In addition to those listed here, there are other faculties of theology or philosophy in state universities and for members of certain religious orders only.

Argentina: Faculties of Philosophy and Theology, San Miguel (Sept. 8, 1932).

Australia: Catholic Institute of Theology, Sydney (Feb. 2, 1954).

Austria: Theological Faculty, Linz (Dec. 25, 1978).

International Theological Institute for Family Studies (Oct. 1, 1996).

Brazil: Philosophical and Theological Faculties of the Company of Jesus, Belo Horizonte (July 15, 1941 and Mar. 12, 1949).

Ecclesiastical Faculty of Philosophy "John Paul II," Rio de Janeiro (Aug. 6, 1981).

Cameroon: Catholic Institute of Yaoundé (Nov. 15, 1991).

Canada: College of Immaculate Conception – Montréal Section of Jesuit Faculties in Canada (Sept. 8, 1932). Suspended.

Pontifical Institute of Medieval Studies, Toronto (Oct. 18, 1939).

Dominican Faculty of Theology of Canada, Ottawa (1965; Nov. 15, 1975).

Regis College — Toronto Section of the Jesuit Faculty of Theology in Canada, Toronto (Feb. 17, 1956; Dec. 25, 1977).

Congo (formerly Zaire): Catholic Faculties of Kinshasa, Kinshasa (theology, Apr. 25, 1957; philosophy, Nov. 25, 1987).

Côte d'Ivoire (Ivory Coast): Catholic Institute of West Africa, Abidjan (Aug. 12, 1975).

Croatia: Philosophical Faculty, Zagreb (July 31, 1989).

France: Centre Sèvres — Faculties of Theology and Philosophy of the Jesuits, Paris (Sept. 8, 1932).

Germany: Theological Faculty of the Major Episcopal Seminary, Trier (Sept. 8, 1955).

Theological Faculty, Paderborn (June 11, 1966).
Theological-Philosophical Faculty, Frankfurt (1932; June 7, 1971).
Philosophical Faculty, Munich (1932; Oct. 25, 1971).
Theological Faculty, Fulda (Dec. 22, 1978).
Philosophical-Theological School of Salesians, Benediktbeuern (May 24, 1992).
Philosphical-Theological School, Vallendar (Oct. 7, 1993).
Great Britain: Heythrop College, University of London, London (Nov. 1, 1964). Theology, philosophy.
Hungary: Faculty of Theology (1635), Institue on Canon Law (Nov. 30, 1996), Budapest,
India: *Jnana Deepa Vidyapeeth* (Pontifical Athenaeum), Institute of Philosophy and Religion, Poona (July 27, 1926).
Vidyajyoti, Institute of Religious Studies, Faculty of Theology, Delhi (1932; Dec. 9, 1974).
Satya Nilayam, Institute of Philosophy and Culture. Faculty of Philosophy, Madras (Sept. 8, 1932; Dec. 15, 1976).
Pontifical Institute of Theology and Philosophy at the Pontifical Interritual Seminary of St. Joseph, Alwaye, Kerala (Feb. 24, 1972).
Dharmaram Vidya Kshetram Pontifical Athenaeum of Theology and Philosophy, Bangalore (theology, Jan. 6, 1976; philosophy, Dec. 8, 1983).
Pontifical Oriental Institute of Religious Studies, Kottayam (July 3, 1982).
Faculty of Theology, Ranchi (Aug. 15, 1982).
St. Peter's Pontifical Institute of Theology, Bangalore (Jan. 6, 1985).
Indonesia: Wedabhakti Pontifical Faculty of Theology, Yogyakarta (Nov. 1, 1984).
Ireland: The Milltown Institute of Theology and Philosophy, Dublin (1932).
Israel: French Biblical and Archeological School, Jerusalem (founded 1890; approved Sept. 17, 1892; canonically approved to confer Doctorate in Biblical Science, June 29, 1983).
Italy: Theological Faculty of Southern Italy, Naples. Two sections: St. Louis Posillipo (Mar. 16, 1918) and St. Thomas Aquinas Capodimonte (Oct. 31, 1941).
Pontifical Theological Faculty of Sardinia, Cagliari, (Aug. 5, 1927).
Interregional Theological Faculty, Milan (Aug. 8, 1935; restructured 1969).
Faculty of Philosophy "Aloisianum," Gallarate (1937; Mar. 20, 1974).
Pontifical Ambrosian Institute of Sacred Music, Milan (Mar. 12, 1940).
Theological Faculty of Sicily, Palermo (Dec. 8, 1980).
Theological Institute Pugliese, Molfetta (June 24, 1992).
Theological Institute Calabro, Catanzaro (Jan. 28, 1993).
Theological Faculty of Central Italy, Florence (Sep. 9, 1997).
Japan: Faculty of Theology, Nagoya (May 25, 1984).
Kenya: Catholic Higher Institute of Eastern Africa, Nairobi (May 2, 1984).
Lebanon: Faculty of Theology, University of the Holy Spirit, Kaslik (May 30, 1982).

Madagascar: Superior Institute of Theology and Philosophy, at the Regional Seminary of Antananarivo, Ambatoroka-Antananarivo (Apr. 21, 1960).
Malta: Faculty of Theology, Tal-Virtù (Nov. 22, 1769), with Institute of Philosophy and Human Studies (Sept. 8, 1984).
Mexico: Theological Faculty of Mexico (June 29, 1982) and Philosophy (Jan. 6, 1986), Institute of Canon Law (Sept. 4, 1995), Mexico City.
Nigeria: Catholic Institute of West Africa, Port Harcourt (May 9, 1994).
Peru: Pontifical and Civil Faculty of Theology, Lima (July 25, 1571).
Poland: Pontifical Theological Faculty, Warsaw (May 3, 1988) with two sections: St. John Baptist (1837, 1920, Nov. 8, 1962) at the "Metropolitan Seminary Duchowne," and "St. Andrew Bobola" – "Bobolanum" (Sept. 8, 1932).
Philosophical Faculty, Krakow (1932; Sept. 20, 1984).
Theological Faculty, Poznan (1969; pontifical designation, June 2, 1974).
Spain: Theological Faculty, Granada (1940; July 31, 1973).
Theological Faculty of San Esteban, Salamanca (1947; Oct. 4, 1972).
Theological Faculty of the North, of the Metropolitan Seminary of Burgos and the Diocesan Seminary of Vitoria (Feb. 6, 1967).
Theological Faculty of Catalunya, (Mar. 7, 1968), with the Institutes of Fundamental Theology (Dec. 28, 1984), Liturgy (Aug. 15, 1986) and Philosophy (July 26, 1988), Barcelona.
Theological Faculty "San Vicente Ferrer" (two sections), Valencia (Jan. 23, 1974).
Theological Faculty "San Damaso" (Sept. 19, 1996), Madrid.
Switzerland: Theological Faculty, Lucerne (Dec. 25, 1973).
Theological Faculty, Chur (Jan. 1, 1974).
Theological Faculty, Lugano (Nov. 20, 1993).
United States: St. Mary's Seminary and University, School of Theology, Baltimore (May 1, 1822).
St. Mary of the Lake Faculty of Theology, Mundelein, Ill. (Sept. 30, 1929).
Weston Jesuit School of Theology, Cambridge, Mass. (Oct. 18, 1932).
The Jesuit School of Theology, Berkeley, Calif. (Feb. 2, 1934, as "Alma College," Los Gatos, Calif.).
Faculty of Philosophy and Letters, St. Louis, Mo. (Feb. 2, 1934).
St. Michael's Institute, Jesuit School of Philosophy and Letters, Spokane, Wash. (Feb. 2, 1934).
Pontifical Faculty of Theology of the Immaculate Conception, Dominican House of Studies, Washington, D.C. (Nov. 15, 1941).
Also located in the United States are:
The Marian Library/International Marian Research Institute (IMRI), U.S. branch of Pontifical Theological Faculty "Marianum," University of Dayton, Dayton, OH 45469 (affil. 1976, inc. 1983).
John Paul II Institute for Studies on Marriage and the Family, U.S. section of Pontifical John Paul II Institute for Studies on Marriage and Family at the Pontifical Lateran University, 487 Michigan Ave. NE, Washington, DC 20017 (Aug. 22, 1988).

Pontifical College Josephinum (Theologate and College) at Columbus, Ohio, is a national pontifical seminary. Established Sept. 1, 1888, it is directly under the auspices of the Vatican through the Apostolic Pro-Nuncio to the U.S., who serves as the seminary's chancellor.

Vietnam: Theological Faculty of the Pontifical National Seminary of St. Pius X, Dalat (July 31, 1965). Activities suppressed.

PONTIFICAL UNIVERSITIES AND INSTITUTES IN ROME

(Source: *Annuario Pontificio*.)
Pontifical Gregorian University (*Gregorian*) (1552): Piazza della Pilotta, 4, 00187 Rome. Associated with the university are: **Pontifical Biblical Institute** (May 7, 1909): Via della Pilotta, 25, 00187 Rome; **Pontifical Institute of Oriental Studies** (Oct. 15, 1917): Piazza S. Maria Maggiore, 7, 00185 Rome.
Pontifical Lateran University (1773): Piazza S. Giovanni in Laterano, 4, 00184 Rome. Attached to the university is the **Pontifical Institute of Studies of Marriage and the Family**, erected by Pope John Paul II, Oct 7, 1982; a section of the Institute was established at the Dominican House of Studies, Washington, D.C., by a decree dated Aug. 22, 1988; sections were opened in Mexico in 1992 and Valencia, Spain, in 1994.
Pontifical Urbaniana University (1627): Via Urbano VIII, 16, 00165 Rome.
Pontifical University of St. Thomas Aquinas (*Angelicum*) (1580), of the Order of Preachers: Largo Angelicum, 1, 00184 Rome.
Pontifical University *Salesianum* (May 3, 1940; university designation May 24, 1973), of the Salesians of Don Bosco: Piazza dell'Ateneo Salesiano, 1, 00139 Rome. Associated with the university is the **Pontifical Institute of Higher Latin Studies**, known as the

Faculty of Christian and Classical Letters (June 4, 1971).
Pontifical University *della Santa Croce* (of the Holy Cross) (Jan. 9, 1985), of the Personal Prelature of Opus Dei: Piazza S. Apollinare, 49, 00186 Rome.
Pontifical Athenaeum of St. Anselm (1687), of the Benedictines: Piazza Cavalieri di Malta, 5, 00153 Rome.
Pontifical Athenaeum *Antonianum* (of St. Anthony) (May 17, 1933), of the Order of Friars Minor: Via Merulana, 124, 00185 Rome.
Athenaeum *Regina Apostolorum* (Queen of the Apostles), of the Legionaries of Christ: Via Aurelia Antica, 460, 00165 Rome.
Pontifical Institute of Sacred Music (1911; May 24, 1931): Via di Torre Rossa, 21, 00165 Rome.
Pontifical Institute of Christian Archeology (Dec. 11, 1925): Via Napoleone III, 1, 00185 Rome.
Pontifical Theological Faculty *St. Bonaventure* (Dec. 18, 1587), of the Order of Friars Minor Conventual: Via del Serafico, 1, 00142 Rome.
Pontifical Theological Faculty, Pontifical Institute of Spirituality *Teresianum* (1935), of the Discalced Carmelites: Piazza San Pancrazio, 5-A, 00152 Rome.
Pontifical Theological Faculty *Marianum* (1398), of the Servants of Mary: Viale Trente Aprile, 6, 00153 Rome. Attached to the university is **The Marian Library/International Marian Research Institute** (IMRI), U.S. branch of Pontifical Theological Faculty *Marianum*, University of Dayton, Dayton, Ohio, 45469 (affil. 1976, inc. 1983).
Pontifical Institute of Arabic and Islamic Studies (1926), of the Missionaries of Africa: Viale di Trastevere, 89, 00153 Rome.
Pontifical Faculty of Educational Science *Auxilium* (June 27, 1970), of the Daughters of Mary, Help of Christians: Via Cremolino, 141, 00166 Rome.

APOSTOLIC LETTER: *INTER MUNERA ACADEMIARUM*

On Jan. 28, 1999, the Feast of St. Thomas Aquinas, Pope John Paul II issued the apostolic letter Inter Munera Academiarum *renewing the statutes of the Pontifical Roman Theological Academy and the Pontifical Academy of St. Thomas Aquinas, commonly called the Angelicum. Excerpts follow:*
Among the tasks of the Academies founded over the centuries by the Roman pontiffs, research in philosophy and theology holds pride of place. In my recent Encyclical Letter, Fides et Ratio, I put great importance on the dialogue between theology and philosophy and clearly expressed my appreciation of the thought of St. Thomas Aquinas, recognizing its enduring originality (cf. Nn. 43-44). St. Thomas can rightly be called "an apostle of the truth" (n. 44). In fact, the insight of the Angelic Doctor consists in the certainty that there is a basic harmony between faith and reason (cf. N. 43).... At the dawn of the third millennium, many cultural conditions have changed. Very significant progress has been made in the field of anthropology, but above all substantial changes have occurred in the very way of understanding the human being's condition in relation to God, to other human beings and to all creation. First of all, the greatest challenge of our age comes from a grow-

ing separation between faith and reason, between the Gospel and culture. The studies dedicated to this immense area are increasing day by day in the context of the new evangelization. Indeed, the message of salvation encounters many obstacles stemming from erroneous concepts and a serious lack of adequate formation.
A century after the promulgation of the Encyclical Letter Aeterni Patris of my Predecessor Leo XIII, which marked the beginning of a new development in the renewal of philosophical and theological studies and in the relationship between faith and reason, I would lime to give a new impetus to the Pontifical Academies working in this area, in accordance with the thought and tendencies of the present day as well as the pastoral needs of the Church.
Therefore, recognizing the work carried out for centuries by the members of the Pontifical Roman Theological Academy and the Pontifical Academy of St. Thomas Aquinas and the Catholic Religion, I have decided to renew that attached Statutes of these Pontifical Academies, so that with greater effectiveness they can increase their involvement in the philosophical and theological field, in order to further the pastoral mission of the Successor of Peter and of the universal Church.

CATHOLIC PRESS

Statistics

The 1999 *Catholic Press Directory*, published by the Catholic Press Association, reported a total of 645 periodicals in North America with a circulation of 25,361,036. The figures included 198 newspapers with a circulation of 5,928,216; 268 magazines with a circulation of 14,639,408; 140 newsletters with a circulation of 4,078,758, and 39 other-language periodicals (newspapers and magazines) with a circulation of 714,654.

Newspapers in the U.S.

There were 186 newspapers in the United States, with a circulation 5,741,316. Five of these had national circulation; 167 were diocesan newspapers; 14 were Eastern Catholic Church publications.

National papers included: **National Catholic Register**, founded 1900; **Our Sunday Visitor**, founded 1912; **National Catholic Reporter**, founded 1964; **Catholic Twin Circle**, founded 1967 and **The Wanderer**, founded 1867.

The oldest U.S. Catholic newspaper is **The Pilot** of Boston, established in 1829 (under a different title).

Other Diocesan Newspapers: There were four other diocesan newspapers located outside continental North America (Puerto Rico, Samoa, U.S. Virgin Islands, West Indies), with a circulation of 83,700.

Magazines in U.S.

The Catholic Press Directory reported 248 magazines in the U.S. with a circulation of 13,801,728. In addition, there were 139 newsletters; circulation, 4,064,458.

America and **Commonweal** are the only weekly and biweekly magazines, respectively, of general interest.

The monthly magazines with the largest circulation are **Columbia** (1,490,417), the official organ of the Knights of Columbus, **Catholic Digest** (501,024) and **St. Anthony's Messenger** (339,086).

Other-Language Publications: There were an additional 25 publications (newspapers and magazines) in the U.S. in languages other than English with a circulation of 445,354.

Canadian Statistics

There were 8 newspapers in Canada with a circulation of 103,200. These included two national newspapers (**The Catholic Register**, founded 1893; **Catholic New Times**, founded 1976) and 6 diocesan. There were 20 magazines with a circulation of 837,680; one newsletter with a circulation of 14,300; and 14 publications in languages other than English, circulation, 269,300.

CATHOLIC NEWSPAPERS, MAGAZINES, AND NEWSLETTERS IN THE U.S.

(*Sources:* Catholic Press Directory; The Catholic Journalist; Almanac *survey; Catholic News Service.*) *Abbreviation code: a, annual; bm, bimonthly; m, monthly; q, quarterly; w, weekly.*

CATHOLIC COMMUNICATIONS

Newspapers

Acadiana Catholic, m; 1408 Carmel Ave., Lafayette, LA 70501; Lafayette diocese.

A.D. Times, biweekly; 2141 Downyflake Lane, Allentown, PA 18103-4724. Allentown diocese.

Agua Viva, m; 1280 Med Park Dr., Las Cruces, NM 88005-3239; Las Cruces diocese.

Alaskan Shepherd, 6 times a year; 1312 Peger Rd., Fairbanks, AK 99709; Fairbanks diocese.

America (Ukrainian-English), 2 times a week; 817 N. Franklin St., Philadelphia, PA 19123. Providence Association of Ukrainian Catholics in America.

Anchor, The, w; P.O. Box 7, Fall River, MA 02722; Fall River diocese.

Arkansas Catholic, w; P.O. Box 7417, Little Rock, AR 72217; Little Rock diocese.

Arlington Catholic Herald, w; 200 N. Glebe Rd., Suite 607, Arlington, VA 22203; Arlington diocese.

Bayou Catholic, The, w; P.O. Box 9077, Houma, LA 70361; Houma-Thibodaux diocese.

Beacon, The, w; P.O. Box 1887, Clifton, NJ 07015-1887. Paterson diocese.

Bishop's Bulletin, m; 523 N. Duluth Ave., Sioux Falls, SD 57104-2714. Sioux Falls diocese.

Byzantine Catholic World, biweekly; 66 Riverview Ave., Pittsburgh, PA 15214; Pittsburgh Byzantine archdiocese.

Catholic Accent, 40 times a year; P.O. Box 850, Greensburg, PA 15601; Greensburg diocese.

Catholic Advance, The, w; 424 N. Broadway, Wichita, KS 67202-2377; Wichita diocese.

Catholic Advocate, The, w; 171 Clifton Ave., Newark, NJ 07104-9500; Newark archdiocese.

Catholic Calendar, semi-monthly; 411 Iris St., Lake Charles, LA 70601; one page in local newspaper twice a month; Lake Charles diocese.

Catholic Chronicle, biweekly; P.O. Box 1866, Toledo, OH 43603-1866; Toledo diocese.

Catholic Commentator, The, biweekly; P.O. Box 14746, Baton Rouge, LA 70898-4746; Baton Rouge diocese.

Catholic Connector, The, m; 660 Burton, SE, Grand Rapids, MI 49507; Grand Rapids diocese.

Catholic Courier, w; P.O. Box 24379, Rochester, NY 14624-0379. Rochester diocese.

Catholic East Texas, biweekly; 1015 ESE Loop 323, Tyler, TX 75701-9663. Tyler diocese.

Catholic Explorer, w (biweekly July, Aug.); 402 S. Independence Blvd., Romeoville, IL 60446-2264; Joliet diocese.

Catholic Exponent, biweekly; P.O. Box 6787, Youngstown, OH 44501-6787; Youngstown diocese.

Catholic Faith and Family, w.; 33 Rossotto Dr., Hamden, CT 06514; national, established 1998.

Catholic Family News, m.; MPO Box 743, Niagara Falls, NY 14302.

Catholic Free Press, w; 51 Elm St., Worcester, MA 01609; Worcester diocese.

Catholic Herald, The, m; 109 Pawnee Ave., Manitou Springs, CO 80829; Colorado Springs diocese.

Catholic Herald, w; P.O. Box 07913, Milwaukee, WI 53207-0913; Milwaukee archdiocese. Also publishes editions for Madison and Superior dioceses.

Catholic Herald — Madison Edition, w; P.O. Box 44985, Madison, WI 53744-4985.

Catholic Herald — Superior Edition, w; P.O. Box 969, Superior, WI 54880.

Catholic Herald, biweekly; 5890 Newman Ct., Sacramento, CA 95819; Sacramento diocese.

Catholic Islander, m; P.O. Box 301825, St. Thomas, USVI, 00803-1825; Virgin Islands diocese.

Catholic Key, 44 times a year; P.O. Box 419037, Kansas City, MO 64141-6037; Kansas City-St. Joseph diocese.

Catholic Lantern, m; P.O. Box 4237, Stockton, CA 95204; Stockton diocese.

Catholic Light, biweekly; 300 Wyoming Ave., Scranton, PA 18503; Scranton diocese.

Catholic Lighthouse, m; P.O. Box 4070, Victoria, TX 77903; Victoria diocese.

Catholic Messenger, w; P.O. Box 460, Davenport, IA 52805; Davenport diocese.

Catholic Mirror The, m; P.O. Box 10372, Des Moines, IA 50306. Des Moines diocese.

Catholic Missourian, w; P.O. Box 1107, Jefferson City, MO 65102; Jefferson City diocese.

Catholic Moment, The, w; P.O. Box 1603, Lafayette, IN 47902; Lafayette diocese.

Catholic New York, w; P.O. Box 5133, New York, NY 10150; New York archdiocese.

Catholic News, w; P.O. Box 85, Port-of-Spain, Trinidad; West Indies.

Catholic News and Herald, The, w; P.O. Box 37267, Charlotte, NC 28237. Charlotte diocese.

Catholic Northwest Progress, The, w; 910 Marion St., Seattle, WA 98104; Seattle archdiocese.

Catholic Observer, biweekly; Box 1730, Springfield, MA 01101-1730; Springfield diocese.

Catholic Post, The, w; P.O. Box 1722, Peoria, IL 61656; Peoria diocese.

Catholic Register, biweekly; 126 C Logan Blvd., Hollidaysburg, PA 16648; Altoona-Johnstown diocese.

Catholic Review, w; P.O. Box 777, Baltimore, MD 21203; Baltimore archdiocese.

Catholic San Francisco, biweekly; 441 Church St., San Francisco, CA 94114; San Francisco archdiocese.

Catholic Sentinel, w; P.O. Box 18030, Portland, OR 97218-0030; Portland archdiocese, Baker diocese.

Catholic Spirit, The, w; 244 Dayton Ave., St. Paul, MN 55102-1893; St. Paul and Minneapolis archdiocese.

Catholic Spirit, The, w; P.O. Box 5247, Kendall Park, NJ 08824-5247; Metuchen diocese.

Catholic Spirit, The, m; P.O. Box 13327, Austin, TX 78711; Austin diocese.

Catholic Spirit, The, m; P.O. Box 951, Wheeling, WV 26003-0119; Wheeling-Charleston diocese.

Catholic Standard, w; P.O. Box 4464, Washington, D.C., 20017; Washington archdiocese.

Catholic Standard and Times, w; 222 N. 17th St., Philadelphia, PA 19103; Philadelphia archdiocese.

Catholic Star Herald, w; 1845 Haddon Ave., Camden, NJ 08101; Camden diocese.

Catholic Sun, The, semimonthly; P.O. Box 13549, Phoenix, AZ 85002; Phoenix diocese.

Catholic Sun, The, w; 421 S. Warren St., Syracuse, NY 13202; Syracuse diocese.

Catholic Telegraph, w; 100 E. 8th St., Cincinnati, OH 45202; Cincinnati archdiocese.

Catholic Times, w; 197 E. Gay St., Columbus, OH 43215-3229; Columbus diocese.

Catholic Times, The, w; P.O. Box 4248, Flint, MI 48504. Lansing diocese.

Catholic Times, w; 1615 W. Washington St., P.O. Box 3187, Springfield, IL 62708-3187; Springfield diocese.

Catholic Transcript, w; 467 Bloomfield Ave., Bloomfield, CT 06002; Hartford archdiocese; Bridgeport and Norwich dioceses.

Catholic Universe Bulletin, biweekly; 1027 Superior Ave. N.E., Cleveland, OH 44114-2556; Cleveland diocese.

Catholic Virginian, biweekly; Box 26843, Richmond, VA 23261; Richmond diocese.

Catholic Vision, m.; P.O. Box 31, Tucson, AZ 85702; Tuscon diocese.

Catholic Voice, The, biweekly; 3014 Lakeshore Ave., Oakland, CA 94610; Oakland diocese.

Catholic Voice, The, biweekly; P.O. Box 4010, Omaha, NE 68104-0010; Omaha archdiocese.

Catholic Week, w; P.O. Box 349, Mobile, AL 36601; Mobile archdiocese.

Catholic Weekly, The, w; 1520 Court St., Saginaw, MI 48602; Saginaw diocese.

Catholic Weekly, The, w; P.O. Box 1405, Saginaw, MI 48605. Gaylord diocese.

Catholic Witness, The, biweekly; P.O. Box 2555, Harrisburg, PA 17105; Harrisburg diocese.

Catolico de Texas, El (Spanish), m; P.O. Box 190347, Dallas, TX 75219; Dallas diocese.

Centinela, El (Spanish), m; P.O.Box 18030, Portland, OR 97218-0300.

Central Washington Catholic, 6 times a year; 5301-A Tieton Dr., Yakima, WA 98908. Yakima diocese.

Challenge, The, semimonthly; 2530 Victory Pkwy., Cincinnati, OH 45206. St. Maron diocese.

Chicago Catolico (Spanish), m; 1144 W. Jackson Blvd., Chicago, IL 60607; Chicago archdiocese.

Chronicle of Catholic Life, bm; 109 Pawnee Ave., Manitou Springs, CO 80829; Pueblo diocese.

Church Today, twice a month; P.O. Box 7417, Alexandria, LA 71306-0417; Alexandria diocese.

Church World, w; Industry Rd., P.O. Box 698, Brunswick, ME 04011; Portland diocese.

Clarion Herald, biweekly; P.O. Box 53247, New Orleans, LA 70153; New Orleans archdiocese.

Compass, The, w; P.O. Box 23825, Green Bay, WI 54305-3825; Green Bay diocese.

Council of Major Superiors of Women Religious, w; P.O. Box 4464, Washington, DC 20017; Washington archdiocese.

Courier, The, m; P.O. Box 949, Winona, MN 55987-0949; Winona diocese.

Criterion, The, w; P.O. Box 1717, Indianapolis, IN 46206; Indianapolis archdiocese.

Cross Roads, 26 times a year; 1310 W. Main St., Lexington, KY 40508-2040. Lexington diocese.

Dakota Catholic Action, m (exc. May and Aug.); P.O. Box 1137, Bismarck, ND 58502; Bismarck diocese.

Denver Catholic Register, w; 1300 S. Steele St., Denver, CO 80210-2599; Denver archdiocese.

Dialog, The, w; P.O. Box 2208, Wilmington, DE 19899; Wilmington diocese.

Diocese of Orange Bulletin, m; P.O. Box 14195, Orange, CA 92867-1999.

East Tennessee Catholic, The, biweekly; P.O. Box 11127, Knoxville, TN 37939-1127; Knoxville diocese.

East Texas Catholic, semimonthly; P.O. Box 3948, Beaumont, TX 77704-3948; Beaumont diocese.

Eastern Catholic Life, biweekly; 445 Lackawanna Ave., W. Paterson, NJ 07424; Passaic Byzantine eparchy.

Eastern Oklahoma Catholic, biweekly; Box 690240, Tulsa, OK 74169-0240; Tulsa diocese.

Evangelist, The, w; 40 N. Main Ave., Albany, NY 12203; Albany diocese.

Fairfield County Catholic, m; 238 Jewett Ave., Bridgeport, CT 06606; Bridgeport diocese.

Florida Catholic, The, w; P.O. Box 609512, Orlando, FL 32860; Orlando diocese. Publishes editions for Miami archdiocese and Palm Beach, Pensacola-Tallahassee, St. Petersburg and Venice dioceses.

Florida Catholic — Miami Edition, w; 9401 Biscayne Blvd., Miami, FL 33138.

Florida Catholic — Palm Beach Edition, w; 9995 N. Military Trail, Palm Beach Gardens, FL 33410.

Florida Catholic — Pensacola-Tallahassee Edition, w; P.O. Drawer 17329, Pensacola, FL 32522.

Florida Catholic — St. Petersburg Edition, w; P.O. Box 43022, St. Petersburg, FL 33743.

Florida Catholic — Venice Edition, w; P.O. Box 2006, Venice, FL 34284.

Four County Catholic, m; 1595 Norwich New London Turnpike, Uncasville, CT 06382. Norwich diocese.

Georgia Bulletin, w; 680 W. Peachtree St. N.W., Atlanta, GA 30308-1984; Atlanta archdiocese.

Glasilo KSKJ Amerikanski Slovenec (Slovenian), biweekly; 708 E. 159th, Cleveland, OH 44110; American Slovenian Catholic Union.

Globe, The, w; P.O. Box 5079, Sioux City, IA 51102; Sioux City diocese.

Gulf Pine Catholic, w; P.O. Box 1189, Biloxi, MS 39533-1189; Biloxi diocese.

Hawaii Catholic Herald, biweekly; 1184 Bishop St., Honolulu, HI 96813; Honolulu diocese.

Heraldo Catolico, El (Spanish), biweekly; 5890 Newman Ct., Sacramento, CA 95819; Sacramento diocese.

Hlas Naroda (Voice of the Nation) (Czech-English), biweekly; 2340 61st Ave., Cicero, IL 60650.

Horizons, twice a month; 1900 Carlton Rd., Parma, OH 44134-3129; Parma Byzantine eparchy.

Idaho Catholic Register, twice a month; 303 Federal Way, Boise, ID 83705; Boise diocese.

Inland Catholic, m; 1201 E. Highland Ave., San Bernardino, CA 92404-4607. San Bernardino diocese.

Inland Register, every 3 weeks; P.O. Box 48, Spokane, WA 99210-0048; Spokane diocese.

Inside Passage, biweekly; 419 6th St., Juneau, AK 99801; Juneau diocese.

Intermountain Catholic, w; P.O. Box 2489, Salt Lake City, UT 84110-2489; Salt Lake City diocese.

Jednota (Slovak-Eng.), w; 6611 Rockside Rd., Independence, OH 44131; First Catholic Slovak Union.

Lake Shore Visitor, w; P.O. Box 10668, Erie, PA 16514-0668; Erie diocese.

Leaven, The, w; 12615 Parallel Parkway, Kansas City, KS 66109; Kansas City archdiocese.

Long Island Catholic, The, w; P.O. Box 9009, Rockville Centre, NY 11571-9009; Rockville Centre diocese.

Maronites Today, m; 1320 East 51st St., Austin, TX 78723; Maronite Epachy of Our lady of Lebanon of Los Angeles.

Message, The, w; P.O. Box 4169, Evansville, IN 47724-0169; Evansville diocese.

Messenger, The, w; 2620 Lebanon Ave., Belleville, IL 62221; Belleville diocese.

Messenger, The, 45 times a year; P.O. Box 18068, Covington, KY 41018; Covington diocese.

Michigan Catholic, The, w; 305 Michigan Ave., Detroit, MI 48226; Detroit archdiocese.

Mirror, The, w; 601 S. Jefferson Ave., Springfield, MO 65806-3143; Springfield-Cape Girardeau diocese.

Mississippi Today, w; P.O. Box 2130, Jackson, MS 39225-2130; Jackson diocese.

Monitor, The, w; P.O. Box 5309, Trenton, NJ 08619-0309; Trenton diocese.

Montana Catholic, The, 16 times a year, P.O. Box 1729, Helena, MT 59624; Helena diocese.

Narod Polski (Polish Nation) (Polish-Eng.) semi-monthly; 984 Milwaukee Ave., Chicago, IL 60622.

National Catholic Register, w; 33 Rosotto Dr., Hamden, CT 06514; national.

National Catholic Reporter, w; P.O. Box 419281, Kansas City, MO 64141; national.

New Catholic Miscellany, The, w; 119 Broad St., Charleston, SC 29401; Charleston diocese.

New Earth, The, m; 244 Dayton Ave., St. Paul, MN 55102. Fargo diocese.

New Star, The, every 3 weeks; 2208 W. Chicago Ave., Chicago, IL 60622; St. Nicholas of Chicago Ukrainian diocese.

New World, The, w; 1144 W. Jackson Blvd., Chicago, IL 60607; Chicago archdiocese.

Newsletter, The, 9 times a year; 215 N. Westnedge, Kalamazoo, MI 49007; Kalamazoo diocese.

NC Catholic, 26 times a year; 715 Nazareth St., Raleigh, NC 27606. Raleigh diocese.

North Country Catholic, w; P.O. Box 326, Ogdensburg, NY 13669; Ogdensburg diocese.

North Texas Catholic, w; 800 West Loop 820 South, Fort Worth, TX 76108; Fort Worth diocese.

Northwest Indiana Catholic, w; 9292 Broadway, Merrillville, IN 46410; Gary diocese.

Northwestern Kansas Register, w; P.O. Box 1038, Salina, KS 67402; Salina diocese.

Observer, The, m; P.O. Box 2079, Monterey, CA 93942; Monterey diocese.

Observer, The, twice a month; 921 W. State St., Rockford, IL 61102; Rockford diocese.

One Voice, w; P.O. Box 10822, Birmingham, AL 35202; Birmingham diocese.

Our Northland Diocese, semi-monthly; P.O. Box 610, Crookston, MN 56716; Crookston diocese.

Our Sunday Visitor, w; 200 Noll Plaza, Huntington, IN 46750; national.

People of God, m; 4000 St. Joseph Pl. N.W., Albuquerque, NM 87120; Santa Fe archdiocese.

Pilot, The, w; 49 Franklin St., Boston, MA 02110; Boston archdiocese.

Pittsburgh Catholic, w; 135 First Ave., Suite 200, Pittsburgh, PA 15222-1506; Pittsburgh diocese.

Prairie Catholic, m; 1400 6th St. North, New Ulm, MN 56073-2099. New Ulm diocese.

Pregonero, El (Spanish), w; P.O. Box 4464, Washington, DC 20017; Washington archdiocese.

Providence Visitor, The, w; 184 Broad St., Providence, RI 02903. Providence diocese.

Record, The, w; Maloney Center, 1200 S. Shelby St., Louisville, KY 40203-2600; Louisville archdiocese.

Redwood Crozier, The, m; P.O. Box 1297, Santa Rosa, CA 95402; Santa Rosa diocese.

Rio Grande Catholic, The, 12 times a year; 499 St. Matthews St., El Paso, TX 79907; El Paso diocese.

St. Cloud Visitor, w; P. O. Box 1068, St. Cloud, MN 56302-1066; St. Cloud diocese.

St. Louis Review, w; 462 N. Taylor Ave., St. Louis, MO 63108; St. Louis archdiocese.

Seasons, q; 5800 Weiss St., Saginaw, MI 48603-2799.

Slovak Catholic Falcon, (Slovak-English), w; 205 Madison St., P.O.Box 899, Passaic, NJ 07055; Slovak Catholic Sokol.

Sooner Catholic, The, biweekly; P.O. Box 32180, Oklahoma City, OK 73123; Oklahoma City archdiocese.

Sophia, q; 11245 Rye St., North Hollywood, CA 91602; Newton Melkite eparchy.

South Plains Catholic, twice a month; P.O. Box 98700, Lubbock, TX 79499-8700; Lubbock diocese.

South Texas Catholic, m; 1200 Lantana St., Corpus Christi, TX 78407-1112; Corpus Christi diocese.

Southern Cross, semimonthly; P.O. Box 81869, San Diego, CA 92138; San Diego diocese.

Southern Cross, The, w; 601 E. Liberty Street, Savannah, GA 31401; Savannah diocese.

Southern Nebraska Register, w; P.O. Box 80329, Lincoln, NE 68501; Lincoln diocese.

Southwest Catholic, m; P.O. 411 Iris St., Lake Charles, LA 70601, Lake Charles diocese.

Southwest Kansas Register, biweekly; P.O. Box 137, Dodge City, KS 67801; Dodge City diocese.

Sower (Ukrainian and English), biweekly; 14 Peveril Rd., Stamford, CT 06902. Stamford Ukrainian diocese.

Star of Chaldeans (Arabic and English), bm; 25585 Berg Rd., Southfield, MI 48034. St. Thomas the Apostle Chaldean diocese.

Steubenville Register, biweekly; P.O. Box 160, Steubenville, OH 43952; Steubenville diocese.

Tablet, The, w; 653 Hicks St., Brooklyn, NY 11231; Brooklyn diocese.

Tautai, bi-weekly; P.O. Box 532, Apia, Samoa; Samoa-Apia archdiocese.

Tennessee Register, The, biweekly; 2400 21st Ave. S., Nashville, TN 37212; Nashville diocese.

Texas Catholic, biweekly; P.O. Box 190347, Dallas, TX 75219; Dallas diocese.

Texas Catholic Herald, The, twice a month; 1700 San Jacinto St., Houston, TX 77002; Galveston-Houston diocese.

Tidings, 11 times a year; 153 Ash St., Manchester, NH 03105-0310.

Tidings, The, w; 3424 Wilshire Blvd, Los Angeles, CA 90010; Los Angeles archdiocese.

Times Review, The, w; P.O. Box 4004, La Crosse, WI 54602-4004; La Crosse diocese.

Today's Catholic, w; P.O. Box 11169, Fort Wayne, IN 46856; Fort Wayne-S. Bend diocese.

Today's Catholic, biweekly; P.O. Box 28410, San Antonio, TX 78228-0410; San Antonio archdiocese.

UNIREA (The Union) (Romanian) (10 times a year), 1121 44th St. N.E., Canton, OH 44714-1297; Romanian diocese of Canton.

U. P. Catholic, The, semi-monthly; P.O. Box 548, Marquette, MI 49855; Marquette diocese.

Valley Catholic, m; 900 Lafayette St., Suite 301, Santa Clara, CA 95050-4966; San Jose diocese.

Vermont Catholic Tribune, biweekly; P.O. Box 526, Burlington, VT 05402; Burlington diocese.

Visitante de Puerto Rico, El (Spanish), w; Apartado 41305 – Minillas Sta., San Juan, PR 00940-1305. Puerto Rican Catholic Conference.

Voice of the Southwest, m; 414 N. Allen, Farmington, NM 87401; Gallup diocese.

Voz Catolica, La (Spanish); m; 9401 Biscayne Blvd., Miami, FL 33138; Miami archdiocese.

Wanderer, The, w; 201 Ohio St., St. Paul, MN 55107; national.

The Way (Ukrainian-Eng.), biweekly; 827 N. Franklin Sts., Philadelphia, PA 19123; Philadelphia archeparchy.

West Nebraska Register, w; P.O. Box 608, Grand Island, NE 68802; Grand Island diocese.

West River Catholic, m; P.O. Box 678, Rapid City, SD 57709; Rapid City diocese.

West Tennessee Catholic, w; P.O. Box 341669, Memphis, TN 38184-1669; Memphis Diocese (replacing **Common Sense**, 1997).

West Texas Angelus, m; P.O. Box 1829, San Angelo, TX 76902; San Angelo diocese.

West Texas Catholic, biweekly; P.O. Box 5644, Amarillo, TX 79117-5644; Amarillo diocese.

Western Kentucky Catholic, m; 600 Locust St., Owensboro, KY 42301; Owensboro diocese.

Western New York Catholic, m; 795 Main St., Buffalo, NY 14203-1250; Buffalo diocese.

Witness, The, w; P.O. Box 917, Dubuque, IA 52004; Dubuque archdiocese.

Wyoming Catholic Register, m; P.O. Box 1308, Cheyenne, WY 82003; Cheyenne diocese.

Magazines

AIM: Liturgy Resources, q; P.O. Box 2703, Schiller Park, IL 60176.

America, w; 106 W. 56th St., New York, NY 10019. Jesuits of U.S. and Canada.

American Benedictine Review, q; Assumption Abbey, Box A, Richardton, ND 58652.

American Catholic Philosophical Quarterly (formerly **The New Scholasticism**), Institute of Philosophical Studies, Univ. of Dallas, Irving, TX 75062. American Catholic Philosophical Assn.

THE ANNALS of St. Anne de Beaupre, m; P.O. Box 1000, St. Anne de Beaupre, Quebec, GOA 3CO.

Anthonian, The, q; c/o St. Anthony's Guild, Paterson, NJ 07509; St. Anthony's Guild.

Apostolate of the Little Flower, bm; P.O. Box 5280, San Antonio, TX 78201; Discalced Carmelite Fathers.

Association of Marian Helpers Bulletin, q; Eden Hill Stockbridge, MA 01263. Congregation of Marians.

Atchison Benedictines, q; Mount St. Scholastica Convent, 801 S. 8th St., Atchison, KS 66002.

Barry Magazine, 2 times a year; 11300 NE 2nd Ave., Miami Shores, FL 33161; Barry Univ.

Bible Today, The, bm; Liturgical Press, Collegeville, MN 56321.

Bolletino, m; 675 Hegenberger Rd., Suite 110, Oakland, CA 94621; Italian Catholic Federation.

Bright Ideas; P.O. Box 432, Milwaukee, WI, 53201-0432.

Brothers' Voice, 5 times a year; 1337 W. Ohio St. Chicago, IL 60622; National Association of Religious Brothers.

Carmelite Digest, q; P.O. Box 3180, San Jose, CA 95156.

Carmelite Review, The, m; 6725 Reed Rd., Houston, TX 77087-6830. Canadian-American Province of Carmelite Order.

Catechist, The, 7 times a year; 330 Progress Rd., Dayton, OH 45449.

Catechumenate: A Journal of Christian Initiation, 6 times a year; 1800 N. Hermitage Ave., Chicago, IL 60622-1101.

Catholic Aid News, m; 3499 N. Lexington Ave., St. Paul, MN 55126.

Catholic Answer, The, bm; 200 Noll Plaza, Huntington, IN 46750; Our Sunday Visitor.

Catholic Biblical Quarterly; Catholic University of America, Washington, DC 20064; Catholic Biblical Assn.

Catholic Cemetery, The, m; 710 N. River Rd., Des Plaines, IL 60016; National Catholic Cemetery Conference.

Catholic Digest, m; 2115 Summit Ave., St. Paul, MN 55105-1081.

Catholic Dossier, bm; P.O. Box 591120, San Francisco, CA 94159.

Catholic Faith, The, bm; P.O. Box 591120, San Francisco, CA 94159.

Catholic Health World, semimonthly; 4455 Woodson Rd., St. Louis, MO 63134-3797. Catholic Health Association.

Catholic Heritage, bm; 200 Noll Plaza, Huntington, IN 46750. Our Sunday Visitor.

Catholic Historical Review, q; 620 Michigan Ave. N.E., Washington, DC 20064.

Catholic International, m; Cathedral Foundation, P.O. Box 777, Baltimore, MD 21203.

Catholic Journalist, The, m; 3555 Veterans Highway, Unit O, Ronkonkoma, NY 11779; Catholic Press Association.

C.K. of A. Journal, m; 1850 Dalton St., Cincinnati, OH 45214; Catholic Knights of America.

Catholic Lawyer, q; St. John's University, Jamaica,

NY 11439; St. Thomas More Institute for Legal Research.

Catholic Library World, 4 times a year; 9009 Carter Ave., Allen Park, MI 48101; Catholic Library Association.

Catholic Near East Magazine, bm; 1011 First Ave., New York, NY 10022; Catholic Near East Welfare Assn.

Catholic Outlook, m; 2830 E. 4th St., Duluth, MN 55812; Duluth diocese.

Catholic Parent, bm; 200 Noll Plaza, Huntington, IN 46750; Our Sunday Visitor.

Catholic Peace Voice, q; 532 W. 8th St., Erie, PA 16502-1343; Pax Christi USA.

Catholic Pharmacist, q; 1012 Surrey Hills Dr., St. Louis, MO 63117-1438; National Catholic Pharmacists Guild.

Catholic Press Directory, a; 3555 Veterans Highway, Unit O, Ronkonkoma, NY 11779; Catholic Press Assn.

Catholic Quote, m; Valparaiso, NE 68065.

Catholic Review (Braille, tape, large print), bm; 154 E. 23rd St., New York, NY 10010; Xavier Society for the Blind.

Catholic Rural Life, twice a year; 4625 Beaver Ave., Des Moines, IA 50310.

Catholic Singles Magazine, two times a year; 8408 S. Muskegon, Chicago, IL 60617.

Catholic Southwest: A Journal of History and Culture, annual; 1625 Rutherford Lane, Bldg. D, Austin, TX, 78754-5105.

Catholic Telephone Guide, a; 210 North Ave., New Rochelle, NY 10801.

Catholic University of America Law Review, q; Washington, DC 20064.

Catholic War Veteran, bm; 441 N. Lee St., Alexandria, VA 22314-2344.

Catholic Woman, bm; 1275 K St. N.W., Suite 975, Washington, DC 20005. National Council of Catholic Women.

Catholic Women's Network, bm; 877 Spinosa Dr., Sunnyvale, CA 94087.

Catholic Worker, 7 times a year; 36 E. First St., New York, NY 10003. Catholic Worker Movement.

Catholic Workman, m; 111 W. Main, P.O. Box 47, New Prague, MN 56071.

Catholic World Report, The, 11 times a year; P.O. Box 1328, Dedham, MA 02027 (editorial office). Ignatius Press.

Celebration, m; 115 E. Armour Blvd., Kansas City, MO 64111; National Catholic Reporter Publishing Co.

CGA World, q; P.O. Box 3658, Scranton, PA 18505. Catholic Golden Age.

Charities USA, q; 1731 King St., Suite 200, Alexandria, VA 22314.

Chicago Studies, 3 times a year; 1800 N. Hermitage Ave., Chicago, IL 60622-1101.

Christian Renewal News, 4 times a year; 411 First St., Fillmore, CA 93016-0547. Apostolate of Christian Renewal.

Christianity and the Arts, 4 times a year; 1100 N. Lake Shore Dr., Apt. 33A; Chicago, IL 60611.

Church, q; 18 Bleeker St., New York, NY 10012; National Pastoral Life Center.

international review of monastic and contemplative spirituality, history and theology.

Columban Mission, 8 times a year; St. Columbans, NE 68056; Columban Fathers.

Columbia, m; One Columbus Plaza, New Haven, CT 06510; Knights of Columbus.

Commonweal, biweekly; 475 Riverside Dr., Room 405, New York, NY 10115.

Communio — International Catholic Review, q; P.O. Box 4557, Washington, D.C. 20017-0557.

Company, q; 3441 N. Ashland Ave., Chicago, IL 60657. Jesuit Magazine.

Consecrated Life, semi-annually; P.O. Box 41007, Chicago, IL 60641; Institute on Religious Life. English edition of *Informationes*, official publication of Congregation for Institutes of Consecrated Life and Societies of Apostolic Life.

Consolata Missionaries, bm; P.O. Box 5550, Somerset, NJ 08875.

Cord, The, m; P.O. Drawer F, St. Bonaventure, NY 14778; Franciscan Institute.

Counseling and Values, 3 times a year; Dept. of Educational Psychology and Special Education, Southern Illinois Univ., Carbondale, IL 62901.

Credo, 26 times a year; P.O.Box 504, Ann Arbor, MI 48106.

Crescat, 3 times a year; Belmont Abbey, Belmont, NC 28012; Benedictine Monks.

Crisis, 11 times a year; 1814-1/2 N St., NW, Washington, D.C. 20036; Journal of lay Catholic opinion.

Critic, The: A Journal of American Catholic Culture, q; 205 W. Monroe St., 6th floor, Chicago, IL 60606. Thomas More Assn.

Cross Currents, q; College of New Rochelle, New Rochelle, NY 10805; interreligious; Association for Religion and Intellectual Life.

CUA Magazine, 3 times a year; 620 Michigan Ave. N.E., Washington, DC 20064; Catholic University of America.

Darbininkas (The Worker) (Lithuanian), w; 341 Highland Blvd., Brooklyn, NY 11207; Lithuanian Franciscans.

Desert Clarion, 10 times a year; P.O. Box 18316, Las Vegas, NV 89114; Diocese of Las Vegas.

Diakonia, 3 times a year; Univ. of Scranton, Scranton, PA 18510; Center for Eastern Christian Studies.

Divine Word Missionaries, q; Techny, IL 60082.

Ecumenical Trends, m (exc. Aug.); Graymoor, Route 9, P.O. Box 306, Garrison, NY 10524-0306; Graymoor Ecumenical Institute.

Eglute (The Little Fir Tree) (Lithuanian), m; 13648 Kikapoo Trail, Lockport, IL 60441; children ages 5-10.

Emmanuel, 10 times a year; 5384 Wilson Mills Rd., Cleveland, OH 44143; Congregation of Blessed Sacrament.

Envoy, bm; P.O. Box 640, Granville, OH 43023. Journal of Catholic apologetics and evangelization.

Eternal Flame (Armenian-Engish), 110 E. 12th St., New York, NY 10003; Armenian exarchate.

Explorations, q; 321 Chestnut St., Philadelphia, PA 19106; American Interfaith Institute.

Extension, 12 times a year; 150 S. Wacker Dr., 20st Floor, Chicago, IL 60606; Catholic Church Extension Society.

Faith and Reason, q; 134 Christendom Dr., Front Royal, VA 22630.

Family Digest, The, bm; P.O. Box 40137, Fort Wayne, IN 46804 (editorial address).

Family Friend, q; P.O. Box 11563, Milwaukee, WI 53211; Catholic Family Life Insurance.

Fidelity, m; 206 Marquette Ave., South Bend, IN 46617.

F.M.A. Focus, q; P.O. Box 598, Mt. Vernon, NY 10551; Franciscan Mission Associates.

Forefront, q; Box 219, Crestone, CO 81131-0219; Spiritual Life Institute of America.

Franciscan Studies, a; St. Bonaventure, NY 14778; Franciscan Institute.

Franciscan Way, q; 1235 University Blvd., Steubenville, OH 43952.

Fraternal Leader, q; P.O. Box 13005; Erie, PA 16514-1305; Loyal Christian Benefit Association.

Fraternally Yours (Eng.-Slovak), m; 24950 Chagrin Blvd., Beachwood, OH 44122; First Catholic Slovak Ladies Assn.

Fuente de Misericordia, q; Eden Hill, Stockbridge, MA 01263; Congregation of Marians of the Immaculate Conception.

Glenmary Challenge, The, q; P.O. Box 465618, Cincinnati, OH 45246-5618; Glenmary Home Missioners.

God's Word Today, m; P. O. Box 64088, St. Paul, MN 55164. Univ. of St. Thomas.

Good News, m; P.O. Box 432, Milwaukee, WI 53201-0432. Liturgical Publications.

Good News for Children, 32 times during school year; 330 Progress Rd., Dayton, OH 45449.

Good Shepherd (Dobry Pastier) (Slovak-English), a; 8200 McKnight Rd., Pittsburgh, PA 15237.

Greyfriars Review, 3 times a year; St. Bonventure Univ., St. Bonaventure, NY 14778; Franciscan Institute.

Growing with the Gospel, weekly; Publications Division, P.O. Box 432, Wisconsin, WI, 53201-0432.

Guide to Religious Ministries, A, a; 210 North Ave., New Rochelle, NY 10801.

Health Progress, bm; 4455 Woodson Rd., St. Louis, MO 63134-3797; Catholic Health Association.

Hearts Aflame, q; P.O. Box 976, Washington, NJ 07882. For youth (13-23).

HNPeople, bm; 127 W. 31st St., New York, NY 10001 Holy Name Province, OFM.

Holy Smoke — Our Lady of the Hills Church, six times a year; 2700 Ashland Rd. Columbia, SC 29210.

Homiletic and Pastoral Review, m; P.O. Box 591810, San Francisco, CA 94159-1810.

Horizon, 4 times a year; 5420 S. Cornell Ave., Chicago, IL 60615-5604.

Horizons, 2 times a year; Villanova University, Villanova, PA 19085. College Theology Society.

Horizons/Crossroads with the Catholic Evangelist, five times a year; P.O. Box 2009, Tulsa, OK, 74101.

Human Development, q; c/o St. John's Seminary, 127 Lake St., Brighton, MA 02135-3898.

Immaculata, 6 times a year; 1600 W. Park Ave., Libertyville, IL 60048.

Immaculate Heart Messenger, q; P.O. Box 158, Alexandria, SD 57311.

In a Word, m; 199 Seminary Dr., Bay Saint Louis, MS 39520-4626; Society of the Divine Word.

Inside the Vatican: See under International Catholic Periodicals.

Jesuit Bulletin, 3 times a year; 3601 Lindell Blvd., St. Louis, MO 63108; Jesuit Seminary Aid Association.

Jesuit Journeys, 3 times a year; 3400 W. Wisconsin Ave., Milwaukee, WI 53208-0287.

Josephite Harvest, The, q; 1130 N. Calvert St., Baltimore, MD 21202-3802; Josephite Missionaries.

Jurist, The, semiannually; Catholic University of America, Washington, DC 20064; Department of Canon Law.

Kinship, q; P.O. Box 22264, Owensboro, KY 42304; Glenmary Sisters.

Knights of St. John International, q; 89 South Pine Ave., Albany, NY 12208.

Law Briefs, 12 times a year; 3211 Fourth St. N.E. Washington, DC 20017; Office of General Counsel, USCC.

Lay Witness, monthly; 827 North Fourth St., Steubenville, OH, 43952; Catholics United for the Faith.

Leaflet Missal, 16565 South State St., S. Holland, IL 60473.

Leaves, bm; P.O. Box 87, Dearborn, MI 48121; Mariannhill Mission Society.

Liguorian, m; 1 Liguori Dr., Liguori, MO 63057; Redemptorists.

Linacre Quarterly; P.O. Box 757, Pewaukee, WI 53072; Catholic Medical Association (National Federation of Catholic Physicians Guilds).

Liturgia y Cancion (Spanish and English), q; 5536 NE Hassalo, Portland, OR 97213. Oregon Catholic Press.

Liturgy, q; 8750 Georgia Ave., Suite 123, Silver Spring, MD 20910. Liturgical Conference.

Liturgy 90, 8 times a year; 1800 N. Hermitage Ave., Chicago, IL 60622; Liturgy Training Publications.

Liturgy Planner, The, semi-annual; . P.O. Box 13071, Portland, OR 97213.

Living City, m; P.O. Box 837, Bronx, NY 10465; Focolare Movement.

Living Faith: Daily Catholic Devotions, q; 10300 Watson Rd., St. Louis, MO 63127.

Living Light, The, q; 3211 Fourth St. N.E., Washington, DC 20017; Department of Education, USCC.

Marian Studies, a; Marian Library, Dayton, OH 45469; Mariological Society of America (proceedings).

Marriage, 6 times a year; 955 Lake Dr., St. Paul, MN 55120; International Marriage Encounter.

Maryknoll, m; Maryknoll, NY 10545; Catholic Foreign Mission Society.

Mary's Shrine, 2 times a year; 400 Michigan Ave., N.E., Washington, DC 20017-1566; Basilica of National Shrine of the Immaculate Conception.

Matrimony, q; 215 Santa Rosa Pl., Santa Barbara, CA 93109. Worldwide Marriage Encounter.

Medical Mission News, q; 10 W. 17th St., New York,

NY 10011; Catholic Medical Mission Board, Inc.
Medjugorje Magazine, q; P.O. Box 99, Bloomingdale, IL 60108.
Merciful Love, q; 5654 E. Westover, No. 103, P.O. Box 24, Fresno, CA 93727.
Migration World, 5 times a year; 209 Flagg Pl., Staten Island, NY 10304; Center for Migration Studies.
Miraculous Medal, q; 475 E. Chelten Ave., Philadelphia, PA 19144; Central Association of the Miraculous Medal.
Mission, q; 1663 Bristol Pike, Bensalem, PA 19020; Sisters of the Blessed Sacrament.
MISSION Magazine, 4 times a year; 366 Fifth Ave., Ne York, NY 10001; Society for Propagation of the Faith.
Mission, The, q; 90 Cherry Lane, Hicksville, NY 11801-6299; Catholic Charities, Diocese of Rockville Center.
Mission Helper, The, q; 1001 W. Joppa Rd., Baltimore, MD 21204; Mission Helpers of the Sacred Heart.
Missionhurst, 6 times a year; 4651 N. 25th St., Arlington, VA 22207.
Mission Update, six times a year; 3029 Fourth St., NE, Washington, D.C. 20017.
Modern Liturgy, 10 times a year; 160 E. Virginia St., No. 290, San Jose, CA 95112.
Modern Schoolman, The, q; 221 N. Grand Blvd., St. Louis, MO 63103; St. Louis University Philosophy Department.
Momento Catolico, El; 205 W. Monroe St., Chicago, IL, 60606.
Momentum, 4 times a year; Suite 100, 1077 30th St., N.W., Washington, DC 20007; National Catholic Educational Association.
Mountain Spirit, The, 6 times a year; 322 Crab Orchard Rd., Lancaster, KY 40446; Christian Appalachian Project.
My Daily Visitor, bm; 200 Noll Plaza, Huntington, IN 46750; Our Sunday Visitor, Inc.
My Friend, 10 times a year; 50 St. Paul's Ave., Jamaica Plain, Boston, MA 02130; for children, ages 6-12.

National Apostolate with People with Mental Retardation, q; 4516 30th St., NW, Washington, DC 20008.
National Catholic Forester, q; 320 S. School St., Mt. Prospect,IL 60056.
National Jesuit News, m; 1616 P St. N.W., Suite 400, Washington, D.C. 20036.
NETWORK Connection, bm; 801 Pennsylvania Ave. S.E., Washington, DC 20003; Network.
New Covenant, m; Our Sunday Visitor, Inc., 200 Noll Plaza, Huntington, IN 46750.
New Oxford Review, 10 issues a year; 1069 Kains Ave., Berkeley, CA 94706.
Notebook, The, q; 31 Chesterfield Rd., Stamford, CT 06902. Catholic Movement for Intellectual and Cultural Affairs.
Notre Dame Magazine, q; Notre Dame Univ., Notre Dame, IN 46556.
Nova-Voice of Ministry, bm; P.O. Box 432, Milwaukee, WI 53201. Liturgical Publications.

Oblate World and Voice of Hope, bm; 486 Chandler St., P.O. Box 680, Tewksbury, MA 01876; Oblates of Mary Immaculate.
Observer, The, m; 4545 W. 63rd St., Chicago, IL 60629; Lithuanian Roman Catholic Federation of America.
Old Testament Abstracts, 3 times a year; Catholic University of America, Washington, DC 20064.
Origins, 48 times a year; 3211 Fourth St. N.E., Washington, DC 20017; Catholic News Service.
Ozanam News, The, ba; 58 Progress Parkway, St. Louis, MO 63043-3706; Society of St. Vincent de Paul.

Palabra Entre Nosotros, La, bimonthly; 9639 Dr. Perry Rd., Unit 126N, Ijamsville, MD, 21754.
Parish Arts Magazine, biannually, P.O. Boc 13071, Portland, OR 97213.
Parish Liturgy, q; 16565 S. State St., S. Holland, IL 60473.
Passionists' Compassion, The, q; 526 Monastery Pl., Union City, NJ 07087.
Pastoral Life, m; Box 595, Canfield, OH 44406; Society of St. Paul.
Pastoral Music, bm; 225 Sheridan St., N.W. Washington, DC 20011; National Association of Pastoral Musicians.
Philosophy Today, q; De Paul University, 1150 W. Fullerton Ave., Chicago, IL 60614; Philosophy Department.
PIME World, m (exc. July-Aug.); 17330 Quincy St., Detroit, MI 48221; PIME Missionaries.
Plenty Good Room, 6 times a year; 1800 N. Hermitage Ave., Chicago, IL 60622.
Pope Speaks, The: Church Documents Bimonthly; Our Sunday Visitor, Inc., 200 Noll Plaza, Huntington, IN 46750.
Poverello, The, 10 times a year; 6832 Convent Blvd., Sylvania, OH 43560. Sisters of St. Francis of Sylvania.
Praxis Press, 10 times a year; P.O. Box 508, San Jose, CA 95103.
Prayers for Worship, q; P.O. Box 432, Milwaukee, WI 53201.
Praying, 6 times a year; P.O. Box 419335, Kansas City, MO 64141.
Priest, The, m; 200 Noll Plaza, Huntington, IN 46750; Our Sunday Visitor, Inc.
Proceedings, a; Catholic Univ. of America, Washington, DC 20064; Journal of the American Catholic Philosophical Association.
Promise, 32 times a year; 330 Progress Rd., Dayton, OH, 45449.

Queen of All Hearts, bm; 26 S. Saxon Ave., Bay Shore, NY 11706; Montfort Missionaries.

Reign of the Sacred Heart, q; 6889 S. Lovers Lane, Hales Corners, WI 53130.
Religion Teacher's Journal, m (Sept.-May); P.O. Box 180, Mystic, CT 06355.
Renascence, q; Brooks Hall - P.O. Box 1881, Marquette University, Milwaukee, WI 53201-1881.
Report on U.S. Catholic Overseas Mission, biannually; 3029 Fourth St. N.E., Washington, DC 20017. United States Catholic Mission Association.
Response: Volunteer Opportunities Directory, a; 4121 Harewood Rd. N.E., Washington, DC 20017; Catholic Network of Volunteer Service.

Review for Religious, bm; Room 428, 3601 Lindell Blvd., St. Louis, MO 63108.

Review of Politics, q; Box B, Notre Dame, IN 46556.

Review of Social Economy, 4 times a year; Marquette University, Milwaukee, WI 53233. Association for Social Economics.

Revista Maryknoll (Spanish-English), m; Maryknoll, NY 10545; Catholic Foreign Mission Society of America.

Roze Maryi (Polish), m; Eden Hill, Stockbridge, MA 01263; Marian Helpers Center.

Sacred Music, q; 548 Lafond Ave., St. Paul, MN 55103.

St. Anthony Messenger, m; 1615 Republic St., Cincinnati, OH 45210; Franciscan Friars.

St. Augustine Catholic, bm (Sept-May), P.O. Box 24000, Jacksonville, FL 32241-4000. St. Augustine diocese.

St. John's News, six times a year; School Street, Quincy, MA 02169.

St. Joseph's Messenger and Advocate of the Blind, biannual; St. Joseph Home, 537 Pavonia Ave., Jersey City, NJ 07303.

St. Paul's Family Magazine, q; 14780 W. 159th St., Olathe, KS 66062.

Salesian Directory, q; 148 Main St., P.O. Box 639, New Rochelle, NY 10802; Salesians of Don Bosco.

Salesian Missions of St. John Bosco, q; 2 Lefevre Lane, New Rochelle, NY 10801-5710; Salesians of Don Bosco.

SALT/Sisters of Charity, BVM, q; 1100 Carmel Dr., Dubuque, IA 52001.

Scalabrinians, 4 times a year; 209 Flagg Pl., Staten Island, NY 10304.

School Guide, a; 210 North Ave., New Rochelle, NY 10801.

SCN Journey, bi-monthly; SCN Office of Communications, P.O. Box 9, Nazareth, KY 40048; Sisters of Charity of Nazareth.

SCRC Spirit, The, bm; 2810 Artesia Blvd., Redondo Beach, CA 90278; Southern California Renewal Communities.

Seeds, 32 times a year; 330 Progress Rd., Dayton, OH 45449.

Serenity, q; 601 Maiden Choice Lane, Baltimore, MD 21228; Little Sisters of the Poor.

Serran, The, bm; 65 E. Wacker Pl., Suite 1210, Chicago, IL 60601; Serra International.

Share Magazine, q times a year; 10 W. 71st St., New York, NY 10023; Catholic Daughters of the Americas.

Share the Word, bm; 3031 Fourth St. N.E., Washington, DC 20017-1102; Paulist Catholic Evangelization Association.

Silent Advocate, q; St. Rita School for the Deaf, 1720 Glendale-Milford Rd., Cincinnati, OH 45215.

Sisters Today, bm; Liturgical Press, St. John's University, Collegeville, MN 56321.

Social Justice Review, bm; 3835 Westminster Pl., St. Louis, MO 63108-3409; Catholic Central Union of America.

Soul Magazine, bm; P.O. Box 976, Washington, NJ 07882; World Apostolate of Our Lady of Fatima.

Spinnaker, 5 times a year; 610 W. Elm, Monroe, MI 48161; IHM Sisters.

Spirit, biannually; Seton Hall University, South Orange, NJ 07079.

Spirit, w; 1884 Randolph Ave., St. Paul, MN 55105. For teens.

Spirit & Life, 6 times a year; 800 N. Country Club Rd., Tucson, AZ 85716; Benedictine Srs. of Perpetual Adoration.

Spiritual Life, q; 2131 Lincoln Rd. N.E., Washington, DC 20002; Discalced Carmelite Friars.

Star, 10 times a year; 22 W. Kiowa, Colorado Springs, CO 80903.

Studies in the Spirituality of Jesuits, 5 times a year; 3700 W. Pine Blvd., St. Louis, MO 63108.

Sunday by Sunday, w; 1884 Randolph Ave., St. Paul, MN 55105.

Sword Magazine, 2 times a year; P.O. Box 1238, Niagara University, NY 14109-1238; Carmelite Fathers.

Theological Studies, q; 37th and O Sts. NW, Washington, DC 20057-1136.

Theology Digest, q; P.O. Box 56907, St. Louis, MO 63156-0907; St. Louis Univesity.

Thomist, The, q; 487 Michigan Ave. N.E., Washington, DC 20017; Dominican Fathers.

Today's Catholic Teacher, m (Sept.-April); 330 Progress Rd., Dayton, OH 45449.

Today's Liturgy, q; 5536 NE Hassalo, Portland, OR 97213.

Today's Parish, m (Sept.-May); P.O. Box 180, Mystic, CT 06355.

Together in the Word, biannual; Box 577, Techny, IL 60082-0577; Chicago province Society of Divine Word.

The Tower, w; The Catholic University of America, Univ. Ctr. W. , Michigan Ave., Ste. 400 A, Washington, D.C. 20064.

Tracings, q; Gamelin St., Holyoke, MA 01040; Sisters of Providence.

Trinity Missions Magazine, q; 9001 New Hampshire Ave., Silver Spring, MD 20903.

Turnaround, The, five times a year; Cardinal Newman Society, 207 Park Ave., Ste. B-2, Falls Church, VA 22046.

TV Prayer Guide; 19 Second Ave., P.O. Box 440, Pelham, NY 10803-0440.

Ultreya Magazine, 6 times a year; 4500 W. Davis St., P.O. Box 210226, Dallas, TX 75211. Cursillo Movement.

L'Union (French and English), q; P.O. Box F, Woonsocket, RI 02895.

Universitas, q; 221 N. Grand, Room 39, St. Louis, MO 63103; St. Louis University.

U.S. Catholic, m; 205 W. Monroe St., Chicago, IL 60606; Claretians.

U.S. Catholic Historian, q; 200 Noll Plaza, Huntington, IN 46750.

Venture, 32 times during school year; 330 Progress Rd., Dayton, OH 45449, Intermediate grades.

Verelk (Armenian-English), bimonthly; 1327 Pleasant Ave., Los Angeles, CA 90033.

Vincentian Heritage, twice a year; 2233 N. Kenmore Ave., Chicago, IL 60614.

Vision, annually, 205 W. Monroe St., Chicago, IL 60606; Claretian Publications in conjunction with National Religious Vocation Conference.

Vision, 3 times a year; 7202 Buchanan St., Landover Hills, MD 20784. National Catholic Office for the Deaf.

Vision (Spanish-English), P.O. Box 28185, San Antonio, TX 78228. Mexican American Cultural Center.

Visions, 32 times during school year; 330 Progress Rd., Dayton, OH 45449. For students in grades 7 to 9.

VOCATIONS and Prayer Today, q; 9815 Columbus Ave., North Hills, CA 91343. Rogationist Fathers.

Waif's Messenger, q; 1140 W. Jackson Blvd., Chicago, IL 60607; Mission of Our Lady of Mercy.

Way of St. Francis, bm; 1500 34th Ave., Oakland, CA 94601; Franciscan Friars of California, Inc.

Wheeling Jesuit University Chronicle, 3 times a year; 316 Washington Ave., Wheeling, WV 26003.

Word Among Us, The, m; 9639 Dr. Perry Rd., No. 126, Ijamsville, MD 21754.

Word and Witness; P.O. Box 432, Wisconsin, WI, 53201-0432.

World Lithuanian Catholic Directory, 50 Orton Marotta Way, S. Boston, MA 02127.

Worship, 6 times a year; St. John's Abbey, Collegeville, MN 56321.

YOU! Magazine, 10 times a year; 31194 La Baya Dr., Suite 200, Westlake Village, CA 91362-4022. Catholic youth magazine.

Newsletters

Act, 10 times a year; Box 272, Ames, IA 60010; Christian Family Movement.

Action News, q; Pro-Life Action League, 6160 N. Cicero Ave., Chicago, IL 60646.

Angel Guardian Herald, 4 times a year; 6301 12th Ave., Brooklyn, NY 11219.

Annual Report, The, 2021 H St. N.W., Washington, DC 20006. Black and Indian Mission Office.

Archdiocesan Bulletin, bm; 827 N. Franklin St., Philadelphia, PA 19123; Philadelphia archeparchy.

Aylesford Carmelite Newsletter, q. 8501 Bailey Rd., Darien, IL 60561.

Baraga Bulletin, The, q; P.O. Box 550, Marquette, MI 49855.

Benedictine Orient, twice a year; 2400 Maple Ave., Lisle, IL 60532.

Bringing Religion Home, 10 times a year; 205 W. Monroe St., Chicago, IL 60606.

Call Board, The, 12 times a year; 1501 Broadway, Suite 518, New York, NY 10036; Catholic Actors' Guild.

Campaign Update, bm; 1513 Sixteenth St., NW, Ste. 400, NW, Washington, DC 20036. Catholic Campaign for America.

Cantor, m; 115 E. Armour Blvd., Kansas City, MO 64111; National Catholic Reporter.

CARA Report, The, bi-monthly; Georgetown Univ., Washington, DC 20057-1203; Center for Applied Research in the Apostolate.

Caring Community, The, m; 115 E. Armour Blvd., Kansas City, MO 64111.

Catalyst, 10 times a year; 1011 First Ave., NY, NY, 10022; Catholic League for Civil and Religious Rights.

Catechist's Connection, The 10 times a year; 115 E. Armour Blvd., Kansas City, MO 64111.

Catholic Communicator, The, q; 120 East Colonial Hgwy., Hamilton, VA 20158-9012; Catholic Distance University Newsletter.

Catholic Connection, The, m (Aug.-May); 2500 Line Ave., Shreveport, LA 71104. Shreveport diocese.

Catholic Trends, biweekly; 3211 Fourth St. N.E., Washington, DC 20017; Catholic News Service.

Catholic Update, m; 1615 Republic St., Cincinnati, OH 45210. ·

CCHD News, q; 3211 Fourth St., NE, Washington, DC 20017-1194; Catholic Campaign for Human Development.

C.F.C. Newsletter, 5 times a year; 33 Pryer Terr., New Rochelle, NY 10804. Christian Brothers.

Chariscenter USA Newsletter, 5 times a year; P.O. Box 628, Locust Grove, VA 22508-0628.

Christ the King Seminary Newsletter, 3 times a year; 711 Knox Rd., Box 607, E. Aurora, NY 14052.

Christian Beginnings, 5 times a year; 200 Noll Plaza, Huntington, IN 46750. Our Sunday Visitor.

Christian Response Newsletter, P.O. Box 125, Staples, MN 56479-0125.

Christopher News Notes, 10 times a year; 12 E. 48th St., New York, NY 10017; The Christophers.

Clarion, The, 5 times a year; Box 159, Alfred, ME 04002-1059; Brothers of Christian Instruction.

Comboni Mission Newsletter, q; 8108 Beechmont Ave., Cincinnati, OH 45255.

Commentary, 6 times a year; 1010 11th St., Suite 200, Sacramento, CA 958143817.

Context, 22 issues a year; 205 W. Monroe St., Chicago, IL 60606.

CPN Newsletter, 8108 Beechmont Ave., Cincinnati, OH, 45255-3194.

Crossroads, 8 times a year; 300 College Park Ave., Dayton, OH 45469. Catholic Campus Ministry Association.

CRUX of the News, w; 24 Wade Rd., Latham, NY 12210.

Cycles of Faith, P.O. Box 432, Milwaukee, WI 532010432.

Damien-Dutton Call, q; 616 Bedford Ave., Bellmore, NY 11710.

Dimensions, m; 86 Front St., Hempstead, NY 11550; National Catholic Development Conference.

Diocesan Dialogue, two time a year; 16565 South State St., South Holland, IL, 60473.

Diocesan Newsletter, The, m; P.O. Box 2147, Harlingen, TX 78551; Brownsville diocese.

Environment and Art Letter, m; 1800 N. Hermitage Ave., Chicago, IL 60622-1101.

Envisioning; 555 Albany Ave., Amityville, NY 11701. Sisters of St. Dominic.

Ethics and Medics, m; 159 Washington St., Boston, MA 02135.

Eucharistic Minister, m; 115 E. Armour, P.O. Box 419493, Kansas City, MO 64141.

Evangelization Update, 6 times a year; 3031 Fourth St. NE, Washington, DC 20017.

Explorations, q; American Interfaith Institute, 321 Chestnut St., Philadelphia, PA, 19106.

Family Connection, The, 6 times a year; 3753 MacBeth Dr., San Jose, CA 95127.

Father Flood, q; P.O. Box 432, Milwaukee, WI 53201.

Fatima Findings, m; 8600 Caliburn Ct.; Pasadena, MD 21122. Reparation Society of the Immaculate Heart of Mary.

Fellowship of Catholic Scholars Newsletter Quarterly; Jacques Maritain Center, 714 Hesburgh Library, Notre Dame, IN 46556.

Fonda Tekakwitha News, P.O. Box 627, Fonda, NY 12068.

Food for the Poor, 3 times a year; 550 SW 12th Ave., Deerfield Beach, FL 33442.

Foundations Newsletter for Newly Married Couples, six times; P.O. Box 1632, Portland, ME, 04104-1632.

Franciscan Reporter, annually; 3140 Meramec St., St. Louis, MO 63118; Franciscan Friars of Sacred Heart Province.

Franciscan World Care, 4 times a year; P.O. Box 29034, Washington, DC 20017. Franciscan Mission Service.

Frontline Report, bm; 23 Bliss Ave., Tenafly, NJ 07670. Society of African Missions.

Graymoor Today, m; Graymoor, Garrison, NY 10524.

Guadalupe Missioners Newsletter, m; 4714 W. 8th St., Los Angeles, CA 90005.

Happiness, q; 567 Salem End Rd., Framingham, MA 01701; Sons of Mary, Health of the Sick.

Harmony, 3 times a year; 800 N. Country Club Rd., Tucson, AZ 85716. Benedictine Srs. of Perpetual Adoration.

Heart Beats, 169 Cummins Hgwy, Roslindale, MA 02131.

HNP Today, w; 127 W. 31st St., New York, NY 10001. Franciscans of Holy Name Province.

HLI Reports, m; 4 Family Life, Front Royal, VA 22630. Human Life International.

Holy Name National Newsletter, 6 times a year; 1169 Market St., No. 304, San Francisco, CA 94103.

Immaculate Heart of Mary Shrine Bulletin, 3 times a year; Mountain View Road, P.O. Box 976, Washington, NJ 07882.

In Between, q; 1257 E. Siena Hts. Dr., Adrian, MI 49221; Adrian Dominican Sisters.

Initiatives, 6 times a year; 10 E. Pearson St., Chicago, IL 60611; National Center for the Laity.

Interchange, P.O. Box 4900, Rochester, MN 55903. Rochester Franciscan Sisters,

It's Our World, 4 times during school year; 1720 Massachusetts Ave. N.W., Washington, DC 20036. Young Catholics in Mission.

Journey, The, 4 times a year; 210 W. 31st St., New York, NY 10001; Province of St. Mary of Capuchin Order.

Joyful Noiseletter, The, m; P.O. Box 895, Portage, MI 49081; Fellowship of Merry Christians.

Knightline, 18 times a year; 1 Columbus Plaza, New Haven, CT 06510-3326; Knights of Columbus Supreme Council.

Laity and Family Life Updates, bi-monthly; 7800 Kenrick Rd., St. Louis, MO, 63119.

Land of Cotton, q; 2048 W. Fairview Ave., Montgomery, AL 39196; City of St. Jude.

Law Reports, q; 4455 Woodson Rd., St. Louis, MO 63134; Catholic Health Association.

LCWR Update, m; 8808 Cameron St., Silver Spring, MD 20910; Leadership Conference of Women Religious.

Lector, m; 115 E. Armour Blvd., Kansas City, MO 64111.

Legatus, m; 30 Frank Lloyd Wright Dr., Ann Arbor, MI 48105.

Let's Talk! (English edition), **Hablemos!** (Spanish edition), 6 times a year; 3031 Fourth St. N.E., Washington, DC 20017-1102; prison ministries of Paulist National Catholic Evangelization Assn.

Letter to the Seven Churches, bi-monthly; 1516 Jerome St., Lansing, MI 48912.

Life at Risk, 10 times a year; 3211 Fourth St. N.E., Washington, DC 20017. Pro-Life Activities Committee, NCCB.

Life Insight, m; 3211 Fourth St. N.E., Washington, DC 20017; Committee for Pro-Life Activities, NCCB.

Liturgical Images, m; P.O. Box 2225, Hickory, NC 28603.

Loyola World, 22 times a year; 820 North Michigan Ave., Chicago, IL, 60611.

Magnificat, three times a year; Star Route 1, Box 226, Eagle harbor, MI, 49950.

Markings, m; 205 W. Monroe St., Chicago, IL 60606.

Maronite Voice, The, m; 4611 Sadler Rd., Glen Allen, VA 23060; Eparchy of St. Maron of Brooklyn.

Maronites Today, m; 1320 East 51ˢᵗ St., Austin, TX 78723. Eparchy of Our Lady of Los Angeles.

Medical Mission Sisters News, 4 times a year; 8400 Pine Road, Philadelphia, PA 19111.

Men of Malvern, q; Malvern, PA 19355-0315.

Messenger of St. Joseph's Union, The, 3 times a year; 108 Bedell St., Staten Island, NY 10309.

Mission Messenger, The, four times a year; P.O. Box 610, Thoreau, NM, 87323; St. Bonaventure Indian Mission and School.

Missionaries of Africa Report, q; 1624 21st St. N.W., Washington, DC 20009; Society of Missionaries of Africa (White Fathers).

Mission 2000, four times a year; 9480 North De Mazenod Dr., Belleville, IL, 62223-1160.

Mission Update, bi-monthly; 3029 Fourth St. NE, Washington, DC, 20017.

NCCB/USCC Currents, 10 times a year; 3211 Fourth St., N.E., Washington, DC 20017.

NCPD National Update, q; P.O. Box 29113, Washington, DC 20017; National Catholic Office for Persons with Disabilities.

NCSC Commitment, biannually; 1275 K St. N.W., Suite 980, Washington, DC 20005-4006. National Catholic Stewardship Council.

NCSC Resources; 1275 K St., N.W., Ste. 980, Washington, DC 20005-4006.

News and Ideas, four times a year; 9480 North De Mazenod Dr., Belleville, IL 62223-1160.

News and Views, q; 3900 Westminster Pl.; St. Louis, MO 63108; Sacred Heart Program.

Newsletter of the Bureau of Catholic Indian Missions, 10 times a year; 2021 H St. N.W., Washington, DC 20006.

Northern Nevada Catholic Newsletter, m; P.O. Box 1211, Reno, NV 89504; Reno diocese.
Nuestra Parroquia (Spanish-English), m; 205 W. Monroe St., Chicago, IL 60606. Claretians.

Oblate Mission-Friendship Club News, four times a year; 9480 North De Mazenod Dr., Belleville, IL 62223-1160; Missionary Oblates of Mary Immaculate.
Oblates, bm; 9480 North De Mazenod Dr., Belleville, IL 62223-1160; Missionary Oblates of Mary Immaculate.
Overview, m; 205 W. Monroe St., 6th Floor, Chicago, IL 60606; Thomas More Assn.

Pacer, m; P.O. Box 34008, Seattle, WA 98124; Providence Medical Center.
Paulist, Today, q; 997 Macarthur Blvd., Mahwah, NJ 07656.
Peace Times, 3-4 times a year; P.O. Box 248, Bellevue, WA 98009-0248.
Perpetual Eucharistic Adoration Newsletter, 3 times a year; P.O. Box 84595, Los Angeles, CA 90073.
Perspectives, q; 912 Market St., La Crosse, WI 54601.
Pilgrim, The, q; Jesuit Fathers, Auriesville, NY 12016; Shrine of North American Martyrs.
Press Conference, q; 1615 Republic St., Cincinnati, OH 45210.
Priests for Life, bm; P.O. Box 141172, Staten Island, NY 10314.
Proclaim, 10 times a year; 3211 Fourth St., N.E., Washington, DC 20037.

Quarterly, The, q; 209 W. Fayette St., Baltimore, MD 21201; Catholic Relief Services.

Religious Life, m (bm, May-Aug.); P.O. Box 41007, Chicago, IL 60641; Institute on Religious Life.
RSCJ Newsletter, m; 1235 Otis St., N.E., Washington, DC 20017; Religious of Sacred Heart.

St. Anthony's Newsletter, 12 times a year; Mt. St. Francis, IN 47146; Conventual Franciscans.
St. Joseph's Parish Life Quarterly, q; 1382 Highland Ave., Needham, MA 02192.
Sacred Ground, three times a year; 1 Elmwood Ave., Kansas City, KS 66103-3719; Christian Foundation for Children.
San Francisco Charismatics, m; 2555 17th Ave., San Francisco, CA 94116.
Savio Notes, q; Filors La, W. Haverstraw, NY 10993.
SCJ News, 9 times a year; P.O. Box 289, Hales Corners, WI 53130; Sacred Heart Fathers and Brothers.
Spirit & The Bide, The, m; 7800 Kenrick Rd., St. Louis, MO 63119.
Spiritual Book Associates, 8 times a year; Notre Dame, IN 46556-0428.
Squires Newsletter, m; One Columbus Plaza, New Haven, CT 06510-3326; Columbian Squires.
SSPS Mission, q; P.O. Box 6026, Techny, IL 60082-6026; Holy Spirit Missionary Sisters.

Tekakwitha Conference Newsletter (Cross and Feather News), q; P.O. Box 6768, Great Falls, MT 59406.

Touchstone, 4 times a year; 1337 W. Ohio St., Chicago, IL 60622; National Federation of Priests' Councils.
Trinity Review, m; P.O. Box 68, Uniconi, TN 37692.

Unda USA Newsletter, 4 times a year; 901 Irving Ave., Dayton, OH 45409-2316.
Union Update, 3 times a year; Washington Theological Union, 6896 Laurel St., N.W., Washington, DC, 20012.

Vision — National Association of Catholic Chaplains, 10 times a year; 3501 S. Lake Dr., Milwaukee, WI 53207.
Visions, 2 times a year; Victory Noll, P.O. Box 109, Huntington, IN 46750; Our Lady of Victory Missionary Sisters.
Voice Crying in the Wilderness, A, q; 4425 Schneider Rd., Fillmore, NY 14735; Most Holy Family Monastery.
Voices, 2 times a year; 1625 Rutherford Lane, Bldg. D, Austin, TX 78754. Volunteers for Educational and Social Services.

Woodstock Report, q; Georgetown Univ., Box 571137, Washington, DC 20057. Woodstock Theological Center.
Word One, 5 times a year; 205 W. Monroe St., Chicago, IL 60606; Claretians.
Word of Hope Newsline, q; P.O. Box 526, Houma, LA 70361-0526.
World Parish, 6 times a year; Maryknoll Fathers; Maryknoll, NY 10545.

Xaverian Missions Newsletter, six times a year; 101 Summer St., Holliston, MA 01746; Xaverian Missionary Fathers.

Your Edmundite Missions Newsletter, bm; 1428 Broad St., Selma, AL 36701; Southern Missions Society of St. Edmund.
Youth Update, m; 1615 Republic St., Cincinnati, OH 45210.

Zeal Newsletter, 3 times a year; P.O. Box 86, Allegany, NY 14706; Franciscan Sisters of Allegany.

BOOKS
The Catholic Almanac, annual; Our Sunday Visitor, Inc., 200 Noll Plaza, Huntington, IN, 46750; publisher; editorial offices, 9165 W. Desert Inn Rd., N-202, Las Vegas, NV, 89117. First edition, 1904.
The Official Catholic Directory, annual; P.J. Kenedy & Sons in association with R.R. Bowker, a Reed Reference Publishing Company, 121 Chanlon Rd., New Providence, NJ 07974. First edition, 1817.

BOOK CLUBS
Catholic Book Club (1928), 106 W. 56th St., New York, NY 10019. Sponsors the Campion Award.
Catholic Digest Book Club (1954), 2115 Summit Ave., St. Paul, MN 55105-1081.
Spiritual Book Associates (1934), Ave Maria Press Building, P.O. Box 428, Notre Dame, IN 46556.
Thomas More Book Club (1939), Thomas More Association, 205 W. Monroe St., Sixth Floor, Chicago, IL 60606.

CANADIAN CATHOLIC PUBLICATIONS

(Principal source: 1999 *Catholic Press Directory*.)
Newspapers

B. C. Catholic, The, w; 150 Robson St., Vancouver, B.C. V6B 2A7.

Catholic New Times (national), biweekly; 80 Sackville St., Toronto, Ont. M5A 3E5.

Catholic Register, The (national), w; 1155 Yonge St., Suite 401, Toronto, Ont. M4T 1W2. Lay edited.

Catholic Times, 10 times a year; 2005 St. Marc St., Montreal, Qué. H3H 2G8.

L'Informateur CatholiQué, semimonthly; 6550 Rte 125, Chertsey, Qué. J0K 3K0.

Monitor, The, m; P.O. Box 986, St. John's, Nfld. A1C 5M3.

New Freeman, The, w; 1 Bayard Dr., St. John, N.B. E2L 3L5.

Pastoral Reporter, q; 290 The Iona Building, 120 17th Ave., S.W., Calgary Alberta, T2S 2T2.

Prairie Messenger, w; Box 190, Muenster, Sask. S0K 2Y0.

Teviskes Ziburiai (The Lights of the Homeland) (Lithuanian), w; 2185 Stavebank Rd., Mississauga, Ont. L5C 1T3.

Magazines, Other Periodicals

L'Almanach Populaire Catholique, y; P.O. Box 1000, St. Anne de Beaupre, Québec, G0A3C0.

ANNALS of St. Anne de Beaupre, The, m; Box 1000, Ste. Anne de Beaupre, Qué. G0A 3C0; Basilica of St. Anne.

Apostolat, bm; 8844 Notre-Dame Est, Montréal, Qué. H1L 3M4. Oblates of Mary Immaculate, CMO (*Centre Missionnaire Oblat*).

Bread of Life, The, 6 times a year; 209 MacNab St. N, P.O. Box 395, Hamilton, Ont. L8N 3H8.

Canadian Catholic Review, The, St. Joseph's College, University of Alberta, Edmonton, Alberta T6G 2J5.

Canadian League, The, 4 times a year; 1-160 Murray Park Rd., Winnipeg, Man. R3J 3X5. Catholic Women's League of Canada.

Caravan, 4 times a year; 90 Parent Ave., Ottawa, Ont. K1N 7B1. Canadian Conference of Catholic Bishops.

Casket, The, w; 88 College St., Antigonish, N.S. B2G 2L7.

Celebrate! (Novalis), 6 times a year; St. Paul University, Suite 604, 9816-112 St., Edmonton, AB T5L 1L5.

Chesterton Review, The, q; 1437 College Dr., Saskatoon, Sask. S7N 0W6.

Companion Magazine, m; 695 Coxwell Ave., Suite 600, Toronto, Ont. M4C 5R6; Conventual Franciscan Fathers.

Compass – A Jesuit Journal, bm (Jan.-Nov.); Box 400, Stn F, 50 Charles St. East, Toronto, Ont. M4Y 2L8.

CRC Bulletin (French-English), q; 219 Argyle Ave., Ottawa, Ont. K2P 2H4; Canadian Religious Conference.

L'Église Canadienne (French), 11 times a year; 6255 rue Hutchison, Bureau 103, Montreal, Qué. H2V 4C7.

Fatima Crusader, 4 times a year; P.O. Box 602, Fort Erie, Ont. L2A 4M7.

Global Village Voice, The, q; 10 St. Mary St., Suite 420, Toronto, Ont. M4y 1P9; Canadian Organization for Development and Peace.

L'Informateur CatholiQué (French), twice monthly; 6550 Rte 125; Rawdon, Québec, J0K 1S0.

Kateri (English-French), q; P.O. Box 70, Kahnawake, Qué. J0L 1B0.

Le Messager de Saint Antoine (French), 10 times a year; Lac-Bouchette, Qué. G0W 1V0.

Messenger of the Sacred Heart, m; 661 Greenwood Ave., Toronto, Ont. M4J 4B3. Apostleship of Prayer.

Mission Canada, 4 times a year; 201-1155 Yonge St., Toronto, Ont. M4T 1W2.

Missions Étrangères (French),6 times a year; 180 Place Juge-Desnoyers, Laval, Qué. H7G 1A4.

Oratory, 6 times a year; 3800 Ch. Queen Mary, Montreal, Qué. H3V 1H6.

Our Family, m; P.O. Box 249, Battleford, Sask.; S0M 0E0; Oblates of Mary Immaculate.

Prête et Pasteur (French), m; 4450 St. Hubert St., Montreal, Qué. H2J 2W9.

Prieres Missionaires, m; Missionaires de la Consolata, 2505 Boulevard Gouin oust, Montréal, Qué. H3M 1B5.

Relations (French), 10 times a year; 25 Rue Jarry Ouest, Montreal, Qué. H2P 1S6.

Restoration, 10 times a year; Madonna House, Combemere, Ont. K0J 1L0.

Reveil Missionaire, 6 times a year; Missionaire de la Consolata, 2505 Boulevard Gouin oust, Montréal, Qué. H3M 1B5.

La Revue d'Sainte Anne de Beaupre (French), m; P.O. Box 1000, Ste. Anne de Beaupre, Québec G0A 3C0.

Scarboro Missions, 9 times a year; 2685 Kingston Rd., Scarboro, Ont. M1M 1M4.

Spiritan Missionary News, 4 times a year; 121 Victoria Park Ave., Toronto, Ont. M4E 3S2.

INTERNATIONAL CATHOLIC PERIODICALS

Principal source: *Catholic Almanac* survey. Included are English-language Catholic periodicals published outside the U.S.

African Ecclesial Review (AFER), bm; Gaba Publications, P.O. Box 4002, Eldoret, Kenya.

Australasian Catholic Record, q; 99 Albert Rd., Strathfield 2135, New South Wales, Australia.

Christ to the World, 5 times a year; Via di Propaganda 1- C, 00187, Rome, Italy.

Christian Orient, q; P.B. 1 Vadavathoor, Kottayam 686010, Kerala, India.

Doctrine and Life, m; Dominican Publications, 42 Parnell Sq., Dublin 1, Ireland.

Downside Review, q; Downside Abbey, Stratton on the Fosse, Bath, BA3 4RH, England.

East Asian Pastoral Review, q; East Asian Pastoral Institute, P.O. Box 221 U.P. Campus, 1101 Quezon City, Philippines.

Furrow, The, m; St. Patrick's College, Maynooth, Ireland.

Heythrop Journal, q; Heythrop College, Kensington Sq., London W8 5HQ, England (Editorial Office). Published by Blackwell Publishers, 108 Cowley Rd., Oxford, OX4 1JF, U.K.

Holy Land Magazine, q; P.O. Box 186, 91001 Jerusalem, Israel. Illustrated.

Inside the Vatican, 10 times a year; Rome office:

Via della Mura Aurelio 7c, 00165 Rome, Italy; USA Office: St. Martin de Porres Community. 3050 Gap Knob Rd., New Hope, KY 40052; the only current journal that focuses exclusively on Rome, the impact of the papacy worldwide, and the functioning, travels, and activities of the Holy Father and the Roman Curia.

Irish Biblical Studies, The, q; Union Theological College, 108 Botanic Ave., Belfast BT7 1JT, N. Ireland.

Irish Journal of Sociology, The, a; St. Patrick's College, Maynooth, Ireland.

Irish Theological Quarterly, q; St. Patrick's College, Maynooth, Ireland.

L'Osservatore Romano, w; Vatican City. (See Index.)

Louvain Studies, q; Peeters Publishers, Bondgenotenlaan 153, B-3000, Leuven, Belgium.

Lumen Vitae (French, with English summaries), q; International Center for Studies in Religious Education, 186, rue Washington, B-1050 Brussels, Belgium.

Mediaeval Studies, annual; Pontifical Institute of Mediaeval Studies, 59 Queen's Park Crescent East, Toronto, Ont., Canada M5S 2C4.

Month, m; 114 Mount St., London, WIY 6AH, England.

Music and Liturgy, 6 times a year; The Editor, 33 Brockenhurst Rd., Addiscombe Croydan, Surrey CRO 7DR, England.

New Blackfriars, m; edited by English Dominicans, Blackfriars, Oxford, OX1 3LY, England.

Omnis Terra (English Edition), m; Pontifical Missionary Union, Congregation for the Evangelization of Peoples, Via di Propaganda 1/c, 00187 Rome, Italy.

One in Christ, q; Edited at: Turvey Abbey, Turvey, Beds. MK43 8DE, England.

Priests & People (formerly **The Clergy Review**), 11 times a year; Blackfriars, Buckingham Rd., Cambridge CB3 0DD, England.

Recusant History, biannual; Catholic Record Society, 12 Melbourne Pl., Wolsingham, Durham DL13 3EH, England.

Religious Life Review, bm; Dominican Publications, 42 Parnell Sq., Dublin 1, Ireland.

Scripture in Church, q; Dominican Publications, 42 Parnell Sq., Dublin 1, Ireland.

Southwark Liturgy Bulletin, q; The Editor, 10 Claremont Rd., Maidstone, Kent ME14 5L2, England.

Spearhead, 5 times a year; Gaba Publications, P.O. Box 4002, Eldoret, Kenya.

Spirituality, bm; Dominican Publications, 42 Parnell Sq., Dublin 1, Ireland.

Tablet, The, w; 1 King Street Cloisters, Clifton Walk, London W6 0QZ, England.

Way, The, q; 114 Mount St., London W1Y 6AN, England.

CATHOLIC NEWS AGENCIES

(Sources: International Catholic Union of the Press, Geneva; Catholic Press Association, U.S.)

Argentina: *Agencia Informativa Catolica Argentina* (AICA), av. Rivadavia, 413, 40 Casilla de Correo Central 2886, 1020 Buenos Aires.

Austria: *Katholische Presse-Agentur* (Kathpress), Singerstrasse 7/6/2, 1010 Vienna 1.

Belgium: *Centre d'Information de Presse* (CIP), 35 Chausée de Haecht, 1030 Brussels.

Bolivia: *Agencia Noticias Fides*, ANF, Casilla 5782, La Paz.

ERBOL, Casilla 5946, La Paz.

Chile: *Agencia informativa y de comunicaciones* (AIC Chile), Brasil 94, Santiago.

Croatia: *Christian Information Service*, Marulicev 14, PP 434, 410001 Zagreb.

Germany: *Katholische Nachrichten Agentur* (KNA), Adenauer Allee 134, 5300 Bonn 1.

Greece: *Agence TYPOS*, Rue Acharnon 246, Athens 815.

Hong Kong: *UCA-News*, P.O. Box 69626, Kwun Tong (Hong Kong).

Hungary: *Magyar Kurir*, Milkszath ter 1, 1088, Budapest.

India: *South Asian Religious News* (SAR-News), PB 6236, Mazagaon, Bombay 400 010.

Italy: *Servizio Informazioni Religiosa* (SIR), Via di Porta Cavalleggeri 143, I-00165 Roma.

Centrum Informationis Catolicae (CIC-Roma), via Delmonte de la Farina, 30/4, 00186 Roma.

Peru: ACI-PRENSA, A.P. 040062, Lima.

Switzerland: *Katholische Internationale Presse-Agentur* (KIPA), Case Postale 1054 CH 1701, Fribourg.

Centre International de Reportages et d'Information Culturelle (CIRIC), Chemin Clochetons 8, P.O. Box 1000, Lausanne.

United States of America: *Catholic News Service* (CNS), 3211 Fourth St. N.E., Washington, DC 20017.

Zaire (now Congo): *Documentation et Information Africaine* (DIA), B.P. 2598, Kinshasa I.

Missions: *Agenzia Internazionale Fides* (AIF), Palazzo di Propagande Fide, Via di Propaganda I-c, 00187 Rome, Italy.

U.S. PRESS SERVICES

Catholic News Service (CNS), established in 1920 (NC News Service), provides a worldwide daily news report by satellite throughout the U.S. and Canada and by wire and computer links into several foreign countries, and by mail to other clients, serving Catholic periodicals and broadcasters who follow Vatican Radio in about 40 countries. CNS also provides feature and photo services and a weekly religious education package, "Faith Alive!" It publishes "Origins," a weekly documentary service, and "Catholic Trends," a fortnightly newsletter, the weekly TV and Movie Guide and Movie Guide Monthly. CNS maintains a full-time bureau in Rome. It is a division of the United States Catholic Conference, with offices at 3211 Fourth St. N.E., Washington, DC 20017. The director and editor-in-chief is Thomas N. Lorsung.

Spanish-Language Service: A weekly news summary provided by Catholic News Service is used by a number of Catholic newspapers. Some papers carry features of their own in Spanish.

Religion News Service (RNS) provides coverage of all religions as well as ethics, spirituality and moral issues. Founded in 1934 (as the Religious News Service) by the National Conference of Christian and Jews as an independent agency, RNS became an editorially independent subsidiary of the United Methodist Reporter, an interfaith publishing company, in 1983. It was acquired by Newhouse News Service in 1994. Address: 1101 Connecticut Ave. NW, Suite 350, Washington, DC 20036.

RADIO, TELEVISION, THEATER

Radio

Catholic Views Broadcasts, Inc.: 10 Audrey Place, Fairfield, NJ 07004. Produces weekly 15-minute program "Views of the News." Also operates Catholic community TV stations in Chicago and Minneapolis.

Christopher Radio Program: 14-minute interview series, "Christopher Closeup," weekly and "Christopher Minutes," daily, on 400 stations. Address: 12 E. 48th St., New York, NY 10017.

Father Justin Rosary Hour (Radio): P.O. Box 454, Athol Springs, NY 14010. Founded in 1931. Polish Catechetical Radio Network. Rev. Marion M. Tolczyk, O.F.M. Conv., director.

Journeys Thru Rock (Radio): Produced in cooperation with the Department of Communication, NCCB/USCC. A 15-minute weekly program currently employing a youth-oriented music and commentary format (ABC).

Radio Maria (Italian): Italian Catholic radio station founded in 1992, 352 W. 44th St., New York, NY 10036. Rev. Mariano Cisco, C.S., executive director.

Vatican Radio: See under Vatican City State; see also Index.

Television and Communications Services

Black Catholic Televangelization Network: Consists of production organizations that promote the evangelization of the Black community and share the gifts of Black Catholics. The member production groups are: Black and Catholic (TV); This Far by Faith (Radio); Search; and Catholic African World Network; Pres., Rev. Clarence Williams, C.Pp.S., Ph.D. Address: P.O. Box 13220, Detroit, MI 48213.

Catholic Communications Foundation (CCF): A foundation established by the Catholic Fraternal Benefit Societies in 1966 to lend support and assistance to development of the communications apostolate of the Church. The CCF promotes the development of diocesan communications capabilities and funds a scholarship program at the Annual Institute for Religious Communications. CCF officers include Bishop Anthony G. Bosco, chairman of the board. Address: 11420 U.S. Highway One, Suite 126, North Palm Beach, FL 33408.

Catholic Television: Instructional TV operations or broadcasts of Masses have been established in the following archdioceses and dioceses. Archdioceses are indicated by an asterisk.

Boston,* MA: Rev. Francis McFarland, Director, P.O. Box 9109, Newton, 02160.

Brooklyn, NY: Rev. Msgr. Michael J. Dempsey, Director, 1712 10th Ave. 11215.

Chicago, *IL: Mr. Joseph Loughlin, Director, Radio/TV Office, Archdiocese of Chicago, 155 E. Superior. 60611.

Corpus Christi, TX: Mr. Martin L. Wind, 1200 Lantana St., Corpus Christi, 78407.

Dallas, TX: Mr. Michael McGee, 3725 Blackburn, P.O.Box 190507. 75219.

Detroit,* MI: Mr. Ned McGrath, Director, 305 Michigan Ave., Detroit, 48226.

Los Angeles,* CA: Mr. David Moore, 3424 Wilshire Blvd. 90010.

New York,* NY: Mr. Michael Lavery, Director, 215 Seminary Ave., Yonkers, 10704.

Oakland, San Jose, San Francisco,* CA: Shirley Connolly, Director, 324 Middlefield Rd., Menlo Park, 94025.

Orlando, FL: Rev. Robert Hoeffner. Director, P.O. Box 1800, Orlando 32802.

Rockville Centre, NY: Rev. Msgr. Thomas Hartman, Director, 1200 Glen Curtiss Blvd., Uniondale, 11553.

San Bernardino, CA: Caritas Telecommunications, Clare Colella, Director, 1201 E. Highland Ave. 92404.

Youngstown, OH: Rev. James Korda, P.O. Box 430, Canfield, 44406.

Christopher TV Series, "Christopher Closeup": Originated in 1952. Half-hour interviews, weekly, on commercial TV and numerous cable outlets. Address: 12 E. 48th St., New York, NY 10017.

Clemons Productions, Inc.: Produces "That's the Spirit," a family show for television; "Thoughts for the Week," on the ABC Satellite Network and "Spirituality for Today" on the internet. Available to dioceses, organizations or channels. Address: P.O. Box 7466, Greenwich, CT 06830.

Eternal Word Television Network (EWTN): 5817 Old Leeds Rd., Birmingham, AL 35210. America's largest religious cable network; features 24 hours of spiritual-growth programming for the entire family. Offers documentaries, weekly teaching series and talk shows, including the award-winning "Mother Angelica Live." Also features live Church events from around the world and devotional programs such as "The Holy Rosary." Mother M. Angelica, P.C.P.A., foundress.

Family Theater Productions: Founded by Father Peyton. Video cassettes, films for TV. Address: 7201 Sunset Blvd., Hollywood, CA 90046. Pres., Rev. John P. Phalen, C.S.C.

Franciscan Communications: Producer of video and print resources for pastoral ministry. Address: St. Anthony Messenger Press, 1615 Republic St., Cincinnati, OH 45210.

Hispanic Telecommunications Network, Inc. (HTN): Produces Nuestra Familia, a national weekly Spanish-language TV series. Address: 1405 N. Main, Suite 240, San Antonio, TX 78212.

Jesuit Productions/Sacred Heart Program, Inc.: Produces and distributes free of charge the weekly "CONTACT" program in 30-, 15-, and 5-minute formats to more than 400 stations in North America. Address: 3900 Westminster Pl., St. Louis, MO 63108. Exec. Dir., Gary Kolarcik.

Mary Productions: Originated in 1950. Offers royalty-free scripts for stage, film, radio and tape production. Audio and video tapes of lives of the saints and historical characters. Traveling theater company. Address: Mary Productions, 212 Oakdale Dr., Tomaso Plaza, Middletown, NJ 07748. Dir., Mary-Eunice.

Oblate Media and Communication Corporation: Producers, Broadcast syndicators and distributors of Catholic and value-centered video programming. Address: 7315 Manchester Rd., St. Louis, MO 63143.

Odyssey-Interfaith Cable Television Channel: Policies shaped by consortium of 28 members representing 64 faith groups from Roman Catholic, Jewish, Protestant and Eastern Orthodox traditions. Address: National Interfaith Cable Coalition, 9th Floor, 74 Trinity Place, New York, NY 10006.

Passionist Communications, Inc.: Present Sunday Mass on TV seen in U.S. and available to dioceses and channels; publish "TV Prayer Guide," semi-annually. Address: P.O. Box 440, Pelham, NY 10803-0440.

Paulist Media Works: Full service audio production in syndication to dioceses, religious communities and church groups. Address: 3055 4th St. NE, Washington, DC 20017. Exec. Prod., Rev. John Geaney, C.S.P.

Paulist Productions: Producers and distributors of the INSIGHT Film Series (available for TV) and educational film series. Address: 17575 Pacific Coast Hwy., Pacific Palisades, CA 90272.

Religious Specials (TV): The NCCB/USCC Catholic Communication Campaign produces two one-hour Catholic specials a year and additional seasonal liturgical services. The specials cover a variety of topics and are broadcast on the ABC and NBC television networks.

Unda-USA: A national professional Catholic association for broadcasters and other allied communicators in church ministry; organized in 1972. It suc-ceeded the Catholic Broadcasters Association of America which in 1948 had replaced the Catholic Forum of the Air organized in 1938. It is a member of Unda-International, the international Catholic association for radio and television (Unda is the Latin word for "wave," symbolic of air waves of communication). In addition to providing support and network opportunities in church communications the organization works to encourage the secular media to produce value-oriented programs and stories. Unda-USA sponsors an annual general assembly and presents the Gabriel Awards annually for excellence in broadcasting. It publishes six newsletters for its membership. President, Frank Morock. Address: Unda-USA, 901 Irving Ave., Dayton, OH 45409.

Theater

Catholic Actors' Guild of America, Inc.: Established in 1914 to provide material and spiritual assistance to people in the theater. Has more than 500 members; publishes *The Call Board*. Address: 1501 Broadway, Suite 510, New York, NY 10036.

CATHOLIC INTERNET SITES

Specific Web site addresses change periodically. Our Sunday Visitor's site is http://www.osv.com.

Holy See Sites

Vatican Web Site: http://www.vatican.va

L'Osservatore Romano: http://www.vatican.va/ news_services/or/or_eng/or_eng.htm

VatRadio: http://www.wrn.org/vatican-radio/ audio.html

Catholic Megasites, Directories and Links

A la Padre: http://alapadre.net/

Biblical Evidence for Catholicism: http://ic.net/ ~erasmus/erasmus.htm

Catholic Information Network: http://www.cin.org

Catholic Internet Directory: http://www.catholic-church.org/cid

Catholic Internet Network: http://www.catholic-internet.org

Catholic Kiosk: http://www.aquinas-multimedia.com/arch/index.html

Catholic Media Directory: http://www.nd.edu/ ~theo/RCD/Directory5.html

Catholic Mobile: http://www.mcgill.pvt.k12.al.us/ jerryd/cathmob.htm

Catholic.Net Periodicals: http://www.catholic.net/ RCC/Periodicals/index.html

Catholic Pages: http://www.catholic-pages.com

Catholic Press Association: http:// www.catholicpress.org//index.htm

Catholic Publications: http://www.catholic.org/ media/publications/index.html

McGill Search Engines: http:// www.mcgill.pvt.k12.al.us/jerryd/cm/engines.htm

St. Jane's: http://www.stjane.org

Totally Catholic Link Directory: http:// www.public.usit.net/merlin

Catholic Movements and Organizations

Adoremus: http://www.adoremus.org

Catholic Charismatic Center: http:// www.garg.com/ccc

Catholic Doctrinal Concordance: http:// www.infpage.com/concordance

Catholic Family and Human Rights Institute: http://www.cafhri.org

Catholic Health Association USA: http:// www.chausa.org/CHAHOME.ASP

Catholic League: http://www.catholicleague.org

CHA Wisconsin: http://www.execpc.com/~chaw

Focolare Movement: http://www.rc.net/focolare

Friendship House: http://www.friendshiphouse.org/

Madonna House: http://www.madonnahouse.org

Nat'l Bioethics Center: http://www.ncbcenter.org

Opus Dei: http://www.opusdei.org

Pax Christi International: http://www.pci.ngonet.be/

Pax Christi USA: http://www.nonviolence.org/pcusa

Preservation Press: http://www.preservationpress.com

Saints Alive: http://home.earthlink.net/~saintsalive/

Schoenstatt: http://www.schoenstatt.org/

Seton Home Study School: http:// www.setonhome.org/generic.htm

Catholic Newspapers and Magazines

Catholic Digest: http://www.catholicdigest.org

Catholic New York Online: http://www.cny.org

Catholic Worker: http://www.catholicworker.org

First Things: http://www.firstthings.com

Houston Catholic Worker: http://www.cjd.org

The Tablet, U.K.: http://www.thetablet.co.uk/ tablethm.cgi

The Universe, U.K.: http://www.the-universe.net

The Wanderer: http://www.thewandererpress.com

Religious Orders and Apostolates

Apostolates\Apostolates\Orders: http:// www.catholic-forum.com/orders.html

AU Links: http://listserv.american.edu/catholic

CathLinks: http://www.cs.cmu.edu/People/spok/ catholic/organizations.htmldioceses

EWTN: http://www.ewtn.com

RCNet — Apostolates: http://www.rc.net/org

Religious Orders: http://communio.hcbc.hu/ rel_ord.html

Colleges and Universities

Colleges: http://alapadre.net/cathcoll.html

Universities: http://alapadre.net/cathuniv.html

HONORS AND AWARDS

Pontifical Orders

The Pontifical Orders of Knighthood are secular orders of merit whose membership depends directly on the pope.

Supreme Order of Christ (Militia of Our Lord Jesus Christ): The highest of the five pontifical orders of knighthood, the Supreme Order of Christ was approved Mar. 14, 1319, by John XXII as a continuation in Portugal of the suppressed Order of Templars. Members were religious with vows and a rule of life until the order lost its religious character toward the end of the 15th century. Since that time it has existed as an order of merit. Paul VI, in 1966, restricted awards of the order to Christian heads of state.

Order of the Golden Spur (Golden Militia): Although the original founder is not certainly known, this order is one of the oldest knighthoods. Indiscriminate bestowal and inheritance diminished its prestige, however, and in 1841 Gregory XVI replaced it with the Order of St. Sylvester and gave it the title of Golden Militia. In 1905 St. Pius X restored the Order of the Golden Spur in its own right, separating it from the Order of St. Sylvester. Paul VI, in 1966, restricted awards of the order to Christian heads of state.

Order of Pius IX: Founded by Pius IX June 17, 1847, the order is awarded for outstanding services for the Church and society, and may be given to non-Catholics as well as Catholics. The title to nobility formerly attached to membership was abolished by Pius XII in 1939. In 1957 Pius XII instituted the Class of the Grand Collar as the highest category of the order; in 1966, Paul VI restricted this award to heads of state "in solemn circumstances." The other three classes are of Knights of the Grand Cross, Knight Commanders with and without emblem, and Knights. The new class was created to avoid difficulties in presenting papal honors to Christian or non-Christian leaders of high merit.

Order of St. Gregory the Great: First established by Gregory XVI in 1831 to honor citizens of the Papal States, the order is conferred on persons who are distinguished for personal character and reputation, and for notable accomplishment. The order has civil and military divisions, and three classes of knights.

Order of St. Sylvester: Instituted Oct. 31, 1841, by Gregory XVI to absorb the Order of the Golden Spur, this order was divided into two by St. Pius X in 1905, one retaining the name of St. Sylvester and the other assuming the title of Golden Militia. Membership consists of three degrees: Knights of the Grand Cross, Knight Commanders with and without emblem, and Knights.

Papal Medals

Pro Ecclesia et Pontifice: This decoration ("For the Church and the Pontiff") had its origin in 1888 as a token of the golden sacerdotal jubilee of Leo XIII; he bestowed it on those who had assisted in the observance of his jubilee and on persons responsible for the success of the Vatican Exposition. The medal, cruciform in shape, bears the likenesses of Sts. Peter and Paul, the tiara and the papal keys, the words *Pro Ecclesia et Pontifice*, and the name of the present pontiff, all on the same side; it is attached to a ribbon of yellow and white, the papal colors. Originally, the medal was issued in gold, silver or bronze. It is awarded in recognition of service to the Church and the papacy.

Benemerenti: Several medals ("To a well-deserving person") have been conferred by popes for exceptional accomplishment and service. The medals, which are made of gold, silver or bronze, bear the likeness and name of the reigning pope on one side; on the other, a laurel crown and the letter "B." These two medals may be given by the pope to both men and women. Their bestowal does not convey any title or honor of knighthood.

Ecclesiastical Orders

Equestrian Order of the Holy Sepulchre of Jerusalem: The order traces its origin to Godfrey de Bouillon who instituted it in 1099. It took its name from the Basilica of the Holy Sepulchre where its members were knighted. After the fall of the Latin Kingdom of Jerusalem and the consequent departure of the knights from the Holy Land, national divisions were established in various countries.

The order was re-organized by Pius IX in 1847 when he reestablished the Latin Patriarchate of Jerusalem and placed the order under the jurisdiction of its patriarch. In 1888, Leo XIII confirmed permission to admit women — Ladies of the Holy Sepulchre — to all degrees of rank. Pius X reserved the office of grand master to himself in 1907; Pius XII gave the order a cardinal patron in 1940 and, in 1949, transferred the office of grand master from the pope to the cardinal patron. Pope John XXIII approved updated constitutions in 1962; the latest statutes were approved by Paul VI in 1977.

The purposes of the order are strictly religious and charitable. Members are committed to sustain and aid the charitable, cultural and social works of the Catholic Church in the Holy Land, particularly in the Latin Patriarchate of Jerusalem.

The order is composed of knights and ladies grouped in three classes: class of Knights of the Collar and Ladies of the Collar; Class of Knights (in four grades); Class of Ladies (in four grades). Members are appointed by the cardinal grand master according to procedures outlined in the constitution.

Under the present constitution the order is divided into national lieutenancies, largely autonomous, with international headquarters in Rome. Cardinal Carlo Furno is the grand master of the order.

There are nine lieutenancies of the order in the United States and one in Puerto Rico. Address of Vice Governor General: F. Russell Kendall, 309 Knipp Rd., Houston, TX 77024.

Order of Malta

The Sovereign Military Hospitaller Order of St. John of Jerusalem of Rhodes and of Malta traces its origin to a group of men who maintained a Christian hospital in the Holy Land in the 11th century. The group was approved as a religious order — the Hospitallers of St. John — by Paschal II in 1113.

The order, while continuing its service to the poor, principally in hospital work, assumed military duties in the twelfth century and included knights, chaplains and sergeants-at-arms among its members. All the knights were professed monks with the vows of poverty, chastity and obedience. Headquarters were located in the Holy Land until the last decade of the 13th century and on Rhodes after 1308 (whence the title, Knights of Rhodes).

After establishing itself on Rhodes, the order became a sovereign power like the sea republics of Italy and the Hanseatic cities of Germany, flying its own flag, coining its own money, floating its own navy, and maintaining diplomatic relations with many nations.

The order was forced to abandon Rhodes in 1522 after the third siege of the island by the Turks under Sultan Suleyman I. Eight years later, the Knights were given the island of Malta, where they remained as a bastion of Christianity until near the end of the 18th century. Headquarters have been located in Rome since 1834.

The title of Grand Master of the Order, in abeyance for some time, was restored by Leo XIII in 1879. A more precise definition of both the religious and the sovereign status of the order was embodied in a new constitution of 1961 and a code issued in 1966.

The four main classifications of members are: Knights of Justice, who are religious with the vows of poverty, chastity and obedience; Knights of Obedience, who make a solemn promise to strive for Christian perfection; Knights of Honor and Devotion and of Grace and Devotion — all of noble lineage; and Knights of Magistral Grace. There are also chaplains, Dames and Donats of the order.

The order, with six grand priories, three sub-priories and 40 national associations, is devoted to hospital and charitable works of all kinds in some 100 countries.

Under the provisions of international law, the order maintains full diplomatic relations with the Holy See — on which, in its double nature, it depends as a religious Order, but of which, as a sovereign Order of Knighthood, it is independent — and 68 countries throughout the world.

The Grand Master, who is the head of the order, has the title of Most Eminent Highness with the rank of Cardinal. He must be of noble lineage and under solemn vows for a minimum period of 10 years, if under 50.

The present Grand Master is Fra' Andrew Willoughby Ninian Bertie, member of the British aristocracy, who was elected for life Apr. 8, 1988, by the Council of State. His election was approved by the Pope.

The address of headquarters of the order is Via Condotti, 68, Palazzo Malta, 00187 Rome, Italy. U.S. addresses: American Association, 1011 First Ave., New York, NY 10022; Western Association of U.S.A., 465 California St., Suite 524, San Francisco, CA 94104; Federal Association of U.S.A., 1730 M St. N.W., Suite 403, Washington, DC 20036.

Order of St. George

The Sacred Military Constantinian Order of St. George was established by Pope Clement XI in 1718. The purposes of the order are to work for the preaching and defense of the Catholic faith and to promote the spiritual and physical welfare of sick, disabled, homeless and other unfortunate persons. The principal officer is Prince Carlo of Bourbon-Two Sicilies, duke of Calabria. Addresses: Via Sistina 121, 00187 Rome, Italy; Via Duomo 149, 80138 Naples, Italy; Address of United States Delegation, 3731 Olympia Dr., Houston, TX 77019.

1999 CATHOLIC PRESS ASSOCIATION AWARDS

Catholic Press Association Awards for material published in 1998 were presented at the annual Catholic Press Association Convention in Chicago from May 26-28, 1999; awards included:

Newspapers – General Excellence

National Newspapers: *Our Sunday Visitor* (First Place); *National Catholic Reporter* (Second Place); *National Catholic Register* and *The Catholic Register* (Tie, Third Place).

Diocesan Newspapers, 40,001+ Circulation: *Catholic New York* (New York, N.Y.), First Place; *The Catholic Review* (Baltimore, Md.), Second Place; *The Record* (Louisville, Ky.), Third Place.

Diocesan Newspapers, 17,001-40,000: *The Catholic Herald* (Colorado Springs, Colo.), First Place; *The Florida Catholic* (Miami, Fla.), Second Place; *The Southern Cross* (San Diego, Calif.), Third Place; *The Catholic Advocate* (Newark, N.J.) and *The Sooner Catholic* (Oklahoma, Okla.), Honorable Mentions.

Diocesan Newspapers, 1-17,000: *Tennessee Register* (Nashville, Tenn.), First Place; *The Catholic Observer* (Springfield, Mass.), Second Place; *Today's Catholic* (Fort Wayne, Ind.), Third Place; *The Message* (Evansville, Ind.), Honorable Mention.

Magazines – General Excellence

General Interest: *Envoy* (Granville, Ohio) First Place; *St. Anthony Messenger* (Cincinnati, Ohio), Second Place; *Liguorian* (Liguori, Mo.), Third Place.

Mission Magazines: *Catholic Near East* (New York, N.Y.), First Place; *Maryknoll* (Maryknoll, N.Y.), Second Place; *Extension* (Chicago, Ill.), Third Place.

Religious Order: *The Anthonian* (Paterson, N.J.), First Place; *SALT/Sisters of Charity, BVM* (Dubuque, Iowa), Second Place; *Marian Bulletin* (Stockbridge, Mass.), Third Place.

Professional/Special Interest: *Catholic Heritage* (Huntington, Ind.), First Place; *Catholic Parent* (Huntington, Ind.), Second Place; *Today's Catholic Teacher* (Dayton, Ohio), Third Place.

Magazines for Clergy and Religious: *Review for Religious* (St. Louis, Mo.), First Place; *Emmanuel* (Cleveland, Ohio), Second Place; *The Priest* (Huntington, Ind.), Third Place.

Scholarly: *Horizon* (Chicago, Ill.), First Place; *Grail* (Ottawa, Ont.), Second Place.

Prayer and Spirituality: *Roze Maryi* (Stockbridge, Mass.), First Place; *Forefront* (Crestone, Colo.), Second Place; *Bible Today* (Collegeville, Minn.), Third Place.

Newsletters

General Interest: *Youth Update* (Cincinnati, Ohio) and *Christopher News Notes* (New York, N.Y.), Tie, First Place; *Sacred Ground* (Kansas City, Kans.),

Second Place; *Catholic Update* (Cincinnati, Ohio), Third Place.

Special Interest: *In Between* (Adrian, Mo.), First Place; *Comboni* (Cincinnati, Ohio) Second Place; *Millennium* (Cincinnati, Ohio), Third Place.

Books — First Place Awards
Popular Presentation of the Catholic Faith: Doubleday, Patrick Ahern, *Maurice & Thérèse, The Story of a Love.*

Spirituality: Softcover: Crossroad Publishing, Co., Diarmuid O'Murchu, *Reclaiming Spirituality.* **Hardcover:** Augsburg Fortress, Shawn Madigan, C.S.J., Editor, *Mystics, Visionaries & Prophets.*

Theology: Liturgical Press, Edward J. Kilmartin, S.J., *The Eucharist in the West*; Orbis Books, Peter Phan, *Mission and Catechesis* (Tie).

Scripture: Doubleday, Joseph A. Fitzmyer, S.J., *The Acts of The Apostles.*

Liturgy: Liturgical Press, Normand Bonneau, O.M.I., *The Sunday Lectionary.*

Pastoral Ministry: Liturgical Press, Robert Howes, *Bridges.*

Professional Books: Ave Maria Press, Loughlan Sofield, Rosine Hammett, Carroll Juliano, *Building Community.*

Educational Books: The Crossroad Publishing Co., Timothy E. O'Connell, *Making Disciples, A Handbook of Christian Moral Formation.*

Design and Production: The Crossroad Publishing Co., Caroline H. Ebertshauser, Herbert Haag, Joe H. Kirchberger, Dorothee Solle, *Mary – Art, Culture, and Religion Through the Ages.*

Children's Books: St. Anthony Messenger Press, Philip D. Gallery, *Can You Find Bible Heroes?*

First Time Author of a Book: The Liturgical Press, Molly Wolf, *Hiding in Plain Sight, Sabbath Blessings.*

Family Life: Augsburg Fortress, Dr. Michael Obsatz, *Raising Nonviolent Children in a Violent World.*

History/Biography: The Liturgical Press, Heinrich Schipperges, *The World of Hildegard of Bingen.*

Gender Issues: Liguori Publications, Mitch Finley, *For Men Only.*

Hispanic Titles: Liguori Publications, *El Matrimonio En Perspectiva, Incluye La Misa de la Boda.*

Reference: The Liturgical Press, John C. Endres, William R. Millar, John Barclay Burns, Editors, *Chronicles and Its Synoptic Parallels in Samuel, Kings, and Related Biblical Texts.*

1999 CHRISTOPHER AWARDS

Christopher Awards are given each year to recognize the creative writers, producers and directors who have achieved artistic excellence in films, books and television specials affirming the highest values of the human spirit. The 1999 awards were presented Feb. 25, 1999, in New York.

Books: *The Children*, by David Halberstam (Random House); *The Endurance: Shackleton's Legendary Antarctic Expedition*, by Caroline Alexander, photos by Frank Hurley (Knopf); *Free and Faithful: My Life in the Catholic Church*, by Bernard Häring (Liguori/Triumph); *Free the Children: A Young Man's Personal Crusade Against Child Labor*, by Craig Kielburger, with Kevin Major (HarperCollins); *The Gifts of the Jews: How a Tribe of Desert Nomads Changed the Way Everyone Thinks and Feels*, by Thomas Cahill (Nan A. Talese/Doubleday); *The Life of Thomas More*, by Peter Ackroyd (Nan A. Talese/ Doubleday); *Love's Harvest: Family, Faith, Friends*, by Christopher De Vinck (Crossroad); *Maurice and Therese: The Story of a Love*, by Patrick Ahern (Doubleday); *Walking with the Wind: A Memoir of the Movement*, by John Lewis, with Michael D'Orso (Simon & Schuster).

Books for Young People: *Raising Dragons*, by Jerdine Nolen, illustrated by Elise Primavera (Ages 6-8, Harcourt Brace/Silver Whistle); *The Summer My Father Was Ten*, by Pat Brisson, illustrated by Andrea Shine (Ages 8-10, Boyd Mills Press); *Mary on Horseback: Three Mountain Stories*, by Rosemary Wells, illustrated by Peter McCarty (Ages 10-12, Dial Books for Young Readers); *Shipwreck Season*, by Donna Hill (Ages 12 and up, Clarion Books); *Holes*, by Louis

Sachar (Young Adult, Straus & Giroux/Frances Foster Books).

Television Specials: *About Sarah* (CBS), Jeffrey S. Grant, Tim Reid, Joel S. Rice, executive prods., Jonathan Bernstein prod., Roseanne Leto, Debbie Martin, Michele Sacharow, co-prods.; Susan Rohrer, prod./dir./writer, Nancy Silvers, writer; *Grace and Glorie* (CBS), Richard Welsh, Brent Shields, exec. prods., Grace McKeaney, writer; Arthur Allan Seidelman, dir.; *Nicholas' Gift* (CBS), Lorenzo Minoli, Judd Parkin, exec. prods., Russell Kagan, prod., Matthew Mitchell, co-prod., Christine Berardo, writer; Robert Markowitz, dir.; *Ruby Bridges* (ABC), Marian Rees, exec. prod., Anne Hopkins, prod., Euzhan Palcy, co-prod./dir., Toni Ann Johnson, writer; *Travis* (ITVS/PBS), Richard Kotuk, exec. prod./dir./ writer, Jean Tsien, writer.

Films: *Down in the Delta* (Miramax), Reuben Cannon, Victor McGauley, Rick Rosenberg, Bob Christiansen, Wesley Snipes, prods., Terri Farnsworth, Alfre Woodard, co-prod., Myron Goble, co-prod./writer, Maya Angelou, dir.; *Life is Beautiful* (Miramax), Elda Ferri, Gianluigi Braschi, prods., Vincenzo Cerami, writer, Roberto Benigni, dir./ writer; *Saving Private Ryan* (DreamWorks), Ian Bryce, Mark Gordon, Gary Levinsohn, prods., Bonnie Curtis, Allison Lyon Segan, co-prods., Robert Rodat, writer; Steven Spielberg, prod./dir.; *Smoke Signals* (Miramax), David Skinner, Carl Bressler, exec. prods., Larry Estes, Scott Rosenfelt, prods., Sherman Alexie, co-prod./writer, Chris Eyre, co-prod./dir.

Miniseries: *From the Earth to the Moon* (HBO).

ECUMENISM

(*Sources: Brother Jeffrey Gros, F.S.C. and Rev. Ronald Roberson, C.S.P., associate directors, Secretariat for Ecumenical and Interreligious Affairs, NCCB.*)

The modern ecumenical movement, with roots in nineteenth-century scholars and individuals began its institutional life in 1910 among Protestants and Orthodox and led to formation of the World Council of Churches in 1948, developed outside the mainstream of Catholic interest for many years. It has now become for Catholics as well one of the great religious facts of our time.

The magna carta of ecumenism for Catholics is a complex of several documents which include, in the first place, *Unitatis Redintegratio*, the Decree on Ecumenism, promulgated by the Second Vatican Council Nov. 21, 1964. Other enactments underlying and expanding this decree are *Lumen Gentium* (Dogmatic Constitution on the Church), *Orientalium Ecclesiarum* (Decree on Eastern Catholic Churches), and *Gaudium et Spes* (Pastoral Constitution on the Church in the Modern World).

The Holy See has more recently brought together Catholic ecumenical priorities in *Directory for the Application of Principles and Norms on Ecumenism* (1993) and *The Ecumenical Dimension in the Formation of Pastoral Workers* (1998). These, in addition to Pope John Paul II's encyclical letter, *Ut Unum Sint* (1995), provide a guide for Catholic ecumenical initiatives.

VATICAN II DECREE

The following excerpts from *Unitatis Redintegratio* cover the broad theological background and principles and indicate the thrust of the Church's commitment to ecumenism, under the subheads: Elements Common to Christians, Unity Lacking, What the Movement Involves, Primary Duty of Catholics.

Men who believe in Christ and have been properly baptized are brought into a certain, though imperfect, communion with the Catholic Church. Undoubtedly, the differences that exist in varying degrees between them and the Catholic Church — whether in doctrine and sometimes in discipline, or concerning the structure of the Church — do indeed create many and sometimes serious obstacles to full ecclesiastical communion. These the ecumenical movement is striving to overcome (No. 3).

Elements Common to Christians

Moreover some, even very many, of the most significant elements or endowments which together go to build up and give life to the Church herself can exist outside the visible boundaries of the Catholic Church: the written word of God; the life of grace; faith, hope, and charity, along with other interior gifts of the Holy Spirit and visible elements. All of these, which come from Christ and lead back to Him, belong by right to the one Church of Christ (No. 3).

[In a later passage, the decree singled out a number of elements which the Catholic Church and other churches have in common but not in complete agreement: confession of Christ as Lord and God and as mediator between God and man; belief in the Trinity; reverence for Scripture as the revealed word of God;

baptism and the Lord's Supper; Christian life and worship; faith in action; concern with moral questions.]

The brethren divided from us also carry out many of the sacred actions of the Christian religion. Undoubtedly, in ways that vary according to the condition of each church or community, these actions can truly engender a life of grace, and can be rightly described as capable of providing access to the community of salvation.

It follows that these separated Churches and Communities, though we believe they suffer from defects already mentioned, have by no means been deprived of significance and importance in the mystery of salvation. For the Spirit of Christ has not refrained from using them as means of salvation which derive their efficacy from the very fullness of grace and truth entrusted to the Catholic Church (No. 3).

Unity Lacking

Nevertheless, our separated brethren, whether considered as individuals or as Communities and Churches, are not blessed with that unity which Jesus Christ wished to bestow on all those whom he has regenerated and vivified into one body and newness of life - that unity which the holy Scriptures and the revered tradition of the Church proclaim. For it is through Christ's Catholic Church alone, which is the all-embracing means of salvation, that the fullness of the means of salvation can be obtained. It was to the apostolic college alone, of which Peter is the head, that we believe our Lord entrusted all the blessings of the New Covenant, in order to establish on earth the one Body of Christ into which all those should be fully incorporated who already belong in any way to God's People (No. 3).

What the Movement Involves

Today, in many parts of the world, under the inspiring grace of the Holy Spirit, multiple efforts are being expended through prayer, word, and action to attain that fullness of unity which Jesus Christ desires. This sacred Synod, therefore, exhorts all the Catholic faithful to recognize the signs of the times and to participate skillfully in the work of ecumenism.

The "ecumenical movement" means those activities and enterprises which, according to various needs of the Church and opportune occasions, are started and organized for the fostering of unity among Christians. These are:

• First, every effort to eliminate words, judgments, and actions which do not respond to the condition of separated brethren with truth and fairness and so make mutual relations between them more difficult.

• Then, "dialogue" between competent experts from different Churches and Communities [scholarly ecumenism].

• In addition, these Communions cooperate more closely in whatever projects a Christian conscience demands for the common good [social ecumenism].

• They also come together for common prayer, where this is permitted [spiritual ecumenism].

• Finally, all are led to examine their own faithfulness to Christ's will for the Church and, wherever necessary, undertake with vigor the task of renewal and reform.

It is evident that the work of preparing and reconciling those individuals who wish for full Catholic communion is of its nature distinct from ecumenical action. But there is no opposition between the two, since both proceed from the wondrous providence of God (No. 4).

Primary Duty of Catholics

In ecumenical work, Catholics must assuredly be concerned for their separated brethren, praying for them, keeping them informed about the Church, making the first approaches toward them. But their primary duty is to make an honest and careful appraisal of whatever needs to be renewed and achieved in the Catholic household itself, in order that its life may bear witness more loyally and luminously to the teachings and ordinances which have been handed down from Christ through the Apostles.

Every Catholic must aim at Christian perfection (cf. Jas. 1:4; Rom. 12:1-2) and, each according to his station, play his part so that the Church may daily be more purified and renewed, against the day when Christ will present her to himself in all her glory, without spot or wrinkle (cf. Eph. 5:27).

Catholics must joyfully acknowledge and esteem the truly Christian endowments from our common heritage which are to be found among our separated brethren.

Nor should we forget that whatever is wrought by the grace of the Holy Spirit in the hearts of our separated brethren can contribute to our own edification. Whatever is truly Christian never conflicts with the genuine interests of the faith; indeed, it can always result in a more ample realization of the very mystery of Christ and the Church (No. 4).

Participation in Worship

Norms concerning participation by Catholics in the worship of other Christian Churches were sketched in this conciliar decree and elaborated in a number of other documents such as: the Decree on Eastern Catholic Churches, promulgated by the Second Vatican Council in 1964; Interim Guidelines for Prayer in Common, issued June 18, 1965, by the U.S. Bishops' Committee for Ecumenical and Interreligious Affairs; a Directory on Ecumenism, published in 1967, 1970 and 1993 by the Pontifical Council for Promoting Christian Unity; additional communications from the U.S. Bishops' Committee, and numerous sets of guidelines issued locally by and for dioceses throughout the U.S.

The norms encourage common prayer services for Christian unity and other intentions. Beyond that, they draw a distinction between separated churches of the Reformation tradition and of the Anglican Communion, and separated Eastern churches, in view of doctrine and practice the Catholic Church has in common with the separated Eastern churches concerning the apostolic succession of bishops, holy orders, liturgy and other credal matters.

Full participation by Catholics in official Protestant liturgies is prohibited, because it implies profession of the faith expressed in the liturgy. Intercommunion by Catholics at Protestant liturgies is prohibited. Under certain conditions, Protestants may be given Holy Communion in the Catholic Church (see Intercommunion). A Catholic may stand as a witness, but not as a sponsor, in baptism, and as a witness in the marriage of separated Christians. Similarly, a Protestant may stand as a witness, but not as a sponsor, in a Catholic baptism, and as a witness in the marriage of Catholics.

The principal norms regarding liturgical participations with separated Eastern Churches are included under Eastern Ecumenism.

DIRECTORY ON ECUMENISM

A *Directory for the Application of the Principles and Norms of Ecumenism* was approved by Pope John Paul II on Mar. 25, 1993, and published early in June. The Pontifical Council for Promoting Christian Unity said on release of the document that revision of Directories issued in 1967 and 1970 was necessary in view of subsequent developments. These included promulgation of the Code of Canon Law for the Latin Church in 1983 and of the Code of Canons of the Eastern Churches in 1990; publication of the *Catechism of the Catholic Church* in 1992; additional documents and the results of theological dialogues. In 1998, *The Ecumenical Dimension in the Formation of Pastoral Workers* was published by the Holy See to give practical and detailed guidance in the implementation of Chapter 3 of the *Directory*.

The following excerpts are from the text published in the June 16, 1993, English edition of *L'Osservatore Romano*.

Address and Purpose

"The Directory is addressed to the pastors of the Catholic Church, but it also concerns all the faithful, who are called to pray and work for the unity of Christians, under the direction of their bishops."

"At the same time, it is hoped that the Directory will also be useful to members of churches and ecclesial communities that are not in full communion with the Catholic Church."

"The new edition of the Directory is meant to be an instrument at the service of the whole Church, and especially of those who are directly engaged in ecumenical activity in the Catholic Church. The Directory intends to motivate, enlighten and guide this activity, and in some particular cases also to give binding directives in accordance with the proper competence of the Pontifical Council for Promoting Christian Unity."

Outline

Principles and norms of the document are covered in five chapters.

"I. The Search for Christian Unity. The ecumenical commitment of the Catholic Church based on the doctrinal principles of the Second Vatican Council.

"II. Organization in the Catholic Church at the Service of Christian Unity. Persons and structures involved in promoting ecumenism at all levels, and the norms that direct their activity.

"III. Ecumenical Formation in the Catholic Church. Categories of people to be formed, those responsible for formation; the aims and methods of formation; its doctrinal and practical aspects.

"IV. Communion in Life and Spiritual Activity among the Baptized. The communion that exists with other Christians on the basis of the sacramental bond of baptism, and the norms for sharing in prayer and other spiritual activities, including, in particular cases, sacramental sharing.

"V. Ecumenical Cooperation, Dialogue and Common Witness. Principles, different forms and norms for cooperation between Christians with a view to dialogue and common witness in the world."

ECUMENICAL AGENCIES

Pontifical Council

The top-level agency for Catholic ecumenical efforts is the Pontifical Council for Promoting Christian Unity (formerly the Secretariat for Promoting Christian Unity), which originated in 1960 as a preparatory commission for the Second Vatican Council. Its purposes are to provide guidance and, where necessary, coordination for ecumenical endeavor by Catholics, and to establish and maintain relations with representatives of other Christian Churches for ecumenical dialogue and action.

The council, under the direction of Cardinal Edward I. Cassidy (successor to Cardinal Johannes Willebrands), has established firm working relations with representative agencies of other churches and the World Council of Churches. It has joined in dialogue with Orthodox Churches, the Anglican Communion, the Lutheran World Federation, the World Alliance of Reformed Churches, the World Methodist Council and other religious bodies. In the past several years, staff members and representatives of the council have been involved in one way or another in nearly every significant ecumenical enterprise and meeting held throughout the world.

While the council and its counterparts in other churches have focused primary attention on theological and other related problems of Christian unity, they have also begun, and in increasing measure, to emphasize the responsibilities of the churches for greater unity of witness and effort in areas of humanitarian need.

Bishops' Committee

The U.S. Bishops' Committee for Ecumenical and Interreligious Affairs was established by the American hierarchy in 1964. Its purposes are to maintain relationships with other Christian churches and other religious communities at the national level, to advise and assist dioceses in developing and applying ecumenical policies, and to maintain liaison with corresponding Vatican offices — the Councils for Christian Unity and for Interreligious Dialogue.

This standing committee of the National Conference of Catholic Bishops is chaired by Archbishop Alexander J. Brunett of Seattle. Operationally, the committee is assisted by a secretariat with the Rev. John F. Hotchkin, director; Dr. Eugene J. Fisher, executive secretary for Catholic-Jewish Relations; Dr.

John Borelli, Jr., executive secretary for Interreligious Relations, the Rev. Ronald Roberson, C.S.P., and Brother Jeffrey Gros, F.S.C., associate directors.

The committee co-sponsors several national consultations with other churches and confessional families. These bring together Catholic representatives and their counterparts from the Episcopal Church, the Lutheran Church, the Polish National Catholic Church, the United Methodist Church, the Orthodox Churches, the Oriental Orthodox Churches, the Alliance of Reformed Churches (North American area), the Interfaith Witness Department of the Home Mission Board of the Southern Baptist Convention. (See Ecumenical Dialogues.)

The committee relates with the National Council of Churches of Christ, through membership in the Faith and Order Commission and through observer relationship with the Commission on Regional and Local Ecumenism, and has sponsored a joint study committee investigating the possibility of Roman Catholic membership in that body.

Advisory and other services are provided by the committee to ecumenical commissions and agencies in dioceses throughout the country.

Through its Section for Catholic-Jewish Relations, the committee is in contact with several national Jewish agencies and bodies. Issues of mutual interest and shared concern are reviewed for the purpose of furthering deeper understanding between the Catholic and Jewish communities.

Through its Section for Interreligious Relations, the committee promotes activity in wider areas of dialogue with other religions, notably, with Muslims, Buddhists and Hindus.

Offices of the committee are located at 3211 Fourth St. N.E., Washington, D.C. 20017.

World Council of Churches

The World Council of Churches is a fellowship of churches which acknowledge "Jesus Christ as Lord and Savior." It is a permanent organization providing constituent members — 330 churches with some 450 million communicants in 100 countries — with opportunities for meeting, consultation and cooperative action with respect to doctrine, worship, practice, social mission, evangelism and missionary work, and other matters of mutual concern.

The WCC was formally established Aug. 23, 1948, in Amsterdam with ratification of a constitution by 147 communions. This action merged two previously existing movements — Life and Work (social mission), Faith and Order (doctrine) — which had initiated practical steps toward founding a fellowship of Christian churches at meetings held in Oxford, Edinburgh and Utrecht in 1937 and 1938. A third movement for cooperative missionary work, which originated about 1910 and, remotely, led to formation of the WCC, was incorporated into the council in 1971 under the title of the International Missionary Council.

Additional general assemblies of the council have been held since the charter meeting of 1948: in Evanston, Ill. (1954), New Delhi, India (1961), Uppsala, Sweden (1968), Nairobi, Kenya (1975), Vancouver, British Columbia, Canada (1983) and Canberra, Australia (1991). The 1998 general assembly was held in Harare, Zimbabwe, with the regular Catholic delegation in attendance, led by Bishop Mario Conti from St. Andrew's, Scotland.

The council continues the work of the International Missionary Council, the Commission on Faith and Order, and the Commission on Church and Society. The work of the council is carried out through four program units: unity and renewal; mission, education and witness; justice, peace and creation; sharing and service.

Liaison between the council and the Vatican has been maintained since 1966 through a joint working group. Roman Catholic membership in the WCC is a question officially on the agenda of this body. The Joint Commission on Society, Development and Peace (SODEPAX) was an agency of the council and the Pontifical Commission for Justice and Peace from 1968 to Dec. 31, 1980, after which another working group was formed. Roman Catholics serve individually as full members of the Commission on Faith and Order and in various capacities on other program committees of the council.

WCC headquarters are located in Geneva, Switzerland. The United States Conference for the World Council of Churches at 475 Riverside Drive, Room 915, New York, N.Y. 10115, provides liaison between the U.S. churches and Geneva, a communications office for secular and church media relations, and a publications office. The WCC also maintains fraternal relations with regional, national and local councils of churches throughout the world.

The Rev. Konrad Raiser, a Lutheran from Germany, was elected general secretary, Aug. 24, 1992.

National Council of Churches

The National Council of the Churches of Christ in the U.S.A., the largest ecumenical body in the United States, is an organization of 34 Protestant, Orthodox and Anglican communions, with an aggregate membership of about 52 million.

The NCC, established by the churches in 1950, was structured through the merger of 12 separate cooperative agencies. Presently, the NCC carries on work in behalf of member churches in overseas ministries, Christian education, domestic social action, communications, disaster relief, refugee assistance, rehabilitation and development, biblical translation, international affairs, theological dialogue, interfaith activities, worship and evangelism, and other areas.

Policies of the NCC are determined by a general board of approximately 270 members appointed by the constituent churches. The board meets once a year.

NCC presidents: Bishop Craig B. Anderson (1998-99), Rev. Andrew Young (2000-2002). General secretary: The Rev. Joan Brown Campbell.

NCC headquarters are located at 475 Riverside Drive, New York, N.Y. 10115.

Consultation on Church Union

(Courtesy of Rev. David W.A. Taylor, General Secretary.)

The Consultation on Church Union, officially begun in 1962, is a venture of American churches seeking a united church "truly catholic, truly evangelical, and truly reformed." The churches engaged in this process, representing 25 million Christians, are the African Methodist Episcopal Church, the African Methodist Episcopal Zion Church, the Christian

Church (Disciples of Christ), the Christian Methodist Episcopal Church, the Episcopal Church, the Presbyterian Church (U.S.A); the United Church of Christ, the United Methodist Church and the International Council of Community Churches.

At a plenary assembly of COCU in December, 1988, a plan of church unity was unanimously approved for submission to member churches for their action. The plan is contained in a 102-page document entitled "Churches in Covenant Communion: The Church of Christ Uniting." It proposes the formation of a covenant communion of the churches which, while remaining institutionally autonomous, would embrace together eight elements of ecclesial communion: claiming unity in faith, commitment to seek unity with wholeness, mutual recognition of members in one baptism, mutual recognition of each other as churches, mutual recognition and reconciliation of ordained ministries, celebrating the Eucharist together, engaging together in Christ's mission, and the formation together of covenanting councils at each level (national, regional, and local). At its January 1999 plenary in St. Louis, the churches proposed a 2002 decision to come into full communion as the *Churches Uniting in Christ*.

Vivian U. Robinson, Ph.D., a lay member of the Christian Methodist Episcopal Church, was elected president in 1988. The Rev. Lewis Lancanster is interim general secretary. Offices are located at 258 Wall St., Princeton. N.J. 08540.

Graymoor Institute

The Graymoor Ecumenical and Interreligious Institute is a forum where issues that confront the Christian Churches are addressed, the spiritual dimensions of ecumenism are fostered, and information, documentation and developments within the ecumenical movement are published through *Ecumenical Trends*, a monthly journal. Director: The Rev. Elias D. Mallon, S.A. Address: 475 Riverside Dr., Rm. 1960, New York, N.Y. 10115-1999.

INTERNATIONAL BILATERAL COMMISSIONS

Anglican-Roman Catholic International Commission, sponsored by the Pontifical Council for Promoting Christian Unity and the Lambeth Conference, from 1970 to 1981; succeeded by a **Second Anglican-Roman Catholic International Commission**, called into being by the Common Declaration of Pope John Paul and the Archbishop of Canterbury in 1982.

The International Theological Colloquium between Baptists and Catholics, established in 1984 by the Pontifical Council for Promoting Christian Unity and the Commission for Faith and Interchurch Cooperation of the Baptist World Alliance.

The Disciples of Christ-Roman Catholic Dialogue, organized by the Council of Christian Unity of the Christian Church (Disciples of Christ) and the U.S. Bishops' Committee for Ecumenical and Interreligious Affairs, along with participation by the Disciples' Ecumenical Consultative Council and the Unity Council; since 1977.

The Evangelical-Roman Catholic Dialogue on Mission, organized by Evangelicals and the Pontifical Council for Promoting Christian Unity; from 1977.

The Lutheran-Roman Catholic Commission on Unity, established by the Pontifical Council for Promoting Christian Unity and the Lutheran World Federation; from 1967.

The International Catholic-Orthodox Theological Commission, established by the Holy See and 14 autocephalous Orthodox Churches, began its work at a first session held at Patmos/Rhodes in 1980. Subsequent sessions have been held at Munich (1982), Crete (1984), Bari (1987), Valamo (1988) and Freising (1990).

Pentecostal-Roman Catholic Conversations, since 1966.

The Reformed-Roman Catholic Conversations, inaugurated in 1970 by the Pontifical Council for Promoting Christian Unity and the World Alliance of Reformed Churches.

The International Joint Commission between the Catholic Church and the Coptic Orthodox Church, since 1974. Established officially in the Common Declaration signed by Pope Paul VI and Coptic Pope Shenouda III in Rome in 1973.

The Joint International Commission between the Roman Catholic Church and the Malankara Orthodox Syrian Church, since 1989.

The Joint Commission between the Catholic Church and the Malankara Jacobite Syrian Orthodox Church, since 1990.

The Assyrian Church of the East-Roman Catholic Dialogue, officially established in the Common Declaration signed by Pope John Paul II and Mar Dinkha IV in November 1994. Has been meeting annually since 1995.

U.S. ECUMENICAL DIALOGUES

Representatives of the Bishops' Committee for Ecumenical and Interreligious Affairs, National Conference of Catholic Bishops, have met in dialogue with representatives of other churches since the 1960s, for discussion of a wide variety of subjects related to the quest for unity among Christians. Following is a list of dialogue groups and the years in which dialogue began.

Anglican-Roman Catholic Consultation, 1965; Eastern Orthodox Consultation (Theologians), 1965; Eastern Orthodox and Roman Catholic Bishops, Joint Committee, 1981; Lutheran Consultation, 1965; Oriental Orthodox Consultation (with Armenian, Coptic, Ethiopian, Indian Malabar and Syrian Orthodox Churches), 1978; Polish National-Catholic Consultation, 1984; Presbyterian/Reformed Consultation, 1965; Southern Baptist Conversations, 1969; United Methodist Consultation, 1966; Faith and Order National Council of Churches.

ECUMENICAL REPORTS

(Source: Rev. John F. Hotchkin, Secretariat of the Bishops' Committee for Ecumenical and Interreligious Affairs, National Conference of Catholic Bishops.)

Common Declarations of Popes, Other Prelates

The following ecumenical statements, issued by several popes and prelates of other Christian churches, carry the authority given them by their signators.

Paul VI and Orthodox Ecumenical Patriarch Athenagoras I, First Common Declaration, Dec. 7, 1965: They hoped the differences between the churches would be overcome with the help of the Holy Spirit, and that their "full communion of faith, brotherly concord and sacramental life" would be restored.

Paul VI and Anglican Archbishop Michael Ramsey of Canterbury, Mar. 24, 1966: They stated their intention "to inaugurate between the Roman Catholic Church and the Anglican Communion a serious dialogue which, founded on the Gospels and on the ancient common traditions, may lead to that unity in truth for which Christ prayed."

Paul VI and Patriarch Athenagoras I, Second Common Declaration, Oct. 27, 1967: They wished "to emphasize their conviction that the restoration of full communion (between the churches) is to be found within the framework of the renewal of the Church and of Christians in fidelity to the traditions of the Fathers and to the inspirations of the Holy Spirit who remains always with the Church."

Paul VI and Vasken I, Orthodox Catholicos-Patriarch of All Armenians, May 12, 1970: They called for closer collaboration "in all domains of Christian life. . . . This collaboration must be based on the mutual recognition of the common Christian faith and the sacramental life, on the mutual respect of persons and their churches."

Paul VI and Mar Ignatius Jacob III, Syrian Orthodox Patriarch of Antioch, Oct. 27, 1971: They declared themselves to be "in agreement that there is no difference in the faith they profess concerning the mystery of the Word of God made flesh and become really man, even if over the centuries difficulties have arisen out of the different theological expressions by which this faith was expressed."

Paul VI and Shenouda III, Coptic Orthodox Pope of Alexandria, May 10, 1973: Their common declaration recalls the common elements of the Catholic and Coptic Orthodox faith in the Trinity, the divinity and humanity of Christ, the seven sacraments, the Virgin Mary, the Church founded upon the Apostles, and the Second Coming of Christ. It recognizes that the two churches "are not able to give more perfect witness to this new life in Christ because of existing divisions which have behind them centuries of difficult history" dating back to the year 451 A.D. In spite of these difficulties, they expressed "determination and confidence in the Lord to achieve the fullness and perfection of that unity which is his gift."

Paul VI and Anglican Archbishop Donald Coggan of Canterbury, Apr. 29, 1977: They stated many points on which Anglicans and Roman Catholics hold the faith in common and called for greater cooperation between Anglicans and Roman Catholics.

John Paul II and Orthodox Ecumenical Patriarch Dimitrios I, First Common Declaration, Nov. 30, 1979: "Purification of the collective memory of our churches is an important fruit of the dialogue of charity and an indispensable condition of future progress." They announced the establishment of the Catholic-Orthodox Theological Commission.

John Paul II and Anglican Archbishop Robert Runcie of Canterbury, May 29, 1982: They agreed to establish a new Anglican-Roman Catholic commission with the task of continuing work already begun toward the eventual resolution of doctrinal differences.

John Paul II and Ignatius Zakka I, Syrian Orthodox Patriarch of Antioch, June 23, 1984: They recalled and solemnly reaffirmed the common profession of faith made by their predecessors, Paul VI and Mar Ignatius Jacob III, in 1971. They said: "The confusions and the schisms that occurred between the churches, they realize today, in no way affect or touch the substance of their faith, since these arose only because of differences in terminology and culture, and in the various formulae adopted by different theological schools to express the same matter. Accordingly, we find today no real basis for the sad divisions which arose between us concerning the doctrine of the Incarnation." On the pastoral level, they declared: "It is not rare for our faithful to find access to a priest of their own church materially or morally impossible. Anxious to meet their needs and with their spiritual benefit in mind, we authorize them in such cases to ask for the sacraments of penance, Eucharist and anointing of the sick from lawful priests of either of our two sister churches, when they need them."

John Paul II and Orthodox Ecumenical Patriarch Dimitrios I, Second Common Declaration, Dec. 7, 1987: Dialogue conducted since 1979 indicated that the churches can already profess together as common faith about the mystery of the Church and the connection between faith and the sacraments. They also stated that, "when unity of faith is assured, a certain diversity of expressions does not create obstacles to unity, but enriches the life of the Church and the understanding, always imperfect, of the revealed mystery."

John Paul II and Anglican Archbishop Robert Runcie of Canterbury, Oct. 2, 1989: They said: "We solemnly re-commit ourselves and those we represent to the restoration of visible unity and full ecclesial communion in the confidence that to seek anything less would be to betray our Lord's intention for the unity of his people."

John Paul II and His Holiness Mar Dinkha IV, Catholicos-Patriarch of the Assyrian Church of the East, Nov. 11, 1994: They acknowledged that, despite past differences, both churches profess the same faith in the real union of divine and human natures in the divine Person of Christ.

Pope John Paul II with Ecumenical Orthodox Patriarch Bartholomew I, June 29, 1995: (See under Common Declaration in Eastern Ecumenism.)

Pope John Paul II with Anglican Archbishop George Carey, Common Ecumenical Declaration, Dec. 5, 1996: The pontiff and archbishop praised the work of the Anglican-Roman Catholic International Commission and stated that "In many parts of the world Anglicans and Catholics attempt to witness together in the face of growing secularism, religious apathy and moral confusion."

Pope John Paul II with Karekin I, Catholicos of All Armenians, Dec. 13, 1996. (See under Common Declaration in Eastern Ecumenism.)

Pope John Paul II with Aram I, Armenian

Catholicos of Cilicia, Jan. 25, 1997: The common declaration declared that "the two spiritual leaders stress the vital importance of sincere dialogue.... The Catholic Church and the Catholicate of Cilicia also have an immense field of constructive cooperation before them."

ECUMENICAL STATEMENTS

The ecumenical statements listed below, and others like them, reflect the views of participants in the dialogues which produced them. They have not been formally accepted by the respective churches as formulations of doctrine or points of departure for practical changes in discipline. (For other titles, see U.S. Ecumenical Dialogues, Ecumenical Reports.)

• The "Windsor Statement" on Eucharistic doctrine, published Dec. 31, 1971, by the Anglican-Roman Catholic International Commission of theologians. (For text, see pages 132-33 of the 1973 *Catholic Almanac*.)

• The "Canterbury Statement" on ministry and ordination, published Dec. 13, 1973, by the same commission. (For excerpts, see pages 127-30 of the 1975 *Catholic Almanac*.)

• "Papal Primacy/Converging Viewpoints," published Mar. 4, 1974, by the dialogue group sanctioned by the U.S.A. National Convention of the World Lutheran Federation and the U.S. Bishops' Committee for Ecumenical and Interreligious Affairs. (For excerpts, see pages 130-31 of the 1975 *Catholic Almanac*.)

• An "Agreed Statement on the Purpose of the Church," published Oct. 31, 1975, by the Anglican-Roman Catholic Consultation in the U.S.

• "Christian Unity and Women's Ordination," published Nov. 7, 1975, by the same consultation, in which it was said that the ordination of women (approved in principle by the Anglican Communion but not by the Catholic Church) would "introduce a new element" in dialogue but would not mean the end of consultation nor the abandonment of its declared goal of full communion and organic unity.

• "Holiness and Spirituality of the Ordained Ministry," issued early in 1976 by theologians of the Catholic Church and the United Methodist Church; the first statement resulting from dialogue begun in 1966.

• "Mixed Marriages," published in the spring of 1976 by the Anglican-Roman Catholic Consultation in the U.S.

• "Bishops and Presbyters," published in July, 1976, by the Orthodox-Roman Catholic Consultation in the U.S. on the following points of common understanding: (1) Ordination in apostolic succession is required for pastoral office in the Church. (2) Presiding at the Eucharistic Celebration is a task belonging to those ordained to pastoral service. (3) The offices of bishop and presbyter are different realizations of the sacrament of order. (4) Those ordained are claimed permanently for the service of the Church.

• "The Principle of Economy," published by the body named above at the same time, concerning God's plan and activities in human history for salvation.

• "Venice Statement" on authority in the Church, published Jan. 20, 1977, by the Anglican-Roman Catholic International Commission of theologians.

• "Response to the Venice Statement," issued Jan. 4, 1978, by the Anglican-Roman Catholic

Consultation in the U.S.A., citing additional questions.

• "An Ecumenical Approach to Marriage," published in January, 1978, by representatives of the Catholic Church, the Lutheran World Federation and the World Alliance of Reformed Churches.

• "Teaching Authority and Infallibility in the Church," released in October, 1978, by the Catholic-Lutheran dialogue group in the U.S.

• "The Eucharist," reported early in 1979, in which the Roman Catholic-Lutheran Commission indicated developing convergence of views.

• "The Holy Spirit," issued Feb. 12, 1979, by the International Catholic-Methodist Commission.

• A statement on "Ministry in the Church," published in March, 1981, by the International Roman Catholic-Lutheran Joint Commission, regarding possible mutual recognition of ministries.

• The Final Report of the Anglican-Roman Catholic International Commission, 1982, on the results of 12 years of dialogue.

• "The Mystery of the Church and of the Eucharist in the Light of the Mystery of the Holy Trinity," issued by the Mixed International Commission for Theological Dialogue between the Catholic Church and the Orthodox Church at Munich, Germany, in July 1982.

• The Final Report of the Anglican-Roman Catholic International Commission, 1982, on the results of 12 years of dialogue.

• "Justification by Faith," issued Sept. 30, 1983, by the U.S. Lutheran-Roman Catholic dialogue group, claiming a "fundamental consensus on the Gospel."

• "Images of God: Reflections on Christian Anthropology," released Dec. 22, 1983, by the Anglican-Roman Catholic Dialogue in the United States.

• "The Journeying Together in Christ — The Report of the Polish National Catholic-Roman Catholic Dialogue (1984-89)."

• "Salvation and the Church," issued Jan. 22, 1987, by the Second Anglican-Roman Catholic International Commission.

• "Faith, Sacraments and the Unity of the Church," issued by the Mixed International Commission for Theological Dialogue between the Catholic Church and the Orthodox Churches in June, 1987.

• "The Sacrament of Order in the Sacramental Structure of the Church, with Particular Reference to the Importance of Apostolic Succession for the Sanctification and Unity of the People of God," issued by the Mixed International Commission for Theological Dialogue between the Catholic Church and the Orthodox Church in Valamo, Finland, in 1988.

• "The Presence of Christ in Church and World" and "Toward a Common Understanding of the Church" (developed between 1984 and 1990), by the Reformed-Roman Catholic Conversations, under the auspices of the Pontifical Council for Promoting

Christian Unity and the World Alliance of Reformed Churches.

• "Uniatism, Method of Union of the Past, and the Present Search for Full Communion," issued by the Mixed International Commission for Theological Dialogue between the Catholic Church and the Orthodox Church at Balamand, Lebanon, in 1993.

• "Common Response to the Aleppo Statement on the Date of Easter/Pacha," issued by the North American Orthodox-Catholic Theological Consultation in Washington, D.C., Oct. 31, 1998.

• "Baptism and 'Sacramental Economy'," issued by the North American Orthodox-Catholic Theological Consultation at Crestwood, New York, in June 1999.

• "Guidelines Concerning the Pastoral Care of Oriental Orthodox Students in Catholic Schools," issued by the Oriental Orthodox-Roman Catholic Theological Consultation in the United States at New Rochelle, New York, in June 1999.

• "Joint Declaration of the Catholic Church and the Lutheran World Federation on the Doctrine of Justification," issued July 8, 1999 by the International Roman Catholic-Lutheran Joint Commission.

(See Special Report on Justification.)

ANGLICAN-ROMAN CATHOLIC FINAL REPORT

The Anglican-Roman Catholic International Commission issued a Final Report in 1982 on 12 years of dialogue on major issues of concern, especially the Eucharist and ordained ministry.

In 1988 the Lambeth Conference called parts of the report on these two subjects "consonant in substance with the faith of Anglicans." In 1991 the Congregation for the Doctrine of the Faith and the Pontifical Council for Promoting Christian Unity called the Report a significant milestone not only in relations between the Catholic Church and the Anglican Communion but in the ecumenical movement as a whole. They said, however, that it was not yet possible to state that substantial agreement had been reached on all the questions studied by the commission, and that important differences still remained with respect to essential matters of Catholic doctrine regarding the Eucharist, ordination and other subjects. Clarifications were requested.

The Anglican-Roman Catholic Commission II responded in 1994, saying that its members were in agreement regarding:

• the substantial and sacramental presence of Christ in the Eucharist;

• the propitiatory nature of the Eucharistic Sacrifice, which can also be applied to the deceased;

• institution of the sacrament of order from Christ;

• the character of priestly ordination, implying configuration to the priesthood of Christ.

In 1994 Cardinal Edward I. Cassidy, president of the Pontifical Council for Interreligious Dialogue addressed a letter to the Catholic and Anglican co-chairmen of the commission, responding to the clarifications, stating that "no further work" seems to be necessary at this time on Eucharist and ministry. Questions still remained to be answered about a number of subjects, including the authority in the Church, ordination of women, infallibility and Marian doctrine. (See Special Reports.)

SEPARATED EASTERN CHURCHES

THE ORTHODOX CHURCH

This is a group of Eastern churches of the Byzantine tradition that were in full communion with Rome during the first millennium, and which all recognize the Patriarch of Constantinople as the first Orthodox bishop. In spite of the division between Catholics and Orthodox, often symbolized by the mutual excommunications of 1054, the Catholic Church considers itself to be in almost full communion with the Orthodox Churches. According to Vatican II, they "are still joined to us in closest intimacy" in various ways, especially in the priesthood and Eucharist. The Orthodox Churches recognize the first seven ecumenical councils as normative for their faith, along with the Scriptures and other local councils that took place in later centuries.

The Orthodox Churches are organized in approximately 15 autocephalous (independent) churches that correspond in most cases to nations or ethnic groups. The Ecumenical Patriarch of Constantinople (modern Istanbul) has a primacy of honor among the patriarchs, but his actual jurisdiction is limited to his own patriarchate. As the spiritual head of worldwide Orthodoxy, he serves as a point of unity, and has the right to call Pan-Orthodox assemblies.

Top-level relations between the Churches have improved in recent years through the efforts of Ecumenical Patriarch Athenagoras I, John XXIII, Paul VI and Patriarch Dimitrios I. Pope Paul met with Athenagoras three times before the latter's death in 1972. The most significant action of both spiritual leaders was their mutual nullification of excommunications imposed by the two Churches on each other in 1054. Development of better relations with the Orthodox has been a priority of John Paul II since the beginning of his pontificate. Both he and Orthodox Ecumenical Patriarch Bartholomew have made known their commitment to better relations, despite contentions between Eastern Catholic and Orthodox Churches over charges of proselytism and rival property claims in places liberated from anti-religious communist control in the recent past.

The largest Orthodox body in the United States is the Greek Orthodox Archdiocese of America consisting of nine dioceses; it has an estimated membership of 1.9 million. The second largest is the Orthodox Church in America, with more than one million members; it was given autocephalous status by the Patriarchate of Moscow May 18, 1970, without the consent of the Patriarchate of Constantinople. An additional 650,000 or more Orthodox belong to smaller national and language jurisdictions. Heads of orthodox jurisdictions in this hemisphere hold membership in the Standing Conference of Canonical Orthodox Bishops in the Americas.

JURISDICTIONS

The Autocephalous Orthodox Churches

Patriarchate of Constantinople (Ecumenical Patriarchate), with jurisdiction in Turkey, Crete, the Dodecanese, and Greeks in the rest of the world outside Greece and Africa. Autonomous churches linked to the Ecumenical Patriarchate exist in Finland and Estonia. Several other jurisdictions of various ethnicities in the diaspora are also directly under the Patriarchate.

Patriarchate of Alexandria, with jurisdiction in Egypt and the rest of Africa; it includes a native African Orthodox Church in Kenya and Uganda.

Patriarchate of Antioch, with jurisdiction in Syria, Lebanon, Iraq, Australia, the Americas.

Patriarchate of Jerusalem, with jurisdiction in Israel and Jordan. The autonomous church of Mount Sinai is linked to the Jerusalem Patriarchate.

Russian Orthodox Church, the Patriarchate of Moscow with jurisdiction over most of the former Soviet Union. Autonomous churches in Japan and China are linked to the Moscow Patriarchate.

The Serbian Orthodox Church, a patriarchate with jurisdiction in Yugoslavia, Western Europe, North America and Australia.

The Romanian Orthodox Church, a patriarchate with jurisdiction in Romania, Western Europe and North America.

The Bulgarian Orthodox Church, a patriarchate with jurisdiction in Bulgaria, Western Europe and North America.

The Georgian Orthodox Church, a patriarchate with jurisdiction in the republic of Georgia.

The Orthodox Church of Cyprus, an archbishopric with jurisdiction in Cyprus.

The Orthodox Church of Greece, an archbishopric with jurisdiction in Greece.

The Orthodox Church of Poland, a metropolitanate with jurisdiction in Poland.

The Orthodox Church of Albania, an archbishopric with jurisdiction in Albania.

The Orthodox Church in the Czech and Slovak Republics, a metropolitanate with jurisdiction in the Czech and Slovak Republics. Its autocephalous status was granted by Moscow in 1951; Constantinople recognizes it only as an autonomous church.

The Orthodox Church in America, a metropolitanate with jurisdiction in North America and a few parishes in Latin America and Australia. Its autocephalous status was granted by Moscow in 1970; Constantinople and most other Orthodox churches have not recognized this.

Population

The Division of Archives and Statistics of the Eastern Orthodox World Foundation reported a 1970 estimate of more than 200 million Orthodox Church members throughout the world. A contemporary estimate put the number close to 220 million. Many Orthodox today claim a total membership of about 300 million.

Conference of Orthodox Bishops

The Standing Conference of Canonical Orthodox Bishops in the Americas was established in 1960 to achieve cooperation among the various Orthodox jurisdictions in the Americas. Office: 8-10 East 79th St., New York, N.Y. 10021.

Member churches are the: Albanian Orthodox Diocese of America (Ecumenical Patriarchate), American Carpatho-Russian Orthodox Greek Catholic Diocese in the U.S.A. (Ecumenical Patriarchate), Antiochian Orthodox Christian Archdiocese of North America, Bulgarian Eastern Orthodox Church, Greek Orthodox Archdiocese of America (Ecumenical Patriarchate), Orthodox Church in America, Romanian Orthodox Archdiocese in America and Canada, Serbian Orthodox Church in the United States and Canada, Ukrainian Orthodox Church in the United States (Ecumenical Patriarchate), Ukrainian Orthodox Church of Canada (Ecumenical Patriarchate).

ANCIENT CHURCHES OF THE EAST

The Ancient Eastern Churches, which are distinct from the Orthodox Churches, were the subject of an article by Gerard Daucourt published in the Feb. 16, 1987, English edition of *L'Osservatore Romano*. Following is an adaptation:

By Ancient Eastern Churches one means: the Assyrian Church of the East (formerly called Nestorian), the Armenian Apostolic Church, the Coptic Orthodox Church, the Ethiopian Orthodox Church, the Syrian Orthodox Church (sometimes called Jacobite) and the Malankara Orthodox Syrian Church of India.

After the Council of Ephesus (431), the Assyrian Church of the East did not maintain communion with the rest of the Christian world. For reasons as much and perhaps more political than doctrinal, it did not accept the Council's teaching (that Mary is the Mother of God, in opposition to the opinion of Nestorius; see Nestorianism. For this reason, the Assyrian Church of the East came to be called Nestorian.) It is well known that in the 16th century a great segment of the faithful of this Church entered into communion with the See of Rome and constitutes today, among the Eastern Catholic Churches, the Chaldean Patriarchate. The Patriarch of the Assyrian Church of the East, His Holiness Mar Dinkha IV, in the course of his visit to the Holy Father and to the Church of Rome of 7 to 9 November, 1984, requested that people stop using the term "Nestorian" to designate his Church and expressed the desire that a declaration made jointly by the Pope of Rome and himself may one day serve to express the common faith of the two Churches in Jesus Christ, Son of God incarnate, born of the Virgin Mary. The labors of Catholic historians and theologians have, moreover, already contributed to showing that such a declaration would be possible.

The other Ancient Churches of the East (today known as the Oriental Orthodox Churches) for a long time have been designated by the term "Monophysite Churches" (see Monophysitism). It is regrettable to find this name still employed sometimes in certain publications, since already in 1951, in the encyclical *Sempiternus Rex*, on the occasion of the 15th centenary of the Council of Chalcedon, Pius XII declared with regard to the Christians of these Churches: "They depart from the right way only in terminology, when they expound the doctrine of the Incarnation of the Lord. This may be deduced from their liturgical and theological books."

In this same encyclical, Pius XII expressed the view that the separation at the doctrinal level came about "above all, through a certain ambiguity of terminology that occurred at the beginning." Since then, two important declarations have been arrived at in line with the ecumenical stance taken by the Church at the Second Vatican Council and the labors of the theologians (particularly in the framework of the Foundation "Pro Oriente" of Vienna). One was signed by Pope Paul VI and Coptic Patriarch Shenouda III on 10 May, 1973, and the other by Pope John Paul II and the Syrian Patriarch Ignatius Zakka II was, on 23 June, 1984. In both of these texts, the hierarchies of the respective

Churches confess one and the same faith in the mystery of the Word Incarnate. After such declarations, it is no longer possible to speak in general terms of the "Monophysite" Churches. The Armenian Apostolic Church has communicants in the former Soviet Union, the Middle and Far East, the Americas. The Coptic Orthodox Church is centered in Egypt and has a growing diaspora overseas. The Syrian Orthodox Church has communicants in the Middle East, the Americas, and India. Members of the Assyrian Church of the East are scattered throughout the world, and the Patriarch now resides near Chicago, Illinois.

It is estimated that there are approximately 10 million or more members of these other Eastern Churches throughout the world. For various reasons, a more accurate determination is not possible.

EASTERN ECUMENISM

The Second Vatican Council, in *Orientalium Ecclesiarum*, the Decree on Eastern Catholic Churches, pointed out the special role they have to play "in promoting the unity of all Christians." The document also stated in part as follows.

The Eastern Churches in communion with the Apostolic See of Rome have a special role to play in promoting the unity of all Christians, particularly Easterners, according to the principles of this sacred Synod's Decree on Ecumenism first of all by prayer, then by the example of their lives, by religious fidelity to ancient Eastern traditions, by greater mutual knowledge, by collaboration, and by a brotherly regard for objects and attitudes (No. 24).

If any separated Eastern Christian should, under the guidance of grace of the Holy Spirit, join himself to Catholic unity, no more should be required of him than what a simple profession of the Catholic faith demands. A valid priesthood is preserved among Eastern clerics. Hence, upon joining themselves to the unity of the Catholic Church, Eastern clerics are permitted to exercise the orders they possess, in accordance with the regulations established by the competent authority (No. 25).

Divine Law forbids any common worship (*communicatio in sacris*) which would damage the unity of the Church, or involve formal acceptance of falsehood or the danger of deviation in the faith, of scandal, or of indifferentism. At the same time, pastoral experience clearly shows that with respect to our Eastern brethren there should and can be taken into consideration various circumstances affecting individuals, wherein the unity of the Church is not jeopardized nor are intolerable risks involved, but in which salvation itself and the spiritual profit of souls are urgently at issue.

Hence, in view of special circumstances of time, place, and personage, the Catholic Church has often

adopted and now adopts a milder policy, offering to all the means of salvation and an example of charity among Christians through participation in the sacraments and in other sacred functions and objects. With these considerations in mind, and "lest because of the harshness of our judgment we prove an obstacle to those seeking salvation," and in order to promote closer union with the Eastern Churches separated from us, this sacred Synod lays down the following policy:

In view of the principles recalled above, Eastern Christians who are separated in good faith from the Catholic Church, if they ask of their own accord and have the right dispositions, may be granted the sacraments of penance, the Eucharist, and the anointing of the sick. Furthermore, Catholics may ask for these same sacraments from those non-Catholic ministers whose Churches possess valid sacraments, as often as necessity or a genuine spiritual benefit recommends such a course of action, and when access to a Catholic priest is physically or morally impossible (Nos. 26, 27).

Again, in view of these very same principles, Catholics may for a just cause join with their separated Eastern brethren in sacred functions, things, and places (No. 28). Bishops decide when and if to follow this lenient policy.

RECENT DOCUMENTS

Three recent documents of importance with respect to relations between Catholic and separated Eastern Churches are the apostolic letter, *Orientale Lumen*, issued May 5, 1995; the encyclical letter, *Ut Unum Sint*, issued May 30, 1995; and the Christological Declaration signed Nov. 11, 1994, by Pope John Paul and His Holiness Mar Dinkha IV, Catholicos-Patriarch of the Assyrian Church of the East. The text of the Christological Document follows.

CHRISTOLOGICAL DECLARATION

Following is the text of the "Common Christological Declaration" between the Catholic Church and the Assyrian Church of the East, signed Nov. 11, 1994, by Pope John Paul II and His Holiness Mar Dinkha

IV, Catholicos-Patriarch of the Assyrian Church of the East. The declaration acknowledges that, despite past differences, both churches profess the same faith in the real union of divine and human natures in the divine Person of Christ. Backgrounding the declaration was the Assyrian Church's adherence to the teaching of Nestorius who, in the fifth century, denied the real unity of divine and human natures in the single divine Person of Christ.

The text was published in the Nov. 16, 1994, English edition of *L'Osservatore Romano*:

As heirs and guardians of the faith received from the Apostles as formulated by our common Fathers in the Nicene Creed, we confess one Lord Jesus Christ, the only Son of God, begotten of the Father from all eternity who, in the fullness of time, came down from heaven and became man for our salvation. The Word of God, second Person of the Holy Trinity, became incarnate by the power of the Holy Spirit in assuming from the Virgin Mary a body animated by a rational soul, with which he was indissolubly united from the moment of conception.

Unity of Two Natures in One Person

Therefore our Lord Jesus Christ is true God and true man, perfect in his divinity and perfect in his humanity, consubstantial with the Father and consubstantial with us in all things but sin. His divinity and his humanity are united in one person, without confusion or change, without division or separation. In him has been preserved the difference of the natures of divinity and humanity, with all their properties, faculties and operations. But far from constituting "one and another," the dignity and humanity are united in the person of the same and unique Son of God and Lord Jesus Christ, who is the object of a single adoration. Christ therefore is not an "ordinary man" whom God adopted in order to reside in him and inspire him, as in the righteous ones and the prophets. But the same God the Word, begotten of his Father before all worlds without beginning according to his divinity, was born of a mother without a father in the last times according to his humanity. The humanity to which the Blessed Virgin Mary gave birth always was that of the Son of God himself. That is the reason the Assyrian Church of the East is praying the Virgin Mary as "the Mother of Christ our God and Savior." In the light of this same faith the Catholic tradition addresses the Virgin Mary as "the Mother of God" and also as "the Mother of Christ." We both recognize the legitimacy and rightness of these expressions of the same faith and we both respect the preference of each Church in her liturgical life and piety.

Confession of the Same Faith

This is the unique faith that we profess in the mystery of Christ. The controversies of the past led to anathemas, bearing on persons and on formulas. The Lord's Spirit permits us to understand better today that the divisions brought about in this way were due in large part to misunderstandings. Whatever our Christological divergences have been, we experience ourselves united today in the confession of the same faith in the Son of God who became man so that we might become children of God by his grace. We wish from now on to witness together to this faith in the One who is the Way, the Truth and the Life, proclaiming it in appropriate ways to our contemporaries, so that the world may believe in the Gospel of salvation. The mystery of the Incarnation which we profess in common is not an abstract and isolated truth. It refers to the Son of God sent to save us. The economy

of salvation, which has its origin in the mystery of communion of the Holy Trinity — Father, Son and Holy Spirit — is brought to its fulfillment through the sharing in this communion, by grace, within the one, holy, catholic and apostolic Church, which is the People of God, the Body of Christ and the Temple of the Spirit.

The Sacraments

Believers become members of this Body through the sacrament of Baptism, through which, by water and the working of the Holy Spirit, they are born again as new creatures. They are confirmed by the seal of the Holy Spirit who bestows the sacrament of anointing. Their communion with God and among themselves is brought to full realization by the celebration of the unique offering of Christ in the sacrament of the Eucharist. This communion is restored for the sinful members of the Church when they are reconciled with God and with one another through the sacrament of Forgiveness. The sacrament of Ordination to the ministerial priesthood in the apostolic succession assures the authenticity of the faith, the sacraments and the communion in each local Church.

Sister Churches But Not Full Communion

Living by this faith and these sacraments, it follows as a consequence that the particular Catholic Churches and the particular Assyrian Churches can recognize each other as sister Churches. To be full and entire, communion presupposes the unanimity concerning the content of the faith, the sacraments and the constitution of the Church. Since this unanimity for which we aim has not yet been attained, we cannot unfortunately celebrate together the Eucharist which is the sign of the ecclesial communion already fully restored. Nevertheless, the deep spiritual communion in the faith and the mutual trust already existing between our Churches entitles us from now on to consider witnessing together to the gospel message and cooperating in particular pastoral situations, including especially the areas of catechesis and the formation of future priests.

Commitment to Unity Efforts

In thanking God for having made us rediscover what already unites us in the faith and the sacraments, we pledge ourselves to do everything possible to dispel the obstacles of the past which still prevent the attainment of full communion between our Churches, so that we can better respond to the Lord's call for the unity of his own, a unity which has of course to be expressed visibly. To overcome these obstacles, we now establish a Mixed Committee for theological dialogue between the Catholic Church and the AssyrianChurch of the East. Given at Saint Peter's on Nov. 11, 1994.

COMMON DECLARATIONS

John Paul II and Bartholomew I

Pope John Paul and Ecumenical Orthodox Patriarch Bartholomew I, after several days of meetings, signed a common declaration June 29, 1995, declaring: "Our meeting has followed other important events which have seen our Churches declare their desire to rel-egate the excommunications of the past to oblivion and to set out on the way to establishing full communion. "Our new-found brotherhood in the name of the Lord has led us to frank discussion, a dialogue that seeks understanding and unity. This dialogue — through the Joint International (Catholic-Orthodox) Commission — has proved fruitful and has made substantial progress. "A common sacramental conception of the Church has emerged, sustained and passed on in time by the apostolic succession. In our Churches, the apostolic succession is fundamental to the sanctification and unity of the People of God. Considering that in every local church the mystery of divine love is realized and that this is how the Church of Christ shows forth its active presence in each one of them, the Joint Commission has been able to declare that our Churches recognize one another as Sister Churches, responsible together for safeguarding the one Church of God, in fidelity to the divine plan, and in an altogether special way with regard to unity."

John Paul II and Karekin I

Pope John Paul and His Holiness Karekin I, Supreme Patriarch and Catholicos of All Armenians, signed Dec. 13, 1996, a common declaration in which they said in part: "Pope John Paul II and Catholicos Karekin I recognize the deep spiritual communion which already unites them and the bishops and clergy and lay faithful of their churches. It is a communion which finds its roots in the common faith in the holy and life-giving Trinity proclaimed by the Apostles and transmitted down the centuries. . . . They rejoice in the fact that recent developments of ecumenical relations and theological discussions . . . have dispelled many misunderstandings inherited from the controversies and dissensions of the past. Such dialogues and encounters have prepared a healthy situation of mutual understanding and recovery of the deeper spiritual communion based on the common faith in

the holy Trinity that they have been given through the Gospel of Christ and in the holy tradition of the Church. "They particularly welcome the great advance that their churches have registered in their common search for unity in Christ, the Word of God made flesh. Perfect God as to his divinity, perfect man as to his humanity, his divinity is united to his humanity in the Person of the only-begotten Son of God, in a union which is real, perfect, without confusion, without alteration, without division, without any form of separation.

"The reality of this common faith in Jesus Christ and in the same succession of apostolic ministry has at times been obscured or ignored. Linguistic, cultural and political factors have immensely contributed toward the theological divergences that have found expression in their terminology of formulating their doctrines. His Holiness John Paul II and His Holiness Karekin I have expressed their determined conviction that because of the fundamental common faith in God and in Jesus Christ, the controversies and unhappy divisions which sometimes have followed upon the divergent ways in expressing it, as a result of the present declaration, should not continue to influence the life and witness of the Church today. They humbly declare before God their sorrow for these controversies and dissensions and their determination to remove from the mind and memory of their churches the bitterness, mutual recriminations and even hatred which have sometimes manifested themselves in the past, and may even today cast a shadow over the truly fraternal and genuinely Christian relations between leaders and the faithful of both churches, especially as these have developed in recent times. "The communion already existing between the two churches and the hope for and commitment to recovery of full communion between them should become factors of motivation for further contact, more regular and substantial dialogue, leading to a greater degree of mutual understanding and recovery of the community of their faith and service."

POPE'S MESSAGE TO KAREKIN I PUBLISHED POSTHUMOUSLY

Courtesy, Vatican Information Service. In conjunction with the funeral of Patriarch Karekin I, Catholicos of all the Armenians, the Holy See issued a message from the Holy Father to the late patriarch.

A delegation from the Holy See led by Cardinal Edward Cassidy, president of the Pontifical Council for Promoting Christian Unity attended the funeral in Etchmiadzin, Armenia on July 8, 1999. Cardinal Cassidy had been scheduled to visit Karekin I from July 1 to 3, bearing a Message from the Holy Father, but the patriarch died on June 29, following a long illness. The Pope's Message was made public, written in English and dated June 29.

In the message, the Holy Father expressed his "spiritual closeness at this difficult time of ill health," and recalled the two visits that Karekin I had paid him in Rome. The Holy Father also highlighted how "the Christian faith has shaped Armenian culture, just as Armenian culture has contributed to enriching the understanding of the Christian faith in new and unique ways.... The Armenian Apostolic Church developed its own identity

in a spirit of great openness to the different ecclesial traditions around it.... (Its) present contribution to the ecumenical movement is part of a long tradition of openness and fraternal exchange."

John Paul II underscored the need to proceed on the path of dialogue in the search for Christian unity, writing that "the one condition necessary for union ... is the truth of faith in charity. May we come to rediscover one full communion precisely in the truth of faith in charity!"

"A crucial question on the path towards full communion concerns the ministry of the Bishop of Rome," wrote the Pope. "Since my election to the See of Peter, I have sought to exercise this ministry as an effective service to the communion of all the Churches. Inspired by the mission of Peter, I have striven to be the servant of unity, and I shall continue to do so."

He emphasized the importance of "concentrating efforts so that ... we may restore the fabric of the undivided Church. Where we cannot at the present time find a way forward, the future will surely show us new paths."

REFORMATION CHURCHES

LEADERS AND DOCTRINES OF THE REFORMATION

Some of the leading figures, doctrines and churches of the Reformation are covered below. A companion article covers Major Protestant Churches in the United States.

LEADERS

John Wycliff (c. 1320-1384): English priest and scholar who advanced one of the leading Reformation ideas nearly 200 years before Martin Luther — that the Bible alone is the sufficient rule of faith — but had only an indirect influence on the 16th century Reformers. Supporting belief in an inward and practical religion, he denied the divinely commissioned authority of the pope and bishops of the Church; he also denied the Real Presence of Christ in the Holy Eucharist, and wrote against the sacrament of penance and the doctrine of indulgences. Nearly 20 of his propositions were condemned by Gregory XI in 1377; his writings were proscribed more extensively by the Council of Constance in 1415. His influence was strongest in Bohemia and Central Europe.

John Hus (c. 1369-1415): A Bohemian priest and preacher of reform who authored 30 propositions condemned by the Council of Constance. Excommunicated in 1411 or 1412, he was burned at the stake in 1415. His principal errors concerned the nature of the Church and the origin of papal authority. He spread some of the ideas of Wycliff but did not subscribe to his views regarding faith alone as the condition for justification and salvation, the sole sufficiency of Scripture as the rule of faith, the Real Presence of Christ in the Eucharist, and the sacramental system. In 1457 some of his followers founded the Church of the Brotherhood which later became known as the United Brethren or Moravian Church and is considered the earliest independent Protestant body.

Martin Luther (1483-1546): An Augustinian friar, priest and doctor of theology, the key figure in the Reformation. In 1517, as a special indulgence was being preached in Germany, and in view of needed reforms within the Church, he published at Wittenberg 95 theses concerning matters of Catholic belief and practice. Leo X condemned 41 statements from Luther's writings in 1520. Luther, refusing to recant, was excommunicated the following year. His teachings strongly influenced subsequent Lutheran theology; its statements of faith are found in the Book of Concord (1580).

Luther's doctrines included the following: The sin of Adam, which corrupted human nature radically (but not substantially), has affected every aspect of man's being. Justification, understood as the forgiveness of sins and the state of righteousness, is by grace for Christ's sake through faith. Faith involves not merely intellectual assent but an act of confidence by the will. Good works are indispensably necessary concomitants of faith, but do not merit salvation. Of the sacraments, Luther retained baptism, penance and the Holy Communion as effective vehicles of the grace of the Holy Spirit; he held that in the Holy Communion the consecrated bread and wine are the Body and Blood of Christ. The rule of faith is the divine revelation in the Sacred Scriptures. He rejected purgatory, indulgences and the invocation of the saints, and held that prayers for the dead have no efficacy. Lutheran tenets not in agreement with Catholic doctrine were condemned by the Council of Trent.

Ulrich Zwingli (1484-1531): A priest who triggered the Reformation in Switzerland with a series of New Testament lectures in 1519, later disputations and by other actions. He held the Gospel to be the only basis of truth; rejected the Mass (which he suppressed in 1525 at Zurich), penance and other sacraments; denied papal primacy and doctrine concerning purgatory and the invocation of saints; rejected celibacy, monasticism and many traditional practices of piety. His symbolic view of the Eucharist, which was at odds with Catholic doctrine, caused an irreconcilable controversy with Luther and his followers. Zwingli was killed in a battle between the forces of Protestant and Catholic cantons in Switzerland.

John Calvin (1509-1564): French leader of the Reformation in Switzerland, whose key tenet was absolute predestination of some persons to heaven and others to hell. He rejected Catholic doctrine in 1533 after becoming convinced of a personal mission to reform the Church. In 1536 he published the first edition of Institutes of the Christian Religion, a systematic exposition of his doctrine which became the classic textbook of Reformed — as distinguished from Lutheran — theology. To Luther's principal theses — regarding Scripture as the sole rule of faith, the radical corruption of human nature, and justification by faith alone — he added absolute predestination, certitude of salvation for the elect, and the incapability of the elect to lose grace. His Eucharistic theory, which failed to mediate the Zwingli-Luther controversy, was at odds with Catholic doctrine. From 1555 until his death Calvin was the virtual dictator of Geneva, the capital of the non-Lutheran Reformation in Europe.

CHURCHES AND MOVEMENTS

Adventists: Members of several Christian sects whose doctrines are dominated by belief in a more or less imminent second advent or coming of Christ upon earth for a glorious 1,000-year reign of righteousness. This reign, following victory by the forces of good over evil in a final Battle of Armageddon, will begin with the resurrection of the chosen and will end with the resurrection of all others and the annihilation of the wicked. Thereafter, the just will live forever in a renewed heaven and earth. A sleep of the soul takes place between the time of death and the day of judgment. There is no hell. The Bible, in fundamentalist interpretation, is regarded as the only rule of faith and practice. About six sects have developed in the course of the Adventist movement which originated with William Miller (1782-1849) in the United States. Miller, on the basis of calculations made from the Book of Daniel, predicted that the second advent of

Christ would occur between 1843 and 1844. After the prophecy went unfulfilled, divisions occurred in the movement and the Seventh Day Adventists, whose actual formation dates from 1860, emerged as the largest single body. The observance of Saturday instead of Sunday as the Lord's Day dates from 1844.

Anabaptism: Originated in Saxony in the first quarter of the 16th century and spread rapidly through southern Germany. Its doctrine included several key Lutheran tenets but was not regarded with favor by Luther, Calvin or Zwingli. Anabaptists believed that baptism is for adults only and that infant baptism is invalid. Their doctrine of the Inner Light, concerning the direct influence of the Holy Spirit on the believer, implied rejection of Catholic doctrine concerning the sacraments and the nature of the Church. Eighteen articles of faith were formulated in 1632 in Holland. Mennonites are Anabaptists.

Arminianism: A modification of the rigid predestinationism of Calvin, set forth by Jacob Arminius (1560-1609) and formally stated in the Remonstrance of 1610. Arminianism influenced some Calvinist bodies.

Baptists: So called because of their doctrine concerning baptism. They reject infant baptism and consider only baptism by immersion as valid. Leaders in the formation of the church were John Smyth (d. 1612) in England and Roger Williams (d. 1683) in America.

Congregationalists: Evangelical in spirit and seeking a return to forms of the primitive church, they uphold individual freedom in religious matters, do not require the acceptance of a creed as a condition for communion, and regard each congregation as autonomous. Robert Browne influenced the beginnings of Congregationalism.

Disciples: From a nineteenth century revival movement and desire for the unity of the Christian churches, a network of congregations developed which desired to be called simply "Christian churches." These churches opened their communion and membership to all, celebrated the Eucharist each Sunday and baptized only adults. From this movement the Christian Church/Disciples of Christ, the Churches of Christ and the independent Christian Churches emerged.

Methodists: A group who broke away from the Anglican Communion under the leadership of John Wesley (1703-1791), although some Anglican beliefs were retained. Doctrines include the witness of the Spirit to the individual and personal assurance of salvation. Wesleyan Methodists do not subscribe to some of the more rigid Calvinistic tenets held by other Methodists.

Pentecostals: Churches that grew up after the 1906 enthusiastic revival, accompanied by the phenomena of speaking in foreign tongues and the experience of baptism in the Holy Spirit. From this revival churches of a Methodist or Baptist theological emphasis emerged, such as the Church of God in Christ or the Assemblies of God. In the midtwentieth century, the charismatic experience began to be shared by some members of the classical churches, including Roman Catholic.

Puritans: Extremists who sought church reform along Calvinist lines in severe simplicity. (Use of the term was generally discontinued after 1660.)

Presbyterians: Basically Calvinistic, called Presbyterian because church polity centers around assemblies of presbyters or elders. John Knox (c. 1513-1572) established the church in Scotland.

Quakers: Their key belief is in internal divine illumination, the inner light of the living Christ, as the only source of truth and inspiration. George Fox (1624-1691) was one of their leaders in England. Called the Society of Friends, the Quakers are noted for their pacificism.

Unitarianism: A 16th century doctrine which rejected the Trinity and the divinity of Christ in favor of a uni-personal God. It claimed scriptural support for a long time but became generally rationalistic with respect to "revealed" doctrine as well as in ethics and its world-view. One of its principal early proponents was Faustus Socinus (1539-1604), a leader of the Polish Brethren.

A variety of communions developed in England in the Reformation and post-Reformation periods.

Universalism: A product of 18th-century liberal Protestantism in England. The doctrine is not Trinitarian and includes a tenet that all men will ultimately be saved.

Anglican Communion: This communion, which regards itself as the same apostolic Church as that which was established by early Christians in England, derived not from Reformation influences but from the renunciation of papal jurisdiction by Henry VIII (1491-1547). His Act of Supremacy in 1534 called Christ's Church an assembly of local churches subject to the prince, who was vested with fullness of authority and jurisdiction. In spite of Henry's denial of papal authority, this Act did not reject substantially other principal articles of faith. Notable changes, proposed and adopted for the reformation of the church, took place in the subsequent reigns of James VI and Elizabeth, with respect to such matters as Scripture as the rule of faith, the sacraments, the nature of the Mass, and the constitution of the hierarchy. There are 27 provinces in the Anglican Communion. (See Episcopal Church, Anglican Orders, Anglican-Catholic Final Report.)

MAJOR PROTESTANT CHURCHES IN THE UNITED STATES

There are more than 250 Protestant church bodies in the United States. The majority of U.S. Protestants belong to the following denominations: Baptist, Methodist, Lutheran, Presbyterian, Protestant Episcopal, the United Church of Christ, the Christian Church (Disciples of Christ), Evangelicals.

See Ecumenical Dialogues, Reports and related entries for coverage of relations between the Catholic Church and other Christian churches.

Baptist Churches

Baptist churches, comprising the largest of all American Protestant denominations, were first established by John Smyth near the beginning of the 17th century in England. The first Baptist church in America was founded at Providence by Roger Williams in 1639.

Largest of the nearly 30 Baptist bodies in the U.S. are:

The Southern Baptist Convention, 901 Commerce St., Suite 750, Nashville, Tenn. 37203, with 15.7 million members.

The National Baptist Convention, U.S.A., Inc., 915 Spain St., Baton Rouge, La. 70802, with 8 million members;

The National Baptist Convention of America, Inc., 1320 Pierre Ave., Shreveport, La. 71103, with 4.5 million members.

The American Baptist Churches in the U.S.A., P.O. Box 851, Valley Forge, Pa. 19482, with 1.5 million members.

The total number of U.S. Baptists is more than 29 million. The world total is 33 million.

Proper to Baptists is their doctrine on baptism. Called an "ordinance" rather than a sacrament, baptism by immersion is a sign that one has experienced and decided in favor of the salvation offered by Christ. It is administered only to persons who are able to make a responsible decision. Baptism is not administered to infants.

Baptists do not have a formal creed but generally subscribe to two professions of faith formulated in 1689 and 1832 and are in general agreement with classical Protestant theology regarding Scripture as the sole rule of faith, original sin, justification through faith in Christ, and the nature of the Church. Their local churches are autonomous.

Worship services differ in form from one congregation to another. Usual elements are the reading of Scripture, a sermon, hymns, vocal and silent prayer. The Lord's Supper, called an "ordinance," is celebrated at various times.

Christian Church (Disciples of Christ)

The Christian Church (Disciples of Christ) originated early in the 1800s from two movements against rigid denominationalism led by Presbyterians Thomas and Alexander Campbell in western Pennsylvania and Barton W. Stone in Kentucky. The two movements developed separately for about 25 years before being merged in 1832.

The church, which identifies itself with the Protestant mainstream, has nearly one million members in almost 4,000 congregations in the U.S. and Canada. The greatest concentration of members in the U.S. is located roughly along the old frontier line, in an arc sweeping from Ohio and Kentucky through the Midwest and down into Oklahoma and Texas.

The general offices of the church are located at 130 E. Washington St., Indianapolis, Ind. 46204.

The church's persistent concern for Christian unity is based on a conviction expressed in a basic document, Declaration and Address, dating from its founding. The document states: "The church of Christ upon earth is essentially, intentionally and constitutionally one."

The Disciples have no official doctrine or dogma. Their worship practices vary widely from more common informal services to what could almost be described as "high church" services. Membership is granted after a simple statement of belief in Jesus Christ and baptism by immersion; most congregations admit un-immersed transfers from other denominations. The Lord's Supper or Eucharist, generally called Communion, is always open to Christians of all persuasions. Lay men and women routinely preside over the Lord's Supper, which is celebrated each Sunday; they often preach and perform other pastoral functions as well. Distinction between ordained and non-ordained members is blurred somewhat because of the Disciples' emphasis on all members of the church as ministers.

The Christian Church is oriented to congregational government, and has a unique structure in which three sections of polity (general, regional and congregational) operate as equals rather than in a pyramid of authority. At the national or international level, it is governed by a general assembly which has voting representation direct from congregations and regions as well as all ordained and licensed clergy.

Episcopal Church

The Episcopal Church, which includes 113 dioceses in the United States, Central and South America, and elsewhere overseas, regards itself as part of the same apostolic church which was established by early Christians in England. Established in this country during the colonial period, it became independent of the jurisdiction of the Church of England when a new constitution and Prayer Book were adopted at a general convention held in 1789. It has approximately 2.5 million members worldwide.

Offices of the presiding bishop and the executive council are located at 815 Second Ave., New York, N.Y. 10017.

The presiding bishop is chief pastor and primate; he is elected by the House of Bishops and confirmed by the House of Deputies for a term of nine years.

The Episcopal Church, which is a part of the Anglican Communion, regards the Archbishop of Canterbury as the "First among Equals," though not under his authority.

The Anglican Communion, worldwide, has 70 million members in 36 self-governing churches.

Official statements of belief and practice are found in the Book of Common Prayer. Scripture has primary importance with respect to the rule of faith, and authority is also attached to tradition.

An episcopal system of church government prevails, but presbyters, deacons and lay persons also have an active voice in church affairs. The levels of government are the general convention, and executive council, dioceses, and local parishes. At the parish level, the congregation has the right to select its own rector, with the consent of the bishop.

Liturgical worship is according to the Book of Common Prayer as adopted in 1979, but details of ceremonial practice vary from one congregation to another.

Lutheran Churches

The origin of Lutheranism is generally traced to Oct. 31, 1517, when Martin Luther — Augustinian friar, priest, doctor of theology — tacked "95 Theses" to the door of the castle church in Wittenberg, Germany. This call to debate on the subject of indulgences and related concerns has come to symbolize the beginning of the Reformation. Luther and his supporters intended to reform the Church they knew. Though Lutheranism has come to be visible in separate denominations and national churches, at its heart it professes itself to be a confessional movement within the one, holy, catholic and apostolic Church.

The world's 61 million Lutherans form the third largest grouping of Christians, after Roman Catholics and Orthodox. About 57 million of them belong to church bodies which make up the Lutheran World Federation, headquartered in Geneva.

There are about 8.5 million Lutherans in the United States, making them the fourth largest Christian grouping, after Roman Catholics, Baptists and Methodists. Although there are nearly 20 U.S. Lutheran church bodies, all but 100,000 Lutherans belong to either the Evangelical Lutheran Church in America (with 5.2 million members and headquarters at 8765 W. Higgins Rd., Chicago, Ill. 60631), The Lutheran Church-Missouri Synod (with 2.61 million members and headquarters at 1333 S. Kirkwood Rd., St. Louis, Mo. 63122), or the Wisconsin Evangelical Lutheran Synod (with 420,000 members and headquarters at 2929 N. Mayfair Rd., Milwaukee, Wis. 53222).

The Evangelical Lutheran Church in America and the Lutheran Church-Missouri Synod carry out some work together through inter-Lutheran agencies such as Lutheran World Relief and Lutheran Immigration and Refugee Services; both agencies have offices at 390 Park Ave. South, New York, N.Y. 10010.

The statements of faith which have shaped the confessional life of Lutheranism are found in the *Book of Concord*. This 1580 collection includes the three ancient ecumenical creeds (Apostles', Nicene and Athanasian), Luther's Large and Small Catechisms (1529), the Augsburg Confession (1530) and the Apology in defense of it (1531), the Smalkald Articles (including the "Treatise on the Power and Primacy of the Pope") (1537), and the Formula of Concord (1577).

The central Lutheran doctrinal proposition is that Christians "receive forgiveness of sins and become righteous before God by grace, for Christ's sake." Baptism and the Lord's Supper (Holy Communion, the Eucharist) are universally celebrated among Lutherans as sacramental means of grace. Lutherans also treasure the Word proclaimed in the reading of the Scriptures, preaching and absolution.

Generally in Lutheranism, the bishop, or a pastor (presbyter/priest) authorized by the bishop, is the minister of ordination. Much of Lutheranism continues what it understands as the historic succession of bishops (though without considering the historic episcopate essential for the church). All of Lutheranism is concerned to preserve apostolic succession in life and doctrine.

Lutheran jurisdictions corresponding to dioceses are called districts or synods in North America. There are more than 100 of them; each of them is headed by a bishop or president.

Methodist Churches

John Wesley (1703-1791), an Anglican clergyman, was the founder of Methodism. In 1738, following a period of missionary work in America and strongly influenced by the Moravians, he experienced a new conversion to Christ and shortly thereafter became a leader in a religious awakening in England. By the end of the 18th century, Methodism was strongly rooted also in America.

The United Methodist Church, formed in 1968 by a merger of the Methodist Church and the Evangelical United Brethren Church, is the second largest Protestant denomination in the U.S., with more than nine million members; its principal agencies are located in New York, Evanston, Ill., Nashville, Tenn., Washington, D.C., Dayton, O., and Lake Junaluska, N.C. (World Methodist Council, P.O. Box 518. 28745). The second largest body, with just under two million communicants, is the African Methodist Episcopal Church. Four other major churches in the U.S. are the African Methodist Episcopal Zion, Christian Methodist Episcopal, Free Methodist Church and the Wesleyan Church. The total Methodist membership in the U.S. is about 15.5 million.

Worldwide, there are more than 73 autonomous Methodist/Wesleyan churches in 107 countries, with a membership of more than 33 million. All of them participate in the World Methodist Council, which gives global unity to the witness of Methodist communicants.

Methodism, although it has a base in Calvinistic theology, rejects absolute predestination and maintains that Christ offers grace freely to all men, not just to a select elite. Wesley's distinctive doctrine was the "witness of the Spirit" to the individual soul and personal assurance of salvation. He also emphasized the central themes of conversion and holiness. Methodists are in general agreement with classical Protestant theology regarding Scripture as the sole rule of faith, original sin, justification through faith in Christ, the nature of the Church, and the sacraments of baptism and the Lord's Supper. Church polity is structured along episcopal lines in America, with ministers being appointed to local churches by a bishop; churches stemming from British Methodism do not have bishops but vest appointive powers within an appropriate conference. Congregations are free to choose various forms of worship services; typical elements are readings from Scripture, sermons, hymns and prayers.

Presbyterian Churches

Presbyterians are so called because of their tradition of governing the church through a system of representative bodies composed of elders (presbyters).

Presbyterianism is a part of the Reformed Family of Churches that grew out of the theological work of John Calvin following the Lutheran Reformation, to which it is heavily indebted. Countries in which it acquired early strength and influence were Switzerland, France, Holland, Scotland and England.

Presbyterianism spread widely in this country in the latter part of the 18th century and afterwards. Presently, it has approximately 4.5 million communicants in nine bodies.

The two largest Presbyterian bodies in the country — the United Presbyterian Church in the U.S.A. and the Presbyterian Church in the United States — were reunited in June, 1983, to form the Presbyterian Church (U.S.A.), with a membership of 2.7 million. Its national offices are located at 100 Witherspoon St., Louisville, Ky. 40202.

These churches, now merged, are closely allied with the Reformed Church in America, the United Church of Christ, the Cumberland Presbyterian Churches, the Korean Presbyterian Church in America and the Associate Reformed Presbyterian Church.

In Presbyterian doctrine, baptism and the Lord's

Supper, viewed as seals of the covenant of grace, are regarded as sacraments. Baptism, which is not necessary for salvation, is conferred on infants and adults The Lord's Supper is celebrated as a covenant of the Sacrifice of Christ. In both sacraments, a doctrine of the real presence of Christ is considered the central theological principle.

The Church is twofold, being invisible and also visible; it consists of all of the elect and all those Christians who are united in Christ as their immediate head.

Presbyterians are in general agreement with classical Protestant theology regarding Scripture as the sole rule of faith and practice, salvation by grace, and justification through faith in Christ.

Presbyterian congregations are governed by a session composed of elders elected by the communicant membership. On higher levels there are presbyteries, synods and a general assembly with various degrees of authority over local bodies; all such representative bodies are composed of elected elders and ministers in approximately equal numbers. The church annually elects a moderator who presides at the General Assembly and travels throughout the church to speak to and hear from the members.

Worship services, simple and dignified, include sermons, prayer, reading of the Scriptures and hymns. The Lord's Supper is celebrated at intervals.

Doctrinal developments of the past several years included approval in May, 1967, by the General Assembly of the United Presbyterian Church of a contemporary confession of faith to supplement the historic Westminster Confession. A statement entitled "The Declaration of Faith" was approved in 1977 by the Presbyterian Church in the U.S. for teaching and liturgical use.

The reunited church adopted "A Brief Statement of Reformed Faith" in 1991 regarding urgent concerns of the church.

United Church of Christ

The 1,501,310-member (in 1994) United Church of Christ was formed in 1957 by a union of the Congregational Christian and the Evangelical and Reformed Churches. The former was originally established by the Pilgrims and the Puritans of the Massachusetts Bay Colony, while the latter was founded in Pennsylvania in the early 1700s by settlers from Central Europe. The denomination had 6,362 congregations throughout the United States in 1988.

It considers itself "a united and uniting church" and keeps itself open to all ecumenical options.

Its headquarters are located at 700 Prospect, Cleveland, Ohio 44115.

Its statement of faith recognizes Jesus Christ as "our crucified and risen Lord (who) shared our common lot, conquering sin and death and reconciling the world to himself." It believes in the life after death, and the fact that God "judges men and nations by his righteous will declared through prophets and apostles."

The United Church further believes that Christ calls its members to share in his baptism "and eat at his table, to join him in his passion and victory." Each local church is free to adopt its own methods of worship and to formulate its own covenants and confessions of faith. Some celebrate communion weekly; others, monthly or on another periodical basis. Like other Calvinistic bodies, it believes that Christ is spiritually present in the sacrament.

The United Church is governed along congregational lines, and each local church is autonomous. However, the actions of its biennial General Synod are taken with great seriousness by congregations. Between synods, a 44-member executive council oversees the work of the church.

Evangelicalism

Evangelicalism, dating from 1735 in England (the Evangelical Revival) and after 1740 in the United States (the Great Awakening), has had and continues to have widespread influence in Protestant churches. It has been estimated that about 45 millon American Protestants — communicants of both large denominations and small bodies — are evangelicals.

The Bible is their rule of faith and religious practice. Being born again in a life-changing experience through faith in Christ is the promise of salvation. Missionary work for the spread of the Gospel is a normal and necessary activity.

Additional matters of belief and practice are generally of a conservative character. Fundamentalists, numbering perhaps 4.5 million, comprise an extreme right-wing subculture of evangelicalism. They are distinguished mainly by militant biblicism, belief in the absolute inerrancy of the Bible and emphasis on the Second Coming of Christ. Fundamentalism developed early in the 20th century in reaction against liberal theology and secularizing trends in mainstream and other Protestant denominations.

The Holiness or Perfectionist wing of evangelicalism evolved from Methodist efforts to preserve, against a contrary trend, the personal-piety and inner-religion concepts of John Wesley. There are at least 30 Holiness bodies in the U.S.

Pentecostals, probably the most demonstrative of evangelicals, are noted for speaking in tongues and the stress they place on healing, prophecy and personal testimony to the practice and power of evangelical faith.

Assemblies of God

Assemblies (Churches) of God form the largest body (more than 2 million members) in the Pentecostal Movement which developed from (1) the Holiness Revival in the Methodist Church after the Civil War and (2) the Apostolic Faith Movement at the beginning of the 20th century. Members share with other Pentecostals belief in the religious experience of conversion and in the baptism by the Holy Spirit that sanctifies. Distinctive is the emphasis placed on the charismatic gifts of the apostolic church, healing and speaking in tongues, which are signs of the "second blessing" of the Holy Spirit.

The Assemblies are strongly fundamentalist in theology; are loosely organized in various districts, with democratic procedures; are vigorously evangelistic. The moral code is rigid.

INTERRELIGIOUS DIALOGUE

JUDAISM

Judaism is the religion of the Hebrew Bible and of contemporary Jews. Divinely revealed and with a patriarchal background (Abraham, Isaac, Jacob), it originated with the Mosaic Covenant, was identified with the Israelites, and achieved distinctive form and character as the religion of the *Torah* (Law, "The Teaching") from this Covenant and reforms initiated by Ezra and Nehemiah after the Babylonian Exile.

Judaism does not have a formal creed but its principal points of belief are clear. Basic is belief in one transcendent God who reveals himself through the Torah, the prophets, the life of his people and events of history. The fatherhood of God involves the brotherhood of all humanity. Religious faith and practice are equated with just living according to God's Law. Moral conviction and practice are regarded as more important than precise doctrinal formulation and profession. Formal worship, whose principal act was sacrifice from the Exodus times to 70 A.D., is by prayer, reading and meditating upon the sacred writings, and observance of the Sabbath and festivals.

Judaism has messianic expectations of the complete fulfillment of the Covenant, the coming of God's kingdom, the ingathering of his people, and final judgment and retribution for all. Views differ regarding the manner in which these expectations will be realized — through a person, the community of God's people, an evolution of historical events, an eschatological act of God himself. Individual salvation expectations also differ, depending on views about the nature of immortality, punishment and reward, and related matters.

Sacred Books

The sacred books are the 24 books of the Masoretic Hebrew Text of The Law, the Prophets and the Writings (see The Bible). Together, they contain the basic instruction or norms for just living. In some contexts, the term Law or *Torah* refers only to the Pentateuch (Genesis, Exodus, Leviticus, Numbers, Deuteronomy); in others, it denotes all the sacred books and/or the whole complex of written and oral tradition.

Also of great authority are two *Talmuds*, which were composed in Palestine and Babylon in the fourth and fifth centuries A.D., respectively. They consist of the Mishna, a compilation of oral laws, and the Gemara, a collection of rabbinical commentary on the Mishna. Midrash are collections of scriptural comments and moral counsels.

Priests were the principal religious leaders during the period of sacrificial and temple worship. Rabbis were originally teachers; today they share with cantors the function of leaders of prayer. The synagogue is the place of community worship. The family and home are focal points of many aspects of Jewish worship and practice.

Of the various categories of Jews, Orthodox are the most conservative in adherence to strict religious traditions. Others — Reformed, Conservative, Reconstructionist — are liberal in comparison with the Orthodox. They favor greater or less modifica-

tion of religious practices in accommodation to contemporary culture and living conditions.

Principal events in Jewish life include the circumcision of males, according to prescriptions of the Covenant; the bar and bat mitzvah which marks the coming-of-age of boys and girls in Judaism at the age of 13; marriage; and observance of the Sabbath and festivals.

Observances of the Sabbath and festivals begin at sundown of the previous calendar day and continue until the following sundown.

Sabbath: Saturday, the weekly day of rest prescribed in the Decalogue.

Sukkoth (Tabernacles): A seven-to-nine-day festival in the month of Tishri (Sept.-Oct.), marked by some Jews with Covenant-renewal and reading of The Law. It originated as an agricultural feast at the end of the harvest and got its name from the temporary shelters used by workers in the fields.

Hanukkah (The Festival of Lights, the Feast of Consecration and of the Maccabees): Commemorates the dedication of the new altar in the Temple at Jerusalem by Judas Maccabeus in 165 B.C. The eight-day festival, during which candles in an eight-branch candelabra are lighted in succession, one each day, occurs near the winter solstice, close to Christmas time.

Pesach (Passover): A seven-day festival commemorating the liberation of the Israelites from Egypt. The narrative of the Exodus, the Haggadah, is read at ceremonial Seder meals on the first and second days of the festival, which begins on the 14th day of Nisan (Mar.-Apr.).

Shavuoth, Pentecost (Feast of Weeks): Observed 50 days after Passover, commemorating the anniversary of the revelation of the Law to Moses.

Purim: A joyous festival observed on the 14th day of Adar (Feb.-Mar.), commemorating the rescue of the Israelites from massacre by the Persians through the intervention of Esther. The festival is preceded by a day of fasting. A gift- and alms-giving custom became associated with it in medieval times.

Rosh Hashana (Feast of Trumpets, New Year): Observed on the first day of Tishri (Sept.-Oct.), the festival focuses attention on the ways of life and the ways of death. It is second in importance only to the most solemn observance of Yom Kippur.

Yom Kippur (Day of Atonement): The highest holy day, observed with strict fasting. It occurs 10 days after Rosh Hashana.

Yom HaShoah (Holocaust Memorial Day): Observed in the week after Passover; increasingly observed with joint Christian-Jewish services of remembrance.

CATHOLIC-JEWISH RELATIONS

The Second Vatican Council, in addition to the Decree on Ecumenism (concerning the movement for unity among Christians, stated the mind of the Church on a similar matter in *Nostra Aetate*, a Declaration on the Relationship of the Church to Non-Christian Religions. This document, as the following excerpts indicate, backgrounds the reasons and directions of the Church's regard for the Jews. (Other portions of the document refer to Hindus, Buddhists and Muslims.)

Spiritual Bond

As this sacred Synod searches into the mystery of the Church, it recalls the spiritual bond linking the people of the New Covenant with Abraham's stock.

For the Church of Christ acknowledges that, according to the mystery of God's saving design, the beginnings of her faith and her election are already found among the patriarchs, Moses, and the prophets. She professes that all who believe in Christ, Abraham's sons according to faith (cf. Gal. 3:7), are included in the same patriarch's call, and likewise that the salvation of the Church was mystically foreshadowed by the Chosen People's exodus from the land of bondage.

The Church, therefore, cannot forget that she received the revelation of the Old Testament through the people with whom God in his inexpressible mercy deigned to establish the Ancient Covenant. Nor can she forget that she draws sustenance from the root of that good olive tree onto which have been grafted the wild olive branches of the Gentiles (cf. Rom. 11:17-24). Indeed, the Church believes that by his cross Christ, our Peace, reconciled Jew and Gentile, making them both one in himself (cf. Eph. 2:14-16).

The Jews still remain most dear to God because of their fathers, for he does not repent of the gifts he makes nor of the calls he issues (cf. Rom. 11:28-29). In company with the prophets and the same Apostle (Paul), the Church awaits that day, known to God alone, on which all peoples will address the Lord in a single voice and "serve him with one accord" (Zeph. 3:9; cf. Is. 66:23; Ps. 65:4; Rom. 11:11-32).

Since the spiritual patrimony common to Christians and Jews is thus so great, this sacred Synod wishes to foster and recommend that mutual understanding and respect which is the fruit above all of biblical and theological studies, and of brotherly dialogues.

No Anti-Semitism

True, authorities of the Jews and those who followed their lead pressed for the death of Christ (cf. Jn. 19:6); still, what happened in his passion cannot be blamed upon all the Jews then living, without distinction, nor upon the Jews of today. Although the Church is the new People of God, the Jews should not be presented as repudiated or cursed by God, as if such views followed from the holy Scriptures. All should take pains, then, lest in catechetical instruction and in the preaching of God's Word they teach anything out of harmony with the truth of the Gospel and the spirit of Christ.

The Church repudiates all persecutions against any person. Moreover, mindful of her common patrimony with the Jews, and motivated by the Gospel's spiritual love and by no political considerations, she deplores the hatred, persecutions, and displays of anti-Semitism directed against the Jews at any time and from any source (No. 4).

The Church rejects, as foreign to the mind of Christ, any discrimination against men or harassment of them because of their race, color, condition of life, or religion (No. 5).

Bishops' Secretariat

The American hierarchy's first move toward implementation of the Vatican II Declaration on the Relationship of the Church to Non-Christian Religions (*Nostra Aetate*) was to establish, in 1965, a Subcommission for Catholic-Jewish Relations in the framework of its Commission for Ecumenical and Interreligious Affairs. Its moderator is Cardinal William H. Keeler of Baltimore. The Secretariat for Ecumenical and Interreligious Relations is located at 3211 Fourth St. N.E., Washington, D.C. 20017. Its Catholic-Jewish efforts are directed by Dr. Eugene J. Fisher.

According to the key norm of a set of guidelines issued by the secretariat Mar. 16, 1967, and updated Apr. 9, 1985: "The general aim of all Catholic-Jewish meetings (and relations) is to increase our understanding both of Judaism and the Catholic faith, to eliminate sources of tension and misunderstanding, to initiate dialogue or conversations on different levels, to multiply intergroup meetings between Catholics and Jews, and to promote cooperative social action."

Vatican Guidelines

In a document issued Jan. 3, 1975, the Vatican Commission for Religious Relations with the Jews offered a number of suggestions and guidelines for implementing the Christian-Jewish portion of the Second Vatican Council's Declaration on Relations with Non-Christian Religions.

Among "suggestions from experience" were those concerning dialogue, liturgical links between Christian and Jewish worship, the interpretation of biblical texts, teaching and education for the purpose of increasing mutual understanding, and joint social action.

Notes on Preaching and Catechesis

On June 24, 1985, the Vatican Commission for Religious Relations with the Jews promulgated its "Notes on the Correct Way to Present Jews and Judaism in Preaching and Catechesis in the Roman Catholic Church," with the intent of providing "a helpful frame of reference for those who are called upon in the course of their teaching assignments to speak about Jews and Judaism and who wish to do so in keeping with the current teaching of the Church in this area."

The document states emphatically that, since the relationship between the Church and the Jewish people is one "founded on the design of the God of the Covenant," Judaism does not occupy "an occasional and marginal place in catechesis," but an "essential" one that "should be organically integrated" throughout the curriculum on all levels of Catholic education.

The Notes discuss the relationship between the Hebrew Scriptures and the New Testament, focusing especially on typology, which is called "the sign of a problem unresolved." Underlined is the "eschatological dimension," that "the people of God of the Old and the New Testament are tending toward a like end in the future: the coming or return of the Messiah." Jewish witness to God's Kingdom, the Notes declare, challenges Christians to "accept our responsibility to prepare the world for the coming of the Messiah by working together for social justice and reconciliation."

The Notes emphasize the Jewishness of Jesus' teaching, correct misunderstandings concerning the portrayal of Jews in the New Testament and describe the Jewish origins of Christian liturgy. One section addresses the "spiritual fecundity" of Judaism to the present, its continuing "witness — often heroic — of its fidelity to the one God," and mandates the development of Holocaust curricula and a positive approach in Catholic education to the "religious attachment which finds its roots in biblical tradition" between the Jewish people and the Land of Israel, affirming the "existence of the State of Israel" on the basis of "the common principles of international law."

Papal Statements

(Courtesy of Dr. Eugene Fisher, associate director of the Bishops' Committee for Ecumenical and Interreligious Affairs.)

Pope John Paul II, in a remarkable series of addresses beginning in 1979, has sought to promote and give shape to the development of dialogue between Catholics and Jews.

In a homily delivered June 7, 1979, at Auschwitz, which he called the "Golgotha of the Modern World," he prayed movingly for "the memory of the people whose sons and daughters were intended for total extermination."

In a key address delivered Nov. 17, 1980, to the Jewish community in Mainz, the Pope articulated his vision of the three "dimensions" of the dialogue: (1) "the meeting between the people of God of the Old Covenant and the people of the New Covenant"; (2) the encounter of "mutual esteem between today's Christian churches and today's people of the Covenant concluded with Moses"; (3) the "holy duty" of witnessing to the one God in the world and "jointly to work for peace and justice."

On Mar. 22, 1984, at an audience with members of the Anti-Defamation League of B'nai B'rith, the Pope commented on "the mysterious spiritual link which brings us close together, in Abraham and through Abraham, in God who chose Israel and brought forth the Church from Israel." He urged joint social action on "the great task of promoting justice and peace."

In receiving a delegation of the American Jewish Committee Feb. 14, 1985, the Holy Father confirmed that *Nostra Aetate* "remains always for us a teaching which is necessary to accept not merely as something fitting, but much more as an expression of the faith, as an inspiration of the Holy Spirit, as a word of the divine wisdom."

During his historic visit to the Great Synagogue in Rome Apr. 13, 1986, the Holy Father affirmed that God's covenant with the Jewish people is "irrevocable," and stated: "The Jewish religion is not 'extrinsic' to us, but in a certain way is 'intrinsic' to our own religion. With Judaism, therefore, we have a relationship which we do not have with any other religion."

Meeting with the Jewish community in Sydney, Australia, Nov. 26, 1986, the Holy Father termed the 20th century "the century of the Shoah" (Holocaust) and called "sinful" any "acts of discrimination or persecution against Jews."

On June 14, 1987, meeting with the Jewish community of Warsaw, the Pope called the Jewish witness to the Shoah (Holocaust) a "saving warning before all of humanity" which reveals "your particular vocation, showing you (Jews) to be still the heirs of that election to which God is faithful."

A collection of Pope John Paul's addresses, On Jews and Judaism 1979-1986, prepared by the NCCB Secretariat was sent to the Pope Aug. 12, 1987. In a response of Aug. 17, the Pope reiterated his Warsaw statement and added: "Before the vivid memory of the extermination (Shoah), it is not permissible for anyone to pass by with indifference. The sufferings endured by the Jews are also for the Catholic Church a motive of sincere sorrow, especially when one thinks of the indifference and sometimes resentment which have divided Jews and Christians."

In 1995, an updated edition of the collection of papal texts entitled Spiritual Pilgrimage won the National Jewish Book Award and became the third best-selling "Jewish" book, according to the Jewish Book News.

Meeting with Jewish leaders Sept. 11, 1987, in Miami, the Pope praised the efforts in theological dialogue and educational reform implemented in the U.S. since the Second Vatican Council; affirmed the existence of the State of Israel "according to international law," and urged "common educational programs on the Holocaust so that never again will such a horror be possible. Never again!"

In an apostolic letter on the 50th anniversary of World War II (Aug. 27, 1989), the Pope stressed the uniqueness of the Jewish sufferings of the Shoah, "which will forever remain a shame for humanity."

On Aug. 14, 1991, during a visit to his home town of Wadowice, Poland, the Pope recalled with sadness the deaths of his Jewish classmates at the hands of the Nazis during World War II: "In the school of Wadowice there were Jewish believers who are no longer with us. There is no longer a synagogue near the school. It is true that your people (the Jews) were on the front lines. The Polish Pope has a special relationship to that period because, together with you, we lived through all that in our Fatherland."

On Apr. 7, 1994, the eve of Yom HaShoah, the Jewish day of prayer commemorating the victims of the Holocaust, Pope John Paul II hosted a memorial concert at the Vatican. It was, he noted, a moment of "common meditation and shared prayer," as the Kaddish, the prayer for the dead, and the Kol Nidre, the prayer for forgiveness and atonement, were recited.

Speaking Apr. 10, 1997, to Aharon Lopez, Israel's second ambassador to the Holy See, the Pope said: "The Catholic Church as a whole is committed to cooperating with the State of Israel in combating all forms of anti-Semitism, racism and religious intolerance, and in promoting mutual understanding and respect for human life and dignity. There can be no question that in these areas more can and must be done. It is precisely such renewed efforts that will give to the Great Jubilee of the Year 2000 a truly universal significance, not limited to Catholics or Christians but embracing every part of the world."

The Pope addressed members of the Pontifical Biblical Commission Apr. 11, 1997, saying: "Jesus' human identity is determined on the basis of his bond with the people of Israel, with the dynasty of David and his descent from Abraham. This does not mean only a physical belonging. By taking part in the synagogue celebrations where the Old Testament texts were read and commented on, Jesus nourished his mind and heart with the. . . . From her origins, the Church has well understood that the Incarnation is rooted in history and, consequently, she has fully accepted Christ's insertion into the history of the people of Israel. She has regarded the Hebrew Scriptures as the perennially valid word of God addressed to her as well as to the children of Israel. It is of primary importance to preserve and renew this ecclesial awareness."

To the Jewish people of Sarajevo on Apr. 13, 1997, the Pope declared: "The great spiritual patrimony which unites us in the divine word proclaimed in the Law and the Prophets is for all of us a constant and sure guide. . . . We (together are) the witnesses of the Ten Commandments. . . . Let us therefore go forward courageously as true brothers and heirs of the promises on the path of reconciliation and mutual forgiveness. This is the will of God."

International Liaison Committee

The International Catholic-Jewish Liaison Committee was formed in 1971 and is the official link between the Commission for Religious Relations with the Jewish People and the International Jewish Committee for Interreligious Consultations. The committee meets every 18 months to examine matters of common interest.

Topics under discussion have included: mission and witness (Venice, 1977), religious education (Madrid, 1978), religious liberty and pluralism (Regensburg, 1979), religious commitment (London, 1981), the sanctity of human life in an age of violence (Milan, 1982), youth and faith (Amsterdam, 1984), the Vatican Notes on Preaching and Catechesis (Rome, 1985), the Holocaust (Prague, 1990), education and social action (Baltimore, Md., 1992), family and ecology (Jerusalem, 1994).

Pope John Paul, addressing in Rome a celebration of *Nostra Aetate* (the Second Vatican Council's "Declaration on the Relationship of the Church to Non-Christian Religions") by the Liaison Committee, stated: "What you are celebrating is nothing other than the divine mercy which is guiding Christians and Jews to mutual awareness, respect, cooperation and solidarity. The universal openness of *Nostra Aetate* is anchored in and takes its orientation from a high sense of the absolute singularity of God's choice of a particular people. The Church is fully aware that Sacred Scripture bears witness that the Jewish people, this community of faith and custodian of a tradition thousands of years old, is an intimate part of the mystery of revelation and of salvation."

Family Rights and Obligations

The Liaison Committee, at its May, 1994, meeting in Jerusalem, issued its first joint statement, on the family — in anticipation of the UN Cairo Conference subsequently held in September.

The statement affirmed that "the rights and obligations of the family do not come from the State but exist prior to the State and ultimately have their source in God the Creator. The family is far more than a legal, social or economic unit. For both Jews and Christians, it is a stable community of love and solidarity based on God's covenant."

Vatican-Israel Accord

On Dec. 30, 1993, a year of dramatic developments in the Middle East was capped by the signing in Jerusalem of a "Fundamental Agreement" between representatives of the Holy See and the State of Israel. The agreement acknowledged in its preamble that the signers were "aware of the unique nature of the relationship between the Catholic Church and the Jewish people, and of the historic process of reconciliation and growth in mutual understanding and friendship between Catholics and Jews." Archbishop William H. Keeler, president of the National Conference of Catholic Bishops, welcomed the accord together with the Israeli Ambassador to the United States at a ceremony at the NCCB headquarters in Washington. (See also News Events for recent developments.)

In 1996, the Anti-Defamation League published a set of documents related to the accord, entitled *A Challenge Long Delayed*, edited by Eugene Fisher and Rabbi Klenicki.

U.S. Dialogue

The National Workshop on Christian-Jewish Relations, begun in 1973 by the NCCB Secretariat, draws more than 1,000 participants from around the world. Recent workshops have been held in Baltimore (1986), Minneapolis (1987), Charleston, S.C (1989), Chicago (1990), Pittsburgh (1992), Tulsa (1994) and Stamford (1996).

In October, 1987, the Bishops' Committee for Ecumenical and Interreligious Affairs began a series of twice-yearly consultations with representatives of the Synagogue Council of America. Topics of discussion have included education, human rights, respect for life, the Middle East. The consultation has issued three joint statements: "On Moral Values in Public Education" (1990), "On Stemming the Proliferation of Pornography" (1993) and "On Dealing with Holocaust Revisionism" (1994).

Ongoing relationships are maintained by the NCCB Secretariat with such Jewish agencies as the American Jewish Committee, the Anti-Defamation League of B'nai B'rith, the Union of American Hebrew Congregations, the American Jewish Congress and the National Jewish Community Relations Council.

In June, 1988, the Bishops' Committee for Ecumenical and Interreligious Affairs published in Spanish and English Criteria for the Evaluation of Dramatizations of the Passion, providing for the first time Catholic guidelines for passion plays.

In January, 1989, the Bishops' Committee for the Liturgy issued guidelines for the homiletic presentation of Judaism under the title, "God's Mercy Endures Forever."

When the Synagogue Council of America dissolved in 1995, the Bishops' Committee for Ecumenical and Interreligious Affairs initiated separate consultations with the new National Council of Synagogues (Reform and Conservative), chaired by Cardinal William H. Keeler, and the Orthodox Union/Rabbinical Council, chaired by Cardinal John J. O'Connor. The former consultation was occupied with issues of how the two communities might jointly celebrate the Millennium/Jubilee Year 2000; the latter was working on issues relating to aid for private education.

WE REMEMBER: A REFLECTION ON THE SHOAH

On Mar. 16, 1998, the Commission for Religious Relations with the Jews under Cardinal Edward Idris Cassidy, issued a long-awaited white paper on the Holocaust, entitled "We Remember: Reflections on the Shoah."

The document was ten years in preparation, and, at its heart, it seeks to offer repentance for the failures of many Christians to oppose the policies of Nazi Germany and to resist the extermination of the Jews during the years of the Third Reich. It analyzes the history of anti-Semitism in the Church, but differentiates between historical anti-Semitism in the Christian community that may have led some Christians to ignore or even participate in the terrible persecutions of Jews in Nazi Germany or Occupied Europe, and the ideology of Nazism that climaxed with the Holocaust.

Defense of Pope Pius XII

We Remember also defends Pope Pius XII and his efforts on behalf of the Jews during World War II, using an extended footnote (No. 16) to mark the praise given to the Pontiff by Jewish leaders after the war. The footnote and the mention in the text of Pius's efforts are in part a reply to the recent criticism that the Pontiff did not do enough to prevent or oppose the Holocaust, a claim strongly repudiated by the Jesuit historian Father Pierre Blet. The scholar was one of the editors of eleven volumes of Vatican archival material documenting Pius's policies concerning the deportation of Jews and his coordination of nunciatures and bishops' conferences to limit the persecution of Jews in Europe.

Nevertheless, We Remember is unequivocal in seeking repentance for the failure of Catholics to do more: "... alongside ... courageous men and women, the spiritual resistance and concrete action of other Christians was not that which might have been expected from Christ's followers ... For Christians, this heavy burden of conscience of their brothers and sisters during the Second World War must be a call to penitence ... We deeply regret the errors and failures of those sons and daughters of the Church."

Five Part Document

We Remember begins with a letter from Pope John Paul II expressing his hope that the document "will indeed help to heal the wounds of past misunderstandings and injustices" and "enable memory to play its necessary part in the process of shaping a future in which the unspeakable iniquity of the Shoah will never again be possible."

Part I, "The Tragedy of the Shoah and the Duty of Remembrance," looks at the call by Pope John Paul II in Tertio Millennio Adveniente: "The Church should become more fully conscious of the sinfulness of her children," lamenting that the 20th century "has witnessed an unspeakable tragedy which can never be forgotten: the attempt by the Nazi regime to exterminate the Jewish people ... We ask all Christians to join us in meditating on the catastrophe which befell the Jewish people, and on the moral imperative to ensure that never again will selfishness and hatred grow to the point of sowing such suffering and death."

Part II, "What We Must Remember," declares that "such an event cannot be fully measured by the ordinary criteria of historical research alone," requiring a "reflection" on the conditions that made it possible. One important point is that the Shoah was perpetrated in Europe, raising the question of a relationship between Nazism and historical Christian anti-Semitism.

Part III, "Relations Between Jews and Christians," traces the "tormented" history of Christian-Jewish relations. The section explores the historical failure of Christians to follow Christ's teachings right up to the 19th century. It is noted that in that century, "there began to spread in varying degrees throughout most of Europe an anti-Judaism that was essentially more sociological and political than religious," in connection with ideas that "denied the unity of the human race." Of these, National Socialism was the most extreme expression, an ideology resisted, as the paper documents, by Church leaders in Germany and by Pope Pius XI.

Part IV, "Nazi Anti-Semitism and the Shoah," stresses that Nazism's anti-Semitism "had its roots outside of Christianity and, in pursuing its aims, it did not hesitate to oppose the Church and persecute her members also." Further, "the Nazi Party not only showed aversion to the ideas of divine Providence ... but gave proof of a definite hatred directed at God ... such an attitude led to a rejection of Christianity, and a desire to see the Church destroyed...."

Part V, "Looking Together to a Common Future," expresses Catholic hopes that by this act of repentance (teshuva), a new relationship will be possible. It calls upon all peoples to reflect upon the Shoah and resolve that "the spoiled seeds of anti-Judaism and anti-Semitism must never again be allowed to take root in any human heart."

Reactions

Response to the paper was mixed, with many prominent rabbis and Jewish leaders expressing disappointment that the Church did not go far enough in making a full apology or in admitting greater complicity on the part of Catholics. One notable dissenting opinion was that of Professor Marc Saperstein, of George Washington University, who wrote in the Washington Post that Nazi ideology had a non-Christian origin and the Catholic Church was limited in its capacity to prevent the Nazis — then dominating Europe — from massacring any who opposed its policies: "The fundamental responsibility for the Holocaust lies with the Nazi perpetrators. Not with Pope Pius XII. Not with the Church. Not with the teachings of the Christian faith."

ISLAM

(Courtesy of Dr. John Borelli, executive secretary for Interreligious Relations, NCCB.)

Islam, meaning grateful surrender (to God), originated with Muhammad and the revelation he is believed to have received. Muslims acknowledge that this revelation, recorded in the Quran, is from the one

God and do not view Islam as a new religion. They profess that Muhammad was the last in a long series of prophets, most of whom are named in the Hebrew Bible and the New Testament, beginning with Adam and continuing through Noah, Abraham, Moses, Jesus and down to Muhammad.

Muslims believe in the one God, Allah in Arabic, and cognate with the Hebrew Elohim and the ancient Aramaic Elah. According to the *Qu'ran*, God is one and transcendent, Creator and Sustainer of the universe, all-merciful and all-compassionate Ruler and Judge. God possesses numerous other titles, known collectively as the 99 names of God. The profession of faith states: "There is no god but the God and Muhammad is the messenger of God."

The essential duties of Muslims are to: witness the faith by daily recitation of the profession of faith; worship five times a day facing in the direction of the holy city of Mecca; give alms; fast daily from dawn to dusk during the month of Ramadan; make a pilgrimage to Mecca once if possible.

Muslims believe in final judgment, heaven and hell. Morality and following divinely revealed moral norms are extremely important to Muslims. Some dietary regulations are in effect. On Fridays, the noon prayer is a congregational (*juma*) prayer which should be said in a mosque. The general themes of prayer are adoration and thanksgiving. Muslims do not have an ordained ministry.

The basis of Islamic belief is the *Qu'ran*, the created word of God revealed to Muhammad through the angel Gabriel over a period of 23 years. The contents of this sacred book are complemented by the *Sunna*, a collection of sacred traditions from the life of the prophet Muhammad, and reinforced by *Ijma*, the consensus of Islamic scholars of Islamic Law (*Shariah*) which guarantees them against errors in matters of belief and practice.

Conciliar Statement

The attitude of the Church toward Islam was stated as follows in the Second Vatican Council's Declaration on the Relation of the Church to Non-Christian Religions (*Nostra Aetate*, No. 3).

"The Church has a high regard for the Muslims. They worship God, who is one, living and subsistent, merciful and almighty, the Creator of heaven and earth, who has also spoken to men. They strive to submit themselves without reserve to the hidden decrees of God, just as Abraham submitted himself to God's plan, to whose faith Muslims eagerly link their own. Although not acknowledging him as God, they venerate Jesus as a prophet, his virgin Mother they also honor, and even at times devoutly invoke. Further, they await the day of judgment and the reward of God following the resurrection of the dead, For this reason, they highly esteem an upright life and worship God, especially by way of prayer, alms-deeds and fasting.

"Over the centuries many quarrels and dissensions have arisen between Christians and Muslims. The sacred Council now pleads with all to forget the past, and urges that a sincere effort be made to achieve mutual understanding; for the benefit of all men, let them together preserve and promote peace, liberty, social justice and moral values."

Dialogue

Pope John Paul II has met with Muslim leaders and delegations both in Rome and during his trips abroad. He has addressed large gatherings of Muslims in Morocco, Indonesia, Mali and elsewhere. The Pontifical Council for Interreligious Dialogue has held formal dialogues with Islamic organizations from time to time. In the U.S., the bishops' Secretariat for Ecumenical and Interreligious Affairs has held consultations on relations with Muslims and several special dialogues with Muslims related to international issues. Dialogue with participation of Catholics and Muslims from several U.S. cities was initiated in October, 1991. These continue, and in 1996 a dialogue between representatives of the ministry of W.D. Mohammed and the National Conference of Catholic Bishops began.

In 1995, the American Muslim Council presented its Mahmoud Abu-Saud Award for Excellence to Cardinal William H. Keeler for his leadership in promoting Christian-Muslim relations during his term as president of the National Conference of Catholic Bishops/United States Catholic Conference.

1999 'Id al-Fitr Message

Christians and Muslims: Witnesses of God's Love and Mercy

The following message was issued by Cardinal Francis Arinze, President of the Pontifical Council for Interreligious Dialogue, and was addressed to the Muslim community on the occasion of the observance of the Muslim feast of 'Id al-Fitr at the end of Ramadan, the month of fasting.

Dear Muslim Friends,

1. The great feasts, such as 'Id al-Fitr which you celebrate at the end of Ramadan, are special times both for God and for humanity. They are a special time for God, reminding us with more force, and in a community fashion, of God's presence and action in human history and in our own personal and family life. Such feasts are also a special time for us human beings, a time of rest from daily work, a time for prayer and reflection, a time for ourselves and also for meeting our relatives, friends and neighbors.

2. God loves all human beings, excluding no one. He is the source of all love in the family, in society, in the world. It is from God that we learn to love one another in a gratuitous manner, without expecting any reward here below. God is the Merciful One. He is close to his servants. He hears their prayers. So we can say that belief in God impels us to an attitude of good will towards our brothers and sisters.

3. There are many ways of showing love, expressions of our faithfulness to the Merciful One: almsgiving — the alms on the occasion of 'Id al-Fitr have special importance for you — care for orphans, the aged, the sick, for strangers, as also the commitment to promote human dignity and in favor of human rights, commitment to development, to the fight against many evils of our societies such as illiteracy, the influence of drugs, the abuse of minors, violence against women. Pardon, reconciliation, reopening dialogues that have broken down, the promotion of peace, education in respect for others — all these are different ways of expressing love. There exists, between our two religions, a considerable degree of

agreement with regard to effectively showing mercy to one's neighbor. Is there not here a wide field for collaboration between Christians and Muslims which needs to be developed ?

4. Offenses against the love of neighbor are also numerous: ignoring the needs of others, refusing the duty of solidarity, hatred, discrimination based on sex, race or religion, injustice in all its forms. There is great convergence between our two religions in condemning such faults.

5. God's love for humanity is universal, going beyond political frontiers, beyond the differences of race, culture or religion, beyond political or ideological options, independent of any particular social situation. We are therefore invited, on the basis of our belief, to love one another. True love is indeed at the heart of the believer's way of acting.

6. I am addressing to you this message fully conscious that we, both Christians and Muslims, have not always loved and respected one another as God requires of us. Unfortunately this lack of mutual love is not only a fact of past history, but is also part of present reality. Nevertheless it is important at the same time to note and to make known the numerous situations where Christians and Muslims live peacefully and fruitfully together. Such examples encourage us to do all we can so that Christians and Muslims everywhere may live together in this way. We are invited to examine the nature of our relations, both in the past and in the present, and above all to make a decision to become more and more what God calls us to be: witnesses of his goodness and mercy, especially towards the weaker members of society.

7. Wishing you, my dear Muslim Friends, an abundance of divine blessings, on my own behalf and on behalf of Catholics throughout the world, I renew my expressions of friendship and esteem.

HINDUISM AND BUDDHISM

(*Courtesy of Dr. John Borelli.*)

Hinduism and Buddhism — along with Confucianism, Taoism, Shinto, Native American Traditions and other religions — unlike Judaism, Christianity and Islam, are called non-Abrahamic because in them Abraham is not shared as a father in faith.

Common elements among Judaism, Christianity and Islam are more extensive than each has with any other religion. All three are scriptural religions, with Christian scripture making reference to Jewish scripture and Islamic scripture making references to the earlier two. The life of the religious community of each religion is defined through the content and use of its scripture. More common elements among the three religions can be discovered through the study of religious law, liturgy, spirituality and theology.

Two of the principal non-Abrahamic religions are Hinduism and Buddhism.

In its Declaration on the Relation of the Church to Non-Christian Religions, the Second Vatican Council stated: "In Hinduism men explore the divine mystery and express it both in the limitless riches of myth and the accurately defined insights of philosophy. They seek release from the trials of the present life by ascetical practices, profound meditation and recourse to God in confidence and love." (2)

Catholics, especially in India, have sought good relations with Hindus and have engaged in numerous dialogues and conferences. In papal visits to India, Paul VI in 1964 and John Paul II in 1986 addressed words of respect for Indian, particularly Hindu, religious leaders. Pope John Paul said to Hindus in 1986: "Your overwhelming sense of the primacy of religion and of the greatness of the Supreme Being has been a powerful witness against a materialistic and atheistic view of life."

In 1995, the Pontifical Council for Interreligious Dialogue began sending a general message to Hindus on the occasion of Diwali, a feast commemorating the victory of light over darkness.

"Buddhism in its multiple forms acknowledges the radical insufficiency of this shifting world. It teaches a path by which men, in a devout and confident spirit, can either reach a state of absolute freedom or attain supreme enlightenment by their own efforts or by higher assistance." So stated the Second Vatican Council in its Declaration on the Relation of the Church to Non-Christian Religions.

Numerous delegations of Buddhists and leading monks have been received by the popes. At the 1986 World Day of Prayer for Peace at Assisi, the Dalai Lama, principal teacher of the Gelugpa lineage, was placed immediately to the Holy Father's left. Numerous dialogues and good relations between Catholics and Buddhists exist in many countries.

In 1995, the Pontifical Council for Interreligious Dialogue organized a Buddhist-Christian colloquium hosted by the Fo Kuang Shan Buddhist order in Taiwan. Also in 1995, the council began sending a message to Buddhists on the feast of Vesakh, the celebration of Gautama Buddha's life.

In 1996, Cardinal Arinze, in a letter to "Dear Buddhist Friends," wrote: "The pluralistic society in which we live demands more than mere tolerance. Tolerance is usually thought of as putting up with the other or, at best, as a code of public conduct. Yet, this resigned, lukewarm attitude does not create the right atmosphere for true harmonious coexistence. The spirit of our religions challenges us to go beyond this. We are commanded, in fact, to love our neighbors as ourselves." The cardinal wrote in the same vein to Muslims on the occasion of their 1996 celebration of Id al-Fitr.

Formal dialogues in the Archdioceses of Los Angeles, San Francisco, Chicago and the Diocese of Honolulu are held from time to time. The Monastic Interreligious Dialogue, a consortium of Catholic monastics, has enjoyed rich exchanges with Buddhist monastics since 1981. In 1989, the bishops' Secretariat for Ecumenical and Interreligious Affairs convened its first national consultation on relations with Buddhists; a second consultation was held in 1990.

SPECIAL SUPPLEMENT

AD LIMINA APOSTOLORUM

(Sources: Bill Ryan, Communications Office, NCCB; L'Osservatore Romano.) Nineteen ninety-eight was the year for each bishop of the United States to undertake an ad limina visit to Rome — the required pilgrimage every five years by all diocesan bishops and apostolic vicars to the tombs of Sts. Peter and Paul. The name ad limina is from the Latin for "to the threshold."

The Ad Limina

During the pilgrimage, the bishops normally have an audience with the Holy Father, meet with relevant officials of the Roman Curia, and give report (*relatio*) about the state of their dioceses. The formal report is normally to be provided approximately six months and not less than three months in advance of their scheduled visit. It should detail all relevant statistics pertaining to the diocese, as well as all institutions, personnel, and activities undertaken within diocesan limits. In those cases where the diocesan bishop is unable to attend, he is permitted to send his coadjutor, if one is present, or some other duly appointed representative from among the clergy.

The Holy Father customarily uses the gatherings of bishops from each region to impart some teachings or deliver an exhortation that may pertain to the specific circumstances of the regions or countries in which the bishops serve. Following are the *ad limina* visits that took place throughout 1998:

February 22-28, 1998

Province of New York: Archdiocese of New York; suffragan sees of Albany, Brooklyn, Buffalo, Ogdensburg, Rochester, Rockville Centre, Syracuse. **Lithuanian Catholics of the Roman Rite. Antiochene Tadition:** Maronite Rite, Diocese of Saint Maron; **Armenian Tradition:** Armenian Catholic Exarchate of USA and Canada. **Diocese of Cleveland.**

March 8-14, 1998

Province of Newark: Archdiocese of Newark and suffragan sees of Camden, Metuchen, Paterson, Trenton. **Province of Philadelphia:** Archdiocese of Philadelphia and suffragan sees of Allentown, Altoona-Johnstown, Erie, Greensburg, Harrisburg, Pittsburgh, Scranton. **Constantinopolitan Tradition: Ruthenian Rite,** Metropolitan Archdiocese of Pittsburgh and Eparchy of Passaic (N.J.); **Ukrainian Rite,** Metropolitan Archdiocese of Philadelphia.

March 15-26

Province of Atlanta: Archdiocese of Atlanta and suffragan sees of Charleston, Charlotte, Raleigh, and Savannah. **Province of Baltimore:** Archdiocese of Baltimore and suffragan sees of Arlington, Richmond, Wheeling-Charleston, Wilmington. **Province of Miami:** Archdiocese of Miami and suffragan sees of Orlando, Palm Beach, Pensacola-Tallahassee, St. Augustine, St. Petersburg, Venice. **Province of Washington:** Archdiocese of Washington, D.C., and suffragan see of St. Thomas (Virgin Islands).

Ordinariate for Military Services. Diocese of Kansas City-St. Joseph.

March 27-April 4

Province of Louisville: Archdiocese of Louisville (Ky.) and suffragan sees of Covington, Knoxville, Lexington Memphis, Nashville, and Owensboro. **Province of Mobile:** Archdiocese of Mobile, Ala., and suffragan sees of Biloxi, Birmingham, and Jackson. **Province of New Orleans:** Archdiocese of New Orleans and suffragan sees of Alexandria, Baton Rouge, Houma-Thibodaux, Lafayette, Lake Charles and Shreveport.

May 17-23, 1998

Province of Cincinnati: Archdiocese of Cincinnati and suffragan sees of Columbus, Steubenville, Toledo, Youngstown. **Province of Detroit:** Archdiocese of Detroit and suffragan sees of Gaylord, Grand Rapids, Kalamazoo, Lansing, Marquette, Saginaw. Geographical area: Michigan. **Chaldean Tradition:** Eparchy of St. Thomas the Apostle. **Constantinopolitan Rite: Romanian Rite,** Diocese of St. George's in Canton. **Ruthenian Rite,** Diocese of Parma; **Ukrainian Rite,** Diocese of St. Joseph in Parma.

May 24-June 1, 1998

Province of Chicago: Archdiocese of Chicago and suffragan sees of Belleville, Joliet, Peoria, Rockford, Springfield. Geographical area: Illinois. **Province of Indianapolis:** Archdiocese of Indianapolis and suffragan sees of Evansville, Fort Wayne-South Bend, Gary, Lafayette. Geographical area: Indiana. **Province of Milwaukee:** Archdiocese of Milwaukee and suffragan sees of Green Bay, La Crosse, Madison, Superior. **Constantinopolitan Rite: Ukrainian Rite,** Diocese of St. Nicholas.

June 1-8, 1998

Province of St. Paul and Minneapolis: Archdiocese of St. Paul and Minneapolis and suffragan sees of Bismarck, Crookston, Duluth, Fargo, New Ulm, Rapid City, St. Cloud, Sioux Falls and Winona.

June 8-15, 1998

Province of Dubuque: Archdiocese of Dubuque and suffragan sees of Davenport, Des Moines, Sioux City. **Province of Kansas City (Kans.):** Archdiocese of Kansas City and suffragan sees of Dodge City, Salina, Wichita. **Province of Omaha:** Archdiocese of Omaha and suffragan sees of Grand Island, Lincoln. **Province of St. Louis:** Archdiocese of St. Louis and suffragan sees of Jefferson City, Springfield-Cape Girardeau.

June 21-27, 1998

Province of Oklahoma City: Archdiocese of Oklahoma City (Okla.) and suffragan sees of Little Rock and Tulsa. **Province of San Antonio:** Archdiocese of San Antonio (Tex.) and suffragan sees of Amarillo, Austin, Beaumont, Brownsville, Corpus Christi, Dallas, Fort Worth, Galveston-Houston, Lubbock, San Angelo, Tyler and Victoria.

September 27-October 5, 1998

Province of Los Angeles: Archdiocese of Los Angeles and suffragan sees of Fresno, Monterey, Orange, San Bernardino, San Diego. **Province of San Francisco:** Archdiocese of San Francisco and suffragan sees of Honolulu, Las Vegas, Oakland, Reno Sacramento, San Jose, Santa Rosa and Stockton. **Antiochene Tradition: Maronite Rite,** Diocese of Our Lady of Lebanon. **Constantinopolitan Rite: Ruthenian Rite,** Diocese of Van Nuys; **Syrian Rite,** Diocese of Our Lady of Deliverance of Newark. **The Holy Father addressed the Bishops on Oct. 2, 1998:**

"Above all, society must learn to embrace once more the great gift of life, to cherish it, to protect it, and to defend it against the culture of death, itself an expression of the great fear that stalks our times. One of your most noble tasks as Bishops is to stand firmly on the side of life, encouraging those who defend it and building with them a genuine culture of life.

"Thirty years after *Humanae Vitae*, we see that mistaken ideas about the individual's moral autonomy continue to inflict wounds on the consciences of many people and on the life of society. Paul VI pointed out some of the consequences of separating the unitive aspect of conjugal love from its procreative dimension: a gradual weakening of moral discipline; a trivialization of human sexuality; the demeaning of women; marital infidelity, often leading to broken families; state-sponsored programs of population control based on imposed contraception and sterilization (cf. *Humanae Vitae*, 17). The introduction of legalized abortion and euthanasia, ever increasing recourse to *in vitro* fertilization, and certain forms of genetic manipulation and embryo experimentation are also closely related in law and public policy, as well as in contemporary culture, to the idea of unlimited dominion over one's body and life."

October 5-10, 1998

Province of Anchorage: Archdiocese of Anchorage and suffragan sees of Fairbanks, Juneau. **Province of Portland:** Archdiocese of Portland and suffragan sees of Baker, Boise, Great Falls-Billings and Helena. **Province of Seattle:** Archdiocese of Seattle and suffragan sees of Spokane, Yakima. **The Holy Father addressed the Bishops on Oct. 10, 1998:**

"To look back over what has been done in the field of liturgical renewal in the years since the Council is, first, to see many reasons for giving heartfelt thanks and praise to the Most Holy Trinity for the marvelous awareness which has developed among the faithful of their role and responsibility in this priestly work of Christ and his Church. It is also to realize that not all changes have always and everywhere been accompanied by the necessary explanation and catechesis; as a result, in some cases there has been a misunderstanding of the very nature of the liturgy, leading to abuses, polarization, and sometimes even grave scandal. After the experience of more than thirty years of liturgical renewal, we are well placed to assess both the strengths and weaknesses of what has been done, in order more confidently to plot our course into the future which God has in mind for his cherished People."

October 11-19, 1998

Province of Denver: Archdiocese of Denver and suffragan sees of Cheyenne, Colorado Springs, and Pueblo. **Province of Santa Fe:** Archdiocese of Santa Fe and suffragan sees of Gallup, Las Cruces, Phoenix, and Tucson. **Diocese of Salt Lake City. Diocese of El Paso. The Holy Father addressed the Bishops on Oct. 17, 1998:**

Ecclesiastical law gives form to the community or social body of the Church, always with a view to that supreme objective which is the salvation of souls (cf. *Canons* 747, 978, 1752). Since this ultimate end is attained above all through the newness of life in the Spirit, the provisions of the law aim at safeguarding and fostering Christian life by regulating the exercise of faith, the sacraments, charity and ecclesiastical government.

3. The common good which the law protects and promotes is not a mere external order, but the sum of those conditions which make possible the spiritual and internal reality of communion with God and communion between the members of the Church. Consequently, as a basic rule, ecclesiastical laws bind in conscience. In other words, obedience to the law is not a mere external submission to authority but a means of growing in faith, charity and holiness, under the guidance and by the grace of the Holy Spirit. In this sense canon law has particular features which distinguish it from civil law and which preclude the application of the legal structures of civil society to the Church without the necessary modifications. Appreciation of these particularities is necessary in order to overcome some of the difficulties which have arisen in recent times regarding the understanding, interpretation and application of canon law.

October 19-26, 1998

Province of Boston: Archdiocese of Boston and suffragan sees of Burlington, Fall River, Manchester, Portland, Springfield, and Worcester. **Province of Hartford:** Archdiocese of Hartford and suffragan sees of Bridgeport, Norwich, and Providence. **Constantinopolitan Rite: Melkite-Greek Rite,** Diocese of Newton; **Ukrainian Rite,** Diocese of Stamford. **The Holy Father addressed the Bishops on Oct. 24, 1998:**

"Nowhere is the contrast between the Gospel vision and contemporary culture more obvious than in the dramatic conflict between the culture of life and the culture of death. I do not wish to end this series of meetings without once more thanking the Bishops for their leadership and advocacy in support of human life, particularly the lives of the most vulnerable. The Church in your country reaches out in the defense and promotion of human life and human dignity in numerous ways. Through countless organizations and agencies she is an immensely generous provider of social services to the poor; active in support of laws more favorable to the immigrant, present in the public debate on capital punishment, aware that in the modern state the cases in which the execution of an offender is an absolute necessity are very rare, if not practically nonexistent (cf. *Evangelium Vitae*, 56; *Catechism of the Catholic Church*, No. 2267).

His Holiness John Paul II

paternally imparts his
Apostolic Blessing
as a pledge of divine graces and favors on the

Staff of Our Sunday Visitor's
Catholic Almanac

on the occasion of the Year 2000 Edition
of the Publication, 1999.

Ex Aedibus Vaticanis, 31 - III - 1999

+ Oscar Rizzato

Archiepiscopus Eleemosynarius Apostolicus

ABOUT THE AUTHOR

A writer for almost 10 years, Matthew Bunson was born in Germany and grew up in Hawaii. He is the author or coauthor of about 20 books, including **Our Sunday Visitor's Encyclopedia of Catholic History, John Paul II's Book of Saints, Our Sunday Visitor's Encyclopedia of Saints, Encyclopedia of the Roman Empire, Encyclopedia of the Middle Ages, Papal Wisdom,** and many others. In addition to delivering lectures on a variety of topics related to his books, Matthew has appeared on numerous radio and television programs.

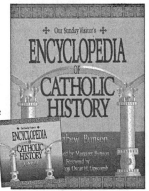
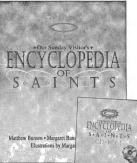

Our Sunday Visitor...
Your Source for Discovering the Riches of the Catholic Faith

Our Sunday Visitor has an extensive line of materials for young children, teens, and adults. Our books, Bibles, booklets, CD-ROMs, audios, and videos are available in bookstores worldwide.

To receive a FREE full-line catalog or for more information, call **Our Sunday Visitor** at **1-800-348-2440**. Or write, **Our Sunday Visitor** / 200 Noll Plaza / Huntington, IN 46750.

Please send me: ___ A catalog
Please send me materials on:
___ Apologetics and catechetics   ___ Reference works
___ Prayer books   ___ Heritage and the saints
___ The family   ___ The parish

Name_____

Address_____Apt._____

City_____State ___Zip_____

Telephone (   ) _____

A93BBABP

Please send a friend: ___ A catalog
Please send a friend materials on:
___ Apologetics and catechetics   ___ Reference works
___ Prayer books   ___ Heritage and the saints
___ The family   ___ The parish

Name_____

Address_____Apt._____

City_____State ___Zip_____

Telephone (   ) _____

A93BBABP

 Our Sunday Visitor
200 Noll Plaza
Huntington, IN 46750
1-800-348-2440
osvbooks@osv.com

Your Source for Discovering the Riches of the Catholic Faith